CW01185817

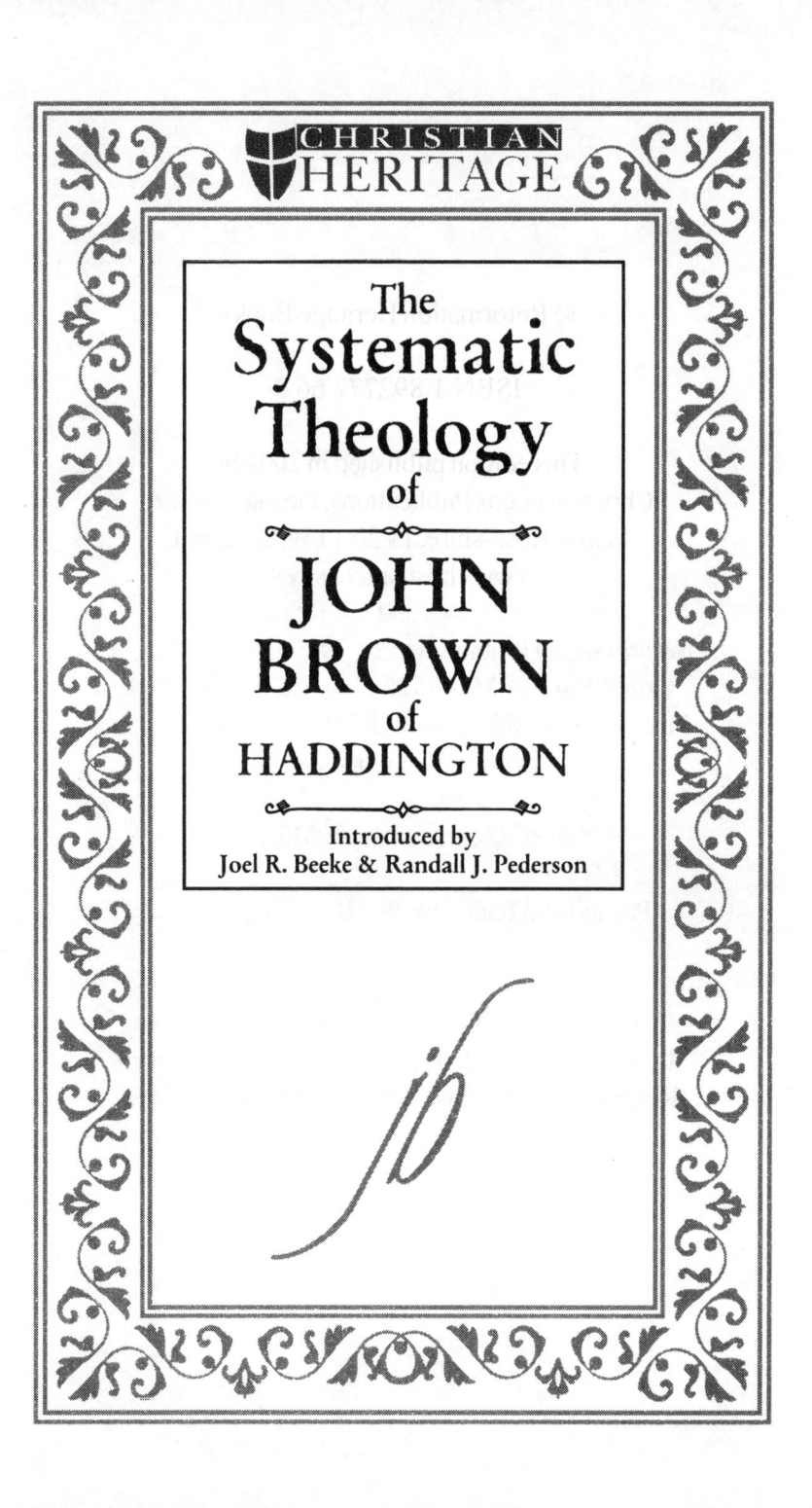

CHRISTIAN HERITAGE

The Systematic Theology of

JOHN BROWN of HADDINGTON

Introduced by
Joel R. Beeke & Randall J. Pederson

© Reformation Heritage Books

ISBN 1 892777 66 5

This edition published in 2002 by
Christian Focus Publications, Geanies House,
Fearn, Ross-shire, IV20 1TW, Scotland.
www.christianfocus.com
and
Reformation Heritage Books, 2919 Leonard St., NE
Grand Rapids, MI 49525 phone 616-977-0599/
Fax 616-977-0889/e-mail: RHbookstore@aol.com
www.heritagebooks.org

Cover design by Alister MacInnes

Printed and bound by WS Bookwell, Finland

For additional volumes of Reformed persuasion,
both new and used, request a free books list from
Reformation Heritage Books at the above address

A COMPENDIOUS VIEW

OF

NATURAL AND REVEALED RELIGION.

IN SEVEN BOOKS

BOOK I. Of the Standard of all Religion, the Law of Nature, in its Foundation and Contents; the Insufficiency of the Light of Nature to render a Man truly virnous and happy; the Possibility, Desirableness, Necessity, Propriety, Reasonableness, Credibility, Divine Authority, Properties, and Parts of that Revelation which is contained in the Scriptures of the Old and New Testament.

BOOK II. Of God, the author, object, and End of all Religion, in his Perfections, persons, Purposes, and Works.

BOOK III. Of the Bonds of Religious Connection between God and Men, the Covenant of Works and Grace, in their Origin, Parties, Parts, and Administrations in time and through eternity.

BOOK IV. Of Christ, the Mediator of the Covenant of Grace, in his Person, Offices, and States.

BOOK V. Of the Blessings of the Covenant of Grace, Effectual Calling, Justification, Adoption, Sanctification, Spiritual Comfort, Eternal Glory.

BOOK VI. Of the Dispensation of the Covenant of Grace by means of the Law, the gospel, and Ordinances thereof.

BOOK VII. Of the New Covenant Society or Church, in her Constitution, Members, Offices, and Government.

BY THE REV. JOHN BROWN,
LATE MINISTER OF THE GOSPEL OF HADDINGTON

The Life and Writings of John Brown of Haddingotn

Eighteenth-century Scotland produced many noted ministers, scholars and educators, but none greater, or so greatly loved, in his own day or afterwards, as John Brown of Haddington. He was a devout Christian, an able preacher, and a prolific theological writer. He was a shining soldier of the cross, who did not falter in the face of opposition. In the course of his life he saw his beloved church torn by painful conflicts, especially in the great breach that divided the Seceders, but he never lost faith that Jesus Christ is King of His church. As a faithful steward, Brown felt his highest calling was to shepherd Christ's flock and defend the truths of the Reformed faith.

Brown's life and career are all the more remarkable for the fact that he began life in obscurity and poverty, with no advantages of wealth, position, title, or education. Yet God had favored him with unusual gifts, and an enormous capacity for hard work, and providentially opened a way before him. Best of all, God favored him with a profound experience of the truth of the Gospel as "the power of God unto salvation." That experience left its indelible stamp on every aspect of John Brown's many-sided ministry.

Early Life and Education
John Brown, named after his father, was born in 1722, in the village of Carpow, near Abernethy, in the county of Perth, Scotland. His mother was Catherine Millie. His parents were poor (his father was a weaver) and could not afford an education for their son, though the father did teach his son how to read. His parents also taught him the basics of true Christianity and conducted family worship every morning and evening.

The year of his birth, 1722, is remembered in Scottish church history as the year in which the General Assembly of the Church of Scotland reaffirmed its previous act of 1720, condemning a book, *The Marrow of Modern Divinity,* and rebuked twelve ministers who had defended the theology of the book. Included among the twelve was the minister of the parish church of Abernethy, Rev. Alexander Moncrieff. Moncrieff and his colleagues were permitted to return to their charges, but the Marrow Controversy set in motion forces that would later divide the Scottish church. Born under the shadow of this controversy, Brown's faith and work were deeply impacted by all that resulted from it. When Brown was eight years old, he pushed through a large Sabbath crowd outside the church at Abernethy and discovered that the Lord's Supper was going to be administered. Since non-communicants were excluded from such services, he was forced to leave but not before he heard a minister who spoke highly of Christ. Brown later wrote, "This in a sweet and delightful manner captivated my young affections, and has since made me think that children should never be kept out of the church on such occasions."

Brown's formal training was sparse, but he did manage to study Latin. He also enjoyed memorizing catechisms. "I had a particular delight in learning by heart the Catechisms published by Vincent, Flavel, and the Westminster Assembly, and was much profited by them," he wrote. His mother noted his eagerness to learn and envisioned him one day standing among Scotland's preachers.

In 1733, Ebenezer Erskine (1680-1745), James Fisher (1697-1775), Alexander Moncrieff (1695-1761), and William Wilson (1690-1741) seceded from the Church of Scotland. Banding together as the Associate Presbytery, they fathered a new organization which came to be known as the Secession Church. As a member of Moncrieff's flock in Abernethy, Brown joined the Secession Church early on and stayed in it until his death.

When Brown was eleven years old, his father died, and then his mother, leaving him an orphan at the age of thirteen. He stayed with various families but was separated from his two brothers and sister. "I was left a poor orphan, and had nothing to depend on but the providence of God," he wrote, "and I must say that the Lord hath been 'the father of the fatherless, and the orphan's stay.'"

In his thirteenth and fourteenth years, Brown was irresistibly attracted to the gospel. He read the major religious books of the period, such as Joseph Alleine's *An Alarm to the Unconverted*, William Guthrie's *The Trial of a Saving Interest in Christ*, William Gouge's *Christian Directions Shewing How to Walk with God All the Day Long*, and the letters of Samuel Rutherford. Though Brown profited by what he read, and was often convicted by it for several days, he resisted resting on free grace alone. "Such was the bias of my heart, under its convictions, that I was willing to do any thing rather than flee to Christ, and trust to his free grace alone for my salvation," he wrote.

Shortly after his mother died, Brown himself became very ill and nearly died. Everyone but his sister thought he would not recover. While praying for her brother, the sister was struck with the promise "With long life will I satisfy him, and show him my salvation." That set her mind at ease. Her brother became well again.

A Teenage Shepherd Converted

John Ogilvie, an elderly man with little education, employed Brown to tend his sheep. Ogilvie asked Brown to read to him, and Brown did so on numerous occasions. They soon became friends and met often to read the Word of God, to pray, and to sing psalms. Brown treasured those times.

After a severe fever in 1741, Brown became greatly concerned about his soul's eternal welfare. While his sheep were resting in the fold, he went to hear a sermon two miles away, running to and from the church. He heard three sermons in this manner, the last of which was preached on John 6:64, "There are some of you that believe not." That sermon pierced his conscience. He was convinced that he was the greatest unbeliever in the world.

The next morning he heard a sermon on Isaiah 53:4, "Surely he hath borne our griefs, and carried our sorrows." That greatly eased his anxiety. "I was made, as a poor lost sinner, as the chief of sinners, to essay appropriating the Lord Jesus as having done all for *me*, and as wholly made over to *me* in the gospel, as the free gift of God; and as my all-sufficient Saviour, answerable to all my folly, ignorance, guilt, filth, slavery, and misery," he later wrote.

Through this sermon and another on Isaiah 45:24, "Surely in the Lord have I righteousness and strength," he was drawn to the Lord Jesus Christ. He was given a clearer view of the freeness of God's grace and the exercise of taking hold of the promises of God.

False Accusations

In his nineteenth year, Brown was personally attacked after learning several foreign languages without a tutor. Through diligent self-study he had acquired some fluency in Latin, Greek, and Hebrew. He had learned the Greek alphabet by poring over notes in his copy of the Latin poems of Ovid, which contained Hellenic words, and by analyzing the Greek forms in the English Bible. Some of the Seceding students were suspicious of Brown's amazing feat and accused him of having learned Greek from the devil!

Rumors about Brown and alleged dealings with the devil circulated for years. Brown agonized about that, though the Lord provided seasons of comfort. He especially found comfort in Psalm 42:8, "The Lord will command his loving-kindness in the day-time, and in the night his song shall be with me, and my prayer to the God of my life." In later years, he remarked that affliction is one of God's kindest blessings to the believer.

While still under suspicion, Brown went to a bookshop in St. Andrews and asked for a Greek New Testament. As the story goes, a professor in the university was struck with Brown, whose shabby clothes announced his deep poverty, asking for such a book. The professor declared that if Brown could read it, the professor would purchase the volume for him. So Brown obtained the New Testament at no cost.[1]

Peddler and Soldier

For several years Brown was a peddler, shouldering a pack and traveling into neighboring counties to sell odds and ends at cottage doors. He was not a great success in this line. The books in people's homes and lengthy discussions would often divert him from selling merchandise.

During this time Brown traveled great distances to attend Communion services. Once he traveled over twenty-five miles to attend a Communion Season at Ebenezer Erskine's church. It was customary at that time for the Lord's Supper to be administered only once or twice a year in any one congregation, and many people would come from afar to take part in the several days of services devoted to the sacrament.

In 1745, Charles Edward Stuart, a staunch Roman Catholic, made an unsuccessful attempt to recover the British throne in Scotland. The Seceders were loyal to the Protestant faith, of course, and to the reigning House of

---

1. That story has never been verified; however, Robert Mackenzie, biographer of John Brown in the early twentieth century, considered it true. Brown's grandson, however, questioned its authenticity in his edition of his grandfather's *Memoirs*.

Hanover. They took up arms to defend their church and country. John Brown fought alongside other Seceders in defense of Edinburgh Castle.

Afterwards Brown returned to peddling but soon was dissatisfied with his work. From his earliest days, he had felt called to proclaim God's truth from the pulpit, but lacked a university education. The next logical step for him was to assume the role of teacher, which he did in 1748.

The Breach in the Associate Synod

In April 1747, a division called "The Breach" took place in the Secession Church over the legitimacy of the Burgess oath. Citizens of Edinburgh, Glasgow, and Perth were required to take the oath in 1744. Taking this "loyalty oath" was a prerequisite to engaging in trade, belonging to one of the artisans' guilds, or voting in elections. Included in the oath was this clause: "Here I protest before God, and your Lordships, that I profess, and allow with my heart, the true religion presently professed within this realm, and authorized by the laws thereof... renouncing the Roman religion called papistry."

Those who condemned the oath believed that it was an endorsement of the Church of Scotland, with all its prevailing errors and corruptions. They were known as Antiburghers. Those who supported the oath were called Burghers, holding that the oath merely required one to profess to be a Protestant, over against Roman Catholicism. Brown and the Erskines sided with the Burghers. Twenty-three church leaders of the Antiburgher party, under the leadership of Alexander Moncrieff and Adam Gib (1714-88), declared that they were the rightful continuation of the Secession. They formed the General Associate Synod.

Teaching and Studying

John Brown first taught at Gairney Bridge, near Kinross, then at Spittal, a village in the parish of Penicuik. One of his students during this time was Archibald Hall (1736-1778), who later became the well-respected minister of Wall Street, London.

During this period Brown learned much about divinity and literature. He committed large portions of Scripture to memory. He acquired a working knowledge of Arabic, Syrian, Persian, Ethiopian, and major European languages, including French, Spanish, Italian, Dutch, and German. He studied long into the night, regularly sleeping no more than four hours. Much later he confessed the error of such unhealthy habits.

The secession of the General Associate Synod forced the Associate Synod to form a new seminary to train pastors for the ministry. The Associate Synod appointed Ebenezer Erskine to begin training students for the ministry at Stirling. Erskine only reluctantly accepted the appointment because he was already sixty-seven years old. The Synod therefore chose James Fisher of Glasgow as an alternate. Fisher is remembered for his *Exposition of the Shorter Catechism,* published in two parts beginning in 1753.

The first student to present himself at Stirling was John Brown. A university education was an entrance requirement, but Brown had already distinguished himself as a scholar through self-education. Some members of the Presbytery questioned those credentials, but Ralph Erskine (1685-1752), Ebenezer's younger brother, came to Brown's defense, saying, "I think the lad has a sweet savor of Christ about him."

Brown was approved for theological studies and started training for the Associate ministry under Ebenezer Erskine. The basic theology text used at the time was Francis Turretin's (1623-1687) *Institutes of Elenctic Theology*. Erskine's method was to read from Turretin and comment on its major doctrines. He also taught homiletics, a field in which he excelled.

After two years James Fisher took over the professorship in Glasgow. Brown moved there to sit under Fisher's teaching. Fisher was often compared to an eagle, due to the keenness of his mental vision and the swiftness with which he swooped down upon fallacies and heresies. Brown learned much from Fisher and so refined his preaching skills that on November 14, 1750, at the age of twenty-eight, he received his license to preach from the Presbytery of Edinburgh.

Pastor in Haddington
A short time after his ordination, Brown received a call to be the minister of the Associate congregation of Haddington, the county town of East Lothian. He received another call from Stow, Mid-Lothian. He accepted the call to Haddington, the smaller of the two congregations.

Brown served the small church in Haddington for thirty-six years, from 1751 until his death. He preached three times every Lord's Day, and visited and catechized his flock during the week. With all his learning, he tried to preach as if he had never read any book but the Bible. He often quoted Archbishop Ussher's saying, "It will take all our learning to make things plain."

During the course of his pastorate Brown suffered many trials in his personal life, including the loss of a wife and several children. He was married eighteen years to Janet Thomson, a God-fearing daughter of a Musselburgh merchant. They had eight children, of which only two survived. After his first wife died, Brown married Violet Croumbie, of Stenton, East Lothian, who outlived him by thirty-five years.

Brown often agonized that he was a trial to his congregation. He begged God to help him lead this flock, but if his ministry was not for God's glory, to remove him by death. He strongly disapproved of ministers who frequently switched pastorates.

On the other hand, he found great pleasure in studies that prepared him for the coming Sabbath. Personal spiritual experience also enriched his sermons. As he said, "Any little knowledge which I have had of my uncommonly wicked heart, and of the Lord's dealing with my own soul, hath helped me much in my sermons; and I have observed, that I have been apt to deliver that which I had experienced, in a more feeling and earnest manner, than other matters." Against the backdrop of man's wretched depravity, Brown's main focus in preaching was the beauty and glory of Christ. He wrote, "Now after near forty years preaching of Christ, and his great and sweet salvation, I think that I would rather beg my bread, all the labouring days of the week, for an opportunity of publishing the gospel on the Sabbath to an assembly of sinful men, than, without such a privilege, to enjoy the richest possessions on earth."

Brown loved to study the great theologians. He was particularly fond of the old divines, Francis Turretin, Benedict Pictet, Petrus VanMaastricht, John Owen—and contemporary writers such as Thomas Boston, James Hervey, Ebenezer and Ralph Erskine.

Brown was a lifetime scholar. As Thomas Brown noted, "He was never more in his element than when in his study, and here he spent the greater part of his time." He would often rise at four or five o'clock in the morning before discharging the day's duties. During that time, Brown fervently prayed for his dear flock, though he often lamented his deficiency in doing so.

Brown delighted in prayer, often setting aside entire mornings for it. His tender love for God would often spring up spontaneously, such as his response to an extra loud peal of thunder. "That's the love-whisper of my God," he would say.

Brown also organized group prayer meetings. For some years he held prayer meetings with seven or eight children in his parsonage. He also led a prayer meeting for adults from both the Church of Scotland and the Seceder congregations. In later years, he wrote guidelines for how prayer meetings should be conducted.

In 1758, Brown published his first book, *An Help for the Ignorant: Being an Essay Towards an Easy, Plain, Practical and Extensive Explication of the Assembly's Shorter Catechism, composed for the Young Ones of his own Congregation.* The book offers thousands of questions about the Shorter Catechism. The answers are succinct, practical, and supported by Scripture. Brown prefaces his book with an introduction to children, urging them to serve the Lord, flee the world, and trust in Christ alone for salvation.

The book was, for the most part, well-received. Some Antiburghers, however, charged Brown with heresy because he wrote that, though Christ's righteousness is of infinite value in itself, it is imputed to believers only in proportion to their need. The Antiburghers maintained that the righteousness of Christ is imputed to believers in its full infinite value so that God's people are infinitely righteous in Christ.

The debate appeared more speculative than edifying. Nonetheless, Brown responded the following year with his *A Brief Dissertation concerning the Righteousness of Christ* (1759), in which he wrote, "Let them do to or wish me what they will, may their portion be redemption through the blood of Jesus.... [Let them] call me what they please, may the Lord call them 'the holy ones, the redeemed of the Lord.'"

That response was typical of Brown. He seldom spoke a negative word about anyone. He also treated rumor as rumor, saying that when it was spoken of those in public office, it usually was not true.

Brown once wrote to Rev. Archibald Bruce, a respected professor of divinity with the Antiburghers: "Our conduct on both sides of the Secession I have often thought to be like that of two travelers, both walking on the same road, not far from one another, but in consequence of a thick mist so suddenly come on they cannot see one another, and each supposes the other to be off the road. After some time the darkness is removed, and they are quite surprised to find that they are both on the road, and had been all along so near one another."

That proved true of the Burghers and the Antiburghers. In 1820, thirty-three years after Brown died, the two denominations were reconciled as the United Secession Church. In 1847 a union was forged between the United Secession Church and the Relief Church, founded in 1761. The new body was known as the United Presbyterian Church.

Brown's ministry was blessed by God. People in his congregation grew in grace under the Word and sacrament. So did others who heard him preach wherever he traveled. Many regarded him as their spiritual father.

Professor of Divinity

After the death of John Swanston of Kinross in 1767, Brown was appointed Professor of Divinity by the Associate Church Synod. For twenty years he filled that position with distinction. He taught theological students in the Associate Church for nine weeks each year, packing in 160 hours of instruction, examination, and student presentations.

Brown taught about thirty students a year in languages, theology, church history, and homiletics. Some of those lectures are included in his publications, such as *A General History of the Christian Church* (2 vols.; 1771), and most importantly, his systematic theology, *A Compendious View of Natural and Revealed Religion* (1782). This book, republished several times in the nineteenth century, was a work of great merit. Other lesser known works that grew out of his theological teaching are *Letters on Gospel Preaching* and *Ten Letters on the Exemplary Behaviour of Ministers,* printed in Brown's *Select Remains* (1789).

In his teaching, Brown continually stressed the necessity of heart-religion. He taught students as a father teaches his children, loving them and admonishing them for their good. After hearing a practice sermon, he said to one student, "I hope never to hear such a sermon again while I live." To another, he wrote, "I hope the Lord has let some of the wind out of you that I thought was in you when first I knew you. Beg of Him to fill its room with Himself and His grace." Such severity, however, was tempered with kindness. His concern for students earned their affection and respect. Many of his lectures stirred their souls. His annual closing address particularly searched their consciences. Here is an example:

> What state you are in, what are the reigning principles in your breasts, what are the motives by which you are influenced, and what are the ends you have in view—whether you are, indeed, what you profess, and what your outward appearance would indicate—all is known to God. To commend a Saviour for whom one has no love; to preach a gospel which one does not believe; to point out the way to heaven and never to have taken one step in that way; to enforce a saving acquaintance with religion, and to be an entire stranger to it one's self—how sad, how preposterous!

One biographer wrote of Brown, "Many of his sayings at those times, it is believed, will never be forgotten by those who heard him. The many able, useful, and acceptable ministers, both in Great Britain and Ireland, whom he trained up for the sacred office, evince the ample success with which the Lord crowned his labours." Some of the students Brown trained were George Lawson (1749-1820), John Dick (1764-1833), and his eldest son, John Brown (1754-1832), later minister of Whitburn.

During his years as professor, Brown was also busy in the work of his denomination. For the last twenty years of his life he served as clerk of the Synod. He missed only two of forty-one synodical meetings in those years. He also served on many denominational committees.

Sickness and Death
In early 1787 Brown suffered from indigestion, which became more acute as months passed. His health could no longer sustain the ruthless workload he had carried most of his life. But he was determined to keep working. "How can a dying man spend his last breath better than in preaching Christ?" he asked.

February 25, 1787, was his last Sabbath in the pulpit. In the morning, he preached from Luke 2:26, "It was revealed unto him by the Holy Ghost, that he should not see death, before he had seen the Lord's Christ." In the evening, his text was Acts 13:26, "To you is the word of this salvation sent." He told his congregation these were his last sermons and commended them to the grace of God.

While his health continued to decline, the man who had always been reluctant to speak of his own religious experience, seemed to become as a little child. The doors of his affections sprung open. He said loving things to his children, urging them to persevere in the faith. Forty-five pages of deathbed expressions conclude his *Memoir* edited by his son William. Here is a sampling of what Brown said:

• If Christ be magnified in my life, that is the great matter I wish for.

• O! to be with God! to see him as he is in Christ! to know him even as we are known! It is worth not merely *doing* for, but *dying* for, to see a gracious God.

• I have served several masters; but none so kind as Christ. I have dealt with many honest men; but no creditor like Christ. Had I ten thousand hearts, they should all be given to Christ; and had I ten thousand bodies, they should all be employed in labouring for his honour.

• Oh! commend Jesus. I have been looking at him for these many years, and never yet could find a fault in him. Many a comely person I have seen, but none so comely as Christ.

• Oh! what must Christ be in himself, when he sweetens heaven, sweetens Scriptures, sweetens ordinances, sweetens earth, and sweetens even trials!

- Once I got a ravishing sight of the necessity of his loving me, *the sinner.* He said, "Other sheep I have; them also I *must* bring."

Brown had a powerful sense of his own sinfulness. He degraded his weakness as thoroughly as he exalted Christ. Here are some samples of that self-knowledge:

- My life is and has been a kind of almost perpetual strife between God and my soul. He strives to overcome my enmity and wickedness with his mercies, and I strive to overcome his mercy with my enmity and wickedness. Astonishingly kind on his side, but worse than diabolically wicked on mine! After all, I wish and hope that he, not I, may obtain the victory at last.

- I know the outrageous wickedness of my heart; such wickedness as would have provoked any but a God of infinite love to have cast me into hell.

- I have no more dependence on my labours than on my sins.

- It has been my comfort these twenty years, that not only *sensible* sinners, but the most stupid, are made welcome to believe in Christ.

- Since Christ came to save sinners, even the chief, why, thought I, should I except myself?

In a letter to his congregation, Brown wrote movingly of these two themes of a hellworthy sinner and a precious Christ:

I see such weakness, such deficiency, such unfaithfulness, such imprudence, such unfervency and unconcern, such selfishness, in all that I have done as a minister or a Christian, as richly deserves the deepest damnation of hell. I have no hope of eternal happiness but in Jesus' blood, which cleanseth from all sin—in "redemption through his blood, the forgiveness of my sins, according to the riches of his grace."

Ordinarily Brown went to the congregation in Stow during June to take part in their Communion season. A friend who realized that the ailing Brown wasn't planning to go to Stow asked, "You are not journeying thither this year?" Brown answered, "No, I wish to be traveling to God, as my exceeding joy." Some days later he uttered his last words, "My Christ," and died on June 19, 1787. He was sixty-five years old.

After Brown died, this "Solemn Dedication to the Lord," dated June 23, 1784, was found among his papers:

LORD! I am now entering on the 34th year of my ministry; an amazing instance of sovereign mercy and patience to a cumberer of the ground! How strange that thou shouldest have, for more than sixty years, continued striving to exercise mercy and loving-kindness upon a wretch that hath all along spoken and done all the evil that I could; nor ever would yield, but when the almighty influence of free grace put it out of my power to oppose it. Lord! how often have I vowed, but never grown better; confessed but never amended! Often thou hast challenged and corrected me, and yet I have gone on forwardly in the way of my heart. As an evil man, and seducer, I have grown worse and worse.

But where should a sinner flee but to the Saviour? Lord! all refuge faileth me, no man can help my soul. Nothing will do for me, but an uncommon stretch of thy almighty grace. To thee, O Jesus! I give up myself, as a foolish, guilty, polluted and enslaved sinner; and I hereby solemnly take thee as mine, as made of God to me wisdom, righteousness, sanctification, and redemption. I give up myself, as a poor, ignorant, careless and wicked creature, who hath been ever learning, and yet never able to come to the knowledge of the truth. To thee, O Lord! that thou mayest bestow gifts on the rebellious, and exalt thy grace, in showing kindness to the unworthy.

O Saviour! come down, and do something for me, before I die. I give up myself and family, wife, children, and servant, to thee, encouraged by thy promises, Gen. xvii. 7; Jer. xxxi. 1; Isa. xliv. 3, lix. 21. I commit my poor, weak, withered congregation, deprived by death of its pillars, that thou mayest strengthen, refresh and govern it. I commit all my students unto thee, that thou, O Lord! mayest train them up for the ministry. May never one of them be so unfit as I have been! Lord! I desire to take hold of thy new covenant, well ordered in all things, and sure. This is all my salvation, and all my desire.

A Prolific Writer
Brown published thirty books. He was best-known for his *Self-Interpreting Bible* (2 vols., 1778) and, to a lesser extent, *A Dictionary of the Holy Bible* (2 vols., 1769). "Brown's Bible" contains history, chronology, geography, summaries, explanatory notes, and reflections—in short, it is a miniature library that covers everything that a typical reader desires. It was reprinted twenty-seven times in Britain and America, often increasing in size through editors' additions. The latest and best edition (4 vols., 1914) contains more than 2,200 pages. Its numerous aids include a system of marginal cross-references. This library in itself became nearly as common in eighteenth-century Scottish households as Bunyan's *Pilgrim's Progress* and Thomas Boston's *Fourfold State*. It incorporated material from the *Dictionary*, which explained English vocabulary and grammar, making it useful for home schooling. It also applied the Scriptures practically and personally. The complete work is exemplary in its directness and accuracy.

Robert Mackenzie's book, *John Brown of Haddington*, devotes an entire chapter to commending *The Self-Interpreting Bible*. MacKenzie writes:

> No work carried the reputation of the author so far afield as his *Self-Interpreting Bible*.... Its success from the first was extraordinary.... It will be evident that an extraordinary amount of valuable material was thus placed

at the command of the ordinary reader. It was the information that a student of the Scriptures hungered for, who had not access to the learned works dealing with such subjects.... Brown states that his avowed aim in his publication is not to depreciate the valuable commentaries of these writers (referring to some of the most famous Reformed commentators of the past), but "to exhibit their principal substance with all possible advantage"... and in referring particularly to the New Testament, he adds that "there the explication is peculiarly extensive, and attempts to exhibit the substance of many learned and expensive commentaries."

Charles Simeon of Cambridge (1759-1836) used Brown's book in his devotions early in the day. He wrote to Brown, "Your *Self-Interpreting Bible* seems to stand in lieu of all other commentaries; and I am daily receiving so much edification and instruction from it, that I would wish it in the hands of all serious ministers."

Brown's audience was remarkably diverse. He wrote for children and young people. *The Young Christian; or, The Pleasantness of Early Piety* (1782) encourages the fear of God in youth. The catechism books for children that were first published under one cover as *Two Short Catechisms, mutually connected* (1764) came to be known as "Little Brown" and "Big Brown." "Little Brown" contains 202 questions, many of which are short and personal and designed for young children, whereas "Big Brown," written for older children, contains 743 questions based on the Shorter Catechism.

Brown also wrote a trilogy of books over a fifteen-year period on the figures, types, and prophecies of Scripture titled: *Sacred Tropology; or A Brief View of the Figures and Explication of the Metaphors contained in Scripture* (1768), *An Evangelical and Practical View of the Types and Figures of the Old Testament Dispensation* (1781), and *The Harmony of Scripture Prophecies, and history of their fulfillment* (1784). He wrote the books, he said, because "In the first, we observe the surprising eloquence of Heaven, and discern, in almost every form of nature, a guide to and an illustration of inspired truth. By the second, we perceive the whole substance of the Gospel of Christ, truly exhibited in ancient shadows, persons, and things: in laws apparently carnal and trifling. In the third, we observe how astonishingly inspired predictions, properly arranged, and compared with the history of nations and churches, do illustrate each other; and modern events, as with the evidence of miracles, confirm our faith in the oracles of God."

He also loved writing biographies and church history. For ministers, he wrote, *The Christian, the Student, and Pastor, exemplified in the lives of nine eminent Ministers* (1781). *Practical Piety Exemplified* (1783) presents the lives of thirteen eminent Christians, illustrating various cases of conscience. *Casuistical Hints, or Cases of Conscience* (1784) was originally written for personal use, but later Brown offered it as "an appended illustration of *Practical Piety Exemplified,* or an appendix to my system on the head of sanctification." It deals with the art of spiritual casuistry, including how to handle temptations, indwelling sin, heresy, and division in the church. His last published work was

The Most Remarkable Passages in the Life and Spiritual experiences of Elizabeth Wast, a Young Woman, sometime Matron of the Trades Hospital, Edinburgh (1785). As for church history, in addition to his two-volume overview, he wrote *An Historical Account of the Rise and Progress of the Secession* (1766) and *A Compendious History of the British Churches in Scotland, England, Ireland, and America* (2 vols.; 1784).

At times, Brown wrote polemically to defend or attack a position. He attacked the papacy and Roman Catholic emancipation in *The Oracles of Christ and the Abominations of Antichrist Compared; or, A Brief View of the Errors, Impieties, and Inhumanities of Popery* (1779) and *The Absurdity and Perfidy of All Authoritative Toleration of Gross Heresy, Blasphemy, Idolatry, and Popery in Britain* (1780). He defended the Burgher position in *The Re-exhibition of the Testimony vindicated, in opposition to the unfair account of given it by the Rev. Adam Gib* (1780). Gib was a prominent anti-Burgher minister, who had written *An Account of the Burgher Re-exhibition of the Secession Testimony*.

Brown also published the following sermons: *Religious Steadfastness recommended* (1769), *The Fearful Shame and Contempt of those professed Christians who neglect to raise up spiritual Children to Christ* (1780), and *The Necessity and Advantage of Earnest Prayer for the Lord's Special Direction in the Choice of Pastors* (1783).

Brown published a journal, too, titled *The Christian Journal; or, Common Incidents Spiritual Instructions* (1765). The journal is divided into five parts: a day in spring, summer, harvest, winter, and the day of rest. Lessons from nature and the Sabbath are applied to spiritual life. He also wrote a bit of fiction. *Letters on the Constitution, Government, and Discipline of the Christian Church* (1767) contains nineteen letters addressed to a fictitious person named Amelius, who lacks understanding of the constitution of the church and how members are accepted into the church. Brown offers scriptural groundwork and weighty arguments to promote a strong view of the organized church and its Solemn League and Covenant.

The Psalms of David in Metre (1775), recently reprinted, include Brown's notes on the Psalms. *A Brief Concordance to the Holy Scriptures* (1783) was useful in its time. *Devout Breathings,* which emphasized experiential faith, was printed sixteen times by 1784. *The Awakening Call: Four Solemn Addresses, to Sinners, to Children, to Young Men and Women, and to Aged Persons,* sometimes bound with *Devout Breathings,* also was widely circulated.

When he died, Brown's name was a household word among Presbyterians in Scotland as well as throughout the English-speaking world. His books, pamphlets, tracts, and catechisms were read by increasing numbers of people. Even after his death, additional works continued to be published. *Select Remains* (1789), which includes some of Brown's voluminous correspondence, a number of tracts, and his dying advice, was edited by his oldest son, John. *Posthumous Works* (1797) and *Apology for the more Frequent Administration of the Lord's Supper* (1804) were also published. In *Apology,* Brown argued for more frequent observation of the Lord's Supper, countering those who taught that infrequency safeguarded solemnity with, "Why not pray seldom, preach seldom, read God's Word seldom, that they may become more solemn too?"

A Spiritual Dynasty

Brown had many children, some of whom became prominent Christian leaders. Of his sons, John (1754-1832) was minister of Whitburn for fifty-five years and was a prolific devotional writer; Ebenezer (d. 1836) was a prominent preacher at Inverkeithing, Fife, for fifty-six years; Samuel (1779-1839) helped start circulating libraries; and William (1783-1863) was a historian of missions and an excellent biographer of his father. Grandson John Brown (1784-1858) served as pastor at Broughton Place United Presbyterian Church, Edinburgh, and was Professor of Exegetical Theology in the United Secession and United Presbyterian College, Edinburgh. Great-grandson Robert Johnston (d. 1918) was a professor in the United Presbyterian College, Edinburgh, and United Free Church College, Aberdeen. Another great-grandson, John (Rab) Brown (1810-82), became a medical doctor and writer. And great-great-grandsons John (1818-92) and David Cairns (1862-1946) became outstanding Presbyterian teachers and writers. Brown's descendants so respected him that some traveled to Scotland from the United States in 1987 for events marking the bicentennial of Brown's death.

Brown's *Compendious View*

Brown's systematic theology, printed in 1782 at the request of theological students, includes seven books and twenty-four chapters. It offers biblical focus, exegetical insights, a covenantal theme, experiential depth, and compelling applications. Brown's style is methodological and includes numerous divisions and sub-points to aid students.

Like Johannes Cocceius (1613-1669) and Herman Witsius (1636-1708), Brown felt that Reformed systematic theology should emphasize the historical activity of God in time rather than His eternal decrees. That activity was grounded pre-fall in the covenant of works and post-fall in the covenant of grace. Consequently, Brown's theology is organized around the doctrine of the covenant.

Address to Students of Divinity

In the 16-page prefix to the work, titled "Address to Students of Divinity," Brown says *A Compendious View* was not written "to make you read, but to make you *think much*," and "to impress your minds with the great things of God." He thus offers a plethora of Scripture verses and references (26,819 in all) in order to "render you mighty in the Scriptures, readily able to support the several articles of our holy religion by the self-evidencing and conscience-commanding testimony of the Holy Ghost, and accustomed to express the things of God in his own language." Brown expected students to move from paragraph to paragraph, committing as many texts as possible to memory.

With eternity in mind, Brown instructs students to do the following:

1. See that ye be *real Christians* yourselves.
2. Ponder much, as before God, what proper *furniture* you have for the ministerial work, and labour to increase it.
3. Take heed that your *call* from Christ and his Spirit to your ministerial work be not only *real* but *evident*.
4. See that your *end* in entering into, or executing your office, be single and disinterested.
5. See that your minds be deeply impressed with the *nature, extent*, and *importance* of your ministerial work.
6. See that ye take heed to your spirits, that ye deal not *treacherously* with the Lord.
7. See that ye, as workmen who need not be ashamed, earnestly labour *rightly to divide* the word of truth, according to the capacities, necessities, and particular occasions of your hearers, giving every one of them their portion in due season.
8. See that ye be judicious, upright, constant, and faithful in your profession.
9. Always improve and live on that blessed encouragement which is offered to you as Christians and ministers in the gospel.

Brown closes his preface with these words: "There is no master so kind as Christ; no service so pleasant and profitable as that of Christ; and no reward so full, satisfying, and permanent as that of Christ. Let us, therefore, begin all things from Christ; carry on all things with and through Christ; and let all things aim at and end in Christ."

The Regulating Standard of Religion
The first book in Brown's work provides the foundation for the rest of the work by addressing the prolegomena of theology. It consists of three chapters: the first, the law of nature; the second, the insufficiency of the law and nature to lead man to true and lasting happiness; the third, an elaborate treatment of the divine character of Scripture.

Brown's opening chapter covers the principles of natural religion as well as the elements of natural morality. In chapter two, he addresses ethics more directly, denouncing the slave trade as criminal, yet allowing for its lawfulness under prescribed circumstances. He also advocates limited monarchy over democracy. And he addresses issues that relate to family life, employers and employees, and wrongs inflicted on the weak.

Next, Brown discusses the insufficiency of natural theology. He meets the Deists on their own turf, crosses swords with David Hume, and exposes the weaknesses of Rationalism.

Brown is a master of examination. For example, commenting on the properties of memory, Brown writes, "The human memory is an intellectual power of *recollecting* or *retaining* our ideas, and is called *good*, when it quickly recollects and strongly retains them. Its condition much depends on that of our body, whether it be in health, free from sleep, etc."

Brown addresses issues that are rarely found in modern systematic theologies. Commenting on social virtues, he notes, "Humanity towards brutes, in carefully forbearing every form or degree of cruelty to them, is implied in social virtue. In this we imitate God, who is good to all, and show a proper regard to his creatures, and our fellow-partakers of his bounty in creation and providence."

Enlarging on the nature of revelation, Brown observes apologetically, "The contents of the Scriptures of the Old and New Testaments are *perfectly agreeable to reason.*" For Brown, scriptural doctrines, such as the Trinity and the mercy of God, transcend the most narrow and laborious search of reason. Brown's arguments, however, are weakened by the lack of a presuppositional apologetic. Brown also refused to admit the possibility of a gradual development of spiritual and ethical truth.

In his closing section on the doctrine of Scripture, Brown urges: "Ponder now, my soul! Are these oracles of God, these testimonies and testaments of Jesus Christ, my heritage, and the word upon which he hath caused me to hope? Are they my divine charter for my everlasting life?" He concludes, "Let me not dare to proceed to the contemplation of his nature and works, till I believe his word, and receive His *unspeakable gift*, that I may, on that ground, all along say of Him, *My Lord and my God*—My God and My All."

God, the Author, Object, and End of All Religion
The second book moves into theology proper. It includes four chapters on God's names, nature, and perfections; persons in the Godhead; the decrees of God; and the execution of His decree.

After discussing the knowledge, wisdom, power, sovereignty, holiness, justice, goodness, and truth of God, Brown challenges readers to say:

> My Soul, stop thy contemplation of the Most High, and ask thyself, as in his presence: If God be a *Spirit*, am I spiritually minded, and a worshipper of Him in spirit and truth? Do I detest and banish every carnal imagination of him from my heart? Do I live in perpetual wonder, that his infinite equity can suffer such a sinner to live; nay, will save me? Do I reckon all things, as coming from His hand, as good—very good for me? Is He my Saviour, my Father, my Husband—my Friend, my Master, my Portion, my Pattern, my God—my All?

As a strong federal Calvinist, he says of God's decrees, "God acts on Himself in contemplating, loving, delighting in Himself; and in the persons of the Godhead, knowing, loving, delighting in, and consulting with each other." Brown then explains how providence works through election and reprobation. Election is always *in Christ,* who is the representative and covenant Head of the elect, Brown says. Like other federalists, Brown sees an essential connection between election and atonement, which limits the atonement to God's elect.

There is some question whether Brown supported a supralapsarian scheme of the decrees. In his discussion of reprobation, he uses the phrases *left un-elected* and *passed-by,* which sound infralapsarian. But Brown also wrote: "But it must be remarked, that though men's sins be foreseen and viewed in God's pre-appointment of them unto wrath, as the cause of their condemnation and punishment, yet they are not the cause of his leaving them un-elected to perish in their sin." Whatever Brown's sentiments concerning the order of the decrees, he clearly taught that foreseen sins are the "cause of their condemnation," but not "the cause of his leaving them un-elected."

In harmony with his federal Calvinistic forebears, Brown asserted that the "awful doctrine of Reprobation, as well as of the Election of men, ought, with great prudence and holy awe, be taught in the church." His reasons for doing so are as follows:

1. It hath been proved that the Holy Ghost hath plainly taught it in His Word.
2. Every thing taught in the Scripture, lawfully used, tends to promote men's holiness in heart and life.
3. Election and reprobation being so closely related and contrasted, the former can neither be taught nor conceived of, separately from the latter.
4. In His providence, which every man ought to observe, God copies out of His decree of reprobation, in the life and in the death of the wicked.
5. A proper knowledge of this decree promotes right and reverential views of the sovereignty, power, wisdom, justice, and goodness of God.
6. The doctrine of reprobation, if duly taught, tends to alarm the wicked and render their conscience uneasy, till they obtain proper evidence that they are not included in it, and to render sin terrible to them: And it excites saints to self-examination, and to lively gratitude to God their Redeemer, in a course of gospel holiness.

Brown refutes eight objections against the doctrine of reprobation and concludes with a personal reflection.

The Covenant Bonds of Religious Connection between God and Men
Brown's theological work includes a notable explanation of God's covenantal relation to man. He says covenant is "an agreement made between different persons on certain terms" and that all covenants require a condition, a promise, and a penalty. For the sake of man's happiness, God exercises His providence toward His creatures "in the form of covenant-connection."

Book three, divided into two main chapters—the covenant of works and the covenant of grace—discusses this "covenant-connection." The first chapter examines in detail topics such as the freedom of Adam's will, the headship of Adam for all, and the curse of a broken covenant—all from a typical federalist perspective. In the second chapter, dealing with God's covenant of grace, Brown writes that the covenant of grace originates, "from the mere grace of God, and contracted between two divine persons, it was *made from all eternity*."

The purpose of the covenant of grace, Brown says, is, "first, to display the glory of God's own perfections, wisdom, power, holiness, justice, and truth—especially the exceeding riches of His grace, and second, to bring elect men out of an estate of sin and misery into an estate of salvation."

Brown rejects the idea of a covenant of redemption separate from the covenant of grace. In characteristic *Marrow* fashion, he distinguishes between the contracting and administering of the covenant of grace. The former is accomplished in eternity, between the Father and the Son, and the latter in time, between the Triune God and fallen humanity, though in its secret decree with the elect only. Brown explains, "The covenant of grace is, in many things, administered indefinitely to men in general, without any consideration of them as either elect or as reprobates." Christ is granted to all as a warrant to those who believe, else men would have no more hope for faith than devils. If the covenant were not administered in such a general way, sinners could not be condemned for unbelief. This general administration of the covenant to all men, however, serves primarily for the salvation of the elect.

Brown teaches that the covenant of grace is essentially conditional in nature. Since Christ fulfils all its conditions, however, the covenant is entirely free to believers. God gives believers, in and through Christ and by His Spirit, whatever the covenant requires. All proper conditions, therefore, are satisfied through Christ's righteousness. Faith can only be spoken of as a condition of the covenant when it is understood to mean a "condition of connection" or an instrument through which we receive God's blessings. Even then, such language is risky. Neither faith nor repentance is a proper condition of the covenant, since, Brown says, "the admission of any act or quality of ours as the condition, would destroy the whole form and grace of" this covenant, which "stands opposed to the covenant of works."

Participation in the covenant of grace can only be understood in terms of spiritual union with Christ, Brown says. He stresses that only the elect are included in the covenant of grace. They come to a saving interest through Christ as their head. Brown fortifies his argument in this chapter with 1,792 Scripture references.

Christ, The Mediator of the Covenant of Grace
In book four, Brown considers Christ's role as Mediator of the covenant. He discusses Christ's mediatorial person, Christ's general and particular offices (such as prophet, priest, and king), and Christ's states of humiliation and exaltation.

Brown emphasizes the unique personhood of Christ, showing the essential incommunicability of any of the distinctively human properties to the divine nature, or of the distinctively divine attributes to the human nature. Next, he discusses the offices of Christ, marshalling hundreds of proof-texts to support limited atonement. His page on the intercession of Christ is comforting. His division of Christ's kingship into a kingdom of power, grace, and glory is succinct and scriptural.

Brown's chapter on Christ's states includes a remarkable list of twenty-four ways in which Christ's humiliation was attended by "honourable circumstances." He asserts that Christ's humiliation and exaltation were joined between His death and resurrections, His body lying in the grave (humiliation) while His soul fled to heavenly mansions (exaltation). He concludes by asking, "If God so exalt Jesus Christ, why hath he not an higher—a far higher place in my heart?"

The Principal Blessings of the Covenant of Grace
Book five discusses the blessings of the eternal covenant of grace in six chapters: union with Christ and effectual calling, justification, adoption, sanctification, spiritual consolation, and glorification.

Brown rightly considers union with Christ as preceding yet inseparable from effectual calling. Scripturally and experientially he explains the Spirit's work in establishing that union and making it effectual through an internal calling. He carefully refutes objections. But his chapters on justification and sanctification are the masterpieces of his soteriology.

Brown's emphasis on the "Surety righteousness" of Christ is clear and helpful. He shows how Christ fulfilled the broken covenant of works in the stead of believers, and how that becomes their justifying righteousness before God. Brown rejects faith as a condition of justification and asserts that justification as God's act is antecedent to the believer's faith.

Faith itself does not justify the believer, though he is justified through the instrument of faith. Faith is the believer's act—an act of his will that consents to the covenant of grace and receives Christ and His righteousness. Faith, which is seated in the will and the affections, is inseparably related to Christ. To walk by faith is to walk in union with Christ.

Brown carefully avoids preparationism. Evangelical repentance is the fruit of justification and never precedes it, he says. It is required of believers in sanctification but is never a ground for our justification.

Dr. George Lawson advised his theological students, "Read Brown on sanctification." MacKenzie also greatly admired this chapter. "The writer's life and character shine through every sentence of it," he said. "The study awakens admiration for the religious life which interpreted and expressed itself in the exposition here given of the secret source and mystic development of the divine life in the Christian soul. The survey of the mystery of divine grace in personal experience is the work of one who has searched the inner depths." Brown backs his points with 2,481 Scripture proofs.

Brown's chapter on spiritual consolation focuses on the perseverance of the saints, indwelling of the Spirit, assurance of God's love, peace of conscience, and joy in the Holy Ghost. Faith is always sure—hence assurance is of the essence of faith—but the believer's sense of having faith may waver. A solid sense of assurance, Brown asserts, comes when faith is repeatedly active in claiming the promises of the gospel, when there is earnest study of fellowship with God in Christ and of universal gospel holiness, and when there is a careful cherishing of the Spirit's activity and frequent exercises of self-examination. In proper self-examination, the Spirit bears witness of our heavenly adoption by directing us to "proper marks of grace." To make our calling and election sure, such examination must be "deliberate, judicious, impartial, earnest, and thorough," Brown says.

The External Dispensation of the Covenant of Grace by the Law and Gospel
Book six discusses the external dispensation of the covenant of grace through law and gospel. The book includes three parts: the law of God, the gospel of

Christ, and the ordinances of the covenant of grace. Those ordinances include reading, meditation, preaching and hearing God's Word; spiritual conference, prayer, ministerial blessing, singing of psalms, vowing, fasting, thanksgiving, and the sacraments.

In a chapter that provides 3,133 proof-texts—more than any other—Brown explains each commandment, showing how it is conducive to spiritual life. He then shows how the gospel magnifies and vindicates the law, and provides an impressive double-column list which affirms that the gospel "promises preparation for, assistance in, and a gracious reward of every duty which the law, *as a rule*, requires." The Ten Commandments, he says, shouldn't be seen only as a law of nature or a reflection of the covenant of works, but as the law of Christ and rule of life.

One neglected ordinance today that Brown describes is "spiritual conference." On a personal level, that involves "communing with our own heart; putting serious questions to our conscience concerning our state, temper, and conduct, in order to have them compared with, and adjusted by God's word." Socially, it includes communing with other believers, formally or informally, and catechizing one's family. Ecclesiastically, it entails "ministerial visiting and catechizing persons and families, or the sick."

Brown's comment on the partaking of the Lord's Supper is notable: "*All professed Christians,* come to years of discretion, are *bound* by the law of God to *partake* of the Lord's Supper, and it is their sin, if they be incapable of regular admission to it." He lists three things necessary for a right partaking of the sacrament:

1. A worthy *state* of union with Christ as our husband, father, righteousness and strength.
2. A worthy *frame* in the actual exercise of all the graces of the Spirit, [such as] knowledge, faith, repentance, and love, etc.
3. A worthy *end* of honouring Christ, glorifying God, and receiving spiritual nourishment to our soul.

The Church Society, for, and to which, the Covenant of Grace is Dispensed
In his last book, Brown discusses ecclesiology. In chapter one, he deals with the nature, formation, and fellowship of the Christian church; in chapter two, the role of church power and where it resides within the church body; and in chapter three, the divine warrant, work, and accountability of ecclesiastical courts—their divine warrant, work, and accountability.

Brown defines the church as "a society of believers and holy persons whom God by the Gospel hath called from among mankind to fellowship with His Son, Jesus Christ." The church is called to be holy, spiritual, and orderly, Brown says, and orderliness is best seen in a carefully organized Presbyterian system of church government involving sessions, presbyteries, and synods.

"Doctrine is heaven!" Martin Luther wrote. Brown would concur. Doctrine was the lifeblood of his salvation. Brown's reflections at the end of nearly every chapter are a unique feature of his systematic theology. In these warm reflections he teaches us how to apply doctrine to our souls to examine whether God's grace and holiness truly shine in us. Only when this is done can we understand the beauty of sound biblical doctrine.

A Word on the Reprint

Brown's method of organization is attractive and his content full of evangelical piety. This systematic theology, said to be "one of the most profound, and at the same time perspicuous, views which have been given of the theology of the Westminster Confession," is an indispensable tool for the student, pastor, and professor of theology. It was used as a textbook in several colleges and seminaries, including the Countess of Huntingdon's college at Trevecca. Its Christ-centeredness is aptly reflected in Brown's last letter to the Countess:

> There is none like Christ, none like Christ, none like Christ.... There is no learning nor knowledge like the knowledge of Christ; no life like Christ living in the heart by faith; no work like the service, the spiritual service of Christ; no reward like the free-graces wages of Christ; no riches nor wealth like "the unsearchable riches of Christ"; no rest, no comfort, like the rest, the consolation of Christ; no pleasure like the pleasure of fellowship with Christ. Little as I know of Christ, I would not exchange the learning of one hour's fellowship with Christ for all the liberal learning in ten thousand universities, during ten thousand ages, even though angels were to be my teachers.

Brown's last words, "my Christ," summarize his systematics, for his one great aim was to cultivate love for Christ in the soul of the believer. "If my soul love not this Lord Jesus, let me be Anathema, Maranatha, *accursed at his coming*," are his closing words.

Joel R. Beeke and Randall J. Pederson

2919 Leonard NE
Grand Rapids, Michigan 49525
February, 2002

ADDRESS

TO

STUDENTS OF DIVINITY.

MY DEAR PUPILS,

FOR my assistance in instructing you, this *Compendious View of Natural and Revealed Religion* was formed. To gratify a number of you, it is now published. Being formed, not to make you read, but to make you *think much*, it must now appear dry and meagre, as stript of its additional remarks: and no doubt some of its expressions admit of a sense which I never intended. To render you mighty in the Scriptures, readily able to support the several articles of our holy religion by the self-evidencing and conscience-commanding testimony of the Holy Ghost, and accustomed to express the things of God in his own language, multitudes of texts are ordinarily quoted, which I have laboured to lodge in your memories. To manifest the extensive connection of divine truths, some leading articles relative to the *perfections of God*, the *person of Christ*, &c. are traced through many others, in a manner which will perhaps be accounted a digression. Few insignificant, local, or dormant controversies, have been brought on the field: Nor, that I know, have the enemies of the truth been unfairly represented or indiscreetly answered, in others. The deceit or wrath of man worketh not the righteousness of God.

While I have been occupied in instructing you, your consciences must bear me witness, that my principal concern was to impress your minds with the great things of God. Now, when I am gradually stepping into the eternal state, to appear before the judgment-seat of Christ, permit me to beseech you, as you wish to promote his honour, and the eternal salvation of your own and your hearers' souls,

1. See that ye be REAL CHRISTIANS yourselves. I now more and more see, that nothing less than REAL, REAL Christianity, is fit to die with, and make an appearance before God. Are ye then indeed *born again, born from above, born of the Spirit? created in Christ Jesus unto good works?—new creatures in Christ Jesus,* having *all old things passed away, and all things become new?* Are ye indeed the circumcision which *worship God in the Spirit,* habitually reading, meditating, praying, preaching, conversing with your hearts, under the influence of the Holy Ghost? Have you no *confidence in the flesh,* no confidence in your self-righteousness, your learning, your address, your care and diligence, your gifts and graces;—but being emptied of self in every form, are *poor in spirit, less than the least of all saints,* and the least of all God's mercies; nay, the very *chief of sinners* in your own sight? Has it pleased God *to reveal his Son in* you? and to instruct you with a strong hand, to count all things but loss for the excellency of the knowledge of Jesus Christ as your Lord, and to count them but dung, that you may win him, and be found in him, not having your own righteousness, but the righteousness which is of God by faith,—and to know the power of his resurrection, and the fellowship of his sufferings, —and to press toward the mark for the prize of the high calling of God in Christ Jesus, John iii. 3, 5, 6. Eph. ii. 10. 2 Cor. v. 17. Gal. vi. 15. Phil. iii. 3. Matth. v. 3. xvi. 24. Eph. iii. 8. Gen. xxxii. 10. 1 Tim. i. 15. Gal. i. 15, 16. Phil. iii. 7—14. If you be, or become either *graceless* preachers or ministers of the gospel, how terrible is your condition! If you open your Bible, the sentence of your redoubled damnation flashes into your conscience from every page. When you compose your sermon, you but draw up a tremendous indictment against yourselves. If you argue against, or reprove other men's sins, you but aggravate your own. When you publish the holy law of God, you but add to your rebellion against it, and make it an awful witness against your treacherous dissimulation. If you announce its threatenings, and mention *hell* with all its insupportable torments, you but infeoff yourselves in it, and serve yourselves

heirs to it as the inheritance appointed you by the Almighty. When you speak of Christ and his excellencies, fulness, love, and labours, it is but to trample him under your feet. If you take his covenant and gospel into your mouth, it is but to profane them, and cast them forth to be trodden under foot of men. If you talk of spiritual experiences, you but do despite to the Spirit of grace. When you commend the Father, the Son, and the Holy Ghost, and invite sinners to new-covenant fellowship with them, you but treacherously stab them under the fifth rib, betray them with a kiss, and from your heart cry, This is the heir, the God, come let us kill him. While you hold up the glass of God's law or gospel to others, you turn its back to yourselves. The gospel, which ye preach to others, is hid,—is a savour of death unto death to you, the vail remaining on your hearts, and the god of this world having blinded your minds.—Without the saving, the heart-transforming knowledge of Christ and him crucified, all your knowledge is but an accursed *puffer up*, and the murderer of your own souls. And unless the grace of God make *an uncommon stretch* to save you, how desperate is your condition! Perhaps no person under heaven bids more unlikely to be saved, than a *graceless Seceding minister;*—his conscience is so overcharged with guilt, so seared as with an hot iron, and his heart so hardened by the abuse of the gospel.—Alas! my dear pupils, must all my instructions, all the strivings of the Holy Ghost, all your reading, all your meditations, all your sermons, all your evangelical principles, all your profession, all your prayers, as traps and snares, take and bind any of you, hand and foot, that, as *unprofitable servants, you* may be cast into *utter darkness*, with all the contents of your Bible and other books,—all your gifts and apparent-like graces, as it were, inlaid in your consciences, that, like fuel, or oil, they may for ever feed the flames of God's wrath upon your souls! After being set for a time at the gate of heaven, to point others into it,—after prophesying in Christ's name, and wasting yourselves to show others the way of salvation, and to light up the friends of our Redeemer to their heavenly rest,—must your own lamp go out in everlasting darkness, and ye be bidden, *Depart from me, I never knew you, ye workers of iniquity?*—Must I,—must all the churches behold you at last brought forth and condemned as arch-traitors to our Redeemer? Must you, in the most tremendous manner, for ever sink into the bottomless pit, under the weight of the blood of the great God, our Saviour,—under the weight of murdered truths, murdered convictions, murdered gifts, murdered ministrations of the gospel, and murdered souls of men!

2. Ponder much, as before God, what proper FURNITURE you have for the ministerial work, and labour to increase it. To him that hath shall be given. Has Jesus bestowed on you the Holy Ghost? What distinct knowledge have you of the mysteries of the kingdom? What aptness have you to teach, bringing out of the good treasure of your own heart *things new and old?* What ability to make the deep mysteries of the gospel plain to persons of weak capacities, and to represent things delightful or terrible in a proper and affecting manner? What proper quickness in conceiving divine things; and what rooted inclination to study them, as persons devoted to matters of infinite importance? What peculiar fitness have you for the pulpit, qualifying you, in a plain, serious, orderly, and earnest manner, to screw the truths of God into the consciences of your hearers? With what stock of self-experienced truths and texts of inspiration did, or do you enter on the ministerial work? Of what truths, relative to the law of God,—or relative to sin, Satan, or the desertions and terrors of God, has your soul not only seen the evidence, but felt the power? What declarations, promises, offers, and invitations of the glorious gospel, have ye, with joy and rejoicing of heart, found and eaten, and therein tasted and seen that God is good? Of what inspired truths and texts can you say, *Even so we have believed, and therefore we speak:* what we have seen and heard with the Father, and tasted and handled of the word of life, that we declare unto you. Thrice happy preacher, whose deeply-experienced heart is, next to his Bible, his principal note-book! John xx. 22. Matth. xiii. 22, 12, 52.

1 Tim. iii. 2. Tit. i. 9. 2 Tim. ii. 2. Isa. l. 4. xlix. 2. Jer. xv. 16. 2 Cor. iv. 13. 1 John i. 1—3. John viii. 34.

3. Take heed that your CALL from Christ and his Spirit to your ministerial work be not only REAL but EVIDENT. Without this you can neither be duly excited or encouraged to your work; nor hope, nor pray for divine success in it; nor bear up aright under the difficulties you must encounter, if you attempt to be faithful. If you run unsent by Jesus Christ and his Spirit, notwithstanding the utmost external regularity in your licence, call, and ordination, you, in the whole of your ministrations, must act the part of a sacrilegious thief and robber, a pretended and treacherous ambassador for Christ and his Father, and a murderer of men's souls, not profiting them at all. What direction,—what support,— what assistance,—what encouragement,—what reward can you then expect? Ponder, therefore, as before God: Have you taken this honour to yourselves? or, Were ye called of God as was Aaron? Has Jesus Christ sent you to preach the gospel, and laid upon you a delightful and awful *necessity* to preach it? While he powerfully determined you to follow providence, and avoid every selfish and irregular step towards entrance into the office as a mean of *eating a piece of bread*, or enjoying carnal ease or honour, did he breathe on you, and cause you to receive the Holy Ghost,—filling you with deep compassion to the perishing souls of men, and a deep sense of your unfitness for such arduous work, and fervent desire, that if the Lord were willing to use you as instruments of winning souls, he would sanctify you, and make you meet for his work?—Perhaps, providentially shut out from other callings to which you or your parents inclined, did you, in your education, go up *bound in the Spirit* by the love of Christ burning in your hearts, and constraining you cheerfully to surrender yourselves to poverty, reproach, and hatred of men, for promoting his name and honour, and the salvation of men in the world?—What oracles of God, powerfully impressed on your soul, have directed and encouraged you to his work? —Know you in what form Jesus Christ gave you your commission? Whether to *open the eyes of the Gentiles, and turn*

them from darkness to light, and from the power of Satan unto God,—that they may receive forgiveness of sins, and an inheritance among them who are sanctified by faith in him :—Or to go *make the heart of this people fat, their ears heavy,* and to *shut their eyes?* Jer. xxiii. 21, 22, 32. Isa. xlix. 1, 2. Jer. i. Ezek. ii. iii. xxxiii. Mat. x. Luke vi. x. John x. Acts i. Heb. v. 4. Rom. x. 15. 1 Cor. i. 17. ix. 16. Acts xxvi. 17, 18. Isa. vi. 8, 9.

4. See that your END in entering into, or executing your office, be single and disinterested. Dare you appeal to him, whose eyes are *as a flame of fire,* and who *searcheth the hearts and trieth the reins,* to give to every man according to his works, that you never inclined to be put into the priest's office, that you might *eat a piece of bread, and look every one for his gain from his quarter;* that ye *seek not great things for yourselves;* that ye *covet no man's silver, gold,* or *apparel;* that ye seek not men's property, but *themselves,* that you may win them to Christ for their eternal welfare; that ye seek not your own honour, ease, or temporal advantage, but the things of Christ and his people; that ye *seek not honour* or *glory of men,* but the honour of Christ or his Father, in the eternal salvation of souls; and have determined to prosecute this end through whatever distress or danger the Lord may be pleased to lay in your way? Jer. xlv. 5. 1 Sam. xii. 3. Acts xx. 33. Isa. lvi. 11. 2 Tim. iv. 10. 1 Cor. ix. 12, 16. 2 Cor. vii. 2. xi. 9. xii. 13, 14. vi. 4—19. Phil. ii. 21. 1 Thess. ii. 4—9. John vii. 18.

5. See that your minds be deeply impressed with the NATURE, EXTENT, and IMPORTANCE of your ministerial work,— that therein it is required of you, as *ambassadors for Christ,* as *stewards* of the mysteries and manifold grace of God,—*to be faithful;*—to serve the Lord with your spirit, and with much humility in the gospel of his Son :—to testify repentance towards God, and faith towards our Lord Jesus Christ, not keeping back or shunning to declare every part of the counsel of God, or any profitable instruction, reproof, or encouragement; and not moved with any reproach, persecution, hunger, or nakedness,—to be ready not only to be

bound, but to die for the name of the Lord Jesus, in order to finish your course with joy. Bearing with the infirmities of the weak, and striving together in prayer, that the word of the Lord may have free course, and be glorified, and your messages provided by God, and made acceptable to your hearers, you must labour with much fear and trembling, determined to know, to glory in, and make known, nothing but Jesus Christ, and him crucified,—preaching the gospel, *not with enticing words of man's wisdom*, as men-pleasers, but with great plainness of speech, in demonstration of the Spirit and with power,—speaking the things which are freely given you by God, not in the words which man's wisdom teaches, but in *words which the Holy Ghost teaches*, comparing spiritual things with spiritual,—as having the mind of Christ, always triumphing in HIM,—and making manifest the savour of the knowledge of him in every place, that you may be a sweet savour of Christ in them who are saved, and in them who perish;—as of sincerity, as of God, in the sight of God, speaking in Christ, and through the mercy of God, not fainting, but renouncing the hidden things of dishonesty;—not walking in craftiness, nor handling the word of God deceitfully, or corrupting the truth, but manifesting the truth to every man's conscience, as in the sight of God;—not preaching yourselves, but Christ Jesus the Lord, and yourselves servants to the church for his sake, alway bearing about his dying, that his life may be manifested in you;—and knowing the terror of the Lord, and deeply impressed with the account which you and your hearers must give to him of your whole conduct in the day of judgment,—awed by his infinite authority, constrained and inflamed by his love, you must persuade men, beseeching them to be reconciled unto God, and making yourselves manifest to God and to their conscience,—and, as their edification requires, changing your voice, and turning yourselves every way, and becoming all things to all men, in order to gain them to Christ,—jealous over them with a godly jealousy, in order to espouse them to him as chaste virgins,—travailing in birth, till he be formed in their hearts. You must take heed to your ministry which you have received in the Lord, that you may fulfil it;—stir up the gifts which were given you,—give yourselves wholly to reading, exhortation, and doctrine;—and perseveringly take heed to yourselves and to the doctrine which you preach, that you may save yourselves and them that hear you;—watching for their souls, as they who do, and must give an account for them to God,—rightly dividing the word of truth, and giving every man his portion in due season, faithfully warning every man with tears, night and day, teaching every man, particularly *young ones*, and labouring to present every man perfect in Christ Jesus,—and warring, not after the flesh, nor with carnal weapons, but with such as are mighty through God to the pulling down of strong holds and casting down imaginations, and subduing every thought and affection to the obedience of Christ. Having him for the end of your conversation, and holding fast the form of sound words in faith in, and love to him,—not entangling yourselves with the affairs of this life, nor ashamed of the Lord, or of his cause or prisoners, but ready to endure hardships as good soldiers of Jesus Christ, and to endure all things for the elect's sake, that they may obtain salvation with eternal glory;—ye must go forth without the camp, bearing his reproach, and, exposed as spectacles of sufferings to angels and men, must not faint under your tribulations, but feed the flock of God which he has purchased with his own blood, and over which the Holy Ghost has made you overseers,—preaching the word in season and out of season, reproving, rebuking, and exhorting with all long-suffering and doctrine,—taking the oversight of your people, not by constraint, but willingly, not for filthy lucre of worldly gain, or larger stipends, but of a ready mind,—neither as being lords over God's heritage, but as examples to the flock,—exercising yourselves to have a conscience void of offence towards God and towards man,—having a good conscience, willing in all things to live honestly,—exercised to godliness,—kindly affectioned, disinterested, holy, just, and unblameable,—prudent examples of the believers in conversation, in charity, in faith and purity,—fleeing youthful lusts, and following after righteousness, peace, faith, charity,—not striving, but being gentle unto all men,—in meekness, instructing them who oppose themselves, avoiding foolish and unlearned questions, and old wives' fables,—fleeing from perverse disputings and worldly mindedness, as most dangerous snares; and following after righteousness, godliness, faith, love, patience, meekness;—fighting the good fight of faith, and laying hold on eternal life,—keeping your trust of gospel truth and ministerial office, and, without partiality or precipitancy, committing the same to faithful men, who may be able to teach others; —and, in fine, faithfully labouring, in the Lord, to try, and confute, and censure false teachers, publicly rebuke or excommunicate open transgressors, restore such as have been overtaken in a fault in the spirit of meekness,—and having compassion on them, to pull them out of the fire, hating even the garment spotted by the flesh, and never conniving at, or partaking with any in their sins. Who is sufficient for these things? May your sufficiency be of God; and as your days are, so may your strength be, Ezek. ii. 7. iii. 9, 17—21. xxxiii. 7—9. Isa. lviii. 1. Jer. i. 17, 18. xv. 19, 20. Mic. iii. 8. Mal. ii. 6, 7. Matth. x. 16—39. xix. 28, 29. xx. 25—28. xxiii. 3---12. xxiv. 42---51. xxviii. 18---20. Acts xviii. 24---28. xx. 18---35. xxiv. 16. xxvi. 16---23. 1 Cor. ii. 1---5, 9, 12, 13. i.---v. ix. xii.---xiv. 2 Cor. ii.---vi. x.---xiii. Rom. i. 9, 16. ix. 1, 2. x. 1. xii. xv. Gal. i. 8---16. iv. 19. Eph. iii. 7, 8, 9. iv. 11---15. vi. 19, 20. Col. iv. 7, 17. i. 23---29. ii. 1, 2. 1 Thess. ii. iii. v. 12. 1 Tim. iii.---vi. 2 Tim. i.---iii. Heb. xiii. 7, 17, 18. 1 Pet. iv. 10, 11. v. 1---4. Jude 22, 23. Rev. ii. iii. xi. 3---7. xiv. 6---11.

6. See that ye take heed to your spirits, that ye deal not TREACHEROUSLY with the Lord. In approaching to, or executing the ministerial office, keep your hearts with all diligence; for out of it are the issues of eternal life, or death to yourselves and others. Building up yourselves in your most holy faith, and praying in the Holy Ghost, keep yourselves in the love of God, looking for the mercy of our Lord Jesus Christ unto eternal life. If you do not *ardently* love Christ, how can you *faithfully* and *diligently* feed his lambs—his sheep? Alas! how many precious sermons, exhortations, and instructions are quite marred and poisoned by coming through

the cold, carnal, and careless heart of the preacher, and being attended with his imprudent, untender, and lukewarm life? If you have not a deep-felt experience of the terrors of the Lord,—of the bitterness of sin, vanity of this world, and importance of eternity,—and of the conscience-quieting and heart-captivating virtue of Jesus's bleeding love, how can you be duly serious and hearty in preaching the gospel? If, all influenced by a predominate love to Christ, your heart be not fixed on everlasting things, and powerfully animated to an eager following of peace and holiness, how can you, without the most abominable treachery, declare to men their chief happiness, and the true method of obtaining it? If your graces be not kept lively, your loins girt, and your lamps burning, all enkindled by the heart-constraining love of Christ, how cold, how carnal, and blasted must your sacred ministrations be? If your work, as ambassadors of Christ, be to transact matters of everlasting importance between an infinite God and immortal, but perishing, souls of men; if the honours and privileges of it be so invaluable, what inexpressible need have you of habitual dependence on Christ by a lively faith? What self-denial, what ardent love to Christ and his Father, what disinterested regard to his honour, what compassion to souls, what prudence, what faithfulness and diligence, what humility and holy zeal, what spirituality of mind and conversation, what order, what plainness, what fervour, what just temperature of mildness and severity,—is necessary in every part of it!——If, while you minister in holy things, your lusts prevail and are indulged, you have less of real or lively Christianity than the most weak and uncircumspect saints under your charge;—if your evil heart of unbelief fearfully carry you off from the living God, and you can live unconcerned while the powerful and sanctifying presence of God is withheld from yourselves or your flocks,—how sad is your and their case!—If your indwelling pride be allowed to choose your company, your dress, your victuals, nay, your text, your subject, your order, your language;—if it be allowed to indite your thoughts, and, to the reproach and blasting of the gospel of Christ, to deck your sermon with tawdry ornaments and fancies, as if it were a stage-play, to blunt and muffle up his sharp arrows with silken smoothness and swollen bombast;—if it be allowed to kindle your fervour, and form your looks, your tone, your action;—or to render you enraptured or self-conceited, because of subsequent applause;—or sad and provoked, because your labours are contemned, how dreadful is your danger and that of your hearers! How can ministerial labours, originating in pride, spurred on by the fame of learning, diligence, or holiness,—hurt the interests of Satan, from whose influence they proceed:—If pride be allowed to cause you to envy or wound the characters of such as differ from, or outshine you, or to make you reluctant to Christian reproof from your inferiors, how fearful is your guilt and danger! Pride indulged is no more consistent with a Christian character, than drunkenness and whoredom.—— If you take up or cleave to any principle or practice in religion, in the way of factious contention, how abominable to God is the *sower of discord among brethren!* If you undervalue the peace and prosperity of the church of Christ, and are not afflicted with her in all her afflictions, how cruel and unchrist-like your conduct! If, in justly proving your opponents deceivers and blasphemers, you, by your angry manner, plead the cause of the devil, will God accept it as an offering at your hands? If you are slothful in studying or declaring the truths of Christ,—if, to save labour or expence, you are inactive or averse to help such as have no fixed ministrations, or to contrive or prosecute projects for advancing the kingdom of Christ, and promoting the salvation of men, how great is your baseness, how dreadful your hazard?—Think, as before God, did Jesus Christ furnish you for, and put you into the ministry, that you might idle away, or prostitute your devoted time, tear his church, conceal or mangle his truths, betray his interests, or starve and murder the souls of men? Are not your people the *flock of God, which he purchased with his own blood?* Will you then dare to destroy his peculiar property and portion, and attempt to frustrate the end of his death? Did Jesus die for men's souls? And will you grudge a small labour or expence to promote his honour in their eternal salvation? If the Son of God was crucified for men,—crucified for you, will you refuse, through his Spirit, to crucify your selfishness, your pride, your sloth, your worldly and covetous disposition, in order to save yourselves, and them that hear you.—While your own salvation, and the salvation of multitudes, are so deeply connected with your faithfulness and diligence,—while the powers of hell and earth so set themselves in opposition to your work, that, in your falls, they may triumph over Christ, your Master, and his church, —while so many eyes of God, angels, and men are upon you, why do you ever think or speak of eternal things, of heaven and hell, of Jesus's person, offices, righteousness, love, and free salvation, without the most serious and deep impression of their importance? While perhaps you preach your last sermon, and have before you, and on every hand of you, hundreds or scores of perishing souls, suspended over hell by the frail thread of mortal life, not knowing what a day or an hour may bring forth,—souls already in the hands of the devil, and, as it were, just departing to be with him in the lake which burns with fire and brimstone,—souls already slain by the gospel of our salvation blasted and cursed to them, partly by your means, why do not tears of deep concern mingle themselves with every point you study, every sentence you publish in the name of Christ?—When multitudes of your hearers, some of them never to hear you more, and just leaping off into the depths of hell, are, in respect of their needs, crying with an exceeding bitter cry, *Minister, help, help, we perish,—we utterly perish,—pluck the brand out of the burning fiery furnace,*—why spend your devoted time in idle visits, unedifying converse, useless reading, or unnecessary sleep?—What, if while you are so employed, some of your hearers drop into eternal flames, and begin their everlasting cursing of you for not doing more to promote their salvation? When Jesus arises to require their blood at your hand, how accursed will that knowledge appear, which was not improved for his honour who bestowed it! that ease, which issued in the damnation of multitudes!—that conformity to the world which permitted, or that unedifying converse which encouraged your hearers to sleep into hell in their sins!—that pride or luxury which restrained your charity, or disgracefully plunged you into debt!——Since, my dear pupils, all the truths of God, all the ordinances and privileges of his church,—the eternal salvation of multitudes, and the infinitely precious honour of Jesus Christ and his Father, as connected with *the present and future ages* of time, are intrusted to you, how necessary, that, like Jesus your Master, you should be faithful in all things to him who appointed you?——If you do the work of our Lord deceitfully,—in what tremendous manner shall your parents who devoted and educated you for it,—your teachers who prepared you for it,—the seminaries of learning in which you received your instruction,—the years which you spent in your studies,—all the gifts which were bestowed upon you,—all the thoughts, words, and works of God in the redemption of men,—all the oracles, commands, promises, and threatenings of God, which direct, inculcate, or enforce your duty,—all the examples of Jesus Christ, and all his apostles, prophets, and faithful ministers,—all the leaves of your Bible,—all the books of your closet,—all the engagements you have come under,—all the sermons which you preach,—all the instructions which you tender to others,—all the discipline which you exercise,—all the maintenance which you receive,—all the honours which you enjoy or expect,—all the testimonies which you give against the negligence of parents, masters, ministers, or magistrates,—all the vows and resolutions which you have made to reform,—and all the prayers which you have presented to God for assistance or success,—rise up against you as witnesses, in the day of the Lord!

7. See that ye, as workmen who need not be ashamed, earnestly labour RIGHTLY TO DIVIDE the word of truth, according to the capacities, necessities, and particular occasions of your hearers, giving every one of them their portion in due season. Never make your own ease, your inclination or honour, but the need of souls, and the glory of Christ, the regulator in your choice of subjects. Labour chiefly on the principal points of religion: To bring down the fundamental mysteries of the gospel to the capacities of

your hearers, and inculcate on their consciences the great points of union to and fellowship with Christ, regeneration, justification, and sanctification,—these will require all your grace, learning, and labour. Never aim at tickling the ears or pleasing the fancies of your hearers, but at convincing their consciences, enlightening their minds, attracting their affections, and renewing their wills, that they may be persuaded and enabled to embrace and improve Jesus Christ as freely offered to them in the gospel, for wisdom, righteousness, sanctification, and redemption. Labour to preach the law as a broken covenant,—the gospel of salvation,—and the law as a rule of life,—not only in their extensive matter, but also in their proper order and connection. It is only when they are properly connected, that the precious truths of God appear in their true lustre and glory. It is at your infinite hazard, and the infinite hazard of them that hear you, if you, even by negligence, either blend or put asunder that law and gospel which Jesus Christ has so delightfully joined together. No where is it more necessary to take heed, than in preaching up the *duties of holiness*. Let all be founded in union to and communion with Christ, all enforced by the pattern, love, righteousness, and benefits of Christ, Eph. iv. v. vi. Col. iii. iv. 1 Pet. iii. iv. See Diction. art. Gospel and Sabbath Journal.

8. You have stated yourselves public witnesses for Jesus Christ, who profess to adhere to, and propagate his *injured truths*,—and to commemorate with thankfulness the *remarkable mercies* which he has bestowed on our church and nation,—and to testify against, and mourn over our own and our fathers' *fearful backslidings* from that covenanted work of reformation once attained in our land. See that ye be judicious, upright, constant, and faithful in your profession. I now approach death, heartily satisfied with our excellent Westminster *Confession of Faith, Catechisms,* and *Form of church-government,*—and cordially adhering to these *Covenants,* by which our fathers solemnly bound themselves and their posterity to profess the doctrines and practise the duties therein contained. I look upon the Secession as in-

deed the cause of God, but sadly mismanaged and dishonoured by myself and others. Alas! for that pride, passion, selfishness, and unconcern for the glory of Christ, and spiritual edification of souls, which has so often prevailed!—Alas! for our want of due meekness, gentleness, holy zeal, self-denial, hearty grief for sin, compassion to souls in immediate connection with us, or left in the established church, which became distinguished witnesses for Christ. Alas! that we did not chiefly strive to *pray better, preach better,* and *live better* than our neighbours.—Study to see every thing with your own eyes, but never indulge an itch after novelties: most of those which are now esteemed such, are nothing but *old errors* which were long ago justly refuted, varnished over with some new expressions. Never, by your peevishness, contentions, eagerness about worldly things, or the like, make others think lightly of the cause of God among your hands. If I mistake not, the churches are entering into a fearful cloud of apostacy and trouble. But he that endures to the end shall be saved. Be ye faithful unto the death, and Christ shall give you a crown of life. But if any man draw back, God's soul shall have no pleasure in him.

9. Always improve and live on that blessed encouragement which is offered to you as Christians and ministers in the gospel. Let all your wants be on Christ. *My God shall supply all your need, according to his riches in glory by Christ Jesus.* Cast all your cares on him, for he careth for you. Cast all your burdens on him, and he will sustain you. If your holy services, through your mismanagement, occasion your uncommon guilt, his blood *cleanseth from all sin.* You have an *Advocate with the Father, Jesus Christ the righteous, who is the propitiation for your sins.* If you be often difficulted how to act, he hath said, *The meek will he guide in judgment: the meek will he teach his way.—I will instruct thee, and teach thee in the way which thou shalt go. I will guide thee with mine eye set upon thee. I will lead the blind in a way which they know not.*—If you be much discouraged because of your rough way and your want of strength, he has said, *When the poor and needy seek water and there is none,*

and their tongue faileth for thirst, I the Lord will hear them, I the God of Israel will not forsake them. I will open rivers in high places. Fear not, for I am with thee: be not dismayed, for I am thy God. I will strengthen thee: Yea, I will help thee: I will uphold thee with the right hand of my righteousness. Fear not, worm Jacob,—I will help thee, saith the Lord thy Redeemer. I will make thee a new sharp thrashing instrument, and thou shalt thrash the mountains. My grace shall be sufficient for thee: for my strength is made perfect in weakness. As thy days are, so shall thy strength be.—If your troubles be many, he hath said, *When thou passest through the waters I will be with thee:—the rivers shall not overflow thee: When thou walkest through the fire, thou shalt not be burnt, nor shall the flame kindle upon thee.*—If your incomes be small and pinching, *Ye know the grace of our Lord Jesus Christ, that though he was rich, yet for our sakes he became poor, that we through his poverty might be rich. He shall see his seed,—the travail of his soul, and be satisfied:* and he has promised, *I will abundantly bless her provision, and satisfy her poor with bread. I will satiate the soul of her priests with fatness.* A salary of remarkable fellowship with Christ, and of success in winning souls, is the most delightful and enriching.—If your labours appear to have little success, be the more diligent and dependent on Christ. *Never mourn as they that have no hope.* Let not *the eunuch say, I am a dry tree.* Jesus hath said, *I will pour water on him that is thirsty, and floods on the dry ground. I will pour my Spirit on thy seed, and my blessing on thine offspring. A seed shall serve him. The whole earth shall be filled with his glory. The kingdoms of this world shall become the kingdoms of our Lord and his Christ.* Believe it on the testimony of God himself: believe it on the testimony of all his faithful servants; and, if mine were of any avail, I should add it, That there is no Master so kind as Christ; no service so pleasant and profitable as that of Christ; and no reward so full, satisfying, and permanent as that of Christ. Let us, therefore, *begin all things from Christ; carry on all things with and through Christ; and let all things aim at and end in Christ.*

CONTENTS.

BOOK I.

Of the Regulating Standard of Religion.

CHAPTER I. Of the *Law of Nature*, as correspondent with the nature of man its subject, and of God its author; chief end of obedience to it; its matter and form; duty required by it, religion towards God :—Virtue, personal, and social towards men,—kindness, —equity,—truth,—relative duties respecting married persons, children, servants,—civil societies:—Advantages of religion and virtue, - - - - - - - - - - - - - - - Page 1—29

CHAP. II. Of the *insufficiency of the law*, and *especially of the light of nature*, to conduct men to true and lasting felicity, because of its obscurity, inefficacy, deficiency, and unsuitableness to the condition of sinful men, - - - - - - - - - - - - - 29—39

CHAP. III. Of the *revealed standard* of religion contained in the *scriptures* of the Old and New Testament, in the possibility, desirableness, necessity, propriety, reasonableness, credibility, divine authority, perspicuity, perfection, contents, and means of explaining it, - - - - - - - - - - - - - - - - - - 39—98

BOOK II.

Of GOD, the *Author, Object, and End of all Religion*.

CHAP. I. Of God's *names, nature, and perfections*, knowledge, wisdom, power, sovereignty, holiness, justice, goodness, and truth; self-existence, independence, simplicity, infinity, eternity, unchangeableness, unity, and subsistence in three distinct persons, 99—130

CHAP. II. Of *Persons in the Godhead*, what they are; their characteristics, plurality, and being precisely THREE.—Proofs of the distinct personality and equal supreme deity of the Father, the Son, and the Holy Ghost; and how they are distinguished.—General observations concerning this mystery, - - - - 130—146

CHAP. III. Of the *decrees of God;* what they are; their exact correspondence to his works of creation and providence; their objects; their properties; principal contents of *election* and *reprobation* of particular angels and men, - - - - - - - - - 147—170

CHAP. IV. Of God's *execution of his decrees* in his *creating* of all things, particularly angels and men; and his upholding and governing them in his *providence*, natural, miraculous, moral, and peculiar, - - - - - - - - - - - - - - - 170—191

CONTENTS.

BOOK III.

OF THE COVENANT BONDS OF RELIGIOUS CONNECTION BETWEEN GOD AND MEN.

CHAP. I. Of the *covenant of works;* its nature; reality; parties; parts; condition; promise; penalty; seals.—That it was broken; by what means, and in what respects; breach chargeable on all men; in what respect this covenant remains in force; all men naturally under it; what power it has over them; how it is administered in God's execution of his curse upon them, in their soul, body, person, or relative concerns, in time and through eternity,
Page 192—225

CHAP. II. Of the *covenant of grace.* Propriety of God's recovering part of mankind; necessity of a new covenant in order to it.—Occasion; origin; date; parties; making it; parts; condition, and promise; but not a penalty;—ought not to be divided into two.—The administration of it by Christ as the Trustee, Testator, and Executor of it, in the characters of Intercessor, Prophet, and King.——Its properties: Who are personally instated in it;—how sinful men are, by means of the word and Spirit of God, and by faith, instated in it, and improve their fixed state in it, - - - 226—255

BOOK IV.

OF CHRIST, THE MEDIATOR OF THE COVENANT OF GRACE.

CHAP. I. Of Christ's *Mediatorial Person.*—Requisites of the Mediator.—Reason and time of the Son of God's becoming man.—Jesus of Nazareth, the true Messiah and Most High God, assumed a true manhood; formation of his manhood, and union to his divine person; pretended and true effects of this union; necessity of his being God and man in one person.—The grace of his person God-Man, and its relative glory, as connected with the nature, perfections, purposes, covenants, and revealed truths of God, and with believers' graces, exercises, fellowship with God, worship of him, and obedience to him, - - - - - - - - - - 256—279

CHAP. II. Of Christ's *general and particular offices:*—His anointing:—His being a reconciling *Mediator,* according to both natures, only for men; *only* Mediator between God and men:—His particular offices, and their order:—His *prophetical* office proved; his fitness for it; and his personal and mediate execution of it: the transcendent excellence, and the effects of his instructions:—Truth and peculiar honours of his *priesthood;* matter, oblation, necessity, propriety, and perfection of his *sacrifice* to satisfy God's law and justice; effects produced by it; offered for elect men:—His *intercession,* its necessity, nature, and efficacy.—His Mediatorial *royalty* explained and proved: extent, spirituality, and everlasting duration of his kingdom:—His kingdom of power, of grace, and of glory; and his management of each, - - - - - 280—316

CHAP. III. Of Christ's *States:*—His *humiliation,* in being made under the law, and having its curse executed upon him; necessity

CONTENTS.

of it, and honours attending it:—His *exaltation* mixed,—and unmixed in his resurrection from the dead, ascension to heaven, sitting at his Father's right-hand, and coming to judge the world,—preparation for,—the judgment itself,—and execution of the sentences passed:—Necessity of Christ's exaltation, - - - Page 316—335

BOOK V.

OF THE PRINCIPAL BLESSINGS OF THE COVENANT OF GRACE.

CHAP. I. Of UNION *with Christ*:—Its necessity; kinds; similitudes; illustration; and production of it by the external CALL of the gospel, and almighty influence of the Holy Ghost in EFFECTUAL CALLING:—effect of it, communion with Christ, - - 336—358

CHAP. II. Of JUSTIFICATION; its true nature; objects; contents; perfection at first; delightful influence through Christ's bearing the curse; ground of it, not men's grace or good works, but Christ's surety-righteousness, imputed by God, and received by faith, 358—393

CHAP. III. Of ADOPTION, in its nature; objects; honours; privileges; date; mean; and marks, - - - - - - - 393—397

CHAP. IV. Of SANCTIFICATION; its meaning; importance; double form; necessity; difference from, and connection with justification; causes; standard; pattern; contents of *inherent graces, Christian tempers*, and *holy exercises;* imperfection in this life; not meritorious.—Rules for promoting it, - - - - - - 398—437

CHAP. V. Of SPIRITUAL CONSOLATION; conservation and perseverance in grace; indwelling of the Holy Ghost as an almighty Comforter; sensible assurance of God's love and friendship; peace of conscience; joy in the Holy Ghost, - - - - - - 437—446

CHAP. VI. Of Believers' GLORIFICATION in this life; at death; at the last day; and through all eternity, - - - - - 446—449

BOOK VI.

OF THE EXTERNAL DISPENSATION OF THE COVENANT OF GRACE, BY THE LAW, THE GOSPEL, &c.

CHAP. I. Of the LAW of God; its nature; kinds; permanency; manifestation; qualities; obedience to it summarily considered; order of commandments; rules of understanding them; duties required and sins forbidden in each:—threefold form of the moral law; and its several uses to men, to sinners, and to saints, - 450—500

CHAP. II. Of the GOSPEL of Christ, in its matter, uses, differences from, and connections with the moral law, - - - - 500—517

CHAP. III. Of the INSTITUTED ORDINANCES of the covenant of grace:—*Reading; meditation; preaching* and *hearing* God's word; *spiritual conference; prayer; ministerial blessing; singing of psalms; vowing; fasting; thanksgiving;* sacraments of BAPTISM and the LORD'S SUPPER.—*Harmony* and *difference* between those under the Old Testament and those under the New, - - - - 517—549

BOOK VII.

Of the Church or Society, for, and to which, the Covenant of Grace is dispensed.

CHAP. I. Of the *nature, formation,* and *fellowship* of the Christian Church, - - - - - - - - - - - - - - - 550—556

CHAP. II. Of *Church-power,* and the *subjects* in which it resides, head and officers, - - - - - - - - - - - - 556—570

CHAP. III. Of ecclesiastical *judicatories,* their divine warrant, work, and censures, - - - - - - - - - - - - - - 570—576

A COMPENDIOUS VIEW OF NATURAL AND REVEALED RELIGION.

BOOK I.

OF THE REGULATING STANDARD OF RELIGION, NATURAL AND REVEALED.

CHAP. I.

Of the LAW of NATURE.

AS the law of nature must necessarily correspond with the nature of God, who imposeth it, and of men, who are subjected to it, and with their relations to each other; these must be carefully considered, in order to our obtaining a proper knowledge of it.

Beginning with our *own nature*, as next to us:—We can form no idea of a *substance* distinct from its most obvious essential qualities, as they are necessarily included in every adequate conception of it.—— By reflection upon that which passeth in our own minds, we obtain the simple idea of *thought*, and so conceive of SPIRITS as *thinking substances:* and, by sensation, we perceive body to be a *solid* and *extended* SUBSTANCE. Thus knowing the *essential properties* of spirits as well as of bodies, and being incapable to comprehend the inward constitution of both, we have at least as much certainty of the existence of spirits as of bodies,—though by our more habitual attention to the surface of matter, we are apt to imagine, that we more thoroughly understand its nature.

From inward consciousness, and from our observation of the actings of others around us, we perceive, that the *human soul* is a spirit endowed with powers of *perception, judging,* and *reasoning,* as well as of recollecting and retaining ideas;—and with a power of *willing,* choosing, desiring, *delighting* in, or disliking and hating;—and even a power of moving at least the external parts of our body by means of the nerves,—and of receiving impressions from them, when objects around appear *rare, good,* or *evil.* Nevertheless, it must not be imagined, that our *understanding* and *will* are *different parts* of our soul, but are the same soul considered as exercising *different powers.*

It is evident that our soul is most closely *united* with our body, though we cannot comprehend the mode of it. Motions in our brain and nerves excite ideas in our mind; and passions in our soul excite motions in our body. The indisposition of our body often disqualifieth our mind for exercising its powers in a regular and lively manner. In sleep, in frenzies of our brain, or in some nervous distempers, our mind acts in a disorderly manner.—On the other hand, intense thinking disqualifies our body for acute and ready sensation.—But we cannot determine whether human souls be formed with different degrees of spiritual powers; or, whether the difference of capacity observable among men ariseth from the different constitution of their bodies, and climates in which they live. Nor can we say, whether our soul is immediately united with and resides in the *brain,* in which, 1. All these nerves on which our sensation depends, do terminate. 2. All the diseases that deprive us of our sensation are seated. 3. A small disorder in the brain renders the agency of the soul very weak or irregular, as in the case of idiots and madmen. 4. When any nerve is cut or hard tied, it retains its sensation only in that part which is next to the brain. 5. If our brain be lost or sore wounded, our life ceaseth:—Or, whether the soul be immediately united to and reside in the *heart,* in which the last remains of life are perceived.

Some learned men contend, That all our ideas of material objects are produced by *sensation,* and our ideas of spiritual objects by *reflection,* the latter rectifying the mistakes of the former;—and that we have no *innate ideas,* as we gradually acquire new ideas; and can form none of sensible objects, without the exercise of the correspondent senses of seeing, hearing, smelling, tasting, or touching. Others contend, That all our ideas have their origin in our mind itself; and that our sensation and reflection are no more than means of exciting them. ——It is certain, that our mind cannot forbear assenting to several primary axioms of knowledge: as, *that nothing can be, and not be, at the same time; that nothing can give that which it hath not; that there is a God,* &c. It is no less certain, that the same external qualities of objects often excite different ideas in different persons; or, in the same persons at different times.

OF THE LAW OF NATURE. 3

That which is pleasant, comely, &c. to one, may be disagreeable to another, or even to the same person at another time.

Some contend, That human souls neither do, nor can exist *without actual thinking*, any more than bodies can exist *without extension*, and that no soul can awaken or excite itself to the *actual exercise* of thought. Others maintain, That they can cease from thinking for a time, as in deep sleep, strong apoplectic or paralytic distempers,—as infants, who have few ideas, sleep much.——It is certain, that in our present mortal state our soul thinks worst when it seems most abstracted from our body, as in dreams, &c. and that *personal identity* cannot consist in *continued consciousness* of thinking or of the same actions; for, none are conscious of their lying in their mother's womb or of their being born, and nevertheless were the *same persons* as they are afterward at full age: But it must consist in our having the same soul united with a body, which is the same in some essential respects.——No wonder that I know so little of God, when the most learned men appear to know so little of themselves. Never let me dare to make my weak and indistinct perceptions a standard for judging of his unbounded excellencies.

The human MEMORY is an intellectual power of *recollecting* or *retaining* our ideas, and is called *good*, when it quickly recollects and strongly retains them. Its condition much depends on that of our body, whether it be in health, free from sleep, &c. It is best in youth, or when we are brisk and lively; or, when our ideas are attended with remarkable pleasure or pain. Nay, the pleasure or pain which attends our ideas, when conceived in our mind, renders our time or duration sensible shorter or longer. A violent blow upon the head, which disorders the brain, sometimes erazeth all former ideas, that nothing which hath been experienced can be remembered.

The AFFECTIONS or PASSIONS of the human soul are its dispositions toward, or in opposition to, those objects of which it thinks. They originate from, or are exerted by sensation or reflection;—by ideas recollected, or by apprehensions of approaching good or evil: and cannot be excited, or hindered, by an act of our will, any more than the internal parts of our body can be governed by it.—They are diversified and distinguished into love, hatred, joy, grief, hope, fear, wonder, astonishment, &c. according as the objects which excite them appear to us *good, evil, rare, dreadful*, &c: and according to the apprehended *degrees* of that goodness, evil, or rarity, &c. and according to the apprehended presence, absence, or futurity of these objects.

An *acquired mental habit* is that easiness and readiness of thinking or willing in such a particular manner, which is produced by frequency of thinking and willing in that form. It depends much on our memory's furnishing us with recollected ideas, and with views of the relation between causes and effects, antecedents and consequents, &c. and on its readily presenting the motives which influence us to such particular forms of thinking. Hence, if our memory be weakened or ruined, so, ordinarily, are our mental habits.

FREEDOM of WILL is either *natural*, when we are not invincibly determined in our choice towards this or that particular thing; or *external*, when no forcible restraint put on our body or mind, hinders our choice; or *philosophical*, when we have a prevalent disposition to act according to the dictates of our reason; or *moral*, when no superior, by his forbidding or commanding authority, interferes in the regulation of our acts.—— Our common and continued consciousness, that we have by nature a *liberty of choice*, or of acting agreeably to our own apprehensions or inclinations;—our frequent preferring of one thing to another, even without well knowing why we do so; and the rewardableness and punishableness of our actions by God, plainly manifest that we have this *freedom of choice* in our will.

The human soul is *immediately* created by God in that very act which unites it to its respective body. No man ever remembered of his being in a pre-existent state, in which, had it been, it behoved his unembodied soul to have been very active. It is absurd to pretend, that it pre-existed in animalcules of generating matter. The existence of such, or the formation of the human body from them, hath never been proved; nor can be, without supposing a stifling or extinction of millions of souls in the conception of every infant.

The human soul is *immortal*, existing and acting in a future state. 1. It is immaterial. Thoughts, even about the most trivial objects, can never proceed from matter, be it formed, figured, and circumstantiated as it will. 2. Equity requires that men be rendered happy or miserable, according as they are virtuous or vicious. Since, therefore, there is so little obvious difference between the righteous and wicked in their present life in this world, there must be a future, an eternal state, in which every man shall receive the reward of his conduct. 3. The inward joys which attend virtue in this life cannot sufficiently and openly vindicate God's present form of providence, in prospering the wicked and afflicting the virtuous. 4. Good men, especially under sufferings, are encouraged in virtue by the prospects of a future, an eternal reward of it. 5. Human souls being formed capable of great improvements, and having an eager desire after happiness, it cannot be thought that they were thus formed merely for their transient, and almost half brutal condition in this world. 6. Men have *generally*, if not *universally*, believed the existence of a future state, even when it promised little happiness to themselves. On this belief much of their idolatry, necromancy, &c. depended. 7. Since men's consciences chiefly impress them with the apprehensions of future rewards and punishments, it is inconsistent with God's infinite wisdom, equity, and truth, that there should be nothing at all answerable to these apprehensions. 8. If there were no future state of rewards and punishments, wicked men would have it in their power to rob the virtuous of much of their reward by quickly murdering them;—and to prevent God's punishment of vice, by quickly dispatching themselves or their fellows in wickedness.——Nor would it be proper that God should be obliged, by miraculous preservation, to prevent their robbing others of, or avoiding themselves, their correspondent reward.

The EXISTENCE OF GOD is no less evident than our own. 1. All nations, Heathens, Jews, Mahometans, and Christians, harmoniously consent that there is a God, who created, preserves, and governs all things. Even the most stupid Hottentots, Saldanians, Greenlanders, Kamtchatkans, and savage Americans, are, upon the most accurate inspection, found to believe this.—This persuasion of the existence of God is least discernable where, and in those, that through ignorance are almost similar to beasts, which plainly manifests it to be an inseparable ingredient of Reason.——Now, what prejudice of fear, of fancy, or of education, could answer the taste of every nation, every person, in every age of the world, in favour of this persuasion, if it were not well founded? How could any one Prince impose it on all men? Or, When and where did several princes meet to contrive and establish it? Or, If princes or priests imposed the belief of this on others, as a state-trick to keep them in awe, how came they also to believe it themselves? 2. There is a natural impression of the existence of God on the minds of all men, *i. e.* an indistinct idea of a *Being of infinite perfection*, and a readiness to acquiesce in the truth of his existence, whenever they understand the terms in which it is expressed. Whence can this impression proceed, but from the power of truth itself, even in the minds of such, whose affections and carnal interests dispose them to believe the contrary? 3. The creation of all things plainly manifests the existence of God. The innumerable alterations and manifold dependence, every where observable in the world, manifest that the things which exist in it, neither are, nor could be, *from eternity:*—It is self-evident, that they never could form themselves out of nothing, or in any of their respective forms: and that CHANCE, being nothing but the *want of design*, never did, nor could, form or put into order any thing, far less such a marvellous and well connected system as our world is.——Though we should absurdly fancy MATTER to be *eternal*, yet it could not change its own form, or produce Life or Reason, nothing being capable to confer that which it hath not in itself, either formally or virtually. Moreover, when we consider the diversified and marvellous forms of creatures in the world, and how exactly their forms and stations correspond with their respective ends and uses;—when we consider the marvellous and exact machinery, form, and motions of our own bodies, and especially when we consider the powers of our soul,—its desires after an infinite good, and its close union with, and incomprehensible operations on our bodies, we are obliged by the light of evidence to admit a Creator of infinite wisdom, and power, and goodness.—— Though we can conceive a succession, a very long succession of animal production, we cannot conceive how that production could be effected by the animals themselves, independently of any other; and still less, how that successive production could extend unto a proper eternity, or commence without the agency of a self-existent, self-sufficient, almighty, infinitely wise and benevolent Creator.—It is further observable, that a tradition of the Beginning of the world hath every where prevailed among mankind. 4. The providential upholding and government of all things;—the motions of the heavenly luminaries, exactly calculated for the greatest advantage of our earth, and its inhabitants;—the exact balancing and regulating of the meteors, winds, rain, snow, hail, vapour, thunder, and the like;— the regular and never-failing returns of summer and winter, seed-time and harvest, day and night;—the astonishing and diversified formation of vegetables,—the propagation of herbs, almost every where, that are most effectual to heal the distempers of animal bodies in that place;—the almost infinite diversification of animals and vegetables, and their pertinents, that, notwithstanding an amazing similarity, not any two are exactly alike; but every form, member, even feather or hair of animals, and every pile of grass, stalk of corn, herb, leaf, tree, berry, or other fruit, hath something peculiar to itself;—the making of animals so sagaciously to prepare their lodgings, defend themselves, provide for their health, produce, protect, and procure food for their young;—the direction of fishes and fowls to, and in such marvellous and long peregrinations, at such seasons, and to such places as best correspond with their own preservation and the benefit of mankind:—the stationing of brute animals by sea or land, at lesser or greater distances, as is most suited to the safety, subsistence, or comfort of mankind,—and preventing the increase of prolific animals, which are hurtful, and making the less fruitful ones, which are useful, exceedingly to abound;—the so diversifying the countenances, voices, and hand-writings of men, as best secures and promotes their social advantages;—the holding of so equal a balance between males and females, while the number of males, whose lives are peculiarly endangered in war, navigation, &c. is generally greatest;—the prolonging of men's lives when the world needed to be peopled, and now shortening them when that necessity hath ceased to exist;—the almost universal provision of food, raiment, medicine, fuel, &c. answerable to the nature of particular places, cold or hot, moist or dry;—the management of human affairs relative to societies, government, peace, war, trade, &c. in a manner different from, and contrary to, the carnal policy of those concerned;—and especially the strangely similar, but diversified, erection, preservation, and government of the Jewish and Christian churches,—clearly manifest the existence of an infinitely wise, patient, and good God, who preserves and governs the world, and every thing in it. 5. The miraculous events which have happened in the world, such as the overflowing of the earth by a flood,—the confusion of languages,—the burning of Sodom and the cities about by fire and brimstone from heaven,—the plagues of Egypt,—the dividing of the Red Sea,—raining manna from heaven, and bringing streams of water from flinty rocks;—the stopping of the course of the sun,—quenching of the violence of fire,—shutting of the mouths of hungry lions,—raising of the dead,—healing of diseases, even the most desperate, without any application of natural remedies,—terrible apparitions in the air, or on the earth, before the overthrow of cities or nations,—also irrefragably demonstrate the existence of God. 6. His existence no less clearly appears from the exact fulfilment of so many, and so particularly circumstantiated predictions, published long before the events took place, viz. predictions concerning mankind in general;—the descendants of Noah, Lot, and Abraham;—Canaanites, Syrians, Assyrians, Chaldeans, Persians, Greeks, Romans,—Arabs, Turks,——Jesus Christ; Antichrist; New Testament church. It is impossible that these predictions, which were so exactly fulfilled in their respective periods, and of the fulfilment of which there are, at present, thousands of demonstrative and sensible documents in the world, could proceed from any but an all-seeing, and infinitely wise, and almighty Governor of the world. 7. The existence of God further appears from the fearful punishments which have been inflicted upon persons, and especially upon nations, when their immoralities became excessive, and that by very unexpected means and instruments,—as in the drowning of the old world,—destruction of Sodom and Gomorrah,—plagues of Pharaoh and his servants,—overthrow of Sennacherib and his army,—miseries and ruin of the Canaanites, Jews, Syrians, Assyrians, Chaldeans, Persians, Egyptians, Greeks, Romans, Saracens, Turks, Tartars, and others. 8. The existence of God may be further argued from the terror and dread which wound the consciences of men, when guilty of crimes, which other men do not know, or are not able to punish or restrain; as in the case of Caligula, Nero, and Domitian, Roman emperors; and while they earnestly labour to persuade themselves, or others, that there is no God. Hence their dread of thunder, or to be alone in the dark, &c.

This God, who maketh, upholds, and governs all things, must necessarily be SELF-EXISTENT, INDEPENDENT, and absolutely ETERNAL. Being the cause of every thing besides himself, he can neither be produced by them, nor depend on them.—As he existed before, and gave being to every one of them, he must be all-sufficient in, of, and to, himself, and to each of them.—None of them, particularly man, whose origination is so late,—whose dependence on inferior creatures is so great,—whose form of body and temper of mind are so changeable, can profit Him, who is the Universal Maker and Manager of ALL things.

God is UNCHANGEABLE. Being *self-existent* and *absolutely eternal*, he can have no principle of change in himself. The existence, essence, and agency, of all other beings being derived from Him, none of them can, in the least, operate towards any change in, or of Him.—Without supposing Him to have been once deficient, and so not God, He cannot be changed to the better. Without becoming deficient, and so ceasing to be God, He cannot be changed to the worse.—Both are equally absurd.

God is ALMIGHTY. 1. He hath never shewed any mark of weakness. 2. He made, upholds, and governs multitudes of creatures, nay of mighty creatures. 3. By the influence of his power, even in an act of his will, he made all things of nothing; and by it he upholds and governs them. 4. His power cannot be limited *from within* himself, as he is *all-sufficient;* nor from without himself, as all the power of creatures proceeds from, and is subordinated to him, and oweth its whole efficacy in the production of effects to his concurrent influence. No creature can retain or exert any power, independently of God, without becoming God, and so depriving him of his godhead:——and no effect can exist without his willing of it.

God is INFINITE. 1. Being self-existent and independent, he is as great, in every respect, *as he can be.* 2. All creatures depending on him, none of them can set bounds to his excellency. 3. His upholding and governing of all creatures necessari-

ly requires his presence with them all, and every where. 4. Being from all eternity, his nature is infinite in duration, and so must necessarily be infinite in every other excellency. 5. His forming of all things from nothing, necessarily required an *infinity* of wisdom, power, and goodness;—the distance between *nothingness* and their present existence being *infinite.*
———The belief of God's infinity, instead of discouraging, strongly encourageth us to the diligent contemplation of Him, —as much important and delightful truth concerning him, may be known, though he can never be fully and comprehensively known by us.

God is INCOMPREHENSIBLE in his excellency, purposes, and works. 1. We have but very imperfect knowledge of ourselves,—What our soul or our body is;—and how the one is united to, or acts upon the other;—how our ideas are treasured up or recollected in our memory;—whether we always think or not;—how dreams are produced;—how all the difficulties relative to human liberty may be solved;—how our nerves affect our soul in frenzies;—how we breathe;—how the motion of our blood and muscles is effected, &c. Nay, we cannot so much as discern the inward substance, or all the properties, of any creatures.—How absurd then the hope to have comprehensive conceptions of the infinite excellencies of God! 2. God's perfections are infinitely superior to those of creatures, even where there is some similarity between them. 3. In his *self-existence, absolute eternity, omnipresence,* of which we certainly know him to be possessed, and his being determined to act from himself, God is infinitely unlike to us, as well as infinitely transcends our comprehension. 4. No reason of ours can controvert, but God may have in his nature millions of excellencies or perfections which are not in the least marked in his works of creation or common providence.

There is but ONE GOD. 1. The light of nature affords no marks of a plurality of Gods. 2. The remarkable unity of design which appears in the works of creation and providence, manifest, that the Creator and manager of all things is but ONE. 3. As God necessarily possesseth infinite excellency, no independent excellency is left to any other. 4. One Being of infinite perfection being sufficient for the making and management of all things,—no necessary and self-existence, and so no godhead, is left for another. 5. God being unchangeable, he can have no rival or competitor of equal power or wisdom.

God is a SPIRIT possessed of an infinite understanding and will. 1. Of necessity it behoved him to be self-moved in the creation of all things. 2. The form of every creature, and of all taken together, plainly manifests deep thought exercised in the contrivance and formation of them. 3. Nothing material could produce such thought, or form such thinking substances, as we find ourselves to be. 4. Nothing but a spiritual and incorporeal substance could be every where present to uphold and govern all things.—Hence it follows, That though God may appear in a visible form, his nature is not visible, nor ought any human passions to be ascribed to him; for, 1. Some passions, as Fear or Grief, &c. imply weakness and present imperfection in happiness. 2. The excitement or operation of our passions is inseparably connected with some commotion of our animal nature.

God hath a perfect KNOWLEDGE of himself and all things else. 1. He is an infinite Spirit, and therefore must have an understanding infinitely extensive. 2. He makes, upholds, and governs all things,—and therefore must necessarily know his own fulness of excellency and influence, and their respective conditions, and the most proper manner of adapting his influences to them, answerably to their need and advantage. 3. To suppose him ignorant of any thing, would reflect dishonour on him unworthy of godhead.——He knows *future contingencies.* 1. If he knew them not, his wisdom and knowledge must be gradually enlarged, as these events shall occur, which is contrary to his infinity and unchangeableness. 2. Without the exact knowledge of them, he could not have exactly foretold them, as he hath often done. 3. If he knew them not, his providential regulations concerning them, and every thing connected with them, must depend on the free will of his rational creatures, or even on mere chance. 4. If sagacious men shrewdly foresee future events, how can they be in any respect hid from God, our infinitely wise Maker, preserver, and governor?

God is infinitely WISE. 1. In creation he hath clearly formed all things most answerable to their manifold and diversified ends. 2. In providence every thing is so managed, as to accomplish the most important purposes, and to promote the most important ends: and great events are effected by the most unlikely means. 3. There is not the least mark of folly or weakness of judgment in any thing he doth.

God is perfectly HOLY, and his nature infinitely contrary to all impurity and vice. 1. There is real virtue found among his rational creatures, which must necessarily originate from him. 2. Holiness is the highest perfection of rational creatures, rendering them happy in themselves, and amiable and useful to others. 3. God, having a perfect knowledge of all the relations of things one to another, cannot deviate from holiness, through ignorance. 4. Being infinitely powerful, God hath nothing to deter or hinder him from the possession or pursuit of holiness. 5. Being perfectly happy in himself, he hath nothing to expect by the indulgence of moral evil. 6. Having therefore no temptations to unholiness, he could not without drawing on himself the most uneasy reflections and the highest dishonour, altogether inconsistent with godhead, indulge it in the least, or in any respect deviate from moral rectitude.

God is infinitely GOOD and BENEVOLENT, inclined to promote the happiness of his creatures, in every proper form and method. 1. Much goodness and benevolent instinct is to be found among his creatures, in this world. 2. Innumerable instances of kindness to his creatures appear in his providence. 3. We know of no bad thing in this world, from which real good may not be extracted: nor have we any evidence that God would have permitted *moral evil*, if he had not intended to bring good out of it. 4. All the evil which we observe in this world, originates from men's abuse of the freedom of their own will. And if men by their own fault introduce moral evil, that penal evil, which follows, becomes a real good to God's creatures in general,—even as the punishment of malefactors is necessary for the real advantage of a state. 5. God may be good, nay, infinitely good, though he be not bound to render every creature happy to the uttermost. A magistrate may be very good and benevolent, though he do not adopt all his subjects to be his children or heirs. 6. Reason admits that there may be many and large regions of creation, perfectly free from all evil, moral or penal, and that this world in its present situation is good enough for sinful men. 7. Benevolence and goodness, being the glory of rational creatures, must also be the glory of the godhead. 8. Being self-sufficient, GOD can have no reason or temptation to promote the causeless misery of his subjects, nor can his perfections and happiness admit of his having any inclination, or making any attempt towards it.

As God's making and upholding of all things necessarily infer his right to be their sole *supreme governor*,—He is perfectly JUST in all his dealings with men. 1. He imposeth no law upon them, but that which originally they had full power to obey. 2. Equity therefore requires, that He, as their Supreme Governor, should treat them with kindness or severity, as their virtue or their vice demands. 3. Having no temptation to it, God cannot act unjustly without defiling his nature, and dishonouring himself to the uttermost, which is absolutely incompetent with godhead. 4. Already, in manifold instances, we see the virtuous rewarded and the wicked punished. 5. Though some of God's dispensations of providence appear to smile on the wicked and frown on the virtuous, yet it must be admitted, that we often mistake with respect to men's real characters, and that we are apt to think there is a great deal more happiness in ease, wealth, or honour, and more unhappiness in afflictions, than really is

6. A future eternity of rewards or punishments may sufficiently balance any apparent inequality of providences in this life.

God is perfectly TRUE, sincere in all his declarations, and inviolably faithful to all his engagements of promises or threatenings. 1. His holiness in himself, and his goodness and equity toward his creatures, require such candour and faithfulness. 2. All the sincerity, truth, and faithfulness, or disposition of heart or conscience to approve it, found among rational creatures, necessarily originate from God. 3. God hath no temptation to dissimulation, falsehood, or treachery; and hence could not indulge it in his conduct, without an inconceivable vitiosity of nature, absolutely inconsistent with godhead.

From these views of the nature of God and man, and of the relations betwixt them, it necessarily follows, that his honour and our enjoyment of him ought to be aimed at, as our CHIEF END, in every thing we do,—in due subordination to which the advancement or maintenance of our own life, health, honour, pleasure, or profit, may and ought to be intended.—— The CHIEF GOOD proper to be proposed for the end of our conduct must necessarily be desirable in itself;—must be complete, including deliverance from all evil, and the fruition of all possible felicity;—must be sufficient to satisfy all reasonable desires, and render its possessors perfect in every thing truly excellent;— must be of infinite value and usefulness, capable to render all men happy at once;—and must be evidently eternal, that there may be no ground to fear that it should fail or he lost.——It is therefore manifest, that *riches* cannot be this *chief good*, as they are not desirable for themselves,—do not enter into our souls,—do not render men either virtuous or happy,—nor is the enjoyment of them either certain or perpetual. Nor can worldly *honours* be this *chief good*,—as we have not these so much in ourselves, as in the imagination of others: nor doth the enjoyment of them render us either better or safer; nor is it either certain or permanent. Nor can *bodily pleasures* be this *chief good*,—as these are often inconsistent with our true honour and usefulness, and enervate and corrupt our body while they weaken and vitiate our mind. Nor can *knowledge* be this *chief good*, as, of itself, it neither renders men virtuous nor happy. It cannot protect from a multitude of real evils; nor is the permanent continuance of it certain. Nor can even *virtue* itself be this *chief good*, as, though it render our mind better, and make us more useful in the world, it doth not exempt us from a multitude of real disasters, inward or outward.——It therefore remains, that God alone, who is infinitely perfect,—desirable in himself,—sufficient to render all rational creatures happy,—and is absolutely unfading and eternal,—of whom the full enjoyment includes perfect freedom from all evil, and possession of every thing good,—and so necessarily renders us perfect in virtue, honour, and happiness,—must be our CHIEF GOOD.

FROM the preceding hints concerning our own nature, and the nature of God, and our absolute dependence on him as our Creator, Preserver, and Governor,—it is no less manifest, that the *declared will* of God as our moral Governor, must be the *sole standard* and *rule* of all our qualities and actions, religious and moral; and that there can be no lawful authority in the world, but what is *derived* from him, and that no laws or engagements of men can bind themselves or others, but *in subordination* to his authority and will.——By virtue of the perfection of his nature, God cannot but will that we should be and act in agreeableness to those relations, in which we stand connected with himself, or with our fellow-creatures. Such deportment is manifestly reasonable, comely, profitable, and honourable. But, some things which are very proper and necessary in some circumstances, may be very unfit and even vicious in other circumstances. That which is proper in health, may be unlawful in trouble. That which is duty in necessary self-defence, may be very criminal in any other case. That which is very becoming in magistrates, as enacting of laws, punishing of criminals, and raising of armies and the like, would be very improper in private persons.——This will of God *manifested to men's reason*, and representing the moral fitness of their qualities, thoughts, words, or actions, is called the LAW OF NATURE. And to be and act according to it, is ordinarily called VIRTUE; and to be and act contrary to it, is called VICE. But some by VIRTUE mean only the duty which we owe to ourselves and fellow-creatures; and call the duty which we owe to God, RELIGION.

To render any of our actions *truly virtuous*, 1. We must have a knowledge of the moral fitness of things, and even of the moral fitness of that particular act. 2. We must have a formed design to act according to that moral fitness, from regard to the authority of God. 3. The act must be performed freely and of choice, and with affection and delight. 4. A good act performed, notwithstanding much opposition, is *not a little* virtuous; but it is most virtuous, when there is no inward opposition at all made to the performance of it. 5. The less selfish our views be, in performing good acts, and the more regard to the authority and honour of God and the real good of our fellow-creatures, they are the *more virtuous*.——Thus, to constitute an act *truly virtuous*, it must originate from a virtuous *principle* or *habit*, be influenced by right *motives*, performed in a right *manner*, and directed to a right *end*.

The principal exercises of RELIGION, or virtue, respecting God, which the law of nature requires, are, 1. To contemplate him as the *reason* and *pattern* of our conduct. 2. To adore him with our soul and body as one *possessed of infinite perfection.* 3. To love him as one *infinitely amiable* and *benevolent.* 4. To observe and acknowledge his manifold and diversified providences, and act answerably to them. 5. To acquiesce in the whole of his will as wise and good. 6. To consider and trust in his power, wisdom, and goodness. 7. To be chiefly careful to please him, and to imitate him in his moral excellencies, who is infinitely perfect in himself, and on whose favour and the enjoyment of him, our true happiness wholly depends. 8. Cordially to listen to, believe, receive, and obey every further declaration of his will, which he is pleased to make to us.

VIRTUE respecting men is either *personal* or *social.* In PERSONAL VIRTUE, I. Great care must be taken to fill our mind with useful knowledge. II. In order to prevent both moral and penal evil, we ought frequently to examine and consider our circumstances and conduct. III. We must never allow our body to want any thing that is necessary for its real preservation and welfare, and never indulge it in any excess of meat, drink, ease, or pleasure.—SELF-MURDER, whether it be instantaneous or gradual, directly or indirectly committed, hath a dreadful criminality in it. It implies the want of all proper reverence of God, the Lord of our life: It injures the church or state, by robbing it of a member, and introducing a pernicious example. It entails distress and infamy upon living relations. It manifests a mind shamefully weak and incapable of bearing adversity; and dying in an act odious to God, we presumptuously rush on eternal misery.——No intention of thereby avoiding torture, disgrace, or lascivious rapes can excuse it. Patient enduring of torture or disgrace, in a good cause, is a glorious instance of virtue; patient bearing of them in the just punishment of our crimes, is a debt, which we owe to the laws, the justice, and the welfare of our country. The suffering of a *real rape* hurts neither our conscience nor our character; and therefore ought to be borne as a *trial of virtue.*———GLUTTONY in eating too much,—in eating without proper appetite,—in eating with too much greed or delight,—or indulging improper inclinations towards delicacies,—is a most beastly vice, in which men live as if they were destitute of souls,—gradually murder their body,—stupify their mind,—abuse their food, to the dishonour of God the bestower of it,—and rob the poor and their relations, of that which was laid out to gratify their lust.

——DRUNKENNESS, in the too indulgent, too frequent, or too extensive use of intoxicating liquor, includes every evil of gluttonny. It also produceth furious passions, improper discoveries of secrets, reproach of neighbours, reviling or affronting of God and religion. It leads to profane swearing, cursing, quarrelling, uncleanness, dishonesty, and murder. IV. Great care ought to be taken for the proper management of our passions, which are merely natural, and for the mortification of those that are vicious. These passions include, 1. ADMIRATION, which is excited by things apprehended as marvellous or rare. It is useful, when it leads to meditation and cordial choosing of God;—when it imprints the remembrance of useful things on our mind,—or disposeth us to an earnest application to proper studies. But it is hurtful, when it is excessive;—when it leads to the choice of insignificant trifles, or of any thing before due examination of it;—when it hinders our application to more useful objects or exercises;—or, when we admire ourselves, or admire even useful things, chiefly for their novelty. 2. LOVE, which disposeth our heart towards union with, kindness to, and delight in its objects. It fixeth only on such persons or things, as, and in so far as, we apprehend them agreeable, and so renders our soul courageous and pleased in the prosecution of its purposes. But it becometh criminal, when we esteem, desire, or delight in, creatures, more, or as much as, in God himself; or in a manner which tends to lessen our love to him, or, as if they were any part of our chief good;—or, when bad things are loved; or good things, more than is meet;—or, when it hinders our impartial examination of ourselves, or makes us overvalue that which belongs to us; when it tempts us to procure that which we think good for ourselves, at the expence of our neighbours, or renders us too indulgent of our own desires, and too susceptible of flattery from others. Love to our neighbours, when fixed and mutual, is called *friendship*, which mightily promotes reciprocal sympathy, assistance, supply, and comfort. As it ought to be founded upon clear conviction of proper excellency and usefulness, we ought never to choose any for our friends, who are unknown, impious, debauched, outrageous, loquacious, selfish, covetous, ambitious, luxurious, inconstant, contentious, quarrelsome, or whimsical. And, when we have fixed on friends, we ought to rejoice in their welfare, approve them in every thing laudable, indulge them in every thing safe, readily offer them our best advice and assistance, whenever it is necessary, study to please them in all things lawful, carefully keep their secrets, kindly and seasonably warn them of their dangers, faithfully reprove their faults, judge very charitably of all their actions, never unnecessarily complain of them to others, especially behind their back,—and never neglect or contemn old friends for the sake of new ones.——LOVE OF GLORY or power, when it exceeds due bounds, is called *Ambition*, which, by feeding on airy applause, renders men proud; frequently produceth contentions, and leads to base, cruel, or fraudulent methods of obtaining the things desired. Excessive *love of riches* in studying to obtain them, is called *Avarice;* and in retaining of them is called *churlishness.* In either of these forms it placeth them in God's room, marks discontentment with his providence, injures our neighbour, taking or withholding his right from him, torments and enslaves our own soul, opposeth all proper love to God, or trust in him, and all love and equity towards our neighbour; and hence produceth much folly and ruin.——Love of corporeal, or even intellectual pleasure, when it exceeds due bounds, marks great pride, selfishness, and meanness of spirit, and often issueth in fearful mischief to ourselves, or our neighbours. 3, 4, 5, 6. Joy and grief, hope and fear, which are virtuous, when they are fixed on proper objects and duly proportioned to them. 7. Pity to the distressed, which originates from mistakes of that which these objects endure, or from a natural tenderness of constitution, or from true love and friendship;—and is only virtuous, when it leads us to sympathize with proper objects, to help and comfort them in a proper manner. 8. Shame, which proceeds from fear of blame or contempt—and is virtuous, when it disposeth us to blush on account of that which is sinful, indiscreet, imprudent, or unsuitable to our character and circumstances in the world,—and when it makes us diligent in well-doing, and cheerful in necessary suffering for righteousness sake. 9. Emulation, which is good in so far as it means a desire to be equal, and superior, to others, in virtuous tempers or actions;—but is most wicked and abominable, in so far as it means an envying or grieving at the virtue, honour, wealth, pleasure, or other advantages, of our neighbours,—as it improves the honour or happiness of others, as a mean of tormenting ourselves,—condemns God's most holy, wise, just, and good distribution of his favours,—wastes our natural constitution, and tempts us to murder ourselves or others, &c. 10. Hatred, unless in so far as it is fixed upon sin as its object, is the reverse of God's infinite benevolence, banisheth love, meekness, humility, and patience, from our heart; and it is a fearful source of our contempt, reproach, and murder, of our neighbours. 11. Resentment of indignities done to God, or of injuries done to churches or nations, answerable to our stations, and conducted in a proper manner, is good; but resentment of private injuries real or supposed, manifests much weakness and baseness of spirit, fills our mind with tormenting fears, cares, and contrivances;—robs us of the delightful pleasure and high honour, of forgiving affronts and injuries, and of returning good for evil, and often hurrieth us into fearful disorders and dangers. 12. Anger is criminal, when it is not directed against, and exercised in a manner destructive to *vice;*

and especially when it kindles into *wrath, rage,* and *fury.*—Sinful anger originates from pride, suspicious humour, excessive credulity, selfish and carnal affections—and it discomposeth our mind, and disfigures our body, and being awakened by mere trifles, it frequently issueth in murder, blasphemy, and like horrible mischiefs. 13. PRIDE, if placed among the passions, is a most mischievous one. It can take occasion from virtue, or any other good thing, as well as from ignorance and self-love, to exercise itself. It disposeth us to exalt ourselves at the expence of our neighbours, and even of God himself, and to attempt to pull down every opposer,—and strongly tempts to rashness, error, insolence, wilfulness, presumption, despair, and even self-murder.—— *Wilfulness*, is that form of pride, through which we obstinately adhere to persons, principles, or practices, without any consciousness of their excellency. It is always *vicious*, manifesting much ignorance and self-conceit, and ordinarily disposing men to a malicious persecution of their opponents. V. In order to prevent the hurt of our soul or body from *idleness*, we ought alway to choose and diligently employ ourselves in some honest and useful business, answerable to our circumstances of knowledge, ability, wealth, and inclination, and calculated to promote the honour of God, and the real happiness of our neighbours around. VI. To prevent our rashly engaging in arduous or dangerous enterprizes,—vain expectation of excessive regard from others, and immoderate sense of injuries received,—we ought carefully to cultivate an humble opinion of ourselves, and, for this purpose, frequently and seriously to ponder our own wants, weaknesses, follies, and faults.——— These six Rules represent the personal virtues of Prudence, Consideration, Temperance, Chastity, Fortitude, Contentment, Meekness, Moderation, Diligence, and Humility.

SOCIAL VIRTUE consists, 1. In carefully forbearing, preventing, or removing, every thing that may be grievous or hurtful to our fellow-creatures, except when it is necessary to promote some greater good. 2. In earnestly labouring, in our respective stations, to promote their real welfare.—This virtue is called *disinterested*, when we prefer the advantage of others to our own.

HUMANITY towards brutes, in carefully forbearing every form or degree of cruelty to them, is implied in social virtue. In this we imitate God, who is good to all, and shew a proper regard to his creatures, and our fellow-partakers of his bounty in creation and providence. We may, nevertheless, in a duly tender manner, kill these animals for our own nourishment. 1. The happiness of men, who are more important animals, is hereby promoted. 2. By this means these slaughtered animals obtain a more quick and easy death. 3. To balance that pain which they suffer from men in their death, many of them are treated more kindly and nourished more delicately, in order to render them more agreeable food. 4. By increase of eatable animals, and giving their flesh so agreeable a relish to our taste, God seems to indicate the lawfulness of our killing them for food. 5. If none of them were killed for food to man, their excessive increase might deprive us of other means of our subsistence, and even endanger our health and life.

But social virtue much more strongly requires KINDNESS toward men, in doing every thing which can promote their life or health, except when the public welfare requires particular persons to be punished. 1. Human life is too valuable to be taken away, without a reason more honourable to God the giver, and more advantageous to the public, which is interested in it, than the preservation of it could be. 2. Natural instinct, if not terribly debauched, shrinks with horror from shedding of human blood without absolute necessity. 3. No man, except in a frenzy, wishes his own life or health taken from him. 4. The taking away our neighbour's life unjustly, robs his relations and neighbours of the important advantages which they might have received from the preservation of it.

Social virtue requires EQUITY towards all men, in doing to them every thing respecting their property, as we could reasonably wish they would do unto us in similar circumstances. But here it must be remarked, 1. That before property be fixed by any possession or agreement, every man may justly claim that which he first finds. And, if there be not enough to satisfy all, the first seizer ought to give portions to those that need them. And, if necessary supplies be denied to any one, he may justly take a necessary portion from the present possessors. 2. Equality of wealth is in no respect necessary among mankind. Particular persons ought to reap the fruits of their lawful care and industry. And, it is not for the hurt, but for the advantage, of the public, that some be richer than others. 3. Any persons may, as they have need or opportunity, seize on things which are still common, as light, air, sea-water, wild beasts, or the like; or which have been abandoned by the former proprietors. 4. In ordinary cases, antiquated claims ought not to be revived, as it tends to produce contention, perjury, and war. Nor is a man faulty in holding the property of another, which upon prescription or other probable grounds, he thought to be his own, till he find the contrary clearly evinced.

Social virtue requires the strictest regard to TRUTH and CANDOUR in all our conduct. Our thoughts, words, and actions ought exactly to correspond with each other, as well as with their objects. 1. Exact adherence to truth in our words much promotes mutual trust and happiness among men. 2. Without truth in our words, speech becomes unsuitable, useless, and ensnaring. 3. Lying, falsehood, and even ambiguity of speech or behaviour, have alway been held infamous by all good men.——In no case doth the law of nature allow of *lying*, as it is contrary to the nature and honour of God, and the safety and happiness of mankind; were it allowed in any one instance, dissimulation, fraud, perjury, &c. must be allowed in other instances.

It therefore follows, that *our promises ought to be carefully and exactly performed.* 1. Truth and candour require that we should really intend doing every thing to which we engage. 2. They to whom any thing is promised, thereby acquire a right to it. 3. They cannot therefore honestly be deprived of it without their own free consent. 4. If property depending on promises uttered, written, sworn, or sealed, were held uncertain, it would introduce the most perplexing confusion, and would ruin all mutual trust among men. 5. Breach of our promises tempts our neighbours to suspect that we were not candid in making them, or that we are very inconstant in our temper and resolutions, and so hurts our character and usefulness in the world.——But, if our promises have been obtained by fraudulent imposition, they are not in every case binding. And promises made by persons destitute of the due exercise of reason, or which engage to any thing sinful, are never binding.

The violation of promises and oaths to men, or vows to God, is exceedingly criminal. 1. It is a horrid abuse of that authority deputed to us by God, in the exertion of which we make our promises, oaths, and vows. 2. It pours the highest contempt on God, to whom vows are made, and who is solemnly stated the witness and guarantee of oaths;—and renders a solemn ordinance of his own the mean of basely affronting him. 3. If perjury were once allowed, all mutual faith and trust among men would soon be utterly ruined. 4. Perjured persons have always, among all nations, been held the pests and scandals of human societies. And no less can we reckon those who, by artful dissimulation, evade the charge of bribery or perjury, in the election of officers or governors in commonwealths; or who, in churches, solemnly avouch or subscribe *Articles* and *Confessions of faith*, without believing or maintaining the *whole doctrines* therein contained.——But, if a promise or covenant be *conditional*, an essential breach of it by one party frees the other from his obligation.

Social virtue requires the propagation of mankind only in a married state. 1. If women were common, it would prevent all tender and faithful friendship between the sexes, and degrade them to beasts. 2. It would occasion much jealousy and strife. 3. It would much counteract the propagation and health of children. 4. It would expose women with child to great danger and distress. 5. Proper provision for, and the regular education of children, would be neglected, and they left to perish, or at best to grow up as wild savages. 6. No property could be bequeathed by fathers to children, and thus a notable encouragement and spur to sobriety and honest industry would be removed.

Hence it follows, that *every form of fleshly lust*, which tends to prevent or dishonour marriage, ought to be detested and mortified as highly criminal,—as dishonourable to God who made us, and to our souls, bodies, and characters,—as a source of the prodigal dissipation of our substance,—an indirect murder of ourselves and our posterity,—an occasion of strife and hatred among accomplices in wickedness,—a grievous and irreparable injury to them and their friends with whom unchastity is committed;—a most effectual mean of rendering our souls stupid, atheistical, or idolatrously attached to filthy objects.——In ADULTERY men commit the most criminal dishonesty, in depriving their neighbour of that which is most dear, precious, and honourable to him;—involve themselves in a most vile and perjurious breach of marriage-vows,—introduce disorder and confusion into families,—and tempt to the commission of idolatry, murder, and every thing horrid.—In civilized nations, it hath been punished with death; and indeed, as it entangles two at once in a crime so ruinous to their souls, bodies, and families, it is in some respects worse than murder itself.

As it therefore follows, that married persons ought earnestly to promote the happiness of their yoke-fellows and children, none ought to have more than one wife or husband at the same time. 1. As God, in his providence, alway maintains so near an equality in the number of males and females among mankind, polygamy must occasion castration, self-pollution, sodomy, bestiality, or the like abominable conduct, wherever it much obtains. 2. It promotes contention among those who affect a plurality of wives, in their respective families. 3. Continued succession of new amours hinders the affections of husbands from duly fixing on their wives. 4. Multiplicity of wives prevents that propagation of mankind which is necessary to their common welfare. Solomon, by all his thousand, appears to have had very few children.

Marriage being a transaction of great importance, on which the welfare of persons, families, and nations, and even the happiness of the future state so much depends, ought never to be contracted, 1. By such as, on account of their non-age, or from want of the exercise of their reason, cannot perform the duties of marriage; nor, 2. By such as are incapable of procreation, unless with such as are in the like condition: nor, 3. By those that are infected with such lothesome distempers as would probably be communicated to, and injure their yokefellows or their children: nor, 4. By those that are already married to another, or that have no proper certainty of their former partner's death or wilful desertion: nor, 5. By those that are too near of kin,—as this would confound the duties of preceding relations,—prevent the extension of friendship in the world,—and produce various other improprieties.

As children have so much dependence on parents,—and as the happiness of the parties and their offspring so much depend on the propriety of their marriage-connection, none ought to enter into it without *consulting their parents*, if alive, and obtaining their consent. And, as marriage can never be dissolved but by death, or on account of adultery or wilful desertion, none ought to be forced into it by parents or others,— or to enter into it without *great deliberation* and *solemn consulting of God*, the supreme and general *Parent* of mankind.

Social virtue requires the *most tender and natural affection* among those who are related to one another.——Parents ought tenderly and carefully to *educate their children*, that they may honour God, and be useful to mankind. And, if possible, mothers ought to suckle their own children. 1. Children when young cannot provide for themselves, and so must perish, if parents neglect them. 2. The more carefully children are educated, the more ready are they to love, obey, and be an honour and comfort to their parents. 3. Careful and prudent education of children is of great importance to the public welfare of the church and nation. 4. The education of children, when it is wholly trusted to others, is very often fearfully neglected.— Children ought to be portioned according to their apparent merit, rather than according to their age.—It is absurd, that one child should carry off almost the whole of his parents' property, for no other reason but because he is a male, or came into the world some months before the rest.——In ordinary cases, an *eldest son* may have the largest portion, as it is expected that he will have most skill to manage it, and will be a protector and director to the rest of the children. But, if he be *notoriously wicked*, he should be disinherited,—it being unreasonable that an inheritance should be put into his hands, while it is most probable that he will use it to his own ruin. —— To mark their gratitude and respect to parents, as the representatives of God to them, children ought to love them affectionately,—reverence and honour them,—obey all their lawful commands,—consult them in every matter of importance,—and, if needful, supply their wants.

SERVANTS in families ought to be considered as *secondary children*,—and have due instruction, wages, and kind and affable entertainment; and they ought to reverence and obey their masters, and to be faithful and diligent in their service.—— Persons who are justly condemned to slavery, as a punishment of their dishonesty or other crimes, may be lawfully bought for slaves: and prisoners may be bought from conquerors, if it be in order to preserve their lives. But to make war upon neighbours, or encourage others to it, in order to procure slaves,—or to trade in buying slaves,—is altogether unmerciful, and shocking to right reason and humanity,—natively entailing upon these merchants the blood of the souls and bodies of their fellow-creatures.

To promote the happiness of mankind it is necessary that they form themselves into CIVIL SOCIETIES. 1. Controversies concerning property or injurious conduct may happen between different families, which need to be determined. '2. Hence some general rules of determination must be established. 3. These contests ought to be determined by one or more judges or arbiters, unbiassed to either party. 4. These judges ought to have authority and power in their hand sufficient to enforce a proper compliance with their decisions.—In forming these civil societies and their government, it is natural to think, 1. Parents, originally, were the sole governors, under God, of their children, mediate or immediate. This is the only form of government which is *merely natural*. 2. No man being naturally any part of inheritance, the government of younger children could not necessarily devolve upon the eldest son. 3. Each family therefore became a small sovereignty or state by itself, in which parents were governors. 4. In order to an amicable decision of contests between families, several of them formed themselves into larger societies. 5. Disputes between lesser societies introduced a coalescence of several of them into one. 6. It thus became necessary that power and authority should be lodged in the hand of some general arbiter of their differences,—to whom, if he managed well, they all gradually submitted. 7. In submitting themselves to one or more, who had no natural right to govern them, men, no doubt, demanded from these rulers, an engagement to protect them in their lives, liberties, and property. 8. If ambitious persons, by force or fraud, obtained this governing power, the submitters, no doubt, insisted on the best terms for their obedience, which they could obtain from their conquerors. Hence some *original contract* between governors and governed, *expressed* or *understood* is the *foundation* of all government among men, that of parents over their children only excepted. And nothing can be more absurd than claims of *indefeasible right* to supreme power, invested in eldest, or other sons, in any families whatsoever, or of *absolute power* to dispose of the property, lives, or liberties of others of mankind.

God, as Creator and Governor of the world, is the author of all civil government. Nor have either subjects or magistrates the smallest degree of liberty or power, but what they derive from him, and for which they must be accountable to him. Not, therefore, the will of subjects, or the consciences of magistrates, but the *Law of God*, as Supreme Governor, must be the *real standard* of all laws enacted by men.—Nor must men's civil interests, but the glory of God, as Founder and Supreme Governor of nations, be intended as their *chief end*, in all civil subjection and government.———To maintain the contrary, necessarily involves in the depths of atheism.

All men being naturally born in a state of *equal freedom*, none of them can be bound to submit to the laws of their country, any further than these are calculated to promote the general welfare of their society, in subordination to the glory of God. 1. None but God hath any *natural right* to rule over any such society. None but he hath any just claim to absolute power in governing. None hath any real power but what is derived from him,—or any power to enact any statutes contrary to his benevolent law. 2. Few parents would by voluntary contract bind either themselves or their children to an unlimited subjection to men; and if they did, the contract could be valid, as they have no power to make any such disposal of themselves or their children,—no power to dispose of either the lives or liberties of children.

If, therefore, magistrates command that which is prejudicial to the general welfare of the society, or dishonourable to God, the Supreme Governor of it, they ought to be disobeyed. And, if they be habitually cruel and tyrannical, they ought to be resisted and deposed, if circumstances permit. 1. When the great body of the subjects are much alienated in affection, a revolution may be accomplished without much hazard or hurt. 2. By resisting tyrannical princes in proper circumstances, nations have often preserved their lives as well as their liberties from impending ruin. 3. Such resistance, prudently managed, is an effectual warning to other magistrates to beware of abusing and oppressing their subjects. 4. In mixed forms of government, the propriety of resistance is most clear as well as most easy: as when a parliament resists a king, or a king resists a parliament, in defence of the common liberties of the nation.—Nevertheless, as princes are exposed to many and uncommon difficulties, and are apt to be imposed on by their confidents;—and as their real designs are not easily penetrated, and often not to be pryed into by their subjects;—and as resistance ordinarily occasions much bloodshed and misery,—subjects ought to put the best construction upon the conduct of their governors that it can justly admit,—and never proceed to violent measures but where it is absolutely necessary, and where there is an hopeful prospect of success.

In some cases, Conquest may confer, or contribute to confirm, civil authority. 1. Kings, to prevent perpetual wars with some neighbouring princes, may subdue a particular country; but, till the inhabitants have directly or indirectly engaged themselves, they are not bound to submit. 2. To prevent more misery and bloodshed, a conqueror may be lawfully submitted to, till the rightful prince become capable to assert his own rights: but imposition of oaths of fidelity or allegiance in such cases, fearfully ensnares men's consciences, and rarely proves of any advantage to the interests of the imposers. 3. When rightful princes long neglect to assert their own claims, permanent possession and tame subjection confer a kind of right on conquerors and their successors,—that nations may not be ruined by once regnant families renewing their antiquated claims. 4. In ordinary cases, conquerors ought to restore what they have conquered to the rightful sovereigns, when they have wrested it from such as had formerly seized it by violence or fraud. 5. Nothing is more absurd, than to detest and punish petty thefts or personal injuries, and yet approve or extol the robbing, enslaving, or murdering of nations.

Except in the case of the Jewish nation, God permits civil societies to establish what particular form of government they find most agreeable to their circumstances, if it be not contrary to his law. But no particular form now in being is absolutely perfect. If kings were perfectly wise and virtuous, ABSOLUTE MONARCHY, in which their will is the only rule of government, would be best. But, as the most of men in high stations are very imperfect, and none of them faultless, it would be unsafe to lodge so much power in one man: Hence oppression and tyranny have generally prevailed, wherever it hath been attempted.——ARISTOCRACY, in which some few principal men have the whole power in their hand,——and DEMOCRACY, in which adult males in general bear rule,—leave too much room for cabals of crafty men,—render the dispatch of business too slow,—the affairs of government too open,—and the cure of contentions very difficult.——MIXED MONARCHY, in which king, nobles, and commons, have their joint shares in the government, therefore, seems best. And, as *election* of kings, though it might sometimes prevent the advancement of improper persons, would afford much occasion for cabals and factions,—a *limited succession* is in many cases preferable to it. As the arbitrary and occasional will of imperfect governors would be an extremely precarious and unsafe standard of government, all civilized societies have, in or after their establishment, formed laws by which they incline to be ruled. Of human laws the most remarkable are, 1. The *Law of nations*, containing those regulations which are tacitly adopted by all civilized societies; as, That no ambassador ought to be ill used,—no prisoners killed, but exchanged or ransomed,—and no women, children, or other unarmed persons, to be abused or killed in time of war,—and should also bear, that no private property, except warlike stores, should be seized. 2. *Laws of shipping*, relative to landing, sailing, loading, or unloading contraband goods, hoisting or striking of colours, &c. 3. The *Civil Law*, which comprehends the statutes once of public and permanent authority in the Roman empire. 4. The *Feudal Law*, introduced by the conquering Goths into a great part of Europe, for regulating superiorities, vassalages, and the like. 5. *National Laws* of France, Spain, England, Scotland, &c. consisting of public immemorial customs, and statutes of the supreme courts of judicature. 6. *Municipal Laws*, regulating the immunities of cities and burghs. 7. *Society Laws*, regulating the privileges and mutual behaviour of merchants, craftsmen, or the like;—to which we may add, 8. The *Canon Law*, formed from the decisions of ancient doctors, and of popes and councils, for the regulation of the Romish church,—even as the Talmud, formed from the dictates of their ancient Rabbins, is *canon law* to the modern Jews. 9. Protestant *Ecclesiastical Laws*, comprehending their Confessions, Articles, Formulas, Canons, Acts of Assemblies, &c. which become civil laws, in so far as they are adopted by the supreme authority of States.——As none of these human laws reach the inward dispositions of men's hearts,—few of them have any rewards, and none of them any rewards or punishments of a spiritual or eternal nature annexed to them, they must all be of infinitely less importance than, and subordinated to, the law of nature, which proceeds immediately from God himself, and are to be obeyed only in so far as consistent with it.

Human life being very precious, and the loss of it irrecoverable, capital punishments ought never to be inflicted, when others are adequate to the crime, or can answer the great end of the glory of God in the general advantage of the society. But some malefactors ought to be punished with death. 1. If the common tranquillity ought to be carefully preserved, notorious disturbers of it must be cut off. 2. Notwithstanding of capital punishments threatened or inflicted, some wickedly commit the most shocking enormities against the welfare of their state, and the honour of God, its Supreme Governor. 3. No loss of property, liberty, or honour, is adequate to the criminal depriving others of their precious life, &c. 4. If the more shocking enormities were not severely punished, the commission would become more and more frequent.——Hence the execution of malefactors ought to be as public and solemn as possible, in order more effectually to deter others from the like crimes. ——It is even sometimes necessary, that innocent persons should suffer in their honours and estates along with the guilty.—For the security of nations, and the more effectually to deter others from such wickedness, the children of traitors may be deprived of their parents' estates, that thus they may be impressed with the treason, and disabled from avenging the traitor's death on the nation.

In necessary self-defence men have a right to kill their assailants. But DUELLING is unlawful and murderous, a remain of the ancient Gothic barbarity. Men by it discover the most abominable pride and passion,—presumptuously usurp the power of the civil magistrate in avenging themselves, and madly risk their own death and damnation, in attempting to murder their neighbour, or even friend.

In no case ought men to deprive their neighbour of his life, and plunge him into an eternity, perhaps of inexpressible misery, if, consistent with equity and the public welfare, it can be avoided. But in some cases WAR is lawful and necessary, upon one side, though never on both. 1. Some men are so unjust that there is no securing our own property or life, but by opposing force to force. 2. Violent injurers of others being public pests of society, their restraint or destruction becomes necessary, not only for securing our own life and property, but also to prevent their injuring or murdering of others.—Though war ought never to be undertaken without urgent necessity, when the matter in dispute is of great importance in itself, or in its consequences,—and never till after the most earnest attempts to retain or recover our property by milder methods,—yet it may be sometimes lawful to take arms before we are attacked, and over-run the country of our implacable opponent, in order to render him incapable of further mischief,—even as we may bind a madman before he hath actually hurt us. Nay, it may be lawful for private persons to take arms of their own accord, in case of invasions or sudden assaults; or when the force of public laws is suspended by public confusions.——But as wars are always *unlawful* and murderous, upon one side, and frequently on both, no man ought to assist in war without an impartial examination and well-grounded satisfaction concerning its lawfulness. No command of superiors can sanctify rage and murder: Nay, even in lawful war, violence and bloodshed ought to be avoided as far as can possibly consist with the good end proposed;—and, though it may be lawful to impose on an enemy by feigned marches, declining of battle, or other doubtful acts, it is always unlawful to deceive him by lies, false promises, or oaths.—But to violate truces, treaties, safe conduct, or injure ambassadors or messengers;—and to hire any to betray or assassinate their princes or generals, or to disclose their secrets, is base and wicked, and often tends to prolong the war, or render it more furious.

As magistrates derive their whole power and authority from God himself, and are bound as his deputies to exercise it for his honour and the welfare of their nation in subordination to it, they cannot lawfully establish any religion but that which is of God,—they cannot *authoritatively tolerate* a FALSE RELIGION, which at once robs, affronts, and blasphemes God, the King of nations, draws down his wrath upon the encouragers and embracers of it, corrupts the morals and disturbs the peace of the nation,—any more than they can lawfully authorize calumny, theft, murder, adultery, or the like.——But, by their own eminently virtuous example, by proper encouragement of orthodox and faithful teachers, and by enacting of prudent and good laws in its favour, they ought to promote the open profession and practice of the TRUE RELIGION in their dominions, and to restrain, or even seasonably and suitably punish any open affront to it. Nevertheless, they ought never to FORCE men to religious acts, especially such as suppose real saintship, by any *civil penalties*. 1. Real religion doth not chiefly consist in external performances, but in the proper frame, and exercise of the heart. 2. Such convulsive force, instead of convincing men of the truth, hardens them against conviction, and prevents impartial examination. 3. It cannot therefore render men *truly religious*, but only base dissemblers in religion. 4. It is hurtful to society. It obliges those that are *conscientiously* persuaded of the propriety of that which is contrary to the will of the magistrate, either to endure the stings of their own conscience, if they comply, or to see themselves and their families ruined, if they do not.—It prejudices others in favour of the prosecuted, as if no other argument than violence could be produced against their opinions. And this is apt to increase their adherents, if not to create public disorders, and revolutions in the state.

In order to a general promotion of religion and virtue, all men ought earnestly to addict themselves to, 1. An attentive reading, hearing, and meditating upon the nature of God and men, and of the connections between them, as they have opportunity afforded them. 2. The utmost regularity and reverence in their external worshipping of God, which mark their own regard to him, and stir up others to the like. 3. The most sincere and fervent prayer to God, that he would teach, incline, and enable them to a right performance of their duty. 4. A religious assembling together in the social worship of God, corresponding to their social temper of mind, and that at proper times, fixed either by God himself, or by their common consent that no civil business may hinder or disturb such associations. 5. All, in their particular relations and circumstances, as *men, women, husbands, wives, parents, children, brothers, sisters, masters, servants, magistrates, subjects, teachers, taught, lawyers, physicians, soldiers, craftsmen, merchants,—rich or poor, noble or ignoble,—natives or strangers,—old or young, prosperous or afflicted in soul, body, property, or relations,*—ought with great attention to fulfil those duties which particularly correspond with their diversified conditions. 6. The present and future advantages of religion and virtue, and the disadvantages of vice, ought carefully to be pondered, and deeply laid to heart.

In this life, the circumspect cultivation of religion and virtue promotes men's health and honour, and their after reflections on their conduct, and their reasonable hopes of a future reward in the prosecution of it, give them a most substantial though secret satisfaction: and what is profitable to every individual must be profitable to the *whole society*.——It is most absurd to pretend, that private vices are public benefits, and that a general reformation of manners would ruin vast multitudes, whose subsistence depends on the common pride and debauchery of others. For, 1. What greater good was ever produced or even occasioned by vice, than hath, or could be by virtue. How easily might that money, which is spent is gaming, drunkenness, whoredom, or prodigality, be better circulated by the inventions and exercises of virtue? 2. To promote the circulation of money, and the support of the industrious, religion and virtue allow men the use of many things not absolutely necessary, if their stations do suit, and their incomes can afford them. 3. A general reformation to temperance and other virtues would prevent the disgrace and ruin, if not the eternal damnation of many thousands of persons and families. The time and money spent in gaming, drunkenness, and whoredom, &c. might be far better employed in forming children or others to some useful business. 4. Many who enjoy splendour and wealth are unhappy amidst them, and might be far happier, even in poverty, if they had but a virtuous temper of mind. 5. Men temperate and virtuous would defend and promote the welfare of their country, with more conscience, care, and courage, than vicious and abandoned wretches can be supposed to do. 6. Nations and other societies have often become great and powerful by virtue, but have been weakened and ruined by vice.

In the future state, men, who live and die religious and virtuous, bid fair to be eternally happy, and those that are vicious to be miserable. 1. God does, and for ever will love, true religion and virtue, and hate profligacy and vice. 2. The pleasures and profits which attend religion and virtue, and the miseries which accompany vice in this world, appear to be an earnest of something correspondent in a future state. 3. The small difference, to appearance, that God makes in his dealings with the virtuous and the notoriously wicked, in this life, induces our rational minds to expect a far greater difference in the next.

CHAP. II.

Of the INSUFFICIENCY of the LAW, and especially of the LIGHT of NATURE, to conduct Men to true and lasting felicity.

THE *Law of Nature*, which hath been imperfectly exhibited in the preceding chapter, ought never to be confounded with the *light of nature as now enjoyed.* The *law of nature* is comprehensively known to God alone, to whom the whole number and forms of relations between himself and men are naked and open, it is stable, permanent, uniform, and every where binding. The *light of nature* is that knowledge of the nature of God and of themselves, and of the duties resulting from the connections between them, which men *actually* possess. It is exceedingly diversified in its extent and degree, according to the different capacities, opportunities, and inclinations of men;—so that, in some parts of Tartary, Africa, America, and the Isles, where it receives no assistance or improvement from Divine Revelation, it appears little superior to the sagacity of some brutes.

Nevertheless, multitudes of our high pretenders to knowledge have extolled it as sufficient, nay, the *only guide* of mankind to true virtue and happiness. Having had their understandings informed and enlarged by means of revelation, and often pretending the highest regard to Christianity, they, in the most uncandid manner, endeavour to undermine its authority, and render it an object of ridicule;—or even to attack the fundamental principles of natural religion, because of their subserviency to it. None of these deistical, or more properly infidel, and often atheistical writers, that I know of, except Lord Herbert, and Blount his plagiary, have so much as pretended to exhibit a *system* of their law or religion of nature; but have contented themselves with rambling, crafty, or insolent attempts to render the oracles of God ridiculous in their matter or manner.

To ramble after them in all their manifold absurdities and whims, would be very impertinent here. We shall only review their principal or more common pretences, extracted from Tindal's *Christianity as old as the creation*, viz. 1. That the light of nature is absolutely sufficient to conduct men to all that virtue and happiness which is suited to their nature. 2. That the light of nature, proceeding from an infinitely wise, perfect, and unchangeable God, MUST be absolutely perfect and unchangeable, and that therefore all revelations from God must be unnecessary, except perhaps to remove prejudices. 3. That by the light of nature, we perceive God to be just, wise, good, and merciful,—happy in himself,—making and upholding nothing for his own honour, nor requiring any service from any creature for that end,—but doing all, chiefly in order to render them happy. 4. That God, influenced by his own infinite natural goodness, takes care to have this law of nature, which regulates the fitness of human deportments, implanted in, and sufficiently known to every man, as his circumstances require. 5. That the obligations of this law of nature are enforced with no sanction of future rewards or punishments, but merely with that pleasure or pain which attends human actions or the reflection on them, in this life. This creed of their long famous chief is a mixture of *infidelity* and *atheism*. But,

I. Our infidels never plainly or self-consistently inform us what their *law of nature* is, but represent it as *reason, sentiment,* or *moral sense,* by which men discern *good* from *evil, virtue* from *vice,* in much the same manner as our taste discerns *sweet* from *bitter,* or our sight *black* from *white, beauty* from *deformity.* Now, 1. This cannot be a law at all. If both God and men, as they pretend, be under it, from whence doth it derive its authority?—If it hath no authority from an enacter, how can it be either obeyed or transgressed? If it could be transgressed, there is no proper penalty enforcing it, to seize on the disobedient subject. If God himself be a subject of this law of nature, conscience, as his deputy, cannot punish men for breaking it. And, unless every man, at once, have *two,* and not *one* person, his own nature cannot at once punish, as the principal judge, and be punished as the guilty criminal.—— Besides, the more any man is accustomed to any vice, his inward remorse, on committing it, becomes less, and perhaps his pleasure the greater.——If then the pleasure or pain attending actions in this life, be all the possible sanction of rewards or punishments annexed to this law of nature, then the more multiplied and aggravated the transgressions of it become, they will be the less punished, if not the more largely rewarded.——No human laws can supply this defect. They reach but to a few more gross and public transgressions, —and often, at least as executed, bear more hard upon the virtuous, than upon the most notoriously vicious.—Even in polite and learned Athens, how few distinguished themselves in excellency, real or apparent, without hazarding their own banishment, imprisonment, or death? 2. If it should be insisted, that this moral sense, sentiment, or reason, as in every man's heart, is a law, men's diversified conduct, where they have been no way biassed by revelation, would manifest it to be either not self-consistent, or very obscure and unknown to men. The ancient Germans and the Siberians, almost to our own times, cast their newly born infants into rivers, lakes, or ponds, that by their swimming or sinking, it might be determined which should be brought up, or suffered to perish. The ancient Ammonites, and others, burnt their children in sacrifice to Moloch and other idols. The African Giagas murdered most of their babes, and one of their queens pounded her only son in a mortar, and then anointed her body with his substance. The Caffres still expose their infants in woods,—while multitudes of other parents have been, and are, inwardly disposed to love, protect, and provide for their children:—While many nations of ancient Celts or Gauls were exceedingly kind to strangers. Some Scythian nations murdered their guests,—admitted none to marriage or to their solemn festivals, who had not killed one or more of a different tribe; and at their solemn banquets drank out of the skulls of the persons whom they had murdered.—— In ancient times, the Gauls, Greeks, Spaniards, Egyptians, Carthaginians, and many others, offered human sacrifices to their idols. Not many ages ago, the Mexicans are said to have sacrificed 64,000 persons at the dedication of one temple. Many of the ancient Goths, Saxons, &c. thought that violent death by their own or some other hand, was absolutely necessary to introduce them to future happiness, at least of the higher kind. The ancient Gauls and others founded property on strength of hand, and pretended that every person had a just right to that which he could force from his neighbour, especially of another tribe. The Spartans held theft to be innocent, if it was but shrewdly committed. The enlightened Romans battered down the temples of their gods, to punish them for not preserving the life of their beloved prince and general, Germanicus. When the wise Chinese cannot obtain the favours which they have requested from their idols, they prosecute them at law, in order to recover the presents with which they had courted their kindness. Notwithstanding all their high reputation for wisdom, the ancient Egyptians worshipped plants, cats, dogs, crocodiles, pyed bulls, and the like; and many of the Africans do much the same to this day. The learned Greeks had about 30,000 gods, and the Romans, who knows how many.——Had all these in their breast a *law of nature, moral sense, sentiment,* or *reason*, altogether different from, and opposite to that which is in the breast of men otherwise minded? Or, have the wild Arabs, who will hazard their life to protect strangers and guests by night, whom they would have willingly murdered in their fields by day, one law of nature for the day, and another for the night? —Nor was it the mere vulgar, for and from whom nevertheless, as most numerous, the standard law of nature ought to be drawn, that discovered such *strange* reason, sentiment, or moral sense. No: It is recorded that Lycurgus, the famed lawgiver of Sparta, authorised sodomy and artful or bold theft;—that Socrates abounded in profane swearing, practised sodomy, and for gain prostituted his wife to his lecherous friends; and, notwithstanding his belief of one God, professed before his judges his acknowledgment of the gods of his country, and in his last moments, ordered a cock to be sacrificed to them;—that Plato practised sodomy, and was a notorious liar; —that one of the famed Catos principally promoted the Romans' villanous destruction of Carthage; another of them villanously robbed of his kingdom the rightful, but young King of Cyprus, whom the Romans were in honour bound to protect, —was dupe to the profligate Clodius, and at last killed himself;—that Cicero, the famed philosopher, when his daughter died, cried out, in a rage, I *hate the gods;*—that on losing the battle of Philippi, the virtuous Brutus exclaimed, that he had been long following virtue, and had at last found it to be a *mere empty name;*—that Seneca, with all his famed morality, was exceedingly covetous, encouraged Nero to murder his mother, and believed good men, and no doubt himself, to be better than the gods, these being good by nature, those by their own care and labour;—that the sagacious Blount murdered himself.—— Nay, notwithstanding all their pretences to superlative wisdom and knowledge, our modern infidel doctors do not appear to know what the law of nature requires,—whether virtue consists in *acting according to some moral instinct*, leading men to practise it themselves, and approve it in others, without any regard to its reasonableness or advantages,—or in acting according to the reason and truth, or real circumstances of things; or, in acting according to some *inward feeling*,—or, in acting that which is *beautiful*.—Hume, the great modern pillar of infidelity, who perhaps neither believed a God, a heaven, or a hell, places virtue in that which is *useful and agreeable* to natural inclinations, as in broad shoulders, well-shaped legs, if not also in pride, adultery, &c. 3. This pretended law of nature can make no proper impression on men's minds.——From the above, and a thousand like instances, it is plain, that multitudes, instead of being deeply awed and affected by its all-determining power, seem to find pleasure in doing that which is *most vile, horrid, hurtful*, and *unnatural*. The most of the conduct of the enlightened Egyptians, Greeks, and Romans, in their worship and wars, amounted to almost nothing else.—Now, if human nature be still good and uncorrupted, how extremely weak must the determining influence of this perfect law of nature be, as engraved on every man's heart, if, when assisted by so very many extrinsic inducements, it cannot excite one of a thousand to the actual study of virtue. If human nature be *morally vitiated*, men's moral sense, sentiment, or reason, must proportionally be corrupted with ignorance and vicious inclination : And if so, how can it be a proper and unerring guide to true virtue and lasting felicity ?—In vain it is pretended, that our Reason will sufficiently assist our moral sense or sentiment; for, as Lord Shaftesbury, an Infidel doctor, observes, " Few men can think, and of those who do, few can guide their thoughts."—None act more plainly contrary to Reason, than our high pretenders to *free* and *deep thinking*. While Reason strongly inculcates temperance as a salutary virtue, how many of them adventure on the intoxicating glass,—or risk their honour, their wealth, their health, and even their life, with an abominable harlot?—While Reason suggests it to be more virtuous, honourable, and profitable to converse with their Maker, listening to his word, and pouring forth their hearts to him in prayer and praise,—how many of them prefer grunting like swine over the stupifying or inebriating bowl, or to lie wallowing in their vomit !—While Reason dictates the propriety of candour and decency,—how many of them abandon themselves to the basest villany, grossest falsehood, most glaring self-contradiction, or most scurrilous abuse, in their attacks upon the sacred oracles, or the professed ministers of Christ? Nay, how inconsistent with common sense, is their attempting to diminish the motives to virtue or determents from vice, in taking off men the chain of divine authority with the apprehensions of future rewards and punishments,—thus sounding an alarm to all around, that they may safely fall on themselves, their friends, or their property, without any danger of the eternal vengeance of God ?—In vain it is pretended, that human laws and instructions may assist men's moral sense or sentiment, in directing them to virtue; for, if human nature itself be corrupted, human laws and instructions bid fair to be tainted with this corruption; and if, as infidels pretend, God be subject to the law of nature, they can have no proper authority.—Besides, human laws reach only to externals, in which neither the principal substance nor parts of virtue, nor the rewards of it, nor the punishments of vice, consist.—And, notwithstanding all these laws and instructions, as well as all the external providences of God, and their tendency to promote virtue, the far greater part of men continue notoriously vicious.—In vain it is retorted, That neither doth the Christian law restrain its professed subjects from vice;—for, according to God's own revealed declaration, it is but written on the hearts of *a few* of those called Christians, and that but very imperfectly, while they live in this world.—No wonder then that many who bear that name, are a reproach to their profession,—especially as our infidel doctors, and their numerous friends, in order to disgrace and undermine the Christian religion, basely pretend to profess it, and presume to partake of its sealing ordinances 4. This infidel-law of nature provides no proper method, nay leaves no possibility, of rooting out the wrong prejudices of education or custom. For, though my moral sense, sentiment, or Reason, should be really corrupted, how can that be documented? If the law of nature be implanted in my heart, as well as in that of my neighbour, how can he prove that my moral sense is not as pure and as much to be trusted as his own? Or, if I should grant that mine is corrupted, what authority has either God or man to correct my mistakes, if they be under the same Law of nature? Or, if, on account of God's superior goodness and wisdom, I allow him a power to correct my errors, yet what assurance have I, that he will rectify my judgment and vicious inclinations, after I have willingly, if not wilfully, corrupted myself? If he should graciously offer me this favour, how can I believe either him or his messengers, without sufficient credentials of divine wisdom, goodness, power, and authority? If such credentials be produced, I have already slipt off from the mere law of nature, and am entered into the Revelation scheme. —To avoid these embarrassing difficulties, it is pretended, *That God can require no more of men, than what they see to be their duty, and are able to perform.* But, how absurdly! Must men, by indulging in sloth or vice, procure for themselves a right to diminish their duty to God or men, as they please?—and yet God be obliged to accept of their conduct as a perfect obedience to his law,—and of themselves on account of it?—Must men have power to abridge or alter the absolutely perfect law of nature, as they please, and God be obliged to accept of unnatural lust, theft, murder, worshipping of leeks, onions, bulls, serpents, cats, dogs, &c. as virtue, because some men have thought them lawful and good?

II. After the evidence which has been given of the obscurity, weakness, imperfection, or inconsistency of the light or infidel-law of nature, it is highly absurd to pretend, that it either must be, or is *absolutely perfect*, because it originates from *an absolutely perfect author.*—Why must all effects produced by perfect causes be absolutely perfect? Must Clodius, Catiline, Tiberius, Nero, Heliogabalus, necessarily be as virtuous and perfect as Socrates, Epictetus, and Antoninus,—because the same infinitely wise and perfect God made them all? Must all creatures, or even all men, be infinitely, or even equally perfect, because God, their common parent, is so? Are unborn infants as perfect men and women as their parents? Are thieves and murderers, whores and whoremongers, absolutely perfect, because an infinitely perfect God formed them?——Nay, might not a law be absolutely perfect in itself, and yet not calculated to promote men's happiness, in some particular circumstances?—Nay, though the circumstances of mankind were unchangeable, as well as the nature of God, yet what natural obligation can lie upon God, to reveal the whole of his mind and will to them at the very first, more than lies upon a master to give his whole possible directions to a servant, that moment he enters on his service?—Though the relations between God and men should remain unaltered, yet might not men be imperfectly acquainted with some of these relations, or through mistake or prejudice neglect or too slightly perform the duties of them? In such a case, might not God reveal to them some new hints, which might more fully instruct, excite, or enable them, to the right performance of such duties? If he did, might he not require their attention to these intimations of his will, and mark his displeasure with such as contemned them?——If men's circumstances be changed from what they were at first, why may not new duties, suited thereto, be necessary;—even as many things relative to eating and drinking, &c. are necessary to sick persons, which are not to those that are in health?——If new relations take place between God and men, why may not some new duties, or new forms of duty, be enjoined on them by him?—If, notwithstanding all the innumerable changes of his creatures, God still continue the same, absolutely perfect and unchangeable, why may not he continue such, notwithstanding he institute some temporary laws suited to the circumstances of mankind?—Must he be an arbitrary tyrant, if, as a wise Governor, he issue forth some new laws or instructions to his subjects, or at least, in a new manner, when he observes, that their altered circumstances require it?

III. It is readily granted, and hath been formerly proved, that the uncorrupted light of nature manifests the wisdom, power, goodness, equity, and some other perfections of God. But it is irrefragably evident, that the light of nature, as possessed by every man in his present corrupted state, amidst so many powerful vicious inclinations and customs, doth not afford proper views of them.—Who knoweth not, how fearfully the wise Egyptians, the learned Chaldeans, the intelligent Greeks, and the enlightened Romans, became vain in their imaginations?—and that, at least the vulgar, who, being most numerous, ought to have had the law of nature peculiarly adapted to them, and who certainly had it in their breasts as well as others, looked on their gods as exceedingly numerous, and many of them as absolute monsters of cruelty, unchastity, theft, low revenge, and other abominations, in which they themselves delighted.——If all the notions of the modern Siberians, Kamtschatkans, Hottentots, and Patagonians, which are very little corrupted by Revelation, —or even of the ancient Sabians, Magians, and Hellenists, relative to religion, were collected, What a fine system of theology should we have?—How many thousand gods?—How many antic ceremonies, more resembling the ridiculous ape, the cruel tiger, or the nasty sow, than a rational creature worshipping his God?——Meanwhile, how could ever men's inward law of nature infallibly assure them of the *infinite* power, wisdom, goodness, or equity of the sun, moon, and stars,—or of pyed bulls, serpents, dogs, cats, leeks, onions, stones, stocks, &c. which it is certain they worshipped as gods, and instead of the true God.——Nay, had our infidel doctors been nothing indebted to that Revelation which they so uncandidly abuse, it is not probable, that their knowledge would have much transcended that of some brutes.

It hath never been proved that the light of nature manifests God never as *merciful to the transgressors of his law.*—In his common providence, there are manifold instances of his patience. But who knows but he may be enduring with much long-suffering the vessels of wrath fitted to destruction?——If men be still in their *original state*, they cannot be *miserable*, and so not proper objects of mercy.—If they have fallen from it, they must have done so, by their deviation from the law of their *infinite Sovereign*, and from attention to the infinitely important end of his honour, and the general good of his creatures,— and hence their crime must be infinitely heinous.—Now, what certain proof doth the Light of nature afford us, That God will forgive an infinite crime, without full satisfaction to his justice;

or that he will render men happy to the uttermost, if, for the time to come, they do the best, that their corrupt nature, which is enmity against him, deceitful above all things, and desperately wicked, is capable of?—Must God trample on his own infinite majesty and honour, or on his own infinite equity to himself and his creatures, that his mercy may be exercised on treacherous rebels?——Can even a magistrate, consistent with wisdom, goodness, and equity, save murderers from punishment, and promote them to honour, providing they become penitent?——Doth not the almost universal oblation of sacrifices among heathens clearly prove, that their consciences dictated to them, That God cannot be merciful and kind to transgressors, even though penitent, without receiving a proper atonement to his justice for their crimes.

Meanwhile, if it be considered that, in those countries where men have had least access to Revelation, they have been, and still are, little better than a kind of sagacious, but savage brutes; and that men's knowledge hath increased in proportion to their immediate access to, and improvement of it; it appears probable, that every proper sentiment concerning the nature of God or of man, and concerning moral virtue, among the Chaldeans, Egyptians, Phenicians, Greeks, Romans, Celts, Chinese, Indians, or others, owed its rise or revival to the diffused sparks of revelation.

Neither the law nor the light of nature teacheth *that God proposeth the highest happiness of his creatures as his sole or principal end in making and managing them, without ever intending his own glory; or that, in consequence of this, rational creatures are under no obligation to aim at his honour as their chief end, in all their conduct; and that he cannot be offended with them if they act according to their own inclinations.*——If the advancing men's happiness to the highest were God's *sole*, or even *chief* end, in his creating, upholding, and governing them, Why, notwithstanding all his infinite power, wisdom, and goodness, is this end so much defeated, and men for the most part miserable?— Why are not all of them in Africa, Tartary, Greenland, and America, and Britain, equally happy, honoured, healthy, intelligent, and useful, being equally the work of his hands?— Hath he formed in them a *free will*, which he cannot govern to promote their own welfare? Or, have the villanous priests been capable to defeat his kind intentions, wise purposes, and almighty influences?—In vain it is pretended that the salutary corrections of a future state may rectify the miseries into which men bring themselves, by their mistakes in this. For, what if God should reckon it folly to lavish his favours, in a future state, upon such as obstinately die in their crimes?—Or, what if he should have determined to be favourable no more to them?—Or, if men, or any thing else, can defeat all his endeavours to promote his chief, his sole end, in this life, why may they not be capable to do it for ever?—Nay, if rendering men happy to the uttermost was his principal or sole end, how can he, consistent with his infinite power, wisdom, and goodness, permit them ever to be, in the least, miserable?—Not therefore the advancing their happiness to the highest, but the manifesting the glory of his own perfections, must have been his *chief end*, in making and managing of men, and of every other creature.—If so, every attempt to defeat or deviate from that important end, must be *infinitely criminal*.——Is it then to be supposed, that men ought never to regard this end or their own eternal welfare, as dependent on it?—Or, that God will sit unconcerned at their pouring contempt on it, and their thus attempting to murder himself, the infinite Maker, Upholder, and Governor of the world; and to ruin the welfare, the existence of all his creatures, which depend on him for every thing?—Nay, though we could suppose that God's own honour had not been his *chief end* in making and managing the world, it might be our duty to make it our chief end in our whole conduct.—Though a benevolent friend should not chiefly, or even not at all, have in view his own honour in freely supplying our wants, it might be our duty to regard chiefly his honour, in testifying our thankfulness.

IV. It is readily admitted, that God's infinite goodness determines him to make his law of nature sufficiently known to his innocent rational creatures. But it hath been sufficiently proved, that he neither doth, nor is obliged to make it perfectly and clearly known to mankind in their present state. And, if he were obliged to render it sufficiently known to them, why might he not restore the knowledge of it by revelation, if its natural impressions be lost?

V. We readily grant that future rewards of virtue, which depend not on any *natural relation* betwixt God and men, but on *federal agreements*, cannot be proved to be an enforcement of the law of nature. But we can never admit, that future punishments of vice are not a penal, nay the principal penal sanction of the law of nature.——How can God, in justice to himself or to his creatures, forbear to point his indignation against the man who attempts to be their common destroyer?—If he duly regard his own infinite excellencies, how can he mark the horrid blasphemer, the bloody murderer, and the rapacious thief, as no less his favourites, than the most virtuous and devout persons?—If he be infinitely displeased with sin, why may not he punish it, when, where, and how he pleaseth?—By what right or power can any limit his patient long-suffering towards the guilty?—If they persist in their sin till their death, why may they not be punished in a future state?—If they sin as long as they can, why may not God punish their sin as long as he can?—If sin, as committed against infinite perfection and authority, in opposition to an infinitely important end, and as an attempt to dishonour, to destroy an infinitely precious- God, be infinitely criminal, how can any punishment of it less than infinite be adequate?—And, how can it be executed on a finite person, but in his eternal damnation?—If the justice of God require the infliction of such punishment, it is needless to inquire how it can be useful to other creatures.——And yet, who knows how the future punishment of sinners may enhance the everlasting happiness of the virtuous;—how much it may impress their minds with a delightful sense of God's goodness to them;—or with a complacent acquiescence in the eternal vindication of his own infinite excellencies, in the punishment of those impious wretches that on earth contemned them?——Moreover, though we should suppose future troubles to be no more than salutary corrections, no more than probable, or even possible, the law of nature which direct men to provide food, raiment, houses, and the like, for a future period, which they will perhaps never enjoy, must also direct them to use every known and proper mean of preventing or escaping them.

CHAP. III.

Of the REVEALED STANDARD *of Religion contained in the Scriptures of the Old and New Testament, in its* POSSIBILITY, DESIRABLENESS, NECESSITY, PROPRIETY, REASONABLENESS, CREDIBILITY, DIVINE AUTHORITY, *and* CONTENTS.

I. A REVELATION of God's mind and will to men is POSSIBLE.— Being infinite in wisdom and knowledge, God cannot but know many things which we do not.—Being absolutely sovereign, he cannot be bound to reveal all his mind at once to us,—nor even all that we are capable of knowing.—There is no greater necessity for his disclosing things relative to religion, than for his discovering things relative to arts and sciences, but as he sees fit.—Though his infinite wisdom and goodness should influence him, at the first, to manifest all that is absolutely necessary to be known, in order to promote real virtue and happiness,—why may not he afterwards make new manifestations, which may promote superior happiness?——If he has given us a power of communicating our thoughts to others around us,—how can he be incapable to communicate his own? ——If he hath enstamped upon every creature the marks of his infinite perfections;—if he mark every creature with a distinguishing form, colour, countenance, or voice, &c.—and give to every man a peculiar style, manner of writing, &c. how can he be incapable to reveal his mind to men in a manner that will sufficiently mark it his own?—And, if he make merciful additions to the law of nature, why may they not be received upon sufficient evidences of their divine authority?——And, why may not men who, before they received this revelation, were very ignorant,—by the plain articles of it, and the uncontrouled miracles and power attending it, be awakened, and enabled to perceive its divine authority.—Though this revelation cannot forbid any thing which the law of nature requires, or require any thing which the law of nature forbids,—why may it not disclose some things which the law, at least the light, of nature, as enjoyed by us, did not? or require some things not required; or forbid some things not forbidden by it?——And, why any more need of *mathematical demonstrableness* to prove a revelation to be from God, than to prove the law of nature to be from him?

II. A supernatural revelation from God is DESIRABLE.— Though the law of nature was perfectly sufficient to conduct men to happiness, while they continued in the estate in which they were created,—the entrance of sin, by putting things out of order, may have rendered it insufficient. Ignorance may have darkened their mind, sense of guilt terrified their conscience, and vicious inclinations biassed their will and affections:— their whole spiritual constitution may be so weakened, as to render helps necessary to excite and enable them, to know and obey, even the law of nature.——And, if human instructions and excitements may be useful, why may not divine ones be much more so?—If then they be offered, why should they not readily and thankfully be received and practised?——In vain it is pretended, that rationality will render men sufficiently religious: for generally the high pretenders to rationality have least appearance of devotion or virtue. Nay, though men should know somewhat relative to their duty and interest, might not a larger measure of wisdom and knowledge render them still more virtuous, useful, and happy? Will our infidels pretend, that the most stupid savages, who are endowed with rationality, bid fair to be as useful and happy as Socrates, Epictetus, Antoninus, Seneca, &c.?—Though men should know their duty in no inconsiderable degree, may they not need excitements to and direction in practising it?—Though sound reason were sufficient to direct men, how God is to be honoured and worshipped, and his creatures used,---corrupted reason cannot.------Though it were sufficient to direct them how to deal with God as a friend, it cannot direct them how to procure his friendship when they have rendered him their enemy.---Nay, if reason alone be sufficient to direct and duly excite men to virtue and happiness, why did Socrates, Plato, Cicero, Seneca, and innumerable others of the like complexion, distress the world with their costly and tedious instructions?---It is absurd to pretend, that men's *innate benevolence* similar to that of God, will sufficiently assist their reason in influencing them to virtue, and leading them to happiness. It is foolish to talk of men's *innate benevolence*, when such atheism, such indevotion, and such malevolence, prevail in every part of the world.---It is equally absurd to pretend, that philosophy will, or can, correct the errors of mankind.---Very few of the heathen philosophers professed to be teachers of morality.---Such of them as did could produce no divine warrant for their commencing instructors to their neighbours.---None of them appear to have given a single lecture against idolatry, sodomy, and other reigning vices of their country. And seldom did their lectures on any point of morality appear to have any good influence on their own behaviour. ---They never touched upon the higher points of virtue in men's loving God with all their heart, soul, mind, and strength, or loving their neighbours as themselves. They never enforced their instructions with the principal motives to true virtue, drawn from the excellency, authority and kindness of God, or from clear and distinct views as to a future eternity of inexpressible happiness and misery. They neither did, nor could, give men any proof, that God would accept their imperfect, or even perfect virtue, unless they first made full satisfaction for their sinful defects.---Their sentiments were also so diversified, that none could certainly learn from them, what was either virtue, or vice.---And even now, how little reformation would a philosophical harangue upon the beauty of chastity, honesty, benevolence, or serious devotion, have upon an assembly of rakes, robbers, and infidels?

Though the light of nature in itself, were still sufficient to point out every thing necessary to our true and lasting happiness, yet our indolence, passion, prejudices, and deep-rooted habits of vice, render us very unfit for an impartial search after truth. Most men from their worldly employments, and their manifold connexions one with another, cannot spare the time that is necessary for inquiring into the principles of natural religion. Few have ever actually undertaken such a laborious task, or succeeded in it.------And after all the search they could make, what certain proof could they give, that God will pardon sin, or that there is a future state of everlasting felicity?—both which must necessarily be known and firmly believed, in order to our attaining to perfection in virtue, nay to any real degree of it, or any satisfactory comfort of mind.——Though some great genius should arise, and find out every thing necessary to be known, in order to perfection in virtue and happiness, how could he, in a clear and efficacious manner, unfold his discoveries to others, who are so ignorant, and so much biassed to the contrary?—By what conscience-awing authority could he give out? or how could he enforce his instructions?—Though the magistrates' power were exerted in his favour, that extends only to the externals of actions, and not at all to the *true form and essence* of virtue.——To add no more, the desires and the hopes of Socrates, Plato, and other heathen philosophers, for some divine revelation to solve their doubts;—the manifold pretences to revelation among Heathens, Mahometans, Jews and Christians;—and even the ready application of medicines providentially provided for our diseased bodies—prove that revelation, the medicine of diseased minds, is *desirable* in order to make us understand and obey the law of nature, or at least to render us more, or more easily happy than otherwise we could be,—if not *really existent.*

Though reason be necessary to examine the authority of divine revelation, Revelation itself is not therefore unnecessary and useless. Even in this very examination, it is useful for the excitement and assistance of our reason.——Though reason be judge and manager in all the methods of learning the arts and sciences, these are so far from being unnecessary and useless, that reason itself is much improved by them.—The external evidence to the divine authority of revelation may strike the mind of an Atheist, convince him that there is a God, and cause him attentively to consider the principles of natural religion, and thus prepare him for examining the internal evidences of the divinity of revelation.——The attesting revelation by miracles, and the accomplishment of its predictions, confirm good men in their former belief of the unchangeable purposes, and of the unerring, wise, and all-powerful providence of God.—— The internal evidence as to the divinity of some revealed doctrines, and the miracles which attest and procure credit to the publishers, as faithful messengers of God, warrant men to receive their other doctrines, though they should not at first clearly perceive the internal evidence of their divine original.—Nor is any remarkable insight into the law of nature necessary to qualify men for embracing divine revelation, as it brings light along with itself, and is as sufficient to procure the assent of their mind, or consent of their will, as the law of nature is.—— Though reason be exceedingly useful in finding out the sense of revelation, that will no more infer, that it is its judge or foundation, than that the hand which brings nourishment to my mouth, is the nourishment itself; or that the eye which perceives the gold in the mine, and the hand which brings it out, are the cause or essence of the gold.——Nay, the true and *saving faith* of divine revelation is not at all founded on *mere rational proofs* of its divine original, but on its *self-evidencing light and power*, displayed in the almighty application of it to our heart, by the Holy Ghost.

III. In the present state and condition of mankind, to conduct them to true virtue and happiness, a supernatural revelation of God's mind and will is absolutely NECESSARY. 1. It is evident, that men are now in a fallen state, in which they want much of that goodness which they originally possessed.—The multitude of civil laws and their sanctions, the multitude of legal securities, bonds, writs, oaths, pledges, and of bolts, locks, keys, &c. are unanswerable documents of the necessity and even the difficulty of restraining men from vice. Notwithstanding all these restraints, much more vice than virtue appears in the world.—The histories of all nations, the most enlightened and civilized not excepted, consists of little else than malevolence, deceit, strife, war, murder, robbery, brutish or whimsical idolatry, and superstition.—Scarce any thing at all fills the annals of the Goths, Hunns, Tartars, African and American savages, but brutality, cruelty, robbery, murder, and the like, their minds not having been impressed by the light of revelation.——Nay, unless men's nature be corrupted, why, notwithstanding much pains to prevent it, is there any vice at all in the world?—Why, at the expence of inward remorse, and the hazard of temporal and eternal punishments, doth any man commit crimes, even the most contrary to the law of nature? ——If men have corrupt inclinations they could not, in their original formation, receive them from God, who is infinitely holy, just, wise, and good. 2. If men be in such a corrupt state, they must have fallen into it by some breach of the law of nature, which is founded on God's *infinite authority*, and is a transcript of his *infinite excellency*,—some deviation from the *infinitely important end* of creation and providence;—and hence their crime, objectively considered, must be *infinitely heinous*, and so must deserve nothing less than *infinite punishment*. God cannot discover a proper regard to his own excellencies and laws, when they are contemned, hated, and trampled on, or to his creatures when they are abused and injured, unless he execute due punishment on the transgressors.—It is not *mean* but *proper* for him to punish those base wretches, whom all the charms and rewards of virtue could never attract,—whom neither his excellency and kindness could allure, nor all his majesty, authority, and justice could awe. 3. If, in proportion to the heinous nature of their crimes, their punishment be infinite, impossible to be endured by them at once, it must be extended through an everlasting duration. Unless also, their nature be changed, they, under their punishment, will offend more and more.—Nay, though their nature were got once changed, how could mere creatures love a *wrathful*, a *condemning*, a *punishing* God, with all their heart, soul, mind, and strength? How could their holiness of nature be preserved under his curse, and the execution of it? Fallen men must therefore continue for ever in their sinfulness and misery, unless some *infinite* and *almighty deliverer* be found, who can give *infinite satisfaction* to an offended God for their sins, and restore them into favour with him and conformity to his image.—No such deliverer can be found, unless there be more than one person in the godhead, and these graciously agree, that one of them shall undertake the arduous work. It is highly absurd to pretend that repentance will *atone for crimes*, where *infinite satisfaction* is due.—It would effectually ruin civil societies, if repentance were admitted as a sufficient satisfaction for crimes against men. The vilest traitor, murderer, or robber, rather than rot in a prison or hang on a gibbet, would pretend to repent, and none could see his heart. ——The repentance of a man who continued under the dominion of sinful lusts, could imply no real hatred of sin itself, but only amount to *mere rage* against it, on account of its consequences; or rather to mere grief and rage, that God should be so holy and just, that he will not suffer sin to pass unpunished. How could this be an acceptable satisfaction to God?—In the future state no troubles suffered by a finite creature could ever amount to an *infinite satisfaction*. Nor have we the least proof, that the torments of that state ever did, or will, or can, in the smallest degree, extinguish men's sinfulness or misery. What, if there be millions of rational creatures, that have been tormented almost ever since the creation, without being in the least bettered by it? 4. If any proper method of recovering fallen men be found out by God, it is proper that it should be unfolded. Without a divine revelation of the subsistence of three persons in one godhead, reason will pronounce the redemption of sinners impossible. A concealed method of salvation could never sufficiently vindicate the justice of God, in punishing an innocent, a divine Redeemer, in our stead, and justifying us, who are guilty sinners, on his account.—A revelation of the method of our redemption is necessary to make us consider it, and give our cheerful consent to it; necessary to make us know our Redeemer, and how to receive his blessings and testify our thankfulness, in suitable forms of duty, not prescribed by the law of nature,—and even necessary to vindicate our behaviour towards God and men, when it is so different from that of the world around us.

IV. No revelation relating to the redemption of mankind could answer its important ends, unless it was sufficiently supported with internal and external evidences of its divine authority, or origination from God.——In its INTERNALS, my reason would induce me to expect, that it should contain nothing unworthy of God's perfections, or inconsistent with his law of nature;—that it would elucidate and confirm the laws of nature, and awaken men's attention to them, especially in their leading articles;—that it would unfold some new and important mysteries concerning God's redeeming mankind;—and clearly exhibit some remarkable truths, not at all, or at least very darkly, pointed by the law of nature, relative to the pardon of sin, future happiness, and the like;—that all the principal points of truth should, in some passages, be so plainly expressed, that every unbiassed reader of ordinary capacity might readily perceive them;—in fine, that it should exhibit a most exalted and amiable representation of God as *wise, holy, just, gracious, merciful,* and *faithful,*—should mightily check the pride and selfishness of men;—and that all its parts should harmoniously concur to promote solid virtue.——In its EXTERNAL circumstances, I would expect, that all or most of those employed in first publishing it should be men of distinguished virtue, practically exemplifying their instructions;—that some principal publisher should, in his own exemplification of the virtues which he enjoined, give an absolutely perfect pattern to others; —that neither he, nor any subordinate publishers, should have such worldly honour, power, wealth, or influence as might bias themselves, or engage others without proper examination to believe them;—that the first publication, or the more noted revivals thereof, should be attended with public, plain, and uncontrouled miracles, for attesting the publisher's commission from God, and for awakening mankind to attend to, examine, and embrace their messages;—that the principal publishers should be remarkably owned of God, in their labours and sufferings.—I would expect that revelation should be gradually exhibited as men needed it, or were able to bear it;— that it should be chiefly exhibited in such seasons, if not also in such places, as were most proper for a thorough examination of its divine marks, manner, and contents;—that its principal exhibitions should be attended with a remarkable influence upon men's hearts and practices, and with alarming events in nations and churches, that the date and other circumstances of it, might lie the more open to an after examination. I would expect, that the principal histories of it should be attested by enemies as well as by friends;—that God, by his providence, should discover a singular care in the preservation and safe conveyance of it from one generation or place to another;—and that, as miracles too frequently repeated lose their alarming influence, it should contain many circumstantiated predictions, the exact accomplishment of which, from age to age, might supply the place of miracles.

The Heathen, Mahometan, and Popish revelations, if examined by these desirable, and some of them absolutely necessary marks of a revelation from God, clearly appear to be mere impostures. They nevertheless indirectly suggest the reality of some genuine and authentic revelation of the mind and will of God; otherwise, why should so many attempt to counterfeit it?—But, the more narrowly that revelation, which is contained in our Bibles, is examined by these or any other proper characteristics, the more clearly will its excellency, suitableness, and divine authority appear.

V. The contents of the scriptures of the Old and New Testaments are PERFECTLY AGREEABLE TO REASON. Indeed, the leading doctrines concerning the *Trinity of persons in one godhead;*—the *origin of moral evil;*—the *mercy of God;*—the *method of our redemption, effectual calling, justification, sanctification, and eternal glorification, through the Son of God in our nature, as Mediator between God and men;*—and concerning *our union and communion with him, and our worshipping of God in him;*—and concerning *the true grounds of our comfort under the troubles of life, or against the fears of death;*—the *certainty and form of the general resurrection and last judgment*, are not unfolded by reason. Nay, it is proper that they should transcend its most narrow and laborious search. Otherwise it were improper, that God should reveal them with so much solemnity and such full attestation.—But, when they are manifested by divine revelation, every one of them appears perfectly consistent with right reason.

Nothing can more transcend the investigation or comprehension of human reason, than the mystery of *three persons in one godhead*, revealed in our Bible, yet it is entirely agreeable to it. It is perfectly reasonable, that an infinite substance, whose fulness is unbounded, should subsist in a plurality of persons at once, though a created and finite substance cannot. The substance of one numerical or individual divine substance in a *plurality of persons* equal in power and in glory, or the reason of its subsisting precisely in *three distinct persons*, is not, in the least, more incomprehensible to our reason, than the self-existence, unsuccessive eternity, and absolute infinity of God, all which we cannot, without trampling on and unhinging our reason, but own to be *essential properties* of his nature. Though mere reason afford us no hint of this *subsistence of one God in three distinct persons*, it loudly suggests, that *in an infinite God*, there may be ten thousand excellencies, which our finite, our weak, and disordered minds, may not have perceived.—— Though there be no vestige of God's subsistence in three persons in his works of creation and providence, reason suggests that it may nevertheless be true. Both reason and experience attest, that men may have many real excellencies, piety, benevolence, and the like, which are not visibly marked in the common productions of their hands. Even the deformed hints of *three persons in one godhead* given by Pythagoras, Plato, Trismegistus, and some Chinese philosophers, which, I doubt not, were derived from revelation, concur to represent this mystery as agreeable to reason. My reason loudly demands, that I admit that an infinite God *knows himself infinitely better* than I can pretend; and that, therefore, I ought readily to believe every representation which he makes of himself, however incapable I be fully to understand it.——Nay, without supposition of this mysterious subsistence of the godhead in distinct persons, reason attests, that the redemption of sinful and miserable men is absolutely impossible. For, how could the same divine person be *Sender* and *Sent; Creditor* and *Debtor; Judge* and *condemned Criminal in law; Punisher* and *Punished?* ——Is it reasonable to damn every individual of mankind, rather than admit that God may possess a perfection which I cannot comprehend, and of which I do not perceive any marks in his works of nature? How shocking the thought!

Upon the supposition of God's purposing to recover all or any of mankind from their *fallen estate*, Reason pronounces the whole mediatorial scheme, when revealed, as not merely agreeable to itself, but most of it absolutely necessary, and all of it highly becoming the perfections of God.——Infinite satisfaction for sin being necessary to purchase its pardon, none but an infinite person could give it.---How reasonable then, that the second person in the godhead should become our Surety and assume our nature, not only that he might endear God to us, and as our pattern exemplify to us a course of the most unblemished and exalted virtue, but chiefly, that in the very nature which had sinned, he might obey the law and satisfy the justice of God, and act as our interceding advocate with Him, providing that all this was necessary for recovering mankind,---and that the honour of God, and of our divine Surety should not, on the whole, suffer, but be proportionally advanced.——Both Reason and experience attest, that no easier method could effectually recover fallen men.---Notwithstanding all the philosophy of the Egyptians, Chaldeans, Persians,

Greeks, Romans, Indians, and Gauls,---all the costly ceremonies of the Jews and their proselytes,---all the engaging deliverances, and alarming corrections of Divine Providence, men had, for several thousand years, become worse and worse, deceiving, and being deceived.------By this method of redemption, the honour of God and of the Mediator is sufficiently secured, and gloriously advanced.---The divine Redeemer's life being properly his own, he readily surrendered it to his Father's justice, in the room and for the benefit of sinful men. Neither he nor the world suffered any injury by his death. To balance his debasement, labours, and sufferings, he was quickly raised from the dead, and rewarded with everlasting glory and honour, as Head over all things to his church.---Though wicked men instrumentally robbed him of his life, his own *voluntary surrender* of it constituted his sufferings and death a *proper atonement* for men's sin.------Hereby the perfections of God are gloriously displayed:---If he had rendered sinful men happy without a *proper* and *adequate satisfaction* for their sins, they would be tempted to think the breaches of his law scarcely criminal, and be encouraged to offend him more and more. But when he fully punishes all their sins on his own Son, constituted their Surety, and charged in law with their crimes,---how possibly can this tempt men to think that he hates the innocent and loves the guilty!---Nay, it discovers Him to be *so infinitely holy and just*, that he cannot but hate iniquity, and cannot suffer his own Son, when legally charged with it, to pass unpunished.------This *atonement* is necessary, not in order that God may love men, but that his love may be honourably manifested to, and upon them :---It renders pardon of sin *due to us* for the Mediator's sake, and yet altogether of God's free grace, as we are considered in ourselves.---Our having a Mediator between God and us imports not any absence of him, or his having any inclination to ceremony ; but it imports our unworthiness, and his infinite greatness and purity, that he neither will, nor can have any immediate favourable and friendly dealing with sinful creatures.---It encourages us in approaching boldly to God to ask and receive every thing that we need, notwithstanding all our weakness, guilt, and pollution.---It unfolds the exceeding riches of his grace, in freely providing for us an effectual mean of fellowship with himself suited to our sinful and wretched condition.------How possibly then can Reason teach men to hazard, nay, insure their own eternal damnation, rather than acquiesce in such a scheme of redemption,---such a Mediator,---such a substitution,---such a mediation, devised and established by God for their everlasting and inconceivable happiness.

Upon the rational supposition of such a reasonable scheme of redemption, nothing can be more reasonable, than that every person for whom it is intended, should be particularly chosen in the Mediator, as their saving Head, that he may have every one, for whom he undertook, as his fellow-sharers of eternal blessedness.----If, in consequence of his engagement for them, and assumption of their nature, their sins were charged on, and satisfied for, by Him, Reason demands that, in consequence of their union to Him as their Surety and Husband, his righteousness fulfilled in their stead should judicially be placed to their account, and all the blessings of justification, adoption, sanctification, spiritual comfort, and eternal glory be communicated to them as in Him.

This revelation contained in our Bibles suggests no *unworthy apprehensions* of God. Human parts, members, affections, passions, or acts, are ascribed to Him, merely in condescension to our weakness, as without them, the deistical Collins justly observes, " many could not conceive of God at all," and they are to be understood in a figurative and spiritual manner.---God is never represented as *unholy*.---When he is said to *harden* or *deceive* men, it means no more than that he permits them to harden and deceive themselves, or to be hardened and deceived by Satan and their wicked companions.---Jeremiah's charge of God with *deceiving* him is probably the language of his unbelief and passion; or, his words might be translated, *Thou hast persuaded me, and I was persuaded, i. e.* to prophecy, Jer. xx. 7. God is the author of the *evil* of punishment, but not of the *evil* of vice, Amos iii. 6. Isa. xlv. 7.---God did not *break* his promise to the Israelites in the Arabian wilderness. He never promised that that particular generation, which came out of Egypt, should enter into Canaan.---Their continuance and their ruin in the wilderness were but a just *interruption* or *delay* of the fulfilment of his promise occasioned by their sin. And when their children had got possession of Canaan, it clearly appeared how unjustly God had been charged with any breach of his promise, Num. xiv. 34.

Nothing which is approved in Scripture is *contrary to the Law of nature*. The Jewish laws prohibited every kind of immorality, and particularly drunkenness and disobedience to parents, Deut. xxix. 19. and xxi. 18—21. They discouraged every kind of whoredom and uncleanness.---Priests' daughters, who committed whoredom, and every person chargeable with adultery, incest, sodomy, bestiality, were appointed to death. If a young woman had been defiled and concealed it, or if a wife secretly committed adultery, they exposed themselves to the utmost hazard of a shameful death, Lev. xviii. xx. Deut. xii. 20, 21. Num. v. He that defiled a slave paid the value of her ransom, and she was scourged, Lev. xix. 20, 21, 22. Bastards were excluded from the congregation of the Lord, Deut.

E

xxiii. 1—8.——Honesty and benevolence were strongly inculcated;—that men should love their neighbours as themselves,—should deal kindly with the oxen and asses of their enemies,—and carefully protect and provide for strangers, widows, and fatherless children, Exod. xxii. 21, 22. Lev. xix. 10, &c.——
Indeed, some laws were singular and obscure ; but these ought to be explained by others, which are more plain ; and the rather, that in so compendious an history many things are certainly omitted which might have illustrated their meaning and propriety.——It was highly reasonable that Abraham, when commanded by God, the sovereign proprietor, Lord, giver and restorer of human life, should willingly attempt to offer his only son Isaac in sacrifice. Besides, God intended, by this command, merely to prove and honour Abraham's faith and obedience ; whenever this was done, he stopt the execution, and loaded them with his blessings, Gen. xxii. Heb. xi. 17—19.
——It was highly reasonable, that the Israelites, when commanded by God, the primary and supreme proprietor of all things, and judge of the world, should ASK (not BORROW) and carry off that wealth which their long hard service had deserved as wages, and to which the Egyptians had forfeited all their right before God, Exod. iii. 22. and xii. 35, 36——As the Midianites, Canaanites, and Amalekites had, by their adulteries, idolatries, and murders, forfeited their lives and substance, into the hands of his justice, God had full right to appoint whom he pleased to deprive them thereof: and it was very proper to appoint the Israelites to do it, in order to deter them from the commission of such crimes, Num. xxv. xxxi. Deut. vii. Lev. xviii. xx. Josh. vi.—xii. Num. xxi. Judg. iv. Exod. xvii. 1 Sam. xv.——Phinehas, Ehud, Elijah, and Jehu, acting as deputies under God, the supreme magistrate of their nation, might justly punish malefactors or act hostilely against declared enemies, Num. xxv. Judges iii. 1 Kings xviii. 2 Kings i. ix. x.
——Idolatry, blasphemy, and witchcraft, being high treason against God as King of nations, as well as King of Israel, it was highly proper, that these and other like crimes should be punished by death. And had that penalty effectually deterred the Jews from these abominations, it had been exceedingly profitable to them and to the heathens around, and had prevented much misery.

God never punisheth children for the sins of their parents, but when they are involved in their guilt, or have by other sins deserved the punishment inflicted, though on account of their parents' wickedness, they met with it in a particular form, Exod. xx. 5.—The innocent children of Korah did not suffer in his punishment. The children of Dathan, Abiram, and Achan, who perished with their parents, were most probably partakers

with them in their crimes, Num. xxvi. 10, 11. and xvi. 27—
—33. Josh vii. 24, 25. Perhaps the descendants of Saul, that
were hanged by the Gibeonites, had wickedly justified his perfidious murder of these strangers, who were dedicated to the
service of God. It is certain, the case was extraordinary,
warning all the Israelites to beware of violating any of their
engagements materially lawful, 2 Sam. xxi. 1—9.——Uncircum-
cised Hebrew children were not liable to death till, by their
own fault when come to the years of discretion, they had con-
temptuously neglected the seal of God's covenant, the badge of
his peculiar people; and perhaps cutting off from God's people
means no more than exclusion from his church, Genesis xvii.
10—14.——But after all, it is certain, that children often suffer in the punishment of their parents' sin—from the hands of
men in the forfeiture of the estates of traitors;—and from the
hand of God, when multitudes of infants perish in inundations,
earthquakes, fires, massacres, overthrows of nations or cities,
&c. And, in ordinary cases, how often do children suffer in
their bodies, minds, and estates, through the sloth, prodigality,
and other wickedness of parents, as well as the bad education
which they receive from them.

No resentfulness of temper is allowed, but strictly forbidden
in the Scriptures, Prov. xxv. 21. Rom. xii. 17.---21. Mat. v.
45---48. Luke vi. 26---36.——Elijah and Elisha acted by extraordinary warrant from God, and punished none but ringleaders in idolatry and blasphemy, if not also murderers of the
godly, who therefore deserved death by the civil magistrate, 1
Kings xviii. 19---40. 2 Kings i. 9---12. and ii. 24. and ix. 7,
8. Jeremiah did not resentfully wish the ruin of his persecutors, but, as directed by God, foretold it as a warning to others,
Jer. xi. xviii, xx, xxviii, xxix, xxxvi, xliv. Several expressions of the Psalms might be translated, and are to be understood *not as resentful wishes* but as *awful predictions* of that punishment which should befal the implacable enemies of David,
and especially the incorrigible enemies of Jesus Christ, of whom
he was a type.—Moreover, as God was in a peculiar manner
the king of the Jewish nation, these petitions for judgments on
offenders may be considered as reasonable applications to him
for proper protection and redress, Psal. v. vi, vii, xxxv, xl,
lvii, lix, lxiv, lxx, lxxix, cix, cxl. And as the Jews lived under a more uniform influence of outward providence, and had
not such distinct revelations of future rewards and punishments
as we have, the exercise of external severities, especially upon
ringleaders in wickedness, was in some cases more necessary.

Neither Samuel nor Jeremiah uttered any falsehood, but
merely concealed that which they had no call to declare, 1 Sam.
xvi. 1, 5. Jer. xxxviii. 26, 27. Nor is there any evidence, that

the Egyptian midwives uttered any falsehood concerning the easy childbirth of the Hebrew women, Exod, i. 19.—Rahab did not betray her country, but merely provided for her own and her friends' safety when she saw the inevitable ruin of her country to be at hand. Nor is she ever commended for her lie concerning the Hebrew spies, but for her faith in receiving them, Heb. xi. 31.

Nothing ridiculous or absurd is ever enjoined in Scripture. The conferences of God with Satan, concerning Job and Ahab, may be figuratively understood. And yet, God might as well converse with Satan, as with Cain, Balaam, &c. Job i, ii. 1 Kings xxii. Hosea's marriage might be figuratively transacted. Or, he might very honourably marry a woman, whose character was good, but after marriage played the harlot: or an whorish woman, who had become remarkably penitent, Hos. i. iii. Isaiah's walking *naked* and *barefoot*, means no more than his going without his upper garment and shoes, Isa. xx. Ezekiel's besieging a tile on which Jerusalem was pourtrayed, 430 days lying on his sides, and living on coarse bread fired with dung,—and other symbolical actions of prophets, had no oddity before God; and if the people reckoned them strange, they were so much the better suited to alarm them, Ezek. iv, v, viii, xii. xxi, xxiv. Jer. xiii, xviii, xix, xxxv, &c.

Christ's parables were not calculated to impose on his hearers, but, according to the manner of the ancients, and of the East, particularly to make them carefully listen to, easily remember, and deliberately consider, what he said, before they either received or rejected it.——A *sword* and *contention* were not strictly the proposed ends and proper effects of his coming into the world; but merely the consequences occasioned by men's rejection of his salutary instructions, Mat. x. 34. Luke xii. 49. He never allowed of any other eunuchism, but a voluntary and chaste abstinence from marriage, Mat. xix. 12. He never declared poor men happy, or rich men miserable, but on certain grounds perfectly agreeable to the Law of nature. Men's giving *all that they have* to the poor, is in some cases agreeable to the Light of nature, and if they do it in obedience to the will of their benevolent God, he will not suffer them to be losers. *Forgiveness of injuries* is an high degree of benevolence recommended by Confucius, a famed Chinese philosopher.---Moreover, Christ's expressions ordinarily alluding to things well known among them, could not but be much more clear to them, than they are to us, Luke xi, xii, xv, xvi. Mat. xix, v, vi, vii, xviii.

No *positive institutions* of worship, or any thing else in Scripture, are contrary to the perfections of God, or injurious to the interests of men.

1. God may know sufficient reasons for such institutions, though our weak minds do not perceive or cannot comprehend them.—It would indeed be improper for him to exert his sovereignty in appointing every ceremony or law, that could be devised, as that would mar his worship, and produce the utmost confusion. But it is very proper, that he manifest his own sovereignty, to prove men's obedience, by some laws founded on his mere will, since he of his mere will formed man. If magistrates, for the greater welfare of their subjects, may enact some statutes which are not absolutely necessary in themselves, Why may not He, whose authority is absolutely independent and infinite, whose wisdom and goodness is unbounded, enact some positive laws for the advantage of his rational creatures,—especially in religious matters, which most directly relate to his own honour, and hence are the less fit to be left to the direction of men's corrupt fancy or choice.

2. The Jewish ceremonies were not instituted at, but most of them after their departure from Egypt, Jer. vii. 22, 23. Nor were they ever enjoined, as of equal importance with the duties of morality, Hos. vi. 6. Nor are they ever represented as *bad* in themselves, though the Jews' manner of observing them, or their adhering to them after the resurrection of Christ, be highly condemned, Hos. xi. 12. Isa. i. 11—15. and xxix. 13. and lxvi. 3. But, when attended to according to God's appointment, they were *lasting* and *public memorials* of the mighty works which he had done for that nation;—and, by separating them from their heathen neighbours, checked their fondness for their abominable idolatry and superstition, to the rites of which, no doubt, some obscure Jewish ceremonies alluded. They also contributed to preserve his oracles from corruption.—Some of these ceremonies represented his infinite majesty, and regulated their affairs under him, as their dread sovereign. But most of them were intended to prefigure Jesus Christ in his person, offices, estates, kingdom, and blessings,—to produce a longing for, and to prepare them to receive him, upon a due examination of his character. Even the burdensome load of these ceremonies tended to enlarge their convictions of guilt, to make them sensible of their extensive dependence on God, and earnestly to desire the promised deliverer with his easy yoke.——Not one of these instituted ceremonies was dangerous. Without any danger, circumcision sealed the covenant of grace, and that covenant of peculiar relation to God with them,—distinguished them from other nations, and probably promoted their cleanliness, health, and fruitfulness. —Most, if not all the prohibited flesh, was unwholesome in that warm climate.—Their numerous purifications promoted their health and their vigour.—These, and their limited food, em-

blematically instructed them to avoid the contagion of vices.— Their sacred oblations prefigured good things to come, promoted a sense of, and humiliation for sins, as also maintained their priests. The sin-offerings also served as a fine imposed on the offender.—No human sacrifices were allowed, but severely prohibited.—The Levites had an original right to the twelfth part of Canaan; and as their sacred labours, and want of fields, prevented their gains by cultivation or civil business, it was meet they should have the *Tithes* from their brethren as their wages for their public service.

The positive institutions of Christianity are but very few and evidently *reasonable.* Reason requires, that men who are endowed with social dispositions, should worship God in a social manner; and Revelation prescribes but one day in seven for that purpose. The ancient Sabbath on the seventh day of the week, commemorated God's finishing his work of *Creation,* and represented the order of labour and rest in the covenant of works. The Christian Sabbath, on the first day of the week, commemorates the resurrection of Christ, and represents the order of rest, comfort, and service in the covenant of grace.— These Sabbaths being *made for man,* God on them allows his own worship to give place to works of necessity and mercy to men.—Religion being the principal business and the distinguishing characteristic of mankind, it is highly proper that it should be explained and inculcated by stated ministers regularly called, and wholly addicted to teach and watch over others, in order to promote virtue among them.—Neither the Old, nor the New Testament, will allow any of these, to introduce a single law or rite of their own invention into the doctrine, worship, discipline, or government of the church; but requires them to explain, inculcate, and apply the general and particular prescriptions of Jesus Christ; and admonishes their hearers to receive nothing from them *implicitly,* but carefully to examine all their doctrines and appointments by the oracles of God. And to render it their interest, as well as their duty, to detect every attempt to impose on them, the burden of a minister's maintenance is laid upon them, and in ordinary cases falls heaviest on those that are, or ought to be most capable of trying them.—Church officers are also expressly forbid to usurp any *secular dominion,* or to act as *spiritual lords* over their people.— The sacraments of the New Testament are *but two,* and easily understood,—they clearly commemorate what Christ is to us, and hath done, and will do for us; they represent, seal and apply his spiritual purification and nourishment to our souls,—of which the material symbols, *water, bread, wine,* or other usable liquid, if wine cannot be had, are every where to be found.

3. It is impossible that God's prescribing a few positive institutions relative to things indifferent in themselves, but calculated to promote his glory and our good, can be inconsistent with his mild government, which is infinite goodness. Instead of an *infinitely high* and supreme governor, he would rather be a slave, if he be allowed no power to forbid or require any thing indifferent, or to appoint a few rites in his own worship, to render it more solemn and striking to our senses.—It can never be inconsistent with his infinite wisdom to order a few helps of instruction to his subjects in their imperfect state.— His wisdom and his power can render them sufficiently useful: though our weak minds should not discern how, yet positive institutions, as well as thousands of things in nature, may be very useful.—If God never enact positive institutions but for a season, and never set them aside till his end in appointing them be gained, they can never *disparage his immutability*, any more than the changes of seasons, summer and winter, day and night, do.—If these positive institutions represent God's displeasure with sin, in the most striking manner, and his infinite condescension to men's weakness, in the forms of his own worship, it is impossible that they can encourage unworthy thoughts of him.

4. As these positive institutions clearly represent God's absolute authority over us, and, in our fallen state, excite as well as assist us to observe the *law of nature*,—they can never derogate from its authority or honour, or substitute superstition in the room of the important duties which it requires.— Being appointed by God for promoting his own honour and the welfare of mankind, they can never be arbitrary or tyrannical.—Am I an enemy to reason, because I obey my Maker's commandment;—or to virtue, because I use the means which he hath appointed for its advancement;—or to the law of nature, because I observe his directions, for the better fulfilling of it? Doth the Scripture extrude the divine law of nature for the sake of positive institutions, when it expressly represents the observance of them as much less important than the duties required by that law of nature, nay, as of no importance, but in so far as they promote that which is absolutely moral and virtuous? Hos. v. 6. and vi. 6. 1 Cor. vi. 13. Col. ii. 20. Gal. v. 6. and vi. 15. 1 Pet. iii. 21. Rom. ii. 28, 29.— Or, how can the exact observation of rites prescribed by God himself, in his own worship, either tempt to, or necessarily introduce our observance of human inventions in it? Knoweth not God better than men, what rites are proper in his own worship? Doth not his appointment of some self-indifferent rites clearly exclude men from all power to appoint any such? Doth not his appointment of them more effectually prevent

our idolatrous esteem of them, than if they were our own inventions?—Ought we to reject his institutions, on which we may crave and expect his blessing, in order to introduce the foolish, the unhallowed, but more numerous inventions of men?—And ought the power of instituting rites in his worship to reside in weak and wicked men, rather than in the infinitely wise, powerful, and sovereign God?

5. Though these positive institutions, as well as every other blessing, may be abused by men, to their own hurt, that does not render them *hurtful in themselves.*—Astonishing! Must regard to institutions, which lead men to fellowship with and imitation of an infinitely gracious God, necessarily prompt men to anathematize and damn one another for trifles?—Can zeal for the *ordinances of God* render men furious bigots for *human inventions,* which are set up in opposition to them?—Whether have the zealous adherers to God's institutions, or the contemners of them, been the most furious persecutors, from age to age? Was it a zealous attachment to the rites prescribed in the gospel of Christ, that rendered the Emperors of Rome and Germany, the Kings of Persia, of France, and even of Britain, or the Dukes of Savoy, &c. furious persecutors of the Christians, Waldenses, Protestants, &c.?——How can our reception of God's institutions, upon sufficient evidence of his having appointed them, lead us to embrace diabolical or human delusions? Are quakerish rejecters of God's positive institutions the least susceptible of delusion in the world?——How can these positive ordinances of God be a real burden to men, and render them miserable, when they are *real helps* in their observing the law of nature?—If all the advantages of life be attended with corresponding hazards, why ought not men's having these helps to be attended with proper punishment, if they abuse them?—Are *reasonable* creatures more miserable than brutes, because, if they abuse their reason, they are in danger of inward grief and the like in this world, and of eternal damnation in the next?——Being clearly prescribed by God, these institutions expose no man to distressful doubts concerning them.—Even the authority of their administrators is for the most part easily discernible. By their fruits we may know them.—And though several of their circumstances, time, place, &c. be incapable of *demonstration*, many of the laws of nature are equally incapable of it. And it is certain, that our infidel opponents believe and practise many things, the propriety of which is infinitely less capable of demonstration.

The revelation contained in our Bibles is not only reasonable in its MATTER, but also in its FORM. The *principal arti-*

cles on which they rest depend are so plainly declared in some passages or other, nay, in several, that every serious inquirer under the influence of the Holy Ghost, may understand them sufficiently to his own salvation. But some less important truths are obscurely represented, that the most learned may find reason before God to blush because of their ignorance; and that the friends of revelation, notwithstanding their different views of them, may be excited to exercise mutual charity.——Scarcely one of the more important truths is *fully declared* in one passage,—that men may be obliged to search the whole Scripture, and carefully compare all the passages together, which treat of a subject.—In order to make men carefully observe the providences of God, and that their fulfilment may never be prevented or counterfeited, it was proper, that many of the predictions should be considerably obscure. And to make us diligently search and compare one passage with another, it was also proper, that some precepts should not be altogether plain. Some hints are repeated without apparent necessity, and some less important things, which might be of more use to the Jews than to us, are more clearly revealed than some more important ones. The same may be found in the writings of Homer, and other celebrated authors. —Indeed, the dictates of revelation are not laid down in regular propositions, or are they mathematically demonstrated. But no more are the laws of nature. And some trifling propositions of Euclid are more capable of such demonstration than either of them.—Revelation doth not exhibit the *rules of morality* in a loose manner, but gives directions to persons in every station of life, to magistrates and subjects, to husbands and wives, to parents and children, to masters and servants, &c.—It supposeth men under the civil and municipal laws of their country, and exhibits general rules, so framed by infinite wisdom, as to suit all particular cases. Nor, without becoming useless for bulk, could it descend to every particular duty. Even the many figurative and parabolical expressions of Scripture point out its antiquity, and that the Hebrew and Greek copies of it are the true originals.—Being drawn from things well known to the Jews and to the Greeks, who were accustomed to such figures, they exhibited their matter in a most obvious and striking manner.—And whatever appears obscure in them, is elsewhere more clearly expressed. Our infidels do not reckon the works of Homer, Cicero, Quintilian, Ossian, &c. one whit the worse, that they abound with figurative language.—Commentators and divines have indeed contended about the sense of several texts: but their own pride, prejudice, and itch after novelties, not the obscurity of revelation, have occasioned their dissensions.—But, have not our heathen doctors had their own contests in almost every article of the law of nature? Had they not 280 different sentiments concerning that *fundamental* point of the *chief good* and *principal end* of all human actions? Never did divines annex as many interpretations to a text of Scripture.—The Scriptures are not laid down in a *systematical form*, though some of Paul's epistles come near to it. Such a form would neither comport with the majesty of God their author, nor with the weak capacities of some men.—It would not shut up men to a diligent comparison of Scripture texts. It would not admit of such delightfully diversified connections of divine truths, nor represent them so suitably to the diversified conditions of men; nor could they be so usefully illustrated with a variety of historical facts.

The revelation contained in our Bibles is also reasonable in the *manner of its exhibition.* As wickedness prevailed in the world, God enlarged his supernatural oracles, and illuminations, in opposition to it. In the infancy of the world, little of revelation was granted: and as the men to whom it was given, lived many hundreds of years, the conveyance of it was entrusted to their memories. When larger portions of it were exhibited, and the lives of the receivers shortened, it was committed to writing for its more effectual preservation and propagation. It was gradually bestowed to make men long after its increase, and especially for the promised Messiah to usher in its full blaze.---Before his incarnation, multitudes of promises, prophecies, and tokens were given, by which men might be prepared to discern and receive him.---The most of it was exhibited at seasons, and in places, where multitudes were awakened by miracles or alarming providences,—or had peace and quietness to examine it, and when the church had peculiar need of comfort and instruction.—The whole New Testament was published when the world, far and wide, by benevolent miracles, and by the terrible calamities of the Jewish nation which rejected it, were awakened.

NOTWITHSTANDING the revelation contained in our Bibles be thus REASONABLE in its MATTER, FORM, and EXHIBITION,—yet if a doctrine be once revealed with proper marks of its divine authority, we ought to embrace it, even though we be incapable to perceive its reasonableness, as it is certain, that God may know and reveal many things, which our reason, while it is so weak and so corrupted, cannot distinctly apprehend.—If any declaration have sufficient evidence of its originating from God, it is horrid presumption for us to suspend our belief till we have examined and found it corresponding to our own apprehensions of reasonableness. Bolingbroke, a noted infidel, excellently observes, "That it would pass for downright madness, if we were not accustomed to it, to hear creatures of the lowest intellectual form, pretend to penetrate the designs, fathom the depths, and unveil the mysteries of infinite wisdom."

VI. The revelation contained in our Bibles is perfectly CREDIBLE. The several parts of it are so connected, that we cannot receive any one without receiving the whole,—every part tending to establish the credit of another.—In the New Testament we have the history of the fulfilment of the typical and verbal predictions of the Old. Nay, in each Testament, we have not a little historical fulfilment of some preceding predictions.—If, therefore, we receive the *predictions*, we must receive the history of their fulfilment as *credible*. If we accept the history of the fulfilment, we cannot reject the predictions as forged.

As the transactions of the New Testament lie nearest our times, let us first examine its *credibility*.—That Christianity is no modern invention, but was professed about 1700 years ago, is attested by Clemens Romanus, Ignatius, Polycarp, Justin Martyr, Irenæus, and Tatian, Christians,—and by Tacitus, Sueton, Tiberianus Serenus, Pliny the younger, Epictetus, Celsus, Porphyry, Hierocles, Marcus Antoninus, and Julian, heathens.—The once extant *acts of Pilate*,—Tacitus, Sueton, Lampridius, Porphyry, Celsus, Hierocles and Pliny, as well as Josephus the Jew, mention Jesus Christ as then living and heading a sect of followers.—Nor could such multitudes have agreed to profess his *self-denying* religion, if they had not had the fullest conviction of his existence.—Many authors of that period wrote on other subjects, which did not lead them to speak of these things. And many more which perhaps mentioned them, are irrecoverably lost.

It is sufficiently credible, that some principal publishers of the Christian religion wrote books bearing the designations of those contained in our New Testament. As that age was very remarkable for an itch of writing, we cannot reasonably imagine that the zealous Christians of it, took no care to record the amazing transactions of Jesus Christ their Lord, and his followers.—In the writings ascribed to Barnabas, Clemens-Romanus, Hermas, Ignatius, Papias, Justin Martyr, Diognetus, —churches of Smyrna, Lyons, Vienne,—Dionysius of Corinth, Tatian, Hegesippus, Melito, Irenæus, Athenagoras, Miltiades, Theophilus, Pantænus, Clemens-Alexandrinus, Polycrates, Quadratus, Aristides, Apollinaris and Symmachus,—who flourished before A. D. 200, while the apostolical manuscripts were still extant, we find multitudes of passages quoted from, or allusions made to the New Testament. Even the epistle to the

Hebrews, the 2d of Peter, the 2d and 3d of John, and that of Jude, which being wrote to private persons, or to Jews, were the last known publicly by the churches, are quoted or acknowledged, though not so much as other books, by the earliest of the Christian writers.——Celsus, the furious opposer of Christianity, about A. D. 150, produces a vast number of quotations from the New Testament, in order to render it ridiculous.—Moreover, the most of these books being written for, or to, societies of Christians, could not possibly be forged or easily corrupted.— Their temporary doubts concerning some of them, till they got full proof of their apostolical original;—their zealous rejection of spurious productions,—and their putting the greatest distance between these inspired books and those of their principal doctors, —fully manifest their care to admit nothing for divinely inspired, without sufficient proof. Whenever they discovered a forgery of a sacred book, such as the pretended acts of Paul and Thecla, they speedily warned all the churches around to prevent their being imposed on. They were so remarkably zealous for their *sacred books*, that no, not the most exquisite tortures could force them to destroy or give them up to destruction. Nor did their most inveterate enemies pretend to dispute their genuineness.

It is no less evident, that the Jewish religion in its extensive form was introduced by Moses, and continued in Canaan for 1500 years, before it gave place to the Christian. Philo, Josephus, and many other Jewish writers, who lived about sixteen or seventeen hundred years ago,—Strabo, Justin, Pliny the elder, Tacitus, Juvenal, Longinus, Numenius, Chalcidius, the Orphic verses, Diodorus, Manetho, Cheremon, Apollonius, Lysimachus, Hermippus, Dion Cassius, Philemon, Polemon, Appion, Ptolemy, Hellanicus, Philocorus, Castor, Thallus, and Polyhistor, heathens, mention Moses or the Jewish antiquities. ——The Jews had sacred books among them of the same designations and contents with those in our Old Testament.— The general division of them into *Moses and the prophets*, or *Moses and the prophets, and Psalms*, is expressly mentioned in the New Testament, Luke xvi. 29, 31. and xxiv. 27, 44. Acts xxvi. 22. and xxviii. 23. John i. 45. And in it, we have quotations from all of them except Judges, Ezra, Nehemiah, Esther, and perhaps Chronicles, Ruth, Ecclesiastes, and the Song of Solomon,—to the expressions of which last, there are sundry allusions.——Josephus the Jew, Melito, Origen, Athanasius, Epiphanius, Jerome, and other Christian doctors, that lived near to the apostolic age, in their LISTS, more or less expressly include all the books of our Old Testament, Ruth being comprehended in Judges, and Nehemiah reckoned the 2d book of Ezra.——Moses' zeal and faithfulness naturally led him to write his own laws, which were so numerous and so important.—The ancient heathen authors sufficiently attest that he did write books. Later passages of Scripture prove that he wrote these very five books ascribed to him in our Bibles. 2 Chron. xxiii. 18. Dan. ix. 11, 13. Mal. iv. 4. Mark vii. 10. and xii. 19. Luke xvi. 29, 31. and xx. 28, 37. and xxiv. 27, 44. John i. 45. and v. 46, 47. Acts xxvi. 22. and xxviii. 23.

The writings of both Old and New Testament have been FAITHFULLY CONVEYED to us. Those of the Old possess sufficient marks of the purity of their ancient Hebrew or Chaldaic originals. In the Talmud and other Jewish writings, we find multitudes of passages quoted as they stand in our Hebrew Bibles. Even in translations, these books retain manifold marks of their Eastern origin. For many ages the Jews had prophets, biassed by no temporal considerations, able and ready to detect every corruption of their sacred books, had it been attempted. Almost three thousand years ago, the Israelites were divided into the two contending parties of Israel and Judah, which ordinarily hating each other, would not have failed to raise horrible outcries, had their opponents dared to vitiate the laws of their God, and the writings of their darling prophets, Moses, Samuel, David, &c.—Scarcely had the Israelites been carried captive to Assyria, when the Samaritans, who peopled their desolated country, procured for themselves a copy of the books of Moses, which, to this day, generally continues the same as the Hebrew. The hatred and contention which afterward subsisted between the Pharisees and Sadducees, rendered it still more impossible for any to attempt to corrupt the oracles of God, without bringing a public odium upon himself.——About two thousand years ago, a Greek translation of these books was published and spread, which, in the main, agrees with our Hebrew ones.—The Chaldaic paraphrases, particularly the literal one of Onkelos, which was composed about eighteen hundred years ago, farther tended to secure these books from corruption. Notwithstanding all that Christ and his apostles inveighed against the wickedness of the Jews, they never charged them with losing or corrupting a single text in their Bible.——The animosity which has ever since prevailed between the Jews and the Christians hath rendered it impossible for either to vitiate these sacred originals, without being shamefully detected.——When a Romish printer, about two centuries ago, attempted but to alter a single letter for one almost similar, HU' into HI', Gen. iii. 15. what a dreadful noise did the Jews and others raise through almost all Europe!

Had the Jews attempted to corrupt their sacred books, it would certainly have been in those passages in which the fearful wickedness of their nation is represented, and Jesus of Nazareth, not any temporal deliverer, is revealed as the promised Messiah. But in none of these can we find any evidence of concealment or corruption. Nay, though, since the spread of Christianity, the Jews have been set upon explaining these Scriptures in favour of their own delusions, they have been zealous, even to superstition, for preserving them in their originals, pure and entire.—About A. D. 500, when, through the general ignorance of the Christian doctors, they had a fair opportunity of corrupting them, we find their Masorite Rabbins zealously occupied in numbering and marking the letters, that so not one of them might be lost or altered, in that or any future age.

The corrupting the originals of either the Old or New Testament by Christians, is absolutely incredible. Such were the multitudes of copies, readers, hearers, and even sects among them, that none could have succeeded, unless he could have made his alterations to have suddenly started into all the many thousands of different copies and into all the different memories of hearers and readers at once.—When Macedonius attempted to vitiate them in the 5th century, how quickly was the alarm sounded far and wide,—and the few corrupted copies detected, and corrected, or destroyed?——As all the furiously opponent sects of Christianity pretended to bring their proofs in religion from Scripture, &c. how could they ever have suffered one another to forge or alter it, without raising an horrible outcry, and a wide-spread accusation!—None of the terms, about which they so much contended, as HOMOOUSION, HOMOIOUSION, METER THEOU, or even FILIOQUE, are found in our Bibles.—— Besides, so many quotations of Scripture, the same with respect to sense as in our books, still remain in the writings of Christian Fathers before A. D. 600, as could almost restore the whole contents of the Bible, though every copy of it were lost.

Perhaps indeed all the apostles were dead before the canon of Scripture was fully fixed in the Christian church; but their original autographs might be extant and well known. It is certain, that in the 2d century of the Christian Æra, Theophilus of Antioch in Syria, Irenæus in France, Tertullian of Carthage, and Clemens of Alexandria in Egypt, quote the very same sacred books which we now have; which proves, that copies of them were then spread through all the Christian churches in Asia, Africa, and Europe. In the 3d and 4th centuries, we have eleven catalogues of these canonical books, seven of which are the same as in our Bibles. Origen, about A. D. 210, hath them all but James and Jude. Eusebius, about 315, hath them all; but says that, though generally received, some doubted of the epistles of James and Jude, 2d by Peter, and 3d by John. Cyril, about 346, and the council of Laodicea, in 364, have them all but the *Revelation*. Athanasius, about 315, Nazianzen, 375, Jerome, 382, Ruffin, 390, Augustine and the council of Carthage, in 394, have them all; but the act of council, if genuine, gives too much honour to some apocryphal books.

The transcribers of these sacred books being no more infallibly inspired than our printers of them, the comparer of a multitude of copies cannot therefore fail to find a number of *various readings*. By a comparison of some of the best Hebrew copies we were long ago informed of eight or ten hundred in the Old Testament. By a comparison of about 600 copies, Dr. Kennicot hath furnished us with many thousands more. From about 125 copies, Dr. Mill hath produced not a few thousands in the New Testament, which have been reduced and improved by Kuster, and especially by Bengelius. The collections of various readings by professed Christians, mark their zeal in examining the books which they adopt as inspired; and too often not a little of their itch after novelties, multitudes of their various readings being collected from manuscripts, and even translations of very little importance or exactness, if not sometimes from their own mere fancy and supercilious inclination to criticism. Meanwhile, a judicious comparison of many copies, which are tolerably exact, is an excellent method for correcting a book. Terence, in the different manuscripts of which 20,000 various readings have been found, is reckoned the most correct of all our Latin classics. Had 125 copies of it been compared, the variations might have amounted to 50,000, though it be scarcely larger than a 3d part of our New Testament. None of all the various readings detected in the Hebrew and Greek copies of our Bible deprive us of one article of our faith, or establish a contrary error, but chiefly relate to letters, accents, and the like. It is even an evidence of God's marvellous preservation of the Scriptures, that the transcribers have been permitted to fall into so many trifling mistakes, and notwithstanding preserved from capital blunders.

It is absurd to imagine, that length of time in the conveyance of a book, *diminishes its credibility.* From what hath been observed, the safe conveyance of our sacred Scriptures is ten thousand times more probable, than the safe conveyance of Homer, Herodotus, Thucydides, or Xenophon, who all represent Greece in a state very different from the present. If then these authors have not, for more than two thousand years past, lost one ten thousandth part of their original credibility, doubtless the Scriptures have not either lost one ten thousandth part of theirs. And meanwhile, the exact accomplishment of prophecies hath much increased the evidence of their divine origination.

Printed copies of our Bible are of as much authority as any manuscripts extant, or any other not taken from the *autographs* of the prophets and apostles. Scarce ever a transcriber took the *tenth* or *twentieth* part of care and pains, in comparing copies, or in correcting his work, which hath been taken on the principal editions of the Hebrew and Greek Testaments.—To promote their own gain, and in the case of *private writs*, securing civil property, which may be easily corrupted, lawyers do not admit *copies of copies* as authentic. But that can by no means prove, that copies of the most public and incorruptible copies of writings, which relate to the most public interests, should not be sustained as *authentic.*——If such copies be not admitted proofs of a correspondent original, and the mistakes of one copy allowed to be corrected from others more exact, every ancient writing in the world, and most of the modern ones, must pass for forgeries; as few can produce, or even swear that they saw the *originals.*

The conveyance of Revelation *by words* written or unwritten, doth not render it *changeable, uncertain, unintelligible,* or *useless.* Dead languages, as those in which the Scriptures are written, are not changeable in their meaning. Nay, supposing these languages were still used, and so the meaning of their words more changeable, the sense of disputed phrases or terms might be traced up to that age in which the Scriptures were written. —Nor can varying the sense of a few words, any more than a mistake of a transcriber, prove that Revelation is not credible, or of divine authority,—any more than the smallest mistake in human writings, or in our apprehensions of them, can prove that no regard is to be paid to them.——Writing is so far from corrupting Revelation, that it is a most excellent mean for the safe conveyance of it, as well as of the dictates of Socrates, Plato, &c.

Our revealed religion is not *founded on mere sounds.* We have the law of nature in our breasts as well as infidels have. But, why may not God communicate his will to us, in a manner like to that in which he enableth us to communicate ours, one to another? If we can procure certain knowledge by conference with philosophers, why may we not procure it as certain by perusing the oracles of God?—If it require skill in languages and customs of nations, to translate the Scriptures rightly, is not this also necessary to render the dictates of Socrates, Plato, Aristotle, Seneca, Epictetus, and Antoninus, relative to the law of nature, plain to an English reader or hearer?—If the translators of Revelation differ about the meaning of some of its words, the inquirers into the law of nature differ much more with respect to the forms, motives, manner, and ends, of that virtue, which it requires.—Though the common people be not capable to judge as to the exactness of a Scripture translation, they who are peculiarly interested in detecting impostures may be capable enough.—Nay the *reasonableness, credibility,* and *divine authority* of the Scripture are so deeply marked, that no translation can conceal them.—Though I should not be capable of accurately tracing *the safe conveyance* of Revelation, common sense may enable me to discern the reasonableness, credibility, or even divine authority of that matter, which is contained in the translation which I understand.—And it is no despicable evidence of the credibility and safe conveyance of Revelation, and of the rectitude of our *public translation* of it, that our infidel doctors, who pretend to so much sense and learning, have hitherto produced nothing but such uncandid and pitiful quibbles, in opposition to them.

Revelation can no more be hurt, by clergymen believing and spreading it, than the light of nature can be, by their possession of it.—Revelation requires every man to see for himself,—*to try all things and hold fast that which is good.*—It doth not force men into religion by clerical influence, but enlightens their minds, and attracts their hearts, by the manifestation and application of its truths. Nor, numbers compared, will it be found, that more Christians are *implicit followers,* than are among infidels.

The FACTS recorded, and the DOCTRINES taught in our Bibles, are *credible in themselves.* The writers of the Old Testament were concerned in many of the transactions which they relate. They published their accounts, while the facts were fresh in men's memory. In the simplicity of their representations, and in recording their own and their friends shameful mistakes, they discover the utmost candour. They never appear to have had hopes of, or to have aimed at worldly advantage, in their writings; but would have exposed their character, if they had forged any thing.—Many of the facts which they relate, were so extraordinary, that they could never have been credited, without the fullest evidence. Nevertheless their report was firmly believed by that very nation, whose carnal interest and honour strongly tempted them to disprove and reject it as a reproach to them, and as binding on them an intolerable load of ceremonies.

The *divine legislation of Moses,* being the most remarkable fact of that dispensation, and a foundation of many others,—his character and narrative are most clearly and fully established.' He always appears most candid and disinterested. He honestly relates his own incestuous descent,—his opposition to God's call of him to be the deliverer of Israel,—his froward speeches to God, or to the people, Exod. iii. iv. vi. Num. xi ; xx. Though he might have been prince, if not king, of Egypt; and might have had his family multiplied into a great nation at

F

the expence of his Hebrew brethren, he declined it, and left his sons no higher than *mere Levites.* He represents his beloved nation as monsters of ingratitude, of perverse, murmuring, and outrageous rebellion against God; and foretells, that after his death, they would become still more wicked and wretched. What then, but the irresistible force of truth could prompt the Jews then, and ever since, tenaciously to adhere to his writings?—How possibly could he, and about two or three millions more, Israelites and strangers, have been *firmly persuaded* by *mere fancy,* that they had seen the land of Egypt smitten with ten dreadful plagues,—of water turned into blood;—of frogs; —lice;—flies;—murrain of cattle;—boils;—hail;—locusts; darkness;—and death of the first-born;—that they had seen the Red-sea divided, and had walked safely through the midst of it, while the Egyptians, who pursued them, were every one drowned;—that they had seen the most terrible lightnings, and heard the most dreadful thunders, at Mount Sinai, and heard God himself, in the most awful manner, proclaim the ten commandments,—that they had lived forty years in the Arabian wilderness, in tents, fed with manna from heaven and with water from flinty rocks,—their clothes never waxing old, or their feet becoming unfit for travel;—and that their repeated murmurings against God had been there punished with the most dreadful plagues?—Or, how, without the fullest persuasion of these strange events, could they have so readily and so long submitted to the most expensive oblations and the most burdensome rites of worship, as a thankful commemoration?
—— In fine, notwithstanding all the care of the Jews to conceal their revelations from their heathen neighbours, Berosus, Abydenus, Hecatæus, Hesiod, Herodotus, Xenophon, Nicolas-Damascenus and Polyhistor, if not also Sanchoniatho, have furnished us with remarkable hints as to the *creation* and *fall* of man,—the division of time into *weeks,*—the *giants,—deluge,—*and *tower of Babel;* the *destruction of Sodom* and cities adjacent; *circumcision;—Abraham, Joshua, David, Solomon, Sennacherib, Nebuchadnezzar, Cyrus,* &c.

Jesus Christ is the Founder and principal subject of the New Testament revelations. Corresponding to the types and predictions of the Old Testament, he appeared as the Messiah, God in our nature. Notwithstanding his external meanness and debasement, Zacharias, Simeon, Anna, John Baptist, nay, angels and God himself, avowed him to be the Son of God and the Saviour of mankind. He not only declared himself such, but, by his marvellous and authoritative instructions, his benevolent miracles, almost innumerable,—his resurrection from the dead and ascension to heaven,—his miraculous effusion of the Holy Ghost upon his disciples,—the subsequent spread of his gospel, with the tremendous ruin of his Jewish opposers and murderers, all in an exact fulfilment of his predictions,—he fully attested it.—Notwithstanding the most dreadful and often repeated abuse, which he suffered from men, his whole behaviour was so holy, harmless and undefiled, and so benevolent, that neither Judas, nor his Jewish prosecutors, nor Pilate, nor Herod, could find any fault in him.——Nay, such is the draught of his character by the Evangelists, so candid and so simple, and yet so sublime and suitable to a God in our nature and a surety for us, that in such circumstances, the incarnation, obedience, suffering and death of the Son of God, however astonishing, appear much more credible to reason,—than that such a sublime and virtuous character, of which there hath never been an adequate pattern in the world, should be forged by persons who had never seen or heard of any thing similar;—nay, by persons who had no education, and whose natural capacities, perhaps were very weak.

His RESSURRECTION, which is the principal point in the Christian scheme, and which proves all the rest, was, and is supported by every proof,—from enemies,—from friends,—from angels,—and from subsequent events, to this day.—Multitudes saw him nailed to, and hanging on his cross. The soldiers found him dead, when they came to break his legs. Multitudes saw without much labour and noise, his corpse interred in a new grave, hewn out of a rock, which could not be entered but by the door.—While a large stone, solemnly sealed by the rulers of Judah, shut him up, a strong watch of enemies deprived his friends, even had they been willing, of every opportunity to carry off his dead body.—Early, on the 3d day, a dreadful earthquake, and an apparition of angels terrified the guard and made them run off. Mean while his body was gone, and his grave clothes left in good order, as by a deliberate remover. Many virtuous persons arose from their graves in Jerusalem, and appeared to the citizens. The guard, having informed the Jewish rulers of what they had seen, heard, and felt, they largely bribed them to conceal the truth, and to pretend, that Jesus's disciples had stolen away his dead body, while they were sleeping. Nothing could be more evident falsehood: for how durst any of them,—how could all of them sleep on a watch,—a watch of so great importance? If they were all asleep, how could they know when or who, carried off his dead body?

Notwithstanding repeated warnings and predictions, his disciples were so exceedingly averse to believe the truth of his resurrection, that scarcely their missing his body in the grave, the testimony of angels, the attestation of brethren, and even the sight of their own eyes could convince them till his repeated appearances to them, and familiar converse with them, and at last, the miraculous descent of the Holy Ghost on them, rendered them incapable to doubt.—Had he not risen from the dead, they had had the strongest grounds to be highly offended with, and incensed against him, as one who had deceitfully exposed them to so much disappointment, reproach, hatred and danger.—But, finding themselves suddenly qualified to work miracles, discern spirits, speak divers languages, and to discourse of religion and virtue in a manner infinitely superior to Socrates, and all his philosophical brethren ;—finding, that they, who just before, on the slightest temptations, had deserted or denied him, were filled with such zeal and boldness in his cause, as to fear nothing but sin,—they, contrary to every temptation of worldly honour, profit and pleasure, and deliberately rushing upon loss, reproach, hatred, poverty, persecution, and death,— in the most plain, and public manner, on the spot where, and in a few weeks after it happened, published *his resurrection*, and charged the Jewish rulers and people with the murder of their own promised and divine Messiah.—Notwithstanding they had no carnal power nor influence, but had been held absolutely contemptible, multitudes, who had the strongest inclination, and the fullest opportunity to detect any imposture in this point, firmly believed their report, confessed themselves the murderers of the Son of God, and humbly applied to him for forgiveness and eternal salvation.—Notwithstanding all their craft, malice and fury, the Jewish rulers could find no other refutation of the report, than imprisonments, scourgings, threatenings, and murders of the publishers.

These preachers declared, that which they had seen and heard, in which common sense will not admit of their being deceived. For, how could they *fancy* themselves into a number of meetings and conversations with their risen Master? How could they, by mere fancy, fix themselves in the most distinct assurance, that they had heard him, in a manner peculiar to himself utter so many gracious words, and had seen him work so many miracles in such different times, places, and persons? How could they fancy themselves into an actual and evident possession of the miraculous gifts and graces of the Holy Ghost? How could Saul of Tarsus, a man of great learning and sense, dream himself into a belief of his miraculous conversion, into the knowledge of languages which he had never learned, into the possession of apostolic powers ; into an humble but bold zeal for the interests and glory of Jesus Christ, whom just before in his cause and members, he had so heartily hated and furiously persecuted. Their exalted instructions and prudent conduct sufficiently prove, that none of them were such idiots, as to be the fit dupes of imposture.—The marks of integrity, simplicity, benevolence, and virtue, so conspicuous in their conduct, sufficiently prove, that they had no disposition to deceive others, in matters so injurious to the honour of God and the souls of men. Could ever the certain, the sole prospect of hatred, reproach, imprisonment, tortures, and violent death,—of rebukes of conscience,—and of eternal damnation, have prompted them, with all their might, to propagate that which they knew to be false and uncertain? The number of those preachers was considerable, and of their followers *many ten thousands* about Jerusalem. Notwithstanding repeated solicitations, threatenings, tortures, &c. none of them, however unfit they were to keep secrets, proposed to discover any fraud.—Judas indeed betrayed his Master, but quickly repented, publicly and solemnly protesting his innocence, and then he hanged himself under desperate convictions of his wickedness.

It is not asserted that every one employed in publishing the mind of God to men, was faultless.—We allow Balaam, the old prophet of Bethel, and Caiaphas, to have been wicked men, Num. xxii.—xxiv. 1 Kings xiii. John xi. Such may enjoy transient inspirations, as well as the permanent light of nature. But the penmen of Scripture appear to have been *holy men of God.* Even their enemies never appear to have been able to charge them with any thing, but what was included in their faithful observance of the laws of their God. It is from the Scripture itself, and often from their own ingenuous and candid pens, that we have any account of their failings. Neither David nor Solomon were *primary publishers* of revelation. Nor can several failings disqualify men from being declarers of facts, or witnesses to the truth.—Paul's having had some contention with Barnabas about the impropriety of taking Mark, who had formerly deserted them, along with them to visit the churches, will not so much as prove that he was in the wrong. His confessing that he was far less holy than he wished, and stating that he could be content with nothing less than perfect holiness, can never unfit him to be a preacher of, and a witness for Christ, Acts xv. Rom. vii.

VII. The revelations contained in our Bibles are DIVINELY INSPIRED, proceeding from an infinitely wise, holy, just, good, true, and infallible God.——Of old, God spake to men *by voices,* as at Sinai, &c. Exod. xix.—xxxiv. Lev. i.—xxvii. Num. i.—xxxvi. Deut. xxxi;—by *visions and dreams,* as to the patriarchs and prophets, Gen. xii, xiii;—xxii, xxvi, xxviii, xxxi, xxxii, xxxv, xxxvii, xlvi. Job iv. Isa. vi. Ezek. i.—xi. xl,—xlviii. Dan. vii, viii, ix, x.—xii. Amos vii.—ix. Zech.

i.—vi. But his mind comes to us by the inspiration of the Holy Ghost on the penmen of the Scriptures, which infallibly taught them what they knew not before, rendered the knowledge which they had of divine things absolutely certain, and directed them to proper words, to express their conceptions of them. While he allowed them the use of their own language and natural abilities, he instructed and directed them in a manner which transcended them. Nor can we sufficiently understand what heart-composing, humbling, and sanctifying influences *marked* his inspirations.

In the inspiration of the Scriptures, while the penmen themselves concurred in exercising their own reason and judgment, Ps. xlv. 1. Mark xii. 36. Luke i. 3. 1 Pet. i. 11, the Holy Ghost, 1. Stirred them up to write, 2 Pet. i. 21. 2. Appointed each his share, correspondent to his natural talents, and the necessities of the church, 2 Pet. i. 21. Mat. xxv. 15. 3. Enlightened their minds, and gave them a distinct view of the truths they were to deliver, Jer. i. 11—16. xiii. 9—14. Ezek. iv. 4—8. Amos vii. 7, 8. viii. 2. Zech. i. 19, 21. iv. 11—14. v. 6. Dan. x. 1, 14. ix. 22—27. viii. 15—19. xii. 8, 11. 1 Pet. i. 10, 11. Eph. iii. 3, 4. John xvi. 13. But this was not given all at once to the twelve apostles, Mark iv. 34. Luke xxiv. 17, 45. John xx. 22. Acts ii. 4. x. 9—15. xxviii. 34; but perhaps all at once to Paul, 2 Cor. xii. 4. Strengthened and refreshed their memories to recollect whatever they had seen or heard, which he judged fit to be inserted in their writings, John xiv. 26. 5. Amidst a multitude of facts, he directed them what to write, and what not, as the edification of his church did or might require, John xx. 30, 31. xxi. 25. Rom. xv. 4. 1 Cor. x. 6—12. Rom. iv. 23, 24. 6. He stirred up and called forth in their minds such images and ideas as were treasured up in their memories, to other ends and purposes than they themselves would have ever done; hence Amos draws his figures from the herd or flock, or field; Paul makes use of his learning, Acts xvii. 28. 1 Cor. xv. 33. Tit. i. 12. 7. He immediately suggested and imprinted on their minds all such things as were matter of pure revelation, Isa. xlvi. 9, 10. xii. 22, 23. xlv. 21. and that whether of things past, as Gen. i. & ii. or to come, or mysteries, 1 Tim. iii. 16. 8. He so superintended every particular writer, as to render him infallible in matter, words, and arrangement; and superintended the whole writers in connection, as to render the whole Scripture, at a given period, sufficient for instruction and correction, to render the man of God perfect, thoroughly furnished unto every good work, 2 Tim. iii. 15—17.

Some distinguish this inspiration of the Holy Ghost into SUGGESTION, which infallibly directed them in the declaration of things secret, mysterious, and future;—and SUPERINTENDENCY, which secured them against gross blunders in representing that which they knew before, leaving them to express their thoughts in the manner they judged best. But, if such superintendency be admitted as the whole of inspiration in lesser matters, 1. Thousands of things, which from plain language of Scripture we apprehended to be true, may be nothing but blunders of less importance. 2. The most peremptory, clear, and certain testimonies of the Holy Ghost may be easily rejected, under pretence that they are lesser blunders of penmen. 3. If the penmen had been left to the choice of their words, the meaning of Scripture must be altogether uncertain. The prophets and apostles might have had very proper ideas, and yet their words be very improper to express and convey them to us. Erroneous persons may assert, whenever they please, that such words of Scripture are not proper to express the inspired ideas, and substitute others, which they judge more meet, in their stead.—Indeed Paul hints, that *not* he, *but the Lord*, or *he, not the Lord*, directed in some cases relative to marriage. But there he only means, that our Saviour had *expressly taught* such things, or *not*, in the days of his flesh, 1 Cor. vii. 10, 12. Some expressions have an appearance of unfixed meaning, to teach us, never to be too peremptory in that which relates to mere circumstances of things, 1 John vi. 19. 1 Pet. v. 12.

Concerning this inspiration of Scripture, it must be remarked, 1. It doth not require, that every sentence which is inserted in Scripture, should be attributed to God as its author. Many bad, or even some good expressions of devils or men are therein recorded, of which nothing but the infallible narration and the *praise* or *dispraise are of divine inspiration*. 2. The different parts of Scripture being so connected, and supporting each other,—Christ and his apostles approving the whole of the Old Testament, and the New being but a more clear declaration of that which had been more darkly expressed by Moses and the prophets,—it is not necessary that all the marks of divine authority should equally appear in every verse, chapter, or book.—Some passages are but circumstantial introductions to, or explications of other passages, which are more essential and important.—But that, taken in their proper connection, the books of the Old and New Testaments are of DIVINE INSPIRATION, is abundantly evident.

1. The matter of them requires a divine inspiration. The history of the *creation* and in part that of the *flood*, &c. which are recorded in them, were known only to God. Mysteries concerning the *Trinity of persons in the Godhead*,—the *covenant of grace*,—the *undertaking, incarnation, offices*, and *states of the*

Son of God as our Mediator,—our union with him, and *justification, adoption, sanctification, spiritual comfort,* and *eternal blessedness in him,* are therein declared, which God alone can comprehend, or unfold. The scheme of religion prescribed is so pure, benevolent, spiritual, and so extensive as God only could devise or appoint. While it represents himself as every where present, infinitely perfect, powerful, wise, holy, just, good, true, and faithful,—as an infinitely gracious lover of righteousness, and an inflexible hater of iniquity,—as our bountiful Creator and Preserver, and as our infinitely merciful Redeemer, by the infinitely precious obedience and death of his only begotten Son,—it requires us to know, believe in, trust on, and revere him, with our whole heart, soul, mind, and strength, as our Father, Friend, Husband, Saviour, and Portion in Christ,—confidently to depend on, and to supplicate from him, every thing that we need in time or in eternity,—and to obey him in every thing which he commands, as children whom he hath begotten again to a lively hope, and made joint heirs with Christ, of himself and his heavenly inheritance. We are taught how our nature may be truly improved, may be perfected in virtue and happiness, by our believing reception of Christ, as made of God unto us wisdom, righteousness, sanctification, and redemption,—as an effectual root and principle of true holiness,—and by our living and walking in him by faith, denying ungodliness and worldly lusts, living soberly, righteously, and godly, patiently, contentedly, and cheerfully,—and through his word, Spirit, and blood, mortifying every selfish and sinful inclination, and setting our affections on things above, where he is, and looking for his glorious appearance to judge the world.—We are taught to be followers of God as dear children, and to walk in love, as Christ hath loved us,—to love our neighbours as ourselves, fulfilling the duties of every possible relation or condition;—to lay aside all malice, envy, hatred, revenge, and other malevolent dispositions or passions;—and to love our enemies, rendering good for evil, and praying for them that despitefully use us. These laws of universal purity and benevolence are prescribed with an authority proper only to God,—and extended to such a compass, as God only can demand; and sins are forbidden which he only can discern or prohibit.
——The most powerful motives to virtue and dissuasives from vice,—drawn from the divine nature, his promises, threatenings, mercies, and judgments, particularly from his kindness in the work of redemption, and his new covenant-relations to us in Christ, and from manifold advantages, temporal, spiritual, and eternal, are most wisely proposed, and earnestly urged: While the most excellent means of directing, exciting, and enabling us to all the exercises of piety and virtue,

OF THE REVEALED STANDARD OF RELIGION. 73

are established in the most prudent form and authoritative manner,---the most perfect and engaging patterns are set before us, in the example of Christ our Redeemer, and of God as reconciled in him, and through him reconciling the world to himself, Exod. xx. 1---17. Lev. xviii.---xx. Deut. iv.---xxv. Matth. iv.---xxvii. Rom. vi. xii.---xv. Eph. iv.---vi. Col. iii. iv. 1 Thess. i.---v. Tit. ii. iii. Heb. xii. xiii. Jam. i.---v. 1 Pet. i.---v. 2 Pet. i.---iii. 1 John i.---v. Rev. ii. iii.

2. The MANNER in which these points are exhibited in Scripture, is manifestly divine, wise, condescending, and yet majestic. The discoveries of them have been gradual, as suited the necessities of mankind, or their condition required, Gen. iii. xii. xvii. xxii. xxviii. xlvi. xlix. Exod. iii.---xxxiv. Lev. i.---xxvii. Num. i. v. vi. viii. xv. xvii. xviii. xix. xxviii. xxix. Deut. iv.---xxxiii. Job i.---x. Rev. xxii.------The principal points relating to God's satisfaction with Christ as our mediator,---his new covenant-grants of himself to us in him as our God,---and his law of the ten commandments were proclaimed by himself from heaven, with the greatest solemnity. Matth. iii. 17. and xvii. 5. Exod. xx. 1---17. While these and other truths are delivered in a most plain and simple style, it is marked with an inexpressible sublimity and majesty.---While the declarations, laws, promises, and threatenings, &c. are authorized by a *thus saith the Lord*,--- the stile, particularly in Scripture *Songs, Job, Psalms, Lamentations, Isaiah*, &c. is surprisingly suited at once to the dignity of the author,---the nature of the subject, and the condition of the persons addressed.

3. The obvious SCOPE of the Scripture is to humble men, to reform them from their beloved lusts and sinful practices, and to exalt and glorify God. No good angel or man could dare to personate God, in the manner of the Scripture. No bad angel or man could devise, publish, and so warmly inculcate that which is so remarkably contrary to their own vicious inclinations, honour, and interest. God alone must therefore be the *Author* or *Inditer* of Scripture.

4. Notwithstanding the contents of Scripture are so exceedingly contrary to the natural corrupt inclinations of mankind, were published without any concert, and by so many persons of very different conditions, and in different ages and places, yet such is the marvellous HARMONY of all its parts, in their matter and scope, as irrefragably proves the penmen to have been all infallibly guided by the same Spirit of God. Its parts are so connected, that we cannot reasonably receive any one, nor so much as one noted doctrine or law, without receiving the whole. All the predictions, histories, laws, doctrines, promises and threatenings, explain, or confirm one another. An attentive reader may every where perceive the same facts implied, re-

corded, or prepared for;—the same doctrines of our gracious redemption through Jesus Christ, exhibited or supposed to be true;—the same rules and exemplifications of virtue or motives enforcing them;—the same kind promises of mercy or just threatenings of misery to persons or societies, held forth, without a single contradiction. Where any such thing seems to appear, an *accurate comparer* of the discordant-like passages may perceive that they do not relate to the *same persons* or *things*, in the *same respect*, and in the *same circumstances* of *time, place*, and *manner;* and so there is no contradiction at all. Suppose that a transcriber or printer should have inadvertently altered a letter, number, or point, that cannot be allowed to constitute a contradiction, or to invalidate the authority of the Bible or of any other book.

5. The unblemished CHARACTER of the PENMEN further demonstrates the divine original and authority of the Scriptures. They every where mark the utmost candour and disinterestedness,—candidly publishing their own and their friends infirmities and guilt. None of them ever acquired any thing in this world by their work, but trouble and vexation. According to their own declared principles, deceit and imposture could procure them nothing in the next, but everlasting destruction. The matter and manner of their work infinitely transcended their abilities. Beside their predictions, how could men of the least and especially men of no education, form such an exalted system of sense, piety, and virtue! How could wicked men, though inspired by Satan, have devised, published, and propagated, as well as fervently exemplified such a scheme of mystery, majesty, and holiness? Or, how could their account of the incarnation, obedience, sufferings, and death, of the Son of God, have been drawn up with such simplicity and undoubted candour, if it had not been taken from real facts.

6. GOD'S marvellous PRESERVATION of the Scriptures of the Old and New Testament, from being lost or corrupted, while, perhaps millions of writings, once of considerable fame in the world, and which no man hated or sought to extirpate, are lost and forgotten, proves them to have been inspired by his Spirit. Notwithstanding they were in part written before any other books, and Satan with his innumerable instruments have hated, and, with all their united fraud and force laboured to destroy or corrupt them, God, in his providence, still preserved them in their purity. By appointing the original tables of his moral law, and an original copy of the other laws of Moses to be kept in the *Holy of Holies*,—by appointing every Hebrew king to write a copy of these laws for himself,—by appointing the public and private reading of them and teaching them to their children,—and making the opponent parties that enjoyed them,

mutual checks upon each other, &c. he, in his infinite wisdom and goodness, secured their safe preservation. By tremendous judgments he restrained Antiochus Epiphanes, the Syro Grecian monarch, Dioclesian, the Roman emperor and others, who attempted to destroy all the copies of them, in order to extirpate the Jewish or Christian religion. And in what amazing forms, hath he upheld and comforted such as risked or parted with their lives, rather than deny the dictates of Scripture, or in the least contribute to their dishonour.

7. MULTITUDES of MIRACLES, which could only be effected by the infinite power of God, have been wrought for confirmation of the doctrines and facts recorded in Scripture, and for attestation of the divine commission of the primary publishers of it.—God's infinite wisdom and goodness required him, especially when, as in the days of Moses and the apostles, he was introducing new forms of worship, to mark the important declarations of his will with distinguishing tokens, which might awaken men to consider them. Nothing appears more proper for promoting this end, than a series of uncontrouled miracles which supported nothing but what was consistent with reason. Neither reason nor experience admits, that God's infinite wisdom and goodness will permit one, much less thousands of uncontrouled miracles to be wrought for the confirmation of falsehood. In the miracles which confirm the Scripture, we find every probatory circumstance. They were almost innumerable, and all of them calculated to answer some great end. Corresponding to the nature of the broken law and its curses, many of those wrought by Moses and Elias, were tremendous and wrathful, Exod. vii.---xiv. Num. xvi. 1 Kings xvii. xviii. 2 Kings i. ii. Congenial to the spirit of the Gospel, which Jesus Christ and his apostles published, the miracles which they performed were generally of a benevolent nature and tendency, Matth. iv. viii. ---xxi. Mark i.---xi. Luke iv.---xix. John ii.---xxi. Acts iii.---xx. xxviii. Most of these miracles were wrought in so public a manner, that both friends and enemies had the fullest opportunity of thoroughly examining them, and when the concurrent circumstances of providence loudly called them. Most of them, as the safe passage of the Israelites through the Red Sea and Jordan,---their living forty years on manna from heaven and water from the flinty rocks,---the standing still, or retrograde motion of the sun,---the feeding of several thousands on a few loaves and fishes,---the raising of the dead or buried, and the like, were of such a nature, that common sense cannot allow the witnesses to have been mistaken concerning them; or that any power less than infinite, could have performed them. Even the inveterate enemies of the gospel, Jews or Heathens, in part attest, that these miracles were really wrought. And it is plain, that they

were wrought in confirmation of a religion the most pure and benevolent, and the most of them by persons of distinguished piety and virtue.

In vain it is pretended, that the *common experience* of mankind being against the existence of miracles, ought to be laid in balance with the positive proofs in favour of them; and it ought to be considered, whether it be not more probable, that all the witnesses of them have been deceived, than that those miracles have been really wrought; for, 1. Nothing can be a miracle at all, which is not contrary to the common experience of mankind. 2. *Negative* proof is of very little force in opposition to that which is *positive*, as it can merely bear, that the deponents did not observe that which others affirm they did. If two creditable persons depone, that they heard me utter such expressions, or saw me commit such crimes, the testimony of ten thousand millions, deponing that they did not observe me say or do such things, will not overbalance it. If negative evidence be not directly opposite to that which is positive, with respect to time and place, it is of no force at all. Millions of mankind could truly depone, that they never saw frozen water,—never observed the load-stone vary its influence under excessive cold,—never saw an animal when cut into an hundred pieces propagate into as many animals of that kind,—never saw a *white man*, or a *negro*, &c. But will it therefore follow that these things never existed, and were never really seen by others? Because thousands of millions, who did not live in the age or place of miracles, never saw them, will it follow, that those who lived in that age and place, when and where they are said to have happened, never saw or felt them? 3. If God be the infinitely powerful Maker and Manager of all things, he can easily work miracles by controuling the ordinary operation of second causes, which himself hath established. And if there be an occasion and end demanding the interposal of his infinite power, reason teacheth that his wisdom and goodness will determine him to exert it. 4. Unless it be proved, that God is incapable to mark out his own interposals as divine, and that the human senses are, in every case, altogether unfit to be trusted, and so all human fellowship undermined, these senses must be allowed sufficient judges as to the reality of the miracles recorded in Scripture.

It is highly absurd, to compare these miracles with those which have been ascribed to Esculapius, Vespasian, Adrian, or Apollonius, Abbé Paris the Jansenist. The miracles ascribed to the first three are only reported by heathens, on distant hear-says, who might be prompted by worldly interest to flatter them. The record of those ascribed to Apollonius was not formed till about a hundred years after his death,—from *secret* memoirs, which the recorder confesses to have been written in a *bombast* style, and stuffed with *romances*,---and was formed in order to confront the evangelical history of Jesus Christ, and to please a romantic lady; and not one of Apollonius' few disciples pretended to have received from him a power of working miracles. The wonderful cures ascribed to Abbé Paris, or his tomb, obtained only among his admirers, and respected diseases, the crisis of which occurring in the order of natural causes, connected with a strong imagination of the Abbé's power and the use of natural remedies, real cures might be effected in some;---while many others, by the examination of the magistrates, were detected to have been mere impostures.

It is no less absurd to assert, that miracles cannot confirm a doctrine which cannot be demonstrated; for, 1. If nothing but what can be formally demonstrated, must be regarded, how little of the Law of nature will be known, or ought to be obeyed? Or, why must *formal demonstration* be required to ascertain the *doctrines of Revelation*, any more than to ascertain the *Laws of Nature?* 2. If all the affairs of common life among men be ascertained without formal demonstration, why may not God ascertain his revelations without it, and in a manner much more suited to their capacities and experience. 3. A demonstration of the reasonableness of any thing cannot sufficiently prove its divine original or appointment. None can prove it unreasonable to observe two days in every week in the public service of God. Yet it will not follow, that he *requires* any such thing. Something higher than demonstration, must therefore mark the divine authority of a revelation. 4. Though some men had real revelations from God, and were certain of it, these could be of no use to mankind in general, unless they had marks of their divine original, which others might perceive. 5. As revelation supposeth men rational creatures, as well as endowed with outward senses, miraculous appearances are not to be taken as a *sole proof* of the divine authority of missions or doctrines, but as co-ordinate with the suitableness of these things to the perfections of God and the natural rules of virtue;—which being more striking to weak minds are more effectual to bear down their prejudices, to procure their attention, and thus lead, and add to the force of the internal evidence which is in the doctrines themselves. 6. Where the doctrines thus correspond with the perfections of God, and our connections with him, we are in no danger of being imposed on by miraculous appearances, through our ignorance of the physical causes of nature, or our inability to examine the extent of created powers. No evil spirits would work wonders for establishing a scheme worthy of God or beneficial to men, whom they so heartily hate. No such pious and virtuous men, as the prophets and apostles, would attempt to work miracles in confederacy with Satan, or deal in deceitful arts. No good spirit would work any miracles to confirm an imposture. Nor would an infinitely wise, powerful, and good God, permit his rational creatures to be seduced into errors by a multitude of uncontrouled miracles. 7. Most of the miracles recorded in Scripture could not possibly have been counterfeited.

8. The SCHEME of reforming mankind by the revelation of Scripture, and its evident SUCCESS, are a continued miraculous proof of its divine original.—Nothing but certain evidences of his divine commission could have made Moses risk his character, that on the 6th day of the week, his whole nation in the wilderness should always have manna sufficient for two days, rained from heaven upon them; and that in Canaan their fields should always produce double crops on the 6th year,— and on that supposition make a standing law, that they should never attempt to gather manna on the 7th day, or cultivate their fields in the 7th year. Nothing but the most infallible assurance that God would then protect them from their inveterate enemies on every side, would have made him require, that all their males, capable of travel, should thrice every year leave their homes, and attend sacred festivals in the midst of their country. Nothing but the clearest warrant from God could have made him hope, that in the family of Aaron, there would always be a sufficient number of males to execute the office of priesthood for all Israel, free of all the exclusive blemishes, which he states;—or could have made him hope, that their small country would supply his numerous nation with sufficient provision, exclusive of all the prohibited flesh, and of all the oblations required for the Lord. Nothing but certain evidence of a divine institution, attended with a divine influence, could have made the Israelites submit to so many burdensome ceremonies, Exod. xvi. Lev. xxv. Deut. xv. Exod. xxiii. xxxiv. Lev. xxi.—xxiii. xi. i.—vi. Num. xviii. xxviii. xxix.

The *scheme* of Christianity and its *success* are still more amazing, and could proceed from nothing less than a divine warrant and influence. Without these, how could ever a few weak or illiterate men, altogether unaided by worldly influence, form a scheme of reforming the whole world, from principles and practices deeply rooted in their inclinations, and firmly established by the extensive customs and long-confirmed laws of all nations, and that not by force or fraud, but by mere declarations of what they thought true; or, of what they knew to be false, if they were impostors?——How could crafty villains, or even the weakest fools, choose for their HERO, one who had made his ignominious sufferings his distinguishing characteristic,—one, who had been always contemned, and had lately been crucified between two thieves, as a noted and base malefactor,

OF THE REVEALED STANDARD OF RELIGION. 79

by the common consent and outcry of his countrymen,—one, who, if he was not God in our nature, had abused his disciples' confidence, and drawn them into a train of temporal and eternal miseries,—one, who had never encouraged them to expect any thing in this world, in following him, but crosses, hatred, imprisonment, tortures, and death,—nor for any thing in the next, but everlasting destruction, if they indulged themselves in any fraudulent promoting of his cause?—How possibly could a few villanous projectors of a general reformation begin their work, in the very place where, and in a few weeks after, even amidst these very multitudes, by whom their Hero had been ignominiously crucified, and in the face of dangers and death, publicly proclaim him to be the Son of God, the true Messiah, who had risen from the dead and ascended to heaven, and sat down at the right hand of God?—How could they, amidst the deepest poverty, cruellest hatred, most calumnious reproach, and most inhuman persecution of enemies unnumbered, in every place carry on their design with unwearied zeal, astonishing toil, and unceasing cheerfulness, never appearing to covet any worldly wealth or honour?—How could they form a system of doctrines and laws, infinitely superior in sense, dignity, and sanctifying virtue to all the productions of the most renowned heathen philosophers?—How astonishing, that those few, most of them illiterate preachers, without the least aid or encouragement from any earthly power, should so triumph over the craft, the rage, and the power of enraged Jews;—over all the pride, policy, and power of the Roman empire, when in its full strength and sagacity; over the pride of learning, and the obstinacy of ignorance, hatred, prejudice, and lust; over the hardened inclinations, deep-rooted customs, and long fixed laws of both Jews and heathens;—and that, notwithstanding every form of danger, loss, and opposition, the gospel should, within a few years after Christ's death, be preached in almost every corner of the Roman empire, and countries around it;—and that multitudes, at the hazard of every thing dear to them, should readily believe it, stedfastly adhere to it, and cheerfully practise it? How astonishing that, for more than 1700 years past, notwithstanding unnumbered persecutions, and all the profane naughtiness of many professors, the base indifference or inconceivable villanies of many clerical instructors, this scheme hath been more or less successful in reforming the hearts and lives of multitudes, and civilizing the manners, in almost every nation of importance, under heaven?

9. Nothing more clearly demonstrates the divine inspiration and authority of the Scriptures than the *exact fulfilment* of the typical and verbal PREDICTIONS, which they exhibited, in the most circumstantiated manner, hundreds or thousands of years,

before that fulfilment, or any appearance of it, took place. Predictions, especially as above circumstantiated, necessarily require a looking with certainty, through an *infinity* of possible events, and seeing and determining which shall certainly happen, and which shall not. Such foresight and determination are only competent to God, the *Omniscient* and *Almighty* governor of the world. To mark him as their author, the Scriptures are crowded with predictions: their exact fulfilment is recorded in the inspired and other histories, which have been since written. Almost every historical passage in our Bible is a record of something antecedently foretold. The New Testament is little more than a representation of the fulfilment of the types and prophecies of the Old, concerning Jesus Christ, and his gospel-church. Nay, the histories of churches and nations from the beginning to the end of the world do, or will, to judicious readers, represent little more than the fulfilment of Scripture predictions concerning the families of Adam and Noah, Canaanites, Amalekites, Ammonites, Moabites, Edomites, Philistines, Egyptians, Ethiopians, Syrians, Assyrians, Chaldeans, Persians, Greeks, Romans, Saracens, Tartars, Goths, Hunns, and Turks, and especially concerning the Jews, Jesus Christ, the New Testament church, and Antichrist.——This proof, drawn from the *fulfilment* of predictions, still continues, and increases in clearness and force, as it takes place and is observed.—The dispersion and misery of the Jewish nation, so often repeated, and long continued;—the progress, continuance, and success of the Gospel among the Gentiles;—the long continued and extensive domination of popery, and partial revolt from it at the Reformation;—the past and present condition of the Roman and Turkish empires;—the present state of Assyria, Chaldea, Arabia, Phenicia, Canaan, Egypt, &c. in exact correspondence with those predictions,—are standing testimonies to the divine inspiration of our Bibles, no less conclusive and striking, than if we had miracles wrought before us, every day.——And it is remarkable, that not only was our Saviour's divine character displayed in his incomparable behaviour, miracles, instructions, and institutions, but also in the striking fulfilment of his predictions relative to the miseries of his Jewish contemners, and the spread of his Gospel-church;—and that Josephus their historian was almost miraculously preserved to write an history of that fulfilment.

No prediction emitted by any true prophet mentioned in Scripture ever failed of accomplishment.—But if a condition be expressed or understood in the annunciation, it is rather a warning than a prediction, and so no fulfilment falls due, unless the condition be implemented.—— In *that* very *day*, nay moment, in which Adam ate the forbidden fruit, he became legally and spiritually dead; his temporal and eternal death commenced, as far as the making of the covenant with his posterity in him permitted, Gen. ii. 17.——God no more than *warned* David, that if he continued there till Saul should come up, the men of Keilah would deliver him up, 1 Sam. xxiii. 12.—Elisha's declaration concerning Benhadad might be translated, *Thou shalt certainly live.* And, according to our English version, it means no more, than that his disease was *not mortal.* Now it is certain that he did not die of his disease, but by Hazael's stifling of him, 2 Kings viii. 10.—The Ninevites were no more than threatened with ruin within forty days if they did not repent, Jonah iii.—Nay, unless threatenings be universal or confirmed by an oath, they generally imply an exception in case of repentance. Agreeable to Huldah's prediction, Josiah died *in peace* with God and his conscience, and before the war which ruined his nation broke out, 2 Kings xxii. 20.—Jehoiakim was buried *like an ass*, though it be not recorded in Scripture, Jer. xxii. 18, 19, and xxxvi. 30.—Zedekiah's eyes being put out at Riblah, he went to Babylon *without seeing it*, where he died, and was honourably buried by his friends, though we have not the history of his funeral, Jer. xxxiv. 4, 5.—The *last days* denote future time in general, or that which followed our Saviour's ascension; or, the last years of the Jewish constitution, Gen. xlix. 1. 2 Tim. iii. 1. 1 John ii. 18.—It was the coming of Christ to execute judgment on the Jewish nation, not his coming to judge the world, which these in the apostolic age were warranted to expect in their own time, Mat. xxiv. with 2 Thess. ii. 2.—Paul considered himself as a member of that mystical body of Christ, whose fellow-members will be alive at Christ's second coming, 1 Cor. xv. 51, 52. 1 Thess. iv. 15, 17.

10. Though the above or like arguments be sufficient to silence gainsayers, and produce a rational conviction, that the Scriptures of the Old and New Testament are indeed the word of God,—yet it is only the Holy Ghost's effectual application of them to our mind, conscience, and heart, in their self-evidencing life, light, and power, which can produce a cordial and saving persuasion of it.—The word of God thus applied, brings along with, and in itself, such light, such authority, and such convincing, quickening, sanctifying, and comforting power, that there is no possibility of shutting our eyes or hardening our heart against it, of continuing blind or unconcerned about it; but all the faculties of our soul are necessarily affected with it, as impressed with evidences of its divinity, attended by almighty influence, 1 Thess. i. 5. and ii. 13. John vi. 63. Jer. xxiii. 29. And hence, without seeing any miracles, or other external evidence of its divine authority, many of the primary hearers of revelation were obliged to believe it on a mere *Thus saith the Lord,*

Isa. i. Mal. iv. Jer. xxiii. 28, 29, 31. 1 Cor. xiv. 24, 25. Heb. iv. 11, 12. 1 Thess. ii. 13. John vii. 17. and x. 3, 4. Acts xiii. 48, 51. This is the true, the formal ground and reason of our faith. And hence, while many of great parts and learning, who understand, and can urge on others the merely rational proofs of the divine inspiration and authority of the Scriptures, never cordially believe them, to the saving of their soul; others, who are of weak capacities, having them applied by the Holy Ghost to their heart, believe them so firmly, as to trust their eternal salvation on a single sentence of them; and to be ready, patiently and cheerfully, to undergo all manner of sufferings, rather than deny the smallest truth contained in them. The sun's effectual probation of his own existence by his own light and warmth seen and felt by us, may shadow forth this present proof of the divine authority of the Scripture. But it can only be understood by our experiencing it.

Such objections of Infidels against the divine original and authority of the Scriptures as have not been formerly anticipated, or removed, must now be considered.

Objec. I. "The revelations contained in the Old and New "Testament, which are known to so few, cannot be from God, "who is good to all men." Answ. 1. God's goodness to all men doth not bind him to promote all men to equal happiness, notwithstanding their most hateful rejection and abuse of his benefits. It doth not bind him to keep prodigal rakes as rich, healthy and honourable, as if they had been frugal and virtuous. —Nay, in fact, God doth not render every man equally rich, honourable, healthy in body and mind, benevolent, contented, or even equally acquainted with the Laws of nature. 2. If men, through sloth or vicious inclinations, have forgotten, contemned, corrupted, or banished, those revelations which God made to all alive in the days of Adam and Noah, Is he bound to preserve them among them clear, pure, and entire, and to add to them, whether they will or not? Is a Lawgiver tyrannical, if he publish not his statutes in every man's chamber?—or, if he do not repeat his publication of them at every year's end, when his subjects have, through their sloth and wickedness, forgotten them,—and meanwhile punish none for disobedience to them, but in proportion to the means of information concerning them which they enjoyed? 3. Revelation might indeed have prevented that gross ignorance and barbarity which prevail among many nations: But it is not their want of it any more than their having the Law of nature in their breasts, but their own inward corruption, and the bad education and example they had, which are the cause of that ignorance and barbarity:—even as, though proper medicines might often prevent diseases and premature death, yet it is not the want of them, but the inbred corruption of the body or external violence, which is the cause of such diseases and death. 4. Certainly God gives a more illustrious display of his infinite goodness, in revealing his will for the salvation of some, nay multitudes of men, than he could do, in suffering them all to perish for ever in their ignorance. Revelation allows every man to retain all the privileges which he hath by the Light of nature; adds not a few to many who are not saved in Christ, vouchsafes multitudes of blessings to them that are saved;—and thus manifests the goodness of God much more clearly than the Light of nature.——Would our benevolent Infidels rather have all mankind eternally unhappy, than a part?

OBJEC. II. "Jesus of Nazareth having observed the then "general rumour and expectation of an appearance of the Son "of God in human nature, as a promised Messiah, laid hold of "the opportunity, and pretended to be Him." ANS. He indeed appeared in the proper season, when men were looking for the Messiah, and ready to examine his characteristics. But, in these circumstances, his appearance in so debased and spiritual a form, so contrary to the carnal wishes and expectations of his countrymen, though perfectly conformable to the ancient predictions, strongly marked his candour and his being the true Messiah. And it is remarkable, that every other claimant of that character hath, to his utmost, conformed his appearances and pretences, to the prevalent hopes and carnal inclinations of the Jewish nation.

OBJEC. III. "If Jesus Christ had been the Saviour of mankind, the universal and equal goodness of God could not have "admitted of the delay of his coming in the flesh, till four "thousand years after the creation." ANS. 1. God might have been infinitely good, though never a man had been formed or a Saviour heard of. And it hath been repeatedly demonstrated, that God doth not manifest *equal* kindness to all men. 2. If our Saviour had appeared in the flesh, immediately after the Fall of man, or much sooner than he did,—the wisdom and goodness of God had been far less manifested therein. The absolute need of him, and of the abounding of grace through him, had been far less evident.—It would not have been clearly manifested, that neither overwhelming floods,—destructive showers of fire and brimstone,—tenfold plagues,—captivity,—desolation,—nor philosophers,—nor prophets, endowed with miraculous powers,—nor repeated and awful appearances of God himself,—could reform the world, but after all it had rather become more and more wicked.——Moreover, men would not have been sufficiently warned of his coming, or prepared to examine his credentials. Multitudes could not have been found to witness his instructions, miracles, death, and resurrection, or to be his opponents and murderers. His gospel could not have had opportunity of clearly manifesting its divine efficacy in triumphing over so much opposition. Millions of incorrigible Jewish enemies could not have been found, or multitudes of nations to scatter them among, as public and permanent documents and witnesses of his Messiahship, by their own inexpressible miseries for rejecting him.

OBJEC. IV. " Jesus Christ made choice not of learned " and wise men, but of weak and simple wretches, whom he " could easily deceive, for his apostles and agents. Such only, " and they in small numbers, were the witnesses of his resur- " rection; whereas a single walk through the streets of Jeru- " salem, or appearance before the Sanhedrim, would have put " the matter beyond doubt, and procured the attestation of men " of high rank and credit." ANSW. 1. The instance of Paul, the most active, zealous, and successful among his apostles, proves, that they were not all simple and ignorant. But if they were so, they were the more unfit to promote an imposture; they could not, like Zoroaster, Apollonius, and other cheats, insinuate themselves into the affections of men, chiefly the great and rich; they were the readier to be every where treated with contempt and persecution, instead of regard and belief, to discover an imposture trusted to them; and without divine assistance, the less capable to form such an incomparably exalted scheme of doctrines and morals, or make it so remarkably triumph over all opposition from hell and earth. 2. It was not proper that he should appear to the Jewish rulers, or in public streets, after his resurrection, and thus again expose himself to their cruelty. After sufficient proofs of his Messiahship, in his miracles, doctrines, and conduct, they had condemned and crucified him. They had exhausted their wits and emptied their purses, to stifle the proofs of his resurrection, which the soldiers that watched his sepulchre had given them. Such obstinate criminals had no claim to be the distinguished favourites of heaven, or honoured publishers of the gospel.—They were soon to have the irrefragable testimony of the Holy Ghost, in his miraculous and heart-conquering influences, which were a thousand times more convincing than a transient view of a body restored to life.—In fine, if any worldly influence had appeared in the rise and primary propagation of the report of his resurrection, the almighty power and wisdom of God had been less clearly manifested in its spread and success.

OBJEC. V. " Few of the Jews, the only people that under- " stood the ancient types and predictions relative to the Mes- " siah, believed in Jesus of Nazareth, but held him for an im- " postor." ANSW. This very thing verified these ancient types and predictions, and marked him out as the *true Messiah*. It was expressly foretold, that he should be despised, rejected, and crucified by his countrymen. Nor, could an opposite conduct have answered his end in coming into the world to be a sacrifice for sin. Nor, without such wickedness, could they and their seed have been qualified to be the wretched witnesses of his Messiahship, and of the truth of his gospel among all nations. And their often repeated readiness to receive every pretended Messiah, makes their rejection of him the more striking.

OBJEC. VI. " The facts of Revelation depend wholly on *faith*, " which is the lowest kind of evidence." ANSW. 1. It is nevertheless the most common evidence, and the best adapted to every capacity, weak or strong. It is not by intuition, or by rational demonstration, but by faith in the testimony of others, that all our dealings with men are managed, nations governed, pleas decided, knowledge of the world procured, and trade with persons and places, which we never saw, carried on. 2. The credibility of Scripture, as hath been repeatedly hinted, depends upon the strongest attestations of friends and enemies, from age to age, nay, upon the *self-evidencing testimony* of an infallible God, which is more clear and strong than demonstration itself.

OBJEC. VII. " The divisions which prevail among Chris" tians, concerning the number of their inspired books and " their meaning, with the doctrines and rules therein contained, " manifest that Revelation cannot be from God, who hath " the hearts of all men in his hand." ANSW. 1. For about 1600 years past, few Christians have had either debates or doubts concerning any book really inspired. Nor have many that deserve the name of Christians, ever contended for the divine authority of the apocryphal books. 2. The divisions among Christians are but a counterpart of those which take place among the extollers of the light of nature,—are a fulfilment of these Scriptures, and are by the providence of God, made useful in preserving them in their original perfection and purity, and are a remarkable evidence of their truth, as not one of the contending parties have prevailed in discovering a cheat in them.

OBJEC. VIII. " Revelation, particularly that which relates " to the Christian religion, hath not reformed the world. " Many of its most noted professors habitually contemn its " plain and fundamental rules,—in not *washing* one another's " feet,—in taking usury for the money which they lend,—in " eating things strangled in blood, in swearing assertory " or promissory oaths. Their own candid authors represent " most of their clergy as consummate villains, and many of " their people as worse than heathens." ANSW. 1. It is too true, that many professors of revealed religion, of whom our infidel doctors are ordinarily a part, habitually disregard the fundamental doctrines and laws of it;---and that even true Christians come not near to that perfection which is required of them. But, 2. The rules pointed at in the objection were never reckoned either *fundamental* or *unlimited*. *Washing of feet*, as a part of kindness to strangers, being common in warm countries, where they walked without shoes, is put for kind and humble behaviour toward brethren, John xiii. 15. 1 Tim. v. 10. ---The eating of things strangled, and of blood, was merely forbidden only for a time, in condescension to the Jewish Christians, who, till their city and temple were destroyed, retained an ill-grounded zeal for their ancient ceremonies, Acts xv. 20, 29.---The Christian law never prohibited *oaths necessary* in witness-bearing, or in self-engagement,---but the swearing vainly, falsely, or in common conversation, or by creatures, Matth. v. 33—37. Jam. v. 12.---As the Israelites, in order to preserve them from infection by their idolatrous neighbours, had little traffic,—and as their possessions reverted to the original proprietors in every year of jubilee, God forbade them to take usury from one another, at least if poor, but allowed them to take it from others, Deut. xxxii. 19. Lev. xxv. 36, 37. Christians still hold it unlawful to take usury from such as are poor, and can make no gain by their money. 3. In every place where Christianity hath properly prevailed, idolatry and savage barbarity have been proportionally extirpated, and humanity, honesty, and benevolence, have taken place.—History, indeed, records the clerical crimes; but it mentions few but noisy bustlers in the church, whose practice is seldom the best, and overlooks multitudes who had silently followed the example of Christ. Besides, most of these infamous clergymen had nothing of Christianity but the mere name. Christian authors sometimes exaggerate the faults of their professed brethren, in order to make them ashamed; and compare only the worst of them with the best of the heathens.—But it is certain, that Christianity hath produced among the clergy and people, multitudes of amiable characters, with which the best of the heathens are altogether unworthy to be compared. 4. If the corruptions of Christians be sufficient to prove that their revelation is not from God, the horrible corruptions of the Greeks, Romans, &c. under the meridian lustre of their philosophy and researches into the *law of nature*, must as effectually prove that it is not from God. And I suppose the true disciples of the mere light of nature in the north-east of Asia, or south of Africa, or in America, &c. are not much superior in virtue to the wicked Christians in Britain. 5. This objection turns out to be a proof of the divine original of the Christian revelation. It represents the Christian clergy and people exactly answerable to the Scripture predictions concerning many of them, 2 Tim. iii. 1—6, 13. and iv. 3, 4.

1 Tim. iv. 1—3. Acts xx. 29, 30. 2 Thess. ii. 3—12. Rev. xiii. xvii. Matth. xxiv. 1 Pet. ii. iii. Jude 4—19. And, since these wretches never attempt to conform revelation to their inclinations and practices, it is evident that God, from regard to it, must keep them under some infallible restraint.

FROM the above proofs of the divine authority of the revelation contained in our Bibles, it is evident that the apocryphal books of Esdras, Tobit, Judith, &c. are not to be reckoned any part of it. 1. The Jews, to whom the keeping of the oracles of God was committed, Rom. iii. 2. Psalm cxlvii. 19, 20. never received or acknowledged these books as divinely inspired, and have always considered *Malachi* as the *seal* or *last* of their prophets. And indeed, he himself hints, that no prophet should arise after him, till John Baptist, Mal. iv. 4, 5. 2. There is no approbation of these books in the New Testament, nor a single sentence of them quoted. 3. The writers of them plainly hint, that themselves were not prophets, nor inspired, but liable to mistake, and did need the pardon of the reader, Eccles. i. 1, 3, 5. 1 Mac. ix. 27. 2 Mac. ii. 24, 27. and xiii. 39. 4. There is not, in these books, that stamp of divine wisdom, majesty, goodness, and holiness, as in the books which we admit for *canonical*. 5. In all of them there are things false, or disagreeable to the oracles of God.——On these or the like accounts, they were not admitted into the list of canonical books, by Melito, Origen, Eusebius, Athanasius, Cyril, Nazianzen, Epiphanius, Amphilochius, Tertullian, Ruffinus Philastrius, Jerome, and other ancient Fathers, or by the councils of Laodicea and Constantinople. Nor, for ought I certainly know, by any council except that infamous one of Trent, that of Florence being properly none; nor, till the ninth and tenth centuries, in which men were plunged into popish darkness and stupidity, were they of much repute.

SEVERAL books mentioned in Scripture, as of *Jasher*,—*The wars of the Lord,* &c. are not now extant, at least under the ancient names. But, if their contents have not been ingrossed in those that we still have, we ought not to suppose that they had been divinely inspired. 1. The Scripture assures us of God's preservation of all the inspired writings of the Old Testament, Matth. v. 18. Luke xvi. 29, 31. and xxiv. 27, 44. Rom. xv. 4. 2. It is altogether inconsistent with the wisdom and goodness of God, to suppose that his providence would permit a book to be lost, which he had intended for standing use in the church. 3. The zeal of the Jews for their sacred books rendered the losing of any of them almost impossible. Nor does Christ or his apostles ever blame them for either losing or corrupting any of them.

The Old Testament doth not now bind men to an observance of typical ceremonies, or laws strictly judicial. But in so far as it instructs them in revealed truths, or inculcates moral duties, it continues its whole binding force, till the end of time. 1. Christ came not to destroy the law or the prophets, but to fulfil them, Matth. v. 17, 19. 2. The Scriptures of the Old Testament are recommended as a rule in the New, Luke xvi. 29, 31. John v. 39. Rom. xv. 4. 2 Tim. iii. 15—17. 2 Pet. i. 19. Acts xvii. 11. and xxvi. 22. Matth. xxii. 29. 3. The writings of the prophets, as well as of the apostles, are the *foundation* of the New Testament church, Eph. ii. 19, 20. 4. Our knowledge and faith of the creation, fall of man, and of Christ being the promised Messiah, &c. much depends on the books of the Old Testament, Luke xvi. 16. and xxiv. 27, 44. John i. 45. Acts x. 43. xiii. 47. xxvi. 22. xxviii. 23. Rom. x. 4. and iii. 21. 2 Cor. iii. 3, 7. Eph. ii. 19, 20.

While no more but a small portion of divine truth, easy to be remembered, was revealed;—while the principal teachers of it lived many hundred years, in which they had opportunity to communicate it to multitudes;—and while delusions were less known in the world,—God exhibited his will *only in words.*— But, when his revelations became so extensive, that men's memories could not easily retain them all;—when the teachers' lives were exceedingly shortened;—when his peculiar people had exceedingly multiplied;—when he intended to render the manifestations of his mind in dreams and visions less frequent,—it became necessary, for the better preservation and propagation of his revelations, that they should be committed to writing.— The penmen did not write them of their own accord, but as expressly or implicitly commanded by God, Exod. xvii. 14. and xxxiv. 27. Deut. xxxi. 19. Isa. viii. 1. xxx. 8. Jer. xxx. 2. xxxvi. 2. Ezek. xliii. 11. Dan. xii. 4. Hab. ii. 2. Rev. i. 11—19. xiv. 13. ii, iii. Isa. vi. 9. Mat. xxviii. 19.—Nevertheless, a divine commission to teach, bound none to write, unless the Holy Ghost directed and determined them to it. And hence several prophets and apostles never wrote any part of Scripture.

The church is, 1. The keeper and guardian of the oracles of God, Rom. iii. 2. 2. The public director to, and exhibiter of what is truly his word, Isa. xxx. 21. 1 Tim. iii. 15. 3. The protector of it against the assaults of adversaries, 1 Tim. iii. 15. But perhaps the *pillar and ground of truth,* there mentioned, may mean not the church, but the great mystery of godliness represented in ver. 16. 4. The preacher and publisher of the contents of Scripture, 2 Cor. v. 18, 19, 20. Rom. x. 15, 17. 5. The explainer of the meaning of Scripture, Acts xiii. 15—41, 47. Neh. viii. 8.——But the Scriptures do not DERIVE their AUTHORITY from the church, but *from God alone.* 1. The church hath all her authority from the Scriptures being founded on them, and so can give no authority to them more than to God himself, Eph. ii. 20. John v. 39. Acts xvii. 11. 2. If we believe the Scripture on the ground of church-authority, we subordinate the authority of God to that of the church, contrary to Acts iv. 19. and v. 29. John xx. 29, 31. Isa. viii. 20. 2 Chron. xx. 20. 3. If we admit the authority of the church, as the foundation of the truths revealed in Scripture, our faith is but human, standing in the wisdom and veracity of men, not in the power of God, contrary to 1 Cor. ii. 5. 2 Cor. iv. 2. and i. 24. 1 Thess. i. 5. and ii. 13. 4. Even Christ and his apostles submitted their authority to be tried by the Scriptures, John v. 39. Gal. i. 8, 9. 2 Pet. i. 16—19. Acts xvii. 11. and xxvi. 22. 5. From what church doth the Scripture derive its authority? Is it from the ancient or the modern church?—from the collective or the representative church?—from the church universal or particular?—from the pope, or a council?—Papists do not know.

The Scriptures are PLAIN and PERSPICUOUS. Every thing necessary to be known, believed, or practised, in order to our salvation, is so clearly and plainly revealed in some passages of them, that every serious inquirer of moderate capacity, may, by diligent consideration, understand it. 1. God himself expressly declares the Scriptures to be plain, Deut. xxx. 11—14. 2 Cor. iv. 2—4. Rom. xvi. 26. 2. They are represented as a *lamp* and a *light*, for the instruction of the *simple*, Psalm xix. 7, 8. and cxix. 105, 130. Prov. vi. 23. and i. 4. 2 Pet. i. 19. 3. All adult persons, however weak, are commanded to read and meditate on them, that they may receive instruction, John v. 39. Luke xvi. 29, 31. Acts xvii. 11. Deut. vi. 6—9. Isa. viii. 20. and xxxiv. 16. Rev. i. 3. Psalm i. 2. and cxix. 97—100. Mat. xxii. 29. 4. The many repetitions, explications, with the multitude of figures and emblems drawn from common things, manifest, that God really intended to speak intelligibly to men: nor could he fail in his design.——But, as the mysteries contained in the Scripture cannot be comprehended by our finite and weak minds; and there are hard passages, chiefly in history and prophecies, which do not so nearly concern our salvation, 2 Pet. iii. 16. Rev. v. 1, 3. the diligent use of means is necessary in order to understand it. And, even the plainest passages of it cannot be spiritually and savingly understood, without the special illumination of the Holy Ghost. 1. Spiritual blindness reigns or prevails in men's minds, while they remain on earth, 1 Cor. ii. 14. 2 Cor. iii. 5, 14. iv. 4. Eph. v. 8. Rev. iii. 17, 18. Psal. cxix. 18. and cxxxix. 6. lxxiii. 22. Prov. xxx. 2,' 3. 2. In the declarations and promises of God, and in the prayers of his saints, this special illumination is represented as necessary to our savingly understanding the mind of God, Psalm xxv. 8, 9, 14. and cxix. 18, 27, 33, 34. Isa. xlviii. 17. and liv. 13. and lix. 21. and xxix. 18, 24. and l. 4. Luke xxiv. 45. John vi. 44, 45. 1 Cor. ii. 10, 12. 2 Cor. iv. 6. Eph. i. 17, 18. and iii. 14—19. 1 John ii. 20, 27, John xvi. 7—14. and xiv. 26. Prov. i. 23.

Not merely the EXPRESS WORDS of Scripture, but also the CONSEQUENCES justly deducible from them, are included in the regulating standard of our faith and practice. 1. All Scripture is profitable for *doctrine,—*for *instruction, correction,* and *comfort;* all which ends cannot be obtained but by deduction of consequences, 2 Tim. iii. 16, 17. Rom. xv. 4. John xx. 31. 2. God's wisdom requires, that he should speak to his rational creatures in a manner answerable to their reasoning faculties; and that he should intend whatever meaning may be reasonably deduced from his words, Prov. viii. 4. with 1 Cor. x. 15. and ii. 15. 3. The Scriptures must be *searched*, in order to find their meaning, Isa. xxxiv. 16. John v. 39. Acts xvii. 11. Prov. ii. 2—4. Psalm i. 2. and cxix. 97. 4. Christ and his apostles often reasoned from Scripture-consequences, Mat. xxii. Rom. iii. ix, x. xi. Gal. iii. iv. Heb. i.—xiii.———In our deduction of Scripture-consequences, our reason is the instrument, by which we discern them in the text, and draw them out; but it is not the ground of our believing them,—even as seeing and hearing are instrumental in our attaining the knowledge of the Scriptures, but are not the ground of our faith in them.

The Scriptures, including the necessary consequences of their express words, are a PERFECT and COMPLETE RULE of our FAITH and PRACTICE, informing us of every thing which we ought to believe or do, in order to our entrance into the glorified state. 1. The Scripture is represented as *perfect*, fitted to answer every necessary end, and to bring us to everlasting happiness, Psalm xix. 8, 9. John xx. 31. 1 John v. 13. Rom. xv. 4. 2 Tim. iii. 15—17. Psalm cxix. 97—100. Gal. vi. 16. 2. We are solemnly prohibited to add to, or take from it, in the least, Deut. iv. 2. and xii. 32. Gal. i. 8, 9. Rev. xxii. 18, 19. 3. All doctrinal traditions of men relative to our faith or practice in religion are plainly condemned and rejected by God, Mat. xv. 2, 3, 9. Isa. viii. 20. 1 Cor. iv. 6.———Indeed, many of Christ's expressions are not mentioned in Scripture, but in it we have the substance of them, and all that God requires us to know concerning him, John xxi. 25. and xx. 31.—— The *traditions* which the Thessalonians are required to hold fast and observe, were the doctrines of faith and the rules of conversation held forth to them in the apostolical sermons and writings, at that time, when the greater part of the New Testament was unwritten, 2 Thess. ii. 15. iii. 6.———The *trust committed* to Timothy

OF THE REVEALED STANDARD OF RELIGION.

was not oral traditions, but the *gospel* and *form of sound words*, and the excellent gifts with which God had qualified him for preaching it, 1 Tim. vi. 20. 2 Tim. i. 13.――――The Popish as well as the Jewish traditions, are so uncertain in their origin, and in their conveyance, and most of them so plainly disagreeable to the word of God, as to merit none of our regard.

No *new revelations* are to be added to the oracles of God contained in the Scriptures. 1. Though particular favourites of God may enjoy his private suggestions relative to private events or duties,—no private Spirit is to be regarded as a director to the church, Gal. i. 8, 9. 2 Thess. ii. 2. Acts xviii. 28. Isa. viii. 20.—And, even private suggestions from God are ordinarily conveyed in some scripture. 2. The deceitfulness of Satan and our own hearts render private revelations very uncertain to ourselves, and much more so to others, Jer. xvii. 9. Prov. xxviii. 26. 2 Cor. xi. 14. and ii. 11. 2 Thess. ii. 9, 10. Mat. xxiv. 24.—And it is observable, that none plead for the authority of private revelations, but such as, by the contrariety of their opinions and practices to the Scripture, manifest themselves to be led by a Spirit of delusion. 3. The Scriptures expressly foretel the rise of false prophets, under a mask of high attainments in religion, Mat. vii. 15. and xxiv. 11, 24. Acts xx. 29, 30. 2 Thess. ii. 8, 9. 1 Tim. iv. 1—3. 2 Tim. iii. 2—6, 13. 1 John iv. 1. and ii. 18.――――To anticipate objections it may be observed, 1. That the word of God is spiritual, quick, and powerful, and becomes a *dead letter*, only through the corruption of men's hearts, Rom. vii. 6, 14. Heb. iv. 12. 2 Cor. iii. 6. 2. That the Scripture-promises *of the Spirit* relate either to his extraordinary influences in the Apostolic age, or his ordinary operations in other ages, by means of the Scripture—which are sometimes expressed in figurative language, Joel ii. 28. Acts ii. 16—18. Rom. viii. 16. 1 Thess. v. 19. John xiv. 26. and xvi. 14. 1 John ii. 20, 27. and v. 6.

The perfection of the Scripture also excludes all *dictates of Fathers* or writers of the primitive church after the apostles, from all place in the regulating standard of our faith and practice. 1. All these fathers were fallible men, and often changed their opinions. Augustine, one of the most judicious of them all, wrote a whole book retracting his mistakes. 2. In their writings, especially if extensive, they often contradict themselves, as well as one another. 3. Sensible of their readiness to err, they earnestly warn their readers against an implicit believing or following of themselves. 4. Several productions ascribed to them, are not really theirs. And such as they formed have been exceedingly corrupted by the ignorance, inadvertence, or villany of the transcribers.――――Most of these reasons equally militate against our receiving the decrees of Popes or Councils, as any part of our Rule in religion.

The Scriptures being our only rule of faith and practice, in order to eternal life, ought to be read both publicly and privately, in a language that is understood. 1. The Lord commands and encourageth all adult persons of every age and rank to read them, Deut. vi. 6. xi. 19. xvii. 18, 19. xxxi. 11, 12. Josh. i. 8. Isa. viii. 20. xxxiv. 16. Luke xvi. 29, 51. John v. 39. Psalm i. 2. 1 Tim. iv. 13. Rev. i. 3. Acts xvii. 11. —and reproves men for their ignorance of them, Mat. xxii. 29. Hos. iv. 6. and viii. 12. Isa. xxvii. 11. 2. The approved practice of saints exemplifies the reading of Scripture, Neh. viii. 3, 6, 8. Luke iv. 16. Acts xiii. 27. and xv. 21. and xvii. 11. and viii. 28. 2 Tim. iii. 15. 3. The Scripture is formed and appointed by God for the use of all men in general, Heb. ii. 1. Rom. i. 2. Eph. iii. 9; and the several uses of it, mentioned by the Holy Ghost, are necessary for all men, 2 Tim. iii. 15—17. Rom. xv. 4. John xx. 31. Eph. vi. 17. 2 Cor. iii. 4. 1 Pet. i. 23. ii. 2. Psal. cxix. 9, 11. 2 Pet. iii. 1. Jude, verse 3. 1 John i. 4. ii. 26. and v. 13. 4. The saints' characters of *prophets, priests,* and *judges* require them all to be thoroughly acquainted with God's mind and law, Psal. cv. 15. 1 Pet. ii. 5, 9. 1 Cor. ii. 15. vi. 2. 5. The Scriptures were originally written in languages, which were then understood by the people of God and others to whom they came, clearly with a view that all might read them, and therefore ought still to be translated into the vulgar languages, that every one may read and understand them. And indeed, till Antichrist prevailed in the church, great care was taken to have them both translated and read.

Every passage of Scripture may be applied to the different purposes of instruction, direction, reproof, consolation, and the like, 2 Tim. iii. 16, 17. Rom. xv. 4.—Many have a *complex* meaning relating first to the type, and then to the antitype. The Jews, being a typical nation, much of their history hath such a complex sense. Many prophecies have a complex meaning, including several steps of fulfilment in the Jewish nation, Christian church, and heavenly state, the former steps being *types* or earnests of the latter,—or, in both church and state. ——In the *Song of Solomon*, and similar allegories, the spiritual things intended by the Holy Ghost are the only meaning, which the emblems are used merely to represent. But no Scripture hath two or more meanings strictly different. 1. The Scripture is fitted to render men *wise unto salvation*; and therefore must exhibit the mind and will of God in a certain, clear, and determinate manner, 2 Tim. iii. 15. Psalm xix. 7. cxix. 97—100. 2. Its uncorrupted purity and perspicuity proves, that the same passages cannot have several different meanings,

Psalm xii. 6. 1 Pet. ii. 2. 3. None of its texts being of *private interpretation*, no meaning ought ever to be affixed to any, but that which was certainly intended by the Holy Ghost, 2 Pet. i. 20, 21. iii. 16. 2 Cor. ii. 17.——The apostles indeed sometimes quote, or seem to quote, passages of the Old Testament, in a sense which we apprehend not to be literal. But these either relate to things typical, and have their fulfilment in different steps: or, they are quoted merely by accommodation to the apostle's subject: or, perhaps are not quoted at all, but merely alluded to, in expressions almost similar.

All men, particularly all Christians, have a right to judge for themselves of the meaning of Scripture, with a *judgment of discretion*. And their exercising it is both commended and commanded by God; nor could their reading or hearing of Scripture be profitable to their souls without it, Acts xvii. 11. 1 Cor. ii. 15. and x. 15. and vii. 23. 2 Cor. iv. 2. Heb. v. 14. Gal. i. 8. 1 John iv. 1. 1 Thess. v. 21. Rom. xv. 4. John v. 39. Isa. xxxiv. 16.——Church rulers have a *definitive public ministerial* power to judge the meaning of Scripture, that they may declare and apply it to others, Mal. ii. 7. Matt. xxviii. 19, 20. 2 Tim. ii. 15, 16. and iv. 2. Neh. viii. 8. Acts ii. 29, 36, 39. and viii. 35. and xx. 20, 21, 24, 27—32. 1 Cor. xv. 1, 3, 4, 11, 12. and iv. 1, 2. and ii. 4, 5. and i. 24. 2 Cor. i. 24. Heb. v. 12. 1 Cor. xiv. 29, 32, 33.——But no mere man, neither church, nor fathers, nor popes, nor councils, are *infallible judges* as to the meaning of Scripture, or supreme determiners of controversies in religion. But the Holy Ghost himself speaking in the Scripture, is the *only supreme* and *infallible judge*. 1. All churches and councils consist of, and all popes and fathers are, fallible men. They have often erred and contradicted themselves, or one another, and are sometimes the parties to be judged. Nor are men capable of judging in causes which were never before them, or did not exist in their particular form, till many years after their death. 2. The Scripture never mentions any such infallible judge on earth. 3. The command of God, and the example of Christ and his apostles, require us to appeal the determination of every dispute relative to faith and practice in religion to the Scripture itself, Deut. xvii. 10. Isa. viii. 20. and xxxiv. 16. Luke xvi. 29, 31. John v. 39. 1 John iv. 1. 2 Pet. i. 19. Acts xvii. 11. James iv. 11, 12. Mat. xxiii. 8—10. and iv. 2—10. and xxii. 29—33. John v. vii. viii. x. Luke xxiv. 27. Acts xv. 15—20. and xviii. 28. and xxvi. 22. And the Pharisees and Sadducees are condemned for departing from the Scripture as their standard of judgment, Mat. xv. 3, 9. and xxii. 29.

HUMAN REASON is of great use to examine the Scripture marks of its divine authority;—to defend it against enemies who attempt to deny, corrupt, or wrest it;—to draw out the consequences, and trace out the manifold connection between the divine mysteries contained in it;—to compare scriptures one with another, or even with the laws of nature;—to illustrate divine truths by hints taken from philosophy, natural history, &c. and thus to discover whether such a meaning affixed to a text be contrary to common sense, or to other passages of Scripture, Mat. vii. 15. and xvi. 6. Col. ii. 8. 1 Thess. v. 21. Heb. v. 14. Acts xvii. 11. 1 Cor. ii. 15. x. 15. xi. 13. Gal. iii. 15—17. 2 Tim. iii. 16. Tit. i. 9.——But human reason is not to be admitted to JUDGE what parts of revelation are to be believed and practised, what not; or even as an *infallible mean* of understanding the meaning of Scripture; for, 1. The reason of unregenerate men is *wholly*, and that of regenerate men *partially* blind and corrupt, Eph. iv. 17, 18. Rom. i. 27, 28. viii. 7, 8. Jer. xvii. 9. Eph. v. 8. 1 Cor. ii. 14. i. 19, 21. iii. 19, 20. Deut. xxix. 4. 2 Cor. iv. 3, 4. iii. 5, 14, 15. xi. 3. 1 Cor. xiii. 12. 2. The mysteries of Revelation infinitely transcend our reason, and are incomprehensible by it, 1 Cor. i. 19, 20. ii. 9. iii. 18, 19. Rom. xi. 33. 1 Tim. iii. 16. John i. 18. Mat. xvi. 17. xi. 25. 3. God represents our faith, in the matters of religion, as not founded upon the authority of men, but only on his oracles of truth, Deut. iv. 1. Isa. viii. 20. John v. 39. xx. 31. 2 Tim. iii. 15. Rom. x. 14—17. 1 Thess. ii. 16. 2 Pet. i. 19. Acts xvii. 11. 2 Cor. i. 24. iv. 2. 1 Cor. ii. 4, 5.—Our religion is nevertheless a *reasonable service*, not outward and carnal like the Jewish ceremonies, but spiritual, performed in the gracious exercise of our reason, Rom. xii. 1.

The *proper means of understanding* and *explaining* the Scriptures, are, 1. Much fervent prayer for the powerful illumination and direction of the Holy Ghost, who indited them, and for his effectual application of them to our heart, Psalm cxix. 18. Eph. i. 18, 19. and iii. 14—19. 2. Frequent attentive reading of them, and meditating on them, with a single and earnest desire to know the mind of God by them, laying open and submitting our consciences to it, that we may believe and practise it, John v. 39. Acts xvii. 11. Psalm i. 2. cxix. 97—100. 1 Tim. iv. 13, 15. Mat. vi. 22. 3. Careful comparison of scriptures one with another, that they may illustrate one another, and that we may never affix any sense to a particular text, but that which is agreeable to the *analogy of faith* or general scheme of gospel truth, and also to the context, Rom. xii. 6. 4. We must carefully attend to the occasion and scope of the book, and particular passage, which we incline to understand or explain, that the sense on which we fix may be corresponding. 5. We must never depart from the *true literal sense* of a text, in order to fix on that which some call the spiritual meaning, without the most evident and forcible reasons. Nor ever fix a *carnal sense* upon any text which is clearly allegorical.—Spiritual improvement may and ought to be drawn from every passage: but no plain historical one ought to be wrested into any mystical meaning. —If histories relate to types, the history of the type and the mystery of the antitype, ought to be conjunctly considered. 6. Especially they, who profess to explain the scripture to others, ought to understand it in its original languages, in which the truths of God appear with incomparable light and emphasis.— Such as cannot read the originals, ought carefully to peruse the best translations and their marginal readings. 7. The figures of Scripture language ought to be carefully observed, and the customs alluded to, and sects and offices mentioned, to be thoroughly known. 8. To understand the histories, and especially the predictions, we ought to be furnished with a considerable knowledge of geography and of the history of the nations, and especially of the church. 9. We must never rest in a general knowledge of a text, but diligently search out what is chiefly and emphatically represented in it;—the discernment of which often depends upon our accurate attention to a single and insignificant-like particle in it, as IN, BY, OF, THROUGH, WHEN, THEN, BUT, YET, THEREFORE, &c. 10. Careful, but never implicit perusal of judicious commentaries, especially such as are most evangelical and practical, which earnestly attend to the connection, and lead us to compare one text with another. 11. In perusing the Scriptures, we ought always seriously to remember, that we are in God's presence, listening to his voice, and searching his word, in which the eternal salvation of our soul is contained. Scarcely any thing more effectually hardens the heart, than a mere notional or philosophical perusal of the Scriptures.

In general, the Scripture is DIVIDED into the Old Testament, which, representing Christ as to come in the flesh, was published before his incarnation:—and the New, which represents him as already come in the flesh, humbled in his obedience and sufferings, and exalted in his resurrection and ascension to heaven, and hath been since published, and is far more clear and spiritual, and directed to the Gentiles as well as to the Jews.——In both Testaments, at least in the translations, we have first the *historical* books, which are generally plainest; next the *doctrinal*, many passages of which need to be illustrated from the historical; and lastly, the *prophetical*, which are generally most obscure, and need to be illustrated from the preceding classes.—— In respect of their matter, the revelations contained in Scripture may be distinguished into, 1. *Histories*, which represent the past circumstances of cities and countries, and what hath been done by God or men. 2. *Predictions*, in which God foretels what should happen in some future periods. 3. *Doctrines*, which declare the permanent nature of persons and things,—as of God in his perfections, persons, purposes, and works; of angels, in their qualities, states, and work;—of man in his innocent, fallen, recovered, and eternal states;—or concerning the covenants of work and of grace, in their origin, making, parties, parts, and administration, &c. 4. *Laws*, in which the nature and parts of our duty to God, to ourselves, and to our neighbours, and the means of our salvation, are exhibited and appointed. 5. *Promises*, in which God intimates his will to confer benefits on men; and, 6. *Threatenings*, in which he declares his will to punish or correct men for their transgressions of his law. Both these last are related to predictions, and are sanctional enforcements of his laws; and many of them are *conditional*, the promises supposing some good quality or behaviour in the promisees, or persons to whom they are made;—and the threatenings supposing continued impenitence in sinning: hence their fulfilment is not to be expected or feared, unless the supposed conditions first take place.——Some promises and threatenings are *running* or *permanent*, respecting blessings or miseries, which are common to men in every nation or age. Others are *restricted* to particular periods, persons, or societies.

All things delivered in Scripture are *equally true*, Psalm xii. 6. xix. 9. cxix. 128. Prov. xxx. 5. But they are not all of *equal importance*, Mat. xxiii. 23. Mark xii. 30—34. Some being *fundamental* truths, without the knowledge, faith and practice of which, no adult person can be saved; others *not fundamental* in this sense;—and others so connected with both kinds, that it can scarcely be determined to which of them they chiefly belong.—It is certain, that nothing can be a fundamental article of revealed religion, which is not *plainly* as well as really contained in the Scripture, 2 Tim. iii. 15—17. 1 Cor. i. 24, 25. Mat. xi. 25. Heb. v. 11—14. vi. 1, 2. It is no less clear, 1. That every truth, without the knowledge of which there can be no faith in Christ, repentance unto life, or worship of the true God, must be *fundamental*, Heb. xi. 6. xii. 14. Tit. ii. 11, 12. Mark xvi. 16. Rom. x. 14. John xvii. 3. v. 23, 24. with x. 30. 1 John ii. 23. 2 John, ver. 9. 2. Every truth, to the cordial belief of which eternal salvation is annexed in Scripture; and with the ignorance or unbelief of which eternal damnation is connected, must be *fundamental: as, That Christ is come in the flesh, and is risen from the dead; and that we are saved by God's free grace, and justified through the imputed righteousness of Christ*, 1 John iv. 2, 3. John viii. 24. iii. 18, 36. Rom. x. 3, 9, 10. Gal. i. 8, 9, ii. 19—21. v. 2, 4. 1 Cor. xv. 14. 3. Every truth, which the Scripture represents as a *foundation*,—as the doctrines concerning Christ's mediatorial person, offices, and states, must be *fundamental*, 1 Cor. iii. 11. Eph. ii. 20. Mat. xvi. 16, 18. 1 Tim. iii. 15, 16. 1 Cor. i. 24. ii. 2. Phil. iii. 8. 1 Cor. xv. 14. 2 Tim ii. 8. 4. Every truth, without the knowedge of which, other fundamental truths cannot be known or believed, must be held as *fundamental*.—Thus the knowledge of our sinfulness and misery as declared by God, is necessary to our knowledge of Christ and his salvation, and our believing on him as our Saviour, 1 John i. 8, 10. 1 Tim. i. 15. Mat. ix. 13. xviii. 11. Rev. iii. 17, 18. Hos. xiii. 9.

As God hath given us no *precise list* of fundamental truths;— as some truths which perhaps are not strictly fundamental, lie very near the foundation, and some truths in an advanced state of the church may be fundamental, which were not so in her infant-state,—as all the truths of Revelation are of unspeakable importance, and even *essentially necessary* in their own place,— and as all attempts to determine which are fundamental, and which not, are calculated to render us deficient and slothful in the study of religious knowledge;—To fix precisely what truths are fundamental and what not, is neither *necessary*, nor *profitable*, nor *safe*, nor *possible*.—But it is certain, that the whole of the Christian religion doth not consist in the temper of mind, or in the observance of God's commands, and having a hope in his promises, without regard to orthodoxy of principles. 1. God in his word, besides precepts and promises, hath plainly revealed many things, which, it cannot be supposed, he hath done in vain, Rom. i.—xi. Gal. i.—iv. 2 Cor. v. Eph. i.—iv. Col. i. ii. Heb. i.—x. &c. 2. Knowledge of, and soundness in the principles of revealed religion, are commanded, recommended, promised, and prayed for, in Scripture, as a necessary part of religion, 1 Tim. ii. 4. 1 John iii. 23. ii. 23. John xvii. 3. and xx. 31. 2 Tim. iii. 15. ii. 8. i. 1. 1 John 9, 10. Isa. i. 3. xxvii. 11. Hos. iv. 6. 2 Thess. i. 8. 2 Cor. iv. 3, 4. Isa. xi. 9. xxix. 18, 24. 2 Pet. i. 2. Col. ii. 2. iii. 16. Eph. i. 18. iii. 17—19. iv. 14. 3. There can be no acceptable obedience to God's precepts, or hope in his promises, without the sound knowledge of them, and the true faith of other divine truths, Rom. x. 9, 10. xiv. 23. Heb. xi. 6. John vi. 29, 39, 40. 4. Such as obstinately maintain opinions contrary to the fundamental truths of the gospel are *accursed* by God, and condemned to everlasting destruction, Tit. iii. 10. 1 John ii. 22, 23. Gal. i. 8, 9. v. 20.

REFLECT. Ponder now, my soul! Are these oracles of God, these testimonies and testaments of Jesus Christ, my heritage, the words upon which he hath caused me to hope? Are they my divine charter for my everlasting life?—Are they even now my food, and the rejoicing of my heart?—Are they sweeter than honey to my taste, and more gladdening than great spoil?—Are they my counsellors, with whom I converse by day and by night,—in the house, or on the way,—when I lie down and when I rise up?—Do I, in very deed, understand their delightful contents? Do I believe their exceeding great and precious promises?—Do, or can I, sing their new songs in the house of my pilgrimage?—While I speak or write of them, are they to me a *vailed*, a *dead letter?* Or, Are they indeed the self-evidencing word of God,—*spirit and life*,—quick and powerful, piercing to the dividing asunder of my joints and marrow?—What passages have particularly affected my soul; and in what manner?—What have I hid in my heart, that I might not sin against God? What promises have I received, and held fast as my enriching bonds on the Bank of Jesus, and his Father's infinite grace?—What have I laid up for cordials to my soul, in her departing moments?—Dare not, my soul, to commence or continue a preacher of these divine truths, while I myself have no spiritual knowledge of their power.—Alas! how shall I hold up my face at Jesus's tribunal, if I wickedly take his covenant in my mouth,—publishing it to others, before my own heart say of it, *This is all my salvation, and all my desire.*—Blush deep, O my soul,—that I have so long enjoyed this scripture glass, and turned my back to it;—so little beheld Jesus and his salvation in it!—that I have had in my house this treasure, this live coal of infinite, of redeeming love, and yet my heart so little moved, melted, and inflamed by it!—that I have so long had this table, richly furnished with the flesh, the blood, nay all the fulness of God, and yet have scarcely *tasted* that the Lord is gracious;—that I have so long had my hands full of this *grace and truth*,—full of redemption through Jesus's blood, full of a three-one God of infinite and everlasting excellency and love,—and yet my heart still so empty.——Let not me dare to proceed to the contemplation of his nature and works, till I believe his word, and receive his *unspeakable gift*, that I may, on that ground, all along say of him, *My Lord and my God*,—MY GOD and MY ALL.

BOOK II.

Of God, the Author, the Object, and End of all Religion, in his Perfections, Persons, Purposes, and Works.

CHAP. I.

Of the NATURE or PERFECTIONS of GOD.

THE Scripture represents mankind as instructed in the knowledge of God by his works of creation and providence, Psalm xix. 1—6. Rom. i. 19, 20, 32, and ii. 14, 15. Acts xiv. 15—17. and xvii. 23. And, while it supposes, it also solemnly asserts and proves, his existence, and represents his *Names, Nature, Perfections, Persons, Purposes,* and *Works.*

The *proper names* which are ascribed to God in the Old Testament, are, EL, which denotes him the *strong and powerful God,* Gen. xvii. 1. Isa. ix. 6. ELOAH, which represents him as the *only proper object of worship,* Gen. i. 1. Psalm. xlv. 6, 7. SHADDAI, which denotes him to be *all-sufficient* and *all-mighty,* Gen. xvii. 1. Exod. vi. 3. HHHELJON, which represents his *incomparable excellency, absolute supremacy over all,* and his peculiar residence in the *highest* heavens, Psalm l. 14. and lvi. 2. ADON, which marks him the great *Connecter, Supporter, Lord* and *Judge* of all creatures, Psalm cx. 1. xvi. 2. JAH, which may denote his *self-existence* and *giving of being* to his creatures, or his infinite *comeliness* and *answerableness,* to himself and to the happiness of his creatures, Exod. xv. 2. Psalm lxviii. 4. cxxx. 3. Isa. xxvi. 4. EHJEH, I AM, or I WILL BE, which denotes his self-existence, absolute independence, immutable eternity, and all-sufficiency to his people, Exod. iii. 14. Rev. i. 4, 8. JEHOVAH, which denotes his *self-existence, absolute independence, and unsuccessive eternity,* with his *effectual and marvellous giving of being* to his creatures, and fulfilling his promises, Gen. ii. 4, 7, 8, 16, 19, 21, 22. iii. 1. x. 9, 10. xii. 1, 4, 7.— This name of God was known in the earliest ages of the world, Gen. iv. 1. ix. 26. v. 29. xiv. 22. xv. 7. xxiv. 7. And so God not being known to the patriarchs by it, means no more than that he had not demonstrated the propriety of it in any remarkable fulfilment of promises, Exod. vi. 3. This name often, in part, composes the names of persons or things; in that state, it merely denotes a relation to Jehovah, but taken simply by itself, it is never ascribed to any but God. 1. He alone is Jehovah, Psalm lxxxiii. 18. Isa. xxxvii. 20. xlv. 5, 6. 2. This name is represented as a distinguishing name of God, Isa. xlii. 8. Exod. xv. 3. Hos. xii. 5. Amos v. 8. and is his great and terrible name, Psal. xcix. 3. 3. The excellency which it denotes is applicable to none but God, Psal. xcvi. 5. Isa. xliv. 24.—Wherever an angel is called JEHOVAH, or LORD, in capitals in our translation, he must be understood to be the Son of God, who is the Messenger of Jehovah, or Messenger-Jehovah, Gen. xvi. 13. xviii. 13, &c.

In the New Testament, God is called KURIOS or LORD, which denotes his *self-existence*, his *establishment* of, and his *authority* over all things;—and THEOS, which represents him as the *Maker*, the *Pervader*, and the *governing Observer* of all things.— This name THEOS, as well as EL and ELOAH, which we render God, is a name which represents his divine nature, not merely his power or office. 1. All persons having power and authority are not truly Gods, 1 Cor. viii. 5, 6. 2. God is represented as a *God by nature*, to distinguish him from idols, Gal. iv. 8. 3. He was God before his power had formed any creatures, or he had any to govern, Rom. i. 20. xvi. 26. Psal. xc. 2. 4. THEOTES, or THEIOTES, *godhead*, means not power, or office, but a divine nature, Acts xvii. 29. Rom. i. 20. Col. ii. 9. 5. No creature is called GOD without some limitation annexed, which plainly imports, that they are not so by nature: angels and magistrates are called *gods*, because of their being his deputies in his government of the world, and resembling his majesty, wisdom, power, and equity, Psal. xcvii. 7. lxxxii. 6. John x. 34. Exod. iv. 16. vii. 1. xxii. 28.—Idols, devils, and men's bellies, are called *gods*, because they are often regarded or worshipped instead of the true God, Psal. cxv. 4. 2 Cor. iv. 4. Philip iii. 19.

God is represented by a multitude of *metaphorical names*, as a Man, a Lion, a Rock, &c.—Besides the names which represent the divine nature, there are others which represent particular persons in the godhead, as Father, Son, Jesus Christ, Holy Ghost or Spirit, Matth. xxviii. 19. 2 Cor. xiii. 14.—The TITLES which denote what relation God hath to others, belong to his name.—Some of them, as *Creator of all the ends of the earth*, Isa. xl. 28. *Preserver of men*, Job vii. 29. *King of nations*, Jer. x. 7. *Lord of Hosts*, belong to him as the *God of nature*.—Others as the God and Father of Christ, Eph. i. 3. 1 Pet. i. 3. John xx. 17. 2 Cor. i. 3. The *God of Abraham, of Isaac, and of*

OF THE NATURE OR PERFECTIONS OF GOD.

Jacob, Exod. iii. 6.—The God and the *Holy One of Israel*, 2 Sam. xxiii. 3. Isa. xlviii. 17.—*King of saints*, Rev. xv. 3.—*Father of mercies, and God of all comfort*, 2 Cor. i. 3.—The *God of mercy*, Psal. lix. 17.—The *God of grace*, 1 Pet. v. 10.—The *God of peace*, Rom. xvi. 20. 2 Cor. xiii. 11. Heb. xiii. 20.—The *God of salvation*, Psalm lxviii. 20.—The *hearer of prayer*, &c.—belong to him as *God in Christ, reconciling the world to himself.*

In respect of his substance, God is a most pure SPIRIT, having an understanding and will, without any bodily parts, any affections or passions. 1. He is expresly represented as a *Spirit*, John iv. 24. Num. xxiv. 2. Judg. iii. 10. Ezek. xi. 24. 2 Cor. iii. 17, 18. and as the *God, the Father, and the former of spirits*, Num. xvi. 22. Heb. xii. 9. Zec. xii. 1. with Luke xxiv. 39. 2. He is represented as altogether incorporeal and invisible, Job x. 4. ix. 11. iv. 16, 17. xxiii. 3, 4, 8. Isa. xl. 18. Deut. iv. 15, 16. Exod. xxxiii. 20. John v. 37. i. 18. Rom. i. 20, 23. 1 Tim. i. 17. vi. 16. Heb. xi. 27. 3. Immortal life is ascribed to him, Deut. xxxiii. 40. Jer. x. 10. 2 Cor. vi. 16. 1 Thess. i. 9. 1 Tim. i. 17. iv. 10. vi. 16. Acts xiv. 15. Rom. i. 23. Rev. i. 18. Gen. xvi. 13. Psal. xviii. 46. Which life is manifested in his giving and preserving that natural or spiritual life which his creatures enjoy, Acts xvii. 25—29. Psal. xxxvi. 9. 1 Tim. vi. 13. Rom. iv. 17. 1 John v. 20. John v. 21, 25, 26, 28. xiv. 19. 4. Spiritual acts of *thinking* and *willing* are ascribed to him, Psal. xxxiii. 11. xl. 5. cxxxix. 2. cxlvii. 4, 5. xcii. 3. Isa. lv. 8. Jer. xxix. 11. Psal. cxv. 3. Rev. iv. 11. Dan. iv. 35. Isa. xlvi. 10. xiv. 24, 27. Eph. i. 11. Phil. ii. 13. Rom. ix. 16, 18. 5. The power, wisdom, holiness, justice, goodness, and truth, the persons, purposes, and works, hereafter proved to belong to him, harmoniously manifest him a *most pure Spirit.*——The bodily members attributed to him in Scripture, are but instructive *emblems* of his spiritual perfections and acts,--used in condescension to our weakness, Hos. xii. 10.—In this manner also, all the affections or passions of *desire, joy, hope, fear, grief, anger*, &c. ascribed to him are to be understood. Moreover, God having always dealt with men, in the way of covenant-connections, many of these affections are intended to represent him as a friend, or enemy, according to the tenor of these covenants. And the changes seemingly attributed to him, really import the change in, or on us, from being under the covenant of works, to be in the covenant of grace.

The ATTRIBUTES, PERFECTIONS, or EXCELLENCIES of God, are the essential and absolutely inseparable properties of his spiritual substance or nature. These may be distinguished into those called *communicable*, of which some faint, but infinitely defective resemblances, may be found among his creatures,—as *knowledge, wisdom, power, holiness, justice, goodness,* and *truth*— and INCOMMUNICABLE, of which no resemblance can be found among his creatures,—as *self-existence, absolute independence, absolute simplicity, infinity, unsuccessive eternity, unchangeableness, necessary oneness,* and *subsistence in three distinct persons.*

I. The KNOWLEDGE of God is that *intellectual* perfection, by which he discerns objects.——He knows *all things,* Psal. cxlvii. 5. John xxi. 17. 1 John i. 5. iii. 20. Heb. iv. 13. Job xxxiv. 21, 22. xxxvi. 4, 5. Psalm xciv. 7—10. cxxxix. 4—7. Jer. xxiii. 24.——He knows, 1. Himself in all his unbounded perfections and mysterious purposes, Matth, xi. 27. John i. 18. x. 15. 1 Cor. i. 10. Jer. xxix. 11. Acts xv. 18. 2. All his creatures, great and small, possibly or really existent, Psal. cxlvii. 4. Mat. x. 30. Acts xv. 18. Deut. xxix. 29. Job xii. 22. xxviii. 8, 10, 24. xxvi. 4—6. xxiv. 1. xxxiv. 21, 22. 2 Chron. xvi. 9. Prov. xv. 3. Psal. xxxiii. 13--15. xi. 4. cxxxviii. 6. Jer. xxiii. 24. 2 Tim. ii. 19. 3. All the actions of his creatures, good and bad, Prov. v. 21. xv. 3. Job xxxiv. 21, 22. Psal. lxix. 5. xc. 8. cxxxix. 7—13. xxxiii. 13—18. xxxiv. 15. i. 6. lvi. 8. Neh. i. 7. 1 Sam. ii. 3. Jer. xvi. 17. xxxii. 19. Isa. xxvi. 7. Hab. i. 13. 4. All the secret properties and thoughts or desires of human hearts, Gen. vi. 5. Heb. iv. 12, 13. Psal. cxxxix. 1—4. vii. 9. xxxviii. 9. 1 Chron. xxviii. 9. 1 Sam. xvi. 7. Deut. xxxi. 21. Prov. xv. 11. xvi. 2. xxi. 2. Luke xvi. 15. Amos iv. 13. Jer. xvii. 5, 9, 10. xvi. 17. Acts i. 24. Rev. ii. 23. Rom. viii. 27. 2 Chron. vi. 30. John ii. 24, 25. 1 Cor. iv. 5. 5. All future things, Psal. cxxxix. 3, 4. Isa. xlv. 20, 21. xli. 21—24. xlii. 9. xlvi. 9, 10. Jer. xxix. 11. Dan. ii. 20—22. Acts xv. 18. and hence he hath foretold most of them, Gen. iii. 14—19. and vi. 9. ix. xii. xiii. xlix. Lev. xxvi. Deut. xxvii.—xxxiii, &c. 6. The connections between possible things, which never actually happen, as he knows what his power can produce, and what dependence one circumstance must have upon another, Ezek. iii. 6, 7. Mat. xi. 21, 23.

God knows all these things. 1. Necessarily from himself, Psal. cxlvii. 5. 1 John i. 5. Dan. ii. 20—22. 2. Intuitively, by a simple glance, not as we know things, by any course of reasoning or succession of ideas, Heb. iv. 13. Job xxviii. 23—28. 3. Independently of all instruction from objects or teachers, Isa. xl. 13, 14. Rom. xi. 33, 34. Job xl. 2. 4. Distinctly and comprehensively,—in their nature, number, properties, and conditions, 1 John i. 5. Isa. xl. 21. Psal. cxlvii. 4. cxxxix. 12, 13, 14. 5. Infallibly, Matth. y. 18. Isa. xiv. 24, 26, 27. Acts xv. 8. Psal. cxxxix. 1—4. xi. 4. 6. Unchangeably,— let the created objects change as much as they will; for all these changes proceed from his sovereign will, Acts xv. 18. Isa.

xlvi. 10.—But conditional declarations of his will must be carefully distinguished from predictions, 1 Sam. xxiii. 11, 12. Jonah iii.

II. The knowledge of God, 1. As proposing the most proper ends for his conduct, Rom. xi. 36. Prov. xvi. 4. Isa. xliii. 21. 2. As choosing suitable means, 2 Sam. xiv. 14. 3. As leading him to act by those means in proper circumstances of time and place, Gal. iv. 4. Eph. i. 10. Ezek. xvi. 8. xxviii. 25, 26. xxix. 21. 4. As leading to act by a right rule or plan, Eph. i. 11. Isa. xlvi. 10. Jer. xxix. 11. is called his WISDOM.

It appears that God is WISE. 1. The Scriptures plainly declare that he is *wise*, Job xii. 13, 16. xxxvi. 4, 5. xxxviii. xxxix. xxviii. 12, 22—28. Prov. viii. Rom. xi. 33, 34. Isa. xl. 13, 14. Dan. ii. 20. 1 Cor. i. 21—25. iii. 18. Eph. iii. 10. 1 Tim. i. 17. Jude 25. Rom. xvi. 27. 2. He gives much wisdom to his creatures, 1 Kings iii. 12. iv. 29. Ezra vii. 25. Job xxxv. 10, 11. xxxvi. 22. xxxviii. 16. Prov. ii. 6, 7. viii. 12. Eccl. ii. 26. Eph. iii. 10. Jam. i. 5. Isa. xxviii. 26. Job xxxii. 8. Matth. xvi. 17. Isa. xlviii. 17. xxix. 24. Jer. xxxi. 34. 3. His wisdom is extensively and clearly manifested, 1. In his PURPOSES,—in forming so perfectly exact a plan of all that comes to pass in time and eternity,—and of every thing in such perfect correspondence with his principal and subordinate ends, Isa. xl. 13, 14. xlvi. 10. xiv. 26, 27. Eph. i. 8—11. 2. In his CREATION of all things, Prov. viii. 22—31.—In the amazing variety of creatures, seeds, instincts, members, endowments, vegetative, sensible, or rational,—and of dispositions, quantities, forms, voices, &c. Psal. civ. 24. Gen. i.—In their beauty, and in their order, with respect to themselves, and in their situations and motions, Eccl. iii. 11.—In their fitness to answer their respective ends,—and in so connecting things one with another, in an almost infinity of forms, Hos. ii. 21, 22. 3. In his PROVIDENCE, in 1. His upholding and governing every creature and all its actions and motions, in exact correspondence to the ends appointed in every particular moment of time, Heb. i. 3. Eph. i. 11. 2. In making awful and threatening providences an introduction to the most glorious and delightful events. Thus Sarah's long continued barrenness introduced her becoming the mother of multitudes of nations. Jacob's dishonourable exile introduced his receiving of singular manifestations from God; his wrestling and lameness, his reception of the invaluable blessing, Gen. xxi. xxviii. xxxii.—Horrible wickedness, fearful sorrow and anguish, and lasting debasement, introduced the glorious advancement of Joseph, and the entrance and happiness of Jacob with his children into Egypt, Gen. xxxvii.—xlvii. The terrible miseries of the Israelites under their Egyptian oppressors, and under Saul,

&c. introduced their most glorious deliverances and happiness, Exod. i.—to Josh. xxiv. 1 Sam. iv.—xxxi.—to 2 Sam. x. 1 Chron. xi.—xxix. 1 Kings i.—x.——Ignorance and wickedness, carried to the uttermost, did, as it were, prepare the world for the incarnation and atonement of Christ, and the honourable spread of his gospel, Rom. i.—iii. v. 20, 21. Tit. iii. 3—5. The persecution and murder of the Son of God, in our nature, by men, were instrumental in promoting the salvation of men through him, John xi. 47—52. Horrible power and progress in impiety and filthiness, have, as it were, introduced distinguished favours from God, and the most singular holiness of life, Rom. v. 20, 21. Acts ix. 22, 26. Gal. i. 12—24. 1 Cor. xv. 9, 10. 1 Thess. ii. 1—10. 1 Cor. vi. 10, 11. 3. In promoting his own holy and glorious ends amidst all the different, contrary, or wicked ends of his instruments, Isa. x. 5—12. xliv. 28. xlv. 1—5.—Thus, while the Egyptians hastened the Israelites out of their country, that they might get rid of their plagues, God hastened them out that he might fulfil his promise to Abraham *to a day*, if not to a minute, Exod. xii. 41, 42. with Gen. xv. 13—16. Contrary to the intention of Augustus, the Roman emperor, war or other accidents retarded the enrolment of his subjects in Canaan, till it could bring the virgin Mary from Nazareth to Bethlehem to bring forth her divine child, that he, herself, and her husband, might all be enrolled in the public imperial registers of the world, as descendents of David and citizens of Bethlehem, where they resided but a short time, Luke ii. Mat. ii. Mic. v. 2. Is. xi. 1. 4. In his promoting multitudes of ends in one act. Thus the selling of Joseph for a slave, saved the Egyptians and their neigbours from perishing by famine,—corrected Jacob's sinful indulgence of his children,—promoted Joseph's honour,—and drew his father's family into Egypt, Gen. xxxvii.—xlvii. Psalm cv. 5. In promoting ends which are exceedingly remote. Balak's hiring of Balaam to curse the Israelites, and Balaam's predictions thus occasioned, served to spread the report of the future incarnation of Christ among the eastern nations.—This, about 1500 years after, led the wise men to observe *his Star*, and come by its direction to worship him at his birth. Their presents supported Him, his mother, and supposed father, while they were exiles in Egypt, Num. xxii.—xxiv. with Mat. ii. 6. In easy counterplotting his most crafty enemies, and making their most violent opposition of his will the very mean of promoting it, Prov. xxi. 30. Psal. xxxiii. 10. Job v. 12, 13. xii. 16—20. Isa. xxix. 14. 1 Cor. i. 20, 25, 27. Thus the hardness of Pharaoh's heart rendered the deliverance of the Israelites from Egypt more honourable and God-like. The alarming invasions of Judea in the days of Jehoshaphat and Hezekiah, issued in the glory and the enrichment of the Jews, 2 Chron. xx. Isa. xxxiii. 3, 7. xxxvi. xxxvii. 7. In his exact timing of events. The Israelites were restrained from entering Canaan, till the rebellious despisers of it were all dead,—till the iniquity of the Canaanites was full, and they had weakened themselves by their intestine wars, Num. xiv. 26. Gen. xv. 16. Judges i. The incarnation of Christ was delayed, till the need of him to save men was fully manifest; —till repeated and wide-spread warnings had raised a sufficient expectation of him;—till the Jews had become wicked enough to persecute and murder him;—and till they had fallen under the power of the Romans, who *crucified* their slaves, Gal. iv. 4. Mat. ii.—xxvii. John v.—xix. The church, or her true members, seldom meet with remarkable deliverances till their troubles have come to an extremity, Micah iv. 10. Psalm xii. 5. Deut. xxxii. 36. Isa. xxxiii. 10. xli. 17, 18. Daniel xii. 1. Psalm cxlii. 4, 5. cxxiv. Acts xii. 6—14. Rev. xi. 7—15.

More particularly, God's wisdom appears in his providential *government of irrational creatures.* 1. In guiding them all to promote ends, which are subservient to the general good of the world, as well as to his own glory, Prov. xvi. 4. Psalm civ. cxlviii. 2. In thus guiding them without their own design, and yet agreeably to their diversified instincts. 3. In promoting his government by such means and instruments, as seem to take all the honour of the work, and yet reserving it all for himself, Rom. xi. 36. Rev. iv. 11—13.——It more abundantly appears in his *government of mankind.* 1. In giving them laws suited to their nature, their condition, their conscience, and their comfort, Rom. vii. 12, 14. 1 Tim. i. 8. Psalm xix. 7—10. cxix. 2. In giving them sufficient ability, inclinations, and assistance to obey these laws, unless a curse procured by their disobedience prevent it, Phil. ii. 12, 13. i. 6. Isa. xxvi. 12. 2 Thess. i. 11. 3. In affording them proper motives and encouragements to obedience suited to their condition, Isa. lv. 1—7. Jer. iii. Hos. xiv. 1 Cor. xv. 58. Heb. x.—xiii. 4. In the amazing suitable intimations of his will to them. Christ was long exhibited in promises and types before he appeared in the flesh. He uttered several undervaluing-like words to his mother, whom, he foresaw, the Papists would idolize. He peculiarly rebuked and recorded the faults of Peter, whom, he foresaw, they would blasphemously avow to be the infallible Head of their church. The doctrine of Justification by free grace, through faith in Christ's imputed righteousness, is chiefly delivered in an Epistle to the church at Rome, where, he foresaw, it would be peculiarly corrupted and denied, John ii. 4. Luke xi. 27, 28. Mat. xii. 48, 49. xiv. 31. xvi. 22, 23. xxvi. 34, 35, 69—75. Luke v. 8. John xiii. 6—10. xviii. 19, 11. xix. 26. xxi. 20—22. Gal. ii. 11—14. Rom. i.—x. 5. In limiting their sinfulness, and bringing glory to himself, and good to them, out of it; and in making the rage and power of sin contribute to destroy itself, and advance the glory of his free grace, Psalm lxxvi. 10. Rom. v. 20, 21. 6. In that manner, the means, the tendency, and even the timing of every change made upon their state, nature, or condition, harmoniously concur to mark his displeasure with sin, and to manifest the exceeding riches of his grace, Rom. v. 12---21. 2 Thess. i. 6---11. Acts xxii. 6. 1 Tim. i. 11---17. 1 Cor. 8---10. Gal. i. 15, 16, 22, 23. Eph. i. 3---10. ii. 1---10.

But, 4. In nothing doth the wisdom of God appear so much as in our REDEMPTION through Christ. It appears in the *person of the Redeemer*. 1. In choosing him, who was the middle person in the godhead, and the Son of God, to mediate between God and us, and make us the friends and children of God, that thus the order of mission and operation might correspond with that of the subsistence of the divine nature, John iii. 16. Rom. viii. 16, 17. Isa. lxi. 1. xlviii. 16. 2. In so uniting his finite and infinite natures, that they delightfully subsist in *one person*, without any confusion, composition, or opposition, 1 Tim. iii. 16. Jer. xxxi. 22. Isa. vii. 14. ix. 6. Zech. xiii. 7. John i. 14. Phil. ii. 6, 7. 3. In investing him with mediatorial offices, infinitely well calculated to promote his own glory in the honour of Christ and our everlasting happiness, Isa. xlix. 1—9. xlii. 1, 8. lxi. i. 3. Phil. ii. 6—13. Luke ii. 10—14. Eph. iii. 21. 1 Pet. iv. 11. 4. In the form and order of his states of abasement and exaltation, infinitely answerable to our guilty, polluted, and wretched condition,—to the covenants and honour of every divine person, Luke ii. 10—14. Phil. ii. 6—11. Luke xxiv. 26. Heb. ii. 10. xiii. 20.——It appears in the purchase of *our redemption* by the obedience and satisfaction of Christ, 1. In reconciling the seemingly discordant perfections of the Deity, by the abasement and death of him, in whom they dwell, Psalm lxxxv. 10. Mat. iii. 15. Heb. ii. 10. with Col. ii. 9. 2. In at once manifesting his greatest hatred of sin, and his greatest love to sinners, Rom. v. 6—10. iii. 24—26. viii. 3. 3. In executing his infinite wrath on Christ, from infinite love to him and to us in him, Mat. iii. 17. xvii. 5. Isa. liii. 10. 1 John iv. 9, 10. 4. In rendering the shame, ignominy, suffering, and death of Christ the grand mean of honour, happiness, and life to him, as Mediator, and to us in him, Phil. ii. 6—11. Heb. ii. 8—10. Isa. liii. 10—12. Rom. v. 9—11, 15—21. 5. In making men's contempt, abuse, and murder of his Son, the mean of finishing transgression, making an end of sin, bringing in an everlasting righteousness, and destroying the dominion of Satan in the world, Dan. ix. 24. 1 John iii. 5, 6, 8. 1 Peter ii. 24. iii. 18. Rev. v. 9. 6. In thus making every one of his perfections promote its own glory, by the strangest means.—Justice, by punishing the innocent Messiah, and by procuring pardon, peace, and happiness for sinful guilty men,—Mercy, by drawing down fearful punishment on God's beloved Son, that it might bestow everlasting favours upon the children of Satan,—rebels against God, and heirs of hell.—— It appears in the *publication of our redemption*, in that, 1. All the reports included in it exactly correspond with our necessities, and with the ends for which they were intended and appointed, 1 Tim. i. xv. 2. The publication was gradual, as men could bear it, Heb. i. 1. 3. The form of it was suited to the infant, or more adult, state of the church, and so was less or more spiritual, Heb. i. 1. x. 1. John i. 17. Col. ii. 17. 4. Imperfect hints relative to the incarnation of the Son of God, and his atonement for sin, were preserved or spread among the heathens, as a mean of facilitating the spread and belief of the gospel, Acts xvii. 23. 5. God took particular care to have all the leading facts of revelation singularly attested. 6. The more noted declarations of divine truth were remarkably well-timed. Those by Moses were published, when the Israelites in the wilderness had the utmost leisure to consider them. The reports of Christ's resurrection were published fifty days after it, when the murderous Jews had time to come to themselves, when the facts were exactly remembered, and when a part of fourteen nations, who attended the feast of Pentecost, were present to hear and spread them, Acts ii. 7. In choosing such instruments and opportunities for this *publication*, as rendered his own power and goodness in the success of it more obvious, 2 Cor. iv. 7.——It also appears in the *application of our redemption*. 1. The persons to whom it is ordinarily applied, are such as we would least expect should have his singular regard; and yet that is made to manifest his glory, 1 Cor. i. 25—31. 1 Tim. i. 13, 16. 2. Their own or their neighbour's sinful conduct or misery often occasions the application. Thus Onesimus' theft and deserting his service, occasioned his conversion to Christ, Philem. 10—16. 3. Even the rage of lust and overwhelming trouble are made the means of applying it, Rom. v. 20, 21. vii. 8—13. Isa. xxxiii. 12—24. 2 Chron. xxxiii. 11, 12. Hosea ii. 7, 14. v. 15. Job xxxiii. 14—30. 4. All things, especially such as they most dislike, are made to work together for the good of the elect, and particularly of believers, Rom. viii. 28. 2 Cor. iv. 17. 1 Cor. iii. 22.

III. The POWER of God is that essential perfection of his nature, by which he can do every thing not base or sinful.——It is no disparagement but honour to his power, that he cannot do that which implies a contradiction in its very nature,—as to satisfy an immortal soul with earthly portions, or make one under the reigning power of sin relish spiritual delights;—or that he cannot do that which is contrary to his own existence, —as to die,—become weak,—sleep, &c. or which is contrary to his moral perfections,—as to lie,—love sin,—deny himself; —or which is contrary to his own fixed purpose.—But it may be observed, that God's purpose doth not limit his power itself, but the exercise of it. His power ought therefore never to be distinguished into *absolute* and *ordinate*. His power itself cannot be *bounded*, and the exercise of it cannot be *inordinate*.

That God is ALMIGHTY, is evident, 1. From express declarations of Scripture, Gen. xvii. 1. xviii. 14. xlviii. 3. Deut. xxxii. 39. iii. 24. Job ix. 4, 10, 19. xxxvi. 5. xxxviii. 22, 23. xli. 10. Psalm xlv. 3. lxviii. 34. lxxxix. 13. lxxii. 18. xxiv. 8, 10. xcvi. 2—7. cxv. 3. xciii. 1. lxii. 11. Isa. ix. 6. xxvi. 4. xl. 28, 29. lxiii. 1. Jer. xxxii. 17. Mat. xix. 26. Luke i. 35, 37, 49. Rom. i. 20. Eph. i. 19. iii. 20. Rev. i. 8. xix. 15. 2. From that abundant power which he hath communicated to his creatures, luminaries, vegetables, brutes, men, and angels, Job xxxvi.—xli. Judges xv. xvi. 2 Sam. xxi. xxiii. 1 Chron. xi. xx. Psalm ciii. 20. 2 Thess. i. 7. 3. From the manifold and amazing displays of his power in his works of Creation, Providence, and Redemption.

In CREATION, his almighty power appears, 1. In making all things of nothing, Heb. xi. 3. Gen. i. Col. i. 16. Rom. xi. 36. 2. In forming such multitudes of creatures at once, Psalm xxxiii. 6. Col. i. 16. Gen. i. Psalm cxlvii. Exod. xx. 11. 3. In forming them of the same nothing, or of unfit matter, in so many diversified forms, Gen. i. Psalm civ. cxlviii. 4. In forming them all with the greatest ease, by his mere word, Psalm xxxiii. 6, 9. Gen. i. ii. 7. Heb. xi. 3. 5. In making them all without any instrumental cause, Gen. i. Psalm xxxiii. 6, 9. Heb. xi. 3. 6. In forming them as instantaneously as his glory admitted, Psalm xxxiii. 6, 9. Gen. i. ii. 7. Exod. xx. 11.

In PROVIDENCE, his almighty power appears, 1. In his preservation of all things in their different nature, forms, stations, motions, or rest, Psalm cxlviii. cxxxvi. civ. cxix. 90. Col. i. 17. Rev. iv. 11. 2. In the propagation of vegetables in the ground, and especially of animals in the womb, or in eggs, or from pieces of dissected ones,—and by means of heat, moisture, &c. Psalm civ. cxlvii. cxlviii. cxxxix. 14. Job x. 8—12. 3. In exciting and producing all their motions or actions, Psalm cxlvii. 15—18. civ. 10—14, 27, 30. cxxxv. 7. cxxxvi. 5—9. Job xxxviii.—xli. Dan. iii. 17. iv. 17. ii. 21. Acts xvii. 28. Rom. xii. 36. 4. In restraining unruly beasts, wicked men, and devils, at his pleasure, Psalm lxv. 7. and lxxvi. 10. Prov. xxi. 1. Rev. xx. 2. 5. In changing men's dispositions and inclinations, as

OF THE NATURE OR PERFECTIONS OF GOD. 109

he pleases, Gen. xxxiii. 4. xxxv. 5. 1 Sam. x. 9, 26. xxiv. 17, 18. Esther vi. 1, 2. Psalm cv. 25. cvi. 45. 6. In making so many millions of unruly inclinations harmoniously promote his *one* design, notwithstanding all their own different or contrary ones, Exod. ii.—xiv. Isa. x. 5—7. xxvii. 9. 7. In destroying his and his people's enemies, when they are at their strongest, and delivering his favourites when most weak and distressed, Deut. xxxii. 33, 35, 36, 41, 42, 43. Isa. xxxvii. 6, 7, 35. xxxiii. 10. xliii. 17, 18. and xlv. 13. Esther iii.—x. Exod. i.—xiv. xviii. 11. Ezek. xxxvii. 1—14. Mic. iv. 10. Dan. xii. 1. Rev. xi. 7—15. xx. 9. 8. In effecting the greatest events by weak means, or by none at all, Isa. xli. 15, 16. 1 Kings xx. 14. Judges vi. 15. vii. 2—22. 2 Chron. xiv. 11.—or by means merely casual. Thus the lighting of a viper on Paul's hand, brought about the conviction of the Maltese, Acts xxviii. 3—10. Moses, the deliverer of the Israelites, was preserved from death and fitted for his work, by the daughter of their oppressor coming to wash herself in the Nile, Exod. ii. 11. A post, with tidings of an invasion, preserved David, the anointed king of Israel, from being murdered by Saul, 1 Sam. xxiii. 26; —or by means calculated and intended for an opposite purpose by the agents. Thus Joseph's abasement promoted his exaltation to be lord over his father and brethren, Gen. xxxvii.—xlvii. The fall of mankind, the abasement and murder of Christ, promoted the eternal happiness of men, the honour of Christ, and the glory of God, Rom. v. 12—21. Phil. iii. 6—11. The building of Babel hastened the dispersion of mankind through the world, Gen. xi. 9. In the strangely diversified success of human affairs. Persons poor, weak, or inactive, perform things, which others of great wealth, parts, powers and activity, cannot, Psalm lxxviii. 71, 72. Amos v. 9. Acts i.—viii. 10. In making bad men befriend his people and his cause, contrary to all the dictates of carnal policy. Thus Cyrus, Darius, Artaxerxes, &c. gave part of their wealth to rebuild the Jewish temple, or promote the worship at it, Ezra i. iv. v. vii. Neh. ii. In the days of Cicero, gold was carried from Rome to adorn it. 11. In marvellously infatuating or defeating the best counsellors or counsels of men, Isa. xliv. 25. xxxiii. 11. 2 Sam. xvii. 8. Job v. 12, 13. Psalm xxxiii. 10. Isa. viii. 10. 12. In working such multitudes of miracles, both under the Old, and under the New Testament, Gen. vii. viii. xix. 24. xxi. 1, 2. Exod. iii.—xx. Num. xi. xvi. xvii. Josh. iii. iv. v. x. Judges vi. 1 Kings xvii. xviii. 2 Kings i.—viii. xiii. xix. xx. Matth. ii. 2. iv. 24, 25. xi. 5. xiv. xv. xvii. xx. xxi. Acts i.—xx. xxviii. Rom. xv. 19. Heb. ii. 4. 13. In raising the dead, and making all men and devils appear before his awful tribunal to receive their final sentence, Mat. xxv. 30—45. Rev. xx. 12, 14. 14. In the everlasting execution of his sentences, in punishing the wicked and glorifying the righteous, and in supporting both under their respective weights of wrath or blessedness, 2 Thess. i. 9, 10. 2 Cor. iv. 17. 15. In the terrible conflagration and the glorious renovation of our lower world at the last day, 2 Pet. iii. 10, 12.

But the almighty power of God chiefly appears in his work of REDEMPTION, Eph. i. 19, 20.——It appears on Christ the *Redeemer*, 1. In the miraculous conception of his manhood by a virgin, Isa. vii. 14. Jer. xxxi. 22. Luke i. 35. Mat. i. 20. 2. In the more than miraculous union of his two natures, which are infinitely different in substance and dignity,—and yet in such manner, that all human personality was prevented, John i. 14. 1 Tim. iii. 16. Isa. ix. 6. Zech. xiii. 7. Rom. ix. 5. 3. In the miracles which he wrought, Acts x. 38. Mat. iv.—xxi. Mark i.—vi. Luke iv.—xx. John ii.—xi. 4. In the tremendous punishment inflicted on him, and in the full support of him under it, Zech. xiii. 7. iii. 9. Isa. liii. 4—10. l. 6, 7, 9. xlii. 1. Psalm xxii. lxix. Mat. xxvi. xxvii. 5. In enabling him to such patience and resignation under his sufferings, of which he had a perfectly quick sense, Isa. liii. 7. Heb. xii. 2, 3. John xviii. 11, 12, 27. Mat. xxvi. 39, 42. 6. In raising him from the dead, justifying and glorifying him, Rom. i. 4. vi. 4. iv. 25. 1 Tim. iii. 16. Eph. i. 19, 20, 23. Psalm cx. 1—7. Phil. ii. 7—11. Heb. ii. 8, 9. 1 Pet. i. 20, 21.—— It appears in the *Publication of Redemption*, 1. In the propagating doctrines so contrary to the carnal reason, the common customs, the deep-rooted lusts, and strongly supported laws of mankind, 1 Cor. i. 20—24. iii. 18. Tit. iii. 3. Rom. i. 21—32. iii. 10—18. 2. In propagating the gospel by so unfit-like instruments, that just before had manifested so much cowardice, ignorance, or wickedness, Mat. xxvi. Acts i.—ix. 3. In propagating it by simple declarations, enforced with no temporal authority or worldly influence, 2 Cor. x. 4, 5. Zech. iv. 6. 4. In the amazing spread and influence of these declarations had on the hearts and lives of millions of ignorant, outrageous, and obstinate sinners, for convincing, converting, and sanctifying them, Acts ii.—xxi. xxvi. 17, 18. Rom. i. 8. xv. 19. 1 Cor. vi. 10, 11. Col. i. 5, 6. Eph. iii. 8, 9. 2 Cor. x. 4, 5. 1 Thess. i. 5, 9. ii. 12, 13. Tit. iii. 3—7.—— It also appears in the *Application of our Redemption.* 1. In the thorough conviction of the most stupid, hardened, and biassed consciences, John xvi. 9—11. Rom. iii. 19. Heb. iv. 12. Psalm xlv. 5. 2. In uniting men to Christ, and thus implanting in them *a divine nature*, or new habits or principles of grace, in opposition to the whole power of Satan, the world, and indwelling lusts, Deut. xxx. 6. Ezek. xxxvi. 26. Psalm c. 3. 2 Cor. x. 4, 5. Luke viii. 24. xi. 21, 22. Eph. i. 19. 1 Thess. i. 5. 2 Thess. i. 11. 3. In the preservation of weak graces in men's souls,

OF THE NATURE OR PERFECTIONS OF GOD. 111

amidst an infinity of corruptions and temptations to sin, 1 Pet. i. 5. Jude 1. 4. In pardoning such multitudes of heinous offences, at, and after our union to Christ; and in applying these pardons with such almighty influence as to quiet our consciences, however fearfully awakened, Num. xiv. 17—19. Isa. xliii. 24, 25. xliv. 22. xlv. 22, 24, 25. lvii. 18, 19. 5. In the mortification of almost almighty corruption by his word, and the agency of his spirit, Rom. viii. 13. Gal. v. 17, 24. 6. In the miraculous exploits which his people have, or do perform through faith, Phil. iv. 13. Col. i. 10, 11, 28, 29. Gal. i. 16. ii. 20. 2 Cor. xii. 7—9. Heb. xi. Mat. xvii. 20. Mark ix. 25. 7. In conferring abundant comfort, and everlasting happiness upon all his people, notwithstanding all that sin, Satan, and the world can do to distress and ruin them, Isa. lxv. 18. Psalm li. 10, 11. Rom. viii. 15—18, 28—39. 2 Cor. iv. 17, Psalm xxxi. 19. lxxiii. 23—26, Isa. xxxv. 10. xlv. 17. lx. 19, 20.

IV. Not only hath God an almighty power of ability, but also a power of unbounded SOVEREIGNTY,—by which, as one free from all obligation of law or force, of motive or influence without himself, he may form, support, and govern his creatures in what manner he pleaseth, Dan. iv. 34, 35.—His sovereign dominion over his creatures is founded on the infinite dignity and excellency of his nature, Psalm lxxxvi. 8. lxxxix. 6—8. and on his being the Contriver, Creator, Preserver, and last end of them, Psalm xcv. 3, 5. Isa. i. 2, 3. xliii. 12. 1 Cor. vi. 19, 20. Prov. xvi. 4. Rom. xi. 36.—It extends over all creatures, 1 Tim. i. 17. vi. 15. Whether in heaven, Isa. xlv. 12. Psalm ciii. 19, 20. cxlviii. 1—4. Or in earth, Job xii. 15, 18. Psalm xlvii. 7—9. xxiv. 1. l. 10. Prov. xxi. 1. Hag. ii. 8. Dan. iv. 35. Psalm. civ—cvi. cxlvii. cxlviii. Or in hell, Psalm lxxviii. 49. 1 Kings xxii. 22. Luke xxii. 31. Rev. xx. 2, 7.

It is evident, that God hath an absolute sovereignty over all things. 1. From express declarations of Scripture, Exod. xxxiii. 10. Rom. ix. 16, 18—23. Math. xx. 15. Psalm. xcv. 3, 4. xcvi. 6. cxv. 3. cxxxv. 6. lxxv. 6, 7. xxii. 28, 29. Job xxv. 2. Dan. iv. 34, 35, 36, 37. ii. 21. Eph. i. 11. Acts xvii. 24, 26. 2. From the characters ascribed to him in Scripture, as *Lord of hosts; King of nations; King of the whole earth; Only Potentate; King of kings; Lord of lords; Most High*, &c. Psal. lxxxiv. 12. lxxx. 4, 14, 19. xlvii. 7. Jer. x. 7—10. 1 Tim. vi. 15. Rev. xvii. 14. xix. 16. Exod. xviii. 11. Deut. x. 17. Gen. xiv. 18—22. Psal. l. 14. lvi. 2. lxxxiii. 18. 3. All the liberty, property, or authority, which creatures have, with respect to themselves or others, is derived from God, Acts xvii. 28. Prov. viii. 15, 16. Psal. lxxxii. Rom. xiii. 1—6. 1 Cor. iv. 7. Rom. xi. 36. 4. His sovereignty is displayed in his works of creation, providence, and redemption.—In CREATION, it appears in his forming such diversified creatures of the same nothing, or of the same unfit matter, and with so many and diversified connections among themselves, Gen. i.——In PROVIDENCE it appears, 1. In the diversified degree and duration of that support which he affords to his creatures. 2. In the forms, extent, and continuance, of his positive laws, and their binding influence on men's consciences. 3. In the manner, time, place, or objects, to whom his laws are published; or of the writing of them on men's hearts;—and in the, at first, unperceived exceptions of his law, as in Abraham's offering up his son, or in a man's marrying the childless widow of his brother. 4. In the objects, instruments, forms, degrees, and seasons of his favour. 5. In the nature, seasons, degrees, instruments, and objects, of his corrections and punishments,—and their proportion to, and correspondence with the sins, on account of which they are inflicted, Dan. iv. 35. Psal. cxv. 3. cxxxv. 6. Matth. xi. 25, 26. xx. 15. —In REDEMPTION,—it is manifested, 1. On the *Redeemer*,— in God's calling him to be our surety to pay our debt;—and to be our spiritual Head;—in fixing the time of his payment,— the place of his birth, life, and death,—the parts, forms, degrees, and continuance of his sufferings, and the forms, degrees, and periods of his exaltation in his own person, or in the happiness of his people, Isa. xlii. 6. Luke xi. 13. xiii. 32, 33. John xviii. 11. Heb. ii. 10. Phil. ii. 7—11. 2. On the persons of the *redeemed*,—in choosing any at all;—in choosing some, while others, no worse, are passed by;—and in alloting to them such particular means, opportunities, seasons, forms, and degrees of gifts and grace; and such intermixed temptations, troubles, deliverances, and comforts, Matth. xi. 25, 26. Rom. ix. 18, 23. Exod. xxxiii. 19. Matth. xx. 1, 15. 1 Cor. i. 26—30. 3. In qualifying such particular persons, of those that remain unregenerate, and at such particular seasons, with such individual forms and measures of gifts, and common graces, to render them useful in promoting the honour of the Redeemer, and the conversion and edification of his redeemed, John vi. 70. Heb. vi. 4, 5. Num. xxiii. xxiv.

V. The HOLINESS of God is that essential perfection of his nature, which lies in perfect freedom from, and hatred of all sin, and in perfect love to every thing holy and pure.——That God is *infinitely holy* appears, 1. From express declarations of Scripture, Josh. xxiv. 19. 1 Sam. ii. 2. Exod. xv. 11. Psal. lxxxix. 35. xi. 7. xcix. 9. Prov. xxx. 3. Hab. i. 12, 13. Isa. vi. 3. Rev. iv. 8. John xvii. 11. Dan. ix. 24. Psal. xvi. 10. Acts iii. 14. Rom. i. 4. Luke i. 35. Nay, holiness is represented as his *beauty*, Exod. xv. 11. Psal. xxvii. 4. his *grandeur*, Psal. lxxxix. 35.

Amos iv. 2. and more than forty times he is called the *Holy One* of Israel or Jacob, Hab. iii. 3. i. 12. Isa. i. 4, 10, 20. xliii. 14. xxix. 23, &c. 2. Every thing relating to God is called *holy*, on account of its connection with and conformity to him;—as the manhood of his Son, Luke i. 35. Acts iv. 27, 30; —his name, Psal. cxi. 9. Lev. xx. 3;—his arm or power, Psal. xcviii. 1;—the place where he manifests himself,—heaven or the temple, Psal. xx. 6. Isa. lvii. 15. Jonah ii. 4. Psal. xcix. 9. Exod. iii. 4. Rev. xxi. 10;—his Sabbaths, Exod. xvi. 23. Isa. lviii. 13; —his covenant and promise, Dan. xi. 28, 30. Luke i. 72. Psal. cv. 42;—his word, law, and gospel, Rom. i. 2. vii. 12. 2 Tim. iii. 15;—his work, Psal. cxlv. 17;—his angels, Rev. xiv. 10. Matth. xxv. 31;—his prophets, 2 Pet. i. 21. iii. 2. Luke i. 70. Rev. xviii. 20. xxii. 6;—his ministers, 1 Thess. ii. 10. Rev. xviii. 20;—his people, Exod. xix. 6. Col. i. 22. iii. 12. Heb. iii. 1. 1 Thess. v. 27. 1 Pet. ii. 9. 3. His holiness is manifested in his works of creation, providence, and redemption, Psal. cxlv. 7.

In CREATION it appears, in forming every creature, which was capable of holiness, perfect in it, Gen. i. 20, 27. Rev. xiv. 10. with Jude 6.—In PROVIDENCE, it appears, 1. In giving to all his rational creatures a moral law, requiring the most perfect and uninterrupted holiness of heart and life,—and enforced with the most powerful sanction of rewards and punishments, Rom. vii. 12. Matth. xxii. 37, 39. Rom. xii. xiii. Col. iii. iv. Eph. iv. v. vi. 1 Thess. iv. v. 1 Pet. 1—5. Exod. xx. 3—17. 2. In prescribing the most proper means of promoting holiness, Gen. ii. 17. Tit. ii. 11, 12. Matth. xxviii. 19. 2 Cor. xi. 23—29. Even all the sacrifices, purifications, and punishments, prescribed by the Jewish laws, marked the holiness of God, Lev. i.—xxiii. Num. v. vi. xv. xix. xxviii. xxix. Lev. x. 1—3. 3. And so permitting sin as not to have any active hand in, or give any encouragement to it, Hab. i. 12, 13. Psal. iv. 5, 6. Jer. xliv. 4. Prov. xvi. 16—19. 4. In fixing standing marks of his detestation of sin upon the first introducers of it, or any particular form of it; as on devils, women, Cain, the old world, the builders of Babel, Sodomites, oppressors of the church, profaners of God's worship, presumptuous rebels against his established government, despisers of his promised favours, &c. Jude 6. 2 Pet. ii. 4, 5. Gen. iii. iv. vii. xi. xix. Exod. i.—xiv. Lev. x. Num. xiv. xvi. Isa. v. 16. 5. In publicly manifesting his detestation of men on account of their most secret sins, Psal. l. 21. x. 8. 11, 14. Ezek. xiv. 3—8. viii. 7—18. 2 Sam. xii. 11, 12. Jer. xvi. 17, 18. 6. In marking all the wicked with the most shameful distance and disgrace in the last judgment, 1 Thess. iv. 16, 17. Matth. xxv. 33. Psal. i. 5. cxxxviii. 6. 7. In his everlasting exclusion of unholy angels and men from his presence, and marking them with the most tremendous tokens of his detestation, Matth. xxv. 41, 46. Psal. ix. 17. Rev. xx. 10, 15. xiv. 10, 11. 2 Thess. i. 8, 9. Even these providential acts, which we are apt to imagine impure, are *perfectly holy*. He *tempts* men, merely by *trying* their obedience, or in permitting them to be enticed to sin, by Satan, evil men, or their own sinful lusts, 2 Sam. xxv. 1. Matth. vi. 12. James i. 13, 14. He *bids* men *curse*, merely by giving them an opportunity of doing it, 2 Sam. xvi. 12. He *hardens* men in sin, when he justly withholds his heart-softening grace, and permits Satan, their neighbours, or their own lusts, to render them more stupid, perverse, and obstinate, Exod. iv.—xiv. Isa. lxiii. 17. vi. 9, 10. He delivers men up to vile affections, a reprobate mind, or strong delusions, or to their own lusts, when he justly withholds his restraining or sanctifying influences, and permits their sinful corruptions to decoy or drag them into wickedness, error, and folly, Rom. i. 24—28. 2 Thess. ii. 9—11. Isa. lxvi. 4. Psal. lxxxi. 12. His *deceiving* of men imports his abandoning them to the temptations of Satan and their own deceitful heart, Jer. iv. 10. Ezek. xiv. 9. 1 Kings xxii. 19—22.—Thus, in all these, he wisely, holily, and justly renders sin its own punishment.——In REDEMPTION, the holiness of God appears, 1. In his choosing men, that they might be holy, Eph. i. 4. 2 Thess. ii. 13. 1 Pet. i. 2. ii. 9. 2. In exhibiting his own Son, in the likeness of sinful flesh, even under the curse, which is the strength of sin, and amidst infinite temptations, as an incomparably perfect and glorious pattern of holiness in heart and life, Luke i. 35. Matth. iii. 15. John viii. 29. xvii. 4. xviii. 11. Heb. v. 8. vii. 26. 3. In punishing, even without mercy upon his own Son, sin imputed, withdrawing his comfortable smiles from him, and shutting out his prayers as if he had been a real sinner, Matth. xxvi. xxvii. Psal. xxii. lxix. lxxxix. 38. Isa. liii. Rom. viii. 3, 32. Heb. ii. 10. 4. In giving Christ to purchase holiness for men, and making him to them, *wisdom, righteousness, sanctification*, and *redemption*, Tit. ii. 14. 1 Pet. i. 18, 19. 1 Cor. i. 30. 5. In so forming the gospel in all its declarations, promises, and invitations, as may best convey, and encourage us to holiness in heart and life, 1 Tim. vi. 3. iii. 16. 2 Pet. i. 4. Tit. ii. 11, 12. 2 Cor. vii. 1. John xv. 3. xvii. 17. Luke i. 74, 75. Psal. cxix. 9, 11, 26. 6. In so framing the whole scheme of our redemption, that holiness of our heart and life is the end of every thing in it, Eph. i. 3, 4. Heb. xiii. 12. ix. 14. 1 Cor. vi. 11. Tit. ii. 14. iii. 8, 14. Ezek. xxxvi. 25—27. Luke i. 74, 75. 1 Thess. iv. 3, 7. v. 23. Rom. vi. 14. vii. 4, 5, 6. Eph. iv. 11—13. Isa. xxvii. 9. Heb. xii. 10, 11. 2 Cor. iii. 18. 1 John iii. 2. 7. In effectually rendering men holy by the manifestations of his own holiness in the gospel, 2 Cor. iii. 18. iv. 4, 6. 8. In the sharp correction of his peculiar favourites for their unholiness, and even

OF THE NATURE OR PERFECTIONS OF GOD. 115

for sins which appear far less criminal than some others, Amos iii. 2. Rev. iii. 19. Heb. xii. 6—11. Psalm xcix. 8. cxix. 67, 71. lxxxix. 31—34. lxxiii. lxxvii. lxxxviii. 1 Sam. ii. iii. Num. xii. xx. 12. Deut. xxxii. 51. 9. In making perfect holiness a principal ingredient of our eternal happiness, Eph. v. 25—27. 1 John iii. 3. Jude 25.

VI. The JUSTICE of God is that essential property of his nature, which disposes him to render to himself, and to all his creatures, that which is right and equal.——It is evident that God is JUST or RIGHTEOUS: 1. The Scriptures expressly declare this, Psal. xi. 7. xxv. 8. vii. 9. ix. 8. xcii. 15. xcix. 4. cxix. 75, 137. Exod. ix. 27. xxxiv. 7. Gen. xviii. 25. Deut. x. 17. xxxii. 4. Jude 1, 7. 1 Sam. iii. 18. 2 Chron. xix. 7. Job viii. 3. ix. 15. xxxiv. 10—12, 19. xxxv. 6—8. xxxvi. 3. xxxvii. 23. Jer. xii. 1. Isa. xxvi. 7. Dan. ix. 16. 2 Thess. i. 6, 7. 2 Tim. iv. 8. Heb. vi. 10. Acts x. 33, 34. Rom. iii. 4, 26. ix. 13, 14. 2. The remains of equity among men proceed from, and are beloved by God, 2 Sam. xxii. 26—28. Psalm vii. 9. xi. 7. Hos. xiv. 9. Gen. xviii. 23, 25. 3. His infinite justice and equity appear, 1. In his giving the most righteous laws to his creatures, suited to their original abilities, and requiring the most perfect equity towards God, their neighbours, and themselves,—insisting chiefly on the principal points of equity; and that such as bear rule over others, should shew themselves distinguished patterns of it, Neh. ix. 13. Rom. vii. 12. Psal. cxix. 75, 137, 138, 142. xix. 8—11. Hos. xiv. 9. Isa. xxvi. 7. Matth. xxiii. 23. xxii. 37, 39. Deut. xvi. 18, 19. 2 Sam. xxiii. 3. 2 Chron. xix. 6, 9. Psal. lxxxii. 2. In annexing to those laws proper sanctions of rewards and punishments, Psal. xi. 5—7. vii. 9—14. ix. 8, 17. Isa. i. 19, 20. iii. 10, 11. Rom. ii. 6—10. 2 Thess. i. 6—10. 3. In rewarding men's good behaviour in the most proper time, manner, and degree, Psal. xix. 11. 1 Cor. xv. 58. Rev. xiv. 13. 2 Tim. iv. 7, 8.—In his rewarding the resemblances of good works performed by wicked men, 1 Kings xxi. 29. 2 Kings x. 30. Jon. iii.—In rewarding the imperfect graces and works of his people, Rev. i. 3. ii. 7, 11, 19, 26, 27. iii. 5, 12, 20, 22. xiv. 13. xxii. 14. Col. iii. 24, 25. 1 Cor. xv. 58. ix. 24, 25. 2 Tim. iv. 7, 8. Matth. v. 3—10.—and in largely rewarding the meritorious service of Christ as our Surety, Isa. xlix. 5, 6. liii. 10—12. Phil. ii. 7—11. Heb. ii. 8, 9, 10. xii. 2. John xvii. 4, 5. Psal. xxii. 27, 31. 4. In bestowing all the purchased blessings of the new covenant upon the most vile, guilty, and rebellious men, on account of that righteousness which Christ, their Surety, performed in their stead, Rom. iii. 24—26. iv. 25. v. 6—11, 15—21. viii. 1—4, 33, 34. 2 Cor. v. 14—21. 1 Thess. v. 9, 10. Eph. i. 3—8. ii. 1—8, 14. 1 Pet.

i. 18—21. ii. 24. iii. 18. Heb. ix. 12, 14, 15. x. 10, 14. 1 John i. 7, 9. ii. 1, 2. iv. 9, 10. Rev. i. 5, 6. v. 9, 10. 2 Tim. iv. 8. 5. In his seasonable, severe, and well-proportioned chastisements of his people, which, *as disagreeable*, are due to them for offending their gracious Father,—and as calculated to promote their sanctification and comfort, are due to them as represented by their law-fulfilling Surety, Christ, Job xxxvi. 7—10. Psal. lxxxix. 30—34. xcix. 8. xciv. 12. Prov. iii. 12. Heb. xii. 6—11. Rev. iii. 19. 6. In afflicting innocent animals, only in so far as they are connected with guilty sinners. And, who knows how far their present suffering may be balanced in their future restoration into the glorious liberty of the children of God? Isa. xxiv. Hos. iv. 2, 3. Jer. xii. 4. xiv. 5, 6. Job i. 16. with Rom. viii. 20—23. 2 Pet. iii. 13. 7. In infallibly punishing national sins with national judgments in this world, as there is no opportunity of punishing societies, as such, in the future state;—and in marking their sins in their punishments,—as in the case of the old world,—Sodomites, Egyptians, Assyrians, Chaldeans, Jews, Papists, &c. Gen. vi. vii. xix. Exod. i.—xiv. Isa. xxxiii. xxxvii. Jer. xxv. xlvi.—li. Judg. i.—xii. 2 Kings xvii. xxv. Matth. xxiii. 32—39. xxiv. Rev. vi.—xx. 8. In punishing wicked men in this life, in a form, though not in a degree proportioned to their sins, and often by permitting them to fall into other sins, Job xviii. xx. xxvii. Psal. xcii. 7. xxxvii. 20. xxxv. 26. vii. 10—16. lviii. 9, 10. Ezek. xviii. Psal. lxxiii. 18—20. xxxi. 12. Gen. iv. ix. 25. Isa. lxvi. 4. lxiii. 17. Hos. iv. 13—17. 2 Thess. ii. 9—11. Rom. i. 18—32. 9. In publicly condemning wicked angels and men, and punishing them in hell for ever, Matth. xxv. 41, 46. 2 Thess. i. 8, 9. Rev. xiv. 9, 10, 11. xx. 10, 12. 10. Especially in exacting from his only and infinitely beloved Son, as our Surety, the very same obedience and satisfaction which were due from us to his broken law,—in the very same nature which had sinned, and under the very same overwhelming curse, Mat. iii. 15. Luke xxiv. 26. Isa. liii. Psal. xxii. lxix. Matth. xxvi. xxvii. Rom. iii. 24—26. v. 6—10. viii. 3, 32. Isa. xlii. 21. Heb. ii. 10. v. 8. 2 Cor. v. 21. 1 Pet. i. 18, 19. ii. 24. iii. 18. Gal. iii. 13. Phil. ii. 7, 8.

Such is the infinite holiness and justice of God's nature, that he cannot suffer sin to pass without adequate punishment. 1. The Scripture represents him as so infinitely holy and just, that he cannot but hate and detest sin, and mark his abhorrence of it, Exod. xxxiv. 7. Hab. i. 12, 13. Psal. v. 4—6. xi. 5, 6, 7. ix. 5. l. 21. Jer. xliv. 4. Neh. i. 2, 3. Prov. vi. 16—19. xvi. 5. Zech. xi. 8;—and as a Governor and Judge, who cannot but maintain the honour of that law which sinners trample on, and do right to his innocent creatures, which are hurt by their wickedness, Isa. xlii. 21. 2 Thess. i. 6—8. Rom. i. 18, 32. ii. 2, 6—10. Gen. xviii. 25. 2. Men's consciences represent him thus holy and just; and hence accuse and torment them when they offend him, and push them to appease him by sacrifices, services, &c. Acts xxviii. 4. Rom. i. 32. ii. 14, 15. 3. The law of God manifests this truth. Most of his moral precepts depending on his very nature and indispensible prerogative of government, must to the violations of them, have an adequate sanction annexed; as otherwise, haters and blasphemers of God would appear as much beloved by him, as the most pious and virtuous persons, contrary to Rom. ii. 7—10. Isa. iii. 10, 11. i. 19, 20.—All the ceremonial laws manifested, that without satisfaction to God's justice, there could be no remission of sin, Heb. ix. 22. And, if God's nature had not required an adequate punishment, the ceremonial offerings might have made atonement for sin, contrary to Heb. x. 3, 4. 4. If God's holiness and justice did not necessarily require him to punish sin in an adequate manner, how could his infinite mercy and goodness admit any punishment of it, as without real necessity, all punishment is an approach towards wanton cruelty? 5. If it had not been necessary to the honourable egress of his mercy towards sinful men, how could God have so fearfully punished his holy, his only begotten, and infinitely beloved Son? Or how could there be such distinguishing love, in giving him for a propitiation for our sins,—as the Scripture represents, Luke xxiv. 26. Rom. iii. 25, 26. 2 Cor. v. 21. Gal. iii. 13. Tit. ii. 14. Heb. ii. 10. 1 Pet. i. 18, 19. ii. 24. iii. 18. John iii. 16. Rom. v. 6—10. viii. 32. 1 John iv. 9, 10. Eph. v. 2. Gal. ii. 20. Rev. i. 5.

To anticipate OBJECTIONS, it may be observed, 1. That God's mercy and justice are not contrary perfections, though the one cannot be exercised to the dishonour of the other. 2. That the effects of God's mercy and grace, being absolutely free and gratuitous, may be restrained, if he please; but the effects of his justice being a debt due to the honour of his nature and law, or the general welfare of his creatures, cannot be justly restrained, Gen. xviii. 25. Deut. xxxii. 4. Psal. xi. 5—7. cxix. 137. Dan. ix. 16. 2 Thess. i. 6—9. Isa. v. 10. 3. Though God's *sovereign* will regulate the circumstances of deserved punishment, the punishment itself is necessary. Magistrates may, by their own will, regulate the time, place, and manner of executing a murderer, but cannot, without flagrant injustice to their character, their laws, or their country, dismiss him unpunished. 4. Though God may delay the full punishment of sinners,—the longer he does so, it must be the more dreadful when it comes, Rom. ii. 4, 5. ix. 22. Heb. x. 26—31. 5. God's substitution of his own Son to bear the punishment due to his elect, instead of proving, that he could have dispensed with it, strongly proves the contrary, Rom. iii. 25, 26. 2 Cor. v. 21. Gal. iii. 13, 14. Heb. ii. 10. Luke xxiv. 26.

VII. The GOODNESS of God is that essential property of his nature, which inclines him to regard and delight in himself, and to deal kindly with his creatures.—As it inclines him to affect, esteem, and delight in himself, or one divine person in another,—and to care for, to promote the welfare of creatures, and delight in and rejoice over them, it is called LOVE, because love to himself and to his creatures, gives rise to, and animates his whole conduct, particularly his work of redemption, 1 John iv. 8, 9, 10, 16, 19. Rom. v. 8. John iii. 16.—His love, in respect of the objects of it, may be distinguished into that which he bears to himself, Isa. v. 16. Lev. x. 3. Mat. xi. 27. John i. 18. iii. 35; that which he bears to all his creatures as such, Psalm civ. 31. Gen. i. 31. and that redeeming love which he bears to his chosen of mankind, Deut. vii. 7, 8. xxxiii. 3. John iii. 16. xv. 9—15. xvi. 27. xvii. 23, 26. Rom. v. 8, 21. viii. 32. Gal. ii. 20. Eph. i. 3—8. ii. 1—9. iv. 8, 9, 10, 19. Rev. i. 5. —His love to creatures is distinguished into his love willing their welfare, Rom. ix. 16, 18. Exod. xxxiii. 19. Psalm lxxxvi. 15. his love doing them good, John iii. 16. Rom. viii. 32—39. Psalm v. 12. Isa. lxiii. 7. lix. 8—10. Eph. v. 2. 1 John iii. 1. iv. 9, 10. his love delighting in them, Psalm cxlvii. 11. cxlix. 4. xxxv. 27. Isa. lxii. 5. Zeph. iii. 17. These are but the same love exercising itself in different forms.——God's goodness, as it inclines him to make or supply his creatures, to none of which he owes either being or any thing else, is called BOUNTY, Psal. cxvi. 7. cxix. 17. 1 Kings iii. 6.—As it inclines him to do good to those that are undeserving or ill-deserving, it is called GRACE, or free favour, Rom. iii. 24. v. 20, 21. Eph. ii. 5, 7, 8. i. 6, 7. 2 Cor. 8, 9. Psalm v. 12. As it inclines him to pity, help, and provide for, persons in misery, it is called MERCY or COMPASSION, Psalm cii. 8, 11—17. lxxxvi. 5, 15. lxxxix. 1, 2, 28. cxi. 4. cxii. 4. Rom. ix. 16, 18.—And as he takes peculiar pleasure in thus manifesting his goodness, in the redemption of men, mercy is attributed to him several hundred times in Scripture, Psalm cxxxvi. c. &c. he hath *bowels* ascribed to him, Isa. lxiii. 7, 15. Jer. xxxi. 20. Hos. xi. 8. and is represented as *full of compassion*, Psalm lxxviii. 38. lxxxv. 15. cxi. 4. cxii. 4. cxlv. 8.—And, as his goodness inclines him to forbear for a time, punishing the affronts done him, it is called PATIENCE and LONGSUFFERING, Rom. ii. 4. ix. 22. xv. 7. 2 Pet. iii. 9, 15. Exod. xxxiv. 6. Psal. lxxxvi. 15.

It is most evident, that God is GOOD. I. The Scriptures in passages innumerable represent him as good,—as only good,— as kind,—gracious, merciful, and long-suffering, Psalm xxv. 8.

OF THE NATURE OR PERFECTIONS OF GOD. 119

xxxvi. 7. cxix. 68. cxlv. 7—9. Mat. xix. 17. Isa. lxiii. 7. Zech. ix. 17. Psalm xxxiii. 15. cvii. cxxxvi. xxxiv. 8. cxliv. 2. lxiii. 3—6. xl. 11. lxix. 16. Joel ii. 12, 13. Jer. iii. 13. Eph. ii. 5, 7. i. 6, 7, 8. Mic. vii. 18, 19, 20. Neh. ix. 17. 2 Pet. iii. 9, 15. Exod. xxxiv. 6, 7. 2. All that goodness which is to be found among creatures, animate or inanimate, rational or irrational, originates from God, Rom. xi. 36. Psalm cxix. 68. James i. 17. 1 Cor. iv. 7. Gen. i. ii. 3. The goodness of God, is most extensively and clearly manifested in his works of creation, providence, and redemption.

In CREATION it appears, 1. In his forming all creatures in order, that they might share of his kindness and bounty,—he having no need either of their existence or service, Psalm xvi. 2. 2. In forming such vast multitudes of creatures,—in such diversified qualities, situations, orders, connections, and mutual dependencies, that the goodness of all might contribute to the advantage of each, Gen. i. 3. In creating angels so many in number, so high in dignity, so excellent in quality, and so capable of enjoying himself, Psalm civ. 4. ciii. 20, 21. 4. In forming man—his body so beautiful, so marvellously compacted of a multitude of members, and fitted to promote his true happiness,—his soul endowed with so many excellent faculties, qualifying it for the enjoyment of God himself, as his *chief good*, and marvellously united to his body, that he might at once partake of an earthly and an heavenly felicity, Gen. ii. 6, 7. and that, by a particular consultation of the divine persons, he was formed in the image of God, Gen. i. 26, 27. ix. 6. and that his formation was so timed as to come into a world fully fitted and furnished for his immediate happiness, Gen. i. and ii.

In PROVIDENCE, God's goodness appears, 1. In his upholding innumerable numbers of creatures in order to render them partakers of his favours, Psalm xxxvi. 6, 7. Zech. ix. 17. Psalm civ. cvii. cxlv. cxlviii. 2. In governing them all, to the best advantage of all in general, Psalm cxix. 68. civ. cv. cvii. cxxxvi. cxlv. cxlvii. cxlviii. Job xxxvii. xli. 3. In so distributing his goodness among them, that they may all depend on, and taste it, in each other; and even worms may teach angels and men the mysteries of the Godhead, Job xii. 8, 9. 4. In his peculiarly kind deportment towards angels and men, while they kept their first estate,—giving them good laws, suited to their natures, and conducive to their happiness; in entering into a covenant of friendship with men; if not also with angels, though not by a representative, Job xxxviii. 7. Gen. ii. 16, 17. 5. In permitting sin to enter into the world, *chiefly*, that it might afford an occasion of opening his infinite treasures of redeeming love and grace, Rom. v. 8, 20, 21. Eph. ii. 1—8. i. 6—8. Gen. iii. 6. In his amazing patience toward sinful men, —in not smiting and even damning them in the very act of sinning, but deferring his vengeance as long as the vindication of his own perfections and good of his creatures in general can permit, Gen. vi. 3. xv. 13, 16. Rom. ix. 22.---In repeating his warnings, before he punish or correct, Lev. xxvi. Deut. xxvii.—xxxii. Judges ii. 2 Kings xvii. Psalm lxxviii. cvi. Isa. i. Ezek. xx. Mal. iv. Mat. xxiv. Rev. viii.—xx. &c.---In inflicting his judgments by progressive degrees, and with an apparent reluctancy, Isa. ix. x, Ezek. xx. Amos iii. iv. vi. Ezra ix. 7. Joel i. 3. Judges x. 16. Isa. i. 24. Lam. iii. 33. Hos. vi. 4, 5. xi. 8. Psalm lxxviii. 38.—And in moderating his judgments, loading men with his favours, notwithstanding many and great provocations, Psalm ciii. 10. Ezra ix. 13. Job xi. 6. xxxiii. 27. Isa. lvii. 17—19. xliii. 24, 25. Lam. iii. 22, 31, 32. Mat. xxvi. xxvii. with Acts ii.—ix. Tit. iii. 3—7. 7. In working an infinity of wonderful and miraculous works for the welfare of persons and nations, Exod. ii.—xx. Deut. xxxii. 6. Ezek. xx. Neh. ix. Ezra i.—x. Esther i.—x. Mat. i.—xxviii. Luke i.—xxiv. John i.—xxi. Acts i.—xxviii. Rom. xv. 19. Heb. ii. 4.——The histories or predictions of Scripture are full of them. 8. In his wonderful care of our world, notwithstanding its present defilement with sin,—as of irrational creatures, Psalm cxlv. 9. cxlvii. 8, 9. civ. 11—22. Deut. xxii. 7. xxv. 4. Lev. xxii. 28.—of slaves, Exod. xxi. 2—10, 27. Deut. xxiii. 15.—of criminals, Deut. xxi. 22, 23. xxv. 1—3.—of the poor, of widows, and fatherless children, Exod. xxiii. 11. Lev. xix. 13, 33, 34. xxv. 35, 39, 47. Psalm ix. 18. x. 14, 18. xii. 5. xxxv. 11. xli. 1—3. lxviii. 5, 10. lxxxii. 3. lxix. 33. lxxii. 4, 13. cvii. 41. cix. 31. cxxxii. 15. cxlvi. 9. Exod. xxii. 22. Deut. xiv. 29. x. 18. xvi. 11, 14. xxiv. 17, 19—21. xxvi. 12, 13. Prov. xv. 25. xix. 17. xxiii. 11, 18. Isa. i. 17, 23. Jer. vii. 6. Zech. vii. 10. Jer. xlix. 11. Hos. xiv. 3. James i. 27.—of wicked men, Mat. v. 45. Ezek. xx. Acts xiv. 16, 17. Jon. iii. iv. 11. 1 Kings xxi. 29. Ezek. xxix. 18—20.—of societies, in dictating or suggesting proper rules of government to them, putting part of his own honour and authority on their magistrates for their benefit, Psalm cvii. 31, 32. Jer. xviii. 9. Rom. xiii. 1—6. 1 Tim. ii. 1, 2. Tit. iii. 1. 1 Pet. ii. 13, 14, 17. Psalm lxxxii. 9. In so timing his favours, particularly deliverances, that they become doubly valuable.—Delays of them till we be brought to an extremity, afford us opportunities of acting faith, and encouraging ourselves in him alone, John xi. 15—44. 2 Chron. xx. 7, 12. Psal. xlii. xliii.—and granting them in the very crisis of extremity, stirs us up to improve our new covenant interest in him, Psalm cxxiii. 3. xliv. 23—26. Exod. xv. 1, 2. Psal. ciii. cxvi. cxviii. xl. xiii. xviii.---Earthly comforts are cut off, to prepare us for his intended spiritual favours, Psalm cii. 23, 24. cxlii. 4, 5.---And remarkable deliverances afforded to prevent future calamities. Thus, the destruction of the Egyptians, and Israel's deliverance at the Red Sea, made the hearts of the Canaanites to melt, Josh. ix. 9, 10. ii. 9—11.

In the origin, the impetration, and the application of REDEMPTION, the goodness of God still more gloriously appears. ——In its origin, it appears, 1. In that absolutely free and infinitely abundant grace in God himself is the only primary cause of it, John iii. 16. 1 John iv. 9, 10, 19. Rom v. 8, 20, 21. Eph. ii. 4, 7. 2. In that the redeeming work was begun an infinity of ages before we were ruined, Eph. i. 4, 5. 2 Tim. i. 9. Tit. i. 2. 1 Pet. i. 19, 20. Prov. viii. 23, 31. Mat. xxv. 34. 3. In that, moved by mere free love, all the divine persons heartily joined in the contrivance and plan of it, and took their respective share of the work,---the Father to exert the grace,---the Son to advance the merit,---and the Holy Ghost to apply the purchased benefits;---the Father to make the exceeding great and precious promises,---the Son to ratify them in his obedience and death, and purchase the things promised,---and the Holy Ghost to put them, and all the blessings which they contain, into our possession;---the Father to adopt us for his children,---the Son to redeem us for his mystical members,---and the Holy Ghost to renew and sanctify our heart, and make us meet habitations for God, Prov. viii. 23—31. Psalm xl. 6—8. Isa. xlviii. 16. liii. 10—12. lxi. 1—3. xlix. 1—6.——In the IMPETRATION of our redemption, God's goodness appears, 1. In that the deliverance is infinitely more important, costly, sure, and delightful, than creation itself, Eph. i. 3—8. ii. 1—8. Rev. i. 5, 6. v. 9, 10. 2. That, not fallen angels, whose nature is of more importance and dignity, but fallen men are delivered, Heb. ii. 14, 16. Jude 6. 3. That the only begotten Son of God is *the Redeemer and Surety* of such mean, sinful, and infamous creatures, John iii. 16. 1 John iv. 9, 10. 4. That he, by the most complete obedience, and the most dreadful, but voluntary sufferings, magnified his Father's law, and satisfied his justice, that he might open an abundant egress for displaying his favours to us-ward, Heb. ii. 10. v. 8. xiii. 12. i. 3. Gal. iii. 13. 2 Cor. v. 21. Isa. liii. 4, 5, 10. xlii. 21. Rom. viii. 3, 4. x. 4. 5. That he thus manifested his love, after men had, for four thousand years, continued in the most uninterrupted, horrid, outrageous, and progressive rebellion against him, Gal. iv. 4. Gen. iii. to Mal. iv. Rom. iii. 10—19. i. 18—32. v. 6---10, 20, 21. 6. That notwithstanding God's most dreadful curse lay upon Christ from his conception till his death, the Holy Ghost marvellously furnished him for, and supported him under his arduous work, John iii. 34. Heb. ix. 14. 7. That God accepted this satisfaction due from us, from his own Son in our stead,—justified and glorified him as our Representative, and constituted him our advocate, that our faith and hope might be in himself, Rom. iii. 25, 26. v. 6---11, 15---21. viii. 3, 4, 32---34. iv. 25. x. 4. Isa. l. 7, 9. lii. 13---15. liii. 2---12. John iv. 9, 10. ii. 1, 2. Eph. v. 2. Gal. ii. 20. 1 Pet. i. 18---21. 1 Tim. iii. 16. Heb vii. 25.——In the APPLICATION of this purchased redemption, the goodness of God is manifested, 1. In that all the blessings of it are lodged in the hands of Christ, our elder brother, as Administrator of the new covenant, Col. i. 19. Psal. lxviii. 18. Mat. xi. 27. xxviii. 18. John iii. 35. Isa. xlix. 6. Psalm lxxii. 17. xxi. 4. 2. That Christ is exalted to the right hand of God, solemnly to take infeftment on, and possession of eternal happiness, in our name; to intercede for us, and pour down the Spirit on us; to apply to us all the benefits of his purchase, John xiv. 2, 3, 26. xvi. 7.--14. Eph. ii. 5---7. Heb. vi. 19, 20. vii. 25. iv. 14---16. 1 John ii. 1, 2. 3. That in him all the blessings of redemption lie ready for us, in exceeding great and precious promises, which are published to us in the gospel, Mat. xxii. 4. 2 Pet. i. 4. 2 Cor. i. 20. Isa. lv. 1—7. Rev. xxii. 17. Prov. i. 20—23. viii. 4. ix. 5. John vi. 39. 4. That these prepared blessings are so infinitely great and many, and MUST be bestowed upon us, Psal. xxxi. 19. xxxvi. 6—10. lxv. 4. lxviii. 10, 18—22. Eph. i. 3—8. ii. 4—10. iii. 17—19. 5. That the offers of these blessings in the gospel are so particularly directed to sinners, even of the worst kind, Ezek. xxxvi. 25—31. Isa. xliii. 24, 25. xlvi. 12, 13. i. 18. lv. 1—7. Jer. iii. Mat. ix. 13. xviii. 11. 1 Tim. i. 15. 6. That these offers of salvation are granted and continued, notwithstanding men's multiplied and dreadful provocations, fearful abuse, contempt, and opposition to them, Acts iii. 15, 26. Isa. i. 3—18. lvii. 17, 18. 7. That these offers are so great, so earnest, so engaging, so free, and condescending, Psalm xxxiv. 8, 11. l. 7. lxxxi. 8---10. Prov. i. 20, 23. viii. 4---36. ix. 1—6. xxiii. 26. Song iii. 11. iv. 8. v. 2. Isa. i. 18. xlv. 22—25. xlvi. 12, 13. xlix. 1—12. lv. 1—7. lxv. 1, 2. Zech. ix. 9, 12. Mat. xi. 5, 28—30. xxii. 1—9. Luke xiv. 16—23. John vii. 37---39. vi. 37—40. 2 Cor. v. 18---21. Rev. xxii. 17. 8. That many, if not most, of those who have these offered blessings conferred upon them, in respect of their former outward circumstances, tempers, or morals, were of the very dregs of mankind, Luke xix. 10. Matt. xxii. 9. ix. 13. 1 Cor. i. 25---31. 1 Tim. i. 13, 15, 16. 9. That God taketh such pleasure in the application of redemption, Isa. lxv. 1, 2. lxii. 5, 11. lxi. 1, 2, 10. Jer. xxxii. 38---41. xxxi. 18---20. Mic. vii. 19. Zeph. iii. 17. 10. That the most outrageous sinners are often received by God with distinguished marks of compassion and kindness, Luke xv. 20---22. vii. xxiii. John iv. Acts ii. iv. vi. ix. xxii. xxvi. 1 Cor.

OF THE NATURE OR PERFECTIONS OF GOD.

xv. 8---10. Gal. i. 15, 16. 1 Tim. i. 13---16. 11. That amidst strange and furious opposition, Christ and his Spirit enter into men's hearts, in order to apply his benefits, Rom. vii. 8---25. Luke xi. 21, 22. Psalm cx. 2, 3. 2 Cor. x. 4, 5. 12. That he deals so tenderly with his people when they offend him, Psalm ciii. 12, 13. Isa. lvii. 17, 18, 19. Jer. xxxi. 18---20. iii. Hos. vi. 4. xi. 8. 13. That he closely adheres to them, sympathizes with them under all their troubles, and delivers them as soon as it can be for their real advantage, Zech. ii. 8. Isa. lxiii. 9. xl. 11. xli. 10, 14, 17, 18. xlvi. 4. Luke xviii. 8; delights to converse with them, and to hear and answer their prayers, Jer. xxxii. 41. xxxiii. 3. Zeph. iii. 17. Isa. lxii. 4, 5. xxx. 18, 21. lviii. 9. lxv. 24. xlv. 11. Luke xi. 9. Mat. vii. 7. Psal. l. 15. xci. 15. lxxxv. 6, 8. Song ii. 14. viii. 13.——In fine, God's goodness appears in manifold respects, in all the particular blessings of our election, union with Christ, justification, adoption, sanctification, spiritual comfort, and eternal glory;---and in all the means of grace, ordinary or solemn, Eph. i. 3---8. ii. 1---10. Rom. v. 15---21.

VIII. The TRUTH of God is not here taken for the reality of his existence, and the necessary possession of infinite excellency, on account of which he is called the TRUE GOD, in opposition to such as are gods only in respect of name, but have no infinite or independent perfection, Jer. x. 10. but it means that essential property of his nature, by which he is infinitely free from, and abhors all deceit and falsehood. It may be distinguished into his *sincerity*, *uprightness*, or *candour*, which consists in the exact agreement of his words and works with his thoughts, inclination, or will; and his *veracity* or *faithfulness*, which consists in the exact correspondence of his works with his declarations, predictions, promises, and threatenings, and with all these relations in which he stands to his creatures.

It is most evident, that God is TRUE in these respects: 1. The Scriptures expressly represent him as a God of truth, that cannot lie or fail to perform his word, Num. xxiii. 19. 1 Sam. xv. 29. Tit. i. 2. Heb. vi. 17, 18. x. 23. 2 Tim. ii. 13. 1 Thess. v. 24. 1 Cor. i. 9. x. 13. Deut. vii. 9. xxxii. 4. Neh. ix. 8. Psal. xxxiii. 4. lxxxix. 1, 2, 5, 8, 14, 35. xxxvi. 5. cxix. 38, 49, 70, 160. cxi. 7, 8. c. 5. xxv. 10. xxxi. 5. Isa. xxv. 1. lxv. 16. John xvii. 17. Rom. iii. 3, 4. 1 Pet. iv. 19. Rev. i. 5. iii. 15. John xiv. 16, 17. 2. His independence, infinite holiness, equity, power, and majesty, set him above all possibility of, or temptation to deceit or falsehood, Num. xxiii. 19. 1 Sam. xv. 29. Heb. vi. 16—21. 2 Tim. ii. 13. 3. All that candour and faithfulness which is among mankind, or regard to it, proceed from him, James i. 17. 1 Cor. iv. 7. 4. This candour or faithfulness is manifested in, 1. The self-consistency of all his words, notwithstanding their being spoken on very different occasions, Psalm cxix. 30, 31, 43, 86, 87, 90, 104, 128, 138, 142, 160, 163. 2. None of his words are contrary to the discoveries of his perfections, which are made by the light of nature or by Revelation, 2 Tim. ii. 13. Deut. xxxii. 4. 3. His whole work of providence, with all the dispositions and actions of mankind, plainly confirm the leading truths of his word, compare Exod. xxxiv. 6, 7. Deut. xxxii. 4. with the history of his works, Gen. iii. to Esther x. Isa. i. to Mal. iv. Mat. i. to Rev. xxii. Psalms lxxviii. ciii. cvii. cxxxvi. cxlv.—cxlix. Jer. xvii. 9. Rom. iii. 10—20. viii. 7, 8. i. 24—32. Mat. v. 19. with the history of mankind, Gen. iv. vi. xi. 2 Kings xvii. Neh. ix. Ezek. xvi. xx. xxiii. Isa. lix. Jer. ii.—xxiii. xliv. &c. 4. All the principal acts of his providence in the world are a manifest fulfilment of his inspired predictions. 5. He hath, or doth, accomplish those promises, threatenings, or predictions, which, to us, appear most unlikely to be fulfilled, or which he had the strongest-like reasons to shift, as of the incarnation, sufferings, and death of his Son, the calling of the Gentiles,—and the Justification, Sanctification, and Glorification of sinful men, Gal. iv. 4—6. Isa. liii. Mat. i. to Acts xxviii. 1 Cor. vi. 9—11. Eph. i. ii. iii. Rom. i.—xi. Col. i. ii. 6. His truth and faithfulness will be most fully manifested in the *last judgment*, when all the works of God and men shall be exactly compared with his word,—and in the everlasting happiness or misery of angels and men, Rev. xx. 12—15. Mat. xxv. 31—46. 2 Thess. i. 6—10. Rom. ii. 6—10.

To anticipate objections, it must be observed, 1. That God may declare to men what is their duty, without manifesting his own secret intentions. His law is the only rule of our duty; and his purpose the only rule of his own conduct, Mic. vi. 8. with Deut. xxix. 29. Isa. viii. 20. lv. 8—11. Eph. i. 11. 2. That God may permit others to deceive, or be deceived, without having any deceit in himself, or in his conduct, 1 Kings xxii. 22, 23. Ezek. xiv. 9. with Deut. xxxii. 4. Psal. xxv. 8, 10. 3. That when promises, threatenings, or predictions, have in them a condition expressed or understood, the fulfilment of them doth not fall due, and ought not to be looked for, unless that condition be first fulfilled, Mark xvi. 16. Jon. iii. 1 Sam. xxiii. 11, 12. Isa. xxxviii. 1.

My Soul, stop thy contemplation of the Most High, and ask thyself, as in his presence: If God be a *Spirit*, am I spiritually minded, and a worshipper of Him in spirit and in truth? Do I detest and banish every carnal imagination of him from my heart?—Is he the *all-knowing* and *only wise God?* Do I then behave as one ever naked and open to his view? Do I reverently avoid all prying into his secrets? Do I relish all his oracles, as the storehouse and fountain of all true wisdom and knowledge to my heart? Do I cordially approve all his ordinances, and admire his whole word, purpose, and work? Do I acknowledge him in all my ways, that he may direct my paths; and in the most perplexing cases, trust to his skill and power for my deliverance?—If he be *Almighty*,—a *Sovereign Ruler*, am I, in the view of my own weakness, still blushing, still trembling before him? Do I alway labour to check the very first risings of my heart in rebellion against Him? Do I, without staggering, rest the whole burden of my salvation upon Him? Do I rejoice in Him, and firmly expect deliverance from Him, when I apprehend all things working against me? Do I ascribe all that I am and have, except my sinfulness, to Him? And am I contented with all that I meet with in providence, as the doing of my Lord?——Am I *holy* as he is *holy*; pure as he is pure? Do I abhor myself and all my righteousness in his sight? Do I chiefly delight in his holiness? And doth even the contempt of it by others excite my love to, and esteem of it? Do I, in all my dealings with Him, labour to act under a deep impression of his holiness? Do I, above all things, hate sin?—my own sin?—my most refined and secret sin? Do I alway labour in the gospel-glass to behold his holiness, that I may be changed into the same image, from glory to glory, even as by the Spirit of the Lord?——Under the affecting views of his *Justice*, Do I revere every dispensation of his providence, and kindly acknowledge, that unto him as my Lord belongeth righteousness, and unto me shame and confusion of face? Do I live in perpetual wonder, that his infinite equity can suffer such a sinner to live; nay, will save me? Do I continually flee from all my own righteousness to that of Jesus Christ, and rest on it alone for my eternal salvation?—If God be good,—be *Love*, Am I, with amazement, believing his loving-kindness, and applying it to my own heart? Am I opening my mouth wide, that he may fill it? Am I satisfied with his goodness, as the source and the substance of all my happiness? Do I reckon all things, as coming from his hand, as good,—very good for me? Do I, above all, desire to be an eternal debtor and unparalelled miracle of his redeeming goodness? And, all inflamed herewith, how burns my heart with love to Him that first loved me, and gave his Son for me?——Do I love them that hate me? and do good to, and pray for them that despitefully use me?——If he be the God of *truth*, Have I set to my seal, that he hath given me eternal life in his Son? Have I found his promises and eaten them; have they been to me the joy and rejoicing of my heart? Do I hold them fast, and refuse to let them go? Have I rejoiced at finding them, as one that findeth great spoil,—and chosen them to be my heritage for ever?—Is this God, who is manifested in all around me,—in all before, behind, above, or below me, for ever in mine eye, and in all the powers of my soul?—Is he my Saviour, my Father, my Husband,—my Friend, my Master, my Portion, my Pattern, my God;—my ALL?

The inimitable or incommunicable perfections of God are,

I. His SELF-EXISTENCE and ABSOLUTE INDEPENDENCE, in respect of which, his being and nature are necessary. He cannot but be; and be what he is; and is altogether in and of himself, Exod. iii. 14. Rev. i. 8. xvi. 5. xxii. 6. He hath no dependence on any creature; but every creature, in its existence, nature, and operation, is wholly dependent on him, Psal. cii. 26, 27. xvi. 2. Job xxii. 2. xxxv. 6, 7.—And, from this his absolute sovereignty and dominion doth proceed, Dan. iv. 34, 35. ii. 20, 22. Mat. xi. 26. xx. 15.

II. His absolute SIMPLICITY, in respect of which he is absolutely free from all composition, and every thing in him is God himself. 1. He is represented as a simple abstract, as,—LIGHT, —LOVE,—LIFE, 1 John i. 5. iv. 8, 16. v. 20. 2. Being the *independent* and *absolutely first* being, he could have none to unite compounding parts in him, Isa. xli. 4. xliv. 6. 3. Being incorruptible and unchangeable, he cannot consist of divisible parts, Rom. i. 23. 1 Tim. i. 17. vi. 16. Mal. iii. 6. 4. Being infinite, there cannot be any thing added to another in him, Jer. xxiii. 23. 1 Kings viii. 27. 5. Being perfect in the highest degree, he cannot be compounded of things which, taken separately, would be imperfect, Job xi. 7.

III. His INFINITY, which denotes him as great and excellent in every respect, as he can be. It includes the *unbounded excellency* of his nature. Hence he is represented as *great*, Deut. xxxii. 3. 1 Chron. xvi. 25. Ezra v. 8. Job. xxxvi. 26. xxxvii. 22. Tit. ii. 13. Psalm xxix.—greater than all men,—than all nations, Psalm xxxv. 10. civ. 1. lxxxvi. 8. lxxxix. 5—8. Dan. iv. 32. Isa. xl. 12—22.—greater than all things, greater than all gods, Job xi. 7—9. 1 Kings viii. 27. Psalm lxxxvi. 8. Exod. xviii. 11.—as transcending all possible limits of excellency, Job xi. 7. Psalm cxlv. 3. cxlvii. 5.—It also includes the *unbounded extent* of his presence. The being of his essence, wherever space or any creature could be, is called his *immensity*, 1 Kings viii. 27. and its being wherever creatures actually are, is called his *omnipresence*, Psalm cxxxix. 7—10. Jer. xxiii. 23, 24. Eph. iv.

6. 1 Cor. xii. 6.—God is peculiarly present with Christ. His nature in the person of the Son is united to, and dwells with his manhood, Col. ii. 9. 1 Tim. iii. 16. Rom. viii. 3. Gal. iv. 4. And he delightfully dwells in him as God-man Mediator, 2 Cor. v. 19.—He is present with his saints, graciously dwelling in their heart, and thus affording them his peculiar favour, help, and comfort, John xiv. 16, 23. 2 Cor. xiii. 14. Rom. viii. 14—17, 26, 27. Gal. iv. 6. 1 Cor. iii. 16, 17. vi. 18, 19. 2 Cor. vi. 16. Rev. xxi. 3. Eph. ii. 19—22. 1 John iv. 4, 16. iii. 24. John xvii. 21—23, 26. Psalm xxxix. 12.—He was present with his prophets and apostles, in his infallible inspiring influence on their minds, in their declaration of his will to men, 1 Pet. i. 11. 2 Pet. i. 21. 2 Sam. xxiii. 2. Heb. i. 1.—He is present in his church, in his oracles, and in the instituted ordinances of his worship, in the representatives of his authority, and in the influences of his Spirit, Matth. xviii. 20. xxviii. 20. Exod xx. 24. John xvii. 21. 1 Cor. xii. 12, 13, 28. Eph. iv. 11—13. 1 John i. 3, 5, 7. 1 Pet. i. 12.—He was present in the Jewish tabernacle and temple at Jerusalem, or at Bethel, Sinai, &c. in the manifested symbols of his glory, power, and grace, and in his solemn ordinances of worship, Exod. xxv. 8, 22. xxix. 43. 1 Kings v. 5. viii. 11. Gen. xxviii. 16, 17. xlviii. 3. Exod. iii. 4. xix. 11. Psalm lxviii. 17. cxxxii. 5. lxxx. 1, 2.—He is present in heaven in the most glorious manifestation of his excellencies, Isa. lxvi. 1. Psalm cxv. 3. Matth. vi. 9. Heb. xii. 23. Phil. iii. 20. John xiv. 2, 3. iv. 14. viii. 1.—He is present in hell, in the most dreadful execution of his wrath, Psalm cxxxix. 8. 2 Thess. i. 9. Rev. xiv. 10, 11. Mark ix. 44, 46.—He is present with all creatures, in observing, supporting, and governing them, Heb. i. 3. iv. 13. Psalm cxxxix. 12, 13. Jer. xxiii. 23, 24. Col. i. 17. 1 Cor. xii. 6.

IV. His absolute ETERNITY consists in his being without beginning, ending, or succession of duration, which indeed is nothing else than his infinity as it respects duration. It is manifest, that he is ETERNAL in this manner. 1. The Scripture expressly represents him as eternal or everlasting, without any limitation, Gen. xxi. 33. Deut. xxxiii. 29. Psal ix. 7. lv. 19. Prov. viii. 23, 25. Isa. xl. 28. lvii. 15. Dan. vi. 26. Jer. x. 10. Rom. xvi. 26. Rev. iv. 8, 9. Hab. i. 12.—And, *he alone* is eternal, without beginning or succession of duration, Psalm xc. 2, 4. xcii. 8. cii. 24—28. 2 Pet. iii. 8. Rom. i. 23. 1 Tim. i. 17. vi. 16. Isa. ix. 6. lvii. 15. James i. 17. He alone is the First and the Last, Isa. xli. 4. xliv. 6. xlviii. 12. Rev. i. 8, 11. xxi. 6. xxii. 13. 2. The *days, years*, and succession, competent to his creatures, are represented as unapplicable to him, Job xxxvi. 26. x. 4. Psal. xc. 4. 2 Pet. iii. 8. Dan. vii. 9, 24.

Psalm cii. 24, 27. Job x. 5. Isa. xliii. 13. 3. Many eternal things, as *eternal life,—strength,—mercy,—dominion,—throne,* &c. are ascribed to him, Deut. xxxii. 40. xxxiii. 27. Rev. iv. 9. v. 14. Isa. xxvi. 4. Psalm ciii. 17. cxxxvi. Dan. iv. 3, 34. vi. 26. Psalm xciii. 2. Lam. v. 19. Isa. li. 6—8. Psal. xxxiii. 11. cxxxv. 13.——And we can as easily conceive how God's unsuccessive eternity co-exists with the successive duration of his creatures, as we can conceive how his omnipresence co-exists with all material substances, without having any corporeal extension in himself.

V. His UNCHANGEABLENESS is that essential property of his nature, by which he is from eternity to eternity, without any alteration, always the same; and it is often expressly ascribed to him in Scripture, James i. 17. Mal. iii. 6. 1 Tim. i. 17. Rom. i. 23. Psalm cii. 24—27. Heb. i. 11, 12. xiii. 8. vi 18. Isa. xlvi. 4. lvii. 15. Exod. iii. 14. Num. xxiii. 19. Tit. i. 2. 2 Tim. ii. 13.—He is unchangeable, 1. In his *existence,* that he cannot cease to be, 1 Tim. i. 17. vi. 16. Rom. i. 25. Psalm cii. 24—27. 2. In his *essence* or *nature,* that he cannot cease to be whatever he is, in his perfections of wisdom, power, holiness, justice, goodness, or truth, &c. 2 Tim. ii. 13. Isa. xxvi. 4. Deut. xxxii. 4. Psalm ciii. 17. xc. 2. Exod. iii. 14. 3. In his *actual knowledge* of things, 1 Cor. ii. 16. Acts xv. 18. Heb. iv. 13. Job xi. 7—9. 4. In his *will* and *purpose,* Heb. vi. 17, 18. Isa. xiv. 24, 27. xlvi. 10. Psalm xxxiii. 11. Rom. ix. 11. Job xxiii. 13. 5. In his *words,*—his doctrines, laws, promises, threatenings, or predictions, Num. xxiii. 19. 1 Sam. xv. 29. Heb. vi. 18. Psal. cxix. 87. 6. In his *essential presence,* that he cannot properly remove from one place to another, 1 Kings viii. 27. Jer. xxiii. 23, 24. 7. In his duration, which is neither less nor greater. He hath never existed longer, nor hath any less future duration to enjoy, Psalm xc. 2, 4. 2 Pet. iii. 8.—His formation of his creatures from nothing, or his changing of their forms in his providence, infers no change in himself. His power and will to create, preserve, or govern them, in such a manner, being the very same from all eternity.—New relations between him and his creatures infer not a change in him, but in them.

VI. His ONENESS, in respect of which, on account of his infinite perfection, there neither is, nor can be any other *like* to, or *equal* with him. This doth not mean, that there is but one *Supreme God,* as Arians and Socinians profess, who admit *subordinate gods.* Nor that there is but *one specific divine nature,* which different beings may possess, as Tritheists pretend: Nor that there is but *one divine person* exhibited in different characters, and by different names, as Sabellians contend. But it means, that there neither is, nor can be any more than *one individual,* or as others speak, *numerical divine substance*. This the necessary self-existence of God, his absolute eternity, infinity, omnipotence, and sovereignty, which exclude every rival partaker, demonstrate. And multitudes of scriptures expressly declare it; Deut. iv. 35, 39. vi. 4. xxxii. 39. xxxiii. 26. 1 Sam. ii. 2. 2 Sam. vii. 22. 1 Kings viii. 23. 2 Kings xix. 15. 1 Chron. xv. 20. Psalm xviii. 31, xxxv. 10. lxxxvi. 8. cxlviii. 13. lxxxix. 6, 8. cxv. 4—8. Isa. xliii. 10—15. xliv. 26. xlv. 5, 18—22. Jer. x. 8—15. xiv. 22. Hos. xiii. 4. Exod. xx. 3. John xvii. 3. Rom. iii. 30. 1 Cor. viii. 6. Eph. iv. 6. James ii. 19. iv. 12. 1 Tim. ii. 5.—But none of these texts exclude the Son, or the Holy Ghost, from true and supreme godhead. Nay, the very characters ascribed to the one *only true God*, are ascribed to each of these two persons, compare Isa. xliv. 6. with Rev. i. 8, 11.— Isa. xlv. 22, 23. with Rom. xiv. 9, 10. Phil. ii. 10, 11.—John xvii. 3. with 1 John v. 20, 21.—Rom. iii. 30. with Isa. liii. 11.—In 1 Cor. viii. 6. 1 Tim. ii. 5. *One God* means the divine nature, as distinguished from Christ the Mediator.——Nor are the distinct persons in the godhead represented as having *similar*, but the *very same* names, attributes, counsel, will, and work, compare Psalm xxxiii. 6. Isa. xliv. 24.—Rom. x. 12. Luke ii. 11. Rom. xi. 34. Isa. xl. 13. 2 Cor. iii. 18.—Deut. vi. 4. Psal. lxxxiii. 18. Jer. xxiii. 6.— Ezek. viii. 3. Matth. xv. 31. Luke i. 16, 17. 2 Sam. xxiii. 3.—Rom. vii. 25. Gal. vi. 2. Rom. viii. 2. Deut. vi. 16. 1 Cor. x. 9. Acts v. 9.—1 Cor. ii. 16. Rom. viii. 27.—1 Thess. iv. 3. Acts xxii. 14. ix. 15, 17. 2 Pet. i. 21.——Ezek. xxxvii. 3—14. 2 Cor. xii. 9. Rom xv. 19.— Rom. xvi. 26. Rev. xxii. 13. Heb. ix. 14.—John vii. 28. Rev. iii. 7. 1 John v. 6. John xiv. 17.—Rev. xv. 4. Acts iii. 14. Dan. ix. 24. 1 John ii. 20. John xiv. 26.—Jer. xxiii. 24. Ezek. i. 22. Psalm cxxxix. 7.—Deut. xxx. 20. Col. iii. 4. Rom. viii. 10.--- Psalm c. 3. John i. 3. Job xxxiii. 4.—John v. 21. 1 Cor. xv. 45. John vi. 63. Rom. viii. 11.—John vi. 45. Gal. i. 12. John xiv. 26.—1 John i. 3. 2 Cor. xiii. 14.—1 Cor. xiv. 25. 2 Cor. xiii. 5. John xiv. 17. 2 Cor. vi. 16. Eph. iii. 17. Rom. viii. 11. ---Phil. iii. 15. Gal. i. 12. Luke ii. 26. Heb. i. 1. 2 Cor. xiii. 3. Mark xiii. 11.---Isa. xlix. 7, 8. Acts xiii. 3.---1 Cor. vi. 14. John ii. 19. 1 Pet. iii. 18.---Isa. xlviii. 17. John x. 3. Rom. viii. 14.---2 Cor. iii. 5, 6. 1 Tim. i. 12. Acts xx. 28.—Jude 1. Heb. ii. 11. Rom. xv. 16.---1 Cor. xii. 16. Col. iii. 11. 1 Cor. xii. 11.—In which texts, in about twenty-four instances, that which is ascribed to God in the first, is ascribed to the Son and the Holy Ghost in those that immediately follow.

VII. His subsistence in three distinct persons, the first the FATHER, the second the SON, and the third the HOLY GHOST, proceeding from both.—It is evident, from the independence, simplicity, eternity, and unchangeableness of the divine nature, that in whatever form it subsists, that form must be a necessary perfection or excellency of it, without which it could not at all exist.—The personal properties of these persons being thus as absolutely necessary, as the existence of the divine nature itself,—and each having that whole nature which necessarily subsists in such persons, as above related to one another, there neither is, nor can be, an inferiority in, or dependence upon, one person, more than another. But of this mystery in the following chapter.

CHAP. II.

Of the PERSONS *in the Godhead.*

A PERSON is *a thinking substance, which can act by itself.* Or, it is *an intelligent agent, which is neither a part of, nor sustained by another.*---The characteristics of a person are, 1. That it be possessed of a rational understanding and will. 2. That the pronouns HE, and especially I and THOU, be applicable to it, not merely in figurative, but in the most plain and simple language. 3. That *thinking, speaking, judging, sending,* and other personal acts, be competent to it. 4. That it be capable of personal offices or stations, as prophet, priest, king, teacher, advocate, captain, &c.——But, as the divine nature infinitely differs from a created one, so a divine person infinitely differs from a created one. 1. All created persons are separate or separable in their substance one from another: but divine persons, in their substance, are perfectly *one* and the *same* with, and in one another, John x. 30. xiv. 9, 10. 2. Different created persons can have only a substance of the same kind, not the same individual one. But divine persons have, and must have, each of them the very same *individual* or *numerical* substance, 1 John v. 7. John x. 30. 3. Every created person is a distinct being, in, or by, though not from itself. But all divine persons are, and must be, *one being.*

It hath been formerly proved, that the infinite nature of God can subsist in a *plurality* of persons. The Scripture manifests that it doth so. 1. ELOHIM, which means God in the plural, or the *worshipful ones,* is used in the Old Testament about two thousand times, to denote the true God. And, it is often connected with a verb in the singular number, Gen. i. 1, 3, &c.— and sometimes with a verb or adjective plural, Gen. xx. 13. xxxv. 7. Deut. iv. 7. Josh. xxiv. 19. 1 Sam. xvii. 26, 36. Psalm lviii. 11. Jer. x. 10. Dan. v. 18, 20.---Even in Psalm xlv. 6. ELOHIM may denote Christ, who is the express image of the invisible God: and in ver. 7. it may denote the Father and Spirit who anoint him. Nay, though in one passage it should mean but one divine person, it will not follow, that in some thousands it should lose its natural signification.——Angels, Magistrates, Moses, and idols, are called *Elohim*, because they occupied the place of these divine persons, as messengers, deputies, or rivals, Psalm xcvii. 7. lxxxii. 1, 6. Exod. xxii. 28. vii. 1. Judg. ii. 12.   2. The true God is often represented as more than one person, Gen. i. 26. iii. 22. xi. 7. Job. xxxv. 10. Psalm lxxviii. 25. (ABIRIM) Eccl. xii. 1. v. 8. Prov. ix. 10. xxx. 3. Hos. xi. 12. Isa. xlv. 15. liv. 5. vi. 8. with John xii. 39. Acts xxviii. 25, 26.—Isa. xli. 21—23. Song i. 11. viii. 9. Dan. iv. 17. (the decreeing watchers being the same as the Most High, ver. 24.)—Mal. i. 6. John iii. 11. xiv. 21, 23. xvii. 21, 22.   3. More persons than one are represented as JEHOVAH or GOD, Gen. xix. 24. Psalm xlv. 6, 7. lxviii. 17, 18. Jer. xxiii. 5, 6. xxxiii. 15, 16.   4. Many passages of Scripture represent Jehovah as an *Angel* or *Messenger*,—which are to be understood of the Son of God, sent forth to announce and officiate in the work of our redemption, Gen. xvi. 7—12. xviii. 12, 13, 20, 26—32, xxii. 11, 12. Heb. vi. 13—18. Gen. xlviii. 16.   Exod. iii. 2—15. xxiii. 20, 21. 1 Cor. x. 9.— Zech. ii. 3, 5, 8, 10. iii. 1, 2.

It is fully evident, that there are precisely THREE persons in the one godhead, or divine essence or substance, from, 1. The scriptural account of God's creation of all things, Gen. i. 1—3. Psalm xxxiii. 6. with Eph. iii. 9. Acts iv. 24, 27. Heb. i. 2. John i. 3. Job xxvi. 13. Psalm civ. 30.   2. From the account of his creation of man, Gen. i. 26. Psalm xcv. 6—8. Heb. iii. 6, 7. Isa. liv. 5. Eccl. xii. 1. Job xxxiii. 4.   3. From the account of his common providence, John v. 17. Heb. i. 3. Psalm civ. 30. Isa. xxxiv. 16.   4. From the account of the Israelites' deliverance from Egypt, Isa. lxiii. 9, 10, 14.   5. From the account of his covenanting with the Israelites, Hag. ii. 4—7.   6. From the account of his general plan as to our redemption from our sinfulness and misery, Eph. i. 3—14. 1 Pet. i. 2.   7. From the account of his mission of Christ to be our Mediator, Isa. xlviii. 16. with verses 12, 13, 17. 8. From the account of Christ's incarnation, Luke i. 35. 9. From the account of God's anointing Christ and his people, Isa. xi. 2. lxi. 1, 2. 2 Cor. i. 22.   10. From the account of Christ's baptism, Mat. iii. 16, 17. John i. 32—34.   11. From the account of his ministrations and assistance therein, Isa. xlii. 1. Mat. xii. 18.   12. From the account of his offering himself in sacrifice to God, Heb. ix. 14.   13. From the account of his and his people's resurrection, Rom. i. 4. viii. 11.

14. From the institution of baptism, Mat. xxviii. 19. 15. From Christ's promises of the Spirit to his apostles and followers, John xiv. 16, 17, 26. xv. 26. xvi. 5—15. 16. From the account of God's changing our spiritual state and nature, Rom. viii. 2, 3. 1 John iii. 20, 24. 1 Cor. vi. 11. Tit. iii. 4—7. 1 Pet. i. 2, 3. 17. From the account of our adoption into God's family, Gal. iv. 6. Rom. viii. 14—17. 18. From the account of our supplies of sanctifying grace, Eph. i. 17—20. 2 Cor. i. 21, 22. iii. 14—16. 1 Thess. iii. 11—13. 2 Thess. iii. 5. 19. From the account of our prayer and access to God, Zech. xii. 10. Rev. i. 4, 5. Eph. ii. 17, 18. 20. From the account of our glorification, John xiv. 2, 3. with Eph. i. 14. 2 Cor. i. 22. 21. From the account of God's giving of gifts to church-officers, 1 Cor. xii. 3—6. 22. From the account of the inspiration of Scripture, 2 Sam. xxiii. 2, 3. 2 Pet. i. 17—21. 23. From the account of the unity of the church, Eph. iv. 4—6. 24. From the triple repetition of the name or epithets ascribed to God, Num. vi. 24—26. Isa. xxxiii. 22. Dan. ix. 19. Isa. vi. 3. Rev. iv. 8. But this is not so evidently conclusive. 25. From the account of the subject preached by faithful ministers, and their assistance in their work, 1 John iv. 2. Rom. xv. 16, 19, 30. 1 Cor. xii. 3. 26. From the account of Christ's manner of working miracles, Mat. xii. 28. 27. From the account of the marvellous efficacy of the gospel, 2 Cor. iii. 3. 1 Thess. i. 4—6. 28. From the account of the dreadful nature of unbelief, Heb. x. 29. 29. From the representation of believers' earnest study, Jude 20, 21. 30. From the account of their spiritual comforts, Rom. viii. 9. 1 Pet. iv. 14. 31. From the apostolical benediction, 2 Cor. xiii. 14. 32. From the heavenly attestation of the gospel record, 1 John v. 7.—— In which multitude of inspired texts we find one person under the name of Jehovah, God, Father, or represented as primary agent; a second under the name of the Word, Son, Servant, Angel, Anointed, Jesus Christ, Desire of all nations, and represented as the Saviour of men; and a third, called the Spirit, Holy Ghost, God, Lord, &c.

Indeed, the Socinians, modern Arians, and some others, contend that the last-mentioned text, John v. 7. is spurious; because, 1. " Many Greek manuscripts want it." But many of these also want other texts: and the similarity of the 7th and 8th verses made a careless transcriber apt to overleap one of them. 2. " Many of the ancient translations want it." But none of these translations are of great weight in this matter, for they want much more of the New Testament. Nor are any of them, except the Syriac and Jerome's Latin one, much worth. 3. " The ancient Fathers do not quote it, " when, in their disputes with heretics, it would have been

" much to their purpose." But that might be, because they had deficient copies, or cared not to adduce a text which their opponents might have rejected.——Let it be further observed, 1. The orthodox had no temptation to forge it, having plenty of proof for their faith concerning the Trinity beside. But the Antitrinitarians had strong temptations to drop it out of their copies, which is also more easily done. And yet perhaps it originated from no design, but from the hurry of a transcriber, amidst the rage of persecution. 2. About 1400 years ago, we find complaints of some Antitrinitarians attempting to corrupt the Scripture: but never, till of late, that the orthodox had done so. 3. This text is referred to by Tertullian about A. D. 200, quoted by Cyprian about 250, and by Athanasius, or one in his name, about 350. Jerome hath it in his translation about 400, and admitting it to be in all the best Greek copies, he severely blames the want of it in the old Latin version. Soon after, it is quoted by Eucherus and Vigilius. In 484 the African bishops quote it in the Confession of their faith which they presented to Hunneric their Arian king; and about thirty years after, Fulgentius, when required by an Arian king to produce his objections against the Arians, quoted it three times. When the Vulgate Latin translation was solemnly, and with great care, corrected from Greek and Latin manuscripts, by order of Charles the Great, about A. D. 800, and again by the famed University of Sorbonne, about two hundred years after, this text was retained. Erasmus, who inclined to Arianism, first suspected it, and dropt it out of his first edition of the New Testament: but restored it in his subsequent editions, upon the credit of an old British copy. It is said, that nine of Stephen's sixteen manuscripts from which he printed his excellent edition of the Greek New Testament, had this text. No doubt, many of the manuscripts, from which other principal editions were formed, are now lost. A printed copy is even more authentic than almost any manuscript extant, the oldest of which were written some hundred years after all these of the apostles were either worn out, or lost: for, more learning and care have been exercised to render some printed editions correct, than perhaps was taken on all the manuscripts written for a thousand years before the Reformation. 4. The passage appears deficient and unconnected if this verse be dropt. Mill and Bengelius have therefore honestly retained it, in their excellent editions, notwithstanding they have fairly, and with much more candour than Michaelis, represented the objections against it.

I. The character of FATHER, ascribed to God, sometimes equally respects all the divine persons, and marks their creation and kind preservation of persons or things, Mal. ii. 10. Heb. xii. 9. But, most frequently and emphatically, it denotes the first person of the Godhead, as related to the second, as his son.——It is evident, that the Father, in this view, is a distinct person: 1. He is expressly called a person, Heb. i. 3. 2. He subsists by himself, and hath life in himself, John v. 26. 3. He is a thinking and willing agent, John v. 17, 22. 4. Manifold personal relations and acts are ascribed to him. He from all eternity begat the second person as his only co-essential Son, Psal. ii. 7. He consulted with him concerning our redemption, Zech. vi. 13. He fore-ordained and set him up for our Mediator, 1 Pet. i. 20. Prov. viii. 23. and entered into a covenant of grace with him, Psalm lxxxix. 1—37. xl. 5—8. Isa. liii. 10. xlix. 6—9. He promised, sent, and brought him into the world, Jerem. xxxi. 22. Zech. iii. 8, 9, 10. Luke i. 35. Heb. i. 6. He gave him his commission to, and furniture for his work, John x. 18. xx. 21. Isa. xi. 2, 3. xlii. 1, 6. xlix. 1—6. lxi. 1—3. Mat. iii. 16, 17. John i. 32, 34. iii. 34, 35. Col. i. 19. He stood by him in his love, care, power, and providential assistance and comfort, during his abasement, Isa. xlii. 1—7. xlix. 2—8. l. 7, 9. He spoke in him, wrought by him, and bore witness to him, Heb. i. 1. 2 John v. 19—22, 32. viii. 16—19. Acts x. 38. He gave him to the death, and in due time raised him from it, Rom. viii. 32. Acts ii. 23, 24. 1 John iv 9, 10. 1 Pet. i. 21. He crowned him with glory and honour, exalted him to his own right hand, gave him as Mediator all power in heaven and on earth, and made him head over all things to his church, John xvii. 5. Heb. ii. 9. Psal. cx. 1. Acts ii. 32, 33, 36. Phil. ii. 9—11. Mat. xxviii. 18. John v. 22. Eph. i. 20—22. 1 Cor. xv. 24—27. He promised, and sends the Holy Ghost, who proceeds from him, to anoint Christ as man and Mediator, and to send and qualify his prophets and apostles, ministers and people, Psal. xlv. 7. Joel ii. 28. Luke xxiv. 49. John xiv. 26. xv. 26. He predestinated elect men to everlasting holiness and happiness, Rom. viii. 28—30. Eph. i. 4, 5. Luke xii. 32. Mat. xx. 23. He proposed the new covenant as terms of their salvation to his Son, Isa. liii. 10—12. Psal. lxxxix. 3, 4. Heb. ii. 10. Having accepted his atoning and reconciling righteousness in their stead, he savingly discovers him to them, draws them to him, and in him justifies and reconciles them to himself, Jer. xxxi. 32—34. Mat. xi. 25. Gal. i. 16. John vi. 44, 45. 2 Cor. v. 18—21. Rom. viii. 11, 14—18. Tit. iii. 5, 6. He, by his Spirit, confirms and comforts them, and brings them to complete and everlasting happiness, 2 Cor. i. 21, 22. Eph. iii. 20, 21. John

x. 28, 29. xvii. 11, 24. xiv. 16, 17, 21, 23. 2 Thess. ii. 16, 17. Heb. ii. 10. Rev. vi. 17.

It was never denied by any but Atheists, that the Father is the MOST HIGH GOD. And, 1. The Scripture expressly declares it, Rom. xv. 6. 2 Cor. i. 3. Phil. ii. 11. Eph. i 3, 17. Heb. i. 1, 3. 1 Pet. i. 2, 3. John xx. 17. And he is called JEHOVAH, Jer. xxiii. 5. xxxiv. 15. Psalm cx. 1. Isa. xliii. 5, 6, 8. xlix. 1, 4, 5, 7, 8. l. 4, 5. liii. 6, 10. lxi. 1. 2. Divine perfections are ascribed to him, as self-existence, John v. 26. Eternity, Rev. i. 4. Eph. i. 4. Absolute all-sufficiency, 1 Cor. xv. 28. Omnipresence with all his saints, 1 John i. 3—7. John xiv. 21, 23. Omniscience, 2 Cor. xi. 31. Almighty power, Mark xiv. 36. Absolute sovereignty, Mat. xi. 25—27. xxvi. 53. John iii. 35. x. 29. xiv. 28. 1 Cor. xi. 3. xv. 24, 27, 28. Eph. iv. 6. 3. Divine works are ascribed to him, as Creation, Eph. iii. 9. Isa. xlii. 5. Providence, John v. 17. Mat. xi. 25. —forgiving sin, Luke xxiii. 34. Eph. iv. 32; raising up Christ and his people from the dead, John v. 21 Heb. xiii. 20 Rom. viii. 11. 4. Divine worship is performed to him by Christ and his people, John xi. 41. xii. 27, 28. xiv. 26. xvii. Eph. i. 17. iii. 14. Mat. xxviii. 19.

II. The second person in the Godhead is called the WORD, or *Word of God*, because he is the perfect resemblance of his Father, even as our words are of our mind. He is the great Speaker for us to God, in his ancient engagements and his continual intercession. He is the subject-matter and end of all divine revelations, and their principal publisher, Luke i. 2. 2 Pet. i. 16. Acts xx. 32. Heb. iv. 12. John i. 1, 2, 14. 1 John i. 1. v. 7. Rev. xix. 13.—He is called the SON of God on account of his relation to the Father, by whom he is begotten, Psalm ii. 7. John i. 14. iii. 10. Rom. viii. 3, 32. i. 3. Gal. iv. 4.——That he is the *Son of God*, hath been attested by his Father, in repeated declarations from heaven, Mat. iii. 17. xvii. 5.—by himself, John v. 16, 17. x. 30, 36. xvii. 11, 24, 25. xix. 7. Mark xiv. 61, 62. Mat. xi. 25, 26.—by the Holy Ghost, in forming his human nature, and in his baptismal unction, Luke i. 32, 35. Mat. iii. 16. John i. 33, 34.—by John the Baptist, and by apostles and saints, John i. 33, 34.—Mat. xvi. 15, 16. John vi. 69. xi. 27. Acts iii. 7. 1 John v. 5.——It hath been confessed by devils, Mat. viii. 28, 29. Mark iii. 11. v. 7. Luke iv. 41. and by wicked men, perhaps just then converted, Mat. xiv. 33. Mark xv. 39.

But he is *not the Son of God*, by his miraculous conception and birth: 1. The Holy Ghost is never represented as his Father, nor could be, without admitting two fathers in the Godhead. That *holy thing born* is the called, the *Son of God*, because his manhood subsisted in the person of the Son of God, Luke i. 35. 2. He had the character and relation of Son of God, long before his conception or birth, Prov. xxx. 4. Psalm ii. 7. Gal. iv. 4. John iii. 16, 17. 3. According to his human nature or *flesh*, he is the *Son of man*,—of Abraham, of David, and not the Son of God. 4. His being *made of a woman*, was subsequent to his being the Son of God, Rom. viii. 3, 32. Gal. iv. 4. 5. His extraordinary conception and birth could never render him the *only begotten* Son of God, as he is termed, John i. 14. iii. 16, 18. 1 John iv. 9. since Adam was his son by creation, and Isaac, Jacob, Joseph, Samson, Samuel, and John the Baptist, were procreated by extraordinary influence,— though indeed very different from that which was exerted in the production of Christ's manhood.——Nor is he called the Son of God on account of God's raising him from the dead; for, 1. He was the Son of God long before, Mat. iii. 17. xvii. 5. John v. 16, 17. x. 30, 36. Mark xiv. 61, 62. Mat. xvi. 15, 16. John vi. 69. i. 49. 2. If his resurrection had rendered him the only Son of God, he would have been his own father, as he raised himself, John x. 17, 18. ii. 19. 3. This could not have rendered him the *only begotten* Son of God, as millions beside have or shall be raised from the dead, Mat. xxvii. 52, 53. John v. 28, 29. 1 Thess. iv. 14, 16. Rev. xx. 12. Nor doth Acts xiii. 33. import, that he became the Son of God by his resurrection, but that his Sonship was manifested by it, compare Rom. i. 3, 4.—and that his resurrection publicly proved, that the word of salvation, particularly that in Psalm ii. 7, 8. was then exhibited, given, and fulfilled to men.——Nor, doth his mediatorial office constitute him the Son of God. 1. A mission on an errand, or an appointment to service, cannot, in the nature of things, constitute Sonship. 2. His Sonship is represented as prior to his commission to, or execution of his mediatorial office, John iii. 16. Gal. iv. 4. 1 John iv. 9, 10. iii. 8. Heb. v. 8. 3. His mediatorial office derives virtue from his divine Sonship, and so his Sonship cannot depend on it, Heb. iv. 14. 4. His being *from the Father*, in respect of his Sonship, is expressly distinguished from his being *sent* to execute his mediatorial office, John vii. 29.

But he is the Son of God by *necessary and eternal generation;* —that is, by such necessity, that the divine nature cannot at all exist, without subsisting in him, in the form and relation of *a Son* to the first person. 1. In many texts of Scripture, he is simply called the *Son of God*, and in that character represented as the Most High God,—the Lord God of his people,—the Lord God,--God the Saviour, Luke i. 16, 17, 32, 35, 46, 47. —as coming from heaven, and above all, John iii. 31. Mat. xi. 27.—and as the object of faith and worship, John iii. 18, 36. ix. 35—38. Mat. iv. 33. xxvii. 54; or, as the same with God,

OF THE PERSONS IN THE GODHEAD. 137

Heb. i. 8. 1 John iii. 8. with 1 Tim. iii. 16.—and as equal with his Father, Mat. xxviii. 19. John v. 21. 2. God hath given the most solemn and emphatic testimonies to his divine Sonship, Mat. iii. 17. xvii. 5. The first of these texts, literally translated, runs, *This is that my Son,—my beloved one, in whom I am well pleased.* And in the other, we are commanded to *hear him*, as infinitely superior to Moses and Elias, his then visitants, who had been the most extraordinary of all the Old Testament prophets. This manifests, that he was *Judah's God*, and the *Lord God*, Isa. xl. 9.—And, it is observable, that in all his instructions he never professed to teach in the name of another, but in his own: Verily I say unto you, or the like, plainly importing, that he himself was that Jehovah, in whose name the prophets had delivered their messages, Mat. v.—vii. John iii. v.—viii. x. &c. 3. The Scriptures represent him as God's *own Son,—his proper Son,—his Son of himself*, John i. 14, 18. iii. 16, 18. Rom. viii. 3, 32. 1 John iv. 9, 12. If these expressions do not represent him as the Son of God by natural generation, what can do it? 4. His being the Christ, Messiah, or Mediator, is plainly distinguished from his being the Son of God, John i. 49. vi. 69. Mat. xvi. 16. Heb. v. 8. 1 John iv. 14. 5. When he was charged with blasphemy in making himself equal with God, by calling himself *the Son of God*, he plainly acquiesced in their interpretation of his words; and instead of shewing them that his claim of Sonship to God did not infer his claim of *equality* with God, he took occasion further to assert and demonstrate his supreme Godhead, John v. 16---29. x. 30---36. xix. 7. Mat. xxvi. 63---65. Nay, perhaps *making himself equal with God*, John v. 18. are not the words of the persecuting Jews, but of the inspired Evangelist. 6. It was not from acts properly *mediatorial*, but from *divine* acts, that he was concluded to be the Son of God, Mat. iv. 3, 6. xiv. 33. xxvii. 40, 54. John i. 49. 7. If the title, *The Son of man*, import his possession of a real manhood, his character, *The Son of God*, God's *proper Son,—Son of himself*, and *only begotten Son* of God, must certainly import his possession of the *divine nature,—of true and supreme Godhead*.——Now, if he be the Son of God by nature, he must be his eternal Son, begotten from all eternity; for nothing that is not necessarily eternal in the highest sense, can be natural to God. Nor is there the least impropriety in God's calling his own eternity THIS DAY, as with him an unsuccessive eternity is ever present, Psalm ii. 7. with Isa. xliii. 13. Mic. v. 2. Nor is the generation of his Son there represented as an event decreed, but as antecedent to, and fundamental of God's grant of the Gentiles to him for his mediatorial inheritance, ver. 8, 9.

The Son of God is a distinct person from the Father and the Holy Ghost. 1. Personal powers of rational understanding and will are ascribed to him, Mat. xi. 27. John i. 18. v. 21. xvii. 2, 24. 2. He subsists as a person by himself, John v. 26. Heb. i. 3. 3. The personal epithets I, THOU, HE, are ascribed to him in the most plain passages of Scripture, Mat. v. John iii. Isa. xlix. 1—9. xlii. 1—7. 4. He is invested with, and executes the personal offices of Mediator, Surety, Prophet, Priest, King, &c. 1 Tim. ii. 5. Heb. vii. 22. Acts iii. 22. Psalm cx. 4. ii. 6. Mat. xxiii. 8—10. 5. Multitudes of personal acts are ascribed to him,—as, engaging his heart, Jer. xxx. 21. taking our nature upon him, Heb. ii. 14. fulfilling all righteousness in our stead, Mat. iii. 15. Luke xxiv. 26. rising from the dead, John ii. 19. x. 17, 18. ascending to heaven, Heb. i. 3. making continual intercession for us, &c. Heb. vii. 26. Rom. viii. 34.

It is no less evident, that the Son is *God equal with the Father*. 1. The names, which are proper to none but the Supreme God, are ascribed to him, as I AM, or I AM THAT I AM, Exod. iii. 14. Rev. i. 8 ——JEHOVAH, Exod. xvii. 7. 1 Cor. x. 9.— Isa. vi. 1—9. John xii. 39, 40, 41.—Isa. xl 3, 9, 10. Mat. iii. Luke i. 16, 17, 76. iii.—Jer. xxiii. 5, 6. xxxiii. 15, 16. 2 Cor. v. 21. 1 Pet. ii. 24. iii. 18.—Zech. xii. 10. John xix. 19, 34, 37. Rev. i. 7. Zech. xi. 12, 13. Mat. xxvii. 9.—Zech. xi. 8, 11. Isa. viii. 13, 14. 1 Pet. ii. 6.—8. Luke ii. 34. Psalm cxviii. 22. Mat. xxi. 42.—Isa. xliv. 6. Rev. xxii. 13.—Isa. xliii. 11. 2 Pet. i. 1. iii. 18. ——GOD, Psalm xlv. 6. Heb. i. 8.—Isa. xlv. 22, 23. Rom. xiv. 10—12. Phil. ii. 9—11.—Isa. xxv. 8, 9. 2 Tim. i. 10.—Isa. xxxv. 4, 5. Mat. xi. 3, 5.—Isa. vii. 14. Mat. i. 23. 1 Tim. iii. 16. John i. 14.—John xx. 28. 2 Pet. i. 1. Jude 4. in which last two texts, as well as in some others; KAI ought to be translated EVEN,—*God even our Saviour—Lord God even our Lord Jesus Christ.*—*God, the First and the Last*, Isa. xliv. 6. xli. 4. Rev. i. 8, 17, 18. ii. 8. xxi. 6. xxii. 6, 13, 16, 20.—the *living and the true God*, 1 John v. 20, 21. Rev. i. 18. Jer. x. 10. —the *great and the mighty God*, Tit. ii. 13. Isa. ix. 6.—the *most high God*, Psalm lxxviii. 56. 1 Cor. x. 9. Luke i. 76.—the *only wise God*, Jude 4, 24, 25. Rom. xvi. 27. 1 Tim. i. 16, 17.—the *God of glory*, Acts vii. 2.—the *only Lord God*, Isa. xliv. 6. xlv. 15, 22, 23. Rom. xiv. 11. Jude 4.—*God over all blessed for ever*, Rom. ix. 5.—the *God of Abraham, Isaac, and Jacob*, Exod. iii. 6. Acts vii. 30—32.—the *God of Israel*, Luke i. 16, 17. Mat. iii. 11. Psalm c. 3. John x. 3. xxi. 16, 17. Acts xx. 28. 1 Pet. v. 2.—*King of kings and Lord of lords*, Rev. xvii. 14. xix. 13— 16. 1 Tim. vi. 14, 15.—*King of glory*, Psalm xxiv. 7—10.—the *Lord of hosts*, and the *God of the whole earth*, Isa. liv. 5. John iii. 29. Mat. ix. 15. 2 Cor. xi. 2.—*Jehovah the shepherd*, Psalm xxiii. 1. John x. 2, 16. Heb. xiii. 20. 1 Pet. ii. 25. v. 4.

OF THE PERSONS IN THE GODHEAD.

2. Such properties or attributes as belong only to the Most High God, are ascribed to him, as, The *fulness of the Godhead*, Col. ii. 9. John xvi. 15.—the *form of God*, and *equal* with God, Phil. ii. 6. Zech. xiii. 7. Heb. i. 3. Col. i. 15. John v. 18.— *Oneness* with the Father, John x. 30. xiv. 9, 10. 1 John v. 7. —*Eternity*, Rev. i. 8, 11. Prov. viii. 23—31. Mic. v. 2. John i. 1. viii. 58. vi. 62. xvii. 5. Isa. ix. 6. Heb. vii. 3, 24, 25. Rom. xvi. 26. Mark xvi. 15.—*Unchangeableness*, Heb. xiii. 8. i. 12. Psalm cii. 24—27.—*Almighty power*, Phil. iii. 21. Rev. i. 8. xi. 17, 18. xxii. 12, 13, 20. Isa. ix. 6. lxiii. 1. xlix. 26.—*Omnipresence*, Mat. xviii. 20. xxviii. 20. Col. i. 17. Heb. i. 3. John i. 8. iii. 13.—*Omniscience*, John i. 18. ii. 25. iv. 29. vi. 64. xxi. 17. Mat. ix. 4. xii. 25. xi. 27. Rev. ii. 23. Heb. iv. 13. Col. ii. 3. ——It was his created manhood which, during his humiliation, knew not the time of the *last judgment*, Mark xiii. 32.——Nay, he could not have executed any of his mediatorial offices of prophet, priest, or king, unless he had had the perfections of God in him, Deut. xviii. 15—18. Mat. xvii. 5. John i. 18.— Heb. vii. 25. ix. 14. Psalm cx. 4, 5. ii. 6—9, 12. 3. The works proper only to God are ascribed to him, as *decreeing* all things, Prov. viii. 22, 30. Gen. i. 26. Rev. i. 8. John xiii. 18. xv. 16.— *creating* all things, Psalm xxxiii. 6. John i. 3. Eph. iii. 9. Heb. i. 2, 10. And hence he is called the *beginning of the creation* of God, and the *first begotten* of every creature, Rev. iii. 14. Col. i. 15, 10.—*preserving* and *governing* all things, Col. i. 17, 18. Heb. i. 3. John v. 17, 19.—*working miracles*, in his own person, in his own name, and by his apostles as moral instruments, Mat. iv. 24, 25. xi. 5. John v. 21, 36. xxi. 25. Luke vi. 19. viii. 46. x. 9, 10. Acts iii. 6, 16. iv. 10, 29, 30. ix. 34.— *erecting* a church and appointing her officers, Heb. iii. 3, 14. Eph. iv. 11, 12. Mat. xvi. 18. xxviii. 18—20.—*instituting* sacraments and other ordinances, Mat. xxviii. 19. 1 Cor. xi. 23— 29.—*redeeming* sinful men, Hos. i. 7. Isa. xlv. 17, 22, 24, 25. Mat. xx. 28. Acts xx. 28. Tit. ii. 14.—*sending* the Holy Ghost to apply his redemption, John xiv. 26. xv. 26. xvi. 7.—the *effectual calling* of rebellious sinners to himself, John v. 21, 25. x. 16. xv. 16.—*justifying* guilty sinners, Mat. ix. 6. Isa. liii. 11. 1 Cor. vi. 11. Col. iii. 13. Rev. i. 5.—*adopting* men into the family of God, John i. 12. Jer. iii. 19. 2 Cor. vi. 18.—*sanctifying* their nature and life, Eph. v. 26, 29. Heb. ii. 11. xiii. 12. ix. 14.— the *almighty preservation* of them in their gracious state, nature, and course, John x. 10, 28. xiv. 6. Col. iii. 3. Jude 1.—*Raising* himself and other dead, John ii. 19. x. 17, 18. v. 21, 28, 29. Rom. i. 4. 1 Pet. iii. 18.—*Judging* the world, bestowing eternal glory upon his saints, and executing everlasting punishment on his wicked enemies, John v. 22, 28, 29. Acts xvii. 31. Heb. ii. 10. vii. 25. Rev. iii. 21. 2 Thess. i. 6—10. Rev. xiv. 9—11.

4. That divine worship and honour which is due only to the Most High God, is ascribed to him, Mat. viii. 2. The same worship which is due to the Father, John v. 23.—As *faith* in him, John xiv. 1. xvii. 3. 1 Pet. i. 21. Psalm ii. 12. Jer. xvii. 5.—*Supreme love* to him, 1 Cor. xvi. 22. John xxi. 15---17. Eph. vi. 24. Mark xii. 30, 32, 33.—*Obedience* and *subjection of soul* to him, Exod. xxiii. 21. Psalm ii. 9---12. xxii. 7---31. xlv. 5. 11. Mat. xvii. 5.—*Baptism* in his name, as equal, and one with that of the Father, Mat. xxviii. 19. Acts xix. 5. x. 48. 1 Cor. i. 13.—*Calling upon* his name in prayer and praise, Heb. i. 6. Phil. ii. 10. Acts vii. 59, 60. 1 Cor. i. 2. Thess. ii. 16, 17. 2 Cor. xii. 8, 9, 10. Rev. i. 5. v. 9, 13. vii. 10, 12.

The Son of God became our Mediator, and assumed our nature; hence those scriptures which represent him as inferior to God, sent or rewarded by him, or, as bearing any character, or performing any work not proper to the Most High God, are to be understood of him *as Man and Mediator*,—and there are generally other texts almost parallel proving his Supreme Godhead, John xiv. 28. 1 Cor. xi. 3. xv. 28. John x. 30. Phil. ii. 6. Zech. xiii. 7. Mat. xix. 17. (read, *there is none good but one God*) Mark ii. 7. 1 John v. 20. Jude 4. Col. ii. 9.—1 Cor. xv. 24, 28. Luke i. 53.—Acts x. 42. xvii. 31. Psalm l. 6. vii. 8.—Acts x. 40. John ii. 13.—John iii. 16. Eph. v. 2, 25.—Eph. iv. 32. Col. ii. 13.—John vi. 38. John xx. 28.—Mat. xxiii. 9, 10. Isa. ix. 6. Rev. xxi. 7.—Luke xx. 36. John xi. 25.—Mark xiii. 32. John xxi. 17.—John i. 18. xiv. 8, 9.—1 Cor. xv. 27. Phil. iii. 20, 21.—Mat. 26, 39. Heb. v. 7, 8.—Mat. xxviii. 18. John vii. 16. xi. 41. Isa. xlii. 1. lxi. 1. xlix. 3, &c.—As God, he doth nothing but in joint operation with his Father, and nothing but what the Father is interested in, John v. 19.—All attempts to prove his inferiority to the Father, from his being *begotten* by him, perhaps proceed from men's ignorance of the true nature of human generation, or rather chiefly from making animal nature and generation a standard, by which they judge of what belongs to an infinite Spirit, than which nothing can be more absurd and blasphemous.

III. It is sufficiently manifest that the Holy Ghost is a real and distinct person in the Godhead. 1. Personal powers of understanding and will are ascribed to him, 1 Cor. ii. 10, 11. xii. 11. Eph. iv. 3. 2. He is joined with the other two divine persons as the object of worship and the fountain of blessings, Mat. xxviii. 19. 2 Cor. xiii. 14. Rev. i. 4, 5. 1 John v. 7. John xiv. 16, 17. xv. 26. xvi. 7. 3. In the Greek a masculine article or epithet is joined to his name PNEUMA, which is naturally of the neuter gender, John xiv. 26. xv. 26. xvi. 13. Eph. i. 13, 14. 4. He appeared under the emblem of a dove, and of cloven

OF THE PERSONS IN THE GODHEAD. 141

tongues of fire, Mat. iii. 16. Acts ii. 3, 4. 5. Personal offices of an Intercessor, Rom. viii. 26, 27.—a Witness, John xv. 26. Heb. x. 15.—a Comforter or Advocate, John xiv. 16, 17. xv. 26. xvi. 7.—a Teacher and Guide, John xiv. 16, 17, 26. xvi. 13, 14. are ascribed to him. 6. He is represented as performing a multitude of personal acts, as teaching, speaking, Mark xiii. 11. Acts xxviii. 25; witnessing, Acts v. 32. xx. 23. Rom. viii. 15, 16; dwelling, John xiv. 17. 1 Cor. vi. 19. 2 Tim. i. 14. sending of ministers, Acts xiii. 2—4. xx. 28. Mat. ix. 38. judging what is meet, Acts xv. 28. forbidding, Acts xvi. 6, 7.—As from all eternity he acted in the counsels of God, particularly in approving the new covenant plan of our redemption, and taking his proper share in its execution, so, in time, he acts distinctly, though not separately, from the Father and Son, in their whole work.---In respect of order, he finished the work of creation, Psalm xxxiii. 6. Job xxvi. 13. He qualified Moses, Bezaleel, Aboliab, Othniel, Ehud, Barak, Deborah, Gideon, and his three hundred soldiers, Samson and others, with uncommon strength of body, wisdom, or courage of mind, for their respective work, Deut. xxxiv. 7. Exod. xxxi. 3—6. Judg. iii. 10, 15. iv. 9, 14, 21. vi. vii. xiii.—xvi. He inspired the prophets and apostles with an infallible knowledge of the will of God, 1 Pet. i. 11. 2 Pet. i. 21. He endowed Balaam, Caiaphas, and others with prospects of future events, Num. xxiii. xxiv. John xi. 50—52. 1 Kings xiii. 11—20. He wrought miracles unnumbered by Moses, Elijah, Elisha, Christ, the apostles, and others, Exod. iv.—xvii. Num. xvi. xvii. 1 Kings xviii.—xx. 2 Kings i.—vii. xiii. Matth. xii. 22—28. Heb. ii. 4.— He framed the body, and created the soul of Christ in union to his divine person, Luke i. 34, 35. He sanctified his manhood, forming it with every gift and grace of which it was capable, Isa. xi. 2, 3. John iii. 34. He increased this grace in proportion to the growing faculties of that manhood, Luke ii. 40, 52. He solemnly anointed and qualified him for his ministerial work, Mat. iii. 16. Isa. lxi. 1, 2, 3. xi. 2—4. Luke iv. 18. John iii. 34. He directed him into and carried him through all his temptations from Satan, Mat. iv. 1. He assisted him in his working miracles, Mat. xii. 28. and in offering up himself a sacrifice to God, Heb. ix. 14. He raised him from the dead, Rom. i. 4. viii. 11. vi. 4. He justified him, as our public Representative, 1 Tim. iii. 16. He filled his manhood with heavenly joys, Psalm xlv. 7. Acts ii. 28. By miraculous and saving influences, he vindicated him, as perfectly righteous in all his conduct,—as the fulfiller of all righteousness for men,— and as ascended to his Father's right hand, Acts i.—xix. Luke xxiv. 49. John xvi. 7—17. xv. 26.——He calls men to, and fits them with gifts and graces for public office in the church, Acts

ii. xiii. 2—4. xx. 28. Mat. ix. 38. 1 Cor. xii. xiv. He directs, assists, and succeeds them in their work, Acts xvi. 6, 7. Heb. ii. 4. 1 Pet. i. 11, 12. 1 Thess. i. 4. Acts viii. 17. x. 44. xix. 6, 7. Rom. xv. 16, 19.—He convinces men of their sin and misery, John xvi. 8, 9. He enlightens their minds in the knowledge of Christ, John xiv. 26. xv. 26. xvi. 13, 15. Eph. i. 17, 18. iii. 17—19. 1 Cor. ii. 10—12. He renews their will, John iii. 5, 6. Tit. iii. 5. He justifies them, 1 Cor. vi. 11. He sanctifies them, 2 Thess. ii. 13. 1 Pet. i. 2. Rom. xv. 16. He comforts them, John xiv. 16, 26. xv. 26. xvi. 7. Acts ix. 31. He directs, leads, and draws them, 2 Thess. iii. 5. John xiv. 16, 17. Psalm cxliii. 10. Rom. viii. 1, 4, 14. Gal. v. 18, 25 He enables them to mortify their sinful corruptions, Rom. viii. 13. He upholds their graces in their spiritual life and courage, Psalm li. 11, 12. Gal. v. 18, 25. He actuates and enables their new nature to bring forth fruits of holiness, Eph. v. 9. Gal. v. 22, 23. Ezek. xxxvi. 27. He directs and assists them in prayer, Rom. viii. 15, 26, 27. Jude 20. Gal. iv. 6. Zech. xii. 10. He assists them in self-examination, bears witness with their spirits, that they are the children of God,—and marks them as such by his presence in them, Rom. viii. 9, 16. 1 John iii. 24. He, as an earnest, seals them to the day of redemption, Eph. i. 13, 14. iv. 30. 2 Cor. i. 21, 22. He teaches them spiritual mysteries, 1 John ii. 20, 27. 1 Cor. ii. 10—12, 15. He is vexed and grieved, when his influences are not cherished, Isa. lxiii. 10. Eph. iv. 30. 1 Thess. v. 19. He will raise their dead bodies at the last day, Rom. viii. 11.

It is no less evident, that the Holy Ghost is a divine person equal in power and glory with the Father and Son. 1. Names proper only to the Most High God are ascribed to him, as JEHOVAH, 2 Sam. xxiii. 2. Num. xii. 6. 1 Pet. i. 11. 2 Pet. i. 21.---Deut. xxxii. 12. Isa. lxiii. 10.---Isa. vi. 8---10. Acts xxviii. 25.---Exod. xvii. 7. Heb. iii. 9.---Lev. xvi. 2. Heb. ix. 7, 8.---Jer. xxxi. 31---34. Heb. x. 15, 16.——GOD, Isa. lxi. 1. Ezek. xi. 5. Heb. i. 1.—Acts v. 3, 4. 1 Cor. iii. 16. vi. 19. 2 Tim. iii. 16. 2 Pet. i. 21.——The *Most High God*, Psalm lxxviii. 56. Heb. iii. 7, 9.—— The LORD, 2 Thess. iii. 5. Matth. ix. 38. 2 Cor. iii. 17, 18. the conclusion of which may be read, " by the Lord the Spirit." 2. Attributes proper only to the Most High God are ascribed to him,—as *Eternity*, Gen. i. 1, 2. Heb. ix. 14. *Omnipresence*, Psalm cxxxix. 7. 1 Cor. iii. 16. vi. 19. 2 Tim. i. 14. Rom. viii. 9. John xiv. 17. *Omniscience*, 1 Cor. ii. 10, 11. John xvi. 13. 2 Pet. i. 21. 1 Pet. i. 11. *Almighty power* and *sovereign dominion*, Isa. xi. 2. Luke i. 35. Acts vi. 10. *Divine holiness*, Isa. lxiii. 10, 11. Rom. i. 4. 3. Works competent only to God are ascribed to him,—as *creating* all things, Gen. i. 2. Psalm xxxiii. 6. civ. 30. Job xxvi. 13.

OF THE PERSONS IN THE GODHEAD. 143

xxxii. 4. *Preserving* all things, Psal. civ. 30. Isa. xxxiv. 16. *Working miracles,* Matth. xii. 28. 1 Cor. xii. 4. Heb. ii. 4. *Forming Christ's human nature,* Luke i. 35. Jer. xxxi. 22. *Anointing* Christ, Isa. xlii. 1. xi. 2. lxi. 1. Psalm xlv. 7. John iii. 34. and perhaps *sending* him, Isa. xlviii. 16. *Governing* the church, Matth. ix. 38. Acts vii. 51. xiii. 2, 4. xx. 28. xv. 28. *Bestowing* extraordinary spiritual gifts, 1 Cor. xii. Heb. ii. 4. *Foretelling* contingent futurities, John xvi. 13. Acts xi. 28. xx. 23. xxi. 11. 1 Pet. i. 11. *Convincing* men's consciences of their most secret sins, John xvi. 9. *Enlightening* their mind in the knowledge of spiritual things, Eph. i. 17, 18. iii. 16—19. 1 Cor. ii. 10, 12, 15, 16. *Justifying* Christ and his people, 1 Tim. iii. 16. 1 Cor. vi. 11. *Regenerating* and *sanctifying* men's hearts, John iii. 5, 6. 1 Cor. iv. 11. Tit. iii. 5, 6. 2 Thess. ii. 13. iii. 5. 1 Thess. iii. 12, 13. 1 Pet. i. 2. Ezek. xxxvii. 1—14. *Comforting* saints, and *preserving* them in grace, John xiv. 16, 26. xv. 26. xvi. 7. Eph. i. 13, 14. iv. 30. 2 Cor. i. 21, 22. Psalm li. 11, 12. *Quickening* saints and churches, when under fearful degrees of spiritual death, John vi. 63. Rom. viii. 2. Ezek. xxxvii. 1—14. Rev. xi. 11. and *raising* of the dead at the last day, Rom. viii. 11. Acts xxvi. 8. 4. Worship proper only to God is required and ascribed to him. *Prayer* to him is exemplified, Song iv. 16. Rev. i. 4. 2 Thess. iii. 5. and commanded, Matth. ix. 38. Acts xiii. 2, 4. xvi. 5, 7. xx. 28. 1 Cor. xii. 4—11. ii. 4, 11, 12. *Solemn appeals* are made to him, Rom. ix. 1. Deut. vi. 13. Jer. xvii. 10. In his name *baptism* is administered, Matth. xxviii. 19. Church judicatories meet and act, Acts xv. 28. xiii. 2, 4. and *solemn benedictions* are emitted, 2 Cor. xiii. 14.——The sin which is peculiarly committed against him is stated as unpardonable, though the worst of those against the Father and Son are not, Matth. xii. 32. Heb. vi. 4—8. x. 26—31.

In all these texts of Scripture, in which something not proper to an intelligent and eternal person is ascribed to the Spirit or Holy Ghost, his name must be understood as meaning not himself, but his gifts and influences, John vii. 39. Joel ii. 28. Acts ii. 17. x. 44. xix. 6. Heb. ii. 4.—And wherever he is represented as inferior to, or sent, or given by the Father or Son, the text is to be understood of his station or agency in the work of our redemption,—of which, with his own choice, he is constituted the applier, John xiv. 26. xv. 26. xvi. 7. Ezek. xxxvi. 27. 1 John iii. 24.

The Holy Ghost *proceeds from the Son,* as well as from the Father. 1. He is represented as the Spirit of the Son as well as of the Father, Gal. iv. 6. 1 Pet. i. 11. Phil. i. 19. 2. He is sent and communicated by the Son, as well as by the Father, John xvi. 7, 13—15. xx. 22. Prov. i. 23. But whether he proceeds from the Son, precisely in the same manner as from the Father, we know not.

These three divine persons are distinguished from one another, 1. By their *names* of Father, Son, and Holy Ghost, Matth. xxviii. 19. 2 Cor. xiii. 14. Mat. iii. 16, 17. 1 John v. 7. John xiv. 16, 17. 2. By their *order of subsistence;* the Father the first; the Son the second; and the Holy Ghost the third, 1 John v. 7. Matth. xxviii. 19. But to mark their equality, they are sometimes mentioned in a different order, 2 Cor. xiii. 14. Rev. i. 4, 5. 1 Thess. iii. 5. 3. By their different *order of operation.* The Father acts from himself through the Son and by the Spirit. The Son acts from the Father and by the Spirit: And the Spirit acts from both the Father and the Son, John iii. 16. i. 1—3. v. 17, 19. xv. 26. xiv. 26. xvi. 7. 4. By their different *stations*, which, in a delightful correspondence with their natural order of subsistence, they have voluntarily assumed in the work of our redemption:—the Father as the Creditor, Judge, Master, and Rewarder;—the Son as the Mediator, Surety, Servant, Pannel, &c.;—and the Holy Ghost as the Furnisher, Assistant, and Rewarder of the Mediator, and the Applier of the redemption purchased by him, Zech. iii. 8. xiii. 7. Isa. xlii. 1, 6, 7. xlix. 1—9. liii. 2—12. John xvi. 8, 15. Eph. i. 17, 18. iii. 16—19. iv. 30. Ezek. xxxvi. 27. 5. And chiefly by their personal properties.—The Father is neither *begotten* by, nor *proceeds* from any other person, but, being first in order, he *begets* the Son, and hath the Holy Ghost *proceeding* from him. The Son is begotten by the Father, and hath the Holy Ghost proceeding from him. The Holy Ghost neither begets, nor is begotten, but proceeds from both the Father and the Son, John i. 14, 18. iii. 16. xiv. 26. Gal. iv. 4—6. 1 Pet. i. 11.——To contend that these properties belong only to these divine persons, as connected with man's redemption, is really to admit the Sabellian heresy, which represents the Father, the Son, and the Holy Ghost, as but *one divine person*, manifested in three different forms in that work: For, if no known differences be admitted, no real distinction of those persons can be admitted. If we assert that these properties must belong to the redemption-scheme, because they are ordinarily found in near connection with something pertaining to it; we must, for the same reason, give up all the evidences as to the true godhead of the Son and Holy Ghost. Mean while these properties are so mysterious, that we can no more comprehend or explain them, than we can do the *self-existence, infinity,* and *unsuccessive eternity* of God.

To prevent or obviate objections against this deep mystery of three distinct persons in one godhead, it may be observed,

1. That the doctrine concerning it, being unfolded only by Revelation, we ought to use as few words as possible concerning it but such as are scriptural. We are certain that God perfectly knows himself, though we do not; and that his expressions concerning himself, though we should not understand them, are *just* and *safe;* whereas those of human invention may be neither; and may lead us, unawares, into blasphemous views or representations of Him.   2. This doctrine of the Trinity of persons in the Godhead, being wholly derived from Revelation, though learned men may know better what *cannot be true* with respect to it, yet they can have no more *positive* knowledge of it, than any diligent searcher of the Scriptures, who is of a moderate capacity. No human learning therefore can, in the least, authenticate either apprehensions or expressions concerning it.   3. It being plainly evident from God's own word, that each of these three persons is equally the Most High and the only true God, no term or phrase must be admitted, in the explication of their personal properties, which can in the least interfere with the divine equality or absolute independence of any one of them.— Subordinate Godhead is no Godhead at all, nor any thing but a mere chimera in men's brain. By calling the Father the *fountain* of the Deity or of the Trinity, by saying that the divine essence is *communicated,*—or the Son and Spirit are *produced,*—or that they have a *personal* though not an *essential* dependence on the Father, learned men have inadvertently hurt this mystery, and given occasion for its enemies to blaspheme. 4. It is certainly absurd to attempt an explication of the personal properties, BEGET,—BEGOTTEN,—PROCEEDING,—by terms which are more unintelligible: and, how to find clearer ones, I know not.   5. As God himself hath no where exemplified any explication of this mystery of the subsistence of three persons in one godhead by any similitude drawn from natural things, it must in itself be very daring, and very hurtful and darkening to the truth, for any man to attempt it.   6. As nothing more concerning this mystery can be known or believed, than is plainly revealed in Scriptnre by God, who hath an infinitely perfect knowledge of himself, and who cannot lie, the cordial belief of this doctrine is very properly required of every adult person, as absolutely necessary to salvation. Nor can any man, without the belief of it, have any true knowledge of the covenant of grace,—of the incarnation of Christ, of his satisfaction for sin, or of any thing else in the work of our redemption. 7. The doctrine of the Trinity of persons in one Godhead is so far from being *merely speculative,* as some pretend,—that without the spiritual knowledge of it, no motive to, or exercise of piety or virtue, can be rightly understood or practised.—The whole of practical religion consists in distinct fellowship with these

divine persons,—*with the Father*, in discerning, believing, and admiring his LOVE, and in returning it, in grateful desires after, delight in, reverence of, and obedience to him ;—*with the Son*, in receiving him, as God-man full of grace and truth, as our Head, Husband, and Saviour, in resting on his righteousness, and in receiving and improving all his purchased blessings, to render us lovers of God and of men for his sake ;—*and with the Holy Ghost*, in preparing for, receiving, co-operating with, and improving his personal presence and manifold gracious influences, for the sanctification and comfort of our heart, and the rendering our life truly pious and profitable.

REFLECT. Now, O my soul, think what an insignificant nothing I am before this infinite, this eternal, this all-mysterious God!—How little a portion I have known or even heard of him!—How astonishing, if he be a Saviour,—an Husband,—a God,—an ALL IN ALL, to mean,—to vile,—to monstrous,— murderous ME!—Alas, why did, why do I, ever exchange this inestimable pearl of great price,—this unbounded treasure of godhead itself,—this infinite Lover, nay, LOVE,—for that which is of no, of worse than no value?—Why despise eternal LOVE, for the sake of a transient shadow?—of a taste of gall and wormwood?—of vanity and vexation of spirit?——Alas, why doth ever my heart turn from him? Why do my desires after him ever cool or flag?—Why is my love, my life, ever unanswerable to his unchangeable excellency and kindness?—— When these INFINITE THREE are ever with me,—are all my own,—why am I not always ravished with their loves?—Why am I not ever listening to their voice, and pouring out my heart into their bosom? Why doth not my soul talk with them, when I sit down, and when I rise up?——Have these honoured, these true and faithful, these unchangeable THREE, by solemn oath, attested and confirmed every promise of the new covenant, that I might have strong consolation and good hope through grace? Dare I then stagger at the promises through unbelief, and not be strong in the faith, giving glory to God? ——O thrice happy new-covenant state, in which the Father, the Son, and the Holy Ghost undertake all for ME,—perform all for, and in ME,—and are ALL IN ALL to ME!——Thrice happy heaven, where the glittering vanities of creation shall be for ever forgotten, and a three-one redeeming God shall be for ever seen,—for ever known,—for ever immediately enjoyed as MY GOD, and MY ALL IN ALL.

CHAP. III.

Of the DECREES *and* PURPOSES *of* GOD.

GOD acts on himself in contemplating, loving, and delighting in himself; and in the persons of the Godhead knowing, loving, delighting in, and consulting with each other, Mat. xi. 27. John i. 17. iii. 35. Col. i. 13. Zech. vi. 13. Isa. xlviii. 16. But few hints of this agency on himself, except in so far as it terminates on his creatures, are revealed to us in Scripture.——His agency respecting his creatures includes his *forming a plan* of his conduct in his own mind in his *purpose* or *decree*,—and his *execution of that plan* in his works of *Creation* and *Providence.*

Nothing can be more evident, than that God, in his purpose, has fixed the whole plan of his works. 1. From the perfection of his nature. If his knowledge be infinite and unchangeable, he must from eternity have known every thing as perfectly as he ever can do in time. If the whole existence, nature, form, and every motion or act of every creature, depend on his sovereign will, he could have no knowledge how to make and manage them but from his own purpose. Abstracting from it, they might have been, or not been,—might have existed in this, or in a thousand other different forms, or conditions.—No placing of creatures in any supposable circumstances can infallibly secure any particular behaviour.—Of the angels who attended Jehovah in heaven, some stood fast, and others fell from their first estate of perfect holiness and happiness, 1 Tim. v. 21. Psal. ciii. 20. Jude 6. 2 Pet. ii. 4. How many men have, like Jacob and Esau, lain in the same womb, even at the same time, and had the same patterns and education, and yet their behaviour and their end have been exceedingly different, Gen. xxv. —xxviii. Rom. ix. Heb. xii. 15—17. Mal. i. 2, 4. If God be *infinitely wise*, how could he, in a random manner, commence and carry on such an important work, so closely connected with an infinitely glorious end? How could he but so plan his work, that all the parts of it might harmoniously promote his general and particular ends? If he be of one mind, which none can change, he, in his purpose, must have unalterably fixed every thing which he effects in his work, Job xxiii. 13. If he be *almighty*, no apprehended opposition could deter him from peremptorily fixing his plan; and no unruly free-will could defeat his intentions. 2. The manifold, marvellous, comely, and profitable connections of an infinity of dissimilar creatures, and the exact answerableness of each to its respective ends; nay, all the marks of infinite wisdom, power, holiness, justice, goodness, and truth, which are to be found in the works of creation and providence, fully manifest, that they have been regulated by a fixed plan, which is exactly executed. 3. In Scripture, we find God's fixed plan of conduct frequently mentioned under the several designations of his WILL; APPOINTMENT; DECREE; PURPOSE; FORE-ORDINATION; GOOD PLEASURE; THOUGHT; COUNSEL; FORE-KNOWLEDGE, Dan. iv. 35. Eph. i. 5, 9, 11. Rev. xvii. 17.——1 Thess. v. 9. 1 Pet. ii. 8. Acts ii. 23. iv. 28. Luke xxii. 22, 29.——Psalm ii. 7. cxlviii. 6. Dan. iv. 17, 24. Zeph. ii. 2. Job xxxviii. 10.——Rom. viii. 28. ix. 11. Eph. i. 9, 11. iii. 11. 2 Tim. i. 9. Jer. iv. 28. xlix. 20. Isa. xiv. 24, 27. xlvi. 10.——Rom. iii. 25. viii. 29, 30. ix. 23. 1 Pet. i. 20. Mat. xxv. 34.——Eph. i. 5, 11. Luke xii. 32. Phil. ii. 13. 2 Thess. i. 11.—Psal. xxxiii. 11. xl. 5. xcii. 5. Isa. lv. 8, 9. xiv. 24. Jer. xxix. 11.——Isa. v. 19. xxviii. 29. xl. 13, 14. xlvi. 10, 11.—— Rom. viii. 29. xi. 2. Acts xv. 18. 1 Pet. i. 2. 4. Nothing more clearly manifests the existence of a divine decree, than God's circumstantiated predictions of an infinity of future events even the most contingent, and his exact fulfilment thereof, for almost six thousand years past, Amos iii. 7. Mat. viii. 17. John xix. 36, &c.

The inseparable connection between God's plan and his execution of it, with the necessarily exact conformity of the one to the other, which his perfections require, his word asserts, and his works plainly manifest, render it utterly impossible to offer any objection against his decrees, which will not equally militate against the actual facts in his works of creation and providence. On this, therefore, we ought particularly to insist in answering every cavil against the peremptory nature of his purpose.——If we find it undeniably manifest, that, in his providence, he hath permitted sin to enter into, or abound in the world; and that particular persons, by far the greatest part of mankind, apparently die in their sins, multitudes of them having never so much as heard of the way of salvation through Christ,—how absurd to deny, that God purposed to permit sin thus to enter and abound?—or to contend, that all men are equally predestinated to everlasting life?—or, that Christ died equally for them all, in order to purchase it for them?—If thousands of men be dying every day, and thus entering into an eternity of inconceivable happiness or misery, how absurd to assert, that God, in his plan, hath fixed nothing relative to the circumstances or the issue of their death?—How can we, without blasphemy, ascribe headlong unconcerted work to the Most High?——This inseparable connection between God's purpose and the execution of it, also manifests, that, in both, he must carry on the same design of *glorifying* himself and *doing good* to his creatures, especially to his favourite people, Prov. xvi. 4.

OF THE DECREES AND PURPOSES OF GOD.

Rom. xi. 36. ix. 22, 23. viii. 28, 30. Eph. i. 6. Isa. xliii. 3, 4, 21. xliv. 28. 2 Pet. iii. 9. 1 Cor. iii. 22.——God's plan, though first in order of nature, being only manifested to us by his word and works, our whole conduct must be regulated by these, not in the least by his unknown purpose.

Every thing which was made in creation, or which happens in providence, was fore-ordained in the decree of God in that precise form, Acts xv. 18. xvii. 26. Eph. i. 11. Isa. xlvi. 10, 11. xiv. 24, 27.—the most contingent and wicked not excepted, Gen. l. 20. xlv. 5, 7. Acts ii. 23, 24. iv. 27, 28. And hence so many of them were foretold, Gen. iii. 14—19. iv. 12. vi. vii. viii. ix. xii. 2, 3, 7. xiii. 15—17. xv. 4—7, 13—21. xvi. 10—12. xvii. 4—8, 16—21. xviii. 10, 14, 18. xix. 13. xx. 12, 13. xxii. 17, 18. xxv. 23. xxvii. 28, 29, 39, 40. xxviii. 13—15. xxxvii. 7—10. xl. 13, 19. xli. 25—32. xlviii. xlix. Exod. iii.—xvii. Lev. xxvi. Deut. xxviii.—xxxiii. Josh. i. Judges ii. iv. vi. vii. 1 Sam. ii. iii. viii. xiii. xv. xvi. 2 Sam. vii. 1 Kings ix. xi. xiii. xiv. xvi. xvii. xix. xxii. 2 Kings vii. x. xiii. xxi. Psal. ii. xxi. xxii. xlv. xlvii. lxvii.—lxix. lxxii. xlvi. —c. cx. cxxxii. Isa. i. to Mal. iv. Mat. xxiii.— xxv. 1 Tim. iv. 2 Tim. iii. iv. 2 Pet. ii. iii. 2 Thess. i. ii. Rev. v.—xxii.

The form and duration of every man's life, with the time and manner of his death, are precisely fixed in the decree of God. 1. The Scripture plainly affirms this, Job vii. 1. xiv. 5. Acts xvii. 26, 28. Eccl. iii. 1, 2. v. 17. ix. 12. Psal. xxxi. 15. cxxxix. 16. xxxix. 4, 5. 2. God hath frequently foretold the manner, the time, and the means of man's life or death,—as *of the life* of Ishmael, Gen. xvi. 12. Isaac, Gen. xvii. xviii. Jacob and Esau, Gen. xxv. 23. Moses, Exod. iv. Israelites after his death, Deuteron. xxviii.—xxxiii. Samson, Judg. xiii. Saul, 1 Sam. viii. ix. x. xiii. xv. Solomon, 2 Sam. vii. 12—15. Josiah, 1 Kings xiii. 2; Cyrus, Isa. xliv. 26—28. xlv. 1—4, 13. xlvi. 11. and especially of CHRIST, Isa. vii. 14. Jer. xxiii. 5, 6. xxxi. 22. Mic. v. 2. Mal. iii. 1, 2, &c.——And of the death of the wicked inhabitants of the old world, Gen. vi. 3, 7. of the Sodomites, Gen. xix. 13, 17. of the murmuring and rebellious Israelites, Num. xiv. xvi. of David's infant, 2 Sam. xii. 14. of Abijah, 1 Kings xiv. 12. of Ahab and Jezebel, 1 Kings xxii. 28. xxi. 22, 23, 29. of Ahaziah, 2 Kings i. 4. of Belshazzar, Dan. v. 25, 26. of Peter, John xxi. 18. of Paul, 2 Tim. iv. 6, 7. of CHRIST, Luke xiii. 32. xviii. 32, 33. John vii. 30. xii. 33. xiii. 1. xviii. 1, 13. Psal. xxii. lxix. Isa. liii. of Eli's sons, 1 Sam. ii. 34. of David's subjects, 2 Sam. xxiv. 15. of Sennacherib's army, Isa. x. xxix.—xxxiii. xxxvii. xxx. 27—33. of the Jews by the Romans, Isa. lxv. 12. Deut. xxviii. 16—68. Lev. xxvi. Psal. xxi. 8—12. Mat. xxiii. xxiv. of the heathen emperors of Rome, and their armies, Psal. cx.

5, 6. Rev. vi. 12—17.———But, to prevent objections, it must be observed, 1. That men's life is said to be *shortened*, when it doth not extend to an ordinary length, or to that of which their constitution seemed capable, Job xv. 32. xvii. 1. Psal. lv. 23. cii. 23, 24. Prov. x. 27. Eccl. vii. 17. 2. That *prolonging* of men's life, denotes merely the long enjoyment of it, but not any lengthening of it beyond the measure or period fixed for it in God's purpose, 1 Kings iii. 14. Exod. xx. 12. Deut. iv. 40. xxx. 18. Prov. x. 27.—Hezekiah had fifteen years added to his life, after a mortal disease had threatened his dissolution,—but not one moment added to the time of his life, as allotted him in God's decree, Isa. xxxviii. 1, 5.

All things which come to pass in creation or in providence, were decreed by God, 1. *From all eternity*, Acts xv. 18. All of them, in innumerable respects, are connected with our redemption through Christ, which, from all eternity, was purposed and prepared for by God, 1 Cor. ii. 7. Eph. i. 4. Rom. viii. 28—32. 1 Cor. iii. 22, 23. 2. *Most wisely*, the most proper and important ends being fixed together with all the forms and connections of things, in that manner which might best promote these ends, Prov. xvi. 4. Rom. xi. 33, 34. Hence the decrees are called a *counsel*, Isa. xlvi. 10, 11. Eph. i. 11. Heb. vi. 17. 3. *Most absolutely*, according to his own good pleasure, without any dependence on the free will or agency of any creature, as a cause of his purpose, Jer. xviii. 4, 6. Mat. xi. 26. Rom. ix. 20, 21. Eph. i. 5, 9. Isa. xlvi. 10. But as men's moral behaviour is often a mean for its execution, his promises and threatenings in his word, often run in a conditional form, Isa. i. 19, 20. Lev. xxvi. Deut. iv.—xxx. Ezek. xviii. xxxiii. 4. In a *fixed* and *unalterable* manner, that every thing and every circumstance of it must necessarily happen precisely according to the plan of the decree, Psalm xxxiii. 11. cxv. 3. cxxxv. 6. Prov. xix. 21. xxi. 30. Num. xxiii. 19. 1 Sam. xv. 29. Heb. vi. 17. Eph. i. 9, 11. Acts xv. 18. Mat. xviii. 7. 1 Cor. xi. 19. Acts ii. 23, 24. iv. 28. Isa. xiv. 24, 27. xlvi. 10.

The PREDESTINATION of angels and men to their everlasting state of holiness and happiness, or of sin and misery, and fixing all the diversified means thereof, are the principal matter of the divine decree.—The Scriptures plainly manifest, that some, nay many, particular ANGELS, were predestinated to everlasting holiness and happiness, to the praise and glory of God's bounty and love, though, as they sinned not, they were not chosen *in* Christ, nor *to salvation*, 1 Tim. v. 21. Dan. vii. 10. Rev. v. 11. Psal. ciii. 20, 21;—and that others were passed by,—to be permitted to fall into sin, and continue, and more and more abound in it; and on account of it, to be for ever justly punished with everlasting destruction, to the praise of the glory of his holiness and justice, Mat. xxv. 41. By this purpose, as well as by their own sinful corruption and guilt, and the curse of God lying upon them on account of it, they are reserved as in chains till the last judgment, Jude 6. 2 Pet. ii. 4. But the predestination of men, in which we are more immediately concerned, is more fully revealed in the Scriptures.

It is not agreed among divines, how God considered men in his predestinating purpose,—Whether as *creatable* and *fallible;* or as *to be created* and *to fall;* or as *created* and *fallen;* or as *converted;* or as having persevered in holiness till their death. The absurdity of the two last views will hereafter be exposed. The difference of the first three views, appears to me to originate in men making their own manner of thinking on the point, an exact exemplar to that of God's, and to be really reconcileable. In God's infinite mind, his whole purpose of predestination is but one simple thought, which, by our finite and weak minds, may be apprehended in the four following steps: 1. His purpose of manifesting the glory of his own perfections, particularly of his mercy and justice in his dealings with men. In respect of this, men can only be considered as *creatable* and *fallible*. 2. His purpose of creating men and permitting them to fall in their common Head, in order to promote or occasion the glorification of his mercy or justice. In respect of this step, men must be considered as *to be created* and *to fall*. 3. His fore-appointment of some particular men for the manifestation of his *mercy*, and others as objects of the manifestation of the glory of his *justice*. In respect of this step, men must be viewed as *created* and *fallen*. 4. His fixing the proper means for rendering the former vessels of mercy, and the latter vessels of his everlasting, but just indignation. In respect of this step, men must be considered as *chosen* or as *passed by*.——In these views, Supralapsarians, who reckon the objects of predestination, men, as *creatable* and *fallible*, or to *be created* and *to fall*,—and Sublapsarians, who reckon men as *created* and *fallen* to be the *formal objects* of it, may cordially agree.—The glory of God's perfections, as the last end of the whole purpose, is first presented to view; and the decree appears as *whole* and *uniform* as Supralapsarians need wish. And men, as sinners, are chosen to salvation in Christ, as Sublapsarians contend.——The above representation also plainly distinguishes God's predestinating purpose into its two important branches, ELECTION and REPROBATION.

In Scripture we find God *electing* men to some particular *office*,—Saul, David, and Cyrus, to be kings, 1 Sam. x. 1, 24. xv, 17. xvi. 1, 6—13. 2 Sam. vii. 8. Psalm lxxviii. 70. Isa.

xliv. 28. xlv. 1;—Bezaleel and Aholiab to frame and rear up his tabernacle, and Solomon to build his temple, Exod. xxxi. 2—6. 1 Kings v. 5. viii. 19. 1 Chron. xvii. 11, 12. xxii. 9, 10;—Aaron and his sons to be priests, Exod. xxviii. Heb. v. 4;—the Levites to be ministers of his sanctuary, Num. i. 49, 50. iii. iv. viii. xvii. xviii. Peter and Andrew, James and John, &c. to be his apostles, Mat. x. 1—4. John vi. 70. Acts ix. 15. Eph. iv. 11.—We also find him electing the whole Israelitish nation to be his peculiar people, typical of the gospel church, and of his redeemed multitude, Exod. xix. 5, 6. Lev. xx. 26. Deut. vii. 6. xvi. 15. xxvi. 18. Isa. xlviii. 10. 1 Pet. ii. 9. Rev. vii. 9.——— But there is also a *divine election* of some men to *everlasting life*, to the praise of the glory of his grace. 1. Some men plainly appear as chosen to more than membership in the visible church. Before the Jewish nation was completely unchurched, some of them were a chosen generation, while others, according to the determination of God, stumbled at Jesus Christ, to their own everlasting ruin, 1 Pet. ii. 8, 9. Mat. xxiv. 22, 24, 31. Luke xviii. 7. Rom. ix. 27. xi. 5, 7. Isa viii. 14, 15, 16, 18. Some poor in this world were chosen, rich in faith, and heirs of the heavenly kingdom, James ii. 5. 2. *Many,* who were called by the gospel to salvation in their external church-state, were not chosen, while a *few* were, Mat. xx. 16. xxii. 14. 3. Some men are by God remarkably distinguished from all others,—as *enrolled* in the Lamb's *book of life,* and *in heaven,* Isa. iv. 3. Dan. xii. 1. Luke x. 20. Phil. iv. 3. Rev. iii. 5. xiii. 8. xx. 12. xxi. 27;—as separated from this, and pertaining to another world or kingdom, John xv. 19. xvii. 9, 16. Mat. xiii. 38. Mark iv. 11. Num. xxiii. 9. Isa. xliii. 21. lxiii. 18. 1 Pet. ii. 9. Luke xx. 35;—as persons, of whom the Jews, when called *children of the kingdom,* are types, Mat. viii. 12.———They are represented as sprung from another root, and of another race or kindred; being of God, 1 John iv. 4---6. v. 19. John viii. 42, 44, 47;— of *the light* or *day,* Luke xvi. 8. 1 Thess. v. 5.---*from above,* John iii. 3, 5, 6. viii. 32.---as subject to another Head, Christ, and God reconciled in him, Isa. lxiii. 19. Mat. xxiii. 8, 10. John x. 3, 26, 27. vi. 37. v. 40;—as perfectly secured from condemnation, and inseparable from the love of Christ and his Father, Rom. viii. 33—39. John x. 28, 29. xiii. 1. Jude 1. 2 Tim. ii. 19. Isa. xlix. 15, 16;—as appointed to salvation, 1 Thess. i. 4, 5. v. 9. 2 Thess. ii. 13. 2 Tim. ii. 9, 10, 19. Mat. xx. 23. xxiv. 31. xxv. 34. Luke xii. 32. and appointed to faith as the mean of receiving it,—and hence men believe or not, as they are elected to eternal life or not, Tit. i. 1, 2. 2 Thess. iii. 2. Acts xiii. 48. John x. 26, 27. Rom. xi. 7. viii. 28—30. 2 Tim. i. 9. ii. 19. 2 Thess. ii. 13. 1 Thess. i. 4, 5.

—— It was not merely in their posterity, or in their external circumstances, but primarily in their persons, as connected with spiritual and eternal salvation, that God made a difference between Jacob and Esau, and he made Esau's behaviour promote the spiritual, if not also the temporal happiness of Jacob as well as of his seed, Gen. xxv. 23, 33. xxvii. xxviii. xxxii. xxxiii. xxxvi. 6. Mal. ii. 2, 3. Rom. ix. 11—13.

In the *decree of election*, God doth not fix *conditions* of eternal life, and choose such as will fulfil them; but he sets apart *particular persons* to be infallibly made partakers of eternal salvation. 1. Particular persons, as hath been just stated, have their *names written in the book of life*, Luke x. 20. Rev. xiii. 8. xx. 12. xxi. 27. Isa. iv. 3, &c. 2. Some men are represented as particularly and personally chosen to everlasting life, Eph. i. 4, 5, 6. Mat. xx. 16. xxii. 14. John x. 3, 26, 27. xiii. 18. xvii. 9. vi. 37. Acts xiii. 48. xviii. 10. Rom. viii. 28—30. ix. 13, 23. xi. 5, 7. 1 Thess. i. 4. v. 9. 2 Thess. ii. 13. 1 Pet. i. 2. ii. 9. 2 Tim. i. 9. ii. 10. 3. The infallible and unalterable connection between election, redemption, and eternal salvation, necessarily requires that those very persons, who are actually saved, must have been elected to obtain that salvation, Psalm xxxiii. 11. Isa. xiv. 24, 27. xlvi. 10. Rom. viii. 28—39. ix. 11—13, 23. John x. 15, 16, 27—29.

God's election of these particular persons is ABSOLUTE, proceeding wholly and only from his own infinitely wise and sovereign will and good pleasure; and altogether independent on their foreseen faith or good works. 1. The Scripture represents his election of them as merely depending on his own will, and as purposed in himself, Luke xii. 32. x. 21. Mat. xi. 25, 26. Rom. ix. 11—13, 16, 18. xi. 5, 6. Eph. i. 5, 9, 11. Deut. vii. 8. ix. 4. x. 15. 2 Tim. i. 9. 2. God, who chooses them, is absolutely sovereign in his disposal of his favours, Gen. vi. 5. viii. 21. Dan. iv. 35. Isa. lvii. 17, 18. xliii. 24, 25. Rom. v. 20, 21. ix. 15, 16, 18, 20, 21. Psalm cxv. 3. cxxxv. 6. Job xxxiii. 13. 3. He could foresee no moral goodness in fallen and corrupted men, as moving Him to elect them to everlasting happiness, Gen. vi. 5. viii. 21. Psalm v. 9, 10. xiv. 1—4. Isa. lix. 1—15. Rom. i. 21—32. iii. 10—19, 23. v. 12. viii. 7, 8. Tit. iii. 3. Jer. xiii. 23. xvii. 9. Eph. ii. 1—3. iv. 17—19. Job xiv. 4. xv. 14, 16. Mat. xv. 19. 4. No true faith or holy obedience, but what God himself works in them, can be found in any man, Phil. i. 29. ii. 13. Eph. ii. 4—10. 2 Thess. i. 11. James i. 17. 1 Cor. iv. 7. 2 Cor. iii. 5. Isa. xxvi. 12. Psalm lvii. 2. Now God's own work in time can never be the condition of his choosing us before time to eternal life. 5. Our faith and holiness are the fruits of God's election of us; and hence can never be the cause or condition of it, Acts xiii. 48. 1 Thess. i. 4, 5. 2 Thess. ii.

13. John viii. 47. x. 26, 27. Eph. i. 4. 1 Pet. i. 2.   6. Our faith and holiness are properly parts of our salvation largely taken, and evidences that we are in the state and begun possession of it. And hence they are not so much as *proper conditions* of salvation, but means of receiving or improving it, and of preparing for the full enjoyment of it, Tit. iii. 5—7. Rom. vii. 4. vi. 14. How absurd then to suppose them conditions of God's electing us to that salvation! 7. If God's election of men to everlasting life depended on his foresight of their faith and good works, his redeeming love could be no such distinguished favour as the Scripture represents it, John iii. 16. 1 John iii. 1. iv. 9, 10, 19. Jer. iii. 19. xxxi. 3. Job xxxv. 7. xli. 11. Deut. x. 11. 1 Cor. i. 29. iv. 7. Eph. i. 6. ii. 7. Rom. ix. 15, 16, 18. v. 8, 20, 21.   8. So far are our good works from being the conditions upon which God elected us to everlasting life, that the making them procuring causes of our salvation is represented as altogether eversive of the grace of God therein manifested, Rom. iv. 4. xi. 6. ix. 16. Gal. ii. 21. v. 2, 4.

Men are chosen by God to everlasting life *in Jesus Christ*, as their representing Head. 1. Our election is expressly represented as IN him, as our new-covenant Head, and the great mean of the execution of that decree, Eph. i. 4. iii. 11. 2 Tim. i. 9. Tit. i. 2.   2. The effects of our election are all enjoyed in Christ—as redemption, Eph. i. 7. Col. i. 14. 1 Cor. i. 30. Rom. iii. 24, 25;—effectual calling, Phil. iii. 14.—justification, Isa. xlv. 24, 25. 1 Cor. i. 30. 2 Cor. v. 21.—adoption, Gal. iii. 26. —regeneration and sanctification, Eph. ii. 10. 1 Cor. i. 2. Acts xxvi. 18. 1 Cor. i. 30.—preservation in grace, Jude 1. Col. iii. 3. John xiv. 19. x. 28. xv. 5, 7.—spiritual comfort, John xiv. 18. 2 Cor. i. 5. 2 Thess. ii. 16, 17.—and glorification, Rom. viii. 15—18. Eph. ii. 6. Isa. xlv. 17, 25. lx. 19. Col. iii. 3, 4.   3. Without supposing our election to everlasting life in Christ as our Head, God's putting our stock of holiness and happiness in Adam, as our covenant-head, could not be so clearly vindicated, Rom. v. 12—21. 1 Cor. xv. 21, 22.—Nor does it appear, how we could have been recovered, quickened, justified, or sanctified by him, if we had not been chosen IN him, Rom. iii. 10—26. John v. 25, 26. Acts iii. 15, 26. Rom. viii. 1, 2. 1 John v. 12. John xiv. 19. Col. i. 19. ii. 9, 10, 13. Eph. ii. 10. iii. 17, 19. Heb. ii. 12—16. 1 Cor. vi. 17. Tit. iii. 5.——But, though we were chosen IN Christ as our Head, yet his mediatorial office and work are not the cause of our election, but only the cause of that salvation which we were chosen to obtain. 1. It hath been proved, that our election proceeds from the mere sovereign will of God.—It was of his mere free favour, that any men were elected to everlasting life. It was of his mere good pleasure, that such particular persons, and not others, were elected, Mat. xi. 25, 26. Luke xii. 32. Rom. ix. 11—23. 1 Cor. iv. 7. i. 25—30. 2. While Christ himself is, in God's electing purpose, chosen as our Head, his mediation is appointed in it, as the mean of executing it, and as the purchasing, procuring, and applying cause of our salvation therein decreed, Isa. xlii. 1—7. xlix. 1—6. 1 Pet. i. 18—21. John iii. 16—18. 1 John iii. 5, 8. iv. 9, 10. 3. Christ died for men considered as sinful in themselves, but loved of God, and elected to everlasting life,—that they might obtain it in a way consistent with his honour, Mat. i. 21. John x. 10, 14, 15. xv. 13. Eph. v. 2, 23, 25. Isa. xlix. 3. xlii. 21.

Men were thus elected in Christ to everlasting life *from all eternity.* 1. It hath been proved, that God decreed all things from all eternity, Acts xv. 18. 2. Christ was set up as the mediatorial Head of elect men from all eternity, Psalm ii. 7, 8. 1 Pet. i. 20. Prov. viii. 23—31. Mic. v. 2. John xvii. 24. 3. Elect men were foreknown and chosen to salvation before the foundation of the world, Rom. viii. 29. ix. 11, 23. Eph. i. 4. 2 Tim. i. 9. Tit. i. 2. Mat. xxv. 34. Rev. xiii. 8. Jer. xxxi. 3. 2 Thess. ii. 13.——How daring then to give God the lie, and contend, that he elects them only in time, at their death, &c. as their behaviour deserves! And how absurd to assert, that *the beginning* from which the Thessalonians were chosen, means the beginning of the gospel period.--It is certain, they did not hear the gospel, till not a few years after our Saviour's ascension, and the first erection of the gospel church, Acts ii.—xvii.

God's purpose of election is *unchangeable,*—none who are elected can fall short of the grace or glory decreed for them, and none that are not elected can obtain it. 1. No unforeseen reason of alteration can occur; nor can any change happen in his own love, power, wisdom, or equity, Acts xv. 18. Psalm cxlvii. 5. Isa. xlvi. 10. Mal. iii. 6. James i. 17. 2. The Scripture peremptorily declares, that all those very persons that were elected, shall obtain that salvation to which they were chosen, Rom. viii. 28—39. 2 Thess. ii. 13. 1 Thess. v. 9, 10. iv. 17. v. 23, 24. Eph. i. 4. John vi. 37. xvii. 9, 12. Rom. xi. 7. Acts ii. 47. xiii. 48. 2 Tim. ii. 19. Isa. xlvi. 10. xlix. 14, 15. xlv. 17. liv. 8--10. Rev. iii. 4, 5. Mat. xxv. 34. Luke x. 20. John x. 27—29. Heb. vi. 17—20.——But to anticipate objections, it must be observed, 1. That men whose names were never written in the *book of life,* may have that plainly manifested, Rev. xxii. 19. 2. Men may be really blotted out of the *book of the living* on earth,—out of God's comfortable providential care,—out of the number of the visible members of his church,—or out of temporal life, Psalm lxix. 28. cxxxix. 16. lxxxvii. 6. Ezek. xiii. 9. Neh. vii. 64. Exod. xxxii. 32. without any blotting them out of God's purpose of election to everlasting life. 3. By frequent and vigorous actings of faith,—by an holy conversation, —and by much impartial self-examination, we may render our election more certainly evident to our own souls, while we thus enjoy the fruits of it, 2 Pet. i. 4—10. 1 Thess. i. 4, 5. Eph. i. 3—9.—But nothing can render it more certain and fixed *in itself*, as a purpose of the unchangeable God, Job xxiii. 13. Psalm xxxiii. 11. Isa. xiv. 24, 27. xlvi. 10. Rom. ix. 11. Heb. vi. 17, 18.

God's decree of election may, therefore, be thus described: An act, in which the eternal, unchangeable, infinitely wise, gracious, powerful, faithful, and sovereign God, intending to manifest to men the glory of his own perfections, particularly of his power, wisdom, sovereignty, and free grace, Rom. xi. 33. Eph. iii. 10. Mat. xi. 26. xx. 15, 16. Rom. ix. 15, 16, 18—23. xi. 35, 36. Eph. i. 5, 6. 1 Pet. ii. 9.—hath in his love foreknown and fore-chosen to the enjoyment of eternal salvation and all its benefits, Rom. viii. 29, 30. 1 Pet. i. 2. 2 Tim. ii. 19. John iii. 16. Rom. v. 8, 21. ix. 13. 1 John iv. 9, 10. Isa. xlv. 17. 1 Cor. i. 30.—some persons of mankind,—the smaller number,—and whom he pleased,—as permitted, or to be permitted to fall into sin and misery, from which they could not recover themselves, Mat. xx. 16. xxii. 14. 2 Tim. ii. 19. John x. 26— 28. xiii. 18. xvii. 6, 9, 12. iii. 16. xv. 19. Rom. viii. 29. ix. 16, 18. v. 8. 10.—and hath predestinated them unto fellowship with, conformity to, adoption through, and joint heirship and eternal happiness in Christ, Eph. i. 3, 4, 5. Rom. viii. 29.— and without being, in the least, moved to it, by any foreseen qualities or acts of theirs, natural or moral,—hath of his own mere will, sovereign grace, and good pleasure, Mat xi. 25, 26. Luke xii. 32. Rom. ix. 11, 15, 16. Eph. i. 5, 6. 2 Tim. i. 9. 1 Cor. i. 26—28.—from all eternity, Mat. xxv. 34. Eph. i. 4. 2 Tim. i. 9. Rev. xiii. 8.—chosen them in Christ as their Head, Prov. viii. 23, 31. Eph. i. 4. 2 Tim. i. 9.—in infinite mercy and compassion hath unalterably ordained and appointed them to be partakers of eternal salvation, life, and happiness through him, Rom. ix. 11, 15, 16, 18, 23. 2 Tim. i. 9. ii. 19. Acts xiii. 48. 1 Thess. v. 9, 10. iv. 17. Isa xlv. 17. Rom. xi. 29.—and hath inscribed their names in his book of life, Luke x. 20. Rev. iii. 5. xvii. 8. xiii. 8. xx. 12. xxi. 27. Phil. iv. 3. Isa. iv. 3.— thus distinguishing them from the rest of mankind, who are left to perish in their sinfulness and misery, 1 Cor. iv. 7. Rom. ix. 11—13. Eph. i. 4.—and hath in that same wise and unchangeable counsel, appointed the mediation of Christ, an interest in his righteousness, effectual calling, faith, and holiness, as means of their obtaining and improving that eternal life,— that so his inflexible justice and infinite mercy may harmoniously shine forth therein, John iii. 16, 17. 1 John iii. 5, 8. iv.

9, 10. John x. 10, 11, 15, 26—29. xvii. 4, 6, 9. Eph. i. 4. v. 2, 23—27. Col. i. 19. ii. 3, 9—13. 2 Tim. i. 9. ii. 10, 19. Isa. xlv. 17, 22, 24, 25. Acts xiii. 48. 2 Thess. ii. 13. Rom. iv. 16. Mark xvi. 16. Heb. xi. 6. xii. 14.

Objec. I. " Such a scheme of election renders God a *respec-*
" *ter* of persons, contrary to Acts x. 34. Job xxxiv. 11, 19.
" Deut. x. 17, 18. 2 Chron. xix. 7. Col. iii. 24, 25. Rom. ii.
" 11. 1 Pet. i. 17." Answ. 1. It no more represents him as a *respecter of persons* than his actual saving of some men, and not of any devils, and his giving to some temporal privileges or eternal salvation, which he doth not bestow on others as deserving. 2. In his purpose of election, God shews no respect to persons on account of their being Jews or Gentiles, poor or rich, great or small, in the world, which is the meaning of these texts, but acts from his own sovereign love and free grace. 3. If God should choose or reprobate, save or damn men, as their free will is pleased to exert itself, then, indeed, he would be a respecter of persons.

Objec. II. " In the declarations of the gospel, which are an
" extract of God's purpose of election, eternal salvation is sus-
" pended on our faith, sincere obedience, and final perseverance
" in holiness, Mark xvi. 16. John iii. 16, 18, 36. Rev. xxii.
" 14. ii. 7, 11, 17, 26, 27, 28. iii. 5, 12, 21. Gal. vi. 9. Mat.
" xxiv. 13. Rom. ii. 7, 10. Isa. i. 19. iii. 10." Answ. 1. Not one of these declarations represents God's electing decree in the conditions of its establishment, but merely exhibits the connection fixed in it between the different fruits of it, or the parts and degrees of salvation. 2. Faith, sincere obedience, and perseverance in holiness, are not *proper conditions* on which our eternal happiness is *suspended;* but being necessary fruits of election, means of, and preparations for happiness, they *characterize* the persons who have been elected and shall be glorified, John x. 27—29. Acts xiii. 48. 1 Thess. i. 4, 5. 2 Thess. ii. 13. 1 Pet. i. 2. Eph. i. 4. Rom. viii. 29, 30.

Objec. III. " An absolute, unconditional, and unchangeable
" election of particular persons to eternal happiness, enervates
" and renders altogether unprofitable the whole preaching and
" ordinances of the gospel, with all the good endeavours of
" mankind, and encourages them to sloth and wickedness,—
" for, if they be elected, they will certainly be saved, do what
" they will; and if they be not elected they will not be saved,
" let them do what they can." Answ. 1. As in this decree the means of happiness are fixed along with, and inseparably from the end, it is highly absurd to contend, that the fixing the end will render the means unnecessary or unprofitable. 2. Even in the common affairs of life, they who believe that God hath unal-

terably fore-ordained all things which come to pass, are as diligent in their lawful employments, and as careful to provide and use food, raiment, houses, medicine, &c. as others who do not. 3. No man hath any reason to expect eternal happiness, but in the way of a diligent attendance on, and improvement of the ordinances of the gospel, public, private, and secret, according to his capacity and opportunity,—and of earnest and persevering endeavours to perfect holiness in the fear of the Lord. Rom. x. 17. Isa. lv. 1—7. Mat. vii. 7, 13, 14. vi. 33. Luke xiii. 24. Prov. viii. 17, 34—36. 2 Pet. i. 3---11. Heb. xi. 6. xii. 14. 1 Cor. xv. 58. 2 Cor. vii. 1. 4. No man can have any evidence of his being elected by God, without an active study of holiness in all manner of conversation, 2 Pet. i. 3---10. 2 Tim. ii. 19. Eph. i. 4. Col. i. 22. 2 Thess. ii. 13. 1 Pet. i. 2. 5. Though our diligent attendance on gospel ordinances, our faith, repentance, or new obedience, cannot, in the least, promote God's making choice of us, and electing us to eternal life, as that was fixed long before we existed,—yet they mightily promote the execution of his electing purpose in our actual enjoyment of all the benefits of that salvation to which we were, from eternity, elected, Phil. ii. 12, 13. 1 Cor. ix. 24---27. xv. 58. Rom. v. 1--- 5. Psalm xix. 11. lxxxiv. 7, 11, 12. Job xvii. 9. Prov. iv. 18. 2 Tim. iv. 7, 8. Rev. iii. 7, 12, 21. 6. It is impossible for men *cordially* to believe the giving, the redeeming, the electing love of God, without being thereby delightfully constrained, and effectually animated to an earnest care of their salvation, and an active study of faith and holiness. Nor are we, the friends of unconditional election, afraid to compare practices with our opponents when they please, if they will but admit the exceeding broad law of God, in both its tables, to be the rule and standard of judgment, 1 Thess. i. 3---10. Gal. ii. 19, 20. 2 Tim. i. 9. ii. 19. 1 Cor. xv. 10. 1 Thess. ii. 1—10.

OBJEC. IV. " An unconditional unalterable election of par-
" ticular persons of mankind to everlasting life, is inconsistent
" with the wisdom, goodness, and integrity of God." ANSW.
1. If God, in providence, bring particular persons of mankind to everlasting life, it is but absurd blasphemy to rail at his fixed election of them to it in his eternal purpose, as if that were contrary to his nature. 2. If it be consistent with the perfections of God to choose particular angels, and render them eternally happy, how can it be inconsistent with them, that some particular men should be elected and rendered eternally happy? 3. Not an *unconditional*, but a *conditional* election of men is manifestly inconsistent with, and disgraceful to God's wisdom, goodness, and integrity. His wisdom is infinitely more brightly displayed in that election which, without hurting a single creature, infallibly secures the salvation of thousands of millions,

Rev. vii. 9. than in that which leaves matters so loose and undetermined, that Christ may die for all men,—intercede to his uttermost for them, and bestow all his ordinances upon them, and the Holy Ghost, with all his might, strive with each of them to no purpose,—their whole happiness depending on the proper exertions *of their free will*, a *carnal mind, enmity against God*, a *heart deceitful above all things, and desperately wicked.—* It is infinitely more kind and gracious, unalterably to purpose to exert his almighty power, and other perfections, in order effectually to bestow that grace and glory, which are necessary to make them for ever holy and happy, upon unnumbered millions, than merely to resolve to give all men an infinitely improbable, nay impossible chance of being happy,—that is, to prepare happiness for them, upon condition that their desperately wicked heart convert itself to believe the gospel, love God, and persevere till death in all holy obedience to him; and meanwhile scarcely give the hundredth part of them the smallest hint of his proposals.—God in his word hath candidly declared, that of the *many* who are called by the gospel, *few* are chosen, and that *few* find the way that leadeth to eternal life, while *many* walk in the broad way which leadeth to destruction, Mat. xx. 16. xxii. 14. vii. 13, 14. and in Christian countries *few, very few*, bear the characters of saintship marked in his word.—How can our affirming that which is so manifest in his word and in his providence, be an impeachment of his candour?—If, in the declarations of the gospel, he assure men that it is both their duty and interest to believe in Jesus Christ for their eternal salvation, how is it an impeachment of his candour, to maintain that this indispensable rule of our duty to him is not necessarily the rule of his providential conduct toward us?—or to maintain, that he cannot inform us of our duty, without divulging to us his most secret purposes? It is time enough for us to claim the same rule of conduct with Jehovah, when our free will hath transformed our mean and desperately wicked nature into true Godhead.

II. With respect to the REPROBATION of men, it may be observed, I. That God purposed to *permit sin*. 1. This the Scripture expressly affirms, Gen. l. 20. Acts ii. 23, 24. iv. 27, 28; hence, 2. He hath foretold multitudes of evil actions, Gen. xv. 16. Deut. xxxi. 16, 20, 29. xxxii. 6, 15—21. Isa. i. v. x. Jer. xxv. Rev. vi. viii. ix. xi.—xiii. 2 Tim. iii. 1—6, 13. 2 Thess. ii. 3—12. 3. In time God actually permits much sin, Acts xiv. 16. 2 Thess. ii. 9—11. Gen. l. 20. xlv. 5, 7. Psalm lxxxi. 12. Rom. i. 21—32. No sin, which hath been, or is in the world, can be said to have happened without his foreknowledge of it, Acts xv. 18. Isa. xlvi. 10, 11. Psalm cxlvii. 5. or, notwithstanding all that his infinite power could have done to prevent and hinder it, Gen. xviii. 14. Jer. xxxii. 17, 27. Matth. xix. 26. Nay, his permission of it tends to the honour of his absolute sovereignty, infinite wisdom, holiness, and justice,—and to the advantage of established angels and men. II. God in his predestinating purpose, left some men UNELECTED to perish in their sin, to the praise of the glory of his justice. 1. The Scriptures plainly declare this, Prov. xvi. 4. (where PAHHHAL, *hath made*, signifies to *appoint, ordain, prepare*, Exod. xv. 17. Psal. xxxi. 19. even as POIEO, Mark iii. 14. Heb. iii. 2.) 1 Pet. ii. 8. (where *stumbling* denotes sinning) Jude 4. (where KRIMA, *condemnation*, denotes the sinful cause of condemnation or what is *criminal*) John ix. 39. Rev. xiii. 8. 2 Cor. iv. 3, 4. Rom. ix. 13—22. 1 Thess. v. 9. 2 Thess. ii. 10—12, 13. 2. In God's providence, which is an exact copy of his decree, Acts xv. 18. Isa. xlvi. 10. Eph. i. 11. Psalm xxxiii. 11. multitudes appear plainly left to perish in their sin, Matth. vii. 13, 14. 2 Thess. ii. 10—12. i. 8, 9. Rev. xiii. 3, 8. xvii. 17. Psalm ix. 17. Millions of fallen angels had never a Saviour provided for them, Jude 6. 2 Pet. ii. 4. Hundreds of millions of men, for many ages, have never been informed of the method of redemption through Christ, Psalm cxlvii. 19, 20. Prov. xxix. 18. Eph. ii. 12. Acts xiv. 16. xvii. 30.—The far greater part of those that hear the gospel, or at least are called Christians, are, by their rejection of it, ripened for hell, Matth. xx. 16. xxii. 14. vii. 13, 14. John x. 26. xii. 39, 40. 2 Cor. iv. 3, 4. Isa. vi. 9, 10. Acts xxviii. 26, 27. Phil. iii. 18, 19. 2 Tim. iii. 1—5. Rev. xiii. 3, 8. xiv. 9—11. III. It follows that certain particular persons have been, in God's decree, appointed to wrath, Mal. i. 2, 3. Rom. ix. 11—18. 1 Thess. v. 9. Jude 4. were never favourably known by God, Matth. vii. 23. were never appointed or ordained to eternal life, Rev. xiii. 8. xvii. 8.—Nay, particular election of some necessarily infers a particular reprobation of others.—In which act of reprobation is included, 1. God's *passing by* certain persons, leaving them unelected, Matth. vii. 23. Rev. xiii. 8. xvii. 8. 2. A pre-appointment of them to undergo his just wrath, to be inflicted on them as the punishment of their foreseen sinfulness, 1 Thess. v. 9. But it must be remarked, that though men's sins be foreseen and viewed in God's pre-appointment of them unto wrath, as the cause of their condemnation and punishment, yet they are not the cause of his leaving them unelected to perish in their sin; for, 1. Reprobates are no worse by nature than those that are elected, 1 Cor. i. 26, 27. iv. 7. John xiii. 18. Eph. ii. 1—3. 2. Their practice was foreseen as no worse than that of many elected persons before their conversion, 1 Cor. vi. 9, 10, 11. Eph. ii. 1—13. 1 Tim. i. 13, 16. Tit. ii. 3—6. 3. The wicked-

OF THE DECREES AND PURPOSES OF GOD. 161

ness of unelected men is represented as the consequence, though not the proper effect of their reprobation, 2 Cor. iv. 3. John x. 26. xii. 39. 1 Pet. ii. 8, 9. Jude 4. Rev. xiii. 8.

REPROBATION may therefore be described, " A simple act of an independent, sovereign, infinitely wise, powerful, righteous, and holy God,—whose thoughts are infinitely high, his judgments unsearchable, and his ways past finding out, Isa. lv. 9. xl. 13. Rom. xi. 33, 34. Psalm xcii. 5. cxlvii. 5.—in which he, in his eternal and unchangeable counsel, Matth. xxv. 34, 41. Rom. ix. 11. Jam. i. 17. Isa. xlvi. 10. Heb. vi. 17. Eph. i. 11. Psalm xxxiii. 11.—intending to manifest the glory of his absolute sovereignty, almighty power, unsearchable wisdom, unconceivable patience,—and particularly of his infinite holiness and avenging justice, Rom. xi. 36. ix. 11, 15—22. Mat. xx. 15. Rom. xi. 33, 34. ii. 4. Isa. v. 4, 16. Prov. xvi. 4.—did, according to his own good pleasure, purpose in himself, to leave many particular men, no worse in themselves than others,—in their estate of sin and misery, into which they were to be permitted to fall, Rom. ix. 6, 7, 11, 15—18, 29, 21. xi. 20, 21, 22. v. 12. Eph. ii. 3. Matth. xxiv. 40, 41;—and never to know them in the way of peculiar regard, or love them with any good will, or pity them in order to their effectual recovery,—nor to choose, predestinate, distinguish from others, or ordain them to eternal life, Matth. vii. 23. Rom. viii. 29, 30. ix. 13, 15. Mal. i. 2, 3. John xiii. 18. 1 Cor. iv. 7. Acts xiii. 48. 1 Thess. v. 9, —or write their names in his *book of life*, or set them apart for his *sheep, people, children*, or *vessels of mercy*, John x. 26. Rom. ix. 6, 7, 23. Hos. i. 6, 9. Mal. iii. 17;—and hence purposed to withhold from them all his undeserved favours of redemption and reconciliation through Christ,—of effectual calling, faith, justification, adoption, and sanctification, John x. 15, 26. xvii. 9. xii. 37—40. Matth. xi. 25, 26. xiii. 11, 13. Rom. viii. 28—33. 2 Thess. iii. 2. Eph. ii. 8;—though not from them all his favours of common providence, gospel ordinances, spiritual gifts, or strivings of the Holy Ghost, by which they are rendered useful to his elect people, Acts xiv. 17. xvii. 30. Rom. ii. 4. ix. 22. Exod. vii. 16, 17. Lev. xxvi. 3—13. Deut. xxviii. 1—14. Isa. v. 4. Matth. xiii. 9. xxiii. 37. Heb. vi. 4, 5. x. 26, 29. 2 Pet. ii. 20, 21. 1 Cor. xii. 10. Gen. vi. 3. Isa. lxiii. 10. Acts vii. 51;—and further determined in himself, that they, having rendered themselves miserable by their sin, original or actual, against law or gospel,—and become abusers or despisers of his benefits offered to, or bestowed on them, Rom. v. 12. Eph. ii. 1—3, 12. Rom. ii. 12, 14, 15. Mark xvi. 16. John iii. 18, 36. iv. 40. Rom. ii. 4, 5. xi. 7, 8. Matth. x. 15. xi. 21, 22. Job viii. 4. ix. 4. Psalm lxxxi. 13. Acts xiv. 16.—should,—in an

M

infinitely wise, sovereign, just, and holy manner, answerable to their own freedom of will and their rebellious inclinations, Deut. xxxii. 4. Psalm xlv. 7. Jer. xii. 1. James i. 13. Matth. xxiii. 37, 38. John v. 40. viii. 12. Acts vii. 51,—be, for the punishment of their preceding sins,---spiritually blinded, hardened, and given up to strong delusions, vile affections, and a reprobate sense, Rom. ix. 22. Exod. xiv. 4. John xii. 40. Rom. ix. 15, 17. xi. 7, 8. i. 24, 28. 2 Thess. ii. 11. Isa. lxvi. 4;—and that they, persevering in their wickedness, and convicted by their own consciences of final impenitence, neither able to blame the just severity of God, nor to excuse their own ignorance, or their inability to accept of his offered salvation, Matth. xxvii. 4. Luke xvi. 24. Matth. xxv. 25, 26, 44. Rom. ii. 14, 15. i. 20. ix. 19, 20. Luke xxii. 22. John v. 40; should be eternally damned for their sins, Hos. xiii. 9. Matth. xxv. 41, 42. Isa. v. 11. Ezek. xviii. 4. Rom. ii. 8, 9. vi. 23. Eph. v. 5, 6. Col. iii. 6. 1 Cor. vi. 9, 10. Gal. v. 19, 20, 21.—as vessels of wrath fitted to destruction,—children of wrath,—children of perdition,—hated of God,—appointed to evil and wrath,—separated, and before-ordained to condemnation, Rom. ix. 22. Eph. ii. 3. 2 Thess. ii. 3. John xvii 12. Lam. iii. 37, 38. Mal. i. 3. Rom. ix. 13. Prov. xvi. 4. 1 Thess. v. 9. 1 Pet. ii. 8. Jude 4."

This awful doctrine of Reprobation, as well as of the Election of men, ought, with great prudence and holy awe, to be taught in the church. 1. It hath been proved that the Holy Ghost hath plainly taught it in his word, Rom. ix. 11—22. xi. 1—7. 2. Every thing taught in the Scripture, lawfully used, tends to promote men's holiness in heart and life, Rom. xv. 4. 2 Tim. iii. 16, 17. 1 Pet. ii. 1, 2. James i. 21. Psalm cxix. 9, 11. 3. Election and reprobation being so closely related and contrasted, the former can neither be taught nor conceived of, separately from the latter. 4. In his providence, which every man ought to observe, Psalm cvii. 43. Hos. xiv. 9. Isa. v. 12. God copies out his decree of reprobation, in the life and in the death of the wicked, Jude 4. 1 Pet. ii. 8. Isa. xlvi. 10, 11. Eph. i. 11. Psalm xxxiii. 11. Acts ii. 23. iv. 27, 28. i. 16---18, 25. Luke xxii. 22. Phil. iii. 18, 19. 5. A proper knowledge of this decree promotes right and reverential views of the sovereignty, power, wisdom, justice, and goodness of God, Matth. xi. 26. Rom. ix. 13, 22, 23. Eph. i. 5, 6. 6. The doctrine of reprobation, if duly taught, tends to alarm the wicked and render their consciences uneasy, till they obtain proper evidence that they are not included in it, and to render sin terrible to them :---And it excites saints to self-examination, and to lively gratitude to God their Redeemer, in a course of gospel holiness, Matth. xxv. 41. Rom. i. 18. 1 Thess. v. 9, 10. 2 Cor. v. 10, 11. Psalm cxvi. 16. Luke i. 74, 75.———To

OF THE DECREES AND PURPOSES OF GOD. 163

render the whole decree of predestination as odious as possible, our opponents strain every nerve to run down that of Reprobation, which is so unpleasant to men's unrenewed heart.

OBJEC. I. " Since the infinite perfections of God's nature
" necessarily requires, that all men should love and fear him,
" he cannot, in a consistence with that perfection, or even with
" common candour, lay any of them under an incapacity to do
" so." ANSW. 1. Though the almighty operation of God's grace be absolutely necessary to remove men's incapacity of loving him, —yet, as his decree, in no respect, forced or drew that incapacity upon them, but they, in their first parents, voluntarily contracted it, in direct opposition to his commandment,—and do as early as possible personally approve of, and delight in it, He can be under no obligation to deliver them from it, especially, as his leaving them under it is but the just punishment of their sin. 2. God's purpose to permit men to fall into, or continue under a sinful incapacity of loving and fearing him, can never be more contrary to his perfection and sincerity, than his actual providential permission of both devils and men to fall into sin and continue in it.—To suppose that his purpose and providence are not perfectly correspondent, is to charge him with ignorance in forming his plan, or with folly, weakness, and changeableness, in the execution of it, Psalm l. 21.

OBJEC. II. " God, being infinitely merciful, good to all, his
" tender mercy over all his works, taking no pleasure in the
" death of the wicked, but willing that all men should be
" saved, and come to the knowledge of the truth, Psalm ciii. 8.
" cxlv. 9. Ezek. xxxiii. 11. 1 Tim. ii. 4. 2 Pet. iii. 9,—can-
" not by an act of his will, fix so many thousands of his ra-
" tional creatures, who are no worse than others, in sinfulness,
" or require them to receive his salvation, while their inward
" corruptions, permitted by himself, render them incapable."
ANSW. 1. By what TIE is this infinitely merciful God bound to preserve all his rational creatures in this original perfection of holiness, whether they will or not?—By what TIE is he bound to shew favour to one sinner, who hath offended him, and sought his life?—By what TIE is he bound to shew more favour to sinful men, than to fallen angels, who are his own rational creatures of a far higher rank? 2. What avails that infinite mercy, which is supposed to have predestinated all men (and why not all devils?) to everlasting happiness, if it bring but a few of them to it, nay, can bring none of them to it, but as their wicked free will pleases; nay, if it do not so much as inform the hundredth part of mankind of the only method of their salvation through Christ? 3. Of the small part of mankind who are properly invited by the gospel as preached, to re-

ceive this salvation, multitudes, not by any influence of God's decree, but by their own self-approved enmity against it, obstinately reject it, John v. 40. Psalm lxxxi. 11. Hos. xi. 2, 7. Rom. viii. 7, 8. Jer. xvii. 9. Zech. vii. 11, 12. xi. 8. Gen. vi. 5. viii. 21. 4. A scheme, which infallibly secures the eternal happiness, perhaps of many thousand millions of mankind, is infinitely more merciful than one which secures it for none, but suspends all upon the *proper exertions of a free will*, a carnal mind, *enmity against God,—a heart deceitful above all things and desperately wicked*.—We allow, that every man that hears the gospel is warranted,—is solemnly called, and earnestly entreated by God to believe on Jesus Christ for salvation. We allow, that one single act of believing, which is ten thousand times less than perseverance in faith and holiness till death, will render a man's state unalterably happy for ever more.—We allow of God's giving, even to reprobates, the largest measures and highest degrees of the common influences of his Spirit to assist them towards acts of faith. Our opponents dare not pretend, that they allow more to their elect,—nay, to their choicest saints.—If men's free will can therefore turn the scale in their favour, and make them believe in Christ, we allow a method of eternal salvation a thousand times more easy to reprobates, than our opponents do to any man.

Objec. III. " How can it consist with the infinite wisdom " of God, to fix on the objects of his favour or of his abhor- " rence, without regard to their moral behaviour as the cause? " —or, to appoint means of salvation for those to whom he " hath decreed never to give that which is absolutely necessa- " ry to render these means effectual ?—or, to require or expect " the conversion of reprobates, when he himself hinders it by " his unalterable decrees ?" Answ. 1. God abhors no creature, but on account of his sin, Gen. i. 31. Psalm civ. 31. It would be very unwise in God to fix upon any of mankind as his favourites, from respect to their behaviour, since, in their unconverted state, not one of them can do any thing but what is abominable to him, in matter or manner, Psalm xiv. 1—4. Rom. viii. 7, 8. iii. 10—20. Jer. xvii. 9. Eph. ii. 1—3. Tit. iii. 3.—But, both his wisdom and sovereignty are highly glorified in his choosing of many, the most unpromising, that so his almighty power and infinite mercy may the more abundantly shine forth in his qualifying them for the most familiar fellowship with himself, and for his service, 1 Cor. i. 25—29. 1 Tim. i. 13—16. Rom. v. 20, 21.——2. God hath not granted the means of eternal salvation to the most of mankind:—nor doth his granting them to any exhibit his decree of saving them, but the true method of obtaining salvation, and their duty to comply with and improve it, Mark xvi. 16. Acts xvi. 31. ii. 37—39. John iii.

14—18. 3. The Scripture never represents God as *expecting* the conversion of reprobates. To assert that he *expects* any thing which never happens, is to deny his infinite wisdom and knowledge. 4. God's requiring from gospel hearers their proper duty, is his appointed mean of effectually converting his elect,—even as Christ's calling of Lazarus to *come forth*, and the widow's son and ruler's daughter to *arise*, was his decreed mean of actually raising them from the dead:—and mean while it renders reprobates much more useful and happy in this world, than otherwise they would be.

OBJEC. IV. " If God, by a secret and unchangeable act of
" his will, hath consigned multitudes of mankind to everlasting
" ruin, how can he, in a consistence with uprightness and sin-
" cerity, openly declare, that he is not willing that any should
" perish, but that all should be saved and come to the know-
" ledge of the truth, Ezek. xxxiii. 11. 1 Tim. ii. 4. 2 Pet.
" iii. 9? How can he impose a law upon them, to be obeyed
" under pain of damnation, while he himself is unalterably re-
" solved to withhold from them all power and ability to keep
" it? How can he be serious and earnest in calling men to re-
" pentance and salvation, if by his own unalterable purpose,
" he hath rendered both utterly impossible? How can he pro-
" fess to wish their welfare, or promise them eternal life upon
" conditions which are infallibly hindered by his own decree;
" —or to offer it to them, upon whom he is unalterably deter-
" mined never to bestow it?" ANSW. 1. The Scripture never declares, that God is inclined to have every individual of mankind, Judas, Antichrist, &c. saved, but the contrary, John xvii. 9, 12. 2 Thess. ii. 4, 11, 12. Rom. ix. 22. Now, if one be appointed to wrath, it will affect the sincerity of God, in the sense of the objection, as much as if it were ten thousand millions. 2. We readily grant, that men of all nations, ranks, and conditions, are actually saved, than which the Scripture never affirms any thing more universal on this point, 1 Tim. ii. 4. 2 Pet. iii. 9. Joel ii. 28. John xii. 32. xvi. 9. Rev. vii. 9. 3. Be the purpose of God what it will, his holy, just, good, and exceeding broad law, binds, and will for ever bind, both devils and men to holiness, nay to perfection in holiness; otherwise they could not commit sin, Rom. iv. 15. v. 13. 1 John iii. 4.—And, men's attempts to obey it are rewarded in this life, or in the next, with, at least, less degrees of punishment, Matth. xi. 21—24. xii. 41, 42. 4. As, in ordinary cases, no man, in this life, can certainly know that he is included in God's reprobating decree,—and as it, in no case, lays any restraint or force upon men's will, it cannot be it, but their own inward corruption and enmity against God, which hinders their care or endeavours to promote their eternal happiness. 5. Most

of those scriptures, in which God appears to wish men's welfare, and to promise them happiness on condition of their obedience, directly relate to the felicity of the Jews in Canaan, which they held upon the foot of such reformation and behaviour, as was partly in their own power, without any assistance of saving grace, Deut. v. 29. xxxii. 29. Psalm lxxxi. 13. Isa. i. 19, 20. Ezek. xviii. 30—32. xxxiii. 11. Jer. vi. 8. 6. Spiritual pardon and salvation are never secured by promise to any but such as have true faith, and that not as a proper condition, but as a mean of receiving them,—and hence as a fruit of election, 2 Thess. ii. 2, 13. Tit. i. 2. Acts ii. 47. xiii. 48. 7. The gospel is so far from declaring that God intends to save all men, that it plainly affirms, that he intends to save but the smaller part of gospel-hearers, Matth. vii. 13, 14, 15, 23. xx. 16. xxii. 14. But it peremptorily declares, that Jesus Christ is able to save to the uttermost all them that come unto God by him;—that he and his salvation are equally suited to the needs of every hearer;—that, by the gracious appointment and infinitely free gift of God, he is the *Official Saviour* of mankind indefinitely considered, and will in no wise cast out any that come to him for salvation;—that it is the duty and interest of all gospel-hearers, as lost and self-ruined sinners, to exert all the powers of their soul to the uttermost, in essaying to believe on and receive him and his salvation, as fully, freely, earnestly, and indefinitely offered to them;—that, not knowing but they are elected, they all ought, earnestly and repeatedly, to attempt this believing, in order to have certain proof that they are so; —that by means of gospel declarations, offers, and invitations, under the influence of the Holy Ghost, the adult elect are brought into their state of salvation, and many reprobates are qualified with spiritual gifts, which render them useful companions and assistants to the elect in this world. 8. Unless, in providence, God actually should save all men, especially all that hear the gospel, which it is manifest he doth not, the whole charge of the objection will fall upon him, with all its weight, if it have any.

Objec. V. " It is inconsistent with God's infinite holiness to " decree the permission of sin, or to command men to be holy " as he is holy, while, by his unalterable purpose, he renders " it impossible for them to be holy." Answ. 1. Let our opponents reconcile the actual entrance of sin into the world, and the long continuance and spread of it, among devils and men, with the infinite holiness of an all-wise and almighty God,—and all the pretended inconsistency of his decree of permitting it will evanish of course. 2. Since God's decree of reprobation neither inclines nor forces men to sin, and is very rarely known to any particular person in this world, it is at once extremely uncandid and absurd, repeatedly to contend, that it renders any man sinful or retains him such. 3. Since, notwithstanding God's all-wise and almighty government of the world, there is *very much sin in it*, it is manifest, that his infinite holiness and nature doth not require him to do his uttermost to prevent it, or the ruin of devils or men by means of it,—though both it and his wisdom require him to glorify himself by means of sin, if it be permitted.

OBJEC. VI. " It is inconsistent with the equity of God to " consign innocent persons to eternal damnation, or to im- " pose on men a law, which his own purpose renders him in- " capable of fulfilling." ANSW. 1. God hath not decreed to inflict damnation upon either angels or men, but as the due wages of their sin, Hos. xiii. 9. Ezek. xviii. 4. Rom. ii. 8, 9. vi. 23. viii. 13. Psalm ix. 16, 17. 2. If, as hath been repeatedly hinted, God neither tempt, incline, nor force men to sin;—nay, if, by his law, he solemnly forbid it, and by his providence deter and dissuade from it, why may he not justly damn men, if they will involve themselves in it? 3. It is highly absurd to imagine, that men's sinful disabling of themselves to obey the law of God deprives him of his right to require their obedience;—that their wickedness strips the Most High of his authority over them, and renders them independent governors of themselves in his room;—that sinful ignorance, perpetual drunkenness, or the like, can render blasphemy, hatred of God or men, murder, whoredom, theft, perjury, &c. altogether innocent, and can free men from all obligation to duty.

OBJEC. VII. " As God can reap no advantage by it, it is " shocking to suppose, that he fixed upon any of his rational " creatures for the manifestation of his mercy or justice,—or " that he made Adam, whose fall he foresaw, men's Repre- " sentative,— or that he brings any of them into being in or- " der to damn them." ANSW. 1. Reprobation is in no respect founded upon God's imputation of Adam's first sin to his posterity, but altogether antecedent to it. 2. God's *proper* end in making men and every thing else was neither their damnation nor salvation, but his own glory. Is this unworthy of him? Rom. xi. 36. Prov. xvi. 4. 3. If God did not from eternity foresee what multitudes of angels and men would fall into and perish in sin, where was his infinite knowledge, Psalm cxlvii. 5. Acts xv. 18. Isa. xlvi. 10? If he foresaw this, and yet created them, as it is certain he hath done, wherein is he a whit more benevolent than the above-described decree of reprobation admits? 4. If the actual entrance of sin and damnation among angels and men be not shockingly unworthy of God, how is it possible that his purpose relative thereto can be so?

OBJEC. VIII. " Men in general are called by God to be-
" lieve the gospel, and to make *sure their election*, which ne-
" cessarily supposes that none of them are irreversibly repro-
" bated." ANSW. 1. None but the hearers of the gospel, who
are not perhaps the hundredth part of mankind, are *called* to
make sure their election, 2 Pet. i. 10. 2 Cor. xiii. 5. 2. God's
command to *make sure* our *election*, proves that only some, not
all men, are elected to everlasting life: For, why labour, with
all diligence, to make sure that which is common to *every one*,
as common to their very rational nature? 3. If men's election be suspended on their final perseverance in faith and holiness, as our opponents contend, it cannot be *made sure* in this
life, nor perhaps in that which is to come. Some angels no
more persevered in heaven, than Adam did on earth, Jude 6.
2 Pet. ii. 4.

OBJEC. IX. " If faith and holiness be the conditions of
" men's eternal salvation; if men's unbelief and impenitence
" be the conditions of their damnation, they must necessarily
" be the conditions of that decree which fixes their salvation
" or damnation." ANSW. 1. Faith, repentance, and new obedience, are not *proper conditions* of our salvation; but proceed
from our being united to Christ, and interested in him and his
salvation. They are first fruits of that salvation by which we
receive and improve begun salvation, and are prepared for
complete salvation in heaven, Phil. i. 29. Eph. ii. 10. Rom.
vii. 4. vi. 14. viii. 2. 2. It is extremely absurd to insist that
the causes of a purpose, and the means of executing it, must
be the very same. The Jews' murder of Christ was a mean
of rendering him our atoning sacrifice. Was it therefore the
cause of God's purpose, to set him forth to be our propitiation? Acts ii. 23, 24. iv. 27, 28. Heb. ii. 10. v. 8. Luke xxiv.
26. John iii. 16. Rom. v. 8. 1 John iv. 9, 10, 19. Paul's persecuting rage, and Onesimus's theft, were occasional means of
their remarkable conversion to Christ. Were they therefore
causes of their election to eternal life?—*All things*, sins, devils,
troubles, &c. work together for believers' spiritual and eternal
advantage, Rom. viii. 28. 2 Cor. iv. 17. Were therefore sins,
devils, and troubles, the causes and conditions of believers'
election to spiritual and eternal happiness?—Can fruit on trees
be the cause of their root? or water in cisterns, vessels, or
streams, be the cause of the fountain?

REFLECT. Having thus reviewed the mysterious purposes
of Jehovah, think, O my soul! if even the supposed possibility
of his having loved me,—having so early loved me, and thought
on me, in my low estate,—ought not this, in the earliest periods
of my life, to have excited and animated me to exercise my

utmost care and diligence in improving the gospel method of certainly knowing that these things were so?—Upon the apprehension of a mere possibility of future existence in this world, what thoughts,—what cares,—what labours have I exercised about the concerns of it, from time to time?—Why then so few, and these so languid, so lifeless, about things of infinitely greater importance?—things of infinite—of everlasting consequence?——But, hath the great, the eternal God, thought,—always thought on, and loved me! And have I spent so many moments,—so many hours,—so many years of my short life,—without thoughts,—without high, fixed, and heart-inflaming thoughts of him?—without love, without superlative love, without an all-subjecting,—all-assimilating, love to him!——Hath the infinite JEHOVAH, with all his heart, chosen ME to be his *vessel* of *mercy*, his *jewel*, his *portion*, his *friend*, his *child*, his *bride!*——Ought not I, if I had ten thousand hearts,—ought not I, with them all, to choose Him?—Choose Him, who is infinite LOVELINESS and LOVE, for my SAVIOUR, my FRIEND, my FATHER, my HUSBAND, my GOD, my ALL?——Passing by millions, not one of them worse, did he set me apart for himself! And shall not my soul prefer him to every trifle!—Whom, my INFINITE ALL, have I in heaven but THEE? what on earth do I,—dare I, desire besides THEE?—Hath he, in his persons and perfections, so exerted himself in the establishment of my election,—my eternal salvation!—Let me work together with Him, giving all diligence to *make* my *calling and election sure.*——Did he choose me to *holiness,—*to *love?* Let me follow hard after it, as a part, a mean of my eternal felicity.—Hath his unchangeable purpose infallibly fixed me and my everlasting salvation, in himself!—Let me be stedfast, immoveable, alway abounding in the work of the Lord.——But, Is there a tremendous purpose of reprobation? Break not through, my soul, unto the Lord to gaze. But, if I be uncertain with respect to my state, let me exceedingly fear and quake.—Let me escape for my life. Arise, O my sleeping soul!—cry mightily to thy God, thy offered Saviour, that he may think on me, that I perish not. Let me give him no rest, till my salvation go forth as a lamp that burneth; till he say, *Fear not, I am with thee; be not dismayed, I am thy God.—I have loved thee with an everlasting love, and therefore with loving-kindness have I drawn thee.*—But have I, in God's light, perceived, that he hath not appointed me to wrath, but to obtain salvation through our Lord Jesus Christ?—Let me, then, for ever admire,—for ever adore, his sovereign mercy and grace, that left not me to perish in my sin, when he passed by thousands,—nay, millions of my brethren in iniquity, whose crimes, he foresaw, would be fewer, and far less aggravated, than mine.—Many, O Lord my God, are thy gracious thoughts to me-ward: they are gone above all thought: when I speak of them, they are more than can be numbered.

CHAP. IV.

Of God's EXECUTION *of his Decrees in his Works of* CREATION *and* PROVIDENCE.

GOD's execution of his decrees includes his giving a being to all things in CREATION, and his upholding and governing that being in PROVIDENCE. His work of creation was chiefly performed by him, without making use of any instruments, in the first six days of time. His work of providence, in which he employs instruments, hath been, is, and constantly will be, carried on through all eternity. As his decrees had *no beginning*, the execution of them will have *no end*.

I. The world did not exist from eternity. The actual infinity of the duration of matter or any other finite being, is altogether inconceivable. The late invention of useful arts;—the short reach of history into past periods of but a few thousand years;—the room on the earth for many more inhabitants, though they have been generally on the increase;—the remaining heights on the surface of it, notwithstanding they are gradually washed down by the rain, &c. prove that it cannot be eternal. But from Scripture we learn, that it had its beginning little more than 5780 years ago.—Common sense plainly dictates, that the world could not make itself, or be formed by a fortuitous concourse of atoms. But the Scripture informs us, That God, Father, Son, and Holy Ghost, by the word of his power, created all things in six days,—in the most distinct and orderly manner,—all very good in themselves, and marvellously fitted to answer their respective ends and their manifold connections, Gen. i. ii. Exod. xx. 11. xxxi. 17. Heb. i. 2. xi. 3. Prov. iii 19. Col. i. 16. Rom. xi. 36. Job ix. 8, 9. xxvi. 10—13. xxxviii. Psalm xxiv. 1, 2. xxxiii. 6—9. xcv. 1—6. cii. 25, 26. civ. 3—6, 19, 24. lxxxix. 11, 12. lxxiv. 16, 17. viii. 1—4. cxix. 73, 89, 90, 91. cxlv. 8. cxlvi. 5, 6. c. 3. cxlviii. 1—6. cxxxvi. 5—9. Neh. ix. 5, 6. Prov. xxx. 4. xvi. 4. Isa. xl. 12, 26. xlii. 5. xliii. 5, 15, 21. xliv. 24. xlv. 7, 11, 12, 18. xlviii. 13. li. 12, 13. lxiv. 8. Jer. x. 11—16. v. 22. xxii. 5. xxxi. 35. xxxii. 17. Amos iv. 12, 13. Zech. xii. 1. John i. 1—3. Acts xvii. 24—26. iv. 24. 1 Pet. iv. 19. Rev. iv. 11. Heb. iii. 4.

IN HIS WORK OF CREATION.

and that angels in heaven, and men upon earth, were the principal creatures which he formed, Job xxxviii. 6, 7. Psalm ciii. 19, 20, 21. civ. 4. Gen. i. 26, 27. ii. 7, 22. v. 1.

ANGELS, properly so called, are spiritual creatures, which God formed for his particular attendants and ministers, Psalm civ. 4.—These hosts of heaven were created during the first six days, Gen. ii. 1. Exod. xx. 11. Before that, nothing but absolute eternity had place, Psalm xc. 2. Prov. viii. 23, 24. Eph. i. 4. Mat. xxv. 34.——It is most probable, that they were created on the *first day*, as they praised God when he laid the foundations of the earth, Job xxxviii. 6, 7.——Being creatures, they must be finite in their faculties, endowments, and presence, Mark xiii. 32.—none of them can be in different places at once, Dan. ix. 21—23. x. 13, 14, 20. They are represented as now either in heaven or hell, Mat. xviii. 10. xxii. 30. 2 Pet. ii. 4. Jude 6.

They are *unembodied spirits*, endowed by God with a very extensive understanding and an active will. And though they can assume bodies of condensed air, in which they may appear to men, Gen. xviii. 2. xix. 1, 5. xxxii. 1. yet no body is ever personally united to their spiritual substance, Psalm civ. 4. Heb. i. 7, 14. Eph. vi. 12. Luke xxiv. 39. xx. 35, 36. Col. i. 16.——They have a very extensive knowledge, natural, acquired, or revealed, 2 Sam. xiv. 17. xix. 27. 1 Cor. xiii. 1, 2. 2 Cor. xi. 5, 14. 1 Kings xxii. 23. Dan. vii. viii. ix. x. xi. xii. Zech. i.—vi. Rev. i. 1. Eph. iii. 10. 1 Tim. iii. 15. 1 Pet. i. 12. ——Their knowledge resembles ours, in their manner of increasing and exercising it:—and being *finite*, it never extends to future events which God hath not revealed,—or to the depths of divine mysteries, Isa. xli. 22, 23, 26. xlvi. 10. Mark xiii. 32. Eph. iii. 10. 1 Pet. i. 12.—nor to any immediate discernment of men's thoughts or inward dispositions, 1 Kings viii. 39. Psal. cxxxix. 2, 4. Prov. xvi. 2. 1 Sam. xvi. 7. Jer. xvii. 10. John ii. 25. Acts i. 24. 1 Cor. ii. 11. Rev. ii. 23. 1 Chron. xxviii. 9. xxix. 17.——Their freedom of will, dependent on God, but now fixed with respect to the objects of its choice, is evidently marked in the voluntary obedience of holy angels, and the rebellion of bad ones against God their Maker, Psalm ciii. 20. Mat. vi. 10. Luke xv. 7. 1 Pet. i. 12. John viii. 44. Jude 6. 2 Pet. ii. 4. 1 Pet. v. 8. 2 Cor. ii. 11, xi. 3. 1 Kings xxii. 22. ——The greatness of their power is manifest from express declarations of Scripture, Psalm ciii. 20. 2 Thess. i. 7. 2 Pet. ii. 11. Eph. vi. 12. Rev. xviii. 1, 2. from their many mighty exploits, —as slaying all the first born of Egypt in one night, Exod. xii. 29. Psalm cxxxv. 8.—killing seventy thousand Israelites in a few hours, 1 Chron. xxi. 14, 15.—and an hundred and eighty-five thousand valiant Assyrians in one night, 2 Kings xix. 35. Isa. xxxvii. 36. x. 34. 2 Chron. xxxii. 21. But it is *finite*, limited by God, Job i. 12. ii. 6. Mat. viii. 31. Rom. viii. 31.—and cannot, by any immediate influence, bow men's hearts, Prov. xvi. 1, 9. xxi. 1. Psalm cx. 3. Deut. xxx. 6; though, by impressions and suggestions, they may much influence their conduct, Eph. ii. 2. Acts v. 3. Luke xxii. 3, 4. John xiii. 2, 27.—nor can it perform any thing *properly* miraculous, Psalm lxxii. 18. lxxxvi. 8. cxxxvi. 4. Exod. xv. 11.

Angels are exceedingly numerous, Psalm lxviii. 17. Deut. xxxiii. 2. Mat. xxvi. 53. Jude 14. Dan. vii. 10. Rev. v. 11. Mark v. 9.——Their being called *armies*, *principalities*, *powers*, *thrones*, *dominions*, &c. denotes their orderly arrangement, and probably also their difference of rank or station, Gen. ii. 1. Col. i. 16. ii. 10. 1 Pet. iii. 22. Eph. i. 22. vi. 12. Col. ii. 15. But what their order or ranks are, we know not;—nor whether the name *Archangel* be ascribed to any but Christ, 1 Thess. iv. 16. Jude 9. Dan. xii. 1. Rev. xii. 7.—who is often called an *Angel*, or the *Angel—Jehovah*, Gen. xlviii. 16. Acts vii. 30. Isa. lxiii. 9. Mal. iii. 1. Exod. xxiii. 20, 21. Job xxxiii. 23. Gen. xvi. 7, 9, 10, 11, 13. xviii. 2, 17, 22. xxii. 11, 12, 15, 16. xxxii. 24. Hos. xii. 3, 4. Judges ii. 1—4. vi. 11, 12, 14, 20—23. xiii. 3, 9, 13, 16, 17, 18—22. Zech. i.—vi. Rev. vii. 2. viii. 3. x. 1, 5, 9.

All the angels were created in an *holy and happy state*. 1. The infinite holiness and goodness of God require that every rational being be formed in perfect moral rectitude, unless an incumbent curse, which could not have place here, prevent it, Psalm cxix. 68. civ. 31. 2. The finished creation was all *very good*, Gen. i. 31.—But they were fallible.———Multitudes of them being chosen by God to be for ever happy in the enjoyment of himself, still retain their original knowledge, righteousness, and holiness, 1 Tim. v. 21. Dan. vii. 10. Mat. xxvi. 53. Rev. v. 11. Psalm lxviii. 17. Deut xxxii. 2. Jude 14. Zech. xiv. 5. Luke ii. 13. Heb. xii. 22. Mat. xxv. 31. vi. 10;—and are confirmed by him in their holy and happy state, Mat. xviii. 10. xxii. 30; but not in Christ, whose reconciliation by his death they need not, Eph. i. 10. Col. i. 20; and who is not their Mediator, but man's, Isa. ix. 6. Zech. ix. 9. Luke ii. 11. 1 Tim. ii. 5. Heb. ix. 15. ii. 16.———Though heaven be their peculiar residence, in which they are perfectly blessed in the full and immediate enjoyment of God,—they are often employed on earth, to execute his purposes, Mat. vi. 10. xviii. 10. Heb. i. 14. Psalm xxxiv. 7.———Their work is, 1. To worship God in high praises, suited to their nature and state, Psal. cxlviii. 2. ciii. 20, 21. Isa. vi. 3. Heb. i. 6. Luke ii. 14. Rev. v. 11. 2. To minister to, attend upon, and serve Jesus Christ as

Mediator, Zech. i.—vi. Mat. iv. 11. Luke xxii. 43. ii. 10, 13. Dan. vii. 10. Psalm lxviii. 17. xlvii. 5, 6. 1 Tim. iii. 16. Acts i. 10. Phil. ii. 9, 10. 1 Pet. iii. 22. Rev. i. 1. xxii. 16. Heb. i. 14. 3. To minister to,—protect, admonish, deliver, instruct, rejoice over, comfort, and transport to heaven, the saints, and to separate them from the wicked at the last day, Heb. i. 14. Psalm xxxiv. 7. xci. 11. Gen. xix. 12, 13. xxxii. 1. Acts xii. 7—10. 1 Kings xix. 5. Gen. xxiv. 7, 40. Acts x. 5. Dan. vii.—xii. Zech. i. 9—14. ii. 3, 4. Acts xxvii. 23, 24. Luke xv. 10. xvi. 22. Mat. xiii. 41. xxiv. 31. 4. To restrain and punish the wicked, Dan. x. 20. Gen. xix. 11. Exod. xii. 39. 2 Sam. xxiv. 15, 16. 2 Kings xix. 35. Acts xii. 23. Psalm xxxv. 5, 6. —But it doth not appear, that every particular saint hath a *particular guardian angel*, but angels in general, as directed by God, attend them, Psalm xxxiv. 7. Heb. i. 14. Nor will the Jews' notion of a *guardian angel*, if they had it, or an angel attending an *apostle*, be any proof, Acts xii. 15.

But many angels, abusing the freedom of their will, by pride or some other sin, quickly fell from that holy and happy state in which they were created, 2 Pet. ii. 4. Jude 6. 1 Tim. iii. 6. ——They are real persons, not horrors of conscience. 1. Personal qualities, as *wiles, subtilty, devising*, &c. are ascribed to them, Eph. vi. 11, 12. 2 Cor. ii. 11. xi. 3, 14. 2. They tempt, lie in wait for, and destroy men, Gen. iii. 1—8. 1 Kings xxii. 22, 23. Mat. iv. 1—10. 1 Pet. v. 8. John viii. 44. James iv. 7. 1 Cor. vii. 5. Zech iii. 1—3. Psalm cix. 6. 3. They believe the existence of God, and tremble at it,—and shall be eternally punished, James ii. 19. Mat. viii. 29. xxv. 41.——Their punishment began with the first moment of their sinning, in their being expelled heaven and shut up in chains of darkness; but they were not so confined to hell, as to hinder their acting on earth, 2 Pet. ii. 4. Jude 6. 1 Kings xxii. 22, 23. Job i. 7—12. ii. 2—7. Psalm lxxviii. 49. Mat. iv. 1—10. viii. 29, 31. xvi. 18. Eph. vi. 11, 12, 16. 2 Cor. ii. 11. xi. 3, 14. Luke x. 18. Rev. xii. 7—9. xx. 1—9.—It was increased by the incarnation, public ministrations, and death of Christ, by the spread of the gospel, and the erection of the Christian church, Gen. iii. 15. Col. ii. 15. Heb. ii. 14. 1 John iii. 8. Mat. xii. 43; and will be completed at the last day, Mat. xxv. 41. viii. 29. Rev. xx. 10, 14.——In this world, these fallen angels, or devils, exert themselves to their utmost, 1. In taking away the truths of God's word from men, particularly in hearing the gospel, Mark iv. 15. 2. In tempting, accusing, and molesting the saints, Mat. xvi. 23. 1 Cor. vii. 5. 2 Cor. ii. 10, 11. xi. 3, 14. Luke xxii. 31. Rev. xii. 9, 10. Zech. iii. 1—3. 1 Thess. ii. 18. 2 Cor. xii. 7. 1 Pet. v. 8. Rev. ii. 10. xii. 7. 3. In seducing the wicked, and retaining them in their corrupt and miserable estate, John xiii. 2, 27. Acts v. 3. Mat. xii. 43.—leading them into error and delusion, 2 Cor. iv. 3, 4. 2 Thess. ii. 9, 10. Rev. xx. 3, 8, 10.—or entering into familiar fellowship with them, Exod. xxii. 18. Lev. xix. 31. xx. 6, 27. Deut. xiii. 1. xviii. 10, 11, 14. Isa. viii. 19, 21. Exod. vii. 11, 12, 22. viii. 7, 18. Num. xxiv. 1. 1 Sam. xxviii. 7—9. 4. In entering into men's bodies to render them delirious, furious, &c. 1 Sam. xvi. 14. Mat. iv. 25. ix. 32. xii. 22. xv. 22. xvii. 15. Nor, 5. Do we know what influence they have in raising storms, producing diseases, &c. Eph. ii. 2. Job i. 19. ii. 7.

MANKIND was the other more excellent class of God's creatures, in which the angelical and animal natures were marvellously united, Gen. ii. 7. Eccl. xii. 7. Adam and Eve were the first of this class, and parents of all the rest, Acts xvii. 26. 1 Cor. xv. 45. Rom. v. 12. Gen. ii. v. x. 1 Chron. i.——The parts of their nature were, 1. An erect body of unparalleled comeliness, formed to point them out as lords of this lower world, under God, and qualified for the contemplation of heavenly things, Psalm cxxxix. 14, 15. Eccl. xii. 2—4. Isa. lxiv. 8. Gen. ii. 7, 22.——2. A rational soul, one of which is united to every human body, Heb. iv. 12. 1 Thess. v. 23. Gen. ii. 7. Mat. x. 28. xvi. 26. 1 Cor. vi. 20. Zech. xii. 1. Psal. xxii. 20. xxxv. 3. xix. 7. xxv. 1.—It is not in any respect corporeal, but spiritual, Eccl. xii. 7. Isa. lvii. 16. Luke xxiv. 39. Mat. x. 28. Acts xvii. 29.—It is only in a figurative manner, that it is represented as *seen*, or as having hands, a tongue, or the like.

Human souls are not generated by parents, but immediately created by God. 1. The souls of Adam and Eve were not formed of dust, but immediately created by God, Gen. ii. 7. 2. God alone is represented as the father or former of souls, Eccl. xii. 7. Isa. lvii. 16. Psalm xxxiii. 15. Zech. xii. 1. Heb. xii. 9. Num. xvi. 22. Acts xvii. 28, 29. 3. Souls cannot perish along with generated bodies, Mat. x. 28. 1 Cor. xv. 42, 53. Luke xii. 20. Acts vii. 59, 60.—4. Souls being indivisible, parents cannot communicate any part of theirs to their children in begetting them.——In Gen. xlvi. 26. and many other places, souls are put for human persons, including both soul and body; or for the body, Gen. xlvi. 22. Lev. xix. 28.——Nor can souls die with their bodies, but are *immortal*. 1. Being not constituted of parts, they are naturally incapable of dissolution, Mat. x. 28. 2. Though their capacities be very extensive, they make small improvements in this life, Prov. xxx. 2, 3. Psal. lxxiii. 22. Phil. iii. 12. 1 Cor. xiii. 12. 3. Men, chiefly saints, have a great desire after immortality, Luke ii. 25---30. 2 Cor. v. 1---8. iv. 17, 18. Phil. i. 23. 4. God's justice requires the immortality of souls, that they may be punished, or rewarded, in a future state, Eccl. iii. 16, 17. 5. Scripture represents souls as surviving those bodies with which they had been personally united, Matth. x. 28. Eccl. xii. 7. Luke xxiii. 43, 46. xvi. 22, 23. Acts vii. 59, 60. Gen. ii. 7. 1 Cor. xv. 45, 18, 19. 1 Pet. iii. 19. Rev. vi. 11. Matth. xxii. 32. 2 Cor. v. 1—8. Phil. i. 21, 23. 6. One soul is of inexpressibly more importance than the whole world, Matth. xvi. 26:—It is only in respect of their body, that men's death is like to that of beasts, or renders them incapable to know things, or to praise God, Eccl. iii. 17, 20. ix. 5. Psalm xxx. 9. cxv. 17. Isa. xxxviii. 18.—But, this immortal soul continues closely united to one person with its body, while it is capable of being its residence, Job iv. 19. 2 Cor. v. 1. Phil. i. 23. 2 Pet. i. 14. Acts xx. 10.

Man was created *after the image of God*, in spiritual knowledge, righteousness, and holiness, his mind duly discerning every proper object, and his conscience, will, and affections awing or inclining him to perform every part of duty towards God or his fellow-creatures, Eccl. vii. 29. Gen. i. 26, 27. v. 1. Col. iii. 10. Eph. iv. 24.—Even since the fall, men somewhat resemble God in the spirituality, intelligence, and immortality of their souls, Gen. ix. 6. James iii. 9. But nothing of that original moral wisdom, righteousness, and holiness, in which the image of God properly consisted, is to be found in them, till it be restored in regeneration, Rom. iii. 23. viii. 7, 8. Eph. v. 8. ii. 1—3. iv. 23. Col. iii. 10. ii. 11. 2 Cor. v. 17. iii. 18. Acts xxvi. 18. 1 Pet. i. 23. 2 Pet. i. 4.—This moral conformity to God, though not essential to, or inseparable from, man's soul, is called *natural*, as it was concreated with, and in him, agreeable to his nature, necessary to answer God's end in making it, and to be conveyed along with it in the propagation of mankind, Gen. i. 31. Eccl. vii. 29.—And the remaining resemblance of our soul to God in respect of its spiritual substance and agency is still *natural*, Rom. ii. 14. i. 20. Gen. ix. 6. 1 Cor. xi. 7.— But our evil concupiscence, not being from God, cannot be *natural* in the primary meaning of that word,—though our nature be now infected with it, in its very formation.—Having this moral image of God concreated with his whole soul, Adam had full ability to have believed on Christ, if he could have been exhibited to him in his innocent state, Eccl. vii. 29. And it is by this very image of God, imperfectly restored in them, that the elect are qualified to believe on, and receive Christ, in the day of his power, Eph. iv. 24. Col. iii. 10.

As God is immortal in, and of himself, 1 Tim. i. 17. vi. 16. Isa. lvii. 15. and angels and human souls are immortal in, but not of themselves,—man was at first created without any tendency toward the separation of his soul from his body, or any tendency of his body towards death, as the means of that separation. Adam's body, though made of dust, and capable of becoming mortal, had no seeds of death in it. And hence death, in Scripture, is alway represented as the fruit and wages of sin, Rom. v. 12. vi. 23. 1 Cor. xv. 21, 56. Ezek. xviii. 4. Gen. ii. 17. iii. 19. Job xxiv. 19. John viii. 44.———At his creation, man was constituted lord of all other creatures on earth,—to manifest which, all the animals, by God's direction, repaired to him, and received their names from him, Psal. viii. 6, 7. Gen. i. 28. ii. 19, 20. But whether in that state, he had any allowance to kill any of them for food, we know not.———Immediately after the fall, animals were slain for sacrifices typical of Christ, the promised Saviour. But, till after the flood, we never find men warranted by God to eat their flesh, Gen. iii. 21. iv. 4. ix. 3, 4.———But as spirituality of nature is retained by devils and unregenerate souls, and an immutable immortality of body awaits damned men after the resurrection,—and dominion over this lower world is partly retained by wicked men,—it is manifest, that the image of God, in which man was created, did not *properly* consist in these, but in moral perfection, Eph. iv. 24. Col. iii. 10. 2 Cor. iii. 18.

God's work of creation is to be improved in contemplating, as we have access, his creatures, in their almost infinitely diversified natures, qualities, and uses: as, light and celestial luminaries, in their mysterious nature, extensive range, fit distances, rapid motion, and powerful influence:—Air, fixed and unfixed, inflammable and uninflammable; in its fluidity, weight, elasticity, and usefulness:—Water, in its fluidity, plenitude, dispersion, saltness or freshness, penetration, and fitness for the formation of rains, dews, marine productions, and promoting of trade:—Earths, stones, metals, moulds, in their adhesion, divisibility, forms, colours, and uses:—Vegetables, in their structure, growth, curious parts, manifold uses, and almost infinitely diversified forms:—Animals, in their curious parts, their connected structure, life, dependence on food, motions, instincts, fitness for self-preservation, beautiful forms, melodious or awful sounds, exquisite but diversified taste: ———and along with these, the unbounded divisibility of matter, laws of attraction, gravitation, electricity, magnetism, and of air, fixed and unfixed, muscular motion, nervous influence;—rational spirits, in their power of thinking, willing, recollecting, sociality or union with bodies, as proofs of the existence and manifestations of the mysterious nature and manifold perfections of God, even our God in Christ, Rom. xi. 36. 2. In viewing them as memorials of the operations of God, and as heart-awing means of impressing our minds with his presence, observation, and influence, Jer. xxxii. 27. Psal. lxxv. 3. In viewing multitudes of creatures, as instituted emblems for representing the Most High, in his persons, perfections, stations, relations, and operations, in the work of our redemption, Hos. xii. 9, 10. 4. In considering all creatures as formed in order to, and fit for subserving God's principal and most glorious work of redemption, Rom. viii. 28. 5. In taking out a particular new-covenant claim to them all in Christ, as means of our present discernment of the glory, and tasting the goodness of God in him, and as pledges and earnests of our eternal enjoyment of him as our all in all, 1 Cor. iii. 21—23. Rev. xxi. 17. 6. In, as a consequence of all this, using them as means of exciting us to an habitual meditation on, admiring, adoring, and praising him as our own God and portion, and living to his glory in this world as his lower temple or sanctuary, Psalm civ. 1—34. cxlviii. 7. In a due regard to all creatures, as the fellow production of God, even our God.

II. God, by a continued work of PROVIDENCE, upholds and governs all things which he created. 1. As he is infinitely more perfect than they, and hath brought them into existence, he hath an undoubted right, and all-sufficient fitness, to uphold and govern them. Having infinite knowledge to discern all their qualities and connections,—infinite wisdom to conduct them to their proper ends,—infinite power to uphold and manage them, notwithstanding all their strength, mischievousness, jarring passions, instincts, or immediate aims,—infinite holiness and equity to prevent culpable partiality or impropriety in his conduct,—infinite patience to bear with offenders, while it can be for his glory and their good,—and omnipresence, rendering him equally near to each of them, he cannot but be infinitely fit for this work. 2. His own perfections require him to uphold and govern all his creatures. His independency requires him to hold all things in perpetual and immediate dependence on himself. His wisdom requires him to make all his creatures answer the ends for which he formed them. His goodness requires him never to forsake the work of his hands. Even his equity forbids, that they should be brought into being, and then left to shift for themselves. 3. Their very nature obliges them to a constant dependence on God. They cannot subsist a moment without new support from his infinite power, wisdom, and goodness. And having formed them to be *receivers* from, not *givers* to him, his providence must supply them according to their necessities, as far as his own glory, the chief end of their creation, can permit. 4. The regular motions of the heavenly bodies,—the regular ebbing and flowing of the sea,—the regular returns of day and night, summer and winter, seed-time and harvest,—the periodical retirements of many animals to places suitable to the season, their sagacity in defending or providing for themselves, and in forming their lodgings, hatching or nourishing their young,—the near approaches of those animals which are useful to mankind, and retirement of hurtful ones into woods and deserts, deep or distant places of the sea; —the multiplication of the more useful animals, while noxious ones, which are naturally more prolific, are not suffered to abound;—the astonishing variety observable in animals, vegetables, and other things, seemingly similar;—the amazing diversification of men's faces, voices, tempers, and forms of writing, taken as connected with the order and safety promoted by it;—the constant proportion of men and women answerable to their circumstances;—the frequent counterplotting of man's most sagacious projects, and defeating his most forcible and promising attempts;—the many miraculous counteractions of the ordinary laws of nature;—and a thousand other like actions, irrefragably manifest a Divine Providence managing the world. 5. The exact correspondence of thousands, I had almost said of every event, relative to persons, families, or nations, and especially relative to Christ and his church, with the predictions of Scripture, plainly demonstrate, that God, the predicter, hath the upholding and government of all things in his own hand. 6. The Scriptures no less plainly declare that God, Father, Son, and Holy Ghost, by the agency of his own will, upholds and governs all his creatures, John v. 17. Heb. i. 3. Col. i. 17. Job xxxiii. 4. Psalm civ. 30. Dan. iv. 34, 35. Rom. xi. 36. Eph. i. 11. Rev. iv. 11. Isa. xli. 4. xlv. 5, 6. xlvi. 4, 10—13. Job xxxvii. 6. xii. 9. xxxviii.—xli. Psalm xxxviii. ix. xix. 1—6. xlviii. lxv. lxvi. lxviii. lxxviii. ciii. civ. cv. cvi. cvii. cxiv. cxxxv. cxxxvi. cxlv. cxlvi. cxlvii. cxlviii. Ezek. ix. xx. &c.

In this work of providence God upholds and governs ALL *his creatures*, and ALL their ACTIONS, Heb. i. 3. Rom. xi. 36. Eph. i. 11. Col. i. 17. Isa. xlvi. 10. Rev. iv. 11. 1. All *irrational creatures*—animate or inanimate, great or small, Neh. ix. 6. Psalm xxxvi. 6. civ. 19—21. Dan. iv. 35. Job xxxvii. —xli. Psalm viii. civ. cv. cvi. cvii. cxxxvi. cxlv.—cxlviii. Hos. ii. 18, 21, 22. Ezek. xxxiv. 25. Mat. vi. 28—33. x. 28—31. Exod. viii. 16, 17. x. 12. Deut. xxviii. 28. Joel ii. 20, 25. Hence stars and rivers fought as his troops, in destroying Jabin's army, Judg. v. 20, 21; frogs, flies, and lice, plagued the Egyptian oppressors of his people, Exod. viii.—x.; serpents punished the murmuring Israelites, Num. xxi.; hornets drove out the wicked Canaanites, Exod. xxiii. 28; mice plagued the profane and murderous Philistines, 1 Sam. v. 5; bears and lions executed his vengeance on the profane scoffers of Bethel, the disobedient prophets, and idolatrous Samaritans, 2 Kings ii. 24. xvii. 25. 1 Kings xiii. 24. xx. 36; unclean ravens provided pure food for his favourite, Elijah, 1 Kings xvii.

6; pity to cattle partly moved him to dry up the waters of the flood, and to spare the city of Nineveh, Gen. viii. 1. 1 John iv. 11. 2. All *reasonable creatures*,—holy angels, Psal. ciii. 18—21. civ. 4. Heb. i. 14.—fallen angels, Luke xxii. 31, 32. 1 Kings xxii. 21, 22, 23. Job i. 12. ii. 6. Psalm lxxviii. 49. Matth. viii. 28—32. xii. 27, 28. iv. 24, 25. Rev. ii. 10. xii. 7. xiii. 7. xx. 2, 7—10;—men, and all their members, are written in this book of providential care, Exod. xxxii. 32. Psal. lxix. 28. cxxxix. 16. xxxiii. 13—15. Prov. viii. 15, 16. xvi. 1, 9. xxi. 1. Dan. ii. 21, 22, 44, 47. iv. 35. Job xii. 10. Acts xvii. 28. He governed the fate of Jacob, a very mild man, and his offspring, Gen. xxviii. 13—15; of Ishmael and Esau, very wild men, and theirs, Gen. xvi. 12. xxv. 16, 23;—the concerns of Jesus Christ, God-man, and his church, which is his body, Isa. xlii. 1—7. l. 4. xlix. 1—12. liii. Rom. viii. 28—39. 1 Cor. iii. 21, 22. 2 Cor. iv. 17. Heb. xiii. 5.——By his providence he managed the haughty and obstinate Egyptians, Exod. i.—xiv. xviii. 11; the oppressed and dispirited Israelites, Gen. xv. 13—18; the proud and atheistical Syrians, 1 Kings xix. 15; the powerful and furious Assyrians, Chaldeans, Persians, Greeks, and Romans, Isa. x. xxx. xxxiii. xxxvii. Jer. xxv. l. li. Dan. ii.—xi. Zech. vi.; the savage Tartars and Turks, Ezek. xxxviii. xxxix. Rev. vii. viii. ix. xx.; the crafty, wicked Papists, Dan. vii. xi. 36—43. Rev. ix.—xix.;—nay, the whole earth, Isa. xxiv. Psalm xxii. 27—31.——His providence extends to men's birth, Job x. 3, 8—12. xxxiii. 4. Psalm cxxxix. 14—16. xxii. 10. lxxi. 6;—their manner of life, Gen. xv. 13. xvi. 12. Deut. xxx. 9, 19, 20. xxxii. 10. Job xii. 10. Psalm lvi. 8. cxxxix. 2. cxvi. 9, 12. lxxi. 17, 18. Prov. xxii. 2. xvi. 9. Isa. xlvi. 3, 4. Mat. x. 29, 30; and their death, Job xiv. 5. John vii. 4. Psal. xxxix. 5. 1 Sam. xxvi. 10. Jer. xxxiv. 4, 5. xxii. 19. xxxvi. 30. 3. *All the actions or motions* of his creatures, Isa. xlv. 6, 7. Lam. iii. 38. Amos iii. 2, 6, 7.—1. All *natural* motions of inanimate, or actions of animate creatures, Psalm lxxiv. 16, 17. cxxxvi. 8, 9. civ. Gen. viii. 21, 22. Isa. lv. 9, 10. Jer. xxxi. 35, 36. Matth. v. 46. Job xxxvii.—xli. Hence plants fixed between a fruitful and barren soil direct all their roots toward the former,—and fishes and fowls, at stated seasons, travel and station themselves to their own or mankind's advantage:—— 2. All *preternatural* motions. By his influence the waters overflowed the earth, and after they had drowned the ungodly inhabitants, were dried up, Gen. vi.—viii.;—Sodom was destroyed by fire and brimstone, Gen. xix. 24;—Egypt was plagued, and the Red Sea and Jordan divided, Exod. vii.—xiv. Psal. lxxv. 14, 15. lxxxix. 10. lxxviii. 12—14. lxxvii. 14—20. cxiv. cxxxvi. cxxxv. cv. cvi. lxxviii. Josh. iii. iv. 2 Kings ii.—

manna and quails were rained about the Hebrew camp, and water brought from flinty rocks, Exod. xvi. xvii. Num. xi. xx. Psalm lxxviii. 15---28;—the earth swallowed up Korah and his companions, Num. xvi.;—the thunders roared and lightnings flashed at Sinai, Exod. xix. xx. xxiv. 16, 17;—the sun and moon stood still, Josh. x. 12, 13. Hab. iii. 11;—the sun went backward ten degrees, Isa. xxxviii. 8;—a drought of forty-two months scorched the land of Israel, 1 Kings xvii. xviii. James v. 17;—ravens, which feed on carrion, regularly provided Elijah with clean flesh, 1 Kings xvii. 6;—a whale swallowed up Jonah, and after three days landed him in a proper place, Jon. i. 17. ii. 10;—an outrageous fiery furnace burnt the bonds of Shadrach, Meshach, and Abednego, while it did not singe their clothes or hair, Dan. iii. 19---37;—hungry lions attended Daniel a whole night, without hurting him in the least, but furiously devoured his accusers, Dan. vi. 22, 23, 24.—3. All *accidental* motions, as the slipping of an axe-head,—falling of a lot,—or fixing of a random arrow in the joint of a coat of mail, &c. Exod. xxi. 13. Deut. xix. 5. Prov. xvi. 33. 1 Kings xxii. 17, 28, 34. Ezek. xxi. 19---27. Jer. li. 16. Psalm cxlvii. 15---18. Matth. x. 29. Gen. xxii. 8, 13.—4. All free actions, which depend on men's will, Prov. xvi. 1, 9. xx. 24. xxi. 1. Jer. x. 23. Phil. ii. 13. Gen. xxiv. 7. xlv. 5, 7. l. 20. Isa. xlvi. 10, 11. x. 5---7. Acts iv. 28.—5. All *civil* actions, even the management of armies in the hottest battles, Isa. x. 5, 6, 7. Psalm xlvii. 9. Jer. xxxvi. 19. Prov. viii. 15, 16. Isa. x. xiii. Jer. xlvi.---li. Mic. ii. 13.— 6. All *moral* actions, *good* or *evil*, Isa. xxvi. 12. 1 Cor. iv. 7. Phil. ii. 13. Jam. i. 17. 2 Cor. iii. 5. Exod. x. 1. Deut. xi. 3, 6. 2 Sam. xii. 11, 12. xvi. 10. xxiv. 1. 1 Kings xi. 14, 26. xxii. 22. Psalm lxxxi. 12. Isa. vi. 9, 10. xxix. 14. Jer. iv. 10. Ezek. xiv. 9. xx. 25, 26. Rom. i. 24---28. ix. 17. xi. 8, 32. 2 Thess. ii. 10, 11, 12.—— In respect of his operation about these creatures and their actions, his providence may be distinguished into his *natural, miraculous, moral,* and *peculiar* providence.

God's NATURAL dispensation of providence includes, 1. His upholding all creatures in their existence and particular forms, and in their powers of action, motion, or passion,—and in the actions or motions themselves, Job xii. 10. Heb. i. 3. Col. i. 17. Rev. iv. 11. Neh. ix. 6. Psalm xxxvi. 5, 6. cxlv. 15, 16. cxlvii. 8, 9. Matth. vi. 26---30. 2. His government of them,— which includes, 1. His fixing certain laws or rules, called *ordinances of heaven, covenant with day and night,* or the like, according to which he ordinarily regulates his influence, Jer. xxxi. 35, 36. xxxiii. 25. Psalm cxix. 90, 91. 2. His co-operating with, and directing the motions of his creatures, according to these stated rules and his own purpose, Gen. viii.

22. ix. 11. Isa. x. 15. Jer. x. 23. Psalm lxxiv. 16, 17. cxv. 3. Acts xvii. 28. 1 Cor. xii. 6. Eph. i. 11. Isa. xlvi. 10, 11. Dan. iv. 35.——In this he applies his creatures to *act*,—and on *such* particular *objects*,—and in *such a manner*, Isa. x. 5. Ezek xxi. 21—23. Job i. 12. ii. 6. Acts i. 26. Exod. xxi. 12, 13. 1 Kings xxii. 34; and he accurately directs them to their proper ends, Prov. xix. 21. xvi. 1, 9. xxi. 1. Gen. xlix. 10.

In his *ordinary* managements of providence, God allows second causes to have their full influence, and acts in, and by them agreeably to their nature as inferior agents or instruments in his hand :—But his co-operating influence or concourse is *not merely general*, fixing a particular impression upon second causes, and then leaving them to move and act of their own accord; but it is *particular* with every particular creature, and producing every particular motion or act, in its particular form. 1. The Scripture represents God as exerting particular influences,—in giving victories, Psalm xxxiii. 16. xviii. 43. cxliv. 1;—in giving direction or satisfaction, Psalm xiii. 1—5;—in sending Joseph into Egypt, Gen. xlv. 5, 7. 1. 20;—in employing the Assyrians, Chaldeans, and Persians, as his *rod*, *axe*, *hammer*, and *host*, Isa. x. 5, 15. xiii. 14. Jer. li. 22, 23. And sometimes his terror, falling on their enemies, procured victory or deliverance for the Jews, Judg. vii. 14—22. 2 Chron. xiv. 11—14. xx. 22, 23. 2 Kings vii. 6. How absurd to imagine, that all these were owing to impressions made upon certain atoms, at the creation! 2. If God only made a general impression of whatever kind on things, at the first, all things must now be carried on by necessity of nature, independent of his will;—and either that impression hath necessarily produced sin in angels and men; or they, in sinning, have counteracted his almighty influence impressed. 3. Such a general concourse exempts his creatures from all continued dependence upon him in their operations, while they are allowed to depend upon him in their existence, Acts xvii. 28. Prov. xvi. 1, 9. xxi. 1,——But concerning this divine co-operation, it must be observed, 1. It is not any power transmitted from God to his creatures, in order to move them; but an agency of his own will, by which he makes second causes to act, when and how he pleases. 2. The acting of God, and that of his creature upon which he acts, are not separable, or different, but he makes it to act, not by its own independent energy, but by the influence of his will. 3. No creatures are left to determine the influence of God's concourse with them, as they please, as the nature of the objects upon which the sun shines, determines his influence to melt, harden, scorch, or fructify them, &c.—If they were thus left to determine it, his agency would be subjected to theirs, and they would do more in an action than he did;—he could be no more the author of good than of evil; no decree could be certain of execution, or any prediction, promise, or threatening, of fulfilment. 4. The agency of God's will in order of nature, not of time, must always precede that of his creature, in every motion or act, Rom. xi. 36.

God's MIRACULOUS providence is that in which his agency surpasses, or is contrary to the influence of second causes, and stated rules of his common operation;—as in stopping the course of the sun,—dividing seas,—raising dead persons,—or giving sight to such as were born blind, &c.—God does not exert more power in working miracles, than in common providence, but merely suspends his ordinary influence, or counteracts the natural or common influence of second causes.—And herein no creature can be any more than a moral instrument of declaring the will of God, by some word or token, that such a miracle should be wrought.——If we consider the infinite wisdom, power, holiness, justice, goodness, truth, and majesty of God, we may, in *real miracles,* expect, 1. That the moral instruments will make no *fantastic* or *absurd* application to superior powers. In working miracles, Christ and his prophets and apostles never did any thing but what was exceedingly simple, as pronouncing a few proper words, touching the objects, stretching out a rod towards it, &c. which imported an authoritative declaration of God's will. 2. As it would be unworthy of God to perform an almighty operation for no, or even an insignificant end, every miracle may be expected to answer some very important end. 3. As it would be unworthy of God's wisdom, goodness, and infinite Majesty to work miracles merely to manifest his strength, they must also tend to vindicate his holiness, equity, goodness, and truth;—and hence none bid fair to be ordinarily moral instruments in working them, but men sound in their religious principles, and holy and virtuous in their practice. 4. That the miraculous operations shall be so many and so openly wrought, that both friends and enemies will have full opportunity to try their reality.——Counterfeits of miracles may be performed, 1. By the powers of second causes unknown to common people, as in *electricity, natural magic,* &c. 2. By deceitful slight of hand, which imposes on the sight of the beholders. 3. By diabolical impressions on matter, or on men's mind, making them think or speak in an uncommon manner.——Of these kinds are the boasted miracles of papists. But those of the Egyptian magicians were the most extraordinary. Nor can we certainly tell how they were wrought:—whether by some Satanical perturbation of the air, imposing on the sight of the spectators;—or by Satan's moving the rods in the manner of serpents, and at the same time perturbing the air, to make them seem real serpents;—or by indiscernibly removing the rods, and placing real serpents in their stead.—But it is certain, that these magicians' apparently-transformed rods were swallowed up by the really transformed one of Aaron, and that their other pretended miracles did not remove but enlarge the punishment of their country.

God's MORAL providence is that by which he manages the *morally good or evil* dispositions and actions of his reasonable creatures. It, in general, includes, 1. His establishing for them a law to be the rule and standard of their disposition and behaviour towards him, themselves, or their fellow creatures, correspondent with his perfections and will. 2. His influence on them relative to their good and evil dispositions, thoughts, words, and deeds.---This influence, though infallibly efficacious, never interferes with the real liberty of rational creatures. 1. Except in miracles, God always acts on second causes answerably to their nature. 2. The liberty of rational beings doth not lie in any indifferent bent towards good and evil; otherwise neither God nor men, nor angels, ever did, or can have it; but it lies in a power of acting with knowledge and inclination, without being forced by any other. 3. Though God often bend their will to that which he wills and commands, he never puts any force upon the will of any. Nay, indeed the will cannot properly be forced.

In *good actions*, 1. God upholds men's natural powers of acting, and the gracious dispositions which he hath implanted in them. 2. He presents to them objects, which are calculated to move them to the good action which he intends they should perform. 3. He removes or restrains such objects or influences as, he knows, would hinder that action. 4. By his word he commands and encourages them to act in such a particular good matter and manner. 5. By his spirit he influences their heart and corrects their indisposition. 6. He bends their mind and affections toward the reasons, which enforce the good action. 7. He makes them feel a peculiar pleasure in such a particular form of acting. Thus, in alms-giving, 1. He furnishes a man with somewhat to give. 2. He presents a needy object to him. 3. He restrains such thoughts as might make him overlook or conceive harshly of that needy object. 4. He impresses on his mind the scriptural exhortations and motives to charity. 5. He powerfully excites his pity and compassion. 6. He fills his mind with pleasure in resolving on or bestowing his alms.

In *sinful actions* God PERMITS them; and herein, 1. He forbears doing that which would hinder them:---he doth not deprive the actors of life, of sight, of reason, or the like, as Exod. xiv. 28. Gen. xix. 11. 2 Kings vi. 18, 19;---he doth not oppose superior force to their inclination or power to commit the sinful deed:---he does not remove out of their way or hand the occasions or instruments of such a sin :---he does not stir up in their mind such thoughts of the wickedness and danger of the sin as would deter them from it: he does not cure their ignorance by spiritual instruction, nor their malice by renewing their heart, nor their sloth and unconcern, by awakening fear and care in their soul. 2. As, in every rational act, there is something *natural, moral,* and *influential;* so in every sinful act there is something *natural,* which renders it the opposite of *nothing,*—a *moral disconformity* to God's law, and an influential tendency to hurt the agent or others.—In the first and last of these, God actually concurs by his co-operating influence; he produces what is natural in the act with which the sinful disconformity to his law is connected;—and he makes that act tend to the hurt of the actor, if not also of its object. 3. He excites in men's mind thoughts which, though good or indifferent in themselves, their inward corruptions improve to a wrong purpose. Thus Joseph's brethren improved their remembrance of his father's love to him, and of his dreams, to inflame their hatred and rage against him, Gen. xxxvii.—and the Jewish rulers improved their thoughts of Christ's success and esteem among the people, and of his raising Lazarus from the dead, to animate and increase their malice and fury against him, John xi. 47—57. 4. He, in a holy manner, lays before them opportunities of sinning. Thus the Babylonish garment and wedge of gold were laid before Achan, Josh. vii. 21. Bathsheba washing herself before David, 2 Sam. xi. 2.——This presentation of the occasion or object neither binds, nor inclines, nor forces men to commit sin;—nor doth God present them for promoting it, but for the glory of his own perfections,—and frequently to punish men for some former wickedness, or to discover their wicked inclinations to themselves or others.

Though, in consequence of such permission, the sinful act infallibly happen, the sinfulness of it is not in the least chargeable on God. For, 1. He influences his rational creatures precisely according to the freedom of their own will. 2. Though he produce that which is natural in the act with which their sinfulness is connected, yet that sinfulness of the act or disconformity to his law proceeds wholly from their self-corrupting or self-corrupted abuse of the inward freedom of their will. Thus hatred, as a *natural affection,* is good, and from God; but the direction of that hatred in opposition to God himself is sinful, and proceeds not from his permission or precourse, but from the corrupted disposition of him that hates him. 3. Sin ought carefully to be considered as not only an *offence* to God and *breach* of his law, but also as a just *punishment* of preceding sinfulness. It is in the *latter respect* that God's providence hath a most remarkable concern in the permission of it, in *blinding* the mind, and *hardening* the heart of sinners, Rom. xi. 7,

8. 2 Cor. iv. 3, 4. iii. 14. 2 Thess. ii. 9—12. Isa. lxiii. 17. Exod. iv. 21. vii. 3, 14, 22.——In *blinding men's minds*, 1. God permits them to conceive such thoughts as occasion or lead to error and mistake. 2. He gives them up to the seduction of Satan and his instruments, 1 Kings xxii. 21, 22, 23. 1 Cor. iv. 3, 4. 2 Thess. ii. 9—12. Acts v. 3. John xiii. 2, 27. 3. Outward providences appear to enforce their temptations, Psalm lxxiii. 2—15. Jer. xii. xx. Job i.—iii. 2 Thess. ii. 9—12. Rev. xi. 2. xiii. 4. They are left to themselves to abuse, to contrary purposes, every thing which might tend to their instruction or conversion, John vi. 64—66. x. 30—40. Acts vii. 54. xxii. 22. xxvi. 24. 5. The powerful working of their inward wickedness disposes them to believe or not believe things, as best answers to promote its reign in their heart, Jer. xliii. xliv. 6. They take all the outward prosperity which they meet with in their evil course, as a token that God is well enough pleased with them in it, Rom. ii. 4. Deut. xxxii. 15, 16. Jer. xliv. 17, 18. 7. If they meet with outward calamities, they either overlook them, or view them as produced by mere natural causes, Isa. xxvi. 11. 2 Chron. xxviii. 22. Jer. v. 3. Isa. i. 5.——In *hardening men's heart*, 1. God justly withholds his grace, which would effectually soften it, Hos. iv. 17. Rev. xxii. 11. 2. He withdraws that common grace, or even in part that special grace, which had once softened it, Isa. lxiii. 17. 3. He permits their sinful lusts to prevail and rage without any remarkable restraint, Psalm lxxxi. 11, 12. 4. He permits them to fall among wicked companions, who, by their example, instruction, or influence, encourage them in sin, Judg. xi 4. 1 Kings xii. 10, 11. Prov. ix. 6. xiii. 20. xxviii. 19, 24. 5. He heaps outward favours upon them, which occasionally increase their pride, atheism, and sinful unconcern, Luke xii. 16—20. xvi. 19. Job xxi. 14, 15. Ezek. xvi. 49. Deut. xxxii. 15. Luke xviii. 24, 25. Psalm lxxiii. 5—9. Isa. v. 11, 12. Hos. xiii. 6. 6. He either forbears to afflict them, or afflicts them very slightly ; or the time, manner, or instrument of their afflictions is such, that their corrupt heart despises them, rages against them, or improves them as excitements to sin, Isa. i. 5. Jer. v. 3. 2 Kings vi. 33. 2 Chron. xxviii. 22. 7. By Satanical or other influence, their conscience is restrained from reproving them, or is so ignorant or biassed, that it calls evil good and good evil, Gen. vi. 3. Hos. iv. 17. Isa. v. 18—23. xxx. 10. Ezek. xiii. 10, 22. Mal. ii. 17. Mic. ii. 11.

The above account of God's *blinding men's mind and hardening their heart*, may be illustrated from the instance of Pharaoh, king of Egypt. 1. God, by exalting him to an high station, afforded him an opportunity of remarkable pride. 2. He withheld from him that gracious influence, which would have humbled his heart, and rendered him obedient and willing to let the Israelites go. 3. He sent him peremptory orders to allow them to depart, which, on account of his claim to them, and of the messengers he sent to demand their liberty, and perhaps also on account of their throng of work, tended to irritate the spirit of the proud king. 4. His mandate was delivered in such a form as could lead Pharaoh to reason upon it in this manner: "If the God of the Israelites be more powerful than I, why should he request my dismission of his people? And if he be weaker, why should I submit to his will, in a point so exceedingly detrimental to my kingdom?" 5. A biassed consideration of the messengers, who made the demand in God's name, tempted him to suspect that the Israelites were too idle, or cherished some superstitious whim, if not a seditious design. —— 6. The first miracles which Moses and Aaron wrought were but objects of sight, and did no hurt. 7. The magicians' ready counterfeits of these first miracles, natively tempted him to look on the whole as a diabolical farce, and Moses and Aaron as jugglers. 8. The distinguished safety of the Israelites and their property under the several plagues inflicted on his kingdom, tended to irritate his proud spirit. 9. The easy, sudden, and often repeated removals of the plagues, tempted his proud, carnal, and wicked heart to despise both plagues and deliverances. 10. The miracle which his magicians could not counterfeit, being seemingly more insignificant than those which they had, might tempt him to think that Jehovah could inflict no worse plagues than had already happened. 11. Moses's peremptory refusal to leave a single beast belonging to his enslaved nation, when he granted them allowance to go off themselves, was very provoking to his proud spirit. 12. The Israelites carrying off the Egyptians' gold and silver, strongly tempted his haughty and covetous heart to pursue them. 13. Their travelling to the south-east, where they were miserably entangled by mountains and seas, instead of going straight to Canaan, tempted him and his servants to think them under no divine, nay, no rational direction; and so might be easily forced back to their servitude, which was exceedingly profitable to his kingdom. 14. Meanwhile, God all along gave him up to the influence of his own corrupt lusts,—to the temptations of Satan, and, no doubt, to the remonstrances of wicked courtiers, who could suggest a multitude of reasons against his allowing the Israelites to leave the country.

2. God LIMITS sinful dispositions and actions, Psalm lxxvi. 10. 1. In their *degree*, that they are so sinful and no more,—so vigorous and no more, &c. Gen. xx. 6. Jer. iii. 5. 2. In their *extent* and influence, that it reaches so far and no farther, Isa. x. 32. xxxvii. 29. Psalm lxxvi. 10. Rev. xx. 2. 3. In their

duration, permitting men to continue them just so long, and no longer, Gen. vi. 3. xv. 13, 16. Dan. vii. 25. Rev. xi. 2. xiii. 5.
——He thus limits men's sinning, 1. By withholding from them an ability or opportunity to commit particular sins, by laying them under poverty, sickness, or the like, 2 Chron. xxi. 16—19. xvi. 10, 12. 2. By cutting them off by death in the beginning or progress of their sinful course, 1 Kings xvi. xxii. 2 Kings i.—xvi. xxiv. xxv. 3. By severely correcting or punishing them for their sin, Job xxxiv. 31, 32. 4. By powerfully convincing them of the evil and danger of it, Judg. ii. x. 5. By converting and changing their heart, Acts ii. ix. 1 Cor. vi. 9—11.

3. God OVERRULES the sinful dispositions and actions of men and devils, 1. To his own glory, in making them occasions for the manifestation of his patience, goodness, or revenging justice,—and especially in rendering them occasions of promoting redemption-work, in which all his perfections are glorified to the highest, Psalm lxxvi. 10. Rom. v. 20, 21. 2. To the good of his people, in making them, or the troubles procured by them, means of awakening, convincing, converting, humbling, reforming, or sanctifying them, Rom. vii. 14—24. Heb. iii. 12, 13. xii. 29. Isa. lxiv. 6. 1 Pet. ii. 1. Heb. i. 14, 25, 28. x. 24, 25. 1 Cor. v. 1—5. Rom. v. 20, 21. with vi. 1, 2.

By God's PECULIAR providence, we mean that which is especially exercised about Christ, as man and mediator, and his church. That these are a peculiar object of divine providence is manifest : 1. All God's dispensations of providence promote the glory of his grace in Christ, whose *fulness* the church is, Eph. i. 10, 22, 23. 2. All power in heaven and on earth is lodged in the hand of Christ, in order to be exercised for the good of his church, Eph. ii. 22. Mat. xi. 27. xxviii. 18. John iii. 35. v. 22. 3. The perfections of God are most gloriously displayed in Christ and his church, Eph. iii. 10, 21. She is God's hill, Psalm ii. 6. lxxxvii. 1; his throne, Jer. xvii. 14; the firmament of his power, Psalm cl. 1; his academy for instruction, Eph. iii. 10. iv. 11, 12, 13. Psalm cxlvii. 19, 20; his temple or house, Eph. ii. 20—22. 1 Pet. ii. 5. Heb. iii. 6.—She is, as it were, Christ, the rose of Sharon spread,—Christ furnished with members,—in whom there is glory to God in the highest, 1 Cor. xii. 12. Eph. iii. 21. Luke ii. 10—14. 2 Cor. iv. 6. 4. The church hath a more near and dear relation to God through Christ, than any thing else, being his bride, his sister, his friend, his flock, his jewels, his rest, his garden, his portion, &c. Isa. liv. 5. lxii. 4, 5. Song v. 1, 2. Ezek. xvi. 8—14. xxxiv. xxxvi. xxxvii. John x. Mal. iii. 17. Psalm cxxxii. 13, 14. Song iv. 12—16. vi. 2. Deut. xxxii. 9. Psalm cxxxv. 4. 5. God hath a peculiar esteem of, love to, and delight in his church, as connected with Christ, Isa. xlv. 15, 19. xli. 14. xliii. 4, 15, 21. xliv. 1, 2, 6. lxii. 3—5. Jer. xxxii. 39---42. Psalm lxxxvii. 1, 2. cxlvii. 11. cxlix. 4. cxxxii. 13, 14. Zeph. iii. 17. Notwithstanding unnumbered sinful blemishes and provocations, he loves one saint more than all the world besides, Isa. lvii. 15—18. lxvi. 2. Gen. vi. 8. 6. He is peculiarly present with Christ and his church, 2 Cor. v. 19. Rev. xiv. 1. Ezek. xlviii. 35. Hag. ii. 4, 5. 7. The prayers of Christ and his people have a peculiar influence in forming the dispensations of his providence, John xi. 42. Zech. i. 12—15. Rev. viii. 3—5. xi. 3—6. Isa. xlv. 11. Psalm cvi. 23. Ezek. xxii. 30. James v. 16, 17. 8. Under the management of God's providence, all things work together for the glory of Christ and the good of his church, Rom. viii. 28.—For this purpose the world is so long continued in its present form, Acts xvii. 30. 2 Pet. iii. 9; and by the presence of Christ and his church in it, it is preserved from utter corruption and ruin, Prov. x. 25. Psalm lxxv. 3. Isa. vi. 13. lxv. 8.——All *natural* things and all *miraculous* events are directed to, and promote this glory of Christ and good of his people, Hos. ii. 18—23. Exod. iii.—xx. Num. xi. xii. xvi. xvii. xx. Josh. vi. x. Hab. iii. 1 Kings xvii. xviii. 2 Kings i.—vii. xiii. John ii. 11. Mat. iv. 24, 25. xi. 5.—All the interests, and the whole fate of nations, in every age and place, are directed to, and really promote this end; though, by reason of our ignorance, we cannot distinctly trace their tendency to it, 2 Kings ix. 6, 7. 1 Kings xix. 15—18. Isa. xliv. xlv. Jer. xlvi. —li. Ezek. xxi. 27. Hag. ii. 6—8. Rev. vi.—xxi.——All *good things* of importance are given to the church as connected with Christ;—all the oracles and ordinances of God, Psalm cxlvii. 19, 20. Rom. iii. 2. Eph. iv. 11—13. 1 Cor. xii. 28.—all the gifts and common graces of wicked men, Balaam, Judas, Demas, &c. Num. xxii.---xxiv. John vi. 70. Mat. x. Philem. 24.--- all true and spiritual gifts and graces, Col. i. 25. 1 Cor. xii. xiv. Eph. i. 3.---all holy angels and men, saints, ministers, Heb. i. 14. Psalm xxxiv. 7. 1 Cor. iii. 22. xii. 28. Eph. iv. 11---13. ——All *bad things* in the world are made to promote the honour of Christ and welfare of the church;---all commotions and destructive judgments are made subservient for relieving, awakening, purging, or preparing for the spread of the church, Psalm xxix. 10, 11. Isa. xlvi. 11---13. Hag. ii. 6, 7. Rev. xi. 12, 13. xvi. xviii.---xxi. Ezek. xx. 36, 37. xxi. 27. Hos. ii. 6, 7, 14. Dan. xi. 35. Isa. xxvii. 9. Mic. vi. 14. Zeph. iii. 8—20. Gen. xlix. 5. Deut. xxxiii. 10.—Contentions in the church are made means of fixing men in the truth, or of spreading the knowledge of it, Acts xv. 36, 37. and persecution is useful for purging or extending the church, Jer. xxiv. 5---7. Phil. i. 12. Acts viii. 3, 4. xiii. xvi.---xix.——Wicked men are made of great use to the church, 1. In spreading the knowledge of divine truths. By the influence of Ptolemy, king of Egypt, or some renegade Jews, part of the Old Testament was translated into Greek, a wide-spread language, to prepare the nations for the spread of the gospel.---Augustus's enrolment of his subjects, Herod's consultation, and his murder of the babes, solemnly marked Bethlehem the place, and that, the date of our Saviour's birth, Luke ii. 1—7. Mat. ii. 1—18. 2. In protecting or providing for the church or her members, Gen. xii. 10. Isa. xvi. 3, 4. Rev. xii. 16. 3. In advancing some of her principal friends and pillars to great power and influence.—Thus Saul and Abner promoted David, 1 Sam. xvi. 2 Sam. iii. v. Pharaoh promoted Joseph, Gen. xli. Another Pharaoh and his daughter, Moses, Exod. ii. Nebuchadnezzar and Darius, Daniel, Dan. i.—vi. Ahasuerus, Esther and Mordecai, Esther ii. viii. Artaxerxes, Ezra and Nehemiah, Ezra vii. Neh. ii. 4. In delivering and enriching the church, Isa. xlv. 3, 4, 13. xlv. 11— 13. 5. In purging the church of her corrupt members, by the terrors of persecution, or even by sucking the blood of saints till she be cured, 1 John ii. 19. Isa. xxvii. 9. xxxi. 9. Ezek. xx. 38.—Even devils are made to work together for the good of the church. By taking possession of such multitudes in the time of Christ and his apostles, they occasioned multitudes of miraculous confirmations of the gospel and Messiahship of Christ. By entering into the Gadarene swine, they justified God's law, which prohibited the eating of these animals, and punished the transgressors of it,—they manifested Christ's almighty power and sovereignty, and proved the truth and great importance of his miraculous cures.——Nay, sin itself is made to promote the honour of Christ, and welfare of his people, Rom. v. 20, 21. Eph. i. 7. 1 John i. 7, 9. Sarah's passion promoted the promised restriction of Abraham's blessed seed to Isaac, Gen. xvi. xxi. Onesimus's theft occasioned his conversion to Christ, and Paul's *furious* persecution of the saints hastened his, Philem. 10. Acts viii. ix. xxii. xxvi. Gal. i. 1 Tim. i. 13. Papal fury, clerical horrid impieties, and licentious indulgences, occasioned the Protestant reformation; and King Henry's pride and lewdness occasioned his promoting it in England.—The Jews' rejection and murder of Christ were instrumental in his ransoming his elect, Isa. liii. Mat. ii.—xxvii.—— But, 6. God, in his providential work, manifests an amazing regard to his church as connected with Christ, 1. In sometimes, as it were, preferring the exercise of his mercy towards her to the vindication of his own honour, and providing for her safety, before he step forth to execute his just vengeance on outrageous offenders, Isa. xxvi. 20. Rev. vii. 1—3. Gen. xix. 22. 2. In taking peculiar care of his own people amidst the most terrible executions of his wrath, Ezek. ix. 6. Jer. xv. 11. xxxix. 11—18. xlv. 5. Amos ix. 9, 10. 3. In stating the injuries done to his people, as the *sole* or *principal* ground of his most terrible judgments on nations, 1 Sam. xv. 2. Jer. xlviii.—li. Ezek. xxv.—xxxv. xxxviii. xxxix. Obad. Mat. xxiv. xxv. 41—45. Rev. vi. viii. ix. xi.—xx. 4. In taking such honourable notice of the meanest of them, while he leaves the great ones of the earth unmentioned, or loaded with infamy and contempt. How large and honourable the history of Jacob, in comparison with that of Cain, Ishmael, Esau, and their families? How much more honourable the history of Ebedmelech and the Syrophenician woman, than of all the kings and princes of their age, Jer. xxxviii. 7—12. xxxix. 15—18. Mat. xv. 22—28. The pins of the tabernacle are more noticed than all the glories of Nineveh, Babylon, Persepolis, Rome, &c. 5. In delaying his more remarkable providential work, till he have laid the plan of it before his people, and obtained their approbation of it, Gen. xviii. 17. xli. Dan. ix.—xii. Exod. xxxii. 9, 10. Isa. xlv. 11. 6. In bestowing all his choicest things,—his Son,—his word,—his grace,—his glory, only upon his church, Isa. ix. 6. ii. 5. Psalm cxlvii. 19, 20. Rom. iii. 2. Hos. viii. 12. Eph. iv. 11—13. 1 Cor. xii. Psalm lxxxiv. 11.

All the providential dispensations of God towards ourselves or our fellow-creatures ought to be CAREFULLY OBSERVED, Psal. cvii. 43. Hos. xiv. 9. Psalm cxi. 2. cxliii. 5. cxlv. 5, 7. lxxvii. 5, 10, 11. Isa. v. 12. lxiii. 7. 1. How they are *timed* with the frame of our spirit, Psalm cxxvi. 1; or with our circumstances, Psalm xciv. 18. Job xx. 23. xxix. 18. 2. How they *begin*, Psalm cxxx. 6. Luke i. 66; *go forward*, Luke ii. 19, 51. Hos. vi. 3; *turn about*, Zech. xiv. 7. Gen. xli. 14. Esther vi. 3, 4. Gen. xxi. 17.—and *end*, James v. 11. Job xlii. 10, 12. 3. How they are *mixed*, sweet and bitter, dark and plain, Lam. iii. 22, 32. Isa. xxvii. 8, 9. Hab. iii. 2. 4. How they *meet together*, Job i. ii. xlii. John xvi. 33. Eccl. vii. 14. 5. What they *teach*, Mic. vi. 8, 9. Psalm lxxiii. 16, 17. Jer. vii. 7. 6. How they *harmonize* with Scripture doctrines, Psalm xlviii. 8. 1 Cor. i. 26. Jer. xvii. 9. Mat. xxii. 14; with Scripture prophecies, 1 Tim. i. 18. Amos iii. 7; with Scripture promises, Josh. xxi. 45. Psalm cxix. 65. Gen. viii. 22. Mark x. 29, 30. Exod. xx. 24. Prov. x. 9. xvi. 7; with Scripture threatenings, Lev. x. 3. Hos. vii. 12. Mic. iv. 11, 12. 1 Sam. ii. 30. Deut. xxxii. 35. and with Scripture examples, Psalm cxliii. 5. Jer. xii. 1, 2. Psalm xcii. 6, 7. Eccl. viii. 14. 1 Cor. iv. 9. Gen. xlvii. 9.——and how they harmonize with each other, in their parts, form, and end, 1 Cor. x. 13. 1 Pet. iv. 12. Eccl. i. 9—11. or with their own particular or common end, Deut. xxxii. 4. Eccl. iii. 11. Rom. viii. 28.—or with the prayers of saints, Gen.

IN HIS WORKS OF PROVIDENCE.

xxxii. 24—26. xxxiii. 10. 1 Chron. iv. 10. Psalm xviii. 4—50. xxxiv. 1—6. cxvi. 1—6. xli. 11. Mic. vii. 7—10. Ezek. xxxvi. 37. Gen. xxiv. 45. 2 Cor. xii. 8, 9. Psalm lxv. 5. Exod. xvii. 11. Rom. viii. 26, 27. Dan. ix. x.—and how they *correspond* with those sins which they punish,—in time,—in kind, —in similarity,—or in contrariety, 1 Kings xiii. 4. Judges i. 7. Gen. xix. 24. Lev. x. 1, 2. 1 Cor. xi. 30. Gen. iii. 5, 6. Psal. xlix. 20.—Gen. xxx. 1. xxxv. 16—19.—Gen. xxvii. 1, 6—24. xxix. 23.—John xi. 48. Luke xix. 43, 44. xxi. 24.

REFLECT. Having thus traversed the spacious fields of creation and providence, think, O my soul! Am I,—are all these beings around me, visible and invisible, the workmanship of God, and constantly preserved and governed by him? Why do I not, then, always consider myself as the temple of the living God, and all places as his residence?—Why do not I constantly perceive him in all things, and enjoy him in all that I meet with?—Why do not I cast all my care, and the care of all the churches, upon him?—Why do not I take every event as a demonstration of his love to my soul, and of his hatred of my sins? —Why do I undervalue any thing which Jehovah reckons worthy of his making, support, and government?——O his unfathomable wisdom!—his almighty power!—his amazing grace! —his perpetual mindfulness of his covenant,—that makes all these creatures work together for his glory and my good!—— And Oh, the horrid guilt of abusing a single creature to the service of my sinful lusts!

BOOK III.

Of the Covenant Bonds of Religious Connection between God and Men.

CHAP. I.

Of the COVENANT of WORKS, in the MAKING, BREACH, and RUINOUS CONSEQUENCES of it.

To render men more happy, and their obedience more cheerful, God hath all along exercised his providence towards them, in the form of covenant-connection. BERITH, the Hebrew word for *covenant*, denotes an establishment in general; and hence we read of God's covenant with day and night, Jer. xxxiii. 25. The Greek DIATHEKE, also signifies an *establishment*, particularly one by agreement or testament, Heb. vii. 22. ix. 15.——A *real* covenant in general is, *an agreement made between different persons on certain terms.*—Its necessary requisites are *parties,*—a *condition,*—a *promise,*—and a *penalty,* if any of the parties be fallible.—The covenants which God hath contracted for promoting the eternal happiness of mankind are TWO,—of WORKS, and of GRACE, Gal. iv. 24.* Rom. iii. 27. Gal. ii. 21. v. 4. Rom. vi. 14. viii. 2. Phil. iii. 19. &c.

---

* This text perhaps immediately respects the *two dispensations* of the covenant of grace,—though not without some reference to the two covenants themselves.——On the one hand, HAGAR, a bond-maid,——first pregnant in,—and at last with her son cast out from, Abraham's family,—denotes the legal dispensation as a state of ceremonial bondage, and of much inclination to the works of the law,— as first in order bringing forth professed children to God,—and at last expelled from the church of God and the hearts of his people.——SINAI, a barren mountain covered with thorns,—once terrible with thunders and lightnings,—and far distant from Canaan, the promised land, represents the covenant of works and legal dispensation, as pricking men's consciences with charges of guilt, and terrifying them with proclaimed commands and curses;—but altogether unfit to bring them into the evangelical and the heavenly rest.——ISHMAEL is an emblem of the Jews and other legalists, as early children of God in their open profession; but continuing under their spiritual bondage, and persecuting his Christian people, and therefore at last expelled from his church.——SARAH, a free woman, late and supernatural in her conception and child-birth, but continuing in Abraham's family till she died, prefigured the Christian dispensation and covenant of grace, as free,

OF THE COVENANT OF WORKS. 193

No party with whom God enters into covenant, can be at liberty to refuse his terms, or to propose terms to him, as in covenants between equals of mankind. No terms, which God, who is infinitely wise, holy, kind, and sovereign, proposes to his creatures, can be refused in a consistency with perfect purity of nature.——Nay, Jesus Christ could not have refused any terms which were proposed to him. He could not refuse them, *as the Son of God;* his will being the very same with that of his Father. He could not refuse them as Mediator, without disobedience to Jehovah's infinite authority. Nay, his manhood could not have refused them without sinning, which its immediate union to his divine person rendered absolutely impossible.—To pretend, therefore, that because Adam durst not refuse the terms which God proposed, there could be no covenant at all made with him, but a *mere law* imposed on him, plainly includes a denial that God can enter into any covenant at all, even with Christ.—If a father who hath a prior, a natural claim to the whole obedience of his son, require him to perform some particular service in order to obtain a particular reward, and mean while, furnish him with food, raiment, tools, and every thing necessary in carrying on the work,—he cannot lawfully refuse the terms; and nevertheless, when the required service is fulfilled, he hath a right, by his father's promise, to claim the reward. And if so, there is manifestly a real covenant between them. The application to our present point is obvious.

It is sufficiently evident, that a real covenant of this kind was made by God with Adam, in his innocent state. 1. In his transaction with him we have all the *requisites* of a covenant,— proper *parties*,—proper and real *terms*,—a condition, promise, and penalty, in case of a breach on Adam's side, who was fallible,—and proper *seals*, as will be afterwards more fully manifested, Gen. ii. 17. iii. 22. 2. This transaction between God and Adam is in Scripture expressly called a *covenant*, Gal. iv. 24. Here we have two *covenants*, one of which *gendereth to bondage*, which the broken covenant of works doth, in a fearful manner, 1 Cor. xv 56. Gal. iii. 10, 13. the other must therefore gender to spiritual and everlasting freedom and liberty, which it is certain the covenant of grace no less remarkably

---

late, but supernaturally productive of children to God, and remaining in his church till the end of time.——Mount ZION, pleasant and comely, the residence of God in his temple, and near the middle of Canaan, represented that covenant and dispensation, as singularly pleasant and beautiful,—blessed with God's peculiar presence,—and bringing men to heaven.—— ISAAC figured out Christian and other believers,—last in order,—born of the Spirit,—made free by Christ,—persecuted by Jews and other legalists,—but fixed and everlasting members of God's family, and heirs of himself.

O

doth, Rom. viii. 2. vi. 14. John viii. 32, 36.—Besides the covenant of grace, which is plainly a *remedial* one, being published immediately after Adam's FALL, necessarily supposeth the breach of an antecedent covenant of works, Gen. iii. 15, 22. Rom. v. 12—21.—In Hos. vi. 7. we have also mention of this covenant with Adam. KEADAM, here rendered *as men*, is only found in other two texts of Scripture.—In Job xxxi. 34. our translation renders it *like Adam*. In Psalm lxxxii. 7. a similar translation would make the passage appear much more emphatic. Ye shall die *like Adam*, whose honours were once so great, but quickly ruined.—In Hosea our translation renders the charge remarkably flat. But if it be rendered, " They, *like Adam*, have transgressed the covenant," *i. e.* have rebelled against the highest authority, manifested in the most solemn and engaging manner, —against the strongest motives,—and in violation of the most solemn engagements,—against the most express warnings, and upon the slightest temptations, and to the ruin of themselves and their posterity;—how nervous and striking! 3. As the infinite goodness of God determines him to lay no unnecessary burden on his creatures, his prescription of a positive command to Adam, and annexing the most dreadful death to the breach of it, naturally infers his annexing of a reward to his obedience,—in which the reality of a covenant-agreement is plainly manifested, Gen. ii. 17. 4. When we observe that God hath ordinarily appended some visible token for establishing or sealing his covenants with men,—as the seal of the *rainbow* to the covenant of safety made with Noah,—the seal of *circumcision* to the covenant of peculiar friendship and promise of Canaan with Abraham,—the seals of the *passover* and *sacrifices* to the covenant of peculiar adoption with the Israelites,—the seals of *baptism* and *the Lord's supper* to the new covenant-dispensation of the gospel period,—we are naturally led to look on the trees of *knowledge* and of *life* as seals annexed to a covenant-transaction with Adam ; the former representing him as on trial for everlasting happiness, and the latter suggesting, that, upon his fulfilment of the obedience required, he should obtain a more perfect life and happiness, than that which he enjoyed. 5. The law, imposed on Adam in his creation-state, hath been frequently published in the form of a covenant, Lev. xviii. 5. Deut. xxvii. 26. Mat. xix. 17. Gal. iii. 12. Rom. x. 5.—and is represented as a law, which admits of *boasting*, if perfect obedience be fulfilled, and as contrary to the *law of faith*, or covenant of grace manifested in the gospel, which it is only in its covenant form, Rom. iii. 27. 6. Nothing more effectually proves, that God made a real covenant with Adam, than the imputation of his first sin to all his natural posterity, even as the Surety-righteousness of Christ is imputed to all his spiritual seed, Rom. v. 12—21. 1 Cor. xv. 22. His being their natural father or root could not be the foundation of this imputation, otherwise all his sins at least before he begat Seth, our progenitor, must be imputed to us,---whereas all men were constituted sinners by *one offence*, Rom. v. 18.---Moreover, if parental relation inferred imputation of conduct to children, all the sins, if not also all the good works of our progenitors, especially of our immediate parents, must be imputed to us, whereas all men were constituted sinners by *one man's disobedience*, and died *in Adam*, Rom. v. 19. 1 Cor. xv. 21, 22.

The PARTIES contracting in this covenant were, I. GOD the Father, Son, and Holy Ghost, considered as the Creator, Sovereign, Proprietor, and Governor of mankind.---In his proposal of it, he appears as, 1. A God of *supreme, unbounded authority*, stamping his mere will into a law, to be obeyed under the highest penalty, and disposing of eternal life on what terms he pleased. 2. A God of *unbounded goodness*, in establishing with Adam, whom he had newly created, perfectly holy and happy, a most proper method of making him and all his posterity eternally more happy, on the easiest terms. 3. A God of *infinite condescension*, entering into a covenant with his creatures, and requiring that obedience by paction, which he might have required by mere authority. II. Adam, considered, 1. As a man *perfectly holy and righteous*,---perfectly inclined and capable to fulfil whatever obedience God required, Eccl. vii. 29. Gen. i. 27. v. 1. Col. iii. 10. Eph. iv. 24. Nor indeed would a kind and righteous God have required any obedience from him, but what he had made him capable of performing, Mat. xxv. 24. Psalm cxix. 68. lxxxvi. 5, 15. Deut. xxxii. 4. 2. As a common public head of all his natural posterity. His being their common Parent fitted him to be their moral Head or representative in this covenant. Hence all that descend from him by ordinary generation, and perhaps Eve also, were represented by him in it.---Indeed she fell by her own personal transgression, but so might any of the representees have done before the condition was fulfilled, the covenant confirmed, and the state of trial in it finished.---Christ being the Son of God;---being from all eternity constituted the Representative of his own elect seed in the remedial covenant of grace,---having never any human person,---and being descended from Adam, not by natural or ordinary generation, but by the supernatural influence of the Holy Ghost, in virtue of a promise posterior to his fall, John i. 14. Psalm lxxxix. 3, 4, 19, 20. Isa. vii. 14. Luke i. 35. Gen. iii. 15.---he could not be represented by him in it.

It is sufficiently evident, that Adam truly represented and stood bound for all his natural posterity in this covenant. 1. In all the occasional typical covenants which God made with men, the parent in some sense represented his posterity; as Noah, Gen. ix. 9; Abraham, Gen. xvii. 7, 8; David, 2 Sam. vii. 16; Phinehas, Num. xxv. 10---13; the Israelites, Isa. lix. 21. 2. In this matter, Adam is represented as similar to Christ, 1 Cor. xv. 21, 22, 45---49. Rom. v. 12---21. And as Christ and his spiritual seed are called by the same name of *Jacob, Israel, and Christ,*—so Adam's posterity are, in the Hebrew original, called by his name about four hundred and thirty times. 3. Adam's breach of this covenant is by an infinitely righteous God imputed, or stated in law-reckoning, to the account of all his natural posterity,—even though they never live to imitate him in actual sin, Rom. v. 12---19.—How could this take place, but upon the foot of their covenant representation in him? 4. All his natural posterity are constituted sinners, and ruined in law, by the *one offence* of his first sin, Rom. v. 17, 18.

God's entering into covenant with all mankind in Adam was *most reasonable and kind.* 1. It was the shortest way in which they could obtain everlasting happiness. In this method, one man's perfect obedience to God's law for a time, perhaps a very short time, would have secured this happiness to all mankind; —whereas, had each man stood bound for himself, it would have continued in suspense to many of them, who knows how long. 2. It plainly appeared the safest method. Adam, being formed in an adult state, perfectly holy, fully able and inclined to fulfil the whole law of God,—and living while Satan was less crafty, and there were fewer occasions of temptation, —and having the strongest motives,—regard to his own, and to all mankind's happiness, to engage him to care, activity, and perseverance in his work,—promised fairer to retain his perfection and persevere in his obedience, than any of his seed. ——Adam was the most fit person of mankind to be the covenant-head and representative of all the rest. Being their common parent, he was most equally related to them all. He had stronger motives and better opportunities to persevere in perfect obedience, than any other could have.—In fine, an infinitely wise, holy, just, and good God, having chosen him for their Head, and included this representation of them in his proposal of his covenant-favours, none of his posterity, if they had been all alive on the spot, could, without sin against God,—without self-injuring folly, have withheld their consent, Psalm cxix. 68. Gen. xviii. 25. Deut. xxxii. 4. Eccl. iii. 14. vii. 13.

Though this covenant was proposed by God, the great lawgiver, to his newly-created subjects, and on that account is frequently called the *Law,* or *Law of Works,* Rom. vii. 4. vi. 14. iii. 27, &c. Adam could not but consent to the terms of it.

1. Being God's rational creature, subject to his sovereign dominion, he was bound to accept whatever terms he proposed, and to receive his favours, in whatever method he pleased to bestow them.—Not to have desired and embraced the promise, would have implied contempt of God's goodness and bounty.— Not to have readily received the precept, would have implied hatred of his holiness, and rebellion against his authority.— Not to have submitted to the penalty, would have implied a denial of his justice and authority.—Not the smallest degree of any of these could have consisted with perfect innocence. 2. The natural love which uncorrupted man bore to himself, naturally carried him out toward God, as his chief good; and consequently to the only way of enjoying him as such. 3. Adam's pure conscience could not but perceive and attest that the whole tenor of this covenant was very acceptable and gracious, *viz.* That he should hold God as his *chief good*, and seek happiness in him above all things else; that he should cheerfully accept of the everlasting enjoyment of him, *an infinite good*, when offered upon the easiest terms; that he should cheerfully receive that law, which was the will of his Creator, and a transcript of his moral perfections to be the rule of his dispositions and conduct; and that he should submit his guilty head to God's just vengeance, if he contemned his gracious promise, and violated his holy law.——In God's proposal of the terms to Adam, and in his acceptance of them, and thus reciprocally engaging themselves, each to other, the making of this covenant consisted.—Adam's consent to the terms, actually instated him in this covenant, even as our believing consent to the terms of the covenant of grace actually and personally instates us in it.

The PARTS of this covenant of works were the Condition, Promise, and Penalty.——The *Condition* was, that which God required Adam to fulfil in order to acquire a right for himself and his posterity to the promised reward.—The *Promise* was, God's engagement or declaration of his will to bestow eternal life on Adam and all his natural posterity, as the reward of his fulfilment of the condition.—The *Penalty* was, that punishment which God threatened and had to inflict on Adam and his seed, if he did not perfectly fulfil that condition.

OBEDIENCE to God was, and must be, the CONDITION of the covenant of works,—the *Rule*, *Matter*, and *Manner* of which require our consideration.——Concerning the RULE of this obedience, or LAW of the covenant, it may be observed, 1. The natural relation between God as a Creator, Preserver, and Governor, and man as a rational creature, necessarily required that God should prescribe a law to him, which should not only regulate his actions, but also the moral qualities of his nature; and that the leading commandments of it should be founded upon the unchangeable nature of God,—that so all men, at all times, might have their dispositions and behaviour adjusted by the same standard. 2. This law must be duly made known to man, that it might be obeyed without mistake.—It was manifested to Adam before the covenant form of it was proposed to him,—being written in his heart, and inlaid in the image of God, which was concreated with and in his nature, Gen. i. 26, 27.—It summarily required him, as he should have opportunity, to love God with all his heart, soul, mind, and strength, and to love his neighbour as himself, Mat. xxii. 37---40. Mark xii. 29---33. 3. The end of this covenant being to render men more happy than when they were newly created, it was very proper that, to the law of nature written on man's heart in his creation, some *positive precept* should be added, and especially one that might promote his exact fulfilment of the whole condition.——That which God actually prescribed was, that Adam should never eat of the fruit of the tree of knowledge of good and evil, which, growing in the midst of the garden of Eden, where he was lodged, was almost continually in his view. This command was remarkably calculated, 1. To manifest God's high sovereignty over man, as one who could enact his mere will into a law,—and try man's obedience in a point which his enlightened conscience did not dictate, but which manifested his entire subjection to the mere will of God. 2. To render Adam's obedience or disobedience more conspicuous, that God might appear most just in bestowing the reward or inflicting the punishment on him and his seed, Psalm li. 4. Rom. iii. 3, 4, 8---18, 25, 26. 3. To mark that Adam held all that which he enjoyed of God, as his great superior, proprietor, and landlord; and so, even in paradise, durst not meddle with an apple without God's allowance, and ought to consult him in all that he did. 4. To be a perpetual monitor to Adam that he was fallible, and had need to take heed to his ways, to watch against his spiritual enemies; and that he was not come to his complete happiness and rest, since, even in his paradise, there was a want, the fruit of a tree, most delightful, was denied him; and that his chief happiness lay only in God himself, and so nothing was to be desired but only in submission to his will, and for his sake. 5. To be a summary of the law of nature imprinted on his heart,—in obedience to which, he might honour God, loving him with all his heart, soul, mind, and strength, and manifest a proper love to himself and to his posterity.

The MATTER of obedience required from Adam in this covenant, was an observance of the *whole law* of God, *natural* or *positive*, or a *being* and *acting* exactly according to it, from regard to its divine authority. This included, 1. The retaining of his nature in all its original purity. Without this, none of his thoughts, words, or deeds, could have been truly, perfectly, or acceptably performed, Eccl. vii. 29. 1 Tim. i. 5. 2. An exercising all the powers of his holy nature, in thoughts, words, or deeds, answerable to the law of the covenant, Lev. xxvii. 26. Gal. iii. 10, 12.

In respect of its MANNER, Adam's obedience must be, 1. PERFECT in its *principle* and *motive*,—exactly answerable to every precept of the *whole law*,—and correspondent with all the parts and powers of his nature, soul, body, understanding, conscience, will, affections and memory, Luke x. 27, 28.—in the matter, manner, means and end of the *action itself*,—and in *degree*, with all the heart, soul, mind, and strength, Mat. xxii. 37, 39. Mark xii. 29—33. 2. PERPETUAL, till God should release him from under that law, in its covenant form, Gal. iii. 10. Ezekiel xviii. 24. Nor, till he had finished his course of obedience, had he any legal claim to the promised reward, but was merely in a *state of trial*, proper for acquiring it, Gal. iii. 12. This state could not have been eternal, as that would have excluded all reward at the end of his service. But, when God would have removed him from it, and fixed him and his posterity under his law as a *rule of life*, in a manner somewhat similar to the state of believers, who are dead to the law by the body of Christ,—whether when the fruit had wholly gone off the *forbidden tree;*—or when he had begotten his first child;—or when his eldest children were each capable to act for himself, &c.—we know not. 3. PERSONAL,—not that every one of mankind should have obeyed for himself, in order to found his particular claim to the promised reward : for, if death was entailed upon Adam's natural posterity by his disobedience, before any of them had actually sinned, Rom. v. 12 —14. eternal life must have been conferred upon them, on account of *his obedience* to the law *as a covenant*, and their own would have been at once their happy privilege, and their holy gratitude to God, under his law as *a rule of life*. But it was to be *personal*, performed by man himself, not by a surety, and begun and finished by the same person. 4. Performed in a COVENANT-FORM, in Adam's fulfilling the law, not merely as imposed on him by the infinite authority of God, but also as taken upon himself by his own engagement,—and fulfilling it in hopes of God's graciously bestowing the promised reward. If he had not thus regarded the covenant, in which he stood, in all his obedience, he had poured contempt on that graciously formed ordinance of God, in all its concerns, Judg. xi. 35. Psal. cxix. 106. 1. 14. Num. xxx.

A REWARD of life by the PROMISE of God, was annexed to Adam's fulfilment of this obedience. The threatening of death, in case of disobedience, especially, as annexed to the breach of a positive precept, implied, that Adam had no reason to fear the *loss of his life or happiness*, while he continued in his obedience; and that if he persevered in it, he might expect some great reward, sufficient to balance that death which had been annexed to the positive precept in a matter quite indifferent in itself.—God's declaration to Cain concerning acceptance and condemnation, as suspended on his good or ill behaviour,—and every re-publication of the covenant of works to men, plainly hinted, that it contained a promise of reward to finished obedience, Gen. iv. 7. Lev. xviii. 5. Neh. ix. 29. Ezek. xx. 11. Mat. xix. 17. Rom. x. 5. ii. 7, 10. Gal. iii. 12. Nay, his annexing a gracious reward to imperfect obedience to his law as a rule of life, Psalm xix. 11. 1 Cor. xv. 58. Heb. xi. 6, 26. confirms it. And it is observable, that all nations have had a belief of God's readiness to accept of, and reward good works.

——The LIFE with which God promised to reward Adam's fulfilment of the condition of this covenant, comprehended,

1. The continuance of that life which he had while he continued in his course of servile obedience, which includes, 1. The continuance of *natural life* in the *matter* of it; his body having in it no actual principle of death, his continued obedience to the law of the covenant barred out death from it:—in the *vigour* of it without any languor or decay,—though by means of labour, food, rest;—and in the *pure comforts* of it,—there being nothing to embitter, but every thing to sweeten these, Rom. x. 5. Gal. iii. 12. Lev. xviii. 5. Deut. iv. 40. 2. The continuance of a prosperous *spiritual life*,—including the continuance of God's image in its perfection on his soul;—the continuance of his favour and kindness, and of familiar intimacy with him in every ordinance suited to that state, without any hiding or frown,—and the continued comforts of a good conscience, reflecting on that which was past, and on his constant approach toward his complete and eternal reward, 2 Cor. i. 12. 2 Tim. iv. 7, 8.

2. The enjoyment of a *more perfect life*, after he should have finished his servile obedience;—in which, 1. Adam and his posterity should have had their bodies sealed up, and secured against natural death, and every form or degree of approach to it. 2. God would have infallibly confirmed their souls in perfect conformity to himself. 3. Their persons should have been unalterably fixed in a state of favour with him, and made honorary subjects to his law *as a rule*. 4. Without any breach of

the union between soul and body, both should have, in God's time, been *translated to heaven*, there to be for ever blessed with the full and immediate enjoyment of a three-one God.

Their eternal life in heaven, would have been the same in substance with that which believers enjoy there, through Christ. 1. Reason itself suggests, that God would promise to Adam and his seed something better than that happiness which he enjoyed;—and that after his *state of service*, there would probably happen *one of reward;* and that, as the garden of Eden was chiefly calculated to promote the temporal felicity of his body, there would be a future state of happiness, chiefly correspondent with the noble nature of his soul. 2. The everlasting execution of the penalty of death in hell, especially as it was originally annexed to the breach of a merely positive command, strongly infers, that the promise of reward included an eternal life in heaven, Mat. xxv. 46. Rom. vi. 23. 3. Our Saviour plainly represents the eternal life of the heavenly state as annexed to the perfect keeping of God's commandments, Mat. xix. 17. 4. That eternal life connected by the law with the perfect fulfilment of all its demands, is represented as the very same in substance with that which is enjoyed by faith, Rom. x. 5. Hab. ii. 4. Rom. i. 17. Gal. iii. 11, 12. 5. Christ purchased that very life for men, which the law, on account of their sinfulness, could not confer on them, Rom, viii. 3, 4. Gal. iii. 21. ii. 21.—Now, the law was originally ordained to be the instrument of conferring eternal life in heaven, as well as temporal and spiritual life on earth, Rom. vii. 10. Mat. xix. 17. 6. Though justification, which includes an adjudging to eternal life, be by the Scriptures declared now altogether impossible by the works of the law,—it is never hinted, that this ariseth from any other cause than man's inability to satisfy for past offences, and perform the duty which is still required, Rom. viii. 3. iii. 19, 20. Gal. iii. 21. 7. The appending of the *tree of life* as a seal of this covenant, obscurely pointed out, that a more perfect life was implied in the promised reward.—— Nevertheless, that eternal life which was suspended on Adam's fulfilling the condition of this covenant of works, would have been inferior to that which is enjoyed through Christ, in several very delightful adjuncts. 1. It would not have been sweetened by means of any preceding experience of sin, sorrow, fear or trouble. 2. There would have been no God in our nature in the midst of the throne, through whom, as slain and alive for evermore, we might behold God as our ALL IN ALL. 3. Our title to our happiness would not have been confirmed in the person and death of the Son of God,— nor our charter have been a New Testament in his blood. 4. We would have had none of the delightful manifestations of

God's perfections peculiar to the work of redemption. 5. Though we would have lived and reigned with God as his created servants, friends and children,—yet not as the redeemed travail of his soul, sisters, brethren, and bride.

With respect to the connection of this reward of life with Adam's obedience, it is plain, that being God's creature, preserved by him, his whole obedience was due to God, independent of any rewards. Besides, there was an infinite disproportion between the temporary obedience of a finite creature, and the everlasting enjoyment of an infinite God, for himself and all his posterity. This whole connection of such a reward with his obedience must therefore depend on the mere grace and bounty of God. God had become debtor, not properly to Adam, but to his own sovereign kindness, and his faithfulness pledged in his promise. But such is my weakness, that I cannot determine whether the bestowal of this reward, would have proceeded from his natural goodness, or *merely* from his sovereign will.——On the one hand, it is manifest that God could have done no injury to man, though he had reduced him to nothing that moment he had finished any prescribed course of obedience. The reward necessarily attending a course of perfect holiness, would have perfectly marked his goodness and bounty, Psal. xix. 11. 2 Cor. i. 12. But on the other hand, it is certain that man was created with an eager desire after the enjoyment of God, as his chief good,—and that annihilation would have been the more distressing in proportion to his holiness or desire after God.—Now, I cannot conceive of God's forming a desire after himself, never to be fully satisfied, unless where sin interposes, nor of his annihilating a soul in the very moment of its ardent desire after, and delight in himself.—God cannot but love an holy creature. But, I cannot conceive how his infinite love could deny this holy and beloved creature, its wished enjoyment of himself; or, how it could admit of his annihilating such a creature, in its very act of love to him, and eager pressing after the highest degrees of holiness and love.

Death was the PENALTY threatened in the covenant of works, Gen. ii. 17. If death was annexed to the least breach of the positive precept, it could not but be annexed to the breach of the natural law written on man's heart, Rom. vi. 23. Ezek. xviii. 4. Rom. ii. 8, 9. Isa. iii. 11. 1 John iii. 4. The emphatical form of the threatening, *Dying, thou shalt die*, imported the infallible certainty, the unspeakable extent, and the dreadful nature of that death, Gen. ii. 17. It was, in general, 1. LEGAL DEATH, which consists in the curse or condemning sentence of the broken law immediately fixing upon the transgressor, as a cloud hovering over his head, pregnant with God's vengeance, and as cords of death girding him so fast, that God alone can loose him, Gal. iii. 10. John iii. 18, 36. 2. REAL DEATH, which consists in the actual execution of that condemning sentence on him, from the first moment of his sinning. This may be distinguished into,

1. SPIRITUAL DEATH. Sin, and the curse procured by it, separating man from the favour and fellowship of God, the fountain of life, he necessarily becomes dead in trespasses and sins, Isa. lix. 2. Eph. ii. 1.—In the *commencement* of it, in Adam's first act of sin, is included, 1. The loss of God's image on the soul, and the succession of all manner of sinful corruption in its stead,—as of ignorance, pride, vanity, proneness to falsehood and deceit, in the *understanding*;—blindness, stupidity, partiality, and disorder in the *conscience*;—weakness with respect to good, proneness to evil, perverse wilfulness, and enmity against God in his existence, perfections, discoveries of himself, word, ordinances, people, and every other thing bearing his image, in the *will*;—earthliness, disorder, respecting objects and degrees, in the *affections*;—treacherous readiness to forget every thing good, and tenacious retention of that which is trifling and sinful, in the *memory*, Gen. i. 26, 27. Rom. i. 28—31. iii. 10—18. viii. 7, 8. vii. 8, 24. Jer. xvii. 9. Mat. xv. 19. Mark vii. 21—23. Tit. iii. 3. Gen. vi. 5. viii. 21. 2. The complete breach of all friendship and fellowship with God, and the succession of stated indignation, wrath, abhorrence, hidings and frowns instead thereof, Psalm v. 4—6. Eph. ii. 3, 12.——In its *progress* this spiritual death includes, 1. The growing strength of sinful lusts, the increasing number and heinousness of dead works, 2 Tim. iii. 13. 2. The infliction of God's just vengeance on the soul, in many fearful and ruinous strokes, some of them *felt*, as sorrows, crosses, anxieties, vexations, terrors, and despair; others of them *unfelt*, as judicial blindness of mind, hardness of heart, searedness of conscience, strong delusions, a reprobate sense, vile affections, slavery of Satan, &c. 2 Cor. vii. 10. Mat. xxvii. 3, 4. Gen. iv. 14. Deut. xxviii. 65—67. Jer. xx. 4. Luke xxi. 26. Isa. xxxiii. 14. Prov. xviii. 14. Isa. xvii. 11. Heb. x. 26—31.—Eph. iv. 18. 2 Cor. iv. 3, 4. iii. 14. Isa. lxiii. 17. xlii. 25. 1 Tim. iv. 2. Rom. xi. 8. Isa. lxvi. 4. 2 Thess. ii. 9—12. Psal. lxxxi. 12. Rom. i. 26—31. Tit. i. 15, 16. 2 Tim. iii. 8. Psal. cix. 6.

2. NATURAL or TEMPORAL DEATH, which is, 1. *Inward* in a sinner's own body.——In his first act of sinning, man *became mortal* in his constitution, a slave to death, and had the seeds of it implanted in him. Terror and anxiety of mind produced a deathful motion in his blood and animal spirits, Gen. ii. 17. iii. 16, 19. This death marks its *progress* in manifold diseases, Eccl. iii. 20. Gen. iii. 19. Deut. xxviii. 22, 28, 29. Mat. iv. 24. It is *completed* in the separation of the soul from the body under

the curse, Gen. iii. 19. Jer. xxxiv. 18. 2. *Outward* and *relative*, affecting those creatures upon which the natural life or health of men's body depends, Hos. ii. 21, 22.——This *began* in the irrational part of the lower creation falling under the bondage of corruption for the sin of man, its immediate proprietor, Rom. viii. 22. Hence animals are armed against one another, especially against man; fields are turned into barrenness; the air is poisoned with pestilential vapours; the sea rageth in tempests; the winds are bleak, cold, and stormy,—all being fitly framed together for promoting man's death.—It *increases* in their becoming worse and worse. The earth was rendered much more unhealthful by the flood; the air was more thoroughly poisoned; and a shortening of man's life ensued.—Still things grew worse and worse; fertile fields are turned to barrenness, sunk by earthquakes, marred by volcanoes, &c. Hence human life is but about a fourteenth part of what it once was, Psal. cvii. 33—35. xc. 7—10. cii. 26.—It will be completed, when the present frame of this lower world shall be dissolved, the elements melt with fervent heat, and the earth and the works in it be burnt up, Psal. cii. 26. 2 Pet. iii. 10.

3. ETERNAL DEATH, in which natural and spiritual death are united, and the penalty carried to the highest extent; hence it is called the *second death*, Rev. xx. 6, 14.—As this death *proceeds from the penal sanction* of the covenant of works, it includes in it the *complete loss* of every thing good or agreeable, earthly, heavenly, or divine, Luke xii. 20. Rev. xxi. 8. xxii. 15. Matth. xxv. 41. and the *enduring* most tremendous torments in soul and body, till infinite satisfaction be made for sin, Matth. xxv. 41. Mark ix. 49. Rev. xiv. 10, 11. Psalm xc. 11. Luke xii. 58, 59.—As it falls on a *finite* and *sinful* creature, it includes the irrecoverableness of God's image and favour, Hos. ix. 12. Psalm lxxvii. 7—9. Heb. x. 26, 27.—a constant and agonizing despair of relief, Mark ix. 44, 45, 48, 49. a constant subjection to the full power and violence of indwelling lusts, pride, envy, malice, &c. Rev. xvi. 10, 11, 21. and all in eternal duration, 2 Thess. i. 7—9. Rev. xiv. 9, 10, 11. Matth. xxv. 41, 46. Isa. xxxiii. 14.

This penalty of the broken covenant of works flows from the natural perfections of God;—not from any mere act of his will, as the making the covenant doth. 1. The Majesty of God the covenanter, being infinite, every act of disobedience to the law of the covenant must be high treason against infinite dignity and goodness,—a contempt of, and rebellion against infinite authority, and an attempt against the infinitely precious life of God,—and hence can deserve nothing less than infinite punishment. Being thus objectively infinite, and nothing less than the blood of God capable to balance its guilt, or purge from its pollution, it must continue for ever; and so the punishment of it on a finite person must be extended through all eternity.—God, who is EL KANE, a jealous God, ready to resent the injuring any thing dear to him, must avenge himself of such a criminal.—He cannot conceal his majesty, when sinful worms attempt to rob him of it, trample it under foot, and enthrone themselves in opposition to him; but the whole earth ought to be filled with the glory of the Lord, Exod. xx. 5. Isa. li. 4. v. 16. Num. xiv. 21. 2. The holiness of God's nature requires such a penalty annexed to sin. Being infinitely holy, he cannot admit men, defiled and enslaved by sin, to fellowship with him, —nor, in consistence with his own curse lying on them, can he grant them a sanctified nature to qualify them for it.—He cannot, with pleasure, behold that which is an abomination to his soul; nor can he but hate those in whom this abomination is loved and reigns, Psalm v. 4, 5. xi. 6, 7. Hab. i. 12, 13. Jer. xliv. 4. Prov. xvi. 5. vi. 16. Zech. xi. 8.—If holiness be his very image, he cannot, without appearing as sinful, forbear to shew his detestation of sin, Psalm l. 21. and hence is represented as *sanctified* in the punishment of it, Lev. x. 3. Ezek. xxxviii. 16. Isa. v. 16. Josh. xxiv. 19. 3. It hath already been proved, that the justice of God necessarily requires his punishment of sin, he cannot be just without giving every one his due, either in himself, or in his representative and surety, Rom. i. 32. ii. 2. Jer. v. 5, 7, 9. Gen. xviii. 25. Psalm xi. 6, 7.—God's judgments are not called his *strange* act or work, on account of their disagreeableness to his good and merciful nature,—but because they are much less common on earth, than his merciful providences, Isa. xxviii. 21. He hath *no pleasure* in the death or misery of his creatures in itself, Ezek. xxxiii. 11. xviii. 32. Lam. iii. 33. Hos. xi. 8; but he relisheth it as a vindication of his own perfections, Deut. xxxii. 35, 36, 41, 42, 43. Isa. i. 24. Hos. x. 10; refresheth himself with it, Amos v. 9. Dutch Version.

The SEALS of this covenant, by which the promise and threatening in it were confirmed, were, 1. The *tree of knowledge of good and evil*, so called, because God, by it, put man to the trial of his obedience or disobedience; and by eating the fruit of it, man experimentally knew the good which he had lost, and the evil which he had incurred. This, like the seal of the rainbow, in Noah's covenant, might only be looked at; and it sealed eternal happiness to men upon condition of fulfiling the law of the covenant, and infinite misery if it was broken, Gen. ii. 17. 2. The *tree of life*, the fruit of which perhaps invigorated the human body; but certainly was a pledge of an eternal life, in consequence of fulfiling the condition of the covenant, Gen. iii. 22. ii. 9. And hence Christ as enjoyed in heaven is called by its name, Rev. ii. 7. xxii. 2.

Nothing but sin against God, in want of conformity of heart or life, or in transgression of his law, which prescribed the condition of the covenant, could BREAK it, 1 John iii. 4. Rom. iv. 15. v. 13. But, that it hath been broken is evident. 1. Sin, in innumerable forms, rages or reigns every where in the world, Gen. vi. 5. viii. 21. xiii. 13. 2 Kings xvii. 7—23. Psalm xiv. 1—4. liii. 1—4. Isa. lix. 1—15. v. 5—23. Mic. vii. 1—5. Matth. xv. 19. Mark vii. 21—23. Rom. i. 28—32. iii. 10—18. 1 Cor. vi. 9, 10. Gal. v. 19—21. Eph. ii. 1—3, 12. iv. 17—19. v. 5, 6. Phil. iii. 18, 19. Tit. iii. 3. 2 Pet. ii. Rev. xvii. 2. All men are by nature imprisoned for their debts and crimes, Isa. xlii. 6, 7. lxi. 1, 2. Zech. ix. 11, 12. 3. All men have contracted an habit of covenant-breaking, Rom. i. 31. Psalm lxxviii. 10, 37, 57. Isa. xlviii. 8. 4. This world is every where marked with the wrath of God, Rom. i. 18. Gen. vii. xix. Exod. vii.—xiv. Josh. vi.—xii. Isa. i. xxiv. xxxiv. Jer. i.—lii. Luke xix. xxi. Matth. xxiv. Rev. vi.—xx. 5. A new covenant of redemption is revealed by God, Isa. xlii. 6, 7. xlix. 1—12. liii. 10—12. Jer. xxxi. 33, 34. Heb. viii. 10—12. Psalm xl. 6—8. lxxxix. 3, 4. Gen. iii. 15. xvii. 7.

This covenant of works was broken by *Adam's eating the forbidden fruit*, in which sin he, 1. Doubted the peremptoriness and veracity of the threatening, and of God's perfections connected with it. 2. His understanding being darkened, his affections and will conceived a lust after that fruit, imagining that his eating of it would render him wise and happy as God. 3. He completed his offence, in his actual taking and eating of that fruit, Gen. iii. 3—6.——This, his first sin, included, 1. Horrid unbelief, insomuch that Satan, in the form of a serpent, was believed in opposition to God, 1 John v. 10. Gen. ii. 17. iii. 4—6. 2. Pride, ambition, bold and presumptuous curiosity, Gen. iii. 5. Isa. xiv. 13, 14. Our first parents were in paradise, and lords of this lower world; but nothing would content them but to be as God. They knew and enjoyed very much; but they coveted the knowledge and enjoyment of every thing. 3. Shocking ingratitude and discontentment. They had every thing useful or delightful. They were the envy of devils, the companions of angels, lords of animals, of every thing on earth, but one tree; and yet grudged their maker and benefactor that small reserve for his own peculiar property, Gen. ii. 7—25. iii. 5, 8. 4. Contemptuous apostacy from, and open rebellion against God. They renounced his covenant of friendship, and threw off all subjection to, or professed dependence on him, Psalm ii. 3. Gen. ii. 16, 17. iii. 3—6. 5. The whole law of God was broken in this one act. The *authority* of God, which is the foundation of it, was trampled on: That *love* which is the fulfilment of it was neglected, and enmity admitted in its stead. The positive precept which was a summary of, and fence to the moral ones, was contemned, and expressly violated. Nay, in this sin, every particular command of the moral law was broken in many different respects.

Adam's first sin, by which he brake this covenant, was exceedingly aggravated. 1. It was committed by one who had been newly created in the image of God, perfectly holy and righteous, and able to continue such, Gen. i. 26, 27. v. 1. Eccl. vii. 29. 2. It was occasioned by fruit of small importance, of which Adam had not the least need, 2 Sam. xii. 1—14. 3. As it respected that which had been set apart by God for his own service, it amounted to a sacrilegious robbing of him, Mal. iii. 9. 4. It was committed in paradise, where man had every thing delightful and engaging to obedience,—where God dwelt as in his temple, and every thing proclaimed his infinite kindness to mankind, Deut. xxxii. 15. Hos. xiii. 6. 5. It was committed on the very day on which he was created, or not long after, Psalm xlix. 12. 6. It was committed on a single, and but a slight temptation, Gen. iii. 3—6. 7. It was committed against God's express command, and the most plain warning of the danger, Gen. ii. 17. 8. It was committed almost immediately after God had entered into covenant with them.

In this first sin of Adam, I. God *left him to the freedom of his own will.* This freedom of will did not consist in any immutable, though voluntary, attachment to good, like that which God, holy angels, or glorified saints have; nor did it consist in having one inward principle inclined to good, and another to evil, in the manner of believers on earth; nor in a fixed, voluntary inclination to evil, as devils and wicked men have;—nor even in any equal inclination to good and to evil; for man was made upright, and in the image of God, Eccl. vii. 29. Gen. i. 26, 27. v. 1. But, it consisted in his being *seducible to evil*, though he was *inclined only to good.* God created him perfectly holy, and able to keep his whole law, natural or positive, and to resist every temptation. He gave him a heart wholly and only inclined to that which is good, but subject to change, and that only by his own will and deed. Natural immutability in goodness and holiness being the peculiar property of godhead, could not be conferred on Adam, Mal. iii. 6. Psalm cii. 26, 27. James i. 17. God's rendering him immutable in holiness by an act of grace, in the manner of established angels and glorified saints, could not have consisted with the tenor of the covenant made with him; would have confounded his state of service with that of his honorary reward. Being therefore thus actually *changeable*,

God neither forced, nor tempted, nor inclined him to any change, but so left him to himself, that he, and he alone, could change the inclination and choice of his own will from good to evil. II. Satan very craftily tempted him to evil. 1. He chose a subtile and simple-like serpent, or perhaps one very beautiful, which might be taken for an angel, to be his instrument in the temptation; and to mark his triumphant victory over mankind by it, he hath caused multitudes of them, to this day, to worship him in serpents. 2. In the absence of her husband, he tempted Eve, who, perhaps, had heard the terms of the covenant only from Adam. 3. He moved a doubt concerning the prohibition of the fruit of the tree of knowledge, in such ambiguous terms, that it was difficult to know whether he meant to ask, Whether God had really forbidden them to eat of that fruit; or if he meant to insinuate, that the forbidder of that excellent fruit could not be the true God, who had so lately created them to partake of his favours;—or that God, who had forbidden such a thing, was an hard master. 4. Finding that Eve adhered to God's commandment, he laboured to render the truth of the threatening apparently doubtful, if not improbable or impossible. 5. He pretended an earnest desire to promote their knowledge and happiness; and improved the name and sight of the tree to further his temptation. 6. Perhaps he pretended, that he had acquired his own superiority in knowledge above other brutes by eating of that fruit. But he certainly introduced his plain contradiction of God's threatening by a solemn appeal to him concerning the usefulness of the fruit. 7. Having prevailed on Eve, he by her tempted Adam, who was no doubt the more readily deceived, as he saw that she did not immediately die by eating of the fruit. III. Being left by God to the freedom of his will, Adam abused it, and complied with Satan's temptations.—This compliance was entirely his own deed. Though God did not give him such measures of grace, as actually to make him overcome the temptation, yet he gave him as much as was sufficient to have enabled him to withstand it, had it been rightly improved. An infinitely holy, righteous, and good God could neither force, incline, nor tempt him to sin. And as he was fully master of his own will, neither Satan, nor Eve, could force him to it.

By this one offence of Adam, the covenant of works was broken in different respects. I. The law of the covenant was violated in all its parts,—was fully violated, in the sinfulness of man's nature and act, Gen. iii. 11. ii. 17. 1 John iii. 4. Mat. xix. 17. And Adam having sinned as our covenant-head, his sin itself in its fault, and in its guilt or chargeableness by law in order to punishment, is really ours, and accordingly is legally imputed to, and charged upon us, by an holy and righteous God. 1. Scripture plainly represents this sin as imputed to all his natural posterity, Rom. v. 12—19. 2. All men are represented as under a sentence of condemnation on account of Adam's first sin, from which they cannot be delivered but by Christ, 1 Cor. xv. 22. Rom. v. 15—19. Eph. ii. 3. Rom. viii. 1—4, 33, 34. Gal. iii. 13. 3. All men are naturally under the power of spiritual death, in all its ingredients, Gen. vi. 5. viii. 21. Psalm xiv. 2, 3. liii. 2, 3. li. 5. lviii. 3. Job xiv. 4. xv. 14, 15. Jer. xvii. 9. John iii. 6. Mat. xv. 19. Mark vii. 21—23. Rom. v. 12. viii. 7, 8. iii. 9—23. 1 Cor. ii. 14. Eph. ii. 1—3. Tit. iii. 3. 4. Experience loudly attests the universal corruption of mankind. Christ alone excepted, all men, in every age and place, have run into moral evil, as soon, and as far, as their abilities and opportunities permitted; and have proceeded from one evil to another still worse.—Their inclinations to it being early and universal, they have, contrary to the severest laws of God and men,—contrary to the dissuasions and determents of providence,—contrary to their most solemn vows, promises, and oaths,—contrary to their most candid resolutions, and even the largest measures of grace bestowed on earth, spoken and done evil things as they could, and thus marked their mind, conscience, will, affections, and memory, to be dreadfully infected with all the above-mentioned plagues, and their bodily members ready instruments of unrighteousness.—There are manifestly much larger degrees, and measures, and multitudes of sins in this world, than of holiness and virtue. Notwithstanding all the means used, by God and men, to prevent or purge out wickedness, and promote virtue, the most of men, in all ages and places, have been manifestly and often outrageously wicked; and the very best exceedingly defective.——As if fond to testify their approbation of Adam's first sin, men have universally imitated it in their sinful curiosity,—in their rushing upon that which is forbidden,—in their readiness to hearken to seduction,—in their bodily eyes, or other senses, blinding those of their mind,—in their caring for their body, at the expence and eternal hazard of their soul,—in their discontentment with their present lot,—in their being more easily influenced by evil counsel than by good,—in their pitiful shifts to help themselves and cover their shame,—in their attempts to flee and hide themselves from God,—in their aversion to be affected with, or confess their sin,—in their extenuating and excusing their sin, and transferring the blame of it upon others, especially on God himself. 5. Without supposing men chargeable with sin from their very conception, and that their soul is formed under a charge of guilt, and a condemning sentence of God on account of it, it is impossible to conceive how so infinitely righteous, holy, and good God, could create it *destitute of original righteousness;*—or how our nature, in its very formation, becomes corrupted with sin. If we are not formed under guilt and the curse, why is not sinful corruption prevented, and holiness implanted? 6. The misery and death which happen to infants in every age, particularly by the flood, the destruction of Sodom and the cities about, and the manifold ravages and destructions of cities and nations, prove that they are chargeable before God with some grievous transgression: Otherwise God, who is infinitely merciful, would never so early and so wrathfully destroy the most excellent work of his hands. 7. The parallel between Adam and Christ manifestly proves, that as in Christ elect men fulfil the law, and live, so in Adam all men are constituted breakers of the law, and die, Rom. viii. 4. Gal. ii. 20. 1 Cor. xv. 21, 22, 45---49. Rom. v. 14---19. vii. 4. II. The law of the covenant being thus broken by Adam, in his own and in the name of all his posterity, they lost all encouragement to obedience from the covenant-promise of eternal life. The promise being altogether undermined by his sin, all prospect or hope of the reward contained in it, and all capacity of earning a claim to it, upon the foot of that promise, were for ever utterly lost, Rom. iii. 23. viii. 3, 7, 8. III. The blessings of the covenant being lost, the favour of God forfeited, and eternal life by the works of the law rendered impossible, the curse or condemnatory sentence of the covenant seized upon the transgressors, and bound them over to death. It seized on Adam and Eve, in the first moment of their sinning, Gen. iii. 16---19. And it lay ready in the threatening to seize their posterity in the first moment of their personal existence, or even to bring them into existence at their destined moment, in the most wretched condition, Rom. v. 12---14. Eph. ii. 1---3. Gal. iii. 10. IV. The representation in the covenant was dissolved, and every particular person of mankind fell bound for himself. Adam, being now dead in law, and under the begun reign of spiritual death, was no longer fit to continue the head and representative of others, in a covenant which was originally ordained unto life.—Moreover, the displacing him from his covenant headship was necessary, that the covenant of grace might be immediately administered, and that he and Eve, with their seed, might have the most early, and the most unhampered access to it.

Nevertheless, the covenant of works was *not utterly abolished.* The law of it, with respect to every thing moral in itself, still remained unaltered.—And the demand of *infinite satisfaction* for sin, answerable to the threatened penalty, was superadded to the original one of *perfect obedience,* as the absolutely necessary condition of eternal life. The natural law of the covenant, being founded on that relation which subsists between God and men as his rational creatures, it behoved to continue while that relation continued.—The penalty, flowing from the very nature of God, and corresponding with his relation to men as his subjects, must be as unalterable as the law itself. 1. Man's sin could not deprive God of his rightful sovereign dominion over him, or free him from his obligation to due obedience, Psalm lxxxiii. 18. Dan. iv. 35. Job xxxv. 6, 8. 2. The Scriptures never hint that this law, in its federal form, was utterly abolished, but represent it as unalterable, Mat. v. 17, 18. xix. 17. Rom. x. 5. iii. 31. viii. 3, 4. Gal. iii. 10, 12, 13. 3. They represent our inability to fulfil the law, not any detachment of the promise of life to the fulfiller, from it, as the reason that we cannot be justified by it, Rom. iii. 10—20. viii. 3, 4. Gal. iii. 10, 12, 21. 4. Believers' entrance into a state of life, or of deliverance from this law, is founded upon their complete fulfilment of all its demands in Christ their surety, Rom. viii. 3, 4. vii. 4. x. 4. iii. 31. Phil. iii. 9. 2 Cor. v. 21. ——In vain it is objected, that man is not now in a friendly covenant with God; that God cannot demand from men that which they are unable to perform; that it would be unbecoming a sinful and accursed creature to trust in, and love God as his own God. For, though man hath forfeited all friendly connection with God, he is still his rational creature. Man's disqualifying himself for obedience cannot deprive God of his right to demand it. Ought God to be punished with the loss of his authority, if men rebel against it?—Cannot God require obedience of his morally incapable subjects, for wise ends, such as to convince them of their sinfulness, and to make their conscience approve their punishment? If God be presented to men as a suitable Saviour, why may they not trust in, and love him? If any thing in God be terrible to them, they have themselves to blame for it. From the beginning it was not so. Nay, are not the damned in hell for ever bound to love God, on account of those very excellencies which he manifests in their destruction.

ALL men are naturally *under the covenant of works*, in its matter and form. 1. The Scriptures plainly represent them as under it, Gal. iii. 10, 12. Mat. xix. 17. Rom. iii. 19. vii. 8, 9. 2. None but Christ's little flock are represented as delivered from, and dead to the law, or covenant of works; and that never till they be united to Christ, in their effectual calling, John iii. 18. Rom. viii. 1, 2, 4. vii. 4. vi. 14. Gal. ii. 19, 20. iii. 13. iv. 4, 5. Col. iii. 3. It hath been pretended, that if unconverted gospel-hearers be under the command of the covenant of works, they must be required by it to seek justification by their own works, while at the same time the gospel requires them to receive it through the righteousness of Christ. But, 1. Adam was not required to SEEK justification by his *perfect obedience*, but to perform it, in hopes of God's graciously accepting and rewarding him. 2. Though the covenant of works had required him to seek justification by his own perfect obedience, it cannot therefore bind men to seek or expect justification by works, the best of which are an abomination to the Lord, Isa. lxiv. 6. Prov. xv. 8. xxi. 24, 27. xxviii. 9. 3. The covenant of works cannot now bind men to seek justification by their works, when even infinitely valuable obedience cannot satisfy its demands, without full satisfaction for offences already committed, Heb. ix. 22. Rom. iii. 24—26. v. 6, 8, 10. 1 John iv. 9, 10. 4. Since the law of the covenant of works requires men to believe every thing which God reveals, and to receive whatever he offers; it must necessarily require every gospel-hearer, as utterly unable to fulfil it himself,—to believe the gospel record, and receive the law-magnifying righteousness of Jesus Christ offered in it, and that under pain of redoubled guilt and punishment, John iii. 18, 38. 1 John iii. 23. v. 10, 12. Heb. x. 29.

All men by nature, and even believers, in so far as they are unrenewed, *desire to be under the covenant of works*, and to obtain happiness by their own righteousness, or the condition of it. 1. It is natural to men, and hence men of every form or religion, station, office, education, or manner of life, agree in it, Rom. ix. 31, 32. x. 3. Jon. i. 16. Mat. xix. 16. John vi. 28. Acts ii. 37. Luke xv. 19. 2. Our own working or suffering, in order to obtain happiness from God, is exceedingly suited to the pride of our corrupt nature, and makes us to look on God as our debtor, Rom. x. 3. vii. 9, 13. John v. 45. Isa. lviii. 3. It is like pangs of death to quit our hold of the law, Rom. vii. 4, 9. Gal. ii. 19. 3. Men's ignorance of the extensive and high demands of the broken law, and of their own utter inability to keep it,—or their care to abridge their apprehensions of them, and to enlarge their conceit of their own ability, mightily promote their desire to be under it, Rom. vii. 9—13. x. 3. Gal. iv. 21. 4. Men have naturally a peculiar enmity against God and his gracious method of redemption,—against Jesus Christ and his whole mediation, particularly his sacrificing work; and hence love to oppose the honour of it by cleaving to legal methods of obtaining happiness, Rom. viii. 7. John xv. 24. Rom. x. 3. ix. 32. v. 21. Gal. ii. 21. v. 2, 4.

Not only doth the Spirit of God make use of the broken law in the awakening, conviction, and illumination of sinners' consciences, but even in itself it hath a manifold power over them. 1. It still retains its federal *commanding* power over them, binding them to fulfil the most perfect obedience, under pain of infinite punishment for the smallest offence,—even while the curse of it allows them no spiritual strength, but subjects them to the dominion of indwelling sin, Luke x. 27, 28. Gal. iii. 10. 2. It hath an *excluding* power, by which it shuts out men from all happiness or solid hopes of it, unless its, to them impossible, condition of perfect obedience and infinite satisfaction for sin be completely fulfilled, Mat. xix. 17. Gal. iii. 10, 12, 21. iv. 24. Rom. x. 5. Mic. vi. 7, 8. It refused to justify Christ upon any lower terms, Mat. iii. 15. Luke xxiv. 26. Heb. v. 8. ii. 10. ——The convincing and distressful influence of the law upon men's consciences, arises from this *commanding* and *excluding* power of it. 3. It hath an *irritating* power, by which its commands and threatenings, fixing on men's consciences, occasion their becoming more and more wicked,—even as the stirring of wasps' nests makes them rage and sting the more,—the warming of serpents renders them more mischievous,—or the shining of the sun upon dunghills makes them the more noisome, Rom. vii. 5, 7—13. Acts vii. 54. Mat. vii. 6. Hos. xi. 2. In this irritating power, the following things are observable : 1. The commands and threatenings of the law, being closely applied to sinners' consciences, lay them under fearful restraints, acting as an austere master, that, with the lash in his hand, issues forth his commands, Gal. iii. 10. Isa. iii. 11. Ezek. xviii. 4. Rom. ii. 8, 9. 2. It doth not in the least remove their enmity against God, or inability to obey its commands ; but by its curse fixes men under the dominion of indwelling sin, Gal. iii. 22. 1 Cor. xv. 56. Rom. vi. 14. vii. 4. viii. 2. John i. 17. 3. Every felt restraint of their inward lusts awakens their rage against the law, and God the law-giver, on account of the strictness of its precepts, and the dreadful nature of its penalty, Rom. iv. 15. vii. 5, 7—13. Men continuing under the curse, their inward lusts, from the opposition made to them, gather strength,—even as furious horses become worse when they are checked. or wild bulls more outrageous when they feel the net upon them, Rom. vii. 5. Hos. iv. 16, 18. Psalm lxxxi. 11, 12. 4. By viewing the hard and extensive commands, and the dreadful penalty of the law, their corrupt heart, foregoing all its hopes, hardens itself in secret despair, like an over-ridden horse, that will not answer the spur, but turns and bites his rider, Jer. ii. 25. Ezek. xxxvii. 11. 5. Hence follows an inward rage against the holiness of God and his law, a frequent abandoning themselves to wickedness, and an improving the most alarming afflictions to render themselves worse and worse, Prov. xxix. 1. i. 29. Rom. i. 26—32. 2 Chron. xxviii. 22. Isa. i. 5. Jer. v. 3. Isa. xlii. 25.——4. The broken law hath a *retaining* power. Its curse and irritating influence concur in holding men under its dominion and influence. Its connecting eternal happiness with personal righteousness, as apprehended by them, suiting their proud inclinations, they desire to remain under it, notwithstanding its piercing them through with many sorrows. Nor do even its most dreadful demands weaken this desire, though they make men wish for mitigations of them, Gal. iv. 21. Rom. ix. 31, 32. x. 3. Mat. xix. 16, 17. Mic. vi. 6, 7. Hos. v. 6. 5. The commanding power of the law being trampled on, it hath a CURSING or *condemning* power over the transgressor, Gal. iii. 10, 13. Prov. iii. 33. Isa. xxxiv. 5. Deut. xxvii. 15—26. John iii. 18, 36. Now, to be under this curse, includes, 1. to be under the just avenging wrath of God, the great Sovereign, Law giver, and Judge of the world, John iii. 36. Psalm vii. 11. Eph. ii. 3. Mat. xxv. 41. Deut. xxix. 20. 2. To be consigned by an offended and angry God into the hands of his avenging justice, to be dreadfully punished without intermission till full satisfaction for sin be made, Heb. x. 31. 2 Thess. i. 7—9. Luke xii. 58, 59. Mat. v. 25, 26. 3. To be separated to evil, having all happiness destroyed, and being established a mark or butt of all the arrows and plagues of infinite wrath, Psalm vii. 12, 13. xxxvii. 20, 22. xciv. 23.

All men who have not believed in Christ, are *under this curse* or condemning sentence of the broken covenant of works. 1. Sin, being contrary to the law of God, and his perfections therein manifested, richly deserves it, Psal. cxix. 128. Tit. ii. 12. Gen. xviii. 25. 2 Thess. i. 6. Psalm cxix. 142. xi. 5—7. Rom. vi. 23. ii. 2, 8, 9. i. 32. Isa. iii. 11. 2. A sentence of condemnation being annexed to the breach of this covenant, the faithfulness of God must see to its full execution, Gen. ii. 17. 3. If Adam had fulfilled the condition of this covenant, he and all his posterity must have been justified, and adjudged to the full possession of eternal life, according to the promise of it, Lev. xviii. 5. Rom. x. 5. Gal. iii. 12. Matth. xix. 17. A divine sentence of condemnation must therefore necessarily follow upon his non-fulfilment of it, Gen. ii. 17. John iii. 18, 36. Mark xvi. 16. Gen. iii. 7. 4. Even the Son of God, when placed under this covenant, in the room of sinful men, as their surety, was *made a curse*, that is, laid under all the multitudes of curses due to all their sins; and had them fully executed upon him. And it is only through their union to him, as their curse-bearing and law-fulfilling Head, that they are freed from the curse, Gal. iii. 13. iv. 4—6. 2 Cor. v. 21. Rom. x. 4. viii. 1, 3, 4, 33, 34. 1 Cor. i. 30. Isa. xlv. 24, 25, 17.

The condition of those that are under the curse is inexpressibly dreadful, as it infallibly engages the infinite holiness, justice, faithfulness, and power of God, 1. To withhold all real good from them, Isa. lix. 2. Jer. ii. 17, 19, 25. 2. To bring all real evil upon them in such manner, form, period, and by such means as do most contribute to manifest the glory of his avenging wrath, Ezek. xviii. 4. Isa. i. 20, 24. iii. 11. Rom. ii. 8, 9. 2 Thess. i. 7—9. Rev. xiv. 9—11. xxi. 8. xxii. 15. 3. To make all things, however good in themselves, work together to promote their misery, Deut. xxviii. 15, 16, 17, 18. Eccl. i. 18. Isa. vi. 9, 10. Rom. xi. 32, 33. xi. 8. 1 Pet. ii. 8.—And indeed, as the nature of sin lies in disconformity to the commands of God's law,—the nature of punishment lies in its proceeding from the curse of it lying on the sufferer. 4. To lay hold on all opportunities, in time and eternity, to execute wrath upon them in their soul, body, or relatives, Psalm xxxvii. 22. 2 Pet. ii. 3.—In the execution of this curse does the ADMINISTRATION of the broken covenant of works chiefly consist.

I. IN THIS LIFE the curse of the broken law operates on men, and renders their state fearfully sinful and miserable. Even before their birth, it, pregnant with wo, secures their future existence in a natural union with Adam their accursed progenitor, Rom. v. 12. No death of ancestors in wars, diseases, or dangers, is permitted to prevent their existence; nor can their piety prevent the attendance of the curse, Gen. iv. 11, 14, 17—24. vi. 4, 5, 3. Psalm li. 5. In virtue of the curse, God's providence is always making preparations for fixing it on each of Adam's destined and represented posterity. And hence the most atrocious sinners are often spared, and rendered fruitful, Psalm xvii. 14. Job xxi. 11. xxvii. 14.—In the moment fixed for their formation in the womb, the curse, as it were, ushers them into being, loaded with its dreadful weight, and infected with its baleful influence, Eph. ii. 3. Deut. xxviii. 18. In consequence of which, it all along operates on their soul, their body, their person, and their relative concerns.

1. It operates *on their soul.* 1. It separates it from all gracious and happy intercourse with God, in whose favour is life, Psalm xxx. 5. Deut. xxix. 21. Isa. lix. 2. Psalm v. 4—6. Amos iii. 3.—If God form them under this curse, it prevents his communication of any holy endowments to their soul. Hence, being formed under sin imputed, and the curse due to it, infants are destitute of original righteousness, John iii. 6. Job xiv. 4. Psalm li. 5. Eph. ii. 1—3.—Whatever influence the temper of their bodies may have in forming inward corruptions into particular lusts, I know not how sinful corruption could enter into our nature, at our very formation, or how it could so quickly overspread Adam's whole nature in a moment, but by the influence of an incumbent curse, withholding all sanctifying communications from God, and subjecting them to an evil conscience, and the dominion of sin; as the punishment of his com-

menced rebellion against God.——Though, in their adult age, men, under the curse, read or hear Christ's word, they hear not his voice, John v. 37.—Though they pray to God, he heareth not sinners, John ix. 31.—Though they wait at the posts of wisdom's doors, in the ordinances of his worship, they are far from God himself, Eph. ii. 13. 2. The soul being thus separated from God, spiritual death preys on it, and deprives it of all that comeliness it had, and prevents what otherwise it would have had. No spiritual knowledge, holiness, or righteousness, can enter into, or continue in, the accursed soul. Hence how quickly the glory of our first parents, like that of the accursed fig-tree, withered away! Gen. iii. 7, 8. All the powers of the accursed soul are dead while it liveth. The eyes of the understanding are shut, and, as it were, glazed in a ghastly manner; the speech of cordial prayer and praise is laid; the right pulse of affections towards God is stopt; every spiritual sense is locked up, and all within cold and stiff as a stone, Rom. i. 21 —32. Eph. iv. 17, 18. Ezek. xi. 19. xxxvi. 26. 3. In consequence of this death, all the powers of the accursed soul become fearfully infected, in the most lothesome manner. The curse laying it under the strength and dominion of sin as a chief part of its punishment, all its powers, being destitute of true knowledge, righteousness, and holiness, corrupt themselves and one another. As the accursed earth and air had their natural constitution altered to the worse, so is that of the accursed soul, with respect to every thing moral.—The understanding, that eye, or directing power of the soul, is filled with ignorance, delusion, doubting, unbelief, vanity, pride, and proneness to falsehood, 1 Cor. ii. 14. Eph. v. 8. Eccl. iii. 18. No instruction, however important, can thrive on it, Matth. xii. 19—22. Isa. vi. 9, 10. 2 Cor. iii. 14, 15. iv. 3, 4. It is only in the way of removing this curse, that God himself can effectually instruct men, Isa. xlviii. 17. Gal. i. 16. iii. 13. ii. 16—30. The conscience, that deputy of God, which watches over the soul, becomes stupid, dumb, erroneous, calling good evil, and evil good,—partial, easily bribed, in favours of self, or in pure prejudice against others, Judg. xxi. 25. John xvi. 2. Isa. v. 20—22. Matth. xi. 18, 19; or becomes furious, rigid, and desperate, Heb. x. 26, 27. Isa. xxxiii. 14, 15. Matth xxvii. 4. Jer. ii. 25. The will, that governing power of the soul, becomes weak and incapable with respect to every thing good, Rom. v. 6. John xv. 5; utterly averse to it, Psalm lxxxi. 11. John v. 40. Hos. xi. 2, 7. Jer. v. 3; filled with irreconcileable enmity against God, in his being, his perfections, his spirit, his word, his ordinances, and providences: and what is most shocking, is filled with peculiar enmity against Christ as a Saviour, and against every gracious purpose or dispensation of God for our salvation; and the more that his redeeming grace appears in any thing, as in the priesthood of Christ, or the doctrine of free justification and happiness through his imputed righteousness, and the free grant of it to sinners in the gospel, the stronger is our enmity against it, Rom. viii. 7. i. 30. x. 3. ix. 32. John xv. 18, 24.—It is, moreover, perverse with respect to our chief end, fixing on the most trifling and detestable things rather than on God himself, Hos. x. 1. Zech. vii. 5. Phil. iii. 19. 2 Tim. iii. 4. Psalm iv. 6. Rom. viii. 5; and so obstinate, that, till the curse be removed, not all the terrors or pains of damnation, or joys of heaven, can bow or melt it, Hos. xi. 2, 7. Zech. vii. 11, 12. Isa. xlviii. 4. i. 5. Jer. v. 3. Ezek. xi. 19. xxxvi. 26. Acts vii. 51. The affections, those feet and arms of the soul, how slow towards, and averse from God!—How shut against receiving him or his unspeakable gift, and against every spiritual object! But how alert and ready to fly as hungry ravens or eagles on things carnal and sinful, and to grasp them fast as our all in all! Psalm iv. 6. Ezek. xxxiii. 31. Prov. xxiii. 5. Phil. iii. 19. Rom. viii. 5. The memory, that magazine and register of the soul, how strong to retain things trifling or sinful which tend to corrupt! and how treacherous and incapable to retain any thing truly good and important! Jer. ii. 32. Deut. xxxii. 18. Hos. xiii. 6.—— In these three respects, Adam's nature, in the first moment of his sinning, was, and infants' souls in the very moment of their formation are, corrupted. 4. The soul being reduced to this lothesome and dreadful condition, the curse shuts it up from all inclination, care, or ability of attempting any thing proper for recovering itself, or receiving redemption from another. It shuts up men in unbelief as in a prison or grave, Gal. iii. 22, 23. Rom. xi. 32. Isa. lxi. 1. xlii. 6, 7. Ezek. xxxvii. 12, 13. Zech. ix. 11, 12. Being thus buried in sinful corruption, God himself seals them up, and secures their continuance in it, Psalm lxxxi. 11, 12. Isa. lxvi. 4. 2 Thess. ii. 10—12. No door of hope remains, except in the way of his removing the curse, Ezek. xviii. 4. Gal. iii. 10, 13. Rom. ii. 8, 9. Isa. iii. 11. Nay, every attempt to escape any other way doth but fix them more and more in their dreadful estate.—If they hear the gospel, it is to them a *savour of death unto death*, blinding and hardening their heart, 2 Cor. ii. 16. Hos. vi. 5. Isa. vi. 9, 10. xlii. 19, 20, 25. Rom. xi. 7, 8, 9. If they pray, it is an *abomination* to the Lord, and draws down his wrath. If they offer the most costly sacrifices to him, he abhors them, Prov. xxviii. 9. xv. 8. xxi. 27. Isa. i. 11—15. lxv. 13. Hos. v. 6. Mic. vi. 6, 7. 5. The accursed soul, being thus dead and buried in sin, its corruption more and more increases, 2 Tim. iii. 13. ii. 16. Mat. xii. 45. 2 Pet. ii. 20. That sinfulness of nature which dwells, reigns, and works in them, is framed into a multitude of particular *lusts of the flesh and of the spirit*,—correspondent with their bodily constitution, as vitiated by their own or parents' drunkenness, lasciviousness, outrageous passion, &c.—or correspondent with their particular circumstances, opportunities, temptations, &c. 2 Cor. vii. 1. Rom. vi. 12. 1 Pet. ii. 11. iv. 3. 2 Pet. ii. 18. Eph. ii. Gal. v. 19—21, 24. Rom. viii. 13. xiii. 14.—These lusts are the members of the old man or body of sin, Col. iii. 5. Rom. i. 29, 30.— are inward tinder, answering to the sparks of Satan's temptations, John xiv. 30. Prov. xxviii. 26,—filthy matter, gathering into a shameful bile of wickedness, James i. 14. Mat. xv. 19. Mark vii. 21—23. Jer. iv. 14. vi. 7.—and constant opposers of the entrance or outgoing of any thing good, Gal. v. 17. Rom. vii. 23, 24.—They are represented as *diverse*, because of their manifold forms, Tit. iii. 3; *ungodly*, detested by God, contrary to his nature and law, and to the love and fear of him, Jude 18. 1 John ii. 16; *devilish*, introduced and supported by Satan, and his very image on the soul, John viii. 44; *warring* against the providence, Spirit, and grace of God, and against men's souls, and even among themselves, James iv. 1. Gal. v. 17. Rom. vii. 23. 1 Pet. ii. 11; *worldly*, reigning in the hearts of worldly men, and leading them towards the world as their portion and pattern, Tit. ii. 12; *insatiable*, Isa. lvii. 10. Eccl. i. 8; *deceitful*, Eph. iv. 22; *hurtful, piercing* men through with many sorrows, 1 Tim. i. 9, 10; *burning* them up, Rom. i. 27; and *drowning* them in perdition, 1 Tim. vi. 9.—These lusts, receiving their dominion from the curse of the law upon the one hand, and from the choice of the sinner on the other, constantly reign, work, and manifest themselves, as they have opportunity, like an uncultivated garden, which brings forth briars, thorns, nettles, and other noxious weeds, Mat. xv. 19. Mark vii. 21—23. Rom. i. 21—32. iii. 10—18. Gal. v. 19—21. 1 Cor. vi. 9, 10. Eph. ii. 1—3, 12. iv. 17—19. Prov xxiv. 30, 31; they become more and more powerful, till they be altogether uncontroulable, Tit. iii. 3. 2 Pet. ii. 13, 14, 22. And that particular lust, which, from man's constitution, station, or circumstances, most easily besets, and most powerfully influences their conduct, is called their *predominant* lust, Heb. xii. 1. Psalm xviii. 23. 6. For the just punishment of man's progress in wickedness, God, in the execution of his curse, inflicts additional plagues on them. Some of these plagues are not felt, but loved and delighted in, though dreadful in their nature, and answerable to former wickedness, Isa. vi. 9, 10. Psalm lxxxi. 11, 12. Isa. i. 5. Jer. v. 3.——To punish man's not receiving, but rebelling against the light of his word, or of their own conscience, God gives them up to *judicial blindness* of mind, John iii. 18. Job. xxi. 14. Eph. iv. 18. 2 Thess. ii. 10, 11. 2 Cor.

iv. 3, 4. Isa. vi. 9, 10. xlii. 19, 20, 25. Mat. xiii. 11. Acts xxviii. 27. John xii. 40. Rom. xi. 7---10.——To punish their not receiving the love of the truth, but holding it in unrighteousness, he gives them up to *strong delusions* and vile practices, 2 Thess. ii. 10---12. Isa. lxvi. 4. Psalm lxxxi. 11, 12. Hos. iv. 17. Rom. i. 18---32.——To punish their hardening themselves in sin, he gives them up to *judicial hardness* of heart, that neither his word nor his providence affects them, Rom. ix. 18. Isa. lxiii. 17; withholding his grace from them, Deut. xxix. 4; blasting to them his ordinances, these means of softening hearts, Hos. iv. 17. Rom. xi. 8, 9. Isa. vi. 9, 10; exposing them to temptations, Deut. ii. 30. Psalm cix. 6. Rev. xx. 7, 8; and suffering them to prosper in their wickedness, Psalm lxxiii. 2---12. Job xxi. 7---15. Deut. xxxii. 15---18. Jer. xii. 1. xliv. 17. Mal. iii. 15. Psalm xxxvii. 35.—To punish their contempt of, and rebellion against the checks, the alarms and rebukes of their conscience, he gives them up to a *spirit of slumber*, and a conscience *seared as with an hot iron*, which neither feels, nor reproves them for their commission of the most horrid crimes, Rom. xi. 8. 1 Tim. iv. 2. Gen. vi. 3 ---To punish their indulgence of vileness in their affections, even contrary to the strivings of their conscience, he gives them up to *vile affections*, disposing them to the most shocking lewdness, or the like, Num. i. 26, 27. Eph. iv. 19. v. 12. 1 Cor. vi. 9 Gal. v. 19. 1 Pet. iv. 3. 2 Pet. ii. 14. Jude 7.——To punish their sinning against common sense and rational conviction, he gives them up to a *reprobate mind* or *sense*, Rom. i. 27. 2 Tim. iii. 8. Tit. i. 16.— To punish their ready compliance with Satan's temptations, he gives him power to *stand at their right hand*, and reduce them to his peculiar slavery, Psalm cix. 6. 2 Tim. ii. 26.—— Other spiritual plagues, which God inflicts on them, are of the *tormenting* kind, as *discontentment*, which the peace of God not ruling their heart, as it were, draws harrows of iron over their soul, making it impatient, fretful, and given to murmur at every trifle, Jude 16. Psalm xxxvii. 1—7. Esth. iii. 5. v. 13. vi. 12. Col. iii. 15. Phil. iv. 17.——From this inward gnawing hunger and painful thirst after happiness, while the curse debars them from it, proceed inward *wrath* and *rage*, which, like a sword or arrow, pierce them to the heart, and are as fire in their bosom, Job v. 2. Isa. xlviii. 21:——*Anxiety* of mind, which racks their soul, stretching it, as it were, on tenter hooks, men being torn asunder by the contention of inward lusts, Esth. v. 13. Luke viii. 14. Psalm vii. 14; and by their apprehensions of their spiritual or their eternal state, Acts ii. 37. xvi. 30. Heb. x. 27, 27. Isa. xxxiii. 14:—*Sorrow of the world*, occasioned by temporal losses, disappointments, and troubles, 2 Cor. vii. 10; or by their envy at the prosperity of others,

Job v. 2. Col. iii. 5; or *legal sorrow,* arising from slavish fears of death and hell, Mat. xxvii. 3, 4. Isa. xxxiii. 14:—*Terror of heart,* under apprehensions of approaching misery, Gen. iv. 14. Deut. xxviii. 65—67. Jer. xvii. 17. xx. 4. Luke xxi. 26. Heb. x. 26, 27, 31. Isa. xxxiii. 14:—*Horror of conscience,* a rising from awful convictions of guilt, felt impressions of God's wrath inflicted, or views of its certain and speedy approach, Isa. xxxiii. 14. xxxviii. 14. Prov. xviii. 14. Heb. x. 26, 27; which is either more confused, as in Herod, Mat. xiv. 1, 2; transient, as in Felix, Acts xxiv. 25; or abiding and violent, as in Judas, Mat. xxvii. 3, 4:——and in fine, *despair,* Isa. xvii. 11. Heb. x. 26— 31. Isa. xxxiii. 14. Ezek. xxxvii. 11. Jer. ii. 25. 2 Kings vi. 34.

2. *Man's body,* that once glorious habitation of his soul, having partaken of forbidden fruit, swallowed down death, and became suddenly cursed, Deut. xxviii. 16, 18, 19. Hence, 1. There often befals it a deforming variation from the original happy constitution,—by deafness, blindness, lameness, &c. And it is merely owing to the sovereign mercy of God that all our bodies are not affected with it, 1 Cor. iv. 7. John ix. 3. 2. Its animal constitution is changed into a correspondence with the sinful lusts of that soul with which it is united, and hence is called a *vile body* and *sinful flesh,* Phil. iii. 21. Rom. viii. 3. And being corrupted by the soul, it is a snare to it, occasioning such multitudes of filthy lusts, drunkenness, gluttony, and unchastity, that its rational powers are, as it were, depressed into a mire of corrupted flesh and blood, Rom. vii. 14, 23, 24. 3. Being thus changed, man's body, under the influence of the curse, becomes a *vessel of dishonour.* The drunkard renders it a common sewer or sink; the glutton makes it a filthy draught house; the covetous renders it a drudged and weary beast; the passionate renders it a burning slime pit, a lake of fire and brimstone; the unchaste renders it a furious stallion, a lecherous dog, or an abominable swine; the brawler renders it an accursed serpent to hiss forth revenge, Rom. iii. 9—18. i. 26—28. 1 Cor. vi. 9, 10. Gal. v. 19—21. Tit. iii. 3. 1 Pet. iv. 3. Jer. v. 7, 8. Deut. xxiii. 18. 2 Pet. ii. 2, 22. Thus, it is the slave of manifold, cruel, and oppresive lusts, even while it, contrary to nature, appears to command the soul, 2 Pet. ii. 19. 4. The curse from every quarter,—from air, from earth, from sea, from beasts, from men, from angels, both good and bad, darts its empoisoned arrows, and heaps mischief upon men's bodies,—famine, war, pestilence, diseases, desolations, captivities, imprisonments, dangers, wounds, bruises, pains, &c. Deut. xxviii. 15—68. Lev. xxvi. 14—39. 2 Kings i. 2. vii. 29. 2 Chron. xxi. 19. Acts xii. 23. 5. Meanwhile, the accursed body itself is a seed-plot of misery, and its inward corruption, especially when it meets with correspondent outward circumstances, works

into unnumbered diseases, and renders our world a kind of hospital, Deut. xxviii. 22. Lev. xxi. 18—20. Mat. iv. 24. 6. Man's body, being thus infected, becomes a remarkable clog to his soul in all its attempts toward spiritual exercises or happiness. Its weakness or weariness occasions slumber, sleeping, or uneasiness in the worship of God. Cares for its welfare or honour, prevent serious care or thoughtfulness about things spiritual or eternal. Its health and sickness, in different forms, hinder concern about true and everlasting happiness, Mal. i. 13. Mat. xxvi. 40, 43. vi. 26—34. Luke x. 40, 41. xii. 16—20.

3. Men's PERSONS and all their *relative concerns* are affected by this curse. 1. They themselves, soul and body, are thereby, and from their own choice, the subjects and slaves of Satan,—his lawful and sure captives, plagued with his delusions, harassments, and drudgery, 2 Tim. ii. 26. Isa. xlix. 24. lxi. 1; who cannot be delivered from his additional chains and burdens, but by the infinite merits, the almighty power and grace of Christ, Zech. ix. 11. Isa. xlix. 24, 25, 26. Mat. xii. 29. 2. Every thing connected with their accursed person is accursed to them for their sake. Their character is cursed with shame and dishonour, and the higher they rise in the world, this the more remarkably appears, Psalm lvii. 4. Job v. 2. Deut. xxviii. 27. Psalm xxii. 6. lxix. 19, 20.—The employment of their mind or hand, as cursed, issues in vanity or mischief, Deut. xxviii. 17. Hag. i. 6, 7. Eccl. i. 13.—Their substance, being cursed, groans to escape out of their hands, is consumed by a secret fire of God's wrath, or flies toward heaven to bear witness against the abusers of it, Rom. viii. 21. Job. x. 26. Prov. xxiii. 5. Hos. ii. 9.—Their outward lot, whether prosperous or afflicted, as cursed, decoys or drives their soul from God, Job xxi. 8—15. Deut. xxxii. 15—18. Hos. xiii. 6. Luke xii. 16—20. Prov. i. 32. 2 Chron. xxviii. 22. 2 Kings vi. 33. Job xxxv. 10. Isa. i. 5. Jer. v. 3. xliii. xliv.—The word and ordinances of God, these means of grace and salvation, and all the opportunities of attending them, are cursed to them, and tend to their hurt, 2 Cor. ii. 16. Rom. xi. 9. Psalm lxix. 22, 23. Isa. vi. 9, 10. 2 Thess. ii. 11, 12. 2 Pet. ii. 20—22. John xv. 22, 24. Mat. xi. 21—23. 2 Cor. iv. 3, 4.—Their relations being cursed to them, increase their misery in different forms. Magistrates are oppressors, entanglers of conscience, a praise to evil doers, and a terror to them that do well. Ministers are unfaithful, unwatchful, unactive, unsuccessful, or deceiving. Neighbours are unjust, selfish, and mischievous. Being unequally yoked, husbands are such sons of Belial, that one cannot speak to them; and wives such brawlers, continual dropping and rottenness, that one cannot live with them. Children are a reproach and grief to parents, arrows to pierce their hearts, and robbers to

waste their substance. Daughters, like carved palaces in comeliness, and corner-stones in connecting families, fall on parents' heads, and crush them with expences and grief, 1 Sam. viii. 11 —17. Prov. xxix. 2—16. Ezek. xiii. xiv. Isa. ix. 15, 16. Jer. vi. 13, 14. Mic. ii. 11. iii. 11. 2 Cor. ii. 14. 1 Sam. xxv. 17. Mal. ii. 11—16. Prov. xix. 13. xxvii. 15. xxi. 19. xxv. 24. xii. 4. x. 1, 5. xv. 20. xvii. 2, 25. xiii. 1. xix. 26. xxviii. 7, 24. Hos. iv. 13, 14. Mic. vii. 5. Gen. xxxiv. xxxvii. xxxviii. 2 Sam. xiii. xv. xvi. 21, 22. 3. They are in perpetual danger of still greater misery than that which they are under,—being waited for by the sword, the vengeance of God; and having snares every where laid for them, Rev. iii. 17. John iii. 18, 36. Jer. xx. 3, 4. Psalm vii. 11—14. Job xviii. xx. 4. Being in prison and without strength, they cannot escape, but must slide in due time, be suddenly hurried out of their place, driven away in their wickedness, and swept into hell by the storm and flood of God's wrath, Deut. xxxii. 35. Prov. i. 26. xiv. 32.

II. After this life, the curse operates on men in a still more dreadful manner. 1. In consequence of soul and body combining in rebellion against God, the curse, *in death*, makes an unhappy separation between them. It is, 1. A most ruinous stroke from the hand of an angry God. Men, having trusted their life to the broken covenant of works, its curse tumbles them headlong into the hands of his wrath, Job xviii. 18. Heb. x. 31. 2. A final breaking up of all treaty between God and them, relative to their eternal salvation. In death, the curse fixes an impassible gulf between him and them, sets his seal to the proclamation of an eternal war with them, and indissolubly girds itself about them as a dreadful serpent to crush them for ever, Luke xvi. 26. 3. A conclusion of all their comfort, which draws an immovable bar between them and it,—quenches their coal, and puts out all their light, that darkness may for ever dwell in their tabernacle, Luke xvi. 25. Job xviii. 17, 18. 4. The *king of terrors*, armed with all that strength which he can derive from sin, and from the holy and just law of God. When men die under the guilt of sin, God's justice and power must chase them into everlasting fire. When they die under the dominion and pollution of their lusts, these, as tormentors, must attend them to the lowest hell, Job xviii. 14. Prov. xiv. 32. 5. A fearful passage into everlasting misery. By death the curse opens a trap-door under sinners, that they may fall into the bottomless pit, and be swallowed up in unfathomable depths of misery, Luke xvi. 22, 23.

2. Immediately after death, man's soul is, by the power of the curse, haled to the judgment-seat of God, to receive its

OF THE COVENANT OF WORKS.

particular sentence of eternal damnation, Heb. ix. 27. Eccl. xii. 7. Matth. xxv. 41. In this, 1. All their sins are brought forth, as out of a sealed bag, in which they had been carefully preserved, Hos. xiii. 12. Amos viii. 7. Job xiv. 16, 17. 2. Every sin appears drawing a curse after it. Alas, what unnumbered cords of damnation! Gal. iii. 10. Rom. vi. 23. 3. There being no more a throne of grace, or advocate with the Father, for them, they, having sinned by the law, must perish by the law, and be appointed to enter into eternal fire, as workers of iniquity, Luke xiii. 25—28. Psalm xi. 5. Mat. vii. 23. Prov. xiv. 32. Isa. xxxiii. 14.

3. Their condemned soul is lodged in hell by the power of the curse, now irrevocably confirmed by God, Luke xvi. 23. 1. Their soul is lodged here as in a prison, securing it for the last judgment, 1 Pet. iii. 19. 2. All the dregs of God's wrath shall be wrung out by the influence of the curse, and poured into it, Psalm lxxv. 8. 3. It shall be fixed among other damned spirits, devoted to eternal ruin by a like curse, Mat. xxv. 41. 4. The happiness which it hath irrecoverably lost, for a trifle or worse, shall now appear in its full value, as an aggravation of torment, Luke xvi. 23, 25, 26. 5. Conscience being fully awakened to sleep no more, shall fasten upon the damned soul the most terrible convictions of his former sinfulness, and apprehensions of the wrath of God, Mark ix. 44, 46, 48. 6. All the powers of their soul shall lie under the unrestrained influence of its sinful lusts, and the tormenting passions of pride, grief, envy, rage, anguish, despair, which attend them, Prov. xiv. 32. Matth. xxii. 13. viii. 12. Rev. xvi. 10, 21. Isa. viii. 21. 7. While the souls of the wicked are tormented in hell, their sins, in the practice of every one who hath been directly or indirectly drawn into sin by their means, shall, till the last judgment, continue increasing on earth, Mic. vi. 16. 2 Kings x. 29, 31.

4. Mean while, their body, being buried under the curse, 1. The grave is no bed of rest, no hiding-place to it, as to the bodies of saints, Isa. lvii. 2. Rev. xiv. 13. But it is there shut up as a malefactor in a prison till the last judgment, Psalm xlix. 14. 2. Sin and guilt continue upon it, without any possibility of removal, Job xx. 11. Ezek. xxxii. 27. 3. It is corrupted in the grave by the influence of the curse, Job xxiv. 19.

5. No part of their debt to the precept or penalty of the broken covenant of works being paid, the bodies of the wicked shall be raised again to life under this curse, at the last day. 1. By virtue of this condemning sentence, they shall be produced and brought forth, as malefactors, to everlasting punishment, John v. 29. Rev. xx. 13. Dan. xii. 2. 2. Having

in their former life been instruments of unrighteousness, they shall now be marked with sin as unclean vessels, perhaps each with his predominant lust, Isa. lxvi. 24. 3. The union between soul and body shall be renewed with inexpressible anguish to both. 4. Who knows what terrible appearances the anguish of their souls, and the immediate impressions of the wrath of God, may give to these bodies? Rev. vi. 16, 17. Isa. xxxiii. 14. xiii. 8. viii. 21, 22.

6. In the last judgment, sinners shall appear under the power of the curse, as damned malefactors, before the tribunal of Christ. 1. Their station at his left hand shall, with its shame and disgrace, mark them accursed, Dan. xii. 2. Matth. xxv. 33. 2. The curse interposing between him and them, shall render his appearance most terrible,—as a devouring lion,—a consuming fire: and the more curses interpose, his appearance will be the more terrible, Rev. i. 7. vi. 16, 17. Psalm l. 22. 3. To manifest the infinite equity of the curse, in its public proclamation and eternal execution, all the sinful qualities, thoughts, words, and actions of the wicked, and which they have directly or indirectly encouraged or approved in others, shall be plainly stated to their account, Eccl. xii. 14. Rom. xiv. 12. 2 Cor. v. 10. Rev. xx. 12. 4. In consequence hereof, the curse shall be solemnly proclaimed by Christ, and ordered into immediate full execution, Matth. xxv. 41—46. Rev. xx. 12, 13.

7. While, by virtue of the condemnatory sentence now ripe for full execution, the holy angels shall drive, and the devils drag them, from the judgment-seat of Christ, Matth. xiii. 41, 42. xxii. 13, the curse which had all along infected this lower world, shall kindle it into an universal flame, to give the transgressors their last, their terrible adieu. By this means the earth, the sea, and the air, shall get rid of the curse; and all that vanity and corruption, which had long infected them, shall be returned, in inexpressible vengeance, on the wicked, who had occasioned it, and all sin and misery shall thenceforth be confined in hell, 2 Pet. iii. 10, 13. 2 Thess. i. 8, 9. Psalm l. 3. Rom. viii. 21—23. Rev. xx. 14, 15.

8. In hell the curse of this broken covenant of works shall for ever prey upon the united soul and body of the wicked, in its full strength, Psalm lxxv. 8. Rev. xiv. 10, 11. 1. By it the infernal pit, having received them, shall close its mouth upon them, and shut them up as in a fiery oven, Num. xvi. 32. Matth. xiii. 30. Psalm xxi. 9. 2. As a dreadful partition, it shall for ever exclude all exercise of God's mercy and patience from among them, Matth. xxv. 41. Hos. ix. 12. 3. Hence all sanctifying and sin-restraining influences shall be for ever stopt from them; and God shall abandon them to the

full fury of their lusts, while they shall have nothing to satisfy them, Matth. xxii. 13. Rev. xvi. 21.   4. As the breath of the Lord, it shall for ever blow up the fire of his indignation on them; and fix the envenomed arrows of his wrath in them, Isa. xxx. 33. Rev. xiv. 11.   5. It shall prolong their misery into eternal duration, and dreadfully uphold them in bearing it, and perhaps perpetually render it more and more tormenting, Rev. xiv. 11. Luke xii. 59. Matth. v. 26. xxv. 41—46. 2 Thess. i. 9. Mark ix. 44, 46, 48. Isa. xxxiii. 14.

Though the condition of the saints, and of the wicked in death, and that which precedes it, be often apparently similar, yet every thing which the saints meet with, or the management of it by God, proceeds from his love and justifying sentence.—Sinful plagues are the choice and delight of the wicked; but they are the heavy burden of believers, Rom. vii. 14—24. Psalm xxxviii. 4. xl. 12.

Reflect. Having thus far compassed the flaming mount, and traversed the paths of condemnation, hast thou, my soul, believed and trembled? Knowest thou these terrors of the Lord, that thou mayest persuade men? Am I still under? or, have I escaped from this broken covenant?—this tremendous curse? Know I when, and how, Jesus Christ removed it, and all its dreadful effects, from my heart?—when, and how, he plucked me as a brand out of the fire, cleansed and washed me in his blood? What experience have I of the translation of the curse from my person to my Saviour, and through him, to my sins, for their destruction?—Thrice dreadful, but—heart-melting thought, Was Jesus, was Jehovah made a curse—for me? Stop then, my soul, and in the most awful mode, devote thyself to him. Bear me witness, ye listening angels, you Omniscient three, that I consent to be only his,—wholly his,—for ever his, as made of God to me, wisdom and righteousness, and sanctification and redemption. If I love not this Lord Jesus, let me be Anathema Maranatha. Dare not, my soul, to enter on the *sacred work*, without having tasted of the wormwood and the gall:—without having tasted redemption through his blood, the forgiveness of my sins, according to the riches,—the exceeding riches of his grace.——How tremendous the charge of dealing between God and men,—men who are under his awful curse! What deep compassion! What prayers and supplications, with strong cries and tears to him that is able to save them from death! What earnest and unremitting labour! What simplicity of the gospel! What travelling in birth till Christ be formed in their souls, is necessary here!

Q

CHAP. II.

Of the COVENANT OF GRACE, *in the* MAKING *and* ADMINISTRATION *of it.*

MAN's ruin being wholly of himself by his sin, and his damnation being infinitely just, it was impossible, that his recovery should proceed from God by any necessity of nature. He is indeed naturally good and merciful, but it was not necessary that this goodness and mercy should be manifested in the infinitely costly, the eternal redemption of his malicious enemies, that sought his life.—As infinitely holy, righteous, and faithful, he might have punished every sinful creature with everlasting destruction, Psalm xi. 5.—Being infinitely and independently blessed in himself, their ruin could not have impaired his happiness, Exod. iii. 14. John v. 26. 1 Tim. vi. 15, 16. i. 11. Nevertheless, if the whole of mankind had been eternally ruined, his wisdom and goodness in his creation of them, had not so clearly shone forth. To have created a *whole kind* of rational beings, not one of which answered the end of their formation, in glorifying and enjoying himself; or to have been seemingly disappointed of his immediate end, with respect to the whole of them, would not have convincingly manifested his infinite wisdom, at least to his enemies. ——If not one of them had shared his eternal favour, how obscure had the manifestation of his infinite goodness been among them?—In vain it is pretended, that in such a case, God would have immediately swept Adam and Eve into hell, and so prevented the damnation of millions.—As in making the covenant of works with Adam, God had in his view every particular person represented in it,—his equity and faithfulness required, that, if the conditions had been fulfilled, every one of them should be brought into being to receive his share of the promised reward;—even as the covenant of grace secures the same, with respect to those represented by Christ, Isa. liii. 10. Psalm ii. 8. xxii. 27--31. lxxxix. 4.—In like manner, when this covenant of works was broken, God's equity and faithfulness secured the existence of all the representees under the curse, to receive their share of the deserved penalty.

If God, in his sovereign mercy and grace, intended to recover any part of self-ruined mankind, he could not have renewed the covenant of works, or entered into any other with themselves, as immediate parties. 1. Their infamous character, *as sinners*, rendered it dishonourable for him to have any immediate dealings with them. 2. The terms of the covenant of

OF THE COVENANT OF GRACE.

works, through their breach of it, became altogether impracticable; perfect obedience to all its precepts could not be performed, and full satisfaction for the infinitely criminal violation of it could not be rendered;—no part of which could be fulfilled by any finite person, Gal. iii. 10. Psalm xlix. 7. · 3. Partly by the curse of the broken law lying on their conscience, as the strength of sin,—and partly by the reign of corruption in their heart, all men in their fallen state are absolutely incapable of performing any thing spiritually good, or even of ceasing from that which is morally evil, 1 Cor. xv. 56. Rom. viii. 7, 8. Job xiv. 4. Jer. xvii. 9. Matth. xv. 19. xix. 24. Eph. ii. 1—3, 12. 4. The whole structure of the covenant of works being of God, his holiness, equity, and faithfulness were deeply interested in the securing its honour. Infinite holiness could not bear with the wanton violation of the holy and good commandment delivered to Adam, Hab. i. 13. Jer. xliv. 4. Rom. vii. 12. Infinite justice could not forbear punishing so horrid a crime, Gen. xviii. 25. Deut. xxxii. 4. Psalm xi. 5—7. Infinite faithfulness could not dispense with the execution of that death which was doubly secured in the threatening, Gen. ii. 17. Tit i. 2. Num. xxiii. 19. 1 Sam. xv. 29. 2 Tim. ii. 13. It was therefore necessary, that any covenant for the redemption of fallen men should be made with a divine person, who could infallibly secure, and, in the same nature which had sinned, would fully pay the debt, as stated from the broken covenant of works, Psalm xl. 6—8. Isa. liii. 4, 5, 10—12. Rom. viii. 3, 4. 1 Thess. v. 9, 10. Gal. ii. 20. Acts xx. 28. Tit. ii. 14. Heb. ii. 10, 11, 14, 16. vii 22. ix. 15. Matth. xx. 28. 2 Cor. v. 21. 1 Pet. ii. 24. iii. 18. i. 18, 19. Rev. i. 5. v. 9.

That misery into which all men plunged themselves by sin, was the OCCASION of God's making a new covenant for their redemption, Eccl. vii. 29. Gen. iii. 1—19. Hos. xiii. 9. Eph. ii. 1—10. i. 7. Rom. iii. 9—20, 23. viii. 3, 7, 8. v. 12—21. Tit. iii. 3, 4. But his own amazing love and sovereign grace was the CAUSE and spring of it, Psalm xl. 5. cxxxvi. 23. Jer. xxxi. 3, 20, 33. Isa. liv. 8—10. lxiii. 7. John iii. 16. 1 John iv. 9, 10, 19. Luke ii. 14. Eph. i. 6, 7. ii. 4—8. And hence it is commonly called the COVENANT OF GRACE. Originating from the mere grace of God, and contracted between two divine persons, it was *made from all eternity*. Hence, 1. Christ is represented as having his *goings* forth from of old, from everlasting, Mic. v. 2. as set up from everlasting, Prov. viii. 23. and foreordained before the foundation of the world, 1 Pet. i. 20. 2. Grace and eternal life are represented as promised, as given before the world began, 2 Tim. i. 9. Tit. i 2.—and the kingdom of heaven as prepared for men, and their names as enrolled in the book of life,—before the foundation of the world, Mat. xxv. 34. Rom. ix. 23. Rev. xiii. 8.——This covenant of grace is nevertheless called the *second covenant*, because, though it was first made, it is last executed, the breach of the covenant of works necessarily preceding the entrance of this. And it is called the *new covenant* for much the same reason, and because of its everlasting stability and excellency, Heb. viii. 6—13. Jer. xxxi. 31—34.

As this covenant took its rise from the infinite, the equal of all the three divine persons, they were equally employed in the making of it, and took their respective shares in the work of it, John iii. 16. Gal. ii. 20. Rom. xv. 30. It is manifest that the Holy Ghost was concerned in it. 1. His will is the very same with that of the Father and the Son, 1 John v. 7. Deut. vi. 4. 2. Though he be independent and free in his agency, he is sent to execute the plan of this covenant, in publishing the tidings or messages of it,—in forming, anointing, and supporting the manhood of Christ, the Representative of men, in it,—in erecting and governing the church,—and in the effectual application of the blessings purchased by Christ, to man's person and nature, 1 Pet. i. 11, 12. 2 Pet. i. 21. Luke i. 35. Isa. xi. 2, 3. lxi. 1. Heb. ix. 14. Acts xiii. 2—4. xx. 28. John xvi. 7—14. 1 Cor. vi. 11. Rom. viii. 2, 13. xv. 16, 19. Eph. i. 13, 14, 17, 18. ii. 21, 22. Eph. v. 9. Gal. v. 22, 23, 18, 25. And from his concern in the making of this covenant, he hath a right to be Intercessor in the hearts of believers for the blessings of it, Rom. viii. 15, 26, 27. Gal. iv. 6.

But this covenant of grace was, in a peculiar manner, made by God with his own Son, *as Mediator*, between him and men. 1. The Scripture plainly represents God as covenanting with Christ, Psalm lxxxix. 3, 4, 19—36. all which texts have language too emphatic to have their full application to the covenant of royalty over Israel made with David, which was typical of that made with Christ,—Psalm xl. 6—8. Luke xxii. 29. Isa. liii. 10—12. Zech. vi. 13; which text runs in the future time, because the execution of this covenant is never finished.—And hence we read of Christ's connection with a *better covenant*, Heb. viii. 22. vii. 6. ix. 15.—and of its promises being before made or confirmed by God unto Christ, Gal. iii. 16, 17. Tit. i. 2. 2. God is represented as the *God, the Head*, and *Master*, and the *Judge*, of Christ his Son, and as giving, sending, helping, bruising, justifying, and glorifying him, Psalm xxii. 1. xlv. 7. John xx. 17. Eph. i. 3. 1 Pet. i. 3. 1 Cor. xi. 3. John iii. 16. Rom. viii. 32, 3. 1 John iv. 9, 10. Isa. xlviii. 16. xlii. 1. 1. 7—9. liii. 10. Heb. ii. 10. xiii. 20. 1 Pet. i. 21. Eph. i. 20—23. Phil. ii. 9—11. 3. Christ is represented as God's servant, or sent messenger, Isa. xlii. 1—7. xlix. 1—9. lxi. 12. John vi. 27,

29. x. 36.—as a Surety, Heb. vii. 22. Psalm cxix. 22.—as made under the law, Gal. iv. 4, 9. Rom. viii. 3, 4. made obedient, Mat. iii. 15. Phil. ii. 7, 8. Heb. v. 8. John viii. 29. x. 18. xiv. 31. xvii. 4. Rom. v. 19. Psalm xl. 7, 8. made sin, 2 Cor. v. 21. Isa. liii. 6, 11, 12. 1 Pet. ii. 24. made a curse, Gal. iii. 13. made a sufferer for us, 1 Pet. i. 19. ii. 24. iii. 18. Rev. v. 9. Eph. v. 2, 23, 25, 26, 27. Mat. xx. 28. Luke xxiv. 26. Isa. liii. 4, 5, 10. 2 Cor. v. 14, 15. Rom. iii. 24—26. v. 6—11. and as receiving the reward of his work, Psalm ii. 8. xxi. 1—7. xxii. 27—31. cx. Isa. liii. 10—12. xlix. 3—9. Luke xxiv. 26. John xvii. 4, 5. Phil. ii. 7—11. Heb. ii. 9, 10.   4. Solemn confirmations of agreement by oaths and seals are represented as between God and his Son.—To mark the infinite importance, infallible certainty, and the necessary belief of that which he declared, God sware it to Christ, Psalm cx. 4. lxxxix. 3, 4, 35. Heb. vii. 17, 21, 28. and Christ pledged his heart or soul, that he would approach an offended God as an atoning priest and sacrifice, Jer. xxx. 21.—God conferred and Christ accepted, the seals of both dispensations of the covenant of grace. Christ indeed did this in obedience to his Father's law, —and as a solemn avowal of his fellowship with the visible church, and of his readiness and cheerfulness in his work,—and as a mean of exciting and strengthening the graces of his manhood. But these seals were also confirmations of the engagement between him and his Father, relative to the redemption of man.—Thus, in circumcision, God signified and sealed to Christ, that he acknowledged him the promised seed of Abraham, in whom men should be blessed;—that through his being cut off by blood-shedding and death, his mystical body should be preserved and admitted to fellowship with God;—and that they should derive their spiritual circumcision from him, Gen. xxii. 18. xvii. 10—14. Col. ii. 11—13. By receiving circumcision, Christ avowed himself a debtor to fulfil the whole law of God, Gal. v. 3. and that, to preserve us and procure our fellowship with God, he was ready to endure bloody sufferings and death, as our Head, and flesh of our flesh, Psalm xl. 6—8. John viii. 21, 23—30.—In baptism, God solemnly acknowledged Christ as acceptable to him in his person and office,—he secured his furnishing him with all the fulness of the Spirit for himself and his people,—and signified that in due time he should be delivered from, and lifted above all waters of trouble, Mat. iii. 15—17. and Christ avowed his readiness to plunge himself into the depths of divine wrath, in the full assurance of his Father's support under, and deliverance from it, Mat. iii. 15. Isa. l. 7, 9. Luke xii. 50. Mat. xx. 22.—In granting the passover to Christ, God solemnly acknowledged him his *Lamb* without spot, 2 Cor. v. 21. Heb. vii. 26. Isa. liii. 7. and that by his

death, and the application of it to men, deliverance and comfort should be secured for all his spiritual seed, Isa. liii. 10---12. Heb. ix. 28. Exod. xii. Deut. xvi. Num. ix.---In eating it, Christ avowed his immediate readiness to undergo the most tremendous suffering and death, for procuring his people's salvation, Psalm xl. 7, 8. John xviii. 11. Luke xxii. 15.---In Christ's partaking of the holy supper, God sealed to him, that by his death, he should be the eternal nourishment and comfort of his people; that his sufferings and their virtue should be solemnly remembered and experienced among his people on earth till the end of time, and in heaven for ever, Isa. liii. 10---12. Psalm xlv. 17. xxii. 27---31. And Christ solemnly avowed his intention to enter immediately on his last sufferings and death, and signified his unition of his people into one mystical body with himself, Mat. xxvi. 26. 1 Cor. x. 16, 17.

Thus the PARTY on heaven's side is God essentially considered, in the person of the Father as sustaining the majesty and authority of the Godhead. He is to be here viewed, 1. As highly offended with man's sin, Psalm xiv. 2, 3. v. 4, 5, 6. Jer. xliv. 4. Hab. i. 13. 2. As purposing to manifest the exceeding riches of his grace in the redemption of a part of mankind, 2 Tim. i. 9. Tit. i. 2. Psalm cxxxvi. 23. Jer. xxxi. 3, 20. 3. As infinitely just and holy, who cannot but give sin its due recompence, and cannot save sinners, but in a way of magnifying his law, satisfying his justice, and vindicating his holiness, Gen. xviii. 25. Deut. xxxii. 4. Psalm xi. 5---7. Exod. xxxiv. 7. Isa. v. 16. xlii. 21. Mat. v. 18.

The Son of God is the *party contractor* on man's side, 1 Tim. ii. 5, 6. Isa. vii. 14. ix. 6. He was considered, 1. As a person of infinite perfection, having in himself sufficient wisdom, power, holiness, justice, goodness, and truth, for the marvellous and arduous work of our redemption, Psalm lxxxix. 19. Isa. ix. 6. Rev. i. 4. Phil. ii. 6. Zech. xiii. 7. 2. As our rightful proprietor, who might save us, if he pleased, and who had a tender regard and compassion to the work of his hands, Psalm c. 3. Rom. ix. 20---23. Isa. xliii. 21. liv. 5. 3. As a public head and representative of all his elect of mankind, as his spiritual seed, Eph. i. 3, 4, 6, 7. 2 Tim. i. 9. Psalm lxxxix. 3, 4. Isa. liii. 10. 11, 12.

That it was made with him as a *Representative* of his spiritual seed is evident. 1. All these covenants, which were typical or emblematical of it, were made with parents as representatives of their descendants,---as the covenant of preservation from floods with Noah, Gen. ix. 9. the covenant of peculiar friendship and relation with Abraham, Gen. xvii. 7. the covenant of priesthood with Phinehas, Num. xxv. 12, 13. the covenant of royalty with David, 2 Sam. vii. 11---19. the covenant of possession of Canaan, and peculiar relation to God, with Israel, Exod. xix. 5, 6. xxiv. Deut. v. 2. xxix. 11, 15. 2. Christ is, in a peculiar manner, compared with Adam our representative in the covenant of works,—with respect to his connection with his elect members, Rom. v. 12—21. 1 Cor. xv. 21, 22, 45—49. 3. Christ and his spiritual seed are called by the same name of ISRAEL, Isa. xlix. 3. Rom. ix. 6. Gal. vi. 16. Isa. xlv. 17. xliv. 23. JACOB, Psalm xxiv. 6. Isa. xli. 14. CHRIST, 1 Cor. xii. 12. Gal. iii. 16; which plainly infers, that he is their head and they his members, Eph. v. 30. iv. 13, 15, 16. Col. i. 18. ii. 19. 4. The promises of this covenant respecting men were all made to Christ, Gal. iii. 16, 17. and before any of them existed, Tit. i. 2. 2 Tim. i. 9. And hence they are sometimes directed to another person than them, Heb. viii. 9—12. Nay, the first promise was published in a threatening directed to Satan, Gen. iii. 15. 5. Christ was the SURETY of this covenant, Heb. vii. 22. viii. 6. ix. 15. Psalm cxix. 122. And hence, the fulfilling the condition of it was exacted from him instead of the represented covenantees, Isa. liii. 4—12. 2 Cor. v. 21. Eph. v. 2, 25—27. Mat. xx. 28. 1 Pet. i. 19. ii. 24. iii. 18. Rev. v. 9.

It was necessary that this covenant should be made with the Son of God, as our representative, 1. That the infinite love and mercy of God might have an early vent, even from all eternity, while none of those that were chosen to everlasting life had begun to exist, Jer. xxx. 21. xxxi. 3. Tit. i. 2. 2 Tim. i. 9. Prov. viii. 23—30. Even then Christ became their *everlasting Father* and their Husband, to whom they were married by proxy, Isa. ix. 6. John xvii. 6. 2. Unless this covenant had been made with a divine person as our representative, it could not have been made at all. They, whose salvation was intended in it, could only be viewed as weak and wicked,—as nothing but enmity and rebellion against God, so that they could fulfil no conditions of life, Rom. viii. 3, 7, 8. Jer. xvii. 9. Psalm xiv. 1—4. Eph. ii. 1—3. Tit. iii. 3. Matth. xv. 19. Mark vii. 21—23. Meanwhile, the law had raised its terms to perfect obedience, and infinite satisfaction for sin, which none but a divine person could perform, Gal. iii. 10, 13. Rom. vi. 23. Ezek. xviii. 4. Heb. ix. 22. 3. It was thus made, that it might be to us a covenant of exceedingly rich and absolutely free grace, Eph. ii. 7—9. i. 6—8. Rom. iv. 4, 16. v. 20, 21. iii. 24. 4. That righteousness and life might be communicated to us, in as compendious a manner as sin and death were by the covenant of works, and thus the perfections of God justified in his entering into a covenant of life for us with Adam as our representative, Rom. v. 15—21. 1 Cor. xv. 21, 22, 45—49. 5. That the promises of this covenant might be sure to all the elect, Rom. iv. 16.—That mercy might be built up for ever, and God's faithfulness established in the heavens, it was necessary that the representative should be a mighty one, who could not fail, nor be discouraged, nor be seduced by Satan, Psalm lxxxix. 2, 19, 22, 28, 29, 33, 36.

The *party contracted for* in this covenant, were persons of mankind chosen by God to everlasting life. 1. Only they that were *chosen in Christ,* are *blessed in him,* Eph. i. 3, 4. In their election he and they are considered as *one body,* of which he is the head, and they the members, Heb. ii. 11. Isa. xlii. 1, 6. Eph. v. 23, 30. 2. All those whom Christ represented become heavenly men, 1 Cor. xv. 47—49. Col. iii. 1—4. Eph. i 4. ii. 6. 3. Those for whom he undertook are represented as his spiritual seed, in due time begotten again in their regeneration, Gal. iii. 16 Psalm lxxxix. 3, 4. xxii. 30, 31. Psalm liii. 10, 11. James i. 18. 1 Pet. i. 2, 3. 4. Those whom he represented are God's spiritual Israel, Rom ix. 6. Gal. vi. 16. Heb. ii. 16. In this representation these persons are considered, 1. As sinners, lost and undone in themselves, by the breach of the covenant of works, Hos. xiii. 9. Luke xix. 10. Mat. xviii. 11. ix. 12, 13. Rom. v. 6, 8, 10. 2. As altogether unable to help themselves, Rom. v. 6. viii. 7, 8. 2 Cor. iii. 5. John xv. 5. Jer. xiii. 23. Eph. ii. 1. Col. ii. 13. 3. As, in the sovereign purpose of God, distinguished from the rest of the world, Matth. xx. 23. 2 Tim. ii. 19. John xvii. 6, 12. Eph. i. 4. 1 Thess. v. 9. 4. As objects of the redeeming love of God, Father, Son, and Holy Ghost, John xvii. 23, 6. xiii. 18. xv. 15, 16. Eph v. 21, 25. John iv. 9, 10, 19. iii. 1.

It was therefore necessary, that, in representing them, Christ should not only bear the general character of Mediator, but that, in particular, he should be, 1. Our KINSMAN-REDEEMER, Job xix. 25. Isa. xlviii. 17. that he might marry the widowed human nature and the holy law, and raise up to them an offspring of good persons and works, Luke iii. 38. Gen. iii. 15. Heb. ii. 11—16. Matth. iii. 15. Luke xxiv. 26. Rom. vii. 4. Psalm xxii. 30, 31. John xii. 24.---might deliver us from the slavery of the broken law, of sin, Satan, and the world, Gal. iv. 4, 5. iii. 13. Rom. vii. 4. vi. 14. viii. 2. 1 Pet. i. 18, 19. Tit. ii. 14. Heb. ii. 14, 15. 2 Tim. ii. 25, 26. Isa. xlix. 24—26. Gal. i. 4. vi. 14.—might buy back our mortgaged inheritance of eternal happiness, 1 Thess. v. 10. Eph. i. 14. John x. 10. Rev. v. 9.—and avenge our blood upon sin, Satan, and death, our murderers, John viii. 44. Heb. ii. 14. 1 Cor. xv. 56. Rom. v. 12. Dan. ix. 24. 1 John iii. 5, 8. Hos. xiii. 14. Isa. xxv. 8. 2. Our SURETY;—not indeed a *Surety for God* to us, it being impossible to render his engagements by promise more certain, Heb. vi. 17, 18 ;—nor a Surety, merely bound to see our debt to the law and justice of God paid,—or bound together with us the principal debtors,—it being impossible for us to do any thing but increase our debt, Rom. v. 6. viii. 7, 8. i. 28—32. iii. 9—18. 2 Pet. ii. 14 ;—nor a Surety for our faith, repentance, and new obedience, these, *as privileges*, belonging to the promises of the covenant, for the fulfilment of which the Father is engaged, Psalm xxii. 27—31 ;—nor can we suppose Christ a Surety for our performance of these *as duties*, without admitting them into the condition of this covenant, and so obscuring, or rather undermining the grace of it. But he is our Surety, who undertook by himself alone, to pay our whole debt to the broken law, and offended justice of God, Gal. iv. 4, 5. Matth. v. 17, 18. xx. 28. iii. 15. Isa. liii. 6, 10. 2 Cor. v. 21. Rom. iv. 25. v. 19. 1 Pet. i. 18, 19. ii. 24. iii. 18. Luke xxiv. 26. Eph. v. 2, 25. 1 Thess. v. 10. Tit. ii. 14. Rev. v. 9. 3. Our SACRIFICING PRIEST. Having engaged as Surety to satisfy the penalty of the broken law for his elect sinners, it became necessary, that as a Priest, he should offer himself in sacrifice to God, for the atonement of their guilt, Heb. vii. 22, 26. v. 1. ix. 14, 28. x. 5, 10, 14. Isa. liii. Psalm xxii. lxix. Eph. v. 2.

In the MAKING of this covenant of grace, 1. The Son of God was constituted *the second Adam*, and agreed to assume our nature, and become a true man ; and hence a *substantial* Mediator between God and men, capable of subjecting himself to the law binding on us, and to pay our debt of love to God and men,— and of suffering for sin in that very nature which had sinned, Psalm xl. 6-8. Gen. xxviii. 12. John i. 51 ;—in the view of which he was constituted an official Mediator, Head, and Representative of his elect, Isa. xlii. 1, 6. Psalm lxxxix. 19. 1 Cor. xv 47. 1 Tim. ii. 5, 6. Heb. viii. 6. ix. 15. 2. All the particular persons of mankind chosen to everlasting life were, in a manner becoming Jehovah, given to Christ by the Father, accepted by him, and enrolled in his book of life, John xvii. 6, 9, 12. Eph. i. 4. Phil. iv. 3. Rev. iii. 5. xiii. 8. xxi. 27. Luke x. 20. Isa. iv. 3. 3. The terms, and every thing relative to the salvation of these persons, were fully settled ; what ransom should be paid, and in what form and time ;—what furniture for, assistance in, and reward of his surety-service, Christ should have from God the Father ;—and in fine, every circumstance of time, manner, or degree, in which grace or glory should be bestowed on him, and on every one of his members, Isa. liii. 10---12. xlix. 1---12. Psalm xl. 6---8. xxii. 27---31. cxxxix. 16. ii. 6---9.——It was agreed that in executing their plan of our redemption, the Father should act the part of a sovereign Master and Judge, with respect to the Son, and the persons to be saved by him, Isa. l. 4---9. lii. 13---15. xlii. 1---7. xlix. 1---9. Heb. ii. 10. Zech. xiii. 7;---

that the Son should act the part of a Mediator,—of an humbled and honorary servant to his Father, 1 Tim. ii 5, 6. Isa. xlix. 3. lii. 13—15; liii. lxi. 1—3. Psalm cx. lxxii. cxix. ii;—and that the Holy Ghost should act as the publisher of the covenant-declaration, 2 Pet. i. 21. 1 Pet. i. 11, 12. 2 Sam. xxiii. 2.—the furnisher, assistant, and rewarder of Christ, Isa. xi. 2—4. lxi. 1—3. Psalm xlv. 7; the witness of Christ's and his Father's fulfilment of this covenant,—and as an effectual applier of the blessings of it to elect men, Heb. ii. 5. Acts ii.—xix. John xiv. 16, 17, 26. xv. 26. xvi. 7—14.

When CONDITION is improperly taken, and signifies no more than what particular duties as performed must, in the order of nature, precede the enjoyment of particular promised benefits, many things may be called *conditions*; for, holiness must precede eternal happiness, Heb. xii. 14. true repentance of sin must precede God's fatherly pardon of it, Prov. xxviii. 13. 1 John i. 9. And as faith is particularly required in the public dispensation of this covenant by the gospel, Acts xvi. 31. Mark xvi. 16. and is the appointed instrument by which God communicates, and we receive the blessings of it, John i. 12. Isa. xlv. 22. Matth. xi. 28. Rom. v. 1, 2. Eph. ii. 8. it is more frequently called the *condition* of it, by divines: and indeed might be called a condition of connection IN it. But when CONDITION is taken properly for *that which, when fulfilled, gives the covenanters full right to claim the promised reward*, nothing but the finished righteousness of Jesus Christ, by which all the demands of the broken covenant of works are fully satisfied, can be allowed as the *condition* of this covenant. 1. Christ took upon himself the whole debt of his elect world,—all that of which the payment secures them from eternal death, Rom. vi. 23. 1 Thess. v. 10. Matth. xx. 28. 1 Pet. iii. 18. Rev. v. 9. and entitles them to eternal life, Matth. xix. 17. iii. 15. v. 17, 18. Rom. v. 19, 21.—Nothing can therefore remain to be fulfilled by them, as the proper condition of this covenant, Dan. ix. 24. 2 Cor. v. 21. 2. It hath been proved, that the perfections of God's nature required, that the condition of the broken covenant of works should be the condition of any covenant he could make for the recovery of fallen men. Unless his truth and righteousness fail, the penalty must be executed, Gen. ii. 17. Sin must be expiated to the full satisfaction of his infinite majesty and perfection, which can by no means clear the guilty, Exod. xxxiv. 7. Unless the holy commandment be honoured with perfect obedience, no man can enter into life, Gal. iii. 12. Matth. v. 18. xix. 17.—Nothing but the righteousness of the Son of God can answer to these high demands, Matth. iii. 15. Rom. viii. 3, 4. 3. The Scripture plainly represents Christ's fulfilment of all righteousness answerable to the precept and

OF THE COVENANT OF GRACE. 235

penalty of the broken law or covenant of works, as the *proper condition* of the eternal happiness of his spiritual seed, Isa. liii. 10, 11. Luke xxii. 20. Matth. iii. 15. xx. 28. Luke xxiv. 26. Heb. ii. 10. Phil. ii. 8. iii. 9. 2 Cor. v. 21. Rom. iv. 25. v. 10, 15—21. iii. 24—26. 1 Pet. i. 18, 19. ii. 24. iii. 18. 2 Pet. i. 1. Rev. v. 9. Eph. v. 2. Tit. ii. 14. 1 Thess. v. 10. 4. Upon his righteousness alone believers found their plea for, and hopes of eternal salvation, Eph. i. 6, 7. Col. i. 14. Phil. iii. 8, 9. Rom. iii. 20—22. v. 21. Gal. ii. 16. v. 4. and Christ himself founds his continual intercession, John xvii. 4. 1 John ii. 1, 2. Rev. viii. 3, 4. 5. Only the righteousness of Christ, our Surety, as the condition of this covenant, can render eternal life a debt to the covenanter or covenantees, Rom. iv. 4—6. and by it, our eternal redemption is a debt to Christ, founded on his merit, which is both *intrinsic* and *pactional*, he being at once the most high God, and the fulfiller of the condition of this covenant made with him, Isa. liii. 10, 11, 12. Psalm xl. 6—8. Acts xx. 28. 6. As our faith, repentance, and new obedience can, by no means, answer the demands of the broken law, so, instead of being proper conditions of this covenant of grace, they are all inestimable benefits promised in it, upon the footing of its fulfilled condition, Phil. i. 29. Psalm xxii. 27, 31. Acts v. 31. They suppose every person in whom they are, already within that covenant,—none of them being performable under the curse or condemning covenant of works, Gal. ii. 19. iii. 10. 1 Cor. xv. 56. Rom. vii. 4. vi. 14. viii. 2.—Being duties performed, not under the law, *as a covenant*, but under it, as a RULE OF LIFE, they can have no pactional merit, but are founded on union to, and fellowship with Christ, interest in his righteousness, and complete claim to eternal life, Luke i. 74, 75. Heb. xii. 28.—Even faith can no more properly be called the condition of the covenant of grace, than a child's receiving and wearing of his Father's wages of service, can be called the condition which entitles to such wages, and renders the master bound to pay them, Isa. liii. 10—12. Heb. ii. 10—16. Psalm xxii. 30, 31. 7. The covenant of grace excludes all boasting, Rom iii. 27. v. 20, 21. Tit. iii. 3, 5. But it could not do so, if our faith, repentance, and new obedience, were the proper conditions of it, as the weakest acting of any of these graces under the curse of the law and dominion of sin, would be more ground of boasting, than Adam's complete fulfilment of the law, in his state of innocence, would have been.

As the perfections of God required, that this condition of the *surety righteousness* of Jesus Christ should be stated from the broken covenant of works, Mat. v. 17, 18. Rom. viii. 3, 4. Gal. iv. 4, 5. it necessarily included, 1. *The holiness of his manhood* absolutely perfect in parts and degrees, and retained till the end of his humbled life, Heb. vii. 26. Luke i. 35. Man, under the covenant of works, being indispensably bound to retain that perfection of nature which had been given him in his creation, duly improved and strengthened, it behoved Christ to afford it, in the room of those that are saved by him. To suppose that the law of God did not require this holiness of nature, is to suppose, that want of original righteousness, and hence even the contrary corruption of nature, is no sin: for where no law is, there can be no transgression, Rom. iv. 15. v. 13. Nor can the admitting Christ's holiness of nature into his surety righteousness to be imputed to us, any more render our holiness of nature unnecessary, than his obedience of life can render our holy obedience unnecessary. Our holiness of nature is an important part of our happiness purchased by Christ's holiness of nature and life, Rom. v. 10, 15—21. 2. The holy obedience of his life carried to the highest perfection in parts and degrees, and continued till his death, John viii. 29. Heb. v. 8. Mat. iii. 15. v. 17, 18. Phil. ii. 8. Psalm xl. 8. Gal. iii. 10, 12. Rom. x. 4, 5. v. 19. Mat. xix. 17. Lev. xviii. 5. Deut. xxvii. 26. Christ's retaining his holiness of nature, and his persevering in this holy obedience, was infinitely difficult, as he all along continued under the curse of God in our stead, Gal. iii. 13. 1 Cor. xv. 56. 3. Full satisfaction to the penalty of the broken law incurred by man's sin, in voluntarily bearing the very same punishment which we deserved, in all the essential ingredients of it.—In, 1. His being subjected to legal death, or the curse due to us for our sin, Gal. iii. 13. Deut. xxi. 23. Hence God was legally wroth with him, Psalm lxxxix. 38. xxii. 1, 2. He was consigned into the hands of his revenging justice, that it might demand full satisfaction from him for all the sins which were imputed to him, without any pity or abatement, Zech. xiii. 7. Isa. liii. Rom. viii. 32.—and was set up as the butt or mark of all the arrows and billows of his Father's almighty wrath, John xviii. 11. Psalm lxix. 1, 2, 14, 15. 2. The infinite execution of this curse or condemning sentence of the broken law, upon his soul, body, and person, in every thing comprehended in that temporal or spiritual death which flows from the curse itself, Gen. ii. 17. Gal. iii. 10, 13. Luke xxiv. 26. Isa. l. 6. lii. 14. xlix. 7. liii. 2—12. Psalm xxii. 1—21. lxix. 1—21. xl. 2, 6—8. 12, 13, 17. John xii. 27. Acts xx. 28. Heb. ii. 10. v. 7. xiii. 12. Rev. v. 9. Eph. v. 2. 1 Pet. i. 19. ii. 24. iii. 18. 2 Cor. v. 21. Mat. xx. 28. xxvi. xxvii. Mark xiv. xv. Luke xxii. xxiii. John v. viii. x. xviii. xix.—The reign of indwelling lusts, the pollution of sin, and the eternity of punishment, not proceeding from the curse of the law in itself, did not belong to this punishment, when inflicted on an infinitely holy and worthy person. His infinite power and holiness prevented all infection from sin, 2 Cor. v. 21. Isa. liii. 7. The infinite dignity of his person made his temporary sufferings of infinite value answerable to the demands of the law, John xviii. 11. Acts xx. 28. Rom. i. 17. v. 17, 18. 2 Cor. v. 21. And being the only Son of God, who had come voluntarily under this curse for others,—it did not debar him from his Father's necessary support or occasional smiles, Isa. xlii. 1. John iii. 34. Mat. iii. 16, 17. xvii. 1—5. iv. 11. Luke x. 21. xxii. 43. John xii. 28.

Being made with a person infinite, eternal, and unchangeable, in wisdom, power, holiness, justice, goodness, and truth, who could not fail to fulfil whatever he had undertaken, this covenant left no room for a PENALTY in case of breach, Psalm lxxxix. 19, 22. Isa. ix. 6. xlii. 4. Heb. vii. 25. The condition of this covenant being fulfilled by Christ, no proper penalty or punishment to their hurt can be inflicted on any of those represented by him. The chastisements which they suffer are indeed annexed to their sins, to promote their destruction,—but they proceed from God's redeeming love, and are purchased by Jesus' blood, as they are connected with, and ever beneficial to their persons and natures, Rom. viii. 1, 33—39. Psalm lxxxix. 30—35. cxix. 67, 71. Heb. xii. 6—11. Rev. iii. 19. Psalm xciv. 12. Prov. iii. 12.

But the promise of this covenant is of infinite importance in it, and hence it is called the *covenant of promise*, Eph. ii. 12. 1. To usward it is one continued promise, or cluster, or constellation of promises. Not one duty is required of us in the whole of its dispensation, but God in it promiseth to work it in us, accept it from us, and reward us for it, Ezek. xxxvi. 26, 27, 31. Isa. lx. 7. Rom. xv. 16. Isa. iii. 10. 1 Cor. xv. 58.— Nay, even Christ's fulfilment of the condition comes to us in a promise, Gen. iii. 15. Dan. ix. 24. 2. The condition of it was, and is attended with many promises to Christ. His fulfilment of this condition flowed from his receiving his father's promised furniture and assistance, and issued in his reception of his promised acceptance and reward, Isa. xlii. 1—6. l. 4, 7, 9. lii. 13 —15. xlix. 1—9. liii. 10—12. Psalm xxii. 27—31. lxxii. cx.

In their immediate application, some promises of the covenant of grace respect Christ, as the head of his elect, as their object, and others of them respect the elect themselves. But such is that oneness and relation between them, that every promise fulfilled on *him*, terminates in their advantage, and every promise fulfilled on *them*, terminates in his glory and joy, Psalm xxii. 27—31. Isa. liii. 10—12. xlii. 1—7. xlix. 1—12.— The promises, which are immediately fulfilled on Christ himself, were made chiefly, if not solely, to him.—Of these, the the promises of furniture for his work, in having an holy manhood formed for him, and the Holy Ghost plentifully given him, being fulfilled antecedently to his performance of his humbled service, have their foundation in the sovereign love of God along with our election, Heb. x. 5. Isa. xlix. 1---9. xlii. 1---6. lxi. 1. xi. 2---4. l. 4, 7, 9. Psalm lxxxix. 21. Mat. iii. 16. John iii. 34.---But the promises of God's *acceptance of his service*, including the promise of his resurrection from the dead, Psalm xvi. 10. Heb. xiii. 20; and the promise of his justification in the Spirit,---in which he received an ample discharge of all the debt which he had engaged to pay for his people, Isa. l. 8. 1 Tim. iii. 16. Rom. iv. 25. Heb. ix. 28. John xvi. 10;--- and the promises of God's *rewarding* him for it,---including a mediatorial interest in God as his God and portion,---heirship of him, and all things in and with him, Psalm lxxxix. 26, 27. Heb. i. ii. Rom. viii. 17. John xx. 17. Psalm xlv. 7. xvi. 11;--- an exaltation to be God's prime minister, and great manager of all things relative to the church, Acts ii. 36. Psalm cx. 1---7. lxxii. xxi. xxii. 27---29. Isa. xlix. 8. lii. 13. Dan. vii. 14. Mat. xxviii. 18. xi. 27. John. iii. 35. v. 22. Eph. i. 22. Phil. ii. 8--- 11. Isa. ix. 6, 7. xxxii. 1;---a spiritual seed, numerous as the stars of heaven, and blesssed in him to the highest, for ever, Isa. liii. 10---12. Psalm lxxxix. 4, 29, 36. xxii. 30. lxxii. 17. Isa. xlv. 17;---and complete victory over all his and his people's enemies, Psalm cx. 1, 2, 5, 6. lxxxix. 23. xxii. 27, 28. xlv. 5, 6. Mic. iv. 3. ii. 13. v. 4, 5. Zech. ix. 9, 10. xii. 9. xiv. 12. Psalm xviii. xxi. lxxii. depend on his fulfilment of the condition of the covenant.

All the promises which have their immediate fulfilment on the elect were *primarily made* to Christ himself. 1. The Scriptures plainly affirm this, Gal. iii. 14, 16, 17. Psalm lxxxix. 4, 28---36. 2. Christ is the great and primary heir of all things, divine promises not excepted, Heb. i. 2. Psalm lxxxix. 27. John xx. 17. Rom. viii. 17. 3. These promises were made to be fulfilled upon condition of his fulfilling all righteousness, and so contain part of the reward promised to him, Isa. liii. 10---12. Psalm xxii. lxix. Heb. ii. 8, 9, 10. xii. 2. Phil. ii. 8---11. 4. They were made, and the grace contained in them given before the world began, while not one of the elect existed, Tit. i. 2. 2 Tim. i. 9.------It therefore follows, 1. That no conditional promises of this covenant entail any spiritual benefit upon any person, but such as are united to Christ, and clothed with his righteousness, which is the condition of it, Isa. i. 19. iii. 10. 1 Cor. xv. 58. Rev. xiv. 13. xxii. 14. 2. That the very beginnings of grace are conveyed into elect persons in promises, 1 Pet. i. 23. James i. 18. Ezek. xi. 19. xxxvi. 26. Deut. xxx. 6. 3. That spiritual union with Christ gives one an actual interest in, and begun possession of all the promises, as an heir thereof in Christ, 1 Cor. i. 30. 2 Cor. i. 20. 4. That we ought to plead the promises only in the name of Christ, John xiv. 13, 14. xvi. 23, 24. Gen. xii. 3. xxii. 18. Psalm lxxii. 17. Eph. i. 3. 5. That we ought never to dread the failure of any promises. For, however much we have provoked the Lord, Christ, to whom they were primarily made, never gave him any provocation to break them, but an infinite and everlasting ground and cause to fulfil them.

The promises immediately respecting the elect, in general comprehend ETERNAL LIFE, that is, all true happiness in time and through all eternity, and all the means of it, Tit. i. 2. 1 John ii. 25. Isa. xlv. 17.---It might be viewed, as including a *death* to the broken law,---to sin,---and to the world, Rom. vii. 4. viii. 2. vi. 2---14. Col. iii. 3, 4. ii. 20. Gal. i. 4. ii. 19, 20. vi. 14.---and an endless *life*,---from a reconciled God as its cause, ---on him as its upholding support,---with him as a gracious companion,---and to him as the highest and last end of it, Psal. xxvii. 1. cxlii. 5. lxxiii. 24, 26. Col. iii. 3, 4. Rom. vii. 4. Gal. ii. 19. 1 Cor. vi. 20. x. 31.---Or, this eternal life may be considered in three different periods of it;---before the elect's spiritual union with Christ;---between the moment of their union to him and their death; and in their eternal state. In the first of which periods, eternal life is on its way towards them, but they have neither title to, nor possession of it, in their own persons. In the second, they have a full title to eternal life, but no more than imperfect possession of it. In the third, they have the full possession of it, as well as title to it.

But taking all these periods in connection, we may take up the promise of eternal life in the following steps or articles: 1. The promise of security against any thing which tends to hinder their partaking of eternal life;—that they shall be brought into natural life, Isa. liii. 10. While the curse immediately thrusts them into being, as children of fallen Adam, the promise made to Christ, and to them in him, secretly draws them into life, that they may partake of his redemption;—that notwithstanding many and great dangers, their natural life shall be preserved till the appointed moment of their marriage with Christ, Mat. xxiv. 22. Ezek. xvi. 6, 8. Isa. lxv. 8.—that no grave-stone fixing them under spiritual death shall be laid upon them, in order to their passing over their day of grace,— or, in their committing the unpardonable sin, Mark iii. 29;— and that all they meet with, or do, during their alienation from God, by his infinite wisdom, power, and love, shall be managed into occasions or means of promoting their union to Christ, Ezek. xx. 36, 37. Hos. ii. 6, 7, 14. Job xxxiii. 14—30. Luke xv. 11—13. Acts ix. 1—18. xxii. xxvi. Philem. 10—19. 2 Chron. xxxiii. 11. John iv. 6—29. Luke xxiii. 39—43.——

This promise is grafted upon God's promise of preparation

furniture, and assistance to Christ, and on that of preserving his body from corruption in the grave, Isaiah vii. 14. xi. 2. Psalm xvi. 10.——2. The promise of spiritual union to Christ in the moment of love fixed in God's eternal purpose and covenant, Isa. liii. 10. liv. 5. Hos. ii. 19, 20. Ezek. xvi 8. This comprehends the promise of the Spirit to convince, allure, apprehend, conquer, and quicken their souls, by shewing them the things of Christ, and working faith in their hearts to receive him, Isa. xliv. 3—5. John xvi. 7—14. Psalm cx. 3. xlv. 4, 5. Ezek. xxxvi. 26, 27. xxxvii. 5, 9, 14. John vi. 37, 44, 45, 65. Psalm xxii. 31. Rom. xv. 12. Isa. xi. 10. Phil. i. 29. Eph. ii. 4—10. This promise is grafted upon that of God's uniting a real manhood to Christ's divine person, and of his reuniting his soul to his body in his resurrection, Eph ii. 5, 6. Isa. xxvi. 19. Hos. vi. 2. Phil. iii. 10. ii. 3. The promise of a free, full, irrevocable, and everlasting justification, through their union to Christ as the Lord their righteousness, and the imputation of his fulfilment of the condition of the covenant, to their person,—it being theirs, as the free gift of God offered to them in the gospel, and by virtue of their communion with Christ as their surety and husband, Isaiah xlv. 24, 25. liii. 11. xlii. 21. Dan. ix. 24. Rom. v. 16—19. i. 17. iii. 22. Phil iii. 9. 2 Cor. v. 21.—This includes all the promises of full and irrevocable pardon of all their sins, past, present, or future, in so far as they are transgressions of the law as a covenant, Heb. viii. 12. Eph. i. 7. John v. 24. Isa. liv. 9. i. 18. xliii. 25. xliv. 22. Jer. l. 20;—and of a full and irrevocable acceptance of their persons into a state of favour with God, and of a full title to a real eternal life, begun here in grace, and perfected hereafter in heavenly glory, Eph. i. 6. Rom. v. 19. 2 Cor. v. 21. Isa. xlv. 24, 25.—These promises are grafted upon that of a full justification made to Christ, 1 Tim. iii. 16. Isa. l. 8. Rom. iv. 25. John xvi. 10. 4. The promises of a new covenant relation to God as their reconciled and reconciling friend, Ezek. xxxvii. 26. Rom. v. 10. 2 Cor. v. 19.—their adopting Father, Hos. i. 10. Gal. iv. 4, 5. Rom. v. 1, 2. John i. 12. 1 John iii. 1. 2 Cor. vi. 18. Jer. iii. 4, 14, 19, 22.—and as their God,—portion,—and ALL in all, Exod. xx. 2. Psalm l. 7. lxxxi. 8, 10. Jer. xxx. 22. xxxi. 33. Ezek. xxxvii. 23, 27. xi. 20. Heb. viii. 10. Gen. xvii. 7. Rom. viii. 17. Gal. iv. 7.—These promises are grafted upon that of the acceptance of Christ and his work, and of his mediatorial interest in God, and heirship of all things, 2 Cor. v. 19. Eph. i. 6, 7. John xx. 17. Rom. viii. 17. 5. The promises of sanctification of their nature and life, Ezek. xi. 19. xxxvi. 26, 27, 29. Psalm cx. 3. xxii. 30. 1 Thess. v. 23, 24.—as proceeding from their union with Christ, 1 Cor. i. 2, 30. Eph. ii. 10. 2 Cor. iii. 18. v. 17. Gal. iii. 26, 27. vi

15.—from their justification by his blood, Heb. viii. 10, 12. xiii. 12.—and from their relation to God as their Friend, Father, and God, 1 Thess. v. 23.—Rom. viii. 29, 30. Gal. iv. 6. v. 17, 24.—Ezek. xvi. 8, 9. Jer. xxxii. 38—40. As they have in Christ a complete treasure of wisdom and grace, ready to be communicated to them, Col. ii. 10. John i. 14, 16,—there proceeds from him as manifested to them, and from his Spirit dwelling in their heart by faith, a predominant measure of every spiritual grace, issuing in their gradual death to the love and practice of every sin, and in their living to righteousness, performing an obedience to God's law, perfect in all its parts,—tending towards perfection in degrees, and acceptable to God as their reconciled Father in Christ, 2 Cor. iii. 18. Col. ii. 10, 11. iii. 10, 11. Phil. iv. 13. Jer. xvii. 7, 8. Psalm xxviii. 7, 8.—These promises are grafted upon that of the sanctification of Christ's manhood in the womb, and of his being filled with the Holy Ghost, and upon that of his resurrection from the dead, Phil. iii. 10, 11. Rom. vi. 1—12. vii. 4. Col. ii. 11, 12. John i. 14, 16. 6. The promises of their perseverance in their state of union to Christ as their husband, the Lord their righteousness, and their head of influences,—and in their covenant-relation to God in him, Jude 1. Col. iii. 3. Jer. xxxii. 40.—and their possession and exercise of implanted grace, Job xvii. 9. Prov. iv. 18.—to promote which, the continued inhabitation and influences of the Holy Ghost are promised, Ezek. xxxvi. 27. John xiv. 16, 17. xvi. 13, 14. Isa. xxvii. 3. Hos. xiv. 7. Col. ii. 19.—and renewed fatherly pardons of their daily sins of infirmity, upon their renewed actings of faith and repentance, Jer. xxxiii. 8. John xiii. 10. Isa. xliii. 25. John i. 7, 9. ii. 1, 2. Mic. vii. 18, 19.—These promises are grafted upon those of Christ's perseverance in fulfilling his surety righteousness, Isa. xlii. 4. Psalm lxxxix. 22; and of the permanent security of his heavenly life, Psalm xxi. 4. John xiv. 19. Col. iii. 3, 4. 7. The promises of spiritual comfort, which consists in sensible assurance of God's love, peace of conscience, and joy in the Holy Ghost, Isa. xl. 1, 2. xliv. 23. xlix. 10. lxi. 2. lvii. 18.—These are grafted upon that of Christ's being made full of joy with his Father's countenance, Psalm xvi. 11. xvii. 15. Acts ii. 28. Rom. viii. 29. 8. The promise of temporal benefits, Ezek. xxxvi. 28, 29. Hos. ii. 18, 22. Isa. xxxiii. 16. 1 Tim. iv. 8. vi. 8. Psalm xxxvii. cxii. cxxvii. cxxviii.—including new-covenant protection from all things really evil, Psalm xci. 3—13. Zech. ii. 5. Psalm i. 3, 4. xli. 1—4. Job v. 19—22. Isa. xlix. 11. Psalm cxxi. 6. Rev. vii. 16; and provision of all good things, as proceeding through Christ from the redeeming love of God, Psalm xxxiv. 10. lxxxiv. 11. lxxxv. 12. xxxvii. 3, 19. Prov. iii. 2—24. Mat. vi. 30—33. Isa. lxv. 21—23.

R

Rom. viii. 32. This promise is founded on that of Christ's heirship of all things, Psalm lxxxix. 26, 27. Heb. i. 2. 1 Cor. iii. 22, 23. 9. The promise of an happy death,—death disarmed of its sting, Hos. xiii. 14. Psalm xxiii. 4.—death sanctified and sweetened, 1 Cor. iii. 22. Phil. i. 21, 23. Luke ii. 29, 30. 2 Cor. v. 1—5.—and at last destroyed in the resurrection, Isa. xxvi. 19. xxv. 8. 1 Cor. xv. 54. This promise is grafted upon Christ's safety in, and victory over death, and his resurrection from it, Psalm xvi. 10. John xi. 25. Isaiah xxvi. 19. 1 Cor. xv. 10. The promise of an honourable judgment at the last day, Psalm l. 1—6. xcvi. 13. xcviii. 9. Mat. xxv. 31—40. This is founded upon that of Christ's being prime minister of heaven, and having dominion over all, 1 Thess. iv. 15—17. Col. iii. 4. 11. The promise of eternal happiness, beginning in their soul at death, Isa. xxxv. 10. lvii. 2. 2 Cor. v. 1—7. Phil. i. 23. Luke xxiii. 43. Rev. xiv. 13; and completed in both soul and body at the last day, Isa. li. 11. liii. 10. Dan. xii. 2, 3. John v. 28, 29.— This promise is grafted upon that of Christ's exaltation and perpetual sitting at the Father's right hand, Rev. iii. 21. Psalm xvi. 11. cx. 1, 5, 7.

From the above hints of the *parties*, *making*, and *parts* of this covenant of grace, it is manifest that it ought never to be splitted into two, as if one *covenant of redemption* had been made with Christ, and another *of grace* were made with the elect in their own persons. 1. The Scriptures mention none but *two covenants* relating to the eternal happiness of men,—of which the covenant of works, which genders to bondage, is one, and therefore one covenant of deliverance must be the other, Gal. iv. 24.—which two are called the *old* and the *new* covenant, Heb. viii. 6—13; and the *law* and *grace*, Rom. xi. 6. vi. 14; and the *law of works* and the *law of faith*, Rom. iii. 27. 2. The blood of Christ is repeatedly called the blood of the *covenant*, but never—of the *covenants*, as if it were the condition of *a covenant of redemption*, and the foundation of *a covenant of grace*, Exod. xxiv. 8. Zech. ix. 11. Heb. ix. 20. x. 29. xiii. 20. This proves that our salvation depends upon none but one covenant; and that Christ and his people obtain their eternal glory by the same covenant. 3. If that, which some plead for as a distinct covenant of redemption, be detached, there remains no proper covenant at all to be made with the elect; but merely a bundle of precious promises, freely giving and conferring upon them the unsearchable riches of Christ: Nor is any thing required as an apparent condition in one promise, that is not absolutely promised in another, Isa. lv. 1—3. Acts xiii. 34. Rev. xxii. 17. Ezek. xxxvi. 25—31. Isa. i. 18. xliii. 24, 25. lvii. 17, 18. Jer. iii. 19. xxxi. 33, 34. Heb. viii.

OF THE COVENANT OF GRACE. 243

10—12. 4. There is no reason why the new **covenant** should be split into two, more than to assert that one covenant of works was made with Adam, and another with his seed, Rom. v. 12—21. 1 Cor. xv. 21, 22, 45—49.

The END of God,—Father,—Son,—and Holy Ghost, in making this covenant of grace, was, 1. To display the glory of his own perfections,—wisdom, power, holiness, justice, and truth,—and especially the exceeding riches of his grace, Isa. xlix. 3. 2 Cor. iv. 6. Eph. i. 6—8. ii. 7. iii. 20, 21. Rom. v. 20, 21. 1 Pet. iv. 11. 2. To bring elect men out of an estate of sin and misery into an estate of salvation, Luke ii. 10—14. i. 74, 75. Hosea xiii. 9. John iii. 14—18. Isa. lv. 2, 3, 7. xlv. 17, 22—24, 25.

The ADMINISTRATION of this covenant of grace, which includes all that is necessary to be done for making the chosen Representees partakers of its purchased and promised blessings,—is committed to Jesus Christ, 1 Cor. xv. 45. Isa. xlix. 3—9. xlii. 1—7. lxi. 1—3. lii. 13, 15. liii. 11, 12. Mic. v. 4, 5. Zech. ix. 9, 10. Mat. xi. 27. xxviii. 18. John iii. 35. v. 22,— who is to administer it for ever, Heb. i. 8. xiii. 8. Luke i. 32, 33. Isa. ix. 7. xlv. 17. Dan. vii. 14. Hos. ii. 19, 20. Jer. xxxii. 39—41. It is committed to him, 1. For the higher advancement of God's honour,—that he may have no immediate dealing with sinful men, even when perfectly healed; but his holiness, justice, mercy, and love to them, may for ever shine through his Son in their nature, as their Mediator, 2 Cor. iv. 6. Job ix. 33. Psalm lxxxiv. 9. 2. To answer the case, and sweeten the redemption of these sinful men, the whole of their fellowship with God, through time and eternity, being through him, who is both their Brother and their God, John i. 14. x. 7, 9. xiv. 6. Eph. ii. 18. iii. 12. Heb. iv. 14—16. x. 19—22. 1 Pet. ii. 5. iv. 11. 3. As an honorary reward to Christ the Redeemer, that all his ransomed millions, and all the concerns of their eternal salvation, may for ever depend on him, Phil. ii. 7—11. Eph. i. 20—22. Isa. liii. 10—12. lii. 13, 15. Psalm xxi. 5. lxxxix. 27. lxxii. 17, 19.

The covenant of grace is, in many things, administered indefinitely to men in general, without any consideration of them either as elect or as reprobates. 1. God's grant of Christ, as his ordinance for salvation to men, is general and unlimited, John iii. 14—17. Num. xxi. 8. 2. Christ's commission from his Father for administering this covenant is general and unlimited, Isa. lxi. 1—3. xlix. 1—9. Mat. xi. 27. xxviii. 18. John iii. 35. xvii. 2. 3. Christ executes his commission respecting sinful men, in the most general and unlimited manner, Prov. i. 22. viii. 4. ix. 4, 5. Isa. xlv. 22. lv. 1—7. Mat. xi. 28. xxii. 4, 5. xxviii. 19. Mark vi. 15, 16. Luke xiv. 23.

Rev. xxii. 17. 4. Though Christ effectually save none but his elect, Eph. v. 23,—he is by divine appointment, grant, and office, *the Saviour of the world*, fit for all sinful men, and to whom they are all warranted by God to apply for salvation, John iv. 42. 1 John iv. 14. His salvation is a *common salvation*, Jude 3. and his gospel is grace, which *bringeth salvation* in offer *to all men* that hear it, Tit. ii. 11. 1 Tim. i. 15. 5. If Christ's administration of the new covenant were not thus general and indefinite, some men would have no more warrant to hear the gospel, or believe in and receive him for their salvation, than devils have, contrary to Mark xvi. 15, 16. John vii. 37, 38. vi. 37. Rev. xxii. 17. Prov. i. 22. viii. 4. ix. 4, 5. Isa. lv. 1—7. xlv. 22. xlvi. 12, 13.—Nor could they be condemned for their unbelief, according to John iii. 18, 36. Mark xvi. 16. Rev. xxii. 8. Prov. viii. 36.——The foundation of God's general grant of Christ in the gospel as his ordinance to men for their salvation, and of his general administration of the covenant, is, 1. Christ's fulfilling the condition of the covenant, being infinitely valuable in itself, is, intrinsically considered, a sufficient ransom for all men, Acts xx. 28. iii. 15. 1 Cor. ii. 8. 2 Cor. v. 21. Phil. ii. 6—8. 2. Being fulfilled in an human nature equally related or similar to all men, it is equally answerable to all their needs. 3. All men, indefinitely considered, have in them the moral characters of those for whom Christ died, being *unjust, ungodly, sinners, enemies to God*, &c. 1 Pet. iii. 18. Rom. v. 6—10; and the characters with which the absolute promises of the covenant directly correspond,—being *stout-hearted and far from righteousness,—godless,—sinful,—lost,—self-destroyed*, &c. Isa. xlvi. 12, 13. Heb. viii. 10—12. Luke xix. 10. Hos. xiii. 9. Jer. iii. 1, 2, 5, 14.

The ENDS for which Christ administers this covenant are, 1. The bringing of sinful men into the bonds of it, Isa. lv. 3—5. xlix. 6. Mat. xxiii. 37. Luke xiv. 22, 23. 2. The right management of those that are instated in it, while they remain in this world, 1 Pet. ii. 25. Isa. xl. 11. Ezek. xxxiv. xxxvii.; in justifying them, Mat. ix. 2, 6; adopting them, John i. 12; sanctifying them, John xiii. 8. Acts v. 31. Eph. v. 26; caring for them, 1 Pet. v. 7; going with them, Ezek. xlvi. 10; and governing them, Psalm ii. 6. Ezek. xxxiv. 23, 24. xxxvii. 24.—And, as he, in his intercession, deals with God for them, John xvii. 9, 12—24. Heb. vii. 25. Rom. viii. 34,—they must receive all their orders from God through him, Exod. xxiii. 21. Deut. xviii. 18—20. Mat. xvii. 5. Rev. i. 1, 3. Gal. vi. 2. 1 Cor. ix. 21. 3. The completing their eternal happiness in heaven, Eph. v. 26, 27. Jude 24; finishing their faith, Heb. xii. 2; carrying them safe through death, Psalm xxiii. 4. Rev. i. 18; bringing them to glory, Heb. ii. 10. John

xiv. 2, 3; and giving them their heavenly throne and crown, Rev. iii. 21. 2 Tim. iv. 8.——Hence, it is manifest that the *elect only* are the objects of the more special and important administration of this covenant; and that it is administered to others only in order to promote their salvation, 1 Cor. xii. iii. 21, 23. Eph. iv. 11—13.

In the FORM and ORDER of his administration of this covenant, 1. Christ, as a TRUSTEE, receives from God all the purchased and promised blessings of it, for the behoof of his sinful brethren of mankind. 2. Having them all in his hand, he, as a TESTATOR, bequeaths them to sinful men. 3. As EXECUTOR of his own testament, he, as their interceding *Priest*, instructing *Prophet*, and liberal and almighty *King*, confers his legacies on his elect.

I. Christ, being by his Father constituted the TRUSTEE of the covenant of grace, hath all the blessings of it lodged in his hand, Col. i. 19. John iii. 35. Mat. xi. 27. Psalm lxviii. 18. This was done from eternity; and hence Christ was ready to begin his administration on that very day on which Adam fell, Gen. iii. 5—15. But the solemnity of his investiture with that high office, was delayed till his resurrection and ascension, when he had fully paid the price of the benefits committed to him, Psalm lxviii. 18. Matth. xxviii. 18. The blessings committed to his trust are, 1. The unseen guard of the covenant, or preservation of his elect in their unconverted state, Ezek. xvi. 6. Isa. lxv. 8. 2. The uniting and quickening spirit of the covenant, Rev. iii. 1. Rom. viii. 2. John v. 25, 26. 3. The justifying righteousness of the covenant, Jer. xxiii. 6. xxxiii. 16. Isa. xlv. 24, 25. liv. 17. xlvi. 12, 13. lxi. 10. 1 Cor. i. 30. 2 Cor. v. 21. 4. The covenant-relation to God as a Friend, Father. and God, Col. ii. 9, 10. Eph. ii. 14. 2 Cor. v. 19. Mic. v. 5, Psalm lxxxix. 26, 27. John i. 12. xx. 17. Rom. viii. 17. 5. The sanctifying influences of the covenant, Col. i. 19, 22. ii. 2, 6, 7, 10—13, 19. John i. 14, 16. vi. 63. 1 Cor. i. 30. Acts v. 31. 6. The establishing grace of the covenant, Jude 1. John xiv. 19. Col. iii. 3. Gal. ii. 20. 2 Cor. i. 21. Col. ii. 7. Matth. xvi. 18. 7. The consolation of the covenant, Isa. li. 7, 12. Luke ii. 25. John xvi. 33. 2 Cor. i. 5. 2 Thess. ii. 16, 17. 8. The temporal good things of the covenant, Mat. xxviii. 18. xi 27. Hag. ii. 8. Psalm xxiv. 1. 1 Cor. x. 25, 26. 9. All fulness of power over death and the grave, Rev. i. 18. Hos. xiii. 14. Isa. xxv. 8. 10. The everlasting and consummate happiness of the covenant, Isa. xlv. 17. Heb. vii. 25. John x. 28. xvii. 2.——Or, in other words, all the light, life, liberty, honour, &c. of the covenant are lodged in his hand, John i. 9. ix. 5. Luke ii. 32. 1 John i. 1. v. 11, 20. John viii. 12, 36.

Rom. viii. 2. 2 Cor. iii. 17. Prov. viii. 18—21. Col. i. 18, 27, 28. ii. 10, 19.

II. Having, for the behoof of sinful men, received these blessings into his hand, Christ, as a *dying Saviour* or TESTATOR, bequeaths them to them in the form of a *latter will* confirmed by his death, Luke xxii. 28, 29. Heb. ix. 15, 17. 1 Cor. xi. 25. Mat. xxvi. 28.—As none of his legacies were needful before Adam had fallen, Christ did not till then commence a Testator, and on that very day, in paradise, he began to form and publish his testament; and for about forty-one hundred years after, he gradually enlarged it by a more clear and particular bequeathment of his benefits. Both parts of his testament were at first delivered in words, and afterwards committed to writing, in our Bibles, 2 Pet. i. 21. Rom. xv. 4. Heb. ii. 3. Luke i. 3. John xx. 31, &c.—The Old Testament, published before his coming in the flesh, is the declaration of a dying Saviour, freely bequeathing his unsearchable riches to sinful men,—confirmed by his typical death, in innumerable sacrifices and oblations, and sealed by the sacraments of Circumcision and the Passover, Heb. ix. 20. Rom. iv. 11. 1 Cor. v. 7. Luke xvi. 16. The New Testament, published after his coming in the flesh, is his dying declaration, in which he freely bequeaths his unsearchable riches of grace and glory to sinful men,—confirmed by his personal death, and sealed by the sacraments of Baptism and the Lord's Supper, 2 Cor. iii. 6. 1 Cor. xv. 3. Mat. xxviii. 19. 1 Cor. xi. 23—29.—These Testaments are circumstantially different in their time, clearness, fulness, efficacy,—extent of original publication;—and in their easiness, their spirituality of worship, 2 Cor. iii. 6—16. Heb. i.—x. Acts xv. 6—11. But they are the same in substance, exhibiting the same new covenant,—making over the same Saviour and salvation, Heb. xiii. 8. Acts xv. 11. Rom. iv.—conferring the same right to,—assurance of interest in,—and actual enjoyment of eternal salvation, Psalm ciii. 1—6. cxvi. cxvii. xviii. 1—3. xxxii. 1, 2. lxxiii. 24—26. Job xix. 25—27. Gal. ii. 20. 1 Tim. i. 13—16. 2 Tim. i. 12. iv. 7, 8.—and requiring the same duties of faith, repentance, love, and new obedience in the legatees, Psalm ii. 12. Hosea xiv. 1. Jer. iii. 1, 4, 14, 22. Psalm xcvii. 10. xxxi. 23. Deut. xii. 32. Acts xvi. 31. 1 John iii. 23. Rev. ii. 5, 16. iii. 19. 1 Cor. xvi. 22. John xxi. 15—17. Mat. xxviii. 20. ——In these Testaments, the histories and rules of behaviour explain the bequeathments, and direct us to improve them in thankfulness to God.——And to connect the duties of holiness with the privileges which attend them, many clauses run in a conditional form: but these are all reducible to absolute ones, in which God's making us to perform these required duties, is promised as a free privilege without any conditions, Acts xvi. 31. Rom. xv. 12, &c. &c.

Christ's bequeathing his purchased blessings being his fundamental act of administration, upon which every thing relative to the application of them depends;—sinful men, indefinitely considered, must be his LEGATEES, to whom in the offers of the gospel, he dispones them; and all of them, as they hear his Testament published, have full warrant, by faith, to claim and take into possession all his benefits thus disponed.—And hence, in his Testament, they are not denominated from their personal names, arts, callings, or places of earthly abode;— but from general marks, descriptive of their disposition, state, and conversation before God,—as *men, sinful, lost, self-destroyed, stout-hearted and far from righteousness, polluted, wicked, rebellious,* &c. Prov. viii. 4. i. 22. ix. 4, 5. Acts ii. 39. Rev. xxii. 17. John vi. 37. vii. 37—39. 1 Tim. i. 15. 2 Cor. v. 20. Matth. ix. 12, 13. xi. 28. xviii. 11. Luke xix. 10. ii. 10, 11. Hosea xiii. 9. Isa. xlvi. 12, 13. lv. 1—7. lxv. 1, 2. i. 18. Jer. iii. 1—5, 14, 19, 22.—All the absolute promises of the covenant being directed to men, as in such wretched conditions, the elect representees, being, by conviction, made to know their testamentary characters, do, in agreeableness to them, claim and take into possession the bequeathed blessings,—and multitudes of reprobates are rendered useful to them in their spiritual concerns, 1 Tim. i. 17, 19. Mat. vii. 22. Eph. iv. 11—18.

The LEGACIES, which Christ bequeaths in his testament, comprehend every thing necessary for the recovery and eternal happiness of sinful and miserable men, Rom. viii. 32. Psalm lxxxiv. 11. lxxxv. 12. Phil. iv. 19. Particularly, 1. Himself as an Husband,—an effectual Saviour,—Portion,—and a governing Head, Isa. xlii. 6. ix. 6. 2 Cor. ix. 15. John iii. 16. 2. A complete and everlasting righteousness in him for justification of life, Rom. v. 17. i. 17. iii. 22. Isa. xlvi. 12, 13. liv. 17. lxi. 10. xlv. 24, 25.——3. A new covenant-interest in God, as a reconciled Friend, an affectionate Father, and an all-sufficient God, Isa. lvii. 19. 2 Cor. vi. 18. Hos. i. 10. Heb. viii. 10. 4. The Holy Spirit of all grace, for the renovation of our nature and life, into the image of God, and for the consolation of our soul, Prov. i. 23. John vii. 37, 38. Ezek. xxxvi. 26, 27. Zech. xii. 10. John xvi. 7—14. xiv. 16, 17, 26. xv. 26. 2 Thess. ii. 16, 17. 5. A proper portion of the good things of this life, Psalm xxxvii. 3, 16. Matth. vi. 33. 6. An unstinged and sweetened death, John viii. 51. Isa. xxv. 8. Hos. xiii. 14. 7. An eternal life in heaven, John vi. 40—58. x. 28. xvii. 2.

III. Having irrevocably bequeathed his unsearchable riches to sinful men, Christ, though not to the exclusion of his Father, and as co-operating with his blessed Spirit, EXECUTES his own Testament, in effectually conferring upon the elect the blessings therein disponed, answerable to their need, in the character of an ADVOCATE, a PROPHET, and KING.

1. As, on account of their unworthiness, guilt, and ignorance, his legatees cannot prosecute their claim before God the Judge of all, Christ, as *the Advocate,* or *interceding Priest* of the covenant, manages the cause of his chosen, skilfully and boldly pleads on the footing of his finished righteousness in their stead, that his disponed blessings may be conferred upon them, in the appointed moments of grace, 1 John ii. 1, 2. Rom. viii. 34. Heb. vii. 25. ix. 24. John xvii. By this he, 1. Secures their effectual inbringing to a new covenant-state of union and fellowship with himself, and of interest in, of peace and favour with God, John xvii. 20, 21. 2. Takes actual infeftment of all the new covenant blessings in their name, Heb. vi. 20. Col. ii. 10. Eph. ii. 6. John xiv. 2, 3. 3. Maintains the new covenant-peace and friendship between God and them,—answering all accusations laid against them, and removing all real controversies which happen between God and them, Rom. viii. 33, 34. 1 John ii. 1, 2. Isa. liv. 9, 10. xxvii. 4. lvii. 18, 19. 4. Notwithstanding their remaining unworthiness, ignorance, and imperfection, procures them access to God, and acceptance of all their services, which they perform in faith, Eph. ii. 18. i. 6. Rom. xii. 1. 1 Pet. ii. 5. Rev. viii. 3, 4. vii. 14. 5. Procures them an abundant entrance into heaven at death and at the last day,—and an everlasting continuance in that happy state, John xvii. 24. Heb. vii. 25. Psalm cx. 4.

2. As, by reason of their ignorance and weakness, his legatees cannot, of themselves, apprehend the mysteries of his covenant and testament, Christ reveals it to them, in the threefold character of a *Messenger,* an *Interpreter,* and *Witness.* 1. As the truths of his testament are good news from a far country, He, as the *Messenger of the covenant,* brings to us the glad tidings of our marriage with his person, and of our justification, adoption, sanctification, and eternal salvation through his blood, —and deals with us to accept these offered benefits, Mal. iii. 1. Isa. lxi. 1—3. Psalm xl. 9, 10. 2. As we are to unable to conceive aright of the mysterious truths and blessings of his covenant, He, as an *unparalleled Interpreter,* explains to us the terms of his covenant, and the articles of his testament, Job xxxiii. 23. 1 John v. 20. John vi. 45, 46, 63. Heb. v. 2. Isa. xlii. 6, 7. xlix. 6. xlviii. 17. lx. 1. lxi. 1. Luke xxiv. 27, 45. John viii. 12. ix. 5. Eph. v. 8, 14. 3. As we are slow of heart to believe the truths of God, especially those that are contrary to our corrupt self-love, and the dictates of a defiled conscience, Christ, as the *faithful and the true witness* of the covenant, attests them

OF THE COVENANT OF GRACE. 249

to us, Isa. lv. 4. Rev. i. 5. iii. 14. John viii. 18. xviii. 37. 2 Cor. i. 20.—declaring them to us in his word, John xx. 31. Rom. xv. 4, 8.—confirming them by solemn asseverations and oaths, John iii. 3, 5. Matth. xxvi. 63, 64. Heb. vi. 17, 18. Rev. x. 6, 7. Isa. xlv. 23.—exemplifying them in his person and work, John i. 14. xiv. 6. 2 Cor. i. 20.—ratifying them in his sufferings and death, Heb. ix. 16. John xviii. 37. Rom. xv. 8. and sealing them in his sacraments, Matth. xxviii. 19. 1 Cor. xi. 23—29.——Acting in these three characters, Christ, as the prophet of the new covenant, 1. Intimates and offers the covenant-proposals to men in his word, in order to bring them to a personal interest in it. And in this he makes use of angels, prophets, apostles, pastors, teachers, parents, masters, &c. as his deputies or instruments, Dan. ix. 21—27. Luke i. ii. Matth. i. 20, 21. Acts x. 13. 2 Cor. v. 19, 20. Heb. x. 25. xii. 25. Deut. vi. 7. Psalm lxxviii. 4, 5, 6. Isa. xxxviii. 19. Gen. xviii. 19. 2. By his Spirit he makes these intimations effectual for the illumination and conversion of his elect, 1 Pet. i. 12. 1 Thess. i. 5. John xv. 26. xiv. 26. xvi. 7—14. 3. Further, by his word and spirit he instructs and directs his converted people, during their continuance on earth, Psalm xxv. 9, 14. xxxii. 7, 8. lxxiii. 24. Isa. liv. 13. xlviii. 17. 1 John ii. 20, 27. Eph. i. 13, 17, 18. iii. 16—19. 4. Immediately communicates light and knowledge to them in their heavenly state, Psalm xvi. 11. xvii. 15. Isa. lx. 19, 20. Rev. xxi. 23. vii. 17. 1 John iii. 2. 1 Cor. xiii. 12.

3. As his legatees are by nature rebellious, unruly, enslaved, and miserable, Christ, as King of the covenant, powerfully confers his bequeathed blessings to his elect.—Having the kingdom of providence committed to him to be used for the benefit of his church, which is his proper kingdom, John v. 22. Mat. xi. 27. xxviii. 18. Prov. viii. 15, 16. Eph. i. 22, 23. Isa. xliii. 14. John xviii. 36. Psalm ii. 6,—He, 1. Appoints ordinances and officers, for bringing sinful men into a new-covenant state, and establishing them in it, Acts vii. 38. Isa. xxxiii. 22. Eph. iv. 11—13. 2. He emits royal proclamations, warranting and calling men to come and unite with himself by faith, and thus receive a full and an everlasting interest in all his benefits disponed, Mark xvi. 15, 16. Rom. x. 17. Mat. xi. 28. Isa. lv. 1—3, 6, 7. Prov. i. 22, 23. ix. 4, 5. xxiii. 26. Rev. xxii. 17. iii. 20. Isa. i. 18, 19. xlvi. 12, 13. lxv. 1, 2. Jer. iii. 1, 4, 14, 19, 22. iv. 14. vi. 8. Zech. ix. 9, 12. John vii. 37—39. Acts ii. 38, 39. 2 Cor. v. 19, 20. 3. By his word and Spirit he effectually subdues his elect to himself,—giving them a full right to, and a begun possession of his blessings, Psalm cx. 3. xlv. 3—5. Rev. vi. 2. Col. i. 13. Acts xxvi. 17, 18. 4. He gathers his converted elect along with others into a visible church state, in

which, by regulations suited to their circumstances and imperfections, he governs them to his own honour and their advantage, Gen. xlix. 10. Mat. xvi. 18. xviii. 15—20. xxviii. 19, 20. Isa. ix. 6, 7. Gen. xvii. Exod. xii. to Deut. xxxi. 1 Cor. iv.—xvi. Eph. iv.—vi. Col. ii.—iv. 1 Thess. ii.—v. 1 Tim. i. to Tit. iii. Heb. i.—xiii. &c. 5. He, in peculiar manner, governs his true and voluntary subjects, according to the tenor of the covenant, preserving and manifesting his own prerogatives, and firmly securing their privileges, Isa. xxxiii. 22;—in giving them a complete legal and filial right to all the happiness of the covenant, in their justification and adoption, Mat. ix. 2, 6. Acts v. 31. xiii. 39. Isa. liii. 11. Jer. iii. 19;—in giving them the laws of his covenant, the moral law, as a rule of life, and writing them by his Spirit in their heart, Heb. viii. 10. Jer. xxxi. 33. Ezek. xxxvi. 26, 27;—in bestowing upon them, when obedient, the rewards of the covenant, not indeed for the sake or worth of their good works, but as rewards originally due to himself as their Surety, and only due to them as they are united with, and accepted in him, Psalm xix. 11. John xiv. 21, 22, 23. Rev. ii. 7, 11, 17, 26—28. iii. 5, 12, 21. 1 Cor. ix. 24. xv. 58;—in ministering to them, when disobedient, the gracious discipline of the covenant, in bodily trouble, reproach, poverty, family or other relative afflictions,—or in desertion, temptation, prevalence of inward corruption, disquiet of conscience, or the like, on their soul,—all which, in themselves and in their natural influence, are the deserved fruits of their sin, and contained in testamentary threatenings against it; but as managed by his infinite wisdom, power, and love, for promoting their holiness and happiness, are mercies purchased by his death, and contained in promises to their persons as beloved of God in him, 1 Cor. xi. 30, 32. Psalm xxxviii. 4—8. xiii. 1—4. Eph. vi. 16. Isa. lxiii. 17. Psalm lxxix. 30—34. Heb. xii. 5—11. Rev. iii. 19. Isa. xxvii. 9. Psalm cxix. 67, 71, 75;—in repeating his intimations of his judicial pardon, and granting them fatherly pardons, upon their renewed acts of faith and repentance, John v. 22. Luke vii. 48. Acts v. 31. Isa. xliv. 22. xliii. 25;—in granting them the protection of the covenant, Psalm lxxxix. 18. 1 John iv. 4. Rom. vii. 24, 25. 2 Cor. xii. 7, 9; in publicly and authoritatively bestowing upon them the eternal happiness promised in the covenant,—at death, Rev. i. 8. xiv. 13. Acts vii. 59; and at the last day, Mat. xxv. 34—40, 46. Rev. xx. 12. xxii. 12, 14;—and in his eternal government and glorification of them in heaven, Isa. ix. 7. Rev. vii. 17. iii. 21. 6. He restrains and conquers his own and his people's enemies, and punishes them, if rational agents, Psalm lxxvi. 10. cx. 5—7. xviii. 41—46. 2 Thess. i. 6—9. Rev. xx. 10, 15,

OF THE COVENANT OF GRACE. 251

FROM the above hints of the *making* and *administration* of the covenant of grace, it plainly appears to be, 1. Well ordered in all things, 2 Sam. xxiii. 5. 2. Richly stored with all necessary blessings, proper for time and for eternity, 2 Sam. xxiii. 5. Isa. lv. 1, 2, 3. xxv. 6. 1 Cor. i. 30. Col. iii. 11. ii. 10. i. 19. Phil. iv. 19. 3. Altogether of free grace and mercy, Rom. v. 20, 21. Psalm lxxxix. 1—4, 28. xl. 5. 4. Sure, that it cannot be broken, 2 Sam. xxiii. 5. Isa. lv. 3, 10. liv. 8—10. 5. Everlasting, 2 Sam. xxiii. 5. Heb. xiii. 20. Jer. x. xii. 40. Ezek. xxxvii. 26. 6. Much different from the covenant of works, and preferable to it, in the party contracted with,—administrator,—nature,—quality,—condition,—promises,—order of our obedience, and God's acceptance of it,—order of execution,—ends,—and effects, Heb. viii. 6—13. Rom. v. 12—21.

NOTWITHSTANDING Christ's indefinite administration of the covenant of grace, few men are ever actually instated in it by their own personal taking hold of it, Mat. xx. 16. xxii. 14. vii. 13, 14. Luke xii. 32. xiii. 24. 1 John v. 19. Rom. ix. 27. xi. 5. Jer. iii. 14.—No adult persons are instated in it, but those that, under deep convictions of their sinfulness and misery, have fled to it for refuge, Rom. ix. 6. Heb. 6, 18. Psalm cxlii. 4, 5. Acts ii. 37—39;—heartily approve the whole plan of it, 2 Sam. xxiii. 5. Mat. xi. 5. 1 Cor. i. 23, 24. Acts ix. 6. 1 Tim. i. 15. Isa. lv. 3;—gratefully love God the maker of it, 1 John iv. 19. v. 3. 2 Cor. v. 14, 15. Psalm lxxiii. 25, 26. iv. 6, 7. xviii. 1. lxxxiv. 12. xlii. 1, 2, 5, 9, 11. xliii. 4, 5. cxvi. 1. ciii. 1—6;—heartily submit to Christ as their head in it, Hos. i. 11. Gal. ii. 20. Phil. iii. 7—9;—cordially trust their whole salvation to the condition of it, 1 Cor. ii. 2. Phil. iii. 3, 9. Gal. vi. 14. Isa. xlv. 24, 25;—feed with inward satisfaction on the promises of it, 2 Sam. xxiii. 5. Psalm vii. 10. xix. 10. cxix. 72, 97, 113, 127, 162, 167;—and who have the sanctifying, free, ingenuous, and sympathizing Spirit of the covenant dwelling and working in them, Rom. viii. 1, 4, 9, 15, 26, 27. Gal. iv. 6. v. 16, 18. vi. 10. Psalm lxix. 9. cxix. 136, 139. Zech. viii. 23. xii. 10;—and in fine, who approve of, delight in, and conform themselves to, the laws of the covenant, in so far as they know them,—and desire to be taught that which they know not, Rom. vii. 12, 14—25. Psalm cxix. 5, 6, 18, 26, 128. cxxxix. 23, 24. xliii. 3, 4. cxliii. 10. Gal. v. 17. Mat. vi. 22. Tit. ii. 11, 12. 2 Cor. i. 12. Phil. iii. 3. John iii. 21. Job xxxiv. 32.

Men are actually or personally instated in this covenant by their being spiritually united with Christ, their Representative in it, Isa. liv. 5—17. Ezek. xvi. 8. Hos. ii. 18—20. 1 Cor. i. 30. 2 Cor. xi. 2. By this spiritual marriage-union, Christ himself, in his person, offices, and relations, is made ours, Song ii.

16. John xx. 28. Phil. iii. 7, 8, 9; his fulfilling the condition of this covenant, ours in law-reckoning, 2 Cor. v. 21. Rom. viii. 4. v. 19. Isa. xlv. 24, 25. lxi. 10. Jer. xxiii. 6. Phil. iii. 9; and all the blessings of it ours in law-right, 1 Cor. i. 30. iii. 22. —Christ *graciously* brings us into the bond of this covenant by uniting himself to us as our husband, the Lord our righteousness, our father, and sanctifying head, Hos. ii. 19, 20. Ezek. xvi. 8. Isa liv. 5, 17. xlvi. 12, 13. lxi. 10. Jer. iii. 4, 19. xxxi. 10, 20. 1 Cor. i. 30. Eph. ii. 10. 2 Cor. vi. 17. And we *dutifully* enter into the bond of it by faith, Acts xvi. 31. Isa. lv. 3. Mark xvi. 16. John iii. 14—18; which, by receiving all the blessings of it freely, preserves the grace of the covenant, Rom. iv. 4, 5, 16. Eph. ii. 4, 9. i. 6, 7; and, by uniting with Christ the representative, preserves the unity of it, John x. 9, 10. Eph. iii. 17.—This faith includes a belief of the Scripture account of this covenant or testament, upon God's own authority, —and a cordial consent to it, with respect to our own salvation in particular, 1 Tim. i. 15. 2 Sam. xxiii. 5.—or, it is a receiving and resting upon Christ alone for salvation, as he is offered to us in the gospel,—made of God to us, wisdom, righteousness, sanctification, and redemption, John i. 12. iii. 16, 17. vi. 40. 1 Cor. i. 30.

Both law and gospel having their respective stations in the dispensation of this covenant and testament, both must be believed with particular personal application to ourselves. By believing the declarations of the law, we, upon the authority of God impressed on our conscience, become fully persuaded of our own guilt, pollution, condemnation, and absolute inability to do any thing for our own recovery, by the covenant of works, Rom. iii. 9—20, 23. Psalm li. 5. Job xiv. 4. Gal. iii. 10. Rom. v. 6. viii. 7, 8. Jer. xvii. 9. xiii. 23, 27. This persuasion or belief is produced by the Holy Ghost, as a *spirit of bondage*, powerfully impressing on us the precepts and threatening of that broken covenant, John xvi. 8, 9, 10. Rom. vii. 9. iii. 20. Gal. iii. 24. This legal faith is but forced on our soul against our will, and in no wise unites us to Christ; nor is it, or the legal repentance which attends it, any ground of our welcome to him. But, in the hand of the almighty and all-wise Spirit of God, it excites us to flee to him, or rather to flee from all things else, Acts ii. 37. xvi. 29, 30. By it we are persuaded of our absolute need of him and his benefits; and that we have in ourselves those wretched and infamous characters, by which men are invited to him in the gospel, 1 Tim. i. 13, 15. Rom. vii. 9—13. John iv. 29.——In believing the declarations of the gospel, we, upon God's own testimony, are cordially persuaded, That Christ is an all-sufficient Saviour, able to save the very worst sinners of mankind, with a full and everlasting

OF THE COVENANT OF GRACE.

salvation, Eph. iii. 8. Heb. vii. 25. Isa. xxxii. 2. xlv. 22. lxiii. 1. 1 Cor. vi. 9---11. 1 Tim. i. 13, 15, 16. Tit. iii. 3---7;---that he is cordially offered by God to sinful men as his *free gift* for their salvation, and to us in particular, Isa. lv. 1—4, 7. Rev. xxii. 17. Prov. viii. 4. ix. 4, 5. Isa. ix. 6. xlii. 6, 7. xlix. 6, 8; —that, by this divine grant of him in the gospel, he and all the benefits of redemption are really ours, not in actual possession, but to be taken into possession, as God's *free gift* to us, to be used for all the purposes of our salvation, 1 John iv. 13, 14. John iii. 27. iv. 42, 10, 14. 2 Sam. xxiii. 5. xxii. 3. Luke i. 47. viii. 12. Isa. xlvi. 12, 13. Psalm xxvii. 1. John vi. 32. iii. 16. 1 Cor. i. 30. Isa. ix. 6. xlii. 6, 7. Rom. v. 17. 1 John v. 10, 11.—In consequence of which persuasion follows our particular trust in him for our own salvation, Acts xvi. 31. Psalm ii. 12. xxxvii. 3. Rom. xv. 12. Gal. ii. 16, 20. Acts xv. 11. 1 Thess. ii. 13. 1 Cor. ii. 5.——By this particular trust in Christ our heart really desires to be saved from sin and wrath, Rom. x. 10. vii. 24, 25.—renounces all confidence in itself, and every other creature for salvation, Phil. iii. 3. Jer. xvi. 19. iii. 23. xvii. 5. Prov. iii. 5. Acts ii. 37. Mat. v. 3;—cordially approves the new-covenant method of salvation, as infinitely well suited to the honour of God's perfections, and to our particular necessities, 1 Cor. i. 23, 24. ii. 2. Mat. ix. 12;—betakes itself to Christ in all his offices of Prophet, Priest, and King, John vi. 35, 40, 68, 69. Heb. vi. 18. Acts viii. 37;—trusts our whole salvation to him and his righteousness, being firmly persuaded, upon the testimony of God himself, declared in the gospel, and applied by his Spirit, that He, as ours by his Father's gift, will fully execute upon us every saving office, fulfil every new-covenant relation, and accomplish every gospel-promise, John iii. 16. Heb. iii. 6, 14. x. 38. Isa. xxviii. 16. xxv. 9. l. 10. xxvi. 3, 4. xlv. 22—25. 1 Pet. ii. 6. Rom. x. 10, 11. Psalm cxii. 7. 2 Tim. i. 12. Song viii. 5. 2 Chron. xiv. 11. xvi. 8. xx. 20. Heb. xi. 13. 1 Tim. i. 15.——This persuasion is produced by the Holy Ghost as the *Spirit of life in Christ Jesus*, discovering him in the declarations and promises of the gospel, and in and by them conveying him into our heart, as made of God to us wisdom, righteousness, sanctification, and redemption,—in which work, and through which word of the covenant, he from Christ's fulness conveys habitual grace into our heart, by which we are rendered capable to discern, receive, and rest upon him, 1 Thess. i. 5, 6. ii. 13. And hence, he is called the *Spirit of faith*, 1 Cor. iv. 13.

This faith, by which we take hold of God's covenant, includes in its very nature a *real*, though not alway a clear, distinct, or strong *assurance*, or persuasion of the truth of God's declarations and promises with respect to one's self, and of

Christ's acting up to all his characters, offices, and relations, represented in the gospel: and in proportion to the degree of this assurance, is our reception of him and his fulness;—our believing upon God's own testimony, that he therein GIVES us all the fulness of his covenant, being our very reception of it. 1. Such an assurance is included in all the plain or metaphorical descriptions of FAITH in Scripture, as a *persuasion*,—the *substance* of things hoped for,—the *evidence* of things not seen,—*trusting*, *staying*, *leaning*, *receiving*, *resting*, &c. Heb. xi. 1, 13. Psalm xxxi. 14. xviii. 2. Isa. xxvi. 3, 4. xii. 2. 1. 10. Song viii. 5. John i. 12. Psalm xxxvii. 3, 5, 7. Hence faith is opposed to *doubting*, *fearing*, *wavering*, *staggering*, *instability*, Mat. xiv. 31. Mark v. 36. James i. 6, 8. John xiv. 3. Rom. iv. 20. Heb. x. 23, 25. 2. The Scripture strongly commends and encourages us to such assurance of faith, Heb. x. 22. iii. 6, 14, 18. x. 35. Rom. iv. 18—24. Mark xi. 24. 3. By directing his gospel-promises to us, in the manner best calculated to beget such assurance, God affords us sufficient ground for it, in all our dealings with him and with his Christ, Acts ii. 39. iii. 26. xiii. 34. Rom. x. 10, 11. xi. 26. John iii. 14—17. vii. 37—39. vi. 37, 39, 40. Jer. iii. 4, 19, 14, 22. Hos. ii. 19—23. 1 John v. 10—12. Exod. xx. 2. Psalm l. 7. Jer. xxx. 22. Zech. viii. 8. xiii. 9. Ezek. xxxvi. 25—32. 1 Tim. i. 15. Heb. vi. 16—18. x. 23. 1 Thess. v. 23, 24. Tit. i. 2. Num. xxiii. 19.—— Doubts and fears are found in true believers, in proportion to the weakness of their faith, and not in their faith itself: and often, their doubts and fears do not immediately respect the faithfulness of God in his word, but their own past or present experience of his power; and so are more properly opposite to the assurance of sense, than to that of faith. If our heart condemn and oppose our doubting God's truth and faithfulness in his promise, we have a *true*, though not a *full* assurance of faith, Mat. xiv. 29—31. Gal. v. 17. Psalm xlii. 5, 11. xliii. 5. lxxvii. 10.

By this assured faith, we unite with Christ, as the Fulfiller of the condition of the covenant in our stead,—and, as the faithful Administrator of the covenant for our good;—and, as guilty and polluted, we heartily surrender ourselves to him, as the almighty Saviour,—as poor and empty, to him, as our infinitely benevolent Friend, and all-supplying and satisfying Portion;—and as perverse and unprofitable, to him, as our wise and gracious Lord, who can form us for himself to shew forth his praise, Isa. xliv. 5. Psalm cxix. 94. cxlii. 4, 5. cxvi. 16. Rom. v. 20, 21. Phil. iv. 19. Isa. xliii. 21. 2 Tim. ii. 21.—This may be called personal covenanting with God.

None can possibly fall from their new-covenant state: 2 Sam. xxiii. 5. Psalm lxxix. 28—35. Isa. liv. 8—10. Heb. xiii. 5. But all that are in it, ought diligently to improve it, 1. By a

OF THE COVENANT OF GRACE.

continued resting on Christ, and receiving out of his fulness, through the promises of the gospel, all necessary comfort and grace, 2 Chron. xx. 20. Acts xi. 23. Gal. ii. 20. Hab. ii. 4. 2 Cor. iv. 7. 2. In a diligent attendance on, and believing improvement of, all the ordinances appointed by God for the dispensation of the covenant, 1 Cor. xi. 2, 23. Deut. iv. 2. v. 32. xii. 32. Prov. viii. 34. Psalm lxxxiv. 1---12. Mat. xxviii. 19, 20. 1 Cor. xi. 23---29. 3. In a thankful, hearty, and an evangelical obedience to all the laws issued forth in the administration of the covenant, Gal. v. 6, 22, 23. Tit. ii. 11, 12. iii. 8, 14. Deut. xii. 32. 4. In patiently waiting, and earnestly preparing for the everlasting happiness of the covenant, Tit. ii. 13. Heb. vi. 12. 2 Cor. iv. 18. 2 Tim. iv. 7, 8. 1 Pet. i. 13---15. 2 Pet. i. 4---8. Tit. ii. 11---14.

REFLECT. Now, O my soul, think what astonishing displays of Jehovah's perfections appear in this covenant!—Behold how infinite mercy, grace, and love excite!—how infinite wisdom plans!—infinite persons mutually engage!—how all infinite perfections work for the redemption of sinful men,—of sinful ME!——Hath God, in very deed, put to, and made with ME this *everlasting covenant, ordered in all things and sure?*—Durst I risk an appearance before the judgment-seat of God,---an entrance into eternity upon it, as *all my salvation and all my desire?*--- Have I, in my present review of it, looked after him that lives, and sees, and saves me?---Him that loved me, and gave his Son for me?---Him that gave himself for, and to me?——Am I prepared by God, with the saving views and heart-captivating influences of his covenant,---to declare to others, what I have seen, and heard, and tasted, and handled, of the Word of life? ---Or, dreadful thought! Am I to view,---to preach this everlasting covenant,---in its amazing origin, marvellous parties, parts, and administration;---preach it in all it fulness and freedom, and never to share the blessings of it!---If, after repeated inquiries into this infinitely gracious transaction, I preach another gospel,---or, in any form decoy sinners to seek righteousness and salvation by the works of the law, shall I not be, for ever, accursed of God, and detested by angels and saints,---a derision of devils, and abhorred by all flesh?

BOOK IV.

Of the Mediator of the Covenant of Grace, in his Person, Offices, and States.

CHAP. I.

Of the Mediatorial Person of Christ.

THE agency, manifold stations, and relations of the Son of God, in the making, fulfilment, and administration of the covenant of grace, plainly manifest him the MEDIATOR of it;—to which three things were necessary: 1. A *mediatorial constitution of person*, that, having the nature of both parties, he might be a middle person between God and men, and qualified to lay his hand on both, in order to their reconcilement, 1 Tim. ii. 5, 6. Job ix. 33. 2. A *mediatorial office*, authorizing and qualifying him to manage for us toward God,—and from God toward us, every thing necessary to make up the breach, Prov. viii. 23. Heb. ix. 15. viii. 6. 3. A *mediatorial state*, in which his condition might correspond with that which was necessary for purchasing or preserving the reconciliation between God and us, Luke xxiv. 26. Phil. i. 7—11. Heb. ii. 9, 10.

If God had not intended to redeem a part of lost mankind, his Son had never become man. 1. Without this gracious design, God had no end worthy of such a marvellous work as the incarnation of his Son. 2. The Scripture alway represents the love of God to fallen men as the cause of the mission and incarnation of his Son, John iii. 16. Rom. v. 6—18. 1 John iv. 9, 10. 3. It never mentions any other end of Christ's incarnation, but to glorify God in the salvation of men. Nor, till man had ruined himself, did the least appearance of it take place, Gen. iii. 15. Matth. i. 21. Luke i. 67. ii. 34. John i. 29. Matth. ix. 12, 13. xviii. 11. xx. 28. Gal. iv. 4, 5. 1 Tim. i. 15. Heb. ii. 14. 1 John ii. 1, 2. iii. 5, 8. 4. All his offices of Mediator, Redeemer, Surety, Prophet, Priest, and King, respect men as fallen. Such only he instructs and calls to repentance, Isa. lxi. 1—3. Mat. ix. 13.

Heb. v. 2. For such only he offers sacrifice, and intercedes with God, 1 Tim. ii. 5. Isa. liii. 4—12. 1 John ii. 12. John xvii. Heb. vii. 7, 25. Rom. viii 33, 34. Such only he subdues, governs, and protects, Psalm cx. 3. Rom. viii. 2. John x. 27, 28. Ezek. 34, 36.——The natural goodness of God no more required his Son to assume our nature, than it required him to assume the angelic.——Innocent creatures would have had a proper head in God himself.——Christ is not called the *first begotten of every creature*, because men were made after his image as incarnate, but because he is the only Son of God, begotten from all eternity, before any creature was formed; and because of his superior excellence and dominion over every creature, Col. i. 15.—— But, if God intended to redeem fallen men, it was necessary that a divine person should become man. 1. God's justice and other perfections required, that no sinner should be saved, unless an infinite ransom were paid for them, —the law fulfilled, and sin punished in that very nature which had sinned, Heb. ix. 22. Acts xx. 28. Mat. xx. 28. Eph. i. 7. Col. i. 14, 15. Ezek. xviii. 4. 2. If any lower mean could have effected our redemption, God's infinite wisdom and goodness could not have exposed his own Son to such debased obedience and tremendous suffering, Heb. ii. 10. Lam. iii. 33.

It was not till about the four thousandth year from the creation of the world, that in the *fulness of time* fixed in the purpose of God, and marked in his inspired predictions, and when the world was in the most proper condition for it, that the Son of God came in the flesh. But preparations had all along been making for it. 1. The necessary occasion of it, through Adam's fall and his ruining all mankind, was foreseen by God from all eternity, Acts xv. 18. Psalm cxxxvi. 23. 2. In the most astonishing and sovereign love, God purposed to recover part of mankind from that sinful and miserable estate into which, he foresaw, they would reduce themselves, 1 Thess. v. 9. 2 Thess. ii. 12, 13. Eph. i. 4. 3. The Son of God was set up from eternity as their Mediator, and multitudes of men chosen in him to everlasting life, Psalm lxxxix. 19, 20. Prov. viii. 23—30. 1 Pet. i. 20. Eph. i. 4, 5. 2 Tim. i. 9. Tit. i. 2. 4. Hereupon ensued his entrance into mediatorial glory suited to the then state of things, and a peculiar delight in the sons of men and in the habitable parts of the earth, in which he and they were to have their abode, and hold mutual fellowship, John xvii. 4—6. Prov. viii. 31. That delight in his future manhood, and connections with men, perhaps resembled, while it infinitely transcended, that regard which glorified souls have to their dead bodies, and desire of reunion with them, in the resurrection. 5. It was indeed proper, that his coming in the flesh should be deferred,—till the necessity of such a mean of reforming the world should be fully manifested,—ignorance and learning, want of ceremonies, and a multitude of them in religion,—external mercies and judgments, all proving ineffectual;—till sufficient marks for examining his character should be leisurely pre-exhibited,—till men's longings for him should be exceedingly awakened, and so his incarnation more honourable;—till there should be a sufficient number of hell-hardened professors of the true religion to persecute and murder him,—and of friends and enemies to attest his labours, death, and resurrection;—and of men to experience his benevolent miracles, and the conquering power of his gospel. But no sooner had Adam sinned, and ruined himself and all his posterity, than the Son of God, as one eager to discover his mercy and love, intimated his purpose to become man, and suffer for our redemption, Gen. iii. 8—15. 6. His heart being exceedingly set upon his mediatorial work, he, in a multitude of predictory promises, publicly intimated his incarnation, sufferings, resurrection, and gathering of a numerous people to himself, insomuch, that not one important circumstance relative to his appearances, work, or success, was left unforetold, Luke xxiv. 25, 27, 44—47. John i. 45. Acts x. 43. xiii. 27. xxvi. 22. Rom. iii. 21. 1 Pet. i. 11, 12. 1 Cor. xv. 3, 4. 7. Men being dull of hearing, and slow of heart to conceive or believe that which was merely hinted in words, he, in a multitude of personal and real prefigurations of himself and his concerns, addressed the very senses of his peculiar people, Col. ii. 17. Heb. x. 1. ix. 9, 10. 8. To mark his delightful intention, and earnest desire to assume our nature, he often appeared as a man, and conversed with his favourites Abraham, Isaac, Jacob, Joshua, the Israelites at Bochim, Gideon, Manoah and his wife, Daniel, Zechariah, &c. Gen. xviii. 2. xxvi. 2, 24. xxxii. 24. Josh. v. 13. Judges ii. 1—4. vi. 11—22. xiii. 2—19. Dan. x. 5. Zech. i. 8. And perhaps the frequent ascription of human members and affections to God under the Old Testament, was intended to keep men in constant remembrance of the future incarnation of his Son. 9. Multitudes of the persons represented by him were, with his Father's consent, admitted to fellowship with God, not only on earth, but in heaven, and two of them soul and body,—not merely as firstfruits of his chosen people, but as an earnest of his future sitting in the midst of the throne, as the Man God's fellow, and the First-born among many brethren, Heb. xi. 13. Gen. v. 24. Heb. xi. 5. 2 Kings ii. 11.

The Son of God hath long ago BECOME MAN. 1. The Sceptre, Tribeship, or power of supreme government, which was foretold, should continue with Judah, the fourth son of

Jacob, and his posterity, till SHILOH should come, is now long ago departed, Gen. xlix. 10. SHILOH here promised can be no other than the Messiah;—not Moses, who was not of the tribe of Judah, nor had any royal power transferred from it;—nor Saul, who was not anointed at Shiloh, but at Ramah, and had his royalty confirmed to him at Gilgal, and from whom it departed to David of the tribe of Judah, and his descendants, 1 Sam. ix.—xi. xiii. xv. xvi. 2 Sam. i.—v;—nor Jeroboam, who was not crowned at Shiloh, but at Shechem, 1 Kings xii. 12. Chron. x. Nor did the sceptre then, or for many ages after, depart from the tribe of Judah, 2 Chron. x.—xxxvii. Nor can SHEBET, or *sceptre*, here mean a *rod of oppression*, as it is connected with a Lawgiver, and its continuance mentioned as an honour and blessing to Judah. Nor is it true, that a rod of oppression hath alway lain on the tribe of Judah; for under David, Solomon, Asa, Jehoshaphat, Uzziah, Hezekiah, Simon Maccabeus, and John Hircanus, &c. it exceedingly flourished in power and wealth. It must therefore mean, that pre-eminent power of government, which that tribe retained, till about the four thousandth year of the world.——At their departure from Egypt it was most numerous, and in the wilderness marched in the front of the Hebrew nation. It was first and most extensively settled in proper Canaan. It, by God's direction, led the attack upon the remaining Canaanites and rebellious Benjamites, Judges i. 1, 2. xx. 18. For almost 500 years, from David to Zedekiah, all the Hebrew kings whom God authorized by peculiar covenant, were of the tribe of Judah. Even during their captivity in Babylon, its sovereignty was not totally extinguished. Daniel and his companions bore rule. Jehoiachin was exalted above other prisoners, Dan. i.—iii. v. vi. 2 Kings xxv. 27. After their return from Babylon, Zerubbabel, Nehemiah, the Maccabees, and the Sanhedrim, had the government of the nation in their hand.——The sceptre began to depart from Judah, when Pompey the Roman general took Jerusalem about sixty years before Christ's birth. It farther departed, when, about A. D. 10, Archelaus was dethroned, and Judea made a Roman province. It fully departed about A. D. 70, when Titus and his Roman troops utterly destroyed Jerusalem and its temple, and cities around. 2. Daniel's *seventy weeks*, in the end of which Messiah was to appear and be cut off, are long ago expired, Dan. ix. 24—27.—— They must be understood of weeks of years, a day for a year, as in several other predictions, Ezek. iv. 5, 6. Dan. vii. 23. xii. 12, 13. Rev. xi. 2, 3. xii. 6. xiii. 5. in allusion to the Jewish weeks of years, which regulated their Releases and Jubilees, Lev. xxv. Seventy common weeks are too short for such an emphatical prediction. Nor did any important event happen at the end of any such seventy weeks, from any remarkable commandment to restore Jerusalem. The destruction of Jerusalem and its temple, and the desolation of Jerusalem by abominable armies, were foretold as immediately following these seventy weeks, Dan. ix. 23—27.——These seventy weeks, or 490 years, commencing not from any edict of Cyrus or Darius to *rebuild the temple*, but from one of Artaxerxes in the 7th or rather 20th year of his reign to *rebuild the city* of Jerusalem, Ezra i. vi. vii. Neh. ii. expired about A. M. 4036, when Jesus Christ was crucified, not long after which, the Gentiles were brought into the Christian church, Jerusalem and its temple and the country about laid desolate, even unto this day. 3. The Jewish temple built by Zerubbabel, in which the Messiah was foretold to appear, and render it more glorious by his presence and work than Solomon's had been, notwithstanding it wanted several principal ornaments, Hag. ii. 6--9. Mal. iii. 1. is long ago turned into an heap of rubbish. 4. Messiah was to come while the tribe of Judah and family of David continued distinct, and preserved their genealogies, which hath not been the case for about seventeen hundred years past, Gen. xlix. 10. Isa. xi. 1. Jer. xxiii. 5, 6. 5. Messiah's coming in the flesh was to be quickly succeeded by God's admission of the Gentiles into his church instead of the Jews, and by the abolishment of idols, Gen. xlix. 10. Isa. liii. liv. lv. Zech. xiii. 2. Isa. ii. 18, 20. These events began remarkably to take place, more than seventeen hundred years ago.

JESUS of Nazareth was, and is, the TRUE MESSIAH. 1. All the characteristics of Messiah relative to his *forerunner*, Mal. iii. 1. iv. 5. Isa. xl. 3—6. Mat. iii. 3—14. Luke i. iii. John i. 19—34. iii. 23—36.—his *tribe* and *family*, Gen. xlix. 10. Isa. xi. 1, 2. Matth. i. Luke i. 26—36. ii. iii. 22—38.—and to the *time*, Gen. xlix. 10. Dan. ix. 24. Hag. ii. 6, 7. Mal. iii. 1.— *place*, Mic. 2. Matth. ii. Luke ii.—and *manner* of his *birth*, Isa. vii. 14. Jer. xxxi. 22. Mat. i. 18—25. Luke i. 26—35. exactly agree to him. 2. The characteristics of Messiah's *person*, God-man, Isa. ix. 6. vii. 14. Luke i. 16, 17, 35. Rom. i. 4. ix. 5.— *offices*, Deut. xviii. 15—18. Acts iii. 22. vii. 35, 37. Mat. xi. 5. xvii. 5. v.—vii. xiii.——Psal. cx. 4. Heb. iv. 14. v. vii. ix. x. Mat. xxvi. xxvii.—Psal. ii. 6. lxxxix. 3, 4, 19, 20. Ezek. xxxiv. 23, 24. Isa. ix. 6, 7. xxxii. 1. Jer. xxiii. 5, 6. xxx. 21. Dan. vii. 14. John ii. 13—22. xviii. 36. Matth. xxi. 12. x. xvi. 18, 19. xxviii. 18—20. Phil. ii. 8—11. Eph. i. 22, 34. iv. 11, 12.—and *states*, Psal. xxii. lxix. Isa. liii. Luke xxiv. 26. Heb. i. 3. ii. 8—10. 1 Cor. xv. 3, 4. Phil. ii. 7—11. 1 Pet. i. 19—21. exactly answer to him. 3. His doctrines and works are the very same which were ascribed to Messiah by the prophets, and are most proper for him. His *doctrines,* how mysterious and

OF THE MEDIATORIAL PERSON OF CHRIST. 261

holy! how heavenly and divine! and how contrary to the corrupt inclinations of men!---In what simple manner! and by what unpromising instruments were they published and spread! and yet how powerfully effectual in converting the nations!--- His *miracles*, how numerous, public, and benevolent! Isa. ii. 2, 3, 4. xlviii. 17. lii. 15. liv. 13. Mic. iv. 2, 3. v. 3. Mal. iii. 2, 3. Mat. v.---x. xii.---xv. xvii.---xix. Luke iv.---xix. John ii.---xviii. 4. For about 1740 years, the Gentiles have obedientially gathered to him as his people, Psal. ii. 8. xxii. 27---31. xlv. 9. xlvii. lxvii. lxviii. 22. c. cxvii. 2. lxxii. Gen. xlix. 10. Isa. xlii. 6, 7. xlix. 6—12. xi. liv. lv. Mat. ii. John iv. xii. 20. Acts ii. x.---xx. Rom. xv. 16, 19. Eph. iii. 8, 9.——But it must be observed, that the spiritual blessings of Messiah's kingdom are frequently foretold under carnal emblems, answerable to the Jewish dispensation,---as of an high *house* or *temple*, Isa. ii. 2. Mic. iv. 1. great *peace*, Isa. xi. 6, 8. Hos. ii. 18. great *light*, Isa. xxx. 26. ix. 19, 20. a glorious *city* and *temple*, Ezek. xl.---xlviii. great happiness in Canaan, Jer. iii. xxx. xxxi.---xxxiii. Ezek. xxxiv. xxxvi. xxxvii.

It hath already been proved, that Jesus of Nazareth is a divine person, God equal with the Father—Book II. It may be further demonstrated to every professed Christian from the many absurdities which necessarily attend the denial of it. 1. If Christ be not the Most High God, he must have been an introducer of blasphemy and idolatry,---in encouraging men to believe on, and worship himself. And even the Mahometan religion, which aims at the abolishment of all worship of creatures, must be much more excellent than the Christian. 2. If Christ be not the only true and Most High God, the Jews did well in crucifying him as a most infamous and blasphemous impostor, and persecuting his disciples, who publicly and obstinately maintained him to be the true God, and by a multitude of Old Testament oracles proved him to be so. 3. If he be not the Most High God, many leading oracles in our Bible are erroneous or trifling. The mystery of the gospel is altogether insignificant. The love of God in sending Christ to die for us is of no such excellence and virtue as the Scriptures represent. His death is but a metaphorical atonement, unavailable to the redemption of our soul. 4. If Christ be not the Most High God, the language of Scripture is most obscure, seductive, impious, and absurd, in attributing to him the names, perfections, works, and worship of God, &c. And either the prophets must have miserably misrepresented matters concerning him, or the apostles miserably misunderstood them, in applying them to prove the true divinity of Christ. 5. If Christ be not the Most High God, the Christian religion must be a system of mere superstition, appointed by a creature;—a mere comedy, in which one falsely appears in the character of the only true and Most High God. All its miracles, mysteries, and predictions must be magical tricks, or diabolical delusions, calculated to promote faith in, and worship of, a mere creature, instead of the Supreme God.

In his incarnation, the Son of God assumed a TRUE MANHOOD, a human soul, and a true body formed of the substance of the Virgin Mary,—not immediately created or sent down from heaven. 1. God's wisdom and equity required, that the broken law, under which we stood, should be fulfilled in the very same nature that had sinned; and that our Redeemer should be near of kin unto us, that the right of redemption might be his, even in respect of his manhood, Ezek. xviii. 4. Luke i. 71. Rom. vii. 4. Eph. v. 23. 2. He is exceeding frequently called a *Man*, and the *Son of man*, Psalm lxxx. 17. Dan. vii. 13. Zech. vi. 12. xiii. 7. Mat. viii. 20. ix. 6, &c. 3. The Scripture represents him as the *seed* of the woman, Gen. iii. 15; the *seed* of Abraham, Gen. xii. 3. xxviii. 18. xxii. 18; the *offspring* of Jesse, Isa. xi. 1; *seed* of David, and *fruit* of his loins, Rom. ix. 5. i. 3. Luke i. 32; the *seed* of Mary; *made* of her, and the fruit of her womb, Luke i. 31, 32, 35. Gal. iv. 4.— And without admitting this, his double genealogy must be useless, false, and seductive, Mat. i. 1—17. Luke iii. 23—38. The scripture never calls him the Son of Joseph but on one occasion, and that because Joseph acknowledged and educated him, as if he had been his child, Luke ii. 41, 44. iii. 23. 4. If he had received his body from heaven, or by any immediate creation, he had not been like unto us in all things, sin excepted, Heb. ii. 17; or related to us, or marked with the prophetic characters of the lineage of Messiah, Gen. iii. 15. xxii. 18. xlix. 10. Isa. xi. 1, 10. Jer. xxxiii. 15, 16. Isa. vii. 14. 5. The Scripture plainly represents him as having a *true human soul*, Isa. liii. 10. Psalm xxii. 21. Mat. xxvi. 38. John xii. 27; with a finite and limited understanding, Luke ii. 52. Mark xiii. 32; —and a will distinct from, and subordinate to, his divine, Mat. xxvi. 39;—and a *true human body*, Mat. xxvi. 26. Luke xxiv. 39; which partook of flesh and blood, and did eat, drink, hunger, thirst, sleep, become weary, shed tears, and sweat drops of blood, Heb. ii. 11, 14, 16. Mat. xi. 19. iv. 2. John xix. 28. iv. 6. xi. 35. Luke xix. 41. xxii. 44.

In forming the manhood of Christ, the Holy Ghost imparted no substance of his own, and so is not the father of it: but, 1. He formed part of the substance of the Virgin into his human body. 2. He formed his human soul in the closest union with that body, and that in union with his divine nature. 3. He sanctified this manhood in its very formation, and filled his soul with a fulness of gifts and grace correspondent with its then condition, Isa. vii. 14. Jer. xxxi. 22. Mat. i. 20. Luke i. 35.—The fancy of Christ's human soul being created before the foundation of the world, hath no countenance from Scripture; renders his manhood unlike to that of his brethren; and attempts to evade the proofs of his true Godhead drawn from his existence and acting under the Old Testament.

The Son of God assumed this human nature *into his own divine person*. The Scripture represents him as God and man in the *same person;—made flesh*, and yet the *only begotten Son of God*, John i. 14. Gal. iv. 4. Rom. viii. 3;—in the *form of God* and *equal to God*, and yet in fashion *as a man*, Phil. ii. 6, 7. Heb. iv. 14, 15. v. 7, 8;—as God manifested *in the flesh*, 1 Tim. iii. 16;—as made of the *seed of David*, or fathers, and yet the *Son of God—God blessed for ever*, Rom. i. 3, 4. ix. 5; as put to death in the flesh, and quickened in the Spirit, 1 Pet. iii. 18;—as God, and yet shedding his blood for our redemption, Acts xx. 28;—as man, and yet *God's fellow*, Zech. xiii. 7;—as *Jehovah*, and yet a *branch* out of David's root, Jer. xxiii. 5, 6. xxxiii. 15, 16;—as a *child born*, and yet the *mighty God*, Isa. ix. 6. Mic. v. 2;—as Immanuel, and yet born of a woman, Isa. vii. 14. iv. 2. Mat. i. 23, &c. &c.

In the union of Christ's two natures in his divine person, two divine acts are observable: 1. A *forming—uniting* act, by which his manhood was at once formed and united to his *person as the Son of God*. This uniting of his manhood to his person, in the very formation of it, prevented its having any personality of its own, even as the uniting of our soul to our body in the very formation of it, prevents its having any existence, without relation to Adam as a covenant-breaking representative. All the divine persons concurred in this act, the Father and the Son acting in, with, and through the Holy Ghost, Heb. x. 5. ii. 14. Isa. vii. 14. Jer. xxxi. 22. xxiii. 5. xxxiii. 15. Zech. iii. 8. Luke i. 35. 2. An *assuming* act, in which the Son only took to, or into his divine person the human nature, that his Godhead might dwell in it, or be, as it were, clothed with it for ever, Heb. ii. 14. John i. 14. Phil. ii. 6. Rom. viii. 3. Gal. iv. 4. Perhaps it would not have become the Godhead, That the Father should have assumed the manhood, as, being the first person in order of subsistence, he could not, in correspondence therewith, have been sent by the Son and Spirit, and acted as a Mediator towards them;—or being the Father in the Godhead, he could not become a Son in manhood.---Nor, that the Holy Ghost should have assumed it,---as there would have been no divine person posterior, in order of subsistence, to have been sent by him to apply his purchased redemption. But it was infinitely condecent, that *the Son* should become man; that the middle person in the Godhead should be the Mediator between God and man; that he who was Son in the Godhead should be the Son of the Virgin in the manhood; that he, who is the only-begotten and well-beloved Son of God, should reconcile us to God; that he, who is the natural, necessary, and essential Son of God, should render us the adopted sons of God; that he, who is the Father's Word, should declare unto us the Father's mind and will; that he, who is the express image of his Father's person, should restore in us the image of God.

The union of Christ's divine and human natures, or the constitution of his mediatorial person, is produced by these two acts. This union is a permanent relation between both natures, and affects the divine nature which assumed the human, as well as the human which was assumed. And it is, 1. PERSONAL, not that two persons, a divine and a human, are joined into one; but that two natures, a divine and a human, are united in *one person*, who is at once true God and true man, Col. ii. 9. Isa. vii. 14. ix. 6. Jer. xxiii. 5, 6. xxxiii. 15, 16. Zech. xiii. 7. Mic. v. 2. John i. 14. iii. 13. Rom. i. 3, 4. ix. 5. Luke i. 16, 17, 35. Phil. ii. 6, 7. Heb. iv. 14, 15. ix. 14. Acts iii. 15. 1 Cor. ii. 8. 1 Tim. iii. 16. 1 Pet. iii. 18.——The Son of God could not have assumed a *human person*, *which continued to be such.* As no finite substance can subsist in more subjects than one at the same time, Christ's finite manhood could not have subsisted both in his person, and in its own personality. If Christ had a human person, he could not be equally related to all men. He could not have obeyed the law of God under the weight of its curse, nor have borne the infinite load of punishment due to us. Nor could his obedience and suffering have been of infinite value to answer and magnify the broken law for us.---He could not have assumed a human person, the personality of which ceased upon its being assumed by him. Such a notion hath no foundation in Scripture. A human nature formerly possessed by a sinner, or even a mere creature, could not decently be assumed into a personal union with the Son of God. It was not possible for a human person to be formed without original sin. ---But it must be observed, that, 1. The divine personality of the Son of God being in itself as unchangeable as his divine nature, could neither be destroyed nor changed, Heb. xiii. 8. Mal. iii. 6. James i. 17. Exod. iii. 14. 2. Christ's manhood having been united to his divine person in the very formation of it, could never have any personality or particular subsistence of its own; nor did it need it, having, by the uniting act, received a divine personality, instead of its own human one. Nor doth the want of human personality, especially when supplied to infinite advantage, render his manhood less perfect, it being soul and body united, not its mode of subsistance, which constitutes a complete human nature. 3. Christ's manhood is not *immedi-*

ately united to his divine nature, considered *absolutely in itself*,—but as it is characterized, and subsists in the person of the Son: and hence is not *personally* united with it, as it subsists in the Father and Holy Ghost, Rom. viii. 3. Gal. iv. 4. John i. 14. 4. Though, in its immensity, Christ's divine nature infinitely transcend his human, which can be but in one small place at once, yet in its spirituality it is WHOLE every where; and in this view is united with, and dwells in his manhood, 1 Tim. iii. 16. Isa. ix. 6. vii. 14. John i. 14. Col. ii. 4.

2. It is an UNCOMPOUNDING union, both the united natures retaining their distinct essential properties. Hence we find ascribed to Christ, 1. Infinitely different *natures*, Rom. i. 3, 4. viii. 3. ix. 5. 1 Pet. iii. 18. Heb. ix. 14. John i. 14. 1 Tim. iii. 16. Phil. ii. 6, 7. Isa. ix. 6. vii. 14. Gal. iv. 4. 2. Different *understandings* and *wills*,—knowing all things, John ii. 25. xxi. 17; and yet not knowing the time of the last judgment, Mark xii. 32;—having one will with the Father, John v. 19. x. 30. xiv. 9, 10. 1 John v. 7; and yet having a will different from the Father's, Luke xxii. 42. 3. Contrary *circumstances* or *properties*, as, to *leave the world*, in respect of his manhood, John xvi. 7, 28; and yet to be *alway in it*, in respect of his Godhead, Mat. xxviii. 20. xviii. 20: to be a *child born*, and yet the *everlasting Father*, Isa. ix. 6; *Almighty God*, and yet *crucified through weakness*, Gen. xvii. 1. Isa. ix. 6. 2 Cor. xiii. 4.

3. It is an INDISSOLUBLE and EVERLASTING union. 1. If Christ had intended to lay aside his manhood, he had probably done when he had finished his humbled service, in which it was peculiarly necessary. But it is certain that he retained it in his resurrection and ascension, and will retain it in the last judgment, Acts i. 10—12. iii. 20, 21. Rev. i. 7. 2. Christ lives for evermore, in respect of that nature which was once dead, Rev. i. 18. Psalm xxi. 4. 3. The everlasting continuance of his mediatorial office requires his perpetual retention of his manhood, —that, *as the Lamb*, he may be the everlasting light of heaven, Rev. xxi. 23;—that, as a *priest for ever*, he may make continual intercession for us, Psalm cx. 4. Heb. vii. 25. Rom. viii. 34;—and that, as a *king*, he may for ever sit on the throne of his father David, Luke i. 32, 33. Isa. lx. 7. 4. All believers shall have their bodies, as his members, fashioned like unto his glorious body, and be for ever with him, Phil. iii. 21. 1 Thess. iv. 17. His own manhood cannot then be supposed to lose its existence or high station. 5. The everlasting union of his manhood to his divine person is necessary,—*in equity to itself*, that it may receive the due reward of that debased obedience, which it performed, and suffering which it underwent in its united state;—and *in kindness to us*, that it may continue an everlasting monument of God's love to us, and a mean of our familiar knowledge, love, and fellowship with him.

No REAL COMMUNICATION of divine properties, omnipresence, omniscience, omnipotence, or the like, ensues to the human nature from this union. 1. Christ's divine nature being absolutely simple, all its essential properties must be communicated by this personal union to his manhood, or none of them at all. But how absurd would it be to maintain, that his manhood hath an unsuccessive eternity, is self-existent, absolutely independent, or a supreme God. 2. No *distinguishing* properties of any nature can be communicated, as, if they be rendered common to two or more natures, they are no more *distinguishing*. 3. As Christ's divine nature is united to his human as really and closely as the human is to it, the properties of his divine nature can be no more communicable, by virtue of this union, to his human, than the finity, dependence, weakness, &c. of the human nature can be to the divine. 4. Each of the natures being incapable of the properties of the other, there can be no communication of them without compounding the natures and forming one out of both, as Eutychians absurdly supposed. 5. The divine properties, particularly mentioned, cannot be communicated. *Omnipresence* plainly contradicts the very nature of a body: that which is omnipresent could never have been conceived, or born, died, or been buried,—have risen from the grave, ascended to heaven, or return to judgment, —nor could have moved from place to place, as it is certain Christ did, or will do, Luke ii. 1—7. Mat. xxvi.—xxviii. John xx. xxi. vi. 24. xi. 15. xvi. 28. xvii. 11. Mark vi. 6. xvi. 19. Luke xxiv. 51. Acts i. 9—11. iii. 21. Heb. iv. 14. 1 Thess. iv. 14, 17.—It could not be *omniscient*, for it increased in wisdom, Luke ii. 40, 52; and when on earth knew not the time of the last judgment, Mark xiii. 32.—It was not *almighty*, but was weary, amazed, and very heavy,—troubled till it knew not what to say, and needed his Father's help, John iv. 6. Mat. xxvi. 38. John xii. 27. Heb. v. 7. Isa. l. 7, 9. xlii. 1. Nor can it, but God alone, quicken the dead, Rom. iv. 17. 1 Pet. iii. 18. John vi. 63. Psalm xxxvi. 9. Acts xxvi. 8.

But the *true effects* of this personal union of Christ's two natures are, 1. Communion of *mutual interest* in each other, John xii. 27. Psalm xvi. 10. 2. Conjunct *anointing*, which, as it respects his divine nature, includes the sending him and the preparing an human-nature for the personal residence of his godhead, Gal. iv. 4. Isa. xlviii. 16; and as it respects his manhood, denotes the actual bestowal of all necessary gifts and graces upon it. And as these endowments were different in degree, in different periods, while the union was the same, they appear to have proceeded, not immediately from his divine nature, but from the Holy Ghost dwelling in his manhood, and qualifying it according to its growing capacity, and different states of humiliation or exaltation, Luke ii. 52. Mark xiii. 32. 3. Communion in all *mediatorial qualities, offices*, and *acts*,—that, notwithstanding a particular nature be the immediate agent or sufferer, —the person God-man is reputed to have acted or suffered these things; He is reputed to obey the law, satisfy God's justice, rise from the dead, return to judge the world, Mat. v. 17. 2 Cor. v. 21. Rom. i. 3, 4. 1 Thess. iv. 14, 16. 4. The properties of both natures are ascribed to his person, God-man,— and even the properties or pertinents of the one nature are ascribed to him, when he is named from the other.—Thus we say, the blood of God, and that the Son of God was born, died, rose again; that the Lord of glory was crucified, Acts xx. 28. Rom. viii. 3. 1 Cor. ii. 8; and that the man Christ is God's equal, knows all things, is every where, and almighty, Zech. xiii. 7. John xxi. 17. iii. 13. Isa. ix. 6.—For, though these things do not agree to the *whole of Christ*, or both his natures, —they agree to his *whole person*, God-man.

This close union of Christ's *two natures in one person*, was necessary, that the works of both natures might be accepted by God for us, and relied on by us, as the work of his whole person, God-man. None but a God-man, who was at once our Creator and our near Kinsman, could have a full right to redeem us. None but he could pay the price of our redemption, or put us into the actual possession of it.——More particularly, it was necessary that he, who was to be *Mediator* between an offended God and offending men, should partake of the natures of both,—that being nearly related to both, he might be careful for the interests of both, and qualified to do every thing proper for bringing both to an amicable and everlasting reconcilement.——It was necessary to his being our *Redeemer*, that he might have full property in us and relation to us,—might be able to pay a suitable and all-sufficient ransom for us,—and might have proper sympathy with us, sufficient dignity and power to purchase and apply our redemption.——It was necessary to his being our *Surety* and *sacrificing Priest*,—that, *as God*, he might lawfully undertake for us, being absolute lord of his own person, obedience, and life;—might fully secure the payment of all that we owed to God's law and justice;—might do the world no injury by his voluntary death;—might willingly do all that law and justice required of him in our stead;— might add infinite value to his obedience and suffering;—might know every particular person for whom he satisfied, and every circumstance relating to each of them;—and might, by his own power, conquer death, and rise from its prison:——and that, *as man*, the broken law, under which we stood, might, in all its demands of obedience, love to God and to men,—and of sufferings, take fast hold of him, and be exactly fulfilled by him, in the very substance and kind in which we owed them;—and that, in paying our debt, he might contract an experimental feeling of our infirmities, and set before us a perfect pattern of holy obedience and patient suffering.——It was necessary to his being our *Advocate* or *interceding Priest,*—that, *as God,* he might remove himself from his debased state of atonement to that of his honorary intercession;—might, with proper dignity and confidence, appear in the presence of God for us;—might for ever sit with him on his throne, as the all-sufficient pledge of our everlasting peace and friendship with him, and take infeftment of the heavenly inheritance in our name;—might know all the necessities and inward desires of his people;—and might, in his intercession for them, counterbalance all their unworthiness, guilt, and want of earnestness in prayer, with his own dignity of person, fulness of merit, and efficacy of desire:—and that, *as man,* he might present our nature before God, as a complete fulfiller of all righteousness,—and might intercede for us as our compassionate brother, who feels our infirmities.——This conjunction of the divine and human natures in the person of Christ, is also necessary to his execution of his *prophetical office,*—that, *as God,* he might be equally present with all his disciples, in every age, Mat. xxviii. 20;—might have a comprehensive view of all divine truths, and of our need of instruction, John i. 18. Col. ii. 3;—might give full and comfortable evidence of the holiness, infallibility, and divine authority of his instructions, Mat. xvii. 5;—might confirm them by miracles wrought by his own power, John v. 36. x. 38;—might employ the Holy Ghost to concur with him in his teaching, John xvi. 7—14. Prov. i. 23; and render it effectual for the conviction, illumination, regeneration, sanctification, and comfort of his people, 2 Cor. iv. 6. iii. 18:—and that, *as man,* he might instruct us with brotherly affection, and in a manner adapted to our weakness; and might exemplify his doctrines and injunctions in his own person, life, and death, Mat. xi. 29, 30.——It was necessary to his execution of his *kingly office,*—that, *being God,* his subjects might not be reduced lower in their redeemed, than they had been in their created state, Hos. i. 10, 11; and that he might be equally near to, and capable to subdue, rule, and defend all his people in every place and period, Psalm cx. 2, 3. lxxii. 8, 9. xxviii. 9. xxix. 11. Zech. ix. 10. Isa. ix. 7;—might be able to withstand all the power and policy of hell and earth, Mat. xvi. 18;—might be head over all things to his church, Eph. i. 22;—might be able to convince, conquer, renew, comfort, sanctify and govern the hearts of all his elect, and to supply all their wants, Psalm xlv. 3—5. John xiv. 1. xv. 3—5. vi. 63. Phil. iv. 19.—and able to manage the unruly hearts of all his implacable enemies, devils or men, Prov.

xxi. 1. Psalm lxxvi. 10. Rev. xvii. 17; and to call them to account for their conduct, Acts xvi. 31. Rev. xx. 12:—and *being man*, he might not exalt his heart above his brethren subjected to him, but maintain a tender and condescending regard to them, Zech. ii. 8;—and might, by his own example, enforce obedience to that law which he enacts, and by which he will, in a visible manner, fix the eternal state of angels and men at the last day.—— It is necessary to his implementing all his saving *relations* of Father, Husband, Friend, Shepherd, &c.— While his manhood renders them near, delightful, and as it were natural towards men, his godhead renders them infinitely efficacious and comfortable, Song v. 9—16. Psalm xxiii. 1—6. xviii. 1—3. Isa. ix. 6. lxiii. 16. liv. 5.—It is necessary to his *states* of humiliation and exaltation. While his manhood did or doth render them possible, real, and adequately exemplary to us,—his godhead rendered his humiliation infinitely deep, marvellously dignified, and the work of it truly and intrinsically meritorious,—and renders his exaltation inconceivably high, makes him capable to support and rightly to manage his unparalleled glory, and makes it infinitely comfortable and efficacious to usward, 2 Cor. viii. 9. v. 21. Heb. ii. 17, 18. iv. 14—16. vi. 18—20. x. 19—22.

The *grace* and *relative glory* of this mediatorial person of Christ are exceedingly remarkable. His *personal grace* comprehends, 1. The *grace of union*, by which his manhood is graciously exalted to its high state of subsistence in the person of the Son of God, John i. 14. 1 Tim. iii. 16. Rom. viii. 3. Heb. ii. 11, 14. 2. The *grace of unction*, which lies in God's appointment of him to his mediatorial work,—and in his abundant furnishing of his human nature with gifts and graces for it, John x. 36. vi. 27, 29. iii. 34. Isa. xi. 2—4. lxi. 1. xlii. 1. 3. The *grace of fellowship*, which consists in those happy fruits which proceed from the union of his natures, and his unction by the Holy Ghost, 1 Cor. i. 30. Col. i. 19. ii. 3, 10, 19.—— Or, his *personal grace* consists in, 1. His fitness for his work, as God in our nature appointed to it, Col. ii. 9. John iii. 16. 1 Tim. iii. 16. John i. 14. 2. His fulness of grace lodged in him, sufficient for the supply of all his people, Col. i. 19. ii. 10. Phil. iv. 19. 3. His excellency to endear,—he, in his person, offices, relations, and work, being every way suited to the understanding, conscience, desires, or necessities of our immortal souls, Song v. 10—16. Col. ii. 10. iii. 11. 1 Cor. i. 30.

The *relative glory* of the person of Christ, God-man, lies in its manifold connections with the nature, perfections, purposes, covenants, and revealed truths of God;—and with believers' familiar fellowship with God,—and all their saving graces, and exercise of them,—and all their acceptable worship of God, and new obedience to him.

I. In respect of his nature, 1. God is ONE with, or the SAME as Christ,—in his divine nature, John x. 30. 1 John v. 7; in perfection, dignity, work, and worship, John v. 16—29. xvii. 9, 10. xiv. 9, 10; in will, Psalm xl. 8; in affection, John xiv. 21, 23. 2 Thess. ii. 16; in interest and dominion, John xvii. 2, 9, 10. xvi. 15. xiv. 2, 9, 10. 2. God is WITH Christ, co-operating in the same work, John v. 17, 19. xiv. 23. 2 Thess. ii. 16. Prov. viii. 27—30;—in upholding and assisting his manhood, Acts x. 38. Isa. xlii. 1, 6. xlix. 2. l. 7, 9;—in exercising love and favour towards him, John xvii. 24. Mat. iii. 17. xvii. 5;—and in sharing the same honours, Rev. iii. 21. xxii. 1. 3. God is IN Christ,—in mysterious co-existence of person, John xiv. 10, 11, 20. xvii. 21, 23;—in marvellous rest, satisfaction, and delight, Isa. xlii. 21. 2 Cor. v. 19. Psalm lxxx. 17. In him alone he is to be found by sinful and self-ruined men, Isa. lxvi. 1, 2. 2 Cor. v. 19—21. Eph. ii. 18. iii. 12.—In him all things respecting God delightfully harmonize,—as perfections of mercy, justice, and wrath, the exercise of which seems inconsistent:—Names apparently irreconcileable,—as *merciful* and *gracious*, forgiving iniquity, transgression, and sin,—and yet *by no means clearing the guilty*, Exod. xxxiv. 6, 7:—Words apparently contradictory, representing God's detesting the justification of the wicked,—and yet representing his own justification of the ungodly, Exod. xxiii. 7. Prov. xvii. 15. Rom. iv. 6. Isa. xliii. 24, 25. xlv. 24, 25. 2 Cor. v. 21;—— and works apparently contrary, as making men dead to the law, and yet writing the law in their hearts, Gal. ii. 19. Rom. vii. 4. viii. 2. Jer. xxxi. 33. Heb. viii. 10. 4. God is MANIFESTED IN and THROUGH Christ. All the words and works of God cannot give a full, clear, efficacious, saving, and satisfying view of God suitable to sinful men. But Christ being of the same substance with him, and yet a distinct person in our nature, is infinitely fit to represent him to us. As Son of God, he is the *brightness of his Father's glory, and the express image of his person*, Heb. i. 3. John xiv. 9, 10. As God-man mediator, he is the representative *image of the invisible God*, Col. i. 15. 2 Cor iv. 4, 6;—in and through which, the perfections of God shine forth with the most unsullied, amiable, heart-captivating and soul-transforming brightness. 1. His *spirituality*, in framing a covenant, kingdom, and people, not of this world, 2 Sam. xxiii. 5. John xviii. 36. 1 Pet. ii. 5. 2. His *infinity*, in devising and executing an infinitely important plan of our redemption, and in cheerfully giving his infinite Son, an *unspeakable gift*, to be a ransom for us, and then to be an husband, effectual Saviour, and everlasting portion to us, 2 Cor. ix. 15. John iii. 16. 3. His *eternity*, in establishing a covenant with him, and an office in him, which reacheth from everlasting to everlasting, 2 Sam. xxiii. 5. Prov. viii. 23. Psalm cx. 4. Isa. ix. 7. 4. His *immutability*, in all his infallible purposes and providences, relative to Christ, in nothing altering his appearance or work, notwithstanding our innumerable provocations,—and in the everlasting union of our nature to his person, as a fixed pledge of our acceptance and happiness, Mal. iii. 6. Jer. iii. 5, 19. xxiii. 5, 6. xxxi. 3. xxxii. 40. Isa. liv. 8—10. 5. His *independence*, in personally uniting his own Son to manhood, and in that new form, rendering him dependent on himself as his created man and mediatorial servant, Jer. xxxi. 22. Isa. vii. 14. xlii. 1. Jer. xxiii. 5. xxxiii. 15. 6. His *absolute sovereignty*, in giving his only-begotten Son to be Mediator and Surety for hell-deserving sinners; and for men, not for fallen angels;—and for some men, not for others as good and valuable in themselves, and no less necessitous, Psalm lxxxix. 19, 20. Heb. ix. 14, 16. 1 Cor. i. 26. Mat. xi. 25, 26. xx. 15. 7. His *subsistence in three persons*,—plainly marked in Christ's mission, Isa. xlviii. 16; his unction, Isa. lxi. 1; his baptism, Mat. iii. 16, 17; his death, Heb. ix. 14; his resurrection, Rom. viii. 11. i. 3, 4; his intercession, John xiv. 16, 17, 26; and his application of his purchased redemption to us, John xv. 26. xvi. 7—15. 1 Pet. i. 2. 8. His *divine life*, in bestowing such fulness of spiritual and eternal life on Christ, for the quickening, the comfort and everlasting happiness and glory of men dead in trespasses and sins, John v. 25. xi. 25. Rom. viii. 2. Eph. ii. 1—10. 9. His infinite *wisdom* and *knowledge*, in finding a proper person for the infinitely arduous work of our redemption, in bringing him into the world in the most proper time, place, and manner, and endowed with the most proper furniture; and through him bringing the greatest glory to God, and good to men, out of the worst of evils; in punishing sin, and saving sinners; in making Satan's complete-like victory the occasion of his complicated ruin; and in rendering Christ wisdom to the most foolish and ignorant. 10. His infinite *power*, in uniting Christ's natures in one person, and our persons to him; in inflicting most tremendous punishments upon him, and supporting him under them, and even making his manhood flourish in holiness under the pressure of an infinite wrath and curse. In rendering him an overcomer by sufferings and death; in raising him from the dead, and bestowing upon him a super-exceeding and eternal weight of glory,—and in justifying, preserving, comforting, and glorifying his people, through him, 1 Cor. i. 24. 11. His infinite *holiness*, in the inconceivable purity of Christ's human nature, even under the curse, Luke i. 35; in hiding himself from him on account of sin not inherent in him or committed by him, but merely imputed to him, Matth. xxvii. 46; and in his slaying him, his beloved Son, in order that he might destroy sin, Dan. ix. 24. 1 John iii. 5, 8.   12. His infinite *justice*, in his relentless execution of all the vengeance due to our sins, upon his only-begotten and well-beloved Son, and in rewarding his most guilty representees with everlasting grace and glory, on his account, Rom. viii. 32. iii. 24---26. Isa. liii. 10, 11. 1 John iv. 9, 10, 19. i. 9. Rom. v. 21. vi. 23.   13. His infallible *truth*, in fulfilling the most important and difficult-like promises and threatenings, in the constitution of his person, and in his work of satisfying for and saving men, 2 Cor. i. 20. Gen. iii. 15. ii. 17. 1 Thess. v. 18. 1 Pet. iii. 18.   14. His infinite *majesty, greatness,* and *authority*, in sending, commanding, punishing, and rewarding his own infinite equal, in our nature, Isa. xlii. 6. xlviii. 16. Matth. iii. 15. John x. 18. xiv. 31.! Phil. ii. 6---11. Zech. xiii. 7. Isa. lvii. 10---12. Eph. i. 20---23.   15. And chiefly his infinite *grace, mercy, goodness,* and *love*, John iii. 16. 1 John i. 8, 9, 10, 16, 19.

II. God's purposes, and the execution thereof in his works, are deeply connected with Christ. His person, God-man, is, 1. The foundation of them, Col. i. 17.   2. The centre, in which they all delightfully meet, Eph. i. 10.   3. The glory of them, the union of his two natures being the principal contrivance and work of God, Jer. xxxi. 22. 1 Tim. iii. 16. 4. The grand mean of accomplishing the purposes and effecting the great works of God, Heb. xi. 3. i. 2, 3. Isa. xlix. 8. 5. The grand scope and end of them, in connection with the glory of God and the salvation of men, Rev. v. 11---13. 6. The great attractive of God's heart to his purposes and works, that makes him rest and rejoice in them with inexpressible pleasure and delight, Psalm civ. 31. Zeph. iii. 17.

III. With respect to the revealed truths of God, Christ in his person and offices is, 1. The *fountain*, whence they proceed to us, John i. 18. Rev. i. 1. 2 Sam. xxiii. 3. Mat. v.---vii. John iii. 3, 5. Rom. i. 16.   2. The *foundation* of them, John xiv. 6. Isa. xxviii. 16. 1 Cor. iii. 11.   3. The *matter* of them, when taken in their full connection, 1 Tim. iii. 16. 1 Cor. i 24. ii. 2, 6, 7. Col. i. 25—27. iii. 11. John xiv. 6.   4. Their *repository*, in which they are safely, honourably, and mysteriously laid up, John i. 14. Col. ii. 3. Isa. xi. 2. lxi. 1. Eph. iv. 20, 21. 2 Cor. i. 20.   5. Their *centre*, in which all their lines orderly meet, Acts x. 43. Rom. x. 4. iii. 21, 22. 1 Cor. i. 20. Luke xxii.

20. xxiv. 27, 45. John i. 45. Acts xxvi. 22, 23. 1 Cor. xv. 1, 3, 4. 1 Tim. iii. 16.   6. The *great Teacher* and *Interpreter* of them, Mal. iii. 1. Isa. xlviii. 17. l. 4. liv. 13. Job xxxiii. 23. Rom. xv. 8. Song ii. 9—15. 1 John v. 20. Luke xxiv. 27, 45. Mic. iv. 2. v. 4.   7. The *witness* and even the *attestation* of them, Rev. i. 5. iii. 14. Isa. lv. 4. John iii. 3, 5. Psalm l. 7. Ezek. xxxiii. 11. Heb. vi. 16—18. 2 Cor. i. 20. 8. The *exemplification* of them in all their leading articles relative to God or men,—sin or misery,—holiness or happiness,—law or gospel, Eph. iv. 20, 21.   9. The *light* and *glory* of them, Gal. i. 16. 2 Cor. iii. 8, 14, 16, 18. iv. 3, 4, 6.   10. The *life, power*, and efficacy of them. All the perfections, purposes, and agency of God for rendering them effectual, are in him. And, known separately from him, they are undervalued, deserted, perverted, dead, and ineffectual,—nay, a savour of death unto death,—a killing letter,—the ministration of death, 2 Cor. ii. 16. iii. 6, 7; but connected with him they are quick and powerful, Heb. iv. 12. Rom. iv. 17. John v. 25. vi. 63. xi. 25. Rom. viii. 2. Psalm cxix. 50.   11. The *application* of them to men's hearts depends upon his application of his person. No truth can be rightly perceived, till he be spiritually discerned. No truth can be received in the love of it, till he be embraced. We can have no comfortable interest in divine truths, till we be interested in him. No saving virtue of truth can be felt, till we experience his self-uniting touch, Rom. vii. 9. viii. 2. But, in his entrance into our soul, divine truths are applied, never more to be taken from us, Isa. liv. 13. Gal. i. 16. 2 Tim. iii. 15. 2 Cor. i. 24. Eph. v. 8. iv. 24. 2 Cor. iii. 3, 18. Eph. i. 18, 19. iii. 16—19. Jer. xxxi. 32—34. Psalm cxix. 11. Jer. xv. 16.

IV. Nor are the covenants of God less connected with Christ God-man. These particular ones which God made with Noah, Abraham, Phinehas, David, Israel, were framed to represent that which he made with Christ and his people in him, Gen. ix. xvii. xxii. Num. xxv. 2 Sam. vii. Exod. xix. 5, 6. xxiv. Deut. v. 2 xxix.—Christ in his person and work was the real, though at first *unseen* end of God's making the covenant of works with Adam, and the full vindication of his making it with a representative, Rom. v. 12—21. 2 Cor. xv. 21, 22, 45—49. He is the fulfiller and magnifier of it in the room of his elect, Rom. x. 4. viii. 3, 4. Isa. xlii. 1, 21. liii. 4, 5, 6, 10. And he thus renders it harmless, useful, and pleasant to fallen men, Rom. viii. 1—4. vii. 5. Gal. ii. 19—21. iii. 24.—Christ is the Contractor, Mediator, Surety, Sacrificing Priest, Condition-fulfiller, Administrator, Trustee, Testator, Executor, Advocate, Prophet, and King, in, or of, the covenant of grace, Isa. xlii. 6. xlix. 6. Psalm lxxxix. 3. Heb. ix. 15. vii. 22. x. 10, 14.

Rom. v. 16—21. John xvii. 2. Psalm lxviii. 18. Heb. ix. 16. Isa. lv. 4. xlix. 8, 9. 1 John ii. 1. Acts iii. 22. Psalm ii. 6. All the blessings of it are in, and only obtained in union with his person, as election, Eph. i. 3, 4. the Spirit, Rom. viii. 2. Tit. iii. 6. justification, Isa. xlv. 24, 25. new covenant interest in God, 2 Cor. v. 19. Gal. iii. 20. John xx. 17. Rom. viii. 17. regeneration and sanctification, Eph. ii. 10. 2 Cor. v. 17. Gal. vi. 15. 1 Cor. i. 30. vi. 11. spiritual comfort, John xvi. 33. Luke ii. 25. perseverance in grace, Jude 1. Gal. ii. 20. Col. iii. 3. an happy death, Rev. xiv. 13. 1 Thess. iv. 14, 16. and eternal glory, Isa. xlv. 17. lx. 19.—He is the cause, substance, and end of all these benefits. Election is but a separation from others to eternal life, in Christ as our root, with him as our companion and head,—through him as the mean, and on him as our nourishment, Eph. i. 4. Redemption is Christ and all his righteousness and purchased fulness received by us for our deliverance and happiness, Eph. i. 3, 8. Col. i. 14. Rev. v. 9.—Justification is Christ accounted to us by God, that through his holiness, obedience, and suffering, we may be freed from condemnation, accepted into favour, and entitled to eternal life, Isa. xlv. 24, 25. 2 Cor. v. 21. Rom. v. 15—21. Adoption is a being instated together with, and in Christ, and in his right, into the family of God, as heirs of every thing happy or honourable, John i. 12. Rom. viii. 17, 29. Regeneration and sanctification are his purchased image, produced in us by his manifesting himself to us, entering into, and dwelling in us by his Spirit, Gal. i. 16. 2 Cor. iii. 18. Eph. iii. 17—19. iv. 12—16. Col. ii. 6, 7, 19. Gal. ii. 20. Consolation is the delightful apprehensions and tastes of Christ and his fulness secured through, and in him, to our soul, 2 Cor. ii. 14. Gal. vi. 14. Phil. iii. 3. iv. 4. Psalm cxlix. 2. Luke i. 47. Christ as the infinite price of our eternal life, and as our unceasing Intercessor, and as living in, and caring for us, makes us to persevere in grace, Rom. v. 21. John xiv. 19. Col. iii. 3. Eternal life is purchased by Christ's death, procured by his intercession, prepared by his grace, pledged by the enjoyment of him on earth, and consists in nearness to, heart attracting and assimilating views of his glory, and enjoyment of him as God-man, and of God in him, Rev. v. 9. Hos. xiii. 14. Heb. vi. 20. vii. 25. John xiv. 2, 3, 6. xvii. 21, 24. x. 7, 9. 2 Cor. iii. 18. Phil. iv. 19. Psalm xvii. 15. xvi. 11. lxxiii. 24, 26. Isa. xxxv. 10. lx. 19, 20.—The *dispensation* of this covenant in word and ordinances, and by the Holy Ghost, is the institution of Christ, in which he himself is exhibited and applied to men, 2 Cor. i. 20. 1 Cor. i. 23, 24. ii. 2. Rom. x. 4. i. 16, 17. viii. 2.—Christ God-man is the Founder, the Foundation, the Apostle, Head, Governor, and Proprietor of the new-covenant society, the church; and the Spiritual Father,

Husband, and life of all her true members, Matth. xvi. 18. Heb. iii. 1. Eph. ii. 19, 20. iv. 11, 12. Isa. ix. 6. liv. 5. Gal. ii. 20. Col. iii. 1, 3, 4.

V. All the fellowship of believers with God is in and through the person of Christ God-man. Through him we have fellowship with the Father in his love, as the mean and centre of it. Through him the Father vents his preventing, free, infinite, distinguishing, and everlasting love to us. And through him we believe it, and return it, in consequential, grateful, superlative, and fruitful love to him. And through him our faith and love are acceptable to, and accepted by the Father, 1 John iv. 8—10, 16, 19. 1 Cor. xv. 58. Heb. vi. 10. xii. 28. Our fellowship with the Son, in his giving himself to us, and our choosing and accepting him for our Husband, Saviour, and Lord;—in his exercise of esteem, delight, compassion, and bounty towards us,—and our exercise of esteem, delight, chaste affection, and cheerful obedience towards him;—and our fellowship with him in his righteousness as the price of our salvation, in his intercession as the procuring cause,—and in their blessed effects of justification, adoption, liberty and boldness toward God,—chastisement for sin,—sanctification, spiritual comfort, —and right to everlasting happiness, depends on our union to, and beholding and enjoying his person God-man. Our fellowship with the Holy Ghost depends on it. He as the Spirit of Christ, sent by and lodged in him, works in his ordinances, enlightens, excites, and opens our hearts, manifests and conveys Christ and his fulness into it;—dwells in us, and sheds abroad the love of God in our hearts, witnesses with our spirits, seals us up to the day of redemption, and by his sanctifying and comforting influence is the earnest of our eternal inheritance;—in all which work, he leadeth us to the person of Christ, as made of God to us wisdom, righteousness, sanctification, and redemption. And it is from Christ living in us, and regarded by us, that we carefully avoid grieving, vexing, resisting, and quenching the Holy Ghost, and complying with, and cherish, his influences, and esteem, expect, and prepare for, his benefits and comforts, John xvi. 7—15. Rom. viii. Eph. iv. 20—30. Gal. v. 18—26.

VI. The gracious qualities of believers, and exercise thereof, are connected with Christ's person. His righteousness as the righteousness of God-man, purchased their new nature in all its diversified graces, Tit. ii. 14. Heb. xiii. 12. ix. 12, 14. x. 10, 14. All the grace implanted in their heart is originally in him, and through him conveyed to them, John i. 14, 16. Col. i. 19. ii. 3, 19. iii. 11. His uniting of himself to them as their justified and quickening Head, is the foundation and cause of the renovation of their nature after the image of God, Gal. iv. 19. vi. 15. Eph. ii. 10. 2 Cor. v. 17. 1 Cor. iv. 15. The actuating their inward graces proceeds from his dwelling in their heart by faith as the *resurrection and the life*, Eph. iii. 17. Gal. ii. 20. Col. ii. 19. Eph. iv. 16. All these graces have him, in some respect, for their object, John xvii. 3. Heb. xii. 2. Zech. xii. 10. 1 Cor. xvi. 22. And only in, and through him are they and their acts accepted by God, Eph. i. 6. Rom. xii. 1. 1 Pet. ii. 5. 2 Cor. v. 9, 19. More particularly, 1. All *true spiritual knowledge* hath him for its fountain, mean, and summary object, 1 Cor. ii. 2. Phil. iii. 8. All saving *knowledge of God* is obtained only through him. Some divine perfections, as pardoning mercy, &c. appear only in him, 2 Cor. v. 19; other divine perfections, as wisdom, power, holiness, justice, goodness, and truth, cannot be clearly and comfortably perceived, as manifested, and to be for ever manifested in promoting our happiness, who are sinful men, but in him, 2 Cor. v. 19. Gen. xv. 1. Heb. vii. 25. Phil. iv. 19.——All saving *knowledge of sin* is to be had only in and through his person. In him we perceive God's end in permitting sin to enter and abound in the world, Rom. v. 20, 21. In his extraordinary conception, we perceive the conveyance of sinful corruption from Adam to his posterity, Luke i. 35. Psalm li. 5. Job xiv. 4. John iii. 6.——In his mediatorial mission and quickening virtue, we perceive our utter inability to recover ourselves, or perform any thing spiritually good, Rom. viii. 2, 3. vii. 8. v. 6—8. Mic. vi. 6—8. In his death we perceive the dreadful nature, due desert, and necessary punishment of sin, and the true method of destroying it, by a believing application of his death and resurrection, Rom. vi. 3, 4, 14. vii. 4.——All saving *knowledge of righteousness* is had in and through him. In viewing his person God-man, made under the law, and fulfilling his surety-engagements, we perceive the righteousness demanded by God's law from us; and that it cannot be abated, Gal. iv. 4, 5. Rom. viii. 3, 4. Mat. iii. 15. Luke xxiv. 26. Heb. ii. 9, 10. v. 8. 2 Cor. v. 21; and that in him alone is a law-magnifying righteousness for us, Isa. xlv. 24, 25. xlvi. 12, 13. liii. 4, 5, 11. liv. 17. lxi. 10. xlii. 21. Jer. xxiii. 6. xxxiii. 16.—— All saving *knowledge of judgment* is only in and through him. In his death we have an awful proof of its certainty, justness, and tremendous nature: In it we perceive the safety of his friends, and the inevitable destruction of his implacable enemies. In his victory over Satan, we foresee the eternal ruin of his followers and interests. ——If Christ be revealed in us, we know all that is necessary, all that is worthy to be known, in order to our eternal salvation, Gal. i. 16. I Cor. ii. 2. Mat. xi. 25. John xvii. 3. 1 John v. 20. Luke xxiv. 45. Phil. iii. 8. 1 Thess. iv. 9. Jer. xxxi. 33. We are directed to choose the best portion, Lam. iii. 24. Psalm xxvii. 4. cxlii. 4, 5. xci. 2. cxix. 57. and the best way, Psalm cxix. 30. Col. ii. 6. Phil. iii. 8, 9; and to prosecute our choice in the best manner, Eph. vi. 10. 2 Tim. ii. 1. Phil. iv. 8, 13. Zech. x. 12. Mic. iv. 5. Psalm xxvii. 4. lxxi. 14—18. Phil. iii. 3, 7—15, 20. Col. iii. 17. Gal. ii. 20. vi. 14. 2 Cor. v. 7. Heb. xi.—and to the best ends, Phil. i. 20, 21, 23. 1 Pet. iv. 11. 1 Cor. x. 31. vi. 19, 20. Isa. xliii. 21. 1 Pet. ii. 9. 2. All the exercise of *true faith* is closely connected with his person God-man. By faith we believe God's declarations as manifested IN him, Psalm ix. 10. 2 Cor. iv. 4, 6. In thus embracing them, we look to, receive, and cleave to him, Isa. xlv. 22. John i. 12. Acts xi. 23. By faith we receive his righteousness, as fulfilled by, and lodged in his person, Isa. xiv. 24. 2 Cor. v. 21. By faith we, through his word, as in him, live on his person, and extract all necessary supplies of life, strength, and holiness, and comfort, from it, Gal. ii. 20. Phil. iv. 13, 19. 2 Tim. ii. 1. 1 Cor. xvi. 13. 1 Pet. i. 8. v. 9. By faith we present our persons, nature, services, necessities, plagues, and burdens to God, only through his person and mediation, Heb. iv. 14—16. x. 19—24. His person and fulness are *all in all* to faith; and hence perhaps he is called by its name, Gal. iii. 23, 25.——His manhood is the object of faith, only in so far as his invisible Godhead is connected with, and manifested in, its conception, assumption, union, fulness, and work, John i. 14. 1 Tim. iii. 16. 2 Cor. iii. 18. iv. 4, 6. 3. All *saving hope* hath Christ's person in his death, and the perfections of God as glorified in him, and the promises of the new covenant as ratified in his blood, for its foundation, 1 Tim. i. 1. Col. i. 27. Psalm cxix. 81.—Dwelling in us, he is the actuator of it, the pledge and earnest of our full enjoyment of that which we expect, Col. i. 27. He, in his person and fulness, and all the fulness of God in him, to be immediately and eternally enjoyed in heaven, is the consummate object of our hope, 2 Cor. iv. 17, 18. 1 John iii. 2, 3. Psalm xvii. 15; and hence he is called *our hope*, 1 Tim. i. 1. Col. i. 27. Jer. xiv. 8. xvii. 7. 4. All *true love* to God or men is formed in us, and drawn out by believing views of his person, Gal. v. 6. He is loved as God-man, and God is loved in him, John i. 14. 1 Pet. i. 8. 1 John iv. 9, 10, 16, 19. Graces, comforts, scriptures, ordinances, truths and saints, are loved as connected with, and conformed to him, 2 Pet. i. 3—8. Psal. cxix. lxxxiv. xxvi. 8. cxix. 63. xvi. 3. 5. All true *gospel-repentance* is produced by believing views of his person God-man allied to, and suffering for us, as at once the greatest demonstration of the evil of sin, and of God's love to us sinners, Zech. xii. 10.—In him God is apprehended as merciful and gracious, forgiving iniquity, transgression, and sin; and so as one to whom we may with safety and ease turn from sin, 2 Cor. v. 19. Exod. xxxiv. 6, 7. Hos. xiv. 1, 4. His righteousness is that of God in our nature, surety for us, being imputed to us, frees us from the broken law and its curse, and so breaks the power of sin in us, and enables us to draw near to God as a pacified Father, Friend, and Master, 2 Cor. v. 14, 15, 19, 20. Heb. x. 19—22. Isa. xliv. 22. Jer. iii. 1, 4, 14, 22. Hos. xiv. 1, 4.

VII. All the saints' true and acceptable worship of God is closely connected with the person of Christ God-man. His person simply as God is the proper object of it. His divine nature is the formal reason of it, Psalm xlv. 11. ii. 12. John v. 23. Isa. xlii. 8. Gal. iv. 8. His manhood and mediation are the great motives to, and means of it, Eph. ii 18. iii. 12. His righteousness and intercession render it accepted, 1 Pet. ii. 5. Rev. viii. 3, 4. And it affords them no small encouragement in their troubles, wants, weakness, and dying moments, that they have a God in their nature to call and depend on, 2 Cor. xii. 7, 8. Rev. v. 3, 4, 6. Isa. lxiii. 9. Luke xvii. 5. 2 Thess. ii. 16, 17. Acts vii. 56—59.

VIII. All the new obedience of believers, as it is a *walking with God*, is closely connected with the person of Christ God-man. Christ himself and his Father's laws and ordinances, as in, and from him, are our *way*, John xiv. 6. Col. ii. 6. Heb. x. 20. Isa. xxxv. 8. Psalm cxix. 1, 30. Hos. xiv. 9. All the agreement between God and us, necessary to our walking with him, is made and maintained only in and by Christ, Amos iii. 3. Dan. ix. 24. Col. ii. 14. 2 Cor. v. 19, 20. Rom. v. 10. Col. i. 20. Eph. i. 10. All the motives enforcing this walk, drawn from the love of God, and his promised favours, are only in Christ, 1 John iv. 9, 10, 16, 19. 1 Cor. xv. 58. All the knowledge and wisdom necessary for promoting it are in him, John v. 37. i. 18. xvii. 3. 1 John v. 20. 1 Cor. i. 30. Jer. xxxi. 33, 34. All strength necessary for it is in him, Isa. xl. 29—31. Zech. x. 12. John xv. 5. Phil. iv. 13. 2 Tim. i. 1. Eph. vi. 10. All the confidence necessary to it is obtained in and through him, Heb. x. 19—22. iv. 14—16. Psalm xxvii. 1—3. cxviii. 6—17. All harmony of design with God, as our leader and companion, is obtained only in Christ; and all the acceptableness of God's presence and conduct to us, and of ours to him, Col. iii. 17. Rom. vii. 25. Isa. xliii. 21. 1 Cor. vi. 20. x. 31. 1 Pet. ii. 5, 9. iv. 11. Rom. xii. 1.—Even in all our *relative duties*, we must have Christ's person in us for their fountain,—Christ in his love for our pattern and motive,—Christ in his authority for our reason and rule,—and Christ in his honour for our end, Rom. xvi. 2, 3, 7—13. 2 Cor. x. 1. Eph. v. 2, 22, 24, 25, 29. iv. 32. vi. 1, 4, 5, 6, 7, 9. Phil. ii. 1—5. Col. iii. 16, 18, 20, 23, 24. iv. 1, 17.

REFLECT. Have I seen and believed on this all-lovely, all-useful, Lord Jesus Christ? Hath it pleased God to reveal his Son in me? Have I by faith beheld this great mystery of godliness, this new thing created in the earth,—God made manifest in the flesh? Have I turned aside to see this great sight, the *bush burning and not consumed?* Have I beheld the glory of the Word made flesh, and dwelling among men,—dwelling in ME,—as the glory of the only begotten of the Father, full of grace and truth? Have I, in this image of the invisible God, beheld the Father also? Have I seen the glory of God in the face of Jesus Christ?—What think I of Christ? Whose Son? Whose Saviour is he?—What is he to me?—Is he white and ruddy, the chief among ten thousand?—Is he altogether lovely, and my Beloved and my Friend?—Beholding, as in a glass, the glory of the Lord, Am I changed from glory to glory, even as by the Spirit of the Lord?——What would I have Christ to be to me,—to do for and to me?——My soul, I charge thee before God, never dare to preach a single sermon till thou hast cordially perused this truly divine system, JESUS CHRIST, as made of God to me WISDOM!—O the transcendently excellent thoughts,—devices,—and inventions that are here!—how God might pardon sinful men, and put them among his children!—how he might have mercy on his inveterate enemies, the rebellious revolters from his righteous government!—how Grace might much more abound, and reign through righteousness to eternal life!—how mercy and truth might meet together, righteousness and peace kiss each other!—how the prey might be taken from the mighty, and the lawful captive be delivered!——Thoughts!—how many!—how condescending!—how deep!—how high!—how gracious!—how fixed!—how efficacious!—how delightful!—how precious!——To convey them into my heart, Into what new form of person, offices, and relations is the eternal Son of God, as it were, cast and moulded!—What new,—what stupendous manifestations of the manifold wisdom and knowledge of God ensue!—What mysteries of godliness,—mysteries of the kingdom!—What lectures concerning Jehovah and his gracious connections with sinful men,—with sinful ME!

——What things were gain to me, these I therefore count loss for Christ: yea, doubtless, I count all things but loss for the excellency of the knowledge of Christ Jesus my Lord;—and I do count them but dung to win him, and to be found in him. All the heaven I wish below is but to taste his love: and all the heaven I wish above is but to see his face. Oh! for that ETERNITY,—that ETERNITY, when Christ God-man shall be my Teacher!—Christ shall be my system!—Christ shall be my Bible!—Christ shall be my ALL IN ALL!

CHAP. II.

Of the GENERAL *and* PARTICULAR OFFICES *of Jesus Christ.*

To constitute the Son of God in our nature, our *Mediator in office*, he was divinely called, appointed to his work, and furnished for it, Heb. v. 4, 5, 10. Isa. xlii. 6. xlix. 1---9.---In allusion to the anointing of the Hebrew kings, priests, and sometimes prophets, at their instalment into their office, Psalm cxxxiii. 3. Exod. xxix. 7, 9, 21. 1 Sam. x. 1. xvi. 13. 1 Kings i. 34. 2 Kings xi. 12. 1 Kings xix. 16;---his appointment to, and furniture for his work, is called an ANOINTING, and himself MESSIAH, CHRIST, or the ANOINTED, Dan. ix. 24, 25. Mat. xvi. 16. John vi. 69. i. 41. Luke ix. 20. Acts ii. 36. viii. 37. Psalm lxxxiv. 9. 1 Sam. ii. 10. The ANOINTING of Christ largely taken, includes, 1. God's solemn setting him apart to be our Mediator. This was done in his designation of him to that office from all eternity, Prov. viii. 23. 1 Pet. i. 20. Psalm ii. 7, 8. Eph. i. 4. It was proclaimed by angels at his conception and birth, Luke i. 33. ii. 10, 11. Heb. i. 6; and by his Father at his baptism, before he entered on his public ministry, Mat. iii. 17; and again a little before his death, Mat. xvii. 5. John xii. 28. Isa. xlix. 3. 2. God's giving him a fixed commission and authority to execute his mediatorial work: and hence he is represented as *called* by God, Heb. v. 4, 5, 10. Isa. xlii. 6. xlix. 1;---*sent* by God, John v. 38. vi. 29. vii. 28, 29. viii. 26, 29, 42. Isa. xlviii. 16;---God's *servant*, acting in his name, and fulfilling his commandment, Isa. xlii. 1. xlix. 3. John x. 18. xiv. 10, 11, 31;---*sealed* by him, John vi. 27.---This commission was given to him from all eternity, Isa. xlii. 6. Prov. viii. 23. It was confirmed to him at his baptism and transfiguration, Mat. iii. 16, 17. xvii. 5: and with respect to his honorary service, it was, as it were, renewed to him in his resurrection and ascension, 1 Pet. i. 21. Eph. i. 20---22. Acts ii. 36. Mat. xxviii. 18. Dan. vii. 14. 3. God's furnishing him for the execution of his work. This included his preparing for him an undefiled manhood, Heb. x. 5. Jer. xxxi. 22; his furnishing this manhood with proper gifts and graces in its very formation and conception, Luke i. 35. Heb. vii. 26; his enlargement of these in his advancing life, Luke ii. 40, 52. Isa. xi. 2---4. xlii. 1. lxi. 1;---the descent of the Holy Ghost upon him at his baptism, to fit him for his public ministrations, Mat. iii. 16. John i. 32. iii. 34. vi. 27;---the further assistance which he received in his ministerial and suffering work, Isa. xlii. 1, 6. l. 4, 7, 9. Mic. v. 4;---and, in fine, all that fulness of joy which he received in his resurrection and ascension, Psalm xlv. 7, 8. Acts ii. 28; and the lodging of all new-covenant fulness in his hand, that, as administrator, he may bestow it upon men, Psalm lxviii. 18. Col. i. 19. Mat. xi. 27. John iii. 35. xvii. 2.

The GENERAL OFFICES to which the Son of God in our nature was thus anointed, was that of MEDIATOR, to which his characters of SAVIOUR and REDEEMER are reducible, John ix. 33. 1 Tim. ii. 5. Heb. viii. 6. ix. 15 xii. 24. His work as a Mediator is to bring an offended God and sinful offending men to an honourable and happy agreement, 1 Tim. ii. 5, 6. Heb. ix. 15. xii. 24. John ix. 33.—In so doing he removes God's legal enmity against men and the real effects of it, and opens an honourable vent for his mercy and love to them, by his obedience and satisfaction,—and intercedes for the bestowal of his favours on them, Rom. v. 8---10, 19, 21. 1 Tim. ii. 6. Mat. xx. 28. Heb. vii. 25. Rom. viii. 34;—and he removes our sinful ignorance, guilt, pollution, and enmity against God, Tit. ii. 11, 12, 14. Isa. xlii. 6, 7. xlix. 8---12, 24---26. Thus he is a Redeemer or Saviour by the PRICE of his surety-righteousness,— and by the POWER of his intercession, spiritual illumination, conquest, government, and protection, Mat. xx. 28. Acts xx. 28. Rev. v. 9. Tit. ii. 14. 1 Pet. i. 18, 19. ii. 24. iii. 18.---Isa. xlii. 6, 7. lxi. 1—3. xlix. 6, 8, 24—26. Psalm cx. 2, 3. xxii. 27 —31. lxxii.

Christ is not merely a *Mediatorial Inter-messenger*, who intercedes for us with God,—reveals to us the method of salvation, —confirms God's promises and doctrines by his death as a martyr,---and exemplifies to us a course of holy obedience. 1. The Scripture describes him as a Mediator that gave himself a ransom for men, 1 Tim. ii. 6. Mat. xx. 28. Acts xx. 28.——that makes peace by his blood, Col. i. 20. Eph. ii. 14. 1 Pet. i. 19. Heb. xii. 24. xiii. 12;---and who is the Surety of the new covenant, Heb. vii. 22. Psalm cxix. 122. Isa. xxxviii. 14. that by his blood obtains eternal redemption for us, Heb. ix. 12---15. x. 14---18. Rev. v. 9 ; and in allusion to the blood of sacrifices shed for transgressors, his is called the *blood of sprinkling*, Heb. xii. 24. 1 Pet. i. 2. 2. The persons between whom and God he was Mediator, were THEOSTYGEIS, *hated by* and *haters of God*, and so needed a reconciling ransom to be paid for them, Rom. i. 30. viii. 7, 8. Psalm v. 4---6. Zech. xi. 8. Prov. xvi. 5. 3. If Christ had been a Mediator only by his doctrine, example, and intercession, he could not have been the *one only* Mediator between God and men, according to 1 Tim. ii. 5; for prophets, apostles, and preachers, especially such as suffered martyrdom, were useful in these forms, as well as he, Acts xx. 17—24. 1 Tim. iv. 16. 2 Tim. ii. 10.

Christ is Mediator *according to both his natures*, divine and human. Indeed some of his acts, as working of miracles, were merely divine. Others, as eating, drinking, weeping, or the like, were properly human. But his Mediatorial acts, though they more immediately proceed from one of his natures, are considered as the works of his person God-man. 1. The Scripture never refers the mediation of Christ to any one of his natures, but to *himself* or his person, Mat. xx. 28. Acts xx. 28. 1 Cor. ii. 8. Heb. ix. 14. Tit. ii. 14. Gal. i. 4. Rev. v. 9. 1 Pet. ii. 24. iii. 18. 2. He assumed our nature, that he might execute his mediatorial office, and was *made flesh*, without any confounding his natures. His acts and sufferings must therefore be considered as the acts and sufferings of his person God-man, Gal. iv. 4, 5. John iii. 16. 1 John iv. 9, 10. Rom. viii. 3, 4. 3. It hath already been proved, that the execution of all his offices require his two natures united in one person, Isa. xlviii. 17. Heb. ix. 14. Eph. v. 2. Psalm cx. 2, 3. 4. It was peculiarly necessary, that he should be Mediator according to his divine nature. According to that, he chiefly humbled himself, and *took* upon him the form of a bond-servant, Phil. ii. 6—8. and in some respects acted as a Mediator before his incarnation, Zech. i. 8---12. iii. 2---4. Gen. iii. xii. xv. xvii. xxii. xxviii. Nor could our redemption, forgiveness, and eternal life be purchased, procured, or bestowed by a mere man, Isa. xlv. 17, 22, 24, 25. xliii. 25. liii. 11. John xvii. 2, 3. 1 John v. 20.

Christ is appointed *Mediator only for men*. No doubt, the holy angels are confirmed in their happy state by him *as the Son of God*, Heb. i. 3. Col. i. 17. God's grant of them to him for ministering Spirits to his heirs of salvation, secures their continuance in holiness and happiness, Heb. i. 14. Eph. i. 21, 22. 1 Pet. iii. 22. The discoveries of divine perfections, in his redemption work, mightily enlarges their happiness, 1 Pet. i. 12. Eph. iii. 10. But Christ is not a Mediator, even of *confirmation* to angels. 1. The Scripture never represents him as the *Mediatorial Confirmer* of angels, but as the Mediatorial Saviour of men, 1 Tim. ii. 5, 6. Nay, it expressly asserts that he *took not hold of angels*, Heb. ii. 16. 2. No variance hath ever taken place between God and holy angels, and so there can be no need of a Mediator between them. 3. Christ having never assumed the nature of angels, hath no proper fitness to mediate between God and them. 4. Holy angels have no need of Christ's atonement, nor of his intercession founded upon it, —both which are essential parts of his mediatorial work, 1 Tim. ii. 6. 1 John ii. 1, 2. Heb. ix. 15. xii. 24. vii. 22, 25. Rom. viii. 33, 34. 5. If Christ be the mediatorial confirming head of angels, he might have been Mediator of the covenant of works. Innocent Adam had at least as much need of him as they. 6. There is no more need of a Mediator of confirmation, than for one of creation. God can preserve his creatures in happiness, as well as form them perfectly holy.—Indeed angels are subjected to Christ as head of the church; but so are brutes, devils, and every thing else, Col. ii. 10. 1 Pet. iii. 22. Eph. i. 21, 22. Psalm viii. 4—7. The *all things* gathered together in Christ and reconciled through the blood of his cross, are elect men, Jews and Gentiles, saints militant and triumphant. These, being once scattered, and at variance with God, need to be gathered and reconciled to him, Eph. i. 10. Col. i. 20.—And indeed, when these are brought back from their rebellion to a state of friendship with God, and a course of holiness, the holy angels behave towards them, not as enemies, but as members of the same happy family with themselves, Heb. i. 14. Psalm xxxiv. 7. Rev. xix. 10. xxii. 9.

Christ God-man is the *only Mediator* between God and men. 1. The Scriptures expressly declare that there is but ONE EIS, ONE ONLY Mediator between God and men, 1 Tim. ii. 5. Mat. xix. 17. Eph. iv. 6. Rom. iii. 10, 11. 1 Tim. iii. 2, 12. Nor doth the Scripture ever hint, that he is but the only *primary* Mediator, or the *Mediator of redemption;* but represent him as the only Mediator that acts in reconciling men to God. And, in their pretended oblation of Christ in their mass, and in admitting men's works or sufferings, as a satisfaction for sin, Papists certainly make their priests and saints *mediators of redemption.* 2. The Scripture represents him as the *only Advocate* with God for sinful men, and his advocacy as inseparably connected with his fulfilment of all righteousness for them, 1 John ii. 1, 2. Heb. i. 3. viii. 4, 6. ix. 12—24. Rom. viii. 33, 34. 3. There is no salvation from sin or misery, but through Christ, Acts iv. 12. John xiv. 6. x. 7, 9. Eph. ii. 18. iii. 12. Heb. iv. 14—16. x. 19—22. 2 John 9. And Christ requires men to come directly to himself without an introducer, Isa. xlv. 22. Prov. i. 22, 23. ix. 4, 5. Mat. xi. 28. John vi. 37. vii. 37, 38. 4. There is no need of another Mediator. And none can be more fit, powerful, condescending. Heb. vii. 25. ii. 14—18. iv. 14, 15. 5. Neither saints nor angels have any necessary requisites of a Mediator between God and sinful men. They cannot so much as know our most important needs, or our thoughts or desires. How unfit then to be mediators of intercession? Isa. lxiii. 16. Jer. xvii. 9, 10. Rev. ii. 23. 6. The mediation of saints and angels pretended by papists originated from the heathens' idolatrous acknowledgment of secondary gods, who were pretended to mediate between them and their principal gods. 7. Departed saints are never in Scripture represented as praying for any particular person: And saints on earth are companions in tribulation; they know one another's needs; and prayer for one another is a part of their church fellowship, in this imperfect state.

Christ's GENERAL office of Mediator includes his three PARTICULAR offices of PROPHET, PRIEST, and KING,—each of which implies an honourable station, and a charge or burden of work. 1. The Scriptures expressly ascribe these three offices to him, Deut. xviii. 15—18. Acts iii. 22. vii. 37.—Psalm cx. 4. Heb. iii. 1. iv. 14. ix. 11. x. 21.—Psalm ii. 6. Mat. xxviii. 18. Isa. ix. 6, 7. Dan. vii. 14. 2. The anointing, station, and work of those that were typical of him figured him out in this threefold office; Moses, Samuel, Elijah, Elisha, Daniel, John Baptist, &c. typified him as a prophet: Melchizedek, Aaron and his descendants typified him as a priest: David and his successors typified him as a king. And it is observable, that none prefigured him in all his offices in a stated manner. Melchizedek was a king and priest, but not a prophet. David was a king and prophet, but not a priest. Moses and Samuel were stated prophets and civil rulers, but never, except on particular occasions, acted as priests, Exod. xxiv. xxix. 1 Sam. vii. 9, 10. xvi. 2, 3. Psalm xcix. 6. 3. Our threefold misery of ignorance, guilt, and bondage required this threefold office in Christ,—that, as a *prophet*, he might instruct us in the nature and will of God;—that, as a *priest*, he might remove our guilt and bring us into peace with, and nearness to God;—and that, as a *king*, he might deliver us from the bondage of sin and Satan, and make us like to, and happy with God, Eph. v. 8. John i. 18. —Rom. iii. 19—26. Mat. xx. 28. 1 Pet. i. 18, 19. Rev. v. 9. Isa. xlix. 24—26. 1 Cor. i. 2. Rev. iii. 4, 21. 4. The nature of our salvation requires this threefold office, that he might purchase it, as a priest; reveal and offer it, as a prophet; and confer and apply it, as a king, Heb. ix. 12—15. ii. 3. Psalm cx. 2, 3.

In his execution of his offices upon us, Christ's *prophetical* convictions and illuminations of our mind necessarily precede his application of his *priestly* righteousness, and this precedes the subjection of our soul to him, as our *king*, Job xxxiii. 23, 24. 2 Cor. v. 14. Heb. xii. 28. But in the natural order of his offices, Christ's *priesthood* stands first. 1. Our salvation must be purchased and procured before it can be explained, offered, or applied, Psalm xxii.—in which Christ is represented as first purchasing salvation, as a suffering priest; then publishing it, as a prophet, and lastly subduing and governing saved men, as their king. His being the WAY by his blood, precedes his being the TRUTH and the LIFE, John xiv. 6. Heb. x. 19, 20. 2. The sacrificing work of his priesthood belongs to his fulfilment of the condition of the new covenant made with him. But his prophetical and kingly work belong to the administration of it, which is the reward of his service. Nay, even his interceding work is the procuring cause of all that light and life, which he confers upon us as a prophet and king, Isa. liii. 10—12. Heb. vii. 25. Rom. viii. 33, 34. John xvi. 7—15. xvii. 3. In his execution of his prophetical and kingly offices, Christ, in the name of God, deals with men to promote their happiness; but, in the execution of his priestly office, he deals with God for his honour, which ought to be first in order secured, Eph. v. 2. Heb. v. 1. ix. 24, 28. Psalm xxii. Isa. liii.——A proper attention to the form of the covenant of grace plainly manifests that these offices of Christ are not the proper fountain of the promises of the gospel, but only the means of their fulfilment, Tit. i. 2. 2 Tim. i. 9.

I. Christ, by the appointment of God, is a mediatorial Prophet. 1. The Scripture expressly represents him as a prophet, Deut. xviii. 15—18. Acts iii. 22. vii. 37. John i. 45. Isa. lxi. 1—3. Luke iv. 17. John vi. 14. vii. 40, 41. Luke xxiv. 19. Matth. vii. 29. 2. His metaphorical characters of *Angel, Messenger of the covenant, Interpreter, Witness, Counsellor, Wisdom of God, Apostle* of our profession, *Teaching Master, Light of the World, Sun of Righteousness, Bright and Morning Star*, manifest him a prophet, Isa. lxiii. 9. Mal. iii. 1. Job xxxiii. 23. Isa. lv. 4. ix. 6. Prov. viii. ix. 1 Cor. i. 24, 30. Heb. iii. 1. Isa. ii. 2, 3. Matth. xxiii. 8, 10. xvii. 5. Mic. iv. 2, 3. John iii. 2. viii. 12. i. 9. ix. 5. xii. 35. Isa. xlii. 6. ix. 2. lx. 1, 19, 20. Mal. iv. 2. Rev. xxii. 16. ii. 28. 3. The light of the lamps in the Jewish tabernacle and temple,—the blowing of the silver trumpets,—as well as a multitude of typical persons, particularly prophets, typified him in his prophetical office, Gen. v. to Mal. iv. Luke i. iii. John i. iii. 4. The effectual revelation of the mysteries of our redemption, in order to remove our ignorance, necessarily required this office, Matth. xi. 27. John i. 18. Rom. x. 14—17.

Being God in our nature, Christ hath an infinite fitness for being the great prophet of the church. 1. He hath an absolutely perfect and comprehensive knowledge of all things, in their nature, properties, and circumstances, John i. 18. xxi. 17. ii. 25. Col. ii. 3. Heb. iv. 13. Prov. viii. 12, 14. 2. While he is full of infinite patience, kindness, compassion, and care to instruct us in every thing important, he hath a sovereign power over our conscience, James iv. 12. Matth. vii. 29. xvii. 5. 3. Being absolutely infallible, being *truth* itself, the faithful and true witness, he can neither deceive nor be deceived, Heb. xiii. 8. John xiv. 6. Rev. i. 5. iii. 14. 4. He gives furniture and authority to all other teachers of God's revealed truths, 1 Cor. xii. 28. Eph. iv. 11, 12. Matth. xvi. 19. xxviii.

19, 20. Mark xvi. 15, 16. John xx. 21, 23. Acts i. 8. Matth. x. Luke x.

Christ neither needed, nor did ascend to heaven for instruction and furniture, before he began his public ministrations. 1. The Scripture never represents him as ascending to heaven but once after his resurrection, which was after he had come down to our world in his incarnation, and gone down to the grave in his burial, Heb. ix. 12. viii. 1. i. 3. Eph. iv. 9. John vi. 38. xvi. 28. 2. As Christ's divine nature continued as much in heaven, while he appeared on earth, as before, John iii. 13. i. 18. vii. 34. xii. 26. xvii. 24; and his human nature was filled with the Holy Ghost, John iii. 34. Isa. xlii. 1—4. lxi. 1, 2. xi. 2—4. Col. ii. 3, he needed not ascend up to heaven for instruction or furniture. Nay, long before his public ministrations, his wisdom amazed all that saw it in the temple, Luke ii. 46, 47.

Christ began to execute his prophetical office immediately after Adam's fall, in publishing the first promise, and particularly announcing the bad consequences of his sin, and teaching to offer sacrifices, Gen. iii. 14—21. In his own person, he, at different times, and in diversified forms, issued forth manifold instructions and predictions, under the Old Testament, Gen. vi. ix. xii. xv. xvi. xvii. xviii. xxi. xxii. xxvi. xxviii. Exod. iii.—xxxiv. Lev. i.—xxvii. Num. v. vi. viii. x. xi. xii. xiv. xv. xvii. xviii. xix. xxviii. xxix. Josh. i. vi. vii. Judg. ii. vi. xiii. Zech. i.—vi.——In his public ministrations on earth, he executed this office, not by correcting or enlarging the moral law of God, but, 1. In explaining and enforcing its commands, Matth. v.—vii. xv. xxiii. Luke vi. &c. 2. In declaring the truths of the gospel, which is called the *doctrine of Christ*, Acts xiii. 12. 2 John 9. Tit. ii. 10; the *testimony of Christ*, 1 Cor. i. 6; the *gospel of Christ*, Rom. i. 9—16; and which consists of divine truths necessary to be known in order to our salvation, but which could not be known by us without revelation, as the doctrine of the Trinity of persons in the Godhead; and especially those truths that originate in the plan of our redemption, and relate to the *making, parties,* and *administration* of the covenant of grace, Matth. xxviii. 19. xiii. xx. xxi. xxv. Luke viii.—xix. John iii.—xvii. xviii. 36, 37. 3. In foretelling future events,—his own sufferings and death, Matth. xii. 40. xvi. 21. xvii. 9, 22, 23. xx. 18, 19, 28. xxi. 38, 39. xxvi. 2; the treachery of Judas, John vi. 70. xiii. 21, 27. Matth. xxvi. 21—25; Peter's denial of him, John xiii. 36—38. Matth. xxvi. 34, 35; the other ten disciples' taking offence at him, and forsaking him, Matth. xxvi. 31. John xvi. 32; his own resurrection and glory, John ii. 19. Matth. xvi. 21, 27. xvii. 9. xix. 28. xxvi. 32,

OF THE PARTICULAR OFFICES OF CHRIST. 287

64; the cruel persecution which his disciples and followers would meet with, and their support under it, Matth. x. xx. 23. xxiv. 9, 10. xvi. 24. xix. 29. John xv. 20. xvi. 20, 22, 33. xv. 26, 27. xvi. 7—15. Luke xxiv. 49. Acts i. 5, 8; the spread of the gospel, the abolishment of the ceremonial law, and the calling of the Gentiles, Acts i. 8. Matth. xxvi. 13. viii. 11, 12. xxi. 41, 43. xxii. 1—13. xxviii. 19. John iv. 21—24. x. 16. xii. 23, 24. Luke xxiv. 47. Mark xvi. 15, 16; the rejection, ruin, and dispersion of the Jewish nation, Matth. iii. 10. viii. 11, 12. xii. 38—45. xxi. 33—44. xxii. 1—13. xxiii. xxiv. Luke xi. 42—51. xiv. 16—24. xvii. 20—37. xix. 12—27, 41—44. xxi. John viii 21; and the form and procedure of the last judgment, Matth. xxiv. xxv. John v. 28, 29. Matth. xix. 28, 29.—After his resurrection he comforted his disciples, and instructed them concerning the form and ordinances of the gospel-church, &c. Mat. xxviii. 19, 20. Mark xvi. 15—18. Luke xxiv. John xx. xxi. Acts i. 2—8.—After his ascension, he instructed Saul, Ananias, and John, Acts ix. xxii. xxvi. Rev. i.—iii. vi. x. xxii.—In the heavenly state, his immediate displays of his person manifest the perfections of God, Isa. lx. 19, 20. Rev. xxi. 23.

In his personal execution of his prophetical office, 1. Christ, in an authoritative, bold, and perfect manner, declared divine truths, Heb. i. 1. ii. 3. Matth. vii. 29. John vii. 46. He often represented them *in parables*, that he might fulfil Old Testament predictions, Psalm xlix. 1, 2. lxviii. 1, 2; might manifest the spirituality of his own mind, and teach us to improve every common incident as a spiritual instructor, John iii. 12, 13; might effectually reprove the Jews, without enraging them, Matth. xxi. 28—46; might more readily instruct the attentive and thoughtful, illustrating divine truths in a manner delightful to their mind, and easy for their memory, Jer. xiii. xviii. xix. Ezek. iv. v. xii. xv. xvi. xvii. xix. xxiii. Isa. xlviii. 17. l. 4. lvii. 18. Hos. xii 10; and might justly occasion the blindness and ruin of those that hated his instructions, Matth. xiii. 10—15. 2. He exemplified the truths which he taught, in his own person and conduct, Eph. v. 2. 1 Pet. ii. 21. 1 Thess. i. 6. 3. He attested his doctrines by his miracles, his death and sacraments, John v. 36. x. 38. xviii. 36, 37. Matth. xxviii. 19. xxvi. 26—28. 4. He did, and doth, effectually apply his doctrines, laws, promises, and threatenings to men's conscience, Isa. xlviii. 17. John vi. 63.

Christ also executes his prophetical office in a mediate manner, by appointing and furnishing angels, prophets, apostles, pastors, teachers, parents, masters, &c.—to intimate his truths to men's ears, Heb. i. 1. Eph. iv. 11, 12. vi. 4. Gen. xviii. 19. Isa. xxxviii. 19; by sending his Spirit to qualify his messengers; and to explain and apply their instructions to men's hearts, 2 Pet. i. 19—21. Heb xii. 25. Acts vii. 38, 54. Deut. xxxii. 10. Luke ii. 25, 32. 1 Pet. i. 11, 12, 23. 1 Thess. i. 5. ii. 13. Acts ii.—vi. John xvi. 7—14. Isa. lix. 21.—But Christ far excels all created instructors. 1. Being the *wisdom of God*, he had, and hath a comprehensive knowledge of divine truths, and of all the spiritual conditions of his hearers, Prov. viii. Col. ii. 3. Heb. iv. 13. Rev. ii. 23. 2. He neither did, nor doth need any instruction, having all knowledge in, and of himself, John i. 18. ii. 25. iii. 32. viii. 38—40. 3. He can open men's understandings, and make them spiritually to understand and apply his instructions, Luke xxiv. 45. 1 John v. 20. Acts xvi. 14. 4. His exemplification of his instructions in his own person, is absolutely perfect, 2 Cor. iv. 4, 6. Col. i. 15. Mat. xvii. 5. John viii. 29. 2 Cor. v. 21. 1 Pet. ii. 21, 22. 5. He delivered his doctrines, not in the name of Jehovah, as one different from and superior to him, but in his own name, as his own oracles, John iii. 3, 5. vi. viii. x. Mat. v.—vii. xiii. xx. xxiii. xxiv. xxv. 6. He wrought all his miracles, by which he confirmed his mission and doctrine, in his own name, and by his own power, without ever praying for the exertion of any divine power in effecting them, John x. 32, 38. Mat. xi. 5. 7. While his death attested his doctrines, it chiefly served as an *atonement* for the sins of his people, Mat. xx. 28. Tit. ii. 14. 1 Pet. ii. 24. iii. 18. Rev. v. 9.

Christ's execution of his prophetical office produces, 1. Rational knowledge of divine truths by external declarations of them. 2. Experimental, but not saving knowledge of them, by these external declarations attended with awakening afflictions and common operations of the Holy Ghost, Heb. vi. 4, 5. Mat. xiii. 20, 22. Isa. lviii. 2. 2 Pet. ii. 20. 3. Saving, heart-conquering, and sanctifying knowledge of them, by the especial and effectual influence and application of them by the Holy Ghost, John vi. 44, 45, 65. 1 Tim. iii. 15—17. 1 Thess. i. 5. ii. 13. 2 Thess. ii. 13, 16, 17. iii. 5.

II. Christ is a Priest appointed by God to offer sacrifice of atonement for men's sin,—and to intercede with God for their eternal redemption. 1. He is often expressly called a priest in Scripture, Psalm cx. 4. Zech. vi. 13. Heb ii. 17. iv. 14. iii. 1. v. 5, 6, 10. vi. 20. vii. 3, 17, 21, 26. viii. 4. ix. 11. x. 21. 2. Offering sacrifice, and making intercession, which are the work of a priest, are ascribed to him, Eph. v. 2. Heb. ix. 14. vii. 24, 27. x. 7, 10, 14. ix. 24. vii. 25. Rom. viii. 34.——His priesthood being only manifested by Revelation, and being the foundation of his other offices,—and especially because it would be disbelieved and detested by unrenewed hearts, and as he, in the sacrificing work of it, needed peculiar encouragement, he was installed in it by the *oath of God*, and had it prefigured by an uncommon multitude of types, some *personal*, as Melchizedek, Aaron and his sons, &c. and some *real*, as sacrifices, oblations, &c. Gen. xiv. xv. xxii. Lev. i.—xvi. Num. xv. xvii. xxviii. xxix. Heb. v.—x. Psalm cx. 4.

The *Levitical priests* resembled Jesus Christ in their divine call to their work; their preparation for it; their necessary purity and perfection; their work of offering sacrifices to God for men's sin, and pleading for his favours to them, Exod. xxviii. xxix. Lev. xxi. xxii. i.—ix. xvi. Heb. v.—x. But he infinitely excels them,—in the dignity and holiness of his person,—in the solemnity of his call,—in his being the only priest of his order, —the only immediate approacher to God;—in the matter, efficacy, and unity of his sacrifice;—in the infinite prevalence of his intercession;—and in the eternal continuance of his priesthood, Heb. v.—x.

Christ was a priest *on earth* during his humiliation, and continues to be one in heaven for ever. 1. He executed both parts of his priestly work on earth. He offered himself a *sacrifice* for sin, Eph. v. 2, 23—27. Heb. i. 3. vii. 27. ix. 25, 28. x. 10, 14; and made *intercession*, Heb. v. 7. John xvii. 2. None of the typical priests became priests by their entrance into the sanctuary of God, but were priests before they could lawfully present any oblations to him, Heb. v. 1. viii. 3. ix. 11, 12.——Christ's two offices of *Priest* and *King* are so different in their types,— their work,—their object and tendency, that it appears altogether absurd for any to pretend that they are the same.

Christ's offering of himself a sacrifice, includes not only his sufferings, but his *whole obedience to the broken law*, habitual, active, or passive,—or his fulfilling the whole condition of the covenant of grace. He began his sacrifice in his conception,— continued it through his whole life, and completed it on the cross and in the grave. 1. The Scripture never restricts his satisfaction for sin to his sufferings on the cross, but represents it as including all his sufferings, and hence his holiness of nature and obedience of life, as therewith connected, Isa. liii. 2—5, 10. 1 Pet. i. 18, 19. ii. 21, 24. iii. 18. Mat. xvi. 21. Heb. v. 7, 8. x. 8, 9. Rom. v. 19, 17, 18. Phil. ii. 6—8. His agony in the garden was a remarkable part of his sufferings, Mat. xxvi. 38. Luke xxii. 44. Nor doth Zech. iii. 9. confine his giving satisfaction, but his finishing of it to *a day*. Nay, in God's reckoning, *a day* often denotes a whole period, Job xxiv. 1. Psalm xxxvii. 13. 2. Christ was made in the likeness of sinful flesh, that the *righteousness of the law might be fulfilled*, which consists in holiness of nature, and obedience of life, as well as in enduring all the

U

sufferings which God pleases to inflict as the punishment of sin, might be fulfilled in us, Rom. viii. 3, 4. And he was *obedient* unto death, Phil. ii. 8. Psalm xl. 8. John. xvii. 4. x. 18. xiv. 31. 3. Christ's satisfaction, taken in its full latitude, must include every thing which he, as our Surety, undertook to fulfil in our stead,---which must be all that we owed to the broken covenant of works, obedience as well as suffering punishment, Gal. iii. 10, 12, 13; for he came to fulfil the law, that we, by faith receiving his satisfaction as for us, may perfectly fulfil the law in him, Mat. 17, 18. Rom. iii. 31. viii. 4. 4. His sacrifice or satisfaction is the very same as his righteousness, Rom. i. 17. iii. 21, 22. v. 18. Phil. iii. 9. Dan. ix. 24. Isa. xlv. 24, 25. Jer. xxiii. 6. Now this comprehends *obedience* to the precept of the broken law, as well as suffering punishment for sin committed, Mat. iii. 15. Psalm xl. 8. Heb. v. 8. Phil. ii. 8. Luke xxiv. 26. Hence we are *made righteous,—made the righteousness of God in him,*—his righteous qualities and works, as well as his sufferings, being imputed to us as our sins were to him, Rom. v. 19. 2 Cor. v. 21. Isa. liii. 6. 1 Pet. ii. 24. iii. 18. 5. The law of God never promises nor bestows eternal life on men as the reward of mere suffering, but as the reward of obedience, Lev. xviii. 5. Mat. xix. 17. Rom. x. 5. Gal. iii. 12.

But to anticipate objections, it must be observed, that, 1. Though Christ's holiness of human nature, obedience of life, and voluntary suffering, be each of them absolutely perfect in its own place, yet they must be joined together in forming one complete satisfaction answerable to the demands of the broken law, Mat. iii. 15. Luke xxiv. 26. Phil. ii. 7, 8. 2. Wherever our eternal redemption is represented as founded on Christ's *blood* or *death*,—that is, put for his whole righteousness,—and the rather, that he was under a legal death as long as he was fulfilling it, and his death and shedding his blood were the most striking and finishing ingredients in it. 3. Christ never became man but in order to satisfy the whole demands of the *broken covenant of works* for us. He never, *as man*, owed any obedience to *that law* for himself, and therefore, all that he performed under it must be a satisfaction for us, Gal. iv. 4, 5. Rom. viii. 3, 4.—Nor did Adam's owing obedience for himself hinder the imputation of it to his posterity as their legal righteousness, if it had been finished. 4. Believers are not bound to fulfil any holiness of nature, or obedience of life, in the manner that Christ fulfilled them, *i. e.* under the curse, and to the broken covenant of works, Rom. viii. 1. vii. 4. vi. 14. Gal. iii. 13. ii. 19. 1 Cor. ix. 21. Nor to purchase eternal life, as he intended by his whole righteousness, Rom. v. 21. vi. 23. But their holiness of nature and life is an important ingredient in their purchased salvation and eternal life, Phil. iii. 8—14. 1 Thess. v. 23.

OF THE PARTICULAR OFFICES OF CHRIST. 291

In Christ's sacrifice, his person God-man was the *priest:* his human nature as subsisting in his divine person, was the *matter offered:* and his divine nature or person was the *altar which sanctified his gift.* Hence he is represented as *giving himself* in sacrifice; for, though his manhood only obeyed and suffered, it did so as personally united to his divine nature, Tit. ii. 14. Gal. i. 4. Mat. xx. 28. Acts xx. 28. Eph. v. 2, 25. 1 Pet. ii. 24. iii. 18. 2 Cor. v. 21. Gal. iii. 13.——To illustrate his satisfaction for our sin, we may consider sin *as a debt,* for which we owe payment to God as our creditor, Mat. vi. 12;—as *an enmity,* rendering us haters of God and hated by him, Col. i. 21. Rom. i. 30. viii. 7. Zech. xi. 8; and *as a crime,* which renders us guilty before him as a judge, Rom. iii. 19. Job ix. 2. Psalm cxxx. 3.——Proper satisfaction must therefore pay our *debt* to the law and justice of God,—remove his indignation from us, and reconcile us to him,—and make full atonement for our guilt in voluntarily bearing all the punishment due to it.——Answerable to which, Christ's righteousness may be considered as a *ransoming price,*—a *reconciling sacrifice,*—and a *satisfying punishment.*—Or, might we say, Christ, as our Surety, pays our infinite debt, by giving his infinitely precious self for us, Mat. xx. 28. 1 Tim. ii. 5, 6;—as our Mediator, he thereby removes the enmity between God and us, Col. i. 20, 21. 2 Cor. v. 19, 21;—and as our Priest and sacrifice for us, he bears the punishment due to our sins, in order to make atonement for them, 1 Pet. ii. 24. iii. 18. Isa. liii. 5, 6, 10, 11, 12. Gal. iii. 13.

It was necessary in order to Christ's making *proper satisfaction* for us sinners, 1. That he should assume our nature, that our sin might be punished in the same nature in which it had been committed, Heb. ii. 14, 16. Psalm xl. 6—8. Heb. x. 5—9. 2. That he should be perfectly holy, owing no satisfaction for his own sin, Heb. vii. 26. 1 Cor. v. 21. 1 Pet. iii. 18. 3. That he should voluntarily consent to make satisfaction for our sin, Heb. x. 9. Psalm xl. 8. Jer. xxx. 21. 4. That he should have sufficient worth and efficacy to make full satisfaction for our sin, and power to raise himself from the dead, that so he might deliver us without ruining himself, Tit. ii. 13, 14. Eph. v. 2. John x. 18. 5. That he should be absolute Lord of his own life, that he might dispose of it as he pleased, Exod. iii. 14. John x. 18.—If these things be supposed, no injury can happen to any, by his satisfaction for us;—none to God, who planned this method of saving men, and whose perfections are highly glorified by means of it, Luke ii. 14. Eph. i. 6. ii. 7;—none to God's holy law, which is hereby magnified and made honourable, Isa. xlii. 21. Mat. v. 17, 18;—none to Christ himself, who willingly undertook this service, and quickly received his glorious reward, Luke xxiv. 26. Phil. ii. 6—11;—none to the world, which lost no person belonging to it by his death,—from which he was quickly raised, Rev. i. 18;—no hurt done by sparing guilty sinners,—they being sanctified, and made a blessing in the earth, Tit. ii. 14. Isa. vi. 13.

Christ's satisfaction to the law and justice of God was ABSOLUTELY NECESSARY for purchasing the salvation of sinful men. 1. This necessity of it no way derogates from the honour of God's perfections. He may be almighty and free, though he *cannot deny himself*, or mark himself like to, and a lover of, the wicked. He may sufficiently manifest his sovereignty in the circumstances, or the immediate subjects of punishment, though he cannot clear the guilty without an adequate satisfaction. It is infinitely to his honour, that he can render no sinners happy, without full atonement for their offences. It manifests, that such is the holiness of his nature, that he can have no fellowship with them, till his holy law and covenant, that original bond of connection between him and them, be fulfilled and magnified by themselves, or by another in their stead. It shews that such is his *equity* of nature, that he cannot acquit even his own beloved and only begotten Son, of sins imputed to him, without full satisfaction for them. It shews that such is his *majesty*, that he cannot suffer any contempt of himself to pass unpunished;—that such is his *wisdom*, that it could and did contrive an infinitely mysterious method of saving men;—that such is his infinite *grace* and *love*, that when it was necessary for our redemption, he, of his own free will, devoted his Son to be a sacrifice for us, Rom. viii. 32. John iii. 16. 1 John iv. 9, 10. 2. It hath already been proved, that avenging justice is essential to God; and that the condition of the broken covenant of works necessarily must be the condition of the covenant of grace, for the redemption of men, Psal. v. 5, 6. xi. 5, 6, 7. cxix. 137. Gen. xviii. 25. Dan. ix. 7. Hab. i. 12, 13. Josh. xxiv. 19. Rom. i. 18, 32. Exod. xx. 5, 7. xxxiv. 7. Rom. ii. 6, 8, 9. vi. 23. 3. The universally-practised attempts of mankind to make atonement for their sins by sacrifices or the like, manifest that their reason suggests the necessity of satisfaction for sin; and that even when they had lost sight of the real design and meaning of sacrifices, which had been suggested by divine revelation, their consciences still insisted for satisfaction to an offended God, Heb. x. 1, 4, 11. Rom. iii. 19, 20. Mic. vi. 6, 7. 4. The Scriptures represent God's giving Christ to be a ransom for us, as an astonishing effect of his love, which it could not be, if he could have saved us by any easier method, without a full satisfaction for sin, John iii. 16. 1 John iv. 9, 10. Rom. v. 8, 21. Eph. v. 2. 2 Cor. viii. 9. 5. The penal sanction of God's law and covenant of works expressly required full satisfaction for sins committed, Gen. ii. 17. Deut. xxvii. 26. Ezek.

xviii. 4. Rom. i. 18, 32. vi. 23. Without shedding of blood there is no remission of sin, Heb. ix. 22. Without an atoning sacrifice nothing is to be expected but a fearful looking for of fiery indignation to devour the guilty, Heb. x. 26--31. Now, though particular threatenings, not confirmed by oath, may be conditional, general ones are never such, Isa. iii. 11. Rom. ii. 8, 9. 6. God could not have exposed his only Son to such extreme debasement and suffering, if it had not been absolutely necessary for the redemption of elect sinners, Lam. iii. 32, 33. Mic. vii. 18, 19. Isa. liii. 10. Rom viii. 32. Heb. ii. 10. Nay, all this was done to manifest his righteousness in the remission of men's sins, Rom. iii. 24—26. 1 John i. 9. And it *became God* to make him a perfect Captain of salvation *through suffering*, Heb. ii. 10.

In vain it is pretended, I. " That God may abate his right in punishing offences against himself, as men may and often do :" for, 1. Men cannot in every case, as in prosecution of murder, give up with their right, Num. xxxv. 31, 32. Now sin is an intended, an attempted murder of God himself. 2. God cannot give up his claim relative to the just punishment of sin, without doing injury to himself, whose honour and majesty are affronted,—injury to his law, which is contemned and violated,—injury to his creatures under his government, which are hurt, or, if capable, would be tempted to, or hardened in sin. II. In vain it is pretended, " That satisfaction for sin cannot consist with the *merciful* forgiving of it :" for, 1. Sins are not money-debts, in which payment from any hand is all that can be required,—but *crimes*, which, in strict law, ought to be punished on the offender himself. 2. God's mercy shines infinitely brighter in his saving men through the blood of his Son, than if he had saved them without any ransom, Tit. iii. 5—7. John iii. 16. Rom. v. 8, 21. iii. 24. 1 John iv. 9, 10, 16, 19. Eph. v. 2, 25. 2 Cor. viii. 9. Gal. ii. 20, 21. 3. God's providing and accepting a satisfaction from his own Son in our stead, is an act of infinite mercy and grace. And as we contribute nothing to his making that satisfaction, or to his Father's accepting it, his remission of our sins, in respect of us, must be as full and free as if no satisfaction had been made, Rom. iii. 24—26. Eph. i. 6—8. ii. 7. III. In vain it hath been pretended, " That God hath forgiven many sins without regard to a satisfaction; that Abel appeased God by his faith; that God pardoned Ahab on account of his repentance, 1 Kings xxi. 29; that, under the Old Testament, he never required any thing but faith and repentance as the conditions of pardon, Deut. xxx. 1—3. Jer. iii. 12—14, 22. xviii. 7, 8. Ezek. xviii. xxxiii. 11, 14. 1 Kings viii. 33—50. Lev. xxvi. 40—45; and that the gospel-covenant, being still more gracious, confers pardon of sin upon men, without any condition at all, Jer. xxxi. 31—34. Heb. viii. 10—12. Mat. xviii. 27, 35. Luke vii. 41—48. Col. ii. 13. Eph. i. 7. iv. 32. Acts v. 31 :"--for, 1. Most of these passages mentioned in the objection relate immediately to God's removal of temporal judgments from the Israelites, which we do not hold to be any necessary satisfaction to his law or justice. 2. When Abel or any other pleased, not *appeased*, God, by faith, it was because they thus presented to him the righteousness of Christ, as fulfilled in their stead, Rom. iii. 24, 25. Gal. ii. 16. Phil iii. 9. 3. The gospel represents Christ as having fully satisfied for our sins, and so can require no satisfaction at all.—Nor doth the dispensation of it require faith and repentance as *proper conditions* of pardon, but as means of receiving and improving that which Christ purchased by his satisfaction, Isa. liii. 6, 8, 11. Heb. x. 14. ix. 12, 13. 1 John ii. 1, 2. John xiv. 6. i. 29. 1 Pet. i. 18, 19. Luke i. 74, 75. Ezek. xvi. 62, 63. xxxvi. 25, 31. 4. According to the new covenant, believers, under both Testaments, receive a free pardon of their sin without any satisfaction made by themselves, but not without one made by Christ; and hence are represented as forgiven or saved freely by grace, and yet as redeemed with a great price, Rom. iii. 24. Eph. i. 7. ii. 8. v. 2, 25. Phil. i. 29. Acts xx. 28. Mat. xx. 28. 1 Cor. vi. 19, 20. Gal. i. 4. ii. 20. iii. 13, 14. Tit. ii. 14. 1 Pet. i. 19. iii. 18. Rev. v. 9. Rom. v. 8, 21. IV. In vain it is pretended, " That if God so loved the world before he gave his Son to obey and suffer for men, there could be no need of his obedience and death to reconcile him to them." —For though God loved that which was his own about his elect, yet he could have no delight in, or fellowship with them, but in the way of destroying their sin, which could not be done without a proper satisfaction made for it. His love could only vent towards them in an honourable manner. Judges may love criminals whom they cannot dismiss unpunished. V. In vain it is pretended, " That, if God could have shortened Christ's sufferings *one* moment, he might have shortened them *two*, &c. &c. till the whole moments, and hence the whole punishment, would be dropped :"—for though the moments or other circumstances of a murderer's execution may be abridged, yet nothing essential to his punishment can lawfully be dispensed with.

 Christ made a TRUE and PROPER satisfaction to the law and justice of God, for the sins of his people. 1. The Scripture represents him as a Surety charged *in law* with our sins, and bearing their punishment from God, Heb. vii. 22. Job ix. 33. Psalm cxix. 122. Isa. liii. 6, 4, 5, 8, 10, 11, 12. John i. 29. 2 Cor. v. 21. 1 Pet. ii. 24. iii. 18. 1 John ii. 1, 2. iv. 9, 10. Rom. iii. 24—26. iv. 25. v. 6—11, 16—21. 2. It represents him as redeeming us by the price or ransom of his obedience and sufferings, Job xxxiii. 24. Isa. liii. 5, 10, 11. Mat. iii. 15. xx. 28. xxvi. 28. 1 Cor. vi. 20. 2 Cor. v. 15, 21. Rom. v. 6, 7, 8. viii. 32, 33, 34. Gal. i. 4. iii. 13, 14. iv. 4, 5. Eph. i. 7. v. 2, 25. Col. i. 14, 20. 1 Thess. v 10. Tit. ii. 14. 1 Pet. i. 18, 19. ii. 24. iii. 18. 1 John ii. 1, 2. Rev. v. 9. John x. 11, 15. And it must be remarked, that HYPER and ANTI in these Greek texts properly mean INSTEAD OF. 3. It ascribes to the obedience and death of Christ as their native and necessary effects, the *purchasing* men, Acts xx. 28. 1 Cor. vi. 20. Tit. ii. 14. Rev. v. 9. Gal. iii. 13. iv. 4, 5.—the *expiating* and *purging away* their sin, Heb. i. 3. ix. 14. x. 22. 1 John i. 7, 9. Rev. i. 5; *atonement* or *propitiation* for sin, Job xxxiii. 24. Rom. iii. 24—26. v. 11. Heb. ii. 17. 1 John i. 7. ii. 2. iv. 10; their *reconciliation* to God, Rom. v. 10. 2 Cor. v. 18—21. Eph. ii. 16. Col. i. 20, 21; their *deliverance* from sin,—from the curse, and from the law as a covenant, Tit. ii. 14. John i. 29. 1 John iii. 5, 8. Eph. i. 7. v. 25. Gal. iii. 13. Rom viii. 1, 2, 33, 34. vii. 4. vi. 14. Gal. iv. 4, 5. ii. 19, 20; their health and peace, Isa. liii. 5. 1 Pet. ii. 24. Mic. v. 5. Eph. ii. 13, 14. 4. It represents his obedience and death as a *sacrifice for sin*, Isa. liii. 10. John i. 29. Rom. iv. 25. iii. 24, 25. Eph v. 2. 1 Cor. v. 7. Heb. ix. 14, 26, 28. vii. 27. viii. 3. x. 1, 12, 14.——Now, it may be observed, that all the sacrifices, especially the sin-offerings, were ceremonial satisfactions in the stead of transgressors, that God might be reconciled to them in a typical manner,—in order to which, the sin of the offenders was emblematically transferred to the unblemished animal, by the laying on of their hands on its head, before it was slain in sacrifice:—and hence the *sin-offerings* and *trespass-offerings* had the very name of SIN, TRESPASS, or GUILT, given to them by the Hebrews, Lev. i.—vii. xvi. Num. vii. xxviii. xxix. Exod. xxix. &c.— All these sacrifices were typical of that of Christ; and hence quickly ceased after his death, Heb. vii. 11—25. x. 4, 5, 14, 18. xiii. 10. 5. In the obedience and death of Christ we find every thing which the broken law could demand *in a satisfaction for sinful men;* and nothing which could be demanded of him for himself. He was *made under the law*, Gal. iv. 4. He was a bond-servant, obedient unto the slavish, the accursed death of the cross, Phil. ii. 7, 8. He fulfilled all righteousness in answer to the demands of the broken law, Matth. iii. 15. v. 17. Heb. v. 8. Dan. ix. 24. John viii. 29. Being *made sin*, having all the sins of his people imputed to him, 2 Cor. v. 21. Isa. liii. 6. 1 Pet. ii. 24.—he was *made a curse*, Gal. iii. 13;—and hence was treated by God and by creatures, as if he had been a remarkable transgressor, Isa. lii. 14. l. 6. xlix. 7. liii. Psal. xxii. 1—21. lxix. 1—20. Rom. viii. 3, 32. Mat. xxvi. xxvii. John xviii. xix. Heb. ii. 10. 6. He was *crucified for us*, in a manner in which none other ever was,

1 Cor. i. 13; and hence must have died *in our stead* in law reckoning: for if he had but died *for our good*, that had been no more than Paul and others have done, or ought to do, in labouring and suffering for the benefit of the church, Col. i. 24. 2 Cor. i. 6. Phil. ii. 17. 2 Tim. ii. 10. iii. 10, 11. iv. 6, 7. 1 John iii. 16. 7. In consequence of his obedience and suffering fulfilled for, and imputed to us, we become righteous before God in law-reckoning, Rom. v. 16—19. viii. 3, 4. 2 Cor. v. 21. Phil. iii. 9. Isa. xlv. 24, 25; and though by nature children of wrath, are legally reconciled to him, Rom. v. 7, 10. 2 Cor. v. 18—21. Col. i. 20, 21. Eph. ii. 2, 11, 14.

To prevent objections, it must be observed, 1. No passages of Scripture relative to men's *bearing their own iniquity*, interfere with God's demand of satisfaction from his innocent and holy Son in our stead. Those in Ezek. xviii. 4—30. xxxiii. 20. Isa. iii. 11. Rom. ii. 8, 9, either relate particularly to the wicked Jews there spoken of, or merely denote the certain ruin of obstinate sinners.—Children have often suffered from God in the punishment of their parents' sin, Exod. xx. 5. 2 Kings x. Psal. cxxxvii. 8, 9. Hos xiii. 16. Isa. xiii. 16. Jer. xlvii. 3. Lev. xxvi. 39. Luke xxiii. 28, 29. Or subjects in the punishment of their rulers, Judges ix. 1 Sam. ii—iv. xiii. xv. xxviii. xxxi. 2 Chron. xiii. xxi. xxviii. 1 Kings xi. 22.——And, if Christ had not suffered as our Surety, having our sins imputed to him, he could never have suffered at all, especially in so tremendous a manner,—being so holy and virtuous in himself. 2. The Scripture never hints, that Christ suffered *only*, or *chiefly*, to confirm his doctrine, procure experience, learn to sympathize with us, leave us an example of finished virtue, and to purchase eternal life for himself,—but to make atonement for sin, which doth not hinder it from answering other subordinate ends. 3. Though Christ's satisfactory obedience and sufferings be not imitable by us, with respect to his end of satisfying God's law and justice, they are an excellent pattern in their matter and manner, being intended for the glory of God and the benefit of men, Eph. v. 2. 1 John ii. 6. 1 Pet. ii. 21. 4. Christ suffered every natural ingredient of the punishment of our sin, though he did not suffer those which merely flow from the curse and its penal effects, as lying on a finite or sinful creature, as dominion of sin and eternity of punishment. And indeed, had he been capable of these, he could never have made any satisfaction. 5. A judge may demand satisfaction for offences, and yet give it himself. And, though Christ indeed equally satisfied all the divine persons, who were all equally offended, yet the Father peculiarly sustained the character of judge, in the work of our redemption. 6. Instead of encouraging men in sin, Christ's satisfaction effectually redeems them from it, Tit. ii. 14. 1 Pet.

i. 18, 19. Mat. i. 21. Rom. vi. 10—12. The application of his righteousness to their conscience effectually delivers them from the strength and dominion of it, Rom. vii. 4. vi. 14. Gal. ii. 19. 1 Cor. xv. 56. The believing views of it most powerfully determine them to hate sin, to love and practise holiness, Rom. vi. 10, 11, 12. 2 Cor. v. 14, 15. Psalm cxix. 32. cxvi. 16. Luke i. 74, 75. Heb. xii. 28. 7. Our gracious obedience and patient suffering are exceedingly profitable in many respects, though they neither satisfy the justice of God nor purchase our eternal happiness, Psalm xix. 11. Isa. iii. 10. 1 Cor. xv. 58. Rev. xiv. 13. iii. 21. xxii. 14.

Christ's obedience and sufferings are a satisfaction so COMPLETE to all the demands of the law and justice of God, and a price so full for our eternal redemption, that nothing can be added to it. 1. Such is the infinite dignity of Christ's person, that his fulfilment of the broken law is sufficient to balance all the debt of all the elect, nay of millions of guilty worlds, Col. ii. 9. Isa. vii. 14. ix. 6. Jer. xxiii. 6. Zech. xiii. 7. Tit. ii. 13, 14. Acts xx. 28. 2. God hath clearly manifested his acceptance of Christ's satisfaction as perfect, in his raising him from the dead, exalting him to his right hand, and making him head over all things to his church, Rom. i. 4. Phil. ii. 6---11. Heb. ii. 8---10. John xvi. 10. Isa. xlii. 21. liii. 10—12. 3. Christ's offering himself but ONCE, manifests the absolute perfection of his satisfaction by it, Heb. vii. 27. ix. 25—28. x. 1—14, 18. Rom. v. 15—19. 2 Cor. v. 21. 1 Pet. iii. 18. 4. Our complete justification by God, our reconciliation to him, and redemption from all evil to perfect and everlasting happiness, which are the immediate effects of Christ's satisfaction, demonstrate the perfection of it, Isa. xlv. 24, 25 Rom. viii. 1, 33. iii. 24. x. 16—21. 2 Cor. v. 21. Col. i. 20, 21, 22, 28. ii 10. 1 John i. 7, 9. Heb. i. 3. ix. 12, 14. x. 10, 14, 18. ii. 10.—Hence it necessarily follows, 1. That in God's acceptance of Christ's righteousness there neither is nor can be any taking *part for the whole*, or any thing instead of that which is of *greater value*, Isa. liii. 4—12. 2 Cor. v. 21. Isa. xlv. 24, 25. 2. That as the best works of believers cannot satisfy for them in the least before God, as their judge, Isa. lxiv. 6. Phil. iii. 8, 9; so the infinite perfection of Christ leaves no possible room for their making any satisfaction, 2 Cor v. 21. Acts xx. 28. Rev. v. 9.

To prevent objections it may be observed, 1. It is absurd to distinguish between the *guilt of the fault* of sin, and the *guilt of punishment*. If Christ's satisfaction therefore remove the chargeableness of our faults upon us in order to punishment, there can remain no obligation to punishment, Rom. viii. 1. Isa. liv. 9. Rev. v. 9. 2. Though elect men continue in a legal state of wrath, till they be spiritually united to Christ, yet the moment of their deliverance being from all eternity fixed in his covenant with his Father, all that they meet with, even under the curse, is managed by him for the introduction of their happiness; and so can be no part of that satisfaction which they owe for their sin. 3. All that believers suffer in their state of union to Jesus Christ, is but fatherly chastisements, proceeding from his Father's love to them, purchased by his righteousness for them, and secured by his new-covenant promises; and so can be no satisfaction to the penalty of the broken covenant of works, Col. i. 24. 1 Pet. iv. 13. 2 Cor. i. 7. Heb. xi. 26, 27. xii. 6, 11. Rev. iii. 19. 2 Tim. i. 8. Psalm cxix. 67, 71, 75. 4. Mercy and truth exercised prevent notorious vices, and the temporal judgments which attend them, or even manifest the persons pardoned by God, Dan. iv. 27. Prov. xvi. 6; but never satisfy for sin, or purchase absolution from God's avenging wrath on account of it, Heb. ix. 22. 1 Thess. i. 10. Acts iv. 12. 5. Believers giving up themselves and services to the honour of God, is never intended as atoning sacrifices for sin, but as grateful oblations for mercies received and secured, Rom. xii. 1. Phil. ii. 17. 2 Tim. iv. 6. Heb. xiii. 15, 16. 1 Pet. ii. 5, 9. Hos. xiv. 2. Psalm lxvi. cxvi. ciii. cxlv. cxlvi.

By this NECESSARY, TRUE, and PERFECT satisfaction of Jesus Christ, 1. The perfections of God are manifested in the brightest and most heart-engaging manner. His infinite wisdom shines in his justly punishing his infinitely holy Son, that guilty sinners might be justified and saved: His unbounded majesty and authority, in having a God-man for his bond-servant:—his inflexible justice, in his not sparing, but condignly punishing his beloved, his only begotten Son, when but charged with the sins of men:—his holiness, in his being wroth with, and casting off his anointed for our sakes:—his faithfulness, in Jehovah himself assuming the likeness of sinful flesh, serving and dying under a curse, rather than one promise or threatening should fail:—his astonishing grace, in God himself, whom we had offended, becoming man, being made under the law,—obedient, poor, reproached, reviled, tempted, and tormented in both soul and body,—sweating great drops of blood, groaning and dying for us sinful worms, his inveterate enemies, Luke ii. 14. 2 Cor. iv. 6. John xii. 27. xiii. 31. 1 John iv. 9, 10. Eph. v. 2. 2. The infinite debt of an elect world was fully paid, and unspeakable and everlasting glory purchased for them,—and for him as their head, Mat. xx. 28. Rev. v. 9. 1 Thess. v. 10. 1 Pet. iii. 18. Isa. liii. 4—12. Phil. ii. 7—11; and he obtained a new right to them, as his *redeemed*, Tit. ii. 14. Acts xx. 28. 1 Pet. i. 19. ii. 9. 1 Cor. vi. 19, 20. 3. This satisfaction being infinitely excellent in itself, fulfilled in a nature common to men, and thus equally suited to every man's case, a sufficient foundation was laid for a general and indefinite invitation of them to receive and rest on it, as their justifying righteousness before God:—and all of them, according to their degree of connection with the elect, receive manifold gifts, offices, or outward accommodations, which otherwise they would not, Isa. lv. 1—7. xxxv. Mat. xxiv. 22. Eph. iv. 11, 12;—though indeed reprobates enjoy these things as *consequents,* rather than as proper *fruits* of the death of Christ with respect to them. 4. A most effectual fountain of gospel holiness was opened. The law of God was therein manifested in its high and unalterable authority, astonishing extent, and infinite holiness, goodness, and equity, Isa. xlii. 21 ; the horrid nature of sin, as an attempt on the life of Jehovah, an actual murder of his Son in our nature, and as a crime, which entails everlasting destruction upon all them that love it—and which only the blood of God can expiate, Zech. xii. 10. John xvi. 9. Heb. x. 29. By this satisfaction applied to men's conscience and heart, the broken law and its curse, which are the strength of sin, are removed, and inward grace conveyed into them, as a permanent vital principle of good works, Gal. iii. 13. 1 Cor. xv. 56.—2 Cor. v. 17, 21. Col. ii. 13. 1 Pet. i. 2, 3.—In this satisfaction, the most complete and engaging pattern of holiness is exhibited, under the most disadvantageous circumstances of poverty, desertion, temptation, reproach, persecution, Phil. ii. 5—8. Eph. v. 2. Mat. xi. 29. 1 Pet. ii. 21, 22. Rom. vi.—In it the most powerful motives of redeeming love, and its blessed effects are manifested, urged, and applied, for animating men to all manner of holiness, Eph. v. 2. 2 Cor. v. 14, 15. 1 John iv. 9, 10, 19. Psalm cxvi. 16. cxix. 32. Luke i. 74, 75. Heb. xii. 28. 5. Satan and his works are effectually ruined, Heb. ii. 14. 1 John iii. 5, 8. Gen. iii. 15. Col. ii. 14, 15. Dan. ix. 24.

In respect of its intrinsic worth, as the obedience and sufferings of a divine person, Christ's satisfaction is sufficient for the ransom of all mankind, and being fulfilled in human nature, is equally suited to all their necessities. But in respect of his and his Father's intention, it was paid and accepted instead of the elect, and to purchase their eternal happiness. 1. Christ died for those only for whom he undertook, as SURETY, in the covenant of grace, in order to obtain their eternal salvation, Heb. vii. 22. Isa. liii. 6, 8. 2 Cor. v. 21. 1 Pet. iii. 18. Rom. viii. 3, 4. x. 4. Tit. ii. 14. Now they are his *seed,* whom his Father loved and gave unto him out of the world, John xvii. 6, 9, 14, 23; whom he shall see in happiness with pleasure, and who shall be justified and glory in him, Isa. liii. 10, 11. xlv. 24, 25; and who shall experience his quickening virtue in their souls, bear his image, serve him, and become heavenly men, 1 Cor. xv. 45, 49. Psalm xxii. 30, 31. 2. Those men for whom Christ died are, in Scripture, represented as *many*, Mat. xx. 28. xvi. xxii. 14;—as his *elect*, who cannot be condemned, nor separated from the love of God, Rom. viii. 32—39; his *church* and *body*, Acts xx. 28. Eph v. 23, 25;—his *sheep*, who shall infallibly enjoy eternal life, John x. 10, 15, 16, 27—29;—his *people*, who are sanctified and saved, Heb. xiii. 12. Mat. i. 21;—his *friends*, who are reconciled to God, John xv. 13. Rom. v. 10. Col. i. 20, 21;—his *children*, for whom he prays, John xvii. xi. 52. xvii. 9. Isa. liii. 10; and brings to glory, Heb. ii. 9, 10; and whom he calls brethren, and sanctifies, Heb. ii. 9, 11—16. 3. His obedience and sufferings are never represented as intended for putting men into any *salvable* state,—or procuring power and liberty for God, to enter upon lower terms of salvation with them; —but as intended for actually saving them from sin and misery, —redeeming them from an evil world,—and bringing them to eternal happiness with God, Mat. xviii. 11. Luke xix. 10. 1 Tim. i. 15. Mat. i. 21. 1 John iv. 9. Heb. ix 15, 16. Eph. i. 7. v. 23 —27. Tit. ii. 14. Rom. xi. 26. John xvii. 19. x. 10. Gal. iv. 4 —6. iii. 13, 14. i. 14. vi. 4. 2 Cor. v. 21. Heb. ii. 9, 10, 14, 15. 1 Pet. iii. 18. And all these ends are represented as actually obtained by them, Heb. i. 3. ix. 12, 14. 1 Pet. i. 18, 19. ii. 24. Dan. ix. 24. Gal. iii. 13. Col. i. 20—22. Eph. ii. 13—16. Acts xx. 28. Rom. v. 8—11, 16—21. vi. 6. viii. 32—34. Isa. xlv. 24, 25. liv. 17. lxi. 10. 2 Cor. v. 15. 1 Cor. i. 30. xi. 10, 11, 19, 20. Phil. i. 29. Rev. i. 5, 6. v. 9, 10. John vi. 33. x. 15, 28, 29. 2 Tim. i. 10. ii. 10. Heb. x. 14. 1 Pet. i. 2—4. 4. Satisfaction to the law and justice of God is of such a nature, that all supposition of God's again demanding any part of it, from any for whom Christ obeyed and suffered, chargeth the most shocking injustice on God, Isa. liii. 4—12. 2 Cor. v. 21. Gal. iii. 13; especially as he satisfied for ALL their sins, 1 John i. 7, 9. ii. 7. Isa. liii. 6, 4, 5, 8, 10. Lev. xvi. 21. Dan. ix. 24. Eph. i. 2. Acts xiii. 38, 39. 1 Pet. ii. 24:—so that neither unbelief, nor any thing else can condemn a soul united to him, Rom. viii. 1, 33, 34. 5. The Scripture represents Christ's death not merely as a sacrifice to make atonement for sin, but also as a *meritorious price* of inestimable benefits, Isa. liii. 5, 10. Acts xx. 28. Mat. xx. 28. xxvi. 28. And our pardon of sin, reconciliation with God, acceptance into his favour,—freedom from the power and pollution of sin, sanctification of nature and life, victory over devils and death,—resurrection to, and possession of eternal happiness, are represented as its inseparable attendants and just reward, Rom. v. 10. Eph. i. 7. Rom. iii. 24. Heb. ii. 14, 15. Rom. vi. 10, 11, 14. Isa. xxv. 8. Rev. v. 9, 10. 1 Thess. v. 10. 1 Pet. iii. 18. A righteous God cannot therefore deprive any person, for whom they were purchased, of any of these benefits, Gen xviii. 25. Deut. xxxii. 4. 1 John i. 9. Rom. iii. 26. 6. Christ's satisfaction is represented as equally, or more effectually justifying and saving those for whom it was made, than Adam's disobedience was to condemn them. But this it could not be, unless every person for whom it was given were made truly righteous in it before God, and to reign eternally in happiness, even as every person whom Adam represented is made a sinner, and heir of death and wrath through his disobedience, Rom. v. 12—21. 1 Cor. xv. 22. 7. It is manifest that Christ, in his intercession, prays only for his elect, John xvii. 9.—Now, his intercession, in respect of its objects, is of the same extent with his atonement, 1 John ii. 1, 2. Nor will common sense allow, that he would lay down his life for any person for whom he would not intercede. 8. The Scripture alway represents the death of Christ for, or instead of men, as an astonishing evidence of his and his Father's love to them, John xv. 13. Eph. v. 2. 2 Cor. viii. 9. Gal. ii. 20. Rom. v. 6—8. viii. 32. 1 John iv. 9, 10, 16, 19. John iii 16. But it could not be so, if the most of those for whom he died were never a whit the better of it, nay, never informed of his death, till by means of the despisers of him, in hell. 9. The tenet of Christ's dying equally for all men, or for any that are not elected and actually saved, is pregnant with the most glaring absurdities, viz. That as but few of mankind, comparatively taken, are actually saved, God hath in a great measure lost his end, in his principal work of men's redemption;—that either, through want of wisdom, he hath laid his plan extremely ill, or, through want of wisdom, power, or mercy, he is unable to execute it in opposition to the corrupt inclinations of men;—that multitudes of wicked men, for whom he put his Son to death, must be much more wise and powerful than himself; so that he cannot make them willing in the day of his power, or keep them through faith unto salvation;—that Christ, to no good purpose, threw away his infinitely precious life for the most of mankind, who are never saved;—that he threw it away for millions who, at that very time, were in hell, beyond the reach of all mercy,—for millions whom he never informs of it, or of the salvation thereby purchased,—and never calls to believe on him any more than if they were devils, Job xviii. xx. Psalm ix. 17. 2 Pet. ii. 5, 6. Jude 7. Psalm cxlvii. 19, 20. Rom. x. 14—17;—nay, for millions whom he forbade his ministers to call to faith and gospel-repentance, Mat. x. 5. Acts xvi. 6, 7;—and so, who are left without all hopes of redemption, Acts iv. 12. Eph. ii. 12. 2 John 9. Prov. xxix. 18.——To pretend that Christ died for men upon condition of their truly believing and repenting of their sins, which are not only infinitely above, but contrary to their corrupted natural powers, is to represent God as insulting the misery and weakness of men,---and sporting with the death of his Son, in suspending the whole efficacy and good fruits of it upon an infinitely improbable, nay impossible condition.

OBJEC. I. " Christ is represented as the Saviour of ALL MEN, " ---and to have died for ALL. God wills ALL men to be sav-" ed: and ALL that were condemned and died in Adam, are jus-" tified and live through Christ, 1 Tim. iv. 10. ii. 4, 6. 2 Cor. " v. 14, 15. Heb. ii. 9. 2 Pet. iii. 9. Rom. v. 18, 19. 1 Cor. xv. " 22." ANSW. 1. The terms ALL and EVERY, used in Scripture, often denote but a *great many*,---or *of all sorts.* Hence it is said, that ALL Judea went out to John's baptism, and ALL men held him as a prophet, Mat. iii. 5, 6. xxi. 26;---that ALL men came to Jesus, John iii. 26;---while it is certain that multitudes of men, and even of Jews, contemned both John and Jesus, Mat. xi. 18, 19. Luke vii. 30.---It is said, that ALL the cattle in the land of Egypt died, when none but such as were left in the field died, Exod. ix. 6, 3, 19;---that the hail smote EVERY herb, and brake EVERY tree,---while many herbs and trees remained to be afterwards destroyed by the locusts, Exod. ix. 23. x. 15;---that ALL the Israelites gave their ear-rings for making the golden calf, when none but such as had gold ear-rings, and consented to that idolatry, did so, Exod. xxxii. 3, 26. 1 Cor. x. 7;---that ALL the people of Judea were carried captive to Babylon with Jehoiachin, when no more but his queen, princes, warriors, eunuchs, artisans, and a few others, were then carried captive, and multitudes afterwards remained under the government of Zedekiah, 2 Kings xxiv. 14, 15. xxv.---that ALL nations served Nebuchadnezzar, and his son, and grandson; that the sight of him extended to ALL the earth; that ALL flesh was fed by him, when but a few nations within about five or six hundred miles of Babylon submitted to, or depended on him, Jer. xxvii. 7. xxv. 18---26. Dan. iv. 11, 12;---that ALL the beasts of the nations lodged in the ruins of Nineveh, when no more than many of different kinds did so, Zeph. ii. 14;---that ALL lands were plagued with famine in the days of Joseph, and heard of the fame of David and Solomon;---that Ahab sought for Elijah in ALL lands, when no more but a few countries adjacent to Egypt and Canaan are meant, Gen. xli. 17. 1 Chron. xiv. 17. 1 Kings iv. 31. xviii. 10;---that people from EVERY nation under heaven attended Peter's sermon at Pentecost, when none but of about thirteen nations, not far from Judea, were present, Acts ii. 5---11;---that the man cured of blindness saw EVERY man clearly, when none are meant but such as were near to, and looked at by him, Mark viii. 25;---that Paul became a servant, and ALL things to ALL men, when no more than all sorts of men, Jews and Gentiles, bond and free, &c. and all lawful condescensions are meant, 1 Cor. ix. 19---22;---that the flesh of ALL men is given to the beasts, when none but antichristian men are meant, Rev. xix. 19.—— Sometimes the signification of ALL and EVERY is limited by the nature or condition of the thing which is spoken of. Servants are to obey their masters, and children their parents, in ALL things, *i. e.* all things lawful, Tit. ii. 9. Col. iii. 22, 20. The Lord upholdeth ALL that fall, and raiseth ALL that are bowed down, *i. e.* such as trust in him, or are upheld and delivered, Psalm cxlv. 14. Aswerably to these manifold plain limitations of the terms ALL and EVERY, we readily grant that Christ died for MANY men; that he died for men *of all sorts and ranks*, high and low, rich and poor, bond and free, Jews and Gentiles,—and that he died for all that believe on, and are saved by him. But what is that to his dying in the room of all men as their Surety and Representative? 2. Not one text quoted in the Objection proves that Christ died in the law-room of all mankind. It is not said in 1 Tim. iv. 10, that Christ, but that the living God is the *Saviour of all men*, delivering them from manifold troubles and dangers. Nay, Christ, not as Surety, but as Administrator of the new covenant, is the *official Saviour* of all men, to whom they have all full warrant to apply for eternal salvation, 1 John iv. 14. John iv. 42.—In the four next texts ALL and EVERY must be limited agreeably to the context,—to all sorts or ranks of men, 1 Tim. ii. 4, 6, 1, 2;—to the children who are *sanctified* and *brought to glory*, Heb. ii. 9, 10, 11, 13;—to those that are made *new creatures*, and the *righteousness of God*, 2 Cor. v. 14, 15, 17, 21;—to those that are *elect according to the foreknowledge of God*,—that obtain *precious faith*, and are *healed*, 2 Pet. iii. 9. i. 1. 1 Pet. i. 2. Isa. liii. 6, 5. Rom. viii. 32, 33. Moreover, it is certain, that though God, by his law, commands all devils, as well as men, to be perfectly holy, and if they were so, they would be perfectly happy, 1 Pet. ii. 16. Mat. xxii. 37, 39, yet he never intended to render them all either holy or happy. And many men have little more opportunity of gospel-repentance or knowledge than devils have, Eph. ii. 12. Psalm cxlvii. 19, 20. Prov. xxix. 18.——The two last texts in the Objection do but prove, that all Christ's spiritual seed, whom he represented, shall have justification and life through him, even as Adam's natural seed, whom he represented, have sin and death entailed upon them through him; and in the first the comparison is not so much stated between the objects of sin and death, or of righteousness and life, as intended to demonstrate that Christ's righteousness hath much more efficacy to save men, than Adam's sin hath to destroy them, Rom. v. 18, 19. 1 Cor. xv. 22.

OBJEC. II. " Christ died for the WORLD,—ALL the WORLD, " the WHOLE WORLD, John iii. 16, 17. i. 9, 29. iv. 42. vi. 51. " 2 Cor. v. 19. 1 John ii. 2. iv. 14." ANSW. 1. Most, if not all of these texts, might as properly have been produced to prove that all men are actually saved. And indeed, if men will insist that Christ laid down his life for ALL men, they ought, if they want to be consistent with themselves, to hold that not a single soul of mankind is or can be damned, there being as good proof from Scripture for the last as for the first; compare Joel ii. 28. John xvi. 9. Psalm xxii. 27. lxxii. 17. John xii. 32. Luke xvi. 16. Col. i. 28. 1 Cor. iv. 5. And why not also prove from Eph. i. 10. Col. i. 20, that ALL the devils are *reconciled* to God by the death of Christ? 2. If the word WORLD, ALL the WORLD, WHOLE WORLD, be taken in its utmost latitude of meaning, it must include ALL devils as well as ALL men. 3. When WORLD in Scripture means *persons*, it sometimes denotes the Roman Empire and its subjects, Acts xi. 28. Rom. i. 8. Acts xvii. 6. Luke ii. 1; or the Gentiles as distinguished from the Jews, Rom. xi. 12, 13; or even but a small part of the Jews, John xii. 19; or the wicked men of the world, 1 John iv. 4, 5. v. 19. John xv. 18, 19. vii. 7. 1 Cor. ii. 12; or the papists, Rev. xiii. 3, 8, 16. 4. Christ is the *official Saviour* of all men in this world, suited to their necessities, and to whom each of them may warrantably apply, 1 John iv. 14. 5. In some of the texts mentioned in the Objection, *world* may denote the Gentiles chosen in Christ as distinguished from the Jews, John iv. 42. 1 John ii. 2. iv. 14. In others it may denote the elect in general, who are the substance and better part of the world, Isa. vi. 13; and who, under the gospel, are chiefly gathered from among the Gentiles,—and it is limited by the context, to such as are enlightened and have their sins taken away, John i. 9, 29;—are loved of God, and not condemned, but saved, John iii. 16, 17;—are made partakers of eternal life, John vi. 51, 54;—have their trespasses not imputed to them, but are made the righteousness of God in Christ, 1 Cor. v. 19, 21.

OBJEC. III. " Christ died for many of those that eter-" nally perish, Rom. xiv. 15. 1 Cor. viii. 10, 11. 2 Pet. ii. 1. " Heb. x. 29." ANSW. The two first-mentioned texts do not respect men's everlasting destruction in hell, but their hurt, grief, trouble, or stumbling in this life. That of Peter relates not to spiritual or eternal redemption, but to deliverance from heathen ignorance and idolatry, and bestowing of common gifts, as Deut. xxxii. 6. Nor is it certain that Christ is the Lord there spoken of, or that he is called by the name DESPOTES, there used, in all the New Testament.—In Heb. x. 29, not the wicked man there spoken of, but Christ himself is said to be *sanctified* by the blood of the covenant; compare John xvii. 19. Heb. ii. 10.——Besides, men may be apparently *bought* or *sanctified* with Christ's blood, though it had never been intentionally shed for their eternal redemption.

Objec. IV. "If Christ did not die for ALL MEN, none but "elect men could be under any obligation to believe the gos- "pel. None could be exhorted to believe on him, as they "could not be sure that he had died for them; nor could "they be blamed for their impenitence and unbelief, as they "could not know that Christ had died for them, in order to "save them." Answ. 1. Men's obligation to believe on Christ, as offered in the gospel, is not founded upon any secret intentions of God, but upon his openly manifested offers of salvation in the gospel, and his plain command to receive that which he offers, Deut. xxix. 29. Isa. xlv. 22—25. lv. 1—7. Rev. xxii. 17. Matth. xi. 28. John iii. 16, 17. Acts ii. 38, 39. iii. 26. xvi. 31. 1 John iii. 23. v. 10—12. John vi. 27—29. 2. No man is called, at first hand, to believe that Christ, as his Surety, intentionally died for him in particular; but is called to believe his own unspeakable need of him, his fulness and ability to save him; that God hath, by a deed of gift, constituted and offered Christ to sinful men in general, as such, and therefore to him in particular, as an all-sufficient Saviour; —that there is an infallible connection between faith and eternal salvation; that such as come to Christ believing his gospel offers, shall in no wise be cast out; that the invitations of the gospel are directed to him as plainly and particularly as to any other, and ought to be credited and embraced without any inquiry into the intended extent of Christ's death: and therefore to credit and embrace them accordingly.——Nor can elect men know any thing of God's kind intentions towards them; but in believing his gracious promises, and feeling his gracious influences on their soul, 2 Pet. i. 4, 10. 1 Thess. i. 4, 5. Gal. ii. 19, 20. Rom. viii. 28—30. 3. The law of nature would have prohibited and condemned men for all their sinful impenitence, though no Saviour had ever been provided.——Gospel hearers will not be condemned for their not believing untruths or uncertainties, but for not believing that which is plainly declared and offered in the gospel. 4. If, as our opponents must grant, heathens be not condemned for not believing on Christ, of whom they have not heard, Rom x. 17, it must be the *revelation* of him in the gospel, not his intention in dying for all men, that is the immediate ground of our faith.

Objec. V. "Even gospel hearers have not sufficient means "of salvation, unless they be certainly informed that Christ "died for them, before they believe in him." Answ. 1. It is then hoped, that our opponents will no more pretend that heathens, who never hear of Christ's death, have sufficient means of salvation. 2. Gospel revelations and ordinances become unprofitable, not from their insufficiency, but through men's neglect or misimprovement of them. 3. God is no more obliged to render the gospel effectual to all them that hear it, than to bestow it upon all them that want it. 4. Men are and will be condemned, not so properly for what they cannot do or attain, as for what they are and do, in approving their own want of true holiness, John v. 40. Zech vii. 11, 12.

OBJEC. VI. " The doctrine of Christ's dying for some, not " for all men, reflects mightily upon the love, goodness, and " mercy of God, as if, though Christ's death might have " equally availed to redeem *all mankind*, he had by his inten- " tion unkindly limited its efficacy to a *few*." ANSW. 1. Christ's death was not intended in the room of a few, but for innumerable multitudes, perhaps thousands of millions of mankind, Rev. vii. 9. xxi. 24. 2. Who dare reply against God, who is bound to shew mercy to no sinner, but hath mercy on whom he will have mercy, and whom he will he hardeneth? Exod. xxxiii. 19. Rom. ix. 16—23. 3. God had no more reason, without himself, to have mercy on all men, than upon all devils;—for not one of whom it can be pretended that Christ died, Heb. ii. 16. Jude 6. 4. If, notwithstanding Christ's dying for them, most or all of mankind may go to hell; most of them never hear of his death for them, nor receive the Holy Ghost to make them apply it to themselves, where could there be any mercy or love in his so dying for them?—Where could there be either mercy or wisdom in dying for them all, on condition that their deceitful and desperately wicked heart should convert itself, and believe, and repent? What distinguished mercy and love could there be in his doing no more for them who are saved, than for those who are eternally damned—and no more than he did for thousands of millions that were in hell at the time of his death, beyond all reach of mercy, and many more, who, he foresaw, would never be a whit better of his death, as to their spiritual concerns.——How infinitely greater the mercy, in his unconditional dying for many millions, so as to render their eternal salvation absolutely certain!

OBJEC. VII. " The doctrine of Christ's dying uncondition- " ally, in the room of some men only, is *destructive* of all *piety* " and *virtue*,—of all *prayer* and *thanksgiving* for *all men*,— " and of all solid comfort to awakened consciences. But that " of his dying equally for all men, mightily encourages to " these, and all other holy duties: it represents Christ and his " Father as infinitely amiable and engaging patterns of bene-

" volence,—gives inconceivable energy to all the gospel-calls
" to faith and repentance,—and comforts the most notorious
" sinners with grounds of hope, if they repent." Answ. 1.
The friends of particular redemption are willing to risk a comparison in piety and virtue, in prayer and thanksgiving for all men, and in every thing else becoming the gospel, with their opponents, whenever they will, if the law of God be allowed to be the standard of judgment. 2. Particular redemption requires prayer to be made for all sorts of men, nay, for all men, living, or that shall live hereafter, unless one were certainly known to have committed the unpardonable sin against the Holy Ghost,—with submission to the will of God, 1 Tim. ii. 1, 2. 1 John v. 14, 16. Thanksgiving is to be made only for what good things men have received, have a right to, or ground to hope for. It is infinitely greater ground of thanksgiving that thousands of millions are certainly and unconditionally redeemed to everlasting life, and shall, without fail, enjoy it, than if men by the conditional death of Christ for them all, had only an infinitely improbable chance of happiness, if their corrupt free will behaved aright. The choicest saint, according to our opponents, hath no more certainty of obtaining heaven, than we allow to the most profligate wretch that ever lived. Nor have saints in heaven any more ground of thanksgiving than the damned in hell, as Christ died equally for them all. And the Spirit may have exerted himself equally for their welfare. 3. Particular redemption represents God as loving men, even his enemies, effectually, and for ever;—a pattern of the most exalted benevolence. But, where is his engaging pattern of benevolence, if he only do that for us which can avail us nothing, unless we perform the infinitely impossible condition of self-regeneration and perseverance in holiness, by the power of our own carnal mind, which is enmity against God? Besides, the death of Christ being only known to a small part of mankind, it cannot be in it, but in his common providence, that all men can discern him as an universal pattern of benevolence, Matth. v. 45. Psalm cxlv. 9. 4. If an Arminian preacher would candidly tell his audience, " Christ died for ALL men; but he and his Father are altogether careless, or incapable to gain their end of saving men by this means: They seldom inform the hundredth part of mankind of it: The far greater part of those for whom he died, are eternally damned: God himself cannot help it, unless their free will conduct itself aright. Nay, though with power superior to omnipotence itself, you should, under the curse of God's law, and under the dominion of your inward enmity against him, repent, believe, and long persevere in perfect holiness, yet a wrong movement of your free will in your last

moment, may certainly plunge you into everlasting misery." What encouraging energy would this add to the calls and promises of the gospel?— But the preacher of particular redemption, upon God's authority assures his audience, " That Jesus Christ and all his full and everlasting salvation are freely and earnestly offered by God to them; that, in their earnestly attempting to believe, they may expect that he will grant them true faith as his free gift, by the very first act of which, however weak, they will be irrevocably interested in him and his eternal salvation," Isa. xlv. 22, 17, 24, 25. 5. It can be small comfort to troubled souls to hear, " That Christ died no otherwise for them, than for Judas and millions who were in hell before his death; and that they must certainly be damned, unless their own wicked heart convert itself, and persevere in true holiness and virtue till their death." But by the full and free offers of Jesus Christ and his salvation, which includes regeneration and faith,—true comfort and relief are administered, Isa. lv. 1—7. i. 18. xlv. 22. xlvi. 12, 13. Prov. i. 22, 23. ix. 4, 5. xxiii. 26. Matth. xi. 28. John vi. 37, 44, 45, 63. vii. 37, 38. 2 Cor. v. 19, 20. Heb. vii. 25. Rom. viii. 1, 2, 32—39.

CHRIST'S INTERCESSION, the other part of his priestly work, doth not properly include his human sympathy towards his countrymen, Luke xix. 41, 42; nor perhaps in part, his prayer for his murderers, Luke xxiii. 34.—It is represented as an ASKING, PRAYING, pleading as an *advocate*, and offering up INCENSE for us, Psalm ii. 8. John xiv. 16. xvii. 9. Heb. ix. 24. vii. 25. Rom. viii. 34. 1 John ii. 1. Rev. viii. 3, 4. He doth not ask any thing for himself, but as it tends to his people's advantage, John xvii. He intercedes for *his elect only*, John xvii. 9. 1 John ii. 1. Rev. viii. 3, 4; and for each of them and all their cases, John xvii. 9—24. Heb. vii. 25. Luke xxii. 31, 32. Rev. viii. 3, 4.—The accusations of Satan, Rev. xii. 10. Zech. iii. 1; —the multitude of our sins and wants, 1 John ii. 1;—and our own unworthiness and unfitness for immediate appearance before God, or to order our cause before him, render Christ's intercession *absolutely necessary.*—Its being represented as a pleading in the *sanctuary*, Heb. ix. 24, 25;—as an offering of *incense* on the *golden altar*, Rev. viii. 3, 4; and a pleading upon his *propitiatory* sacrifice, 1 John ii. 1, 2; prove that it belongs to his priesthood.—Nor is his godhead any more inconsistent with his intercession, than it is with his offering himself in sacrifice,—or than his manhood is with his high royalty.—Nay, before he assumed his manhood, he, though not in his present manner, interceded for his people, Zech. i. 12; and perhaps Job xxxiii. 24.—In his complete person, God-man, he will continue to intercede for ever, Psalm cx. 4. Heb. vii. 24, 25.

Christ's intercession, in its *present form*, consists in, 1. His presenting himself before God, in our nature, and in the merit of his finished atonement, as the ground of his bestowing upon elect men all the blessings which they need, according to the covenant of grace, Heb. ix. 24. 2. His intimation of his will in thought, if not sometimes in words, that his purchased blessings may be applied to them according to their need and the new covenant-settlement, John xvii Luke xxii. 31, 32. Zech. i. 12. Rev. viii. 3, 4. 3. His answering all accusations laid against them by Satan, the world, or their own conscience, —refuting that which is false, and pleading forgiveness of every thing justly charged, on account of his own completed atonement, 1 John 1, 2. Zech. iii. 1—3. 4. His presenting all their worship and service performed in faith to God, and rendering it acceptable through his own righteousness, Rev. viii. 3, 4. 1 Pet. ii. 5.

The dignity of Christ's person, the merit of his sacrifice, and the wisdom and fervour of his requests, rendering them *alway prevalent*, John xi. 42. xvii. 24. Rom. viii. 34. Heb. vii. 25, they procure for his elect every blessing of the new covenant, in its proper order and time;—for the unconverted, the gift of the Spirit, regeneration, justification, adoption, John x. 16. xvii. 20. Psalm ii. 8;—for believers' growth and perseverance in grace, peace of conscience, and access with boldness to God's throne of grace, and at last eternal glory,—notwithstanding their daily failings, 1 John ii. 1. John xiv. 13, 14. xvii. 17. Heb. iv. 16. vi. 19, 20. John xvii. 24.—And, by his intercession, he effectually counteracts Satan and all his instruments, Luke xxii. 31, 32. Zech. iii. 1—3. i. 12.

III. Besides that natural supremacy and dominion over all things equally with his Father and the Holy Ghost,—Christ hath also a *mediatorial dominion*, or kingdom, which, 1. Was given him by his Father as the *reward* of his offering himself in sacrifice, Psalm ii. 8. Mat. xxviii. 18. Phil. ii. 6—11. Isa. liii. 10—12. lii. 13, 14. 1 Pet. i. 21. Luke xxii. 29. Dan. vii. 14. 2. Belongs to him as God-man, Isa. ix. 6, 7. John v. 22—27. 3. Which chiefly respects his church, and is administered for promoting the eternal salvation of her true members, Eph. iv. 11—14.——1. Multitudes of scriptures ascribe *lordship* and *dominion* to him, Gen. xlix. 10. 1 Sam. ii. 10. 2 Sam. vii. 16. Psalm ii. xxi. xlv. lxxii. lxxxix. xcvi.—c. cx. cxxxii. xlvii. cxlv.—cxlix. xxii. 27—31. lxviii. 17—35. xxiv. 7—10. cxviii. 22. Isa. ix. 6, 7. xi. 4, 5. xxxii. 1, 2. Jer. xxiii. 5, 6. xxxiii. 15, 16. xxx. 21. Ezek. xvii. 22, 23. xxi. 26, 27. xxxiv. 23, 24, 29. xxxvii. 24, 25. xliii. 3. xlvi. 10. Dan. ii. 44, 45. vii.

13, 14. ix. 25. xii. 1. Hos. iii. 5. xiii. 9, 10. Mic. v. 1—6. ii.
13. Zech. vi. 9—13. ix. 9, 10. Mat. ii. 2. xxv. 34, 41. xxviii.
18 John i. 49. xviii. 36, 37. 1 Tim. i. 17. And, even on his
cross, his kingly power was marked in three different langnages,
John xix. 19.——2. Many *kingly titles* are ascribed to him,—
as a made Lord, Acts ii. 36. 1 Cor. viii. 6. Eph. iv. 5; Prince
of life, Acts iii. 15; King of saints, King of kings, and Lord of
lords, Rev. xv. 3. xvii. 14. xix. 16; Head of the church, Eph.
iv 15, 16. v. 23. i. 22. Hos. i. 11. Col. i. 18. ii. 19; the Foundation, 1 Cor. iii. 11. Isa. xxviii. 16. Eph. ii. 20—22; chief corner Stone, Psalm cxviii. 22. Zech. x. 4. Eph. ii. 20; Ruler,
Judge, Leader, Commander, 2 Sam. xxiii. 3. Mic. v. 1, 2. Isa.
xxxiii. 22. lv. 4; Captain of the Lord's host, and of salvation,
Josh. v. 13. Heb. ii. 10; Shepherd, Ezek. xxxiv. 23. Isa. xl.
11, 12. 1 Pet. ii. 25. v. 4. Heb. xiii. 20. 3. Many *symbols of
kingly power* are attributed to him,—as royal unction, Psalm
xlv. 7. ii. 1—3. lxxxix. 19, 20;—royal inauguration commenced
in God's eternal purpose, Psalm ii. 6---9; intimated by angels
at his conception and birth, Luke i. 31---33. ii. 10, 11; and acknowledged by himself and others at his death, John xviii.
33---37. xix. 12---19. Mat. xxvi. 64. Luke xxiii. 42, 43;—solemn investiture with royalty in his resurrection, ascension, and
sitting down at his Father's right hand, Mat. xxviii. 18. Acts
ii. 36. 1 Pet. iii. 22. Eph. i. 20---22. Phil. ii. 9---11;—royal
coronation by his enemies, Mat. xxvii. 29. John xix. 2, 3; by
his church, Song iii. 11; and by his Father, Heb. ii. 9. Phil.
ii. 9---11. Psalm xxi. 3;---a royal throne, Psalm cx. 1, 5. xlv.
6. Heb. i. 5. viii. 1. Rev. iii. 21. Mat. xix 28. xxvi. 64; a
royal sceptre, by which he gathers and governs his people, Heb.
i. 8. Psalm xlv. 6. cx. 2; and destroys his implacable enemies,
Psalm ii. 9. Rev. ii. 27. xix. 15; royal laws, Isa. ii. 3. Rom. iii.
27. 1 Cor. ix 21. Mat. xi. 29, 30. Gal. vi. 2. Prov. viii. 15;---
royal servants or ambassadors, 2 Cor. v. 20. iii. 6. 1 Cor. iv.
1, 2;---royal guards or attendants, Zech. xiv. 5. Hab. iii. 3---7.
Deut. xxxiii. 2. Jude 14. Mat. iv. 11. xxvi. 53. Dan. vii. 10.
Psalm lxviii. 17. xlvii. 5, 6. Mat. xiii. 41, 49. xxv. 31; royal
revenues, Psalm xcvi. 8. xlv. 11;—royal magazines of spiritual
armour, Eph. vi. 10—19;—royal power to judge, acquit, or
condemn, John v. 22. Mark ii. 5—11. Mat. xxv. 31---46.
4. He was *prefigured* in his kingly office by Melchizedek, king
of Salem, Heb. vii. 1---24; Moses, king in Jeshurun, Heb. iii.
Joshua the conqueror of Canaan, David and Solomon, kings of
Israel, and by all the kings of Judah, Jer. xxx. 9, 20. Song
iii. 6---11. Mat. xii. 42.

Christ's mediatorial kingdom is, I. Very *extensive*, reaching
to all creatures, either as conquered enemies, ministers, and instruments of government, or faithful subjects, Mat. xxviii. 18.
Acts x. 36. Psalm cx. 1, 2, 3, 5, 6. viii. 6---8. Heb. i. 14. Eph

iv. 11, 12. 1 Cor. vi. 11. Tit. iii. 5---7. Eph. v. 25---27, 30; to persons of all ages, nations, and conditions, Psalm ii. 8. lxxiii. 10---14. xxii. 27, 28. Gal. iii. 28. Col. iii. 11; and to both body and soul, Phil. ii. 10, 11.---But, though Christ, as Mediator, hath a power to influence the management of all things in heaven and earth for the benefit of his church, Eph. i. 22. John xvii. 2. Mat. xxviii. 18. Prov. viii. 15, 16. 2 Sam. viii. 15, he is not, as Mediator, the moral governor of men, who are without his visible church. 1. The Scripture never represents him as mediatorial moral governor of heathens, but as King of Zion, Zech. ix. 9. Psalm ii. 6; of the house of Jacob, Luke i. 33; of his own house, Heb. iii. 6. His kingdom can have multitudes added to it, Psalm cx. 2, 3. Rev. xi. 15. Obad. 21. Men are not naturally members of his kingdom, but graciously brought into it, Col. i. 13. 2. We find no mediatorial laws without his church, Rom. ii. 14. Eph. ii. 12. Isa. ii. 3; nor any proclamations of his mediatorial authority, Isa. lxiii. 19. Psalm cxlvii. 19, 20. 3. Christ being alway *undivided*, he cannot be the mediatorial governor of Heathens' morals, till he be first their mediatorial prophet or teacher, Psalm cxlvii. 19, 20. Eph. ii. 12. Acts xiv. 16. xvii. 30. 4. Christ cannot be the mediatorial moral governor of Heathens without their being under a dispensation of the covenant of grace, and having the means of their eternal salvation, which it is certain they have not, Eph. ii. 12. Prov. xxix. 18. 2 John 9. II. Christ's mediatorial kingdom is of a SPIRITUAL nature, Luke xvii. 20, 21. John xviii. 36. And hence, in its New Testament form, it is called the *kingdom of heaven*, or *of God*, to mark that its original, form, administration, privileges, and tendency are heavenly and divine, Mat. iii. 2. iv. 17. xxii. xxv. 1. In its more glorious form, it began when the temporal dominion was departed from the tribe of Judah and the family of David, Gen. xlix. 10. Dan. ix. 24—27. 2. It was typified by the temporal government of the Jews, and therefore must be of a more excellent, a spiritual nature, Heb. xi. 40. x. 1. ix. 10, 11. 3. Every thing pertaining to the kingdom is spiritual. The king is meek and lowly,—a root out of a dry ground, that came not to be ministered unto, but to minister,—a servant of rulers, who avoided every appearance of temporal dominion, Zech. ix. 9. Isa. xi. 5. liii. 2. xlix. 7. Mat. xx. 28. John vi. 13. Luke xii. 13, 14; and is a quickening Spirit, 1 Cor. xv. 45. His throne at his Father's right hand, and in the hearts of his people, is spiritual, Psalm cx. 1. Heb. i. 3. Rev. iii. 21. Eph. iii. 17. Col. i. 27. His sceptre is his spiritual word, made the power of God to men's salvation or destruction, Isa. ii. 3. liii. 1. Psalm cx. 2. Rom. i. 16. John vi. 63. Heb. iv. 12. 2 Cor. x. 4, 5. Psalm xlv. 4, 5. ii. 9. 2 Cor. ii. 16. Hos. vi. 5. Rev. ii. 12, 16. xix. 15, 21. His laws are spiritual, Rom. iii. 27. viii. 2. vii. 12, 14. The worship and homage paid him are spiritual, John iv. 24. Rom. xii. 1. 1 Pet. ii. 8, 9. Phil. iii. 3. His true subjects are spiritual men, a willing people, renewed in the spirit of their minds, born from above, not of the will of the flesh, but of the will of God by his Spirit, 1 Cor. ii. 15. Psalm cx. 2. Rom. xii. 2. Eph. iv. 23. John i. 13. iii. 5, 6. James i. 18. 1 Pet. i. 2, 23. ii. 5. Gal. iv. 19 ; and their dwelling and conversation are heavenly and spiritual, Eph. ii. 6. Phil. iii. 20. Col. iii. 1, 2. His manner of government is spiritual, Zech. iv. 6. His ministers, principal enemies, armour, warfare, and principal punishments and rewards, are spiritual, 1 Pet. iii. 22. Heb. i. 14. Psalm ciii. 19, 20, 21. Eph. iv. 11, 12. vi. 10—20. 2 Cor. x. 3—5. John xiv. 27. xvi. 33. Rom. xiv. 17. 2 Cor. iv. 18. 2 Thess. i. 6—10. 4. His ends of erecting his kingdom are spiritual, *i. e.* to destroy the works, power, and kingdom of the devil, 1 John iii. 5, 8. Col. ii. 13 ; and to glorify God in the eternal salvation of men, Gen. xlix. 10. Psalm lxxii. 17. Isa. xlv. 17. Eph. i. 3. 1 Pet. iv. 11. Luke xii. 14. Eph. iii. 21.—It is only in allusion to the Jewish state, and in condescension to men's weakness, that this spiritual kingdom is often represented by the prophets in figures drawn from a temporal kingdom, Deut. xxx. 4, 5. Ezek. xxxiv. xxxvii. Dan. vii. 27. Mic. iv. 6—8. Psalm ii. lxxii. xxi. xlv. III. It is EVERLASTING. Christ was appointed to it from all eternity, Psalm ii. 6—8. Prov. viii. 23. Mic. v. 2. He began to execute his kingly office immediately after the fall, Gen. iii. 8—19. He executed it all along under the Old Testament, in taking Adam, Noah, Abraham, and their families, into a church state, Gen. iii. 24. iv. 3, 4. ix. xii.—xxviii.—in prescribing laws to the Hebrews in the wilderness, Exod. xv. to Deut. xxxi.—in appointing the form and service of Solomon's temple, 1 Chron. xvii. xxii.—xxvi. 1 Kings v.—ix. In his incarnation, he was *born* a *king*, Mat. ii. 2. He was acknowledged as such by the wise men, Mat. ii. 1, 2, 11 ; by Nathaniel, John i. 49 ; and by the Syrophenician woman, Mat. xv. 22 ; by blind men, Mat. ix. 27. xx. 30, 31 ; by mariners, Mat. viii. 27 ; by the crucified thief, Luke xxiii. 42 ; by Pilate, John xix. 19 ; by angels, Luke i. 31—33. ii. 10, 11 ; and by his Father, Mat. xvii. 5. In his state of humiliation, he acted as King of his church, in instituting ordinances, appointing officers, and issuing forth commandments in his own name, Mat. x. xvi. 18, 19. xviii. 15—20. xxvi. 26—28. v.—vii. Luke vi. x. ---in dislodging devils, Mat. iv. 25. xii. 28, &c. ; in repeatedly purging the Jewish temple from buyers and sellers, John ii. 13---17. Mat. xxi. 12, 13 ;---in triumphantly riding to Jerusalem on an ass, Mat. xxi. John xii. Zech. ix. 9 ; in conquering and triumphing over his enemies on the cross, Col. ii. 14, 15.

Gen. iii. 15.---In, and after his resurrection, he was more solemnly invested with royal power, Mat. xxviii. 18---20. Phil. ii. 8---11. Acts v. 31. ii. 36. 1 Pet. i. 21. iii. 18, 21, 22. Eph. i. 20---23. Psalm xlvii. 5, 6, 7. xxiv. 7---10. lxviii. 18. cx. 1---7. In his exalted state of royalty, he appointed the form and laws of his New Testament church, John xx. 21, 22. Mat. xxviii. 18---20. Acts i. 3, 4, 8. Mark xvi. 15---18. 1 Cor. xii. 28, 29. xi. 23---29. Eph. iv. 11, 12; he hath and shall govern her to the end of the world, Mat. xxviii. 20. Psalm lxxxix. 37. 2 Sam. vii. 13. Isa. ix. 7. 1 Cor. xi. 23, 26. At the last day, he will judge the world; and thereafter continue his reign through all eternity, Psalm l. 2---6. Mat. xxv. 31---46. Rev. xx. 11---15. Psalm xlv. 6, 7. lxxxix. 37. 2 Sam. vii. 13. Dan. ii. 44. vii. 14, 27. Luke i. 33. Isa. ix. 7. 1 Thess. iv. 17.----
At the end of the world he will account to his Father for his management in time, present all his redeemed, perfect in holiness and happiness, and change his present form of government, 1 Cor. xv. 24---28; but will for ever retain his kingly power. His enemies, being then all conquered, and under his feet, will not be able to dethrone him, John xvi. 33. Col. ii. 15. Heb. ii. 18. Isa. xxv. 8. Psalm cx. 5, 6. 1 Cor. xv 25. His subjects will not seek to dethrone him, Isa. liv. 9, 10. lxi. 10. xxvi. 2. Jer. xxxii. 39, 40. Nor will his Father attempt it, Psalm xlv. 6. Heb. i. 8. Psalm lxxxix. 3, 4, 28. Nor would it be for the honour of God or the benefit of his people, that he should be deprived of his peculiar honours of reward, while they enjoy the glories which he purchased.

Christ's mediatorial kingdom may be distinguished into, 1. His *kingdom of power*, in which he hath the disposal of all things in heaven and earth, for the good of his church, Mat. xxviii. 18. xi. 27. John iii. 35. v. 22. Eph. i. 20---22. Phil. ii. 9---11. 1 Pet. iii. 22. 1 Cor. xv 25.---David's headship over the heathen nations which he conquered, was typical of this, 2 Sam. viii. 14. xxii. 44. Psalm xviii. 43, 44. 2. His *kingdom of grace*, ---the external form of which consists in men's conjunct profession, worship, and service of God in Christ, by means of officers, and ordinances of his own appointment. In respect of this, men often but *feign* subjection to him, and shall be *cast out*, Psalm xviii. 44. Mat. viii. 12. xiii 47. xxi. 43. The internal form of it consists in the spiritual subordination of true believers to Christ as their Husband, Saviour, and Lord,---and in righteousness, peace and joy in the Holy Ghost, Luke xvii. 20, 21. Isa. xliv. 3---5. xlv. 23. Rom. xiv. 17. Phil. iii. 3. Tit. ii. 14. 3. His *kingdom of glory*, which is also called the *kingdom of the Father*, because he gives it to redeemed men, and reigns in it in a more immediate manner, ordinances and church-officers being laid aside, and the subjection of Christ, as man and Mediator, to him, more fully manifested, Mat. xxv. 34. xiii. 43. 1 Cor. xv. 28.

Christ manages his *kingdom of power*, 1. In appointing or making angels, men, and every other creature, to work together for the good of his church, especially her true members, in their militant state, Heb. i. 14. Psalm xxxiv. 7. lxxviii. 49. Rom. viii. 28. 1 Pet. iii. 13. 2. In permitting evil angels and their instruments to tempt and persecute his professed subjects, 2 Cor. xii. 7. Eph. vi. 12. 1 Thess. ii. 18. Rev. ii. 10. xii. xiii. xx. 7— 9. 3. In restraining and bounding their rage and hatred, in respect of its fervour, duration, or effects, Rev. ii. 10. xii. 10, 12. xx. 1—3. Psalm lxxvi. 10. 4. In making all their temptations, and the harassments of his people, turn out to his glory and their good, Psalm lxxvi. 10. Rom. viii. 28. 2 Cor. iv. 17. Psalm cxix. 67, 71, 65. Heb. xii. 10, 11. Phil. i. 12—14. 1 Cor. xi. 19. Mic. vii. 9, 14. Isa. xxvii. 9. 5. In judging and punishing all his and his people's enemies, Psalm ii. 9. xxi. 8—12. xlv. 5. lxxii. 9. cx. 1, 5, 6. 2 Cor. xv. 25;—particularly his Jewish opposers, Mat. xxiv. 29—51. xxi. 44. xxii. 7; the persecuting heathens of the Roman empire, Rev. vi. 12—17; the Antichristian papists, Rev. ix. xi. xiii. xiv.—xix. 2 Thess. ii. 8; and all wicked angels and men at the last day, 2 Thess. i. 8, 9. Rev. xiv. 11. xx. 12—15. Mat. xxv. 31—46. 6. In rewarding those that had been friendly to his people and interests, as in making most honourable use of angels at the last day, Mat. xxv. 31. Jude 14. 2 Thess. i. 7; and in gloriously renewing this lower world, Rom. viii. 21. 2 Pet. iii. 13.

Christ manages his *kingdom of grace* in its external form, 1. In appointing many different ordinances of worship, common or more solemn, for erecting or preserving his church in her infant or adult state, Gen. iv. 4, 5. xvii. 10---14. Exod. xii.---xl. Lev. i.---xxvii. Num. iii.---vi. xv. xvii.---xix. xxviii. xxix. Deut. iv.---xxxii. Mat. v.---vii. x. xvi. 18, 19. xviii. 15---20. xxviii. 19, 20. Mark xvi. 15---18. 1 Cor. xi. 23---29. xiv. 1 Tim. ii.--- vi. Tit. i.---iii. 2. In instituting offices, qualifying and sending ordinary and extraordinary officers, for erecting and maintaining his church, 2 Chron. xxxvi. 15. Heb. i. 1. Eph. iv. 11---14. 1 Cor. xii. 3. In giving his Spirit, that, by his ordinary and extraordinary influences, accompanying the proclamation of his truth, he may attest his officers and doctrines, gather and preserve his subjects, and make them observe his ordinances and laws, Isa. xxxii. 15---18. xliv. 3---5. lix. 21. Joel ii. 28, 29. John xvi. 7---14. xv. 26, 27. xiv. 16, 17, 26. vii. 37---39. iii. 5, 6, 8. xx. 22. Ezek. xxxvi. 27. Prov. i. 23. Acts i. 5, 8. ii. 1--- 47. iv. 31. Heb. ii. 4. 1 Thess. i. 5. 1 John ii. 20, 27. 4. In providentially protecting his church from being ruined by erro-

OF THE PARTICULAR OFFICES OF CHRIST. 315

neous teachers or naughty professors within her, or by open persecutors without her, Zech. ii. 5. Isa. lxiii. 9. Rev. vi. vii. xi. xii. xiv. 1—5. 5. In enlarging his church at the expence of her Jewish, Heathen, or Antichristian enemies, Psalm cx. 2, 5, 6. Dan. ii. 44. Rev. xii. 10. xi. 15. Isa. xlix. liv. lx. Mic. iv. v. Zech. viii.—xiv. ii. 11.——He manages it in its *internal form*, 1. In effectually calling his elect, and by changing their state and nature, bringing them to himself, thus rescuing them from their slavery to the broken law, sin, Satan, the world, and death, Psalm cx. 3. xxii. 27—31. Isa xxvii. 12, 13. xliv. 3—5. xlv. 24, 25. xlix. 25, 26. Rom. viii. 2. vi. 14. vii. 4. John iii. 5, 6, 8. v. 25. viii. 32, 36. 1 Cor. vi. 11. Tit. iii. 3—7. Col. i. 13. 1 Pet. i. 2, 3. 2. In ruling them by his word published to them in the gospel, and written in their hearts by his Spirit, as their enlightener, directer, quickener, and comforter;—and in subordination hereto, by his providence, correcting them for their disobedience, or pardoning it, on their renewed actings of faith and repentance, Psalm cxlvii. 19. cxix. 11, 18. John xiv. 16, 17, 26. xv. 26. xvi. 13—15. Gal. vi. 8. v. 18, 22. 23. Eph. v. 9. Psalm lxxxix. 30—35. xciv. 12. 1 Pet. i. 6, 7. Mic. vii. 14, 18, 19. Psalm cxix. 67, 71. xcix. 8. Isa. xxxviii. 16. xliv. 22. lvii. 17—19. Hos. ii. 6, 7, 14. Jer. xxxi. 18—27. Heb. xii. 5—11. Rev. iii 19. 3. In protecting them from the hurtful and re-enslaving influence of the broken covenant of works, and of sin, Satan, the world, or death, Col. iii. 3. Jude 1. 1 Pet. i. 5. John x. 28, 29. Psalm xli. Isa. xlvi. 4. lxiii. 9. xxv. 8. Hos. xiii. 14. Heb. ii. 15. Psalm xxiii. 4.

Christ manages his *kingdom of glory*, 1. In giving all his true subjects on earth, a full and irrevocable title to it, and some foretastes of its happiness, 2 Cor. v. 1—7. xii. 1—6. 1 Pet. iv. 14. i. 8. 2. In preparing heaven for them against the appointed moment of their death, as well as them for it, John xiv. 2. 3. In readily admitting their departed souls into the heavenly mansions, Acts vii. 59. Luke xxiii. 43. ii. 29. 2 Pet. i. 11. Rev. iii. 21. xiv. 13. Isa. lvii. 2. Phil. i. 21, 23. 4. In raising the dead, publicly and solemnly judging the world at the last day, John v. 28, 29. Dan. xii. 2. Rev. xx. 11, 12. Mat. xxv. 2 Tim. iv. 7, 8. Tit. ii. 13. 5. In then putting down all temporary power and authority, which had been used in church or state, that every thing may be under the more immediate government of God, 1 Cor xv. 24, 28. 6. In solemnly presenting all his redeemed subjects in one body to his Father, perfect in holiness and happiness, 1 Cor. xv. 24. Heb. ii. 10, 13. 7. In perpetually governing and blessing his saints in their heavenly state with the full and immediate enjoyment of God, 1 Thess. iv. 17. Isa. lx. 19, 20. 1 Cor. xv. 28.

REFLECT. Thrice happy they, in and for whom Jesus Christ executes these offices!—Happy they, whom he teaches the infinitely marvellous, pleasant, powerful, and profitable truths of God, in a manner that enlightens, draws, renews, ravishes, and sanctifies their heart!—Happy they, who, being chargeable with guilt, sinful pollution, impotence, and unskilfulness in prayer, have this sin-expiating, this ever-effectually interceding High Priest between God and them!—How boldly they may come to his throne of grace,—flow together to his goodness, and sing in the heights of Zion, while their soul is like a watered garden, whose springs fail not!—Happy his subjects, who is LOVE itself, whose laws are holy, just, and good,—a perfect law of liberty, and whose whole administration is wisdom, righteousness, condescension, and kindness.—Let me never presume to teach others, till Jesus Christ teach me himself. Let me not dare to touch holy things, till Jesus have washed me in his blood, clothed me with his righteousness, and made me an effectual sharer in the virtue of his intercession.—Let me not dare to commence ambassador for Christ, till he hath subdued my inward enmity against him, and given me a manifest commission.—God forbid, that my ministerial labours should but amount to a stabbing of my Redeemer in all his offices, under the fifth rib;—that I should be a Judas,—by my legal and lifeless sermons, or unedifying practice, betraying him into the hands of sinners to be crucified.

CHAP. III.

Of Christ's STATES of HUMILIATION and EXALTATION.

CHRIST's Person, God-man, is manifested, and his offices are executed, in his two states of HUMILIATION and EXALTATION. It behoved him to pass through the former into the latter. In the first he fulfilled his meritorious service, and in the last he receives his glorious reward, Luke xxiv. 26. Phil. ii. 6—11. Psalm xxii. Isa. liii. His mere possession of manhood implies infinite condescension, but is not properly a part of his humiliation, as he still retains it in his glorified state, Acts iii. 21. vii. 56. Rev. i. 7, 18. But he was HUMBLED in taking flesh of a sinful and mean stock, and in the low and afflicting circumstances of his conception, birth, life, death, and burial, Phil. ii. 6—8. Isa. liii. 2—12. Psalm xxii. lxix. Matth. xii. 40. Matth. i. to John xix.

In these several steps of his humiliation, it may in general be observed, that he was made under the law as our Surety, and had all its demands required from him, without the least pity or abatement, Gal. iv. 4. Matth. iii. 15. v. 17. Luke xxiv. 26. —From all eternity he had engaged himself for our debt; but while he remained merely God, the law could not fix upon him to demand its due. But he no sooner began to assume our nature, than it took fast hold of him, and made his very conception in the form of a bond-servant, and in the likeness of sinful flesh, Phil. ii. 7. Rom. viii. 3. He was made under the *judicial* law, and hence early enrolled a descendant of David. He was made under the *ceremonial* law, and hence was early circumcised, and presented at the temple, and afterward attended the sacred festivals, and required the lepers, whom he healed, to perform their ceremonial purifications, Luke ii. Matth. viii. 4. Luke xvii. 14. But he was more properly and immediately placed under the *moral law, as a broken covenant of works:* Under this, all his elect, whom he came to redeem, are by nature, Rom. iii. 10—20; and from this they are redeemed by his fulfilment of it in their stead, Rom. viii. 2—4. x. 4. vii. 4. vi. 14. Gal. iv. 4, 5. And he was under the judicial and ceremonial laws, only as they were grafted into this moral law. 1. The Most High God, the great Lawgiver, and Lord of all, was made under the commands of this broken law, requiring him to perform perfect, personal, and perpetual obedience, under the infinite weight of its curse, Matth. v. 17, 18. iii. 15. Heb. v. 8. John viii. 29. Isa. xlii. 21. Dan. ix. 24. 2. The infinitely happy God, blessed for ever, was made under the curse of this broken law, which the transgressors represented by him had incurred, Gal. iii. 13. This curse, 1. Laid him under the power of legal death, and retained him under it from the moment of his conception till he had finished his humbled service, and was justified in his resurrection. 2. It shut him up to undergo the wrath of God, in every thing about him, which it could affect, and from every quarter, and agency of every kind.

He underwent the execution of this curse, in, 1. His soul, Isa. liii. 10. It was often tempted, Mat. iv. 1—11. John xiv. 30. Heb. ii. 17, 18. iv. 15;—was grieved with the reproaches cast on himself, and with the sins and miseries of others, Psalm lxix. 19, 20. xxii. 6, 7. Heb. xii. 3. Mark iii. 5, 21. Matth. xi. 19. xii. 24. xxvi. 59—74. xxvii. 29, 39—49. John viii. 48, 52. Luke xix. 41, 42. John xi. 35;—and burdened and tormented with the hidings of his Father's face, and the fears and impressions of his wrath, Matth. xxvii. 46. xxvi. 39. Luke xxii. 43. Heb. v. 7. John xii. 27. Psalm xxii. 1, 2, 14, 21. lxix. 1, 2. 2. In his body,—in circumcision, Luke ii. 21; in labour, Mark vi. 3; in hunger, Matth. iv. 2; in thirst, John xix. 28; in weariness, John iv. 6, 7; in repeated dangers of death, Matth. ii. 16. Luke iv. 18—29. Mark iii. 6, 7. Luke

xiii. 31. John v. 16. vii. 1, 32, 44. viii. 59. x. 39. xi. 53, 54; in bloody sweat, Luke xxii. 44; in apprehension and bonds, Matth. xxvi. 50. xxvii. 30; in being shamefully spitted on by vile miscreants, Isa. l. 6. lii. 14. Matth. xxvi. 67. xxvii. 30; in being buffeted, scourged, and his hair plucked out, Isa. l. 6. Mic. v. 1. Matth. xxvi. 67. xxvii. 30. John xix. 1; in being crowned with thorns, and having his garments painfully torn from his bloody and wounded body, Matth. xxvii. 29, 34, 35. John xix. 2; in receiving gall and vinegar for drink, Psal. lxix. 21. Matth. xxvii. 34, 48; and in dying the most shameful, lingering, and universally tormenting death of the cross, Luke xxiii. 28. John xix. 17. Psal. xxii. 17. Mark xv. 24, 25. 3. In his reputation he was loaded with the most abusive railing and calumny, Matth. xi. 19. xii. 24. John viii. 22, 24, 48, 52. vii. 20. x. 33. Mark iii. 7, 21. xiv. 63, 64. Psal. xlix. 19, 20. xxii. 6; the most false accusations, Matth. xxvi. 59—67. xxvii. 12. Luke xxiii. 2. John xix. 7; and the most ignominious ridicule, Psal. xxii. 6—8. xl. 15. lxix. 7, 12. Matth. xxvi. 68. xxvii. 47. Luke xv. 2. John vii. 35. 4. In his outward lot. He sprang of a very debased, though once royal family, Isa. xi. 1. liii. 2; was conceived by a woman of low estate, Luke i. 27, 28; in Nazareth, a wicked and infamous city, John i. 46. vii. 52; born in Bethlehem, a mean place, Mic. v. 2. Matth. ii. 1—6; in a stable, and laid in a manger,—thus rendered like to a beast, to punish our original hearkening and continued conformity to beasts, instead of God, Luke ii. 7. He, for a time, lived an exile in Egypt, the land of cruel bondage, Matth. ii. 14, 15; and long dwelt and laboured as a mean carpenter in profligate Nazareth, Matth. ii. 23. Luke ii. 51. Mark vi. 3. He was oppressed with poverty, especially while he preached the gospel, and went about healing all manner of diseases, 2 Cor. viii. 9. Mat. viii. 20. Luke ix. 58. Psalm lxix. 29. xl. 17. 5. Though his Godhead could not be affected with sufferings of any kind, yet his person being under the curse, Gal. iv. 4. iii. 13, his divine glory was concealed under the likeness of sinful flesh, Rom. viii. 3; and subsisted in personal union with a manhood, continually affected with sufferings, and was, by that means, exposed to the vilest contempt and insults, Acts xx. 28. iii. 15. 1 Cor. ii. 8. Psalm xxii. 6.

The curse of the broken covenant of works having thus set him up, in all that pertained to him, as a butt of God's indignation, drew sufferings upon him from every quarter. His Father, who loved him infinitely, acting as a righteous judge toward him as our Surety charged in law with our sins, deserted him,—hid his face from him,—was wroth with him,—and executed upon him just vengeance, by himself, by devils, men, and other creatures, as his instruments, Isa. liii. 2—12.

Matth. xxvii. 46. Zech. xiii. 7. John xviii. 11. xix. 11. Acts ii. 23, 24. iv. 27, 28.—While holy angels, shut out by the curse, stood aloof from him, devils permitted, and as it were empowered by it, did tempt and harass him, Matth. iv. 1—11. John xiv. 30.—Of men, his kinsfolk reproached, rejected, and plagued him, Mark iii. 21. John vii. 1—10; his neighbours of Nazareth attempted to murder him, Luke iv. 28, 29; his hearers cavilled at his words, and blasphemed him, Luke xi. xiv. Mark iii. v. John v.—x.; his disciples vexed him with their ignorance, unbelief, presumption, contention, ambition, and unconcern, Luke v. 8. John xiv. 5—9. xvi. 31. Matth. xiv. 31. xvi. 22, 23. xvii. 4, 17. Luke xxii. 23, 46. Judas, one of them, in the most treacherous manner, for a pitiful reward betrayed him, Psalm xli. 9. lv. 13—15. cix. 4. Matth. xxvi. 15, 21, 25, 47, 48. Contrary to his most solemn promises, Peter, upon the slightest temptations, thrice denied him, cursed and swore that he had never known him, Matth. xxvi. 33, 35, 69—74; the other ten forsook him and fled, Matth. xxvi. 31, 56. John xvi. 32. His avowed enemies persecuted him in every form. Herod I. attempted to murder him in his infancy, and for his sake slew all the babes about Bethlehem. Herod II. sought to kill him, when a preacher; and with his men of war abused and contemned him.—After they had for several years persecuted him, the Jewish rulers, priests, scribes, and pharisees apprehended him, procured his crucifixion, and during it, in the vilest manner insulted and abused him. The common people, who had just before loudly extolled him as the promised Messiah, preferred to him a most notorious robber and murderer; insisted for his crucifixion, and abused him under it. Pilate, the Roman governor, condemned him; his heathen soldiers scourged and crucified him, and parted his garments, Psalm ii. 1—4. xxii. 6—21. lxix. 1—22. Matth. ii. xxvi. xxvii. Luke xiii. 31, 32. xxiii. 7—11. Mark iii. John v. vii. viii. x. xi. xviii. xix. Luke xxii. xxiii. And, by slanderous accusations, the Jewish rulers attempted to imprison him in his grave, Matth. xxvii. 63—66.

The humiliation of Christ was necessary, 1. To execute the purpose of God and the covenant-engagements of Christ, Acts ii. 23, 24. iv. 27, 28. Psalm xl. 6—8. 2. To fulfil the manifold types and predictions of the Old Testament, Lev. i.—xvi. Num. xv. xix. xxviii. xxix. Psal. xxii. lxix. Isa. liii. Zech. ix. 9. xiii. 7. The troubles of Abel, Isaac, Jacob, Joseph, Job, Moses, David, and all the sacrifices, with the lifting up of the brazen serpent, prefigured this, Col. ii. 17. Heb. x. 1. 3. To satisfy the broken law of God, and purchase eternal redemption for us, Isa. liii. 4, 5, 6, 8, 10, 11, 12. Heb. ix. 12, 15. x. 10, 14. 1 Pet. i. 18, 19. ii. 24. iii. 18. Rev. v. 9. 4. To give the redeemed an unspotted pattern of holiness and patience under suffering, 1 Pet. ii. 20—24. Eph. v. 2, 25.

REFLECT. Turn aside, my hell-hardened heart, and behold this great sight, the bush of Jesus' manhood burning in the flames of Jehovah's wrath, and not consumed! Behold the power of men's enmity against God, that made them thus hate, reproach, and murder his only begotten Son,—their Saviour, whose instructions had been so edifying, his life so virtuous, and his unnumbered miracles so benevolent! Behold the dreadful punishment,—and in that punishment the heinous nature of sin! What is a deluged world,—a burning Sodom,—a plagued Egypt,—an opened hell,—and all the torments of the damned, when compared with this,—the Son of God cursed,—troubled in soul, till he knew not what to say,—amazed and very heavy,—sorrowful even unto death,—roaring under the hidings of his Father's face,—groaning and dying under the weight of his wrath!—Behold with awful dread, what must quickly be my condition, if I be and continue an unbelieving and impenitent sinner,—a graceless preacher!—Betrayed by Satan, by the world, and my own treacherous, but much trusted heart! Accused by the fiery law! Fast apprehended by a stinging death! Condemned by God, and consigned to be an everlasting butt of his infinite vengeance, and a derision of wicked angels and men! Upbraided by the curses of those whom my careless ministrations, my carnal or trifling converse, and untender example, have seduced towards hell!—— But listen, my soul!—how,—by every reproach,—by every wound,—every groan,—every tear,—every drop of blood, Jesus, the Son of God, invites and obtests me to come to him and be saved!—— Dare I,—can I, contemn or resist such calls from him who loved me, and gave himself for me!—Behold! how completely my debt is paid,—my happiness is purchased,—my peace with God procured and confirmed! Behold a fulfilled, an everlasting righteousness, a finished transgression, an ended sin, a wasted curse, a vanquished death, an extinguished hell, a fulfilled, a magnified, a smiling law, an espousing God! and ALL for ME!—Behold, the mighty debt of love which I owe to Christ and his Father!——Let me prize, prize more than ten thousand worlds, the Man, God's fellow, who, for me, was sold for thirty pieces of silver. Let me cleave with full purpose of heart to my once forsaken Lord. Let me boldly confess my thrice denied Redeemer. Let my heart and soul entertain him who, for me, had not where to lay his head. Let me with hosannas in the highest exalt my once contemned, reproached, but now glorified Christ. Let me take up my cross and follow him.—If I forget thee, O Jesus!

let my right hand forget her cunning, and my tongue cleave to the roof of my mouth.——But, ah! my sins! shamed, detested, crucified, and destroyed let them be.—Nay, lothed and detested be my soul, if I follow,—if I preach Jesus Christ, not from love, but for filthy lucre.

NOTWITHSTANDING the tremendous humiliation of our Redeemer, it was attended by many honourable circumstances. 1. An angel repeatedly foretold his birth, Luke i. 26---36. Matth. i. 20, 21. 2. John Baptist, his forerunner, when yet unborn, leaped in his mother's womb at his approach, Luke i. 41. 3. An host of angels with high shouts of praise proclaimed his birth, Luke ii. 10---14. 4. An angel prevented his falling under a suspicion of bastardy; and directed the preservation of his infant life, Matth. i. 19, 20. ii. 13, 19, 20. 22. 5. When he was presented in the temple, Simeon and Anna, by divine inspiration, proclaimed him the true Messiah, Luke ii. 25---38. 6. An uncommon star directed the wise Gentiles to the place of his birth, in order to worship him, Matth. ii. 2, 9, 10. 7. Being yet a child, he disputed with the most learned doctors, Luke ii. 40—50. 8. His Father by a voice from heaven repeatedly attested his divine Sonship, Matth. iii. 17. xvii. 5. John xii. 28. 9. The Holy Ghost, in a visible manner, descended upon him at his baptism, and rested upon him, Matth. iii. 16. John i. 33, 34. 10. John Baptist repeatedly declared him the Messiah, John i. 29—36. iii. 24— 36. Matth. iii. 11—14. 11. He fasted forty days in the wilderness, vanquished Satan's temptations, and angels ministered to him, Matth. iv. 1—11. Luke iv. 1—10. 12. His body was gloriously transfigured on the mount, and he conversed with Moses and Elias, two glorified saints, Matth. xvii. 1— 14. Luke ix. 28—36. 13. A voice from heaven encouraged him under his fearful apprehensions of approaching death, John xii. 27—29. 14. In his agony, an angel appeared to strengthen and comfort him, Luke xxii. 43, 44. 15. A few days before he was crucified, the solemn hosannas of the children and multitude at Jerusalem proclaimed him the Messias, Mat. xxi. John xii. 16. A supernatural darkness attended his crucifixion, Matth. xxvii. 45. 17. A perplexing dream of Pilate's wife attested his innocence, Matth. xxvii. 19. 18. Pilate, who condemned him, repeatedly pronounced him innocent, and, instead of a crime, resolutely marked his cross with a threefold attestation of his true Messiahship, John xviii. 38. xix. 4. Luke xxiii. 4, 14, 15, 22. Matth. xxvii. 23, 24. John xix. 19---22. 19. While he hung on the cross, a crucified thief and an attending centurion, being then converted, publicly acknowledged him the true Messiah, Luke xxiii. 40—47.

Matth. xxvii. 51.   20. While he expired, an earthquake rent the rocks, and the vail of the temple, if not also opened many graves about Jerusalem, Matth. xxvii. 51, 52.   21. Nicodemus and Joseph of Arimathea, who had hitherto concealed their regard for him, now openly acknowledged him the Messiah, and procured him an honourable burial in Joseph's new sepulchre, lately hewn out of a rock in his garden; thus making his grave *with the rich*, after it had been appointed with the wicked malefactors in Calvary, John xix. 38—42. Isa. liii. 9.   22. While he lay in his grave, fulfilling the sentence of the broken law, Gen. ii. 17. iii. 19; implementing the ancient types and predictions concerning him, and manifesting that he was truly dead, the Holy Ghost preserved his mangled bloody corpse from all corruption, Psalm xvi. 10. Acts ii. 27, 31. xiii. 35, 37.   23. His enemies' attempt to imprison him in his grave, did but render his resurrection more glorious and manifest, Matth. xxvii. 66. xxviii. 4, 11.   24. His amazing instructions, sermons, and conferences, Matth. v.—vii. xiii. xx. xxi. xxii. xxiii. xxiv. xxv. Luke iv.—xxi. John ii.—xvi. 25. His almost unnumbered miracles, Matth. iv. 25. xi. 5. xiv. 35, 36.

His miracles were public and uncontrouled,—manifesting his power—over devils, in dislodging them from men, and granting them liberty to enter into swine, Acts x. 38. Mat. viii. 16. ix. 33. xii. 22—28, &c.—over men, in making the furious band who came to apprehend him, fall backward at his word, John xviii. 6;—over diseases, healing the most inveterate leprosies, palsies, dropsies, fevers, bloody issues, blindness, withered benumbedness, lameness, maimedness, lunacies, &c. Luke iv. 40. Mat. viii. Mark i.—iii. v. vii. ix. x. Luke xiv. John v. ix.—over death, in raising to life the deceased daughter of Jairus, the coffined son of the widow at Nain, and Lazarus, who had been dead four days, and was buried, Mark v. 36—42. Luke vii. 11—15. John xi. 38—44;—over irrational creatures, in cursing the fig-tree, Mat. xxi. 19; multiplying the loaves and fishes, Mat. xiv. 15—21. xv. 31—38; causing multitudes of fish to come into a net, Luke v. 4—7. John xxi. 6—8; and one bring money in its mouth for paying the tribute, Mat. xvii. 27; in walking upon the sea, and making Peter walk upon it, Mat. xiv. 25—29; in calming dreadful tempests by his word, Mat. viii. 26. xiv. 32.—His working miracles differed from that by his prophets and apostles. 1. He wrought all his miracles by his own power, and in his own name, John v. 17. xi. 11; they wrought their's in his name and strength, Acts iii. 6—13. iv. 11. ix. 34.   2. His power of working miracles was constant,—theirs but occasional, and by means of prayer, Mat. iv. 25. xi. 5. 1 Kings xvii. xviii.

2 Kings i.—iv. Acts iii. 3. He communicated this power to others; they could communicate it to none.——By his miracles thus performed, 1. He manifested himself to be the Son of God in our nature, producing the miracle by his divine power, and yet by a word, a touch, or the like, which respected his manhood, Mat. vii. 33, 34. John ix. 6, 17. 2. He manifested in himself one distinguishing mark of the true Messiah, Isa. xxxv. 5, 6. xxix. 18. Mat. xi. 5, 7. And this the more remarkably proved his true Messiahship, as there had been no miracles wrought in the holy land for above 700 years before, nor on earth for about 600 years before. Nor did any but himself work any miracles in the temple, the house of God, Matth. xxi. 14. 3. He confirmed his doctrine to be of God, John v. 36. x. 38. xiv. 11. Luke xi. 20. Matth. xii. 28, 29. 4. He demonstrated his supreme power over all creatures, Mat. xxviii. 18. Eph. i. 21. Psalm xxiv. 1. 5. He testified his compassion and kindness towards men, and his readiness to heal the diseases, and supply the wants of their souls, John vi. 37. Luke ix. 56.——During his private life, Christ wrought no miracles at all, and but one after his resurrection: nor did he ever work any for his own advantage.—He refused the devils' attestation of his miraculous powers, that he might not be suspected of any collusion with them, Mark i. 24, 25.——To fulfil ancient predictions,—to shun the troublesome concourse of multitudes,—to manifest his own humility,—and not irritate the Jews to untimely conspiracies against him,—and that he might not confound them with too many miracles, he sometimes forbade them that had been healed to publish it, Mat. viii. 4. ix. 30. xii. 16. But he never hindered any Gentiles to publish what they had experienced; which, perhaps, prefigured his publication of his gospel among them.

II. Betwixt the death and resurrection of our Saviour, his humiliation and exaltation were conjoined. His humiliation continued in his body's lying in the grave, under the power of death, and in the breach of the union between his soul and body.—His exaltation began in the happiness of his separated soul, in the heavenly mansions. That it went thither is evident. 1. He committed his departing soul into the hands of his pacified Father, Luke xxiii. 46. 2. It retired to paradise, and was there with the soul of the penitent thief that very day on which he died, Luke xxiii. 43. 3. The Papists' Limbus patrum or infantum, or purgatory, are but mere fancies, into which nothing can go. 4. Neither Scripture nor common sense assign any proper end of his soul's retiring to hell after his death.—It needed not go thither to finish its part in his sacrifice, that being completed in his death, John xix. 30. Heb. x. 14;—nor to triumph over devils, having done that on the cross, and being soon to do it more gloriously in his resurrection and ascension, leading captivity captive, Col. ii. 15. Psalm lxviii. 18;—nor to preach the gospel to the damned, their season of grace being for ever gone, Heb. iii. 7, 13---15. Luke xvi. 26.—It was not then, but in the days of Noah, that he preached to the sinners of the old world, whose souls had lived in the prison of an unregenerate state, and after death had gone to the prison of hell, 1 Pet. iii. 19, 20. And though SHEOL, or HADES, sometimes means the place of the damned, Psalm ix. 17. Luke xvi. 23; yet, more frequently it means the grave or separated state of the dead, Job xxi. 13. Gen. xxxvii. 35. xlii. 38. 1 Kings ii. 6. Psalm cxli. 7; or, a state of terrible debasement and trouble, Isa. xiv. 9, 11, 15, 19, 20. Psalm xviii. 5. cxvi. 3. Jon. ii. 2.—Now, Christ's *body*, which is all that NEPHESH or PSYCHE means in some texts, Lev. xix. 28. xxi. 1, 11. Num. v. 2. Luke vi. 9, was not left in SHEOL or HADES, but raised from death and the grave, Mark xvi. 6, 9. 1 Cor. xv. 4, 20. Nor was his soul left in its terrible debasement, or separated from his body, but re-united to it, and exalted to glory, Psalm xvi. 10.——The lower parts of the earth into which Christ descended, was this world, reckoned lower than the heavens,—and his mother's womb, Eph. iv. 9. Isa. lv. 9. Psalm cxxxix. 15.——In the grave he was in the *heart of the earth*, Matth. xii. 40; even as Tyre was in the *heart of the sea*, though very near the shore, Ezek. xxvi. 4.

Christ's unmixed exaltation consists in his being completely glorified, in *rising from the dead, ascending to heaven, sitting at God's right hand*, and *coming to judge the world.* In all these four steps, his person God-man is exalted, though the addition of glory be only made to his human nature.—As, in his humiliation, his person was debased in his manhood, so, in his exaltation, his person was exalted in his manhood. In his humiliation, the glory of his Godhead was eclipsed by the sufferings of his manhood. In his exaltation it shines brightly through the graces of his manhood, Phil. ii. 6---11. Heb. ii. 8---10. Isa. liii. 2---12. lii. 13, 14, 15.

I. Christ's resurrection from the dead on the third day, being a peculiar hinge of the gospel-dispensation, was not only foretold by the prophets, Job xix. 25. Psalm xvi. 10, 11. xxii. 19---21. cx. 7. Isa. liii. 8. xxv. 8. lv. 3. Acts xiii. 34. Zech. iii. 8. Hos. vi. 2;—and typified by Noah's departure from the ark, Joseph's deliverance from prison, Samson's carrying off the gates of Gaza, Daniel's coming out of the lions' den,—the leper's live bird flying away after it had been dipped in the blood of its fellow,—the dismission of the scape-goat, Gen. viii. xli. 14. Judg. xvi. 3. Dan. vi. 23. Lev. xiv. 6, 7. xvi. 21, 22;—and by Isaac's deliverance from death on the third day after he was divinely devoted to it; Hezekiah's going up to the house of the Lord on the third day after he received a divine sentence of death; and Jonah's coming out of the whale's belly on the third day, Gen. xxii. Heb. xi. 19. 2 Kings xx. 5. John ii. 10. i. 17. Mat. xii. 40. 1 Cor. xv. 4;—but we have many, and most manifest proofs, that it actually took place. I. The soldiers who had been appointed to watch his sepulchre, being affrighted by the earthquake, or by the angels who had appeared to roll the stone from the door of it, published the truth of his resurrection, and of the wonders which attended it, that same day in Jerusalem. Nor could their confounded masters, rulers of Judah, invent any thing to discredit it, but a most glaring falsehood, Mat. xxviii. 11—15. II. Holy angels testified that he was risen, to the women that went to visit his sepulchre, Mat. xxviii. 6, 7. III. Many saints, who had been raised together with him, went into Jerusalem, and appeared unto many, Mat. xxvii. 53. IV. Christ himself manifested the truth of it, in eleven or twelve different appearances to his friends. 1. To Mary Magdalene at the sepulchre, Mark xvi. 9. John xx. 11—18. 2. To the women returning from the sepulchre, Mat. xxviii. 9, 10. 3. To Cleophas and his companion going to Emmaus, Luke xxiv. 13—31. 4. To Simon Peter alone, Luke xxiv. 34. 1 Cor. xv. 5. 5. To ten apostles in their chamber at Jerusalem, Luke xxiv. 36—48. John xx. 19—23,—all on the very day of his resurrection. 6. To eleven apostles on the eighth day after, 1 Cor. xv. 5. John xx. 26—29. 7. To seven of them at the Sea of Tiberias, John xxi. 1—21. 8. To eleven apostles on a mountain of Galilee, Mat. xxviii. 16—20. 9. To more than five hundred brethren at once, 1 Cor. xv. 6. 10. To his eleven apostles just before his ascension, Acts i. 4—11. Luke xxiv. 49—51. 11. To James, 1 Cor. xv. 7. 12. After his ascension, to Stephen, Acts vii. 56;—to Paul, 1 Cor. ix. 1. xv. 8. Acts ix. 3—17;—and to John in Patmos, Rev. i.—iii. v. x. xxii. V. After many repeated sights of him, and much converse with him, his twelve apostles, without, nay, contrary to, every consideration of carnal interest, did, within a few weeks after he had been murdered at Jerusalem, when the very same multitudes who had procured and witnessed his death were met together, publish his resurrection to them, in the most bold, steady, and uniform manner. Nor could all the power, learning, craft, rage, and malice of their opponents produce any other refutation but

threatenings, imprisonment, and murder, Acts ii.—viii. xii.
VI. The Holy Ghost, by miraculously descending upon the apostles, and enabling them to preach in languages which they had never learned, discern spirits, and work miracles, and making their report so wonderfully successful on the hearts even of their most outrageous opposers, mightily attested Christ's resurrection, Acts ii.—vi. John xiv. 16, 17, 26. xv. 26. xvi. 7---14. xx. 21. Acts i. 5, 8.

Christ was raised from the dead by the concurring influence of all the three divine persons. 1. By the Father, to whom it is emphatically ascribed, Acts ii. 24. iii. 15, 16. iv. 10. x. 40. xvii. 31. Rom. x. 9. vi. 4. viii. 11. 1 Pet. i. 21. Eph. i. 20. Heb. xiii. 20.—Thus he acknowledged him his beloved Son, adjudged, and called him to his glorious reward, as well as he had done to his debased service, 1 Tim. iii. 16. Heb. v. 4, 5. And, to testify his full satisfaction for his elect, and his solemn justification as their head, he sent an angel to open the grave, his prison, Isa. liii. 8. Mat. xxviii. 2. 2. By the Son, John ii. 19. x. 17, 18. Rom. i. 4. 1 Pet. iii. 18. John v. 21. xi. 25. 3. By the Holy Ghost, who is perhaps on that account called the *Spirit of life in Christ Jesus*, Rom. viii. 2, 11. vi. 4. ——The Father, as a fully satisfied judge, released him from prison. The Son, having finished his humiliation-work, re-united his soul to his body, both having still continued united to his person. The Holy Ghost, who dwelt in both, re-established their natural union.

Concerning the resurrection of Christ, it must be remarked, that, 1. The very *same body* which he had before his death, rose again, in all its essential properties, Luke xxiv. 39. John xx. 20, 27. 2. He rose from the dead very *early* on the *first day* of the week, to mark him the *Hind of the morning*, the *morning Star*, the *Day-spring from on high*, and the *Sun of righteousness*, Psalm xxii. title. Rev. ii. 28. xxii. 16. Luke i. 78. Mal. iv. 2. Mat. xxviii. 1. Mark xvi. 9. Gen. i. 5. 3. He rose again upon the *third* day, after he had lain dead part of the sixth, all the seventh, and a few hours of the first day of the week, Mat. xii. 40. 1 Cor. xv. 4. It was not proper that he should rise too soon, lest the reality of his death should have been doubted; nor proper that he should continue dead very long, lest his followers should have utterly fainted, and his resurrection not be timely published, when the facts were fresh in men's memories. 4. He rose again with great deliberation,—to manifest which, and that his body had not been stolen away, nor should die any more, he left his grave-clothes behind him, decently wrapped together, and orderly placed, John xx. 5---7. 5. He rose with great solemnity: An earthquake shook the place: an angel rolled away the stone from the door of his sepulchre, and sat upon it: two others placed themselves on his grave: multitudes of saints rose along with him, and perhaps ascended to heaven as his harbingers, Mat. xxviii. 2. xxvii. 53. Mark xvi. 4—6. John xx. 12.   6. He rose as a public person, representing an elect world, and, in his resurrection, received from God as the Judge, a complete legal discharge of all their debt, and took possession of eternal life in their name, Rom. iv. 25. Eph. ii. 6.   7. He rose to enjoy a state of everlasting life and happiness, Rom. vi. 9. Col. i. 18. 1 Cor. xv. 23, 37, 38. And though he once ate with his disciples, it was not from natural appetite, but to confirm his resurrection, Luke xxiv. 42, 43. Acts x. 41.

II. Christ, in his manhood, *ascended to heaven.*—Not only had the translations of Enoch and Elias to heaven, soul and body,—the exaltations of Joseph, Moses, Joshua, David, and Daniel, after their trouble and danger,—and the priests' placing the ceremonial ark in the most holy apartment of the tabernacle or temple,—and their carrying the blood and incense into the sanctuary or Holy of Holies, prefigured it, Gen. v. 24. 2 Kings ii. 11. Heb. xi. 5. Gen. xxxvii.—xlviii. Exod. ii. to Deut. xxxiv. Josh. i.—xxiv. 1 Sam. xvi.—xxx. 2 Sam. i.—xxiv. 1 Chron. xi.—xxix. Dan. vi. Exod. xl. 21. xxx. 7, 8. 1 Kings viii. 8—10. Lev. iv. 7, 18. xvi. 12—16;—— and the prophets foretold it, Psal. xxiv. 7—10. xlvii. 5, 6. lxviii. 18. Mic. ii. 13. Psalm viii. 1. Ezek. i. 26, 27. x. 18. 1 Pet. iii. 22.   But, 1. His disciples saw him ascend to heaven, Acts i. 9, 10.   2. Two holy angels testified that he did ascend to it, Acts i. 11.   3. Stephen, Paul, and John saw him in his ascended state, Acts vii. 55, 56. ix. 3, 4, 17. xxii. 6—21. Rev. i. 10—19. v. 6. xii. 5.   4. The marvellous descent of the Holy Ghost, and its effects, demonstrated that he had ascended, John xvi. 7—14. Acts ii. 33.   5. The terrible overthrow and dispersion of the Jewish nation is a standing proof of his ascension, Mat. xxvi. 64. John viii. 21.—And, in this ascension, 1. His Father *took him up* into heaven, to acknowledge him his beloved Son, and to manifest his perfect fulfilment of all righteousness for his elect, Phil. ii. 9. Luke xxiv. 51. Acts i. 11, 22. ii. 33. v. 31. Eph. i. 20. 1 Tim. iii. 16. 1 Pet. i. 21.   2. In improving his purchased glory for himself and his people, Christ *went up* into heaven, John xx. 17. Eph. iv. 8—10. John xiv. 2, 3, 28. xvi. 7, 28. Acts i. 10, 11. Mark xvi. 19. Psal. xlvii. 5. lxviii. 18.

Concerning Christ's ascension to heaven, it may be observed, 1. He ascended *forty days* after his resurrection. He continued so many days on earth before he ascended,—that he might give many repeated proofs of his resurrection to his followers, Acts i. 3.;—that he might sufficiently instruct his apostles in every thing which pertained to the abolishment of the Jewish ceremonies, with the form, order, and worship of the New Testament church, Acts i. 3. Mark xvi. 15---18. Mat. xxviii. 18---20;—that his disciples might have but a few days to wait for the effusion of his Spirit; and that there might be as much time between his glorious birth to immortal life and his entrance into his heavenly temple, as had been between his humbled birth and his presentation in the Jewish temple,—and as much time between his bloody baptism, the attestation of his divine Sonship, and his entrance on his heavenly ministrations, as had been between his water baptism, the attendant attestation of his Sonship, and his entrance on his public ministry on earth, Mat. iii. 14---17. iv. 1---17;—of which spaces, perhaps the long fasts of Moses and Elijah were typical. 2. He ascended from Mount Olivet, perhaps from the very spot where he had suffered his blood agony,—there displaying his power, and setting off as a triumphant conqueror, where his human weakness had chiefly appeared, and where he had sustained a terrible conflict with all the powers of darkness, Acts i. 12. Luke xxiv. 50. 3. He was parted from his disciples while he was solemnly blessing them,—thus labouring in his redemption-work till his very last moment on earth,— shewing that he was the true SEED of Abraham, in whom all nations should be *blessed*,—and that while he left blessings behind him, he had still many more to bestow, Acts i. 9. Luke xxiv. 52. 4. Multitudes of angels attended him in his ascension with solemn shouts of praise, Psal. lxviii. 17. xlvii. 5, 6. Dan. vii. 9---14. 5. In his ascension he triumphed over devils as his captives, and received gifts for sinful men, in order to promote and secure their eternal salvation, Psalm lxviii. 18.

III. Having ascended up into heaven, Christ *sat down at the right hand of God*, which means the most honourable station, the nearest and most familiar fellowship with him, 1 Cor. xv. 27. Psalm cx. 1, 5. Heb. i. 3 iv. 14. viii. 1. Phil. ii. 9. Isa. lii. 13. Eph. i. 20, 21. 1 Pet. iii. 22. God the Father, in rewarding Christ for his humbled service, *set* him down at his right hand, Eph. i. 20. Acts ii. 31, 33; and Christ himself, as taking possession of his glorious reward, *sat* down, Mark xvi. 19. Heb. i. 3. viii. 1. Zech. vi. 13.——His sitting at the right hand of God includes, 1. The endowment of his manhood with inconceivable glory and happiness, Acts ii. Psalm xvi. 11. 2. The high honour of his person God-man, it being the privilege of Lords to sit, Dan. vii. 9. 1 Kings ii. 19. Esth.

i. 13. Job xxix. 25; and the character of servants to *stand*, 1 Kings xvii. 1. Dan. vii. 16. Zech. iii 7. Psalm cxxxiv. 1. Prov. xxii. 29. Thus Christ sits as our Intercessor crowned with glory and honour; and yet, to mark his readiness to act, help, or enter into us, he is represented as *standing* at the right hand of God,—at the right hand of the poor,—or at the door of your heart, Acts vii. 55, 56. Psalm cix. 31. Rev. iii. 20. 3. His refreshful rest after his finished labours, Heb. iv. 10. Psalm cx. 1. Mic. iv. 4, 4. His judicial and royal power and authority, Matth. xix. 28. Zech. vi. 13. 5. The everlasting and undisturbed continuance of his happiness, honour, rest, and authority, 1 Cor. xv. 25. Psalm cx. 1, 5. xlv. 6. Heb. i. 8.

IV. Christ's judging the world at the last day, is not an higher step of exaltation, than his sitting at his Father's right hand; and is by some included in it. But it is a more public and solemn manifestation of his glory, in which we may consider the PREPARATION, the JUDGMENT itself, and the EXECUTION of the sentences.

I. In the PREPARATION for the last judgment, are included Christ's own personal appearance, the raising of the dead, and the assembling and separation of the parties to be judged.

1. Christ will appear in the most exalted manner in his own and his Father's glory, attended by all his holy angels,—will erect his great white throne in the air;—and, in an awful manner, require all men to attend at his judgment-seat. Rev. i. 7. xx. 11, 12. Mat. xxiv. 24, 29—31. xxvi. 64. John v. 28. 1 Thess. iv. 15. 2 Thess. i. 7—10. Psalm l. 1—6.

2. The dead shall be raised from their graves. This pre-supposes the preservation of all the essential particles of their bodies while dead, and preservation of their souls in life, in order to be reunited to them.—It includes the new formation of these particles into bodies fit for the residence of their respective souls, —and the reunion of their souls to these newly formed bodies, in order to the renewal of human life.—All the dead of mankind shall be thus raised. 1. In nature, we have manifold emblems of this resurrection. The day returns after the night.— Vegetables, which are apparently dead in winter, as well as serpents, swallows, and other animals, revive in the spring. And men, as well as brutes, awaken after sleep. 2. While reason manifests that God, by his infinite power and wisdom, is able to preserve, and anew form these particles into human bodies, —it no less clearly suggests, that men not being rewarded in this life according to their deeds, there must be some future state of retribution, in which men's bodies, which had partook

with their souls in their virtue or vice, must share with them in sensible happiness or misery, Eccl. iii. 16, 17. 3. Every leading truth of the Christian religion requires the resurrection of the dead. If the Son of God assumed a human body in order to shew kindness to us, our bodies must be eternal partakers of his fraternal favours. If, in his body, as well as in his soul, he fulfilled all righteousness for us, our bodies must be delivered from death, and partake of his purchased eternal life. If our bodies, in a proper manner, partake of the seals of his covenant, they must share of the eternal happiness therein sealed. If our bodies be temples of Christ and his Spirit, and be washed in his blood, they must not lie in everlasting ruins, Heb. ii. 11—15. x. 5, 22. Mat. xxvi. xxvii. xxviii. 19. 1 Cor. x. 16, 17. xi. 24 —26. vi. 19, 20. Rom. viii. 11. 4. God hath already given almost innumerable pledges of this future resurrection of the dead, —in raising the son of the widow of Zarephath, 1 Kings xvii. 21; the son of the Shunamite, 2 Kings iv. 35; the man cast into the grave of Elisha, 2 Kings xiii. 21; the daughter of Jairus, Luke ix. 49--56; the son of the widow of Nain, Luke vii. 15; Lazarus, John xi. 44; many saints at Christ's resurrection, Mat. xxvii. 53; Dorcas, Acts ix. 40; Eutychus, Acts xx. 10;—but chiefly Christ himself, who is the *first begotten from the dead*, and the *first fruits* of them that slept, 1 Cor. xv. 13—28. Col. i. 18. 2 Cor. iv. 14. 1 Thess. iv. 14. Rom. viii. 11. 1 Pet. i. 3. Rev. i. 5. 5. Scripture plentifully attests this future and general resurrection of men, good and bad, Exod. iii. 6. Mat. xxii. 31, 32.—Deut. xxxii. 39. 1 Sam. ii. 6. Job xix. 25 —27; (the words of which are too emphatical to mean only a temporal deliverance: nor doth Job appear to have had any hopes of such a deliverance, Job vi. 8, 9, 11. vii. 7, 8. x. 20, 29. vi. 22. xvii. 1, 15. xix. 10.) Psalm xvi. 11. xvii. 15. Isa. xxv. 8. xxvi. 19. Dan. xii. 2. Hos. xiii. 14. Luke xiv. 14. John v. 28, 29. vi. 39, 40, 44, 54. xi. 24, 25, 26. xiv. 19. Acts iv. 2. xvii. 18, 31. xxiii. 6. xxiv. 15. xxvi. 8. 1 Cor. vi. 14. xv. 2 Cor. i. 9. iv. 14. 1 Thess. iv. 14—16. 2 Tim. iv. 1. Heb. vi. 2. Rev. xx. 12. Ezek. xxxvii. 1—14.—In Luke xiv. 14. xx. 26. 1 Cor. xv. 23. Phil. iii. 11. John vi. 39—47. 1 Thess. iv. 14, wicked men are excluded from an happy resurrection, but not from a miserable restoration to life.—All men shall be raised in the *same last day;* but the righteous, including the martyrs, shall be raised first in order.—And the *same* human *bodies* which were buried, shall be raised again in all their essential parts. 1. It would not be a resurrection, but a new creation, if the same bodies were not raised. 2. God's justice requires, that the same bodies which assisted in virtue or vice, should be raised to share in their respective rewards or punishments. 3. Christ, who is the pattern of our resurrection, had his very body that was crucified, restored to life, and re-united to his soul, John xx. 20, 26, 27. Luke xxiv. 39. Rom. viii. 11. 4. The very same bodies of men which fell asleep,—which were once mortal, corruptible, weak, dishonourable, vile,—sown in death, lay in their graves, and were devoured by worms, shall be raised again, Dan. xii. 2. 1 Cor. xv. 42—54. Phil. iii. 21. John v. 28, 29. Job xix. 25—27. No possible mixture of particles can render this raising of the same body difficult to God's infinite knowledge, wisdom, and power:—and perhaps no essential particles of human bodies can incorporate with any other animal body.— Nevertheless raised bodies will be very much different in qualities from what they are now, suited to bear the happiness or misery of the eternal state, 1 Cor. xv. 42—44, 52, 54. vi. 13.

3. The righteous and wicked shall, by the angels, be fully separated one from another,—the righteous placed at Christ's right hand in the air; and the wicked, perhaps classed according to their most remarkable crimes, shall be left assembled on the earth, Rev. xx. 12. 1 Thess. iv. 17. Mat. xiii. 41, 49. xxiv. 31. xxv. 32, 33.

II. The general judgment of all mankind will immediately follow these preparations. 1. God's not punishing or rewarding men in this world, according to their deeds, strongly suggests the certainty of some future general judgment, Eccl. iii. 16, 17. 2 Thess. i. 6—8. 2. The consciences of heathens suggest a future judgment, Rom. ii. 15. And hence spring their fables of Eacus, Minos, and Rhadamanthus judging men in the other world. 3. Scripture plentifully attests the reality of a future general judgment, Psalm l. 1—6. xcvi. 11—13. xcviii. 7—9. Eccl. xii. 14. Jude 14, 15. Acts xvii. 31. Mat. xii. 32, 36, 37. xiii. 41. xvi. 27. xxvi. Rom. xiv. 10. 2 Cor. v. 10. 2 Tim. iv. 1. Rev. xx. 11—15. John v. 27—29. Heb. vi. 2.

To render men perpetually watchful, and constantly preparing for this general judgment, in which their qualities and conduct will be thoroughly tried, and their eternal happiness and misery publicly fixed, God hath perfectly concealed the precise time of it, Mark xiii. 32—38. But the destructive vengeance of God on the Jewish nation, and the heathen persecuting empire of Rome,—on Antichrist, and Gog and Magog, are preludes of it, Psalm xxi. 8—12. cx. 5, 6. Mat. xxiv. 29—51. And the general conversion of both Jews and Gentiles to Christ, and the thousand years reign of his saints, are more delightful forerunners of it, 2 Thess. ii. 11—13. Rev. xi. xvi.—xx. Rom. xi.

God, Father, Son, and Holy Ghost will judge the world at the last day, Eccl. xii. 14. Psalm l. 6. Rom. ii. 15, 16. But Christ God-man, as the mediatorial deputy of God, will immediately act in this work, Mat. xxv. 31—46. xix. 28. John v. 22.

Acts xvii. 31. x. 42. Rom. ii. 16. xiv. 10. 1 Cor. iv. 4, 5. 2 Cor. v. 10. 1 Thess. iv. 16. 2 Thess. i. 7---9. 2 Tim. iv. 1. Rev. i. 7. Thus shall the ignominy of his debasement be publicly wiped off, and his victory over his enemies be manifested, Rev. i. 7. Mat. xxvi. 64; and men shall have a visible judge, who, in the hardest circumstances, fulfilled that law by which he judges others, Rev. i. 7. Mat. iii. 15. v. 17, 18. Luke xxiv. 26. Gal. iv. 4. iii. 13. John viii. 29. Isa. xlii. 21.---The saints will not *assist* Christ in judging the world. But they judge others,--- 1. In Christ their Head, in whom they are already risen and sit together, Eph ii. 6. 2. Their good works, especially when publicly mentioned in the last judgment, interpretatively condemn the wickedness of devils and men. 3. They will approve, perhaps with solemn shouts, the sentences which Christ will pass upon wicked angels and men, 1 Cor. vi. 2, 3.—The apostles' sitting on twelve thrones, judging the twelve tribes of Israel, ——-means that gospel-hearers will be judged by those doctrines and laws which they taught; and they will have most exalted fellowship with Christ in heaven, as they had in the church on earth, Mat. xix. 28.

Christ will then judge, 1. All the devils. Jude 6. 2 Pet. ii. 4. Mat. xxv. 41. viii. 29;—and all men, good and bad, 2 Cor. v. 10. Rev. xx. 12. Acts x. 42. 2 Tim. iv. 1. But believers shall not come into the judgment of condemnation, John iii. 18. v. 24. Rom. viii. 1, 33, 34. Nor shall wicked men stand or be justified in the judgment, Psalm i. 5. 2. All the qualities, thoughts, words, and deeds of these devils and men, 1 Cor. iv. 5. Rom. ii. 15, 16. Mat. xii. 36, 37. 2 Cor. v. 10. Eccl. xii. 14. Mat. xxv. 34—45;—and in judging these, Christ will *examine the causes*, and *pronounce the sentences*.

Christ's *trial of causes*, in the last judgment, will be, 1. Most easy,—the judge being possessed of infinite knowledge, wisdom, power, equity, and majesty; and the consciences of the judged being fully awakened and impartial, will readily attest every charge, 1 Cor. iv. 5. Heb. iv. 13. Rom. ii. 15. 1 John iii. 20, 21. 2. Most exact, as if transacted by *opened books*,—the book of God's infinite knowledge, and exact remembrance of every quality, thought, word, and deed, Psalm cxxxix. 16. lvi. 8. Mal. iii. 16;—the book of men's conscience, in which the law, which is the standard of judgment, and every quality, thought, word, and deed, are divinely marked, Rom. ii. 15, 16. 1 John iii. 20, 21. Acts xxiv. 16. 2 Cor. i. 12;—the book of Scripture, according to the declarations of which, the judgment shall proceed, and by which they who had it shall be judged, they who had it not, shall be judged by the law of nature, Rom. ii. 12. Luke xii. 47, 48;—and the book of God's purposes; those who are found in his purpose of election or *book of life*, being through Christ's righteousness imputed to them, and his grace implanted in, and exercised by them, adjudged to eternal happiness; and those who are not, being condemned to hell, Rev. xx. 12. xxii. 12. 3. Most public, every angel and man being present to witness or share in every thing transacted; and hence much different from God's judging men in this life, or at death, Rev. xx. 11, 12. Mat. xxv. 31—45. 4. Most regular, the righteous being first judged, as they were first raised, and must give their solemn assent to the judgment of others,—and to shew them that God delights more in acts of mercy and favour, than in those of dreadful vengeance, Mat. xxv. 34—45. 5. Most solemn, with inconceivable grandeur and majesty, Rev. xx. 11, 12. i. 7. 2 Thess. i. 7. Mat. xxv. 34—45.

The *sentences pronounced*, in consequence of this trial, will be infinitely just and proper, every one receiving sentence according to the nature or desert of the works charged to their account in law, Rev. xx. 12. xxii. 12. Rom. xiv. 12. 2 Cor. v. 10. Mat. xii. 36, 37. Wicked men shall be condemned for the sinfulness of their nature and practice, and particularly for unkindness to poor saints, in which they had manifested their contempt and hatred of Christ and his Father, Mat. xxv. 41—45. Believers shall be adjudged to everlasting life on account of Christ's fulfilment of the law in their stead, Rom. viii. 34. Phil. iii. 9; and their sentence will correspond with the nature, though not with the merit of their gracious qualities and works, particularly their kindness to poor saints, which shall be publicly mentioned as a mark of their union with Christ, filial relation to God, gracious heirship and diligent seeking of his heavenly kingdom, Mat. xxv. 34—40. But, whether their sins will be publicly mentioned in the last judgment, is not so evident. On the one hand, 1. None of their sins are mentioned in the judicial procedure, Mat. xxv. 34—40. 2. God casts all their sins behind his back, into the depths of the sea, and remembers them no more, Isa. xxxviii. 17. xliii. 25. Mic. vii. 18. Jer. xxxi. 34. v. 20. 3. Christ, their judge, being also their propitiation and advocate, would not mention their sins, Rom. iv. 25. 1 John ii. 1, 2. Prov. x. 12. xvii. 9. 4. The public mention of their sins could not but affect them with shame; and could not consist with his presenting them *without spot* or *without wrinkle*, Eph. v. 27. But on the other hand, 1. Every work of men, whether good or bad, is represented as brought into judgment, Eccl. xii. 14. 2 Cor. v. 10. 2. God's justice seems to require, that both sides of a cause should be produced and heard, Gen. xviii. 25. 3. Many of their sins are publicly marked in Scripture. 4. By the public mentioning of their sins, the justifying virtue of Christ's blood will be illustriously manifested, Acts xiii. 39. 5. Many of their sins are so connected with those of the wicked, that the one cannot be publicly mentioned without the other. 6. The belief of such public manifestation of their sins may be of great use to render them circumspect in this life. 7. Such public mention of their sins could not then affect them with disagreeable shame and confusion, as it is not their innocence, but Jesus and his righteousness, which are their comfort and glory, Eph. i. 7.

III. These sentences will immediately be EXECUTED in the wicked going away into everlasting punishment, and the righteous into life eternal, Mat. xxv. 46 2 Thess. i. 8—10. Dan. xii. 2. John v. 28, 29. Rev. xx. 13—15. 1 Thess. iv. 17. Rom. ii. 6—10. Isa. iii. 10, 11.—While the holy angels drive the wicked to hell, and honourably attend the saints to heaven, Mat. xiii. 41, 42, 49, 50, this lower world, by an universal conflagration, shall be purged of all the effects of sin, and its present form changed into one exceedingly pure and glorious, Job xiv. 12. Psalm cii. 26, 27. Isa. lxv. 17, 18. lxvi. 22. Rev. xx. 12—15. xxi. xxii. 2 Pet. iii. 7—13. Rom. viii. 19—21.

Christ's exaltation is NECESSARY, I. *In respect of his Father.* 1. That he might manifest his faithfulness and equity, in rewarding him, as Mediator, according to his deserts, and the promises made to him, Psalm xix. 11. Isa. liii. 10—12. lii. 13. Psalm xxi. xxii. 27—31. Isa. ix. 6, 7. xl. 9, 10. xlix. 1—12. 2. To mark his distinguished love to him, as the darling of his heart, in whose high honour and intimate fellowship he infinitely delights, Isa. li. 13. xlii. 1. Mat. iii. 17. xvii. 5. Psalm xci. 14—16. 3. To manifest his infinite highness, in holding so inconceivably exalted a God-man Mediator still subject to him, John xx. 17. 1 Cor. xv. 27, 28. 4. To manifest the exceeding riches of his grace towards men, in exalting their nature in personal union with his own Son, that they may behold, receive from, and worship God, answerably to their condition. And hence perhaps his exaltation is represented as a *gift*, Phil. ii. 9. II. *In respect of Christ himself.* 1. That his honour might be fully and conspicuously re-established after so remarkable humiliation, John xvii. 5. 2. That, notwithstanding his manhood had a right to great glory by its personal union with his divine nature, he might also enjoy it as the reward of his humbled service, as a public and everlasting mark of the perfection and acceptation of his atonement by God, Isa. xlix. 3, 4. xl. 10. liii. 10—12. Phil. ii. 6—11. John xvi. 10. 3. That in his administration of the new covenant, he might honourably execute his threefold office, take possession of eternal life, prepare heaven for his people, and, by his intercession, word, and Spirit, prepare them for it, and at last manifest his special love to them before the whole world, John xiv. 2, 3, 19. Heb.

vi. 20. 4. That he might effectually subdue, restrain, destroy, and triumph over his and our implacable enemies, Psalm xxi. 8—12. lxviii. 18, 21. cx. 1, 5, 6. 1 Cor. xv. 25. 5. That, in fulfilling the ancient types and predictions, he might manifest himself the true promised Messiah, 1 Cor. xv. 4. Luke xxiv. 26, 27. Heb. viii. 4. III. *In respect of his elect.* 1. In his resurrection he secured their union to him, as his quickened mystical members;—secured their justification, receiving a solemn acquittance and acceptance, in their name, 1 Tim. iii. 16. Rom. iv. 25;---secured their regeneration and sanctification, Col. ii. 11, 12. iii. 1. Eph. ii. 5, 6. Rom. vi. 4---6. Phil. iii. 10. Gal. ii. 20; and secured their resurrection to everlasting life, 1 Thess. iv. 14. 1 Cor. xv. 12, 13, 22, 23. Col. iii. 3, 4. Rom. viii. 11, 13, 29. 2. In his ascension he took possession of heaven in their name,---prepares it for them,---pours down his Spirit upon them,---weans their affections from things of this world, which he hath left, and attracts them to things above, where he is, John xiv. 2, 3. 2 Cor. v. 5. John xvi. 7. xii. 32. Col. iii. 1, 2. 3. His sitting at the right hand of God is their relative glorification,---secures their exaltation in due time, Eph. i. 20---23. Rev. iii. 21. It manifests the perpetual efficacy of his intercession for completing their happiness, and the destruction of their enemies, Heb. i. 3. viii. 1, 2. 1 Cor. xv. 24. Psalm ii. 4. xcvii. 1---5.——It teaches them an holy reverence of him, Psalm ii. 12. xlv. 11. Rev. i. 13---17; an ardent love to him, and a ready opening of their heart to him, Psalm xxiv. 7—10; a contempt of earthly, and an esteem of, and desire after, heavenly things, as seen in HIM, their Head, exalted to the highest, Eph. i. 18—20. 4. In his coming to judgment, he will crown them with glory and honour; and instead of secret pardons, comforts, and attestations by his Spirit,—will publicly, before all angels and men, proclaim them his and his Father's righteous favourites and adopted children.

REFLECT. If God so exalt Jesus Christ, why hath he not an higher,—a far higher place in my heart? Why do not all my thoughts, words, and deeds, concur in exalting him? Why is not my whole conversation in heaven, where Christ is at the right hand of God, and making continual intercession for me? Why am not I alway denying ungodliness and worldly lusts, and living soberly, righteously, and godly in this present world, —and looking for the glorious appearing of the great God my Saviour,—and my being for ever with the Lord?

BOOK V.

Of the Principal Blessings of the Covenant of Grace, Union with Christ; Justification; Adoption; Sanctification; Spiritual Comfort, and Eternal Glorification.

CHAP. I.

Of Union with Christ, and Effectual Calling.

THE general benefit which Christ, by his humiliation, procures and bestows in his exaltation, is our REDEMPTION or SALVATION, which includes the whole of our deliverance from the broken law, from sin, Satan, the world, death, and hell,—our full title to, and possession of grace and glory, to all eternity: Or, it includes the *change of our spiritual state,* in union to Christ, justification through his blood, and adoption into his family, which is perfected in the very first instant; and the *change of our nature and condition* in regeneration, sanctification, consolation, and eternal glory, which is perfected by degrees, Rom. viii. 30.

Christ's purchase of redemption for us doth not profit us, but by its effectual application to us. 1. Its typical representations manifest this.—The water of purification did not remove legal pollution, unless it was sprinkled; nor did the mixture of blood and water purify the leper, unless it was applied to his flesh, Num. xix. Lev. xi. xv. xvi. xiv. 1 Pet. i. 3. Heb. x. 22. xii. 24. 2. The emblematical representations of Christ and his benefits by a garment, Rom. xiii. 14. Isa. lxi. 10; by food, John vi. 53. Isa. xxv. 6; and by medicine, Isa. liii. 5. Rev. xxii. 2, which do not profit unless they be applied, prove this. All the promises of the gospel represent God as making over himself and his blessings to men, Gen. xvii. 7, 8. Isa. xxv. 6. lv. 2, 3. Acts xiii. 34. Ezek. xxxvi. 25—27. 4. If this application were not absolutely necessary, the eternal happiness of all men must be equal, as the price of our redemption is infinite in value, and equally suitable to all men, contrary to John xiii. 18. Acts viii. 21, 23. Mat. vii. 13, 14. 5. Christ's word, sacraments, and other instituted means of salvation, plainly mark the necessity of a spiritual application of it, 2 Cor. v. 18—21. Luke x. 21. Gal. iii. 27. 1 Cor. x. 16, 17.

OF UNION WITH CHRIST. 337

The Holy Ghost is the EFFECTUAL APPLIER of redemption to us, in and by whom Christ and his Father work in us. And he applies it, either *mediately*, through the word and sacraments, to adult persons, or *immediately*, to infants, and in the heavenly state, Isa. xliv. 3—5. John xvi. 7—14. Ezek. xxxvi. 27. Isa. lix. 21. And Christ being the Surety, Trustee, Administrator, Source, and Sum of all the blessings of the new covenant, UNION with him must be a remarkable benefit in itself, and the immediate foundation of all the rest, which are lodged in his person.—There is an *apparent union* between Christ and all the members of the visible church, which is formed by their receiving common gifts and influences from him, and their making an open profession of his truths and service;—and which is easily broken, John xv. 2, 6. Mat. viii. 12. And there is a *moral union* of mutual affection between him and believers, which is more properly *communion*, John xiv. 21.—But that UNION with him, upon which our enjoyment of his benefits depends, includes, 1. A LEGAL UNION between us as guilty and self-ruined *debtors* and *criminals*, and him as our SURETY. This was formed from all eternity, when we were chosen in him. The everlasting love of God and the covenant of grace are the *bonds* of it;—and the placing our sins to Christ's account, that his satisfaction for them might be placed to ours in law-reckoning, is the effect of it, Heb. vii. 22. Eph. i. 4. 2 Cor. v. 21. Rom. v. 19. 2. His PERSONAL UNION with our nature, formed in the *fulness of time*, in order to his fulfilling the requirements which his legal union with us drew upon him, Heb. ii. 11—16. John i. 14. Isa. vii. 14. Rom. viii. 3, 4. Gal. iv. 4, 5. 3. A SPIRITUAL or MYSTICAL UNION, formed in the moment of our regeneration,—in which we, as Christ's purchased Bride, are, by his Spirit entering into our hearts, and by our receiving him by faith, united to him as our Husband and Head of influence, 1 Cor. i. 30. vi. 17. John xvii. 26. Eph. ii. 21, 22. iii. 17.—In attesting the reality of this union between Christ and believers, the Scripture represents him as in them, and them as in him, John xiv. 20. vi. 56. xv. 4, 5, 7. xvii. 21, 26. Col. i. 27. 1 John v. 20. 2 Cor. v. 21. Isa. xlv. 17; and having him for their life, 1 John v. 11, 12. Gal. ii. 20. Col. iii. 3, 4; and being partakers of him, Heb. iii. 14.

This spiritual union between Christ and believers being exceedingly mysterious in itself, is in Scripture illustrated to us by many similitudes, some of which transcend, and others are transcended by it. 1 It is likened to that union which is between the persons of the Godhead, John xvii. 21. xiv. 20. vi. 57. But here it falls infinitely short,—not being absolutely necessary, or self-existent; nor doth it constitute Christ and believers one individual substance. 2. It is likened to the union

Z

of Christ's two natures in his person:—for, as his manhood was conceived by the power of the Holy Ghost, we are born of the Spirit, Mat. i. 20. Luke i. 35. John iii. 5, 6, 8. 1 Pet. i. 3, 23. 1 John iii. 9. v. 18. As Christ, by a sovereign act, assumed our nature,—he by another apprehends our person, Heb. ii. 14, 16. Phil. iii. 12. As, in his manhood dwells all the fulness of Godhead, we, being in him, are filled with all the fulness of God, Col. ii. 9, 10. Eph. iii. 19. He, being made flesh, tabernacled with us,—and we, being united to him, God dwells with us in him, John i. 14. Rev. ii. 13. Eph. ii. 21, 22. iii. 17.—In him, as God-man, there is the grace of union, unction, and headship; and in us, as united to him, there is a gracious union, unction, and membership, John i. 14, 16. Col. ii. 19. i. 18.—Nevertheless, our spiritual union with him falls far short of the union of his two natures,—as it doth not render him and us one person,—nor, for a time, incapable of sin, Gal. v. 17. Rom. vii. 14—25. viii. 13. But it is indeed by that new nature which his self-uniting act forms in us, that he holds fellowship with our soul, 2 Pet. i. 4. 2 Cor. v. 17. Gal. vi. 15; and which, by his gracious influence, mortifies our inward corruption, till it be utterly abolished, Rom. viii. 2, 13. Gal. v. 17, 24. Rom. vii. 14—25. 3. It is likened to the union between a king and his subjects, because he, as our Brother, hath power over, cares for, rules, and protects us; and we are voluntarily subject to him, and have our eternal happiness dependent on his infinite wisdom, power, mercy, and honour, Rev. xv. 3. Mat. xxv. 34—40. But it is much more spiritual, close, and permanent. 4. As it imports mutual knowledge, chusing, solemn self-dedication, and issues in mutual love, delight, and interest, it is likened to the marriage-union betwixt husband and wife, Eph. v. 30, 32. Isa. liv. 5. Ezek. xvi. 8—14. Song ii. 16. vi. 3. But here also it much transcends, as it renders Christ and believers *one spirit*, and can never be dissolved, 1 Cor. vi. 16, 17. Phil. ii. 5. 2 Pet. i. 4. Col. iii. 3. Hos. ii. 19, 20. 5. To mark that their happy connections, support, and glory, depend on him, it is likened to the union of a building with its foundation or corner-stone, Isa. xxviii. 16. 1 Cor. iii. 9, 11, 17. Psalm cxviii. 22. 1 Pet. ii. 4, 5. Eph. ii. 20—22. But here also it far transcends, as Christ is equally near, and communicates life to every believer, 1 Pet. ii. 5. Gal. ii. 20. John xiv. 19. xi. 25. 6. Because through it we receive all our supporting, quickening, beautifying, and fructifying influences, it is likened to the union between the root of a tree and its branches, John xv. 1—7. Col. ii. 7. But here also it far transcends, as Christ, our root, is equally near to all his branches, and not one of them can become altogether withered, barren, or broken off, Rom. vii. 4. vi. 14. viii. 35—39. John x. 28, 29. 7. As we are enlightened, governed, honoured, and receive our spiritual nourishment and breath through Christ, it is likened to the union between our head and other members of our body, Eph. iv. 15, 16. 1 Cor. i. 12. Col. i. 18. ii. 18, 19. But it far transcends this, as Christ is equally near to every member, and none can be separated from him, or become utterly benumbed or mortified, John xiv. 16, 19. Col. iii. 3, 4. Gal. ii. 20. Isa. xxvi. 19.   8. As Christ enters into our soul, and is the very life of it, our spiritual union with him is likened to that of our soul, or of our food with our body, John vi. 56, 57. Col. iii. 4. But it is much more close, as Christ can never be separated from us, or cease to actuate us, Eph. iv. 16. Col. ii. 19. Gal. ii. 28.

Our spiritual union with Christ may be further illustrated from our connection with Adam. In consequence of our legal union with him, formed in the covenant of works, his Fall under the curse drew, that very moment, all his posterity along with him; and lying in threatenings of the broken law, it is ready to pour its vials of wrath upon us, whenever we exist; and hath a baleful influence in drawing us into actual existence; but never, till we become united with him as our natural root or parent, hath it any hold by which it can fix upon us:—so, in consequence of Jesus's fulfilling all righteousness for us, he, as our legal Head and Husband, received a full justification for us, which lies ready for us in the promises of the gospel; but till we be united to him, as our Head of influence, in whom all the promises are YEA and AMEN, we have no actual share in his righteousness and grace.——It may also be further illustrated, from the personal union of Christ's two natures. 1. In the constitution of the *legal union* between Christ and us, a precise moment was fixed for the union of our nature to his divine person, that the debt charged upon him, as our Surety, might be demanded and obtained from him, Gal. iv. 4. Rom. viii. 3, 4. In like manner, a precise moment was fixed in the purpose of God for the spiritual union of our persons to him, that his righteousness fulfilled in our stead might be imputed to us, and the effects of it imparted to us, Ezek. xvi. 8. Psalm cx. 3.   2. Notwithstanding Christ's engagement from all eternity to pay our debt to the broken law, he remained in his Father's bosom, without having it demanded, till he assumed our nature in the *fulness of time:* and, notwithstanding the translation of our debt upon him, and his satisfaction for it long ago, we, though chosen in him, continue under the broken law, *children of wrath*, till in the *time of love* we be spiritually united to Christ, Eph. ii. 2, 3. Ezek. xvi. 5—8.   3. From the creation of the world till the *fulness of time*, God was constantly preparing to demand his undertaken satisfaction from his Son, and his Son repeatedly appeared as in our nature, before he actually assumed it: And, while elect men continue unborn, or in a state of wrath, God is always making preparations for uniting them to Christ in their *time of love*,—and, by common operations of his Spirit, produces apparent unions of many of them to him, Rev. iii. 20. Matth. xiii. 20. Heb. vi. 4, 5. 4. Though the translation of our debt to the broken law upon Christ by his legal union with us as our Surety, was the spring of his actual assumption of our nature, yet the demand of satisfaction, in order of nature, not of time, commenced posterior to that assumption. And, though Christ's righteousness—really ours, as fulfilled by our Surety legally united to us, be the foundation or meritorious cause of God's spiritual union of our persons to his, yet his formal, actual, and judicial accounting that righteousness to our persons, to constitute us righteous in law-reckoning, is in order of nature, not of time, consequential to our spiritual union to Christ, 2 Cor. v. 21. Rom. viii. 1. vii. 4. Isa. xlv. 24, 25.

In infants this mystical union with Christ is formed by the Holy Ghost's application of him, or Christ's spiritual application of himself, as made of God to them wisdom, righteousness, sanctification, and redemption, and thus forming in them a new nature, including faith, love, repentance, and every other saving grace, all which, in answerableness to the natural powers of their soul, are ready to act in due time, as God gives opportunity, John iii. 5, 6, 8. Mark x. 14. But, in persons having the actual use of their reason, this union is formed in the work of EFFECTUAL CALLING, in which Christ, by his word and Spirit, invites, drives, and draws them to himself; and, in his powerfully applied declarations, and offers of the gospel, conveys himself and his grace into their hearts. This effectual calling is the work of God, Rom. ix. 24. viii. 30. xi. 29. 1 Thess. iv. 7; and is ascribed to the Father, 1 Cor. i. 9. 2 Tim. i. 9; and to the Son, Rom. i. 6. 2 Pet. i. 3; but, in a peculiar manner, to the Holy Ghost, as sent by the Father and Son to apply redemption to us, Rom. viii. 2. 2 Cor. iii. 6. Rev. ii. 7. John xvi. 7—13. Ezek. xxxvi. 26, 27. Isa. xliv. 3—5.—Effectual calling being a benefit of the covenant of grace, Jer. xxxi. 33. xxxii. 40. Ezek. xxxvi. 26, 27. Hos. ii. 14, 18—20. 2 Tim. i. 9; purchased by the blood of Christ as a Surety, Tit. ii. 14. Gal. iii. 13, 14. 1 Pet. i. 18—21. ii. 24. iii. 18. Rev. v. 9, *all the elect, and they only*, partake of it, Rom. viii. 28—30. 2 Tim. i. 9. 1 Pet. i. 2. 2 Pet. i. 10; and that in different periods of their life on earth, Mat. xx. 1, 5, 6. 2 Tim. iii. 15. 1 Cor. xv. 8. Luke vii. 37. xxiii. 42, 43.——This effectual work of God is named a CALLING, as it supposes men at a distance from Christ by nature, and implies his dealing with them as reasonable creatures, by convictions, illuminations, and persuasions.

in bringing them to him: and by it they are brought from a state of sin, wrath, darkness, and worldliness, to a state of fellowship with Christ and his Father and the blessed Spirit,—to the kingdom of God, to marvellous light, love, liberty, holiness, and eternal happiness in Christ, Rom. viii. 30, 1, 2. Eph. ii. 1—13, 19—22. v. 8. 1 Pet. ii. 9. John xv. 9. 1 John i. 3, 7. 2 Cor. xiii. 14. 1 Cor. vii. 22, 23. John viii. 32, 36. 1 Thess. ii. 12, 13. 1 Tim. vi. 11, 12. 1 Pet. i. 16. v. 10. 2 Pet. i. 3—10.

The manifestations of God's perfections, in the works of creation and providence, may make men more capable of a rational attention to the invitations of his word, *if enjoyed;* and afflictions may awaken to a seriousness in this attention. But multitudes of mankind have no outward call to the fellowship of Christ. 1. Multitudes of them are destitute of his statutes, and ignorant of his judgments, Psalm cxlvii. 19, 20; are not his people in an external manner, Hos. i. 9. ii. 23. Rom. ix. 25, 26. x. 19; are strangers to the covenants of promise, without God, and without Christ, and without all hopes of future happiness, Eph. ii. 12; are perishing for want of vision, Prov. xxix. 18; are permitted to walk in their own ruinous ways, Acts xiv. 16. xvii. 30. Isa. liii. 6. lv. 7; and are by wisdom ignorant of God, 1 Cor. i. 20. Rom. i. 21—23. 2. The doctrine of salvation is hidden from the heathen world, Eph. iii. 8, 9. Col. i. 26. Rom. xvi. 25. 3. God forbade preaching of the gospel to many men, Mat. x. 5. Acts xvi. 6, 7. 4. An extensive knowledge of the world experimentally demonstrates, that the bulk of mankind are ignorant of the method of salvation through Christ.

OBJEC. I. " The call of the gospel reaches all men, Tit. ii. " 11. 1 Tim. ii. 4. Col. i. 6. Mark xvi. 15. Luke ii. 10." ANSW. It is extended to men of *all sorts*, Jews and Gentiles, and of all ranks, poor or rich, but not to every particular person, Rev. v. 9. vii. 9. A warrant to preach it every where will not prove that it is every where preached.

OBJEC. II. " The voice of nature, which extends to every " man, calls all to repentance and virtue, Psalm xix. 1—5. " Rom. i. 18—21. ii. 14, 15. Acts xiv. 17. xvii. 27." ANSW. It calls them to God as a Creator and Preserver, but affords no hints of him as a Redeemer.

OBJEC. III. " All men have had a double revelation of the " gospel of Christ, in the first promise to Adam and Eve, and " in God's covenant with Noah, Gen. iii. 15. ix." ANSW. Were all men that have, do, or shall live on earth, present to hear these declarations, or capable to understand them? Why not as well maintain that all mankind, in their own persons, lived perfectly happy in Eden, or are just come out of the ark into a scarce dried world?

OBJEC. IV. " Many heathens were endowed with eminent " goodness and virtue." ANSW. 1. They had received many remarkable gifts from God as their Creator and preserving Governor, but no appearances of saving graces. Nay, their pride, selfishness, or indulgence of some particular wickedness, plainly manifested the naughtiness of their apparent virtues. 2. Let them have what goodness they will, there is no salvation without Christ, Acts iv. 12; no saving connection between adult persons and Christ, without knowledge of, and faith in him, John xvii. 3. Eph, iii. 17. John iii. 18, 36; and no knowledge of, or faith in him, without hearing the gospel, Rom. x. 14, 17, Prov. xxix. 18. Eph. ii. 12.

OBJEC. V. " Melchizedek, Job, and his friends, the centu-
" rion, whose faith Christ admired, the Syrophenician woman,
" Cornelius, and many other heathens, had true and saving
" faith. All that in any place call upon the name of the Lord
" shall be saved. All that fear God and work righteousness
" are accepted by him. No more is necessary to our coming to
" our God, than a believing that he is, and is a rewarder of
" them that diligently seek him, Gen. xiv. 18. Job i.—xlii.
" Mat. viii. 5—13. xv. 22—28. Acts x. Rom. x. 12. Acts x.
" 34, 35. Heb xi. 6." ANSW. 1. None of the persons mentioned appear to have wanted divine revelations. Melchizedek, Job, and his friends had access to them by tradition from Noah, or immediately from God, as well as Abraham and his immediate descendants.—The two centurions and Syrophenician woman had access to the Jewish revelations and worship. 2. The works of unregenerate men, which are materially good, are regarded and rewarded in this life by God, 1 Kings xxi. 29. Jon. iii. Mark x. 21. 3. Under the gospel men are accepted by God, without any regard to their family, nation, or outward circumstances: but men never truly fear God or work righteousness, without believing in Christ; or have any true faith in him, but as connected with Christ, 2 Pet. i. 1. Phil. i. 29. Eph. iii. 17. Luke xvii. 5. John xiv. 1. vi. 35, 44, 45. Eph. ii. 18. iii. 12. Nor is acceptance or any other new-covenant blessing promised but in Christ, 2 Cor. i. 20. Psalm lxxii. 17.

OBJEC. VI. " It is inconsistent with the infinite mercy of
" God to leave multitudes of mankind destitute of the neces-
" sary means of salvation." ANSW. 1. We have long ago proved against Deists, that he hath done so in full consistency with all his perfections. 2. God's infinite mercy no more binds him to bestow the means of salvation upon all men, than it binds him to bestow them on all devils, who are his more excellent creatures by nature, Jude 6. 2 Pet. ii. 4. Mat. xxv. 41. 3. Scripture never hints that God bestows any saving mercy, but through Christ, 2 Cor. v. 19. Eph. i. 3. Psalm ciii. 17, xxxi. 19. xxv. 10. lxxii. 17.

OBJEC. VII. " All the heathens must have sufficient means
" of salvation. If God require them to worship him, he must
" afford them the proper laws and motives of acceptable wor-
" ship. If he hath given them immortal souls, he must put
" them into a proper way of obtaining everlasting happiness.
" He cannot, in a consistence with his own infinite wisdom and
" goodness, require that as the condition of their salvation, con-
" cerning which he doth not inform them : in distributing eter-
" nal rewards or punishments, he must deal with men accord-
" ing to the opportunities, manifestations, abilities, and motives
" which he bestowed upon them.—The faithful improvement
" of the smallest talents, shall be rewarded with everlasting
" life, John xx. 29. Luke xii. 47, 48. Mat. xxv. 14—29."
ANSW. 1. God hath afforded heathens some knowledge of the
object of worship, but not of the way of salvation, Rom. i. 19,
20. Eph. ii. 12. Rom. x. 10---17. Acts iv. 12. John xiv. 6. x.
7, 9. 2. God made devils immortal spirits, and yet, never
since their fall, put them into any way of salvation, Jude 6.
2 Pet. ii. 4. Mat. xxv. 41. 3. Sins against the light of nature
are sufficiently criminal to render men eternally miserable,
Ezek. xviii. 4. Rom. vi. 23. i. 18---32. ii. 4---10. iii. 9---20,
23. And, though they be not so heinous, as like sins committed against gospel-light, yet ignorance of God and spiritual
things being a sin in itself, can never make that which is sinful
innocent or virtuous. 4. Though God, for the encouragement
of order and virtue, reward the apparently good works of heathens with temporal benefits, they, when examined by his spiritual and exceeding broad law, appear very unfit to be rewarded by him with eternal happiness, Prov. xv. 8. xxi. 4, 27, xxviii.
9. Psalm xiv. 2—4. Rom. iii. 9—20.

All men who read and hear the gospel contained in the
Scriptures, are called to the fellowship of Christ, and to receive
a full salvation in him, as the *free gift* of God to themselves.
The law, which manifests our sinfulness and danger, and warns
us to flee from the wrath to come, and which, upon a revelation of Christ, binds us to believe in him, is binding upon all
men, Ezek. xxxiii. 11. Rom. iii 10---20. Gal. iii. 10, 24. John
vi. 29. 1 John iii. 23. And the gospel, which exhibits and offers Christ and his salvation, invites every man that hears it
to receive him in it, as *given* to himself, without regarding
whether he be well or ill qualified, elect or reprobate. 1. Christ's
righteousness being infinitely valuable in itself, and fulfilled in
manhood, is equally answerable to the demands of the broken
law on every man ; and all his purchased blessings relative to
their change of state, nature, or condition, are equally sufficient
for and suited to them all, Acts xx. 28. Gal. iv. 4, 5. 1 Cor. i.
30. Ezek. xxxvi. 25---27. Tit. ii. 14. Heb. ix. 12, 14. 2. In

the gospel, Jesus Christ is indefinitely presented and offered to all men that hear it, as the absolutely free gift of God, and the *official Saviour* of mankind, Psalm lxviii. 18. Rom. xi. 26, 27. 1 John iv. 14. John iii. 14---17. iv. 42. vi. 32, 39, 40. 1 Tim. i. 15. Heb. vii. 25. Isa. xlii. 6, 7. xlix. 6, 8. 3. In the gospel men are, in the most general and unlimited manner, called to receive the blessings of salvation, Isa. xlv. 22---25. lv. 1---7. Prov. viii. 4. Mat. xi. 28. John vii. 37, 38, 39. vi. 37. Rev. xxii. 17. 4. Such men as appear most likely to be excluded, are expressly invited to receive Christ and his salvation,---as the *lost*,---the *stupid*,---*foolish*,---*haters of knowledge*,---*scorners*, ---*notorious transgressors*,---*stout-hearted, and far from righteousness*,---*rebellious*,---who have *sinned to their uttermost*,---*self-conceited*,---*insensible of their sinfulness and misery*, &c. Mat. xviii. 11. Luke xix. 10. Hos. xiii. 9. Prov. i. 21---23. ix. 4, 5. Isa. i. 18. xlvi. 12, 13. lv. 7. lxv. 2. Jer. iii. 1, 4, 5, 14, 22. Mat. ix. 13. 1 Tim. i. 15, 16. Rev. iii. 17, 18. 5. The moral law, which requires men to receive and obey God as the only true God, and their God, is precisely of the same extent in its object as his offers of himself to be their God. And it is observable, that, in that moral law, there is a five-fold grant of God by himself to men, as *their God*, Exod. xx. 2—17. Deut. v. 6—21. comp. Deut. xxx. 6. Unless the gospel offers and calls were directed to all men in general that hear it, none durst embrace them, till they were certain of their having the required qualifications.—Nevertheless, it is certain, that the more fully a man is acquainted with himself, he will see the more of his own pride, naughtiness, sloth, insincerity, enmity against God, unworthiness of Christ, and unfitness to receive him;—and that no thoroughly convinced person, especially if tempted by Satan, will be able to see in himself enough of sincerity, sensibility, and willingness, to receive Christ as offered in the gospel.

OBJEC. I. " Only the *thirsty*, the *willing*, the *heavy laden* " *labourers*, are invited to receive Christ and his salvation, Isa. " lv. 1. John vii. 37. Rev. xxii. 17. Mat. xi. 28." ANSW. The *thirsty* in Isa. lv. 1, cannot mean only those who earnestly desire Christ and his righteousness and blessings; for, in verse 2, they are said to be spending money for that which is not bread, and labouring for that which satisfieth not; but must mean such as desire happiness in any form. *Whosoever will*, in Rev. xxii. 17, denotes the universality of the invitation, not the qualification of the persons invited, John vi. 37. vii. 37. The *heavy laden labourers* in Mat. xi. 28, includes such as have fatigued themselves in sinful courses, and are laden with the guilt and enslaving power of sin, Isa. lvii. 10. Heb. ii. 15. 2 Tim. iii. 6.

OBJEC. II. " It would be infinitely unbecoming men, who " had just been wallowing in their wickedness, to approach to, " or receive the holy Jesus, before some change be made upon " them." ANSW. 1. God must indeed make them new creatures, before they be able to receive him; but it is not as *new men*, but as *sinful men*, that they are warranted and required to receive him for their salvation, Mat. ix. 13. xviii. 11. 1 Tim. i. 15. 2. How is it unbecoming the dangerously diseased to approach to, or admit the all-skilful physician, before they be almost cured?—the unclean to apply the purifying water, before they be partially cleansed?—the starving to take any wholesome provision till they be almost satisfied? Exod. xv. 26. Hos. xiv. 4. Ezek. xxxvi. 25. Zech. xiii. 1. Isa. i. 18. Acts iii. 26. Rom. xi. 26, 27. Prov. ix. 5. Isa. lv. 1—3, 7. Rev. xxii. 17. How is it unbecoming ignorant men to come directly to the only-effectual Teacher?—unbecoming guilty men to receive the Lord their righteousness, who is made of God unto them righteousness?—unbecoming lost men to come to the *only*, the *divinely appointed* Saviour of men? Isa. xlviii. 17. xlv. 17, 22, 24. Luke xix. 10. Hos. xiii. 9. 3. It is impossible for men to attain to any true sincerity, humility, or reformation of heart, before they receive Christ, Job xiv. 4. Prov. xx. 9. Psalm li. 5. Eph. ii. 1—3, 10. Rom. viii. 7, 8, 2. John xv. 5. Jer. xvii. 9. xiii. 23. Tit. i. 15. iii. 3—7. 4. In receiving Jesus Christ, as made of God unto us wisdom, righteousness, sanctification, and redemption, we cannot continue cleaving to our sin, as we receive him in order to purge away and destroy it.

OBJEC. III. " God could not be candid, if he called all men " that hear the gospel to receive Christ and his salvation, since " he knows many of them to be reprobates." ANSW. 1. If God intend to cut off one by death, will that justify the man's withholding proper food, medicine, or warmth from himself, or his plunging a knife into his own throat? 2. God, by his gospel, calls no man to believe, any thing but what is important truth, nor to do any thing but what his law requires.

OBJEC. IV. " It is altogether absurd and unprofitable to call " reprobates to believe on Christ, since they cannot believe." ANSW. 1. Indeed they *cannot*, and what is worse, they *will not*, believe on him, John x. 26. v. 40. Isa. lxv. 2. Mat. xxiii. 37. 2. Ministers, being utterly uncertain who are elected, and who not, must invite men in general to Christ, and leave it to the Holy Ghost, who knows all things, to determine such as are elected to believe, to the saving of their soul. 3. By the general invitations of the gospel, many reprobates obtain common gifts and graces,—have many sins prevented,—obtain much temporal happiness,—and are rendered remarkably useful to the elect.

Before their mystical union to Jesus Christ, men, and especially gospel-hearers, may perform that which is naturally or civilly good,—and even the matter of religious duties; and, under common operations of the Holy Ghost, may perform that which resembles *spiritual* goodness. But they can never heartily comply with the gospel-call, believe in Christ, or perform any thing in a truly holy and spiritual manner. 1. We have formerly proved, that all men by nature are under the curse of the broken law, which is the strength of sin. And as, in their conception, that curse keeps them destitute of original righteousness, so it retains them in that condition, while it lies on them. 2. Scripture declares all men *unclean*, which being universal, must be understood of sinful pollution, Job xiv. 4; that David, a child of pious parents, and one of the best of men, was shapen and conceived in sin, Psalm li. 5; that the Jewish people of God were wicked transgressors from the womb, Psalm lviii. 3. Isa. xlviii. 8; and that all men, by nature, are so enslaved by their indwelling corruptions, that they can do nothing spiritually good, Gen. vi. 5. viii. 21. Psalm xiv. 2—4. liii. 2, 3. Prov. xx. 9. Jer. xvii. 9. John iii. 6. xv. 5. Rom. v. 6. viii. 7, 8. Eph. ii. 1—3, 12. Tit. i. 15. iii. 3. 2 Cor. iii. 5. 1 Cor. iv. 7. Mat. xv. 19. 3. If men had any natural inclination or ability to do that which is spiritually good, why, amidst so many thousand powerful motives to virtue, and none at all to vice, are men, every where, so remarkably wicked in their thoughts, their words, and their deeds?—Why do all attentive, and especially the most sanctified men, find such inclinations toward vice, and such difficulty in doing any thing spiritually good? Psalm xiv. 1—4. liii. 1—4. Rom. i. 21—32. iii. 9—19. Mark vii. 21—23. Rom. vii. 5—25. James iii. 2. 1 John i. 8, 10.

OBJEC. I. "Without freedom of will, and ability to perform that which is spiritually good, men can be in no proper state of trial for everlasting happiness or misery; but must be either in the state of devils, or of established angels." ANSW. 1. Believers, while on earth, are not as established angels, being imperfect in their nature, work, and condition: Nor are wicked men as devils, being under a dispensation of God's mercy, which hath and will issue in the eternal salvation of many, Rom. vii. 14—25. 1 Tim. i. 13—16. John iv. Luke vii. 36—50. 1 Cor. vi. 9—11. Tit. iii. 3—7. Eph. ii. 1—22. iii. 8, 9. Acts xxvi. 17, 18. 2. Since Adam's fall, no man hath, or ever will be, in a *proper state of trial* for everlasting happiness. 1. All believers are fixed in a state of everlasting salvation in Christ. Without this, they could have no solid hope of their perseverance or eternal glory, Rom. viii. 28—39. Jer. xxxii. 39, 40. Isa. liv. 8—10. xlv. 17. John x. 27—29. xiv. 19. Col. iii. 3, 4. 2. If all men were in a state of trial for everlasting happiness, they ought all to have equal means and opportunities of grace afforded them, which it is certain they have not, Eph. ii. 12. Prov. xxix. 18. Psalm cxlvii. 19, 20. Acts xiv. 16. xvii. 30. 3. Such a state of trial would suspend men's eternal happiness upon their own inclinations and behaviour, not upon the free grace of God, contrary to 1 Cor. iv. 7. Mat. xi. 25, 26. Rom. ix. 16, 18. xi. 6. 4. The Israelites then stood in a state of trial for their temporal happiness in Canaan, but in none for their eternal happiness, Isa. i. 19, 20. Deut. viii. 2. xiii. 5. Judg. ii. 21, 22. iii. 1, 4. Exod. xvi. 4. xx. 20. 5. For promoting the exercise and evidence of their graces, believers are, in their condition, much tried with temptations, hard services, and sufferings, 1 Cor. iii. 13. 2 Cor. viii. 2. 1 Pet. i. 7. iv. 12. James i. 3, 12. Rev. ii. 10. iii. 10, 19. Psalm lxvi. 10. Dan. xi. 35. xii. 10. Zech. xiii. 9. But their eternal salvation being secured in Christ, is in no wise suspended on their good behaviour, Col. iii. 3, 4. John xiv. 19. x. 27---29. 6. Many warnings, exhortations, promises, and threatenings are directed to sinners in Scripture, not to put them to the trial whether they will, of themselves, do that which is truly acceptable to God, but to awaken their concern to have their state changed by an union to Christ, Acts xxvi. 17, 18. Col. i. 13. Eph. ii. 1---6; or directed to believers, to cause them to walk worthy of that state of salvation in which they are fixed in Christ, Col. ii. 6, 7. 1 Cor. xv. 58. Jer. xxxii. 39, 40. Heb. xii. 28, 29. Phil. i. 27. Col. i. 10. Luke i. 74, 75. 2 Cor. vii. 1. Eph. iv.—vi. Col. iii. iv.

OBJEC. II. " If men have not a freedom of will indifferently to choose good or evil, and power to act accordingly, their qualities and works, not being of free choice, cannot be either virtuous or vicious, deserving praise and reward, or blame and punishment." ANSW. 1. Hath God then no freedom of choice, no liberty? Are all his attributes and works unworthy of praise, because his infinite and unchangeable perfection of nature cannot admit his doing any thing base or sinful? Are the acts of holy angels and glorified saints, and especially of the man Christ, in no wise virtuous or praiseworthy, because their wills were, and are divinely determined towards good only? Are the acts of devils no sins, because their inclination is fixed on mischief? May not all these acts be voluntary, though their will be unalterably bended to that which is good, or to that which is evil? 2. It is highly absurd to pretend, that the more inward holiness one has inclining him to that which is good, the less virtuous and praiseworthy are his good actions;—and the more fixed and propense malice he has determining him to evil, the less bad his evil actions are:—that the better the root be, the less valuable the fruit; and the worse the root, the better the fruit, Matth. vii. 16—18. xii. 33—35. 3. Man's will never was, nor ever will be, placed in an equal bent towards good and evil. In his state of innocence it was inclined only to good, though changeable towards evil, Eccl. vii. 9. Gen. i. 27. v. 1. In his fallen state it is inclined only to evil, Gen. vi. 5. viii. 21. Jer. xvii. 9. Rom. viii. 7, 8. Tit. iii. 3.—In men's state of begun recovery, their new nature is inclined only to good, and their unrenewed, or old man, only to evil, Rom. vii. 14—25. Gal. v. 17, 19—24. In the heavenly state, it will be inclined only to good, 1 John iii. 2. Eph. v. 27.

OBJEC. III. "To suppose men by nature without this free- "dom of will to choose, and ability to perform that which is "spiritually good, is inconsistent with the whole tenor of the "covenant of grace, and all the promises and calls of the "gospel, in which men are supposed capable to believe and "repent." ANSW. 1. The promises of the new covenant plain- ly suppose men to have hard and stony hearts, and to stand in absolute need of God's Spirit being put into them to change their heart, and enable them to choose and perform that which is spiritually good, Ezek. xi. 19, 20. xxxvi. 26, 27. Jer. xxxi. 33. 2. The calls of the gospel do not suppose men's natural ability to perform any thing spiritually good, but are calcu- lated to convince them of their weakness and wickedness, and to bring them to Christ, in whom alone spiritual strength is to be had, John vi. 37, 44, 45, 63, 65. vii. 38, 39. Phil. iv. 19. Zech. x. 12.

OBJEC. IV. "Without an equal bent of their will to good "and evil, men cannot be subjected to any moral law." ANSW. Was then Christ,—and are holy angels, glorified saints,—or even devils and damned men,—under no moral law, because their will is not equally inclined towards good and evil? If so, the blasphemy and murderous malice of the latter are as pleas- ing to God as the love and lively services of the former, Rom. iv. 15. v. 13. 1 John iii. 4.

OBJEC. V. "Scripture attests, that if heathens had enjoyed "proper means of grace, they would have repented and been "saved, Ezek. iii. 6. Matth. xi. 20—23." ANSW. It is not affirmed, that they would have turned to the Lord in a truly hearty and evangelical manner, and been eternally saved; but they would have so turned as to prevent their temporal de- structions, which, it is granted, may be done without special grace, Jon. iii. 1 Kings xxi. 29.

OBJEC. VI. "To deny the equal bent of men's will to good "and evil, or their natural ability to do that which is spi- "ritually good, is a plain adopting the tenets of atheistical

"Hobbes, and of the ancient heathen stoics." Answ. 1. We may safely and honourably adopt the truth, though Satan, and all his emissaries, should, for wicked purposes, do the same, James ii. 19. Mat. viii. 29. xvi. 16. Mark i. 24. 1 John v. 5. Acts xvi. 17. 1 Cor. iv. 1. 2. Hobbes pretended that God, by his grace, cannot determine men's will; that he hath no more hand in their best actions, than in their worst; that infants have no original sin; and being under no law, are capable of no fault; that the first motions of men's minds are not sinful; that no good thoughts are inspired by God, or bad ones by Satan; that men may sufficiently understand their Bible without any assistance of God's Spirit; that the mere belief of Christ's being the true Messiah is sufficient for men's salvation; that saving faith is not the gift of God, but the production of men's own mind; that our faith and obedience justify us before God, he accepting the will for the deed.—Many heathen stoics taught, that human nature is not corrupted with any original sin; that the following right reason is sufficient to render men happy in the highest degree; that men have it in their power to do little or no evil, and to conform themselves perfectly to God in moral goodness; that virtuous men are, in some respect, superior to the gods, as they are perfect by their own choice and care, not by any necessity of nature; and that truly virtuous dispositions once gained, may be totally and finally lost.—Let our opponents, therefore, claim them as their fathers and brethren in sentiment.

If men's eternal happiness do not depend on their own free will, an effectual calling of any of them to a state of fellowship with Christ, must be entirely of God's free grace. 1. Scripture attributes it wholly to God's free grace, James i. 17, 18. Eph. i. 3—8. ii. 1—10. Rom. v. 16—21. ix. 16, 18. xi. 6. iii. 24. vi. 14. Tit. iii. 3—7. ii. 11, 12. 2 Tim. i. 9. 1 Tim. i. 13, 15, 16. 2. This call finds men in a most dreadful state of sin and misery, Tit. iii. 3. Rom. i. 21—32. iii. 10—20, 23. viii. 7, 8. Eph. ii. 1—3, 12. 1 Cor. vi. 9—11. Job xiv. 4. xv. 14, 16. Gen. vi. 5. viii. 21. Jer. iii. 1—5. Psalm xiv. 1—4. 3. God often effectually calls those that are most outrageously wicked, as Manasseh, Mary Magdalene, the harlot of Samaria, the dying thief, the murderers of Christ, Saul the persecutor, 2 Chron. xxxiii. 11—13. Luke vii. 36—50. John iv. Luke xxiii. 42, 43. Acts ii. vi. ix. 1 Tim. i. 13—16. 4. Immediately before his call of them be rendered effectual, men's heart is at the very worst, under the sin-irritating power of his law, Rom. vii. 5, 8—13. 5. Though God, to honour his own ordinances, frequently may bestow his grace upon men while they are attending them, yet he has never promised to reward natural men's most serious attendance with special and saving grace; and when they receive it, it is not as the reward of their attendance, but as the issue of their using God's appointed means of bestowing it. Thus, while Moses stretched out his rod towards it, the Red Sea was divided. In his sevenfold washing in Jordan, Naaman was healed. Such as got first into the troubled pool of Bethesda, were effectually cured.—In attempting to stretch out his withered arm, the impotent man had it perfectly restored to vigour; and in washing his eyes in the pool of Siloam, the blind man had his eyes opened; not as the rewards of their work, but as the issue of their using God's appointed means of effecting these things, Exod. xiv. 16—22. 2 Kings v. 10, 14. John v. 4. ix. 7. Mark iii. 5.

OBJEC. I. " Then men, by the most outrageous sinning, " put themselves as much in the way of effectual calling, as by " the most serious prayer, reading, hearing, or meditating, on " God's word." ANSW. 1. None but the most abandoned men will sin because grace does abound, Rom. vi. 1, 2. ii. 4, 5. Jude 4. 2. Though men by their attendance on God's ordinances, do not prepare themselves for Christ and his grace, yet thereby they give him his usual and beloved opportunities of converting them to himself, even as beggars, who, at the king's command, place themselves on the way which he often passes, that they may receive his charity, Prov. viii. 34---36. Isa. lv. 1---3.

OBJEC. II. " Many conditional promises are made to the " good endeavours of unregenerate men, James iv. 8. Rev. iii. " 20. Matth. vii. 7, 8." ANSW. These texts are addressed to professed saints. And it cannot be proved, that the *drawing nigh* to God, *opening* to Christ, *asking*, *seeking*, and *knocking* there mentioned, mean nothing more than may be found in unregenerate men.

An ALMIGHTY, INVINCIBLE, or as others term it, IRRESISTIBLE, influence of the Holy Ghost, is therefore *absolutely necessary*, in and with the outward call of the gospel, in order to apply it to men's heart, so as to translate them from their state of sin and misery into a state of union to, and fellowship with Christ. 1. Men's natural weakness to that which is good, and their deep-rooted enmity against it, require such an almighty influence, 2 Cor. iii. 5. John xv. 5. Rom. v. 6. viii. 7, 8. Jer. xvii. 9. Tit. iii. 3. Nay, besides their natural corruptions, they are generally under the influence of many additional hindrances from Christ and salvation.—They never seriously consider the certainty, awfulness, and infinitely interesting consequences of their death and last judgment, Deut. xxxii. 29. Psal. x. 13. Eccl. xi. 9. xii. 14;—nor the nature, number, and aggravations of their sins, Jer. ii. 35. viii. 6, 7, 12.---Nor the dreadful nature, certainty, and eternal duration of hell torments, and their own connections with them, Matth. x. 28. xvi. 26. xxii. 13. Luke x. 22---26; nor the necessity, spirituality, extent, excellency, suitableness, and eternity of that salvation which Christ hath purchased for them. They indulge a vain conceit of their easily obtaining salvation; or improve their contrary apprehensions, as an excitement to sloth and despair, 1 Pet. iv. 18. Jer. ii. 25. Ezek. xxxvii. 11. They are inclined to defer their concern about eternal things to some future time, perhaps their dying moments, Acts xxiv. 25. Prov. xxiv. 33, 34. vi. 9---11. i. 22---28. They are closely connected with wicked men, as their patterns and companions, Psalm xlix. 11---20. Prov. xiii. 20. ix. 6. They are enslaved and inflamed by a love of this world, in its diversified contents, appearances, and lusts; and perhaps entangled in an hurry of worldly business, James iv. 4. Luke x. 41, 42. xii. 16---20. Eph. iv. 18, 19. Rom. i. 21. They prefer the care and gratifications of their body to the salvation of their soul, Matth. xvi. 26. Rom. xiii. 14. Eph. iv. 18, 19. They entertain manifold errors, and persuade themselves that an infinitely merciful God will put up with very little religion, at least in those who are not in any ecclesiastical office. 2. Many passages of Scripture plainly affirm, that an almighty influence is necessary in the effectual calling of sinners; and represent it as an exceeding greatness of God's power; a creation work; a raising of the dead, &c. Eph. i. 18, 19. Gal. vi. 15. 2 Cor. v. 17. Isa. lxv. 17, 19. lxvi. 19. Eph ii. 5, 9, 10. iv. 24. Col. iii. 10. John i. 13. iii. 5, 6. v. 25. 1 Cor. ii. 12, 14. 2 Cor. iii. 5. iv. 6. Jer. xxxi. 18, 33. John vi. 37, 44, 45, 63, 65. xv. 5. Phil. ii. 13. Jer. xxxii. 40. Ezek. xxxvi. 26, 27. xi. 19, 20. xxxvii. 1---14. Psalm li. 12. Deut. xxx. 6. Song i. 4. Acts xi. 18. v. 31. xvi. 14. xxvi. 17, 18. 1 Pet. i. 2, 3, 23. Col. i. 13. iii. 1. Rom. iv. 17. viii. 2 Heb. xiii. 20, 21. 1 Cor. i. 26---31. 2 Pet. i. 4. And hence the gospel, through which this powerful influence is exerted, is called the *rod* of Christ's *strength*, *arm* of the Lord, and the *power* of God, Psalm cx. 2, 3. Isa. liii. 1. Rom. i. 16. 1 Cor. i. 24. 3. Unless the influence of the Holy Ghost, in this work, were *invincible*, men's faith, repentance, and good works must be ascribed to their own *free will*, as rendering effectual the influence of God,—contrary to Eph. ii. 8. 1 Cor. iv. 7. Isa. xxvi. 12. Phil. ii. 13. Rom. ix. 6, 16, 18. Tit. iii. 3, 5. 4. Unless God, in this work, could, and did, more than afford men such means, opportunities, and influences, as their free will may rightly improve or not, as it pleases,—these second causes must act independently of God, but dependently on men's free will,— contrary to 1 Cor. iii. 5—7. 1 Thess. i. 5. John vi. 63. 5. If

God's influence in changing men's state and nature, be not almighty and invincible, but dependent on their free will for its efficacy and success,—glorified saints in heaven have no more ground to thank God for their eternal salvation than the damned in hell have to thank him for theirs, as not he, but their own *free will*, was the proper cause of it,—contrary to Ro. v. ix. vii. 10, 12. 6. Unless this heart-changing influence be *almighty* and *invincible*, we can have no comfortable certainty of our eternal happiness, no not in heaven, as even there the free will of many millions of angels gave them a damning slip, 2 Pet. ii. 4. Jude 6. Matth. xxv. 41. 1 Tim. iii. 6. God may choose us in Christ, and prepare heaven for us before the foundation of the world, Eph. i. 4. Matth. xxv. 34. Christ may become man, obey, suffer, and die for us, rise again for our justification, and do all that he can by his intercession, be able to save to the uttermost, Gal. iv. 4, 5. Rom. iii. 25. iv. 25. viii. 3, 33, 34. Heb. vii. 25, 26; the gospel may be preached to us, in every advantageous circumstance, Heb. ii. 3, 4. 1 Pet. i. 11, 12. 1 Thess. i. 5. Rom. i. 16, 17. Tit. ii. 11—14; the Holy Ghost may do all that he can to bring us into, and keep us in, a state of grace, and yet all be to no purpose, unless our free will, which is *enmity against God*, convert itself to him, and, by its influence, more promote our salvation than all the Omnipotent THREE, by love, by wisdom, by power, by blood, by prayer, are capable to do.

OBJEC. I. " These scriptures which represent men's con-
" version to God as an effect of divine power, mean no more
" than that the miracles, which they saw or heard of, de-
" termined or excited them to believe the gospel-doctrines
" thereby confirmed, 1 Cor. iv. 19. 1 Thess. i. 6. Rom. i. 16."
ANSW. In none of these texts doth POWER mean miracles. Miracles are not Christ crucified, 1 Cor. i. 24. Nor did Paul demand knowledge of the miracles of his opposers. Nor are miracles a proof of men's election, as this power was, 1 Thess. i. iv. 5. Matth. vii. 22, 23.

OBJEC. II. " Multitudes of inspired promises, exhorta-
" tions, &c. represent God as unsuccessfully exerting himself
" to his uttermost, for the conversion of men, Isa. v. 34.
" (which words might be rendered, What shall be hereafter
" done to my vineyard,) John i. 7, 9. v. 34, 40. xii. 32—40;
" —and as wishing that they would comply with his calls, and
" bewailing that they did not;—and represent the efficacy of
" his ordinances as dependent on their choice, diligence, and
" care, Deut. xxxii. 29. iv. 29. viii. 2. xxx. 19. x. 16. Psalm
" lxxxi. 10---14. Prov. i. 22---30. Matth. xxxiii. 37. (which
" means that the Jewish rulers and parents hindered their
" subjects and children from attending or improving Christ's

"instructions,) Luke xix. 41—44. Isa. i. 16—20. xxx. 15. lv.
" 1—7. xlv. 22. xlvi. 12, 13. Gen. iv. 7. Jer. iv. 4, 14. vi. 8.
" Ezek. xviii. 30—32. xxiv. 13. xxxiii. 11. Joel ii. 13. Zech.
" ix. 12. Matth. iii. 2. iv. 17. vii. 7, 8. Luke xiii. 24. Acts ii.
" 38. iii. 19. Phil. ii. 12. Tit. ii. 11, 12. Eph. v. 14. James
" iv. 8. Rev. iii. 19, 20. Matth. xxv. 14—29. Luke xix.
" 12—27," &c. ANSW. 1. Though men, in their unregenerate state, can do nothing spiritually good, yet they can do many things which are materially good, as to pray, read, hear, or meditate on the Scripture,—which the Holy Ghost may make the means of his regenerating and quickening influences. And though God cannot accept their labour as coming from their accursed person and corrupt heart, he may, from regard to his own ordinances, meet with them in the use thereof. Nay, perhaps, he never fails graciously to meet with such as, with natural earnestness, persevere in seeking after salvation. 2. God's demands of dutiful obedience do not necessarily suppose men's sufficiency of strength to fulfil them; but for their conviction of their inability, and to drive them to Christ for righteousness and strength,—represent what they owe to God, to themselves, and to their neighbours, under pain of eternal damnation. 3. God may do all that is possible or proper in the bestowal of outward means of salvation upon men, without success, Isa. v. 1—4; but not all that he can do, in the exertion of his spiritual influence, 1 Cor. ii. 4, 5. Rom. i. 16. 1 Thess. i. 5. ii. 13. 4. Many of the texts mentioned in the objection, merely represent God, as in a friendly manner declaring his law; and some of them denote Christ's human sympathy towards his self-ruined Jewish countrymen. Others of them represent what the Israelites were bound to, and capable of performing, as the means of their temporal happiness in Canaan. 5. While some of these texts respect *elect* persons, whom Christ effectually enlightens, and draws to himself and his heavenly throne,—others of them, particularly these last quoted, relate to regenerated persons, in whom the Holy Ghost dwells, and causes them to walk in his statutes.—At least, the *one talent* and *pound* in the parables, mean common gifts and opportunities of doing good granted to church-officers or others, not real grace.

OBJEC. III. " Men are represented as *grieving*, *vexing*, *re-*
" *belling against*, *quenching*, *resisting*, *outstriving*, and *doing de-*
" *spite* to the Spirit of grace, Eph. iv. 30. Isa. lxiii. 10. 1 Thess.
" v. 19. Gen. vi. 3. Acts vii. 51. Heb. x. 29. Amos ii. 13. Ezek.
" xvi. 43." ANSW. All indulgence of sin in heart and life by those in whom the Holy Ghost dwells, or with whom he deals, is a *resisting*, *grieving*, and *vexing*, &c. him. But opposition doth not necessarily infer actual prevalence over his strongest efforts. His influences and evidences in the declarations of the

prophets and apostles, and his common operations may be effectually resisted, quenched, and despitefully used;—but his special and saving influences cannot, Psalm cx. 3. 2 Cor. x. 4, 5. 1 Thess. i. 5—10. ii. 13. 1 Cor. vi. 11. 2. Believers vex, grieve, rebel against, and in some measure quench the Holy Ghost, when, instead of cherishing his influences, they hearken to the temptations of Satan and the world.

Objec. IV. " An almighty and invincible influence of the " Holy Ghost in men's conversion to Christ, excludes all instru- " mentality of his word in it, which can only work by moral " suasion." Answ. 1. Did then the word of God, in the creation of all things, work by mere moral suasion? Gen. i. Psalm xxxiii. 6, 9. Heb. xi. 3. 2. The almighty influence of which we speak, is perfectly answerable to the nature of men's soul, and so is truly and morally, though infinitely powerful to persuade; and so may well be conveyed through the word of God. And, though men may be able to withstand the influence of the word, when spoken by men, they cannot withstand it when savingly applied by the Holy Ghost.

Objec. V. " If men believe the necessity of an almighty in- " fluence of God's Spirit to convert them, they will never be " persuaded to endeavour any reformation in their heart and " practice, till they certainly feel this almighty influence, and " can continue no longer in sin." Answ. 1. Men may reform their outward practice, without any experience of this almighty influence, Phil. iii. 6. 1 Kings xxi. 27—29. Mark vi. 20. Isa. lviii. 2. 2 Pet. ii. 20. 2. It is not men's feelings, but the law of God that is the rule of their duty, Isa. viii. 20. Deut. iv. 2. v. 32. xii. 32. Mat. xxviii. 20. 3. No man acts agreeably to the gospel, who doth not, under convictions of his own sinfulness, apply to Jesus Christ for reformation of heart and life, without making any prior attempts to reform them himself, Prov. xxiii. 26. Ezek. xxxvi. 26, 27. Jer. xxxi. 3, 18, 33. Tit. iii. 3—7. Acts xxvi. 17, 18. John iii. 14—18, 36. Isa. xlv. 22. lv. 1—7.

Objec. VI. " The effectual calling, regeneration, or conver- " sion of men to Christ by mere *moral suasion,* exceedingly glo- " rifies all the perfections of God. He thus, in infinite wisdom, " deals with reasonable men by precepts, promises, and threat- " enings suited to their rational powers. With unblemished " candour, he calls all men to repent and be saved, if they will. " In infinite equity, he punishes men only for the sins which " they could have avoided. Thus the glory of all that is good " redounds to God, and all the guilt and shame of that which " is evil, falls only on the sinners themselves." Answ. How is it for the glory of God, to be represented as if his almighty hands were so tied up, that he can do nothing effectually for the eternal salvation of men, unless their free will, which is *en-*

mity *against* him, *deceitful above all things, and desperately wicked,* assist and succeed his labours in his regenerating and sanctifying work? How hath he the honour and praise of all that is good in men, when their free will alone must determine whether despiteful blasphemy and redoubled damnation, or faith in Christ and eternal salvation, shall be the effect of all that he can do for and with them? 2. Men's conversion by the almighty and invincible influences of God's Spirit, is truly and highly honourable to God. His ordinances, as intended, issue in the eternal salvation of his elect, and render multitudes useful to them on earth, Isa. lv. 10, 11. It encourages men who are convinced of their weakness and wickedness, to seek and expect a thorough change of their nature from the almighty power and grace of God.—While God, in the most affectionate manner, deals with men by his word, his attendant almighty influences enlighten, renew, and draw their hearts to himself, Psalm cx. 2, 3. Phil. iii. 12. Gal. i. 15, 16. 1 Thess. i. 5. ii. 13. —Thus all the conditional declarations of the gospel, and the salvation of the elect only, are harmoniously accomplished, Acts x. 43. v. 31. Isa. liii. 10—12.—And reprobates are left with all their power of *free will,* and so are as salvable as our opponents allow any of mankind to be, if not much more so, as we allow that one, even the weakest act of faith in Jesus Christ, infallibly secures eternal salvation, John iii. 16, 18. vi. 39, 40. Mark xvi. 16.—Nothing but disobedience to the law of God, in which the formal nature of sin consists, is punished, and wilfulness in sinning, rendering crimes more heinous, draws on further punishment. No refuser of Christ is punished for any inability to believe or repent, but what he justified himself in— not doing as well as he might have done.

The Holy Ghost, by his convincing and alluring, but resistible influence, deals with those that enjoy the gospel,—and especially with elect men before their union to Christ. But, in the *time of love,* appointed in the purpose and covenant of God, He, by his almighty and invincible influences, in the declarations of his law applied to their consciences, effectually convinces his elect of the divine authority, indispensable obligation, spirituality, holiness, righteousness, goodness, and inconceivable extent of its precepts, and of the import, equity, and faithfulness of its threatenings,—and by this means convinces them of their sins in heart and life, and of the equity, certainty, dreadful nature, and eternal duration of their deserved punishment, —so as to fill them with shame and fear, and cut off all their hopes of happiness by their own good works; and fixing upon them the infamous characters by which men are invited to Christ in the gospel promises and declarations, Isa. lv. 2, 7. xlvi. 12. Prov. i. 22. ix. 4. Luke xix. 10. Mat. ix. 13. 1 Tim.

i. 15. Hos. xiii. 9. Ezek. xxxvi. 25—27, charges and urges them to believe on him as their offered Saviour, John xvi. 9—12. Rom. vii. 7—13. iii. 19—22. Gal. iii. 24. Acts ii. 37, 38. xvi. 30, 31. 1 John iii. 23.—And, by this same almighty invincible influence, in the declarations, promises, and invitations of the gospel, applied to, or impressed on their hearts, he manifests Christ, in his person, offices, relations, righteousness, and purchased redemption,—as infinitely excellent, all-sufficient, and exactly suited to their case, and by God appointed, presented, and offered unto them, under those very infamous characters which the law had fixed upon them; and in this manifestation of Christ, he conveys him and all his fulness in the promise into their heart, that, as a *prophet*, and made of God to them *wisdom*, he may fill their understanding with spiritual light and knowledge,—as a *priest*, and made of God unto them *righteousness*, he may purify and quiet their awakened conscience,—and as a *king*, and made of God unto them *sanctification* and *redemption*, he may deliver them from sinful slavery, subdue, renew, and rule in their will;—and that as an infinitely lovely, gracious, necessary, and suitable Husband and Saviour, he may change, conquer, captivate, and for ever bind their affections to himself, Gal. i. 15, 16. John vi. 39, 40. Thus they are made *partakers of Christ*, apprehended by, and united to him, Heb. iii. 14. Rom. vii. 4. Hos. ii. 19, 20. Isa. liv. 5. Phil. iii. 12. This act of the Holy Ghost in thus manifesting and conveying Christ and his fulness into our soul, is at once an uniting, justifying, adopting, and regenerating act.—And the word of the gospel, in which he acts, is, as it were, Christ's marriage-vow, the sentence of justification, the adopting deed, and the seed of the new nature,—or mean by which it is conveyed into the soul,—which, in the whole, is a *mere patient*, experiencing the exceeding greatness of the power and grace of God, Eph. i. 18—20. ii. 4—10. Psalm cx. 3. Tit. iii. 5—7. Mat. xvi. 17. John i. 13. iii. 3, 5, 6, 8. 1 John iii. 1, 9. v. 18. 1 Pet. i. 3, 23. Col. iii. 11, 12. Ezek. xi. 19, 20. xxxvi. 25—27. Jer. xxxii. 40.

COMMUNION with Christ is the immediate effect of this uniting act of the Holy Ghost in our effectual calling, Heb. iii. 14. Song ii. 16. This communion is either, 1. Of mutual interest in one another, and what belongs to each, Song ii. 16. Isa. liv. 5. Zech. xiii. 9. 1 Cor. iii. 22. 2. Of mutual communication one to another, John i. 14, 16. Prov. xxiii. 16. Psalm lv. 22. 1 Pet. v. 7. 3. Of mutual intercourse, Song ii. 14. viii. 13. Psalm l. 15. xci. 15. lxxxv. 8. cxviii. 28. Isa. lviii. 9. lxv. 24. Phil. iv. 6. Zech. xiii. 9.—Thus, in virtue of union to, and communion with Christ, our relative and real state are completely changed in a moment. By his uniting himself to us as the Lord our *righteousness*, and the end of the law for righteousness, we obtain *justification*, and have our whole relation to the law as a broken covenant, binding on us, perfectly dissolved, Isa. xlv. 24, 25. Acts xiii. 38, 39. Rom. iii. 21, 22, 24. vi. 14. vii. 4. viii. 1, 4, 33, 34. x. 4. Gal. iv. 4, 5. iii. 13. ii. 16—20. 2 Cor. v. 21. By his uniting himself to us as our everlasting *Father* and *elder Brother*, we obtain *adoption*, Isa. ix. 6. Heb. ii. 13. Gal. iii. 26. Rom. viii. 17. John i. 12. xx. 17. Jer. iii. 4, 19. By his uniting himself, the only begotten Son of God made flesh, to us as a *quickening Spirit*, full of grace and truth, and made of God to us wisdom, righteousness, sanctification, and redemption, we obtain *regeneration*, new creation, spiritual resurrection, or renovation after the image of God, John xi. 25. i. 14, 16. 1 Cor. xv. 45—49. i. 30. 2 Cor. v. 17. Gal. vi. 15. Eph. ii. 1, 5, 10. Col. ii. 11, 12, 13. iii. 10, 11.—In his whole work of convincing men's conscience, enlightening their mind, and renewing their will, the Holy Ghost forms men for *receiving and resting upon Christ as offered in the gospel*, in which he and his fulness are conveyed into their hearts, and hence they are no sooner apprehended and quickened by him, than their soul, upon God's own testimony and *giving* promise, believes God's report concerning him, receives him, and unites itself with him as offered in the gospel, John xvi. 9—12. Isa. lv. 1—7. John vi. 37, 44, 45, 63, 65. vii. 37, 38. 2 Cor. v. 14—21. Acts xxvi. 18. Jer. xxxi. 18. Phil. i. 29. ii. 12, 13.—By virtue of this union to, and communion with Christ, our spiritual condition is also gradually changed and perfected. By union to, and fellowship with him, as our *quickening* and *sanctifying* Head, we obtain our gradual *sanctification* of nature and life, 1 Cor. i. 2. John i. 16. Acts xxvi. 18. 2 Cor. iii. 18. Col. ii. 10, 19. Eph. iv. 15, 16.—By our union to, and fellowship with him, as the Lord our righteousness, mean of fellowship with the Father, and Treasury of all blessings, we obtain spiritual *comfort*, Heb. iv. 14—16. x. 19—22. John xiv.—xvi. Isa. xi. 10. xii. 1—6. Phil. iii. 3. iv. 4. Rom. v. 1—11. By union to, and fellowship with him, as the Conqueror of death, the risen and exalted Saviour, who hath all power in heaven and earth, we obtain our eternal *glorification*, Rev. i. 18. xiv. 13. Hos. xiii. 14. Isa. xxv. 8. lx. 19, 20. xxvi. 19. John xiv. 2, 3, 19. xvii. 24. Rom. viii. 1, 11, 17. Col. iii. 3, 4. Rev. iii. 21.

REFLECT. Have I indeed been called of God with this holy, this high and heavenly calling, and spiritually united to the all-precious Redeemer? Can I appeal to himself, that he is my Beloved, and I am his?——God forbid that I should profess, should preach a Jesus Christ, that is not *my own*. Let union with the Son of God, as effectually made unto me wisdom, righteousness, and sanctification, and redemption, be the root, the foundation of all my religion.——Am I indeed crucified with Christ, and yet live; yet not I, but Christ liveth in me? And is the life which I live in the flesh, by the faith of the Son of God, who loved me and gave himself for me?——O wonder! wonder! wonder!—an espousing God, and I the ugly, wicked, worthless bride!

CHAP. II.

Of Justification.

JUSTIFICATION, in Scripture, never means the *making* of persons inherently holy and righteous, but the *holding* and *declaring* them righteous, as in a court of judgment. 1. In this sense the Hebrew HATSDIK and the Greek DIKAIOUN, which we render *to justify*, are taken, Exod. xxiii. 7. Deut. xxv. 1. Prov. xvii. 15. 1 Kings viii. 32. Isa. l. 8. liii. 11. xlv. 24, 25. Psalm cxliii. 2. Job xxvii. 5. 2 Sam. xv. 4. Psalm lxxxii. 3. Gen. xliv. 16.——Luke x. 29. xvi. 15. xviii. 14. Mat. xii. 37. Rom. ii. 13. iii. 4, 20, 24, 28, 30. iv. 2, 5, 25. v. 1, 9, 16, 18. vi. 7. viii. 30, 33, 34. Gal. ii. 16, 17. iii. 11, 24. v. 4. Tit. iii. 7. Mat. xi. 19. 1 Tim. iii. 16. John xvi. 10. James ii. 22—25.—Now, wherever, in these texts, *Justification* is opposed to *condemnation*;—or it is represented as criminal to *justify* the wicked;—or wherever divine persons are said to be *justified*, it cannot mean *making them holy or virtuous*, but the *holding* or *declaring* them to be so.—Ministers *justify many* in publishing God's sentence of justification revealed in the gospel, and in stirring them up to manifest their justification by good works, Dan. xii. 3 Heb.—even as they *save* men, 1 Tim. iv. 16. 1 Cor. ix. 22. James v. 20. 1 Cor. vii. 16.—Rev. xxii. 11, might be translated, *He that is righteous, let him do righteousness still,—*or *be justified still, i. e.* continue fixed in his justified state, and by good works more and more manifest to other men, and to his own conscience, that he is justified before God, 1 John ii. 29. iii. 7. James ii. 22—25. 2. This also appears from the scriptural representations of justification, or of pardon of sin, a leading ingredient in it,—as a *reconcilement*,—a *receiving the atonement*, Rom. v. 3—11; not *coming into judgment* or *condemnation*, John v. 24. Rom. viii. 1—33. God's *blotting* out sin, Isa. xliii. 25. xliv. 22. Psalm li. 9; *not retaining* anger, but *passing by* transgression, and *casting* sins into the *depths* of the sea, or *behind his back*, Mic. vii. 18, 19. Isa. xxxviii. 17 Psalm li. 9. Jer. xviii. 23. Psalm xc. 8. cix. 14, 15. Jer. xvi

17; *not seeing* sin, Num. xxiii. 21. Jer. 1. 20; *not imputing* or *remembering* sin, but *forgiving, covering, removing* and *purging* it away, Jer. xxxiii. 8. Isa. xliii. 25. Psalm xxxii. 1, 2. lxxxv. 2. ciii. 3, 12. lxxix. 9. Rom. iv. 6. Isa. i. 18. Ezek xxxvi. 25. Rev. i. 5. Col. ii. 13. Heb. viii. 12. 3. Every thing relative to justification is represented in the form of a *trial* in law. Here is a *judgment*, Psalm cxliii. 2; a *judge*, Isa. l. 7, 9; a *judgment-seat*, Heb. iv. 16. Isa. xxx. 18; a guilty *pannel*, Rom. iii. 19; an *accusing* law, conscience, and devil, John v. 45. Rom. ii. 15. Psalm cix. 6. Zech. iii. 2; a *charge* or *hand-writing* exhibited against us, Col. ii. 14; a *plea* of grace reigning through Christ's righteousness, Rom. iii. 24, 25. Dan. ix. 24. Eph. i. 6, 7. ii. 7. Rom. v. 16---21; the accused criminal betaking himself to this plea alone, Job ix. 2, 3. xi. 4. xlii. 5---9. Psalm cxxx. 3, 4. Isa. liii. 4---6. Luke xviii. 13. Rom. iii. 24---26. v. 11, 16---21. viii. 1---4, 33, 34. Heb. ix. 12---15. x. 1---14. 1 Pet. ii. 24. iii. 18. 1 John i. 7, 9; an *advocate*, who improves this plea before God, the judge, for the *justification* of the guilty pannel, 1 John ii. 1, 2; and a *sentence* pronounced by God, upon the foot of this plea insisted on, Job xxxiii. 24. Psalm xxxii. 1, 2. Rom. iii. 21---26. viii. 1, 33, 34. 2 Cor. v. 21. Gal. iii. 13, 14. ii. 16.

Justification largely taken, respects as its OBJECT, either, 1. THINGS, in which some particular act, or series of acts, is declared innocent or righteous. Thus God justified Job's representation of him as more righteous than those of his friends, Job xlii. 7, 8; and counted Phinehas' zealous execution of the two impudent adulterers, for righteousness, Psalm cvi. 31. Num. xxv. 11—13. And David in a particular case pleads, that he would judge him according to his integrity or righteousness, Psalm vii. 8. xviii. 24. And the Israelites justified themselves more than treacherous Judah, in being less wicked, Jer. iii. 11; and the Jews justified the Sodomites, in being more wicked than they, Ezek. xvi. 51, 62. Or, 2. PERSONS, and that either, 1. *Righteous persons*, declaring them innocent of that which is charged upon them; as when God justifies believers against the accusations of Satan;—or sustaining them to have that goodness of heart or life which they really have. Thus God commended Job, chap. i. 8. ii. 3; and Moses, Num. xii. 7; and accepts every one that fears him, Acts x. 34, 35. 1 John iii. 7. Luke i. 6. In this sense, good works justify men, declaring them fearers of God, James ii. 21, 24. Gen. xxii. 12, 16.—If Adam had fulfilled the obedience required, he would have been still more formally justified on that account, declared a complete fulfiller of the condition of the covenant of works, and himself and all his posterity adjudged to everlasting happiness, Rom. ii. 13. Gal. iii. 12. Lev. xviii. 5.—In this sense,

Christ, after he had fulfilled his Surety-righteousness, was *justified, i. e.* judicially declared by God to have perfectly fulfilled all that obedience and satisfaction which his elect owed to the broken covenant of works; and on that account, he, and they in him, discharged of the whole debt, and entitled to their respective shares of eternal life, Isa. l. 8. 1 Tim. iii. 16. Rom. iv. 25. 2 Cor. v. 21; or, 2. *Men guilty* in themselves, through the righteousness of Christ, as their surety, imputed to them, Isa. xlv. 25. liii. 11. 2 Cor. v. 21. Rom. iii. 24—26. v. 16—19. viii. 3, 4, 30, 33, 34.—This justification originated from all eternity, when elect men were chosen in Christ, and their debt to the broken covenant of works was placed to his account, to be demanded *only from him*, Eph. i. 4. Heb. vii. 22. Isa. liii. 6. Its foundation was laid in Christ's finishing transgression, and bringing in an everlasting righteousness, answerable to all the demands of the broken law, Dan. ix. 24. 1 Pet. ii. 24. Isa. liii. 4—12.—In his resurrection Christ was solemnly justified, as the public Head and Representative of all his elect; and in him the sentence lies ready to be extended to them in their respective *times of love* fixed in the purpose of God, Rom. iv. 25. 2 Cor. v. 21. 1 Tim. iii. 16. Isa. l. 8. It is formally transferred to their persons in the promise and act of God, by which they are united to Christ, Rom. vii. 4. viii. 1, 2. Gal. ii. 16. 2 Cor. v. 20, 21. Not only then, but afterwards, it is intimated to their conscience in the powerfully applied word of the gospel, Isa. xliii. 25. xliv. 22. Mat. ix. 2, 6. It is further manifested to their conscience, as well as to the world, by their good works, James ii. 21, 24. It will be most publicly intimated in the last judgment, Acts iii. 19.

Justification, strictly and properly taken, is "*An act of God's grace, in which he freely pardons all our sins, and accepts us as righteous in his sight, only for the righteousness of Christ imputed to us, and received by faith alone.*"—It is an act of God alone, Father, Son, and Holy Ghost, Rom. iii. 26, 30. viii. 30, 33. Gal. iii. 8. Luke v. 21,—as a supreme Lord, Lawgiver, and Judge, offended, but satisfied, Gen. xviii. 25, 30. Deut. xxxii. 39. James iv. 12. Isa. xxxiii. 22. Heb. xii. 23. Psalm li. 4, 6. Matth. vi. 12. xviii. 23—34. Isa. xlii. 21. xliii. 25. xliv. 22. Rom. iii. 24—26. viii. 32—34. Mark ii. 7.—It is ascribed to the Father, as he laid our sins upon Christ, accepted his righteousness in our stead, and imputing it to us as our judge, acquits and accepts us, as in him, Rom. viii. 29, 30. 2 Cor. v. 21. It is ascribed to the Son, as he purchased it with his blood, procures it by his intercession, and as administrator of the new covenant, issues forth the sentence, Mat. xx. 28. 1 John ii. 1, 2. Acts v. 31. Mat. ix. 2, 6. Isa. liii. 11. It is ascribed to the Holy Ghost, as he applies Christ and his righteousness to our person and conscience, intimates the sentence in his word, seals and attests it to our heart, 1 Cor. ii. 10, 11. vi. 11. Tit. iii. 7. Rom. viii. 15. 2 Cor. i. 22. v. 5. Eph. i. 13. iv. 30.——Nothing but God's own free grace and love inwardly moves him to justify sinful men, Rom. iii. 24. v. 20, 21. Eph. ii. 8. Tit. iii. 5—7. He provided our surety, afforded the price, and in our stead accepted it: he freely offers and gives it to us in the gospel,—imputes it to our persons, and gives us faith to receive it,—all according to the exceeding riches of his free grace, John iii. 16. 2 Tim. i. 9. Rom. v. 20, 21. Phil. i. 29. Eph. i. 6---8. ii. 4---8.

ALL the ELECT, and they ONLY, are justified in their respective *times of love*, Isa. liii. 4, 5, 6, 8, 10, 11. Rom. v. 19. viii. 28---34, considered in themselves as *ungodly*, and condemnable to eternal wrath, Rom. iv. 5, 6. v. 6, 8, 10. Those that lived under the Old Testament were as perfectly justified as these under the New. 1. The general promise of the covenant of grace made to them, plainly included complete justification, Gen. xvii. 7. Psalm xxxiii. 12. Num. xxiii. 21. Isa. i. 18. xxviii. 16. xliii. 25. xliv. 22. lvii. 17, 18. Jer. xxxi. 34. xxxiii. 8. Ezek. xxxvi. 25. Mic. vii. 18, 19. Exod. xxxiv. 6, 7. 2. Several believers under the Old Testament, are expressly represented as justified, without any limitation, Rom. iv. 3. James ii. 25. 2 Sam. xii. 13. Psalm xxxii. 1, 2. lxv. 3. lxxxv. 2, 3. ciii. 3, 12. Isa. xxxviii. 17. Mic. vii. 18, 19. 3. All the expressions of God's *not retaining his anger,—not remembering their sin,—not imputing it,—not beholding it,—but forgiving, passing by, covering, expiating, lifting up, cleansing, blotting out,* and *casting sin behind his back,*—prove that their pardon was absolutely perfect, Micah vii. 18, 19. Isa. xliii. 25. xliv. 22. Psalm xxxii. 1, 2. lxxxv. 3. ciii. 12. Num. xxiii. 21. Exod. xxxiv. 6, 7, 9. And it, as well as that which Christian believers receive, is called APHESIS as well as PARESIS, Mat. vi. 12, 14. ix. 2. Mark i. 4. Luke vii. 47, 48. Acts x. 43. Rom. iv. 6. Heb. ix. 22.

Our justification is a *most simple act*, in respect of God our Judge; but, as it respects the precept and penalty of the broken law, and the correspondent change made upon our state, it may be distinguished into PARDON of sin, and ACCEPTANCE with God. PARDON respects the penalty of the broken law, removes the guilt of sin, frees from the curse due to it, on account of Christ's satisfactory sufferings for it.—ACCEPTANCE on account of Christ's holiness of human nature, and obedience to the precept of the broken law, sustains us as fulfillers of it in God's sight, instates us in his favour, entitles and adjudges us to eternal life. This title to eternal life is of a *legal or judicial* nature, such as a man hath to his purchased property, whereas that received in adoption is such as one hath to an inheritance, as his father's son and heir.—In this double title to eternal life, we are conformed to Christ, who, as an obedient servant, and as the Son of God in our nature, hath full right to his eternal glory.——Both pardon of sin and acceptance, which are included in our justifying sentence, respect our persons, change our state with respect to the favour of God and our own safety and happiness; free us from all charges of guilt against, or demands of service to the broken covenant of works; and are never preceded but followed by gospel repentance, Rom. viii. 1, 33. v. 16—21. Eph. i. 6. 1 John v. 11, 12. Ezek. xvi. 62, 63. xxxvi. 25, 31. Paternal pardon and acceptance are founded on, but not included in our justification:—make no change in our state before God, but only in our spiritual condition and comfort, and are granted from time to time, as our sins are committed and repented of, and our obedience of faith performed, and are preceded as well as followed by true evangelical repentance. Paternal pardon forgives our sins, as they are committed against the law as a rule in the hand of Christ, and expose us, not to God's revenging wrath, but to his fatherly anger and chastisement. Paternal acceptance respects not our persons, but our holy services, and introduces us to the enjoyment of God's fatherly smiles and favours, 2 Sam. xii. 13. Mat. vi. 12. 1 John i. 7, 9. Psalm xxxii. 5. Rom. v. 10. Psalm xxiii.

In our judicial pardon, ALL our sins, past, present, or future, are forgiven, in so far as they are, in any sense, transgressions of God's law *as a covenant of works*. 1. The Scripture plainly represents them as ALL forgiven in our justification, Isa. i. 18. xliii. 25. xliv. 22. Jer. xxxi. 34. xxxiii. 8. Heb. viii 12. Ezek. xxxvi. 25. Col. ii. 13, 14. Acts xiii. 39. Num. xxiii. 21. Jer. l. 20. Psalm lxxxv. 2, 3. ciii. 3, 12. Isa. liv. 9. Rom. viii. 1, 33. 2. The sacraments of the new covenant seal the remission of all our sins at once, 1 Pet. iii. 21. Mark i. 14. Acts ii. 38. xxii. 16. Matth. xxvi. 28.——If baptism did only seal the remission of past sins, it had best be delayed till the last moment of our life, contrary to Matth. xxviii. 19. Mark xvi. 16. Acts ii. 38. xxii. 16. Judicial pardon cannot be conditionally sealed, as it is bestowed upon us as an infinitely *free gift*, Rom. iii. 24. v. 16—21. Tit. iii. 7.— Nor is any promise of judicial pardon, or of reconciliation, directed to justified persons; but they are supposed to be fully possessed of these benefits, Rom. viii. 1—4, 15—17, 33, 34. Gal. iii. 26. 3. In their spiritual union to Christ, believers are legally reckoned to have fully satisfied all the demands of the law, as a covenant in him, Rom. x. 4. viii. 3, 4, 33, 34. v. 6, 8, 16—

21. vii. 4. vi. 14. Gal. ii. 19, 20. 2 Cor. v. 21. Isa. xlv. 24, 25; and are represented as dead to, or for sin, as he was, Rom. vi. 10, 11. Gal. ii. 20. 4. Being once spiritually united to Christ, we can never afterward be, for one moment, separated from him. Nor, being ONE with Christ, can any of our sins stand chargeable against us, without supposing him to have left part of our debt unpaid, in his satisfaction, Isa. liii. 6. Heb. ix. 12, 14. x. 10, 14, 18. 2 Cor. v. 21. Rom. viii. 1— 4, 33, 34. x. 4. 5. If God's redeeming love be unchangeable, they who are once instated in such favour cannot be, for a moment, liable to his revenging wrath,, Jer. xxxi. 3, 20. xxxii. 39, 40. Isa. liv. 8---10. Rom. viii. 28---39. Zeph. iii. 17. John xiii. 1. xv. 9, 10. 6. If the after sins of believers be not so pardoned in their justification, as to prevent all legal imputation of them, the same persons at the same time might, or rather must, *as believers*, be dead to the law as a covenant, and not under it, but adjudged to everlasting life by the covenant of grace, Rom. vii. 4. vi. 14. viii. 2. John vi. 40. 1 John v. 10, 12; and yet, *as alway sinning*, be alive to, and under the law as a covenant, and liable to God's revenging and eternal wrath, Ezek. xviii. 4. Rom. ii. 8, 9. vi. 23. 7. Believers' full remission of all their sins at once, with respect to their legal guilt, not only corresponds with their complete translation from under the covenant of works, and exalts the free grace of God, which hath suspended no part of their legal pardon upon their future faith or repentance, but also powerfully excites and promotes their most earnest and persevering study of gospel holiness, Luke vii. 42---47. i. 74, 75. Psalm cxvi. 16. cxix. 32. 2 Cor. vii. 1. Heb. xii. 28.

OBJEC. I. " Believers' after sins cannot be pardoned in their " justification, as they cannot be *blotted* out, and *not remem-* " *bered*, till once they have been committed, and marked, and " remembered." ANSW 1. *Remembering* sometimes respects that which is present or future, Eccl. xi. 8. xii. 1. 2. If Jesus Christ was condemned and punished for, and absolved from, millions of transgressions before they were committed, why may not sins be pardoned, as well as satisfied for, before they be committed? 1 Pet. ii. 24. Dan. ix. 24.

OBJEC. II. " Pardon is plainly restricted to past crimes, " Jer. xxxiii. 8. Ezek. xviii. 22." ANSW. Past sins are particularly mentioned in these texts, for the humiliation of the guilty persons; but pardon is not restricted to them only.

OBJEC. III. " Confession of sin, repentance, and humi- " liation for it, which necessarily follow the commission of " sin, must precede the pardon of it, 2 Chron. vii. 14. Prov. " xxxviii. 13. 1 John i. 9. Acts iii. 19." ANSW. 1. These texts do not relate to legal pardon of sin, but either to the removal of outward judgments, or to fatherly pardon,—or to the public intimation of pardon at the last day. 2. It will be hereafter proved, that, though a rage against sin, or at God's connecting fearful punishment with it, may precede judicial pardon, no truly evangelical repentance or humiliation can.

OBJEC. IV. " If believers' after sins be judicially forgiven in " their justification, they ought not to pray for the pardon of " their sin, as Christ directs, Mat. vi. 12. Luke xi. 4." ANSW. 1. They that are justified, but not distinctly assured of it, ought to pray for pardon of their sin in general, leaving it to God to grant what *kind* is proper. 2. Every justified person ought daily to pray for more clear and powerful intimations of judicial pardon to his conscience, which may be called *pardon*, as well as the manifestation of justification is called by its name, James ii. 21—25. 3. Every justified person ought daily to pray for paternal pardon of his daily infirmities, James iii. 2. 1 John i. 8—10. Eccl. vii. 20. Isa. lxiv. 6.

OBJEC. V. " We must forgive others, in order that God " may forgive us our sins committed after our justification." ANSW. 1. Our hearty forgiving others the injuries which they have done us, must follow after, and proceed from God's judicial pardon of our sins, Mat. xviii. 32, 33. Eph. iv. 31, 32. But our comfortable sense of that pardon frequently follows our being, by his grace, enabled from our heart to forgive others, Luke vi. 37. xi. 4. 2. We must forgive others in order to our receiving fatherly pardon, Mat. xviii. 35.

OBJEC. VI. " The sinful scandals of believers regularly ex- " communicated from the church are *bound, i. e.* not pardoned, " —in heaven." ANSW. 1. Excommunication deprives men of their visible membership in the church on earth, but doth not change the spiritual state of their person, and hence God's ratification of it cannot bind them over to his revenging or eternal wrath. 2. If an excommunicated believer died deeply penitent of the scandalous causes of his censure, without having opportunity of absolution from it, could his want of ecclesiastical absolution exclude him from heaven? Surely not.

OBJEC. VII. " Christ, by his continual intercession, procures " daily pardon of sin to his people." ANSW. But it is only such pardon as they need, 1 John ii. 1, 2. John xiii. 10. Col. ii. 13, 14.

Though therefore the daily sins of believers, being exceedingly aggravated, richly deserve the eternal wrath of God, Rom. vi. 23; and while unrepented of, render them liable to his fatherly chastisements, Psalm xcix. 8. lxxxix. 30—35. Heb. xii. 6—11. Rev. iii. 19,—they cannot bind them over to his revenging wrath, or any *proper* punishment. 1. Nothing can be threatened against them for their sins, that is inconsistent with the perpetual continuance of God's love to their persons, Psalm lxxxix. 28—35. Isa. liv. 8, 10. Hos. xiv. 4. Heb. xii. 6—11. 2. Believers are under no law which can condemn them to God's revenging wrath for their sins, Rom. vii. 4. vi. 14. viii. 2. Gal. iii. 10, 13, 14. ii. 19, 20. v. 4, 5, 18. 3. No possible condemnation remains for them with God, John iii. 18. v. 24. Rom. viii. 1, 33, 34. 2 Cor. v. 21. Isa. xlv. 24, 25. 4. No person united to Christ can, for one moment, be liable to God's revenging wrath, without being bound to pay over again that satisfaction which Christ already paid to the full in his stead, to suppose which is most absurd and blasphemous, Rom. v. 1, 21. viii. 33, 34. Gen. xviii. 25. Deut. xxxii. 4. Rom. ii. 2. iii. 5, 6. 5. Every believer, being united to Christ, hath in him a righteousness meritorious of eternal life, Rom. viii. 3, 4. 2 Cor. v. 21. Isa. xlv. 24, 25. Gal. iv. 4, 5. Rom. vi. 10, 11. iii. 22, 24—26. v. 16—21. How can he, under such a covering, be, for one moment, liable to eternal death? 6. If the sins of believers render them liable to God's revenging and eternal wrath, then, if they die cleaving to some things sinful, which they apprehended to be good and lawful, they must be damned; contrary to 1 Pet. i. 5. John x. 27—29. xiv. 19. vi. 40.—No virtual repentance inlaid in their new nature can be more effectual to preserve them from hell, than it is to prevent all liableness to it. 7. That righteousness on which their judicial pardon is founded, being infinitely perfect and everlasting, the pardon founded on it by a just God, must also be perfect, uninterrupted, and eternal, Rom. xi. 29. viii. 1, 33, 34. Isa. xlv. 17, 24, 25. liv. 8—10.

Objec. I. " Believers are required to repent, in order to ob-" tain the pardon of their sins." Answ. Yes, in order to receive fuller manifestations of their legal or judicial pardon, or to receive fatherly pardons;—but never in order to obtain judicial pardon. The *putting away* of David's sin, on his repentance, 2 Sam. xii. 13, doth not mean any removal of his liableness to God's avenging wrath,—but that God had removed that long before, and would not extend his paternal correction to the cutting off of his natural life, as he deserved.——Part of the due correction is often inflicted on believers, even when their sin is blotted out by paternal pardon, Psalm cxviii. 18. xcix. 8. cvi. 43.

Objec. II. " If the sins of believers while unrepented of do " not render them liable to God's revenging wrath, there is no " need of Christ's intercession." Answ. His continual pleading his righteousness in their favour, prevents all such liableness to God's wrath, 1 John iii. 1, 2. Heb. vii. 25;—procures further manifestations of his judicial pardon;—and procures fatherly chastisements, and the proper removal of them in due time.— Nay, his intercession will be necessary for them in heaven.

OBJEC. III. " Maintaining that believers' sins do not render " them liable to God's revenging and eternal wrath, strongly " encourages them to carnal security and licentiousness."— ANSW. 1. Maintaining the contrary mightily discourages their earnest following holiness; for it represents them as loved by God with no more than a weak and fluctuating affection, and as ready to be ruined by some small mistake at last. 2. How is it possible for one who has any real experience of the new nature in believers, or regard to the Scripture, to think it so *superdiabolically* wicked as to sin because experienced grace doth abound? Rom. v. 20, 21. vi. 1, 2, 5, 10, 11, 14. 2 Cor v. 14, 15. vi. 17, 18. vii. 1, 6. 1 John iii. 2, 3. iv. 9, 10, 16, 19. Luke i. 74, 75. Psalm ciii. 1—6. cxvi. 16. cxix. 32, 166. Heb. xii. 28, 29. 3. It is most terrible to an heaven-born soul to be, by his sins, exposed to the temporary prevalence of indwelling lusts, rage of devils, hidings and frowns of God's face, and other fatherly chastisements, Rom. vii. 14—24. 2 Cor. xii. 7, 8. Psalm xiii. 1—4. lxxxviii. lxxvii. 1—10. lxxiii. 2—19. xlii. 9, 10. cxvi. 3. cxliii. 1—7. Job vi. 4. ix. x. 16, 17. Prov. xviii. 14. Psalm iii. vii. x. xxxv. xxxviii. xlii. liv.—lx. lxiv. cii. Believers' justification, from the very first moment of their mystical union with Christ, is absolutely PERFECT and IRREVOCABLE. 1. It is a judicial act which admits of no degrees, Acts xiii. 38, 39. Rom. viii. 1, 33, 54. vi. 14. vii. 4. Col. ii. 13. Jer. xxxi. 34. xxxiii. 8. Isa. i. 18. xliii. 25. xliv. 22. 2. It is founded on the imputation of an infinitely perfect and everlasting righteousness, Dan. ix. 24. Rom. v. 16—21. Isa. xlv. 24, 25. Jer. xxiii. 6. 2 Cor. v. 21. Acts xx. 28. 1 Pet. i. 18—21. ii. 24. iii. 18. Rev. i. 5. v. 9. 3. All that are justified are perfectly freed from the law as a covenant, Rom. vii. 4. vi. 13. Gal. ii. 19. iv. 4, 5. v. 18. 4. Nothing can be laid to their charge before God as a judge, Rom. viii. 33. Jer. l. 20. Num. xxiii. 21. 5. No curse or condemnation before God remains for them, Rom. viii. 1, 33, 34. John v. 24. Gal. iii. 13. Psalm lxxii. 17. Eph. i. 3, 6, 7. Isa. xlv. 17. 6. God hath no judicial or avenging wrath to pour out upon them, Isa. xxvii. 4. liv. 8—10. lvii. 17, 18. Jer. xxxi. 18, 20. Hos. xiv. 4. 7. They are instated in the favour of God, which is infinitely perfect and everlasting, Isa. liv. 8—10. xlvi. 3, 4. Psalm xxxvii. 24, 28, 33. lxxxix. 24, 28, 33. cxxxvi. Mal. iii. 6. Rom. xi. 29. v. 10, 21. viii. 28—39. 2 Thess. ii. 16, 17.

OBJEC. I. " Believers cannot be perfectly freed from the law " as a covenant of works, without receiving a liberty of sin- " ning." ANSW. They are not hereby delivered from, but much more bound by the moral law as a *rule of life* in the hand of Christ, in whom they have much more abundant and affecting views of the infinitely evil nature and demerit of sin, of the holiness and majesty of God, of the excellency and authority of his commandments, and hence much stronger motives, as well as assistances, to holy obedience, than they could have under the law as a covenant, 1 Cor. ix. 21. Rom. vi. vii. 1--6.

OBJEC. II. " Believers, notwithstanding their justification, " continue at least in part under God's curse. Our first pa- " rents had it denounced upon them after they had believed in " Christ:—men, in every age, toil for their subsistence,—and " women conceive and bring forth their children with pain.— " Their afflictions are called *punishments*, and proceed from " God's wrath or anger : and death is an enemy to them." ANSW 1. We have no proof that our first parents had believed in Christ, before God addressed his threatenings to them. Nor is there, in them, any curse denounced against their persons, Gen. iii. 16—19. 2. Believers' afflictions being of the same matter with those of wicked men, and often suffered in connection with them,—and always procured by their own sin, and tending to its destruction, may be termed a *punishment*,—while, to their persons, they are the invaluably useful discipline of the new covenant, purchased by Christ for them, Heb. xii. 5—11. Rev. iii. 19. Rom. viii. 28. 2 Cor. iv. 17, 18. Isa. ii. 7. Hos. ii. 6, 14. Psalm cxix. 67, 71, 75. xciv. 12. Prov. iii. 12. Job v. 17. 3. From whatever indignation in God against their sins the afflictions of believers proceed,—his love to their persons as united to Christ is the principal spring thereof, Heb. xii. 6, 10. Rev. iii. 19. 4. Death hath an unfriendly appearance to believers, but it is a real benefit to them, transporting their souls to Christ; and hence, the more enlightened of them earnestly desire it, Luke ii. 29. Phil. i. 21, 23. 2 Cor. v. 4.

This sentence of justification being the very reverse of the curse of the broken covenant of works formerly explained,— must be our LEGAL LIFE in the covenant of grace, from which our temporal, spiritual, and eternal life, promised in that covenant, do proceed.—It not only adjudges us to that REAL new-covenant life, but engages all the perfections of God, infallibly to confer it upon us.—Let us therefore, with delightful wonder, observe how, through the operation of the curse on Christ, this justifying sentence operates on believers, in a manner directly contrary to the forementioned influence of the curse on others; and that, as all the dealings of God with the wicked, in time and through eternity, are but his execution of the curse on them ; so all his dealings with believers, in time and through eternity, are but the execution of his justifying sentence passed upon them.

More generally, 1. Christ having fulfilled all righteousness under the curse, he received a sentence of justification as our public Head, 1 Tim. iii. 16. Isa. liii. 8, 9. Rom. iv. 25. viii.

33, 34; which, pregnant with precious blessings, infallibly secured our spiritual and eternal welfare, who are his elect seed, in a state of union with himself, Isa. liii. 4, 5, 6, 8, 10, 11. Rom. v. 10, 15. John x. 10. 2. This virtual justification in Christ, as our Representative, prevents every thing that could effectually hinder our mystical union to, and regeneration by him, Ezek. xvi. 6, 8. Acts ix. Philem. 11, 15, 16. 3. By it the perfections of God are infallibly engaged to make his providences concur in making preparation for, and promoting our spiritual union to Christ, and our receiving of influences from him, Hos. ii. 6, 7, 14, 18—20. Ezek. xx. 37. 4. This sentence being transferred to our person through our spiritual union to Christ, places us in a most delightful state.——Christ having borne the wrath of God, Psalm lxxxix. 38. Isa. liii. 10, we are infallibly instated in his infinite and everlasting favour, Rom. v. 2, 10. Col. i. 20, 21. Isa. liv. 8—10. lvii. 19. xxvii. 4, 5. Psalm v. 12. James ii. 23.—Christ having satisfied his Father's law and justice to the uttermost, Luke xxiv. 26. Isa. liii. 10. Heb. ii. 9, 10. v. 7, 8. 1 Pet. iii. 18. ii. 24. Mat. xx. 28. John xvii. 4, we are solemnly consigned into the hands of infinite mercy, that God may exert all his influence in promoting our happiness, Psalm v. 7, 8. xxiii. 6. lxi. 7. xxxi. 19. Deut. xxxiii. 27—29. Isa. lxiii. 7.—Christ having continued the butt of his Father's wrath, till all of it that was due to our sins was completely exhausted, Isa. liii. 6, 4, 5, 10. Zech. xiii. 7. Acts ii. 23. iv. 27, 28, we are set up as the marks of God's infinite love, that all its blessings may be pointed at, and conferred on us, through all eternity, Psalm lxviii. 18, 19. lxxii. 17. Eph. i. 3—14. ii. 4—10. Rom. v. 17, 18, 20, 21. Tit. iii. 5, 6, 7.— Christ having for our sakes become poor by the curse, 2 Cor. viii. 9. Mat. viii. 20, we, by our justification, have all his unsearchable riches, all the fulness of God, secured for us, Psalm lxxxv. 10—12. lxxxiv. 11. ciii. 4, 5. xxxiv. 8—12. Phil. iv. 19. Eph. iii. 8, 19.—Evils from every quarter having pursued Christ by virtue of the curse, Psalm lxix. 1, 2, 14, 15. Isa. liii. 4, 5, 8, 10. Psalm xxii. 1—21, our justification infallibly secures us from every real evil, and draws blessings on us from every quarter, Psalm xci. 10. ciii. 3. xxxiv. xxxvii. Job v. 15—26. 1 Pet. iii. 13. Job i. 10. Rom. viii. 28—30.—The curse, having deprived Christ of his comforts, and made even his nearest connections distressful to him, John xix. 11. Mark iii. 21. John vii. viii. Mat. xxvi. 69—73, God, in executing his justifying sentence on us, must make all things work for our spiritual and eternal advantage, Rom. viii. 28. 2 Cor. iv. 17. xii. 7—10. Phil. i. 16, 19. Psalm cxix. 71. Isa. xxvii. 9. Mic. vii. 14. Heb. xii. 6—11. James i. 3, 12. 1 Pet. i. 7.—More particularly,—in this life,

I. It operates on our soul. 1. The curse having separated Christ from much comfortable fellowship with his Father, Psalm xxii. 1, 2. Mat. xxvii. 46, justification opens our free access to the most intimate fellowship with all the divine persons, Heb. x. 19—22. 1 John i. 3, 7. Eph. ii. 18. iii. 12. John x. 7, 9. 2 Cor. xiii. 14. Hence, in the very moment of our justification, regenerating influences from God flow into our soul, and renew all its powers after the image of God, notwithstanding all that Satan, the world, and our inward corruptions can do to the contrary, Rom. v. 12, 15, 20, 21. vi. 14. vii. 4. Gal. ii. 19. vi. 15. 2 Cor. v. 17, 18. And thus, in consequence of Christ's divine power and holiness, keeping his manhood perfectly holy even under the curse, we, under the justifying sentence, through fellowship with Him, and his Father and the Spirit, have our primitive beauties of holiness restored, Ezek. xvi. 8—14. Psalm xlv. 11, 13, 14. Song i. 15. ii. 14. iv. 1—5, 7. vi. 4, 5. vii. 1—6. 2. As, notwithstanding his being under the law, made sin, and made a curse for us, Christ continued perfectly free from sinful defilement, and flourished in holiness, 2 Cor. v. 21. 1 Pet. ii. 22. Isa. liii. 9,—we, being justified, and so no more under the law, but under grace, sin hath no more dominion over us, but holiness dwells, reigns, and gradually fills all the faculties of our soul, Rom. vi. 14. Col. ii. 13. John iii. 6. 2 Cor. v. 17; our understanding is made light in the Lord, Hos. ii. 20. Eph. v. 8. 1 Cor. ii. 15; our conscience is made pure and tender, Heb. ix. 14. 2 Kings xxii. 19. 1 Tim. i. 5. Heb. x. 22; our will is inclined to every thing good, Deut. xxx. 6. 2 Cor. v. 19. Psalm cx. 3. Phil. iii. 7—9; our affections are restored to their proper order and bent, Luke vii. 47. Psalm xviii. 2 cxvi. 1. Rom. v. 5. vii. 24. Psalm cxxxix. 17, 20; our memory is rendered retentive of good, and ready to forget injuries and trifles, Heb. viii. 10—12. Psalm xlii. 6. Gen. xlviii. 3. 3. The curse having fixed on Christ, confined him in his humbled estate, till he had fulfilled all the condition of the new covenant, Luke xxiv. 26, 46. Heb. ii. 9, 10. v. 8, justification secures us in our happy state to all eternity, that all his purchased blessings may be fully conferred on us, and all our grateful, holy services completed, Rom. v. 8, 10. viii. 33—39. 1 Pet. i. 5. Satan may tempt, but shall be defeated, 1 Cor. x. 13. Heb. ii. 14, 15; the world may flatter, or frown, but shall be overcome, John xvi. 33. 1 John v. 4; sin may struggle and prevail, but shall never reign, nor push to the unpardonable crime; and shall at last be completely destroyed, Rom. vii. 23, 25. 1 John iii. 8—10. Mark iii. 29. Psalm ciii. 3. Mic. vii. 19. 4. Notwithstanding the increasing of his sufferings under the curse, Christ increased in wisdom and grace, and learned obedience by the things which he suffered, Luke ii.

40, 52. Isa. xlii. 4. xi. 2. Heb. v. 8. And, under the influence of our justifying sentence, our implanted holiness increases, and though simple in itself, Eph. v. 8. John iii. 6, is formed into a number of particular graces, and Christian tempers, which are exercised in good works, Rom. v. 1---5. Gal. v. 22, 23. 2 Pet. iii. 18. i. 4---8. Psalm lxxxiv. 7. Job xvii. 9. Prov. iv. 18; one of which ordinarily predominates in our heart and life, even as some particular sinful lust does under the influence of the curse, Rom. iv. 20. Num. xii. 3. James v. 11. 1 Kings iv. 30. Heb. xii. 1. Psalm xix. 13. xviii. 23. 5. Notwithstanding Christ's increasing holiness of human nature, and his more and more assiduous service of God, the curse increased his sufferings towards the end of his humbled life on earth, 1 Pet. iii. 18. ii. 24. Phil. ii. 8. Heb. v. 7, 8, 26, ii. 10. xii. 23. Mat. iv.—xxvii. Luke iv.—xxiii. John ii.—xix.—And, to reward our believing progress in holiness, our justifying sentence pours down special favours on us, Mat. xiii. 12. xxv. 29. Isa. lxiv. 5. Psalm xix. 11. Isa. iii. 10.—To reward our receiving of the word with all readiness of mind, it secures further illumination, Isa. xxxii. 3. John viii. 32. Hos. vi. 3.—To reward our lowliness and tenderness of heart, softening influences are bestowed, Isa. lvii. 15. Prov. iii. 34.—To reward our holiness of conversation, purifying influences are added, Mat. v. 8. 2 Cor. iii. 18. Rev. iii. 4.— To reward our care, to keep our conscience void of offence, and to maintain a prudent behaviour, further wisdom is granted, Dan ii 21. John vii. 17. Prov. i. 5. ix. 8.—To reward our faithful and stedfast resistance of temptation,—support under, and deliverance from it, are secured, Rev. ii. 10. 1 Cor. x. 13. 6. The curse having filled Christ's soul with most dreadful sorrow and anguish, Isa. liii. 3, 4, 10. Mat. xxvi. 37—39. Luke xxii. 44. Mark iii. 5. John xi. 35. xii. 27; justification having given us a legal right to every thing satisfying, we obtain contentment with our lot, Phil. iv. 11, 12, 18; peace possesses our mind, Phil. iv. 7. Col. iii. 15. Rom. xv. 13. v. 1; joy is diffused through our heart, Rom. v. 1, 2, 11. Phil. iii. 3. iv. 4. Psalm xxxiii. 1. cxlix. 2; and full assurance of eternal life transports it, Rom. xv. 13. 2 Tim. iv. 8 Psalm xxiii. 6. lxxiii. 26. xvi. 5---11. xvii. 15. 2 Cor. v. 1, 2. 2 Tim. i. 12.

II. It operates on our BODIES, 1. As under the influence of the curse, Christ, in his incarnation, assumed the likeness of sinful flesh, Rom. viii. 3; so, being justified, our body is for the Lord, 1 Cor. vi. 13, 15, 19, 20; its tendency to unfit our soul for holy duties is gradually subdued, 1 Cor. ix. 27. Rom. xiii. 11---14; and it will at length be freed from all sinful pollution, Phil. iii. 21. 1 Cor. xv. 44. 2. By virtue of the curse lying on him, Christ's body had no form nor comeliness, his face

OF JUSTIFICATION.

was more marred than any man, Isa. lii. 14. liii. 2, 3;—through justification our body is washed with pure water, and sanctified, Heb. x. 22. 1 Thess. v. 23; is no more under the dominion of sinful flesh, but its members consigned and fitted to be instruments of righteousness,—our ears to hear God's voice,—our eyes to behold his works,—our hands to labour in his service,—our feet to travel in his paths,—and our mouth to utter his praise, Rom. vi. 11, 12. Phil. i. 20. 2 Cor. iv. 10, 11. 1 Cor. vi. 20. 3. The curse having inflicted fearful torments on Christ's body, Isa. liii. 5, 7. lii. 14. 1 6. Psalm xxii. 14, 15.—Justification frees our body from all unblessed troubles, and renders those which we meet with profitable to us, Heb. xii. 10, 11. 2 Cor. iv. 17. Isa. xxvii. 9. Job v. 17. Psalm xciv. 12. cxix. 67, 71, 75., Prov. iii. 12.

III It operates on our whole-PERSON and CONNECTIONS. 1. Under the curse, Christ's manhood, as subsisting in his divine person, was subjected to bondage and oppression, Gal. iv. 4. iii. 13. 2 Cor. v. 21. Through justification, our person is delivered from the dominion and slavery of spiritual enemies, and their prevailing power gradually decreases, John viii. 32, 36. Gal. i. 4. Luke i. 74, 75. Rom. vi. 14. viii. 2, 3, 15, 37. Heb. ii. 15. 2. The curse having brought Christ into most fearful dangers and difficulties, Mat. ii. 16. Mark iii. 6, 7. Luke iv. 29. xi. 54. xiii. 31. John v. 16. viii. 59. x. 31, 39. xi. 53, 54, justification effectually secures believers from all real danger of hurt, 1 Pet. i. 3—5. iii. 13. Rom. viii. 38, 39. Psalm xci. 4, 5, 7. Deut. xxxiii. 26, 27. 3. The curse having rendered Christ's name a reproach, his labours unsuccessful or hurtful, and deprived him of the necessaries and comforts of life, nay, of delightful fellowship with his Father in his ordinances, and turned his friends into enemies, Mat. xi. 19. Psal. xxii. 6. lxix. 20. Isa. xlix. 4. Mat. xiii. 14. viii. 20. xxvii. 36—46. Psalm lxix. 19. Heb. v. 7, 13. Psalm xxii. 1, 2. Luke v. 8. Psalm xli. 9. John xvi. 32, justification renders us honoured and famed, Job v. 21. Prov. x. 7. Zeph. iii. 20; prospers the work of our hands, Psal. cxxvii. 2. cxxviii. 2. xc. 17. Deut. xxviii. 6. xvi. 15. xxiv. 25; secures our outward provision, and blesses our basket and our store, Psalm xxxvii. 16. Mat. vi. 33. Isa. xxxiii. 16. Job i. 10; makes the ordinances of the gospel edifying to us, Isa. xii. 3. Psalm lxxxiv. 9, 10; our relations comfortable, and our enemies useful to us, Psalm cxxviii. 1—3. cxliv. 12. cxxxii. 16. Prov. x. 7. Rom. viii. 28. 1 Pet. iii. 13.

After this life, the justifying sentence will operate on believers, 1. *In death.* The curse having made death a wrathful stroke to Christ, Isa. liii. 10. Zech. xiii. 7, it is a message of love to us that are justified, Psalm xxxvii. 37. Luke ii. 29.

Phil. i. 22, 23.—The curse having excluded God's comforting presence from Christ in his agonies of death, Psalm xxii. 1, 2. Mat. xxvii. 46,—justification secures for us his supporting, if not comfortable, presence and influence, and transports our soul to his immediate fellowship, Psalm xxiii. 4. xlviii. 14. Rev. xxi. 22—24. Psalm xliii. 4. 1 Cor. xv. 28. The curse having exerted all its force upon Christ in his death, and made him expire under the dreadful pressure of divine wrath, Isa. liii. 4—8, 10. Psal. xl. 12. xxii. 14. Zech. xiii. 7; justification will, by death, put an end to all our troubles of body or mind, and introduce us into inconceivable happiness, Rev. xxi. 4. xiv. 13. Isa. lx. 20. 2 Cor. v. 4. Isa. lvii. 1, 2. Psalm lxxiii. 24. Christ's death being stinged by the curse, he met it with agony and terror, Mat. xxvi. 38. xxvii. 46. John xii. 27. Heb. v. 7; —but our death, being disarmed and sweetened by our justifying sentence, we may meet it with composure and joy, Psalm xxiii. 4. Luke ii. 29, 30. 2 Tim. iv. 6—8. 2. In the *removal of our souls to the eternal state.* The curse having led Christ to the slaughter, and made him appear before his Father's tribunal, laden with the sins of all his elect, Isa. liii. 6, 7,—justification will then cover our sins, and make our imperfect obedience of faith to appear and be accepted, Rev. xiv. 13. Mat. xxv. 34—40. Under the curse, every sin imputed to Christ drew along with it its punishment, Isa. liii. 4—6 ;—justification will then make every act of our gospel-obedience draw along with it its gracious reward, Matth. xxv. 21, 23.—The curse having debarred Christ's soul from all deliverance, till he had made full atonement for our sin, and brought in an everlasting righteousness, Mat. xxvi. 39, 42. Luke xxiv. 26, 46, justification, through his atonement and intercession, secures the eternal welfare of our souls, and the readiness of heaven to receive us, 1 John ii. 1, 2. Rom. v. 17, 21. John xiv. 2, 3. 3. In the *separate state of our souls.* The curse having sunk Christ into an horrible pit, Psalm xl. 2. lxix. 1, 2,—justification will place our departed souls on thrones of glory, John xiv. 2. xii. 26. Rev. iii. 21. Christ having had the cup of God's indignation poured into him by the curse, Mat. xxvi. 39, 42. John xviii. 11. xii. 27. Psalm cx. 7. Isa. liii. 3, 4, we, by the justifying sentence, shall, at God's right hand, be filled with fulness of joy, and pleasures for evermore, Psalm xvii. 15. xvi. 11. Isa. lx. 19, 20. The curse having surrounded Christ with ungodly men and devils, and appointed his grave with the wicked, Psalm xxii. 12. Isa. liii. 9, justification shall place our souls among holy angels, the spirits of just men made perfect, and chiefly with divine persons, Heb. xii. 22—24. Phil. i. 23. John xvii. 24. 4. In the *condition of our dead bodies.* The curse having shut up Christ in his grave as in a prison, Isa.

liii. 8. Psalm xl. 2. lxix. 14, justification renders our grave a place prepared and perfumed by God for our security and rest, Isa. lvii. 1, 2. Job xiv. 13.—Some fruits of sin continued fixed by the curse on Christ in his grave, Isa. liii. 9, 12. Matth. xxvii. 65, 66. By justification we will lie in our grave, with all our sins blotted out, and wrapped in his everlasting righteousness, Mic. vii. 19. Isa. xxvi. 19, 20.—Even under the curse, Christ's body saw no corruption in the grave, Psalm xvi. 10. Acts ii. 27, 32. xiii. 34, 35. Under our justifying sentence, our bodies shall be dissolved in our grave, for their purification and glorious resurrection, 1 Cor. xv. 36, 42—45. Job xix. 26, 27. 5. In *our resurrection.* Christ having, under the curse, with his visage more marred than any man, paid all our debt and fulfilled all our legal service, Isa. lii. 14. liii. 2, 3. Dan. ix. 24. 1 Pet. ii. 24. iii. 18. Matth. xx. 28. Tit. ii. 14. Eph. v. 2, we, under the justifying sentence, shall be raised in glory to receive the reward, 1 Cor. xv. 41—44. Phil. iii. 21. Psal. xvii. 15. xvi. 10, 11. Dan. xii. 2, 3. Matth. xxv. 21, 23. Col. iii. 4. Christ having under the curse, endured desertion and ignominy, Matth. xxvii. 46. Isa. l. 5, 6. lii. 14. liii. 3, 4, 7. Matth. xxvi. xxvii, our justification shall place us as his ransomed members, in distinguished honour, Matth. xxv. 33, 34. 1 Thess. iv. 17. Col. iii. 4.—God his judge having, through the interposing curse, appeared in terrible majesty to Christ, Psalm lxxxix. 38. Zech. xiii. 7, Christ our judge will, through our interposing justification, appear to us in the most delightful and engaging form, Job xix. 25—27. 2 Thess. i. 10. Heb. ix. 28. Tit. ii. 13. —The curse having imprinted upon Christ its most visible marks of infamy and woe, Gal. iii. 13. Matth. xxvi. xxvii.— the holy fruits of our justification shall be proclaimed for our, and for Jesus' and for Jehovah's honour, in his redemption work, Matth. xxv. 34—40.—Christ having, by the curse, been publicly condemned and executed, Gal. iii. 13. 1 Pet. iii. 18. Heb. xiii. 12. John xviii. xix. our justifying sentence shall, by Christ, be publicly proclaimed before all angels and men, and ordered into immediate and full execution, Matth. xxv. 34, 46. 6. In *our complete and eternal happiness.* The curse having shut up Christ for a time to lamentation, mourning, and woe, Isa. liii. 2, 3, 10, we, as justified, having returned from the tribunal with songs and everlasting joy on our heads, shall be unalterably fixed in the highest felicity, Rev. iii. 12. 1 Thess. iv. 17.— The curse having for a time debarred Christ from his Father's presence and smiles, we, through our justification, shall be for ever with the Lord and see him as he is,—*all our own*, 1 Thess. iv. 17. 1 John iii. 2. 1 Cor. xiii. 12. xv. 28.—The curse fixed on him, having made God to take pleasure in bruising his own Son, Isa. liii. 10. Zech. xiii. 7; our justification shall have its full execution in God's vouchsafing us an exceeding and an eternal weight of glory, Rom. v. 17, 21 vi. 23. Psal. xvi. 11. xxxi 19. Zeph. iii. 17. Isa. lx. 19, 20. 2 Cor. iv. 17. Rev. ii. 7, 17. iii. 4, 5, 12, 21.

When we consider the infinite knowledge, equity, and faithfulness of God the justifier, we must conclude, that nothing can be the *ground* of our justification, or *justifying righteousness,* but what is answerable to the importance of the sentence, Rom. ii. 2. Deut. xxxii. 4. Zeph. iii. 5. Gen. xviii. 25. Rom. iii. 24—26. v. 21. But men's legal dispositions and their inveterate enmity against the glory of God's redeeming grace, and the sole mediation of Jesus Christ, hath made them to stretch every nerve to corrupt this doctrine of a sinner's justification before God: and as if the one stone, which God hath laid for its foundation, were too narrow, or too weak to bear it, they have collected much dung, dross, sand, hay, and stubble, to support it; which we must now remove.

I. The new nature, which, by the Holy Ghost, is implanted in us in regeneration, cannot be the ground of our justification; for, 1. It is always imperfect while we remain on earth, 1 Kings viii. 46. Eccl. vii. 20. James iii 2. 1 John i. 10. Rom. vii. 14—24. 1 Cor. xiii. 12. Gal. v. 17. 2. Though it were perfect, it could not justify us, as it is not answerable to the whole demands of the law, as a broken covenant, Mat. xix. 17. Gal. iii. 10, 12. Rom. x. 5. vi. 23 Heb. ix. 22. Adam had once a perfectly holy nature, and yet was never justified by the law, even when its demands were infinitely lower than at present. Christ had a perfectly holy nature, and yet could not be justified, till he had finished his course of obedience and suffering, Heb. ii. 10. v. 8. 1 Tim iii. 16 with John xvii. 4. Isa. xlii. 21. 3. As, in our natural formation, the curse in some respect prior, keeps us destitute of original righteousness,—the justifying sentence which removes that curse, which is the strength of sin, must in order of nature, not of time, precede our implanted holiness, which is the beginning of that real eternal life, to which we are adjudged in justification. 4. We have our justifying righteousness, not *in ourselves,* but *in the Lord,* Phil. iii. 9. 2 Cor. v. 21. Isa. xlv. 24, 25. liv. 17. Jer. xxiii. 6. xxxiii. 16.

II. Faith, neither as an habit nor as an act, can be imputed to us for our justifying righteousness; for, 1. Faith, as an holy habit or good act, is obedience to the law, 1 John iii. 23. John vi. 29;—whereas our justification is directly contrary to a justification by the works of the law, Rom. iii. 27, 28. iv. 4, 5. 2. Neither the permanent habit, nor the transient act of faith, can be that righteousness witnessed by the law and the prophets, which is not IN, but UNTO and UPON all them that believe, Rom. iii. 21, 22. 3. If our imperfect habit or act of faith were imputed for our justifying righteousness, how could God be JUST, eminently just, in justifying us? Or, how could boasting be excluded, Rom. iii. 26, 27. 1 John i. 9? How could God justify the *ungodly*, and the reward be *not of debt but of grace*, Rom. iv. 4, 5?—How could it be a righteousness revealed *from faith to faith*, Rom. i 17? —Or, a *gift* of righteousness by grace, *more effectual* to make men reign in eternal life, than Adam's sin was to ruin them, Rom. v. 15—21? 4. If our faith be our justifying righteousness, why is it called the *righteousness of God*, as distinguished from our own righteousness, and even from our faith, Phil. iii. 9. 2 Cor. v. 21. Rom. iv. 24. iii. 22. x. 10. i. 17? Or, how does the obedience of ONE make MANY righteous, Rom. v. 19. Isa. xlv. 24. Jer. xxiii. 6?—How is it imputed to *many*, Rom. iv. 22—24? And how is it a righteousness IN, and put on by the Lord, Isa. xlv. 24, 25. lxi. 10? 5. If our habit or act of faith be imputed to us for our justifying righteousness,—then God must account that a righteousness which does not answer the ten thousandth part of the demands of the broken law:—A very imperfect part of righteousness must be a sufficient foundation for the *pardon of innumerable sins*, and of a *full title* to everlasting happiness:—We must be justified on account of that which is so imperfect, as to need to be pardoned:—God must receive the justifying righteousness from us: And justification must be by works, not by grace,— at least not by grace only: Men may glory in themselves:— than all which nothing can be more contrary to Scripture.

OBJEC. "Faith was imputed to Abraham for his justify- "ing righteousness, Gen. xv. 6. Gal. iii. 6. Rom. iv. 3, 9." ANSW. 1. To understand these texts of the imputation of faith, as an habit or act, for a justifying righteousness, is manifestly contradictory to the scope of the apostle in them, which is to prove that justification is by God's grace, not by the works of the law. 2. Abraham was justified many years before that act of believing mentioned, Gen. xv. 6. xii. 2, 3. Heb. xi. 8. Rom. iv. 3; and so it could not be his justifying righteousness. 3. Abraham's justifying righteousness excluded his obtaining the inheritance by the works of the law, Rom. iv. 13. 4. That which was imputed to Abraham for righteousness, is imputed to all them that believe, and so could not be his act of faith, unless we make him the Saviour of mankind by that act, Rom. iv. 11, 22—24: but, it was the object of that act of faith which he embraced in the promise, *viz.* Christ and his righteousness, who is perhaps called FAITH,

Gal. iii. 23, 25; as well as HOPE, 1 Tim. i. 1. Col. i. 27. Jer. xiv. 8. xvii. 7.

III. True and evangelical REPENTANCE is necessary as an obedience to God's law;—as a fruit of faith;—as a part of begun, and as preparation for complete salvation, Mark i. 15. Zech. xii. 10. Gal. v. 6. Luke xiii. 3, 5. It is necessary as a mean of attaining a comfortable sense of judicial pardon, and as an evidence that we have received it, Psalm lxvi. 18. Ezek. xvi. 62, 63. xxxvi. 25, 31. It is necessary to obtain God's paternal pardons, and remove his chastisements, Isa. xxvii. 9. 1 John i. 9. Jer. xxxi. 18—20. iii. 12, 13. Prov. xxviii. 13. But it is not necessary to obtain judicial pardon, as a ground of our justification before God. 1. Our faith, from which all gospel repentance proceeds, Zech. xii. 10. Ezek. xvi. 62, 63, in its first act, or rather in its very formation, completes our union with Christ, in whom we cannot but be justified, Eph. iii. 17. 1 Cor. vi. 17. Rom. viii. 1. 2 Cor. v. 21. Isa. xlv. 24, 25. 2. Gospel repentance and love to God precede noted intimations of judicial pardon; but they, and all other good works, are fruits, not the condition of it, Luke vii. 47, 48. Ezek. xvi. 62, 63. xxxvi. 25—31. Hos. xiv. 1, 4, 8. Isa. xliv. 22. 3. The admission of repentance as the condition or ground of our justification, detracts from the illustrious manifestation of God's grace in it, Rom. iii. 24. v. 15—21. Eph. ii. 7, 8. i. 6, 7. 4. If repentance be the condition of judicial pardon, none ought to apply it as offered in the gospel, till they be fully certain that their repentance is truly gracious, Rom. xiv. 23. Psalm l. 16. Faith is not prerequired as any necessary qualification, but is the very reception or application of the pardon. 5. None can repent evangelically, while they remain under the law as a covenant, which is the strength of sin, 1 Cor. xv. 56;—nor turn to God with full purpose of heart till they apprehend him gracious and merciful, forgiving iniquity, transgression, and sin, Isa. lv. 7. Hos. xiv. 1—3, 8. Jer. iii. 4, 5, 12—14, 22. Exod. xxxiv. 6, 7.

OBJEC. I. " We are called to turn and repent, in order to " obtain the pardon of our sins, Jer. iii. 12, 13, 14, 22. Isa. " lv. 7. Rev. ii. 4, 5. iii. 19. 'Psalm xxxii. 4, 5. Acts ii. 38. " iii. 19. viii. 22." ANSW. TURNING, in the two first mentioned and other like texts, at least, includes faith or *coming*, which receives pardon, Jer. iii. 22. Isa. lv. 1, 3, 7. The three next texts relate to such as are in Christ, and only need God's fatherly pardon. That text, Acts ii. 38, merely represents that repentance is necessary in adult persons to prepare them for baptism, the seal of pardon. In Acts iii. 19, perhaps *re-*

pentance means but a change of mind, as conversion is subjoined to it. Or, repentance and conversion taken for the same thing, may mean our whole exercise of turning to God by faith and love. Besides, the pardon here mentioned may denote the declarative pardon published in the last judgment. Nay, the words have been rendered, *Repent therefore, because of the blotting out of your sins*. In Acts viii. 22, repentance includes turning to God by faith, as well as by grief for, and hatred of sin.

OBJEC. II. " Many promises and threatenings of Scripture " suspend the pardon of our sins on our true repentance, " 1 Kings viii. 47—50. 2 Chron. vii. 13, 14. Prov. xxviii. 13. " Luke xiii. 3, 5. 1 John i. 9." ANSW. The last of these texts respects believers and fatherly pardons, 1 John ii. 12, 13, 14. All the rest immediately respect the outward happiness of the Jewish nation, which we readily grant to have been not a little suspended on their good behaviour. In Prov. xxviii. 13. Luke xiii. 3, 5, pardon of sin is not mentioned: but it is merely suggested, that repentance is an excellent mean of averting misery and receiving happiness. Nay, in *Luke*, no more but the inseparable connection between final impenitence and fearful ruin is declared. Now, though our wicked works be certainly damning, it will not follow that our good works will certainly save us, Rom. v. 21. vi. 23. Lev. xxvi. Deut. xxviii. Amos i.—iv. Ezek. xviii.

IV. None of our own GOOD WORKS can be our justifying righteousness. 1. The Scripture plainly excludes them from the least room in the ground of our justification, Job ix. 2, 3. Psalm cxxx. 3, 4. cxliii. 2. Rom. iii. 19, 20, 28. iv. 4, 5, 6. Gal. ii. 16, 21. v. 4. Phil. iii. 8, 9. 2. The imperfection of our best works renders them altogether unanswerable to the demands of God's law, 1 Kings viii. 46. Eccl. vii. 20. James iii. 2. Isa. lxiv. 6. Psalm xiv. 1—4. liii. 1—4. Rom. iii. 10— 20, 23. Nay, suppose they were perfect, they could not satisfy for offences already committed, Rom. vi. 23. Heb. ix. 22. 3. Our justification, including *pardon* of sin, and being wholly of *free grace*, excludes all human works from being the ground of it, Tit. iii. 3—7. Eph. i. 7. Col. i. 14. Rom. v. 17—21. iii. 24. xi. 6.

OBJEC. I. " David, Hezekiah, Nehemiah, and other saints, " plead that God would judge them according to their works, " Psalm vii. 8. Isa. xxxviii. 3. Nehem. v. 19. xiii. 14, 22." ANSW. 1. None of these texts relate to the justification of these men's persons, that being completed long before; but represent their desire that God, as king of nations, and particularly of Israel, would manifest and reward their innocence or good deeds with some temporal favours. 2. These very men betake themselves wholly to the sovereign and great mercy of God for their eternal salvation, Psalm cxxx. 4. Neh. xiii. 22. Isa. xxxviii. 17.

OBJEC. II. " Abraham, Rahab, and others, were justified " by their good works, James ii. 21—25." ANSW. 1. James, who maintains justification, and Paul, who denies justification by works, both mean the *same kind of works.* James treats of works, which manifest a true and lively faith, and fear of God in the heart, James ii. 14—25. Paul means works of righteousness, Tit. iii. 5, works required in God's law, Rom. iii. 20, 28. Gal. iii. 10, 11;—good works, to which we are created in Christ, Eph. ii. 10. But, 2. They mean very *different kinds of faith.* In discoursing of justification, Paul always speaks of the faith of God's elect, by which men put on Christ and his righteousness, live in him, and have him in them; and which saves them, and works by love in an universal obedience to God's law, Tit. i. 1. Rom. xiii. 14. Gal. ii. 20. Phil. iii. 9. Eph. iii. 17. ii. 8. Gal. v. 6. 1 Tim. i. 5. But James speaks of a *dead faith,* a mere nominal faith, which worldly men have, and which brings forth no good works. 3. They mean very *different justifications.* Paul, in his epistles to the Romans and Galatians, means only that justification of sinful men *before God,* in which he pardons their sin, instates them in his favour, and gives them a legal right to everlasting happiness: and his scope is to shew guilty men, mad on being justified by their own works, how they may obtain true justification of their persons.—James never mentions justification *before God.* Abraham was justified before God about sixty years before he offered his son, which James mentions as his justifying work. Rahab's receiving of the spies, being performed in faith, Heb. ix. 31, must have followed her justification before God.—But he speaks of men's *manifestation* of their justification to *the world* and *their own conscience,* the *shewing of faith,* which may be as properly called *justification,* as Christ's strength is *perfected, i. e.* hath its perfection manifested in men's weakness. 2 Cor. xii. 9;—and as men are, or become the children of God by their charity and mercifulness, *i. e.* are manifested to be such, Luke vi. 35. And indeed, the Hebrew TZIDDEK properly means, *to shew one's self righteous,* and TZADDIK, *one that shews himself righteous;*—to which not only many Hebrew verbs of the third species, or Greek ones of the middle voice, have a similar signification; and his scope is to convince self-conceited and sin-indulging professors, of the necessity of good works for manifesting themselves true believers, or in a justified state.

OBJEC. III. " Though repentance and good works be not "conditions of our first justification, they are the condition of "our second or continued justification." ANSW. 1. Our justification is indeed repeatedly intimated in this life, at death, and in the last judgment. But neither scripture nor any experience of the saints knows any *second* justification, or fallibility of the *first*. 2. Scripture attributes so much to our *first* justification, that it leaves no place for a *second*, Rom. iv. 6, 7. v. 1, 2, 9, 10, 11, 17, 18, 19 viii. 1, 4, 33, 34. x. 4. Heb. x. 10, 14, 18. Dan. ix. 24. 2 Cor. v. 21. Acts xxvi. 18. xiii. 39. Col. ii. 10, 13. John v. 24. Eph. i. 3, 6, 7. 3. Neither scripture nor experience admits any other foundation of justification than that which is the ground of its first constitution, Rom. i. 17. Gal. ii. 20, 21. Phil. iii. 9. 1 John i. 7. ii. 1, 2. Eph i. 3, 6, 7. Col. i. 14. 4. Ezek. xviii. xxxiii. do not relate to the justification of sinners before God, but to the Jews' temporal happiness in Canaan, as their immediate object. Rev. xxii. 11. suggests no repeated justification or progressive continuance in it, but the irrevocableness of our justification, and our duty to persevere in increasing its evidence.—Nor is the *right*, *power*, or *privilege* to the tree of life, ver. 14. any more than a manifest evidence of right to, and a meetness for, the heavenly felicity.

Now these works excluded from the ground of our justification are not merely or chiefly, *the works of the ceremonial law*, for, 1. The ceremonial law itself, and all obedience to it, were dying out, when the Holy Ghost so strongly decried all justification of sinful men by the works of the law, Rom. i.—x. Gal. ii.—vi. 2. If these works are only or chiefly excluded, why should the Scripture addressed to the Gentile disregarders of these ceremonial works mightily decry them in the matter of justification, Rom. ii—x. Gal. ii. 5; and that addressed to the Jewish boasters of them so highly extol them, James ii. 14—26? 3. The law, by the works of which no man can be justified, is that which stops *every mouth*, and holds *all the world* guilty before God,—that of which the doers are justified,—that which condemns *covetousness*, and gives the knowledge of *sin*, that which was in full force in the days of Abraham,—that of which the fulfilment would warrant boasting before God,—and which curses every one that continues not perfectly to fulfil all its demands, Rom. iii. 19, 20. ii. 13. iii. 27, 28, 31. iv. 13. Gal. iii. 5, 6, 10. 4. If only ceremonial works be excluded from our justifying righteousness, why did the Holy Ghost take such pains to convince the Gentiles of their manifold violations of the moral law of nature, in order to introduce his doctrine of justification, Rom. i. ii. iii? 5. No reason can be produced against the justifying influence of ceremonial works, which will not equally militate against that of other human works.

It is not merely *external* works, or works *not performed in faith*, which are excluded from our justifying righteousness; for, 1. Justification is perfected that very moment in which we begin to believe, Rom. v. 1. iii. 28. Gal. ii. 16. No works, therefore, which proceed from faith, and so follow after our justification, can be the condition of it,—any more than a thief or murderer can be declared innocent, because, after such a sentence, he so offends no more. 2. The best works of believers are very unanswerable in perfection to the demands even of the precepts of the moral law, Isa. lxiv. 5, 6. 1 John i. 8—10. 1 Kings viii. 46. Eccl. vii. 20. James iii. 2. Rom. vii. 14—25. 3. Believers are not under the law as a covenant, by which men must be justified or condemned,—when they perform their obedience of faith, Rom. vii. 2, 4. vi. 13. viii. 2. Gal. ii. 19. iv. 4, 5. v. 18. 4. Believers, renewed in the spirit of their mind, renounce all their works from having any place in their justifying righteousness, Psalm cxxx. 3, 4. cxliii. 2. Job ix. 2, 3. xl. 4. xlii. 5, 6. Isa. lxiv. 6. 1 Cor. iv. 4. Gal. ii. 16. Phil. iii. 8, 9. 5. The noted instances of justification mentioned in Scripture, were *by faith*, in opposition to all human works, Rom. iv. 1—6, 13. Psal. cxliii. 2. cxxx. 3, 4. xxv. 11. 6. All works performed by men, in obedience to any law of God, and particularly the good works of believers performed in faith, are excluded from our justifying righteousness, Rom. iii. 19, 20. x. 3—10. Eph. ii. 8—10. Tit. iii. 5. 7. If inward holiness and works performed in faith, were our justifying righteousness, —how could the righteousness imputed in justification be a righteousness without the law, Rom. iii. 21, 22, 24—26?—or, how could God justify the *ungodly*, and impute righteousness *without works*, Rom. iv. 5, 6?—or, how could the promises be of faith, in opposition to works, that it might be sure to all the seed, Rom. iv. 16?—or, how could believers have inward peace, or assured hope of everlasting happiness, before they had completed the condition of good works performed in faith, Rom. v. 1—5, 10, 11. xv. 13. 2 Tim. i. 12? Or, how could any think the doctrine of justification could encourage licentiousness, Rom. vi. 1, 2. Jude 4? 8. Why should the Holy Ghost so laboriously exclude mere external works, or works not performed in faith, which men never plead to be a sufficient justifying righteousness, Rom. xiv. 23. Prov. xv. 8. xxi. 4, 27. xxviii. 9?

It is not merely *perfect works*, such as Adam performed before his Fall, which are excluded from our justifying righteousness before God; for, 1. Why should the Holy Ghost so laboriously disprove the admission of such works as are not to be found on earth, 1 Kings viii. 46. Eccl. vii. 20. Prov. xx. 9. James iii. 2. Isa. lxiv. 6. vi. 5. Rom. vii. 14—25. Gal. v. 17. Phil. iii. 12? 2. If only imperfect works justify men, why doth the Holy Ghost labour to persuade us, that our works are condemnable, in proportion to their imperfection, Isa. i. 11—15. xxix. 13?— 3. How absurd to exclude perfect works, which fulfil the precept of the law, in order to introduce imperfect works, which, *as such*, break the law, as our justifying righteousness before God, whose judgment is according to truth, Rom. ii. 2?— 4. Paul, David, and other saints, renounced their own works, which they believed to be very imperfect, from being their justifying righteousness, Phil. iii. 8, 9. Rom. vii. 14—25. Psal. cxliii. 2. cxxx. 3, 4. 5. How can imperfect righteousness be the *righteousness of God*,—a righteousness IN *Jehovah*,—*fine linen, clean, and white*, which renders men *all fair*, without spot, *unreprovable* in God's sight, 2 Cor. v. 21. Isa. xlv. 24. Rev. xix. 8. Song iv. 7. Col. i. 22? 6. How could God's justifying men, in an imperfect righteousness of their own, agree with his justifying the *ungodly*,—of mere *grace, not of debt*, and to the exclusion of all *boasting*, Rom. iv. 4—6. iii. 27? Performance of imperfect obedience under the *broken law*, would be an infinitely glorious performance for us, 1 Cor. xv. 56.

It is no less absurd to suppose, that *only the merit* of human works or men's *conceit of it*, is excluded from our justifying righteousness. 1. It was perhaps never imagined, that human merit could wholly exclude the manifestation of God's free grace. 2. No works can be admitted as our justifying righteousness, without supposing them to have at least a pactional merit. 3. The infinitely wise Spirit of God never so much as seems to exclude the *mere* merit of men's works, or their *self-conceit of it*, but always plainly excludes the work themselves from being our justifying righteousness, Rom. iii. 20, 26. Gal. ii. 16. iii. 10. v. 2—4. 4. How could the same works be *our righteousness*, and the *righteousness of God*; the *works of the law*, and the *righteousness of faith*, as the conceit of merit is annexed to them, or not? 5. It is not proud conceit of merit which is a violation of God's law, but obedience to the law,—good works, which mark us godly, and to which we are created in Christ, that are excluded from our justifying righteousness, Rom. iv. 5. Eph. ii. 8—10. But,

V. The SURETY RIGHTEOUSNESS of Jesus Christ, including his holiness of manhood, obedience of life, and satisfactory sufferings and death, must therefore not only be the *meritorious cause* or *price* of our justification, as it is of our adoption, sanctification, and glorification,—but that *justifying righteousness* which constitutes us righteous before God as a judge; as will appear,

I. From a consideration of *that law, by or according to which alone we can be justified.* We were originally under the law of the ten commandments, and could not but be so. This being the RULE of that moral relation, which is between God as a Sovereign, and man as his rational creature and subject, necessarily proceeding from the nature of God, and answerable to the nature of man, must, as hath been formerly observed, continue unaltered, while God remains a Creator, Preserver, and Governor, and man continues his rational creature and subject. And nothing can constitute a man righteous, but what answers all its demands, Gal. iii. 10. Mat. xix. 17.—This law neither is nor can be *abrogated.* 1. God hath never used any means tending to abrogate it. No law is given that makes any thing sinful, which was at first required as duty; or, that declares any thing lawful, which was at first forbidden as sinful. 2. Christ came not to destroy the law, but to fulfil it, Mat. v. 17, 18, 19. iii. 15. Luke xxiv. 26, 46. Rom. viii. 3, 4. x. 4. Gal. iv. 4, 5. Heb. x. 5—10. Psalm xl. 6—8. 3. The gospel does not make void, but establishes the law, Rom. iii. 31. viii. 4. x. 4. Isa. xlii. 21. xlv. 24. 4. No obligation to endure punishment can absolve men from that of the precepts. To imagine that transgression can dissolve obligation to duty, or render criminals independent on God as their moral Sovereign,—and that former injuring God or men, will warrant further injuring them, is most absurd.

There can be no *derogation* from this moral law,—no relaxing its demands with respect either to qualities or degrees of obedience. 1. No such derogation or relaxation is ever hinted in Scripture, but the contrary, Mat. v. 17—19, 20, 48. xxii. 37—40. 1 Pet. i. 15, 16. Rom. iii. 31. viii. 3, 4. x. 4. 2. This law being God's own representation of his holiness and righteousness to men, it cannot be relaxed while he continues the same. 3. If this law be rendered less strict and extensive, no standard of righteousness can be left. To bring it down to *sincerity*, would render it as changeable as the circumstances of mankind, at least of believers, are. If once the centre of all religion become variable, the same thing that is good in one, may be bad in another, in the same station; and the degrees of men's duty must alter as their inward tempers do. 4. What could produce a relaxation of God's law? could length of time, or men's making themselves worse by their own fault, make God to hate that which he once loved, or to love that which he once reckoned sinful,—or make him to pull down his own law, that that they might comply with their sinful inclinations? 5. If such relaxation could be effected, why did not God at first put Adam, his innocent creature, and put Christ, his beloved Son, under this easy law? 6. It hath been formerly proved, that the covenant-form of this law is not changed; and God hath verified it in the difficult obedience and dreadful sufferings of his only begotten Son, Rom. viii. 3, 4. x. 4. 2 Cor. v. 21. Gal. iii. 10, 13. iv. 4, 5. 1 Pet. i. 18—20. ii. 24. iii. 18. Dan. ix. 24, 26. Isa. liii Zech. xiii. 7.—Nay, this law cannot admit of *acceptilation*, in God's taking that which is not fully answerable to its demands, instead of a complete fulfilment. 1. God must always give sentence according to truth and equity, Rom. ii. 2. Gen. xviii 25. Deut. xxxii. 4. 2. He hath fully demonstrated this in the unabated demands which he made on his own Son, as our Surety, Rom. viii. 3, 4, 32. Mat. iii. 15. v. 17, 18. Luke xxiv. 26, 46. Heb ii. 10. v. 8. 3. God could not accept that which is dung, is filthy rags, for a perfect righteousness, Phil. iii. 8, 9. Isa. lxiv. 6.—Now, if the broken law admit of no justification but by a righteousness fully answerable to all the demands of its precept and penalty,—nothing but the righteousness of God, in our nature, can justify us, Rom. iii. 19—22, 24---26. viii. 3, 4. x. 4. Isa. xlii. 21. xlv. 24, 25. Jer. xxiii. 6. xxxiii. 16. Dan. ix. 24, 26 2 Cor. v. 21. Mat. xx. 28. v. 17, 18. Eph. v. 2. Acts xx. 28. Gal. ii. 20. iii. 13. iv. 4, 5. 1 Pet. ii. 24. iii. 18. Rev. v. 8, 9.

It is absurdly pretended, That the gospel is a *new law*, in which God, on account of the mediation of Christ, promises and offers salvation to men, on condition of their faith, repentance, and sincere obedience, which thus become our evangelical justifying righteousness before God.——Indeed the gospel is called a law, and the *law of faith*, as it comes to us marked with the authority of God, and is granted to us for our instruction, Isa ii. 3. Mic. iv 2. Rom. iii. 27; but LAW doth not always mean the declared will of a proper sovereign, binding his subjects to their due obedience; for inward grace and corruption are represented as *laws*, Rom. vii. 23, 25. viii. 2. And that the gospel is no such *new law* as is pretended, is most evident. 1. The gospel is represented as good or glad *tidings* to sinful men, which it could not be if it merely offered them happiness on conditions infinitely exceeding their ability, and contrary to their inclination. 2. The gospel is a manifestation of the exceeding riches of God's grace. It represents the FATHER as abounding in love, grace, and mercy toward his enemies, John iii. 16, 17. 1 John iv. 9, 10, 16, 19. iii. 1. Eph. i. 3—8. ii. 4—9. Isa. xlii. 6, 7. xlix. 1—12. It manifests Christ the Son, in his person, God-man, in his gracious names, offices, relations, work, and fulness, for the benefit of sinful men,—his humiliation as the price, and his exaltation as the immediate cause of our everlasting redemption, Mat. xx. 28. 1 Pet. i. 18—20. Isa. liii. 10—12. lii. 13—15. It abounds with promises, in which he, and all things necessary for their salvation, are freely offered to sinful men, 1 Tim i. 15. Isa. xlii. 6, 7. Ezek. xxxvi. 25—31. It is full of gracious and unlimited invitations and encouragements to them to accept of him and all his fulness, as the free and unspeakable gift of God to them, Isa. lv. 1—7. Mat. xi. 28. 2 Cor. v. 18—21. Rev. xxii. 17. Prov. i. 22, 23. viii. 4. ix. 4, 5. 3. Though the gospel provide for the honourable fulfilment of the law, both as a covenant and as a rule of life, Rom. iii. 31. Isa. xlv. 24. Heb. ix. 14—17. 1 Cor. i. 30. 2 Cor. v 14—17. Tit. ii. 11—14, and connect our privileges with our duties to the honour of God's grace, Luke i. 74, 75. Psalm cxvi. 16. cxix. 32, 166. 1 Cor. vi. 19, 20. 2 Cor. v. 14, 15. vi. 18. vii. 1. 1 John iv. 19. iii. 2, 3. Rom. v 21. vi. 1. Tit. ii. 11—14. iii. 8, 14. Heb. xii. 28;—yet the claims to eternal life by the law and by the gospel, are directly contrary, John i. 17. Heb. iii. 5, 6. xii. 18, 24. Rom. iii. 20, 24. iv. 4, 5. v. 15—21. vi. 23. xi. 6. Gal. ii. 16—21. v. 2, 4. 4. If this *new law* requires the same obedience as the *old*, it is unnecessary.—If it requires a different obedience, we have one law of God against another, and that which is held imperfect by one law, is held perfect by the other. 5. If this new law demand no more than *sincere* obedience, such obedience is not imperfect, but as perfect as God's law demands. 6. What curse is to fix, or punishment to be inflicted, on the breakers of this new law, Gal. iii. 13. Psalm lxxii. 17. lxxxix. 28—35. xciv. 12. Isa. liv. 8—10. Heb. xii. 6—11. Rev. iii. 19. Prov. iii. 12. 7. If we admit this *new law*, we must have a double righteousness to answer the two laws; and that of Christ, which answers the demands of the *old law*, must be subordinated to our own righteousness, which fulfils the new and saving law,—contrary to Phil. iii. 8, 9. Isa. xlv. 24, 25. lxiv. 6. 8. Either this new law must be framed answerable to men's natural abilities, and so can demand nothing but desperate wickedness and enmity against God, Jer. xvii. 9. Rom. viii. 7, 8. Or, it must suppose them endowed with gracious qualities, and why not with ability to be perfectly holy,—as it is certain, the legal righteousness of Christ could purchase the one as well as the other. 9. In the dispensation of the gospel, not *mere sincerity*, but perfection in holiness is loudly demanded, 2 Cor. xiii. 11. James i. 4. Mat. v. 48. 1 Pet. i. 15, 16. Col. i. 28. And the most evangelical Christians, who are fully persuaded of their sincerity, bitterly bewail their want of perfection, Rom. vii. 14—25. Phil. iii. 12—14. Psalm lxv. 3. xix. 11—13. Isa. lxiv. 6. vi. 5. 10. Will this new law of sincere obedience accept of men's sincerity in worshipping dogs, cats, leeks, onions, harlots, stocks, stones, consecrated waters, images, reliques; or in murdering Christ and his saints, and blaspheming his name,---as their justifying righteousness before God? John xvi. 2. Acts xxvi 9, 10. 11. How, in consistence with his infinite holiness, can God enact a law which connives at every degree of sinfulness which is consistent with sincerity? Hab i. 12, 13. Psalm v. 4, 5. xi. 6, 7. 12. How could Christ die to procure a new law, which gives no small indulgence in and to sin?---Is he a Saviour of men in their sin?---a *Saviour of sin* from the ancient opposition made to it by God's law?---a martyr for sin, to make that which was once held sin, to be no more so? For where no law is, there can be no transgression, Rom. iv. 15. v. 13.---13. How could Christ's mediation procure this sin-indulging law? If God's justice and holiness require him to adhere to the terms of the ancient law,---how could the end of Christ's mediation be to destroy that justice and holiness? If God's justice required him to bring down his terms to men's abilities, how could the end of Christ's mediation be to redeem God from adhering to that which was unjust? 14. This new law mightily discourages men's holiness, and hinders their spiritual comfort. For, how hard to know, if we come up precisely to its standard of SINCERITY, without which we are in a state of condemnation? And, if we go beyond it, who knows what may be done with our unrequired supererogation?

II. If the covenant of grace made with Christ and his people be ONE and the SAME, as has been formerly proved, his fulfilment of its condition must be imputed to them, to render them righteous in their new-covenant state before God, as their judge, Gal. iv. 24. Exod. xxiv. 8. Zech. ix. 11. Mat. xxvi. 28. Heb. ix. 20. xiii. 30. Rom. v. 12---21. 1 Cor. xv. 21, 22, 45. It hath been proved, that, in this covenant, every thing has been undertaken for and promised that we can need, Isa. liii. 10---12. Gal. iii. 16. Heb. viii. 10---12; and that all the promises of it with respect to us are either formally or reductively absolute; and that faith, repentance, and sincere obedience, are promised to us as God's *free gifts*, and not required as *proper conditions* of it, Ezek. xxxvi. 25---31. Jer. xxxi. 32---34. xxxii. 38---41. Hos. ii. 19, 20. Eph. ii. 4---9. Acts v. 31;---and that the admission of any act or quality of ours as the condition, would destroy the whole form and grace of it, as it stands opposed to the covenant of works, Rom. xi. 6. Eph. ii. 4---9. i. 3, 6, 7, 8. Tit. iii. 5. Isa. lv. 1---4. Rom. iii. 24. v. 17---21.---It is also manifest, that dying infants are never capable of acting faith, repentance, or sincere obedience.---Further, if God give us faith and repentance, before we enter into the new covenant, why might he not give us the whole blessings of eternal life, without any condition performed by us? If we obtain them after we are in this covenant, how can they be conditions of our entrance into it?---The Scripture never represents the covenant of grace made with us, as purchased by, or founded on the death of Christ, but as flowing from the sovereign will of God. Nor is it conceivable, how a covenant promising eternal life to sinful men, so desperately wicked, on condition of their faith, repentance, or sincere obedience, could either be honourable to God, profitable to them, or worthy of having the death of Christ for its foundation, Jer. xvii. 9. Rom. viii. 7, 8. Gen. vi. 5. Mat. xv. 19.—God's making this covenant with men, means that they are personally instated in it, take hold of it, and acquiesce in the whole tenor of it, Jer. xxxi. 31—34. xxxii. 38—41. 2 Sam. xxiii. 5.

III. In the new covenant, Christ and his people, in law-reckoning, are *one person*, he their SURETY, and they his legal REPRESENTEES, 1 Cor. xii. 12. Heb. vii. 22. Rom. viii. 3, 4, 29, 32---34. Eph. i. 3---7. John xvii. 4, 6. Gal. i. 20. iv. 4, 5. The Hebrew HHHEREB, *Surety*, means one that mingles himself with others, or goes softly under their burden in law, Gen. xliii. 9. xliv. 32, 33. Neh. v. 3. Prov. vi. 1. xvii. 18. xx. 19. Jer. xxx. 21. And the Greek ENGYOS is one that gives hand, and engages to pay for another, Heb. vii. 22. Christ having become our Surety, all the debt which we owed to the broken covenant of works was charged upon him, Psalm xl. 6---8. Gal. iv. 4.——Our *sins themselves*, and not merely the obligation to punishment arising from them, were laid upon him. 1. Scripture expressly affirms this, Isa. liii. 6, 11, 12. 1 Pet. ii. 24. 1 John iii. 4, 5.---Thus he was *made sin* for us, being charged with all the sins of his elect. 2 Cor. v. 21. 2. The ancient offerings, which represented him, had the sins of the offenders, for whom they were offered, laid upon them, by the putting their hands on them before they were sacrificed. Nay, the trespass-offerings and sin-offerings had the very name ASHAM, *trespass*, and HHATAAH, *sin*, given to them, Exod. xxix. 14, 36. xxx. 10. Lev. iv. 3, 8, 14, 21, 24, 26, 27, 29, 35. v. 7, 8---12. vi. 4, 17, 18, 25, 29, 36. vii. 1, 2, 5, 6, 7, 18, 37. viii. 2. ix. 2, 3, 7, 8, 10, 15, 22. x. 16, 17, 19. xii. 6, 8. xiv. 3, 13, 17, 19—31. xv. 15, 30. xvi. 3, 6, 9, 10, 21, 22, 25, 30, 34. xxiii. 19. Num. vi. 11, 12. viii. 11. xviii. 9, 22. xix. 9, 17. vii. xxviii. xxix, &c. Isa. liii. 6, 10, 4, 5, 8. Dan. ix. 24. Rom. viii. 3. 2 Cor. v. 21. 3. The *very ground* of God's displeasure with men was laid upon Christ, in order to his removing it by atonement. Now, that could never be the mere obligation to punishment, which originates from God's own nature and law,—but their sinful transgressions of the law, 2 Cor. v. 18—21. Isa. liii.

6, 4, 5, 8, 10, 11, 12. Dan. ix. 24. 1 Pet. ii. 24. 4. That, which is removed in our justification, was laid on Christ as our surety, which is sin itself, as rendering us obnoxious to punishment,. Heb. ix. 14. x. 18. Psalm xxxii. 1, 2. Mic. vii. 18, 19. 5. If our sins themselves had not been legally charged upon Christ, he had been, in law-reckoning, innocent. And if so, how could his righteous Father punish him? Or, how could he give his life a ransom for many, Isa. liii. 5, 10. Mat. xx. 28. 1 Tim. ii. 6. 1 Cor. vi. 20. Rom. iii. 25, 26. Heb. x. 5, 10, 14. Rom. viii. 3, 4, 32, 33, 34. 2 Cor. v. 19—21. 1 Pet. i. 18—20. ii. 24. iii. 18. Eph. v. 2. Rev. v. 9?—— But this legal charging our sins themselves upon Christ, did not render him the *blasphemer*, the *sinner*, &c. any more than the charging debt to a surety's account, renders him the. prodigal contractor of the debt. Our sins continued ours, as committers or proper proprietors of them; and were made his, only in respect of charge in law, in order to make satisfaction for them.

It is most absurd to allege, that Christ bore our sins and satisfied for them, merely *upon condition* of our fulfilling the new law of sincere obedience. 1. The Scripture never hints that Christ made satisfaction for men upon any such terms, but plainly suggests, that all those for whom he satisfied shall be saved, John x. 10, 14, 26—29. 1 John i. 7. Heb. x. 10, 14. ii. 9, 10. Isa. xlv. 17. 2. Christ could not satisfy conditionally for our sins, but upon the foot of a conditional decree of election, which hath formerly been disproved, Acts xiii. 48. Rom. viii. 30. ix. 15—23. 3. If Christ had satisfied for men conditionally, that condition must be either something to be given us for his sake, and so no proper condition at all, but merely one blessing preceding another equally free;—or something produced by our natural corrupted abilities, and so certainly sinful, Rom. viii. 7, 8. xiv. 23. Jer. xvii. 9. Gen. vi. 5. viii. 21. Job xiv. 4. Prov. xx 9. Mat. xv. 19. Mark vii. 21—23. Tit. i. 15. iii. 3. Eph. ii. 1—3. Gal. v. 19—21. 4. If our begun justification depend on some condition performed by us, it must be continued on the same ground; and then, if free will afterwards misgive, perhaps in heaven itself, we must be again unjustified and condemned to eternal wrath.

If Christ, as our surety, had our sins themselves charged on him, and he satisfied for them without dependence on any condition to be performed by us, his righteousness or satisfaction ITSELF, not merely its effects, must be unconditionally imputed to us. 1. If his righteousness itself be not imputed to us, how can we obtain justification, reconciliation, adoption, sanctification, glorification, or any other effect of it? How can we be justified, reconciled to God, &c. if our offences still stand chargeable, and charged by God, against our persons and consciences, which must be the case, if his sin-removing righteousness itself have not, by imputation, taken their place between God and us? 2. If Christ's righteousness be imputed to us only in its effects, it hath no other influence in our justification, than in our sanctification and glorification, of which it is the alone meritorious price. 3. If Christ's righteousness *itself* be not imputed, there can be no imputation of it at all, as its effects, peace with God, sanctification, spiritual comfort, and eternal glory, are not, cannot be, imputed, but really imparted to us. We are not *relatively* and *legally*, but *really* holy and happy in these. 4. If Christ's righteousness itself be not imputed to us, some other righteousness must be imputed, as an infinitely righteous God cannot sustain and declare us righteous in his sight, but on a proper ground, Rom. ii. 2. 5. If Christ's righteousness itself, not its effects, satisfied the demands of the broken law under which we were held as offenders, that righteousness itself, not its effects, must be imputed to us, that God, as a righteous judge, may be satisfied with us, Rom. viii. 3, 4. x. 4. Gal. iv. 4, 5. 6. If Christ's righteousness itself be the ground on which he pleads for us, in his intercession, and we by faith plead for ourselves, itself, not its effects, must be imputed to us, Rev. viii. 3. 1 John ii. 1, 2. Heb. ix. 24. vii. 25. x. 10—22. 7. If Adam's sin itself was imputed to us, the very righteousness of Christ must be imputed to us, to counterbalance that, and all other transgressions chargeable against us in law, Rom. v. 12—21. 1 Cor. xv. 21, 22, 45—49. —— Now, if Christ, as our surety, be one with us in the view of God's broken law;—if our sins themselves were charged upon, and satisfied for by him, without regard to any condition to be performed by us; and if his righteousness itself be imputed to us, as our sins were to him, it necessarily becomes our justifying righteousness; and being fully answerable to all the demands of that law by which we must be justified, it leaves no room for any thing else, as our justifying righteousness before God, Rom. v. 16—21. 2 Cor. v. 21. Jer. xxiii. 6. xxxiii. 16. Isa. xlv. 24.

IV. The Scripture, in an infinity of texts, represents that righteousness, which Christ fulfilled under the broken covenant of works, in our stead, as our only justifying righteousness before God, Job xxxiii. 23, 24. Isa. xlv. 24, 25. liii. 4, 5, 6, 8, 10, 11, 12. xlii. 21. xlvi. 12. liv. 17. lxi. 10. Jer. xxiii. 6. xxxiii. 16. (which ought always to be read, *He, who shall call her*, is *the Lord our righteousness*,) Dan. ix. 24, 26. Zech. iii. 4. Mat. xx. 28. xxvi. 28. John i. 29. Rom. i. 17. iii. 21—26, 31. iv. 6, 11, 25. v. 10, 11, 12—21. viii. 2, 3, 4, 32, 33, 34. ix. 31, 32. x. 3, 4. 1 Cor. i. 30. 2 Cor. v. 21. Gal. ii. 16, 20, 21. iii. 3, 14. iv. 4, 5. v. 2, 4. Eph. i. 7. v. 2, 25—27. Phil.

iii. 8, 9. Tit. ii. 14. Heb. i. 3. ix. 12, 14, 15, 28. x. 10, 14, 18—22. xiii. 12. 1 Pet. i. 18—20. ii. 24. iii. 18. 2 Pet. i. 1. 1 John i. 7. ii. 1, 2. iv. 9, 10. Rev. i. 5, 6. v. 9. iii. 18. xix. 8. ——Nor are his holiness of human nature and obedience of life less imputed to us, than his sufferings for sin. 1. The law as a broken covenant, by which we must be justified, demanded these as well as his sufferings for sin, Rom. ii. 13. Gal. iii. 12. Heb. ix. 22. Mat. iii. 15. Luke xxiv. 26, 46. 2. Eternal life is never annexed to mere sufferings, but to holy qualities and services, as its condition, Gal. iii. 12. Mat. xix. 17. Rom. x. 5. ii. 13. Lev. xviii. 5. Ezek. xx. 11, 21. 3. Mere enduring punishment is not a righteousness at all, as it doth not answer the commands of God's law, Rom. v. 19. 2 Cor. v. 21. And, in damned angels and men, is no satisfaction at all, as it doth not proceed from any cheerful regard to God's law. 4. That obedience of Christ, which is directly contrary to Adam's disobedience, must be the ground of our justification, and constitute us righteous in law, Rom. v. 19. Phil. ii. 6—8. iii. 9. Eph. i. 6. Dan. ix. 24. 5. Christ never being under the broken law, nor owing it any obedience, for himself, but for us, all his obedience to it must be imputed to us, in whose room he fulfilled it, Gal. iv. 4, 5. Rom. viii. 3, 4. 6. Believers being united to Christ, and clothed with his righteousness, are not bound to perform any obedience to the law as a broken covenant, but merely to obey it as a rule of life, in the hand of Christ, Rom. vi. 14. vii. 4, 6. viii. 2. Gal. ii. 19, 20. v. 18.

OBJEC. I. " If Christ's fulfilment of the broken law be " imputed to us as our justifying righteousness, then our holi- " ness of heart and of life are rendered unnecessary." ANSW. Holiness of heart and good works are necessary fruits and evidences of our justification,—and necessary parts of our salvation, as will hereafter be proved. But they are not necessary conditions of our justification, or of our entrance into a state of salvation: for, 1. Many infants are admitted to union with Christ, justification, and even heaven itself, before they can perform any good works, Mark x. 14. 2. No truly good work can be performed by adult persons, till they be actually entered into a state of salvation, Rom. vii. 4, 6. Eph. ii. 10. 1 Cor. xv. 56. 3. Scripture represents salvation as founded only upon God's free grace reigning through the righteousness of Christ; and as an inheritance *given to us*, not *purchased by us*, Eph. ii. 7, 8. i. 7, 11, 14. Rom. vi. 23. v. 21. viii. 16, 17. John x. 9, 10, 15, 16, 26—29. Tit. iii. 3—7. Gal. iii. 18, 29. iv. 30, 31. 4. If our justification or salvation depend at all upon our good works, it must depend wholly upon them, Gal. v. 2, 4. ii. 21. Rom. xi. 6. iv. 4, 14. 5. All our good works performed in faith, suppose our *preceding*, full, and everlasting justification, and interest in eternal salvation, through Christ's righteousness; and are not performed under that law, by which men are adjudged to eternal happiness, Rom. vii. 4, 6. vi. 14. viii. 2. Gal ii. 19, 20. v. 2, 4, 18. 1 Cor. ix. 21.

OBJEC. II " Though Christ's imputed righteousness justify " us against the demands of the law as a broken covenant, we " must have a righteousness of our own to justify us answer- " ably to the demands of the gospel, as Christ did not satisfy " for our unbelief and final impenitence against it." ANSW. 1. We have already proved that the gospel is *no new law*, demanding duties from men. 2. If where no law is, there is no transgression, Rom. iv. 15. v. 13. 1 John iii. 4;—what can be sin against the gospel, that is not sin against the law! Where doth God's law allow unbelief or impenitence, more than his gospel doth? 1 John iii. 23. Ezek. xxxiii. 11. 3. Christ as little satisfied for the other sins of reprobates, as for their final impenitence and unbelief, John x. 11, 15. Isa. liii. 5, 6, 8, 10, 11. 4. He satisfied for all the sins of his elect, their impenitence and unbelief, which otherwise would have been final, not excepted; and his blood applied to their conscience cleanses from all sin, Isa. liii. 6. 1 Pet. ii. 24. Dan. ix. 24. 1 John i. 7, 9.

CHRIST's surety righteousness being fulfilled in our nature, name, and stead, is OURS in these respects. In consequence hereof, God, in the gospel promise, exhibits and *gives* it to us, in, and with Christ himself, Isa. xlv. 24. xlvi. 12. liv. 13, 17. It is *imputed* to our person in God's act of uniting us to Christ, and is *received* by faith alone, together with, and in him, Isa. lxi. 10. 2 Cor. v 21. Phil. iii. 9. Gal. ii. 16.—IMPUTATION is the reckoning some quality, deed, or suffering, to a person's account, that he may be dealt with accordingly.—It is either of that which he really performed or suffered himself, Gen. xxx. 33. Psalm cvi. 31. 2 Sam. xix. 19. Acts vii. 60. Lev. xvii. 4; or is supposed to have done, 1 Kings i. 21;—or of that which was done or suffered by another, who stood in his room.—As the Israelites bore the iniquities of their fathers and kings, as Jeroboam, Manasseh, Num. xiv. 33. Exod. xx. 5, some have founded imputation on parental magistratical relation. But here, though the bearers, as irrational creatures often do, share in the deserved effects of their parents and governors' sins, they are not thereby constituted criminals in law-reckoning; and so there is no proper imputation at all.——But, all proper imputation of that which is done or suffered by another, must be founded on such a relation between the doer or sufferer, and him to whom his deeds and sufferings are imputed, as constitutes them one person in the view of the law. Hence, when debts, sin, or righteousness, is imputed, the imputee becomes debtor, offender, or righteous in law-reckoning, Philem. 18. Gen. xliii. 9. xliv. 32. Rom. v. 12, 19.—It is therefore plain, 1. That God, who is an infinitely exact judge, can impute nothing to a person, but for that which it really is in itself, perfect or imperfect, Rom. ii. 2. Gen. xviii. 25. 2. That the imputation of that which we do or suffer ourselves, is a mere legal charging that to our account, which was personally ours before: But the imputation of that which was owing, done, or suffered by another, in our stead, imports a legal communication of it to us. 3. That the imputation of that which was our own in every respect before, as well as the imputation of Adam's first sin to us, imports strict justice; but the imputation of our sins to Christ, in order to his making atonement for them, and the imputation of his righteousness to us, is of free grace, to the glory of God's justice. 4. That, in just imputation, no persons can be judged *sinners* or *righteous*, who are not, upon sufficient grounds in law-reckoning, really such. 5. That imputation includes no infusion of sin or righteousness into the nature of the imputees, nor any conferring upon them the rewards or effects of it. But it is a legal charging that debt, sin, or righteousness to us, which was in some respect ours before, that its effects may be applied or imparted to us.— Only in consequence of such imputation could God inflict the punishment due to our sins on Christ, or confer the blessings which he purchased on us, Isa. liii. 6, 4, 5, 8, 10, 11. Eph. i. 3, 6, 7.

It is not perfectly agreed, whether God's act imputing the righteousness of Christ to us, or our receiving it by faith, which are perfectly contemporary, be first in order of nature; nor is either side without its difficulties. My poor thoughts are, 1. That while we continue under the condemning sentence of the broken covenant of works, there can be no real habit of grace or act of faith, any more than perfect holiness or happiness, 1 Cor. xv. 56. Rom. vi. 14. vii. 4. viii. 2. Eph. ii. 10. Gal. iii. 10, 13. iv. 4, 5. 2. That God's circumcision of our heart, and writing his law in it, is the consequence of his pardoning our sins, Heb viii. 10, 11, 12. Col. ii. 13. 3. As in Adam all men die, so in Christ all his elect are made alive, *i. e.* God's imputation of Christ's righteousness issues in his implantation of grace in our heart, even as his imputation of Adam's first sin issues in his withholding original righteousness, in the formation of our soul, and in the subsequent corruption of our nature, 1 Cor. xv. 22. 4. That the beginning as well as the progress and perfection of our real eternal life, depends on the imputation of Christ's righteousness, 1 John v. 12. 5. It is given us on the behalf of Christ to believe, Phil. i. 29; and we obtain precious faith through the righteousness of God our Saviour, 2 Pet. i. 1.   6. God's imputation of Christ's righteousness may as well precede the existence or agency of our faith, in order of nature, as Christ's act of uniting us to himself, and God's act of regenerating us in Christ, may, in in order of nature, precede that faith, by which we receive Christ and all his purchased salvation, Phil. iii. 12. Eph. ii. 10. 2 Cor. v. 17.   7. Might we not safely say, that justification, *as it is God's act*, is in order of nature antecedent to our faith; and our faith is antecedent to it, as it is *passively* received into, and terminated in our conscience?

It is most certain that we are justified BY, or THROUGH faith, Rom. iii. 22, 28, 30. v. 1. Gal. ii. 16. Phil. iii. 9. Rom. iv. 24. —Only the habit of faith can be concerned in the justification of infants; but the act also in adult persons.—And as men, in their reception of justification, stand trembling before the judgment-seat of God erected in their conscience,—deeply convinced of their sinfulness and misery, there is often much confusion and an apparent diversity in their actings of faith,— some fixing their attention on the redeeming mercy of God,— others upon Christ and his mediation,—others on the gospel promises,—and others on the promised pardon and eternal life. But there is always a regard to the whole method of redemption. God is discerned as merciful in Christ. Christ is viewed as the mercy promised, and as the Lord our righteousness. The promises are viewed and embraced as manifesting and offering his person and righteousness, and pardon and eternal life through it, as the free gift of a gracious and merciful God. Thus, in our cordial persuasion of the applied promises, we, in one act, approve God's whole method of salvation, receive Christ and his righteousness, justification and eternal life through it, as the unspeakable and free gift of God in Christ to us, as guilty and wretched in ourselves.

This faith doth not justify us, as a *preparing quality*, or as a *condition* even of the lowest kind. 1. It cannot exist in us while we continue under the law and its curse, which are the strength of sin. Nor is justification more subsequent to the habit and act of faith, than the commencement of salvation, in which faith is formed in our heart, Gal. ii. 16. Eph. ii. 8, 9. Phil. i. 29. 2 Pet. i. 1.   2. Faith, as a disposing qualification or condition, would be a work of the law, and so undermine and tarnish the free grace of God in our salvation.—But faith justifies as a receiving instrument, by which we cordially credit and embrace the word of the gospel, in which Christ is made over to us as the Lord our righteousness, and justification in him. It is not as it is an habit or act answerable to God's command, but as it has a *receiving* quality or agency relative to Christ and his righteousness, and justification through it, that it justifies.—This faith, as it is the door which Christ, in his almighty application of himself, makes for his own entrance into our soul, might be called *God's instrument* of justifying us, Rom. iii. 30. But it is more proper to call the gospel, by which, in spiritual manifestation, he conveys Christ and his righteousness, and justification and regeneration through it, into our heart,—*God's instrument;* and to call faith, by which, in our crediting his giving promise, we, in one act, receive Christ and his righteousness, and justification through it,—our instrument, Gal. ii. 16. Rom. v. 11. Acts xxvi. 18.

CHAP. III.

Of Adoption.

ANGELS are called *Sons of God*, being made after his image, admitted into intimate familiarity with him, and having a kind of authority over inferior creatures, Job xxxviii. 7, and perhaps i. 6. ii. 1. But some take the two last texts to mean professed saints, as Gen. vi. 2. Mat. viii. 12.—In much the same respects, Adam was the *Son of God*, Luke iii. 38; but some apply that text to Christ, who is the Son of God by natural, necessary, and therefore eternal generation, Psalm ii. 7. John i. 14. iii. 16.——Men are called *sons of God*, 1. Because they are created and preserved by him, Mal. ii. 10. Acts xvii. 25, 28. Heb. xii. 9. 2. Because they represent him as his deputies in civil government, particularly in that which was typical, Psalm lxxxii. 6. John x. 34—36. 3. Because of their peculiar relation to him, as his subjects or church members, Gen. vi. 2. Matth. viii. 12. Exod. iv. 22. Deut. xiv. 1. xxxii. 10, 11. Rom. ix. 4.——Believers are *sons of God* in a very exalted manner, 1. By their spiritual marriage-union with Jesus Christ, his only begotten Son, Psalm xlv. 10, 11. John i. 12. Exod. xxi. 9. 2. By regeneration, in which they are spiritually begotten or born in his image, by the renewing power of his Spirit, John i. 12, 13. iii. 3, 5, 6. James i. 18. 1 Pet. i. 3, 23. ii. 2. 1 John iii. 9. v. 18. 3. By adoption, in which they who were by nature children of Satan, of disobedience, and of wrath, are, in consequence of the imputation of Jesus' righteousness to them for their justification, admitted members of his family, by a concurrent and absolutely gracious act of God, Father, Son, and Holy Ghost, 1 John iii 1. Jer. iii. 4, 19. 2 Cor. vi. 18. Eph. i. 5. John i. 12. Rom. viii. 16. Gal. iv. 6.

ALL the ELECT, and they ONLY, are in their respective *times of love* thus adopted, Eph. i. 5. Gal. iii. 26.—These under the Old Testament were God's children, Job xxxiv. 36. Psalm ciii. 13. Isa. lxiii. 16. Jer. iii. 4, 14, 19. xxxi. 20;—by spiritual union to Christ, Hos. ii. 19, 20. Isa. liv. 5. Psalm xlv. 9—14;—by regeneration, Ezek. xxxvi. 26. xi. 19, 20. Psalm li. 10;—and in respect of adoption and spiritual heirship, Gal. iv. 1. Psalm xvi. 5, 6. xvii. 15;—and as children they had fellowship with him, Gen. v. 22, 24. vi. 9. xv. 1. xvii. 1. Lam. iii. 24. Psalm lxxiii. 23—26, 28. cxliii. 10. Heb. xi. 10.—Their adoption was as perfect as ours under the gospel:—But the Lord used them as children under age. He prescribed to them their natural food, and what they might touch, Lev. xi. Deut. xiv. Col. ii. 21. He much concealed himself from them, Isa. xlv. 15. Matth. xiii. 17. The sacrificial tokens of variance between him and them, were yearly, monthly, weekly, and daily renewed. Canaan was but an obscure pledge of their heavenly inheritance; and, though never to forget it in their prayers, they were sometimes driven from it.——Under the New Testament, Christ, having assumed our nature, and paid our debt, sets us, his younger brethren, free from the legal ceremonies and the beggarly elements of this world, John viii. 32, 36. Col. ii. 16, 20. He calls them to more spiritual and reasonable service, Rom. xii. 1, 2. 1 Pet. ii. 5. Heb. ix. 10, 11. Mal. i. 11. Mat. xi. 30. Hos. xi. 4. He gives them more knowledge of, and intimacy with himself and his Father in him, Song viii. 1, 2. John i. 18. xiv. 9, 10. xv. 15. Jer. xxxi. 34. 1 John ii. 20, 27. Isa. liv. 13. xlviii. 17. Eph. ii. 18. iii. 12. 1 John i. 37. He allows them greater boldness in their approaches to God, and equal access to him from every part of the world, Heb. x. 19—22. iv. 14—16. vii. 19. xi. 40. John x. 7, 9. xiv. 6. Rom. v. 1, 2, 3. Eph. ii. 18. iii. 9, 12. Isa. xix. 19. xlv. 22. liv. 5. Psalm xxiv. 1. ii. 8. He bestows his Spirit upon them more abundantly, Rom. viii. 15—17. Gal. iv. 4—6. Isa. xliv. 3, 5. Joel ii. 28. Acts ii. 1 Cor. xii.; and calls them to more direct and immediate views of their spiritual inheritance, Luke xxii. 29.

ADOPTION into the family of God includes, I. *Advancement to great honour.* God, of his mere grace and love, reigning through the righteousness of Jesus Christ, translates us from the family of Satan into his own, in which we have him for our new-covenant Father, Christ, holy angels and saints for our spiritual brethren, 1 John iii. 1. Jer. iii. 19. John xx. 18. Rom. viii. 29. Heb. ii. 11, 12; and are God's prophets, priests, and kings, anointed with the same Spirit as Christ, 1 John ii.

20, 27. 2 Cor. i. 21, 22. 1 Pet. ii. 9. Rev. i. 5, 6. v. 10.——As *prophets*, being enlightened in the knowledge of divine mysteries or even future events, Psalm xxv. 14. lxxiii. 24—26, 28. xliii. 5, we, 1. Openly confess Christ and his truths with our mouth, 2 Cor. iv. 13. Rom. x. 10. Matth. x. 32; entertain our neighbours with holy conference and spiritual instructions, Eph. iv. 29. vi. 4. Phil. ii. 16. Song iv. 11. v. 10—16. vii. 9; sing the praises of God, Eph. v. 19, 20. Col. iii. 16, 17. 1 Sam. x. 5. xix. 24, 25. 1 Chron. xxv. 1, 2, 5.   2. Study an holy, instructive, and exemplary practice, Matth. v. 11. Phil. ii. 16. 1 Pet. ii. 12, 15. iii. 1.   3. Attest the truths of God by our sufferings, Rev. ii. 10. Luke xiv. 26. Matth. xvi. 25.——As *priests*, we live in familiar fellowship with God, and offer up spiritual sacrifices, intercessions, and worship to him, Rom. xii. 1, 2. Col. iii. 5. Heb. xiii. 15, 16. Phil. ii. 17. 2 Tim. iv. 6. Mal. i. 11. Rev. viii. 3, 4. 1 Pet. ii. 5. 1 Cor. xv. 58. Heb. x. 25. xii. 28.——As *kings*, we have generous and noble spirits, Psalm li. 12. Dan. v. 11, 12. Song i. 3. Zech. x. 3. 2 Cor. iv. 17, 18. Phil. iii. 8, 9. Heb. xi. 26, 27; possess royal treasures of God's word and grace, Psalm cxix. 11, 72. Job xxiii. 12. Jer. xv. 16. James ii. 5; and are venerable before God and men, and dangerous to be injured, Isa. xliii. 4. xlix. 23. lx. 14. Song vi. 4, 9. Rev. iii. 9; and spiritually war with, and conquer sin and Satan, and rule the world and our own spirits, Gal. v. 17, 24. Eph. vi. 10—20. Rom. vii. 14—25. vi. 10—14. viii. 37. xvi. 20. Rev. xii. 11. 1 Cor. vi. 1, 2, 12. 1 John v. 4. Rev. ii. 26, 27. Isa. xlv. 11. Prov. xvi. 32.

II. Adoption includes God's vouchsafing a right to all the privileges of his family. 1. A new name, Jer. xiv. 9. 2 Cor. vi. 18. Rev. iii. 12. Isa. lvi. 6. lxii. 12.   2. A new spirit of adoption, the Holy Ghost to comfort and seal us up to the day of redemption, Rom. viii. 9, 15. Gal. iv. 5, 6. Eph. i. 13, 14. iv. 30. 2 Cor. i. 21, 22. v. 5.   3. His own fatherly sympathy, Psalm ciii. 13. Zech. ii. 8. Isa. lxiii. 4, 5, 7, 9, 15. 4. His fatherly protection, Prov. xiv. 26. 2 Chron. xvi. 9. Deut. xxxiii. 27—29. Isa. xlvi. 4. iv. 5, 6. xxvi. 20. Psalm cxxi. 2—8. xli. 1—3. Zech. ii. 5, 8.   5. The ministration of angels to attend, guard, provide for, and direct us, Heb. i. 14. Psalm xxxiv. 7.   6. New-covenant provision of every thing that can be useful to soul or body, Psalm xxxiv. 8—10. Mat. vi. 30—33. 1 Pet. v. 7. Phil. iv. 6, 19. Psalm lxxxiv. 11. lxxxv. 12.   7. Fatherly and kind correction, wisely managed for our spiritual advantage, Heb. xii. 6—11. Prov. iii. 12. Psalm xciv. 12, 13. lxxxiv. 28—35. cxix. 67, 71, 75. Isa. xxvii. 9. Mic. vii. 14. Hos. ii. 14. Zech. xiii. 9. Rom. viii. 28.

2 Cor. iv. 17. 8. Unfailing establishment in this adopted state, and all the happy relations included in it, Lam. iii. 31, 32. Psalm xxxvii. 24, 28. Jer. xxxii. 40. Rom. viii. 35—39. 2 Sam. xxiii. 5. 9. Spiritual freedom from the power of the law as a broken covenant, and from the power of sin, Satan, the world, and death,—attended with a holy pleasure in serving God himself as our Father, John viii. 32, 36. 2 Cor. iii. 17. Hos. xi. 4. Gal. i. 4. iv. 4, 5. Psalm cxvi. 16. cxix. 32, 45, 166. 10. Filial boldness and familiarity with him, as reconciled in Christ, Heb. x. 19—22. iv. 16. Job xxiii. 3. Psalm lxiii. 3—8. Song i.—viii. 11. His fatherly hearing, accepting, and answering our prayers which are presented in faith, Psalm lxv. 2. 1. 15. xci. 15. cxvi. 4—8. xxxiv. 4, 6, 15. John xvi. 23, 24. Mat. vii. 7—11. Isa. lvii. 9. lxv. 24. 12. His fatherly instruction and direction in spiritual things, and holy conversation, Isa. xlvii. 17. liv. 13. Psalm lxxiii. 23, 24. xxxii. 8. Hos. xi. 4. xiv. 2. Jer. iii. 19. Psalm xlviii. 14. 2 Thess. iii. 6. Prov. iii. 5, 6. 13. Fatherly comfort under every adversity, 2 Thess. ii. 16, 17. 2 Cor. i. 3—19. Zeph. iii. 17. Jer. xxxi. 13, 14, 25. Isa. li. 7, 12. lxvi. 13, 14. lxv. 18, 19. lvii. 18, 19. 14. A full, free, and irrevocable right to all happiness in time and eternity, being heirs of promises, —of righteousness,—of the grace of life,—of salvation,—of the world,—of the kingdom,—and heavenly inheritance,—nay, of God himself, Jer. iii. 19. Heb. vi. 17. xi. 7. i. 14. Psalm cxix. 111. 1 Pet. i. 4. iii. 7. Rom. iv. 13. James ii. 5. Rom. viii. 17. Psalm xvi. 5, 6. lxxiii. 26. Lam. iii. 24.——Or, our inheritance by adoption includes, 1. Our happy enjoyment of all temporal good things, that is, our enjoying all that this earth can afford, in so far as it is for our real profit, and our tasting of God's special love in it, 2 Cor. viii. 9. Psalm xxxvii. 16. Prov. xvii. 1; all creatures leading us to God himself as our Creator, Redeemer, and Father, Psalm civ. 24. xxxvi. 7. xcii. 4, 5. viii. 3, 4. cvii. 43. Hos. xiv. 9. ii. 6, 7, 14; and under his directions, working together for our good, Rom. viii. 28. 2 Cor. iv. 17. xii. 7—10. Psalm xci. 11;—and the very earth being preserved and renewed for promoting our happiness, Isa. vi. 13. lxv. 8. Mat. xxiv. 22. 2 Pet. iii. 10, 13. Isa. lxv. 17. lxvi. 22. 2. Our spiritual kingdom, Luke xxii. 29. xvii. 20, 21; which includes our superior excellency among men, Psalm xvi. 3. Prov. xii. 26; our victory, triumph, and dominion over sin, Satan, and the world, Rom. vi. 14. xvi. 20. 1 John v. 4. Gal. vi. 14; our rich treasures of gifts and graces, Psalm xlv. 12—14. Rev. ii. 9. James ii. 5. Isa. liv. 11, 12; and our inward order, peace, purity, and joy in the Holy Ghost, Prov. xvi. 32. Rom. xiv. 17. 3. God himself, as our ALL in all, Rom. viii. 17. Psalm xvi. 5, 6,

lxxiii. 26. cxlii. 5. cxix. 57. Lam. iii. 24; our unfailing security against all evil, Psalm xxiii. xli. Isa. xliii. 1, 2. xli. 10, 14—16; our source and substance of all possible happiness, Psalm lxxiii. 25, 26. lxxxiv. 11. 1 Cor. xv. 28.

All the elect are chosen from all eternity *to be adopted*, and their names enrolled in the book of life, as future members of God's family, Eph. i. 5. Rev. xiii. 8. Mat. xxv. 34. They are *actually adopted* in the moment of their union to Christ, and their regeneration after his image:—and faith, in so far as an instrumental cause, embraces and consents to God's adopting act, as intimated in the heart-renewing truth of the gospel, Jer. iii. 4, 19. John i. 12, 13. Gal. iii. 26, 27. 2 Pet. i. 4.——It is manifested by an holy and heavenly conversation, marking their likeness to God, love to him, and to his word, ordinances, people, and interests in the world, Mat. v. 44—48. Luke vi. 27 —36. 1 Pet. i. 13--17. 2 Pet. i. 4—8. 1 John i. 1—5. And it will be publicly manifested in Christ's acknowledgment of them as his brethren, at the last day, Mat. xxv. 34—40, 45.

REFLECT. Hast thou, my soul, experienced the double change of thy state? Am I, that was once an enemy of Jesus Christ and his Father, now washed in his blood, and justified in his sight? Am I, that was so long a child of the devil, and an heir of hell, made a Son, an heir of God, and joint heir with Christ, and made light and love in the Lord?—God forbid, that I should dare to preach a free justification, of which my soul never felt the need, never received, never delighted in?—a gracious adoption, in which I have no share?——Perhaps, in no lawful station do fewer experience these blessed changes than in that of preachers.—If men intrude themselves into, or even approach the sacred office in their pollutions, how often God consigns them over to spiritual death, that all that they read, think, or speak of Jesus Christ, and his eternal salvation, tends to harden their own hearts? How often do preachers neither pray nor talk about divine things, especially if out of their public ministrations, with the delightful feeling or inward warmth of the private Christian! How often, by affecting-like descants upon the doctrines, offers, and influences of the gospel, they, like Judas, but in a more invisible manner, hasten themselves to the depths of hell! But, if I am justified and adopted, why do not I always believe, wonder at, and praise him for his love? Hath God, in me, shewn to what amazing length his love and grace can go? And shall not I love him, and live to him, with all my heart, and with all my soul, and with all my mind, and with all my strength? And shall not I count all things but loss and dung to win him, and be found in him, and cheerfully contribute toil, expence, reputation, health, and even life, to win souls to him?

CHAP. IV.

Of Sanctification.

SANCTIFICATION, in Scripture, means, 1. An acknowledgment or manifestation of holiness. Thus God is *sanctified*, or his name *hallowed*, when he manifests, and others, actuated by him, acknowledge and declare his holiness, Lev. x. 3. Isa. v. 16. Mat. vi. 9. 1 Pet. iii. 15. 2. Setting apart persons and things to holy services, Isa. xiii. 3. Jer. i. 5. Gen. ii. 2. John xvii 19. Thus every thing pertaining to the ceremonial worship was made holy, Exod. xxix. 1, 27, 44. 3. Purification from ceremonial defilements, or freedom from gross idolatry, error, or profaneness, Heb. ix. 13. 1 Cor. vii. 14. 4. Deliverance from the guilt of sin, John xvii. 19. Heb. i. 3. x. 14. xiii. 12. Ezek. xxxvi. 25. 5. And more properly, That *work of God's free grace, whereby we are renewed in the whole man, after the image of God, and are enabled more and more to die unto sin and live unto righteousness*, 1 Cor. vi. 11. 1 Thess. iv. 3.

This sanctification is of unspeakable importance in itself,—and as it is the end of all the offices of Christ, Mat. i. 21. Tit. ii. 11, 12, 14. Heb. ii. 10, 11. ix. 14. x. 19—22. xiii. 12. Psalm cx. 1—3;—the end of his humiliation and exaltation, Tit. ii. 14. 1 Pet. i. 18, 19, 20. ii. 21, 22. Eph. v. 1—4, 25—27;—the end of the Holy Ghost, in all his work on Christ and his church, John xvi. 7—14. xiv. 16, 17. xv. 26, 27. Tit. iii. 5, 6. Ezek. xxxvi. 26, 27;—the end of all the precepts, promises, ordinances, and providences of God, Mat. xxii. 37—40. 2 Cor. vii. 1. 1 John iii. 2, 3. Rom. ii. 4. Isa. xxvii. 9;—and the end of our election, redemption, effectual calling, justification, adoption, and spiritual comfort, Eph. i. 4, 5. 1 Cor. vi. 19, 20. Tit. ii. 14. 2 Tim. i. 9. Rom. vi. 14. vii. 4, 6. viii. 2. 2 Cor. vi. 18. vii. 1. 1 John iii. 1—3. Heb. xii. 28. Rom. v. 21. vi. 12.

It must be carefully considered in a twofold light, 1. As our *inestimable privilege*, fully purchased with Christ's blood, Heb. xiii. 12. Eph. v. 25—27. Tit. ii. 14; freely exhibited, offered, and given in his promises, Ezek. xxxvi. 25—27. 1 Thess. v. 23, 24; firmly secured by the imputation of his righteousness, Rom. v. 1—5, 10, 21. vi. 14. vii. 4, 6; and graciously effected by his almighty power and Spirit, 1 Cor. vi. 11. Psalm cx. 3. 2. As our *all-comprehensive duty*, commanded by God in his law as a rule, Heb. xii. 14. Mat. v. 48. 1 Pet. i. 15, 16. 1 Thess. iv. 3; delightfully exemplified in his pattern, Mat. v. 44—48. Eph. iv. 31, 32. v. 1, 2. Mat. xi. 29. 1 Pet. ii. 21, 22; effectually enforced by his redeeming love, 1 John iv. 9, 10, 16, 19. 2 Cor.

v. 14. Gal. ii. 20. Psalm cxvi. 12—16. ciii. 1—6;—to the study of which we are qualified, excited, and assisted by his almighty gracious influence, Gal. ii. 20. Phil. ii. 12, 13. iv. 13. Zech. x. 12. John xv. 2---7;—and by which we honour God, 1 Pet. ii. 9. iv. 11. Mat. v. 16. Psalm cxvi. 16. Tit. ii. 10. John xv. 8. Rom. vii. 4, 6; profit our neighbour, Tit. iii. 8, 14. 1 Pet. iii. 1, 5, 16. Phil. ii. 16. 1 Cor. vii. 16. 1 Tim. iv. 16; and obtain for ourselves a FREE, but glorious and lasting reward, Psalm xix. 11. 2 Cor. i. 12. 1 Cor. xv. 58. John xiv. 21, 23. Gal. vi. 8, 16. 2 Tim. iv. 7, 8. Rev. ii. 7, 10, 17, 26. iii. 3, 5, 12, 20, 21. xxii. 14.

Sanctification is *not necessary* in order to found our right of access to Christ as a Saviour,—or to be the ground of our claim to his righteousness, or of our interest in the judicial favour of God, or title to everlasting happiness, Isa. lv. 1. Rev. xxii. 17. Mat. ix. 13. xviii. 11. Luke xix. 10. John iii. 14—17. Tit. iii. 5. Gal. ii. 20, 21. Phil. iii. 8, 9. Rom. v. 1, 2, 15—21. But it is *absolutely necessary* as a part of begun salvation, Mat. i. 21. Rom. xi. 26; necessary to correspond with the nature of the divine persons, in fellowship with whom our happiness consists, Lev. xi. 44, 45. 1 John iv. 8, 16, 19. Heb. xii. 28, 29; and with what they have done and do for us, in our election, redemption, effectual calling, justification, adoption, spiritual comfort, and glorification, Eph. i. 4. Tit. ii. 14. John xvii. 15, 17. Ezek. xxxvi. 25—31. Acts xxvi. 18;—necessary, as an obedience to the will of God, our Creator, Sovereign, and Redeemer, Exod. xx. 2—17. Deut. v. 6—21. Mat. xxii. 37—40. Rom. vi. xii.—xv. Eph. iv.—vi. Col. iii. iv. Heb. x.—xiii. James i. to Jude, Mat. v.—vii;—necessary to express our gratitude to God for his redeeming kindness to us, Luke i. 74, 75. Rom. vi. 1, 2, 15. Psalm c. 2—4. cxvi. 16;—necessary, as fruits and evidences of our union to Christ, faith in him, and justification by his imputed righteousness, Col. ii. 6. James ii. 17—24; —necessary to adorn our profession, and to gain others to Christ, and to an useful and comfortable manner of living in the world, Tit. ii. 10. 1 Pet. ii. 9. iii. 1, 2. 1 Cor. vi. 20. vii. 16; —necessary, as a mean of our present happiness and comfort, 2 Cor. i. 12. 1 John i. 6, 7. Psalm cxix. 6, 165. Prov. iii. 17. iii. iv. xvi. 7;—and necessary as a preparation for heavenly enjoyments and exercises, 1 John iii. 2, 3. Rom. ii. 7, 10. viii. 6, 9, 13. Heb. xii. 14. Gal. v. 22, 23. Rev. xxii. 14.

To prevent our turning the grace of God into licentiousness, or our placing our own qualities and works in the room of Christ's righteousness; or our erroneous judging our state before God by our frames, we ought accurately to observe how our justification and sanctification differ in, 1. Their nature. Justification changes our state in law before God, as a judge:

Sanctification changes our heart and life before him, as our Father, Rom. viii. 1, 4. 2. In their order. Justification precedes, and sanctification follows as its fruit and evidence, Rom. vi. 14. vii. 4, 6. 2 Cor. v. 14, 15. 3. In their matter. The surety-righteousness of Christ imputed, is our justifying righteousness: but the grace of God, implanted, actuated, and exercised, is the matter of our sanctification, Rom. v 19. John i. 16. 4. In their form and properties. Justification, being an *act*, is perfected at first, and always equal on all believers: Sanctification, being a *work*, is unequal in different believers, and even in the same persons at different times, and is never perfect in any till death, Rom. viii. 1, 35. Acts xiii. 39. Prov. iv. 18. Job xvii. 9. 5. In their proper subject of righteousness. Justifying righteousness is IN Christ, and UPON us, as a robe: but sanctification is FROM Christ, and IN us, as a new nature and life, Isa. xlv. 24, 25. lxi. 10. Rom. iii. 22. 2 Pet. i. 4. 2 Cor. v. 17. Eph. ii. 10. 6. In their object and extent. Justification respects our persons, and particularly affects our consciences. Sanctification renews our whole man, Heb. ix. 14. x. 19—22. 1 Thess. v. 23. 7. In their ingredients. In justification the excellencies of God and Christ, particularly the love of God and the righteousness of Christ, are manifested to us. In sanctification, our love to God, and our holiness of nature and life appear, Rom. iii. 24—26. v. 19—21. Eph. v. 1—5. 8. In their discernibleness. Justification is a most secret act. Sanctification manifests itself, and also our justification, on which it is founded, Rev. ii. 17. 2 Cor. xiii. 5. 9. In their relation to sin. Justification removes the guilt of it, as it is a capital damning crime: Sanctification, as a medicine, removes the filth and power of it, as it is a mortal disease, Col. i. 14. ii. 13. 2 Cor. v. 21. vii. 1. 10. In their relation to the law of God. Justification delivers us from the law as a *broken covenant:* Sanctification conforms us to the law as a *rule of life*, Rom. vii. 4, 6. viii. 2, 4, 13. Gal. ii. 19, 20. 2 Cor. i. 12. Phil. iv. 8. 1 Cor. ix. 21. 11. In their relation to God. Justification delivers us from his avenging wrath, and instates us in his favour: Sanctification conforms us to his image, Rom. viii. 1, 33. v. 19, 10, 11. Col. iii. 10. 1 Pet. i. 15, 16. Eph. iv. 24, 32. v. 1, 2. Mat. v. 48. 12. In their relation to the offices of Christ. Justification is immediately founded upon the sacrificing work of his priesthood. Sanctification immediately proceeds from his prophetical instruction, and his kingly subduing, ruling, and defending us, Rom. viii. 1—4, 33, 34. x. 4. Isa. lxi. 1—3. Psalm cx. 2, 3. 13. In their usefulness to us. Justification frees us from all obnoxiousness to the punishments of hell, and entitles us to the happiness of heaven. Sanctification frees us from the pollution and slavery of our lusts, and prepares us for heaven, Rom. v. 21. viii. 30. Col. i. 12. 2 Cor. v. 5.

We must no less carefully observe, how justification and sanctification are inseparably connected, 1. In the purpose of God, Rom. viii. 28, 30; calling and glorifying there including our sanctification. 2. In the mediatorial office and work of Christ, Tit. ii. 11—14. 1 Cor. i. 30. Eph. v. 25—27. 3. In the doctrines and promises of the gospel, Luke i. 74, 75. vii. 47. Ezek. xxxvi. 25—31. Heb. viii. 10—12. Acts v. 31. 4. In the use of God's law, Rom. viii. 1—4. 5. In the experience of all believers, 1 Cor. vi. 11. 1 Pet. i. 2. Rom. viii. 30. Col. ii. 13.— And how justification, being the source and foundation of our sanctification, mightily promotes it. 1. Justification perfectly frees us from the curse of the broken covenant of works, which infallibly binds us under the reigning power and abominable slavery of our sinful lusts, 1 Cor. xv. 56. Gal. iii. 13. Rom. vi. 13, 14. vii. 4, 6. 2. In our justifying sentence, the justice, holiness, love, mercy, faithfulness, wisdom, and power of God are legally engaged to bestow upon us holiness of heart and life, as a principal part of that eternal life, to which we are adjudged by it, 1 John i. 9. Rom. v. 21. vii. 4, 6. vi. 14. 2 Tim. iv. 7, 8. 3. The justifying righteousness of Christ applied to our conscience does, in a real and efficacious manner, purge it from dead works to serve the living God, 1 Tim. i. 5. Heb. ix. 14. x. 22. 4. In our firm belief of our justifying sentence upon God's own testimony and evidence, we perceive the constraining love of Christ, the goodness, greatness, and holiness of God, —the goodness, holiness, and equity of his law, and its high and indispensible obligations on us as a rule of life;—the infinite vileness and tremendous desert and danger of sin,—the beauty, dignity, and usefulness of gospel holiness, and the delightful exemplification of it in Christ, and full provision of strength for it, and gracious reward of it through him; and are hereby effectually enabled and excited to cleanse ourselves from all filthiness of the flesh and spirit, perfecting holiness in the fear of the Lord, 2 Cor. v. 14. Gal. iii. 13, 14. Mat. iii. 15. v. 17. Zech. x. 12. xii. 10. Isa. xlv. 24, 25. xl. 29—31. 2 Cor. vii. 1. Luke i. 74, 75. Heb. xii. 28.

SANCTIFICATION, as a new covenant PRIVILEGE, is the work of God alone as reconciled in Christ, Lev. xx. 8. Ezek. xxxvii. 28. xx. 12. xxxvi. 26, 27. Phil. ii. 12, 13. 1 Thess. v. 23, 24. Deut. xxx. 6.—It is ascribed to the Father, John xvii. 17. Eph. ii. 5. 1 Pet. ii. 5. 1 Pet. i. 2, 3. Jude 1.—to the Son, Eph. i. 1. v. 25—27. Heb. ii. 11—14. xiii. 12. x. 10, 14. 1 Cor. i. 2, 30. 2 Cor. v. 17. Gal. vi. 15. Eph. ii. 10. Col. i. 2, 12. ii. 6, 7, 10—13, 19. iii. 4. Gal. ii. 20. John vi. 33. xi. 25. xiv. 6, 19. 1 Cor. xv. 45—49; but it is peculiarly ascribed to the Holy Ghost, in, and by whom, the Father and Son work it, 2 Thess. ii. 13. Rom. xv. 16. 1 Cor. vi. 21. Tit. iii. 5. Zech. xii. 10. 2 Cor. iii. 18. Rom. viii. 12, 13. Eph. i. 18, 19. ii. 22. Psalm cxliii. 10. John vi. 63. xvi. 13, 14. iii. 5, 6. 1 Pet. i. 2. Ezek. xxxvi. 27. Isa. xliv. 3—5.——Nothing but God's own free grace inwardly moves him to sanctify us, Eph. ii. 4, 5. v. 25, 26. Christ's surety righteousness is the only meritorious cause, or purchasing price or condition of our sanctification, 1 John iii. 5, 8. 1 Pet. i. 2, 18, 19. ii. 24. John xvii. 17, 19. Heb. ix. 12, 14. x. 10, 14. xiii. 12. Rev. i. 5, 6. v. 9. 1 Cor. i. 2. And applied to our heart, it frees from the dominion of sin, introduces new covenant grace, and powerfully stirs us up to the study of holiness, Rom. vii. 4, 6. Heb. ix. 14. x. 22. 2 Cor. v. 14, 15. Psalm cxvi. 16. cxix. 32, 166. Luke i. 74, 75. His intercession is the procuring cause of it, John xvii. 9—26, 15, 17, 21.——In sanctification, considered as our DUTY, we, that are sanctified, work together with God, as enabled and excited by him, Song i. 4. 2 Pet. i. 3—8. Rom. xii. 1, 2. 1 Pet. i. 15, 16, 22. Mat. v. 48. 2 Cor. vii. 1. Eph. iv. 22—24, 31, 32. v. 1, 2, 5. 1 Thess. iv. 3. 1 John iii. 3. Heb. xii. 1, 14, 28.

In both these views of it, ministers are useful in promoting our sanctification, being instruments for conveying it as a *privilege*, through the gospel, directors in, and exciters to the study of it, as a *duty*, 1 Cor. iii. 9. 2 Cor. vi. 1. xi. 2. 1 Tim. iv. 16.— God's word and ordinances promote sanctification, as they shew what is sinful, the abominable nature and hurtful tendency of it; and represent what is lawful and holy, with the motives to, and means of studying and attaining it,—and as they are the means, by which the blood, Spirit, and grace of Christ, are conveyed into our hearts, John xv. 3, 7. xvii. 17. Psalm cxix. 9, 11. James i. 18, 21. 1 Pet. i. 23. ii. 2. Eph. v. 26. Rom. i. 16, 17. Acts xiii. 26, 34. Heb. ii. 3, 4. 2 Thess. ii. 13. Gal. ii. 20. iii. 2. Rom. vi. 4. John vi. 31, 32.—The declarations, promises, and invitations of the gospel, are the means of conveying holiness into our hearts, and of maintaining and increasing it there, Ezek. xxxvi. 26, 27. Isa. ii. 35. The law, in the hand of Christ, directs and binds us to the study of holiness, 1 Pet. i. 15, 16. Mat. xxii. 37—40 Rom. xii.—xv. Gal. v. vi. Col. iii. iv. 1 Thess. iii.—v. Heb. x.—xiii. Mat. v.—vii. Exod. xx.—But it is not of themselves that God's word and ordinances promote our sanctification, but the Holy Ghost, with his saving influences attending them, renders them effectual, for the ends above-mentioned, 1 Cor. vi. 11. Rom. viii. 13. Gal. v. 17, 18, 22, 25.—God's providences, particularly afflictive ones, as subordinated to his word and ordinances, are occasional promoters of our sanctification, as they awaken, allure, or shut up to an earnest study and improvement of them for that end, Psalm cxix. 67, 71, 75. Isa. xxvii. 9. xxxviii. 16. Job xxxiii. 16—30. Ezek. xx. 36, 37. Hos. ii. 6, 7, 14. Isa. xlviii. 10. Mic. vii. 14. Dan. xi. 35. xii. 10. Heb. xii. 6—11. Prov. iii. 12. Psalm xciv. 12. Rev. iii. 19.

The law of God, as a rule of life, in its whole extent, is the regulating *standard* of our sanctification, Matth. xxviii. 20. John xiv. 15. xv. 10, 14. 1 John iii. 3, 4. v. 3. James ii. 8. Deut. xii. 32. v. 32. iv. 2. v. 6—21. Exod. xx. 2—17. And though no saint can attain absolute perfection in holiness in this life, the law peremptorily requires it, both in qualities and practice, Matth. xxii. 37, 39. v. 48. 2 Cor. xiii. 11. 1 Pet. i. 15, 16. 1. The infinite perfection of God's nature renders it impossible for him to give any law, which requires no more than imperfect holiness and virtue, 2 Tim. ii. 13. 2. His love to his people renders it necessary for him to bind them to the highest degrees of holiness, which is at once happiness and a mean of it, 1 John iii. 1—3. John xv. 9, 10. 3. The more perfection in holiness we attain, the more is God glorified, John xv. 8. 1 Cor. vi. 20. x. 31. xv. 58. 1 Pet. iv. 11. 4. This demand of perfection in holiness is necessary to excite our most earnest study of fellowship with Christ, in order that we may abound in holiness, John xv. 3—10. Col. ii. 6, 19. Eph. iv. 16. John i. 14, 16. 1 Cor. i. 30. 5. It is necessary to promote our earnest endeavours after much more holiness and virtue than we have attained, Phil. iii. 12—14. 2 Pet. i. 5—8. iii. 18. Eph. v. 9. Gal. v. 22, 23. 6. It is necessary to promote our humility, self-denial, and daily improvement of Christ's blood for forgiveness, under a sense of our shortcomings, Phil. iii. 8, 9, 11, 12. 1 John i. 7, 9.

The example of former or present saints is to be improved as an excitement to, and mean of regulating our study of holiness by the law of God, Heb. vi. 12. xii. 1, 2. xiii. 7. 1 Cor. xi. 1. But the example of Christ, and of God in him, in that which is imitable by us, is our only perfect pattern of holiness, which we ought to copy, Heb. xii. 1, 2. 1 John ii. 6, 29. iii. 7. Phil. ii. 1—7, 15. Eph. iv. 32. v. 1, 2. 1 Pet. ii. 21, 22. iv. 1. i. 15, 16. Mat. v. 44—48. xi. 29. xvi. 24.— Christ's example, being given under that very law which is our rule, and in circumstances much similar to our own, is a *peculiarly proper pattern*. 1. In his assured faith and trust in his Father, Isa. l. 7, 9. Psal. xvi. 1. xxii. 8, 9, 10. 2. In the universality of his obedience, John xv. 10. viii. 29. Matth. iii. 15. v. 17. Phil. ii. 8. 3. In his solemn and fervent devotion, Matth. iv. 2. xi. 25, 26, 27. Luke vi. 12. xxii. 41—44. John xvii. xi. 41, 42. xii. 27, 28. Heb. v. 7. 4. In his perfect resignation to his Father's will, Matth. xxvi. 39. John xviii. 11.

5. In his most disinterested love to men, 2 Cor. viii. 9. Eph. v. 2. John xv. 9—12. Gal. ii. 20. 6. In his unparalleled humility and meekness, Matth. xi. 29. John xiii. 14, 15. Phil. ii. 1—7. 7. In his constancy and patience under trouble, 1 Pet. ii. 21—24. Isa. l. 6. liii. 7. Heb. xii. 2, 3. 8. In his sincerity, candour, and uprightness, 1 Pet. ii. 22. Isa. liii. 9. 9. In his readiness cordially to forgive injuries, and render good for evil, Luke xxiii. 34. Col. iii. 13. 10. In his constant readiness to do good, temporal or spiritual, to his most inveterate enemies, Acts x. 38. Luke xxii. 50, 51. 11. In the spirituality of his mind, and readiness to improve the most common things for spiritual instruction, John iv. vi. x. Matth. v.—vii. xiii. xvii. xx. xxi. xxii. xxiii. xxiv. xxv. Luke iv.—xx. John ii.—xvi.

Though our faith cannot be a mean of God's implanting grace in our heart, yet, being formed by his regenerating act, it, under the influence of the Holy Ghost,—improving the word of God, and the person, righteousness, fulness, and example of Christ, and the perfections of God as manifested and offered in him, is a noted mean of our increasing in holiness of heart and life. 1. By uniting with Christ, and receiving justification and adoption in him, it lays a proper foundation of holiness and virtue, John xv. 1—10. Rom. vii. 5, 6. Gal. ii. 19, 20. Col. ii. 6, 7, 10, 11. 2. By believing God's declarations, and regarding his example, it powerfully affects our hearts with the odiousness and criminality of sin, and with the nature, excellency, and motives to holiness, John xv. 3. xvii. 17. Eph. v. 26. 1 Thess. ii. 13. 2 Thess. ii. 13. 3. By trusting to Christ and his Spirit, that, according to their characters, they will fulfil their gracious promises, it derives virtue from them, for mortification of sin, and increase of holiness, Col. ii. 19. Eph. iv. 16. Jer. xvii. 7, 8. Psalm xcii. 13, 14, 15.—In managing religious duties for the increase of our sanctification, faith, 1. Improves the Lord Jesus Christ, in his manifold connections with us sinful men, in correspondence to the condition of our souls; and from his fulness, by his Spirit, and through his word, derives grace to form in us proper tempers, and to animate and fit us for proper exercises, John i. 14, 16. 2. It presents our persons and services to God, to be accepted only through the righteousness and intercession of Christ, Col. iii. 17. Eph. iii. 21. v. 20. 1 Pet. iv. 11. ii. 5, 9. Rom. xii. 1.—In managing our common transactions of life for promoting holiness, faith, 1. Enables us to receive all our outward mercies as purchased by Christ, and as the gifts of his free grace, Gen. xxxii. 10. xxxiii. 5. 2. It disposes us to count all things but loss and dung to win Christ and his spiritual blessings, and to a readiness to part with them for his sake, Phil. iii. 7—9. Acts xx. 24.

xxi. 13. 3. It disposes us to look for our success in our civil business, from Christ's new-covenant care of us, 1 Pet. v. 7. Phil. iv. 6. Psalm xxxvii. 3—9. Matth. vi. 26—33. 4. It enables us to improve outward things as means of fellowship with God,—prosperity, for exciting our thankfulness to him, and desire of more full enjoyment of him, 2 Chron. xvii. 5, 6. —and adversity, for weaning our affections from this world, and setting wholly on him, Hab. iii. 17, 18. Psalm cxlii. 4, 5. Hos. ii. 6, 7, 14. 5. By improving the redeeming love of God and everlasting fulness of Christ for us, it disposes us humbly and cheerfully to bestow all the temporal property we have in his service, Rom. xv. 27. 1 Cor. ix. 11. 1 Chron. xxix. 14. Isa. xxiii. 18.—In the commanding temper of our souls, faith hath a peculiarly powerful influence; as, 1. The objects upon which it fixes, are such as are of an universal efficacy when rightly improved. 2. The testimony and authority of God, which it improves, are most powerful and determining. 3. It hath an appointment by God to be the leading principle of our Christian practice, next to Christ and his Spirit. 4. In walking by faith, we walk as always united to Christ, and always resting upon him for grace and strength, and for acceptance, according to his character and promises.

THE sanctification promoted by God's word, ordinances, and influences, and by the faith of his operation, answerably to his law, image, and pattern, includes, 1. *Sanctification of nature*, in which our whole man, soul, body, and spirit, is renewed after the image of God, Eph. iv. 23, 24. 2. *Sanctification* of life, in which we are enabled more and more to die unto sin, and to live unto righteousness, 2 Pet. i. 3—8. iii. 18. Rom. vi. xii. xiii. xiv. Gal. v. vi. Eph. iv.—vi. Col. iii. iv. 1 Thess. v. Heb. xii. xiii. 1 Pet. i.—v. 1 John i.—v. James i.—v. Jude 20—25. —Or, it includes *gracious habits* implanted, *Christian tempers* acquired, and *holy exercises* performed.—In this view, it includes *regeneration*, which properly means God's implantation of gracious or holy principles in our heart, Tit. iii. 5. Eph. ii. x. 1 Pet. i. 3, 23. ii. 2. Ezek. xxxvi. 26. xi. 19. John iii. 3, 5, 6; and *sanctification*, strictly taken, which means the continuance, strengthening, and increasing those gracious principles, and exercising them in holy and virtuous actions, Job xvii. 9. Prov. iv. 18. 2 Pet. i. 4—8. iii. 11, 12, 14, 18;—and which, as it respects our nature, is a continued new creation, in which our regeneration is carried into perfection; on which account, it was called *Regeneration* by our Reformers, and their immediate followers, for almost an hundred years.

IN opposition to that habitual permanent indwelling sinfulness of our nature, a supernatural habit, or vital principle of grace or holiness, is created, infused, and implanted by God, in every saint in his regeneration or effectual calling, which is continued, strengthened, and increased in sanctification, strictly so called, and perfected in glorification,—which being different from, and antecedent to all acts of faith or obedience, doth, under the actuating influence of the Holy Ghost, dispose and enable to such acts. I. Neither God, nor any of his creatures, perform any act or motion, without first having a correspondent life and power, or acting principle, Matth. vii. 17, 18. xii. 33—35. Nothing may as well speak, work, believe, obey, as any act of faith or holiness be performed, without a correspondent gracious permanent principle. II. Adam and angels were created with vital principles or habits of holiness, in order to qualify them for holy acts, Gen. i. 26, 27. v. 1. Eccl. vii. 29. Col. iii. 10. Eph. iv. 24. Jude 6. Psalm ciii. 19—21. This habit or principle, included in it an inclination and power to understand whatever God should make known to them,—believe whatever he should declare,—receive whatever he should give,—and do whatever he should command.—Nay, though Christ had all the fulness of the Godhead dwelling in him bodily, and the Spirit without measure,—he had, in his manhood, a created principle or habit of holiness, capable of being strengthened and enlarged by exercise,—disposing and enabling him to perform acts of faith and obedience;—and which is imputed to us, to balance our want of original righteousness, Luke i. 35. ii. 40, 52. Heb. vii. 26. v. 8. III. Every man, since the fall, has in him a natural habit or principle of wickedness, continually inclining and enabling him to acts of unbelief, hatred of God, and disobedience to him, Gen. vi. 5. viii. 21. Job xiv. 4. Psalm li. 5. 1 Cor. ii. 14. John v. 40. xii. 39, 40. Eph. iv. 18. ii. 1, 2. Tit. iii. 3. Rom. viii. 7, 8. Matth. xv. 19. Jer. xvii. 9. If then no new and contrary supernatural habit or vital principle of grace be implanted in our heart, the new-covenant remedy is not answerable to our sinful malady; nor can even omnipotence itself make us perform one act of faith, repentance, or holy obedience, Rom. viii. 7, 8. xii. 33—35. Luke vi. 43—45.—If Satan mark his malice against us, and mark us his children, by introducing sinful habits, shall not God manifest his infinite love to us, in supernaturally implanting permanent habits or principles of holiness, as his permanent image on his children? Shall not Jesus Christ, by uniting his person, and imputing his righteousness to his members, and putting his Spirit within them, produce in them a permanent conformity to him, in the qualities of their heart? Col. ii. 19. Eph. iv. 16. 1 Cor. vi. 17. IV. The form of God's act or work in converting his people,—his *quickening* or *raising them from the dead*, Eph. ii. 6, 7. John v. 21, 25. Col. ii. 13. John iv. 14. Rom. vi. 4, 5. viii. 2;—his *giving sight* to the blind, Acts xxvi. 18. 2 Cor. iv. 6. Isa. xlii. 7. lxi. 1. xxxv. 5. xxix. 18; *circumcising their heart to love* himself, Col. ii. 11, 12. Phil. iii. 3. Rom. ii. 29. Deut. xxx. 6;

renewing them *after his image*, Tit. iii. 5. Eph. iv. 24; *creating* them *unto good works*, Eph. ii. 10. iv. 24. Col. iii. 10,—manifestly prove, that he produces something permanent, a supernatural habit or vital principle of holiness. V. The inspired descriptions of that which is conferred by God on men in their regeneration, plainly prove it an abiding habit or principle. It is God's *workmanship* created in Christ Jesus, not IN, but UNTO good works, Eph. ii. 10. It is a *new heart*,—a *new spirit*,—a *heart of flesh*,—a *pure heart*,—a *true heart*,—directly contrary to the habit of sinful corruption, which makes an heart old,—stony,—obdurate,—obstinate, polluted, and deceitful, Ezek. xi. 19. xviii. 31. xxxvi. 26. 1 Tim. i. 5. Heb. x. 22;— a *new creature*, 2 Cor. v. 17. Gal. vi. 15;—a *new man*, having spiritual powers directly opposite to those of the *old man*, or sinful corruption of our hearts,—knowledge instead of ignorance,—life instead of spiritual death,—power instead of inability,—faith instead of unbelief,—love instead of enmity, Col. iii. 9, 10. Eph. iv. 23, 24. v. 8, 9. ii. 15. 1 Tim. i. 5. Deut. xxx. 6. 1 John iii. 17;—an inward or *inner man*, which is *renewed* day by day,—and *after which* we *delight* in the law of God,—and which is strengthened with all might, 2 Cor. iv. 16. Rom. vii. 22. Eph. iii. 16;—the *hidden man* of the heart, in that which is not corruptible, 1 Pet. iii. 4.—It is a *divine nature*, 2 Pet. i. 4; the *image of God*, conformed to his moral perfections, and to that likeness of him in which Adam was created, in every essential ingredient, Eph. iv. 23, 24. Col. iii. 9, 10. 2 Cor. iii. 18;—the *image of Christ*, conformed to the permanent holiness of his manhood, Rom. viii. 29. 2 Cor. iv. 4. —It is a *spirit born* of the Spirit of God, conformed to the excellencies which are in him, John iii. 5, 6, 8; a *spirit*, which *lusts against* the sinful corruption of our heart, as being perfectly opposite to it, Gal. v. 17; a *spirit*, which, under the influences of the Holy Ghost, *brings forth* good fruits, Gal. v. 22, 23. vi. 8. Eph. v. 9;—a *spirit after which* believers *walk*,— and *in which* they *walk* and *live*, as wicked men do after, and in the indwelling corruption of their nature, Rom. vii. 1, 4. Gal. v. 18, 25.—It is *grace*, a *freely given*, created, implanted, and permanent comeliness, Zech. xii. 10. 2 Cor. iv. 13. 2 Tim. ii. 1. Heb. xiii. 9. 2 Pet. iii. 18.—It is *life—abiding life*, Gal. ii. 20. 1 John v. 12. iii. 15. Eph. iv. 18. John iv. 14.—It is *circumcision*, an abiding mark of our new-covenant relation to God, directly opposite to our sinful lusts, Col. ii. 11, 12, 13. Phil. iii. 3. Rom. ii. 29.—It is a *law of* our *mind*, which *wars against* our indwelling corruptions, Rom. vii. 23, 25.—It is *fleshly tables of our heart*, on which God's law is written, and we made an *epistle* of Christ, 2 Cor. iii. 3. Jer. xxxi. 33. Heb. viii. 10.—It is an inward *root* or *stock* into which God's word is *ingrafted*,

Job xix. 28. James i. 21; and which produces a plentiful crop of good acts, Mat. xiii. 8, 23. Luke viii. 15. It is *incorruptible seed*, which is conveyed into adult persons BY or THROUGH the word of God, 1 Pet. i. 23;—*seed of God*, which abides in every saint, infant, or adult, 1 John iii. 9. It is represented as *acting, reigning*, &c.—Can any man believe, that all these mean no permanent indwelling habit or principle of holiness, but mere acts of faith, without supposing the Scripture to be altogether unintelligible, and that every effect of God's power represented may be no more than mere acts of men? VI. Even particular graces of faith, love, &c. are represented as habits, qualities, or vital principles. Thus faith is said to be *obtained*, 2 Pet. i. 1; to be *had*, 2 Thess. iii. 2. James ii. 14, 18; to be *kept*, 2 Tim. iv. 7; to *abide*, 1 Cor. xiii. 13; to *dwell in* us, 2 Tim. i. 5; and we in it, as wicked men in the flesh, 2 Cor. xiii. 5. Rom. viii. 8. By it Christ *dwells* in us, Eph. iii. 17, and through it we are *kept*, 1 Pet. i. 5. It *fails* not, Luke xxii. 32. John iv. 14. Men *grow* in it, and it *groweth exceedingly*, 2 Thess. i. 3. 2 Pet. iii. 18. It is increased, Luke xvii. 5. 2 Cor. x. 15. It *fills* the heart, Acts vi. 5. xi. 24. It *works*, Gal. v. 6. James ii. 22. And it is *strong, lively, unfeigned*, &c. Rom. iv. 19, 20. James ii. 17, 20, 26. 1 Tim. i. 5. 2 Tim. i. 5,——Love *dwells in* us, 1 John iii. 17; *abides*, 1 Cor. xiii. 8, 13; and is perhaps *shed abroad*, Rom. v. 5, and *acts* in many different forms, 1 Cor. xiii. 4—7.——But acts of faith and love are sometimes called by the name of the habit from which they proceed. VII. The denial of indwelling graces, supernatural habits, or vital principles of holiness, implanted in believers' hearts, really opposes the whole work of the Spirit of God, and undermines all practical religion; for, if there be no such indwelling, permanent, vital principles created in our soul in regeneration, then, 1. Our free will, *i. e.* our corrupt will, must reign without controul in our heart, having no supernatural principle to check it. And it can never act under Christ as his deputy, Rom. viii. 7, 8. Jer. xvii. 9. 2. Contrary to Christ's most solemn and express declaration, we may enter into heaven without being born again, or born of the Spirit,—by acts of faith, repentance, and new obedience, proceeding from no gracious principle, John iii. 3, 5. 3. If men can act faith or repentance, without supernatural habits of faith and repentance created in them, What need is there of regeneration? or, What is regeneration? Is it our act of believing? 4. If no habitual grace be implanted in regeneration, all infants who cannot hear or believe the gospel must be destitute of God's grace, and dying, must either be all damned, or be admitted to heaven without any inward inherent holiness, Heb. xii. 14. xi. 6. 5. In giving up with supernatural habits of grace, we must either disprove original sin altogether, or maintain that a heart which is only *deceitful above all things, and desperately wicked*, may, under the influences of Christ and his Spirit, act in contradiction to itself, and savingly believe and repent. 6. In giving up with supernatural implanted habits, or principles of grace in believers, we must deny the whole work of the Holy Ghost in the *formation, preservation,* or *perfection* of the new creature.—And all that is left for him, is to act upon the powers of our soul as simply natural, or as sinfully corrupted, to make them perform acts of faith and gospel-holiness, which proceed from no correspondent, but contrary principle. 7. Without indwelling habits of grace, there can be no spiritual union with Christ. He, the *quickening Spirit*, the *resurrection and the life*, cannot be *one spirit* with men destitute of spiritual life, and continuing members of the devil, *dead in trespasses and sins*, John xiv. 19. xi. 25. 1 Cor. xv. 45—49. vi. 17. 8. If there be no implanted habitual grace, there can be no imputation of the surety-righteousness of Christ, which partly consists in holiness of nature, for our justification; as habitual holiness in our heart, must as necessarily proceed from the imputation of Christ's righteousness, as the want of original righteousness, and corruption of our nature, do from the imputation of Adam's first sin. 9. There can be no adoption into God's family, without supernaturally implanted habits of holiness. God cannot be our Father, and permit Satan to hold his whole image and power in our heart. 10. If we deny the inherent holiness of nature implanted in believers, we must reject the whole law of God as a rule; for he neither has nor can give any law, which doth not require inherent holiness, and require that all acts of obedience should proceed from holy qualities and inclinations, 1 Pet. i. 15, 16, 18. 1 Tim. i. 5. Mat. vii. 17, 18. xii. 33—35. 11. Without inherent habits of holiness, there can be no fellowship with Christ or his Father, as there is no likeness to him, no inclination towards him, no fitness to entertain his visits, or ability to hold intercourse with him, Amos iii. 3. 2 Cor. viii. 14. 12. Without indwelling habits of grace, the Holy Ghost and his lively oracles can have no residence in us. How could he dwell in a dead carcase, a Sodom of filthiness?---or his truths be an *engrafted word*, where there was no gracious root or stock for it; or written in our inward parts, where there were no fleshly tables of a new nature, and where they could only be held prisoners in unrighteousness? 13. If God's law require inward holiness, his writing of it in our heart must include it. If his law do not require it, the want of it, and the corruption of nature, which is contrary to it, can be no sin, no ground of grief, confession, or application to the blood of Christ for purification from it. 14. Without implanted habits or principles of grace, there can be no spiritual warfare,---as there is no *law of the mind* to resist the law of our members;---no *spirit to lust* against our flesh, or inward corruption:---but acts of faith, and acts of unbelief; acts of love to God, and acts of enmity against him; acts of pride, and acts of humility,---must proceed from the same corrupt habits, as excited by the Spirit of God, or not.----And yet, an excitement of bad principles by him to perform acts spiritually good, is absolutely inconceivable. 15. Without inherent habitual holiness, there can be no spiritually good acts at all: How absurd to suppose, that they can exist without proceeding from any created principle,---and still more so to imagine, that they can proceed from a desperately wicked principle? Mat. vii. 17, 18. Luke vi. 43—45. Rom. viii. 7, 8. 16. Without inherent habits or principles of grace, there can be no spiritual experience, as we are not fit objects for the Holy Ghost to nourish, cherish, or comfort,—or capable to discern and feel his influence. 17. Without inherent habits or principles of grace, there can be no work of sanctification,---no renovation of the whole man after the image of God; and hence no enabling us to die unto sin, and live unto righteousness. 18. Without permanent habits and vital principles of grace, there can be no examination of our state before God.---There is no indwelling life to be discovered,---no abiding faith for us to have, or be in,---no standing difference between saints and sinners;---and nothing but rootless chimerical acts of faith, to be marks whether we are in Christ or not. Moreover, the Scripture never represents *good like acts*, be their number ever so great, as marks of our gracious state, but in so far as they are connected with, and proceed from inherent graces.---It is not acts, but abiding habits, which constitute the proper difference between the righteous and the wicked. Men's good works do not make them good; but being made good by implantation of inherent graces, they bring forth good works, as the native fruit of their inward renovation, and a manifest proof that it hath taken place. 19. Without inherent habits of grace, there can be no perseverance in grace, there being no gracious quality for God to preserve, or for us to persevere in.---But we must be *in*, or *out of* real grace, as we are actually employed in acts of faith or repentance, or not. 20. Without inherent habits or principles of holiness, there can be no preparation for the Lord's Supper, or for death. Habitual preparation is expressly excluded; and without it there can be no actual preparation but what proceeds from corrupt principles. 21. Without inherent habits of implanted holiness, there can be no growth in grace, in time, or perfection in it at death. Acts being altogether transient, cannot, after they have been acted, be rendered more lively, vigorous, or holy. And indeed, such as proceed from no gracious principles, are not fit to be increased in any respect. 22. Either, then, *acquired* habits of holiness must make us meet for heaven; or God must implant gracious habits, though he never would, or could do it before;---or he must admit us to heaven, in our chimerical acts of faith, which proceed from no inherent grace; or he must damn us all for want of habitual grace and holiness.

This habitual grace implanted by the Spirit of God, in regeneration, inclines our hearts to correspondent acts, with impartiality, evenness, and constancy, and enables us to perform them readily and willingly, to their proper end. And as our indwelling corruption may be considered as one sinful habit, diversified into the several lusts of the flesh and of the spirit, so our implanted and inherent grace may be considered as one *simple habit* of holiness or grace in itself, but diversified in correspondence to the powers of our soul, in which it dwells, or to the manner in which it acts upon its object. 1. Our mind or understanding is renewed, and through the Holy Ghost's all-powerful manifestation of divine truth, is endowed with sight, light, wisdom, and knowledge, that it can think, perceive, judge, esteem, devise, search, reason, and deliberate concerning spiritual things in a just, spiritual, and heart-engaging manner, 2 Cor. iii. 13, 14. Isa. liv. 13. Jer. xxxi. 33, 34. John vi. 44, 45, 65. Heb. x. 32. Rom. viii. 5, 6. Gal. i. 16. Eph. i. 17, 18. iii. 17—19. 1 Cor. ii. 10, 12, 15, 16. Rom. vii. 23, 24. viii. 28—39. 1 Cor. xv. 8, 58. 1 John ii. 8, 13. Mat. xvi. 17, 25, 26. 2 Cor. iii. 18. iv. 6, 18. Col. iii. 10. 2. Our conscience being purged by the blood of Christ, and awed by the majesty of God reconciled in him, is enlightened, directed, quickened, quieted, and made tender, faithful, and impartial, Heb. ix. 14. x. 19—22. 1 Tim. i. 5. Psalm lxxxvi. 11. Job xxxi. 14, 23. Phil. i. 9, 10. Psalm xxv. 4, 5, 7. Eph. i. 7. v. 14. Acts xxiv. 16. 2 Cor. i. 12. Heb. xiii. 18. 3. Our will, captivated with the manifested excellency, love, and fulness of Christ, and of God in him, is renewed in its inclinations, choice, delight, and aim, and endowed with power to govern our soul, and with a readiness to be impressed with spiritual things, Deut. xxx. 6. Psalm cx. 3. Jer. xxxi. 33. Heb. viii. 10. Ezek. xxxvi. 26, 27. xi. 19, 20. 4. Our affections being captivated with the manifested love and loveliness of Christ, and of God in him, are renewed and rectified with respect to their objects, order, and degree, Gal. v. 17, 24. Psalm xviii. 1—3. xxxi. 21, 22. lxxxiv. 1, 2, 10. xlii. 1, 2. cxix. 122, 136. xxxv. 17, 27. lxxiii. 25, 26. 5. Our memory, purged by the Spirit of God, and attracted by important and eternal things, is qualified to forget injuries, errors, and trifles, and to retain God's truths and works, and the impressions thereby made, Luke ii. 51. Lam. iii. 20, 21. Gen. xlviii. 3. Jer. xxxi.

3. Psalm cxix. 49, 52, 93. 6. Our body is renewed in respect of its use, and being governed by our renewed heart, is drawn off from its wonted readiness to be instrumental in wickedness, to a readiness in the exercises of holiness, 1 Cor. vi. 13, 19, 20. ix. 27. Psalm cxli. 3. Job xxxi. 1, 8. Rom. xii. 1. vi. 13, 19.

This newness of nature implanted in our regeneration, or begun sanctification, and carried on to perfection in our increasing sanctification, in respect of its diversified agency towards different objects, may be distinguished into the several permanent habits or graces of *knowledge, faith, love, hope, repentance*, which are the members of our *new man*, or *divine nature*. 1. As this implanted supernatural habit, or new nature, is opposed to sinful ignorance, stupidity, and folly, and as it conceives aright of objects connected with our duty and our everlasting happiness, it is spiritual KNOWLEDGE, *eyes to see, ears to hear*, and an *heart to understand*, Eph. i. 17, 18. 2 Tim. iii. 15. Deut. xxix. 3, 4. This includes *knowledge of ourselves*,—of the worth of our souls,—of our state before God,—of our temper and endowments,—and of our conduct in its principle, motives, manner, and ends, 2 Cor. xiii. 5; and of the manifold deceitfulness and corruptions of our heart, Jer. xvii. 9. Heb. iii. 12. 1 Kings viii. 32;——*knowledge of Christ*, in his person, natures, offices, relations, qualifications, work, and fulness, Gal. i. 16. 1 Cor. ii. 2. Phil. iii. 7, 8, 9. John i. 14;—— and *knowledge of God*, in his perfections, persons, purposes, works, doctrines, laws, promises, and threatenings, as connected with, and manifested in Christ, Jer. ix. 23, 24. Exod. xxxiv. 6, 7. Jer. xxxi. 34. John i. 18. 2 Cor. iv. 4, 6. 2. As this new nature disposes and enables us to believe and rest assured upon the testimony of God, and to receive and rest upon Jesus Christ as revealed, promised, offered, and given in his gospel,—it is called FAITH, Heb. xi. 13. 1 Tim. i. 15. John i. 12. Phil. iv. 6. 1 Pet. v. 7.——There is a *faith of miracles*, or persuasion of God's readiness to work some supernatural effect upon us, or at our request, Acts xiv. 9. 1 Cor. xiii. 2. Luke xvii. 6. Mat. xvii. 20. viii. 10. ix. 2. John xi. 40; —an *historical faith*, or persuasion of the truth of God's declarations, without any cordial application of them to ourselves, John xii. 42. Acts xxvi. 27. James ii. 19, and in part Rom. xiv. 22, 23; ——and a *temporary faith*, or transient persuasion of gospel truths, attended with some slight affectionate application of them to ourselves, Mat. xiii. 20, 21. Mark vi. 20. John v. 35. Heb. vi. 4, 5. x. 26. 2 Pet. ii. 20. Isa. lviii. 2. Ezek. xxxiii. 31. But none of these is the true, saving, unfeigned, precious, most holy, heart-purifying, and love-producing faith of God's elect, which is included in the new nature, James ii. 26. 1 Tim. i. 5. 2 Tim. i. 5. 2 Pet. i. 1. Jude 20. Acts xv. 9. Gal. v. 6. Heb. x. 22. Tit. i. 1. 2 Thess. iii. 2. John. i. 12. Mark xvi. 16.——In the whole exercise of this saving faith, there is included an assured belief of God's declarations, upon his own testimony. But this assurance is stronger or weaker, less or more mingled with doubting and unbelief, in different saints, and in the same saint at different times, Rom. iv. 19, 20. Mat. xiv. 30, 31.—It is *strong* and *full*, when we disregard every objection that presents itself against the testimony of God, Rom. iv. 19, 20. 2 Chron. xx. 20; when Christ is highly prized and firmly trusted, Psalm lxxiii. 25. Job xiii. 15; when great difficulties are cheerfully encountered and gone through, 2 Cor. xii. 7—10. Job i. 21, 22. ii. 10. Acts v. 41. Psalm cxii. 7; when there is a bold, but humble familiarity with God maintained, Heb. iv. 16. x. 22. Phil. iii. 20. Gal. iv. 6. Rom. viii. 15, 16; when the persuasion of his redeeming love is tenaciously retained, notwithstanding fearful hidings and frowns, Gal. ii. 20. Rom. viii. 32—39. Psalm xxii. 1. lxxxviii. 1. xlii. 9—11; and when his promises are held fast, and firmly relied on, while his providence appears very contrary to them, Rom. iv. 19, 20. Heb. xiii. 5. xi. 11, 17—19. Job xiii. 15. Psalm cxxxviii. 7. lxxi. 20, 21. Hab. iii. 17, 18.— This strong and full assurance of faith much honours God, Rom. iv. 19, 20. Mat. xv. 22—28; remarkably supports and comforts believers themselves, Psalm xxvii. 1—3, 13, 14. cxviii. 5—18; and powerfully promotes practical piety, Gal. v. 6. 1 Tim. i. 5. Luke i. 74, 75. 3. As the new nature disposes and enables us to look forward to God's promised benefits, and earnestly to expect and wait for the enjoyment of them, it is called HOPE, Psalm cxix. 81. Rom. viii. 24. 2 Cor. iv. 18. Heb. vi. 18, 19. Faith fixes on all the declarations of God relating to things past, present, or future; and peculiarly regards the *truth* of them, Heb. xi. 3, 13. Acts viii. 37. But hope fixes only upon promises of *future good* things, Rom. viii. 24. Heb. vi. 11, 18, 19. 4. As the new nature disposes and enables us to desire, cleave to, and delight in Christ, and God in him, and what is related to him, or for his honour, it is called love. Christ and his Father are loved for their excellency, relations, and kindness to us; and ordinances, saints, &c. for their sake, Song i. 2—4. v. 10—16. Psalm cxv. 1—3. civ. 34. cxxxix. 17, 18. xxxvii. 4, 7. xviii. 1—3. xlii. 1, 2. lxxxiv. 1, 2, 10. ciii. 1—6. cxvi. cxix. Eph. iv. 30. 1 Thess. v. 19. Psalm cxix. 63. li. 18. cii. 13—22. cxxxvii. 5---7. cxxii. cxxxii. Phil. i. 21. 2 Cor. v. 1---7. 5. As this new nature disposes and enables us to a kindly sorrow for, and hatred of our past and present sinfulness, and to turn from it to God, as our reconciled Father in Christ, with full purpose of, and endeavour after new obedience, it is called REPENTANCE, Acts v. 31. xi. 18. 2 Cor. vii. 11. Jer. xxxi. 18, 19. iii. 13, 21, 23;—the exercise of which proceeds from a true faith of the law and gospel of God,—from a true sense of our sins, as contrary to his nature and law, and as murderous to Christ our Saviour, as defiling and destructive to our immortal souls, Ezra ix. 6, 15. Job xl. iv. xlii. 5, 6. Psalm li, 1—5. Isa. lxiv. 6. vi. 5. Zech. xii. 10. Rom. vii. 14—24;—and from a believing application of God's forgiving them, through the blood of his Son, Ezek. xvi. 62, 63. xxxvi. 25, 31, 32. Jer. xxxi. 18 —20. Zech. xii. 10. Acts ii. 36—38;—and it consists in an hearty, godly, universal, proportioned, superlative, and fixed grief for our sin, Jer. ii. 19. Lam. iii. 28. Psalm vi. 6. li. 3, 5. xxxii. 5. Rom. vii. 24;—in a gracious, self-lothing, constant, universal, proportioned, superlative, and in aim, perfect hatred of sin as such, in every appearance of it, Psalm cxix. 104, 113. Rom. vii. 14, 23, 24. Gal. v. 17, 24. Job xlii. 5, 6. Ezek. xxxvi. 31. Psalm cxxxix. 21—23;—and in an humble, hearty, earnest, and universal turning from it as a pleasure to God in Christ, as our portion and Master, companion and Lord, with full purpose of, and endeavour after true evangelical obedience, *new* in its foundation, principle, motives, manner, and ends, Jer. xxxi. 18—20. Luke xv. 18, 20. Hos. xiv. 1—3, 8. Acts xi. 23. Josh. xxiv. 15. Psalm cxix. 59, 60.

This evangelical repentance is exceedingly different from that *legal* fear, grief for, and rage against sin, which are produced by the convictions of unregenerate men. 1. In their *order*. Legal repentance follows a legal faith of the broken law only; but this evangelical repentance also follows the saving faith of the gospel, Acts xvi. 30. Zech. xii. 10. 2. In their *cause*. Legal repentance proceeds from apprehensions of God's revenging wrath, manifested in his threatenings and judgments, Gen. iv. 10—14. Mat. xxvii. 3, 4. Exod. ix. 27; but evangelical repentance proceeds from apprehensions of God's revenging wrath manifested in Christ's death, and of the free and full pardon of all our sins, Isa. vi. 5. Dan. ix. Ezra ix. Zech. xii. 10. Ezek. xvi. 62, 63. 3. In their *object*. In legal repentance men are chiefly affected with their gross sins, and of the connection of punishments with them, Gen. iv. 13, 14. Mat. xxvii. 4. But, in evangelical repentance, they are chiefly affected with secret and beloved sins, and with sin as odious to God and defiling to their soul, Psalm li. 4, 5. Rom. vii. 14, 23, 24. 4. In their *effects*. Legal repentance turns men only from gross acts of sin, works death, fills with inward rage against God, and often leads to self-murder, 1 Kings xxi. 27, 29. Gen. iv. 13. Mat. xxvii. 4, 5. 2 Cor. vii. 10; but evangelical repentance turns men from the love of every sin, and works salvation and eternal life, 2 Cor. vii. 11. Psalm cxix. 104, 113. Acts xi. 18. 5. In their *connection with divine pardons*. Legal repentance having no spiritual good in it, hath no proper connection with divine pardon, though God often make it an introduction to it, Acts ii. 37. Rom. vii. 8—13;

but evangelical repentance is the necessary fruit and evidence of God's judicial pardon in justification, and the mean of further intimations of it, of fatherly pardons and removals of corrections for sin, Isa. xliv. 22. Jer. iii. 12, 14, 15, 21, 22, 23. Hos. xiv. 1—3, 8.—And, though it be impossible, under legal guilt, which tends to destroy men, and binds them under the dominion of their sin, 1 Cor. xv. 56. Rom. vii. 5, 8—13, it takes place under that guilt which binds over to God's fatherly anger, that is real love to our persons, and tends to make us partakers of his holiness, Jer. iii. 1, 12, 13, 14, 22. xxxi. 18—20. Hos. xiv. 1, 8. Heb. xii. 6—11. Psalm xciv. 12. Prov. iii. 12. Rev. iii. 19.

Evangelical repentance of our sins is most reasonable and necessary. 1. God often expressly requires it, Ezek. xxxiii. 11. Isa. i. 16—18. lv. 7. xliv. 22. Jer. iii. Hos. xiv. 1. 2. His perfections, as manifested in Christ by the gospel, and all promises confirmed in Christ's person and righteousness, mightily encourage to it, Exod. xxxiv. 6, 7. Isa. lv. 7. i. 18. Mic. vii. 18, 19. Hos. xiv. Jer. iii. 3. Christ's execution of all his offices, and all saving discoveries of him, powerfully promote it, Mark i. 14. Acts iii. 26. v. 31. Rom. xi. 26. Zech. xii. 10. Isa. vi. 5, 7. 4. God's providential favours and frowns, as well as our own convictions and pressures of conscience, call to it, Rom. ii. 4. Jer. vi. 8. Hos. ii. 6, 7, 14. v. 15. Acts ii. 38. iii. 19. 5. The approved examples of all the saints powerfully invite and excite to it, Heb. xii. 1. Job vii. 20. xl. 4. xlii. 5, 6. 2 Sam. xxiv. 10. Isa. lxiv. 6. vi. 5. Jer. iii. 21. xvi. 19. xxxi. 18—20. Ezra ix. Psalm li. xxxviii. Dan. ix.— And delay of it is infinitely dangerous,—as the present moment may be our last, Prov. xxvii. 1. Luke x. 20. xiii. 3, 5; all continuance in sin is a reacting all our former sins with new aggravations,—hardens our hearts in sin, increases our inward corruption, and makes repentance more difficult, Rom. ii. 4. Psalm xcv. 7. Heb. iii. 7, 8, 13, 15; provokes God to deny us grace to repent, Hos. iv. 17. Gen. vi. 3. Psalm lxxxi. 11, 12. xcv. 11;—and loses much opportunity of honouring God, and of advancing our own holiness and comfort, Psal. lxxviii. 33. xc. 9. Nor, in 4000 years, have we more than one instance of true repentance in dying moments,—when the Son of God was expiring and triumphing over Satan, on his cross, Luke xxiii. 42, 43.

These graces are jointly exercised in our spiritual acts. Thus, in our reception of Christ, our spiritual *knowledge* discerns him and our warrant to appropriate him; we by *faith* rest on the faithfulness, power, and love of God, manifested in the gospel grant of him, and upon him as able and willing to answer every end of our salvation, for which he is offered in the gospel; we affectionately delight in, desire after, and are satisfied with him, and with God in him; and we are ashamed of, and lothe ourselves as guilty, polluted, and miserable. And hence some divines attribute that to one grace, particularly to FAITH, which properly belongs to another.

From the inbeing and proper exercise of these graces, proceed many delightful CHRISTIAN TEMPERS, *acquired gracious habits*, or fruits of our new Spirit under the influence of the Holy Ghost, Gal. v. 22, 23. Eph. v. 9. As, 1. Christian *wisdom* and *prudence*,—enabling us to propose proper ends of conduct,—choose proper means,—and execute them in a proper place, time, and manner, and by proper instruments;—to discern what enemies are most dangerous, and how we may best prevent their hurting us,—what friends or companions are most proper and useful for us, and how to improve familiarity with them to the best advantage;—when, and how to oppose, or condescend to, our friends and neighbours, or to reprove and warn them most to their and our advantage;—to discern how to attend God's ordinances, and improve his providences to the best advantage, in honouring him, and profiting ourselves or our neighbours;—and how to live most inoffensively and usefully amidst a crooked and perverse generation, Prov. i. 3, 4. Matth. x. 16, 17. Eph. v. 15—17. 2. *Spirituality of mind*, which is manifested in our deliberate esteeming and choosing spiritual things, and in the fixed, and, as it were, natural bent of our affections towards them, and habitual employment of our thoughts upon them,—in our alertness and activity in prosecution of them, and ready preference of them to every temporal concern, Rom. viii. 5, 6. 1 Cor. ii. 15. 3. *Godliness*, manifested in our ready reception of God's testimony, Job xxiii. 12. Psalm lx. 6. Jer. xv. 16. Psalm lxxxv. 8. 1 Thess. ii. 13; fixed trust in, and reverential fear of him, Psalm lxii. 8. lxxxix. 7. Rev. xv. 4.; superlative love of him, and unreserved obedience to him, Matth. xxii. 37. Heb. xi. 8; cordial submission to his disposing will, Matth. vi. 10. 1 Sam. iii. 18. 2 Sam. xvi. 11, 12; and earnest care to imitate and approve ourselves to him, 1 Pet. i. 15, 16. Mat. v. 48. Luke vi. 35, 36. Rom. xvi. 10. 2 Tim. ii. 15. Col. i. 10. 4. *Pureness of heart*, including a conscience sprinkled with Christ's blood, Heb. ix. 14. x. 22. 1 Tim. i. 5; inward hatred and abhorrence of sin, and of all temptations to it, or appearances of it, particularly that which tends towards fleshly lust, Mat. v. 8, 28—31. Rom. vii. 24. xii. 9. 2 Tim. ii. 16, 19, 22. 1 Pet. ii. 11. 1 Thess. v. 22;—and permanent grief on account of past impurities or inherent corruptions, Job xl. 4. Rom. vii. 14—24. 5. *Sincerity*, which includes our singly aiming to please and honour God in all that we do, 2 Tim. ii. 15. Col. i. 22; and impartial desire and endeavour to know the whole of our duty, Job xxxiv. 32. Psalm cxix. 5, 27, 33, 34;—our earnestly practising that which we know, Psalm cxix. 58—60; with an exact correspondence between our inward sentiments and our external conduct, 2 Cor. i. 12. Acts xxiii. 1. xxiv. 16. 6. *Humility*, which includes a low esteem of our own knowledge,—humbly observing the imperfections of our faculties, and our readiness to mistake,—the great attainments of others,—and the small importance of that knowledge which is not attended with a correspondent holy practice;—low thoughts of our goodness, as borrowed from God,—undeserving and insignificant before him,—unanswerable to our opportunities, —and much inferior to that of some fellow-christians;—humble sense of our dependence on God, and even on the meanest of his creatures,—of our infinite meanness before him, and our sinfulness and rebellion against him, and wretched abuse of his favours;—and hence a readiness to receive his distinguishing mercies, walk humbly with him, and always depend on him,—undeservedly accepting all his gospel-grants, and obeying all his commandments;—a fixed disposition to behave humbly toward our neighbours, preferring them to ourselves in love and esteem,—never despising them for their meanness, falls, or infirmities,—meekly reproving their faults,—readily receiving their reproofs, and kindly confessing and amending our mistakes;—an abhorrence of self-praise or preference, and boasting,—and all flattery of others;—and a readiness to receive favours with thankfulness, endure contempt without passion, and to serve in the lowest stations with cheerfulness, James iv. 6, 10. 1 Pet. v. 5, 6. Phil. ii. 3. Luke xiv. 10. xviii. 14. 2 Cor. x. 13, 14. 7. *Meekness*, including a ready and full subjection of soul to God's authority in his word, and cheerful resignation to his providence,—an inward calmness under provocation, and readiness to forgive injuries from men; —carefulness to avoid offending others; a modest comportment of ourselves with our worldly circumstances; and a mild and gentle deportment toward all around us, in temporal and religious concerns, Gal. v. 23. 2 Tim. ii. 23. 1 Tim. vi. 11. 1 Pet. iii. 4. Zeph. ii. 3. 8. *Patience*, which includes a meek bearing of continued injuries from men,—a kindly receiving heavy and manifold afflictions from the hand of God, and a submissive waiting for his promised favours, Psalm xxvii. 13, 14. xxxvii. 1—8. lxii. 1, 5. cxxx. 5. cxxiii. 1—4. Job xxxv. 14. Isa. xxx. 18. xxviii. 16. James i. 4. v. 7, 8, 11. 9. *Peaceableness*, which includes an earnest carefulness to avoid giving, or groundless taking offence;—to maintain peace when enjoyed, and regain it when lost, by satisfying the offended, and by convincing and forgiving offenders, Heb. xii. 14. Psalm xxxiv. 14. Matth. v. 9. Rom. xii. 18. xiv. 19. Gal. v. 22.

10. *Tenderness of heart*, which includes a quick sense of spiritual things,—an inward pliableness to divine influence,—a readiness to engage heartily in known duties, and to mourn for dishonour done to God, and for the falls and afflictions of men, 2 Kings xxii. 19. Eph. iv. 32.   11. *Bravery, Fortitude,* or *Virtue*, which includes ability to suppress slavish fears of seemingly approaching calamities; steady boldness in lawful resolutions; undaunted and lively application to even the most difficult Christian exercises; and uniform stedfastness in prosecution of good purposes and dutiful endeavours, 2 Pet. i. 5. 12. *Zeal*, which consists in an earnest abhorrence of that which is evil, and eager desire to maintain and promote that which is good. It is truly regular, when we are zealous against that which we know to be bad, and for that which we know to be good;—when it is proportioned to the importance of things;—when it influences us to an earnest study of holiness and virtue;—and when, in the exercise of it, we avoid all uncharitableness toward others, and all expedients improper in themselves, or unanswerable to our station, for the advancement of truth or piety, Psal. lxix. 9. cxix. 139. Gal. iv. 18.   13. *Temperance*, which imports a stated aversion from such meat, drink, or bodily pleasure, as would indispose our body for subjection to, and service of our soul, or would not comport with our outward circumstances;—or would mispend our time, mar the due exercise of our reason, promote irregular desires, taint our spirits with a wrong bias, unfit us for Christ's second coming, dishonour that outward property which God has given us, or rob him of that which ought to be expended in his service, 2 Pet. i. 6. Luke xxi. 34. Gal. v. 23.   14. *Equity* or *Justice*, which is a fixed inclination to render to God, to ourselves, and to our neighbours, their respective dues; and to wrong ourselves in worldly claims, rather than wrong our neighbour, Rom. xiii. 7, 8. Mat. xxii. 19, 21, 37, 39. vii. 12. 15. *Mercifulness*, which consists in a tender sympathy with, and pity of those that are in danger, distress, or poverty; and strong inclination to relieve them to the uttermost of our power, Psalm xli. 1. xviii. 25. Matth. v. 7. Col. iii. 12. 1 Pet. iii. 8. iv. 8.   16. *Truth, Candour,* and *Faithfulness*, which include a fixed aversion from every form or degree of deceit or falsehood, and an inclination earnestly to maintain and promote truth on every proper occasion, and to act up to every thing which our character, relations, trust, or engagements require from us, Psalm xv. 2, 3. Luke xvi. 10—12.—— To render all these tempers *truly Christian*, they must be produced in hearts united to Christ, by gracious virtue derived from Christ and his Spirit, through his word dwelling in us richly, in conformity to Christ, and exercised in obedience to the

authority of Christ, and aiming at his honour and the honour of God in him, 1 Pet. i. 4—8. Gal. v. 22, 23. ii. 20. 2 Tim. ii. 1. 2 Cor. i. 12. Phil. iv. 13.

The above-mentioned *implanted Graces* and *acquired Tempers*, are exercised in our *dying to sin* and *living to righteousness*. This gradual dying to sin is necessary, because we are never perfectly purged from our sinful corruption in this life.—Indeed believers are *freed* from the dominion and slavery of sin, Rom. vi. 7, 11, 14, 18. viii. 2. John viii. 32, 36; and are *perfect*, 1. In Christ their Head, Col. ii. 10. 2. They are sound, candid, and sincere,—indulging themselves in no known sin, Job i. 1, 8. Gen. vi. 9. Isa. xxxviii. 3. 3. Every faculty of their soul, and power of their nature, is renewed in part, 1 Thess. v. 23. 2 Cor. v. 17. Gal. vi. 15. 4. They aim at perfect obedience to the *whole* law of God, Luke i. 6. Phil. iv. 8. iii. 14, 15. 5. They are more perfect than other men, Gen. vi. 9. Nay, some of them are more perfect in gifts and graces than other believers,—those under the New Testament than those under the Old, 1 Cor. ii. 6. Gal. iv. 1—3. Phil. iii. 15. Heb. v. 13, 14. 1 John ii. 13, 14. But none of them, in this life, are completely delivered from the pollution and working of indwelling corruption. 1. Scripture represents them all as defiled with, and guilty of sin, 1 John i. 8, 10. James iii. 2. Prov. xx. 9. Eccl. vii. 20. Psalm cxlii. 2. cxxx. 3. 1 Kings viii. 38, 46. Gal. v. 17. Job xv. 14. xxv. 4. 2. None can bear the yoke of God's law, so as to be thereby justified;—perfect obedience to the moral law being much more difficult than to the ceremonial, Acts xv. 10. 3. All believers are taught by Christ to pray daily for the pardon of their sins, Mat. vi. 12. Luke xi. 4. 4. The most eminent saints mentioned in Scripture are charged with sins, even such as were directly contrary to their predominant graces, as Noah, Gen. ix. 21; Abraham, Gen. xii. 13, 19. xx. 2; Job, chap. iii. ix. 3, 20, 28. xv. 5. vii. 20; Moses, Num. xi. 15, 22. xx. 10, 12; Psalm cvi. 33; David, Psalm xxxii. 6. xxv. 11. li. cxxx. 3. cxliii. 2. 2 Sam. xi. xxiv; Solomon, 1 Kings xi. Isaiah, chap. vi. 5. lxiv. 6; Jeremiah, chap. xii. 1. xx. 7—18; Daniel, Dan. ix. 6; John, 1 John i. 8, 10; James, Jam. iii. 2; Paul, Rom. vii. 14—25.—This last passage cannot respect an unregenerate man; for, 1. Paul speaks as plainly of himself as words can express, relative to his condition just when he was writing. 2. In the verses immediately preceding, he had spoken of himself in the past time, representing what he had been; but here he changes the time, and represents himself as *presently* under that powerful influence of sin. 3. This passage respects a person that *willed* that which is good,—that *consented* to, and *delighted* in the law of God, after his inward man, —and that *felt* the remains of indwelling corruption as his *heaviest burden*,—and had an inward man which did *not sin*,—a *law* in his mind, which *warred* against the remains of his indwelling lusts;—none of which things are applicable to unregenerate men. 4. There is nothing in the whole passage which could unfit Paul to be a distinguished example of piety and virtue, Phil. iii. 12—14. 2 Cor. i. 12. Acts xxiv. 16.

To anticipate objections, it must be observed, that, 1. Christ's yoke is easy, and his burden light, and his commandments not grievous to believers,—as they delight therein, and are enabled by him to obey in an acceptable, though imperfect, manner; and his blood covers their defects, Mat. xi. 30. 1 John v. 3. Psalm cxix. 97. Rom. vii. 22. Isa. xl. 31. Zech. x. 12. Phil. iv. 13. Rev. vii. 14. xix. 8. 2. Believers are *free from sin, i. e.* from its legal guilt, dominion, and slavery, Rom. vi. 2, 7, 11, 18; and *do not sin*, do not make a trade of sinning with pleasure and delight. Not being under the law as a covenant, they cannot sin against it,—and their new nature, being born of God, cannot sin at all, 1 John iii. 9. v. 18. John viii. 34. 3. All things are *possible* to them that believe. By the prayer of faith, they can obtain every thing that is for their real advantage; and, in Christ's strength, they can patiently endure all the changes which God's providence makes in their lot, Mark ix. 23. Phil. iv. 13.

God permits the continuance and frequent prevalence of sinful corruptions in believers, while they live on earth, 1. To correct them for former sins, Psalm lxxxi. 11, 12. 2. To manifest to them the abundance and power of their secret sinfulness, Psalm xix. 12, 13. Rom. vii. 14—25. 3. To manifest the deceitfulness and desperate wickedness of sin, and render it more hateful to them, Heb. iii. 12, 13. Rom. vii. 14—24. Psalm li. 4. To make them more deeply sensible of their need of Jesus Christ as their righteousness and strength, Mat. ix. 12, 13. Isa. xlv. 24. 5. To lead them to a constant and close dependence upon him, as made of God to them wisdom, righteousness, sanctification, and redemption; and to much study of familiar fellowship with God in prayer, Heb. xii. 1, 2. Isa. xlv. 24. Psal. xxv. 2. 2 Cor. xii. 7—9. 6. To render them humble, 2 Cor. xii. 7. Isa. vi. 5. lxiv. 6. Phil. iii. 8, 9. Rom. vii. 14—25. 1 Tim. i. 15. 7. To excite them to more activity and watchfulness, in the mortification of sin, Mark xiii. 37. xiv. 38. 2 Pet. ii. 1. v. 8. Heb. xii. 12. James i. 21. Col. iii. 5. 8. To dispose them to extend their charity and Christian fellowship to the weakest followers of Christ, Heb. x. 24, 25. Rom. xiv. 1. 9. To wean their affections from things on earth, and make them long for the heavenly purity and happiness, Gen xlix. 18. Phil. i. 21, 23. 2 Cor. v. 1—7. Tit. ii. 12, 13. 10. That, as in other cases, he may produce great effects gradually.——But, as most of these ends could be otherwise gained, perhaps God, in this dispensation, chiefly intended, 1. To conform our death to sin, to Christ's gradual suffering or death for sin, Gal. ii. 20. Rom. vi. 4, 5, 6. viii. 29. 2. To manifest the exceeding riches of his own grace;—for,—the more numerous and aggravated sins he forgives, the more of his grace, and of the virtue of Jesus' blood, appears in the pardon:—the more deeply sin appears to be rooted in our nature, the more is the grace of God exalted in extirpating it:—the more of our weakness appears, the more abundantly the grace of God is displayed in our supply, support, and victory over sin:—the more difficulty appears in the work of our salvation, the more is the free grace of God manifested in completely perfecting it.

The sinful corruption of our nature, called the *old man*, from its antiquity, craftiness, and dying condition in believers, Eph. iv. 22. Rom. vi. 6;—the *law of the members*, or *law of sin and death*, from its powerful influence in many different forms to defile and ruin us, Rom. vii. 23, 25. viii. 2;—the *flesh*, from its filthiness, earthliness, and exertion of its influences through our body, Rom. viii. 1, 4. Gal. v. 17, 24; and *lust*, from its constant tendency toward sinful acts, Eph. ii. 2,—remains during this life in every believer, in all its *original forms*,—in ignorance, pride, vanity, and falsehood, in their mind;—in stupidity, partiality, and aptness to call evil good, and good evil, in their conscience;—in weakness to, and aversion from good, in enmity against God, and perverseness with respect to their chief end, in their will;—in earthliness, disorder, and inordinacy, in their affections;—in levity and treachery, in their memory;—and in a readiness to be instrumental in unrighteousness, in their bodily members, Rom. vii. 14—25. Isa. lxiv. 6.——The force of this indwelling corruption is weakened, and its dominion destroyed in regeneration; but it must be gradually mortified in sanctification, Rom. viii. 2, 13. Gal. v. 24. Col. iii. 5. Eph. iv. 22.

The MORTIFICATION of this remaining sinfulness of nature doth not consist in concealing it,—or in diverting its particular lusts into some other channel of influence,—or in improving our natural powers in opposition to it,—or in occasional conquests of some particular lust in times of conviction, danger, or distress;—or in the utter extinction of it in this life; but it consists in, 1. An earnest labour to destroy the root of sin, by a continued application of Jesus' blood to our conscience, for the removal of all that guilt which defiles it from time to time, Heb. ix. 14. x. 19—22. 1 John i. 7, 9. 2. Animated by evangelical pain for it, hatred and abhorrence of it, and all its works,—endeavouring to lessen its power and fulness, by an earnest improvement of Christ's death, resurrection, word, and Spirit, in opposition to it, and receiving out of his fulness more and more supplies of grace to take its room in the several powers of our soul, Rom. vii. 14—24. Job xlii. 5, 6. Ezek. xxxvi. 31, 32. Psalm cxliii. 12. Phil. iii. 9—14. Eph. iv. 22—24. v. 15, 14. Rom. xiii. 14. vi. 6. viii. 13. Col. iii. 5, 9, 10.   3. A gradual diminishing of our love to sin, and increase of our hatred against it, and all its appearances, produced by the love of God being shed abroad in our heart, Rom. v. 5. vii. 24, 25. Job xl. 4. xlii. 5, 6. Psalm cxix. 104, 113.   4. By earnest watchfulness against the first motions of sin and all temptations to it, diminishing the workings of it in thought, word, and deed, and our inclinations to them,—through the exercise of inward graces, strengthened and actuated by Christ and his Spirit, Prov. iv. 23. Rom. vi. 12. viii. 13. Eph. vi. 10—19. Phil. iv. 13. 1 Cor. xvi. 13. Col. iii. 5. Gal. v. 17, 24.

Hence follows a constant WARFARE between the indwelling grace and sinful corruption of believers, Song vi. 13. Rom. vii. 23. Gal. v. 17. Eph. vi. 12. This inward warfare is not merely between their inclination and their conscience, or with respect to gross sins only, as often happens in unregenerate men; but their inclinations, as far as renewed, war against their inclinations, in so far as they are not renewed;—even with respect to the most secret sins, Rom. vii. 24, 25. Psalm xix. 12, 13.—In this warfare our indwelling corruptions, assisted by Satan and all the enticements of this world, do, by deceit and violence, often prevail over our inward graces, and make us commit sin in thought, word, or deed, Rom. vii. 14—29. Isa. lxiv. 6. James i. 14. iii. 2; which prevalence hath a native tendency to reduce our soul under the dominion of sin, Rom. vii. 23.—But Christ's complete deliverance of us from under the covenant of works, and his removing the curse, which is the strength of sin, and his effectual assistance of our graces by his intercession, word, blood, and Spirit, and providence, not only checks this dreadful tendency of the motions of sin, but enables us to repent of, and overcome that sin into which we had fallen, Rom. viii. 2. vii. 4, 6, 14. Psal. li. xxxviii.

In this spiritual warfare, nothing is of more importance than a vigorous exercise of SELF-DENIAL, in which we, at once, die to sin and live unto righteousness, Matth. xvi. 24. In this exercise we renounce our natural, civil, and religious, as well as sinful self, in so far as it is apt to take the place of Jesus Christ, his Father, and the blessed Spirit, in our hearts or lives, Matth. xvi. 24. Luke xiv. 26. Tit. ii. 12. We renounce our wisdom and knowledge, as altogether insufficient to guide us to real and lasting happiness, and embrace Christ, as made of God to us wisdom, and his word and Spirit, for our instructor and director, Prov. iii. 5—7. 1 Cor. i. 24, 30. 2 Thess. ii. 13. We renounce our own qualities and works, as altogether unfit to justify us before God, or to be the ground of our hope, and price or condition of our happiness, and heartily submit to, and accept of, the righteousness of Christ alone, Isa. lxiv. 6. Phil. iii. 9. We renounce self, in all its excellencies, relations, and enjoyments, as altogether improper to be our portion; we seek and place our chief happiness in God, as our God in Christ, Phil. iii. 19, 20. 2 Thess. iii. 5. Col. iii. 1, 2. Psal. lxxiii. 25, 26. xvi. 5, 6. cxlii. 5. Lam. iii. 24. Matth. x. 37, 38. xix. 29. We renounce self, as altogether unfit to be our chief end, or any end at all, but in subordination to God,—and direct all that we do, to his glory, 1 Cor. x. 31. vi. 19, 20. Col. iii. 17. 1 Pet. iv. 11. Eph. iii. 21. Psalm cxviii. 28. Exod. xv. 1.— Contrary to the natural corrupt bias of our soul, we subordinate all our care for, and delight in lawful, temporal enjoyments, to a concern for that which is spiritual and eternal, Matth. vi. 33. John vi. 26, 27. 2 Cor. iv. 18. Luke x. 41, 42.— Refusing to obey our own self-will, we submit ourselves wholly to God, as our God and Ruler in Christ, and to his law, as holy, just, and good, Rom. vii. 12, 14. xiv. 8, 9. 1 Cor. vi. 19, 20. Deut. iv. 2. v. 32. xii. 32. Matth. xxviii. 20.— Renouncing our own choice, we cheerfully submit to, and kindly receive whatever God, our Father, and the proprietor of all things, is pleased to distribute to us, Job i. 21. 1 Sam. iii. 8. Psalm xxxix. 9. Matth. xx. 15. Phil. iv. 11—13. Acts xxi. 14. Matth. xxvi. 39, 42. John xviii. 11.—Distrusting self and every other creature, we, without anxiety, depend on God in Christ, as our God, to bestow upon us whatever is truly good and best for us, in his most proper time, place, and manner, Jer. xvii. 5—8. Psal. lxxxiv. 11, 12. iv. 6, 7. xxxiv. 8—10. lxxxv. 12, 13.

To *live unto righteousness*, is more and more to love and abound in inward holiness, and in the practice of good works proceeding from it, Job xvii. 9. Prov. iv. 18. Psalm xcii. 13, 14. 1 Cor. xv. 58.—A *good end* is not sufficient to constitute our works good; for, 1. Men may do that which God has forbidden in his law, with a good intention, John xvi. 2. Acts xxvi. 9. 2. Men may have a kind of good intention without any proper knowledge of the law of God, which is the standard of our actions, Rom. x. 2, 3. xiv. 15. 1 Tim. i. 7, 8. 3. Not merely our intention, but our whole nature and exercise, are bound, and therefore ought to be regulated by the law of God, Deut. iv. 2. xii. 32. Matth. xxii. 37, 39.——It is not sufficient to constitute our works *good*, that they be required in the law of God: They ought also to be performed from proper principles and motives, in a right manner, and to right ends, duly subordinated.——And, to render our works, which are required by the law of God, truly *evangelical*, and *new* obedience, they must be built upon a *gospel foundation*,—the revealed truths of God relative to our free, full, and everlasting salvation, flowing from his free grace, reigning through the imputed righteousness of Christ, and the holy law, as through his fulfilment of it, turned into a perfect law of liberty, to direct our hearts and lives,—received into all the powers of our souls, John viii. 32. xiii. 17. James i. 21. 1 Thess. ii. 13.—They must proceed from vital gospel principles,—a mind enlightened with the knowledge of Jesus Christ, as our Saviour, Portion, and Lord ; a conscience sprinkled with his law-magnifying blood, and a will and affections renewed and actuated by his indwelling Spirit, Mat. vii. 17, 18. xii. 33—35. Luke viii. 15. Gal. i. 16. Heb. ix. 14. 1 Tim. i. 5. Ezek. xxxvi. 25, 26.—They must be influenced by *gospel* motives impressing our heart,—the redeeming love of God, and his authority as our God in Christ, manifested in his law, as our rule,—the example of Christ, and of God in him, as our Father and friend,—and the well-grounded hope of eternal life as his free gift, 2 Cor. v. 14, 15. 1 John iv. 19. 1 Thess. iv. 3. Eph. v. 1, 2. Heb. xii. 1, 2. 1 Cor. xv. 58. They must be performed in a *gospel manner*, in the exercise of faith on Christ, as our righteousness and strength,—and of grateful love to him as dying for us,—and with great humility, reckoning ourselves infinite debtors to his grace, and after all that we do, less than the least of his mercies, 1 Tim. i. 5. Gal. ii. 19, 20, 21. Phil. iv. 13. Zech. x. 12. Psalm cxvi. 16. Mic. vi. 8. Luke xvii. 10. Gen. xxxii. 10.—They must be performed to an *evangelical end*, to render us like God our Saviour, glorify God our Maker and Redeemer, profit our neighbour, and bring him to God in Christ;—and to prepare us for the free, full, and everlasting enjoyment of God, as our redeeming ALL IN ALL, Luke vi. 27—36. 1 Cor. vi. 19, 20. 1 Pet. i. 15, 16. ii. 9. iii. 1. Matth. v. 16. 1 Cor. vii. 16. Rev. iii. 21. xxii. 14.

It is not enough that we have real grace, and have done some truly good works: we ought always to increase and abound in them more and more, 2 Pet. i. 4—8. iii. 11, 13, 18. Tit. ii. 11—14. iii. 8, 14. Phil. iii. 12—14. iv. 8. Heb. xii. 1—3. 1 Cor. ix. 24. Job xvii. 9. Prov. iv. 18. And, notwithstanding inconceivable opposition from their indwelling corruptions, and their assistants, all true believers do increase in the measure, strength, and liveliness of their implanted graces and Christian tempers, and become more earnest and exact in holy thoughts, words, and deeds, Psal. xcii. 13, 14. lxxxiv. 7. Job xvii. 9. Prov. iv. 18. But they do not grow at all times, or alway in in every respect, 2 Sam. xi. 1 Kings xi. Matth. xxvi. 69—74. —Nevertheless, through God's making all things to work together for their good, they sometimes increase in self-acquaintance and humility, when they apprehend themselves growing

OF SANCTIFICATION. 425

worse,—even as cold and storms promote the growth of trees, while they seem to hinder it, Rom. viii. 28. 2 Cor. iv. 17. Jer. xvii. 8. Mic. vii. 14. Hos. ii. 7, 14. Isa. xxvii. 9. Psalm cix. 67, 71, 75. Heb. xii. 6---11. Prov. iii. 12.

But no human works or qualities, however excellent, can DESERVE any favour from God. The best works of unregenerate men *deserve nothing but his wrath.* 1. They want all the former constituents of true goodness. They are not done in faith, Rom. xiv. 23. Tit. i. 15. 1 Tim. i. v.; nor in obedience to the authority of God in his law, Deut. xii. 32. Rom. viii. 7, 8. Zech. vii. 5. 2. Their most useful works are represented as sin, Prov. xv. 8. xxi. 4, 27. xxviii. 9. Isa. i. 11---15. lviii. 3. Nay, sinning in one point renders a man a transgressor of the whole law, James ii. 10. 3. Unregenerate men are represented as fools, atheists, and most wicked, Psalm xiv. 1---4. Eph. ii. 1---3, 12. Tit. iii. 3. Rom. i. 29---32. iii. 9---20. 4. The implantation, or beginning of grace in men, is a free gift of God's grace, Rom. ix. 16. Eph. ii. 4---10. Tit. iii. 3---7. 2 Cor. iii. 3, 5. iv. 7. Rom. xi. 26, 35.——As *proper merit,* of *condignity,* requires, not only that the meritorious works be perfect, but that they be performed in our own strength, and be more than is due from us to God, and be equal in value to the bestowed reward, it is plain, that neither saints nor angels can *thus merit* any thing from God. For, 1. We owe all possible obedience to his law, Psalm xcv. 6, 7. c. 2, 3. Matth. v. 48. xxii. 37, 39. Luke vi. 27---36. Rom. viii. 12. 2. All our works, which are truly good, are the product of God's grace within us, James i. 17. Phil. ii. 13. 2 Cor. iii. 5. 1 Cor. iv. 7. 3. None of our works are answerable to the demands of God's law, Rom. xvii. 18. Gal. v. 17, 18. Isa. lxiv. 6. 4. There is no equal proportion between the good works of finite creatures, and a reward of everlasting happiness, Rom. viii. 18. 2 Cor. iv. 17. Rom. vi. 23. iv. 4. xi. 6.——Nay, believers' good works cannot, even by *pactional merit,* purchase their reward of eternal life. 1. Their works on earth are never perfectly answerable to any law which God can prescribe for them, Matth. v. 48. xxii. 37, 39. 1 Pet. i. 15, 16. Matth. vii. 12. Isa. lxiv. 6. Eccl. vii. 20. 1 Kings viii. 38, 46. James iii. 2. 1 John i. 8, 10. 2. The law of Christ, under which they are placed, being a perfect law of liberty, can constitute no pactional merit, James i. 25. ii. 12. 1 Cor. ix. 21. 3. The grace of God toward them, and the righteousness of Christ imputed to them, leave no place for their pactional merit, Rom. v. 16---21. Heb. x. 10, 14. ix. 12. Eph. ii. 4---9. 4. The principles of faith and love, from which their good works proceed, suppose their full possession of Jesus' righteousness, which is meritorious in every respect, and of a full title to all the grace and glory of the new covenant, 2 Cor.

v. 14, 15, 21. Rom. iii. 24, 31. Gal. ii. 16, 19, 20.---Indeed believers' good works are *rewarded* by God. But, 1. This reward is entirely of his own free grace, Rom. v. 21. xi. 6. vi. 23. 2. It is bestowed upon believers, not for their works sake, but because their persons are united to Christ, and accepted in him, 1 Cor. xv. 58. Isa. xlv. 17. Psalm lxxii. 17. 3. There is a mere connection of order between their good works and their gracious rewards,---the blessing of holy diligence being bestowed antecedently to remarkable happiness;---and the blessings which follow being proportioned to such antecedent ones as admitted of degrees, Rev. ii. 7, 17, 26. iii. 5, 12, 21. Luke xix. 16---19.

To promote right conceptions, and a regular study of sanctification, the following RULES must be carefully observed:

I. *The true nature of sanctification, and its manifold ingredients, must be learned with the utmost care and attention*, Prov. xix. 2. Jer. v. 4. Hos. iv. 1, 2, 6. Isa. xxvii. 11. For many, through ignorance of these, take an outward profession, a blameless behaviour among men, formal devotion towards God, or even popish or heathen superstition, for true holiness, Mat. xix. 20. Gal. i. 14. Rom. vii. 9. Phil. iii. 5, 6. Isa. lviii. 2. Mat. xv. 1---9.---The nature and ingredients of sanctification must be learned from the word of God, which is the regulating standard of it,---from the covenant of grace, which provides it for us as a free and gracious privilege,---and from our condition in this world, relative to ourselves, or to our connections with others, Isa. viii. 20. xxxiv. 16. John v. 39. Isa. lv. 3. 2 Sam. xxiii. 5. 1 Pet. v. 8. Eph. vi. 10---20. iv.---vi. Col. iii. iv.

II. *The proper methods of attaining true holiness of nature and practice must be learned with the utmost accuracy and diligence.* For, 1. The law of God, which prescribes and regulates our sanctification in all its matter, manner, and ends, being *spiritual* and *exceeding broad*, is not, in a proper degree, easily understood, Rom. vii. 14. Psalm cxix. 96. And yet it must be wholly attended to, in our pursuing a course of true holiness, James ii. 10. Mat. xxii. 37---40. vii. 12. Tit. ii. 12. 2. By nature we neither know the proper method, nor have any proper ability to study true holiness, Eph. v. 8. ii. 1---3. Rom. viii. 7, 8. v. 6. John xv. 5, 6. vi. 44. 1 Cor. ii. 14. 3. The proper method of sinful men's attaining true holiness can only be learned from the word of God, Rom. ii. 14, 15. 2 Tim. iii. 15---17. John v. 39. Isa. viii. 20. Deut. xii. 32. 4. No adult persons can justly hope to attain true holiness without using proper methods, Acts xxvi. 17, 18. 2 Pet. i. 2---4. Rom. vi. 6, 17, 18. Eph. vi. 10---19. 5. The true method of sanctification of sinful men being one of the great mysteries of religion, is not easily learned, even out of the Scriptures, 1 Tim. iii. 16. 1 Cor. i. 19---24, 30. ii. 14. Psalm cxix. 5, 18. cxliii. 10. 2 Thess. iii. 5. 6. A proper knowledge of the true method of sanctification is exceedingly useful—for establishing our mind in the truths of the gospel, in opposition to error; for, if a doctrine promote universal holiness, it is certainly true, 1 Tim. vi. 3. John xvii. 17, 18. Mat. vii. 15, 16;—and for making us persevere in the study of holiness, Isa. lxiv. 5. 2 Tim. ii. 5, 15. 7. Through their ignorance of the proper method of attaining true holiness, many content themselves with a mere shadow of sanctification, and others even neglect that;—and not a few, after they have begun an apparent earnestness in religion, suddenly stop, and become profane, or even murder themselves.

III. *There can be no proper study of true holiness, without being first in order, furnished with an inward inclination to it,—a real persuasion of our reconciliation with God through the imputed righteousness of Christ,—a well-grounded hope of eternal life— through his obedience and death,—and a cordial belief that God, by his grace, will enable us to perform our duty in an acceptable manner.* I. We must have a fixed and abiding inclination towards holiness of heart and life implanted in us: For, 1. The duties of the law, such as delighting to do God's will,—loving him with our whole heart, soul, mind, and strength,—loving our neighbour as ourselves, &c. cannot be performed without such an inclination, Psalm xl. 8. Mat. xxii. 37, 39. 1 Tim. i. 5. Luke viii. 15. Gal. v. 16, 17, 24. Job xxiii. 12. Psalm xix. 10. xlii. 1, 2. lxiii. 1, 2. lxxxiv. 2. 2. Both Adam and Christ were formed with such an inclination to qualify them for their study of holiness, Eccl. vii. 29. Gen. i. 27. Luke i. 35. Heb. vii. 26. 3. By nature we have no such inclination, but the contrary in us, Mat. xii. 33. xv. 19. Rom. viii. 7, 8. Jer. xvii. 9. 4. All believers find the receipt of this inclination absolutely necessary to their studying holiness, Psalm li. 10. cxix. 36, 37. 5. God not only requires it, but hath promised to bestow it, in order to our practising holiness, Ezek. xxxvi. 26. xi. 19, 20. II. We must be persuaded, on God's own testimony, of our new covenant reconciliation with him as our friend: 1. Adam was created in high favour with God, that he might exercise himself in the study of holiness, Gen. i. 26, 27. ii. 16, 17; and Christ was God's beloved Son, high in his favour, Mat. iii. 17. xvii. 5. Isa. xlii. 1. Col. i. 13. 2. Our conscience, when thoroughly convinced, dictates, that we can do nothing that is spiritually good, unless God, in his free favour, enable us, 1 Cor. xv. 10. 2 Cor. iii. 5. Phil. ii. 12, 13. 1 Thess. v. 23; which he can only do, in consequence of removing his curse, which condemns us to lie under his displeasure and wrath, Gal. iii. 13. Rom. vi. 14. viii. 2. vii. 4, 6. 3. The duties required by the law, cannot be performed without persuasion of our reconciliation to God, Mat. xxii. 37, 39. John iv. 16—19. 4. Our conscience must be purged from dead works to serve the living God, Heb. ix. 12,

OF SANCTIFICATION.

15. x. 1, 2, 4, 14, 17, 22. 1 Tim. i. 5. For, if sin lie on our conscience, it will dispose us to curse God rather than to serve him, Job i. 5. 5. By manifesting himself as reconciled, God ordinarily encourages and excites to holiness, Jer. iii. 14, 22. Hos. xiv. 1—8. Isa. xliv. 22. Ezek. xvi. 62, 63. xxxvi. 25—31. His sacraments of initiation into his service import reconciliation, Gen. xvii. 7—14. Acts ii. 38, 39. God began the publication of his law at Sinai with declarations of his being a reconciled God, Exod. xx. 2, 5, 7, 8, 12. xix. 5, 6. xxiv. 1—8. All the Jewish priests and Levites were admitted into their holy service by sacrifices and washings, which imported reconciliation, Exod. xxix. Lev. viii. ix. Num. viii. Every Jewish day, month, and year began with one or more sacred festivals of reconciliation with God, Num. xxviii. xxix. Lev. xxiii. Our Christian week begins with a sacred festival, and a sacramental feast of reconciliation, Acts xx. 7. John xx. 20, 26. 1 Cor. xi. 23—26. x. 16. 6. Reconciliation with God is represented as the source of all genuine study of gospel-holiness, Eph. iv. 31, 32. v. 1, 2. 1 John ii. 12, 15. Heb. xii. 28. Psalm cxix. 32. cxvi. 16. Luke i. 74, 75. 2 Cor. v. 14, 15, 19. vi. 18. vii. 1. Tit. ii. 11, 12. III. We must have a well-grounded hope of everlasting happiness in the full enjoyment of God, through the imputed righteousness of Christ, as its proper condition and price. 1. The nature of our duty, particularly our love and gratitude to God, require this, 1 John iii. 1—3. iv. 9, 10, 19. 2. Since the fall, God hath always proposed this hope as men's encouragement to holiness, Heb. xii. 1, 2. 2 Cor. iv. 16—18. Heb. x. 34, 35. xi. 26. 1 Cor. xv. 58. Psalm cxix. 166. Tit. ii. 12, 13. 2 Pet. iii. 11, 14, 18. 3. This the more effectually induces to holiness, as our eternal happiness has perfect holiness as its principal ingredient, 1 John iii. 2, 3. Psal. cxix. 166. Hos. xi. 4. IV. We must have a well-grounded persuasion of God's making us able and willing to serve him acceptably. 1. We have no natural ability or willingness to serve him in this manner, Eph. ii. 1. Rom. v. 6. viii. 7, 8. Jer. xvii. 9. 2 Cor. iii. 5. John xv. 5. 2. The study of true holiness is very difficult, and there are many adversaries, Gal. v. 17, 24. Eph. vi. 10—20. Rom. vii. 14—24. viii. 13. Col. iii. v. Mat. xv. 23—28. xvi. 24. xix. 29. 3. God never sent any a warfare on their own charges; neither Adam, Gen. i. 27. Eccl. vii. 29; nor Moses, Exod. iii. iv.; nor Joshua, Josh. i. v. 13, 14; nor the apostles, Mat. xxviii. 20. John xx. 21, 22. Acts i. 8. xxvi. 17, 18; nor Christ, Isa. xlii. 1. xlix. 1, 2. l. 7, 9. lxi. 1. xi. 2. 4. He hath secured ability for, and willingness in the study of holiness for his people, Rom. vi. 13, 14. Eph. vi. 10, 11. 1 John ii. 13, 14. Phil. ii. 12, 13. iv. 13.

IV. All our furniture for the study of gospel-holiness *must be received from the fulness of Christ*, by *spiritual union to* and *fel-*

lowship with him, John xiv. 20. xvii. 22, 23, 26. xv. 4, 5. 1. All the fulness of new-covenant grace is lodged in him, Col. i. 19. ii. 10—13, 19. Eph. i. 3. 1 Cor. i. 30. 2 Cor. i. 20. Psalm lxxii. 17. Gal. ii. 20. 1 John v. 11, 12; and particularly the forementioned furniture, Rom. viii. 14, 15. 2 Cor. v. 17—21. Rom. v. 19, 21. viii. 33—39. Col. i. 27. Zech. x. 12. Isa. xlv. 24. 2. The scripture-emblems of our union with Christ, import that we must live by him, as he does by his Father, John vi. 57; receive life from him as we do sin and death from Adam, Rom. v. 12—21. 1 Cor. xv. 22, 45; receive influences from him, as our body derives its sensation from, and receives its nourishment by, our head, Col. ii. 19. Eph. iv. 16; bring forth good works by him, as a wife does lawful children by her husband, Rom. vii. 4, 6; derive life and nourishment from him, as a branch does from its root, John xv. 4;—and as our body does from its food, John vi. 51—56; and become a spiritual temple in him, as stones are built in connection with their foundation and corner-stone, 1 Pet. ii. 4—6. Eph. ii. 20—22. 3. Christ's end in his incarnation, death, and resurrection, was to form in himself a treasure of holiness, to be imparted to us through union to, and fellowship with him, John i. 14, 16. Phil. iii. 10, 11. 1 Cor. xv. 45—49. Rom. vi. 4—6. He partook of our nature, and became God with us, that we might be made partakers of a divine nature, and be filled with all the fulness of God, Mat. i. 23. Col. ii. 9, 10. 2 Pet. i. 4. Eph. iii. 19. John i. 14, 16. In his life he purchased life for us, Rom. v. 10, 17—19, 21. Dan. ix. 24. In his death he freed himself, and us in him, from the curse of the broken law, and crucified our old man of inward corruption, which derives its strength from it, Rom. vi. 2, 3, 4, 6, 10, 11. Phil. iii. 10, 11. John xii. 24. Isa. liii. 10. In his resurrection, he solemnly took possession of legal, spiritual, and eternal life in our stead, Rom. iv. 25. vi. 4, 5, 10, 11. vii. 4, 6. Eph. ii. 6. Psalm xxi. 4. 4. All sanctifying influences are from the Holy Ghost working upon and in us, only as first resting upon, and abiding in Christ, and taking of the things which are his, and shewing them unto us, Rom. xv. 16. Gal. v. 25, 26. Isa. xi. 2. John i. 32. iii. 34. 1 Cor. xii. 13. Rom. viii. 2, 9, 10. John xvi. 13, 14. Gal. iv. 5, 6.

V. As God's justification of our persons and renovation of our nature must necessarily precede all our study of holiness, *we must receive Christ in all his offices, as offered in the gospel, in order to our beginning and carrying it on.*—In the gospel, Christ and his fulness are brought near, presented, and offered to us, as sinful, indigent, and miserable, Isa. ix. 6. Acts iii. 26. xiii. 26, 34. Rom. xvi. 26, 27. Eph. iii. 8. Hence it is called the ministration of the Spirit, and of righteousness, 2 Cor. iii. 6, 8. Rom. x. 6—8. Gal. iii. 2—5. And, by faith, we do not merely assent to the truth of the gospel, but therein receive Christ, and God in him, as given to us, John i. 12. 1 John v. 11—13. 2 Cor. i. 20. 1 Pet. i. 21. John xiv. 1, and hereby become one with Christ, Gal. ii. 20. Eph. iii. 17. 1 John v. 11—13. John vi. 56. Rom. viii. 1; and are rooted in him, eat his flesh and drink his blood, Col. ii. 6, 7. Gal. iii. 14, 26, 27. Acts xxvi. 18. John vi. 54—57. vii. 37—39, and receive a full salvation as God's free gift in him, Eph. ii. 8, 9. Rom. iii. 24, 25. Acts x. 38, 43. Rom. xi. 6. And faith in this receiving Christ, hath a peculiar fitness for improving him as a foundation, fountain, or root of holy exercises.—It removes the world, as it is an occasion of sin,—a pretended portion for our soul, or as useful in any other but the new covenant channel;—that we may trust and cleave to him, who, by his Spirit, hath entered into our hearts, 1 John v. 4. Gal. vi. 14. Phil. iii. 7—9. Hos. xiv. 3. 2 Chron. xx. 12. Psalm lxxiii. 25, 26, 28. clxiii. 9. lvii. 1. Isa. xxvi. 3, 4. l. 10. Psalm xxv. 1. xxxvii. 5. lv. 22;—and thus derives from him all the furniture necessary for us, Rom. vi. 2, 4, 6. Gal. v. 22, 23. Psalm xxxi. 14. lxv. 3, 4. Isa. xlv. 24, 25. Phil. iv. 13; and prompts our soul to all holy duties, Col. i. 11, 12. 1 John v. 12. ii. 6. iv. 19. iii. 1, 3. 2 Cor. v. 14, 15. Gal. ii. 20.

But here it must be carefully observed, I. That no true holiness can be attained by us in our natural state of separation from Christ. 1. All the furniture necessary for it is conveyed and produced in us by Christ's entrance into our hearts, 1 Cor. i. 30. Eph. ii. 10. iii. 17—19. 2. In our flesh or natural state, we cannot please God, Rom. viii. 8. John iii. 6. Eph. ii. 1—3; but are under sin, guilt, and the curse on account of it, Eph. ii. 3. Rom. viii. 1, 7; and are blinded by, and bond-slaves to Satan, 2 Cor. iv. 3, 4. 2 Tim. ii. 26. 3. In order to promote the study and practice of holiness, our whole state of person and nature must be changed. We must be renewed, born again, created in Christ, Eph. iv. 21—24. ii. 10. Rom. xiii. 14. Col. iii. 10, 11. ii. 10, 11, 12. 2 Cor. v. 17—21. Gal. vi. 15. Christ did not die for us, to rectify our natural state, but to remove it; nor to rectify our old man, but to crucify and destroy it, Gal. iii. 13. iv. 4, 5. Rom. vi. 2, 6, 10, 11, 14. vii. 4, 6. Gal. v. 24. And it is his being in us, that delivers us from our reprobate or unregenerate state, 2 Cor. xiii. 5. 4. The gospel is preached to unbelievers to awaken and raise them out of their natural state, and to make them *new men*, perfect in Christ, Col. i. 28. 2 Cor. iii. 6. x. 4, 5. John v. 25. 1 Thess. i. 5, 6; even as Christ's addresses to the dead or diseased, tended to bring them out of that condition, Mark v. 41. John xi. 43, 44. Mat. ix. 6. Mark iii. 5. II. All attempts of men to perform sincere obedience, in order to be a foundation of their right to salvation, or of their trust in Christ, are most legal and wicked. 1. They are plainly condemned by the Spirit of God, Rom. ix. 31, 32. Gal. v. 2, 4. ii. 21. Luke xviii. 11—13. 2. Salvation by the grace of God is directly contrary to every form of attaining it by our own works, Gal. iii. 12. v. 2, 4. ii. 16, 19. Rom. iv. 4, 5. x. 3—8. xi. 6. 3. God never intended his gospel to dishonour his law, by offering to it our works, which are but as filthy rags,—but to establish and exalt it by a complete and transcendently glorious fulfilment, Gal. iv. 4, 5. iii. 10—14. Mat. iii. 15. v. 17, 18, 19. Rom. iii. 21—27, 31. iv. 5. viii. 3, 4. x. 4. Isa. xlii. 21. 2 Cor. v. 21. 2 Pet. i. 1. 4. All performance of good works, in order to recommend us to God's favour, or to give us a right to Christ, is contrary to his execution of his saving offices,—as we would be in part saved before we were connected with him, Rom. x. 3. Gal. v. 2, 4. ii. 21. Mat. ix. 13. xviii. 11. III. All attempts to perform holy duties, in order to recommend our persons to God's favour, or to procure a right to salvation, instead of making us more holy before God, render us much worse. 1. The law, as a covenant, was never given since the fall, that men might obey it, but to convince them of sin, and drive them to Christ, Rom. v. 20. Gal. iii. 24. 2. The law, as a broken covenant, allows men no life, no strength for obedience, but is the ministration of death, irritating and strengthening sin, Ezek. xviii. 4. 2 Cor. iii. 6—14. Rom. x. 5. vii. 5, 7—13. 1 Cor. xv. 56. 3. Hence all attempts to obey it in this form, do but fasten the curse upon us, which blasts our knowledge, and all the means of grace and holiness which we enjoy, Gal. iii. 10. Rom. ix. 31, 32. xi. 8, 10. 4. All such attempts toward holiness labour to make Christ's atonement contemptible, useless, and sinful, Rom. x. 3; and exclude all his saving influences from us, Gal. ii. 21. v. 2, 4. Rom. ix. 30—32. Mat. ix. 13. Luke xix. 10; and render the promises of the new covenant of no effect, Rom. iv. 14;—and are but the working of our inward enmity against God, Rom. viii. 7.

VI. To promote the study of true holiness, we,—*depending on no change of our nature or practice, as our warrant and ground of right,—as sinful and wretched* men, *must unite* with Jesus Christ, as made of God to us, in the gospel-offer, wisdom and righteousness, and sanctification and redemption. 1. Till we be united with him, we are under the law, which is the strength of sin, and excludes all the above-mentioned preparations for the study of gospel-holiness, Rom. vii. 4. 1 Cor. xv. 56. Gal. iii. 10. 2. Christ never requires holiness to warrant our receiving him in the gospel, but invites men, the very worst not excepted, but rather particularly called, to come *directly* to him, *as they are,* for whatever wisdom, righteousness, sanctification, and redemption they need, Prov. xxiii. 26. i. 20—23. viii. 4. ix. 4, 5, 6. Isa. i. 18. xlvi. 12. lv. 1—7. Jer. iii. 1, 4, 13, 14, 22. Mat. xi. 28. ix. 13. 2 Cor. v. 19, 20. 1 Tim. i. 15. Rev. xxii. 17. iii. 17. No true repentance is ever required as our qualification warranting us to receive Christ as our Saviour; for it is a turning to God through him as our way, Hos. xiv. 1. Isa. xliv. 22.—Nor willing subjection to God's law; for that proceeds from our deliverance by Christ, Psalm cxvi. 16. Luke i. 74, 75.—Nor humiliation for sin; for that is the fruit of God's application of Christ to us, Ezek. xxxvi. 25, 31. Phil. iii. 7—9.—Nor purity of heart; for that is produced by faith coming to Christ, Acts xv. 9.—Nor love to God; for that must proceed from his loving us, and washing our consciences in Christ's blood, 1 John iv. 19. 1 Tim. i. 5.—Nor filial fear of God; as that must proceed from our having received the kingdom, Heb. xii. 28.—Nor prayer, as a good work; as that proceeds from believing on Christ, Rom. x. 14. Heb. xiii. 10, 15. —Nor forgiving others the injuries which they have done us; as that is a fruit of God's Spirit in us, and of his forgiving our sins in Christ, Eph. iv. 30—32.——All these proceed from faith, which is the first habit and work in order of nature, John vi. 29. Gal. v. 6. Rom. xiv. 23.—Nor is regeneration our warrant or ground of right to receive Christ, as it is effected in him, Eph. ii. 10. 1 Cor. iv. 15. 3. If we could attain any true holiness or virtue before our union to Christ, it would infallibly exclude us from all warrant and access to believe in him, and demonstrate that we were none of those LOST SINNERS whom he came to seek and save, or calls to himself, Luke xix. 10. Mat. xviii. 11. ix. 12, 13. 1 Tim. i. 15. Isa. lv. 7.

VII. *Gospel-holiness must be earnestly sought after by faith, as a necessary and principal part of our salvation,—enjoyed in consequence of our union with Christ, justification by his blood, and reception of his Spirit.* It must be *earnestly* sought after, as it is of great importance, as a necessary mark of our union with Christ, and pledge of, and preparation for our being eternally with him, 1 Cor. i. 30. John xiii. 8. Rom. viii. 1—4. Heb. xii. 14. 2 Pet. iii. 11, 14, 18. i. 3—10. Tit. ii. 11—14. Rev. xxii. 14; and wherever true faith is, it works by love, and pants after progress in holiness, Gal. v. 6. Psal. cxliii. 10. li. 10. cxix. 5, 11. Jer. xxxi. 18. Rom. vii. 14—24.——It must be earnestly sought after, as a *necessary part of salvation*, Matth. i. 21. Tit. iii. 5. Eph. ii. 10. Gal. v. 10, 14. Rom. vii. 4, 6. xi. 26. It is to be sought after in *due order*, consequential to our spiritual union with Christ, justification by his imputed righteousness, and receiving his sanctifying Spirit, John xv. 4, 5. Heb. ix. 14. Gal. v. 18, 25.

OF SANCTIFICATION.

VIII. *Not only at first, but as long as we live on earth, we must always receive the comforts of the gospel, in order to qualify us for obeying the law, as a rule of life.* 1. The necessity of the fourfold furniture for the practice of holiness requires this. 2. Spiritual peace, joy, and hope, are an effectual source of good works, and slavish fear and oppressive grief are an hindrance of them, Psalm iv. 7, 8. 1 Thess. v. 23. Neh. viii. 10. 1 John iii. 3. iv. 18. Psal. cxvi. 16. cxix. 32, 166. Amos iii. 3. Luke i. 75. 3. The Holy Ghost establishes men in every good word and work, by comforting them, 2 Thess. ii. 16, 17. Rom. v. 17—21. vi. 1, 2, 10, 11, 12, 14. vii. 4, 6. viii. 1, 2, 9, 11, 13. Eph. iv. 30—32. v. vi. 2 Cor. v. 14—21. vi. 1, 18. vii. 1, 11. Col. iii. 1—4. Heb. xiii. 5.—And they that are under deep convictions and tormenting fears, have special need of such comfort to strengthen them for holy duties, Luke x. 5. Acts ii. 37—39. iii. 26. v. 31. xiii. 26, 34, 38, 39. xvi. 30, 31. 4. Without such continued comforts, we cannot delight in God, devote ourselves wholly to him, cast all our cares and burdens upon him, deny ourselves, or suffer torture or death for his sake, Mat. xvi. 24. xix. 29. 5. It is God's ordinary method to prepare his servants for their work by proper comforts; as Adam, Gen. ii; David, Psal. cxvi. 16. cxix. 32—166; the Hebrews, Hos. xi. 4; the Christians at Antioch, Acts xiii. 47, 48, and of Thessalonica, 1 Thess. i. 4—6; nay, Christ, Psalm xvi. 8, 9. Isa. xlii. 1—7. xlix. 1, 2. Matth. iii. 16, 17. xvii. 1—5. 6. All attempts to practise holiness in any other form, method, or order, are heartless and burdensome, and so not scriptural, Mal. i. 13. iii. 14. Isa. lviii. 3. Amos viii. 5. Luke ii. 10, 11. John xiv. 16, 17. xv. 11. Isa. lxiv. 5. Prov. iii. 13—18.

IX. *In order to promote our study of true holiness, we must receive these comforts of the gospel, in Christ, by an assured faith in the declarations and promises of it, as offering and giving him, and all his blessings of salvation in him, to us in particular,* Rom. ix. 25, 26. 1 John v. 11—13. 1 Cor. i. 30. 1. Though it be not absolutely necessary that we should have a sensible assurance that we actually possess Christ and his salvation, yet, without a real hearty persuasion of the faithfulness of God, in his giving the promises of the gospel, there can be no receiving or improving Christ, for the purification of our nature and life, Gal. ii. 20. v. 6, 24, 25. Nor can any spiritual doubts or fears be removed, while endeavours after an assured acting of faith on the gospel of God are neglected. 2. Those saints who have most firmly believed the declarations, offers, and promises of God in the gospel, have been most eminent in holiness: as Job, Job xiii. 15. i. 1, 21, 22. ii. 3; Abraham, Isaac, and Jacob, Heb. xi. 8—21; Moses, Heb. iii. 2, 5. xi. 24—29; David, Psalm xviii. 1—3, 23. Acts xiii. 22, 36; and the apostles and primitive Christians, Rom. viii. 15, 38, 39. Gal. iv. 6. 1 Thess. i. 5, 6. Heb. x. 32—34.

X. *In order that our fellowship with Christ in his comforts and grace, and our study of gospel-holiness by means of it, may be begun, continued, and more and more increased, we ought, with great diligence, to exercise this assured faith in a right manner, and to abound in it more and more.* I. We must act this assured faith *with great diligence and earnestness.* 1. The scope of the gospel is to encourage such diligence, Rom. i. 5. 2 Tim. iii. 15. Rom. x. 4. xv. 4. John xx. 31. 2. Even the slothful exercise or indulgence of unbelief, is most criminal and dangerous, Heb. x. 29, 31. John iii. 18, 36. 2 Thess. i. 7—9. 3. All acting of true faith requires almighty power on God's side, and diligent labour on ours, Heb. iv. 11. vi. 11, 12. Eph. i. 17—19. iii. 16—19. 4. Though we cannot truly believe of ourselves, yet it is our indispensible duty; and the Holy Ghost works faith in us, by stirring us up to essay believing, Phil. ii. 12, 13. Rom. x. 17. And, as we know not when he may work it in us, we ought always to be attempting to believe, as our duty, John iii. 8. 1 Chron. xxii. 16. Psalm cx. 3. 5. Though none but elect men truly believe the gospel,—every hearer of it ought to believe it, with application to himself. Nor can any know their election, but by their receiving Jesus Christ for the sanctification of their nature and lives, John iii. 6. vi. 37, 40. Psalm cvi. 4, 5. cx. 3. II. We must thus diligently believe the declarations and promises of the gospel *without delay,* as it is infinitely wicked and dangerous to continue in unbelief and unholiness, so much as a moment, Prov. xxvii. 1. Heb. iii. 7, 8, 12, 15. vi. 18. 2 Cor. vi. 2. Psalm cxix. 59, 60. xviii. 44. III. We must act this assured faith in a *right manner.* It must be faith unfeigned and lively, 1 Tim. i. 5. James ii. 14, 19, 26. It must be complete, including a persuasion founded upon God's infallible testimony, that we are altogether guilty, polluted, miserable, and self-irrecoverable, Rom. iii. 19, 20. Gal. ii. 16. John xvi. 9—11; that Christ and his salvation are infinitely excellent, sufficient, and suitable for us, John i. 14. iii. 16. vi. 33, 34, 68, 69. Phil. iii. 8, 9. 1 John i. 7, 9. Heb. vii. 25. Psalm lxxxix. 19, 20. 1 Tim. i. 15. 1 Cor. vi. 9—11. Isa. xxviii. 16. Matth. ix. 13. xii. 31. 1 Pet. ii. 4, 7; that God's free and full promises and offers of him and it, are only and infinitely suited to our case, Acts iv. 12. John xiv. 6. x. 7, 9. Jer. ii. 13, 22, 23. iii. 23. xvi. 19.——Rom. ix. 30—32. Luke xix. 10. 1 Tim. i. 15. 2 Cor. vi. 2. Rom. iv. 5, 25;—and that he requires us to believe them with particular application to ourselves, 1 John iii. 23. Mark x. 49. Matth. xxiii. 37. Rev. xxii. 17. Isa. lv. 1—7. Ezek. xxxiii. 11;—and our cordial reception of Christ and all his salvation in them, as

God's free gifts to us sinful men. Isa. lv. 1, 2, 3, 7; and trusting that he, and his Father and Spirit, will act towards us, according to their new-covenant characters and promises, 2 Tim. i. 12. Heb. x 22. vi. 18, 19. x. 35. Rom. ix. 33. Isa. xxviii. 16. IV. We must not only continue, but *more and more abound* in the diligent exercise of this assured faith, Col. i. 23. ii. 6, 7. Heb. iii. 6, 14. x. 35. Phil. iii. 12—14; —as the mean of further victory over our spiritual enemies, and growth in holiness by received influences from Christ, Exod. xvii. 11. 1 Pet. i. 5. Eph. vi 10—20. Zech. x. 12. xii. 10. 1 John ii. 1, 2. Luke xxii. 32. Col. ii 6, 7, 19. Eph. iii. 16. John i. 16.

XI We must act this assured faith *only in a manner suited to our state of union with Christ, in order to promote holiness according to it, and not at all according to our legal or natural state.* For true holiness is a *walking*, a *warring*, a *living by faith,* 2 Cor. v. 7. Gal. v. 6. 1 John v. 4. Eph. vi. 16. 2 Cor. x. 3 Hab. ii. 4. Gal. ii. 20; a walking in Christ, Col. ii 6, 7. 1 Pet. iii. 16. Phil. iii. 10—14; a walking by grace, 2 Tim. ii. 1. 2 Cor. i. 12. 1 Cor xv. 10. Heb. xii. 28; a walking in, or after the Spirit, Rom. viii. 1, 4. Gal. v. 18, 24, 25; and a putting off the old man, and putting on the new, Eph. iv. 21—24. Col. iii. 9, 10.—We must therefore, 1. Live always under a deep sense of the remaining corruption of our nature and practice, Mark ix. 24. Eph. iv. 13. 1 Cor. iii. 1 Phil. iii. 8—14. Gal. v. 5. Rom. viii. 9, 13. vii. 14—25. 2. Never satisfy ourselves with a trusting in Christ's grace to assist our endeavours; but, wholly distrusting our own strength and best meant endeavours, we must trust in him alone to perform in and for us every thing necessary for his honour and our happiness, Isa. xxvi. 12. xl. 11. xlvi. 3, 4 lxiii. 9. Psalm lvii. 2. Rom. viii. 26, 37. Gal. ii. 20. v. 24, 25. 1 Thess. v. 23, 24. 2 Thess. ii. 16, 17. 3. Never perform any duty,—in order to obtain God's judicial pardon of our sin, favour, or title to eternal life; but as persons already pardoned, accepted, and entitled to eternal life, and possessed of his Spirit and gospel-comforts, Rom. vii. 4. vi. 14. Gal. v. 18. iii. 2, 3. iv. 6. Col. ii. 10, 19. Eph. iv. 16 4. No consideration of God's perfections, or authority over us, or of the happiness of heaven, or torments of hell, must make us immediately apply to any particular duty, without, first in order, applying Christ and his grace to our soul, Zech. x. 12. 2 Tim. ii. 1. Eph. vi. 10. Psalm lvii. 2. Tit. ii. 14. iii. 8, 14. Heb. xii. 28. Ezek. xxvi. 27. 5. The solid hopes of an everlasting enjoyment of Christ, and of God in him, must excite and strengthen us for every holy exercise, Psalm xvi. 8—11. xvii. 15. lxxiii. 24—28. Rom. vi. 4, 6, 11, 12. viii. 17, 18. 2 Cor. iv. 16—18. 1 John iii. 1—3. 6. Such benefits of the new covenant as most excite love to

God or men,---striving against sin,---diligence in holy duties,---familiarity with and trust in God,---patience under afflictions,---cordial repentance of sin,---or the like, must be peculiarly improved for that purpose, 1 John iv. 18, 19. i. 3. 1 Cor. vi. 11, 15, 19. Gal. v. 25. Eph. ii. 10. 1 Thess. v. 14---24. Rom. v. vi. Col. iii. 1---5. Phil. iii. 12---14. i. 23, 24. Heb. x. 19---25. 1 Pet. v. 7. Psal. lv. 22. lxxxiv. 11, 12. 2 Cor. iv. 16---18. xii. 8, 9, 10. 1 Cor. x. 13. vi. 19, 20. 1 John i. 7, 9. Tit. ii. 11---14. Heb. xii. 28.

XII. *We must diligently attend upon, and improve every gospel ordinance answerable to our condition,—agreeably to our new-covenant state, that we may therein have fellowship with Christ in his blood and Spirit for the sanctification of our nature and lives,* —particularly reading and hearing God's word, self-examination, meditation, prayer, singing of psalms, receiving the sacraments, fasting, vows, church-fellowship, and Christian conference, John v. 39. Acts xvii. 11. Isa. lv. 3. 2 Cor. xiii. 5. Zeph. ii. 1. Psalm i. 2. cv. 5. cxix. 11, 97. John xvi. 23, 24. Matth. vi. 1—13. Col. iii. 16. Eph. v. 19. Matth. xxviii. 19. 1 Cor. x. 16, 17. xi. 23—29. Mat. ix. 15. vi. 14—17. Psalm lxxvi. 11. cxix. 106. Heb. x. 25. Psalm lxxxvii. 1, 2. Mal. iii. 16. Luke xxiv. 23. Song v. vi.

XIII. For our excitement to such earnest and evangelical study of holiness, we ought *carefully to consider and thoroughly to understand the peculiar excellency and advantage of this method.* 1. It exalts all the perfections of God, and all the offices and relations of Christ, 1 Pet. iv. 11. Col. iii. 3, 4, 11. ii. 10, 19. Heb. xiii. 7, 8. 2. It perfectly corresponds with all the scriptural doctrines of original sin, particular election and redemption, union with Christ, justification by his blood, adoption into his family, and the infallible perseverance of his saints, &c. 3. While it alone produces real holiness of heart and life, Isa. l. 10, 11,—it is most delightful and honourable, the easy, plain, peaceful, love-paved, pleasant, costly, but free and highly exalted path, in which, in an high state of union with Christ and favour with God, we walk familiarly with him, as his friends, children, and spouse, to everlasting perfection and glory, Jer. vi. 16. Prov. iii. 17. Isa. xxxv. 8—11.

REFLECT. But am I thus renewed in the spirit of my mind?—thus sanctified wholly in soul, body, and spirit, by the faithful God of peace? Are those promised *graces*, Christian *tempers*, spiritual *lustings* against the flesh, those holy and virtuous *exercises*, produced by the influence of his Spirit, to be found in me?—Are those evangelical *rules* hid in my heart and practised in my life, that I may not sin against him? No where are divine direction and influence, and distinct experience, more necessary than in studying and preaching the doctrine and duty of sanctification, and no where do multitudes of preachers more miserably err and mislead than here.

CHAP. V.

Of SPIRITUAL CONSOLATION, *including the infallible Conservation and Perseverance of Saints;—Indwelling of the Holy Ghost as an Almighty Comforter;—Assurance of God's love and friendship;—Peace of conscience;—and Joy in the Holy Ghost.*

I. GOD's infallible CONSERVATION of his saints in their gracious state and course, and their PERSEVERANCE which proceeds from it, are not formally included in their spiritual consolation, but are an immediate principal ground of it.— Through the power and subtlety of their indwelling corruption and its assistants, believers, if left by God to themselves, would soon fall from all their possession and exercise of grace, and they often do fall into fearful degrees and acts of sin. But being kept by God in Christ, they can never in the least fall from their *happy state* of union with Christ, or of justification and adoption through him; nor can they fall totally or finally from the possession and exercise of spiritual life or saving grace. 1. Scripture represents them as firmly *established;* as an *everlasting foundation;* as *unmoveable* like mount Zion; as a *rock* or *house built on a rock;* as God's *jewels,* which shall not be lost; as a *spring whose waters fail not;* as *trees which shall never wither,* &c. Prov. x. 25. Psalm cxxv. 1, 2. Matth. vii. 24, 25. xvi. 18. Mal. iii. 17. Isa. lviii. 11. lxi. 3. Jer. xvii. 8. Psalm xxxvii. 24. 1 John ii. 17, 19. iii. 9. 2. Many infallible promises of God secure their conservation and perseverance in their gracious state and exercise, Deut. xxxi. 8. Heb. xiii. 5. Isa. xlv. 17. xlvi. 4. liv. 8—10. lix. 21. Jer. xxxii. 39, 40. Hos. ii. 19, 20. John x. 27—29. Psalm xxxvii. 24, 28, 33, 37. xcii. 13, 14. xciv. 14. 3. Many scriptures expressly affirm that they are all infallibly preserved and persevere in their state and exercise of grace, Job xvii. 9. Prov. iv. 18. Psalm lxxxiv. 7. Phil. i. 6. 1 Thess. v. 23, 24. 2 Thess. iii. 3. ii. 16, 17. Col. iii. 3, 4. John vi. 35, 39, 40. xvii. 9, 12, 24. Rom. viii. 28—39. xi. 2, 29. 1 Cor. i. 8, 9. x. 13. 1 John ii. 19. Heb. x. 38, 39. 4. Their total or final fall from their state and exercise of grace is altogether inconsistent with the perfections of God. For, how can he, who is unchangeable, hate those whom he once loved with an everlasting love? Jer.

xxi. 3. John xiii. 1. How can he, who is infinitely just, demand full satisfaction for their sins from Christ, and yet punish them for ever in hell, Job xxxiii. 24. Tit. ii. 14. Rom. iii. 24—26. Gal. iii. 13, 14. 1 Pet. i. 18, 19. ii. 24. iii. 18? How can he, who is infinitely wise and powerful, begin an important work without being able and willing to finish it, Luke xiv 28—30. Phil. i. 6. 2 Thess. i. 11, 12. 1 Pet. i. 5? How can he, who is infinitely faithful, engage himself by promise and oath to do that which he is either unable or unwilling to perform, Num. xxiii. 19. Tit. i. 2. 1 Sam. xv. 29. 1 Thess. v. 24. 1 Cor. i. 9. Heb. x. 23. vi. 14—18. Deut. xxxiii. 27—29. 5. Believers' total or final fall from the state or exercise of grace is perfectly inconsistent with God's unchangeable purpose and new-covenant love to Christ as Mediator, and to them in him, Isa. xlvi. 10. xiv. 24, 27. Psalm xxxiii. 11. Prov. xix. 21. 2 Tim. i. 10. 1 Thess. v. 8, 9. Heb. vi. 17, 18. Rom. viii. 28—30. ix. 11. xi. 29. Isa. liii. 10—12. Psalm xxii. 27—31. lxxxix. 4, 28—35 6. Believers' total or final fall from their state or exercise of grace is absolutely inconsistent with all the honour and new-covenant characters of all the persons in the Godhead. It is inconsistent with the honour of the Father, as the chooser of them,—and giver of them to Christ for a reward of his mediatorial obedience unto death, Rom. viii. 29. John xvii. 6. Psalm ii. 8. Isa. liii. 10— 12. 1 Cor. vi. 19, 20. 1 Pet. i. 18, 19. Rom. v. 9, 10. viii. 32. Rev. v. 9;—or, as their steady friend, Isa. liv. 8—10 Jer. xxxii. 40. Zeph. iii. 17;—and their almighty preserver and safe-guard, John x. 29. 1 Pet i. 5. Col. iii. 3. Psalm xci. Deut. xxxiii. 26—29.—— It is inconsistent with the honour of the Son, who with his blood redeemed and purchased them, Tit. ii. 14. 1 Pet. i. 19. Rom. v. 9, 10. Rev. v. 9. Matth. xx. 28. 1 Cor. vi. 19, 20. 1 Tim. ii. 6. 1 Thess. v. 9, 10;—who, as their advocate, continually intercedes for them, 1 John ii. 1, 2 John xvii. 11, 15, 20, 24. Psalm ii. 8. xxi. 4. John xi. 42. Heb. vii. 25;—who builds them up together, as a church or temple for himself, Heb. iii. 3, 6 Matth. xvi. 18; and is in them as their life and hope of glory, Gal. ii. 20. John xiv. 19. Rev. i. 18. Col iii. 3, 4 i. 27;—and who is their Head, Husband, King, Shepherd, &c. Col. i. 18. ii. 19. Eph. iv. 16. Isa. liv. 5. lxii. 4, 5. Hos. ii. 19, 20. 2 Cor. xi. 2. Isa. xxxiii. 22. Psalm ii. 6. xxiii. 1. John x. 1 Pet. ii. 25. v. 4. Heb. xiii. 20. Isa. xl. 11. Ezek. xxxvii. 24—28,—to suffer them to be ruined and damned.—— It is inconsistent with the honour of the Holy Ghost, who dwells in them as a comforter, John xiv. 16, 17. Rom. xi. 29. 1 John ii. 27;—as a perpetual fountain of quickening influence, John iv. 14 Rom. viii. 2, 10. John xiv. 19;—as an almighty worker of goodness, Eph. v. 9.

i. 17—19. ii. 21, 22;—as an anointing and earnest, 1 John ii. 20, 27. 2 Cor. i. 21, 22; and as a seal, confirming them to eternal happiness, Eph. i. 13. iv. 30. 2 Cor. i. 22. v. 5. 7. Believers' total or final fall from their state or exercise of grace, is inconsistent with the nature of their implanted graces, which are *incorruptible seed*, 1 Pet. i. 23; the *Seed of God*, which *abideth* in them, 1 John iii. 9; their faith crucifies the flesh, Gal. v. 24, and overcomes the world, 1 John v. 54; and fails not, Luke xxii. 32. 1 Cor. xiii. 13; their hope makes not ashamed, Rom. v. 5. viii. 24. Heb. vi 18, 19, and their love never fails, 1 Cor. xiii. 8, 13. But this infallibility of their graces arises wholly from their connection with Christ and his Spirit.

OBJEC. I. " Many Scripture texts plainly suppose that be-
" lievers may fall totally and finally from their state and exer-
" cise of grace; and therefore warn them to watch against it, or
" promise great rewards to their perseverance, Psalm cxxv. 3.
" Ezek. xviii. 24, 26. xxxiii. 12—19. Mat. v. 13. xxiv. 13.
" Rom. xiv. 15. 1 Cor. viii. 11. ix. 27. x. 12. 2 Cor. vi. 1. xi.
" 3. Heb. xii. 12, 13, 16. x. 38. Jude 12, 21. Rev. ii. 7, 11, 17,
" 26. iii. 5, 12, 21. Gal. vi. 9. 2 Pet. i. 4—11." ANSW. 1. Mere supposition of righteous men's falling from their righteousness does not prove that they can do so, as is most evident from the Hebrew form of the oaths of God mentioned in Scripture, Psal. lxxxix. 35. Amos viii. 7. 2. Such as are but apparently holy, may, and often do lose all their appearances of it, and become profane, Mat. xiii. 21, 22. 2 Kings xii. 3. Believers may lose much of their gracious dispositions and practices, and fall into fearful sins and chastisements; and might wholly fall from their grace, if God did not keep them. 4. Our watching over ourselves, and against temptations, is one blessed mean, by which Christ and his Spirit preserve us in our gracious dispositions and exercises, Eph. vi. 10—19. 1 Pet. v. 8. Mark xiv. 38. 1 Cor. xvi. 13.

OBJEC. II. " Some very eminent saints, as David, Solomon,
" Peter, Alexander, Hymeneus, Demas, &c. actually fell from
" their state and exercise of grace, 2 Sam. xi. 1 Kings xi. Mat.
" xxvi. 69—74. 1 Tim. i. 19, 20. 2 Tim. ii. 17, 18. iv. 10.
" Heb. vi. 4, 5. x. 26—30, 38. 2 Pet. ii. 20—22." ANSW. 1. David's fall was not *total;* for God's Spirit remained with him, Psalm li. 11: nor Solomon's; for God's mercy departed not from him, 2 Sam. xii. 24; and his *Ecclesiastes* manifests his repentance, chap. ii. 10, 11, 17. v. 10, 12. vii. 2, 3, 26, 27: nor Peter's; for his faith failed not, Luke xxii. 32. 2. There is no proof that Alexander, Hymeneus, Demas, &c. ever had any real grace more than Judas, John vi. 70. Mat. vii. 22, 23.

OBJEC. III. " The pretence of believers' unfailing perseve-
" rance in grace encourages them to sin, particularly in the
" manner of Noah, Abraham, Jacob, Aaron, David, Solomon,
" Samson, Peter, and other saints." ANSW. 1. The sinful falls
of saints are not recorded in Scripture for our imitation, but for
our warning to take heed to ourselves, to watch against, and
resist temptations. 2. Such as merely imagine themselves saints,
often improve the grace of God into licentiousness; but a truly
regenerated heart cannot but improve grace received and secured, as a powerful excitement to holiness, Phil. ii. 13. Rom.
vi. 1, 2, 12. 2 Cor. vi. 16, 18. vii. 1. 1 Pet. i. 3, 5, 13, 15.
1 John iii. 2, 3. Psalm cxix. 32, 166. cxvi. 16. Luke i. 74, 75.
Heb. xii. 28. Astonishing! Because the love of Christ firmly
believed constrains men to holiness, must their belief of its unchangeable and eternal duration induce them to wickedness?
2 Cor. v. 14, 15.—Because true faith *purifies* the heart, Acts
xv. 9, must the infallible continuance of it *pollute* the heart?—
Because evangelical hope of everlasting happiness makes men to
purify themselves as God is pure, 1 John iii. 3, must the firm
continuance of it prompt them to render themselves worse than
devils?——Can a man who has any real experience of God's
grace in his soul, believe that the new nature formed by and
like to the Spirit of Christ, John iii. 5, 6, is so very *superdevilish*,
that God's powerful discoveries and applications of the exceeding riches of his redeeming grace will encourage it to outrageous rebellion against him?—Even in natural things, do mothers
holding, assisting, and teaching their children to walk, encourage them to stumble and break their necks? Or, do the ledges
of bridges, or battlements of houses, encourage them that walk
along to leap over and drown themselves, or dash themselves
to pieces?

OBJEC. IV. " God's infinite holiness cannot permit him to as-
" sure men of everlasting favour and happiness, notwithstand-
" ing their falls into sin, as that would weaken and invalidate
" all his calls to the study of holiness." ANSW. 1. God himself
hath repeatedly declared the contrary, Psalm lxxxix. 28---35.
Isa. liv. 8---10. lvii. 17, 18. Heb. xii. 5---11, 28. Rom. viii.
28---39. v. 21. vi. 1. 2 Cor. vi. 18. vii. 1. 2. Not our good behaviour, but the surety righteousness of Christ, is the new covenant foundation of our everlasting friendship with God, and
happiness in the full enjoyment of him, 1 John i. 7, 9. ii. 1, 2.
Rev. v. 9, 10. Rom. v. 10, 16---21. Heb. ix. 14. x. 14.

II. The indwelling of the Holy Ghost as an almighty COM-
FORTER. He dwells in the heart of believers, not only in his
influences, but primarily *in his person*, Ezek. xxxvi. 27. Gal. iv.
6. Rom. viii. 9. John xiv. 17. 1 Cor. iii. 16, 17. vi. 19. 2 Tim.

i. 14. Being infinite, and every where present, he can, at once, personally dwell in all the saints in heaven and on earth, all of whom are united to Christ, in whom he primarily dwells, as members of his one mystical body.---In the character of a Comforter, 1. He kindly explains, and by his word manifests to believers the things freely given them of God,---the excellency, fitness, and encouraging characters and blessings of Christ, that with delight they may discern and contemplate the mysteries of the gospel, John xiv. 26. xv. 26. xvi. 13, 14. Mat. xiii. 11. 1 Cor. ii. 10, 12, 15. Psalm xix. 7—10. cxix. 72, 103, 126, 162. Jer. xv. 16. Song v. 10—16 2. He *seals* them up to the day of redemption, bestowing upon them such communications of divine light, purity, life, righteousness, peace, and joy, as mark them his peculiar people, whom he will preserve inviolable for himself,—and certify them of their saving interest in the promises of eternal life, Eph. i. 13, 14. iv. 30. 2 Cor. i. 21, 22. 3. He is the *earnest* of their eternal inheritance, which renders them certain of obtaining it in due time, and gives them pleasant foretastes of it, Eph. i. 14. 2 Cor. i. 22. v. 5. Rom. viii. 23. This includes his shedding abroad the love of God in their hearts,— his attesting the pardon of their sin, and what God is to them, has done, and will do for and in them, Rom. v. 5; and his giving them delightful fellowship with Christ as their *bridegroom* and *hidden manna*, Song ii. 3—5. Rev. ii. 17. 4. To their great comfort, and through their exercise of faith and repentance, he treads Satan and their indwelling corruptions under their feet, Rom. xvi. 20. vii. 25. viii. 2, 13. Mic. vii. 19. 5. As an Intercessor within them, he encourages, directs, and enables them to proper familiarity, distinctness, and earnestness in their prayers to God, Rom. viii. 15, 26, 27. Isa. lxiii. 16. lxiv. 8. Job xxxiv. 36. Jer. iii. 4, 19, 22. Gal. iv. 6. 6. He bears witness with their spirits, that they are the children of God: And herein, 1. He enables them to render their being *such* more evident, by their renewed, lively, and vigorous application of the promises of the gospel to their own souls, 1 Tim. i. 15. Jer. iii. 22. Psalm xxxi. 14. cxlii. 4, 5. Lam. iii. 24. Zech. xiii. 9. 2. He sometimes elucidates some former manifestation of Christ, and shews it to have been true and saving, John xv. 26. xiv. 26. Ezek. xliii. 1—3. 3. He assists them in their examination of their state and experience,—directs them to proper marks of grace, such as likeness to God, purity of heart, poverty of spirit, love to Christ, and to every person and thing bearing his image, Eph. iv. 24. v. 1, 2. Mat. v. 3, 8, 44—48. Isa. lxiv. 6. 1 Kings viii. 38. 1 John iv. 19, 20. iii. 14. Psalm lxxxiv. 1, 2, 10. xxvi. 8;—shines on these marks of grace, that they may truly understand them, 1 Cor. ii. 12;—invigorates their inward graces, and renders them discernible amidst all the remains of corruption, 1 John iii. 14, 22, 24. 2 Cor. i. 12. Phil. iii. 3;—and enables their consciences to compare their qualities and exercises with the marks of grace established in Scripture, Rom. viii. 16. 1 John iii. 20, 21. 4. He confirms their persuasion of the reality of their grace, by a new application of some gospel promise to their heart, Exod. xx. 2. Psalm l. 7. lxxxi. 10. Isa. liv. 5, 6. Jer. iii. 19, 14, 22. xxxi. 3. Hos. xiv. 1. Zech. xiii. 9. Mal. iii. 17. 2 Cor. vi. 18. And the majestic, powerful, self-debasing, sanctifying, and love-kindling influences which attend his declarations, mark them truly divine, John xiv. 17. x. 4. Job xlii. 5, 6. Song ii. 8—15. viii. 6, 7.

III. Sensible ASSURANCE of God's love is a well-grounded persuasion that we are in a state of favour with him, and that therefore he, according to his promises and new-covenant characters, has, and certainly will exert all his perfections for advancing our real and everlasting felicity in Christ. This assurance of sense greatly differs from that which is included in the very nature of faith. The foundation of *that* assurance of faith is wholly without us in the faithfulness of God pledged in his word. The foundation of *this* assurance of sense is partly within us, in the gracious effects of God's word and Spirit upon our heart. By *that* we are persuaded of the truth of God's revealed declarations, particularly in his offering Christ to us in the gospel. By *this* we are certified that the work of God begun upon our soul is truly gracious and saving. By *that* we believe, upon God's own testimony, his candour in giving Christ and his salvation to us. By *this* we certainly know that God hath formed in us the begun possession of salvation.—This assurance of sense indeed implies a belief of the justness and certainty of the marks of grace exhibited in Scripture; but it also depends on our sensible perception of the almighty influences of God's Spirit in changing and actuating our heart, Song ii. 3—5, 8—15; and on the manifested effects of his influence in our gracious qualities and works, 1 John iii. 14, 22, 24. Mat. v. 3—10. Gal. v. 22, 23.

Such assurance of sense is attainable by believers in this life. 1. The work of God's Spirit on their soul manifests this. He *testifies* to their conscience, John xv. 26. xvi. 14. Rom. viii. 16. He *writes* his law in their heart to make them his people, Jer. xxxi. 33. Heb. viii. 10. 2 Cor. iii. 3. He *seals* them up to the day of redemption, Eph. i. 13. iv. 30. As an *earnest* of it, he secures eternal life to them, 2 Cor. i. 22. v. 5. Eph. i. 14. Rom. viii. 23. John iv. 14; and as an *unction*, he prepares them for it, 1 John ii. 20, 27. 2 Cor. v. 5. Col. i. 12. 2 Thess. i. 11. 2. The diligent study of holiness and much self-examination are, by God, inculcated upon us, that we may obtain this sensible assurance, 2 Pet. ii. 5—8, 10. 2 Cor. xiii. 5. 1 Cor. xi. 28. Zeph. ii. 1. 3. Many marks of grace are exhibited to us in Scripture, that by them we may try and know our gracious state, Mat. v. 3—10. 1 John i.—v. i. 4. v. 13. 4. Many saints have actually obtained this assurance, as Job, Job xix 25—27; Jacob, Gen. xlviii. 3. xlix. 18; Moses, Exod. xv. 1; David, Psalm xviii. 1—3. xxxi. 14. xci. 2; Asaph, Psalm lxxiii. 23—26; Heman, Psalm lxxxviii. 1; Isaiah, Isa. lxiii. 16; Jeremiah, Jer. xxxi. 3; Daniel, Dan. ix 4, 18, 19. x. 11; Habakkuk, Hab. iii. 17, 18. i. 12; Simeon, Luke ii. 25—28; Mary, Luke i. 47; Thomas, John xx 28; Paul, Gal. i. 16. ii. 19, 20. 2 Cor. v. 1. Phil. iii. 8, 9. Acts xxvii. 23. 2 Tim. i. 12. iv. 7, 8; and others, John i. 14. 1 John iii. 14. Isa. lxi. 10. 1 Thess. i. 4—6. 5. Believers' inward peace, confidence, and holy gloriation, manifest their having this assurance, John xvi. 22, 33. Rom. v. 1, 2, 11. Heb. vi. 11. Eph. iii. 12. 1 Pet. i. 8.

To attain this sensible assurance of the happiness of our state and the truth of our grace, are necessary, 1. Vigorous and often repeated acts of faith upon the declarations of the gospel, which are directed to us as *sinful men*, 1 Tim. i. 15. Isa. vii. 9. James i. 6, 7. 2. Earnest study of much familiar fellowship with God in Christ, 1 John i. 37. Song i. 4. 3. Diligent study of universal gospel holiness in heart and life, Luke i. 6. vi. 27—36. Mat. v. 44—48. John xv. 14. 4. Careful cherishing of the motions of the Spirit of God, who witnesses with our spirits, that we are the children of God, Eph. iv. 30. 1 Thess. v. 19. 5. Frequent, deliberate, judicious, impartial, earnest, and thorough examination of ourselves, 1 Cor. xi. 28. 2 Cor. xiii. 5. Zeph. ii. 1.—In which we must never admit an outward profession of religion, blamelessness of behaviour, experience of the common influences of the Holy Ghost, or any other thing which may exist without saving grace, as a mark, Mat. vii. 21—23. Phil. iii. 6. Heb. vi. 4, 5. Isa. lviii. 2;—nor admit the tokens of *strong* grace as distinguishing marks of the *truth* of grace, Rom. iv. 19, 20. Hab. iii. 17, 18. Job xiii. 15. Mat. xiv. 31. And, conscious of the deceitfulness of our own heart, we must earnestly plead for the powerful attestation of the Holy Ghost, Psalm cxxxix. 23. xxvi. 1, 2 xvii 3.——Neglect of these things, attended with God's sovereign and severe chastisements thereof, make many real believers wait long before they attain this assurance, or even lose it for a time, Heb. ii. 15. Psalm lxxiii. 2—15. lxxvii. 1—10. lxxxviii.

IV. PEACE of conscience is that inward and delightful calm of spirit, which proceeds from our sensible or believing views of our being in a state of favour, fellowship, and conformity to God, Rom. v. 9, 10. xiv. 17. 2 Cor. v. 19. Isa. liv. 5, 8—10.

lvii. 18, 19. John xv. 14, 15. xiv. 27. Prov. iii. 17. Psalm cxix. 165. 2 Cor. i. 12. Heb. xii. 28. It is attended with delightful contemplation of God as our God, Psalm cxxxix. 17, 18. lxiii. 1---8. xvi. 5---8. ciii. cxlv. cxlvi; and leads to a bold and familiar, but humble dealing with him, Song ii. 14. viii. 13. Heb. iv. 16. x. 19---22; and an affectionate and peaceful disposition towards all his children, Psalm xvi. 3. cxix. 63. Being obtained by the sprinkling of the blood of Jesus, and the sanctification of our whole man, this peace is always the same in its root or state, Isa. liv. 8---10. Ezek. xxxvii. 26. Hos. ii. 18---20; but the sense of it is often, in a great measure, lost or interrupted.

In the *interruptions* of this peace of conscience, Satan and his instruments have a *wicked* hand, seducing and vexing our souls, Mat. xxiv. 24. 1 Pet. v. 8. We have a *sinful* hand, in abusing God's kind favours to us, committing conscience-wasting sins, or indulging formality, sloth, and self-confidence in religious duties, Psalm li. 1---14. Jer. ii. 17, 19. Isa. lxiii. 10. Deut. xxxii. 15---27. Song v. 3---5. Psalm xxx. 6, 7. And God,— to manifest his sovereignty, Dan. iv. 34, 35; correct our sinfulness, Jer. ii. 17, 19. vi. 19; try and exercise our graces, 1 Pet. i. 6, 7; instigate our earnest prayers, Psalm xxii. 1, 2. lxxxiv. 2. cxxx. 1; manifest his love under, or after, such affliction, Isa. lvii. 16---19; and teach us to improve the sense of his favour, Rom. v. 3,—*righteously* hides his countenance, and either mediately or immediately distresses our soul, Isa. viii. 17. xlv. 15. Psalm x. 1. xiii. 1---4. lxxvii. 1---10. lxxx. 4, 5. lxxxviii. Job xiii. 24. 2 Cor. xii. 7.——It is *regained* by repeated applications of Jesus' blood, 1 John i. 7; by serious renewals of our repentance for sin, Lam. iii. 40. Jer. xxxi. 18---20; and by God's repeating his manifestations of love to our soul, Isa. lvii. 16—19. John xvi. 22.——It is *maintained* by an habitual application of Christ's blood to our conscience, 1 John i. 7. Heb. x. 22; by daily devout meditation on the endearing excellencies and relations of Christ, and of God in him, as our God, and on the origin, tenor, and administration of the covenant of grace, Psalm civ. 34. 2 Sam. xxiii. 5. John xiv. 21; by much familiar fellowship with God, Isa. lxiv. 4, 5. Psalm lxiii. 1---8. lxv. 4. Song i. 4. ii. 3; by much candid and earnest study of universal holiness, and watchfulness against beloved lusts, Isa. xxxii. 15, 17. lxiv. 5. Acts xxiv. 16. Heb. xii. 1. Psalm cxix. 165. xviii. 23; by speedily washing off the filial guilt of sin, and repenting of those offences which mar our peace, Psalm li. 6---14. Jer. iii. 22. xxxi. 18; and by much hearty resignation of ourselves and our concerns to the providence of God as our affectionate Father, Philip. iv. 6, 7. 1 Pet. v. 7. Psalm lv. 22. cxii. 7.

V. Joy in the Holy Ghost is a spiritual pleasure in living on, and walking in and with Christ, produced by the inhabitation and influence of his Spirit in our hearts. The grounds of this joy are, 1. What God in Christ is to us, Psalm xviii. 1—3. xxxiv. 1—4. ciii. 1—5. cxviii. 28. Hab. iii. 17, 18. i. 12. John xx. 28. Psalm xxiii. xxvii. xlvii. xci. Isa. xii. 2. What God, the Father, Son, and Holy Ghost have done for and in us, Isa. lxi. 10. Psalm lxxi. 14—24. ciii. cxxxvi. cxlv. Rom. v. 1—11. 2 Cor. i. 12. 3. What his promises and characters secure for us, Psalm xlii. 11. xliii. 5. Rom. viii. 28—39. 2 Tim. i. 12. iv. 8. Psalm lxxiii. 24—26.———Such joy is ordinarily most full, 1. After remarkable grief at conversion, Isa. lxi. 2, 3. lvii. 16—19. lxvi. 2. John xx. 20, 28. Acts ii. 37, 46. 2. After dark nights of desertion, temptation, and trouble, Isa. liv. 6—12. lvii. 16—19. Psalm xvi. 10, 11. xiii. cxvi. xl. 1—5. 3. When entering into, or under much tribulation, especially for the cause of Christ, Acts v. 41. xvi. 25. 1 Pet. iv. 13, 14. 4. When God bestows some remarkable deliverance upon his church, Exod. xv. Judges v. Isa. xlii. 10, 11. lxv. 17—19. lxvi. 10. Jer. xxxi. 12—14. Rev. vii. 9—12. xii. 10. xi. 15, 17. xv. 3. xiv. 1—4. xix. 1—6. 5. When he grants some remarkable favour almost quite unexpected, 1 Sam. ii. 1—10. Luke i. 45—77.

All spiritual comfort differs from that presumptuous confidence of God's love, sleep, or ill-grounded peace of conscience and false joy, which may be found in hypocrites or others,—as it mightily humbles the heart, Gen. xviii. 30, 32. xxxii. 10. 1 Cor. xv. 10; promotes the cheerful and active study of universal holiness, Psalm cxvi. 16. cxix. 32, 166; renders sin more and more hated, Rom. vii. 14—24. Psalm cxix. 104, 128. 2 Cor. vii. 1, 11. Gen. xxxix. 9; animates to an earnest following after fellowship with God, Job xxiii. 3. xxix. 2. Psalm xlii. 1, 2. lxiii. 1—8. xxvii. 4. lxxxiv. 2, 10. xlv. 1. 2 Cor. iii. 18. John xvi. 22; and disposes to impartial self-examination, John iii. 21. Psalm xxvi. 1, 2. cxxxix. 23, 24. xvii. 3.—— It is bestowed upon believers, 1. To qualify them for their proper work, Neh. viii. 10. Isa. lxiv. 5. 2. To reward them in, or after their performing it, Psalm xix. 11. 1 Cor. xv. 58. 3. To manifest the amazing virtue of Christ as the *consolation* of his people, Luke ii. 25. 2 Cor. ii. 14. 4. To manifest the riches of God's redeeming grace, and his delight in the prosperity of his servants, Eph. ii. 7. Psalm xxxv. 27.

Reflect. Hast thou, my soul, these first fruits of the Spirit, these earnests of eternal glory in thee? Has the Holy Ghost thus dwelt in, preserved, attested, assured, quieted, and filled thee with joy unspeakable and full of glory?——Let me take heed, lest my persuasion of God's love should be an ill-grounded fancy,—my inward quietness a mere sleep or delusion of conscience,—and my joy but common, carnal, legal, or delusive.—Alas! that I have been so long named a Christian, and yet have lived so ignorant of Christian experience!---that I have been so long a student,---a preacher,---and yet so ignorant of these deep, these great, these sweet things of God!--- that I am so near eternity, and yet have so little tried how much of God might be enjoyed on earth to prepare me for it!

CHAP. VI.

Of Glorification *begun and perfected.*

GLORIFICATION, more generally taken, includes the whole of believers' honour and pleasure in time and eternity.

I. The commencement of it in this life, which has been considered in the preceding chapters, may be summed up in, 1. Our high state of honour as the spouse and members of Christ, and the friends, favourites, children, kings, and priests of God, in, and together with him, 1 Cor. i. 30. 2 Cor. v. 21. Eph. i. 3—7. 1 John iii. 1. Rev. i. 6. 2. Our spiritual manifestations and knowledge of God in Christ, Psal. xxvii. 4. lxviii. 24. lxiii. 2. Heb. xi. 1, 27. 2 Cor. iii. 18. iv. 18. 3. Our honourable conformity to God in holiness of heart and life, 2 Cor. iii. 18. Exod. xv. 11. 1 Pet. i. 15, 16. Matth. v. 48. 4. Our familiar intercourse with, and communications from God, Psal. cxliv. 15. xxxiii. 12. xvi. 5, 6. xxxiv. 8. xxxvi. 6—9. lxv. 4. xxv. 14. lxxxiv. 11. lxxxv. 12. 5. Our spiritual comforts, arising from certain views of our present and future happiness, Psal. xxxii. 2. ciii. 1—5. xxiii. civ. 34. xxxi. 19. Heb. vi. 17, 18. Isa. xl. 1, 2. li. 7, 12. lx. 19, 20.

II. At death, the souls of believers enter upon the enjoyment of perfect honour and happiness. 1. Their death being unstinged, by virtue of Christ's blood applied to them, Hos. xiii. 14. Isa. xxv. 8, comes to them as an inestimable legacy bequeathed in his testament, 1 Cor. iii. 22. Isa. li. 11, and procured by his infinitely kind intercession, John xvii. 24. 2. Their soul, not being killed with their body, Matth. x. 28, they long for death, Luke ii. 28—30. Phil. i. 23. 2 Cor. v. 1—8, and commit their departing soul to Christ, Psalm xxxi. 5. Acts vii. 59. 3. In its departing moment, it is made perfectly free from

OF GLORIFICATION BEGUN AND PERFECTED. 447

sin, and conformed to God in holiness, Heb. xii. 23. Rev. xxi. 4, 27. 1 John iii. 2. Eph. v. 25—27. Jude 24. 1 Cor. xiii. 12. 4. Being separated from their body, it is immediately conveyed by angels into the heavenly state, in which it is inexpressibly active and happy, Luke xvi. 22, 23. xxiii. 42, 43. Acts vii. 59. 2 Cor. v. 1—8. John xvii. 24. Rev. xiv. 13. Phil. i. 23. These scriptures, together with those that mention only two forms of the future state, or of the way to it, Matth. vii. 13, 14. Rom. ii. 7—10; or, which prove the perfection of Christ's satisfaction for the sins of his people, manifest that there is no *purgatory* or *middle state*, between heaven and hell.

III. At the last day, 1. The bodies of believers having, through their continued union to Christ, rested in their graves perfectly freed from all sin and trouble, Rev. xiv. 13. 1 Thess. iv. 16. Isa. lvii. 2, shall, by virtue of this union, and the powerful influence of his indwelling Spirit, be raised to life, strong, immortal, glorious, and spiritual, Isa. xxvi. 19. Job xix. 25—27. Rom. viii. 11, 23. Phil. iii. 21. 1 Cor. xv. 42—49. 2. Their complete persons shall be publicly acknowledged before all angels and men by Christ, as his redeemed bride, dear children, beloved friends, and obedient people, and acquitted from all the false charges which had been cast upon them, and absolved from all their real faults, Luke xii. 8. Matth. x. 32. xxv. 34—40. 2 Tim. iv. 7, 8. 3. All of them in one assembly or body, shall be publicly and solemnly adjudged and invited, and blessed of the Father, and heirs of his prepared kingdom, to take an everlasting possession of it, Psal. xcvi. 13. xcviii. 9. Matth. xxv. 34. 4. Along with Christ their Head, and attended by millions of angels, they shall be admitted into their heavenly state, while new heavens and a new earth are formed for enlarging the objects of their delightful contemplation, Mat. xxv. 46. Psalm xlv. 15. Isa. xxxv. 10. 2 Pet. iii. 10, 13.

IV. Through all eternity they shall be made perfectly blessed in the full enjoyment of God, Psalm xxxi. 19. 2 Cor. iv. 17. 1. No evil thing, sin, or sorrow, shall ever enter, Rev. xx. 14, 15. xxi. 4, 8, 25, 27. xxii. 3, 5, 15. Isa. xxxv. 10. li. 11. lx. 20. 2. Every thing calculated to promote true happiness shall be enjoyed in full perfection, Rev. vii. 17. Isa. xxxv. 10 lx. 19, 20. 1 Cor. xv. 28. 2 Cor. iv. 17.—Their place of abode shall be inexpressibly delightful,—a *better country*,—a *city*, a *temple*, and an *house, having foundations, built by God*,—a *new Jerusalem*,—*Zion*,—*God's kingdom, palace, throne, paradise, barn, garner*,—*Abraham's bosom*, the *third heaven*, &c. Heb. xi. 16, 10. Rev. xxi. xxii. 1—5. Matth. xiii. 43. v. 34. Psalm xlv. 15. Isa. lxvi. 1. Luke xxiii. 43. 2 Cor. xii. 2, 4. Rev. ii. 7. iii. 21. Matth. iii. 12. xiii. 30. viii. 11. Luke xvi. 22. 2 Cor. v. 1. John xiv. 2.—Their eternally and immutably fixed condition, in this abode, shall be most glorious,—a *treasure, joy, peace, rest, glory,* an *exceeding weight of glory,*—the *joy of the Lord,—light, life,*—an *inheritance incorruptible, undefiled,*—a *walking with Christ in white robes,*—a *sitting with Christ on his throne,* or at a splendid banquet, Matth. vi. 20. Isa. lvii. 2. Psalm lxxiii. 24. 2 Cor. iv. 17. Mat. xxv. 21, 23. Col. i. 12. Matth. xix. 17. Psalm xvi. 11. 1 Pet. i. 4. Rev. iii. 5, 21. ii. 26. vii. 17. Matth. viii. 11.—They shall enjoy the most delightful fellowship with angels and perfected saints, Matth. viii. 11. Heb. xii. 22, 23. Rev. v. 9—13, and with Christ as their elder brother, John xii. 26. xiv. 3. xvii. 24. Psalm xxii. 22. Heb. xii. 24. 1 Thess. iv. 17; and shall enjoy God himself in every known excellency of his nature, manifested through Christ, as their ALL IN ALL, Heb. xii. 24. Psalm xliii. 4. lxxiii. 26. 1 Cor. xv. 28.

In this state of the full enjoyment of God is included, 1. An immediate vision with the eyes of their understanding, of the Father, the Son, and the Holy Ghost, 1 John iii. 2. 1 Cor. xiii. 12. Psalm xvii. 15. John xvii. 24, 25. xiv. 10. 2 Cor. iv. 6;—while their bodily eyes behold the glorified body of Christ and these of his saints. 2. The most full experience of the goodness and love of God, Rev. vii. 17. Isa. lx. 19, 20. 1 Cor. xv. 28. 3. Perfect likeness to God in his imitable, and correspondence of heart with his inimitable perfections, Psalm xvii. 15. 1 John iii. 2. 4. Inexpressible love to God, and to all around for his sake, 1 Cor. xiii. 8, 13. 5. Inconceivable delight and joy, expressed in unceasing and enraptured songs of praise to God, through, and together with Christ, Rev. vii. 17. v. 9—13. Psal. xvi. 11. xvii. 15. xliii. 4. Isa. xxxv. 10. lx. 18—20.——All this happiness will be everlasting, if not perpetually increasing by means of the heart-enlarging influence of such fellowship with God, 1 Thess. iv. 17. Matth. xxv. 46. Isa. lx. 19. li. 11. The everlasting love and covenant of God, the everlasting merit of Christ's righteousness, and the power of his intercession, secure the eternity of it, Jer. xxxi. 3. Isa. liv. 8—10. 2 Sam. xxiii. 5. Dan. ix. 24. Heb. ix. 12. x. 14. vii. 25.—In this happy state there will be different degrees of glory, graciously proportioned to those of their sanctification on earth. 1. Their state is represented as having different degrees of glory, John xiv. 2. 1 Cor. xv. 41, 42. iii. 8, 14, 15. 2 Cor. ix. 5, 6. Matth. xix. 29. 2. There will be different degrees of torment in hell, proportioned to men's sinfulness, Matth. xi. 22, 24.

REFLECT. But, O my soul, in what form am I to die,—to rise again,—and to live for ever? Shall I certainly die *in the Lord?* and, when he appears, shall I appear *with him in glory?* Shall I be for ever with him,—for ever like him, by seeing him as he is? God forbid, that I should either commence or continue a preacher of Christ, before mine eternal interest in him be secured. How dreadful if, after lighting up his friends to their high mansions of bliss, I be turned downward into everlasting darkness, and bottomless pits of woe!—be driven away from Jesus Christ, as a worker of iniquity, into everlasting fire prepared for the devil and his angels!—But, if I am a true, an experienced Christian, having a call from God to the ministerial work, let me bend all my powers,—all my prayers,—all my labours,—all my cares, to try how much Christ may be enjoyed, imitated, and served upon earth.—Let my lot, in earnestly following and preaching him, be as poor and distressful as it will, it is enough, that all be seasoned with the love, the blood, the presence, the influence, of the great God my Saviour.—I had ten thousand times rather be outwardly ruined with Christ, than reign with Cæsars.—But what shall it be to enter into the joy of my Lord!—to reign in life with him! and for ever possess the REDEEMING THREE, as my infinite ALL IN ALL!—MY GOD and MY ALL!—Unquestionably bliss inexpressible, inconceivable!

BOOK VI.

Of the External Dispensation of the Covenant of Grace, by the Word and Ordinances of God.

In Christ's administration of the new covenant, and conferring the blessings of it upon us, there concur, 1. The Word of the covenant, in which God declares his mind to us, and which may be distinguished into the Law and the Gospel. 2. The Ordinances of the covenant, in which God deals with us, and we with him, for the effectual application of his word, and his benefits therein exhibited. 3. The Spirit of the covenant, by whose influences God's word and ordinances are made effectual for bringing us into the covenant,—making us actual partakers of its blessings,—and to receive and improve them for his honour. 4. Faith, by which we, being qualified and actuated, receive and improve the word, ordinances, Spirit, and blessings of the covenant.—The agency of the Spirit and faith having been repeatedly pointed out, and not pertaining to the external dispensation of this covenant, falls not under our present consideration.

CHAP. I.

Of the Law of God, in its Manifestation, Matter, Forms, and Uses to men.

I. The Law of God means either his whole word, Psalm i. 2. xix. 8, 9; or all the books of the Old Testament, John x. 34. 1 Cor. xiv. 21; or the five books of Moses, Luke xxiv. 44. Rom. iii. 21. John i. 45; or the ceremonial dispensation of the new covenant, John i. 17; or the covenant of works as opposed to the covenant of grace, Rom. vi. 14. vii. 4. viii. 2. Gal. iii. 10, 12, 13. But, *properly taken*, the law, as distinguished from the gospel, is the manifested will of God, our infinitely high Sovereign, directing and binding all men what to be, do, or avoid. *Direction* and *obligation* are the two essential constituents of a law. A *sanction* of penalty is never annexed to it, but where the subjects are actually fallible. A promissory sanction is never annexed, but when the law is formed into a covenant, or inlaid in one.

OF THE LAW OF GOD.

The revealed law of God is ordinarily distinguished into the *moral, ceremonial,* and *judicial.* The *ceremonial* law prescribed the rites of worship used under the Old Testament, and was mostly grafted upon the second and fourth commandments of the moral; and these rites, in their intended signification, were an obscure gospel, Col. ii. 17. Heb. x. 1. iii.—x. The *judicial* law directed the civil managements of the Israelites under God, as their principal governor, with respect to their encampments, marches, wars, inheritances, marriages, punishments, rulers, &c. Exod. xxi. xxii. xxiii. Num. i. ii. x. xxvii. xxxiv. xxxv. xxxvi. Lev. xviii. xx. Deut. xvii. xix.—xxv.; and is reducible to the correspondent precepts of the moral, and never bound any but the Jews, in their national establishment, any further than moral equity requires.—The *moral* law is that declaration of God's will which directs and binds all men in every age and place to their whole duty to him, themselves, or their neighbours.—The leading articles of this law, proceeding from the very nature of God, and his relation to men as their Creator, Preserver, and Governor, are altogether unchangeable and indispensable, Mal. v. 17, 19. Rom. iii. 31. xiii. 8, 9. Tit. iii. 8, 14. James ii. 8, 10. And all the ten commandments of it are either more or less directly inculcated in the New Testament. The substance of the *first* is in John iii. 19. v. 42. 2 Pet. i. 5—8. iii. 18. 2 Thess. i. 8. 1 John iii. 23. iv. 19. Matth. iv. 10. Acts ii. 38. Matth. xxii. 37. 1 Pet. ii. 17. Heb. xii. 28. Rom. iii. 18. 2 Cor. i. 6. 1 Tim. iv. 7. vi. 17;—the substance of the *second*, in John iv. 23, 24. v. 39. Rev. i. 3. Rom. xii. 1—6. 1 Thess. v. 17. Col. iii. 16. Eph. v. 19. James v. 13, 14. 1 Cor. x. 14. 1 John v. 21; —of the *third* in Matth. v. 34—37. xv. 9. vi. 7. James i. 23. v. 12. John iv. 24. 1 Cor. xiv. 15;—of the *fourth* in Mark xvi. 2, 9. John xx. 19, 26. Acts xx. 7. 1 Cor. xvi. 2. Rev. i. 10;—of the *fifth* in Eph. vi. 1—9. v. 22—33. iv. 32. Col. iii. 18—25. iv. 1. Tit. ii. 3—10. 1 Pet. ii. 18. iii. 1—8. 1 Thess. v. 12—14. 1 Tim. iii.—vi. And the other *five* commands are repeatedly inculcated together, Mat. xix. 18, 19. Rom. xiii. 9. Gal. v. 14. James ii. 8—11.——Such articles of the moral law as do not immediately proceed from the nature of God or his relations to men, admit of God's excepting particular cases, but of no other. Thus, in Adam's family, brethren lawfully married their own sisters: God might require a brother to marry the widow of a childless brother deceased; or require a man to sacrifice his own son, &c.

God's moral law is manifested, 1. As partly, but obscurely, written in the heart of all men, Rom. ii. 14, 15. i. 19, 20, 32. 2. As summarily contained in the ten commandments, Exod. xx. 3—17. Deut. v. 6—21. 3. As largely held forth and explained in the whole Bible, in every divine requirement or prohibition, direct or indirect, Deut. iv.---xxxi. Mat. v.---vii. Eph. iv.---vi. Col. iii. iv. Rom. xii.---xv. Phil. ii.---iv. 1 Thess. v. Heb. x.---xiii. James i. to Rev. iii.—It was manifested to Adam, its natural demands being wrote on his heart, and its positive requirements revealed to him, Gen. i 26, 27. ii. 16, 17.—It was manifested to the Israelites at Sinai, proclaimed in a most solemn and terrible manner, to represent the danger of those that are under it as a covenant, Exod. xix. xx. Deut. iv. v. Heb. xii. 28, 29.—Wrote upon tables of stone, to mark its perpetual obligation, and the hardness of men's hearts, on which the Holy Ghost writes it, Exod. xxiv. 12. xxxiv. 1, 28.—And the hewing of the latter tables by Moses might import, that we must be convinced by the law as a covenant, before it can be wrote in our heart as a rule of life.---It was thus solemnly published, 1. To confirm the original law of nature. 2. To correct men's mistakes concerning its demands. 3. To supply that which was wanting in it. 4. To convince the Israelites of their need of a Mediator in order to their eternal salvation, or their being the peculiar people of God, Gal. iii. 19, 20.

Christ and his apostles republished and further explained the moral law, and vindicated it from the false interpretations of the Jewish doctors, Matth. v. xv.; but they did not in the least *enlarge* it. 1. It was long before perfect, Deut. iv. 2. v. 32. xii. 32. Psalm xix. 7, 8. cxix. 96; nor could it be corrected, without impeaching the wisdom and equity of God, who framed it. 2. Christ came not to destroy the ancient moral law, but to fulfil it, Matth. v. 17, 18. 3. He and his apostles taught nothing but what Moses and the prophets had done, Matth. xxii. 37---40. vii. 12. Rom. i. 3. Acts xxvi. 22. The *loving of brethren* is an *old* commandment, and from the beginning, in respect of its matter; and only *new*, in respect of its additional enforcement by Christ's death for us, and his clear publication of the gospel, 1 John ii. 8. John xiii. 34. *Self-denial, taking up our cross,* and *imitating Christ,* were required in the Old Testament as well as in the New. In self-denial and taking up his cross, Abraham left his native country, Gen. xii. Heb. xi. 8; the pious Levites slew their idolatrous brethren, Exod xxxii. 27, 28; Job blessed God under his heavy troubles, Job i. ii.; Moses chose affliction with his brethren, Heb. xi. 25, 26.—Almost every prophet and good man appears denying himself and taking up his cross, 2 Sam. xvi. 5---11. 1 Kings xvii. 2 Chron. xxiv. 20---22. Dan. iii. vi. Neh. ii. v.—The loving God *above all*, necessarily requires self-denial and taking up our cross when it is for his glory, Psalm cxv. 1. 1 Cor. vi. 19, 20. 1 Pet. iv. 14.—Christ being

God, the imitation of him in the divine excellencies he then had, was required under the Old Testament, Lev. xi. 44. xix. 2. xx. 7.—Christ added nothing to the three first commandments,—no new form of prayer: That which he taught his disciples contains nothing but what had been long before requested, Isa. lxiii. 16. Psalm lxxii. lvii. 11. cxliii. cxix. Prov. xxx. 8. Psalm xxv. 11. xvi. 1. xvii. 2.—The worshipping Christ, and God in his name, was practised under the Old Testament, Psalm ii. 12. xv. 11. xcvii. 7. Heb. i. 6. Exod. xxiii. 21. Gen. xviii. 23. xlviii. 16. Dan. ix. 17. Psal. lxxxiv. 9; men were forbidden to have images, or frequent idolatrous temples, as well as now, Exod. xxiii. 24. Deut. xii. 23. vii. 2, 3. Psalm xvi. 4; and to swear rashly or irreverently, Deut. vi. 13. x. 20. Eccl. ix. 2. Isa. lxv. 16. Jer. iv. 2. v. 7. Mat. v. 34—37. James v. 12.——Nothing moral in the fourth and fifth command is in the least altered.—Sinful anger, injuring brethren, private revenge, unchaste looks or words, unnecessary divorce, and polygamy, were forbidden before Christ came, as well as since, Gen. iv. 6. xxvii. 41, 43. xxxi. 24. xlv. 8. xlix. 7. Job xxix. 16. xxxi. 1. 2 Kings v. 13. Deut. v. 20, 21. xvii. 5. xxiv. 1. Mal. ii. 14, 15. Lev. xix. 8.

In respect of QUALITY, the moral law is, 1. *Universal*, extending to all men, in every age, in all their dispositions, thoughts, words, and works, Rom. ii. 14. iii. 19, 20. iv. 15. v. 13. 2. *Perfect*, requiring all good dispositions and exercises, in the most perfect degree, and forbidding every thing sinful in any degree, Psalm xix. 7. cxix. 96, 128. 3. *Perpetual*, directing and binding men both through time and eternity, Luke xvi. 17. Mat. v. 18. 4. *Holy*, a transcript of God's infinite holiness, and binding men to perfect holiness, Rom. vii. 12. 5. *Just*, requiring nothing but what we owe to God, ourselves, or our neighbours, and what we, in Adam, had originally strength to perform, Rom. vii. 12. Psalm xix. 8. cxix. 7, 128. 6. *Good*, requiring nothing but what is good in itself, and calculated to promote the happiness of all under it, Rom. vii. 12. ii. 7, 10. Psalm xix. 11. cxix. 165. 7. *Spiritual*, reaching all the powers of men's souls, and requiring all obedience to proceed from spiritual principles, and to be performed in a spiritual manner, and directed to proper spiritual ends, Rom. vii. 14. 8. *Exceeding broad*, extending its requirements and prohibitions to multitudes of things in every moment, place, and circumstance, Psalm cxix. 96.

II. OBEDIENCE to this law consists in our *being* and *acting* answerably to its requirements and prohibitions, from an high regard to its divine authority. Or, it is the making the matter of it our *Rule*, and the authority of God in it the *Reason* of our whole conduct. It must be, 1. *Sincere* and candid, Psalm xviii. 23. Heb. xi. 17. Num. xiv. 40—44. 2. *Constant*, notwithstanding all alterations in our state or circumstances, Psalm cxix. 44. 3. *Tender*, abstaining from the smallest appearance of evil, 1 Thess. v. 22. Judg. ii. 5. Ezek. vi. 9. 4. *Ready* and cheerful, Psalm xviii. 44. Gal. i. 16. Heb. xi. 8. 5. *Universal*, to every precept, in every point, and by every power in us, Psalm cxix. 6. 6. *Absolute*, determined by the revealed will of God, though we perceive no other reason, Heb. xi. 8. Mat. xxiii. 8—10. Acts iv. 19. v. 29. 7. *Perfect*, without the smallest defect, and answerable to the highest demands of holiness, Mat. v. 48. Lev. xi. 44. 1 Pet. i. 13, 15, 16. 8. In our case, *Evangelical*, having Jesus Christ offered and bestowed in the gospel, for its origin, cause, motive, pattern, and end, 1 Tim. i. v. Rom. i. v. 2 Cor. x. 5. Eph. v. 2. Col. iii. 17. 1 Pet. iv. 11.

Love to God, to ourselves, and to our neighbours, is the general duty of obedience required by the moral law. 1. *Love to God* is the source or root of all our obedience to the law, John xiv. 15, 21—24;—the chief stream or branch of obedience, 1 Cor. xiii.; and the all-comprehending substance of it, Rom. xiii. 10.—We must love God with all our heart, soul, mind, and strength, Mat. xxii. 37:—Which includes, 1. A true spiritual knowledge of what he is in himself, and as connected with us, John xvii. 3. 2. A hearty choice of him as our chief good, Psalm lxxiii. 25, 26. 3. A cleaving to him as our God and ALL in ALL, Acts xi. 23. 4. An high esteem of him in all that he is and does, Song v. 10. Psalm xxxv. 10. Exod. xv. 11. Psalm viii. 1, 9. xxxvi. 7. civ. 34. cxxxix. 17, 18. Zech. ix. 17. 5. Ardent desire after familiar enjoyment of him, Psalm xxvii. 4. xlii. 1, 2. lxxxiv. 2. lxiii. 1—8. 6. Delight in him, Song i. 13. Psalm xxxvii. 4. cxlix. 2.——And thus our love to him must be *Judicious*, Mark xii. 33: *Sincere* and hearty, Prov. xxiii. 26: *Pure* and absolute, for the sake of his excellency and kindness to us, Song i. 3. Psalm xxxvi. 7. 1 John iv. 19: *Strong* and vigorous, Song viii. 6, 7: *Superlative*, far transcending that which we bear to other objects, Luke xiv. 26; and *operative* in holy exercises, 1 John iii. 18. Rom. xiii. 10. xiv. 6, 8, 9. II. We ought to *love ourselves*, in valuing ourselves as God's rational creatures, having immortal souls capable of an eternal enjoyment and service of him, and so unspeakably more important than all the irrational world, Mat. xvi. 26.—In humble satisfaction with our particular natural form as the work of God, Psalm c. 3. cxxxix. 14—16; in detesting and avoiding every thing which tends to our real hurt, Rom. xii. 9. Psalm cxix. 104. Acts xvi. 28;—in laying out our whole care, knowledge, ability, and opportunity to promote our own holiness, honour, safety, and comfort, in subordination to the glory of God. Mat. vi. 33. John vi. 27.

Rom. ii. 7, 10. 1 Tim. iv. 8. III. All men on earth being our neighbours, we ought to love them, in duly esteeming them for the gifts, grace, and usefulness with which God hath endowed them, 1 Pet. ii. 17. Phil. ii. 3. Rom. xii. 10. 1 Pet. iii. 8. iv. 8; —and delighting in them in subordination to our superlative delight in God, Psalm xvi. 3. cxix. 63. 1 Pet. i. 22.——We are to love them *as ourselves*, in doing every thing for and to them, which we could reasonably wish them to do to us in like circumstances, Mat. vii. 12; and in loving and doing good to them from true love to their persons, 1 John iii. 17, 18. 1 Pet. i. 22. iii. 8. iv. 8.

The whole moral law, which regulates our love to God and men, and all the actings of it, is contained in the *ten commandments*,—the *first four* of which direct our *love to God*, prescribing the object, means, manner, and peculiar season of our worship;—and the *last six* direct our *love to man*, answerably to relative connections, life, chastity, property, reputation, and inward disposition;—our whole duty to man being thus founded on our relations and duty to God, Exod. xx. 3—17. Deut. v. 6—21.——As these commandments contain very much matter in few words, the following rules must be carefully observed in understanding and explaining them: I. Wherever a duty is required, the contrary sin is forbid; and wherever a sin is forbid, the contrary duty is required. II. Wherever a sin is forbid, every sin of the same kind, and every cause, occasion, and appearance thereof, are also forbid; and where a duty is commanded, every duty of the same kind, and all the means of performing it, are required. III. Whatever we ourselves are bound to be, do, or forbear, we are bound, according to our stations, to do all that we can to make others to be and do the same. IV. That which is forbid is never to be done: but actions required are only to be performed when God gives opportunity. V. The same sin is forbidden, and the same duty required, in different, nay, in all the commandments, in different respects. VI. No sin is ever to be committed in order to avoid a greater; but some duties required must give place to others. Our natural duties to God must be preferred to our natural duties to men, Acts iv. 19. v. 29. And the positive worship of God must sometimes give place to the natural duties of necessity and mercy towards men, Hos. vi. 6.

I. The First Commandment being, as it were, the foundation or corner-stone of the whole law, especially of the first table, is obeyed or disobeyed, in all our obedience or disobedience to any commandment.—It particularly requires, I. Knowledge of God, as God, in his existence, perfections, persons, purposes, and works, 1 Chron. xxviii. 9. John xvii. 3. 1 John v. 7, 20. Psalm cvii. 43;—and as our God in Christ, Exod.

xxxiv. 6, 7, 9. 2 Cor. v. 18---21; not merely speculative but practical, conforming our heart and life to his image, 2 Cor. iii. 18. John xiii. 17. Eph. iv. 32. v. 1, 2. 1 Pet. i. 15, 16. II. AcKNOWLEDGMENT of him as God and our God. I. INWARDLY in our heart. 1. In crediting all that we know concerning him upon his own testimony, John xx. 31. 1 Thess. ii. 13. 2. In believing on Christ as our only Saviour and way to God, and chusing God in him for our everlasting portion and Lord, 1 John iii. 23. Psalm xvi. 2. cxlii. 5. xxxi. 14. xci. 2. cxviii. 28. 3. In deliberate renunciation of every idol, and solemnly surrendering up ourselves to him as our Husband and King, Mat. v. 29, 30. Hos. xiv. 3, 8. Jer. iii. 16, 19. Josh. xxiv. 15. 4. In constant faithfulness to our covenant relations and engagements to him, keeping our hearts from every thing else to him, as our superlatively beloved ALL in ALL, Prov. iv. 23. Psalm lxxiii. 23—26. Song iv. 12. 5. In truly penitent turning from our indwelling lusts and sinful practices to him with grief and hatred of our sin, and with full purpose of, and endeavour after new obedience, Acts xx. 21. Jer. iii. 13, 14, 21—23. xxxi. 18, 19. Hos. xiv. 1—3, 8. 6. In constant correspondence of our inward frame of spirit with the excellencies of God, and the manifestations thereof in Christ,—serving and worshipping him, who is a *Spirit*, in spirit and in truth, John iv. 24. Rom. i. 9. viii. 5. 1 Cor. xiv. 15; enlarging our heart to embrace and enjoy him as *Infinite*, Psalm lxxxi. 10. Isa. xxvi. 8, 9; looking not at things temporal, but at things *Eternal*, 2 Cor. iv. 17, 18; humble and absolute dependence on him as *All-sufficient* and *Independent*, Song viii. 5; unmoved trust in, cleaving to, and imitation of him as *Unchangeable*, Mal. iii. 6. Psal. lxxxix. 34. Deut. iv. 4. x. 20. Josh. xxiii. 8. Acts xi. 23. Prov. xxiv. 21. Job ii. 3. 1 Cor. xv. 58; living alway as in his presence and under his *Allseeing* eye, Psalm xvi. 8. Gen. xvi. 13. Jer. xxiii. 24; filial awe of, and trust in his *Power, Greatness*, and *Equity*, Heb. xii. 28, 29. Job vi. 14. xiii. 15; delight in, and conformity to his unspotted *Holiness*, 1 Pet. i. 15, 16. Lev. xi. 44. Mat. v. 48; humble receiving, admiring, and rejoicing in his *Goodness*, Jer. xxxi. 12. Gen. xxxii. 10; trust in, and imitation of his truth, candour, and *faithfulness*, 2 Chron. xx. 20. 7. In affections correspondent with his word, as manifesting his excellencies,---searching, believing, loving, delighting in, and feeding upon it, as his word of salvation, Psalm cxix. Gen. xxxii. 9---12. 2 Sam. vii. 25. Job xxiii. 12. Jer. xv. 16. Acts xiii. 26. 1 Tim. i. 15. 2 Tim. iii. 15---17; and with his work,---discerning, magnifying, and praising him in it,---as infinitely glorious, wise, powerful, holy, and good, in Creation, Psalm viii. 3. cxxxvi. 5 ;---as just, wise, almighty, faithful, and gracious in afflictive providences, and therefore bearing them patiently, humbly, and thankfully, Job i. 21. ii. 10. Psalm cxix. 67, 71, 75; as gracious and merciful in smiling providences, and therefore exercising love, wonder, and gratitude, Gen. xxxii. 10. 1 Thess. v. 18. Phil. iv. 4, 6. Col. iii. 17;—— as infinitely wise, powerful, just, and merciful in redemption, and hence approving it with our whole heart, and trusting our temporal and eternal happiness wholly to it, 2 Sam. xxiii. 5. Phil. iii. 8, 9.   2. We must also acknowledge him OUTWARDLY, as God and our God, in an open and stedfast profession of him, as such,—and of his truths for his sake,—and in a correspondent practice, 1 Pet. iii. 15, 16. Heb. iv. 14. x. 23. Eph. iv.—vi. Col. i.—iv. 1 Thess. i.—v. Rom. xii.—xv. vi.;—and that in order to glorify him, Phil. i. 20. Luke ix. 26; edify our neighbour, Phil. i. 12, 13. Tit. iii. 8, 14; and to promote our own spiritual advantage, Mark viii. 35, 38. Rom. x. 10. Luke xii. 8.   III. WORSHIPPING and *glorifying* God as God and our God in Christ, 1. INWARDLY, *in our mind*, thinking of him, Mal. iii. 16. Psalm lxiii. 6. cxxxix. 17, 18. civ. 34; esteeming him, Exod. xv. 11. Psalm cxxxv. 10. viii. 1, 9. xxxvi. 7. lxxiii. 25; and believing him, Exod. xiv. 31. 1 Thess. ii. 13;—*in our conscience*,—standing in awe of his authority, Psalm xliv. 20, 21. Job xxxi. 14, 23; subjecting it to him alone, without reserve, Mat. xxiii. 8—10. iv. 10. Jam. iv. 12; receiving his law as marked with his infinite authority, Isa. viii. 20. v. 20. Mat. vi. 22, 23; constant application of Christ's blood for purging it, and as the means of our unceasing familiarity with God, Heb. x. 19—22; self-excitement to duty upon an evangelical foundation, Luke i. 74, 75. Psalm cxvi. 12, 16. ciii. 1—5; and accusing or excusing us according to our state, our practice, and the tenor of his law, Rom. ii. 15. Psalm lxv. 3. cxxx. 3, 4;——*in our will*,—solemnly and repeatedly chusing him, Josh. xxiv. 15. Psalm xvi. 2. lxxiii. 25. cxix. 57. xci. 2. cxlii. 5. Lam. iii. 24; making him our chief end, in every thing we do, 1 Cor. x. 31. 1 Pet. iv. 11. Rom. xiv. 8; denying our natural, civil, and religious self for his sake and honour, Mat. xvi. 24. Luke xiv. 26. xvii. 10; resigning ourselves to his commanding and providential will, Rom. vi. 17. Gen. xxii. 1—18. Luke xxiv. 26. Psalm xlvii. 4. xxxix. 9. cxix. 71, 75; patient bearing his afflicting rods, Psalm xxxix. 9. 1 Sam. iii. 18. 2 Sam. xvi. 10, 11. Lam. iii. 22, 39. Micah vii. 7—10. Isa. liii. 7;—— *in our affections*, —loving him as infinitely excellent and kind, Deut. vi. 5. Psal. xviii. 1—3. cxvi. 1; desiring more full enjoyment of him, Isa. xxvi 8, 9. Phil. i. 23. 2 Cor. v. 4, 8; delighting and rejoicing in him, and what he hath said, done, or will do for us, Psalm xxxii. 11. cxlix. 2. Isa. lxi. 10. Hab. iii. 18. Psalm lx. 6. Luke i. 47; grieving for offences given him, Zech. xii. 10. Psalm cxix. 136; kindly fear of him, Isa. viii. 13. Hos. iii. 5.

Psalm xxxvi. 1. cxix. 120. Mat. x. 28; judicious, prudent, and well governed zeal for his honour and interest in the world, Psalm lxix. 9. cxix. 139; loathing and abhorring ourselves for our sinfulness, as contrary to his nature and will, Ezek. xvi. 63. xxxvi. 31, 32. Job xlii. 5, 6. Isa. vi. 5. lxiv. 6. Jer. xxxi. 18. Rom. vii. 14—24;—*in our memory* delightfully recording and remembering the discoveries which we have had of him in his word and works, Psalm cxix. 11. xxxvi. 6, 7. ciii.—cvii. cxvi. cxxxvi. cxlv.—cl. John ii. 17. Job xxxvi. 24;—— *in our whole soul,* trusting and hoping in him, as our Saviour, Husband, Father and God, for all that we need, Isa. xxvi. 4. Psalm cxxx. 7, 8. cxix. 49, 81;—in humility towards him, Micah vi. 8; and hence, under a deep sense of our own ignorance, weakness, and unworthiness, consulting him in all our ways, and giving him the glory of any good in or done by us, Prov. iii. 5, 6. Isa. xl. 6. 2 Cor. iii. 5. 1 Cor. xv. 10. Psalm cxv. 1; voluntarily undertaking the meanest services to which he calls us, Acts xxi. 13; and restricting ourselves within the limits of our proper station, Psalm cxxxi. 1. 1 Cor. vii. 20, 24; and labouring in internal prayers and praises, Phil. iv. 6. Exod. xiv. 8. Psalm cxix. 58. xlv. 1. cviii. 1. 2. OUTWARDLY, in our due attendance upon the instituted ordinances of his worship, Mat. xxviii. 20. 1 Cor. xi. 2; and a due performance of all that duty which we owe to ourselves or others from a regard to his authority, and answerably to his nature, and to his relations to us, Mat. v. 16. 1 Cor. x. 31. 1 Pet. iv. 11.

The first commandment FORBIDS, I. ATHEISM, which is either *speculative,* in which men flatly and directly deny or doubt God's existence, perfections, and providence, Psalm xiv. 1. liii. 1. Eph. ii. 12. 1 John ii. 23. Ezek. viii. 12. Psalm x. 11. Men are often tempted to this by their prosperity, or outrageousness in wickedness, or by the uncommon afflictions of the godly; but they rather attempt to force themselves into it, than actually to fix it in opposition to the dictates of their conscience, and the manifold proofs to the contrary, Prov. xxx. 9. i. 32. Jer. ii. 5, 25. Mal. iii. 13, 14. i. 13. Psalm lxxiii. 13;—or *practical,* in which men live as if there were not a God; having no knowledge of him, no faith in him, no choice of him, no love to him, no spiritual thoughts of him, no holy desires after him; —no spiritual impressions of his perfections, discernment of him in his word or works, or activity in his worship;—indulging themselves in secret sins, wishing there were no God to punish them, and encouraging others in wickedness, Psalm xiv. 1. Eph. ii. 2, 12. Psalm xxxvi. 3. Mic. vi. 16;—live without any profession of religion, or appearance of regard to the worship of God, Jer. x. 25; or live wickedly under the mask of a profession, Phil. iii. 19. Tit. i. 15, 16. 2 Tim. iii. 2—5; or abandon that religious profession and practice which they once had, John vi. 66. Hos. vi. 4, 5. Heb. vi. 4—6. II. PROFANENESS respecting the *object* of worship, in not worshipping and glorifying him as God and our God;—which, *in our mind*, includes natural, slothful, or wilful ignorance of him and spiritual things, Hos. iv. 1, 6. Isa. xxvii. 11. 2 Thess. i. 8. Job xxi. 14; misapprehensions of him, Acts xvii. 23, 29. Rom. i. 21. 1 Cor. i. 23; neglect and aversion to think of him, Psalm x. 4. Rom. i. 28; want of honourable, and conception of vile thoughts concerning him, Isa. liii. 3, 4. Psalm x. 13. l. 21. Ezek. viii. 12; doubting, unbelief, and error, contrary to his declarations in his word, 2 Kings vi. 33. vii. 19. Deut. xxix. 19. Acts xxvi. 9. Gal. v. 20; rash credulity of others instead of God, 1 John iv. 1. John v. 43. 2 Thess. ii. 11, 12.—In *our conscience*, it includes carnal security, Zeph. i. 12; blindness and misinformation, Isa. v. 20; inactivity, stupidity, senselessness, 1 Tim. iv. 2. Eph. iv. 18, 19; partially, making most ado about lesser matters, and chiefly disapproving other men's sinfulness, Mat. vii. 1—4. xxiii. 23; deceitfulness, pretending regard to God, when it is biassed by bribes, Ezek. xiii. 19; legality, exciting men to follow after righteousness by the works of the law, Rom. ix. 31, 32. x. 2, 3. vii. 9; submission to men's authority instead of God's, 1 Cor. iii. 4, 5. Hos. v. 11. Mic. vi. 16.—*In our will*, it includes rejection of the gospel offers of Christ, and God in him, to be our God, Hos. xi. 2, 7. Psalm lxxxi. 10—12. Heb. x. 26, 29; neglect of surrendering ourselves to God, and not making him our chief end, Eph. ii. 12. Hos. x. 1. Zech. vii. 5; hypocritical dedication of ourselves to him, Mic. iii. 11. Hos. viii. 2; disregard of our solemn engagements to him, Jer. v. 4, 5. Psalm l. 16, 17. lxxviii. 10, 57; inward covenanting against him and his interests, Eccl. v. 6. Hos. v. 11. 2 Cor. xiii. 8; discontentment with, and murmuring against his words or works, Job xxxiv. 33, 37. Jude 16. Psalm xxxvii. 1—8. Jer. xii. 1. xx. 7—18; unsanctified contentment, seeking that satisfaction which we cannot find in one creature, in another,—satisfaction with our lot, without regard to the will of God in it; indolent, fool-hardy, stupid, and brutish patience under our troubles,—and enduring them as just, but not as good,—nay very good for us, Isa. xlii. 25. xxxix. 8. Psalm cxix. 71.—*In our affections*, it includes want or weakness of love to, and desire after, or delight in God, aversion from, and hatred of him, and what pertains to him and bears his image, Rom. i. 30. Psalm xiv. 1. Job xxxiv. 9; deadness in, and weariness of his service, Mal. iii. 13. i. 13. Amos viii. 5; lukewarm indifference about spiritual things, Rev. iii. 16; corrupt, indiscreet, blind, and passionate zeal, not proportioned to the importance of its object; or chiefly against sin in others, Rom. x. 2. Mat. xxiii.

23. vii. 1—4. Gen. xxxviii. 24. 2 Sam. xii. 5; and which carries us out of our station to act from proud and selfish views, without a proper call, and without proper pity to offenders, 2 Sam. vi. 6. 2 Kings x. 16. Luke ix. 54. 2 Cor. ii. 7. 2 Thess. iii. 6, 7;—want of filial reverence of God, rashness and irreverence of heart in his presence, Psalm lxxxix 7. Eccl. v. 1; unconcern at his threatenings, Amos iii. 8. Jer. v. 22. Isa. v. 19; presumptuous rebellion against his warnings, Psalm xxxvi. 1. Ezek. xii. 27. Jer. xliii. 1, 2. xliv. 15, 16. xxiii. 17, 33; hope of impunity in sin, Deut. xxix. 19. Psalm x. 11, 13; obdurate impenitence in sin, manifested in our denying, extenuating, excusing, or transferring the blame of it on others, Rom. ii. 5. Prov. xxviii. 13. xxix. 1. xxx. 20; bold and curious inclination to pry into God's secrets, Deut. xxix. 29; presumptuous confidence that he will support us in that to which he never called us,—tempting or putting him to the trial, what he can or will do, in exercising his patience or inflicting his judgments, Mat. iv. 7. Psalm xcv. 9. Mal. iii. 15; diffidence, anxiety and despair, Jer. ii. 25. Mat. vi. 34. Gen. iv. 13. Ezek. xxxvii. 11. —*In our memory*, it includes our readiness to forget God, his words and works, and aptness to retain that which is trifling and wicked instead thereof, Jer. ii. 32. Psalm l. 22. Deut. xxxii. 18.—In *our whole soul*, it includes pride, Psalm cxxxviii. 6. Hab. ii. 4. Prov. xxx. 12, 13; insensibleness of our weakness and sinfulness, Jer. ii. 31. viii. 6, 12. 1 Cor. x. 12. Mat. vii. 2, 3; contempt of duty, or want of inclination to it, because of its apparent meanness, 1 Sam. ii. 30. 2 Kings v. 11, 12; inward meddling with things above our situation or ability, Psalm cxxxi. 1, 2. Num. xvi. 1; infervency and wandering of heart in religious duties, 1 Thess. v. 19. Eph. vi. 19, 20. Rom. xii. 11; unthankfulness to God for benefits received, and thankfulness for success in sin, Deut. viii. 17. Zech. xi. 5; inward slighting God and his law,—resisting and grieving his Spirit, Psalm l. 17. Deut. xxxii. 15. Isa. lxiii. 10. Acts vii. 51. Eph. iv. 30. Heb. x. 29. Mat. xii. 31, 32;—and, in so far as our inward frame and exercise is not suited to his glorious excellencies, and his new-covenant relations to us, Rom. i. 21.—In our *external appearances*, it includes our not avouching him in our profession as God and our God in Christ, and not attending that profession which we make of him with a suitable practice, 2 Tim. iii. 2—5. Tit. i. 15, 16. III. IDOLATRY, which is the giving that worship and honour to any other, which is due to God alone,—and is either more *gross* or *refined*. In the more *gross idolatry*, heathens worshipped the sun, moon, stars, kings, heroes, benefactors, inventors of arts, nay dogs, cats, crocodiles, serpents, leeks, onions, harlots, &c. Jer. xliv. 3, 8, 18. 1 Kings xi. 2. 2 Kings xvii. 29—33. Rom. i. 21—25. And papists wor-

ship angels, popes, pretended relics of Christ and his saints, consecrated wafers, &c. The sinfulness and absurdity of such worship is evident: 1. No creatures deserve our worship, being at best little superior, and many of them inferior to us. Being weak, or at least finite, they are unfit to be trusted, Jer. xvii. 5. Isa. ii. 22. Rom. x. 14. The most exalted creatures cannot judge of the inward truth or importance of our worship, Rev. ii. 23. Jer. xvii. 10; nor can they grant our requests, or even a blessing on our outward enjoyments, Exod. xxiii. 25. 2. God hath given us no warrant by precept, promise, or approved example, to invoke or adore any creature. 3. He requires, that only himself, as the self-existent God, should be worshipped; and condemns all religious worship of any other, Exod. xx. 2, 3. Matth. iv. 10. Deut. vi. 13. x. 20. 1 Sam. vii. 3. Isa. xlii. 8. Rom. i. 23. Gal. iv. 8. 4. Though Christ, *as God*, be the object of religious worship, and though, *as Mediator*, he is to be received by faith as God's *unspeakable gift*,—and though his mediation be an excitement to worship him *as God*, as well as his Father, and the Holy Spirit in him, yet, as the *Son of man* and the *servant of God*, he cannot be the object of divine worship, unless his finite nature shared the same honour with his godhead, or he have a subordinate and a supreme worship ascribed to him, both of which are equally absurd.—Nor is there any reason to pretend, that the religious worship called LATREIA belongs only to God, but that called DOULEIA may be given to creatures; for DOULEIA is ascribed to God, Gal. iv. 8. 1 Thess. i. 9. Mat. xxvi. 24. Acts xx. 19. Rom. xii. 11. xiv. 18. Eph. vi. 7; and civil homage to men is called LATREIA, Deut. xxviii. 48. Lev. xxiii. 7.—In *more refined idolatry*, we believe, choose, trust, love, esteem, desire, delight in, fear, think on, sorrow for the want of,—are zealous for, or careful to please, or obtain any thing as much or more than the true God, or in opposition to his will.—In this manner men chiefly idolize and worship, 1. Satan,—in entering into covenants with him, practising or encouraging divination, witchcraft, or magic, consulting him or his agents relative to things future, secret, or lost, Deut. xvi. 9—12. Lev. xix. 31. xx. 6. Exod. xxii. 18. Isa. viii. 19. Dan. ii. 2;—embracing his false doctrines, 1 Tim. iv. 1, 2; regarding his pretended miracles, 2 Thess. ii. 9, 10. Rev. xiii. 13. xix. 20;—obeying his laws, Jer. vii. 23. Mic. vi. 16. Hos. v. 11; hearkening to his suggestions, Acts v. 3—10. 1 Kings xxii. 22, 23. John xiii. 27. 1 Chron. xxi. 1; or submitting to his slavery, 2 Cor. iv. 4. 2 Tim. ii. 26. Isa. xlix. 24, 25. 2. The world,—in seeking the enjoyments of it as the portion of our soul, or for themselves, not as they lead to God, Psalm xvii. 14. Col. iii. 1, 2. Rom. viii. 5, 6. Phil. iii. 19. James iv. 4. 1 John ii. 15, 16. iii. 17. Rev. i. 7; making the customs and fashions of it a standard of our faith or practice, Rom. xii. 1, 2. 1 Pet. i. 14, 18; delighting in the fellowship of carnal men, Psal. xv. 4. cxix. 115. Prov. ix. 6. xiii. 20. James iv. 4; or sinfully pleasing men, Gal. i. 10. Rom. xv. 2. 1 Cor. ix. 19---22. 1 Thess. ii. 4---6. 3. Self, natural, civil, or religious,---in having too high an esteem of ourselves, Prov. xxvi. 12, 16. Isa. lviii. 3. Rom. x. 3; loving ourselves, not as subordinated to God, and for his sake, 2 Tim. iii. 2. Luke xiv. 26; or seeking ourselves too much, or as our great end in any thing we do, 2 Kings x. 16. Prov. xxi. 4. xv. 8. Zech. vii. 5, 6. Phil. ii. 21. iii. 19. 4. Sin, in indulging or practising it in any form or degree, as it stands in direct opposition to God, Jer. xliv. 4. Hab. i. 12. 1 John iii. 4; and its reign or prevalence in us renders all that we do a service to and worship of it, Isa. i. 11, 12. lxvi. 3. Prov. xv. 8. xxviii. 9. xxi. 4, 27. 5. Graces and spiritual comforts, in loving, trusting to, desiring, and delighting in them for themselves, and instead of God, 1 John v. 21. 2 Cor. xii. 7.

The REASONS annexed to this commandment are, 1. That the all-seeing God takes special notice of our atheism, profaneness, and idolatry, let them be varnished with as many fair pretences as they will, Psalm xliv. 20, 21. Ezek. viii. 7---12. 2. That he is much displeased with us for them, particularly for idolatry. He has manifested his displeasure in his word, 1 Cor. vi. 9, 10. Gal. v. 19---21. Rev. xxi. 8. xxii. 15. xiv. 10, 11. And few nations, heathens, Jews, or antichristians, have or will be destroyed in his providence, but on account of idolatry, as one principal article of his controversy with them, 2 Kings xvii. Jer. xxv. xlvi.---li. Rev. ix. xiii. xiv. He has often taken away men's idols, Judg. xvii. xviii.; obliged them either to part with them or with their profession of religion, Gen. xxxv. 2; or rendered them a plague to them, as in the case of Eli, and David's idolized children, 1 Sam. ii.---iv. 2 Sam. xiii.---xviii. 1 Kings i.; or has left them shamefully to manifest their idolatry, as in the case of Judas, Matth. xxvi. 15; Demas, 2 Tim. iv. 10.

II. The SECOND COMMANDMENT respects the MEANS of religious worship. Our bodies, as well as our souls, being redeemed with the blood of God, Acts xx. 28. 1 Cor. vi. 19, 20;---everlasting happiness awaiting our bodies as well as our souls, 1 Cor. xv. Matth. x. 28;---our mouth being the interpreter and agent of our heart, Matth. xii. 34; and external worship being of use to promote that which is internal,---God has framed this commandment, immediately to respect it, though as proceeding from our heart.---This external worship, not being strictly natural, but *instituted*, and God having a distin-

OF THE LAW OF GOD. 463

guished zeal for his own worship, and men a remarkable proneness to intrude their own inventions into it, this and the fourth commandment are more largely stated and enforced than any of the rest.

Our whole worship of God, since the fall, being an abomination to him, but in so far as performed in the name of Christ, Prov. xv. 8. xxi. 27. xxviii. 9. Isa. lxvi. 3. i. 11—15. Col. iii. 17. 1 Pet. iv. 11. Eph. iii. 21. He, the true representation and image of the invisible God, may, as Mediator, be considered as the principal mean of it, Col. i. 15. 2 Cor. iv. 4, 6. John xiv. 6, 9, 10. And it must be performed in obedience to his command,—in the exercise of faith in and love to his person God-man Mediator,—in reliance upon his strength,—and presented to his Father through his righteousness and intercession, in order to render it acceptable, John xiv. 6. x. 7, 9. Eph. ii. 18. iii. 12. Col. iii. 17. 1 Pet. iv. 11. ii. 5, 9. —In subordination to, and in order to extensive improvement of Christ, in our worship of, and fellowship with God, he, in his word, has appointed many diversified ordinances; particularly, 1. Prayer, secret, private, and public, Matth. vi. 6. Jer. x. 25. Mal. iii. 16. Acts ii. 46. 2. Singing of psalms, hymns, and spiritual songs, in secret, private, and public, for the praise of God, James v. 13. Col. iii. 16. Eph. v. 19. Psal. xxxiii. 1, 2. xlvii. xcvi.—c. ciii. cv. cvii. cxxxiv.—cxxxvi. cxlv.—cl. 3. Reading and hearing God's word, John v. 39. Acts xvii. 11. xv. 21. 4. Preaching and hearing the gospel, 1 Pet. iii. 19. i. 12. Neh. viii. 8. 2 Kings iv. 23. Mark xvi. 15. 2 Tim. iv. 2. Rom. x. 14, 15, 17. 5. Administration and receiving of the sacraments, Gen. xvii. 9—14. Exod. xii. Num. ix. xxviii. xxix. 1 Cor. x. 1—4. Matth. xxviii. 19. 1 Cor. x. 16, 17. xi. 23—29. 6. Religious fasting and thanksgiving, secret, private, and public, Matth. vi. 17, 18. ix. 15. Zech. xii. 12—14. 1 Cor. vii. 5. Joel ii. 13. Exod. xv. 1 Chron. xvi. 2 Chron. xx. 26. 7. Church government and discipline, including a standing ministry and the maintainance of it, Exod. xxv.—xxxi. Lev. i.—xvi. Num. iii. iv. viii. xv. xvii. xviii. Heb. iii. 5, 6. Matth. xvi. 18, 19. xx. 25, 26. xviii. 15—20. 1 Cor. xii. 28. Eph. iv. 11—14. John xviii. 36. Acts i.—xx. 1 Tim. v. 17. 1 Thess. v. 12. Heb. xiii. 7, 17. 1 Cor. ix. 14. 8. Catechetical and other instruction of children, servants, or people, in the truths of God, Gen. xviii. 19. Deut. vi. 6—9. Gal. vi. 6. 9. Spiritual conference and joint prayer in social meetings, stated or occasional, Mal. iii. 16. Song i. 4. v. 8—16. vii. 1—3. vii. 1—3. vii. 13. iv. 11. vii. 9. iii. 7—11. Psalm lxvi. 16. Luke xxiv. 14—32. 10. Vows of self-dedication to the service of God, personal or social, Isa. xliv. 4, 5. Psalm cxvi. 16. lxxvi. 11. cxix. 106. Eccl. v. 4, 5. Num. xxx. Lev. xxvii. Deut. v.

2. xxix. 2. Josh. xxiv. 15, 25. 2 Chron. xv. 12, 13. xxiii. 16. xxix. 10. xxxiv. 31, 34. Neh. ix. x. Ezra x. 3. Isa. xix. 18, 21. 2 Cor. viii. 5. 11. Oaths, assertory, promissory, and minatory, in which we solemnly call God to witness the truth, and our sincerity in that which we declare or engage, and to avenge himself upon us, if we declare any thing false or unknown to us, or neglect to fulfil that which we engage, Deut. vi. 13. Jer. iv. 2. Heb. vi. 16. Isa. xlv. 23. lxv. 16. Rom. ix. 1, 2. 2 Cor. i. 23. xi. 31. Gal. i. 20. 1 Thess. v. 27. 12. Casting of lots, in which we solemnly appeal to the immediate decision of God in an important matter, in which human prudence cannot, at least peaceably, determine, Prov. xvi. 33. xviii. 18. Lev. xvi. 8. Num. xxxiv. 13. Josh. vii. 13—18. xv.—xxi. 1 Sam. x. 19—24. xiv. 41, 42. 1 Chron. xxiv.—xxvi. Neh. xi. 1. Acts i. 24—26. 13. Collection for the poor, in which we give a part of our substance to the Lord, Matth. vi. 1—5. 1 Cor. xvi. 1, 2. Gal. ii. 10.—All which ordinances this commandment REQUIRES, 1. To be *received* in principle and public profession,—known and assented to as divine by our mind, and embraced as appointed of God by our will, Mic. iv. 5. 2. To be *observed* in all their requirements, as instituted by God, to be means of our fellowship with himself, Mat. xxviii. 30. Psalm xxvii. 4. lxiii. 2. lxxxiv. 2, 10. 3. To be kept *pure* from every human addition, 1 Cor. xi. 2. Psalm xvi. 4. Acts xvii. 16, 17, 22. Deut. vii. 5. xii. 23. Exod. xxiii. 24. Col. ii. 4, 8, 16—23. Matth. xv. 2, 3, 9. 4. To be kept entire, without suffering any thing to be taken from them, Deut. iv. 2. v. 32. xii. 32. Rev. xxii. 19.

This commandment FORBIDS, I. PROFANENESS respecting the *means* of religious worship. 1. In not receiving God's ordinances as his, but as delivered to us by Popes, Councils, Kings, Parents, Teachers, Hos. viii. 12. Isa. xxix. 13. 2. In neglecting the secret, private, or public observance of them, Exod. iv. 24, 25. Jer. x. 25. Heb. x. 25. Rev. ii. 4. 3. In devolving upon others that observance of them which God requires of us,—as when clergymen hold a plurality of charges, and hire curates to officiate for them, or heads of families devolve the whole religious care of them into the hands of chaplains, 1 Kings xii. 31. Judg. xvii. 5, 12, 13. 4. In curtailing them, in respect of parts, time, or frequency, Amos viii. 4, 5. Mal. i. 13. iii. 7—9, 14. 5. In contempt of them disposing us to neglect them, or to use them without due reverence, Eccl. v. 1. Mal. i. 12, 13, 14. 6. In sleepy or careless attendance on them, Acts xx. 9. 7. In valuing ourselves on account of our contempt of them, Job xxi. 14, 15. 8. In making merchandise of church-livings, censures, decisions, sacraments, Acts

viii. 18. Rom. ii. 22. John ii. 16. Mark xi. 15—17. 9. In hindering the free observation of God's ordinances by derision, immoderate and unseasonable worldly business, intrusion of careless and scandalous ministers, establishing or executing iniquitous laws, persecuting men for conscience-sake, Isa. xxviii. 22. 1 Pet. iii. 7. 1 Sam. ii. 17. Mic. vi. 16. 2 Kings xviii. 13. Acts iv.—xxviii. II. IDOLATRY respecting the *means* of worship, in, 1. Forming corporeal representations of God in our mind, John iv. 24. Rom. i. 23. 2. Forming material representations of the divine persons, in order to worship them, or that which they are intended to represent, Acts xvii. 29. Rom. i. 23. Deut. iv. 14, 15. Hab. ii. 18. Rom. xi. 4. Lev. xxvi. 1. 3. Retaining images of divine persons, or even of false gods, for ornaments of houses, &c. Deut. vii. 5. Exod. xxiii. 24. Psalm xvi. 4. 4. Exhibiting images in churches for the instruction of the ignorant, Exod. xxiii. 24. 2 Kings xviii. 4.——To pretend their usefulness is to accuse God of neglecting to give us sufficient means of instruction in his word and ordinances, contrary to Mat. xxviii. 20. Luke xvi. 29, 31. Isa. viii. 20. Such images blasphemously represent God, who is an infinite Spirit, as if he were finite and corporeal. They cannot even represent the body of Christ in connection with his divine person, or in its glorified state, Isa. xl. 18. xlvi. 5. Jer. x. 8, 14, 15. Hab. ii. 18. Zech. x. 2. God condemns and punishes men for making carnal representations of himself, Rom. i. 23, 24; and for their adoration of saints, angels, popes, relics, and images, under pretence of worshipping him by them, Acts x. 25, 26. Rev. xix. 10. xxii. 8, 9. xiii. 4, 8, 15. ix. 20, 21. Nay, for their idolatry, the papists are expressly adjudged to eternal damnation, Rev. xiv. 9—11. III. SUPERSTITION, in adding to or changing God's ordinances of worship, in, 1. Pretending to render that to be sin or duty which God never declared to be so, Mat. xv. 5, 6, 9. Prov. xxx. 6. Col. ii. 16—23. 2. Imagining that virtue in worship arises from places, postures, instruments, or number of acts, contrary to Mal. i. 11. John iv. 20—22. 3. Fancying that the position of stars at the time of birth, the meeting or dealing with particular persons first in the morning, flight of birds, or the like, are declarative tokens of God's will relative to future events, Isa. xliv. 25. xlvii. 8, 13. Jer. x. 2. 4. Adding to God's worship ceremonies, restricted seasons, church-officers, sacraments, apocryphal books, &c. not prescribed in his word, Deut. xii. 32. iv. 2. v. 32. Isa. i. 12. Mat. xv. 3, 9. Col. ii. 16—23. Gal. iv. 10, 11.——Men render themselves guilty of such superstition and idolatry, 1. In devising it, Num. xv. 39. 1 Kings xii. 28—33. 2. In advising or enticing to it, Deut. xiii. 6—8. 3. In commanding it, Hos. v.

11. Micah vi. 16. 4. In using it, 1 Kings xi. 33. 5. In approving or tolerating it, Rev. ii. 14, 15.—Nor will any pretence of the piety of its authors or promoters, Matth. xv. 2—9; or its antiquity, 1 Pet. i. 18; legal establishment or customariness, Jer. xliv. 17; good intention, 1 Sam. xv. 21. xiii. 12; or its seeming tendency to promote devotion, Isa. lxv. 5, excuse their conduct before God.

The REASONS annexed to this commandment for enforcing obedience to it, are, 1. God's *sovereignty*, which entitles him alone to prescribe the ordinances of his own worship, Jer. vii. 31. xxxii. 35. 2. His *propriety* in his people, as his children, servants, and subjects, Isa. xxxiii. 22. 3. His *zeal* for his own worship, in punishing the breakers and rewarding the keepers of this and other commandments, Lev. x. 1, 2, 3. Isa. ix. 7.

III. The THIRD COMMANDMENT respects the NAME of God, which comprehends every thing by which he makes himself known. 1. Proper *names*,—*essential*, as Jehovah, Jah, I am, The Lord, God, Exod. vi. 3. iii. 14. Psalm lxviii. 4. lxxxiv. 11.—Or *personal*,—Father, Son, Word, Jesus Christ, Holy Ghost, &c. 2. *Titles* which mark his relations to us-ward, as The God and Father of Christ, Eph. i. 3. 1 Pet. i. 3; The High and lofty One,—The Holy One of Israel, Isa. lvii. 15. xlix. 7; The God of mercy and grace, and peace, Psalm lix. 10. 1 Pet. v. 10. Rom. xvi. 20; The God of salvation, Psalm lxviii. 20; The God of all comfort, 2 Cor. i. 3; The God and King of glory, Acts vii. 2. Psalm xxiv. 8, 10; The God of gods, Josh. xxii. 22; King of kings, and Lord of lords, Rev. xvii. 14. xix. 16; The God of Abraham, Isaac, and Jacob, Exod. iii. 6; The God of the Hebrews, or of Israel, Exod. v. 3. Psalm lxxii. 18; The God of the whole earth, Isa. liv. 5; The Father of mercies, 2 Cor. i. 3, and of glory, Eph. i. 17; of spirits, Heb. xii. 9. Num. xvi. 22; Creator, Isa. xl. 28; Preserver or Observer of men, Job vii. 20; King, Judge, Lawgiver, Isa. xxxiii. 22. James iv. 12; Saviour, Isa. xlv. 15, 22; Redeemer, Isa. xlviii. 17. xlix. 26. Jer. l. 34. Job xix. 25; Comforter, Isa. li. 7, 12. John xv. 26. 2 Cor. i. 4. vii. 6. 3. *Attributes* imitable and inimitable, Infinity, Eternity, &c. 4. *Ordinances* of worship, Mic. iv. 5. Luke i. 6. 5. *Words*, Law and Gospel, Psalm cxxxviii. 2. 6. *Works* of creation, providence, and redemption, Psalm xix. 1. ix. 16. Acts xiv. 17. Eph. iii. 10, 21. 2 Cor. v. 18---21.

This commandment REQUIRES us, I. To take up the name of God, as it is laid before us in his word,—*in our thoughts*, meditating on it, Psalm civ. 34. cxxxix. 17, 18;—*in our words*, speaking of it, Psalm cv. 1---3. cvii. cxxxvi. cxlv. cxlvi. cxlvii.; —and *in our deeds*, making an open profession of it, adorned with an answerable practice, 1 Pet. iii. 15, 16. Rom. x. 10. Rev. xiv. 1. Heb. iv. 14. x. 23. Matth. v. 16. Phil. ii. 15, 16. iv. 8.—This taking up of God's name is necessary to his honour; and without it we hide, bury, and deny the excellency and usefulness of his name, 1 Cor. x. 31. Lev. x. 3;—necessary to our own advantage, his names, titles, and attributes being precious, reviving, sanctifying, and comforting cordials to our soul,—his ordinances breasts of spiritual nourishment,—his words sweeter than honey, an inheritance better than thousands of gold and silver, an incomparable instructer, Song viii. 6. Psalm xix. 10. cxix. 72, 103, 111, 97—100, 105;—his works a prospective glass, manifesting wonders of wisdom, power, mercy, and goodness, Rom. i. 19, 20. Psalm xix. 1—5. ciii.—cvii. cxxxvi. cxlv.—clvii. xcii. 4. Eph. i. 3—10. ii. 4—10; and necessary to the edification of others, leading them to Christ, salvation, and holiness, Mat. v. 16. John xvii. 26.

——And for gaining these important ends, our profession of God's name ought to be *judicious*, every point of it knowingly founded on his word, Rom. x. 10. Prov. iv. 5—7. Acts xvii. 11; *candid*, perfectly answerable to that which we believe in our heart, Rom. x. 10. Psalm cxvi. 10. 2 Cor. iv. 13; *complete*, extending to every attained truth, Phil. iii. 16. Acts xx. 20, 27; *plain*, without ambiguity or equivocation, Gal. ii. 11, 12. v. 1—4. 2 Cor. i. 12; *meek*, 1 Pet. iii. 15. Matth. xi. 29. 2 Tim. ii. 24, 25; *bold* and *zealous*, Psalm cxix. 46, 139. Acts ii. 14—36. iii. 12—26. iv. 10—13, 19, 20. v. 29, 32. vi. 15. vii. 51—53. Eph. vi. 20; *constant* to the end, 1 Pet. iii. 15. 2 Pet. iii. 17, 18. Rev. ii. 10. iii. 11. II. It requires us to use the name of God in an holy and reverent manner, in spiritual knowledge of it, Psalm ix. 10; faith in it as manifested in Christ, Heb. xi. 6. iv. 2. Rom. xiv. 23; ardent love to it, Psalm lxix. 36. Isa. xxvi. 8; kindly fear and awe of it, Mal. iv. 2. Deut. xxviii. 58. Psalm lxxxix. 7. Rev. xv. 4; in singleness of heart, and to a right end, Psalm xcvi. 7, 8. III. To employ God himself to hallow or glorify his own name, in removing from the world and our heart all that atheism, ignorance, idolatry, profaneness, &c. which tends to dishonour his name, and in disposing all things in nations, churches, and persons, to promote his glory to the best advantage, Mat. vi. 9. Psal. cviii. 5. lxxxii. 8. lvii. 5, 11. lxxii. 19.

This commandment FORBIDS our neglecting to promote God's honour in the matter and manner required, Deut. xxxii. 51. Num. xxvii. 14; and our profaning and abusing his name in using it ignorantly, Acts xvii. 23; lightly or rashly, in exclamations, thanksgivings, prayers, obsecrations, adjurations, and appeals, Acts xix. 13, 14; superstitiously, as when the Israelites carried his ark to the field of battle to render them successful against the Philistines, 1 Sam. iv. 3—5; wantonly, in swearing by him, or creatures in his stead, in our common conversation, Mat. v. 34—37. James v. 12; in angrily or sportfully cursing and devoting ourselves or others to damnation, devils, mischiefs, &c. 1 Kings xix. 2. 2 Kings vi. 31. Num. xxii. 11. Judg. xvii. 2;—perjuring ourselves, attesting that which is false, and not endeavouring to perform that which we have engaged upon oath, Zech. v. 4. Mal. iii. 5. Mat. v. 33. Hos. iv. 2. x. 4;—blasphemously reviling God, or causing others to do so, Rom. ii. 24. Acts xxvi. 11. 1 Tim. vi. 1. 2 Sam. xii. 14. Isa. li. 5; reproaching his ordinances, words, works, or people, because of their relation and likeness to him, 1 Tim. vi. 1. Tit. ii. 5. 1 Cor. iv. 13. Mark iii. 30; ascribing to him that which is dishonourable to him, Mat. xi. 19. xii. 24. John viii. 48, 52. Psalm l. 21. x. 13; denying him that which is true and honourable, and ascribing it to creatures, Job xxxvi. 19—25. Psalm lxxiii. 9. xciv. 7. Ezek. viii. 12. ix. 9. Zeph. i. 12. Acts xii. 22; thinking or speaking against him in a virulent manner, Job ii. 5, 9. Exod. v. 2. 2 Kings vi. 33. vii. 2, 19; and despitefully or maliciously rebelling against the plain and powerful testimonies of his Spirit to our conscience, Mat. xii. 23, 24, 31, 32. Heb. vi. 4, 5. x. 26—29. But,

More particularly, God's names, titles, and attributes are profaned and abused, when they are not thought and spoken of, and improved by inward principles of faith in, and love to Christ, Rom. xiv. 23. Heb. xi. 6. 1 Tim. i. 5; when our inward unbelief works in opposition to them, 2 Kings vii. 2, 19. Ezek. viii. 12. ix. 9. Zeph. i. 12. Psalm x. 11, 13. l. 21. lxxvii. 8, 9. xciv. 7. Jer. xv. 18. xx. 7; when we retain or exercise hatred of them, Rom. viii. 7, 8. i. 30. Psalm cxxxix. 20; and when we use them not to their proper ends, but as encouragements to wickedness, Mal. i. 6. Eccl. viii. 11. Isa. xliii. 24. Rom. ii. 4, 5.—His ordinances are profaned and abused when they are used with unholy hearts, from principles of self-love, pride, regard to human laws or customs, 1 Tim. i. 5. 1 Cor. xii. 3; or in a proud, careless, hypocritical, unbelieving manner, Phil. iii. 3. John iv. 24. Isa. lviii. 3. xxix. 13. Heb. iv. 2; or to promote some sinful or selfish end, Mat. ii. 16. xxiii. 14. Rom. x. 3. ix. 31, 32.—PRAYER is profaned and abused when we do not duly prepare for it by searching and feeling our necessities, emptying our hearts of carnal cares, and by consideration of Christ's mediation and promises, Psalm x. 17. Eph. vi. 18; when we pray in an ignorant, proud, formal, legal, careless, wandering, and unbelieving manner, Isa. xxix. 13. Luke xviii. 11, 12. James i. 6—8. John xvi. 24; when we ask improper things, or for a bad end, Luke ix. 54. James iv. 3; and when we do not observe *whether* and *how* our requests are granted, Psalm v. 3.. cxxiii. 1—4.—SINGING of psalms is profaned when it is performed rashly, Psalm cviii. 1; merely in an outward manner, Psalm cxi. 1; without knowledge of what we sing, 1 Cor. xiv. 15; without proper affection or proper application of the matter to our own case, Eph. v. 19. Col. iii. 16. —READING or HEARING of God's word is profaned and abused when it is performed without due preparation, 1 Pet. ii. 1, 2. Jam. i. 21; without proper attention, Ezek. xxxiii. 30. Prov. xxviii. 9. Acts viii. 30; or in a sleepy and indolent manner, Amos viii. 5. Mal. i. 13; when our consciences are not laid open to it as the candle of the Lord, and we do not receive it into our heart as indeed the word of God, Psalm lxxxv. 8. 1 Thess. ii. 13. 2 Thess. ii. 10, 11; when we do not cordially believe, nor are sensibly affected with it, Heb. iv. 2. Isa. lxvi. 2; when we do not spiritually meditate on, and carefully remember that which we have read and heard, Psalm i. 2. x. 4. Psalm cxix. 11; and reduce into an holy and circumspect practice, Ezek. xxxiii. 31. Jer. xxv. 4—7; or when we regard the truths of God as we affect the preacher, Ezek. xxxiii. 32. 1 Kings xxii. 8.—PREACHING of God's word is profaned when performed by those whom God never called to that work, Jer. xxiii. 32. Rom. x. 15. Heb. v. 4; or in an unbelieving, lazy, unaffectionate, obscure, indistinct, contentious, and unfaithful manner, Isa. lvi. 10, 12. Rom. xvi. 17, 18. Phil. i. 16. Ezek. xiii. 17—19; or to exalt self, and promote carnal gain, 2 Cor. iv. 5. 1 Thess. ii. 4--6.—SACRAMENTS are profaned when they are dispensed by persons not authorised by God, 1 Cor. iv. 1, 2. xi. 23; or to improper persons, or from carnal motives, Mat. vii. 6. 1 Cor. xi. 27—29; when rites not prescribed by God are annexed to them, Isa. i. 12; when they are received without due preparation for them, proper exercise of grace in them, and a correspondent practice after them, 1 Cor. xi. 27, 29. Acts iv. 13. Rom. xii. 1, 2.—Religious FASTING is profaned when we fast for strife and debate, or to promote some bad end, Isa. lviii. 4. 2 Kings xxi. 9—13; without being truly and deeply affected with the mercies which we acknowledge, and with the sins which we confess, or judgments which we bewail and deprecate, Hos. vii. 14. Isa. lviii. 4; when we cleave to our sins, while we profess to mourn over, and supplicate deliverance from them and their effects, Isa. lviii. 4—6. Mic. iii. 11; or when we seek to honour ourselves, and recommend ourselves to God's favour by it, Mat. vi. 16. Zech. vii. 5. Luke xviii. 12. Isa. lviii. 3.—CHURCH-GOVERNMENT is profaned when it is modelled according to the forms of the state, John xviii. 36. Mat. xx. 25, 26; and its affairs regulated, not by the word of God, but by the decrees of councils, parliaments, popes, kings, &c. Isa. viii. 20. Mat. xxiii. 8—10. Mic. vi. 16. Rev. xiii.; or to please the humours of men, chiefly the great, Gal. i. 10. 1 Thess. ii. 4, 5; or when censures are inflicted as civil punishments, or are despised and opposed, or not submitted to as the institutions of Jesus Christ for promoting spiritual edification, Acts xv. 1 Cor. v. 5. 1 Thess. v. 12—14. 2 Thess. iii. 6, 14. Heb. xiii. 7, 17.—RELIGIOUS vows are profaned when we vow in a rash, ignorant, careless, legal, and hypocritical manner, Judg. xi. 30—40. Deut. v. 27—29. Jer. xlii. 5, 20; or engage to that which is sinful, trifling, or not in our power to perform, 2 Kings vi. 31. 1 Kings xix. 2; when we are proud of our vows, John viii. 41. Prov. vii. 14; and when, after lawful vows, we do not speedily, and with the utmost care and diligence, fulfil them, Num. xxx. Judg. xi. 35. Psalm lxi. 8. lxxviii. 8, 57. Eccl. v. 4—6. Prov. xx. 25.—OATHS are profaned when we refuse to swear lawful ones, which tend to glorify God, and put an end to strife, Heb. vi. 16. Deut. vi. 13. x. 20; when we swear without a proper call, James v. 12. Mat. v. 34—37; or give or take oaths which are unlawful or dubious in themselves, or impossible for us to fulfil, Mark vi. 22, 23. Acts xxiii. 14, 21; or swear in an idolatrous or superstitious manner by creatures, kissing the gospels, &c. Psalm xvi. 4. Mat. xv. 9; when we swear *without truth,* what we are uncertain of, or know to be false, or with dissimulation; *without judgment,* not understanding the nature of an oath, or the matter about which, or words in which we take it; or *without righteousness,* engaging to, or intending to promote that which is unlawful and unjust, Jer. iv. 2. Zech. v. 4; or swear lightly and rashly, Eccl. ix. 2; or, when we equivocate in swearing, understanding our expressions in a sense different from that commonly affixed to them, or which is unperceived by the imposer; or, when our swearing does not tend to the honour of God or edification of men, but is merely a compliance with some human law, and intended as a mean of access to some place of civil or ecclesiastical honour and profit; and when the impression of our oath wears off our spirits, and through sloth, inadvertency, wickedness, or specious pretences, we do not labour to perform our oaths, Josh. ix. 18, 19. 2 Sam. xxi. 1. 2 Chron. xxxvi. 19. Ezek. xvii. 12—19; when we pretend the obligation of an oath as a reason of our doing that which is sinful, Mat. xiv. 9; or when, without sufficient new ground, we repeat our oaths at, or near the same time, Exod. xx. 7.—LOTS are profaned when they are used in affairs trifling, or which human prudence might have rightly and peacefully decided, Psalm xxii. 18; or in important matters, without earnest prayer and dependence on God for his decision, Prov. xvi. 33. xviii. 18. Acts i. 24—26; or to obtain knowledge of future events, Deut. xxix. 29; to which heathenish observation of accidents, as ominous, may be reduced, Jer. x. 2. Isa. xliv. 25; or in division of cards, or throwing of the dice, &c.—the sinfulness of which is manifest. It is the common delight of wicked men, whose hearts are filled with enmity against God. It never fits men for religious exercises, but, in a most bewitching manner, diverts from them. It occasions intimate familiarity with graceless persons, few others being inclined to such diversions. As *luck* or *chance*, being mere imaginations, can give no decision, the appeal for division of cards or fall of the dice must be made either to God, or to the devil in his stead. To appeal to God in diversion, how presumptuous and blasphemous! To appeal to the devil in his stead, how horrid!—It renders men *heathenish,—believers of heathenish principles*, as that God has left some events to chance; that fortune changes sides; that some persons are lucky and others not;—*users of heathenish language, luck, chance, good fortune,* &c. influenced by *heathenish affections,* hoping, rejoicing, fearing, or grieving at what fortune has done, or is like to do;—and given to heathenish practices, irreverently disregarding God and his providence in the management of their affairs, 1 Sam. vi. 9.—A PROFESSION of religion is profaned by indulging malignity and hatred of religion, Zech. xi. 8;—by scoffing at it, Isa. xxviii. 22. Psalm i. 1. 2 Kings ii. 23. Psalm xxii. 7, 8. lxix. 10—12; by hypocritical pretences to it, 2 Tim. iii. 5. Tit. i. 16. Isa. xxxiii. 14; by making a profession of religion a cloak for maliciousness, voluptuousness, covetousness, or the like, Mat. xxiii. 14. Ezek. xxxiii. 31, 32. Mic. iii. 11. 1 Pet. ii. 16. Tit. i. 15, 16. 1 Thess. ii. 5; by being ashamed of our profession of Christ's truths, Mark viii. 38; or a reproach to it, in our foolish, untender, unstable, unfruitful, or scandalous practice, Phil. iii. 18, 11, 19. 2 Tim. iii. 1—6. Phil. i. 27. Eph. v. 15. Col. iv. 5. Isa. v. 4. Rom. ii. 4, 5, 22, 25; or by apostacy from it, John vi. 66. Gal. iii. 3. i. 6. 1 Tim. i. 19, 20. 2 Tim. iv. 10. ii. 16, 17. i. 15. 2 Pet. ii. 20—22. 1 John ii. 19.—God's WORD is profaned when we speak lightly of it, insolently against it, or pervert it to jests and bywords, Acts xvii. 18, 20. xxvi. 24. ii. 13. Jer. xxiii. 33, 36; wrest it to support error and wickedness, 2 Pet. iii. 16. 1 Tim. vi. 4. 2 Tim. ii. 14; affix our own fancies to it as the meaning of God's Spirit in it, 2 Pet. i. 20. Mat. v. 21, 33, 43; misapply it for encouragement of the wicked, and discouragement of the godly, Ezek. xiii. 22; or use it in charms, idolatrous kissing, or as a lottery book for spiritual cases, Acts xix. 13; or neglect to search and believe and practise it as indeed the word of God, John v. 39. 1 Thess. ii. 13.—God's WORKS are profaned when we do not discern, love, and admire himself as manifested in them, Rom. i. 18—20. Eph. iii. 10, 21; when we do not improve them for his glory, but for the gratification of our selfish or sinful lusts, 1 Pet. iv. 11. Hos. xiii. 6. Deut. xxxii. 14, 15. Rom. ii. 4, 5. xiii. 12—14. Jude 4. 1 Pet. ii. 8; or when we murmur against, or harden our hearts under them, 2 Cor. x. 10

Jude 16. Jer. v. 3. Isa. i. 5. 2 Chron. xxviii. 22. Zech. vii. 12. Jer. xxv. 4—7.

The profanation of God's name much ABOUNDS, because, 1. Men have so low thoughts of him, that they never discern the high regard which is due to his name, Exod. v. 2. Psalm l. 21. 2. Much abuse of his name being little discerned by unregenerate men, hardens their heart into mere profaneness, Psalm xxxvi. 1, 2. Zech. vii. 5, 6. 3. Sinful customs make multitudes look on many instances and forms of profaning it as lawful, Matth. v. 37. 4. No laws either of church or state can reach many forms of profaning it, Eccl. viii. 11. 1 Sam. xvi. 7. 5. Many ministers and magistrates have so little knowledge of, or regard to the name of God, that they scarcely think the most gross and public profanation of it a fault; and the laws which they make against it are but a mere farce, being never executed. 6. By the example of ministers and magistrates;—by the imposition of sinful, unnecessary, obscure, and dubious oaths; by taking oaths at elections, or in pleas, in so careless and irreverent a manner, the profanation of God's name is mightily encouraged and promoted.—But he will not not suffer it to escape his righteous and most dreadful judgment; for, 1. This sin is committed in direct opposition to his nature and will, Psalm lxxiii. 8, 9. 2. It manifests a most outrageous hatred of him, Psalm cxxxix. 20. 3. It is contrary to the whole tendency of divine revelation, which is to promote an holy fear and awe of him, Prov. i. 7. Psalm cxi. 9, 16. 2 Tim. iii. 15—17.

IV. The FOURTH COMMANDMENT prescribes the proper TIME of God's worship. The precise quantity and part of time proper for the stated and social worship of God depending on his *mere will*, this command is introduced with a solemn charge to *remember* to observe it, and is both positively and negatively expressed, and enforced with manifold *reasons*. The law of nature teaches, that men having bodies as well as souls, and being social creatures, they ought to worship God in an external and social manner; but does not determine what proportion or precise part of time ought to be observed in that stated and solemn worship. But the seventh part of our time being appointed by God for that purpose, his command is universally and perpetually binding or MORAL. 1. This command concerning the sabbath was imposed upon man in paradise before any typical ceremonies. Nor is there any more appearance of Moses mentioning the sabbath, Gen. ii. 1, 2, than of his mentioning the creation of the world, by an anticipation of 2500 years before it took place. 2. The appointment of the sabbath is inserted in the very middle of that moral law which God solemnly published from mount Sinai, and wrote upon two tables of stone, which was not the case with any ceremonial institution, Exod. xx. 8—11. xix. 20. xxiv. 12. xxxiv. 28. 3. Every reason annexed to this commandment, when thus published and written, is of a moral nature, forcible on all men in every age and place; and hence strangers, as well as Israelites, were obliged to observe the weekly sabbath, Exod. xx. 9, 10, 11.

Immediately after the creation of the world, God appointed the seventh day of the week for the weekly sabbath. 1. Nothing can be more plain and express than Moses' declaration on this head, that God, having finished his work of creation in six days, rested on the seventh, and sanctified it to be a sabbath to himself, Gen. ii. 1, 2. 2. All the reasons annexed to this command were as forcible immediately after the creation, as ever, Exod. xx. 10, 11. 3. The sabbath was observed before the giving of the law at Sinai, as a thing which the Israelites well knew to be already appointed, Exod. xvi. 23. 4. In Heb. iv. 3—10, three distinct sabbaths are mentioned, one which commenced from the foundation of the world, which can be no other than that of the seventh day:—another which commenced from the Israelites' entrance into Canaan, when their ceremonial sabbaths received their full force; and a *third* in commemoration of Christ's resurrection and entrance into his glorious rest.—Nay, ancient heathens take notice of the division of time into weeks, and of the *seventh* day, which it cannot be supposed they learned from the contemned Jews, who were then scarcely known at any great distance from Canaan.—— There is no reason to wonder that the observation of the sabbath from Adam to Moses is not mentioned in a history which dispatches the events of 2500 years in a few pages, especially as it is not common for historians to mention ordinary and stated observances, except at the beginning of them. In a much more extensive history of about 480 years, there is no mention made of the weekly sabbath from the second year of the Israelites' travels in the wilderness till the days of David. Nor have we one instance of a child circumcised on the eighth day from Isaac to John Baptist.—God's giving his sabbath to the Israelites for a *sign*, only means, that the law of it was solemnly published and given to them, and a typical signification added to its original moral use, Ezek. xx. 12. Neh. ix. 14. Exod. xxxi. 17.

Nevertheless God's appointment of the sabbath on the *seventh day* of the week was *not strictly moral*, but *alterable* by him. 1. Abstracting from his appointment, it is merely circumstantial whether it be on the seventh day or not. 2. It is not said in this commandment, that God blessed the *seventh* day, but that he blessed and sanctified the *sabbath* day, Exod. xx. 11. 3. The sabbath being made for man, not man for the sabbath, the day of it must be altered, if for the greater good of mankind, Mark ii. 27, 28. 4. Though the fixing it at first on the *seventh*, to commemorate the finished work of creation, was exceedingly proper, a greater event happening on another day, natively rendered it proper to change it to that day. 5. The seventh day sabbath having had a typical signification superadded to it, very properly fell into disuse with the other typical ceremonies, Exod. xxxi. 13, 17. Ezek. xx. 12, 20. Col. ii. 16, 17. The change of the sabbath from the seventh day of the week, on which Christ rose from the dead, is exceedingly proper. 1. Christ being Lord of the sabbath, it is proper that, in consequence of his resurrection, he should manifest his dominion with respect to it, Mark ii. 28. 2. His resurrection, being his entrance into rest from his finished work of redemption, more deserved to be commemorated than God's finishing of creation work did, Eph. i. 19, 20, 21. Rom. i. 3, 4. iv. 25. 1 Cor. xv. 20. Col. i. 18. Rev. i. 5. 3. It was proper that the peculiar time, as well as the nature of Christian worship, should directly relate to his finishing the purchase of our redemption. It was not proper that the day of his birth should be commemorated in the sabbath, as on it he entered on his labour and suffering; nor the day of his death, as on that he was in the heat of his conflicts; nor the day of his ascension, as on that he did not enter, but proceeded into his rest. 4. It was proper that when the covenant of grace was clearly manifested, men's religious rest should, according to the tenor of that covenant, precede their labour, Luke i. 74, 75; even as the order of labour and of rest on the seventh day sabbath, had corresponded with the order of duty and privilege in the covenant of works, Gal. iii. 12. Matth. xix. 17.

God changed the weekly sabbath *from the seventh to the first* day of the week, at the resurrection of Christ. 1. God foretold that the first day of the week should be the Christian Sabbath, Ezek. xliii. 27. Psalm cxviii. 24. 2. This day is expressly called *the Lord's day*. Now, except his healing of persons on the Jewish sabbath, no day of the week is ever ascribed to any of his acts, or events which befel him, but to his resurrection: nor is there any reason why that should be called *his day*, unless he had peculiarly sanctified and set it apart for his public worship, Rev. i. 10. 3. Christ marked his peculiar claim to that day by repeated visits to his disciples, and by the miraculous out-pouring of his spirit on it, John xx. 19, 26. Acts ii. Lev. xxiii. 16. Num. xxviii. 26. 4. His apostles, who were instructed by him in all things relative to the New Testament church, and who had his Spirit to guide them into all truth, observed the first day of the week as the Christian Sabbath. On that day they assembled the Christians to break bread in the Lord's Supper. After tarrying seven days at Troas, Paul preached on the *first day of the week*, and dispensed the Lord's Supper, and continued till midnight, Acts xx. 7. On that day, they required Christians to lay up their collections for the poor, 1 Cor. xvi. 2. xi. 2, 23.—The apostles frequently preached upon the Jewish sabbath, not because they observed it, but because they then found the Jews assembled in their synagogues, Acts xiii. &c.

The Christian Sabbath begins in the morning after midnight. 1. Christ rose early in the morning, Mat. xxviii. 1. Mark xvi. 2, 9. 2. It begins where the Jewish sabbath ended, which was when it *began to dawn* towards the first day of the week, Mat. xxviii. 1, 3. 3. The evening which follows the day of our sabbath pertained to it, John xx. 19.

Men cannot, without sin, appoint any *holy days*. 1. God has marked the weekly sabbath with peculiar honour, in his command and word. But, if men appoint holy days, they detract from its honour: And wherever holy days of men's appointment are much observed, God's weekly sabbath is much profaned, Exod. xx. 8. Ezek. xliii. 8. 2. God never could have abolished his own ceremonial holy days, in order that men might appoint others of their own invention in their room, Col. ii. 16—23. Gal. iv. 10, 11. 3. God alone can bless holy days, and render them effectual to promote holy purposes; and we have no hint in his word, that he will bless any appointed by men, Exod. xx. 11. 4. By permitting, if not requiring us to labour *six days* of the week in our worldly employments, this commandment excludes all holy days of men's appointment, Exod. xx. 8, 9. If it *permit* six days for our worldly labour, we ought to stand fast in that liberty with which Christ hath made us free, Gal. v. i. 1 Cor. vii. 23. Mat. xv. 9. If it *require* them, we ought to obey God rather than men, Acts iv. 19. v. 29.——Days of occasional fasting and thanksgiving are generally marked out by the providence of God: And the observation of them does not suppose any holiness in the day itself, Joel i. 14. ii. 15. Acts xiii. 2. xiv. 23. Mat. ix. 15.

The weekly sabbath is to be SANCTIFIED, 1. By an *holy resting* from all such worldly works as are lawful on other days, whether *servile*, ploughing, sowing, reaping,—*civil*, as buying and selling,—*liberal*, studying of sciences,—or *social*, pleasures and recreations, Exod. xx. 9. Isa. lviii. 13. Neh. xiii. 1 Cor. vii. 5. And our rest ought to be attended with much spirituality of mind and delight in God, Rev. i. 10. Isa. lviii. 13. 2. The whole day, except so much as is necessary for works of necessity and mercy, is to be *spent in* the public and private exercises of *God's worship*, Rev. i. 10. Luke xxiii. 54. Psalm xcii. Mark i. 35—39. Acts ii. 42. xiii. 14, 15, 44. xvi. 13. xx. 7. xvii. 11. Luke xxiv. 14, 17.—And it is PROFANED, 1. By *omitting* the duties required in whole or in part,—not duly remembering it before it come,—omitting the public, private, or secret duties of God's worship on it, or even the works of necessity and mercy, such as visiting and healing the sick, relieving the poor, feeding cattle, and the like, Neh. viii. 12. Mark iii. 3—5. Luke xiii. 16. xiv. 1—4. Mat. xii. 7—12. ·2. By a superficial, carnal, heartless, wearisome performance of the duties required, Mat. xv. 7. Amos viii. 5. Mal. i. 13. 3. By unnecessary sleep, idle talk, vain gadding, slothful rest, Mat. xx. 6. 4. By doing that which is in itself sinful, thrusting wickedness into the place of worship, Jer. xliv. 4. Zech. xi. 8. Ezek. xx. 21. xxii. 26. 5. By unnecessary thoughts, words, or works about worldly employments and recreations, Isa. lviii. 13. Amos viii. 5. Exod. xvi. 23—30. Num. xv. 22—36. Mat. xxiv. 20. Neh. xiii. 16, 17.

The REASONS annexed for enforcing obedience to this commandment are, 1. That God, the original proprietor of all our time, has allowed us enough for our worldly employments, even *six* days in seven; which are sufficient for our earthly business, and to tire us of it, and raise our appetite for the spiritual rest of the sabbath, Exod. xx. 9. xxxi. 15. 2. That the Lord our God has challenged a special propriety in the seventh, and so it must be sacrilegious, ungrateful, and self-ruining to rob him of it, Exod. xx. 10. xxxi. 15. Deut. v. 14. 3. God's own example, which is most honourable and binding; and so we cannot profane the sabbath without pouring contempt on his example, as unworthy of imitation, and on his works of creation and redemption as unworthy of remembrance, Exod. xx. 11. xxxi. 17. 4. God's blessing the sabbath day, in separating it, with peculiar honour, for his public worship, and for bestowing spiritual benefits on his people, and even promoting their temporal happiness; and so we cannot, without disregarding God's honour, and our own true happiness in time and eternity, neglect to observe and sanctify it, Exod. xx. 11. Isa. lvi. 2, 4—7. Lev. xxv. 20, 22.

V. The FIFTH COMMANDMENT, prescribing *relative* DUTIES, comprehends very much practical religion, and is, in so far, the foundation of the five following ones, which are all obeyed in the same proportion as this is.——To manifest his own sovereignty,—to beautify this world, and maintain some order amidst its present corruptions, God has placed men in the different stations of superiors, inferiors, or equals, one to another; and to mark with what tender affection relative duties ought to

OF THE LAW OF GOD. 477

be performed, not only natural parents, but husbands, masters, ministers, and magistrates, and other superiors in dignity, age, gifts, or grace, are named *fathers and mothers*, and wives, servants, people, subjects, and all inferiors are represented as *children*.——The *most exact* performance of duties answerable to all these relations is necessary, 1. To fulfil God's commands, Exod. xx. 12. Eph. iv.—vi. Col. iii. iv. Tit. ii. iii. Rom. xii.—xv. 1 Thess. ii.—v. 1 Pet. ii. iii. 2. To manifest us Christians indeed, Eph. iv. 24, 25. 2 Pet. i. 7, 9. 3. As a part of our conformity to Jesus Christ, 1 John ii. 6, 29. Eph. v. 25. Luke ii. 51. 4. To honour God and his religion, 1 Tim. vi. 1, Tit. ii. 10. Mat. v. 16, 17, 27. xxii. 16—21. Gen. v. 22, 24. xviii. 17, 19. 1 Pet. iii. 6, 16. 5. To gain others to Christ, shewing them a good example, while we do them much service, 1 Pet. iii. 1, 2. 1 Cor. vii. 16. 1 Tim. iv. 12. Phil. ii. 15, 16. Mat. v. 16. 6. To prevent our own shame, promote our personal holiness, render our relations a blessing and an honour to us, and stir them up to pray to, and praise God for us, Psalm cxix. 6. Heb. xii. 14. Job xxxi. 17—20. Gal. vi. 10. Ruth iii. 1. Jer. xxxv. 4. 2 Cor. ix. 11—14. Job xxix. 13.

The duties of PARENTS to their children are, 1. Careful preservation of them in the womb, Judg. xiii. 14. 2. Fervent prayer for them as soon as they have life, Gen. xxv. 21, 22. 1 Sam. i. 11; and afterward, particularly when they are in danger of sin or death, Job i. 5. 2 Sam. xii. 15, 16. Psalm xxii. 10. 3. Earnest care to have them born within the covenant of grace, solemnly and frequently taking hold of it for themselves and their seed, Isa. xliv. 3. Gen. xvii. 7—9. 4. Thankfully to bless God for them, Luke i. 67. Psalm cxxvii. 3—5. cxxviii. 3. 5. After much solemn surrendering them in secret, publicly dedicating them to God in the initiating seal of his covenant, Exod. iv. 24. Luke i. 59. 6. Tender affection and care for them, particularly in their infancy and childhood, Isa. xlix. 15. Hos. ix. 14. 7. Providing proper food and raiment for them, 1 Tim. v. 8. 2 Cor. xii. 14. Eccl. ii. 18, 19. 8. Educating them in good manners, Prov. xxxi. 28. 1 Pet. iii. 8; school learning, 2 Tim. iii. 14; and some useful business, Gen. iv. 2. Ruth iii. 11. Prov. xxii. 29. 9. Instructing them in the knowledge of God's revealed truths, encouraging them to inquire concerning spiritual things, and frequently putting them in mind of their baptismal vows, 1 Kings xviii. 12. Prov. ii. iii. iv. vi. vii. xxxi. 2 Tim. iii. 15. Exod. xii. 25—27. xiii. 14, 15. Deut. vi. 6, 7, 20, 21. 10. Deterring them from evil by serious warnings, and by meek, suitable, and God-glorifying correction, 1 Sam. iii. 13. Eph. vi. 4. Prov. xxix. 15. xiii. 24. xxii. 15. xxiii. 13, 14. 11. Encouraging them in well-doing by example, kind excitements, and rewards, Psalm ci. 2. Prov. iv. 4.

1 Chron. xxviii. 9, 20. xxii. 16. 12. Seasonable disposal of them in marriage suited to their station, temper, consent, and their temporal, but especially their spiritual and eternal welfare, Ruth iii. 1. 1 Cor. vii. 36. Gen. xxiv. xxviii. 13. Careful Christian management of their temporal affairs for their advantage, and timely settlement of them, so as to prevent all contention and alienation of affection among them, 2 Cor. xii. 14. Isa. xxxviii. 1. 14. When dying, solemnly to charge and encourage them to fear God,—and to bless and commit them into the hand of their covenanted God, Gen. xxvii. xxviii. xlix. Jer. xlix. 11.—And the duties of CHILDREN to their parents are, 1. Tender love and affection, Gen. xlvi. 29. Rom. i. 31. 2. Filial awe, fear, and reverence of them, Lev. xix. 3. 3. Respectful behaviour towards them, Lev. xix. 32. Mal. i. 6. Gen. xxxi. 35. 1 Kings ii. 19. 4. Ready obedience to their lawful commands, Col. iii. 20. Gen. xxvii. 13. Luke ii. 51. Eph. vi. 1. 5. Hearty submission to their directions, admonitions, reproofs, corrections, Prov. i. 8. xiii. 1. Heb. xii. 9. 6. Ready compliance with their reasonable advice relative to their calling, marriage, or other things important, Deut. vii. 3. Jer. xxix. 6. 1 Cor. vii. 37, 38. Gen. xxiv. 34. xxi. 21. xxviii. 1, 2. xxix. 19. 7. Affectionate requital of their parental kindness, in providing for them when they become old and infirm, 1 Tim. v. 4. Mat. xv. 4—6. Gen. xlvii. 12. John xix. 27. 8. Living in a manner which tends to honour them, following their good advices and examples, improving their instructions and property in a right manner, and paying their just debts, Psalm xlv. 16. cxxvii. 3—5. cxxviii. 3.

The mutual duties of HUSBANDS and WIVES are, 1. To marry only in the Lord, first giving themselves to him, and marrying with such as apparently fear him, and after much solemn consultation of him, and in a manner honourable to him, and with a single eye to his glory as their chief end, 1 Cor. vii. 39. 2 Cor. vi. 14. Deut. vii. 3, 4. 1 Cor. x. 31. 1 Pet. iv. 11. 2. Most tender marriage-love to one another, Eph. v. 21, 28. 3. Peaceful affectionate dwelling together, 1 Pet. iii. 7. 1 Cor. vii. 5, 10, 15. Gen. xii. 11. 4. Earnest care to please one another, Gen. xxvii. 9. 1 Cor. vii. 33. 5. Cheerful behaviour toward one another, Eccl. ix. 9. Prov. v. 19. 6. Honouring one another, 1 Cor. xi. 7. 1 Pet. iii. 4. Prov. xxxi. 11, 28. Gen. xvi. 6. xviii. 12. 7. Most affectionate sympathy, partaking one another's troubles, burdens, griefs, cares, joys, &c. Gal. vi. 2. Rom. xii. 16. Heb. xiii. 3. 8. Concealing one another's infirmities, as far as it can be done without sin, Prov. x. 12. 1 Pet. iv. 8. 1 Sam. xxv. 25. 9. Faithfulness to one another, in respect of soul, body, reputation, or outward property, 1 Pet. iii. 7. Heb. xiii. 4. Prov. xiv. 1. 10. Deep concern for one another's spiritual welfare, watching over, praying with, kindly admonishing, and living exemplarily before one another, 1 Pet. iii. 7. 2 Kings iv. 1, 9, 10. 1 Cor. vii. 16. 1 Sam. i. 8. 2 Cor. xiii. 9, 10. Job ii. 9, 10. Eccl. iv. 9, 10. 1 Tim. v. 1. Lev. xix. 17. 11. Conjunct care to provide for, and religiously govern the family, 1 Tim. v. 8. Gen. xviii. 19. Josh. xxiv. 15.—The peculiar duties of HUSBANDS to their wives are, 1. Kindly to cherish and protect them, Ruth iii. 9. 1 Sam. xxx. 18. Gen. xvi. 6. 2. To provide for them, 1 Tim. v. 8. 3. To direct them, Prov. ii. 17. 1 Pet. iii. 7.—The peculiar duties of WIVES to their husbands are, 1. Subjection to them in heart, word, and deed, manifested in a ready submission to their will, 1 Tim. ii. 11, 12. Eph. v. 22, 24. Col. iii. 18. 1 Pet. iii. 1, 5. 2. Delightful awe and reverence of them, 1 Pet. iii. 2, 6. Eph. v. 33. 3. Readiness to ask and receive instruction from them, Gen. iii. 16. 1 Tim. ii. 11. 1 Cor. xiv. 35. 4. Frugal management of that which they provide for the family, Prov. xxxi. 29. xiv. 1. Tit. ii. 5, 6. 1 Pet. iii. 3, 4.

The duties of MASTERS to their servants are, 1. To take heed whom they hire, lest they bring God's curse into their family with a wicked servant, Psalm ci. 6. Gen. xxxix. 3, 4. 2. Carefully to consider their abilities, in order to proportion their work to them, Psalm cxii. 5. Gen. xxix. 14, 15. 3. To give them proper directions for their work, Prov. xxxi. 27. 4. To give them proper maintainance and wages for their labour, Prov. xxvii. 27. James v. 4. Lev. xxiii. 43. Deut. xxiv. 14, 15. 5. To keep them in their proper station with respect to familiarity, power, victuals, and the like, lest they become insolent, Prov. xxix. 21. 6. Gentle treatment of them, and readiness to hear their defences or excuses for their conduct, Col. iv. 1. Job xxxi. 32. 2 Kings v. 13. 7. Aversion to hear bad reports of them, Prov. xxix. 11. 8. Tender care of them when they are sick and infirm, Mat. viii. 6. 1 Sam. xxx. 13. 9. Bestowing distinguished favours on those that are remarkably diligent and faithful, Deut. xv. 13, 14, 18. xxv. 17. 10. Earnest care to train them up for God, who brought them into his service for that end, Josh. xxiv. 15. Gen. xviii. 19.—The duties of SERVANTS to masters are, 1. If possible to hire themselves with such as apparently fear God, Prov. iii. 33. Jer. x. 25. 2. Inward reverence and esteem of them, 1 Pet. ii. 18. Mal. i. 6. Eph. vi. 5. 3. External honour of them, Mal. i. 6. 1 Tim. vi. 1, 2. 4. Conscientious care to maintain the honour of the family, Gen. xxiv. 34—41. xxxix. 8, 9. Mic. vii. 6. 5. Strict adherence to their own allotted provision, wages, and rest, Gen. xxx. 33. Prov. xxxi. 15, 18. 6. Meek submission to rebukes and corrections, Tit. ii. 9. 1 Pet. ii. 18—20. Gen. xvi. 9. 7. Conscientious, honest, cheerful, single, faithful, ready, and diligent performance of the business appointed them, Tit. ii. 9, 10. Psal. cxxiii. 1, 2. Col. iii. 23—25. Gen. xxix. 20. Mat. xxiv. 45. Luke xvi. 6. 2 Kings v. 22. Gen. xxxi. 6, 38. Prov. xviii. 9. xxii. 29. Rom. xii. 11. 8. Earnest care to attend family worship, and to profit by family instructions, Prov. iv. 7.

The duties of MINISTERS to their people are, 1. To make sure a proper stock of furniture for their work, 1 John i. 1—3. 2 Cor. iv. 13. 2. To fix among them by a proper call, 1 Pet. v. 3. Jer. xxiii. 21, 22, 32. Rom. x. 15. Heb. v. 4. 3. Prudently to acquaint themselves with their tempers and spiritual estate, that they may regulate their ministrations accordingly, Phil. ii. 19, 20. 4. To abound in, and exercise the most tender love to, and care for their souls, 1 Thess. ii. 7, 8. 5. Faithful, impartial, and diligent administration of divine ordinances answerable to their condition, poor, sick, scandalous, &c. 2 Tim. iv. 2. 1 Thess. ii. 3, 4. 6. Watchfulness over their behaviour for the benefit of their souls, Heb. xiii. 17. 7. Habitual fervent prayer for them, Eph. i. 15—19. iii. 14—19. 8. A lively and shining example of divine truth in their own Christian practice, Heb. xiii. 7, 8. Tit. ii. 7. 1 Tim. iv. 12. 1 Thess. ii. 1—10.—The duties of PEOPLE to their ministers are, 1. Distinguished reverence of them as ambassadors of Christ, 2 Cor. v. 20. 1 Cor. iv. 1, 2. Rev. i. 20. 2. Endeared affection to them for their work's sake, 1 Thess. v. 12, 13. Gal. iv. 14, 15. 3. Much fervent prayer for them, and for the success of their work, Rom. xv. 30, 31. Eph. vi. 19, 20. 1 Thess. v. 25. 4. Diligent attendance on all the ordinances of Christ dispensed by them, Heb. x. 25. Luke x. 16. 2 Kings iv. 22, 23. 5. Submission to them as Christ's deputies in their warnings, reproofs, censures, Heb. xiii. 17. Mat. x. 40.

The duties of MAGISTRATES to their subjects are, 1. To establish good laws, and effectually execute them, Zech. viii. 16. 2 Chron. xix. Psalm lxxii. lxxxii. 2. To govern them with wisdom, equity, and affection, 2 Chron. i. 10. 3. To protect them in their just rights and privileges derived from God, 1 Tim. ii. 2. Prov. xxviii. 16. 4. By good example and righteous laws to promote the true religion, and no other, among them, Isa. xlix. 23. 5. To punish evil doers, and encourage them that do well, Rom. xiii. 3.—And the duties of SUBJECTS to their magistrates are, 1. To respect them as the deputies, image, and ordinance of God, Rom. xiii. 1—6. Psalm lxxxii. 6. 1 Sam. xxvi. 16, 17. Prov. xxiv. 21. 2. Charitable construction of their conduct as far as it can bear it, 1 Sam. xxvi. 19. Exod. xxii. 28. Eccl. x. 20. 2 Pet. ii. 10. Jude 8. 3. Subjection to their just laws, Rom. xiii. 5. Tit. iii. 1, 2. 1 Thess. ii. 4. 4. Cheerful payment of just taxes, Rom. xiii. 6, 7. Luke xx. 25. 5. Defence of them from their enemies, 2 Sam. xviii. 3.

1 Sam. xxvi. 15. 6. Much solemn and fervent prayer for them, 1 Tim. ii. 1, 2. 7. Earnest care to live under their government as an honour, comfort, and blessing to them and others, Isa. vi. 13. lxv. 8.

The duties of SUPERIORS in age, gifts, or graces to their inferiors in these, are, 1. To adorn their superiority by an holy and exemplary conversation, Tit. ii. 2. 2. To take every opportunity of instructing and warning them, recommending Christ and his ways to them, 1 Cor. ii. 2.—The duties of INFERIORS to their superiors are, 1. To give them due honour and respect, Lev. xix. 32. 2. Earnest desire to have their counsels and instructions, and ready submission to them, 1 Pet. v. 5. 3. Earnest imitation of them in that which is good, 1 Cor. xi. 1.—The duties of EQUALS one to another, are, 1. To cultivate the most affectionate love to, and peace with one another, 1 Thess. iii. 13. Heb. xii. 14. Rom. xii. 9, 10—18. xiv. 19. 2 Cor. xiii. 11. 2. To prefer one another in honour and esteem, Rom. xii. 10. Phil. ii. 2, 3. 3. To be courteous and affable, and ready to promote and rejoice in the welfare of one another, 1 Pet. iii. 8. iv. 8. Rom. xii. 10, 15. xiv. 19. 1 Cor. x. 24. 4. Faithfully to warn and reprove one another, Lev. xix. 17. 1 Thess. v. 14. 5. To vie with one another in tender sympathy under trouble, Gal. vi. 2. Heb. xiii. 3. Rom. xii. 15. 6. To provoke one another to love, and in holy and circumspect behaviour, Heb. x. 24. Eph. iv. 31, 32.

The sins against these and similar relations lying either in neglect of, or in acting contrary to the above-mentioned duties, we shall not particularly exhibit them.—This commandment is not only the FIRST in the second table, but is the FIRST, the only one, which has a promise peculiar to itself, *viz.* of long life and prosperity to the upright keepers of it, Exod. xx. 12. Eph. vi. 2. Long life is a blessing, 1. When men grow in grace as they do in age, Psalm xcii. 19. 2. When they retain the full exercise of their reason with some proper measure of bodily vigour, Deut. xxxiv. 7. 3. When they continue useful to others around, Josh. xxiv. 25—29.—In such circumstances old age is *honourable*, Prov. xvi. 31. Lev. xix. 32; and *profitable*, giving us more experience of God's kindness, 1 John ii. 13; more ability to resist the temptations of Satan or the world, 2 Tim. ii. 13. 1 Pet. v. 9 ; and more opportunity to glorify God, edify others, and be ripened for everlasting happiness, Job v. 26. 2 Cor. ix. 6. Phil. i. 23, 24. Josh. xxiv. 31.—Some that neglect relative duties live long, and have much outward prosperity, but not by the virtue of any gracious promise, but by the fearful curse of God, Deut. xxvii. 26. Gal. iii. 10. They enjoy no true comfort, but are ripened for hell, by every thing which they enjoy, Deut. xxxii. 15. Hos. xiii. 6.—Some that conscientiously perform relative duties have their life short and afflicted. But either their performance has some remarkable defect in it before God; or their adversity is remarkably blessed to them, and they enjoy the residue of their years in heaven, Psalm xcix. 67, 71, 75. Heb. xii. 5—11. Job v. 17. Prov. iii. 12. Psalm xciv. 12. Rev. iii. 19. Isa. xxvii. 9. lvii. 1. Phil. i. 23. Rom. viii. 28. 2 Cor. iv. 17.

VI. The SIXTH COMMANDMENT REQUIRES the preservation of temporal, and the promoting spiritual LIFE.—We ought to *promote our own spiritual and eternal life*, 1. By a careful perusing the Scriptures, which are the words of eternal life, and of gospel-ordinances, which are the means of it, John v. 39. Isa. xxxiv. 16. viii. 20. Prov. viii. 34—36. 2. By receiving Jesus Christ as the *resurrection and life* into our hearts by faith, in order to beget, maintain, and perfect spiritual life in us, John vi. 27. xi. 25. 1 Pet. ii. 1—4. 3. By avoiding sin and all appearances of, and temptations to it, Prov. xi. 19. iv. 23. viii. 36. v. 8. 1 Thess. v. 22. Mark xiv. 38. xiii. 31, 37. 1 Pet. v. 8. 1 Cor. xvi. 13.—We ought to preserve our natural life, 1. By instating and confirming it in a new-covenant relation to God, Psalm cxix. 94. xvi. 1. xvii. 8. 1 Sam. xxv. 29. 2. By just and necessary defence of it from such as seek to destroy it, Luke xxii. 30. vi. 29. 3. By furnishing our body with proper food, physic, labour, clothes, rest, recreation, Eph. v. 29. 4. By avoiding drunkenness, gluttony, and lasciviousness, which gradually ruin it, Luke xxi. 34. Prov. v. vii. vi. 26, 32. xxiii. 26—35. ix. 18. 5. By maintaining our inward passions in a proper temper of meekness, peaceableness, patience, and humility, Prov. xvii. 20, 22. xv. 13, 15. xviii. 14.—We ought to *promote the spiritual and eternal life of our neighbours*, 1. By setting before them such an amiable pattern of gospel-holiness as may gain them to Christ, Matth. v. 16. 1 Cor. vii. 16. 1 Pet. iii. 1, 2. Zech. viii. 23. 2. By diligent instruction and excitement to faith and holiness, answerable to our station, accompanied with fervent prayer for them, 1 Thess. v. 14. Gen. xliii. 29. Isa. ii. 3, 5. 3. By earnest endeavours to prevent their sinning, or being tempted to it, Jude 23. 1 Thess. v. 14.—And we ought to *preserve their natural life*, 1. By protecting them from unlawful attempts against it, Psalm lxxxii. 3, 4. Prov. xxiv. 11, 12. 2. By giving them the necessaries of life, as equity or charity require, Prov. iii, 27—29 xxvii. 27. xxxi. 15. xx. 27. xix. 17. James ii. 15, 16. 1 John iii. 17. 3. By labouring to promote and exercise such affection toward them as will hinder our hurting them, and make us do them all the good we can, readily forgiving the injuries they have done us, and by the most kind behaviour, rendering their life comfortable to them, Eph. iv. 31, 32. Rom. xv. 1. 2 Cor. xiii. 5, 7.

Col. iii. 12, 13. Matth. v. 42, 44. Acts xvi. 28.—But we must never lie, deny any truth of Christ, or practise an unlawful trade, or use any sinful shift, for preserving our own or our neighbour's life. 1. No commandment of God must ever be opposed to another, Rom. vii. 12. 2. Their damnation is just who do evil that good may come, Rom. iii. 8. 3. God must be loved, feared, and obeyed, rather than men, Luke xiv. 26. Matth. x. 28. Acts v. 29. iv. 19. 4. Our soul ought not to be murdered, in order to preserve alive our body, Matth. xvi. 25, 26. 5. He that conscientiously dies rather than sin, is a real martyr for Christ, Rev. ii. 10.

Besides inhumanity towards brute animals, Prov. xii. 10. Num. xxii. 27—29. Exod. xxiii. 5, 12, 19. Deut. xxii. 4—7. Luke xiii. 15. xiv. 5, this commandment FORBIDS, I. *Self-murder,* either, 1. *Of our soul,* by neglecting God's appointed means of salvation, Prov. viii. 34—36;—by opposing the mediate or immediate strivings of his Spirit, Prov. xxix. 1. Acts vii. 51. Isa. lxiii. 10. Heb. x. 26—31, 38. 2 Pet. ii. 20—22;—and by continued unbelief, impenitence, and progress in sin, Ezek. xviii. 31, 32. Jer. iv. 14. xiii. 23, 27. vi. 8. Rom. ii. 4, 5.—Or, 2. *Of our body,* in directly attempting to deprive it of life, which at once usurps the prerogative of God, the Lord of life, manifests the most horrid pride, discontentment, impatience and despair, and naturally tends to plunge us headlong into hell fire, 1 Sam. xxxi. 4, 5. 2 Sam. xvii. 23. Mat. xxvii. 4, 5;—or in doing that which tends to destroy our natural life, —as indulgence of thoughts or designs against it, Job vii. 15; envy and rage against others, Job v. 2. Prov. xiv. 30; impatience and discontent under trouble, Psalm xxxvii. 1, 8. Heb. xiii. 5. Prov. xv. 13. xvii. 22; immoderate worldly sorrow, 2 Cor. vii. 10. 1 Sam. i. 15; anxious care about worldly things, Matth. vi. 31, 34. Psalm iv. 6; neglect of our body with respect to food, raiment, medicine, rest and recreation, through superstition, carelessness, covetousness, churlishness, outrageous passion, or temptations of Satan, Col. ii. 23. Eccl. x. 8. vi. 2. 1 Kings xxi. 4;—intemperance, gluttony, drunkenness, sensuality, Phil. iii. 19. Prov. xx .1. xxiii. 1, 21, 9—35. v. 10. vii. 22, 27. ix. 18. Luke xxi. 34. xvi. 19. xvii. 27. Isa. xxii. 12—14. Rom. xiii. 13, 14. 1 Pet. ii. 11; immoderate labour, Eccl. vii. 22, 23; or exposing ourselves to unnecessary dangers, 2 Sam. xxiii. 16, 17. Matth. iv. 5—7. II. *Murder of our neighbours,* in, 1. *Their soul,* by giving them a sinful or imprudent example, Mat. xviii. 6, 7; by neglecting to prevent their sinning, or to reform them from it, Ezek. iii. 18. 1 Sam. iii. 13. Lev. xix. 17. 1 John iii. 15; by co-operating with them in sin, commanding, advising, provoking, tempting, teaching, or assisting them to commit it, or approving and delighting in it,

Hos. v. 11, 12. 2 Sam. xiii. 5. 1 Kings xxi. 25. Prov. vii. 10—27. Psalm l. 18. Acts viii. 1. Rom. i. 32. Psalm. xlix. 13. Prov. xiv. 19;---and by hardening our heart against them on account of their sin, and not mourning over it, or their danger by it, Lam. i. 8, 17. v. 16---22. Ezek. ix. 4. Ezra ix. 5---15. Dan. iii. 19, 20. Jer. ix. 1---21. 2. *In their body,*---not by killing them in lawful war, Josh. vi.---xiii. Num. xxxi. 1 Sam. xv; or in necessary self-defence, or in just punishment of their murder, adultery, idolatry, blasphemy, gross profanation of the Sabbath, &c.; as in these cases, God puts his sword into men's hands to execute his just vengeance according to their stations. ---But we murder their body, in unjustly killing them without, or under colour of law, Gen. iv. 8---11. 2 Sam. xi. 15. 1 Kings xxi. 1---12; in unjust war, Hab. ii. 12; or in private duels, Rom. xii. 19. Prov. xvi. 32. xxv. 28. Mat. v. 39, 44;---or in doing that which tends to murder them---whether *in our heart,* by sinful anger and wrath, Matth. v. 22. Eph. iv. 26, 27. Col. iii. 12, 13, 21; envy, Prov. xiv. 30. xxvii. 4. Job v. 2. Rom. xii. 15. Gal. v. 20, 21, 26; hatred, malice, 1 John iii. 15. Tit. iii. 3; revengeful thoughts, desires, and joys, Matth. vi. 15. Prov. xxiv. 17, 18; unaffectedness with their distress, Prov. xii. 10. Obad. 10—14. Amos vi. 6;—*in our speech,* by quarrelling, bitter railing, reproachful or disdainful scoffing or deriding, angry cursing, Prov. xxiii. 29, 33. Gal. v. 15. 1 Cor. v. 11. Psalm lxiv. 3, 4. lii. 2. lvii. 4. cxl. 3. xxii. 6, 16. cix. 18. Prov. xii. 18. xv. 1. Eph. iv. 31. 2 Sam. xvi. 5, 7. 1 Pet. iii. 9. Matth. v. 22. Heb. xi. 33. John xix. 3. 2 Kings ii. 23, 24; or false accusation, Luke xxiii. 2. Acts xxiv. 5;—in fierce, sullen, or enraged *looks,* which denote inclination to, or pleasure in mischief, Gen. iv. 5. Obad. 12. Acts vii. 54; and in *our acts,* withholding from them their means of life, Luke x. 31, 32. James ii. 15, 16. Job xxxi. 26. Matth. xxv. 42; and hurting their body, or their trade, labour, or property, by which its life and health are maintained, Exod. xxi. 18, 22. Ezek. xxii. 7. Isa. iii. 14, 15. Mic. iii. 3. Matth. xxiv. 9, 10. Isa. v. 8.

VII. The SEVENTH COMMANDMENT REQUIRES, I. The *preserving our own chastity* in heart, speech, and behaviour, Job xxxi. 1. Col. iv. 6. 1 Pet. iii. 2; by studying to have our whole man instated in a new-covenant marriage relation to Christ, and to God in him, Isa. liv. 5—10. Jer. xxxii. 38—41; and to have his Spirit dwelling in us, Isa. xliv. 3, 4. Ezek. xxxvi. 27. Rom. viii. 9, 13; and by a daily and earnest application of his word, blood, and gracious influence for mortifying our inward lusts, and filling our heart with true holiness in opposition to them, John xv. 3. xvii. 17. Psalm cxix. 9. Heb. ix. 14. x. 22. Rom. viii. 13. 2 Cor. vii. 1. Prov. ii. 1—19; an habitual, frequent, and fervent recommending ourselves to God's preservation, Psalm xvi. 1. xvii. 8. xix. 11, 12, 13; lively exercise of our implanted graces, 2 Pet. iii. 18. i. 5—8. 2 Cor. vii. 1; watchfulness over our heart, eyes, and ears, Prov. iv. 23. Psal. xviii. 23. Job xxxi. 1. 2 Sam. xi. 2. Gen. xxxix. 7. Prov. vii. 21, 22. xix. 27; temperance in eating and drinking, or recreations, Luke xxi. 34; a careful avoiding frothy and unchaste company, Prov. ii. 16. ix. 6. v. 8, 9; diligence in lawful business, Rom. xii. 11. 2 Sam. xi. 2. Gen. xxxiv. 1. Ezek. xvi. 49; early and earnest resistance of temptations to unchastity or occasions thereof, Gen. xxxix. 1—9. 1 Cor. vi. 18. Prov. v. 8; marrying in the Lord, when proper, 1 Cor. vii. 2, 9, 39; and dwelling with our yoke-fellow in tender love and affection, 1 Pet. iii. 7. Prov. v. 19, 20. Eccl. ix. 9.——II. The *preserving our neighbour's chastity* in heart, speech, and behaviour, taking care to do nothing that tends to ensnare or defile them, Gen. xxxviii. 14, 15, 26. 1 Tim. ii. 9; and doing every thing we can, by example, instruction, warning, reproof, and prayer for them, to promote and preserve their chastity, Prov. ii. v. vii. ix.

This commandment FORBIDS, I. *Completed acts of uncleanness*, —unnatural, bestial, diabolical, selfish, sodomitical, and incestuous pollutions, Lev. xviii. xx. Gen. xxxviii. 9, 18. Jude 8. Rom. i. 26, 27. Eph. v. 12. 1 Cor. v. 1.—Adultery, to which polygamy may be reduced, as marriage, and far less perjury in the violation of former marriage-vows, cannot sanctify sin, Hos. iv. 18. Gen. ii. 18—24; and concubinage, 1 Kings xi. 1, 3;—fornication between persons both of them unmarried, Col. iii. 5, 6. Eph. v. 5. 1 Cor. vi. 9, 15;—rape or violent defilement of women, Deut. xxii. 25;—immoderate and unseasonable familiarity between married persons, 1 Thess. iv. 3, 4. Heb. xiii. 4. Lev. xv. 10. xviii. 18. 1 Cor. vii. 5.——II. Every thing *that tends towards unchaste* actions,—all *approaches towards them*,—indwelling lustfulness, unchaste imaginations, thoughts, and desires, Mat. v. 28. xv. 19; speaking, hearing, writing, or reading unchaste expressions, Eph. iv. 29. Prov. vii. 18, 21; unchaste looks, receiving temptations into our own heart, or enticing others, 2 Pet. ii. 14. Isa. iii. 16—26; light and immodest behaviour, Isa. iii. 16. Prov. vii. 13; wanton embraces and dalliances, Prov. vii. 13;—and all *incentives to them*, as stage-plays, lewd pictures, Ezek. xxiii. 14—21; immodest apparel, Prov. vii. 10; fellowship of vain persons, Gen. xxxiv. 1. Prov. v. 8—12; idleness, Ezek. xvi. 49; intemperance in eating and drinking, Prov. xxiii. 30. Jer. v. 8. Rom. xiii. 13. James v. 5. 1 Pet. iv. 3; undue delay of marriage, 1 Cor. vii. 7—9; unjust divorce, Mat. v. 32. 1 Cor. vii. 12, 13. Mat. ii. 16; unkindness between married persons, 1 Cor. vii. 5; vows of perpetual single life, prohibitions of marriage, Matth. xix. 10, 11.

1 Tim. iv. 3;—dispensing with unlawful marriages, Mark vi. 18;—tolerating stews, Deut. xxiii. 17. Heb. xiii. 4.—All which forms of unchastity we ought carefully to avoid, because, 1. It exceedingly dishonours God, Gen. xxxix. 9. Psalm li. 4. 1 Cor. iii. 17. vi. 18. Job xxxi. 11. 2. Falls into it are frequently the punishment of some other sin, Prov. xxii. 14. Rom. i. 26, 27. Hos. iv. 14. Amos vii. 17. 3. Few truly repent of it, and these with great difficulty, Prov. ii. 19. xxii. 14. xxiii. 27, 28. Eccl. vii. 26. Acts xxiv. 25. 4. It dishonours and often murders our body, 1 Cor. vi. 18. Prov. v. 11, 12. vii. 22. 5. It fixes a permanent stain upon our character, Prov. vi. 33. 6. It wrathfully consumes our outward estate, Prov. v. 10. vi. 26. Job xxxi. 12. 7. It, in a fearful manner, secures our eternal ruin, Prov. vi. 32. vii. 26, 27. ix. 18. Heb. xiii. 4. 1 Cor. vi. 9, 10. Gal. v. 19, 21. Rev. xxi. 8. xxii. 15. Col. iii. 5, 6. Eph. v. 5, 6.

The EIGHTH COMMANDMENT REQUIRES the promoting our own and our neighbour's WEALTH and outward estate. This command necessarily supposes men's peculiar property in temporal good things; as without that there could be no *stealing*. The Jewish Christians were not required to part with their civil property; but, being apprehensive of the impending ruin of their nation, they inclined to bestow it in the service of Christ and the support of his saints, while they had opportunity. Nor perhaps was the right to it, but the use of it made common, Acts ii. 44, 45. iv. 34—37. I. We ought to promote *our own wealth and outward estate*, 1. By taking a new-covenant right to all things through a spiritual union with Christ the heir of them, 1 Cor. iii. 22. Heb. i. 2. Mat. vi. 33. 2. By depending on and praying to God, as our new-covenant Father, to bestow on us, and keep for us such things as are necessary and convenient, Deut. viii. 18. Psalm cxxvii. 1. cxxviii. 1, 2. Prov. xxx. 8. Mat. vi. 11. 3. By prudent foresight and care to have every thing answerable to our station and ability, 1 Tim. v. 8. 4. By due exercise of our ability or stock in some lawful calling, which is calculated to glorify God, and profit ourselves and our neighbours, Gen. ii. 15. iv. 2. Eph. iv. 28. Prov. xiv. 8. xiii. 4. x. 4. xxii. 29. Isa. xxviii. 26. Gen. ix. 19, 20. 5. By cheerfully allowing ourselves a moderate enjoyment of the fruit of our lawful industry, Eccl. iii. 12, 13. ii. 24. ix. 9. Psalm cxxviii. 2. 6. By frugal management of that which we have to the best advantage, not from a churlish disposition, but as stewards of God's property, taking care to waste nothing upon trifles, and to lose nothing useful, Isa. lv. 2. John vi. 12. Prov. xi. 24. xxi. 20. 7. By careful avoiding unnecessary law-suits, and every other thing that tends to embarrass our outward estate or shame our profession, Mat. v. 40. 1 Cor. vi. 1—8. 8. By necessary prosecution of our civil rights at law, if the matter be of much importance, and can be obtained without rendering our neighbour and his family outwardly miserable, and if softer methods cannot procure us justice, Deut. xxv. 1. 9. Never idolizing, but moderating our affections toward all earthly enjoyments, 1 Tim. vi. 17. 10. By carefully avoiding all haste to be rich, and all mingling of unjust gain with our lawful property as a curse upon it, 1 Tim. vi. 4. Prov. xxviii. 22. James v. 3, 4. 11. By liberal, but prudently directed donations to the poor, and to pious uses, Prov. xix. 17. iii. 9, 10.——II. We ought to *promote the wealth of our neighbours*, 1. By much prayerful endeavours to have them and it secured in a new-covenant connection with God, James v. 16. Phil. ii. 4. 2. By careful endeavours to prevent their loss and damage, Deut. xxii. 1. Exod. xxiii. 4, 5. 3. By universal honesty in dealing with them, rather hurting our own property than theirs, Mat. vii. 12. Psalm xv. 2, 4. Zech. vii. 9, 10. 4. By conscientious restitution of every thing which we have found or wrongfully taken from them, Deut. xxii. 23. Lev. vi. 2—5. Job xx. 10, 18. Ezek. xviii. 7. Luke xix. 8. Num. v. 6—8; or, if the proper owners cannot be found, to restore it to the poor, as factors for the Lord of all things. 5. By charity and equity, in cheerfully but prudently lending to them for their assistance, even without interest or hope of payment, if their circumstances require it, Mat. v. 42. Luke vi. 35, 36. Deut. xxiii. 20. Lev. xxv. 34; and in thankful and timely returning that which we have borrowed, in as good condition as we got it, unless God's providence, not our own prodigality or sloth, render us incapable, 2 Kings iv. 1. 6. By charitable donations of that which is truly our own, and with a real desire to help the poor, and to promote the religious service of God, Luke xi. 41. xvi. 9. Gal. vi. 10. Tim. v. 8. Eph. iv. 28. Eccl. xi. 1. 1 John iii. 17. Prov. iii. 9. xix. 17.—These donations ought to be made conscientiously, under a sense of our debt to God as his vassals and tenants, Prov. iii. 9. Mat. vi. 1, 2; cheerfully, 2 Cor. ix. 7; with secrecy, except when publicity is necessary for exciting others, Mat. vi. 3, 4; in proportion to that which he bestows upon us, —perhaps not less than a *tenth* part of our incomes in ordinary cases, 1 Cor. xvi. 2. Psalm cxii. 5, 9. Gen. xiv. 20. xxviii. 22; and from an honourable regard to Christ and his poor members or brethren of mankind, 1 Cor. xi. 22. Gal. vi. 10.—And thus given, these donations are, 1. Most reasonable, as we hold all that we have of God as his stewards or tenants, Luke xvi. 10 —12. 1 Tim. vi. 17, 18; and hence called righteousness, Psalm cxii. 9. Prov. x. 2. iii. 27. 2. Most honourable, conforming us to the pattern of God in Christ, Acts xx. 35. Luke vi. 35. 2 Cor. viii. 9. 3. Most conducive to secure proper necessaries for us and our posterity, Prov. xxviii. 27. xix. 17. Eccl. xi. 1, 2. Psalm xxxvii. 25, 26; nay, to render us rich, Prov. iii. 9, 10. xi. 24, 25. Psalm cxii. 3. 4. A most remarkable mean of preventing trouble or securing comfort under it, Dan. iv. 27. Psalm xli. 1—3. 5. They will be most honourably proclaimed by Christ in the last judgment, Mat. xxv. 34—40. 6. They shall be abundantly, but graciously rewarded in heaven to all eternity, Mat. v. 7. vi. 4. Luke xvi. 9.

This commandment FORBIDS, I. The *hindering our own wealth*, by, 1. Idleness, living without a business, or not attending to it, 2 Thess. iii. 10, 11. 1 Tim. v. 13. 1 Thess. iv. 11, 12. Ezek. xvi. 49. Gen. iii. 19. 2. Carelessness and sloth, Prov. xxviii. 19. xiv. 1. xiii. 4. xxiii. 21. vi. 10, 11. xxiv. 30—34. 3. Not depending on, and acknowledging God in all our worldly business, Deut. viii. 18. Psalm cvii. 38. 4. Prodigal wasting that which God brings to our hand, Prov. xxi. 17. xxviii. 7. Luke xv. 13, 30. 5. Rash engagement in law-suits and suretyship, Mat. v. 40. 1 Cor. vi. 1—8. Prov. vi. 1—5. xviii. 18. xxii. 26, 27. xxv. 9, 10. 6. Foolish giving to monasteries, overstocked funds, or to such as have no need, or to sluggards, spendthrifts, or imprudent lending to rash schemers, prodigal wasters, or the like, Psalm cxii. 5. 7. Distrustful anxiety in procuring or retaining earthly things, Mat. vi. 31, 34. Prov. xxviii. 22. Eccl. iv. 8. 8. Sordid churlishness, wanting a heart to enjoy in a proper manner or degree that wealth which we have, or to lay out proper expences upon our affairs, Eccl. vi. 1—5. 9. Exercise of unlawful callings,—gamesters, stage-players, puppet-shewers, pimps, pawn-brokers, smugglers, &c. and all grasping at excessive gains, by which God's curse is brought upon that which we have, Zech. v. 4. Hos. v. 12. Hag. i. 6. II. The *hindering our neighbour's wealth and outward estate*, not only by direct theft and robbery of their persons or goods from particular persons, states, or churches, 1 Tim. i. 9, 10. Rom. ii. 22; but by that which is more indirect, in, 1. A covetous inclination to have their property, Heb. xiii. 5. Col. iii. 5. 2. Idleness, Eph. iv. 28. 2 Thess. iii. 10—12. 1 Thess. iv. 11, 12. Mat. xx. 6. 3. Unnecessary begging, laying the burden of our maintainance upon others to the hurt of the liberal and the truly poor's wanting their due share of charity, Eph. iv. 28. 4. Base gain procured by sordid or unlawful methods, Acts xix. 24, 25; of which kind is helping persons to a stock or subsistence by balls, drinking matches, penny weddings, Hab. ii. 15. Prov. xiii. 15. 5. Simoniacal merchandise of spiritual gifts, pardons, church-livings, sacraments, censures, or other sacred things; giving or procuring them on account of money, favour, or the like, Acts viii. 20. Job xv. 34. 6. Family frauds by husbands, wives, children, or servants, 1 Tim. v. 8. Prov. xxxi. 22. xxviii. 24.

Tit. ii. 9, 10. Psalm l. 18. 7. Taking the advantage of our neighbours' ignorance or necessity in buying or selling, Mat. vii. 12. Lev. xix. 11. 8. Improper or false commendation of that which we sell, and dispraise of that which we intend to buy, Prov. xx. 14. 9. Adulterating goods, or selling one kind and delivering another, Amos viii. 5, 6. 10. Using false weights or measures in merchandise, Micah vi. 10, 11. Amos viii. 5. Prov. xi. 1. Lev. xix. 36. 11. Bad payment of debts, neither early nor fully enough, nor in current money, Psalm xv. 4. Acts v. 1—9. Gen. xxiii. 16. Rom. xiii. 8. 12. Dishonest fellowship, taking as much or more of the gain when we have less of the stock or labour in procuring it, 1 Thess. iv. 6. Matth. vii. 12. 13. Bad neighbourhood, removing their land marks, injuring their corns, grass, goods, conveniencies; decoying their servants or customers from them; screwing ourselves into their business, farms, &c. Prov. xxii. 28. xxiii. 10. Isa. v. 8. Jer. ix. 6. Micah ii. 2. vii. 2—4. 14. Dishonesty in trust, particularly to the poor, fatherless, or widows, Prov. xxiii. 10, 11. Luke xx. 47; or perfidy in stewards, overseers, factors, &c. Luke xvi. 1—10. 15. Dishonesty in loans,—borrowing without any probability of power to pay it at the time promised; restoring things borrowed in a worse condition;—refusing to lend to the industrious poor in their necessity, and requiring interest from such as are unable to bear it, Exod. xxii. 14, 25—27. Mat. v. 42. Psalm xv. 5. Luke vi. 35. 16. Dishonest contracting of debt,—without sincere intention or proper appearance of ability to keep our promise of payment,—or without necessity on our part, and to the hurt of others, buying things which we might well want, Rom. xiii. 8. Mat. vii. 12;—neglect to pay just wages or debts at the time appointed, Prov. iii. 27—29. Psalm xxxvii. 21;— unwillingness to pay just debts, and mean while giving our ready money to others; obliging our creditors to sue us at law, in order to have their own,—or leaving our debts to be paid by our sureties, Isa. lviii. 4. 1 Thess. iv. 6. Isa. lix. 14. 17. Fraudulent bankruptcy, when by prodigality, pride, indolence, heedlessness, rashness, or unlawful pushing of business, we plunge ourselves irrecoverably in debt; or stop payments without sufficient cause; or conceal part of our stock from our creditors;— or are unconcerned to pay what part we have promised, or even the whole debt, if ever we be able, Luke xv. 13. Jer. ix. 4—6. 18. Uncharitable use of our property, in engrossing useful commodities, forestalling of markets, unjust inclosures of commons, depopulation of villages, &c. James ii. 13. Prov. xi. 26. Isa. v. 8. Micah ii. 2. 19. Oppression, bearing down our neighbours by our superior wealth, power, or influence, vexatious law-suits, retaining pledges, &c. Micah iii. 2, 3. Ezek. xxii. 7. Mal. iii. 5. James ii. 6. 1 Cor. vi. 1—6. Mat. v. 40, 41. Exod. xxii. 26, 27.

Deut. xxiv. 6. 20. Extortion, proprietors racking their rents, rulers their taxes, servants their wages, lenders their interest, 1 Cor. v. 11. vi. 10. 21. Fellowship with thieves,—tempting them to steal, resetting or concealing that which they have stolen, or not sufficiently checking and punishing them when it is in our power, Psalm l. 18. Prov. xxix. 24. Isa. i. 23. 22. Unmercifulness to the poor, which is real theft, Eph. iv. 28; perfidious ingratitude to God, Mat. xxiv. 41—45. xviii. 23—35. Luke xvi. 10; murder of the poor, 1 John iii. 15. James ii. 16, 17,—a token that we are destitute of God's grace, 1 John iii. 17. Mat. xxv 41—43; provokes God to deal unmercifully with us, James ii. 13. Prov. xxi. 13. James v. 4; imperceptibly wastes our substance, Prov. xi. 24, 25. James v. 2, 3; and, if continued in, will at last damn us, Mat. xxv. 41—43. 23. Withholding from the support of ministers, schools, and other pious uses, that which is answerable to our incomes before God, Neh. xiii. 10. x. 32, 34. Hag. i. 4. Mal. iii. 9. 24. Sacrilegious deficiency in that good example, religious instruction, fervent prayer, and other important usefulness which we owe to our neighbours for promoting their temporal as well as eternal advantage, Rom. xiii. 8. Heb. x. 24.

IX. The NINTH COMMANDMENT, respecting our own and our neighbour's reputation, and the truth connected with it, REQUIRES, I. The *maintaining and promoting truth between man and man*, in, 1. Speaking nothing but truth, as we think, and as things really are, Psalm xv. 2. 2 Thess. ii. 11. 2. Declaring that which is true upon every proper occasion, Zech viii. 16, 19. 3. Bearing witness, when necessary in judicature, freely, plainly, fully, sincerely, and unbiassedly, declaring the truth and nothing else, Prov. xiv. 5. xix. 5. 1 Sam. xix. 4, 5. John vii. 19. 2 Chron. xix. 9. 2 Sam. xiv. 16—20. II. The *maintaining and promoting of our own good name*, in, 1. Taking hold of God's covenant of grace, that we may have his new name put upon us, and have his honour engaged in support of our character, Rev. iii. 12. Isa. lvi. 5. lxii. 4, 12. Jer. xxxii. 40. 2. Studying to have a distinct, certain, and affecting knowledge of our own dignity as rational creatures, members of Christ, and friends of God, Psalm c. 3. 1 Cor. vi. 15, 17, 19, 20. iii. 16, 17, 23. Eph. iv. 30. v. 30. Jer. iii. 4, 14, 19, 22. 3. Entertaining only such thoughts as are honourable to truth and our character, Phil. iv. 8. 4. Speaking nothing of ourselves but what is real truth, either in praise or dispraise, and even that only when we have a due call to it, Prov. xxv. 14. xxvi. 16. xxvii. 2; prudently concealing our secret sins and infirmities, which we have no divine call to confess to men, Prov. xxv. 9, 10; and meekly defending our character when it is unjustly attacked, John v. vii. viii. x. Acts xxii. xxiv. xxvi. 2 Cor. x. xi. 1 Cor. ix. Gal. i. ii. Josh. xxii. 1 Sam. xxii. 15. xxiv. 9---15. xxvi. 18; candidly and readily confessing our faults with grief and shame, when reproved, Prov. xxviii. 13. James v. 16. 5. In our behaviour avoiding every thing sinful or imprudent, and all appearances of it, and constantly following every thing good, and answerable to our station, 1 Thess. v. 22. Eccl. x. 1. Phil. iv. 8. Col. i.---iv. Eph. iv.---vi. 1 Thess. i.---v. Rom. xii.---xv. 1 Pet. i. ---v. 2 Pet. i. 4---8. iii. 11, 14, 18. III. The *maintaining and promoting our neighbour's good name*, in, 1. Earnest care to have them vested with the honourable character of God's friends and children, Gal. iv. 19. James v. 19, 20. Prov. x. 12. 1 Pet. iv. 8. Rom. x. 1. 2. Charitable esteeming of them, 1 Cor. xiii. 8. Phil. ii. 3. Rom. xii. 10. 3. Kind covering their infirmities, 1 Pet. iv. 8. James v. 20. Prov. x. 12. 4. Readily acknowledging their gifts, graces, and good behaviour, 1 Cor. xiii. 4, 5, 7. xiv. 5, 7. xvi. 15---18. 2 Cor. viii. 16---24. Phil. ii. 19---30. Col. iv. 12. 5. Defending their character when it is unjustly attacked, 1 Sam. xxii. 14. 6. Readily receiving good reports concerning them, and aversion to hear that which tends to their dishonour, 1 Cor. xiii. 6, 7. Psalm xv. 3. 1 Sam. xxii. 14, 15. 7. Earnestly discouraging tale-bearers, backbiters, and slanderers, and labouring to bring them to due disgrace and punishment, Psalm ci. 5. Prov. xxv. 23. 2 Cor. xii. 20. 8. Watching over our neighbours, from true love to them, and issuing in proper advice, warning, or reproof to them, Lev. xix. 16, 17. Matth. xviii. 15---17. 1 Thess. v. 14. 2 Thess. iii. 14.

This commandment FORBIDS, 1. *Whatsoever is prejudicial to truth*, 1. In *judicial processes*, uttered or done by parties, witnesses, advocates, or judges, Exod. xxiii. 1---7. Deut. xix. 15 ---19. Lev. xix. 11---16. Prov. xix. 5, 9. xxv. 18. Isa. lix. 13 ---15. Jer. ix. 3---6. Micah vii. 3. Mal. iii. 5. Falsehood and deceit in this case are peculiarly criminal, being committed in that judgment which belongs to God, before, or by judges sitting in his name and authority, as his deputies, and under the form of a solemn appeal to him,—and are peculiarly ruinous to the consciences and interests of mankind. Or, 2*dly*, In *extrajudicial cases*, as, 1. Unfaithfulness, paying no due regard to promises,—rashly making them, or entering into stations and relations which imply them, and want of due concern to remember and fulfil them, Rom. i. 31. 2 Tim. iii. 3. Jer. ix. 3---6. Luke xvi. 10. Deut. xxxii. 20. 2. Undue silence when iniquity requires that we should reprove it ourselves, or complain of it to rulers, Lev. xix. 17. v. 1. Deut. xiii. 8. Mark viii. 38. Eph. v. 7, 11. Mat. xviii. 15---17. 3. Speaking truth unseasonably or maliciously, or perverting it to a wrong meaning, Eccl. iii. 7. Prov. xxix. 11. Psalm lii. 2—4. 1 Sam. xxii. 8, 9. Acts xvi. 16, 17. Matth. xxvi. 60, 67. 4. *Equivocation*, using words of a double signification, in a sense different from that in which we expect our neighbour will understand them; and mental reservation, concealing some words in our mind which give our expressions a different meaning from that which they appear to have, Gen. iii. 3, 4. xx. 2, 12. xxvi. 6, 7. 5. Hypocrisy or dissimulation, appearing to be and do that which we neither are nor do, Matth. xxiii. 13—30. Tit. i. 16. 2 Tim. iii. 5. Isa. xxix. 13; to which may be reduced forgery of writs, counterfeiting of money, &c. 6. Simple falsehood, uttering that which is really false, but we believe to be true, Zech. viii. 16, 19. 7. Rash judging, affirming or denying facts without proper certainty, embellishing stories with circumstances which are not founded on proper information, 1 Cor. xiii. 6. 8. Gross lying, uttering that which we know to be false, with an intention to deceive our neighbour, Hos. iv. 2. Jer. ix. 3, 5. Isa. lix. 13.—All lying, whether in jest, Hos. vii. 3; for profit, Job xiii. 7. 2 Kings v. 22. Rom. iii. 8; for concealment of guilt, Gen. xviii. 15. 2 Kings v. 25. Acts v. 3, 8; for preventing danger, Gen. xii. 11—13. xx. 2. xxvi. 7. Mark xiv. 68—71; or for doing mischief, Prov. vi. 19. Jer. ix. 3, 5. Acts vi. 11, 13. xxiv. 5. Luke xxiii. 2; or from mere rashness and custom, 2 Sam. xiii. 30. Psalm cxxix. 29,—and all deceit, are of the devil, John viii. 44; contrary to the nature of God, Deut. xxxii. 4. 1 Sam. xv. 29; and condemned in his law, as abominable to him, and eternally ruinous to men, Psalm v. 4—6. Prov. vi. 17, 19. xiv. 5. xix. 5, 9. xxix. 12. Eph. iv. 25. Col. iii. 9. Rev. xxi. 8. xxii. 15. But concealing that which men have no call to reveal, figurative expressions, and changes of purpose or conduct, upon sufficient grounds, do not imply any deceit or falsehood, 1 Sam. xvi. 2, 5. 2 Kings vi. 19. Jer. xxxviii. 24—27. John xv. 1. Song ii. 1—3. 1 Kings xviii. 27. xxii. 15. Eccl. xi. 9. Gen. xix. 2, 3. 2 Cor. i. 17. John iii. II. *Whatsoever is injurious to our own good name,* 1. *In our heart,* thinking too highly or too meanly of ourselves, reckoning ourselves less indebted to God for his gifts and graces than we really are, Rom. xii. 16. Prov. xxv. 14. xxvi. 12, 16. Exod. iv. 10, 14. 2. *In our words,* unjustly or unseasonably accusing ourselves, Prov. xxv. 9, 16. Job xxvii. 5, 6; denying truth or affirming falsehood in our own favours, Prov. xxviii. 13. 1 Kings v. 25. Acts v. 8. Gen. xviii. 15. 2 Sam. i. 10; or boasting of ourselves in a vain glorious manner, Luke xviii. 11. Prov. xxv. 14. xxvii. 2. Luke xvi. 15. 2 Tim. iii. 2. 3. *In our behaviour,*—doing that which is sinful or imprudent,—connecting ourselves with infamous or carnal companions,—pushing ourselves into stations and circumstances in which we cannot behave to our own or the honour of God, 1 Sam. ii. 24. Prov. v. 8, 9. 2 Kings viii. 13. III. *Whatsoever is injurious to the good name of our neighbour.* 1. *In our heart*, by *unjust* suspicions, evil surmisings, 1 Tim. vi. 4; uncharitable and rash judging, Mat. vii. 1—4. 1 Cor. xiii. 7. Acts xxviii. 4; making ourselves a standard for judging others, Rom. xiv. 3, 10; judging their conscience, state, or intentions, as if we were God, Rom. xiv. 3, 4; misinterpreting their purposes, words, or deeds, Neh. vi. 6. Rom. iii. 8. Psalm lxix. 10; secret contempt of them, 2 Sam. vi. 16. Luke xviii. 9—11; envy of their just fame, Matth. xxi. 15. Num. xi. 29. John iii. 26; pleasure in their disgrace, Jer. xlviii. 27; or fond admiration of them, 1 Cor. iv. 6. Jude 16. 2. *In our speech*, speaking truth in order to dishonour them, Luke xv. 2. Mark vi. 3; unnecessarily divulging their infirmities, Gen. ix. 22; aggravating their real faults, Matth. vii. 3—5; reviving the infamy of their former falls, of which they had repented, and which had been forgotten, 2 Sam. xvi. 7; betraying their secrets, especially if some difference between them and us has happened, Prov. xvii. 9. xvi. 28. x. 12. xxv. 9. 2 Tim. iii. 4; attempting to undermine or diminish their reputation, Ezra iv. 12, 13. Mat. xii. 22—24; raising, spreading, or receiving false reports concerning them, Exod. xxiii. 1. Neh. vi. 6. Psalm xv. 3. Jer. xviii. 18. xx. 20; falsely slandering them, Psalm l. 20. Heb. x. 33. Psalm xxii. 6. lxix. 7, 20. xlii. 10; false or malicious accusation of them to rulers, Luke xxiii. 2. Acts xxiv. 5. Jer. xxxviii. 4; backbiting, tearing, and undermining their character, in their absence, Rom. i. 29, 38. Psalm xxxv. 15, 16. xv. 3. lxix. 10—13. Prov. xxv. 23. 2 Cor. xii. 20; tale-bearing between different families or persons, Lev. xix. 16. Prov. xi. 13. xx. 19. xviii. 8. xxvi. 20, 22. 2 Thess. iii. 11. 1 Tim. v. 13; encouraging tale-bearers, backbiters, and slanderers, at least in not bringing them to due disgrace and punishment, Prov. xxix. 12. xxv. 23; scornful derision, Gal. iv. 29. Psalm xxii. 7, 8. xxxv. 16, 19. Job xxx. 9. Heb. xi. 36; reviling, calling bad names, Mat. v. 22. 1 Cor. vi. 10. v. 11; passionate railing and brawling, Psalm lii. 2, 4. lxiv. 3. Jer. ix. 23. Jude 9, 10. 1 Tim. iii. 3. 3. *In our behaviour*, by suspicious or contemptuous gestures, Psalm xxii. 7. Prov. vi. 12, 13; turning our back on them as infamous, without sufficient ground, Gal. ii. 12. 2 Tim. i. 15. iv. 10; neglecting to warn and hinder them from what is sinful and imprudent; and by advice, encouragement, or example, drawing them into it, to the hurt of their character, 1 Sam. iii. 13. ii. 13. Ezek. xxxiii. 6, 8. IV. *Whatsoever tends both to the injuring truth and our own and neighbour's good name,* as, 1. An excessive readiness to speak in company; by which we manifest the frothiness and pride of our heart, and mark ourselves fools, Eccl. v. 2, 3. x. 14. Prov. xiv. 23. x. 19. xii. 23. xiii. 3, 6. xv. 2, 14. xvii. 27. xxix. 11, 20. 2. Idle talk, which has no tendency to promote any good end, either civil or religious, Mat. xii. 36. Eph. v. 4. 3. Inordinate jesting, Eph. v. 4. 4. Flattery, which includes much baseness, falsehood, deceit, and treachery in the giver; and marks much baseness and self-conceit in the receiver, Psalm xii. 3. xxxvi. 3. Acts xii. 22, 23.

X. The TENTH COMMANDMENT, which respects the most inward dispositions of our heart, and is, as it were, a guard to the rest, particularly to those of the second table, REQUIRES, I. *A due weanedness of affection from every created enjoyment,* Psalm cxxxi. 1, 2; having our heart habitually indifferent towards them, Luke xiv. 26; expecting nothing from them, but as God puts it into them, Psalm iv. 6, 7. Isa. lvii. 10. xvii. 10; extracting our whole comfort from God himself amidst plenty as well as in poverty, Psalm xviii. 46. 1 Sam. ii. 1—10. Luke i. 47. Psalm cxlii. 4, 5. Hab. iii. 17, 18; using them all as fading and transient, 1 Cor. vii. 29; and mortifying every degree of lustful desire after them, Matth. xxiv. 38. Luke xxi. 34. Gal. vi. 14. James iv. 4. 1 John ii. 16. II. *Full contentment with that condition in which God places us* with respect to gifts, graces, office, honour, wealth, pleasure, &c. in this world, Heb. xiii. 5. 1 Tim. vi. 6. Phil. iv. 11. This contentment doth not exclude, but imply detestation of our sinfulness,—humbly bewailing our distresses and wants,—and earnestness in all regular endeavours to have our condition as comfortable as possible; —and it includes an hearty reconcilement to God's will, as the only and universal standard for regulating our lot, in its form and degree, Psalm xlvii. 4. 1 Tim. vi. 8, 9; an absolute resignation, and entire submission to his will, as wise, holy, just, good, and very gracious, in all his providential disposals of us, or any thing belonging to us,—and hence, an inward easiness under his denials of outward comforts, and a satisfaction in our lot as *good, very good,* nay *best* for us, Matth. xvi. 24. 1 Sam. iii. 18. Phil. iv. 6, 11, 12. Mic. vii. 9. Psalm xxxix. 9. cxix. 67, 71, 75. Lam. iii. 27—39. Job i. 21. ii. 10. Hab. iii. 17, 18. 2 Cor. xii. 10. 2 Sam. xv. 25, 26. xvi. 10—12.—In order to attain this full contentment, we must, 1. Receive God in Christ, as the infinite origin and sum of all that good which can be found in creatures, for our only and eternal portion, and live daily upon him as such, Psalm lxxxi. 8—10. lxxiii. 23—26. cxlii. 4, 5. xvi. 5—11. xxiii. xviii. xci. cxvi. cxvii. cxviii. cxliv. cxlv. cxlvi. 2. Live in the believing consideration, that our new-covenant God, Friend, Father, and Husband, is the maker and manager of all things, Job xxxiv. 33; that he manages our lot in his infinite wisdom and love, Matth. x. 30. vi. 30. Isa. lii. 7. xlvi. 3, 4. 2 Sam. xvi. 10—12. 1 Sam iii. 18. Psalm xxxix. 9. Zech. xiii. 8, 9. iii. 9. Rom. viii. 28—32. 2 Cor. iv. 17. Deut. xxxii. 4. xxxiii. 26—29. Job xxxv. 14. Isa. xxx. 18. l. 10; that we live on his mere grace and bounty, Gen. xxxii. 10. Lam. iii. 22. Isa. lxiii. 7. xlvi. 3, 4. Psalm xxxvi. 6, 7; that the wants and afflictions of our outward lot bid fair to be its most useful part to our soul, Lam. iii. 27, 29, 32, 33. 2 Cor. iv. 17. Psalm cxix. 67, 71. Job xxxiii. 17—30. Isa. xxvii. 9. Ezek. xx. 37. Hos. ii. 6, 7, 14. v. 15. vi. 1, 2. Mic. vii. 14. Rev. iii. 19. Heb. xii. 5—11. Prov. iii. 12. Psalm xciv. 12. Job v. 17; that earthly enjoyments are always very empty and often very hurtful, Eccl. i.—xii. i. 2, 14, 17. Prov. xxiii. 5. i. 32. Deut. xxxii 15. Hos. xiii. 6; that our temptations, burdens, services, and final account, are proportioned to our enjoyments, Matth. xxv. 15—30. Luke xix. 13—26. xii. 47, 48; that Jesus Christ has marked and pathed our way through every trouble, and attends us, to bear, carry, and deliver us, Isa. lxiii. 9. xlvi. 3, 4; and that death and eternity, in which earthly enjoyments can do us no service, and in which we shall reap the happy fruits of our troubles, are at hand, Matth. xvi. 25. xix. 29. 2 Tim. iv. 6—8. Acts xiv. 22. John xvi. 33. Rom. viii. 17, 18, 37—39. 2 Cor. iv. 17, 18. 2 Tim. ii. 10—12. Rev. ii. 7, 17, 26. iii. 5, 12, 21. III. A *right and charitable frame of spirit toward our neighbour, and all that is his*—heartily loving his person for God's sake, Rom. xiii. 9, 10; kindly regarding his property for his, and chiefly for God's sake, Deut. xxii. 1; earnestly desiring and cordially delighting in his welfare, temporal, spiritual, or eternal, Rom. xii. 15. Heb. xiii. 3. Psalm xxxv. 13, 14. Phil. ii. 4. IV. *A perfectly holy frame of spirit*, Rom. vii. 7. 1 Pet. i. 15, 16. Lev. xi. 44. Matth. v. 48. xxii. 37, 39.

This commandment FORBIDS, I. All *discontentment with our own condition*, which includes in it inward rebellion against God's providential will, Hos. iv. 16. xiii. 6; fretfulness or grief at his disposal of our lot, 1 Kings xxi. 4. 2 Cor. vii. 10; inward displeasure against that form or condition which he has allotted to us, Job xviii. 4; inward blasphemy against him, as if he had been guilty of injustice or cruelty in ordering our lot, Job ix. 17, 18. x. 16. xxx. 12. II. *Envy*, grief, and fretfulness, on account of the advantages of our neighbour, in gifts, graces, relations, wealth, honour, pleasure, Job v. 2. John iii. 26. 1 Cor. xiii. 4. Psalm xxxvii. 1, 7, 8. James iii. 14, 16. Jer. xii. 1. Psalm lxxiii. 2—15. Eph. iv. 4, 5, 11. Gal. v. 21, 26. Prov. iii. 31. xxiv. 1, 19. III. *Covetousness* of created enjoyments,

1. In inordinate lusting after those things which we possess, having our heart fixed on them, Col. iii. 5. Luke xiv. 18—21. xii. 21; and hence desiring them for themselves, for a wrong end, or as our chief good, James iv. 3—5; using them with too much avidity, without regard to necessity or expedience, as if we were under their power, 1 Cor. vi. 12; or to the hurt of our soul, and the dishonour of God, James iv. 3, 4. 1 Cor. x. 31. Hos. x. 4. 2. In lusting after that which belongs to our neighbour; desiring that which God has put out of our power, 2 Sam. xxiii. 15. Josh. vii. 21; desiring that which is attainable by lawful means, by such as are unlawful, or for an unlawful end, Jam. iv. 3. 1 Kings xxi. 2—15. Jer. xvii. 11. Job xvii. 10—18; or desiring them so violently as disturbs our mind till we enjoy them, and renders us fretful if we must want them, Gen. xxx. 1. 1 Kings xxi. 4. Psalm iv. 6. xvii. 14. 1 Tim. vi. 9, 10. IV. The corrupt frame of our fallen nature, from which these sinful lustings proceed. This evil concupiscence may be considered, 1. As existing in our heart, but not consented to, Rom. vii. 14—24. 2. As consented to in itself, but not in the execution of its desires, Matth. v. 28. Eccl. vi. 9. 3. As conceiving, contriving, and bringing forth actual sin, in thoughts, words, and deeds, James i. 15. Matth. xv. 19. Mark vii. 21, 22. 4. As having brought forth contrived acts of wickedness to the very point of execution, 1 Sam. xxiii. 26. Esth. iii. v. vi. Acts xvi. 27. xxi. 31, 32. xxiii. 10, 12—24.

REFLECT. Pause now, my soul! How holy must God the giver of this law be, with whom I have to do! How awfully strict and extensive that standard, by which he will judge me, and fix my eternal state!---How inexpressibly guilty before God must I now be, who have so long, in so many forms, and in so aggravated a manner, broken all these commandments!--- How infinitely horrid, abominable, and criminal must sin be, which is in opposition to the law of God, so *holy, just, and good!* ---How absolutely necessary the righteousness of God in our nature, as our Surety, to justify us, who are sinful men, before God! And what an unbounded mercy, to be justified from all the charges of this law, and to be, to its inexpressible honour, adjudged to everlasting happiness! And how important that inward change of nature, in which God writes his law on our heart! How base the traitors, that would improve Jesus's righteousness as a reason of trampling this law under their foot!---But what knows my conscience of its power, in driving me to Christ, or directing me to improve his righteousness, his grace and glory?---Is it the object of my dearest affection,--- my delightful meditation all the day? And, all washed in

Jesus's blood, and animated by his redeeming love, do I daily run in the way of all those commandments?

III. The ten commandments, above explained, may be viewed in a threefold form: I. As a *Law of Nature* antecedent to, and disengaged from any covenant-transaction between God and us. In this form, 1. God, as a Creator and absolute Sovereign, imposed it. 2. It was written upon man's heart in his creation, —it, and full power to fulfil it, being included in the instamped image of God the Lawgiver, Gen. i. 26, 27. Eccl. vii. 29. 3. It contained no positive precept, but obliged all its subjects to believe every thing which God should reveal, and perform every thing that he should command, Deut. xii. 32. 4. Its subjects not being confirmed in holiness of heart and life, it implied a sanction of infinite punishment to every transgressor, as the due reward of his sin, Rom. vi. 23. 5. The most perfect obedience of innocent men, having no proper merit before God, especially of eternal happiness, it implied no promise of any such reward, or that men should ever be confirmed under it as an easy and delightful *rule of life*, Job xxii. 23. Rom. vi. 23. 6. It did not admit of God's accepting any thing less than perfect obedience, Ezek. xviii. 4. Rom. vi. 23. 7. All men, as *rational creatures*, were subject to it, Rom. ii. 14, 15. II. *As a Covenant of Works.* In this form, 1. An absolute God, condescending to friendship, makes alliance and familiarity with holy and perfect man, was the imposer of it, Gen. ii. 17. 2. It included not only all the commands of the law of nature, but also some positive institutions, Gen. ii. 16, 17. 3. It not only denounced infinite punishment against every transgressor of it, Gal. iii. 10. Deut. xxvii. 26. Ezek. xviii. 4; but also promised eternal happiness to the perfect fulfiller of it, Matth. xix. 17. Gal. iii. 12. Rom. x. 5. 4. It binds mankind, not only as authoritatively imposed by God their sovereign, but also as accepted by themselves, in their own self-engagement to fulfil it. 5. The original scope and end of it was, that man might obtain eternal life by his own obedience, as its condition, Rom. vii. 10. viii. 3. x. 5. 6. As it admits not of God's accepting any obedience but that which is absolutely perfect, answerable to all its demands, Gal. iii. 10, 12; so the accepting the fulfiller's person depended on the accepting his obedience, Matth. xix. 17. v. 18. Rom. x. 5. 7. In consequence of God's making this law-covenant with Adam, all his natural descendants, while in their natural state, are under it before God, even though, as hearers of the gospel, they be under the external dispensation of the covenant of grace, Eph. ii. 3. Rom. ix. 30—32. But all true believers being united to Jesus Christ, who, as their Surety, fulfilled it for them, are perfectly delivered from it, and dead to it; so that their sins no

2 K

longer condemn them to endure God's revenging wrath, nor their holy qualities or works in the least entitle them to eternal happiness, Rom vi. 14. vii. 4. viii. 1—4, 33, 34. Gal. ii. 19—21. iii. 13. iv. 4, 5. v. 18. Phil. iii. 9. 1 Tim. i. 9. III. *As the law of Christ, or rule of life.* In this form, 1. It has the whole authority of God as a Creator and Sovereign, as well as a Redeemer, giving to it binding force. His nature being absolutely irreconcileable to every thing sinful, his law, as a transcript of his holiness, must still retain its original obligation, 1 Pet. i. 15, 16. Lev. xi. 44. Matth. v. 48. 2. It proceeds immediately from Jesus Christ, God-man, Mediator, and from God, as our Creator and Sovereign, as reconciled and dwelling in him, 1 Cor. ix. 21. Gal. vi. 2. 2 Cor. v. 19—21. 3. Its precepts are the very same with those of the covenant of works, and demand the same perfection of obedience, Matth. xxii. 36, 37. v. 48. 1 Pet. i. 15, 16. Phil. iv. 8. 4. The subjects of it being fully and irrevocably instated in the favour of God, and entitled to eternal life in Christ, it has no sanction of judicial rewards or punishments, 1 John iii. 14. John v. 24. Rom. v. 21. viii. 1, 33, 34. But while their condition, temper, and practice are changeable, it is enforced with a sanction of gracious rewards, of much freedom from spiritual distress, and much comfortable fellowship with God, and correspondent degrees of glory annexed to their obedience,—and of fatherly chastisement annexed to their disobedience, Psalm xix. 11. Isa. lxiv. 5. iii. 10. 2 Cor. i. 12. 1 Cor. xv. 58. 2 Tim. iv. 7, 8. 1 Tim. iv. 8. Heb. x. 35. xii. 6—11. Rev. iii. 19. Psalm lxxxix. 30—34. xcix. 8;—which sanction corresponds with the spiritual condition of believers, and is founded on their happy new-covenant state. 5. God's end in giving the law as a rule of life, is not that men, by their obedience to it, may procure his favour as a Judge, and a title to eternal life; but to direct, bind, and excite believers in Christ to improve their full and irrevocable justification, and begun possession of eternal life, in cordial gratitude to him, and preparation for complete salvation; so that their obedience, in its highest view, is a part of their happiness here, as well as it will be in heaven, Psalm cxvi. 16. Luke i. 74, 75. Rom. vii. 4, 6. Gal. ii. 19. Heb. xii. 28. Tit. ii. 14. 1 Pet. ii. 9. 6. It supposes all its subjects to have already full strength, motives, and encouragements in Christ: and though it require perfect obedience, it admits of God's accepting our imperfect obedience of faith, not to found any acceptance of our persons, but as a fruit of their being united to, and fully accepted in Christ, Eph. i. 6. 1 Cor. xv. 58. Heb. xiii. 16. 1 Pet. ii. 5. Rom. xii. 1. 1 Thess. iv. 1. 7. All believers, and they only, are the subjects of this law of Christ, 1 Cor. ix. 21. Gal. vi. 2. It binds them as much under the gospel, as before Christ and his apostles inculcated it with additional enforcements, Matth. v.—vii. xxii. 37—40. Rom. xii.—xv. Eph. iv.—vi. Col. iii. iv. 1 Thess. iv. v. Tit. ii. iii. Heb. x.—xiii. Jam. i. to Rev. iii. Their relation to Christ, and to God in him, as their Husband, Father, Friend, and Pattern, requires its continued obligation, Gal. ii. 19, 20. 1 Pet. ii. 4, 5, 9. Matth. xxviii. 20. v. 44, 48. All their new-covenant blessings of union with Christ, justification, adoption, regeneration, sanctification, spiritual comfort, and eternal glorification, require their continued subjection to it, Rom. vii. 4, 6. 2 Cor. vi. 18. vii. 1. Tit. ii. 11—14. iii. 8, 14. Psalm cxvi. 16. cxix. 32, 166. Phil. ii. 12, 13—16. 1 Pet. i. 13—16. ii. 5, 9. Gal. v. 24, 25. Heb. xii. 1, 2, 14, 28. Gal. vi. 7, 8. Rom. viii. 23. Phil. iii. 14, 20, 21.

IV. In one or more of these different forms, the moral law is of USE, I. To *all men* in general. 1. To teach them their duty to God, to themselves, and to their neighbours; and to bind them to it by his infinite authority, Mic. vi. 8. 2. To discover to them the holiness, equity, and goodness of his nature and work, Rom. vii. 12. 3. To restrain them from sin, and to encourage them to virtue, as even the approaches to it, and resemblances of it, are rewarded with freedom from temporal miseries, and with temporal felicity, or non-infliction of the greater punishments in hell, Psalm xix. 11. Ezek. xviii. Isa. i. 19. Deut. iv.—xxx. 4. To convince them of their sinfulness and misery on account of it, and of their utter inability to recover themselves by keeping the commandments, Rom. iii. 19, 20. vii. 8—13. 5. To shew them their need of Christ, his righteousness and grace, and to stir them up to apply them to their soul, Gal. iii. 24. II. It is of use to unregenerate men, 1. To convince and awaken their conscience, Rom. iii. 19, 20. vii. 9. Gal. ii. 19. 2. To denounce the wrath of God against their sin, and thus affect them with a deep sense of it, Rom. iii. 19. ii. 8, 9. vi. 19, 23. 3. To bridle the rage of their lusts, 1 Tim. i. 9. 4. To drive them, as convinced of their sinfulness, misery, and self-irrecoverableness, to Jesus Christ, as their almighty Saviour, Gal. iii. 24. Rom. x. 4. 5. To fix upon their conscience a deep sense of their having those very characters of sinfulness and misery by which men are particularly invited to receive Christ and his salvation, 1 Tim. i. 15. Isa. xlvi. 12. i. 18. lv. 2, 7. lxv. 1, 2. Matth. ix. 13. xviii. 11. xi. 28. Prov. i. 22. ix. 4. Jer. iii. 1, 4, 5. 6. To consign them to redoubled damnation, if they reject him, John iii. 18, 36. Heb. ii. 3. x. 26—31. Matth. xi. 20—24. III. It is of use to believers, 1. To shew them what Christ, from love to their souls, did and suffered in their stead, Gal. iv. 4, 5. iii. 13. Rom. viii. 3, 4. 2. To shew them their inexpressible deficiency in holiness, in order to humble them, cause them to renounce their own righteousness, and rely wholly on Christ, and to make them long for heaven, Phil. iii. 8, 9. i. 23. Rom. vii. 24. 2 Cor. v. 4. 3. To instruct them what grateful service they owe to Christ and his Father, and what perfection of holiness they ought always to aim at, Phil. iii. 12---14. 1 Tim. i. 5. 2 Cor. vii. 1. 1 Pet. i. 13---16. 2 Pet. i. 4---8. Matth. v. 48. 4. To attest the truth of their begun sanctification, and to comfort them as Israelites indeed, who walk in the law of the Lord after their inward man of implanted grace, 2 Cor. i. 12.

REFLECT. Study carefully, O my soul, the wide, but little perceived difference between the law of God, *as a covenant*, and *as a rule of life* in the hand of Christ. Without distinct experimental knowledge of this, I can neither rightly discern nor practise the truth as it is in Jesus.—What powerful experience have I had of these several uses of the holy law?—God forbid that I should preach it up, so as to render it a source and seal of eternal damnation to myself and others.

CHAP. II.

Of the GOSPEL, *in its* MATTER, USE, DIFFERENCE *from, and* CONNECTION *with the Law.*

BY the GOSPEL in Scripture is meant, either the whole system of God's revealed truth, Mark i. 14; or the history of Christ's birth, life, death, resurrection, and ascension, Mark i. 1; or the New-Testament dispensation of the covenant of grace, 2 Tim. i. 10; or the preaching of God's truth, particularly his free offers of Christ, and salvation through him, 1 Cor. ix. 14. But, *strictly taken*, the gospel denotes *the glad tidings of life, of full and free salvation through Christ to sinful men*, Mat. xi. 5. Luke ii. 10, 11. Nothing can more justly be called *gospel*, i. e. *good news*, or a *gladdening message*, than God's free and earnest offers of righteousness, pardon, and acceptance to guilty sinners, adoption to heirs of wrath, sanctification to men dead and defiled in sins, redemption to the most miserable and enslaved, and salvation to the lost,—gifts to the rebellious, that God may dwell among them, 1 Cor. i. 30. Acts v. 31. Luke xix. 10. Psalm lxviii. 18. It is in connection with this view, that the history of Christ's life is called the *Gospel*, because it declares how he, being the Son of God, was made of a woman, was made under the law, obeyed and suffered in our stead, in order to purchase salvation for us, and has ascended to heaven, in order to procure and apply it to us. The general dispensation of God's revealed truth is called *Gospel*, as it is wholly calculated to drive, direct, or draw us to Jesus Christ, as made of God to us wisdom, righteousness, sanctification, and redemption.—The New-Testament dispensation is called *Gospel*, because the glad tidings of salvation through Christ are therein more fully, clearly, extensively, and powerfully held forth and applied to sinful men, Mark xvi. 15. Rom. xv. 19.

I. The gospel, strictly taken, includes, 1. God's doctrinal declarations concerning the salvation of men,—concerning his purpose of election, and the covenant of grace, in its origin, parties, making, parts, administrations,—and concerning the mediator of it in his person, offices, and states, and concerning the blessings of it, union with Christ, justification, adoption, sanctification, spiritual comfort, and eternal glory, Rom. i.—xi. Gal. ii.—v. Eph. i.—v. Col. i.—iii. Phil. ii. 6—11. 1 Tim. iii. 16. Isa. xl.—lxvi. &c. and that whether these declarations be plain or figurative, Exod. xii. xiv. xvi. xvii. xxiv.—xxx. Lev. i.—xvi. xxiii. xxv. xxvii. Num. xv. xvii. xix. xxviii. Heb. iii.—x. Gal. iii. 8. Heb. iv. 2. 2. God's candid and earnest offers of Jesus Christ, in his person, offices, relations, and fulness, and of himself in him, as an absolutely free gift bequeathed to sinful men in his new covenant promises, John iii. 16. Isa. xlii. 6, 7. lv. 4. Jer. iii. 19. xxxi. 31—34. xxxii. 38—41. Ezek. xi. 19, 20. xxxvi. 25—32. 3. His affectionate invitations, in which he calls and earnestly entreats men, under their manifold wretched characters, to receive that which he offers to them, upon the foot of his free grant of it, and to apply it to themselves in particular, Psalm xxxiv. 8. lxxxi. 8, 10. Prov. i. 22, 23. viii. 4. ix. 4, 5. xxiii. 26. Zech. ix. 12. Mat. ix. 13. Isa. i. 18. xlv. 22. xliv. 22. xlvi. 12, 13. lv. 1—3, 6, 7. Jer. iii. 1, 4, 14, 22. Hos. xiv. 1. Ezek. xxxiii. 11. Mat. xi. 28—30. John vi. 37. vii. 37—39. 2 Cor. v. 19, 20, 21. Rev. iii. 17, 18, 20. xxii. 17.—These invitations, in so far as they demand our performance of our duty, are reducible to the law as extended upon the foundation of the offers of the gospel, 1 John iii. 23. John vi. 29; but, in so far as they hold forth God's willingness, readiness, and earnestness to bestow his salvation upon sinful men, and warrant them to receive it to themselves, they belong to the gospel. Notwithstanding they are distinguishable, these declarations, offers, and invitations of the gospel are often contained in the same sentence of Scripture, and ought never to be separated. We never rightly believe any doctrinal declaration of the gospel, unless we, in that very act, receive the good offered, as invited to do so by God himself.

II. The USE, therefore, of these declarations, offers, and invitations, is, 1. To make known Christ in his person, offices, work, and fulness, and God as reconciled in him, 1 Cor. ii. 2. i. 24. 2 Cor. iv. 3, 4, 6. v. 18—21. 1 Tim. iii. 16. 2. To present and offer Christ and his fulness to men, and affectionately call and urge them to fellowship with him, 1 Cor. i. 9. Prov. ix. 4, 5. Isa. xlv. 22. lv. 1—3, 6, 7. 3. To be God's mean of effectually conveying Christ and his fulness into our heart, for the changing our state and nature, Psalm cx. 2, 3. 1 Cor. i. 30. 2 Cor. v. 17. 4. To be God's mean of further applying Christ and his fulness to our renewed heart, for carrying on and completing our holiness and comfort, John i. 14, 16. xx. 31. Psalm xxvii. 13, 14. Gal. ii. 20. Eph. iii. 17—19. ii. 20—22. 5. As a mean of enlarging the knowledge, softening the tempers, and reforming the outward practice of many reprobates, in order to render them useful to the elect, Heb. vi. 4, 5. 2 Pet. ii. 20. Mat. xiii. 19—22. Phil. i. 15—18. Num. xxiii. xxiv.

III. The gospel, strictly taken, differs from the law, in that, 1. The law considers us as God's rational creatures and subjects, who were *originally* formed with sufficient abilities perfectly to obey it, and hence directs and binds us to have such abilities, and to exercise them in a proper manner towards God, ourselves, and our neighbours, as our duty, Mat. xxii. 37—39; but the gospel considers us *as sinful* and *self-ruined men*, graciously pitied by God, and declares what he, according to his infinite mercy and grace, has done, prepared for, and offers to be, and do to and for us, Isa. xlii. 6, 7. xlix. liii. liv. lv. Psalm xxii. lxviii. lxxii. cxlvi. Hence its offers and invitations continue to believers while their sinfulness remains, and no longer. 2. In every essential point the law flows from the very nature of God; but the gospel, both in its matter and manifestation, flows from his sovereign mercy, grace, or good will,—the outgoings of his mercy in the redemption of men, being no more necessary than the exertion of his wisdom and power in the creation of all things, Eph. i. 3—8. ii. 4—9. Tit. iii. 4, 5. Rom. v. 20, 21. 3. The law represents God's blessings as bestowed upon men as *good and obedient*, Gal. iii. 12. Rom. x. 5. Psalm xix. 11. Isa. iii. 10. i. 19; but the gospel represents blessings as bestowed upon men, as in themselves *guilty and sinful*, Rom. v. 5—10, 20, 21. Isa. xlvi. 12, 13 xliii. 24, 25 lv. 2, 7. i. 18. xliv. 22. Jer. iii. 4, 14, 19, 22. Psalm lxviii. 18. Ezek. xxxvi. 25, 26, 27, 31. Hos. xiii. 9. Mat. ix. 13. xviii. 11. Luke xv. 19, 10. 1 Tim. i. 15.

IV. The harmony of the law and gospel is their suitableness and subserviency to each other: the gospel promises, offers, and gives to sinful men every thing which the law, in any form, demands of them. It provides them with the righteousness of the

OF THE GOSPEL.

Son of God, which answers and magnifies all the demands of the law, *as a broken covenant:* and lays an effectual foundation of universal, and at last perfect obedience to it, *as a rule.* Nay, it promises preparation for, assistance in, and a gracious reward of every duty which the law, *as a rule,* requires, as the following and many other texts, if carefully compared, will sufficiently evince:

LAW.	GOSPEL.
Lev. xi. 44. xx. 7. 1 Pet. i. 15, 16. Mat. v. 48.	Lev. xx. 8. xxi. 23. xxii. 32. Isa. xxix. 23. lxii. 12. Heb. ix. 14. xiii. 12. Ezek. xxxvii. 28. 1 Thess. v. 23.
Ezek. xviii. 31. Jer. iv. 4. Rom. xii. 1, 2. Col. iii. 9, 10.	Ezek. xi. 19. xxxvi. 26. Jer. xxiv. 7. xxxii. 39, 40. 2 Cor. v. 17. Rev. xxi. 5. Deut. xxx. 6.
Isa. i. 16. Jam. iv. 8. Jer. iv. 14. 2 Cor. vii. 1.	Ezek. xxxvi. 25, 29. Zech. xiii. 1. Joel iii. 21. Isa. iv. 3, 4.
Deut. xii. 32. James i. 19. Jer. vii. 23. Exod. xxiii. 21. Mat. xxviii. 20.	Ezek. xxxvi. 27. xi. 20. Psalm cx. 3. Jer. xxxi. 33. xxxii. 39, 40.
Exod. xx. 3. 1 John v. 21. 1 Cor. x. 7. Mat. iv. 10.	Exod. xx. 2. Psal. l. 7. lxxxi. 8. Jer. xxx. 22. xxxi. 33. xxxii. 38. xxiv. 7. Ezek. xxxvii. 23, 28. Zech. viii. 8. xiii. 9.
1 Chron. xxviii. 9. John v. 39. 2 Pet. iii. 18. Isa. i. 17. 2 Chron. xx. 20. Isa. xxvi. 4. Acts xvi. 31. 1 John iii. 23. John xiv. 1.	Isa. xlviii. 17. liv. 13. xxix. 24. Jer. xxxi. 34. 2 Cor. iv. 6. Isa. xi. 10. Rom. xv. 12. Zeph. iii. 12. Psalm xxii. 27, 31. John vi. 37. Phil. i. 29. 2 Pet. i. 1. John v. 25.
Isa. i. 16, 17. lv. 7. Jer. vi. 8. vii. 3. Luke xiii. 3, 5. Rev. iii. 19.	Zech. xii. 10. Ezek. xvi. 63. xxxvi. 31. Acts v. 31. Hos. xiv. 8.
Jer. iii. 14, 22. Hos. xiv. 1. Isa. xliv. 22. Ezek. xxxiii. 11. xviii. 30.	Isa. x. 21. Psalm lxviii. 22. Isa. xxvii. 13, 14.
Jam. iv. 10. 1 Pet. v. 5, 6. Jer. xiii. 18.	Isa. ii. 11, 17. Ezek. xvi. 63. xxxvi. 31. Zeph. iii. 11.
James iv. 8. Psal. l. 15. Isa. lv. 6. Amos v. 8. Psalm cv. 4. Mat. vii. 7.	Psal. xci. 15. lxv. 2, 4. Zech. xii. 10. Isa. lviii. 9. lxv. 24.
1 Cor. xvi. 13. Eph. vi. 10. 2 Tim. ii. 1. &c. &c. &c.	Isa. xli. 10, 14. xl. 29, 31. Zech. x. 12. &c. &c. &c.

The law, *as a covenant,* is subservient to the gospel, 1. As a glass to shew us our sinfulness and misery, and thus our need of Christ and his salvation offered in the gospel, Rom. iii. 19, 20. vii. 9. 2. As an infallible witness that we have in us these very ignominious and wretched characters with which the promises, offers, and invitations of the gospel do correspond, and to which they are directed, Rom. v. 20, 21. iii. 9—18. i. 28—32. Rev. iii. 17, 18. Prov. i. 22. ix. 4. Isa. i. 18. xliii. 24, 25. xlvi. 12, 13. lv. 2, 7. lxv. 1, 2. Jer. iii. 1, 4, 5, 19. Hos. xiii. 9. xiv. 1. Zech. ix. 12. Mat. ix. 13. xi. 28. xxii. 9. Luke xiv. 23. xix. 10. 3. As a scourge to lash our conscience with charges of guilt and threatenings of wrath, in order to drive us out of all lying refuges to Christ alone for righteousness and salvation, Rom. vii. 7—13. Gal. iii. 24. 4. As a tremendous charge by God immediately to receive Christ and his salvation offered to us in the gospel,—as a necessary and principal part of that obedience which we owe to him as our Sovereign, whose declarations we ought to believe, and whose gifts we ought to receive,—and as the only method of affording full satisfaction to all its infinite demands,—and as a leading exercise of love to ourselves, John iii. 18. 1 John iii. 23. Rom. x. 3, 4. vii. 4. viii. 3, 4. 5. As an awful commentary upon the mysteries of the gospel, which indirectly manifests the amazing nature of God's redeeming love, the tremendous price of our redemption, and the astonishing happiness of those that are redeemed from under the law to God, 1 John iv. 9, 10. Mat. iii. 15. xx. 28. Luke xxiv. 26. Gal. iii. 10, 12, 13. iv. 4, 5, 6. Heb. xii. 18—24. Dan. ix. 24. 6. As an infallible, a divine security for the eternal happiness of those that are made fulfillers of it in Christ, Rom. viii. 1—4, 32—34. v. 19, 21. 7. In revenging the indignity done to itself, in men's obtruding upon it their own abominable self-righteousness, instead of the law-magnifying obedience and sufferings of Christ, it terribly punishes the indignity and injury they did to the gospel, and all the redeeming blood and grace of God in it, by their unbelieving rejection of its offers, Mal. i. 13, 14. Heb. ii. 3. x. 26—29. xii. 25. John iii. 18, 36. Mark xvi. 16.——As a *rule of life* in the hand of Christ, the law is subservient to the gospel, 1. As an exciter of believers, obedientially to receive more of the gracious privileges of the gospel to qualify them for more full and lively obedience to this law, 2 Pet. iii. 18. i. 4—8. Eph. vi. 10. 2 Tim. ii. 1. 2. As an instructing charge from Christ to improve the abundant grace of the gospel to its honour, Tit. ii. 10. Phil. i. 27. ii. 15, 16. 3. God's impression of it on our heart being a blessing of the gospel, makes us relish, desire, and rest satisfied with the other pure and spiritual blessings of it, 1 Cor. ix. 21. Jer. xxxi. 33. 4. As a glass it shews us the nature of that God, and of that holiness which the gospel promises and gives to us as our eternal happiness, 1 Pet. i. 15, 16. Mat. v. 48. Eph. iv. 32. v.

1, 2. 1 John iv. 8, 16, 19.—Thus the law of God as a *covenant*, and as a *rule*, turns every way to drive, shut up, or allure men to the gospel, and to Christ, and his righteousness and grace in it.

On the other hand, the gospel marvellously promotes the honour of the *law as a covenant*. 1. Its representations of Christ, and his undertaking and righteousness, is a delightful commentary upon its tremendous requirements, Rom. viii. 3, 4. x. 4. Dan. ix. 24. Isa. xlii. 21. 2. It presents in Christ the most clear and persuasive proof of its infinite importance and infallible stability, Gal. iv. 4, 5. Matth. iii. 15. v. 17, 18. xx. 28. Luke xxiv. 26. 3. It presents and offers to us a righteousness proper to be presented by us to this law, as an infinitely high and honourable satisfaction to all its demands on us, Rom. iii. 21, 22, 24—26, 31. 2 Cor. v. 21. Isa. xlii. 21. xlv. 24, 25. liv. 17. Jer. xxiii. 6. xxxiii. 16.—It promotes the honour of the *law as a rule*, in that, 1. It presents, offers, and conveys to us every thing relative to example, motive, endowment, assistance, or reward, which can promote obedience to it in heart or in life, Eph. v. 2. 1 John iv. 9, 10, 19. Hos. ii. 19, 20. Rom. vii. 4. vi. 14. viii. 4. Ezek. xxxvi. 15—27. Phil. ii. 12, 13. Zech. x. 12. 1 Cor. xv. 58. Heb. xii. 28. 2. By the powerful influence of the gospel, the law, as a rule, is written on our heart, Heb. viii. 10—12. Jer. xxxi. 31, 33.

To illustrate the subservience of the gospel to the moral law *as a rule of life*, the powerful influence of its evangelical preface, *I am the Lord thy God, which brought thee out of the land of Egypt*, &c. in enforcing obedience to all its commandments, may be considered. Here all our holy obedience is founded upon the lawgiver, being *Jehovah*, and *our God* and *Redeemer*. His character JEHOVAH represents him as necessarily existent as to himself and every thing else; all-sufficient as the Author of all created being, chiefly of the fulfilment of promises. His being *Jehovah, our God*, imports, that he, in all his fulness and glory, is offered and conveyed to us in the gospel, in all the different relations of Father, Husband, Master, Portion, &c. And it is observable, that in the law given at Sinai, this grant of himself as *Jehovah our God* is five times repeated, Exod. xx. 2, 5, 7, 10, 12.—His typical representation of himself as our Redeemer, presents to us our eternal redemption in its *price*, and in its several *benefits* of union with Christ, justification, adoption, sanctification, spiritual comfort, and everlasting happiness. All these in the most delightful manner enforce obedience to every *table*,—to every *command*.

If he be JEHOVAH, what an infinitely excellent object must he be, of all that *love* which is demanded for him by the *first table!* Mark xii. 30, 33. What an all-sufficient, all-comprehensive, infinite sum of every thing lovely!—If he be Jehovah *connected with us* in every delightful new-covenant relation;—if he gave, and was the *price* of our eternal redemption, what an infinitely strong reason for, and engaging pattern of superlative love to himself, is he!—If, in Christ, we receive such rich and inestimable benefits, how powerfully they demand that we should love God in Christ, and for him, and as Christ loved him, and answerably to the manifestation of his perfections in these benefits, and answerably to the relations into which they bring us to God!

They no less powerfully enforce love to ourselves and to our neighbour, in obedience to the second *table.* If the Lawgiver be JEHOVAH, infinitely glorious and worthy of our superlative love, his creatures ought to be loved in proportion to their excellency. If he be the author of their being, he ought to be loved in them as his offspring, and they loved for his sake, in proportion to their resemblance of him. If he, in infinite kindness, gave men their being,—how becoming to render that being as happy as possible,—and, as his joint progeny, to live joined in love to him, and to each other!—If, in his new covenant of grace, he has connected himself with us in so many delightful relations, and acts according to them,—why, by our inhuman behaviour, condemn his infinitely gracious example, and refuse to extend our goodness to his representatives, and especially his darling saints on earth, Psalm xvi. 2, 3. 1 Pet. iii. 8. iv. 8. Rom. xii.—xv. Eph. v. vi. Col. iii. iv.?—If in Jesus' payment of the infinite price of our redemption, he gave us the most engaging example of, and motive to the most disinterested love to mankind, John xiii. 14. xv. 12. Eph. v. 2. If it was paid, and is applied in order to promote our loving men as well as God, why should we not be powerfully constrained by its influence?—If we be united to Christ, why should not the same spirit and mind be in us that was and is in him, Eph. iv. 21. Phil. ii. 5. 1 Pet. ii. 21? If, notwithstanding our unnumbered and high provocations, we be *justified* freely by his grace, why not love and shew kindness to our brethren that injure us, especially if they appear to have received forgiveness from God, Eph. iv. 32. Matth. xviii. 23—35? If God, in his redeeming love, has brought us into his family, and put us *among his children*, why should we retain or live in our former malice and envy? Why not, to the honour of his house, breathe forth the temper of his sons and daughters, in acts of love to each other, 1 John iii. 11, 14. Tit. iii. 3? If we be *renewed*, and have the sanctifying spirit of God dwelling in us, why strive against him and the new nature which he has implanted, in order to do mischief, 1 Pet. i. 3, 22, 23. Gal. v. 22. Eph. v. 9. Rom. xiii. 8? If we enjoy the *consolations* of God, why not improve them to the comfort of others by acts of love to them, Col. ii. 2? If we expect that *heavenly state* in which *love* reigns in perpetual perfection, why should we not make it our present temper and business on earth? But, more particularly,

I. These reasons strongly demand that we should know and acknowledge, worship and glorify the true God as God and our God, and abstain from and abhor all atheism, profaneness, and idolatry, in obedience to the FIRST commandment.— If he alone be JEHOVAH, how absurd to attempt finding happiness in, or giving his glory to another,—an imaginary, or at best an upstart, dependent, fading, unsubstantial creature, Psalm lxxxiii. 18. cii. 26, 27. Isa. xlii. 8. Jer. x. 10, 11. Heb. xiii. 5, 8. Psalm xlviii. 14. lxxiii. 25, 26? If he be the all-sufficient Jehovah, why not fix all our contemplation, trust, delight, gloriation, and worship on him *alone*, Jer. ii. 13. xviii. 14, 15. 2 Cor. i. 5. 1 Sam. ii. 8? If he be Jehovah, the independent Sovereign, why attempt to pull him down from his high throne, in order to exalt an insignificant creature, or worse, to his place, Isa. xl. 12—26. Psalm lxxxix. 6—8. xxxv. 10. xxxvi. 7? If he be Jehovah, the sole author and preserver of our being, why ought not all that we are and have to be directed to his honour, Psalm c. 3. xcv. 6, 7? If he be the author, upholder, and governor of all creatures, he must possess all their attractive excellency in an infinitely superior degree, and his mere forbearance to communicate to them would render them despicable nothings; why then choose, love, trust in, and adore them in his stead?—If, in his infinite grace, he earnestly offer and freely give himself to us as our God, our infinite ALL, why refuse him, in order to catch at things empty, abominable, and hurtful, Psalm lxxxi. 10—13. Jer. iii. 1, 9. xvi. 19, 20. Isa. xliv. 9—20? If, through condescension, debasement, and suffering, he has so laboured to bestow himself on us, why not abandon every rival to receive and enjoy him, Psalm xlv. 10, 11. cxviii. 28. xviii. 1— 3? If he candidly and kindly grant us himself and all his fulness, why discredit his promise and offer, as if we believed himself a churlish restrainer of all to himself? If, by solemn declarations of his word, and manifold strivings of his Spirit and providence, he has *shut* us *up to the faith* of his being our God, why trample his authority, his faithfulness, and his bowels of mercy under our feet, in order to shift all saving title to, or enjoyment of himself? If Jehovah be our kind, our everlasting Father, why not avouch and glorify him, Mal. i. 6? Why turn away from him, Deut. xxxii. 6? If he be our affectionate husband, why should we, to his and his people's grief, adulterously forsake him, in order to entertain devils and sinful lusts in his room, John vi. 68? If, through suffering and death, he has become our Friend, why live ignorant of, deny, hate, distrust, or displease him, 1 John iv. 19. Prov. xvii. 17. xviii. 24? If he be our Master, who has bought us, and already more than rewarded all our service, and nevertheless reserves infinite rewards of grace for us, why break away from him to serve our murderers, Mal. i. 6?—In Jesus' payment of the *price* of our redemption, we behold every perfection of Jehovah displayed in the most engaging manner,— every promise and grant of him to be our God sealed with the blood of his Son,—the most delightful access and claim to him suited to our sinful condition,—together with full and irrefragable evidence that he will withhold no good thing from us, 2 Cor. iv. 6. v. 19—21. i. 20. Heb. x. 19—22. viii. 10---12. Rom. viii. 32. Why then should we wickedly neglect or refuse to receive, improve, and serve him, Luke i. 74, 75. Gen. xxxix. 9?—Why should not his infinite mercy, from which all his new-covenant blessings proceed, invincibly draw and bind our hearts to an eternal dependence on, and worship of him? And, if we be *united* with Christ, why attempt to dissolve our marriage, put him away, or cause him to hold fellowship with idols, 2 Cor. vi. 14, 15. 1 John v. 20, 21? If we be *justified*, why condemn our Justifier, and tread him under our feet? If God has adjudged us to eternal life, why prefer dead idols to him? If he has *adopted us into his family*, why not live upon him as its provision, join in its worship, and labour to be an honour to its head and members? Why attempt to destroy our gracious adopter, and cut off all life and comfort from ourselves and fellow-children, Jer. ii. 13? If, by *regeneration* and *sanctification*, we have been made temples and living images of God in Christ, why bring idols into his holy place, and deface his honourable image with the mark of the devil in our heart, hand, or forehead? Why act in furious contradiction to the excellent and graciously implanted principles of our new nature, in an unholy and unrighteous forsaking God, for the sake of idols? If we have tasted the everlasting *consolations* of Christ, why, by forsaking the God of all comfort, undermine our happiness, Col. ii. 2. 2 Cor. i. 3—5? If we have experienced much of his mercy and grace, wisdom, power, and faithfulness, why doubt of his existence, or be ashamed or regardless of him? If we have a title to, or solid hope of *everlasting happiness*, why commit idolatry, which tends to exclude us from it? If we expect Jehovah to be our eternal ALL IN ALL, why not rest satisfied with him on earth? If we desire that heavenly happiness, why abandon the preparer of it, and the guide of it, for an idol? why attempt to make our life on earth a hell, through want of fellowship with God?

II. These reasons no less powerfully enforce the receiving, observing, and keeping pure and entire all God's instituted ordinances of his worship, and dissuade from worshipping him by images, or any other way not appointed in his word. If the Lawgiver be JEHOVAH infinitely glorious, how fearfully every carnal imagination and corporeal representation of him must misrepresent and debase him! If he be the author of our, and of all other beings, how absurd for us to encourage false and disgraceful representations of him! if he be all-sufficient, why should not his own ordinances alone be held proper means for the enjoyment and worship of him? If he be an absolute sovereign, why forsake his appointments, in order to subject ourselves to the inventions of men, Col. ii. 16—23?—If he be our divine Father, why not adhere to the rules of his family? If he be our Husband, why not please him in all things, and abhor every reproachful misrepresentation of him,—and every encroachment upon his prerogative of appointing all the means of his own worship? If he be our Friend, why forsake his institutions, or exchange or mix them with those of Satan and the world? If he be our Master and Proprietor, why not receive and adhere to his rules and service? If he be our Portion, why not carefully attend to the only means of enjoying him, Ezek. xxxvii. 26, 27. Psalm lxxxiv. 10—12?—If, to pay the *price*, and secure the conveyance of our redemption to us, Jehovah's own Son became his representing image, why throw him aside as useless or insufficient, in order to view the Godhead in fancies, or in images made by men, Col. i. 15. 2 Cor. iv. 4, 6. John xiv. 9, 10? If, in redeeming mankind, he came to abolish idols, why should they, whom he redeemed, attempt to counteract the end and influence of his incarnation, ministry, and death, Zech. xiii. 2—7? If he has consecrated these ordinances with his own blood, and furnished them with his purchased blessings, why trample on the blood of the covenant, with which they are sanctified, in neglecting, corrupting, or changing them, Eph. ii. 14—18. i. 3? If, by his blood, he has purchased his mediatorial dominion, from which these ordinances immediately proceed, and has purchased the mission and operation of the Holy Ghost to render them effectual, and has redeemed us from infinite sinfulness and misery, that we may be zealous observers of them, why disregard, abuse, or neglect them?—If we be *united* to Christ, that we may live by him, why not improve him, in his own ordinances of fellowship with him and his Father and the Spirit? If God has *justified* us, and adjudged us to eternal life, why not justify his institutions, and use them as means of receiving and increasing our spiritual life? If he has *adopted* us into his family, why introduce the ordinances of hell or earth into his worship, to prevent our enjoyment of fellowship with him, Matth. xv. 2, 3, 9? If we be *sanctified*, why not earnestly look into his erected glass, in which, beholding his image, we may be changed from glory to glory by his Spirit, 2 Cor. iii. 18? If, in holiness and righteousness, we be living images of God, formed by himself, why debase ourselves by falling down to a fancy, or the stock of a tree, 1 Cor. viii. 4. Isa. xliv. 10—20? If there be any new covenant *comfort*, why expect it to be conveyed to us, but through the ordinances of the God of all comfort, Isa. lxvi. 11, 12? If we hope for *eternal happiness*, why not walk to it, and prepare for it, in God's way, Prov. viii. 34? If God, the bestower of all blessings, have instituted these ordinances as the means of conferring his favours on men, how absurd, by our negligence or superstition, to attempt to frustrate his kind intentions, Prov. viii. 34, 36. Matth. xv. 9?

III. In subservience to the THIRD commandment, these reasons powerfully enforce the holy and reverent use of God's names, titles, attributes, ordinances, words, and works, and dissuade from all profanation and abuse of them.—If he be the infinitely glorious JEHOVAH, all contempt or abuse of his name must be infinitely criminal. If he be all-sufficient, how mad and impious to attempt to rob him of his honour and pleasure? If he be the Author of all being, every abuse of that which he has formed or instituted must terminate on him. If he be an independent Sovereign, why not give him the most profound reverence?---If he be our God, our Father, Husband, Friend, Master, and Portion, what ingratitude, impiety, and self-destruction must be included in our dishonouring his name? And how shocking to improve his new-covenant characters as objects of our profanation and blasphemy?---If, in paying the *price* of our redemption, Jesus Christ obeyed, suffered, and died, to sweeten the name of God to us, and give it a glorious manifestation in our deliverance,---died to purchase our souls and bodies to be eternal honourers of it,---and to procure the Holy Ghost's creating the fear and love of it in our hearts,---how shocking to crucify Jesus afresh, and by abusive reproach profane his name?---If his name be the source and security of all our new-covenant privileges, why trample on and tear it? If we be *united* to Christ, why abuse and blaspheme our divine, our dearest Relatives? If we be *justified*, why abuse and blaspheme our merciful and lofty Judge? If we are *adopted* by God, why introduce the language and behaviour of hell into his family? If we be *regenerated* and *sanctified*, why mark our hatred of holiness, and belch forth blasphemy against that worthy God, whose image we bear? If we be *comforted* by God, and through his name, why reward his kindness with the most shocking insult and abuse? If we expect to enjoy and praise him for ever, why disqualify ourselves for that work, and by profaneness prepare ourselves for eternal damnation?

IV. These reasons no less powerfully enforce the keeping holy to God such set times as he has appointed in his word, especially one whole day in seven to be an holy sabbath to himself. —If he be the infinitely glorious JEHOVAH, how can time be better spent than in honouring him, and contemplating his glory? If he be all-sufficient, how profitable the time spent in fellowship with him, and receiving his fulness! If he be the author of beings, how proper to commemorate his astonishing works of creation and redemption, and cheerfully to bestow time, or any thing else, on his service, when he demands it! If he be an absolute Sovereign, how necessary to allow him every thing which he challenges for his property!—If he be our God, our Father, our Husband, our Friend, our Master and Portion, how absurd to refuse him any thing he requires! And how pleasant, profitable, honourable, and dutiful, to spend proper time in fellowship with, and enjoyment of him, in these new-covenant relations!—If Jesus Christ, by his obedience and death, has redeemed us from sin and hell to God, how worthy of our solemn remembrance must the finishing of his purchase be? If, in his death, he purchased for us an everlasting fellowship with, and the enjoyment of God, and procured the applying influences of the Holy Ghost to promote it, why should the peculiar season and means of this fellowship be despised or profaned?—If we be *united* to Christ, why should not we, on the day of his resurrection, awake, that he may give us light? If we be *justified*, why not commemorate that day of the week in which Christ received his justifying sentence for himself and his people?—and prize that day which God has appointed for bestowing or intimating justification to men? If we be *adopted*, why not observe the great birth-day of God's family in Christ their risen Head? If we be *sanctified*, why not delight to keep holy the Sabbath of the Lord our God, and improve it as a mean of our progressive holiness? If we have received the Spirit of *consolation*, why not delight to hold solemn weekly fellowship with the God of all comfort and his people? If, by the covenant, the promise, the oath of God, *eternal salvation* be secured for us, why not take pleasure in weekly foretastes of it, and call the Sabbath a delight?

V. These reasons also enforce the careful performance of all the relative duties required in the FIFTH commandment, and dissuade from every thing contrary.—If the infinitely glorious, all-sufficient, independent, all-creating and governing JEHOVAH, be manifested in the diversified relations of men to each other, and the duties belonging to them, why, by neglect of these duties, should we dishonour his character in his representatives, resist his ordinances, and practically consider ourselves more capable to fix our stations, and regulate our duties in them, than he?—If Jehovah, *as our God*, stand to us in the infinitely gracious new-covenant relations of Father, Husband, Friend, Master, Portion, &c. how richly must we be furnished,—how strongly bound and powerfully excited to give an honourable representation of him, in all our relative behaviour toward men, Eph. v. vi. Col. iii. iv. 1 Pet. ii. iii. Rom. xii.—xv?—If, in paying the *price* of our redemption, Christ fulfilled the duties of every relation in which he stood, as Child, Servant, Subject, Master, Friend, Father, &c. Matth. iii. 17. John viii. 29. Luke ii. 51. Isa. xlix. 3. lii. 13. liii. 11. John xiv. 28, 31. x. 18. xvii. 4. xiii. 1—10. xv. 13, 14. x. 10, 11, 15. Mat. xxiii. 8, 10. Isa. liii. 10. ix. 6. Eph. v. 25---27; why not copy his pattern? If, by his obedience and sufferings, he sanctified and rendered human relations useful and comfortable to us, why should we not honour him in fulfilling the duties pertaining to them, Eph. v. 23, 27?—If we be united to Christ, why not walk as he also walked, 1 John ii. 6. Eph. v. 2. 1 Pet. ii. 21. 1 Cor. xi. 1? If we be *pardoned* and *accepted* to eternal life, why not act tenderly toward all our relatives,—even such as injure us? Matth. v. 44. Eph. iv. 32. If we be *adopted* members of God's family, why not exemplify our good manners before the world? If we be *renewed* and *sanctified*, why not walk in the beauties of holiness, in abiding with God, in our respective stations, and attempting to gain our relations to Jesus Christ? If we have enjoyed spiritual comforts, why, in our whole behaviour towards others, should we not comfort them with the consolation wherewith we are comforted by Christ, 2 Cor. i. 4, 6? If we expect the heavenly state, why not make this world as like it as we can, in social order and happiness, 2 Pet. iii. 11, 14?

VI. No less powerfully do these reasons enforce and urge our preservation of human life required in the SIXTH commandment, and dissuade from every thing contrary. If JEHOVAH be the Author, Preserver, and Proprietor of men's life, what a presumptuous striking at his life, a robbing him of his power and property, and an exposing our own life to his just vengeance, must all unjust taking it away be! If he be our infinitely glorious and absolute Sovereign, why should not the views of his infinite glory and majesty awe and compose our spirits! Why should we vie with him in the power of life and death, or rob him of that life which he might dispose to his own glory?—If he be our all-sufficient God, Father, Husband, Friend, Master, Portion, why, like devils, attempt to render ourselves happier by ruining ourselves or our neighbours?—If, infinite kindness, he has become related to us his enemies, why not imitate his gracious and honourable conduct, in labouring, by every lawful mean, to preserve the life of our enemies,—and in walking in love toward that life, which he may make useful for his honour? Why not, in the whole of our behaviour, exhibit him to the world, as gracious, merciful, and long-suffering? If, with his infinitely precious blood, he has purchased our eternal life, why, by destroying men's lives, should we counteract the end of his death?—Why rob him of an opportunity to glorify himself, by bestowing spiritual and eternal life on our neighbours? And why not follow his example, who prayed for, and promoted the welfare of his betrayers and murderers?—And why not earnestly and hopefully improve all the means of promoting the precious life of our own or our neighbours' souls?—If we be *united* to Christ, why render his members instruments of cruelty, hatred, and murder? If we be *justified*, and adjudged to eternal life, why not mortify every murderous disposition? Or why act as if we had no eternal life abiding in us, or attempt to annul our happy sentence, or rob God of an opportunity of justifying others? Eph. iv. 31, 32. Matth. xviii. 23—33. 1 John iii. 15. Dan. xii. 3. If we be God's *adopted* children, why should not we be kindly affectioned, and ready to lay down our lives for our brethren? 1 John iii. 16. If the Holy Ghost dwell in us in his *sanctifying* and *comforting influences*, why should we not permit, nay, improve him, to purge out all our selfishness, and render us fruitful in all goodness and love? And why not avoid every thing which may provoke or grieve him? —If, at an infinite expence of love, power, and blood, God has conformed us to his own image, why make ourselves like the devil, who was a murderer from the beginning? If he *comfort* us with his kindness, why should we maliciously pain and distress others? If we expect everlasting happiness, why indulge such affections as render us unfit for it, and mark our exclusion from it? If God suffer not bloody men to live out half their days on earth, why should they expect eternal life in heaven?

VII. These reasons no less powerfully enforce the preservation of our own and our neighbour's chastity, in obedience to the SEVENTH commandment. If God be JEHOVAH, the Author and Former both of our body and mind, both ought to be kept pure to his honour. If he, in his everlasting arms, be their upholder and governor, why pollute them? If he be all-sufficient, why, in his stead, seek unlawful and beastly pleasures for our immortal soul? If he be infinitely glorious, why, with abominable filthiness, stain his image on ourselves? If he be our God, our Father, our Husband, our Friend, our Master and Portion, how unnecessary, how infamous, absurd, and provoking, to prefer disgraceful and ruinous pleasures to the most intimate and most delightful fellowship with him?—If Jesus Christ purchased our body and mind with the infinite *price* of his blood, why not glorify him and his Father with both? If he died to redeem us from the filthiness of the flesh and Spirit, why attempt to frustrate the end of his death, and, for nothing, for endless ruin, sell our body and soul to the coarse drudgery of Satan? 1 Cor. vi. 19, 29. Tit. ii. 14. 1 Pet. i. 18, 19. If, in paying the price of our redemption, he marked such contempt of the pleasures of sense, why not, with the same mind, arm ourselves? 1 Pet. iv. 1—3.—If we be *united* to Christ, why make our body and mind, which are his members, the members of an harlot? If, in our *justification*, we be delivered from the broken law, we are no longer debtors to live after the flesh, Rom. vi. 13, 14. viii. 12; why then tempt God to reverse his infinitely gracious sentence? Heb. xiii. 4. 2 Pet. ii. 10. Or why interrupt our new-covenant evidence, or his new intimations of our pardon? If we be the *adopted* children of God, why dishonour him and his family, by our abominable whoredoms? If we have his sanctifying Spirit and a *sanctified* nature in us, why disgrace his temple, debase and oppose his work, by the indulgence of beastly lusts? 1 Thess. iv. 3, 4. Eph. v. 3—6. 1 Cor. vi. 19. Gal. v. 22, 23. If we enjoy the *consolations* of God, and have his love shed abroad in our heart, why abuse them, as if sensual gratifications were a necessary supplement of, or preferable to them? If we be entitled to, or expect heavenly and eternal pleasures, why, by brutal defilements on earth, unfit ourselves for them? If Jesus and his complete salvation be fast approaching to us, why not lay aside chambering and wantonness? Rom. xiii. 11—14. If we expect that he will fashion our body like to his glorious body, why now render it viler than the beasts?

VIII. These reasons no less powerfully urge that universal equity, which is required by the EIGHTH commandment. If God be the sovereign proprietor of all things, how wicked must it be to rob any of that which he has allotted him? If he be the author of all being, all dishonesty in any thing must amount to a robbery committed on God himself, and an attempt to reverse his disposal.—If he be our God, our Father, our Husband, our Friend, and our Master, why not trust him to lay up for his children, and provide for his spouse, his friends, and servants, things earthly as well as eternal, and why blaspheme him, as if he were a resetter of our stolen goods? If he be our all-sufficient portion, why prefer stolen trifles to his infinite fulness?—If, in Jesus's payment of the *price* of our redemption, God has so clearly manifested his infinite regard to equity, why, for trifles, violate a law ratified by the death of his Son? If Jesus Christ, by his death, has purchased for us a new-covenant right to, and possession of every temporal good thing, why rob others, in order to procure that which is bad for us? If he has purchased for himself a mediatorial right to all things, why, by our dishonesty, attempt to disgrace or rob him of the reward of his death, Heb. ii. 8, 9. Hag. ii. 8?—If we be *united* to Christ, why stretch forth our heart or our hands, which are his members, to dishonesty? If we be *pardoned*, and *adjudged* to eternal life, why reproach and condemn God our justifier, as if he permitted and obliged us, on our way to heaven, to procure maintenance from Satan? If we be *adopted* into the family of God, why stain our character with dishonesty, which is not the spot of his children? And, why disgrace our Father, elder Brother, and fellow Saints, as if they connived with our theft? If we be the *sanctified* temples of the Holy Ghost, why debase ourselves with treasures of rapine, Isa. xxxiii. 15, 16? If we enjoy the *consolations* of God, why mix them with, or lose them for, the disgraceful fruits of fraud and violence, Heb. xiii. 18. Luke xvi. 1? If we be certain heirs of God and joint heirs with Christ, and expect *everlasting* riches and *glory*, why dishonour him, and disgrace ourselves, by dishonesty in the things of this world?

IX. These reasons no less forcibly urge the most strict regard to truth, and to our own and our neighbour's good name. If the lawgiver be JEHOVAH the God of truth, who gives being to all his words, why incline to, utter, or encourage falsehood or calumny? If he be the author of all being, why employ the work of his hands in the service of his arch-enemy, who is a *liar*, and the father of lies? If he be our absolute sovereign, why act as if our heart and tongue belonged to the devil? If his name and nature be infinitely glorious, why disgrace him in those creatures in whom his name and image are peculiarly marked? If he be all-sufficient, why prefer calumny and falsehood to the just commendations and high praises of him?—If he be our God, our Father, our Husband, our Friend, our Master, our Portion, what can tempt us to slander and falsehood, either to avert evil or to procure advantage? And, in order to imitate Satan, and retail the poison of asps under our tongue, why dishonour his relations to us, and ours to him?—If, in the *price* of our redemption, God has manifested his inviolable, his infinite regard to the truth of his own promises and threatenings, in the death of his Son, his detestation of Adam's reception of falsehood, and his reproaching his Maker, why ought not lying and reproachful lips to be an abomination to every one interested in that propitiation, and in the New Testament ratified by it?—If we be UNITED to Christ, who is the true and faithful witness, nay truth itself, why render his members instruments of calumny and falsehood, especially to the disgrace of his mystical body, which to him is as the apple of his eye? If God has graciously *blotted out* millions of our crimes and justified us, why should we not for ever detest all slandering others, or delighting in their infamy? And why not pass the most charitable judgment on the conduct of others, particularly of those who, to our shame, may, in the last judgment, have their character solemnly vindicated? If we be *adopted* into God's family, why act as the children of Satan, and as if the spirit of God assisted us to contrive and utter lies and calumny? If the Spirit of truth, by his word of truth, has begotten us again and *sanctified* us, implanting truth in our inward part, why not speak the truth in love growing up into Christ, Eph. iv. 15; and our sanctified tongue be as choice silver, and our lips feed many, rather than pour forth malice and folly? If God's law be written in our heart, why not put away all guile, malice, and evil speaking, 1 Pet. ii. 1. James i. 18, 21. iv. 11? Why should the same tongue bless God, and curse men who are made after his image? If we enjoy the *comforts* of the Holy Ghost, why banish them to introduce infernal pleasure in falsehood and slander? If God has given us so many exceeding great and precious promises sealed with the blood of his Son, why, by such infamous, though too common wickedness, labour to come short of them? If we be entitled to, or expect everlasting happiness, why, by lying and calumny, ripen ourselves for hell, Rev. xxi. 8. xxii. 15?

X. These reasons no less mightily enforce that contentment and charitable frame of spirit required in the TENTH commandment, and dissuade from every thing contrary. If God be the infinitely glorious, all-sufficient author, and independent sovereign of being, why, by discontentment, envy, and covetousness, or corruption of nature, should we deprive him of his honour, and of his proper place in our heart? If he be our God, Father, Husband, Friend, Master, and Portion, why should we be discontented under his care, and our new-covenant enjoyment of him? And why fond to fill his place in our soul with base, vile, empty, or ill-gotten nothings?—If, in paying the price of our redemption, Jesus Christ contented himself with poverty, reproach, distress, and death, that he might render us, his enemies, happy and renowned, why should we imitate devils, who left their first estate, in order to procure what must attend the curse of God?—If we be *united* with Christ, why indulge tempers which are so displeasing and disgraceful to him? If God, in our *justification*, forgive us so many sins, how much less must we be than the least of all his mercies! And why then not contented with so many and great mercies as we possess, or are entitled to? And why refuse to walk in his way to that eternal life to which he has adjudged us? If we be God's *adopted* children, why repine at his all-sufficient and delightful provision, and labour to feed on husks, which swine do eat? If we be *sanctified*, why indulge that evil concupiscence, which renders us carnal, sold under sin? If we be graciously *comforted* by God, why, with discontentment, envy, and covetousness, unrighteously vex our soul from day to day? If we be heirs of eternal life, why fond of that which detains our heart from our heavenly blessedness? If God draw us upward, why should our belly and soul cleave to the earth?

REFLECT. But what do I know of this glorious gospel, and its marvellous influence? Have I understood and believed its declarations, embraced its offers, and complied with its invitations? Have I experimentally discerned and felt its difference from, harmony with, and subservience to the law, as a *covenant*, and as a *rule?* Is my heart filled and inflamed, my loins girt and my feet shod with this gospel of grace and peace? Under its heart-purifying, heart-enlarging, and animating influence, have, and do I, run in the way of all God's commandments?—Here, here, let my knowledge be exact, and my experience powerful and distinct.—A mistake here, even to appearance the most trivial, how greatly may it affect the exercise of my soul, or my preaching Christ!

CHAP. III.

Of the INSTITUTED ORDINANCES *of the Covenant of Grace, and the* HARMONY *and* DIFFERENCE *between those under the Old Testament, and these under the New.*

IN these divinely instituted ordinances, God does not only come near to us, as in his word, but we also draw near to him. Some of them respect the *less* and others the *more immediate* ;—

Some the *solitary;* and others the *social;* and others both the *solitary* and *social;*—some the *occasional;* and others the *stated* and *permanent* worship of God. Some pertained to the *Old Testament dispensation* of the covenant of grace; others to the *New*, or to *both.* Some belong to both saints and sinners; and others of the *sealing* kind belong only to saints. Some pertain to all *church members;* and others only to *church rulers.* The END of them all, as respecting unconverted sinners, is to instruct, convince, and convert them;—and, as respecting saints, to build them up in holiness and comfort, through faith unto complete salvation, John xx. 31. Eph. iv. 11—14. These ordinances are,

I. READING the Scriptures in secret, private, and public, John v. 39. Acts xvii. 11. Neh. ix. 3.—Every person capable by age ought to read the Scriptures. 1. God has plainly warranted them to do so, Deut. iv. 6, 7. xi. 19. xvii. 18, 19. xxxi. 11, 12. Jer. xxxvi. 6. John v. 39. Matth. xxii. 29. Luke xvi. 29, 31. Isa. viii. 20. xxxiv. 16. Rev. i. 3. Col. iv. 16. Mark xiii. 14. 2. The church, with God's approbation, has constantly done so, Neh. viii. 3, 4. ix. 3. Luke iv. 16. Acts xv. 21. viii. 28. xvii. 11. Psalm cxix. 24. Luke x. 26. 2 Tim. iii. 15. 3. God appointed his word to be written that it might be read, Hab. ii. 2. Isa. viii. 1. xxx. 8. Jer. xxx. 2. xxxvi. 2, 6, 28. Rev. i. 3, 11. 2 Tim. iii. 15—17. Rom. xv. 4. 4. The state of men, particularly of believers, on earth, as God's children, prophets, and priests, require their intimate acquaintance with his word, Rom. i. 16, 17. iii. 21, 22. James i. 18, 21. 1 Pet. i. 23. ii. 2. 1 John iii. 1. Psalm cv. 15. Rev. i. 5, 6. 1 Cor. ii. 15.— The Scriptures ought to be read by all, 1. With an high and reverent esteem of them as indeed the word of God, Psalm xix. 10. cxix. 72. Neh. viii. 3. ix. 3. Exod. xxiv. 7. 2 Chron. xxxiv. 17. Isa. lxvi. 2. 2. With a firm persuasion that they are the word of God, necessary to be known by us in order to our eternal salvation, 2 Pet. i. 19, 20; and that he alone can make us savingly understand them, Luke xxiv. 45. 2 Cor. iii. 13—16. 3. With our conscience lying open to God's authority in them, and earnest desire to know, believe, and obey his whole will revealed in them, 1 Thess. ii. 13. Deut. xvii. 18—20. Psalm cxix. 18. lxxxv. 8. 4. With a diligent attention to the matter and scope of them, and of every particular passage in them, John v. 39. Acts xvii. 11. viii. 30, 34. Luke x. 26—28. 5. With particular and earnest application of that which we read to ourselves, Prov. iii. 1, 4. 2 Chron. xxxiv. 21. Jer. xv. 16. Col. iii. 16. Psalm cxix. 6. With a self-denying dependence upon God for his effectual blessing upon that which we read, Prov. iii. 5. ii. 1—7. Psalm cxix. 18. 7. Cordially experiencing, and constantly and earnestly practising that which we read, John xiii. 17. Josh. i. 7, 8. 1 Pet. ii. 2.

II. MEDITATION on the word of God, and on his works as connected with it, Psalm i. 2. cxix. 48, 97. cv. 5. cxi. 2, 4.— In thinking on God's word and works, 1. Our heart ought to be fixed, Psalm cviii. 1. cxxxix. 18. 2. It ought to be deeply affected, Psalm civ. 34. xlv. 1. cxxxix. 17. 3. It ought to be habitually employed in this exercise, Psalm cxix. 97. cxxxix. 17, 18. lxiii. 6. 4. Our thoughts ought to have a sanctifying tendency and influence, 2 Cor. iii. 18. 5. It is proper that they be diversified in their objects and form, and proceed orderly from one point to another.

III. PREACHING the word of God, in explaining his law and gospel, and pointing his truths in the most particular manner to the consciences of hearers, for their conviction, conversion, sanctification, and comfort.——God's word ought to be preached, 1. Regularly, by such only as are duly qualified and called to that work, 1 Tim. iii. 2—6. 2 Tim. ii. 2, 4. Eph. iv. 8—11. Mal. ii. 7. 2 Cor. iii. 6. Jer. xiv. 15. xxiii. 21, 32. Rom x. 15. Heb. v. 4. 1 Cor. xii. 28, 29. 1 Tim. iii. 10. iv. 14. v. 22. 2. Soundly, preaching nothing but what is founded in the word of God, and stated in that very connection in which it states it; nothing but what, and as it is calculated to exalt Christ, humble men, and bring them to God in Christ, Tit. ii. 1, 8. 1 Tim. ii. 7. 2 Tim. iv. 2, 3. 3. Evangelically, rightly arranging Law and Gospel, answerably to their above-mentioned differences and harmony, 2 Tim. ii. 15. Rom. i. 16, 17. 4. Diligently, earnestly watching for and embracing every opportunity of preparing for, or preaching it in order to glorify God in the edification of souls, 2 Tim. iv. 2. Heb. xiii. 17. Acts xviii 25 xvi. 31. Col. i. 28, 29. 5. Plainly, not in the enticing words of man's wisdom, but in words which the Holy Ghost teaches, and with demonstration of the Spirit and of power, manifesting the truths of God to every man's conscience in the most simple and scriptural language, plain order, with obvious proofs and enforcements, 1 Cor. xiv. 19. ii. 4, 13. 2 Cor. iii. 12. iv. 2, 13. xi. 3. Hab. ii. 2. Isa. xxx. 8. 6. Faithfully, giving to saints and sinners that which best answers their diversified states and circumstances, Jer. xxiii. 28. 1 Cor. iv. 1, 2. ii. 1, 2. xi. 1, 2. Acts xx. 27. Ezek. iii. xxxiii. xiii. 19—23. Matth. xxiv. 45. 2 Cor. iv. 1, 2. 7. Wisely, the doctrine and manner of delivering it being suited to the capacities and the circumstances of the hearers, Col. i. 28. 2 Tim. ii. 15. 1 Cor. iii. 2, 10. Heb. v. 11—14. Luke xii. 42. John xvi. 12. 8. Sincerely, not from regard to worldly applause, gain, or like carnal ends, but from a firm faith and deep impression of the truth, directly and principally aiming at the glory of God in the edification of souls; and hence chiefly insisting on the more important truths of the gospel; but never neglecting to manifest and establish those truths which are presently opposed, when an opportunity calls for it, 1 Cor. ii. 17. iv. 2. 1 Thess. ii. 4—6. John vii. 18. 1 Cor. ix. 19.— 22. 2 Cor. xii. 19. Eph. iv. 12—14. 1 Tim. iv. 16. Acts xxvi. 16—18. 2 Pet. i. 12. Rev. iii. 10. 9. Fervently, with a judicious, heart-burning zeal for the glory of God, and deep-felt compassion towards the souls of men, manifested in a grave and affectionate address, Acts xviii. 25, 28. 2 Cor. v. 11, 13, 14. Phil. i. 15, 17. Col. iv. 12. 2 Cor. xii. 15. Gal. iv. 19, 20. 1 Thess. ii. 1—10.

IV. HEARING God's word read or preached, Isa. lv. 3;—to which is necessary, 1. Preparation for hearing it, getting our heart impressed with an awful sense of God's majesty and holiness, into whose presence we come, and whose word we hear, Psalm lxxxix. 6, 7. Acts x. 33. Isa. lxvi. 2; banishing all lawful worldly cares from our heart, Matth. xiii. 7. Gen. xxii. 4, 5; application of Jesus' blood for removing all our guilt, and all controversy between God and us, Amos iii. 3. Psalm xxvi. 6. Rev. iv. 6; purging our heart from corrupt lusts and affections, and stirring it up to spiritual desires of fellowship with God, 1 Pet. ii. 1, 2. James i. 21. 2. Earnest prayer for assistance to the minister, and for edification to ourselves and others by the out-pouring of the Holy Ghost in the ordinance, 2 Thess. iii. 1. Eph. vi. 19, 20. Psalm cxix. 18. Song iv. 16. Ezek. xxxvii. 9. 1 Pet. i. 12. 3. Careful attention to that which is read or preached, diligently waiting on all the opportunities of hearing that come within our reach, as God's appointments with sinful men, 1 Tim. iv. 13. Prov. viii. 34; gravely and composedly bending our ear and mind to that which is spoken, Isa. lv. 3. Luke iv. 20. Prov. ii. 1, 2; observing what we hear, and judging it by the Scripture, Mark iv. 24. Luke viii. 18. Acts xvii. 11; and studying to know the mind of God in his word, Acts xvi. 14. Psalm lxxxv. 8. 4. Cordial reception of that which we find to be the truth of God, in the assured faith of its divine authority, with particular application of it to ourselves, and with esteem of, love to, desire after, and delight in it, and hence with meekness and readiness of mind, Heb. iv. 2. 2 Thess. ii. 10. Eph. iv. 21. James i. 21. 1 Pet. ii. 2. Acts xvii. 11. 1 Thess. i. 5. ii. 13. 5. Hiding it in our heart as a precious treasure, and a continued remembrance, knowledge, and love of it, Psalm cxix. 21, 72, 103, 139, 140. Job xxiii. 12. Col. iii. 16. Isa. xlii. 23. Prov. ii. 1.

iii. 1, 3.   6. Serious meditation and pious conference on that which we have heard, Luke ix. 44. Heb. ii. 1. Luke xxiv. 14—32. Deut. vi. 6, 7.   7. Practising that which we hear, making God's word the *rule* and the *reason* of all that we do; and abounding in holiness answerably to our enjoyment of the means of it, Luke viii. 15. James i. 22, 23, 25. Rev. i. 3. John xiii. 17.

V. Spiritual CONFERENCE, to which may be reduced, 1. Communing with our own heart, Psalm iv. 4; putting serious questions to our conscience concerning our state, temper, and conduct, in order to have them compared with, and adjusted by God's word, 2 Cor. xiii. 5. Zeph. ii. 1; laying solemn charges on it before God, Psalm ciii. 1—5. civ. 1, 35. xlii. 5, 11. xliii. 5; and reciting important facts to it, Psalm xvi. 2. 2. Spiritual conference with neighbours in occasional or stated meetings;—or in catechising of families, Luke xxiv. 13—32—49. Deut. vi. 6, 7. Mal. iii. 16. Col. iii. 16. Song v. 8—16. vi. 1—3. Gen. xviii. 19. 3. Ministerial visiting and catechising persons and families, or the sick, which may also be referred to preaching, Gal. vi. 6. Acts xx. 20, 31.—In such conferences, 1. The matter ought chiefly to be the most important points of divine truth, Matth. xxiii. 23. 1 Cor. ii. 2. 1 Tim. i. 5, 6. Tit. i. 11—14.   2. The glory of God and the edification of souls ought to be earnestly and chiefly intended, Col. iii. 17. 1 Pet. iv. 11. 1 Cor. xiv.   3. We ought always to speak and hear as in God's presence, and in the view of our speedily accounting to him for our conduct, Psalm xvi. 8. Eccl. xii. 14. 2 Cor. v. 10—12. Mat. xii. 36, 37.

VI. PRAYER, by which we, as it were, draw to ourselves the blessings which God communicates by other ordinances. It is sometimes characterized from the postures of our body used in it, as *bowing, kneeling, stretching forth* the hand, &c. Psalm xcv. 6. cxxi. 1. xxviii. 2; or, it is called *meditation, supplication, pouring out the heart, lifting up the soul*, &c. Psal. v. 1, 2. vi. 9. lxii. 8. xxv. 1; to mark the judicious, earnest, and humble manner in which it is or ought to be performed.— It is performed either solitarily by one's self, at stated times, or occasionally, while one is occupied about other business, Matth. vi. 6. Psalm lv. 17.—Neh. ii. 4, 5. Judg. xv. 18. xvi. 28.—Or socially, in families or voluntary societies, Jer. x. 25. Josh. xxiv. 15. Acts x. 2, 30. xx. 36. Mat. xviii. 19, 20; or in public assemblies, 1 Kings viii. 22—54. 2 Chron. xx. 5—13. Acts xiv. 23.

Prayer includes *invocations* of, or addresses to God by his names and titles;—*adoration* of him as possessed of infinite excellencies;—*confession* of our meanness, sinfulness, and wants;—*deprecation* of judgments inflicted or feared;—*petition* for things that we need;—*pleading* with arguments for that which we ask;—*dedication* of ourselves to God and his service;—*thanksgiving* for the mercies which we have received, or have ground to expect;—and *blessing* him for what he is in himself. Or, it consists in, 1. *Confession* of our sins, original and actual, in thought, word, and deed, with their several aggravations, Job xxxiii. 27. Psalm xxxii. 5. xxxviii. 18. Isa. vi. 5. lxiv. 6. Jer. iii. 13. Rom. vii. 14—25. Dan. ix. Ezra ix: This is the duty of all men while on earth, as they are all guilty of, and polluted with sin, Rom. iii. 19, 20, 23. Ezek. xvi. 62, 63; and ought to be made under a deep sense of sin, Rom. iii. 19, 20. vii. 9—24. Psalm xl. 11—13. xxv. 11. lxv. 3. cxxx. 3; in the assured faith of God's mercifully forgiving it through Christ's blood, Psalm cxxx. 3, 4. lxv. 3. Prov. xxviii. 13; with an hearty detestation of sin, and desire to reform from it, Jer. xxxi. 18. 2 Sam. xxiv. 10. Isa. lxiv. 6. vi. 5. Job xl. 4. xliii. 5, 6; and with self-debasing shame and grief for sin, Job xlii. 5, 6. Psalm vi. xxxviii. lxx. li. 2. *Thanksgiving* for mercies received, offered, or secured, whether temporal, spiritual, or eternal, and even the lightness, short duration, or usefulness of troubles, as well as deliverance from them,—to ourselves or others, Psalm xcv.—c. ciii cv. cvii. cxvi. cxvii. cxviii. cxxxv. cxxxvi. cxlv.—cl. Eph. v. 20. Phil. iv. 6. Gen. xxxii. 10. Psalm xxxvi. 6, 7. cxix. 67, 71, 75. 2 Cor. iv. 17. 3. *Petition* to God for what mercies we need, or for what things are agreeable to his will, being required by his law, or contained in his promise;—for whatever tends to the honour of his name, the coming of his kingdom, and the doing of his will on earth; or to our real advantage in temporal provision, pardon of sin, and preservation from it, Mal. vi. 9—13.—Confession supposes our guilt and pollution; thanksgiving our unworthiness; and petition our emptiness and wants. —Confession and petition have place only on earth; but thanksgiving also for ever in heaven.

Prayer is a divine ordinance to be observed by men. 1. It is often commanded in Scripture, Mat. vii. 7—14. Eph. vi. 18. Phil. iv. 6. Rom. xii. 12. Col. iv. 2. Matth. xxvi. 41. James v. 13; to which might be added a multitude of texts, which point out for whom, for what, and in what manner we ought to pray. 2. The characters in which the divine persons are represented to us, require and encourage prayer: God is a gracious hearer of prayer, Exod. xxxiv. 6, 7. Isa. lxiii. 7, 15. Matth. vii. 7—11. Psalm lxv. 2. l. 15. xci. 15. Isa. lviii. 9. lxv. 24. Psalm ix. 18. x. 17. cii. 17. Christ is a kind and an effectual Intercessor, the way to the Father, and an all-comprehen-

OF INSTITUTED ORDINANCES. 523

sive Saviour, Heb. iv. 14—16. x. 19—22. vii. 25 ix. 24. Rom. viii. 34. Rev. viii. 3, 4. Eph. ii. 18. iii. 12. John xiv. 6. Psalm cx. 4. lxviii. 18. 1 John ii. 1, 2 And the Holy Ghost is the Spirit of adoption, and of supplication, and an Intercessor within us, Gal. iv. 6. Zech. xii. 10. Eph. ii. 18. vi 18. Jude 20. Rom. viii. 15, 26, 27. 3. We have many approved examples of prayer by Christ and his saints, Matth. xv. 23. xix. 15. xxvi. 39—45. Luke vi. 12. ix 29. John xvi. Gen. xviii. 25—32. xxv. 22. xxxii. 9—12, 24—28. Exod. xxxii. xxxiii. xxxiv. Deut. ix. Num. xii. xiv. Deut. xxxiii. Joh. vii. 1 Kings viii. 2 Chron. xiv. xx. Ezra ix Neh. i. ix. Psalm iii.—cxliv. Dan. ix. Acts i. 14. ii. 42. xii. 5. xiii. 3. xiv. 23 vi. 4. Rom. i. 9, 10, &c. 4. Believers' new nature and their new-covenant relations to God require it, while they continue in their imperfections on earth, where their sins, their wants, their enemies, their troubles, their mercies bestowed and promsed, and their duties required, are so numerous, Acts ii 42. Gal iv. 4, 5. Rom. viii. 15, 26, 27. 1 Pet. ii. 5. Psalm cxvi. 12 16, 17. cxix. 5. The present state of churches and nations, nagistrates and ministers, &c. with which we are connected on arth, requires it, Matth. vi. 9, 19. Rev. xxii. 20. Psalm lxxii. 5, 19. 1 Thess. v. 25. 2 Thess iii. 1. Eph. vi. 18, 19, 20. 1 Tim ii. 1, 2. Dan. ix. 20. Matth. v. 44. 6. The neglect of prayer is charged as an heinous sin, Isa. xliii. 22. lxiv. 7. Hos. vii. 7 Dan. ix. 13. Psalm x. 4. Jer. x. 25. It is a practical denial, contempt, and robbery of God,—a denial and contempt of Christ as Mediator, and of all the method and blessings of redemption through him, a resisting and quenching the Holy Ghost, and a wilful ruining ourselves and our neighbours in time and eternity.

God alone is the *Object* of prayer and all other religious worship. 1. It is demanded for him, and exclusivey of all others, Matth. iv. 10. Deut. vi. 13. x. 20. 2. He alone is the object of that faith from which all prayer ought to proceed, Rom. x. 14. Jer. xvii. 5. 3. He alone can discern whether our prayers be sincere, proceeding from our heart, Jer. xvii. 10. Rev. ii. 23. Psalm lxvi. 18. 4. He alone can hear and answer our prayers, in forgiving our sins, and bestowing all necessary mercies, Psalm lxv. 2. l. 15. xci. 15. Mic. vii. 18, 19. Psalm xx. cii. Isa. lviii. 9. lxv. 24. lxiii. 16. Nor is our prayer to him unnecessary, though he knows all our sins and wants, and has unalterably purposed what, when, and how he will apply his mercies and judgments; but it is his appointed mean of fulfilling his purposes and promises, and of obtaining his mercies and preventing his judgments, Ezek. xxxvi. 25—37. Psalm xci. 15. l. 15. Jer. xxxiii. 3. Psalm xlv. 11. Mark x. 24.

All men while they live on earth ought to pray to God. Believers, to the delight of Christ and his Father, nake prayer a principal part of their work, 1 Cor. i. 2. Psalm cxiv. 6. Luke

xi. 1—13. xviii. 1—7. Mat. vii. 7—11. John xvi. 24, 26. Song ii. 14. vii. 13. vii. 5. And wicked men ought to pray: 1. Prayer is a duty required by the mere light of nature, Jon. i. 5, 6, 14. Acts xvii. 26. 2. Their neglect of prayer is represented as higlly criminal, Psalm x. 4. xiv. 4. lxxix. 6. Jer. x. 25. Rom. i. 21. Hos. vii. 14. Dan. ix. 13. Job xxxvi. 13. 3. Every thing mentioned in the Lord's prayer is proper to be asked by then, Matth. vi. 9—13. 4. God expressly calls wicked men to pray; and has often answered, though never accepted, their prayers, Acts viii. 22. Psalm cvii. 6, 14, 19, 20, 29. Gen. xxi. 17. Jon. iii.—Though their prayer, as well as their ploughing, be abominable to God, in the manner and end of it, Rom. xiv. 23 Prov. xv. 8, 9. xxviii. 9. xxi. 4, 27. Psalm cix. 17; yet the natter of it being good, the neglect of it is a greater abomination. Their immediate duty, therefore, is to get their state and nature renewed by Christ, that they may pray aright, Matth. vii. 1. Luke xiii. 24; and earnestly to use prayer as a divinely instituted mean of that renovation, Acts viii. 22.

We are not to pray for *the dead*, as their state and condition are unalterably fixed, Luke xvi. 22—27. 2 Sam. xii. 21—23. Nor for the pardon of the sin against the Holy Ghost, or such as we certainly know to have committed it, John v. 16. But we ought to pray for all *sorts of men living, or that shall live hereafter* on earth,—Christians, Jews, Mahometans, Heathens, noble and ignoble, 1 Tim. ii. 1, 2. John xvii. 20. 2 Sam. vii. 29. Psalm xc 14—17; and to abound in prayer for them, according to our connection with them, and the importance of their station and difficulty of their work, Gen. xxxii. 9—12. Psalm iii. iv. r. vi. &c. 2 Cor. xii. 7—9. Isa. xxxviii. 14.—Particularly for the church of Christ, Eph. vi. 18. Psalm xxviii. 9. li. 18. cxxii. l. Amos vi. 1, 6;—for ministers, 1 Thess. v. 25. Rom. xv. 30, 31. Col. iv. 3. 2 Thess. iii. 1. Eph. vi. 19, 20; for magistrates, 1 Tim. ii. 1, 2. Psalm lxxii. 1. xx. Prov. xxi. 1; for the nation and place in which we live, Jer. xxix. 7; for the afflicted, Psalm xxxv. 13, 14. James v. 14. Acts xii. 5; for our families, friends, and relations, Job i. 5. xlii. 10. James v. 16. Eph. i. 16—20. iii. 14—19. 2 Sam. xii. 16. Gen. xvii. 18. xxiv. 12. 2 Kings vi. 17; nay, for our enemies, Matth. v. 44. Luke xxiii. 34. Acts vii. 60. Psalm xxxv. 11—14. And we ought to confess the public sins of past generations, and thank God for their mercies, as well as of the present, Ezra ix. Neh. ix. Dan. ix. Lev. xxvi. 40. Psalm lxxviii. cv. cvi. cxxxvi.

We ought to pray, 1. Under the influence of God's Spirit, and with our own heart deeply engaged, Eph. vi. 18. Jude 20. Phil. iii. 3. 1 Cor. xiv. 15. Jer. xxix. 13. 2. Deliberately, Psalm v. 1. Eccl. v. 1, 2. 3. Judiciously, with true knowledge of our own guilt, pollution, weakness, and wants, and need of

Christ, in his person, offices, fulness, and work, and of God in him,—and of the true object, matter, and manner of prayer, Psalm li. xxxviii. lxv. 2. 1 Cor. xiv. 15. Eph. i. 17. 4. Reverently, under a deep impression of the infinite majesty, holiness, power, mercy, justice, goodness, and truth of God, Psalm lxxxix. 7. Hab. i. 12, 13. Gen. xviii. 25—30. Exod. xxxiv. 6, 7. Num. xiv. 18, 19. 5. *Humbly*, with a deep sense of our unworthiness, sinfulness, and wants, Gen. xviii. 27. xxxii. 10. Luke xv. 17, 18, 19. xviii. 13, 14. Psalm x. 17. cii. 17. 6. *In the name of Christ*,—united to his person,—in obedience to his command,—in the strength of his grace,—with confidence in his promise,—and dependence on his righteousness and intercession, as the ground of God's accepting and answering our prayers, John xv. 7. xvi. 23, 24. Heb. iv. 14—16. Col. iii. 17. 1 Pet. ii. 5. Matth. xxi. 22. 1 John ii. 1, 2. Heb. vii. 25. x. 19—22. Eph. ii. 18. iii. 12. Rev. viii. 3, 4, 34. 1 John v. 14. 7. In the *assured exercise of faith* upon the promises, perfections, and relations of God as in Christ, believing that he will certainly grant our requests, Psalm lxii. 8. James i. 6, 7. Mark ix. 23. xi. 24. Matth. xxi. 22. Rom. x. 14, 15. Heb. xi. 6. 8. *In love to*, desire after, and delight in God, and an affectionate regard to all those for whom we ought to pray, Gal. iv. 6. Isa. lxiii. 15, 16. 1 Tim. ii. 8. 9. With much *brokenness* and enlargement of heart, Psalm li. 17. lxii. 8. Phil. iv. 6. 1 Sam. i. 10, 15. 10. With *sincerity*, inward truth and candour answerable to our confessions, petitions, and thanksgivings, Psalm xvii. 1. civ. 18. Heb. x. 22. Psalm lxvi. 18. xliv. 18—22. 11. With *boldness* and familiarity, Heb. iv. 16. Job xxiii. 3. Rom. viii. 15. Gal. iv. 6. 12. With *fervent importunity*, James v. 16. Luke xi. 8. xviii. 1—7. Mark x. 47, 48. Matth. xv. 22—28. Gen. xxxii. 26. Exod. xxxii. xxxiii. xxxiv. Deut. ix. Num. xiv. 13. With humble *submission to the will of God* with respect to the season, form, or degree of his granting the mercy which we ask, Psalm x. 17. Luke xviii. 9—14. Matth. xxvi. 39. John xii. 27. Rom. viii. 26, 27. 2 Cor. xii. 7—10. 14. With *watchfulness* and *perseverance*, Eph. vi. 18. Luke xviii. 1—8. xi. 5—13. Isa. lxii. 1, 6, 7. Matth. vii. 7—11. 15. *Hopefully*, waiting for a gracious answer in God's granting us the mercy we asked, or another more proper in its stead, in his own time and way, Psalm lxxxv. 8. v. 3. Mic. vii. 7—9. Isa. viii. 17. xxx. 18. Job xxxv. 14. Psalm xxvii. 13, 14. cxxx. 5, 6. Heb. x. 36. vi. 11, 12.—Such submission, persevering, watchfulness, and humble waiting, manifest that God has accepted our prayers in Christ, and will answer them in due time, Psalm vi. 9. lvi. 8. xx. 4. l. 15. xci. 15. Isa. lviii. 9. lxv. 24.

The word of God is our encouragement to, and director in prayer. By its commands, promises, and records of the success of prayer, it encourages us to pray. Its doctrines, laws, histories, prophecies, promises, threatenings, and forms of prayer instruct and direct us concerning the object, matter, and manner of that duty.—That form which Christ taught his disciples is a *superlatively* excellent *pattern* of prayer, representing to us in a few words our encouragement to, and the manner and order of it. But it was not prescribed to be a *stated form* used on almost every occasion. It is differently expressed by the Evangelists Matthew and Luke: In Matthew, where it is most fully recorded, we are only required to pray *after this manner*. Neither Christ nor his disciples appear ever to have used it as a form, but prayed in other words as their occasions required. Nor does it plainly include either confession or thanksgiving.

Forms of prayer which are truly evangelical may be of use to assist children and such as are very ignorant. But *restriction* of men to forms of prayer is unlawful. 1. It cramps our desires, and thus quenches the Holy Ghost, who is our divine and stated assistant, Rom. viii. 26, 27. 2. It inverts the true order of prayer, making our words to regulate our desires, instead of our desires regulating our words, Psalm lxii. 8. 3. It restrains the exercise of our understanding and other inward powers, and obliges us to walk on crutches, whether we need them or not. 4. It naturally leads us into a mere lip-service, cools and flattens our spirits, especially if the prayers be read. 5. It renders us slothful in our observation of providences,—and in our examination of our state, condition, sins, wants, mercies,—or in searching the Scriptures for direction in prayer, or in stirring up our gifts and graces, or in supplicating the assistance of the Holy Ghost. 6. No form can suit every case either of soul or body, as of *Jonah* in the whale's belly, *Daniel* in the lions' den, &c. 7. Even nature teaches the absurdity of such restriction. No children need a book or form to be read, or even repeated, in conversing with their parents, or in asking food, raiment, &c. from them. No naked, hungry, or distressed beggars need a form from which they may read their desires of relief. 8. Though an habitual impression and frequent consideration of our own and others' needs, and of the promises of, and pleas for supply be very necessary before prayer, especially in those that are the mouth of others, yet we have no instance of any restriction to forms of prayer in the Bible, but even they who officiated in public under the influence of the Holy Ghost, and of their own judgment, poured forth their requests suited to the occasion, 1 Kings viii. 22—54. 1 Chron. xxix. 10—19. 2 Chron. xx. 5—12. Neh. ix. Acts i. 24, 25.

The Holy Ghost assists men in their prayer, 1. By disposing them to search the Scriptures, and thus gives them the *gift of prayer*, which lies in a readiness to address God in a grave, decent, and orderly manner, calculated to move their own, or the affections of such as join with them in it.—This is sometimes bestowed upon unregenerate men. 2. By giving them the *grace of prayer*, which lies in an habitual disposition and ability of heart, to pour forth candid confessions of sinfulness and misery, thankful acknowledgment of mercies received or secured, and earnest supplications for necessary favours from God. This is bestowed only upon believers in his powerfully discovering to them their needs, and their encouragement to ask the supply thereof,—and in directing their heart to fix upon that which is fit to be granted, and enabling them to ask it in faith and fervency, and patiently to wait for the bestowal of it.

VII. Ministerial BLESSING people in the name of the Lord, in dismissing them from public ordinances; which is not merely a supplication of divine favours, but chiefly a solemn declaration of God's good-will to them. It is an ordinance of divine appointment, Num. vi. 23—26. 2 Cor. xiii. 14. Rev. xxii. 21; in all which texts every thing necessary to render men holy and happy through time and eternity is comprehended, wished, and announced. This solemn benediction is to be ministered and received, 1. With great reverence, Psalm lxxxix. 7. Lev. ix. 22. Heb. xii. 28, 29. 2. With solid understanding of the blessings announced, and of the manner of their conveyance to us, Hos. iv. 6. Prov. xix. 2. 3. With serious consideration, and humble sense of our need of those blessings implored and offered, Eph. v. 15, 17. 4. With ardent desire of actual and eternal enjoyment of them, Psalm xlii. 1, 2. lxxxiv. 2, 10. 5. With fervent love to all concerned in this benediction, 2 Cor. xiii. 11, 13. 6. In the assured faith and joyful hope of God's fully conferring all these blessings on us and others, 2 Chron. xx. 20. Mark ix. 23. xi. 24. Isa. vii. 9.

VIII. Singing of PSALMS in public, private, and secret, 1 Chron. xvi. Exod. xv. Isa. lii. 7—9. Acts xvi. 25. Mat. xxvi. 30. Psalm cxviii. 15. James v. 13. This is a moral duty. 1. We have the example of Christ, angels, and apostles for it, Matth. xxvi. 30. Job xxxviii. 6, 7. Luke ii. 13, 14. Acts xvi. 25. 2. We have an express commandment of God for it, respecting the New Testament church, Psalm xlvii. 1—6. Col. iii. 16. ii. 16, 17. Eph. v. 19. ii. 14, 15. 3. God's command respecting it extends to Gentiles as well as Jews, Psalm lxvii. 4. lxvi. 1, 2. cxvii. 1, 2. 4. It is distinguished from, and opposed to ceremonial worship, Psalm lxix. 30, 31. 5. It was performed before most of the laws of Moses were given, is, and will be after they are abolished, Exod. xv. 1—22. Isa. xxvi. 19. Rev.

xiv. 3. v. 9. xv. 3, 4. xix. 1, 2.—We ought to sing psalms, 1. With understanding, Psalm xlvii. 7. 1 Cor. xiv. 15. 2. Under the influence of the Holy Ghost, and with our own spirit fixed, 1 Cor. xiv. 15. 3. To the Lord, Col. iii. 16. Eph. v. 19. 4. With inward joy, James v. 13. Luke i. 47. 5. In the name of Christ, Col. iii. 16, 17. 1 Pet. ii. 5, 9. 6. With affections suited to the psalms sung, Psalm xlv. 1. cviii. 1.

IX. VOWING is the making a solemn promise to God, in which *we bind ourselves to do or forbear* somewhat for the promoting his glory. A vow is not a mere acknowledging the obligation of God's law upon us, nor a placing ourselves more directly under any of his commandments than he has done, nor a constitution of any new relation to his law; but it is a laying upon ourselves a *new obligation*, as distinct and different from that of the law of God as that of the commands of parents, masters, or magistrates, or of civil or of sacred bonds between man and man. 1. In his law *God binds* us by his authoritative command. In our vow we, by an act of our own will, *bind ourselves* by a voluntary engagement, Num. xxx. 2. The obligation of God's law must *never be examined*, but in order to know its meaning and extent. But all vows *ought to be tried* in their matter and manner by his law, in order to know whether they be lawful and binding or not, Isa. viii. 20. 3. God's law binds *all men* whether they will or not. Vows bind none but such as *take them*, and those *whom they represent* in that deed, Deut. v. 3. xxix. 14, 15. Num. xxx. 4. God's law binds all men to *absolute perfection* in holiness. Our vows do not bind us to absolute perfection, but to the most sincere and strenuous endeavours we CAN, by the grace of God assisting us, Psalm xliv 17. 5. God's law binds all men to such perfection *for ever*. Our vows bind only to that which is proper in this *present life*.—But, as every lawful vow is made in the right exercise of power and authority over one's self, derived from God and his law; and its obligation formed in an act of obedience to his authority and law; and having his law for the supreme rule and standard of its matter; and the more perfect observance of his law, in order to his glory, for its chief end,—the law of God must necessarily ratify it, and, under the highest pains, require the exact fulfilment of it.

Vowing to God is, 1. Warranted by the very light of nature; nothing being more reasonable than for men rightly to *bind themselves* to serve God better than they have done, Jon. i. 16. 2. The Scriptures expressly command it, Psalm lxxvi. 11. 3. God gives directions concerning it, Lev. vii. xxvii. Num. vi. xxx. Deut. xii. xxiii. 4. God plainly approves it and accepts it, if done in faith, Gen. xxviii. 20. xxxi. 13. Num. xxi. 2.

1 Sam. i. 11, 12. Psalm lvi. 12. lxi. 5. cxix. 106. cxxxii. 2. Isa. xix. 18, 21. xliv. 5. xlv. 21, 24. 2 Cor. viii. 5. 5. God requires our attentive regard to, and exact performance of our vows, Gen. xxxi. 13. Deut. xxiii. 21—23. Job xxii. 27. Eccl. v. 4, 5. Neh. i. 15. Psalm l. 14. Prov. xx. 25. Psalm xxii. 25. lxi. 8. lxvi. 13. cxvi. 14, 18. cxix. 106. Jon. ii. 9.

The matter to which *we bind ourselves* in a vow, must be, 1. That duty which God has commanded in his law, Psal. cxix. 106. 2 Chron. xv. 12, 13. xxxiv. 31. Neh. x. 29, 30, 31. Or, 2. That which in our circumstances conduces to promote holiness, so long and so far as it does so, Num. vi. xxx. Lev. xxvii. Gen. xxviii. 20. 1 Sam. i. 10—18. 3. That which, assisted by the grace of God, is *in our power* to perform, Num. xxx. Eccl. vii. 20. James iii. 2. 1 John i. 8, 10. Gal. v. 17. Rom. vii. 14—25. —And the vow respecting such matter may be made either, 1. Inwardly in our heart, 1 Sam. i. 10—18. Or, 2. By some sign expressive of our self-engagement, as by partaking of the sacraments, Gal. v. 3. 1 Pet. iii. 21. 1 Cor. x. 16, 17. xi. 23—26. Or, 3. In words assented to, or pronounced, written, or sworn, Isa. xliv. 5.—And it may be either *personal*, in which one man solemnly gives up himself as ignorant, guilty, polluted, empty, perverse, and unprofitable to God in Christ, as his Instructor, Forgiver, Sanctifier, Supplier, Portion, and Master, according to the tenor of the covenant of grace; and engages himself, by the assistance of God's Spirit, to manifest his gratitude in universal holy obedience, if not also in some particular parts or means of it, Isa. xliv. 5. xix. 18, 21. xlv. 23, 24. Psalm cxix. 106. lxvi. 13, 14. cxvi. 10—19. lxi. 5, 8. lvi. 12. Gen. xxviii. 20;—or *social*, in which the lesser or greater part of a nation or church jointly and solemnly devote themselves to the Lord, Josh. xxiv. 15. Isa. xix. 18, 21. Exod. xxiv. 7, 8. xix. 5, 6. Deut. v. 2, 3. xxvi. 16—19. xxix. 1—15. Josh. xxiv. 24, 25. 2 Chron. xv. 12, 13. xxiii. 16. xxix. 10. xxxiv. 30--32. Ezra x. 3. Neh. ix. x. Jer. xxxiv. 8—10. 2 Cor. viii. 5.

All vows ought to be made, 1. Deliberately, Eccl. v. 2, 6. 2. Judiciously, knowing their nature and contents, Jer. iv. 2. 3. In truth, candidly resolving to perform them, Jer. iv. 2. 4. In righteousness, fully certain that every thing vowed is lawful in itself, and answerable to our station and circumstances, Jer. iv. 2. 5. Humbly, Psalm cxvi. 16. Luke xvii. 10. Hab. ii. 4. 6. Evangelically, obtruding no covenant of our own upon God, nor pretending to purchase or requite his favours by our services,—but giving up ourselves to him, as sinful and unworthy, to receive his gracious benefits, and even holiness itself, as a free privilege, that we may practise it as our bound duty, Ps. cxvi. 16. cxix. 32. Isa. xliv. 3—5. Luke i. 74, 75. Heb. xii. 28. 7. Our vows, being made, must be quickly and carefully performed, Deut. xxiii. 21—23. Eccl. v. 4, 5. Prov. xx. 25. Psalm lvi. 12. lxi. 8. cxix. 106. lxvi. 13, 14. cxvi. 14, 18.—And being thus made and performed, vows are profitable, 1. As an instituted mean of our fellowship with God, and receiving out of Christ's fulness, Isa. xix. 18, 21. xliv. 4, 5. xlv. 23, 24. lvi. 4, 6. 2. To engage us to a more exact regard for the service of God, Psalm cxvi. 12—19. Job xiii. 15. 3. To increase our love and firm adherence to the truths of God and practice of holiness, Josh. xxiv. 15. Psalm cxix. 106. Phil. i. 27, 28. 4. To fortify us against sinful compliances with temptation, Jude 3, 20, 21.

X. Religious FASTING is an ordinance of God. 1. The light of nature requires it, Jonah iii. 2. God more or less directly commands it, Lev. xxiii. 27. Joel ii. 12. James iv. 9. Matth. ix. 15. 3. He encourages men's practising it, Joel ii. 15—17. Zech. xii. 10—14. 4. He gives direction how to perform it, Joel ii. 15—17. Matth. vi. 16—18. 5. It is closely connected with prayer, one of the most noted duties of the Christian life, Matth. xvii. 21. Acts xiii. 3. xiv. 23. 1 Cor. vii. 5. 6. We have many approved and successful examples of it, 2 Sam. xii. 16. Psalm xxxv. 13. 2 Cor. xi. 27. Deut. ix. Josh. vii. Judges xx. 1 Sam. vii. 1 Kings xxi. 27—29. 2 Chron. xx. Ezra ix. x. Esther iv.—x. Dan. ix. x. Jonah iii. Mat. iv. Acts x.—It includes in it, 1. Partial or total abstinence from food, in order to promote solemn devotion, Jonah iii. 7. Dan. x. 3. 2 Sam. xii. 16, 17. 2. Serious searching our heart, and consideration of our ways, Zeph. ii. 1. 2 Cor. xiii. 5. Hag. i. 5. Lam. iii. 40. 3. Deep humiliation before God on account of our sinfulness and miseries, Joel ii. 12, 13. Isa. lxiv. 6. Job xl. 4. Dan. ix. Ezra ix. 4. Candid acknowledgment of our sin, Neh. ix. 3. Dan. ix. 20, 21. 5. Gospel repentance towards God, Joel ii. 12, 13. Jer. iii. 12—14, 21—25. Ezek. xvi. 63. xxxvi. 31, 32. 6. Earnest prayer for forgiveness of, and cleansing from sin and deliverance from trouble, or for mercies needed, Ezra viii. 21. ix. x. Neh. ix. Dan. ix. 7. Solemn, evangelical covenanting with God, Jer. l. 4, 5. Neh. ix. 38. Deut. xxvi. 17, 18. Psalm cxvi. 16—19. Isa. xliv. 3—5. lvi. 4, 6.

As religious fasting is either, 1. Personal, 2 Sam. xii. 16. Luke ii. 36, 37. Dan. x. 2, 3. Acts x. 30. Matth. vi. 16—18. 2 Cor. xi. 27. 2. Private, in families, Zech. xii. 12—14; or, 3. Public, in congregations, churches, and nations, 1 Cor. v. 2. 1 Sam. vii. 6. 2 Chron. xx. 5,—We are called to it by God, in the appearances of his providence, 1. When he has been remarkably dishonoured, 1 Sam. vii. 6. 1 Cor. v. 2. 2. When we much need some special favour from him, Dan. ix. 1—3. Acts vi. 6. xiii. 2. xiv. 23. Ezek. xxxvi. 37. Mat. xvii. 21. 3. When some fearful judgment is threatened, Jonah iii. 4—7. 2 Sam. xii. 16. 1 Kings xxi. 27. 4. When we or others lie under some remarkable tokens of God's wrath, James v. 13. Psalm xxxv. 13. Neh. i. 3, 4. Joel i. ii. Isa. xxii. 12. Matth. ix. 15. But he has left it to men to fix the particular day or hour of it, by the general rules of doing all things *in charity, decently,* and in order, to the *use of edifying*, and to *his glory*, 1 Cor. xvi. 14. xiv. 26, 40. x. 31. Every person has power to fix the precise time of his own secret fasting or solemn thanksgiving. Heads of families must fix the precise time of private fasts, or thanksgivings. Societies must fix their time for fasting by mutual agreement of, at least, the majority, Zech. xii. 12—14.— Ministers and elders must fix the time of congregational fasts, Acts xiv. 23. xiii. 3.—Church rulers met in the name of Christ have the power of appointing general *ecclesiastical fasts*, Joel i. ii.—Civil rulers, as heads of their political families, and ministers of God for good to them, have power to appoint *national fasts*, for promoting the welfare of the commonwealth, 1 Sam. vii. 6. 2 Chron. xx. 1—13. Ezra viii. 21. x. Neh. ix. Jer. xxxvi. 6. Jonah iii. 5—7.

All religious fasts ought to be observed, 1. To God's glory, Zech. vii. 5. 2. In the name of Christ, Dan. ix. 19. Zech. xii. 10—14. 3. With much tenderness and brokenness of heart, 2 Cor. vii. 9—13. Dan. ix. Ezra ix. Neh. ix. 4. Followed with much humility, deep and lively sense of the sins lamented, and turning from them to God, and active abounding in the fruits of holiness, Luke xviii. 13. Psalm li. 2, 3. Matth. iii. 8.—— The ends of such religious fasting are, 1. To put honour on the perfections and providence of God, Zech. vii. 5. Josh. vii. 19. Jer. xiii. 16. 2. To lament our own and others' sinfulness, unworthiness, and troubles, and to impress our conscience and heart with a deep sense of them, Dan. ix. Ezra ix. Neh. ix. 2 Chron. xxx. 22. Jer. iii. 13, 21—25. Ezek. vii. 16. 3. To mortify our body and the deeds of it, 1 Cor. ix. 27. Rom. viii. 13. 4. To promote the fervour of our supplications, Dan. ix. Jon. iii. 5. To promote our turning to God, Joel ii. 12. Jer. l. 4, 5.

XI. Solemn Thanksgiving to God for his spiritual or temporal mercies is warranted, 1. By the light of nature. 2. By the express command of God, Psalm l. 14. 3. By the approved example of saints, Exod. xv. 1—22. Judges v. 1 Sam. ii. 1—10. 2 Chron. xx. 26. 4. It is one end of God's bestowing his favours, Psalm cvi. 4, 5. 5. The neglect of it much provokes God to withdraw his mercies and annex a curse to them, Hos. ii. 8, 9.—It is either personal, 1 Sam. ii. 1—10. 2 Sam. xxii. Luke i. 46, 47, &c.; or private, Judges v; or public, Exod. xv. 1 Chron. xvi. 2 Chron. xx. 26.——It supposes an observed receipt of God's free favours, Psalm cxvi. xviii. ciii. cv. cvii. cxxxvii. cxxxviii. cxlv.—cl; and implies a grateful sense of them, Psalm xxxvi. 6, 7. cxvi. 12, 16. Gen. xxxii 10; and a solemn return of praises to him for them, Psalm c. ciii. civ. cv. cvii. cxxxvi. Exod. xv. 1 Chron. xvi.——And it ought to be performed, 1. As to the Lord, Rom. xiv. 5, 6. 2. Judiciously, knowing for what, how, and to what end we thank him, Psal. ciii. 1—8. 3. In the Spirit, and not in carnal mirth, 1 Cor. xiv. 15. James v. 13. Psalm cviii. 1. 4. Evangelically, as a cordial expression of gratitude to God for his favours, not with any intention to requite him for them, Psalm cxvi. 12—19. 5. With faith, and in the name of Christ, Eph. v. 20. Col. iii. 17. 1 Pet. ii. 5. Heb. xiii. 15. 6. With cheerfulness of heart, Judges v. 12. 7. To a proper end, viz. 1. To glorify God, ascribing to him the praise of all his undeserved mercies, Psalm l. 23. 2. To promote our own spiritual welfare, rendering our heart more affected with God's kindness to us,—fortifying our mind against dejections, and making our obedience more liberal, Psalm xlii. 5, 6. Hos. ii. 14, 15. 3. To promote the public credit of religion, Isa. ii. 4, 5. Zech. viii. 20—23.

BESIDES the above-mentioned plain ordinances of the new covenant, there are others of a *figurative* nature, which are emblems of Christ and his benefits. These chiefly had place under the Old Testament, and were typical, in so far as they prefigured that which was then future; but sacramental, in so far as they sealed and applied Christ and his benefits to believers.— These typical ordinances included the *extraordinary* sacraments of Noah's ark, Heb. xi. 7. 1 Pet. iii. 21; the rainbow, Gen. ix. 12—18. Isa. liv. 9, 10. Rev. iv. 3. x. 1; the pillar of cloud and fire, Exod. xiii. 20—22. 1 Cor. x. 1, 2; the Israelites' passing through the Red Sea, Exod. xiv. 15. 1 Cor. x. 1, 2; the manna, Exod. xvi. 1 Cor. x. 3. John vi. 31—56; the water-yielding rock, Exod. xvii. 2—8. 1 Cor. x. 4; the sacrifices, Gen. iv. 4. viii. 20; and the *ordinary* sacraments of circumcision and the passover, Gen. xvii. Josh. v. Exod. xii. Num. ix.

Every SACRAMENT, whether of the Old or of the New Testament, is *an holy ordinance instituted by Christ, in which, by sensible signs, Christ, and the benefits of the new-covenant, are represented, sealed, and applied to believers,* and *they are solemnly dedicated to his service.* The MATTER of every sacrament is sensible signs, and spiritual things represented by them. And the FORM is that union which is constituted between the signs and things signified, by the authority, institution, and promise of Christ, 1 Cor. x. 16. Exod. xii. 1 Cor. v. 7.——No sacraments are *absolutely necessary* to salvation, as they do not put men into a state of it, but suppose them already in it: and many have been saved without partaking of them, Rom. iv. 11. 1 Cor. xi. 28. Mark xvi. 16. But it is nevertheless proper that God should appoint them, and that we should receive them. 1. Our bodies as well as our souls being redeemed by the blood of Christ, it is proper that his benefits of redemption should be in part communicated to us under corporeal signs. 2. Amidst our present childhood and weakness, it is proper that God, in gracious condescension, should give us such seals of his covenant as may strike our senses, while they represent the foundations of our redemption, and our interest in it. 3. God, by such visible confirmations of his covenant, makes them similar to those that are used among men in other matters. 4. It is proper that bodies, which are to inherit eternal life, be consecrated to it, by an use of holy things. 5. It is proper that church-members should be distinguished from others, and should edify each other by some visible tokens of their principles, state, faith, and hope.——But the mere administration or partaking of sacraments conveys no saving grace to the receivers. 1. It is not their nature to contain or produce inward grace, but to signify and seal that which God brings along with them. The rainbow gave God's full security against a second universal deluge; but it did not hinder the waters from rising, or rain from falling. Seals annexed to the patents or donative letters of kings do not confer any thing, but merely confirm the royal grants contained in the sealed writs. 2. If the sacraments of themselves conferred or produced inward grace, it must be by some natural power of the corporeal signs, or by some spiritual power infused into them,—both of which are equally absurd. 3. Common sense loudly proclaims, that *material* signs can never produce purification, or nourishment, in a soul. 4. Scripture declares, that mere partaking of sacramental signs is of no avail for securing our salvation, Rom. ii. 25—29. Gal. vi. 15. v. 6. 1 Pet. iii. 21. 1 Cor. xi 27—29. 5. All the blessings which are sealed by the sacraments to believers, are ascribed to the mercy and grace of God, not to the operation of the outward signs, Isa. i. 18. xliii. 25. Ezek. xxxvi. 25—31. Phil. ii. 13. 6. Faith and repentance are pre-required, as necessary to render sacraments effectual for salvation, Mark xvi. 16. 1 Cor. xi. 27—29.

Nevertheless sacraments are not mere marks of our Christian profession, or mere signs of spiritual benefits; but, being made effectual by the blessing of Christ and the working of his Spirit, Exod. xx. 24. 1 Cor. iii. 5—7. 2 Cor. iii. 17. 1 Cor. xii. 13, they are of use, 1. To assist our spiritual meditation, 1 Cor. x. 16. 2. To seal and apply Christ and his benefits to such as receive them by faith, exhibiting these benefits, and directing the promises to us, and conveying that which they contain to us:— God therein giving us a solemn investiture of right to them and infeftment in them; and, along with the signs, conferring the first fruits of eternal happiness, as an earnest of the full communication of it in due time, Rom. iv. 11. 1 Cor. x. 16. 3. To confirm and increase our faith to receive his gifts, Heb vi. 17, 18. 4. To produce and enliven our spiritual experience. 5 To impress our mind with just sentiments of gratitude as a debt which we owe to Christ, and his Father and Spir't; and to make us heartily devote ourselves to him, Eph. v. 2. Psalm cxvi. 12, 16. 6. To distinguish church members from others,— marking at the same time the source of the difference, Gal. iii. 27. 7. To be public bonds of conjunct profession and mutual love among Christians, 1 Cor. x. 16—18.

The sacraments of the New Testament, instituted by Christ, which have come in room of the now abolished ones of *circumcision* and the *passover*, are *baptism* and the *Lord's Supper:* which two agree in their author, age, or period, general signification, solemnity, administrators, and adult subjects; but differ in their immediate end, their fulness of representing Christ and his benefits,—their repetibleness; and that infants are capable of receiving baptism, but not of receiving the Lord's Supper.—To these two, papists have added *ordination, marriage, confirmation, penance,* and *extreme unction,* none of which have any appointment in the word of God *as sacraments:* and the three last, as used by them, have no warrant at all. Ordination belongs only to church officers. Marriage is a common privilege of mankind. But papists exclude their clergy and devotees from it, as a state of unchastity.

None but ministers of the gospel have any warrant from Christ to *administer* his sacraments pertaining to it. 1. He authorises them, and them only, to administer them, Mat. xxviii. 19. 1 Cor. xi. 2, 23. iv. 1, 2. Heb. v. 4. 2. All those that administered them in the apostolic age had either an ordinary or extraordinary call to the ministerial office, Luke i. iii. 1 Cor. xii. 28, 29. Eph. iv. 11, 12.—The candid *intention* of administrators in dispensing sacraments, is absolutely necessary to justify their own conduct before God, but not to render these ordinances true and real sacraments to the receivers. 1. Ministers, in their ministrations, being but the servants of Christ and his people, their intention can neither add to, nor detract from the essence or validity of any divine ordinance, 2 Cor. iv. 5, 7. 2. The efficacy of the word preached does not depend on the intention or importance of the preacher, Phil. i. 18. 1 Cor. iii. 6. 3. If the intention of administrators were necessary to constitute the essence or validity of sacraments, wicked clergymen might, at their pleasure, rob men of the seals of God's covenant, or confer them upon the most unfit receivers. 4. All would be left at an absolute uncertainty, whether they had ever received baptism or the Lord's Supper as a sacrament of Christ or not.—Among papists, for want of this *intention* of administrators, which they pretend to be necessary *in baptism*, almost all may be in an unbaptized state of damnation. For want of it *in the Lord's Supper*, the elements may be unconsecrated; and so mere bread and wine, offered, worshipped, and received as Christ himself; for want of it, *in their ordination* no sacred office may be conferred; and so all their priests, for many ages, but mere laymen.—Through want of it *in marriage*, the parties may but enter on a life of whoredom.—Through want of it *in penance*, there may be no absolution from sin, or the misery entailed on it.—Through want of it in *extreme unction*, there may be nothing in it but a consignation of the dying person to the devil and his angels.—Through want of it, according to their own principles, there may have been no Christianity among them who knows how long.

I. BAPTISM *is a sacrament, wherein the washing with water in the name of the Father, the Son, and the Holy Ghost, does signify and seal our ingrafting into Christ, and partaking of the benefits of the covenant of grace, and our engagement to be the Lord's.*—It was for a long time customary with the Jews to wash or baptize their proselytes when their wound of circumcision was healed. But never till the ministry of John, our Lord's forerunner, was baptism appointed by God as an ordinance of his covenant, Mat. iii. Our Saviour himself baptized none with water, but with the Holy Ghost, which was thereby represented, John iv. 1, 2. Mat. iii. 11. But, during his debased ministrations, he appointed his twelve disciples to baptize multitudes, John iii. 26. iv. 1, 2; and a little before his ascension he gave them a stated commission for life to preach the gospel, and to baptize all nations, Mat. xxviii. 19. John's baptism differed from that of the Christian church, as it related to Christ as not yet manifested, Acts xix. 4; and did not clearly exhibit the mystery of the three persons in one Godhead: But they agreed in their sign of water, Mark i. 4. Acts viii. 36, 38; in their pre-requisites of faith and repentance, Luke iii. 3, 8—14. Acts ii. 38; and in their signification of pardon of sin, regeneration, &c. Mark i. 4. Acts ii. 38. Tit. iii. 5.—And hence our Saviour, in order to initiate himself a member of the New Testament church, partook of John's baptism, Mat. iii. 13—17.

The *outward sign* in baptism is *mere water* solemnly blessed for that purpose, Mat. iii. 11. Acts viii. 36, 38. x. 47. 1 Pet. iii. 20, 21;—which may be applied by dipping the whole body in water, or by sprinkling with it the face, a principal part of the body. For, 1. Eis Hydor, when used with respect to baptism in Scripture, signifies no more than *to the water*, and Ek Hydatos no more than *from the water*. 2. Neither at *Enon*, where there were *many waters* fit for the refreshment of the assembled multitudes; nor at *Gaza*, where the Eunuch was baptized, can I find a probability of their being waters proper for the dipping of multitudes over head and ears, John iii. 23. Acts viii. 26, 36. 3. Nor is it probable that the multitudes that were baptized in Jerusalem were dipt in some pool;—nor, that the jailor at Philippi and his family went off from the prison at midnight, and sought some pool into which they might plunge their whole bodies, Acts xvi. 33. 4. The word *baptize* in Scripture does not always, if ever, denote *plunging* into water, Mark vii. 4, 8. Luke xi. 38. 1 Cor. x. 2. Heb. ix. 10. 5. That which is represented by baptism is called a *sprinkling* the blood of Christ, 1 Pet. i. 2. Heb. x. 22. xii. 24. Isa. lii. 15. Ezek. xxxvi. 25.

Baptism is not *absolutely necessary to salvation*. 1. Mere participation of sacraments does not render men partakers of salvation, 1 Pet. iii. 21. 1 Cor. xi. 27, 29. Rom. ii. 28, 29. 2. If baptism were absolutely necessary to salvation, it would be in the power of men to save or damn others as they pleased, by giving or withdrawing it. 3. The nature of baptism, as a seal of the new covenant, and of the righteousness of faith, imports men's antecedent interest in that covenant. 4. Many have had real grace, and so been in a state of salvation, before they received baptism, as Paul, Gal. i. 16; Cornelius, Acts x. 35, 44, 45, 47; Peter's converts, Acts ii. 41. Those who are regenerated in their mother's womb are in a state of salvation before they are capable of baptism. The converted thief went to heaven without it, for ought appears, Luke xxiii. 43. 5. Others, as Simon the sorcerer, have been baptized, and nevertheless continued in an unregenerate state, Acts viii. 13, 20—23. 1 John ii. 19. 6. It is the want of faith, not of baptism, that damns men, Mark xvi. 16. Where baptism is manifestly omitted in the last sentence, in order to shew that men may be saved without it. But baptism *is necessary*, 1. As an ordinance of Christ, which is to be continued in the church to the end of the world, Mat. xxviii. 19, 20. 2. As an ordinary mean of fellowship with Christ, and of receiving grace from him, and honouring him before the world, Rom. vi. 3—5.

The *washing with water in baptism, in the name of the Father, Son, and Holy Ghost*, does signify and seal, 1. Our solemn admission into Christ's family as members of it, not in order to make us such. In this a three one God and his ministerial deputies solemnly acknowledge us members. The Christians present acknowledge us brethren. And we, when baptized, profess ourselves embodied with them, as a society separated from the world to the service of God in Christ, 1 Cor. xii. 12, 13. Acts ii. 41. 2. Our ingrafting into Christ, by spiritual union with his person as our Root, Head, and Husband, Gal. iii. 27. Rom. vi. 3, 4. 3. Our solemn partaking of the benefits of the covenant of grace, particularly of Christ's righteousness and justification through it, Rom. vi. 4. Acts ii. 38. xxii. 16; Adoption into God's family, and relation to him as our God, Gal. iii. 26, 27. 2 Cor. vi. 18. Acts ii. 38, 39; Regeneration after his image, Tit. iii. 5. 1 Pet. iii. 21. Rom. vi. 3—5. Col. ii. 11 —13. John iii. 3, 5, 6; and a joyful resurrection to everlasting life and happiness, Rom. vi. 4, 5. 1 Cor. xv. 29. 4. Our solemn profession of our faith in the declarations of the gospel relative to the Father, Son, and Holy Ghost, and our interest in them in all their new covenant relations,—and solemn surrender of our persons, and all that we have, to be their property, and disposed of and employed as they please, according to the tenor of that covenant, John iv. 1. Rom. vi. 4. Isa. xliv. 3—5. Acts ii. 39. 1 Cor. vi. 19, 20. Eph. iv. 1. v. 1, 2, 11. 1 Cor. xii. 12—14.

None but regenerated persons have a right to baptism *before God.* 1. The having the Holy Ghost, faith, and repentance, are required as necessary pre-requisites of baptism, Acts x. 47. viii. 36, 37. ii. 38. 2. Sacraments, being *confirming* ordinances, suppose those who receive them to be already instated in the covenant of grace;—and being *seals*, cannot be divinely set to a blank, Rom. iv. 11. Col. i. 11, 12. Gal. iii. 27.——None but such as *appear truly regenerated* have a right to baptism *before men.* 1. If none but real saints have a right to it before God,— none but such as have the *appearance* of saints can have a right to it before the church. 2. That which is holy ought not to be given to dogs, Mat. vii. 6. Prov. xxvi. 11. 2 Pet. ii. 18, 20, 22. Psalm xiv. 1—4. 3. Men ought to be *made* Christ's *disciples* before they receive baptism, John iv. 1. Mat. xxviii. 19. And none ought to be reckoned Christ's disciples but such as appear to have heard and learned of the Father; and manifest their knowledge and faith by their good works, John vi. 44, 45. Mat. vii. 20, 21. Tit. i. 16. 1 Tim. v. 8. 4. The Scripture represents men as baptized upon appearances of saintship, Mat. iii. 6. Acts ii. 41. viii. 12, 13, 37, 38. ix. 18. x. 47, 48. xvi. 14, 15, 32, 33. xviii. 8. 5. Admission of persons manifestly wicked, is a fearful profanation of sealing ordinances, Lev. x. 8—10. Ezek. xxii. 26. xliv. 9.

The *infants* of parents, one or both *visible saints*, have a right to baptism *before the church.* 1. Christ's general charge to baptize all *nations* includes them, Mat. xxviii. 19. Mark xvi. 15, 16, where the *world* and *nations* are opposed to the Jews, whose infants were circumcised. And certainly infants are included in *nations*. 2. The children of believers are in covenant with God, Gen. xvii. 7. Acts ii. 38, 39; and therefore may enjoy the seal of that covenant which is competent for them,—for which no pre-examination of the subjects is necessarily required,—in which no eating or drinking are necessary,—and of the leading blessings represented in which they are capable, viz. union with Christ, justification, adoption, regeneration, and resurrection to everlasting life. 3. Infants in the Jewish church were admitted to circumcision, which represented much the same things as baptism, Gen. xvii. 10—14. And it ought to be observed that Christ came not into the world to curtail the privileges of his church, but to enlarge them;—that infants are as capable of baptism as of circumcision;—and that baptism is represented as a *circumcision*, Col. ii. 11, 12. 4. Infants, such as Christ could carry in his arms, are members of *the kingdom of God*, Mat. xix. 13. Mark x. 14. And if members, why deny them the primary seal of membership? 5. Infants of one or both believing parents are HOLY,—not by legitimacy, for that is not the point there handled; nor is the faith of at least one parent necessary to it;—but *federally holy*, as belonging to God, and separated to his service, 1 Cor. vii. 14. 6. Whole families were often baptized, as of *Lydia*, and of the *jailor of Philippi*, Acts xvi. 15, 33; *Stephanus of Corinth*, 1 Cor. i. 16, &c.; in which families, it ought to be presumed that there were infants, till the contrary be proved. 7. Infants of believing parents were baptized in all the primitive ages of the Christian church. Even Pelegius, whose learning was considerable, and who had travelled through a great part of the Christian world, and whose darling opinions powerfully tempted him to deny infant baptism, declares that he had never heard of any who denied infants' right to baptism; and complains of the report of his denial of it as a vile slander cast upon him.

OBJEC. I. " There is no express warrant in Scripture for " *baptizing* infants." ANSW. 1. There is an express command of God to circumcise infants; and there is equal reason to baptize them, Gen. xvii. 10—14. Col. ii. 11, 12. 2. There is a command to baptize NATIONS, of which infants are a part, Mat. xxviii. 19. 3. There is a new covenant promise respecting the infants of believers, Acts ii. 39. xiii. 46. 4. There is no more express command or reason for observing the *Christian Sabbath*, nor for *women's* partaking of the Lord's Supper, than is for the baptism of infants.

OBJEC. II. " We have no express instance of the baptism of " infants in Scripture in the history of the church for about " thirty years." ANSW. 1. For almost two thousand years, from Abraham to John Baptist, we have not one instance of the circumcision of an infant *on the eighth day.* Will it therefore follow that no infants were circumcised, or none on the eighth day, all that time? There is no instance of baptism in the churches of Antioch, Iconium, Rome, Thessalonica, or Colosse. Were therefore none of their members baptized? It is not common for historians to give particular instances of that which is altogether common. 2. It is incumbent upon our opposers to produce instances of the refusal of baptism to the children of believing parents till they were capable to vow for themselves.

OBJEC. III. " Infants can receive no benefits from baptism." ANSW. 1. If parents can settle upon them an earthly inheritance, what can hinder God to settle upon them an heavenly felicity? What can hinder him to bestow upon them all the blessings represented in baptism? 2. If they received benefit by circumcision, why may they not receive as much from baptism? And can they not be laid under obligations to serve God by the one as well as by the other? Gal. v. 3.

OBJEC. IV. " Faith and repentance, and the profession " thereof, are required as *pre-requisites* of baptism." ANSW. If infants can be saved, what hinders them to have the *habits* of faith and repentance? And as for the profession of them, it is only required of adult persons.

Children derive their *right to baptism from their immediate parents.* 1. If they derived their right to baptism from their *mediate parents,* the children of some, if not all Heathens and Mahometans, would have a right to it, because of their descent from some pious ancestor. Nevertheless they are represented as *aliens from the commonwealth of Israel, strangers to the covenants of promise,* without Christ, *and having no hope,* and *without God in the world,* 1 Cor. vii. 14. Eph. ii. 12. 2. If infants derive their right to baptism from *mediate parents,* they must either derive it from their most remote ancestor; and then all must be baptized as descended from pious Noah, Enoch, &c. Or the extent of the derivation of that right must be fixed; which it no where is in Scripture. If it be pretended that it extends to a *thousand generations,* then all the infants of heathens have a right to it; as perhaps none of them are, or ever will be at the distance of three hundred generations from Noah, Abraham, &c. If that right extend to a *thousand* generations, how can the curse of God lie on the children of wicked men to the third and fourth generation? Or how could the Jews have been unchurched, when scarcely in the sixtieth generation from Abraham, in whom they were taken into covenant with God? 3. Notwithstanding the eminent piety of their ancestors, the infants of the Jews that lived in the apostolic age were unchurched along with their immediate parents. But why, unless the sin of these immediate parents had procured it? Rom. xi.

16, 20. 4. Children are rendered *federally holy* through the faith of their immediate father or mother, 1 Cor. vii. 14. 5. The children of wicked parents are by God, in his word, declared cursed, Deut. xxviii. 18. But how can they, who are visibly cursed by God, have a visible right to the seal of his promise and blessing?

No infants, but such as are *immediately descended* from one or both parents, *visible believers*, have any right to baptism *before the church*. 1. Since they derive their right from their immediate parents, it must either be derived from their being baptized, or from their being visible believers. It cannot be derived from their baptism, as that becomes null and void if they be wicked, Rom. ii. 25. It is quite absurd to allege, that no more is here meant than that circumcision is unprofitable to justify men, except they keep the law: for in that respect it would be unprofitable though millions of good works attended it, Gal. iii. 10. ii. 16. Rom. iii. 20. 2. Parents' right of access to the Lord's table, and their infants' right to baptism, stand or fall together. Such church-members as have offended by one or a few scandalous steps in their conversation, have their right continued; but they are disqualified to use it till their offence be removed. But such as appear unholy in the general tenor of their practice, manifest that they have *no right* at all; and consequently their children have none. In vain it is pretended, that the Holy Ghost may enter into the heart of an infant who is descended from parents both of them manifestly wicked: for though he should, yet that child's right before God to baptism could never be manifested to the church till it could profess and act for itself. 3. The children of parents visibly wicked are declaratively *cursed* by God, Deut. xxviii. 18. How then can he allow them in baptism to be solemnly declared *visibly blessed?* James iii. 10, 11. 4. Such as have no discernible evidence of their being within God's covenant of grace, as is the case with the infants of wicked parents, can have no visible claim to the seal of it. Though these parents had been baptized, nay regularly baptized, yet if their baptism profit not themselves, how can it profit their seed? 5. Faith and repentance are required in parents, to render their children *federally holy* and admissible to baptism, 1 Cor. vii. 14. Acts ii. 38, 39. 6. None but such as are visible believers have any mark of God's being their God and the God of their seed, Gen. xvii. 7. Jer. xxxi. 33. 7. If the children of manifestly ungodly parents have any real right to baptism, the church ought to put them into possession of it. But what could be done in this matter? The parents are incapable to educate these children in a Christian manner. It would be but a solemn mockery of God to bring them under vows relative to it, while their practice continues an habitual contradiction to them.—It would be no better to lay these vows on a sponsor, who could not, or would not, have the children under his power. 8. Baptizing the infants of parents manifestly wicked, renders that solemn ordinance altogether common, and declares those church-members that are not visible saints; and so makes the church a society *not separated* from the world,—contrary to John xviii. 36. 1 Pet. ii. 5, 9. Eph. ii. 12, 19, 20. 1 John v. 19. Rom. ix. 29. 9. If wicked parents have no right to baptism themselves, and their children derive their right from them, as has been proved, the children of such parents can have no right to it. 10. The faithful exclusion of the infants of wicked parents from baptism has a remarkable tendency to promote the ends of the gospel, which calls men to unite with Christ by faith, and so deny *ungodliness* and *worldly lusts*, and live *soberly, righteously*, and *godly*. Parents would not be hardened in their wickedness, by an unlawful admission of them to sealing ordinances. None would be tempted to believe themselves true Christians, merely on account of their being baptized. Hearers of the gospel would not be tempted to indulge themselves in ignorance and wickedness, in hopes of having their infants baptized notwithstanding. Baptism would not be reckoned less solemn than the Lord's Supper, or profaned as a common thing.

OBJEC. I. "All the infants of Christians are within God's "covenant." ANSW. Will that infer that the manifest enemies of God, who have nothing but the name of Christians, or their children, are within God's covenant? Has Christ a confederacy with Satan, when he is but *called* an angel of light?

OBJEC. II. "Children ought never to suffer for their pa-"rents' sins." ANSW. 1. Must then all the infants of heathens, who are born as innocent as those of Christians, be baptized? 2. If no children ought to be excluded from admission to the church for their parents' sins, the Jews must still be the *peculiar* people of God, as well as in the days of Moses, David, &c. 3. Does not God, in manifold instances, visit the iniquities of the parents on their children, Exod. xx. 5? 4. The withholding baptism from the infants of wicked parents is no proper punishment of these infants; but a not giving them that to which they have no right, and which, if given them, would do them no good, but hurt. 5. If magistrates may take occasion to execute both father and son, who were guilty of preceding treason,—from the father's continued repetition of his treason, why may not God justly take occasion, from the wickedness of parents, to punish their children as themselves deserve by their original sin? 6. Must all children, even of Christians, be put into possession of inheritances to which their parents never had any right: or which they had prodigally squandered away? How absurd and wicked the pretence!

OBJEC. III. "The heresy and impiety of wicked parents" "never excluded their children from circumcision." ANSW. 1. If heresy do not exclude men from baptism, neither will *atheism*, 1 John ii. 22. 2. If no heresy or profaneness exclude men from baptism, why did John Baptist and Peter the Apostle require repentance as a *pre-requisite* of it, Matth. iii. 2, 6, 8. Luke iii. 3, 7—14. Acts ii. 38. iii. 19. 3. Where is the proof that the infants of Hebrews, who were notoriously profane, were admissible to circumcision? Did God allow those parents to be sustained members of his church, whom he *cut off* from his people, and did not suffer to live on his earth, Deut. xvii. 12. Num. xv. 30, 35, 36? Had the infants of the profane contemners of the promised land any circumcision allowed them, till, as adult persons, they received it in their own right? And where is the evidence that Joshua circumcised any that were heretical or profane, Num. xiv. Josh. v.?

OBJEC. IV. "John baptized every person that offered himself to his baptism." ANSW. 1. Must then all Heathens and Mahometans be baptized, if they offer themselves to it? 2. John does not appear to have baptized so much as one, but on proper evidence of repentance of former sins, Matth. iii. 2, 6—12. Luke iii. 3, 7—14. 3. He did not baptize the profane Pharisees or Sadducees, Luke vii. 30.

OBJEC. V. "God calls the children of the idolatrous Jews *his children*, Ezek. xvi. 20." ANSW. Perhaps these children were God's peculiar property, being *first born*, Exod. xiii. 12, 13. Num. iii. 13. viii. 17; or, they may be called *his children* in the same sense as the *silver and gold, corn and wine, flax and wool*, are called HIS, Hag. ii. 8. Ezek. xvi. 17—19. Hos. ii. 5, 8, 9.

OBJEC. VI. "If only the infants of visible believers be allowed baptism, then whole families and parishes will be paganized. Nay, as we have no rule to state who are visible believers, many infants of Christians will be robbed of baptism." ANSW. 1. It is no honour for Christ to have profane persons, similar to brutes and devils, openly reputed his members. 2. God's word is a sufficient rule for distinguishing professors from the profane, 2 Tim. iii. 15—17. 3. None can be *visible believers*, who have *no appearance* of faith in their practice: for true Christians are known by their fruits, Mat. vii. 17, 20. Gal. v. 16—24.

OBJEC. VII. "Though many parents be wicked and scandalous, yet they were made Christians by their baptism."

Answ. As a single scandal in parents does not necessarily infer their being destitute of the grace of God, their children may have a right to baptism, though these parents, until their scandal be purged, be disqualified from presenting them. But when parents, by their *habitual* behaviour, manifest themselves graceless,—their being *once baptized* can no more avail their children, than it avails those of a prodigal that their father had once a rich estate.

Baptism ought to be administered, 1. With water, in the simple manner prescribed by Christ, 1 Cor. xi. 2, 23. 2. Expressly in the name of the Father, the Son, and the Holy Ghost, as three divine persons, the same in substance, and equal in power and glory, Matth. xxviii. 19. 3. With preaching the gospel immediately preceding it, Matth. xxviii. 19. Mark xvi. 15, 16. 4. And for this reason, as well as because it is a mystery of God, it ought to be administered by those only who are *stewards* or *ministers* of Christ, 1 Cor. iv. 1, 2. Rom. x. 15. Matth. xxviii. 19. 5. As preaching must attend it;— as it is a solemn declaration of visible church-membership;— as much effectual fervent prayer is necessary to render it efficacious;—as it affords opportunity for others to be impressed with, and renew their baptismal engagements;—and as private administration of it tends to make persons, like the papists, believe it absolutely necessary to salvation, it ought to be publicly dispensed, Matth. xxviii. 19. 6. It ought to be administered with much gravity, and serious, not superstitious solemnity, Psalm lxxxvii. 7.

Baptism ought to be improved by such as have received it, 1. By labouring to have just apprehensions of the nature, use, and ends of it. 2. By serious and deep-fixed remembrance of the mercies and vows represented by it. 3. In fulfilling the vows therein made,—through an exercise of faith on Jesus Christ.

II. The Lord's Supper is a sacrament, *wherein, by giving and receiving bread and wine according to Christ's appointment, his death is shewed forth; and the worthy receivers are not, after a corporal and carnal manner, but by faith made partakers of his body and blood, with all his benefits, to their spiritual nourishment, and growth in grace.* Or, it is the sacrament of our spiritual nourishment, in which, by the divinely appointed use of bread and wine, is represented, sealed and applied, the saints' communion in grace and glory with their once crucified, but now exalted Saviour.—It is called the *Lord's Supper*, 1 Cor. xi. 20; *Blessing*, 1 Cor. x. 16. Matth. xxvi. 26; the *Eucharist* or thanksgiving, Mat. xxvi. 27. 1 Cor. xi. 24; the *Lord's table*, 1 Cor. x. 21; the *breaking of bread*, 1 Cor. x. 16. Acts ii. 42,

46. xx. 7; and the *communion of the body and blood of Christ*, 1 Cor. x. 16.

The outward signs in this sacrament are BREAD of any kind; for Christ took that which was readiest; and WINE of any kind or colour. The *eating* the bread, and *drinking* the wine, being always connected in Christ's example and command, ought never to be separated, Mark xiv. 23. 1 Cor. x. 16. xi. 26. Nor does the disjunctive mention of the *bread* and *cup* infer the dropping the CUP more than the bread. Disjunctive particles are often put for copulatives, Rom. iv. 12. 1 Cor. xiii. 8. Mat. v. 17. Eph. vi. 8.—Besides, the end of this sacrament is to represent the *blood* or death of Christ.—The cup contains in a figure the remission of sins, of which papists think their clergy have as little need as their laity.

The bread and wine in the Lord's Supper are *not changed* into the real body and blood of Christ. 1. Such a transubstantiation of them is contrary to the testimony of our senses; and so completely undermines the whole proof of all the miracles by which God has confirmed his revelations to men: Nay, overturns almost all certainty in the world. 2. According to such a transubstantiation, the same body of Christ is alive and dead at once; is in heaven, and in a thousand or ten thousand different and distant places on earth at once; accidents remain without a substance, and a substance exists without accidents. —The glorified body of Christ is apt to become food for dogs and moths, and with wicked communicants to go into hell fire,— all which are perfectly absurd, contrary to reason and common sense. 3. Such transubstantiation is contrary to the end of this sacrament, which is to represent and commemorate Christ, not to sist him corporally present, 1 Cor. xi. 24, 25. 4. It is contrary to Scripture, which represents Christ's body as whole, and his blood in his veins, when he first administered this sacrament, and declares that it is BREAD that is broken, and WINE that is drunk, Matth. xxvi. 26—30. 1 Cor. x. 16, 17. xi. 23—29; and that the *heavens must contain* Christ's manhood till the last day, Acts iii. 21.

OBJEC. I. " God is almighty, and can do every thing." ANSW. Omnipotence cannot work contradictions and nonsense.

OBJEC. II. " Unless the elements be changed into the very " body and blood of Christ, we receive mere bread and wine in " the Lord's Supper." ANSW. 1. We spiritually receive his body and blood, as well as we do his Spirit and blood in baptism, where no transubstantiation is pretended. 2. Though Christ be not corporally present, yet, as God-man Mediator, he is symbolically and spiritually present.

OBJEC. III. " Christ expressly calls the *bread* his *body*." ANSW. 1. The Jews had no other than the verb AM, IS, ARE,

TO BE, to mean *signify* or *represent;* and this signification of their substantive verb was altogether common among them. Hence *circumcision* is said to be God's covenant, Gen. xvii. 10. *Ears* of corn, and *kine,* are said to be *years* of plenty or famine, Gen. xli. 26, 27. The paschal *lamb* to be the *passover,* i. e. an act of the angel, Exod. xii. 11. The water-yielding *rock* to be Christ, 1 Cor. x. 4. The Sabbath to be the Lord's *covenant,* Exod. xxxi. 13, 17; and *Christ* said to be a *rose, lily,* and *vine,* Song ii. 1. John xv. 1. 2. Our Saviour plainly intimates, that he meant no more, but that the bread and wine *represented,* sealed, and applied his body and blood,—in his words: *This cup is the New Testament in my blood,* which if read without allowing any figure would infer another transubstantiation of his blood into the New Testament; and be read thus, *This my blood is the New Testament in my blood.* What absurd nonsense!

The Lutheran pretence, that the material body and blood of Christ are corporally present WITH, IN, and UNDER the bread and wine, is scarcely less absurd. For, 1. How can a body at once be visible and invisible; felt and unfeelable; present in heaven, and in multitudes of places on earth? Heb. ii. 14. Luke xxiv. 39. Acts iii. 21. 2. In Christ's own administration of this sacrament, how could his body, at once, be present with his disciples giving the bread and wine to them: and yet, IN the bread and wine given and received in *remembrance* of him, 1 Cor. xi. 23—26. 3. How can his body be broken and his blood shed on every sacramental occasion, when he is now glorified. 4. The Scripture represents his manhood as no more in this lower world, but in heaven, Acts iii. 21. Heb. i. 3. viii. 4. John xii. 8. xiv. 28. xvi. 7, 28. xvii. 11.

In the Lord's Supper there is *no oblation of Christ's body and blood as a sacrifice to make atonement for the sins of the quick and the dead.* 1. The Scripture never intimates that there is any sacrifice made in it. 2. Such oblation of sacrifice is inconsistent with the declared design of this sacrament to commemorate Christ's person and work, and hold fellowship with him, 1 Cor. xi. 24, 25. x. 16. 3. It is contrary to the ONENESS of Christ's priesthood and sacrifice, in which he alone offered himself, John x. 18. Heb. vii. 24. ix. 28. x. 10, 14. 1 Tim. ii. 5. Heb. ix. 14, 15. And there is but *one offering* of him, Heb. vii. 27. ix. 12, 28. x. 10, 14. 4. The absolute perfection of Christ's sacrifice of himself excludes all repetition of it, Heb. x. 1—14. ix. 12—15, 28. i. 3. xiii. 12. 1 Pet. i. 18, 19, 20. ii. 24. iii. 18. Rev. v. 9. 2 Cor. v. 21. Rom. v. 9—11, 16—21. viii. 3, 4. x. 4. Dan. ix. 24. 5. In this sacrament, there is nothing like to an oblation of sacrifice;—not an *altar,* but a *table,* 1 Cor. x. 21; no visible substance sacrificed;—no death, but a commemoration of that which had formerly happened;—nor is Christ here given to God, but to men.

To anticipate objections, It must be observed, 1. That Melchizedek brought forth bread and wine for refreshment to Abram's fatigued troops, but not to be offered in sacrifice, Gen. xiv. 18. 2. That the paschal lamb was *not a type* of this sacrament, but of Christ himself. 3. That the daily sacrifice offered under the New Testament is not the Lord's Supper; but prayer, praise, and good works, Mal. i. 11.

All professed Christians, come to years of discretion, are *bound* by the law of God *to partake* of the Lord's Supper, and it is their sin, if they be incapable of regular admission to it.—Only *true believers* have a *right* to it before God.—Only true believers, who *have examined themselves*, and are *actually exercising their faith and love*, can *rightly use* this privilege, 1 Cor. xi. 23—29.—Three things are necessary to a right partaking of the Lord's Supper. 1. A worthy *state* of union with Christ as our husband, father, righteousness, and strength. 2. A worthy *frame* in the actual exercise of all the graces of the Spirit, knowledge, faith, repentance, love, &c. 3. A worthy *end* of honouring Christ, glorifying God, and receiving spiritual nourishment to our soul, 1 Cor. x. 26—31. xi. 23—29.

From the whole nature of this ordinance, and what Christ has required in relation to it, it is manifest that it is a most horrible profanation of it, either to impose or receive it as a condition of civil office or liberty, or as a test of loyalty.

REFLECT. My soul, has God in Christ been at such pains in ordinances and influences to save and sanctify me! Why then do not I stir up myself to take hold of him? In which ordinance, and when, did God Almighty appear unto me and bless me? When and where hath the Lord made me lie down in these *green pastures;* and fed me beside these *still waters?* When saw I my King in these *lattices*, and held him in these *galleries?* Alas! how long I have lien at these pools of mercy without being put in! How long and often I have lien as an ox or ass, at these *wells of salvation*, without drinking their living water!

THE Old and New Testament DISPENSATIONS of the Covenant of Grace AGREE, 1. In their *Author*, God in Christ, Heb. i. 1. 2. In their *matter;* the Law and the Gospel being alway the substance of both, Psalm cxlvii. 19. Gal. iii. 8. Tit. ii. 11—14. iii. 8. Gal. v. 6. 3. In the blessings offered and bestowed;—union with Christ, justification, adoption, regeneration, sanctification, spiritual comfort, and eternal glory, Job xix. 25. xxxiii. 24. Isa. lxiii. 16. Ezek. xxxvi. 26, 27. Psalm lxxxvi. 3. lxiii. 2—7. lxxiii. 24—26. 1 Cor. i. 30. iii. 22. Rom. viii. 29, 30. 4. In requiring the same end, and the same exercise of faith, repentance, love, and new obedience, in attending their ordinances, Isa. lv. 1—7. Psalm xcvi. 6—8. lxxxix. 7. Matth. xi. 28, 29. Heb. x. 22. 5. In their ordinances, having no spiritual efficacy of themselves to save men; and hence often least effectual when best dispensed, as by Moses, Isaiah, Christ, Paul, Deut. xxix. 4. Isa. vi. 9, 10. xlix. 45. liii. 1. Acts xvii. 22—32. 6. In their being rendered effectual for salvation by the same means, viz. 1. The blessing of Christ, which includes his appointment of them for blessings to men, and his rendering them such by his almighty influence attending them, Exod. xx. 24. 2. The working of Christ's Spirit in preparing men for these ordinances, assisting them in their attendance on them, fixing the impression of their contents, inclining and enabling to a proper improvement of them, 1 Cor. iii. 6, 7. xii. 13. 3. The exercise of true faith correspondent with the influences of Christ and his Spirit in them,—in discerning that which God manifests,—in crediting that which God declares,—in receiving that which God offers,—and in improving God's manifestations, declarations, and gifts, to promote that holy obedience which he requires, Heb. iv. 2. xi. 6.

The typical ceremonies of the Old Testament dispensation being more dark, carnal, confined, and representing Christ as to come, continued, as it were, *living* and *vigorous* in their obligation till his incarnation;—*languid* and *dying* during his state of humiliation, and especially of his public ministry;—and became *dead* after his death and resurrection;—and *deadly* and *hurtful* after his full declaration of the gospel, and ruin of the Jewish temple, Heb. vii.—x. Gal. ii.—v.—It is evident that they are now abolished, 1. From many express declarations of Scripture, Acts xv. 18, 28. Gal. v. 2, 4, 5, 13. iv. 11. Col. ii. 14, 17. Heb. vii.—x. 2. From many Scripture-predictions, Isa. lxvi. 3. Jer. iii. 16. xxxi. 32. Dan. ix. 27. Mal. i. 11. Psal. cx. 4. 3. From the very nature of many of these ceremonies. They were not good in themselves; pointed out Christ not as come, but *to come*; and excluded the Gentiles from the church, Heb. x. 1. Col. ii. 17. Gal. iii. 24. v. 1. Eph. ii. 12, 14, 15. 4. From the state of the Jewish nation, which for more than 1700 years past has rendered the observance of these ceremonies at Jerusalem or in Canaan impossible, Luke xix. 43, 44. xxi. 20, 24. Rom. xi. 7—15, 20.

OBJEC. I. " Several of these ordinances were appointed to " continue *for ever*, Gen. xvii. 13. Exod. xii. 24." ANSW. 1. *For ever* and *everlasting* often signify no more than a long time, or the whole time of a particular state of things. 2. These ceremonies continue for ever in their antitypes.

OBJEC. II. " Christ's apostles marked a great regard to the "Mosaic ceremonies." ANSW. Only for a time, and in so far as they thought necessary for the edification of the weak Jews converted to the Christian form of worship, Acts xv. Rom. xiv. 1 Cor. viii. Gal. ii. v. Heb. vii.—x.

OBJEC. III. "Priests, sacrifices, and temples, &c. are foretold "to take place in the New Testament church, Ezek. xl.—xlviii. "Mal. i. ii." &c. ANSW. These typical terms must be understood in a spiritual sense, agreeably to the nature of the gospel dispensation, 1 Pet. ii. 5. Heb. xiii. 15, 16. Rom. xii. 1.

The *peculiar* and transcendent *prerogatives* of the more full, clear, spiritual, extensive, and lasting New Testament dispensation are, 1. The Messiah exhibited as already incarnate, made perfect through suffering, and exalted to glory, John i. 14. Heb. ii. 9, 10. v. 9. Psalm xcvii. 1. xcix. 1. cx. 1—7. Heb. vii.—x. 2. The gospel preached in a new form; revealing and offering Christ, and a finished redemption in him, 1 Cor. ii. 7—10;—exhibiting him and his blessings in a clear manner, 2 Cor. iii. 6—16. Col. i. 25, 26. Rom. xvi. 25, 26. 2 Tim. i. 10;—in which all appearance of severity, even to beasts, is laid aside,—in a manner most delightful and comforting, 2 Cor. iii. 9. 1 Cor. ii. 9. xv. 3, 4. Isa. lii. 7. xl. 1, 2. lxi. 1—3. lxvi. 10—12; and in which the gospel dwells plentifully in men, Rom. x. 8, 18. Col. iii. 16, 17. 3. The calling the Gentile nations into the Christian church, while the Jewish church and state are ruined; in order to wean the believing Jews from their ceremonies, and confirm the Messiahship and gospel of Christ, 1 Cor. ii. 4, 5. 2 Cor. x. 4, 7. Isa. lxvi. 7, 8. Rom. x. 18, 19. xi. 11, 12. xvi. 26. Acts xiii. 46. Mat. xxiv. 14. xxvi. 13. xxviii. 19. Mark xvi. 15, 16. Eph. iii. 8, 9. Col. i. 23. Rev. v. 9. vii. 9. And in the last ages of the world, both Jews and Gentiles shall be almost universally united into one gospel church, Rom. xi. 12—16, 26, 30, 31, 32. Rev. xi. 15. Psal. lxxii. xcviii. 2, 3. 4. A far more plentiful and comfortable enjoyment of the Holy Ghost in his presence and influence, Zech. xii. 10. Joel ii. 28. Isa. xliv. 3—5. John vii. 38, 39. xiv. 16, 26. xv. 26. xvi. 7—14. Acts ii. viii. x. 1 Cor. xii. 5. More remarkable endowments,—more clear and distinct views of divine mysteries, Isa. xi. 9. liv. 13. Jer. xxxi. 34. 1 John ii. 27;—more eminent holiness, Isa. xxix. 24. xxxiii. 24. xxxv. 9. lx. 12, 21, 22. lxii. 12. Zech. x. 5, 12. xii. 8. Isa. liv. 11, 12. lxvi. 12—14. Zech. xiv. 20, 21;—more abundant comfort, John xiv. 16, 26. Acts ix. 31. Eph. i. 13. 2 Cor. i. 22. v. 5. 2 Thess. ii. 16, 17;—much greater boldness and intimacy with God, Gal. iv. 6. Rom. viii. 15, 16. Heb. iv. 14—16. x. 19, 20;—miraculous gifts bestowed on the apostles and others, Acts ii. viii. x. xvi. 19. xxi. 8. 1 Cor.

xii. xiv. 6. Evangelical liberty, consisting in more distinct understanding the saints' freedom from the dominion of the broken covenant of works, and of sin and Satan, Rom. viii. 1. vi. 14. Col. i. 13;—and from all human impositions in the worship of God, James iv. 12. 1 Cor. vii. 23. Mat. xv. 9. Col. ii. 18—23; —and in complete deliverance from the ceremonial law, and from the judicial law of the Jewish nation, in so far as subordinated to it, Acts xv. 10. Gal. v. 1—25. iv. 5, 26. Tit. i. 15. Col. ii. 20, 21. 1 Cor. x. 25. 7. As it relates to things past, it admits of no change till the end of the world, Mat. xxviii. 20. 1 Cor. x. 25, 28.

BOOK VII.

OF THE COVENANT SOCIETY, FOR ERECTING OF WHICH, AND TO WHICH, THE COVENANT IS DISPENSED.

CHAP. I.

Of the NATURE, *F*ORMATION, *and* FELLOWSHIP *of the Christian Church.*

HAVING elsewhere exhibited a representation of the TYPICAL church of the Old Testament, and its ordinances, our present hints shall immediately respect the New Testament CHURCH. The Greek word ECCLESIA, which we render CHURCH, denotes *any assembly* met about business, whether lawful or unlawful, Acts xix. 32—39. But, when it respects the objects of the new covenant, it denotes, 1. The *whole body of the* elect considered in their relation to Christ, those on earth being called the *militant,* and those in heaven the *triumphant church,* Eph. i. 22. v. 25. Mat. xvi. 18. Heb. xii. 23. 2. All those men and women in this world who profess their faith in Christ and obedience to him, and their children, 1 Tim. iii. 15. Eph. iv. 11, 12. 1 Cor. xii. 12, 13, 28. 3. Some particular assemblies of the worshippers of God in Christ united together in special fellowship for their own mutual edification, and subjected to their respective governors, Acts viii. 1. xv. 41. xx. 17. Rev. i. 11, 20. ii. 1, 7, 8, 11, 12, 17, 18, 29. iii. 1, 6, 7, 13, 14, 22. 2 Cor. i. 1. Gal. i. 13, 22. 1 Thess. i. 1. 4. A particular congregation of persons professing faith in Christ, love to him, and regard to his ordinances as distinguished from their spiritual governors, Acts xiv. 23. 5. A particular assembly of the professed followers of Christ that ordinarily meet in one place for the dispensation of gospel ordinances, their rulers being among them, Acts ix. 31. xv. 41. 2 Cor. viii. 1. Gal. i. 2, 22. Tit. i. 5. 1 Cor. xiv. 34. Acts xx. 7. Col. iv. 15. Rom. xvi. 5. Philem. 2. 6. A meeting of church rulers constituted in Christ's name, for ordering of the affairs under their charge, which is often called a *church representative,* Mat. xviii. 17. Acts xv. 3. xviii. 22. xxi. 20.

The church being founded upon *revelation alone*, ought to be wholly regulated by the *measuring reed*, and the *line* of God's word, Eph. ii. 20. Ezek. xliii, 11, 12. Heb. viii. 5. Rev. xi. 1. xxi. Ezek. xl.—xlviii.——The visible church on earth is *a society of believing and holy persons, whom God, by the gospel, has called from among mankind, to fellowship with his Son Jesus Christ*, 1 Cor. xii. 12. Acts ii. 41, 47. Heb. iii. 1, 6. 1 Cor. i 9. xii. 6—28. Eph. ii. 19—22. Col. i. 13. 1 Pet. ii. 5, 9.- This society is, 1. HOLY, Heb. iii. 1. John iii. 3, 5. Eph. ii. 21. Ezek. xliii. 12. 1 Pet. ii. 9. 2. SPIRITUAL, formed by the Holy Ghost,—through, and for, ordinances and services of a spiritual nature,—and of men made spiritual,—blessed with spiritual blessings,—living on spiritual provision, and built up a spiritual house for God, Eph. ii. 22. 2 Cor. x. 3—5. John vi. 63. 1 Cor. ii. 15. x. 3. Eph. i. 3. John vi. 27—57. Rev. ii. 17. 1 Pet. ii. 5. 3. INDEPENDENT of all human wisdom and authority, Isa. xxxiii. 22. Matth. xxiii. 8—10. Psalm ii. 6. Heb. iii. 1. 4. ORDERLY, 1 Cor. xii. xiv. 5. VISIBLE, Matth. vii. 16, 20. xviii. 15—17.

REAL SAINTSHIP is not the distinguishing criterion of the members of this visible church on earth. None, indeed, without it, can honestly offer themselves to church-fellowship. But, for the mere want of it, they cannot be refused admission. 1. God alone can judge men's heart. Deceivers can counterfeit saintship, and often believers doubt of, or deny their real grace, 1 Sam. xvi. 7. Rev. ii. 23. 2. God himself admitted many whose hearts were unsanctified, as members of the Jewish church, Deut. xxix. 3, 4, 13: John vi. 70. 3. John Baptist and the Apostles, in order to baptism, required no more than *outward appearances* of faith and repentance, Matth. iii. 5, 7. Acts ii. 38. v. 1—10. viii. 13—23. 4. Many that were admitted members in the churches of Judea, Corinth, Philippi, Laodicea, Sardis, &c. were unregenerated, Acts v. 1—10. viii. 13—23. 1 Cor. v. xi. xv. Phil. iii. 18, 19. Rev. iii. 5, 15—17. 5. Christ compares the gospel church to a FLOOR, on which corn and chaff are mingled together;—to a NET, in which good and bad fishes are inclosed;—to a FIELD, in which tares grow up with the wheat, Matth. iii. 12. xiii. 24, 47.

But in order to their being received into church-fellowship, it is necessary that men *profess their faith in Christ and obedience to him, and be apparently holy.* 1. They must manifest no prevailing inclination to any kind of wickedness, 1 Cor. vi. 9—11. v. 11. 2 Tim. iii. 2—5. 2. They must have escaped the corruption that is in the world through lust, and manifest a readiness to receive Christian reproof from neighbours or church rulers, Matth. xviii. 15—17. Lev. xix. 17. Prov. xxix.

1. 3. Having received the knowledge of the truths of God revealed in his word, they must profess to esteem and love them, Eph. i. 1. Acts viii. 12. James ii. 14---26. 4. In consistency with the habitual tenor of their practice, they must make an open and judicious profession of the subjection of their conscience to the authority of Christ in the gospel, and of their readiness to yield obedience to all his institutions, Psalm xv. xxiv. 3---5. Isa. xxxiii. 15, 16. Heb. iii. 1. Tit. ii. 11---13. Rom. x. 9, 10. 2 Tim. ii. 19.

The END of such persons uniting in church-fellowship ought to be, 1. The maintaining and exhibiting a system of sound principles, 2 Tim. i. 13. iii. 14. 1 Tim. vi. 3, 4. Rom. vi. 17. 1 Cor. viii. 5, 6. Eph. iv. 21. Col. ii. 2. Rev. ii. 13---15, 20. iii. 2, 3, 10, 15, 16. Gal. i. 6. Prov. xxiii. 23. Heb. ii. 1. 2. The maintaining the ordinances of gospel-worship in their purity and simplicity, Deut. xii. 31, 32. Rom. xv. 6. 3. The impartial exercise of church-government and discipline, Heb. xii. 15. x. 24, 25. Gal. vi. 1. 2 Tim. ii. 24---26. iv. 2. Tit. iii. 10. 1 Cor. v. 1 Tim. v. 20---22. James iii. 17. ii. 1---10. Rev. ii. 4. The maintaining and promoting holiness in all manner of conversation, Phil. i. 27. ii. 15, 16. 2 Pet. iii. 11. Mic. vi. 8. 2 Cor. vii. 1, 10, 11. Tit. ii. 10---14. iii. 8, 14. Phil. iv. 8.

The embracement or profession of nothing but what is really divine truth, and tends to promote peace and holiness, and order, ought ever to be made a TERM of admission to church-fellowship, 2 Cor. xiii. 8. 1 Cor. xiii. 6. xiv. 32, 40. 1 John ii. 23. 2 John 9. Rom. xiv. 19. Heb. xii. 12--14. Psalm xciii. 5. Ezek. xliii. 10, 12.——The forming church-connections upon this ground consists in mutual, *judicious*, and *candid covenanting*, express or implicit, with or without an oath, to make a joint profession of the faith of the gospel, 1 Tim. vi. 3, 4. Jude 3, 20. Phil. i. 27. Col. ii. 2; and to walk together, each in his station, in the order of the gospel, as becomes saints, Rom. xv. 5—7. Eph. ii. 12—22. iv. 1. 2 Cor. viii. 5. Phil. i. 27. Col. i. 10, 11. This plainly appears, 1. From the inspired representations of the Church, as a BODY, Rom. xii. 4, 5; an HOUSE, Eph. ii. 19—22; a CITY, Heb. xii. 22; a KINGDOM, Col. i. 13; a NATION, 1 Pet. ii. 9. 2. An entering into church fellowship is called a *joining to the Lord*, and being *added to the church*, 1 Cor. vi. 17. Acts ii. 47. v. 3, 14; and continuance in it is called a *standing fast in one spirit*, and *striving together*, Phil. i. 27. 3. This connection is represented as a MARRIAGE, Isa. lvi. 4. lxii. 5. 4. None are subjects of church government, unless they be within her communion, 1 Cor. v. 12. 2 Cor. vi. 14—16. Mat. xi. 29. 5. Such covenanting is requisite to found that intimate fellowship which subsists in the church, Eph. iv. 1—6. 6. The general use of *Creeds* and *Confessions of faith*, in

OF CHURCH FELLOWSHIP. 553

all the Christian churches for 1700 years past, is a strong, though subordinate argument in its favour.

The union and communion of the Christian church is of *great importance*.—True believers being, by the inviolable bonds of the Spirit and faith, connected with Christ as their head, and with their fellow-saints as one with him, there can be *no schism in, or separation from* his invisible church, or mystical body, 1 Cor. xii. 25—27. Eph. v. 30. 1 John iii. 14.——The members of the catholic visible church on earth, which comprehends all those in the world who *profess the true religion, and their children*, are united in their acknowledgment of Christ as their *one Head*,—profession of the same *fundamental truths*,—and practice of the same *principal holy duties*, 1 Cor. i. 2. Eph. iv. 3—6. Luke ix. 49, 50.——Members of particular churches are united by a joint profession of adherence to the same faith and order of the gospel, in doctrine, worship, discipline, and government, Acts ii. 41. Eph. iv. 6. Acts iv. 32. Rom. xv. 5—7.

Christian fellowship consists in church-members' conjunction in faith and practice, and joint walking in all the ordinances of God's worship and service, for their mutual comfort and welfare in every thing pertaining to vital, powerful, and sincere religion. ——In order to maintain this Christian fellowship, I. Personal holiness and devotion, attended with purity and uprightness of conversation, must be carefully studied, Tit. ii. 10—14. iii. 8, 14. 2 Cor. i. 12. Acts xxiv. 16. 1 Tim. iv. 8. vi. 11, 12 2 Tim. ii. 22. Phil. iv. 8. II. As families regularly managed are a representation of churches,—religion, with respect to instruction, worship, discipline, order, and edifying example, ought to be carefully promoted in them. 1. The light of nature represents family religion as a just debt due to God,—and as the chief end of the erection of families, and of great advantage to all in them: And hence the heathens had their household gods. 2. God has expressly commanded such diligence in family religion, Col. iv. 2. 1 Pet. iii. 7. Eph. vi. 18. 3. It is recommended by the approved example of many saints, Gen. xviii. 18, 19. Job i. 5. Josh. xxiv. 15. 2 Sam. vi. 20. Rom. xvi. 5. 1 Cor. xvi. 19. Col. iv. 15. Acts x. 2. 4. Many are the advantages which attend it, and the evils which follow the neglect of it, Psalm xxx. ci. Jer. x. 25.—It is therefore mournful, that by their regular constitution of families through marriages not in the Lord, Deut. vii. 3. 2 Cor. vi. 14. 1 Cor. vii. 39; by the neglect or frequent omission of family religion at the first erection of families,—by sinful bashfulness in the heads of them,—by their want of zeal for God,—or by their immoderate inclination to company, or hurry of worldly business,—family worship, and its proper attendants, are so much neglected. III. Christians ought to join in *private societies* for prayer and spiritual conference. 1. The relations of saints to one another require this, Eph. ii. 19. Phil. ii. 25. Rev. vi. 11. Gal vi. 16. Rom. viii. 17. Matth. xxiii. 8, 10. 1 Cor. xii. 12. Rom. xii. 5. 2. God is much pleased with such social meetings, Mal. iii. 16, 17. 3. The Scripture much recommends them, Eccl. iv. 9—12. Gal. vi. 2. Matth. xviii. 19, 20. Col. iii. 16. Heb. iii. 13. x. 24, 25. 4. In Scripture there are approved examples of such meetings, Psalm lv. 13, 14. Song i. 7, 8. Dan. ii. 17, 18. Esth. iv. 16. John xx. 19, 26. Acts xvi. 13. 5. Such social meetings are of great use, if rightly managed,—for promoting the knowledge of divine truths, Col. iii. 16. Psalm cxi. 2;—and Christian sympathy, Gal. vi. 2. Rom. xii. 15;—for mutual encouragement and confirmation of one another in the way of holiness, Heb. x. 24, 25. Esth. iv. 15, 16. Heb. iii. 13;—for mutual communication of one another's gifts and experiences, 1 Pet. iv. 10, 11. Psalm lxvi. 16;—for promoting mutual watchfulness over, and admonishing one another, 1 Thess. v. 14. Heb. iii. 13;—for invigorating their mutual prayers and praises, Matth. xviii. 19, 20;—for recommending religion to others, Matth. v. 16. Phil. ii. 15, 16;—for anticipating the delightful fellowship of the saints in heaven, Heb. xii. 22;—and for shaming the wicked from their social meetings for carnal conversation, drunkenness, idle diversion, &c.

The *duties of church fellowship* are, 1. Earnest study to keep the unity of the Spirit in the bond of peace, Eph. iv. 3. Phil. ii. 2, 3. iii. 15, 16. 2. Bearing one another's burdens, Gal. vi. 1, 2. 3. Earnest and constant endeavouring to prevent all occasion of stumbling, 1 Cor. x. 32, 33. xi. 1. Rom. xiv. 13. 1 Pet. iii. 15, 16. John iii. 21. Phil. ii. 15, 16. James ii. 18. v. 16. Matth. xviii. 15—17. Lev. xix. 17. 4. Stedfast continuance in the faith and worship of the gospel with one another, Acts ii. 42. Phil. i. 27. iv. 1. 1 Cor. xi. 2. Heb. x. 25. Song i. 8. Prov. viii. 34. ix. 5. 5. Strict and conscientious fulfilment of relative duties, which mightily tends to promote order in the church, 1 Cor. vii. 24, 39. 1 Pet. iii. 7. 1 Tim. v. 1—3. Eph. v. 22, 25. vi. 1—9. 2 Sam. xxiii. 3. Rom. xiii. 1—7. Heb. xiii. 7, 16, 17. 1 Tim. v. 17. Acts vi. 1—3. Rom. xii. 6—16. Phil. ii. 3, 4.——These duties are inculcated upon us, 1. By the light of nature rightly understood. 2. By the word of God, Eph. iv. 1—6. Psalm cxxii. cxxxiii. Song i. 7—9. Phil. i. 27. Heb. x. 25. 3. Instead of being needless, selfish, or hurtful, as some pretend, such fellowship prevents much mischief, and produces much good. 1. It encourages particular Christians boldly to profess and practise their religion. 2. Hereby multitudes are instructed at once, and devotion is excited and prayers rendered more prevalent. 3. Every one being a pattern, guide, monitor, and reprover to another, apostacy and sinful stumbling are much prevented. 4. Christians thus mutually connected and acquainted, can better assist one another in duty. 5. It fits us for the heavenly fellowship of angels and saints. 6. Hereby we much glorify Christ, and God in him, as our God, John xvii. 11, 21, 23.

It is chiefly with respect to the union and communion of Christians in particular churches, that SCHISM in the church, or SEPARATION from it, takes place. SCHISM is properly an uncharitableness and alienation of affection among church members, who, in the main, continue in church fellowship with one another, 1 Cor. i. 10, 12. xi. 18. xii. 15. Or, it consists in church members carrying on their religious disputes with sinful eagerness and want of Christian affection to one another, 2 Cor. xii. 20. It proceeds from pride, self-love, jealousy, hatred, evil speaking, &c. James iv. 1. It ought to be prevented by self-denial, taking up our cross and exact following Christ, Matth. xvi. 24. Phil. ii. 1—5. 2 Cor. xiii. 11. Rom. xiv. 19. xv. 5, 6, 7. xvi. 17, 18. Acts iv. 32. Eph. iv. 31, 32. v. 1, 2. Matth. xviii. 21. Mark xi. 25, 26. Rom. xiv. 13. xv. 12. 1 Cor. xiii. 4—7. Gal. vi. 1, 2. Rom. vi. 3—5. 2 Tim. ii. 16, 17, 22, 23, 24. Tit. iii. 9. 1 John iv. 1.

There can be no SEPARATION from the Catholic church without abandoning the *fundamental principles and practices* of true religion, and so becoming no Christian at all. But *separation* from a particular church is a *schism* in the Catholic church, and is sinful, when members separate from the communion of a church, the prevailing part of which appear candidly to endeavour conformity to that system of faith and practice which Christ has, by his word, fixed as a standard of church fellowship, Jude 19. 2. When the prevailing part of a church make any addition to, or alteration of the scriptural system of faith, worship, discipline, or government, an essential condition of fellowship with them: In this case, the *prevailing party* are the *real separatists*, and they who are obliged to withdraw from their communion rather than sin, are the true adherents to the church, cleaving to her constitutional laws, and only forbearing fellowship with offending brethren in public and sealing ordinances, in so far as is consistent with an adherence unto the laws of Christ.

As an individual person, obstinate in notorious wickedness, ought to be *cast out* from church fellowship: So it is only when the prevailing part of a church become obstinate in notorious apostacy from attained reformation in doctrine, worship, discipline, or government, that a separation from a particular church can be lawful. The churches of Corinth,

Galatia, Ephesus, Pergamus, Thyatira, Sardis, Laodicea, &c. which were tainted with several corruptions, not having become *obstinate* therein, the Lord enjoins no separation from them, 1 Cor. i. iii. v. viii. x. xi. xiv. xv. Gal. i. 6. iii. 1. iv. 11. v. 7. Rev. ii. iii.—This *obstinacy* is manifested in a continued disregard of the faith, obedience, and fellowship of the gospel, which had been formerly embraced; and in an incorrigible refusing reproof dutifully offered, which is often attended with severity of edicts, or censures against the modest but faithful remonstrants.—Or, separation from a particular church becomes necessary when we cannot continue in her public fellowship without complying with something sinful as it is circumstantiated, or omitting some necessary duty.—In such a case, the sin of separation is only chargeable upon them that have occasioned the withdrawment, except in so far as the withdrawers mismanage the manner of their conduct.

Schism, properly so called, and separation on insufficient grounds, or forcing others from church fellowship, by making any term of it in any respect sinful, is an *horrible scandal and crime.* 1. Jesus Christ died, intercedes, and bestows his Spirit and grace, in order to promote the unity and peace of his church, Eph. i. 10. ii. 15, 16. Col. i. 20. John xiv. 16, 17, 27. xvii. 21, 23. Jer. xxxii. 39, 40. Ezek. xi. 19. xxxvii. 15—27. 2. God much commands and urges the promoting peace and unity in his church, Rom. xii. 9, 10, 16, 18. xv. 1—6. xiv. xvi. 17, 18. 1 Cor. i. 10. 2 Cor. xiii. 11. Eph. iv. 2, 3—6, 23, 31, 32. v. 1, 2, 30. Phil. i. 27. ii. 1—5. iv. 2. Col. ii. 2. iii. 12—15. 1 Thess. v. 13, 14. Psalm cxxii. cxxxiii. Zech. viii. 19. 3. Schism and sinful separation spring from base lusts, and are very dishonouring to God and hurtful to men, Prov. xiii. 10. xv. 1. x. 12. James iv. 1. iii. 15, 16. 1 Cor. iii. 1—4. Mark iii. 24. Rom. xv. 1, 2. xiv. 19. Jude 19. Isa. lxv. 5. lxvi. 5.

CHAP. II.

Of Church Power, *and the* Subjects *in which it resides, Head and Officers.*

THAT Jesus Christ is the *alone Head* of the church, is manifest, 1. From express declarations of Scripture, John xviii. 36. Col. i. 18. ii. 19. Eph. i. 22. iv. 15, 16. Isa. ix. 6, 7. Luke i. 32, 33. Mic. v. 2—5. Matth. xxviii. 18—20. John iii. 35. v. 22. Phil. ii. 9—11. 1 Cor. xv. 25, 26. Rev. iii. 7. 2. From the princely titles, respecting the church, which are ascribed to him in Scripture: as *Lord,* Acts ii. 36. x. 36. 1 Cor. viii. 6; *Lawgiver,* Isa. xxxiii. 22. James iv. 12; *King,* Psalm ii. 6. xxiv. 7, 9. lxxii. 1. Song i. 4, 12. iii. 9, 11. vii. 5; *Prince,* Ezek. xxxiv. 24. xlvi. 10; *Governor; Ruler,* Jer. xxx. 21. Mic. v. 2. Isa. ix. 6; *Judge,* Mic. v. 1. Isa. xxxiii. 22. ii. 4. xi. 3, 4; *Shepherd,* Isa. xl. 11. Ezek. xxxiv. 23. xxxvii. 24. Heb. xiii. 20. 1 Pet. v. 4. ii. 25; *Bishop* of souls, 1 Pet. ii. 25; *Master,* Mat. xxiii. 8, 10. John xx. 16; *Head,* Col. i. 18. Hos. i. 11; *Apostle, and High Priest of our profession,*—a *Son over his own house,* Heb. iii. 1—6. 3. To him alone are attributed the acts of supreme power in the church, as *enacting of laws* and ordinances, even to her principal officers, Gal. vi. 2. 1 Cor. ix. 21. Acts i. 2. Mark xvi. 15, 16. Matth. x. 7. xxviii. 19, 20. John i. 33. 1 Cor. iii. 5. Matth. xvi. 19. xviii. 18. v. vi. vii. He *qualifies* all her officers, and *prescribes* to them the manner of their call, as well as the matter and manner of their work, Eph. iv. 7, 8, 11. 1 Cor. xii. 28. John xx. 21—23. 2 Cor. x. 8. And *in his name* all her ordinances are dispensed, Mat. xviii. 20. xxviii. 19. Acts xix. 5. John xiv. 13, 14. Col. iii. 17. 1 Cor. v. 4. xi. 23.

It necessarily follows, that the Christian church must, in Christ's word, have a particular form of government appointed. 1. Christ as her Head is not an *author of confusion,* but of order and peace, 1 Cor. xiv. 33. 2. The Scripture, either by particular or general rules, instructs in every good word and work, and renders the men of God *perfect,* 2 Tim. iii. 15—17. 3. Christ, as her King, not only governs his church by the internal influence of his Spirit, but externally, by appointment of ambassadors, assemblies, laws, and ordinances, Eph. iv. 11. Matth. xviii. 20. xxviii. 18—20. 1 Cor. xi. 23—29. xii. 28. John xx. 21—23. 1 Cor. v. 4, 5. 4. The proper end of church power is not mere decency, but the spiritual edification of men,—the confirmation of them that stand; the recovery of them that are fallen; and the salvation of many, 1 Tim. v. 20. i. 20. 1 Cor. v. 5. Jude 22, 23. 5. The laws of Moses manifest that Christ appointed a particular form of government in the Jewish church. But in no respect could they need an express form more than the Christian church, or the Mediator's care of them be greater. Human inventions are now no more wise and holy; or Christ more in love with them than in the days of old, Heb. iii. 1—6. Matth. xv. 1—9. It is absurd to suppose, that after Christ gave himself for his church, he abandoned the forming and manner of governing it to the imaginations of men, which are only evil continually, Gen. vi. 5. viii. 21. 6. The account of the ordinances, officers, and procedure of the Christian church, which we have in Scripture, exhibits every thing necessary to a particular form of government. 7. By attempting to support from Scripture their own particular forms of church government, almost all professed Christians have manifested their belief that some particular form of it is appointed by Christ.

The whole power communicated by Jesus Christ, for the government of his church, is of a SPIRITUAL nature, corresponding to the nature of his kingdom, John xviii. 36. 1. The source and author of it is Christ, the *quickening Spirit*, Mat. xxviii. 18—20. xvi. 19. xviii. 15—20. John xx. 21—23. 1 Cor. xv. 45. 2. The rule of it is not the carnal statutes of men, but the spiritual oracles of the Holy Ghost, 1 Tim. iii. 14, 15. 2 Tim. iii. 15—17. Isa. viii. 20. 3. The matter of it is spiritual: The keys of order and government are not carnal, but *keys of the kingdom of heaven*, Mat. xvi. 19. The doctrine preached relates not to human science, but is spiritual and divine, 2 Pet. i. 19, 20, 21. 2 Tim. iii. 15—17. Tit. ii. 10. Heb. v. 12. vi. 5. Eph. i. 13. iv. 21. vi. 17. 2 Cor. x. 4, 5. 1 Cor. ii. 2. i. 23, 24. Rom. i. 16, 17. The sacraments confirm only spiritual privileges, Rom. iv. 11. vi. 4, 5. 1 Cor. x. 16, 17. xi. 23—29. The discipline is spiritual, reaching neither to body nor purse, but to soul and conscience, Mat. xvi. 19. xviii. 15—20. 1 Cor. v. 4, 5, 13. 2 Cor. ii. 1—7. John xx. 21—23. 4. The objects of this power are spiritual,—men considered not as of this world, but as spiritual members of Christ's mystical body; and their conduct not as *civil*, but as pleasing or displeasing to God in Christ, Gal. vi. 1. 1 Cor. ii. 15. v. 11—13. 2 Cor. xiii. 8. 5. The tendency of it is spiritual,—to gain sinful men to Jesus Christ, destroy their sin, and save their souls, Eph. iv. 11—13. 1 Cor. v. 5.

All church-power is bestowed by Christ for the advantage of all the members of his church, Eph. iv. 11—13. 2 Cor. xiii. 8, 10. x. 8. Acts xxvi. 17, 18. 1 Pet. iii. 21. Rom. iv. 11. 1 Cor. x. 16, 17. Mat. xviii. 15—17. 1 Tim. v. 20. i. 20. Tit. i. 13. 1 Cor. v. 5, 7, 13. 2 Cor. ii. 7; and every one is warranted to improve it to his spiritual advantage, and to try whether that which is dispensed to him be according to the word of God, 1 John iv. 1. Acts xvii. 11. 1 Thess. v. 21. But no power of office for dispensing public ordinances in doctrine, worship, government, or discipline, is lodged by Christ in the *community of the faithful*. 1. Not the Christian people, but particular rulers are, in Scripture, warranted to preach the gospel, administer sacraments, ordain officers, censure or absolve delinquents, Rom. x. 15. Heb. v. 4, 5. 1 Cor. iv. 1. Mark xvi. 15, 16. 1 Tim. iv. 14, 15. Acts xiv. 23. vi. 3, 6. Tit. i. 1 Tim. iii. v. 20. i. 20. Mat. xviii. 18. xvi. 19. 1 Cor. v. 4. 2 Cor. ii. 6. Tit. iii. 10. 2. The gifts necessary for the execution of ecclesiastical offices are no where promised, or represented as given to the community of believers, but only to church officers, Mat. xxviii. 19, 20. xvi. 19. John xx. 21—23. 1 Cor. xii. 7, 8. 1 Tim. iii. 2. 2 Tim. ii. 2. Eph. iv. 11, 12. 3. No where are the Christian people in general, but particular officers, marked by characters which denote *authority* :—Nay, they are represented as the *flock;* the *family;* the *body;* and *subjects;* and are commanded to honour, obey, and submit to their officers, who are represented as *elders, overseers, rulers, guides, governments,* Acts xx. 17, 28. 1 Thess. v. 12. 1 Tim. v. 17. Heb. xiii. 7, 17. 1 Cor. xii. 28. 4. Great absurdity and confusion would ensue, if even all adult believers should be admitted to govern the church. All would be rulers: who then would remain to be ruled? All would be stewards of the mysteries of God to themselves and others: who then could need the dispensation of them?—— Further, unless manhood, which is nothing spiritual, draw all church power to male believers, women, who are prohibited to speak in the church, must be allowed as much authority in government as men, 1 Cor. xiv. 3, 4. 1 Tim. ii. 12.————Moreover, What neglect of business, what disorder must ensue, if all adult believers be equal *triers* and *ordainers* of pastors, or *censurers* of subtle heretics? If elders or deacons offend, their spiritual pupils and children must be their judges and correctors. If a whole congregation fall into error and scandal, who can reclaim them?

Civil magistrates ought to encourage and protect the church: and, in so doing, may, in their station, act in a manner like to parents and masters in theirs. By a proper exercise of their *civil power,* and *for the good of the commonwealth,* they ought to prevent and remove persecution, profaneness, idolatry, superstition, heresy, and every other thing which tends to hinder the pure worship of God, Isa. xlix. 23. lx. 3, 10, 16. Rom. xiii. 3, 4. 1 Tim. ii. 2. 2 Chron. xv. 8, 16. xvii. 3—10. xxxi. 1. xxxiii. 15. 2 Kings xviii. 4. xxiii.—They ought to preserve for the church her fulness of spiritual power allowed her by Christ; and by providing places of instruction, and maintainance for pastors and other instructors, and by encouraging laws, and their own example, they ought to promote the administration of, and attendance upon the ordinances of the gospel, 2 Chron. xv. 9—16. xx. 7—9. xvii. xxix. xxx. xxxi. xxxiv. xxxv. Deut. xvii. 18—20. 1 Chron. xxii.—xxv. Neh. xiii. 10—14.—— As heads of families ought to promote sound principles and holy practices in their families,—magistrates ought to promote and establish the reformation of doctrine, worship, discipline, and government of the church in their dominions, as a mean of promoting their happiness. And for this end, may call synods of church officers for settling and governing her affairs according to the word of God, Exod. xxxii. Josh. xxiii. xxiv. 2 Kings

xviii. 4—7. xii. xxii. xxiii. 2 Chron. xv. xvii. xxxiv. xxxv. 1 Sam. vii. 6. 2 Chron. xx. 3. Jonah iii. 7. Ezra viii. 21.—By their civil authority, they ought to enforce her laws or constitutions which are warranted by the word of God; as observing them tends to promote the welfare of the nation, and ought to excite her rulers and members to an external performance of their duty by every method agreeable to the gospel; and ought to punish open violations of God's law, as crimes which dishohour him, whose deputies they are, and bring a curse on the commonwealth, 2 Chron. xv. xxx. xxxi. xxxiv. xxxv. Neh. xiii. Dan. iii. 28, 29. vi. 26, 27. Deut. xxi. 18—21. Gen. ix. 6. Num. xxxv. 30—32. xv. 30—36. Job xxxi. 9, 11. Lev. xx. 11—25. Exod. xxii. 1—15. Deut. xix. 16. xiii. 1—6. xvii. 1—8. Lev. xvii. 2, 8. 2 Chron. xv. 13, 16. Job xxxi. 26, 27, 28. Lev. xxiv. 15, 16. Rom. xiii. 3, 4. 1 Pet. ii. 13, 14. Heb. x. 28.

OBJEC. I. " In their care about religion they must not act " *as magistrates*, but as Christians." ANSW. Why separate their Christianity from their power? Are not all parents and masters, that are Christians, obliged by the law of God to act *as Christians* in these stations? Why may not magistrates also act as Christians in the execution of their office? In neither of these cases does Christianity add to men's power, but qualifies them for the better exercise of the power which they have, on another foundation.

OBJEC. II. " The above proofs are generally taken from " Jewish magistrates, who were ecclesiastical rulers, and their " nation an ecclesiastical nation." ANSW. Notwithstanding the Jewish magistrates were deputies under God, who was the Supreme King of their nation; yet it never can be proved that they were *church rulers*, till it be demonstrated that proselytes of the covenant and of the gate had equal privileges with Jews in both church and state; that every thing which excluded from church fellowship, excluded also from civil privileges; that fining, burning, stoning, &c. of malefactors were ordinances of Christ, for worship of God, as well as excommunications; and that there is no difference between the *judicial* and *ceremonial* laws.

OBJEC. III. " If magistrates have such power about religion, " they ought, by fines, imprisonment, death, or the like, to force " their subjects to whatever themselves think to be the *true re-* " *ligion;* and so bereave them of their natural liberties, in " which they are bound to protect them." ANSW. 1. Parents and masters can do much to promote true religion in their families, without either starving or hurtfully beating any under their charge. 2. Not the conscience of either magistrates or subjects, but the law of God, is the standard of duty to them. 3. If magistrates act according to the law of God, they can never attempt to propagate the true religion by methods which God never enjoined for that end, or which tend to disparage religion. 4. As all liberty, civil as well as sacred, proceeds from God himself, it can never be a protection of men in idolatry, blasphemy, notorious heresy, or profanation of the Sabbath, which render them open and insolent, dishonourers of, and rebels against God, and plagues to the nation;—any more than protect them in treason, murder, or theft.

But Christ has communicated *no spiritual power* to civil magistrates. 1. No where doth he appear to bestow any such power on magistrates, but on his apostles and their successors, as officers in the church, Mat. xvi. 19. xviii. 18. xxviii. 18—20. John xx. 21—23. Nor, in his establishment of his gospel-church, could he bestow any such power on magistrates, as both Jewish and Heathen were open enemies to him, and the civil power of the former just expiring. 2. For about 300 years the whole power of the Christian church was exercised, while the magistrates of those countries continued heathens and bloody persecutors. The word was preached; the sacraments dispensed; the unruly admonished; the scandalous rebuked; the obstinate excommunicated; the penitent absolved; elders and deacons ordained; synods assembled; and ecclesiastical decrees enacted, Acts iv. 2. 1 Tim. iii. 16. Acts xx. 7. 1 Cor. xi. 17—29. Acts ii. 41, 42. viii. 12. xiii. 1—3. xiv. 23. 1 Tim. iv. 14. Tit. i. 5. Acts vi. 1—6. 1 Tim. v. 20. i. 20. 1 Cor. v. 4, 5. 2 Cor. ii. 6—8. Acts xv. xvi. 4. 3. No where do magistrates appear in the list of church-officers recorded in Scripture. Nay, if *children, women, or heathens*, how could they be capable of ruling the Christian church? Rom. xii. 6—8. 1 Cor. xii. 28. Eph. iv. 11, 12. 1 Cor. xiv. 34. Eph. ii. 12. 4. Church-government is altogether independent on civil government. Church-officers are not set up by the state, but by the Lord, Acts xx. 28. 1 Cor. iv. 1, 2. xii. 28. 1 Thess. v. 12. Eph. iv. 11. They preach the gospel, dispense sacraments, inflict or absolve from spiritual censures, which no magistrates have power to do, Rom. x. 15. 2 Chron. xxvi. 18, 19. They may execute their office, not only without the consent, but contrary to the command of civil magistrates, Acts iv. 19. v. 29. 1 Cor. v. 4, 5. Mat. xviii. 17, 18. Tit. iii. 10. Rev. ii. iii. None can lawfully appeal from an ecclesiastical decision of a spiritual cause to the civil magistrate, Mat. ii. 7. Deut. xvii. 8—10. 1 Cor. xiv. 32. Acts xiv. xvi. 4. Even kings, if disorderly church-members, are to be censured by church-rulers, 2 Thess. iii. 6. Mat. xviii. 15—18. 5. Civil and ecclesiastical power exceedingly differ in many respects: 1. In their proper *origin*. In its general nature civil government flows from God as Creator, Preserver, and King of nations; and, excepting the Jewish theocracy, is, in its particular form, an *ordinance of men*, Rom. xiii. 1—4. 1 Pet. ii. 14. Jer. xxvii. 12. Luke xii. 13, 14. All church power is derived from Christ as mediatorial head of the church, Mat. xvi. 19. xxviii. 18—20. Eph. iv. 11, 12. 1 Cor. xii. 28. 2. In the *formal nature of their object*. The church is a spiritual society, and body and spouse of Christ. The state, which is the object of the magistrate's power, is a carnal and earthly society, Eph. i. 22. v. 25. iv. 8—11. 1 Cor. xii. 28. Acts vi. 3, 4. xiii. 1—4. xiv. 23. 1 Tim. iv. 14. 1 Cor. iv. 12. v. 20. John xviii. 36. Jer. xxix. 7. xxvii. 7, 17. 3. In the *matter* in which they are exercised. Civil power is worldly, and exercised in making and executing civil laws, enforced with rewards and punishments of a *worldly* nature. Church-power is *spiritual*, and exercised in preaching the gospel, dispensing sacraments, and inflicting medicinal censures for the benefit of souls, 2 Cor. x. 4, 5, 8. Heb. xiii. 17. 2 Thess. ii. 3, 4. 3 John 9, 10. 1 Tim. iii. 5. 1 Cor. xiv. 5, 34. xii. 28. v. 13. 4. In the *manner* of exercising them. In exercising civil power, men may make laws, —judge according to human laws,—may act by delegates, or one by himself alone;—must enforce obedience with civil rewards or punishments, from which last repentance is not sufficient to exempt a criminal. In exercising church power we must make no laws, but judge every thing by the word of God. We must always act in the name of Christ: We cannot delegate our power to any other, nor one person exercise it by himself, in acts of government; nor enforce obedience by any thing but what is of a spiritual nature, Mat. xxviii. 18—20. xviii. 17. Acts xxvi. 17, 18. 1 Cor. v. 4, 5. 5. In their *immediate end*. Magistracy is to be executed for promoting the outward welfare of men as members of the commonwealth, Rom. xiii. 1—4. 1 Tim. ii. 1, 2. Church-power must be exercised for promoting the spiritual salvation of men as united to Christ, and members of his church, Eph. iv. 12. Acts xxvi. 17, 18. 1 Tim. iv. 16.

CHRIST has not lodged church-power in the hands of *diocesan bishops*, that bear rule over preaching presbyters. 1. The Scriptures expressly forbid all *lordly* dominion in the church, 3 John 9. 1 Pet. v. 3. Luke xxii. 25, 26. Matth. xx. 25, 26. Not *tyrannical*, but *lordly* dominion, however mild, is here prohibited. The Greek word expressing it is used by the SEVENTY in Gen. i. 28. Psalm lxxii. 8. cx. 2, to express dominion, which none dare pretend to be *tyrannical*.—How absurd to imagine, that the mother of James and John asked a *tyrannical* power for her sons from Christ! Or that he who acknowledged Cæsar's authority, Matth. xxii. 21, would represent all heathen rulers as *tyrants!* 2. Bishops and Presbyters are represented as the very same officers in Scripture. Several *bishops* or *overseers* were at Ephesus, all of whom are called *elders* or *presbyters*,

Acts xx. 17, 28. Several bishops governed the church in Philippi, no great city, having no inferior officers but deacons, Phil. i. 1. 1 Tim. iii. 3. The reason why *elders* or *presbyters* must be of good report is, that *bishops* must be blameless; which marks them the same, Tit. i. 5, 6. Elders must feed God's flock EPISCOPOUNTES, *acting the part of bishops over them*, 1 Pet. v. 2, 3. Judas had a *bishopric*, Acts i. 20. Peter and John, not inferior apostles, were *presbyters*, 1 Pet. v. 1. 2 John i. 3. The power of *ordaining pastors*, which diocesans claim for their distinguishing prerogative, is, by the Scripture, placed in no standing church-officer, but in the presbytery, or *meeting of elders*. Nay, where elders were ordained, even the apostles did not by themselves ordain pastors, but concurred as members of the presbytery, 2 Tim. i. 6. 1 Tim. iv. 14.

To anticipate objections, it must be observed, 1. That the TWELVE and the SEVENTY disciples whom Christ, before his death, appointed to preach the gospel, had all of them *equal* power and authority, and but a *temporary* commission, Mat. x. Luke x. 1—21. 2. The apostleship for life bestowed on several after his resurrection, was an extraordinary office, in which they had no successors. 3. That neither Timothy nor Titus were fixed diocesans, but *itinerant* evangelists, who either travelled with the apostles, or were sent by them to supply their place, 1 Thess. i. 1. 2 Thess. i. 1. Rom. xvi. 21. Heb. xiii. 23. Col. i. 1. Phil. ii. 19. 2 Cor. i. 1. 1 Cor. iv. 17. xvi. 10. 2 Cor. i. 19. iii. 2. 1 Tim. i. 3. 2 Tim. iv. 9, 10, 12. Gal. ii. 3. 2 Cor. ii. 13. vii. 6, 7. viii. 16, 23. xii. 18. Tit. iii. 12. 4. That the *angels* of the Asian churches were not diocesan bishops, but their pastors in general; and hence one angel is sometimes addressed as *several* persons, Rev. ii. 10, 24. 5. That for the first three hundred years of the Christian church, such as moderated in their courts, or were more aged, or had more noted congregations, were often called *bishops:* and, in the last case, had other ordained preachers to assist them, and to officiate in case of their imprisonment or death. But we have no decisive proof of any diocesan lords. Nor do any, except the principal pastors of Rome, seem to have struggled hard for such a pre-eminence. 6. That no Protestant church, except in England and Ireland, is governed by diocesan bishops, properly so called, though indeed the almost nominal ones of Sweden and Denmark would gladly be such. 7. That almost all the noted primitive doctors of the Christian church grant that diocesan Episcopacy has no foundation in Scripture. 8. Scarcely one argument hath ever been produced for the support of diocesan Episcopacy, but hath been effectually overturned by some other learned prelatist; nor indeed can they combat the Popish government without destroying their own. 9. Diocesan bishops, as such, have never been any honour to the church, or centre of unity: but have often been introducers and supporters of Popish abominations.

If Christ has not lodged church-power in the *community of the faithful*, or in *magistrates*, or in *diocesan bishops*, he must have placed it in *officers of his own appointment*, Matth. xvi. 19. xviii. 18—20. 2 Cor. x. 8. Heb. xiii. 7, 17. 1 Tim. v. 17. 1 Thess. v. 12.—Some of these were EXTRAORDINARY, appointed for the first erection of the gospel-church. 1. APOSTLES, who had an immediate commission from Christ equally extended to all nations, as occasions offered,—were privileged with an infallibility in their doctrine;—had a constant power of working miracles as directed by God, and of speaking languages which they had never learned;—had power to confer the miraculous influences of the Holy Ghost on others, and of sending forth evangelists, or by themselves ordaining presbyters and deacons, Mark xvi. 15—20. Acts i.—xxi. 2. EVANGELISTS, who assisted the apostles in planting or watering churches, and, by their direction, ordained presbyters and deacons, and erected judicatories in infant churches. 3. PROPHETS, who explained dark passages of Scripture, and sometimes foretold future events, 1 Cor. xiv. 29—32. Acts xi. 28. xxi. 10, 11.

Others of these officers were ORDINARY, which are divided into BISHOPS, OVERSEERS or ELDERS, and DEACONS. Bishops or elders are subdivided into *pastors,* or *elders that labour in word and doctrine,* and *elders* that only *rule well.* Their name BISHOP or OVERSEER marks their authority over and inspection of others. PRESBYTER or ELDER denotes their gravity, prudence, and experience, and their being but subordinate rulers under Christ to declare and execute his laws. Thus we have three distinct kinds of church-officers, PASTORS, RULING ELDERS, and DEACONS. The office of the first includes the power of the two latter; and that of the second the power of the last, but not the distinguishing power of the first; and the office of deacons includes no power peculiar to either of the two preceding offices.

I. The *pastoral office* is a spiritual relation to the Christian church, empowering men to preach the gospel, dispense the sacraments, and concur in acts of governing church-members. Its divine institution is evident. 1. God furnishes and appoints *pastors, teachers, bishops* or *overseers,* in the church, 1 Cor. xii. 28. Eph. iv. 11. Acts xx. 28. Rom. xii. 6—8. 2. The qualifications of such officers are *divinely* prescribed, 1 Tim. iii. 1—8. v. 21, 22. Tit. i. 5—9. 3. Such characters are, by the Holy Ghost, ascribed to them, as import authority and call to their work, as *pastors, teachers, rulers, stewards, preachers, heralds, ambassadors, bishops,* Eph. iv. 11. 1 Cor. xii. 28. 1 Tim. v. 17.

1 Cor. iv. 1, 2. Luke xii. 42. Rom. x. 15. 2 Cor. v. 19, 20. Acts xx. 28. 1 Pet. v. 2, 3. Rev. i. 20. 1 Thess. v. 12. Col. i. 7. Eph. vi. 21. Matth. ix. 38. 4. The manner of their entrance on their office, by the call of the church and ordination of the presbytery, is divinely prescribed, Acts i. 15—26. xiv. 23. 1 Tim. iv. 14. 5. The work which belongs to this office is divinely prescribed, 1 Pet. v. 2, 3. 1 Tim. iv. 14—16. Acts vi. 2, 4. 2 Tim. iv. 2. ii. 25, 26. 2 Cor. xii. 15. 1 Cor. xiv. 9, 16, 17. Ezek. xxxiv. 2, 4. Heb. xiii. 17. Acts xxvi. 17, 18. Mat. xxviii. 19, 20. 1 Cor. xi. 23—26. 2 Tim. ii. 2. 1 Cor. v. 4, 13. Tit. iii. 10. 2 Cor. ii. 6, 7. 6. People's behaviour towards ministers is prescribed by God, 1 Thess. v. 12, 13. 1 Tim. v. 17. Heb. xiii. 7, 17. Gal. vi. 6. 1 Cor. ix. 7—19. 2 Thess. iii. 1. 7. God has promised them encouragement in, and a reward of their work, 2 Cor. iii. 3, 5, 6. Rev. ii. 1. Matth. xxviii. 20. xvi. 19. John xx. 23. Matth. x. 40—42. Luke x. 16. John xiii. 20. 2 Tim. iv. 7, 8.

The office of the gospel ministry is PERPETUAL, continuing till the end of the world. 1. God has provided nothing to supply its place: Nor can any bestowal of the Holy Ghost exclude it, any more than it did in the apostolic age, Acts i.—xxi. xxvi. 17, 18. Heb. xi. 40. 2. The necessity of it is *perpetual.* Men are in every age ignorant and corrupt; Satan active; heresy and error raging, or ready to spring up; gospel mysteries much unknown; the conversion of sinners, edification of saints, and silencing of gainsayers, still necessary, 1 Tim. iv. 1—3. 2 Tim. iii. 1—7. 2 Thess. ii. 3—12. Acts xxvi. 17, 18. Eph. iv. 12—15. Tit. i. 11. 3. The removal of the gospel ministry is represented as an heavy judgment, which it could not be any more than the abolishing the Jewish ceremonies, unless the perpetual continuance of it were necessary, Rev. ii. 5. 4. God has wonderfully preserved a gospel ministry amidst all the destructive rage and persecution of heathens and antichristians, Rev. vi. xi. xii. xiv. 5. The divine ordinances which are connected with a gospel ministry, are appointed to continue till the end of the world, Eph. iv. 11—13. Mat. xxviii. 19, 20. 1 Cor. xi. 26. 1 Tim. vi. 14.

It is requisite to a man's being a minister of the gospel, that he be divinely qualified with, 1. *Proper abilities,* rendering him apt to teach, which includes rational and experimental knowledge of divine truths, and being able to explain and inculcate them in a manner calculated to enlighten the minds, impress the consciences, and excite the affections of his hearers, Eph. iv. 7—11. 1 Cor. ix. 7. iii. 8. vi. 19, 20. 1 Tim. iii. 2. 1 Cor. xii. 8. Col. iv. 3, 4. 1 Cor. iv. 19. ii. 2, 4, 6, 7, 13. 2 Cor. ii. 14. iv. 2, 5. 2 Tim. ii. 15. Isa. l. 4. xlix. 1, 2. lviii. 1. Mic. iii. 8. 1 Cor. xiv. 24, 25. Acts xxiv. 25. 2. A blameless, holy, and edifying conversation, 1 Tim. iii. 1—8. 2 Tim. ii. 2, 21, 22. Tit. i. 5—9. 3. Distinguished zeal for advancing the glory of God in Christ, and tender compassion to the souls of men, Rev. iii. 19. Psalm lxix. 9. cxix. 139. Gal. iv. 18, 19. 2 Cor. xii. 14, 15. 1 Thess. ii. 8. 1 Pet. v. 2. Jude 22.

All heads of families, teachers of youth, and even neighbours, ought, in a private manner, to instruct those under their charge, in the truths of the gospel. But none, without being *regularly called* to it, however well qualified, ought to exercise any part of the ministerial office. 1. The Scripture plainly distinguishes between *gifts* for, and a *mission* to that office, John xx. 21, 23. Isa. vi. 6, 7, 9. 2. It most expressly declares a call absolutely necessary to render one a public teacher, Rom. x. 15. Heb. v. 4, 6. Jer. xxiii. 21, 32. 3. The character of *preachers, heralds, ambassadors, stewards, watchmen, angels, messengers,* &c. necessarily import a divine call, 1 Cor. ix. 17. 2 Cor. v. 20. 1 Cor. iv. 1, 2. Heb. xiii. 17. Rev. i. 20. 4. Rules prescribed for the qualifications, election, and ordination of gospel ministers, are declared binding until the second coming of Christ, 1 Tim. iii. 1—8. v. 21, 22. vi. 13. 5. God severely punished Korah, Saul, Uzza, Uzziah, and the sons of Sceva, for their intermeddling with the work of the sacred office, Num. xvi. 3—11, 32—38, 40. 1 Sam. xiii. 8—14. 1 Chron. xiii. 9, 10. 2 Chron. xxvi. 16—18. Acts xix. 13—16. 6. To rush into the ministerial office without a proper call, is inconsistent with a proper impression of the awful nature of the work of it, 2 Cor. iii. 5, 6. ii. 16. Ezek. iii. 17—21. xxxiii. 1—20. Rom. i. 1. Gal. i. 15, 16. John iii. 27, 28. Heb. xiii. 17. v. 4, 5; and introduces wild disorder and error, Gal. ii. 5. 7. Christ's manifold connection with this office,— in his being the author of it, Eph. iv. 11, 12; his suspending much of the order and edification of his church on it, Acts xx. 28. 1 Pet. v. 1—3; his including such power and authority in it, Matth. xvi. 19. xviii. 18; his committing such an important trust to ministers, Col. iv. 17. 1 Tim. vi. 20; his enjoining his people to honour and obey them, 1 Tim. v. 17. Heb. xiii. 7, 17; and his promising present assistance in, and future gracious rewards to their faithful discharge of their work,— manifests the necessity of a divine and regular call to it, Mat. xxviii. 20. 1 Pet. v. 4.

The call of an ordinary pastor to his work ought to be *twofold.* 1. A *divine call,* which consists in God's inwardly inclining his heart to it in an humble manner, and by regular means; and which is often attended by a tract of providences shutting him up to it, exclusive of any other. 2 An *ecclesiastical call,* which consists in the election of the Christian people to whom he is to minister, and the ordination of the presbytery. That adult Christians have a right from Christ to choose their own pastors is evident: 1. The church being a voluntary society, none imposed upon her members by men can be related to them as their pastor. 2. None can so well judge what gifts are best suited to their spiritual edification as Christians themselves. 3. If men may choose their servants or physicians, why hinder Christians from choosing the servants and subordinate physicians of their souls? 4. The Scripture allows the election of pastors in ordinary cases to adult Christians, and to none else, Acts i. 15---26. vi. 1—6. xiv. 23. 5. Christ requires his people to *try* the spirits, which supposes their ability to do so, and their power to choose such only as they find most proper to edify their souls, and to refuse others, 1 John iv. 1. 6. The introduction of ministers into their office by *patronage*, of whatever form, has its origin from *Popery;* tends to establish a tyranny over men's conscience, whom Christ has made free;—to fill pulpits with naughty, impious, and indolent clergymen;—encourages simony, sacrilege, and perjury;—and effectually gives Christ the lie, modelling his kingdom after the form of those of this world, Ezek. xxxiv. 2---4. Isa. lvi. 9---12. John xviii. 36.---The ordination of candidates chosen for the ministerial office is not the work of the people, but of the presbytery, 1 Tim. i. 14. 2 Tim. i. 6. ii. 2. Acts xiii. 1---3. xiv. 23. 1 Tim. v. 21, 22.

The work of a pastor when ordained, is, 1. With much inward compassion and zeal for the welfare of their hearers' souls, to feed them with the truths of Christ according to their different necessities, both publicly and privately, whether in the form of sermons, lectures, catechizing, or exhortation, when sick, &c. 1 Pet. v. 3. 2 Cor. v. 11. 1 Cor. ix. 16. Phil. i. 17, 24, 25. 1 Tim. vi. 20. iii. 15. iv. 15, 16. 2 Tim. iv. 2. Gal. vi. 6. Heb. v. 11, 13. 1 Cor. iii. 1. Acts xx. 20, 21, 27, 28, 31, 35. xxvi. 17, 18. Ezek. xxxiv. 1—16. iii. 17- 21. xxxiii. 1—20. Col. i. 28, 29. Isa. xl. 11. l. 4. 1 Thess. ii. 2—12. v. 12. James v. 14. 2 Cor. xi. 28, 29. 2. To administer the sacraments in a proper manner to proper persons, Matth. xxviii. 19, 20. vii. 6. 1 Cor. xi. 23—29. 3. To rule over their people with impartiality, zeal, meekness, and prudence, censuring offenders, and absolving penitents, Heb. xiii. 17. 1 Tim. v. 20, 21. i. 20. Tit. iii. 10, 11. Rev. ii. 2, 14, 20. 1 Cor. v. 4, 5. 2 Cor. ii. 6, 7. 4. To care and provide for the poor, Gal. ii. 9, 10. 1 Tim. vi. 17, 18. 2 Cor. viii. ix. 5. To give himself habitually to *effectual fervent prayer* for the church of Christ in general, and especially for those of his particular charge, Acts vi. 2, 4. Eph. iii 14---19. i. 15---20. Gal. iv. 19. Col. iv. 12. 6. To exemplify his doctrines and exhortations in an eminently meek, humble, holy, and edifying conversation, 1 Thess. ii. 10. 1 Tim. iv. 7, 8, 12, 16. vi. 11, 12. 2 Tim. ii. 1, 15, 16, 21, 22, 23. iii. 14. Tit. i. 7—9. ii. 7, 8. Matth. v. 16—48.

II. It is plain from Scripture declarations, that Christ has appointed *rulers* in his church that are *not appointed to preach the gospel*, Rom. xii. 7, 8. Heb. xiii. 7, 17. Different gifts qualify men for teaching and for ruling, Eph. iv. 7. Such rulers are necessary for the assistance of pastors, Gal. ii. 9, 10. Acts vi. 2—4. Exod. xviii. 17—23.—The complete form of every Christian congregation requires several elders, Acts xx. 17—38. xiv. 23. Christian churches have courts similar to those Jewish ones which had the power of excommunication; and which consisted of *elders* ruling as representatives of the congregation, Matth. xviii. 15—17. Num. xxxv. 24. Deut. xix. 12. Josh. xx. 4, 6. Exod. xii. 3, 21; by comparing of which texts we find that congregation denotes rulers of it. The SEVENTY use the very word ECCLESIA, which is translated *church* in Matth. xxviii. 17.—But the divine appointment of *ruling elders* is still more evident, 1. From Rom. xii. 5—8, where we find in the *one body* of the gospel church PROPHESYING, which includes *teaching* and *exhortation*, which may correspond with teachers and pastors, Eph. iv. 11; and MINISTRY, answerable to the deacon that *gives* out the church's charity, and *shews mercy* in visiting the sick and imprisoned,—and to the elder *that rules* with diligence. Here *different gifts*, given to profit withal, infer different offices, Eph. iv. 7—11. 1 Cor. xii. 7, 8. Here is one *that rules* characterized by different gifts, and different work. 2. From 1 Cor. xii. 28, where we find GOVERNMENTS, that is, *governors,* even as MIRACLES denote workers of miracles,—set by God *in the* Christian *church*. While they are represented as different from HELPS or deacons, Acts vi. 1—6, their designation of *governments* marks that their office is chiefly, if not solely, executed in *ruling*. It much more properly denotes them *rulers* of church members, than mere managers of church money.—It is further observable, that God has set SOME, not ALL, *governments* or *governors* in the church. From 1 Tim. v. 17, where some *elders* are represented as worthy of double honour, though they do no more than *rule well*, while others are represented as more worthy of double honour, because they not only *rule well*, but also *labour in word and doctrine*.—All which elders belong to the church, compare chap. i, 19. iv. 14. iii. 15.—KOPIONTES, *labouring*, doth not denote uncommon diligence, but the common duty of all gospel ministers, 1 Cor. iii. 8. 1 Thess. v. 12. John iv. 38.—MALISTA, *especially*,—always in the New Testament distinguishes persons or things of the same general class, one from another, Acts xx. 38. xxiii. 26. xxvi. 3. Gal.

vi. 10. Phil. iv. 22. 1 Tim. iv. 10. v. 8. 2 Tim. iv. 13. Tit. i. 10. Philem. 16. 2 Pet. ii. 10.——Not only do most of the chief Fathers in the Christian church declare for *ruling elders;* but even Papists and Episcopalians, who inveigh against them, have a shadow of them in their chancellors, officials, commissaries, wardens: and bishops having *no care of souls,* are *lay elders* properly so called.—Independents also manage most of their congregational affairs by a few of their number.

The necessary qualifications of ruling elders are, 1. True piety, 1 Tim. iv. 12. 2 Tim. ii. 21, 22. 2. Capacity for judging causes, 1 Chron. xii. 32. Deut. i. 13. 1 Kings iii. 5—15. Isa. xi. 2—5. Num. xi. 16, 17. 3. Wisdom, prudence, and uprightness of conduct, connected with a good report from others, 1 Tim. iii. 1—8. Psalm ci. 2—8.—Their ordination ought to be transacted in much the same manner as that of *teaching elders* or pastors.—Their duty in general is to *rule well;* particularly, 1. In judging the agreeableness of doctrines to the word of God,—judicially declaring what seems good to the Holy Ghost and to them, in controverted points of principle or practice, Acts xv. 28, 29. xvi. 4. Rev. ii. 2. Acts xx. 17—31. 2. In admitting persons to church-fellowship on proper qualifications, Matth. xvi. 19. 3. In directing or encouraging church-members to observe Christ's laws, for the honour of God and their own mutual edification, Heb. xiii. 7, 17. 4. In taking care that all the ordinances of the gospel be duly preserved in their purity and perfection, Song i. 7, 8. 5. In carefully watching over the moral behaviour of church-members,—instructing, admonishing, exhorting, comforting, or rebuking them, as they find cause, Heb. xiii. 17. 6. In visiting the sick in body, or distressed in mind, Jam. v. 14. 7. In making provision for the poor, or other expences necessary for promoting the *spiritual welfare* of the congregation, Acts xi. 27—30. 8. In judging the case of offenders and penitents, in order to censure the former, and absolve the latter, Matth. xviii. 15—18. xvi. 19. 9. In regulating diets of fasting, thanksgiving, the Lord's Supper, &c. 1 Cor. xiv. 26, 40.

III. The divine appointment of DEACONS in the Christian church is beyond dispute, Acts vi. 1—6. 1 Tim. iii. 8—11. Rom. xii. 8. 1 Cor. xii. 28. Phil. i. 1.—They ought to be men of *honest report, full of the Holy Ghost,* and *of wisdom,* 1 Tim. iii. 8—10. Acts vi. 3.—Their election and ordination ought not, in its manner, to differ from that of elders, Acts vi. 1—6.—Their work is to manage the temporal affairs of the congregation relative to the table of the poor, the table of ministers, and the table of the Lord, Acts vi. 2. 1 Cor. xii. 28. No other work is annexed to their office in Scripture. Hence, though some of the first *seven deacons,* becoming evangelists, might preach and administer sacraments, yet none, *as deacons*, have any right to do so.

There is no hint in Scripture, that the offices of RULING ELDER and DEACON were designed to be *temporary*. Both of them were appointed on moral grounds and necessities respecting every church and period. The rules concerning them both are to be observed till the end of the world, 1 Tim. vi. 13, 14 No congregation can therefore answer to Jesus Christ for *dropping* of deacons, any more than for the *dropping* of ruling elders.

CHAP. III.

Of the SOCIAL EXERCISE *of Church Power in Sessions, Presbyteries, and Synods.*

IN preaching the gospel, and administering the sacraments, ministers exercise their power as single persons. But all jurisdiction relative to admission of members, ordination of officers, censure of offenders, or absolution of penitents, is to be exercised socially, in courts constituted of two or more rulers, in the name of Jesus Christ,—viz. in *Sessions, Presbyteries,* and *Synods.*

I. SESSIONS are church courts constituted of the rulers of a particular congregation. Their appointment by Christ is evident. 1. The light of nature teaches us to decide smaller matters by inferior courts, Exod. xviii. 17—23. 2. The Scripture approves of judging lesser matters by inferior courts, Exod. xviii. 17—26. Matth. v. 22. xviii. 17—20. 3. In the *form of process* against scandals, prescribed by Christ, there is a plain allusion to the courts of the Jewish synagogues or congregational assemblies, Matth. xviii. 15—18. 4. In conformity to the Jewish synagogues, every Christian congregation hath several elders allotted to it by God's warrant, Mark v. 35—38. Luke viii. 41. xiii. 14. John ix. 22. Acts xiii. 15. xviii. 8, 17. xiv. 23. Tit. i. 5. 5. Necessity requires such courts; it being impossible for every thing proper to be judged in congregations, to be got carried to presbyteries and synods.—It belongs to sessions to inquire into the spiritual state or Christian characters of members of the congregation; to admit members to, or suspend them from sealing ordinances; to admonish and rebuke offenders, or absolve them when penitent.

II. PRESBYTERIES are church-courts constituted of different pastors, and ruling elders from different congregations.—Such courts are warranted by Christ. 1. Many affairs of the church, as trial, and ordination of pastors; judging subtle heretics; composing differences in sessions, or between different congregations, require such courts, Rom. xiv. 19. 1 Cor. xiv. 26, 40. 2. The strict connection of Christians in one mystical body of Christ, requires that unity of fellowship among them should be carried as far as possible, Rom. xii. 5. Eph. iv. 3—6. 1 Cor. xii. 12, 27. 4. There is an express mention of a *presbytery* at the ordination of Timothy, 1 Tim. iv. 14. 5. The Scripture exhibits several patterns of one presbytery governing several particular congregations of Christians. 1. At Jerusalem *three thousand* were added to one hundred and twenty members of the then forming church, and others daily adding, Acts i. 15. ii. 41, 47. *Five thousand* were afterwards added to them, and thereafter such *multitudes*, that the twelve apostles, on account of their preaching the gospel, had not time to receive or distribute their charity to the poor. To all these were added a *great number* of priests, and, no doubt, others obedient to the faith, Acts iv. 4. v. 14. vi. 7. All these taken together could scarcely be fewer than forty thousand.——Notwithstanding repeated persecutions, Acts viii. xii. we find them *many ten thousands*, Acts xxi. 20; which could scarcely be fewer than *forty* or *eighty* thousand. Now, in what private house, and they had no other place, could all these assemble to eat the Lord's Supper together.——The twelve apostles, with several other teachers, laboured ordinarily at Jerusalem, for many years, and preached the gospel in different languages. Now, how absurd to pretend, that they did all this in one single congregation, Acts ii. 41, 42. iv. 31—37. vi. 2. viii. 14. xv. 2. ii. 5—12?—Nevertheless, all the Christians in and about Jerusalem are represented as one church, the rulers of which met together for acts of government, Acts xi. 27, 30. xv. 2. vi. 1—6. xxi. 18. 2. At Antioch a *great number believed;* and afterward *much people* was *added to the Lord*, Acts xi. 24, 26. They had a great number of teachers, Acts xi. 20, 23, 26. xiii. 1—3. xv. 35. How could such multitudes amidst persecutors find one place fit to contain them, in their eating the Lord's Supper? Or, how could so many teachers find work in one single congregation? Nevertheless, they are all called one church, Acts xiii. 1—3. xv. 35. 3. At Ephesus the word of God *grew mightily* and *prevailed*. A multitude even of magicians believed, and burnt their devilish books to the value of fifty thousand pieces of silver, Acts xix. 10, 17—20. 1 Cor. xvi. 8, 9. They had Paul, and twelve other teachers, that prophesied at once; and afterwards a considerable number of presbyters or bishops, Acts xix. 1—10. xx. 17, 28, 36.—Nevertheless, all these Christians of Ephesus belonged to one church, the rulers of which are represented as one *Angel*, and met to judge their spiritual affairs, Rev. i. 11. ii. 1. Acts

xx. 17, 28. 4. At Corinth *many believed;* the Lord had *much people,* Acts xviii. 8—10. They had a considerable number of teachers that taught in different languages and churches, 1 Cor. xiv. 20, 26, 29, 32, 34. Nevertheless, all the Christians at Corinth were but one church, the rulers of which met together for government, 1 Cor. i. 2. v. 4, 13. 2 Cor. ii. 6, 9. In none of these places had they then any diocesan bishops, as their uniting heads.

III. Synods are church-courts constituted of several presbyteries, in order to review their sentences when necessary, and to regulate affairs which are too hard for presbyteries, or which affect different presbyteries. The divine warrant for synods appears, 1. From the ecclesiastical sanhedrim of the Jews, which had the supreme power in excommunications, &c. 2 Chron. xix. 11. Mat. xviii. 18. 2. From the greater safety of extensive consultation, Eccl. iv. 9. Prov. xi. 14. 1 Cor. xiv. 32. 3. From the law of necessity in some cases,—as when a whole presbytery or their people are infected with error or scandal; or when disputes arise between different presbyteries. 4. From the unity of the church, Mat. xvi. 18. 1 Tim. iii. 15. Eph. iv. 4—12. 1 Cor. xii. x. 32. 5. From the pattern of the apostolical synod, Acts xv. Here was a proper case for the decision of a synod;—a dispute which could not be composed by the presbytery of Antioch, and which concerned not only the churches of Syria and Cilicia, but also of Jerusalem,—from which the raisers of it pretended to derive their authority. Here the proper members of a synod were convened,—*Apostles* and *elders* at Jerusalem, with *others* deputed from the churches of Syria and Cilicia,—who all, as on the same level, judged, Acts xv. 2, 6, 22—36. xvi. 4.——As it was impossible for all the believers in Jerusalem to meet in this synod, we are uncertain if *the brethren* mentioned in the history of it means any but preaching elders, Acts xv. 22; but we grant that such private Christians as were present signified their consent, and even voted in the election of the commissioners that were to bear the letters of the synod to the churches of Syria and Cilicia, &c.——Here, as in a synod, the Apostles and elders, by reasoning from facts, and especially from the Scriptures, prepared the affair for a decision.——In the decision itself the whole power of a church synod was exercised. The true doctrine was solemnly asserted and declared; the erroneous were publicly stigmatized; and a decree of decency and order was established.——The whole decision was *authoritative,* not mere consultation, and hence is called a *necessary burden* imposed,—*decrees ordained;*—and as such was cheerfully submitted to by the churches concerned,

Acts xv. 28, 31. xvi. 4, 5. 1 Thess. v. 12. 1 Cor. xvi. 16. Heb. xiii. 7, 17.

The subordination of sessions to presbyteries, and of presbyteries to synods, is manifest, 1. From the very light of nature, which requires the subordination of the lesser to the greater. 2. From the gradation prescribed by Christ in the removing offences, Mat. xviii. 15—18. 3. From the reference made by the churches of Syria and Cilicia to the Synod at Jerusalem, Acts xv. 4. From the absurdities which follow on the denial of it, as that no relief is left by the law of Christ for one that is injured by the greater part of a congregation, session, or presbytery;—that no means are left for the reclaiming a greater part of a congregation, session, or presbytery,—nor any means of promoting uniformity between sister congregations. 5. From a consideration of the peculiar advantages of *presbyterian government*. 1. It best restrains the lordly pride of clergymen. 2. It best secures liberty and peace to the people. 3. It best brings offenders to adequate censure. 4. It most effectually answers the purging out of error. 5. It is best calculated to prevent schisms and separations.

In the present imperfect state of the Christian church, Offences will often be both given and taken, Mat. xviii. 7. Offence or Scandal means some thing openly done or neglected by church-members, which in matter or manner is contrary to the law of God, and which tends to decoy others into sin, or mar their spiritual comfort, Isa. xxvii. 11. Hos. iv. 1, 2, 6. 1 Cor. v. 11. vi. 9, 10. Gal. v. 19—21. 2 Thess. i. 8. iii. 6, 14. 1 Thess. iv. 1—8. Rom. xiv. 1 Cor. viii. x. xiv. Mat. vi. 5, 16. Isa. xlviii. 5. Such offences are very bad in their nature and consequences, but are necessarily permitted by God, Mat. xviii. 1—9. 1. To punish hypocritical professors of religion, 2 Thess. ii. 8—12. 2. To occasion spiritual blessings to true saints, Isa. viii. 11, 12. Rom. xiv. 18, 19. 1 Cor. xi. 19. 3. To occasion the spread of the gospel, Acts xv. 37—41. Phil. i. 12—14. Rom. xi. 20—22.

Great prudence and order, as well as faithfulness and zeal, are necessary in the removing offences. 1. If the offence be known to but one, or a few, the offender must be secretly reproved, Lev. xix. 16, 17. Psalm cxli. 5. Prov. xxvii. 5, 6. Eph. v. 3—11. Mat. xviii. 15. 2. If no satisfaction be thus obtained, we are to take with us one or two friends, who may assist us in the reproof, or witness the offender's carriage under it, Mat. xviii. 16. 3. If the offender persist in the obstinate defence of his conduct, or denial of that which can be proved, he must be delated to a church judicatory. 4. If he disregard the dealings and decision of the church judicatories with respect to him, he must be excommunicated from the fellowship of the church, and held as an heathen man and publican, Mat. xviii. 17, 18.

In their whole procedure, particularly in that which relates to scandals, the end of church judicatories must be to support the innocent, condemn the guilty, and edify all concerned, Deut. xxv. 1. Rom. xiv. 19. 1 Cor. xiv. 26. 2 Cor. xiii. 8, 10. x. 8. ——In order to obtain this end, their conduct ought to be, 1. Candid and open, 2 Cor. i. 12. 2 Tim. ii. 15. 2. Regular, 1 Cor. xi. 13, 14. xiv. 40. 3. Moderate and gentle, Phil. iv. 5. Luke ix. 51—56. 2 Tim. ii. 24, 25. 1 Thess. ii. 7, 8. Mat. x. 16. Col. iii. 12—14. 4. Patient and long-suffering, Prov. xviii. 13. Eph. iv. 2, 32. 5. Prudent, Eph. v. 15. Eccl. iii. 1—11. Prov. x. 5. 6. With equity, Prov. xvii. 15. Mat. xxviii. 20. Rev. ii. 2. iii. 2. 2 Sam. xxiii. 3. Luke xvii. 1—12. 7. With impartiality, James ii. 1—14. iii. 17. 1 Tim. v. 21. 8. With an earnest aiming to promote the glory of God in the edification of his church, Psalm lxix. 9. 1 Cor. x. 31. xiv. 26. 1 Cor. x. 8. xiii. 8, 10. 1 Pet. iv. 11.

All the censures inflicted by church-courts proceeding from a spiritual power, must necessarily be of a spiritual nature, affecting neither body nor goods.——Their principal censure of EXCOMMUNICATION is reckoned *two-fold*, the lesser excommunication judicially suspending church-members from partaking of the seals of God's covenant, 2 Thess. iii. 6, 14, 15. Rom. xvi. 17; and the GREATER EXCOMMUNICATION, which shuts them out from church fellowship altogether into the world, or kingdom of Satan, while they continue impenitent, 1 Cor. v. 4, 5, 13. 1 Tim. i. 20. Tit. iii. 10, 11. Mat. xviii. 17.——The relevant ground of such excommunication is not any disobedience to mere human authority, James iv. 12. Isa. lxvi. 5. John xvi. 2, 3; nor any conduct indifferent in itself, Rom. xiv. 5, 6; nor any matter of doubtful disputation, Rom. xiv. 1; nor any slips of mere human infirmity, James iii. 2. Gal. ii. 11.——But either some error subversive of the gospel and our hope towards God, openly advanced and obstinately maintained, Tit. iii. 10, 11. 1 Tim. i. 20; or obstinate perseverance in some scandalous practice, plainly condemned by the word of God, 1 Cor. v. 4, 5, 13.

As this sentence becomes exceedingly dreadful by God's ratification of it, Mat. xviii. 17, 18. John xx. 23; it ought not to be inflicted upon any before their scandalous error or practice be fully proved against them, and they be allowed proper time to consider their conduct, and the nature and design of this awful ordinance, Tit. iii. 10, 11.——The design of such excommunication is, 1. To render offenders sensible and ashamed of their sin, afraid to continue or die in it, and earnestly desirous to repent and be saved, Jude 22, 23. 2 Thess. iii. 14. 1 Tim. i.

20. 1 Cor. v. 5. 2. To prevent others partaking with them in their sin, and to deter them from the like evils, 1 Tim. v. 20. 2 Cor. vii. 12. 3. To vindicate the honour of Christ, and his religion and church, 2 Cor. vi. 14—18. vii. 1, 11. 1 Cor. v. 7, 13.

The power of excommunicating church-members being authoritative, belongs only to her rulers, Mat. xviii. 17, 18. xvi. 19; to the *many* or *more excellent*, 2 Cor. ii. 6. Heb. xi, 4. Luke xi. 31, 32. Their warrant for inflicting this tremendous censure is, 1. *The keys of the kingdom of heaven* are committed to them, Mat. xvi. 19. 2. They have Christ's express command to inflict it, Mat. xviii. 17—20. Tit. iii. 10, 11. 3. They have an approved example of it in the church of Corinth directed by an Apostle,—and another inflicted by that apostle; in neither of which there appears any thing extraordinary in the occasion, matter, manner, effect, or end, 1 Cor. v. 1 Tim. i. 20.——The procedure of church-rulers to inflict this sentence ought to be carried on, 1. With much solemn and earnest prayer, James v. 16. 2. With much deep humiliation and mourning, 1 Cor. v. 2. 2 Cor. xii. 21. 3. With a deep impression of their own approaching appearance before the tribunal of Jesus Christ, 2 Cor. v. 10, 11. Mat. xviii. 18. 4. With great meekness and compassion towards the offenders, Jude 22, 23.

No performance of any natural or necessary moral duty towards excommunicated persons ought to be suspended, 1 Cor. vii. 12, 13. Nor ought church-rulers to forbear dealing with them for their conviction, as God gives them opportunities. But to render them ashamed, all church-members ought, as far as possible, to avoid all familiar civil fellowship with them, 1 Cor. v. 11. Matth. xviii. 17.—None ought to be absolved or relaxed from this censure, and restored to the fellowship of the church, before, by their profession and practice, they have given such evidence of their repentance as would satisfy any impartial and inquiring mind, 2 Cor. ii. 6—10.

REFLECT. Ponder now, my soul! Am I a true member of the church of the living God? Or, am I a branch that shall be withered, and cast out into eternal fire?—In this systematic view of God's truths, have I, last of all, beheld the tremendous sentence of EXCOMMUNICATION and absolution from it? Let me think, as in Jehovah's presence, under what sentence of his I myself now am:—for what I am prepared, or preparing:—what I shall receive from Jesus Christ at his second coming.—Perhaps I must appear before his awful tribunal in the very same state and temper of mind in which I finish this work—this page.——Hearest thou, O my soul, what these thousands of truths which I have been reviewing, bear witness for, or against me?—Alas! Have I reviewed so many precious,—so many saving truths, and seen none in their glory, felt none in their power?—Alas! What an hell-hardened heart must I have now, if the vail still remain, and they have all proved a *killing letter*, a *ministration*, a *savour of death unto death*, unto me! How dreadful, if I leap into eternal flames with all this oil of gospel-truth in my conscience!—To prevent this tremendous event,—and to glorify the God of all grace, let me conclude my work, with a solemn surrender of myself, as a poor, an unparalleled, ignorant, guilty, polluted, and enslaved sinner,—to Jesus Christ, as in the gospel made of God ui. me wisdom, righteousness, sanctification, and redemption.—Let my conscience,—let angels,—let the redeeming THREE, bear me witness, that I consent, heartily consent, that Jesus, and all that he is and has, be mine, and that I be his from henceforth and for ever;—and that in me, the *first-rate sinner*, he may shew, in the ages to come, all his long-suffering, and the exceeding riches of his grace. If my soul love not this Lord Jesus, let me be ANATHEMA, MARANATHA, *accursed at his coming.*

FINIS.